Master Index

BASIC AND CLINICAL SCIENCE COURSE

2012–2013

AMERICAN ACADEMY
OF OPHTHALMOLOGY
The Eye M.D. Association

LEO

LIFELONG
EDUCATION FOR THE
OPHTHALMOLOGIST®

American Academy of Ophthalmology Staff

Richard A. Zorab, *Vice President, Ophthalmic Knowledge*

Hal Straus, *Director, Publications Department*

Christine Arturo, *Acquisitions Manager*

Stephanie Tanaka, *Publications Manager*

D. Jean Ray, *Production Manager*

Ann McGuire, *Medical Editor*

Steven Huebner, *Administrative Coordinator*

Index by Katherine Pitcoff, Fort Bragg, California

**AMERICAN ACADEMY
OF OPHTHALMOLOGY**
The Eye M.D. Association

655 Beach Street
Box 7424
San Francisco, CA 94120-7424

Basic and Clinical Science Course
2012–2013

Gregory L. Skuta, MD, Oklahoma City, Oklahoma, *Senior Secretary for Clinical Education*

Louis B. Cantor, MD, Indianapolis, Indiana, *Secretary for Ophthalmic Knowledge*

Jayne S. Weiss, MD, New Orleans, Louisiana, *BCSC Course Chair*

Section 1   *Update on General Medicine*
   Chair: Eric P. Purdy, MD, Fort Wayne, Indiana

Section 2   *Fundamentals and Principles of Ophthalmology*
   Chair: K. V. Chalam, MD, PhD, Jacksonville, Florida

Section 3   *Clinical Optics*
   Chair: Neal Atebara, MD, Honolulu, Hawaii

Section 4   *Ophthalmic Pathology and Intraocular Tumors*
   Chair: Robert H. Rosa, Jr, MD, Temple, Texas

Section 5   *Neuro-Ophthalmology*
   Chair: Lanning B. Kline, MD, Birmingham, Alabama

Section 6   *Pediatric Ophthalmology and Strabismus*
   Chair: Edward L. Raab, MD, New York, New York

Section 7   *Orbit, Eyelids, and Lacrimal System*
   Chair: John Bryan Holds, MD, St Louis, Missouri

Section 8   *External Disease and Cornea*
   Chair: James J. Reidy, MD, Buffalo, New York

Section 9   *Intraocular Inflammation and Uveitis*
   Chair: Ramana S. Moorthy, MD, Indianapolis, Indiana

Section 10   *Glaucoma*
   Chair: George A. Cioffi, MD, New York, New York

Section 11   *Lens and Cataract*
   Chair: James C. Bobrow, MD, Clayton, Missouri

Section 12   *Retina and Vitreous*
   Chair: Hermann D. Schubert, MD, New York, New York

Section 13   *Refractive Surgery*
   Chair: Christopher J. Rapuano, MD, Philadelphia, Pennsylvania

Master Index

(*f* = figure; *t* = table. Numbers in **boldface** indicate Section numbers.)

A

A constant, in IOL power determination/power prediction formulas, **3**:217, 218, 219, **11**:84
A2E, in fundus autofluorescence, **12**:30
A-pattern deviations, **6**:107–112, 109*f*
  definition of, **6**:107
  esotropia, **6**:107–112, 109*f*
    treatment of, **6**:112
  exotropia, **6**:107–112, 109*f*
    treatment of, **6**:112
  in inferior oblique muscle paralysis, **6**:122*t*
  pulley system pathology and, **6**:23, 109–110, 110*f*
  surgical treatment of, **6**:110–111, 111*f*, 112
A-R syndrome. *See* Axenfeld-Rieger syndrome
A-scan ultrasonography/echography, **3**:273, 273*f*, 274*f*, 275. *See also* Ultrasonography
  for axial length measurement
    in IOL power determination/selection, **3**:213–214, 214*f*, 215*f*, **11**:82–83, 83*f*, 84, 84–85
    in primary congenital glaucoma, **10**:152
  in choroidal/ciliary body melanoma, **4**:276, 276*f*
  in choroidal hemangioma, **4**:291*f*, 292
  in metastatic eye disease, **4**:319
a-wave, of electroretinogram, **5**:109, **12**:34, 34*f*. *See also* Electroretinogram
AA. *See* Arachidonic acid
AAION. *See* Arteritic anterior ischemic optic neuropathy
AAO. *See* American Academy of Ophthalmology
AAP. *See* American Academy of Pediatrics
AAPOX. *See* Adult-onset asthma with periocular xanthogranuloma
Ab externo approach
  for IOL dislocation repair, **11**:164–165, 165*f*
  for trabeculotomy, in children, **10**:152–153, 154
Ab interno approach, for IOL dislocation repair, **11**:164–165, 165*f*
Abacavir, **1**:33
Abatacept, **1**:186
Abbe number (V-number), **3**:50–51
  lens materials and, **3**:161, 162–163
ABC/ABCR transporters. *See* ATP binding cassette (ABC/ABCR) transporters
ABCA4 gene
  in cone–rod dystrophy, **12**:233
  in Stargardt disease, **4**:172, **12**:233, 234
ABCC6 gene, in pseudoxanthoma elasticum, **12**:84
ABCDE mnemonic, in melanoma evaluation, **1**:277
Abciximab, for ischemic heart disease, **1**:103, 109, 109*t*
  non–ST-segment elevation acute coronary syndrome, **1**:112
ABCR. *See* ATP binding cassette (ABC/ABCR) transporters
Abducens nerve. *See* Cranial nerve VI
Abducens nerve palsy/paralysis. *See* Sixth nerve (abducens) palsy/paralysis

Abduction, **6**:33
  extraocular muscles in, **5**:55–56, 56*f*
    inferior oblique, **5**:56, 56*f*, **6**:15, 29, 29*t*, 32, 34*f*
    lateral rectus, **5**:55, 56*f*, **6**:13, 17*t*, 29, 29*t*
    superior oblique, **5**:55, 56*f*, **6**:15, 17*t*, 29, 29*t*, 32, 33*f*
  in Möbius syndrome, **6**:140, 140*f*
  nystagmus and (dissociated nystagmus), **5**:244, 254, **6**:326
  in sixth nerve (abducens) paralysis, **6**:134, 134*f*
Aberrant nerve regeneration. *See also specific nerve*
  cranial nerve III (oculomotor), **5**:232, 232*f*, 273*t*, **6**:132
  cranial nerve IV (trochlear nerve), **6**:142
  cranial nerve VII (facial), **5**:284, 284*f*
  pupillary reactivity disorders and, **5**:273*t*, 274
  superior oblique myokymia and, **6**:142
  synkinesis and, **5**:284, 284*f*, **7**:203, 207, 221
Aberrations, **3**:93–102, 238, 239*f*. *See also specific type and* Wavefront aberrations
  chromatic, **3**:40, 41, 41*f*, 93, 100–102, 102*f*
    duochrome test and, **3**:135–136
    with polycarbonate lenses, **3**:162
    prisms producing, **3**:88
  combining spherocylindrical lenses at oblique axes and, **3**:99
  first-order, **13**:7
  higher-order, **3**:93, 115–116, 240, **13**:7–8, 8*f*, 9*f*
    contact lens masking of, **3**:190
    custom contact lenses for, **3**:195–196
    after LASIK, **13**:7, 95, 96*f*
    after surface ablation, **13**:7, 95
    wavefront-guided/wavefront-optimized ablation and, **13**:7, 8, 25, 69, 95
  irregular astigmatism, **3**:93, 115–116, 164. *See also* Irregular astigmatism
    after LASIK, **13**:7, 95, 96*f*
  lower-order, **13**:6, 6*f*, 7*f*
  monochromatic, **3**:93
  optical, **3**:93–102
  after photoablation, **13**:95
  prism, **3**:88
  refractive surgery and, **3**:99–100, 140, 232, 233*f*, **13**:5–9, 5*f*, 6*f*, 7*f*, 8*f*, 9*f*, 40, 72, 74
  regular astigmatism, **3**:93–97, 93*f*, 94*f*, 95*f*, 96*f*, 97*f*, 98, 98*f*. *See also* Regular astigmatism
  of retinoscopic reflex, **3**:129
  spherical, **3**:99–100, 100, 101*f*, 231, 233*f*, 238, 239*f*, **13**:7, 8*f*. *See also* Spherical aberration
    after LASIK, **13**:7, 95
    after surface ablation, **13**:7, 8*f*, 95
  transposition and, **3**:97–99
  wavefront, **3**:93–100, 238, 239*f*. *See also* Wavefront aberrations
  zero-order, **13**:7
Aberrometers, wavefront. *See* Wavefront aberrometers

1

Abetalipoproteinemia, **12**:260–261
  microsomal triglyceride transfer protein defects
    causing, **2**:298
  retinal degeneration and, **12**:260–261
  vitamin supplements in management of, **2**:232
Ablepharon, **8**:249
ABMD (anterior basement membrane dystrophy).
    See Epithelial/subepithelial dystrophies, basement
    membrane
ABO antigens, transplant rejection and, **8**:407, 411
AbobotulinumtoxinA. *See* Botulinum toxin, type A
ABPM. *See* Ambulatory blood pressure measurement
Abrasions, corneal, **4**:13–14, **8**:372
  in children, **6**:407
  contact lenses causing, **3**:198
  posttraumatic recurrent corneal erosion and, **8**:372
Abrevia. *See* Nedocromil
Abscesses
  in dacryocystitis, **7**:275
  orbital, **7**:43, 43*f*
  subperiosteal, in orbital cellulitis in children, **6**:195,
    196, 196*f*
Absence (petit mal) seizure, **1**:261
Absidia, **8**:140
Absorptiometry, duel-energy radiographic, for bone
    density measurement, **1**:229
Absorption, light, **3**:13
  lasers and, **3**:21, 23*f*
  spectra of, for visual pigments, **12**:337, 338*f*
Absorptive lenses, **3**:159–161, 160*f*. *See also* Sunglasses
Abstinence (withdrawal) syndrome, **1**:250. *See also*
    specific drug
  hypertension and, **1**:87
Abuse
  child
    cataract and, **6**:404
    gonococcal conjunctivitis and, **6**:189
    ocular trauma and, **6**:404–407, 405*f*, 406*f*,
      12:330–331, 330*f*
  elder, **1**:223–224
AC. *See* Accommodative convergence
AC/A esotropia. *See* High accommodative convergence/
    accommodative esotropia
AC/A ratio. *See* Accommodative convergence/
    accommodation ratio
ACA. *See* Anterior cerebral artery
ACAID. *See* Anterior chamber–associated immune
    deviation
Acanthamoeba, **2**:385, **8**:140
  castellani, **4**:85
  keratitis/ocular infection caused by, **4**:54, 84–85, 86*f*,
    8:167–169, 168*f*
    contact lens wear and, **3**:196, **4**:84–85, **8**:167, 168
    herpes simplex keratitis differentiated from,
      8:168–169
    isolation techniques for diagnosis of, **8**:103
    stains and culture media for identification of, **4**:85,
      8:103*t*
    treatment of, **2**:385–386, **8**:168–169
  polyphaga, **4**:85, **8**:140*f*
    stains and culture media for identification of, **4**:85,
      8:103*t*
Acantholysis, definition of, **4**:206

Acanthosis, definition of, **4**:206
Acarbose, **1**:199*t*, 201
ACC. *See* Adenoid cystic carcinoma
Acceptor splice site, **2**:147
Accessory lacrimal glands, **2**:26*f*, 27*t*, 33, 239–240, 239*f*
  of Krause, **2**:23*f*, 26*f*, 27*t*, 33, 239–240, **4**:205, 207*t*,
    7:135*f*, 141, 244
  of Wolfring, **2**:23*f*, 26*f*, 27*t*, 33, 240, **4**:205, 207*t*,
    7:135*f*, 141, 244
Accessory molecules, in immune processing, **9**:39, 40*f*
Accolate. *See* Zafirlukast
Accommodating intraocular lenses, **3**:229, **13**:4*t*, 146,
    159–160
Accommodation, **2**:67, 69*f*, 70, **3**:116–117, 117*f*, 172,
    11:19–20, 19*t*, **13**:149–152, 150*f*, 151*f*, 152*f*
  aging affecting, **2**:67, **3**:117, 142, 143*t*, **11**:19–20,
    13:149. *See also* Presbyopia
  amplitude of, **3**:117, **11**:19–20
    aging affecting, **3**:142, 143*t*, **11**:19–20, **13**:149
    binocular, **3**:145
    cycloplegic refraction and, **3**:137
    measurement of in bifocal add determination,
      3:145–147
    premature loss of (accommodative insufficiency),
      3:142–143
    refractive procedures for improving, **13**:149–161
  changes with, **11**:19, 19*f*
    in nonorganic disorders, **5**:316
  clinical problems of, **3**:142–145, 143*t*
  contact lens correction affecting, **3**:144–145, 172–173
  definition of, **3**:116
  development of, **6**:170
  Helmholtz hypothesis (capsular theory) of, **11**:19,
    13:149–150, 150*f*
  muscarinic drugs affecting, **2**:335
  near point of, measuring, **3**:145–146
  near reflex and, **2**:99, **6**:37, 81
  paralysis of, for refraction in infants and children, **3**:141
  range of, **3**:117
    power of bifocal add and, **3**:146
      occupation and, **3**:157
      selection and, **3**:147
  relaxing. *See also* Cycloplegia/cycloplegics
    in children, **3**:141
    for gradient method of AC/A ratio measurement,
      3:144
  Schachar theory of, **13**:150–152, 151*f*, 152*f*
  spasm of (ciliary muscle spasm), **5**:316
    accommodative excess caused by, **3**:143
  spectacle lens correction affecting, **3**:144–145
  stimulating, for gradient method of AC/A ratio
    measurement, **3**:144
  theories of, **13**:149–152, 150*f*, 151*f*, 152*f*
Accommodative amplitude. *See* Accommodation,
    amplitude of
Accommodative convergence, **6**:37. *See also*
    Accommodative convergence/accommodation ratio
  assessment of, **6**:81
  in refractive accommodative esotropia, **6**:93
Accommodative convergence/accommodation ratio,
    3:143–144, **6**:37
  assessment of, **3**:144, **6**:81–82
  convergence spasm and, **5**:214

high, **6:**94–95
  in intermittent exotropia, **6:**100–101
  management of, **6:**82, 94–95
Accommodative effort, **3:**116–117
Accommodative esotropia, **6:**93–95
  high accommodative convergence/accommodative
    (nonrefractive), **6:**82, 94–95
  infantile esotropia and, **6:**91
  muscarinic agents for management of, **2:**339
  partially accommodative, **6:**95
  refractive, **6:**93
  refractive surgery and, **13:**181
Accommodative excess, **3:**143
Accommodative insufficiency, **3:**142–143
Accommodative intraocular lenses, **11:**137
  complications associated with, **11:**169
Accommodative response, **3:**117. *See also*
    Accommodation
  loss of, aging and, **3:**117
Accommodative rule, **3:**146
ACCORD (Action to Control Cardiovascular Risk in
    Diabetes) trial, **1:**139, 203
AccuNeb. *See* Albuterol
Accupril. *See* Quinapril
Accuracy
  saccadic system evaluation and, **5:**203, 209
  of screening/diagnostic test, **1:**330
Accuretic. *See* Quinapril
Accutane. *See* Isotretinoin
ACD. *See* Anterior chamber, depth of; Granular corneal
    dystrophy, type 2
ACD prediction formula, **3:**217
  personalized, **3:**218
ACE. *See* Angiotensin-converting enzyme
ACE inhibitors. *See* Angiotensin-converting enzyme
    (ACE) inhibitors
Acebutolol, **1:**76t, **2:**345f
Acenorm. *See* Captopril
Aceon. *See* Perindopril
Acephalgic migraine (migraine equivalent), **5:**296–297.
    See also Migraine headache
Acetazolamide, **2:**351, 352t, 353, **10:**156–157,
    163–164t
  in children, **10:**156–157
  for cystoid macular edema, **12:**143
    in retinitis pigmentosa, **12:**230, 230f
  for glaucoma, **10:**156–157, 163–164t
    in children, **6:**243, **10:**156–157
  for idiopathic intracranial hypertension, **5:**124
  sustained-release oral preparation for, **2:**329, 353
  for uveitic cystoid macular edema, **9:**301
Acetohexamide, **1:**199t
Acetylcholine, **2:**259t
  clinical use of, **2:**335–337, 336f
  in iris–ciliary body, **2:**258, 259t
  receptors for
    drugs affecting, **2:**334–344, 335f, 336f, 337f, 339f,
      343f. *See also* Cholinergic agents
    in myasthenia gravis, **5:**328, **7:**209
  sphincter activity affected by, **2:**260
  synthesis/release/degradation of, **2:**335–337, 337f
    botulinum toxin affecting, **7:**218, 219f
  in tear secretion, **2:**240, 242, 242f

Acetylcholine receptor antibody tests, for myasthenia
    gravis, **5:**331, **7:**209
Acetylcholinesterase. *See* Cholinesterase/
    acetylcholinesterase
Acetylcholinesterase inhibitors. *See* Cholinesterase/
    acetylcholinesterase inhibitors
Acetylcysteine, **2:**333
  for filamentary keratopathy, **2:**333, **8:**60
Acetylsalicylic acid. *See* Aspirin
Acetyltransferase, in isoniazid pharmacogenetics, **2:**229
ACh. *See* Acetylcholine
Achromatic automated perimetry, **10:**54
Achromatopsia (monochromatism), **12:**214–215, 214t
  blue-cone, **12:**214, 214t, 215
    in children, **6:**291
    ERG patterns in, **12:**36f
    gene defects causing, **2:**297
    ocular findings in carriers of, **2:**222t
  cerebral, **5:**194
  in children, **6:**291
    incomplete, **6:**291
  gene defects causing, **2:**297
  with myopia, racial and ethnic concentration of, **2:**211
  rod, **12:**214t, 215
  Sloan test for, **12:**50
Achromycin. *See* Tetracyclines
Acid, ocular injuries caused by, **8:**355
  cataract and, **11:**53
  in children, **6:**407
Acid-fast stain, **8:**131
Acidic fibroblast growth factor. *See also* Fibroblast
    growth factor
  in aqueous humor, **2:**270
Acidosis, carbonic anhydrase IOP lowering and, **2:**353
Aciduria, methylmalonic, **6:**398
Acinar cells, lacrimal gland, **2:**32, 33f
  differentiation of, **2:**140
ACIOLs (anterior chamber intraocular lenses). *See*
    Intraocular lenses (IOLs), anterior chamber
ACIP (Advisory Committee on Immunization
    Practices), **1:**280
ACL syndrome, congenital corneal keloids in, **8:**264
ACLS. *See* Advanced cardiac life support
ACMASTER, **3:**218
Acne rosacea. *See* Rosacea
Acoustic interface, in ultrasonography, **3:**273
Acoustic neuromas/neurofibromas, **5:**338, 340–341, **6:**371,
    10:148. *See also* Neurofibromatosis, bilateral acoustic
  Bruns nystagmus and, **5:**250
  seventh nerve (facial) palsy and, **5:**286, 287f
ACPIOL (anterior chamber phakic intraocular lenses).
    See Phakic intraocular lenses, anterior chamber
Acquired esotropia, nonaccommodative, **6:**90t, 95–98
  basic, **6:**95–96
Acquired (adaptive) immunity, **1:**280, **9:**9. *See also*
    Adaptive immune response
Acquired immunodeficiency syndrome. *See* HIV
    infection/AIDS
Acquired ocular motor apraxia, **5:**194, 210
Acquired pendular nystagmus, **5:**244f, 253
Acquired ptosis. *See* Ptosis
Acquired strabismus, **6:**11
ACR. *See* American College of Rheumatology

Acral-lentiginous melanoma, 4:226, 227f
Acrocentric chromosome, 2:147
Acrocephalopolysyndactyly type II, 8:322t
Acrocephalosyndactyly (Apert syndrome), 6:388, 389f, 391f, 7:35, 8:322t
Acrocephaly, 6:383
Acrochordons, 7:157, 157f
Acrodermatitis chronica atrophicans, in Lyme disease, 1:15, 9:251
Acromegaly, 1:215
Acropachy, in thyroid eye disease, 7:51
Acrospiroma, eccrine (clear cell hidradenoma), 7:162
Acrylic
    for intraocular lenses, 3:205, 11:135–136. See also Foldable intraocular lens
        capsular opacification and, 11:170
        for children, 6:259
        dysphotopsias and, 3:224, 224f
        glistenings and, 11:169
        instrumentation for handling, 11:138
        uveitis and, 11:204
    refractive index of, 3:40t
AcrySof IQ intraocular lens, 13:142, 142f, 143, 144
AcrySof ReSTOR intraocular lens, 3:228, 228f, 13:144, 155, 155f
ACS. See Acute coronary syndrome; Anterior ciliary sclerotomy
Actemra. See Tocilizumab
ACTH (adrenocorticotropic hormone), in tear secretion, 2:244
Actin, 2:277
    in immunohistochemistry, 4:33
        in adenoid cystic carcinoma, 4:236
Actin filaments, 2:277
Actinic injury. See Photochemical injury
Actinic (Labrador) keratopathy (spheroidal degeneration), 4:88–89, 90f, 8:334–335, 335f
Actinic keratosis, 4:216–217, 217f, 218f, 7:166, 167f
Actinomyces, 8:137
    canaliculitis caused by, 7:274
    dacryolith formation and, 7:266
Actinomycin-D (dactinomycin), 1:239
Action to Control Cardiovascular Risk in Diabetes (ACCORD) trial, 1:139, 203
Activase. See Alteplase; Tissue plasminogen activator
Activated macrophages, 9:20, 21f, 22–23
Activated neutrophils, 9:17, 19, 19f
Activated partial thromboplastin time (aPTT), 1:152
Activated protein C, 1:151, 152
    deficiency of, 1:152
Activated protein C resistance, 1:157
Activation
    lymphocyte, 9:37–38, 40f, 42
    macrophage, 9:11, 14t, 20–23, 21f
    neutrophil, 9:14t, 17–20, 19f
Activators, 2:332
Active force generation, 6:83
Active immunization, 1:280
Active medium, laser, 3:19, 21, 23, 24f
Active pulley hypothesis, 6:23
Active transport/secretion
    across retinal pigment epithelium, 2:307
    aqueous humor composition affected by, 2:266

in aqueous humor dynamics, 2:254, 255, 10:14
    in lens, 2:278, 11:17–18
        epithelium as site of, 11:17–18
        pump–leak theory and, 11:18–19, 18f
Activities of daily living (ADL)
    assessment of, 1:219–220
    vision impairment/loss and, 1:219, 224, 3:284
Activities of Daily Vision Scale (ADVS), 11:71
Actonel. See Risedronate
Actos. See Pioglitazone
ACTSEB. See Anterior chamber tube shunt to an encircling band
AcuFocus corneal inlay, 13:54, 200
Acuity. See Brightness acuity; Visual acuity
Acuity meter, potential. See Potential acuity meter
Acular. See Ketorolac
Aculeiform cataract, 6:247t
Acute coronary syndrome, 1:101–103. See also Myocardial infarction
    hypercholesterolemia and, 1:100, 131, 132–133, 133t
    hypertension management and, 1:84
    management of, 1:99, 109t, 110–113
    ophthalmic considerations and, 1:128
    risk stratification for, 1:111
Acute disseminated encephalomyelitis, optic nerve involvement and, 4:252
Acute hemorrhagic conjunctivitis, 8:130
Acute idiopathic blind-spot enlargement, 5:112–113, 12:190
Acute idiopathic maculopathy, 12:193
Acute lymphoblastic leukemia, orbital involvement in, 7:90
Acute macular neuroretinopathy (AMN), 9:169, 12:193
Acute posterior multifocal placoid pigment epitheliopathy (APMPPE), 9:148–150t, 155–158, 156f, 157f, 158f, 12:185–187, 186t, 187f
Acute retinal necrosis, 4:151, 151f, 5:359, 9:199–203, 199t, 201f, 12:201–202, 202f
Acute retinal pigment epitheliitis (ARPE/Krill disease), 9:148–150t, 170, 170f, 12:193–194
Acute spastic entropion, 7:194, 195f
Acute zonal occult outer retinopathy (AZOOR), 9:148–150t, 170–172, 171f, 12:186t, 192–193, 192f
Acuvue contact lenses, 3:177t
Acyclovir, 1:55t, 65–66, 2:381t, 382–383, 8:109t
    for acute retinal necrosis, 9:202, 12:201
    for epithelial keratitis, 8:113
    for herpes simplex virus infections, 1:22–23, 65, 2:381t, 382–383, 8:108t, 109t, 113, 115, 9:199, 12:201
    for herpes zoster infections, 1:23, 65–66, 8:121, 9:199, 12:201
    for herpetic uveitis, 9:199
    for iridocyclitis, 8:116
    for progressive outer retinal necrosis, 9:203, 12:201
    for stromal keratitis, 8:108t, 115, 116
Acylureidopenicillins, 1:57
AD. See Alzheimer disease
ADA. See American Diabetes Association
Adalat. See Nifedipine
Adalimumab, 1:186, 9:108t, 114–115
    for uveitis, 9:108t, 114–115
        in children, 6:278

Adamantiades-Behçet disease. *See* Behçet disease
Adaptation
 dark
  sunglasses affecting, 3:159
  testing, 12:46, 47*f*
   in congenital stationary night blindness, 12:215,
    216*f*
 light, 2:294
Adaptive immune response/adaptive immunity, 1:4, 9:9,
  33–55. *See also* Immune response arc
 clinical examples of, 9:34–35
 complement and, 9:23–24, 24*f*
 effector reactivities of, 9:42–43, 42*f*, 44–55, 44*t*. *See
  also specific type*
  antibody-mediated, 9:45–48, 45*f*, 47*t*, 48
  combined antibody and cellular, 9:51–55, 54*f*
  lymphocyte-mediated, 9:42–43, 42*f*, 48–51, 49*f*,
   50*t*, 52–53, 53*f*
  mediators in, 9:23–31, 23*t*
 in viral conjunctivitis, 9:60–61
Adaptometer, Goldmann-Weekers, for dark adaptation
  testing, 12:46, 47*f*
ADC mapping. *See* Apparent diffusion coefficient
  (ADC) mapping
ADCC. *See* Antibody-dependent cellular cytotoxicity
Adduction, 6:33
 elevation deficiency in (double elevator palsy),
  6:123–124, 123*f*, 7:205
 extraocular muscles in, 5:55–56, 56*f*
  inferior rectus, 5:55, 56*f*, 6:14, 17*t*, 29, 29*t*, 31, 32*f*
  medial rectus, 5:55, 56*f*, 6:13, 17*t*, 29, 29*t*
  superior rectus, 5:55, 56*f*, 6:14, 17*t*, 29, 29*t*, 31, 31*f*
 in Möbius syndrome, 6:140, 140*f*
 overdepression in, 6:115
 overelevation in, 6:114
Adefovir, 1:66
Adenine arabinoside. *See* Vidarabine
Adenocarcinoma, 4:10*t*
 of retinal pigment epithelium, 4:184, 288
 sebaceous, 4:215*t*, 221–224, 222*f*, 223*f*, 7:173–175,
  174*f*, 8:233, 234*f*
Adenoid cystic carcinoma (cylindroma)
 of eyelid, 7:162
 of lacrimal glands, 4:236–238, 237*f*, 7:87
Adenoma
 Fuchs (pseudoadenomatous hyperplasia), 4:184,
  288
 pituitary, 1:214–216
  chiasmal syndromes caused by, 5:161*f*, 162–163,
   163*f*
  neuroimaging in evaluation of, 1:216, 5:82*t*
 pleomorphic (benign mixed tumor)
  of eyelid, 7:162
  of lacrimal gland, 4:236, 237*f*, 7:86–87, 86*f*
 of retinal pigment epithelium, 4:184, 288
 sebaceous (sebaceum), 4:215*t*, 221, 222*f*, 7:161
  in tuberous sclerosis, 5:341, 342*f*, 6:372, 372*f*,
   10:28
 thyroid, 1:212, 213
 of uvea/retina, 4:288
Adenomatous polyposis, familial (Gardner syndrome),
  retinal manifestations of, 4:150–151, 12:255, 255*f*
 in children, 6:352

Adenoviruses/adenoviral infection, 8:123–127
 in children, 6:190–191
 conjunctivitis, 8:124–127, 125*f*
  acute hemorrhagic conjunctivitis, 8:130
  epidemic keratoconjunctivitis, 6:191, 8:124, 125,
   125*f*, 126*f*
  follicular conjunctivitis, 4:53, 8:124
  immune response to, 9:60–61
  herpes simplex infection differentiated from, 8:107
  pharyngoconjunctival fever, 6:191, 8:124
Adenylyl/adenylate cyclase
 adrenoceptor binding and, 2:348, 349
 receptor-effector coupling and, 2:262, 262*f*
 tear secretion and, 2:243, 243*f*
Adherence, as microbial virulence factor, 8:98, 159
Adherence syndrome, after strabismus surgery, 6:158
Adhesins, 8:98, 132
Adhesion, in neutrophil recruitment and activation,
  9:18, 19*f*
Adie tonic pupil, 5:54, 265*f*, 270–271, 271*f*, 272*f*, 316,
  6:229
 pharmacologic testing for, 2:338, 5:270–271, 272*f*,
  316
Adipose tissue, in orbit, 6:19, 20*f*
Adipose tumors, of orbit, 4:245
Adits, for neck liposuction, 7:236
Adjustable refractive surgery (ARS), 13:137. *See also*
  Bioptics
Adjustable sutures, 6:148–149
ADL. *See* Activities of daily living
Adnexa. *See* Ocular adnexa
ADOA. *See* Autosomal dominant optic atrophy
Adolescents. *See also* Children
 cystinosis in, 8:313
 hypertension in, 1:69, 86–87
 low vision in, 3:307
Adrenaline. *See* Epinephrine
Adrenergic agents, 2:344–351, 345*f*, 347*f*, 347*t*, 350*f*. *See
  also specific agent and* Alpha (α)-adrenergic agents;
  Beta (β)-adrenergic agents
 angle closure caused by, 10:119
 centrally acting, for hypertension, 1:77*t*, 78*t*, 82
 for glaucoma
  agonists, 2:264*t*, 346–347, 347*t*, 348–349, 10:157,
   163*t*, 168–170
  antagonists/β-blockers, 2:264*t*, 349–351, 350*t*,
   10:156, 162–163*t*, 167–168
  in children, 6:243
 for heart failure, 1:119
 as miotics, 2:260, 348
 modes of action of, 2:264*t*
 as mydriatics, 2:260, 345–346
 systemic absorption of, 2:344
Adrenergic neurons, 2:259
Adrenergic receptors, 2:259, 259*t*
 drugs affecting, 2:344–351, 345*f*
 in iris–ciliary body, 2:259, 259*t*, 260, 262–263, 344
 locations of, 2:344
 signal transduction and, 2:262–263, 262*f*, 263*f*, 264*t*
 in tear secretion, 2:242, 242*f*, 243, 243*f*
Adrenochrome deposition
 corneal pigmentation caused by, 8:337*t*, 348, 348*f*
 epinephrine causing, 10:29

Adrenocorticotropic hormone (ACTH), in tear secretion, 2:244
Adrenoleukodystrophy, neonatal, 6:398, 12:250*t*, 254, 261, 261*f*
  pigmentary retinopathy in, 12:250*t*, 254, 261, 261*f*
Adriamycin. *See* Doxorubicin
ADRP. *See* Autosomal dominant retinitis pigmentosa
Adult gangliosidosis (GM₁ gangliosidosis type III), 6:401*t*
Adult-onset asthma with periocular xanthogranuloma (AAPOX), 7:85
Adult-onset diabetes. *See* Diabetes mellitus, type 2
Adult-onset foveomacular vitelliform dystrophy, 4:175, 176*f*, 12:237–238, 238*f*
  age-related macular degeneration differentiated from, 12:69, 69*f*
Adult-onset myopia, 3:118
Adult-onset vitelliform lesions, 4:175, 176*f*, 12:237–238, 238*f*, 239*f*
Adult-onset xanthogranuloma (AOX), 7:85
Adult Treatment Panel (ATP) reports, 1:131, 132*t*
Advair. *See* Salmeterol, with fluticasone
Advance directives, surgery in older patients and, 1:224–225
Advanced cardiac life support (ACLS), 1:289, 292–293
  pediatric (PALS), 1:289, 293
Advanced Glaucoma Intervention Study (AGIS), 10:107–108
Advanced glycation cross-link breakers, for hypertension, 1:84
Advanced glycosylation end products, diabetes mellitus complications and, 1:189, 205
Advancement flaps, 8:400
  for canthal repair, 7:186
  for eyelid repair, 7:182, 183*f*, 184, 185
Advancing (extraocular muscle insertion), 6:147
Advil. *See* Ibuprofen
Advisory Committee on Immunization Practices (ACIP), 1:280
ADVS. *See* Activities of Daily Vision Scale
Aerial image
  in fundus photography, 3:249, 250*f*
  in indirect ophthalmoscopy, 3:245, 246*f*
AeroBid. *See* Flunisolide
Aerodur. *See* Terbutaline
Aerolate. *See* Theophylline
AF. *See* Autofluorescence
Affective disorders (mood disorders), 1:247–248
  drugs for treatment of, 1:257
Afferent fibers
  somatic, 2:105
  visceral, 2:105
Afferent lymphatic channels, 9:12, 22, 33, 34, 37
Afferent phase of immune response arc, 9:33, 36–37, 36*f*, 38*f*, 39*f*
  response to poison ivy and, 9:34, 35
  response to tuberculosis and, 9:35
Afferent pupillary defects
  relative. *See* Relative afferent pupillary defect
  in traumatic optic neuropathy, 7:105
Afferent pupillary pathway, 2:99
Afferent signal error information, 5:48–49

Afferent visual pathways, 5:27–37, 28*f*
  in cortex, 5:34–37, 35*f*, 36*f*
  in nonorganic ophthalmic disorder, 5:307–314, 308*f*, 309*f*, 310*f*, 311*t*, 313*f*, 314*f*, 315*f*
  optic chiasm, 5:31–32, 32*f*, 33*f*
  optic nerve, 5:29–31
  optic tract, 5:32–33
  pupillary reactivity disorders and, 5:273, 273*t*
  in retina, 5:27–29, 30*f*
Affinity constant (K_m), "sugar" cataract development and, 11:15
aFGF. *See* Acidic fibroblast growth factor
AFL. *See* Anterior focal length
Aflibercept. *See* VEGF Trap
AFMVD. *See* Adult-onset foveomacular vitelliform dystrophy
Afocal systems, 3:80–83, 81*f*, 82*f*, 83*f*
Afterimages/afterimage test
  in palinopsia, 5:191
  in sensory adaptation testing, 6:58, 58*f*
Afterload, 1:117
  reduction of for heart failure, 1:118–119
Against motion, in retinoscopy, 3:123–124, 123*f*
  neutrality and, 3:124, 125, 126*f*
Against-the-rule astigmatism, 3:115
Age/aging, 1:219–233
  accommodative response/presbyopia and, 2:68, 3:117, 142, 143*t*, 11:19–20, 13:149. *See also* Presbyopia
  adaptation to distortion affected by, 3:140, 320
  angioid streaks and, 12:84
  angle closure/angle-closure glaucoma and, 10:10, 113
  antiglaucoma medication use and, 10:176–177
  aqueous tear deficiency/dry eye and, 8:50
  cataracts related to, 11:39–47. *See also* Age-related cataracts
  ciliary body hyalinization and, 4:192
  ciliary muscle affected by, 2:63
  of conjunctiva, 8:331
  of cornea, 8:334
    donor corneas and, 8:411
    stromal corneal degenerations and, 8:336–338, 338*f*, 339*f*
  Descemet membrane/corneal endothelium affected by, 2:45, 251
  ectropion and (involutional ectropion), 7:190–193, 191*f*, 192*f*
  elder abuse and, 1:223–224
  entropion and (involutional entropion), 7:194–196, 195*f*, 197*f*
  ERG affected by, 12:36
  extrinsic, 7:229
  eye dimensions and, 6:167–168, 167*f*, 167*t*, 168*f*
  eyelid changes associated with, 1:221
    orbital septum changes and, 7:138
    skin changes and, 7:136
    SOOF and, 7:141
  facial changes associated with
    cosmetic/rejuvenation surgery and, 7:228–229. *See also specific procedure*
    facial ligaments and, 7:131
    forehead rejuvenation and, 7:232, 233*f*

lower face and neck rejuvenation and, 7:234–238, 237f, 238f
midface rejuvenation and, 7:233–234, 234f, 235f
pathogenesis of, 7:228–229
physical examination of, 7:229
falls and, 1:231–232
glaucoma and
  angle closure/angle-closure glaucoma, 10:10, 113
  antiglaucoma medication use and, 10:176–177
  open-angle glaucoma, 10:8, 75
  surgery and, 10:211–212
hyperopia and, 3:119
hypertension and, 1:86
intraocular pressure affected by, 10:20, 22, 75
intrinsic, 7:228–229
lens changes associated with, 2:67–68, 314, 11:7, 20, 39–47, 40f. See also Age-related cataracts
  presbyopia and, 3:117, 142, 143t
lens proteins affected by, 2:277, 11:13, 39
Lisch nodule prevalence and, 6:225
macular changes associated with, 12:55–56, 56f. See also Age-related macular degeneration
macular holes and, 12:304
medication use and, 1:222
mitochondrial DNA diseases and, 2:173
myopia and, 3:118
normal changes of, 1:225–226
ocular hypertension and, 10:75, 105
open-angle glaucoma and, 10:8, 75
ophthalmic considerations and, 1:227
optic disc size affected by, 10:46
osteoporosis and, 1:227–231
outflow facility affected by, 10:16
outpatient visits and, 1:222–223
parental, chromosomal aberrations in Down syndrome and, 2:201, 202
periorbital changes and, 7:221–222, 221f
pharmacologic principles affected by, 2:323
physiologic/pathologic eye changes and, 1:221, 227
posterior vitreous detachment and, 4:135, 12:274
presbyopia and, 3:117, 142, 143t
preseptal cellulitis and, 7:41
psychology/psychopathology of, 1:225–227
psychosocial assessment of older person and, 1:219–220
refractive status affected by, 3:118–119, 6:169, 169f
refractive surgery and, 13:32–33
  epithelial defects in LASIK and, 13:104
  overcorrection in photoablation and, 13:93–94
  radial keratotomy and, 13:44
of sclera, 4:115, 116f, 8:9, 345–346, 346f
surgical considerations and, 1:224–225
syneresis and, 4:134, 134f
systemic disease incidence and, 1:232–233
trabecular meshwork and, 10:17, 38
transient visual loss and, 5:173
vitreous changes and, 2:84, 84f, 286–289, 12:297
wavefront aberrations and, 13:7
Age-related cataracts, 11:39–47. See also specific type of cataract
  cortical, 11:41–42, 42f, 43f, 44f, 45f
  in diabetes mellitus, 2:279, 11:55

epidemiology of, 11:65–68
genetic contributions to, 11:37–38
nuclear, 4:127, 128f, 129f, 11:39–40, 41f
nutritional deficiency and, 11:57–58
posterior subcapsular, 4:124–125, 125f, 11:42–44, 47f
Age-Related Eye Disease Study (AREDS), 2:314–315, 11:66, 12:61–63
Age-related macular degeneration/maculopathy, 3:284, 4:167–170, 168f, 169f, 170f, 171f, 12:55–80
  antiangiogenic agents for, 12:72–73
  central serous chorioretinopathy differentiated from, 12:60, 70, 71f
  choroidal neovascularization in, 12:23f, 63–64, 64–65f, 65–68, 66f, 67f. See also Choroidal neovascularization
  clinical studies in, 12:61–62, 72, 74, 75, 75f, 76–77, 78. See also specific study
  drusen associated with, 4:168–169, 168f, 169f, 12:57–58, 57f
  fluorescein angiography in, 12:59–60, 64
  genetic factors in, 4:167, 12:56–57
  hyperfluorescent lesions in, 12:59
  hypofluorescent lesions in, 12:59
  incidence/prevalence of, 12:55
  low vision caused by, 3:284
  management of, 12:60–63, 71–80, 75f
  melanoma differentiated from, 4:278, 12:70
  neovascular (wet/exudative), 4:169–170, 171f, 12:63–80
    choroidal neovascularization and, 12:63–64, 64–65f, 65–68, 66f, 67f
    differential diagnosis of, 12:68–70, 68t, 69f, 70f, 71f
    management of, 12:71–80, 75f
    signs and symptoms of, 12:64
  nonneovascular (dry/nonexudative), 4:169, 12:57–63
    differential diagnosis of, 12:60
    management of, 12:60–63
    signs and symptoms of, 12:57–60, 57f, 59f
  photocoagulation for, 12:71, 340
    ineffectiveness of, 12:63
  photodynamic therapy for, 12:71–72, 78, 79, 344
  retinal pigment epithelium abnormalities associated with, 2:309, 12:57, 58–59, 59f
  risk factors for, 12:56
  statin drugs and, 1:131, 139, 325
  submacular hemorrhage in, 12:349, 350f
Agenesis (congenital fibrosis/congenital cranial dysinnervation) syndromes, 5:240–241, 241f, 241t, 6:127, 138–140, 171
  type 1 (CFEOM1), 5:240
Aggrastat. See Tirofiban
Aggrecan, 8:9
Aggrenox. See Aspirin-dipyridamole
Aging. See Age/aging
AGIS (Advanced Glaucoma Intervention Study), 10:107–108
Agnosia
  in Alzheimer disease, 1:268
  object, 5:192
  parietal lobe lesions and, 5:168
Agonist (drug), 2:331
Agonist (muscle), 6:33

Agranulocytosis, clozapine causing, 1:251
Agraphia
    alexia with, 5:194
    alexia without, 5:193–194, 193f
AGV. See Ahmed glaucoma valve/implant
AHC. See Acute hemorrhagic conjunctivitis
Ahmed glaucoma valve/implant, 10:205, 205t
    for childhood glaucoma, 6:241
    for uveitic glaucoma, 9:298
AHWP (Asian Harmonization Working Party), 13:202
AIBSE. See Acute idiopathic blind-spot enlargement
AICA. See Anterior inferior cerebellar artery
Aicardi syndrome, 2:220, 6:292, 292f
AIDS. See HIV infection/AIDS
AIDS-dementia complex (HIV encephalopathy), 1:29,
    5:359–360. See also HIV infection/AIDS
AIDS-related virus (ARV), 1:28. See also HIV (human
    immunodeficiency virus); HIV infection/AIDS
AIM. See Acute idiopathic maculopathy
AION. See Anterior optic neuropathy, ischemic
Air, refractive index of, 3:40t, 8:38
Air cells, ethmoidal (ethmoidal sinuses), 2:7f, 8f, 12, 13f,
    14f, 5:7, 11f, 7:18–19, 18f
Air–cornea interface, reflection at, 3:12
Air–glass interface, reflection at, 3:12
Air-puff (noncontact) tonometers, 10:25
    infection control and, 10:26
Air–tear film interface, 2:43, 44f
Air-ventilated scleral lenses, 3:192
AIRE-deficiency, uveitis in mice and, 9:69–70
Airway disease, 1:142
Airway management, in CPR, 1:290, 291
Airy disk, 3:14–15, 14f, 15f
AJCC (American Joint Committee on Cancer), staging
    of ocular tumors by, 4:329–352t
AK. See Arcuate keratotomy; Astigmatic keratotomy
AK Beta. See Levobunolol
AK-Chlor. See Chloramphenicol
AK-Con. See Naphazoline
AK-Dex. See Dexamethasone
AK-Dilate. See Phenylephrine
AK-Mycin. See Erythromycin
AK-Pentolate. See Cyclopentolate
AK-Poly-Bac. See Polymyxin B, in combination
    preparations
AK-Pred. See Prednisolone
AK-Sulf. See Sulfacetamide
AK-T-Caine. See Tetracaine
AK-Tain. See Proparacaine
AK-Tob. See Tobramycin
AK-Tracin. See Bacitracin
Akarpine. See Pilocarpine
AKC. See Atopic keratoconjunctivitis
Akinetopsia, 5:193
    in Alzheimer disease, 1:268
AKPro. See Dipivefrin
AL. See Axial length
Ala69Ser (LOC387715) gene, in age-related macular
    degeneration, 12:56
Alagille syndrome
    pigmentary retinopathy and, 12:250t
    posterior embryotoxon in, 6:212
Alamast. See Pemirolast

Alaway. See Ketotifen
Albaconazole, 1:65
Albalon. See Naphazoline
Albendazole, for diffuse unilateral subacute
    neuroretinitis, 9:241
Albinism, 2:213t, 214, 308, 4:148, 149f, 6:298–302,
    299–300t, 301f, 12:257–259, 258t, 259f
    in Chédiak-Higashi syndrome, 6:300t, 302
    defective melanin synthesis and, 2:308, 12:257
    in Hermansky-Pudlak syndrome, 6:300t, 302,
        12:258t, 259
    in infants/children, 6:298–302, 299–300t, 301f
    iris transillumination in, 4:149f, 6:231, 298, 301f
    ocular, 2:308, 4:148, 6:298, 300t, 301, 12:258, 258t
        ocular findings in carriers of, 2:222f, 222t, 12:258
        X-linked (Nettleship-Falls), 6:298, 300t, 301,
            12:258
            ocular findings in carriers of, 2:222f, 223, 12:258
    oculocutaneous, 2:195, 308, 4:148, 6:298–301, 299t,
        12:257, 258t
        racial and ethnic concentration of, 2:211
        retinal manifestations of, 12:257–259, 258t, 259f
        tyrosinase activity/defect in, 2:195, 213t, 214, 308,
            6:298, 299t, 12:258, 258t
        X-linked, 6:298, 300t, 301, 12:258
            ocular findings in carriers of, 2:222f, 223, 12:258
Albinoidism, 12:258
Albright hereditary osteodystrophy, 8:322t
Albright syndrome, 7:78
Albumin
    in aqueous humor, 2:268, 10:14
    in vitreous, 2:285
Albuminuria, in diabetes mellitus, 1:206
Albuterol, 1:145t, 2:259t
    with ipratropium, 1:145t
Alcaine. See Proparacaine
Alcian blue stain, 4:30, 31t
Alcohol (ethanol)
    retrobulbar injection of, for pain control, 7:118
    as tissue fixative, 4:29, 29t
    for tissue processing, 4:29
    use/abuse of
        cataract formation and, 11:58–59
        cephalosporins and, 1:58
        esophageal cancer and, 1:275
        intraocular pressure and, 10:21
        maternal, malformations associated with, 1:250,
            2:142–143, 142f, 6:394–395, 395f
        moderation of in hypertension management, 1:75t
        ophthalmic considerations and, 1:250
        optic neuropathy caused by, 5:154
        vitamin A deficiency and, 8:78
Aldactazide. See Spironolactone
Aldactone. See Spironolactone
Aldehyde dehydrogenase, in cornea, 2:248
Aldochlor. See Methyldopa
Aldomet. See Methyldopa
Aldoril. See Methyldopa
Aldose reductase
    in cataract formation, 2:280–281, 11:15
    diabetes mellitus complications and, 1:205, 206
    in lens glucose/carbohydrate metabolism, 2:280, 280f,
        11:14f, 15

Aldose reductase inhibitors
  cataract prevention/management and, **11**:72–73
  for diabetes mellitus, **1**:205, 206
Aldosterone-receptor blockers, for hypertension, **1**:76*t*, 79*t*
Alemtuzumab, **1**:186
Alendronate, for osteoporosis, **1**:230–231
Aleve. *See* Naproxen
Alexander's law, **5**:248, **6**:317, 325
Alexia
  with agraphia, **5**:194
  without agraphia, **5**:193–194, 193*f*
Alfenta. *See* Alfentanil
Alfentanil, perioperative, **1**:309*t*, 311
Alfuzosin
  intraoperative floppy iris syndrome and, **11**:155
  ocular effects of, **1**:301*t*
Alignment
  ocular
    disorders of/unsatisfactory. *See also* Diplopia
      in infant with decreased vision, **6**:414
      nonorganic, **5**:314–315
      after strabismus surgery, **6**:155
      refractive surgery and, **13**:34–35
    tests of, **5**:215–218, 216*f*, 217*f*. *See also specific type*
      in children, **6**:74–80
      Vernier acuity and, **3**:109
    for retinoscopy, **3**:122
Aliskiren, **1**:77*t*, 83
Alizarin red stain, **4**:31*t*
ALK. *See* Automated lamellar keratoplasty
Alkalis (alkaline solutions), ocular injuries caused by
  cataract and, **11**:53
  in children, **6**:407
  glaucoma and, **10**:97
  vitamin C and, **8**:79
Alkapton, corneal pigmentation caused by, **8**:315–316, 337*t*
Alkaptonuria, **2**:212–214, 213*t*, **8**:314*t*
Alkeran. *See* Melphalan
Alkylating agents, **9**:108*t*, 112–113
  for Behçet disease, **1**:180, **9**:195
  for cancer chemotherapy, **1**:240*t*
  for rheumatic disorders, **1**:186–187
  for uveitis, **9**:108*t*, 112–113
    in children, **6**:278
All-*trans*-retinol/all-*trans*-retinaldehyde, **2**:293, 306
Allele-specific marking (genetic imprinting), **2**:154, 169
Allele-specific oligonucleotides, **2**:148
  in mutation screening, **2**:184
Alleles, **2**:148, 194–195
  human leukocyte antigen, **9**:70–71. *See also* Human leukocyte antigens
  null, gene therapy and, **2**:187–188
Allelic association. *See* Linkage disequilibrium
Allelic heterogeneity, **2**:148, 192–193, 193
Allen pictures, for visual acuity testing in children, **6**:72*t*, 73
Allergens, **9**:55. *See also* Allergic reactions/allergies
Allergic aspergillosis, **5**:364
  sinusitis and, **7**:46

Allergic conjunctivitis, **8**:185–187, **9**:55
  in children, **6**:198, 198*t*, 199*t*
  drugs for, **2**:364–366, 365*t*
Allergic fungal sinusitis, orbital involvement and, **4**:234
Allergic granulomatosis and angiitis (Churg-Strauss syndrome), **1**:177*t*, 179–180
Allergic reactions/allergies. *See also specific type and* Hypersensitivity reactions
  to adrenergic agonists, **10**:169, 169*f*
  anaphylaxis, **1**:295, **8**:178*f*, 179–180, 179*t*, 183, 184*f*, **9**:44, 44*t*, 55
  to carbonic anhydrase inhibitors, **10**:171
  in children, **6**:197–200
  conjunctivitis, **6**:198, 198*t*, 199*t*, **8**:185–187, **9**:55
  contact lens wear and, **3**:200, **8**:92
  to cycloplegics, **6**:88
  drugs for, **1**:295, **6**:198, 198*t*, 199*t*. *See also* Antihistamines
    ocular effects of, **1**:301*t*
  in eyelid
    atopic dermatitis, **8**:185
    contact dermatoblepharitis, **8**:183–185, 184*f*
  to fluorescein, **1**:295–296, **12**:24–25
  immunization and, **1**:280
  to indocyanine green, **12**:26
  to insulin, **1**:198
  keratoconjunctivitis
    atopic, **6**:200, **8**:190–192, 191*f*, **9**:55
    vernal, **6**:198–200, 199*f*, **8**:187–190, 188*f*, 189*f*, 191*f*
  to latex, **1**:308–309
  to local anesthetics, **1**:298, 311
  to penicillin, **1**:57, **2**:369
  to suture materials, in strabismus surgery, **6**:156, 157*f*
  to topical medications, **6**:88, **8**:183–185, 184*f*
Allergic shiners, **6**:198
Allesthesia, visual, **5**:195
Allografts
  corneal, **8**:413. *See also* Keratoplasty
    rejection of, **8**:407, 408, 427–430, 428*f*, 429*f*, 436, **9**:63, 64, 64*f*, 65. *See also* Rejection
  limbal, **8**:94, 398
    for chemical injuries, **8**:94
    indications for, **8**:387*t*
  transplantation antigens and, **9**:65
Alloplastic material addition techniques, **13**:22, 22*f*
  corneal inlays
    in keratophakia, **13**:54
    for presbyopia, **13**:53, 54
Alloxygen. *See* Terbutaline
Allylamines, **1**:54*t*, 65
ALMD1 (anterior limiting membrane dystrophy type 1). *See* Reis-Bücklers corneal dystrophy
ALMD2 (anterior limiting membrane dystrophy type 2). *See* Thiel-Behnke corneal dystrophy
ALMS1 gene, mutation in, cone–rod dystrophy and, **12**:233
Alocril. *See* Nedocromil
Alomide. *See* Lodoxamide
Alpha (α)-adrenergic agents, **2**:345–348, 347*f*, 347*t*
  agonists, **2**:347*t*
    direct-acting, **2**:345–346

for glaucoma, **2**:264*t*, 346–347, **10**:157, 163*t*, 169–170, 169*f*
  in children, **10**:157
  suppression of aqueous formation and, **10**:15, 169
for hyphema, **8**:368
indirect-acting, **2**:346–348, 347*f*
for postoperative elevated intraocular pressure, **10**:101
antagonists, **2**:260, 348. *See also* Alpha (α)-blockers
centrally acting, for hypertension, **1**:77*t*, 78*t*, 82
Alpha (α)-adrenergic receptors, **2**:344, 345*f*
blocking, **2**:260
  in iris–ciliary body, **2**:259, 259*t*, 260, 262–263
  signal transduction and, **2**:262–263, 262*f*, 263*f*, 264*t*
  in tear secretion, **2**:242, 242*f*
Alpha₁ (α₁)-antitrypsin, in aqueous humor, **2**:269
Alpha (α)-blockers, **2**:260, 348
  angle closure prevention and, **10**:119
  for heart failure, **1**:119
  for hypertension, **1**:77*t*, 82
    with β-blockers, **1**:77*t*, 82
  intraoperative floppy iris syndrome and, **11**:74, 154–155
  ocular effects of, **1**:301*t*
Alpha chemokines, **9**:28*t*
Alpha (α)-chymotrypsin, for ICCE, **11**:93, 214
Alpha (α)-crystallins, **2**:70, 276, **11**:11–12, 11*f*
Alpha-galactosidase, defective, **2**:213*t*
Alpha-galactosidase A gene, in Fabry disease, **12**:262
Alpha (α)-glucosidase inhibitors, **1**:199*t*, 201
Alpha (α) helix, **2**:166, 167*f*
Alpha (α)-hemolytic bacteria, endocarditis prophylaxis and, **1**:7, 8*t*
Alpha (α)-iduronidase, in mucopolysaccharidoses, **8**:305
Alpha (α)-interferon, **1**:243, **9**:29*t*
  for Behçet disease, **1**:180, **9**:195
  for cancer therapy, **1**:242*t*, 243
  for delta hepatitis, **1**:26
  for hemangiomas, **7**:64, 152
    in children, **6**:340
  for hepatitis B, **1**:281
  for hepatitis C, **1**:26
  for uveitis, **9**:115
Alpha (α)-L-iduronidase, defective, **2**:213*t*
Alpha₂ (α₂)-macroglobulin, in aqueous humor, **2**:269
Alpha (α)-mannosidase, defective, **2**:213*t*
Alpha (α)-melanocyte-stimulating hormone (α-MSH), **8**:177*t*
  in tear secretion, **2**:244
Alpha (α)-thalassemia, **1**:148
Alpha-tocopherol. *See* Vitamin E
Alpha-zone peripapillary atrophy, **10**:50
AlphaCor keratoprosthesis, **8**:432
Alphagan. *See* Brimonidine
Alport disease/syndrome, **4**:121, **6**:302
  lenticonus in, **4**:121, **11**:26
  pleiotropism in, **2**:210
  renal disease and, **12**:254
Alprazolam, ocular effects of, **1**:301*t*
Alrex. *See* Loteprednol
Alström syndrome
  cone–rod dystrophy and, **12**:233
  renal disease and, **12**:254

Altacaine. *See* Tetracaine
Altace. *See* Ramipril
Altafrin. *See* Phenylephrine
Alteplase. *See also* Tissue plasminogen activator
  for ST-segment elevation acute coronary syndrome, **1**:113
Alternate cover test (prism and cover test), **6**:74–75, 76*f*
  for intermittent exotropia evaluation, **6**:100
Alternating cross-over test, **5**:216
Alternating fixation, **6**:11
Alternating gaze deviation, periodic, in comatose patients, **5**:259
Alternating heterotropia, **6**:74
Alternating nystagmus, periodic, **5**:251*t*, 252–253, **6**:322
Alternating skew deviation, **5**:222, 222*t*
  periodic, **5**:223
Alternating suppression, **6**:51
Alternating vision contact lenses, **3**:176, 189, 189*f*
Alternative splicing, **2**:165, 168
Altitudinal defect, in glaucoma, **10**:68, 71*f*
Alu repeat sequence, **2**:148, 166
Aluminum, foreign body of, **12**:327
Alveolar nerve, posterior, **5**:60
Alveolar rhabdomyosarcoma, **4**:243, 243*f*, **6**:335, **7**:77
Alveolar vein, posterior superior, **5**:24*f*
Alzheimer disease, **1**:227, 265, 265–268
  diagnosis of, **1**:267
  etiology of, **1**:266–267
  ophthalmic considerations and, **1**:268
  treatment of, **1**:267–268
Alzheimer's Association, **1**:267
Amacrine cells, **2**:75*f*, 300, **5**:28, **12**:12, 14*f*
  differentiation of, **2**:126
Amantadine, **1**:55*t*, 66
  ocular side effects of, **1**:260
  for Parkinson disease, **1**:259
Amaryl. *See* Glimepiride
Amaurosis
  fugax, **5**:177. *See also* Monocular transient visual loss
    in antiphospholipid antibody syndrome, **1**:172
    carotid artery disease and, **5**:173, 174, 177–183, 179*f*
    in central retinal artery occlusion, **12**:139
    hypercholesterolemia and, **1**:138
  Leber congenital (congenital/infantile/childhood retinitis pigmentosa), **6**:289–291, 290*f*, **12**:229, 251–252
    gene therapy for, **9**:66
    guanylate cyclase mutations causing, **2**:296
    pleiotropism and, **2**:210
    RPE65 gene defects causing, **2**:297, **6**:290
Amber codon, **2**:148
Ambien. *See* Zolpidem
Ambient light toxicity, **12**:334. *See also* Light toxicity/photic damage/phototoxicity
AmBisome. *See* Amphotericin B
Amblyopia, **5**:116, **6**:61–69
  abnormal visual experiences and, **6**:46–48, 47*f*, 61–62
  ametropic, **6**:64
  anisometropic, **3**:116, 142, **6**:63
    refractive surgery and, **13**:178–179
    visual development affected by, **6**:47–48, 61–62
  in capillary hemangioma, **7**:151

in childhood glaucoma, 10:158
classification of, 6:62–64, 63f
compliance with therapy and, 6:66–67, 68
in congenital ptosis, 7:203
contrast sensitivity affected in, 3:113
corneal transplantation and, 6:219, 8:430, 431
in craniofacial syndromes, 6:390
diagnosis of, 6:64–65, 65f. See also Ocular motility,
    assessment of
history/presenting complaint in, 6:71
iatrogenic, 6:67–68
in infantile esotropia, 6:90
meridional, 6:64
in monofixation syndrome, 6:59
occlusion, 6:64, 67–68
    eye trauma and, 6:403
"organic," 6:64
persistent fetal vasculature (persistent hyperplastic
    primary vitreous) and, 12:308
recurrence of, 6:69
refractive errors and, 6:63, 64. See also Ametropic
    amblyopia; Anisometropic amblyopia
refractive surgery and, 13:178–181
in retinopathy of prematurity, 6:287
screening for, 6:61
stimulus deprivation, 6:64
    eye trauma and, 6:403
    visual development affected by, 6:46–47, 47f, 61–62
strabismic, 6:62–63, 63f
    visual development and, 6:48–49, 48f, 61–62
in traumatic ptosis, 7:181
treatment of, 6:65–69
    complications of, 6:67–69
    occlusion/optical degradation and, 6:66–67
    pediatric cataract surgery and, 6:65–66, 255, 259
    refractive correction and, 6:66
    unresponsiveness to therapy and, 6:68–69
Amblyopia ex anopsia. See Deprivation amblyopia
Amblyoscope testing, 6:58–59, 59f, 78, 80
Ambulatory blood pressure measurement, 1:70, 270
AMD. See Age-related macular degeneration
Amebae, 8:140, 140f
Amebic cysts, 8:140, 140f, 169
Amebic keratitis, 4:54, 84–85, 86f, 8:167–169, 168f.
    See also Acanthamoeba, keratitis/ocular infection
    caused by
Amelanotic choroidal masses, 4:266, 278, 278t
Amelanotic conjunctival nevus, 4:65, 8:236, 236f
Amelanotic melanoma, 4:69, 274f, 278, 278t
American Academy of Ophthalmology, 1:129, 139
educational material from, 1:315
on eye examination in diabetes mellitus in children,
    6:297
on fundus examination in premature infant, 6:285, 286t
on monitoring systems, 1:341
on Preferred Practice Patterns, 1:343
on preoperative assessment, 1:304
on vision loss and function, 1:220
on vision rehabilitation, 9:304
    in childhood nystagmus, 6:330
American Academy of Pediatrics
on eye examination in diabetes mellitus in children,
    6:297

on eye examination in juvenile idiopathic (chronic/
    rheumatoid) arthritis, 6:270, 271t, 9:131t
on fundus examination in premature infant, 6:285,
    286t
on immunization, 1:283, 285
American Association for Pediatric Ophthalmology and
    Strabismus, on fundus examination in premature
    infant, 6:285, 286t
American Cancer Society, 1:277
cancer screening recommendations of, 1:272t
American College of Cardiology, 1:129, 139
American College of Rheumatology (ACR), on chronic
    childhood arthritis nomenclature, 6:267–268, 269t
American Council of the Blind, 6:418t
American Diabetes Association, 1:190, 191t, 204, 12:89
American Foundation for the Blind, 6:417t
American Heart Association, 1:129, 133, 139, 289–290,
    292
American Joint Committee on Cancer (AJCC), staging
    of ocular tumors by, 4:329–352t
American Kidney Fund, 6:418t
American Printing House for the Blind, 6:417t
American Red Cross, 1:289
American Standards Institute (ANSI), on corneal
    topography standards, 8:43
Amethocaine. See Tetracaine
Ametropia, 3:113–114, 114f. See also Refractive errors
amblyopia and, 6:64
of aphakic eye, contact lenses for, 3:171–172
correction of
    in children, 3:141–142
    contact lenses for, 3:171–172
    spectacle, 3:138–140, 139f, 140f
        cylindrical lenses for, 3:139–140
        far point concept and, 3:138–139, 139–140, 139f
        spherical lenses for, 3:138–139, 139f
        vertex distance and, 3:139, 140f
overrefraction and, 3:138
Ametropic amblyopia, 6:64
Amicar. See Aminocaproic acid
Amikacin, 1:52t, 61–62, 2:368t, 375–376
for endophthalmitis, 12:354
    after cataract surgery, 11:181
Amikin. See Amikacin
Amiloride
for heart failure, 1:118
for hypertension, 1:76t, 78t
Amino acids
in aqueous humor, 2:255
disorders of metabolism of, 8:313–316, 314t. See also
    specific disorder
    corneal changes and, 8:313–316, 314t
    retinal degeneration and, 12:264–265
in tear film, 2:240
Aminocaproic acid/ε-aminocaproic acid, 2:394
for hyphema, 6:410, 8:368, 10:98
Aminocyclitols. See Aminoglycosides
Aminoglycosides, 1:44, 51–52t, 61–62, 2:372t, 375–376.
    See also specific agent
for Acanthamoeba keratitis, 8:169
ototoxicity of
    mitochondrial DNA mutations and, 2:173, 176
    peripheral vestibular dysfunction and, 5:250

ρ-Aminohippuric acid, in aqueous humor dynamics, **2**:255
Aminopenicillins, **1**:57
Amiodarone
  for arrhythmias, **1**:123*t*
  for cardioversion, **1**:125
  cornea verticillata caused by, **8**:346
  for heart failure, **1**:120
  lens changes caused by, **11**:49
  ocular effects of, **1**:128, 301*t*
  optic neuropathy caused by, **5**:154
  refractive surgery in patient taking, **13**:31, 70
Amitriptyline, for postherpetic neuralgia, **8**:121
Amlodipine
  for angina, **1**:108
  for heart failure, **1**:119
  for hypertension, **1**:77*t*, 78*t*
AMN. *See* Acute macular neuroretinopathy
Amniocentesis, **2**:228–229
  trauma from, infantile corneal opacities and, **6**:219
Amniotic fluid embolism, Purtscherlike retinopathy and, **12**:154, 155*t*
Amniotic membrane transplantation, **8**:389
  for chemical injuries, **8**:358
  for corneal edema after cataract surgery, **11**:148
  as cyanoacrylate alternative, **8**:404
  for eyelid repair, in burn patients, **7**:181
  for graft-vs-host disease, **8**:203
  for herpetic eye disease complications, **8**:117
  indications for, **8**:387*t*
  for ligneous conjunctivitis, **8**:193
  for neurotrophic keratopathy, **8**:88
  for pseudocryptophthalmos, **8**:250
  for pterygium, **8**:394
  for squamous cell carcinoma of conjunctiva, **8**:232
  for Stevens-Johnson syndrome, **8**:197
Amorphous corneal dystrophy, posterior, **8**:268*t*, 270*t*, 288–289, 288*f*
  genetics of, **8**:269*t*, 288
Amoxicillin, **1**:46*t*, 57, **2**:370
  with clavulanic acid, **1**:46*t*, 59
  for endocarditis prophylaxis, **1**:8*t*
  for Lyme disease, **9**:253*t*
Amoxil. *See* Amoxicillin
Amphotec. *See* Amphotericin B
Amphotericin B, **1**:20, 40, 54*t*, 65, **2**:379–380, 379*t*
  for coccidioidomycosis, **9**:280
  for fungal endogenous endophthalmitis
    Aspergillus/mold, **9**:278, **12**:204
    Candida/yeast, **9**:275, **12**:203
  for fungal keratitis, **8**:166
Ampicillin, **1**:46*t*, 57, **2**:368*t*, 370
  for endocarditis prophylaxis, **1**:8*t*
  Haemophilus influenzae resistance and, **1**:9
  intravenous administration of, **2**:329
  with sulbactam, **1**:46*t*, 59
Amplifying cells, transient, in corneal epithelium, **2**:43
Amplitude
  of accommodation, **3**:117, **11**:19–20
    aging affecting, **3**:142, 143*t*, **11**:19–20, **13**:149
    binocular, **3**:145
    cycloplegic refraction and, **3**:137

measurement of in bifocal add determination, **3**:145–147
  premature loss of (accommodative insufficiency), **3**:142–143
  refractive procedures for improving, **13**:149–161
  fusional, **6**:41, 41*t*
  of light wave, **3**:3–4, 4*f*
Ampulla, **7**:245, 245*f*
Ampullectomy, **7**:271
Amsler grid testing, **5**:98–99
  in age-related macular degeneration, **12**:60, 64
  in central visual field assessment, **3**:292, 293
  in chloroquine/hydroxychloroquine toxicity screening, **12**:267
  for choroidal rupture self-testing, **12**:321
  in low vision evaluation, **5**:98–99
AMT. *See* Amniotic membrane transplantation
Amyloid AA, **8**:316, 319
Amyloid AL, **4**:212, **8**:316
Amyloid-β42, in Alzheimer disease, **1**:266
Amyloid-β peptide immunization, for Alzheimer disease, **1**:268
Amyloid degeneration, **8**:341. *See also* Amyloidosis/ amyloid deposits
  polymorphic, **8**:338, 339*f*
Amyloid plaques, in Alzheimer disease, **1**:266
Amyloid precursor protein (APP), in Alzheimer disease, **1**:266
Amyloid SAA, **8**:316
Amyloidosis/amyloid deposits, **1**:153, **4**:139–140, 140*f*, 212, **8**:316–319, 317*t*, 318*f*, **12**:312–313, 313*f*
  conjunctival, **4**:58–59, 60*f*, **8**:317*t*, 318, 318*f*
  corneal, **8**:317*t*, 318–319, 318*f*
    in Avellino dystrophy, **4**:97, 99*f*
    in gelatinous droplike dystrophy, **8**:274–275, 275*f*, 317*t*, 318, 318*f*
    in keratoconus, **4**:91
    in lattice dystrophy, **4**:96–97, 99*f*, **8**:278, 280
  in eyelid, **4**:211–212, 212*f*, 213*t*
  familial
    Finnish-type (amyloidosis IV/gelsolin-type lattice corneal dystrophy), **4**:212, **8**:268*t*, 270*t*, 280, 280*f*, 317*t*, 319
      genetics of, **4**:212, **8**:269*t*, 280, 317*t*
    primary of cornea (subepithelial amyloidosis/ gelatinous droplike dystrophy), **8**:268*t*, 270*t*, 274–275, 275*f*, 317*t*, 318, 318*f*
      genetics of, **8**:269*t*, 274, 317*t*
    vitreous opacification in, **12**:312–313, 313*f*
  orbital, **4**:235
  primary localized, **8**:317*t*, 318–319, 318*f*
  primary systemic, **8**:317*t*, 319
  secondary localized, **8**:317*t*, 319, 341
  secondary systemic, **8**:317*t*, 319
  vitreous involvement in, **4**:139–140, 140*f*, 141*f*, **12**:312–313, 313*f*
ANA. *See* Antinuclear (antineutrophil) antibodies
Ana-Kit, **1**:296
Anabolism, glucose, **1**:190
Anaerobes, as normal ocular flora, **8**:97*t*
Anaerobic glycolysis, in glucose/carbohydrate metabolism
  in cornea, **2**:248–249
  in lens, **2**:278, **11**:13–15, 14*f*

Anakinra, 1:186, 9:108*t*, 115
  for uveitis, 9:108*t*, 115
Analgesics. *See also specific agent*
  ocular effects of, 1:301*t*
  rebound headache and, 5:298
Anamnestic immune response, 9:43–44
Anaphase lag, mosaicism caused by, 2:203
Anaphylactic hypersensitivity (immediate/type I)
    reactions, 8:178*f*, 179–180, 179*t*, 9:44, 44*t*, 54–55.
    See also Allergic reactions/allergies; Anaphylaxis
  allergic conjunctivitis and, 8:185, 9:55
  fluorescein angiography and, 12:24
  topical medications/substances and, 8:183, 184, 184*f*
Anaphylactoid reactions, 1:295
  fluorescein angiography and, 12:24
  penicillin causing, 2:369
Anaphylatoxins, 9:24
Anaphylaxis, 1:295–296, 8:178*f*, 179–180, 179*t*, 9:44,
    44*t*, 55. *See also* Anaphylactic hypersensitivity
    (immediate/type I) reaction
  local anesthetics causing, 1:298
  penicillin allergy causing, 2:369
  slow-reacting substance of, 8:179*t*
Anaplasmosis, human granulocytic (human
    granulocytic ehrlichiosis), 1:15
  Lyme disease coinfection and, 9:254
Anaplastic carcinoma, of thyroid gland, 1:214
Anaprox. *See* Naproxen
Anatomical reattachment surgery, for retinal
    detachment, 12:290–291
ANCA. *See* Antinuclear (antineutrophil) antibodies
ANCA-associated granulomatosis vasculitis (Wegener
    granulomatosis) , 1:177*t*, 179, 7:32, 56–58, 57*f*,
    9:145–146, 146*f*
  choroidal perfusion abnormalities and, 12:179, 180*f*
  eyelid manifestations of, 4:213*t*
  scleritis/retinal vasculitis and, 7:56, 9:145, 146*f*
Ancef. *See* Cefazolin
ANCHOR (Anti-VEGF Antibody for the
    Treatment of Predominantly Classic Choroidal
    Neovascularization in AMD) study, 12:73–74, 75,
    75*f*
Ancobon. *See* Flucytosine
Ancotil. *See* Flucytosine
Ancrod, for stroke, 1:94
Ancylostoma caninum (dog hookworm), diffuse
    unilateral subacute neuroretinitis caused by, 9:239,
    12:210
Anderson-Kestenbaum procedure, 5:258, 6:328–329,
    329*t*
Androgens, in tear secretion/Sjögren syndrome, 2:244,
    8:63–64
Anemia, 1:148–150
  aplastic
    carbonic anhydrase inhibitors causing, 2:354,
        10:171
    chloramphenicol causing, 1:63, 2:375
  of chronic disease, 1:148
    iron deficiency differentiated from, 1:147
  diabetic retinopathy and, 12:94
  folic acid deficiency causing, 1:149
  hemolytic, 1:149–150
    autoimmune, 1:150

iron deficiency, 1:147, 148
  in older patients, 1:232
  pernicious, 1:149
  sickle cell. *See* Sickle cell disease
  sideroblastic, 1:149
  vitamin B$_{12}$ deficiency causing, 1:149, 232
Anestacaine. *See* Lidocaine
Anesthesia, corneal
  congenital, 8:264–265
  herpes simplex epithelial keratitis and, 8:110
  neurotrophic keratopathy/persistent corneal defects
      and, 8:86, 87
Anesthesia (anesthetics)
  for blepharoplasty, 7:224
  for cataract surgery, 11:98–102, 99*f*, 100*f*, 101*f*
  for corneal transplantation in children, 8:430
  for dacryocystorhinostomy, 7:268
  ERG affected by, 12:40
  examination under. *See* Examination, ophthalmic,
      under anesthesia
  for extraocular muscle surgery, 6:160–162
  general
    balanced, 1:310
    for cataract surgery, 11:101
      in arthritis, 11:188
    for extraocular muscle surgery, 6:161
  for intraocular pressure measurement in infants and
      children, 10:151
  for lacrimal probing, 7:251
  local (topical/regional), 1:311–312, 2:386–390, 387*t*
    abuse of, 8:90, 91*f*, 359
    adverse reactions to, 1:298–299, 311–312,
        8:359–361, 359*t*, 361*f*
      allergic, 1:298, 311
      toxic overdose, 1:298–299, 311, 312
    for anterior segment surgery, 2:389–390
    for blepharoplasty, 7:224
    for cataract surgery, 11:99–100
    for extraocular muscle surgery, 6:160–161
    for foreign-body removal in children, 6:5
    keratoconjunctivitis caused by, 8:359, 359*t*
    maximum safe dose of, 1:298*t*
    in patients taking cholinesterase inhibitors, 2:340
    for phakic IOL insertion, 13:129
    after surface ablation, 13:86
    malignant hyperthermia caused by, 1:312–313, 313*t*,
        6:161–162
  for perforating injury repair, 8:376
  peribulbar, for cataract surgery, 11:99, 100*f*
  for phakic IOL insertion, 13:129
  for photocoagulation, 12:339
  for refractive lens exchange/clear lens extraction,
      13:139
  retrobulbar
    adverse reactions to, 1:298–299, 311
    for cataract surgery, 11:98–99, 99*f*
      hemorrhage and, 11:176, 189
    for extraocular muscle surgery, 6:160–161
    strabismus after, 6:143
  tear production affected by, 8:66*t*
Aneuploidy, 2:148. *See also specific disorder*
  of autosomes, 2:199–203
  of sex chromosomes, 2:199

Aneurysmal bone cyst, orbital involvement and, **6**:343
Aneurysmal telangiectasia (type 1 parafoveal retinal
   telangiectasia), **12**:145*f*, 146
Aneurysms
   basilar artery, **5**:350, 350*f*
   berry (saccular), **1**:97, **5**:350
   cerebral, **5**:349–353, 350*f*, 351*f*, 352*f*
      neuroimaging in diagnosis of, **5**:77, 79*f*, 80, 82*t*
      ruptured, **5**:351, 351*f*
         intracranial hemorrhage caused by, **1**:97, 98,
            5:351
         third nerve (oculomotor) palsy and, **5**:228, 228*f*,
            273, 351
            aberrant regeneration and, **5**:232
            divisional palsy and, **5**:231
            pupil-involving palsy and, **5**:229, 229*f*, 273, 351
            pupil-sparing palsy and, **5**:230
            in younger patients, **5**:231
   cranial nerve III (oculomotor) affected by, **2**:99
   giant, **5**:350, 352
   internal carotid, **5**:164, 350, 350*f*, 351
      chiasmal syndromes caused by, **5**:164
      third nerve (oculomotor) palsy and, **5**:229, 273, 351
   intracavernous carotid, **5**:351
   Leber miliary, **12**:146
   neuroimaging in evaluation of, **5**:82*t*
   ophthalmic artery, **5**:350–351
   retinal arterial
      idiopathic vasculitis and neuroretinitis and
         (IRVAN), **12**:141
      macroaneurysms, **12**:147–148, 147*f*
         age-related macular degeneration differentiated
            from, **12**:68–69, 69*f*
      microaneurysms, **4**:160–162, 162*f*, 164
         in diabetes mellitus
            in children, **6**:297
            in diabetic macular ischemia, **12**:103
            in nonproliferative diabetic retinopathy, **4**:166,
               12:104, 104*f*
Angelman syndrome, imprinting abnormalities causing,
   2:154, 169
Angiitis
   allergic granulomatosis and (Churg-Strauss
      syndrome), **1**:177*t*, 179–180
   cutaneous leukocytoclastic, **1**:177*t*
Angina pectoris, **1**:101. *See also* Ischemic heart disease
   ECG changes in, **1**:104
   heart failure and, **1**:114
   stable, **1**:101
      hypertension management and, **1**:84
      management of, **1**:108–110, 109*t*
   unstable, **1**:101–102
      hypertension management and, **1**:84
   variant (Prinzmetal), **1**:101
Angioedema, **8**:196*t*
Angiofibromas, facial, in tuberous sclerosis, **5**:341, 342*f*,
   6:372, 372*f*
Angiogenesis
   in age-related macular degeneration/choroidal
      neovascularization, **12**:72
   in retinopathy of prematurity, **12**:162
   vitreous as inhibitor of, **2**:287
Angiogenesis inhibitors. *See* Antiangiogenic agents

Angiographic cystoid macular edema, **12**:143
   after cataract surgery, **11**:182
Angiography/arteriography
   in arterial dissection, **5**:354
   in carotid stenosis, **5**:180
   in cerebral aneurysm, **5**:351–352
   in cerebral ischemia/stroke, **1**:93
   computed tomographic, **5**:69, 78–80
      advantages/disadvantages/contraindications and,
         5:86*t*
      in aneurysm detection, **5**:229, 229*f*
      in carotid artery evaluation, **5**:180
      in cerebral aneurysm, **5**:352
      in cerebral ischemia/stroke, **1**:93
      in ischemic heart disease, **1**:107
      in orbital evaluation, **7**:31
   conventional/catheter/contrast, **5**:77, 79*f*
      in aneurysm detection, **5**:229
      in cerebral ischemia/stroke, **1**:93
   coronary, **1**:106, 107
   fluorescein. *See* Fluorescein angiography
   indocyanine green. *See* Indocyanine green angiography
   magnetic resonance, **5**:69, 77–78, 79*f*
      advantages/disadvantages/contraindications and,
         5:86–88, 86*t*
      in aneurysm detection, **5**:229
      in carotid evaluation, **5**:180
      in cerebral aneurysm, **5**:352, 352*f*
      in cerebral ischemia/stroke, **1**:93
      in orbital evaluation, **7**:31
   in orbital evaluation, **7**:31
   retinal, **12**:20–26, 23*f*, 24*f*. *See also* Fluorescein
      angiography; Indocyanine green angiography
   in subarachnoid hemorrhage, **1**:98
Angioid streaks, **12**:84–85, 84*f*
   in pseudoxanthoma elasticum, **12**:84, 84*f*
   in sickle cell hemoglobinopathies, **12**:84, 120
Angiokeratoma corporis diffusum (Fabry disease),
   2:213*t*, **6**:399, 400*t*, **8**:310, 311, **12**:262–263, 264*f*
   cataract and, **6**:247*t*
   ocular findings in carriers of, **2**:222*t*
   plasma infusions in management of, **2**:231
   retinal degeneration and, **12**:262–263, 264*f*
Angiomas (angiomatosis). *See also* Hemangiomas
   (hemangiomatosis)
   cerebrofacial/encephalofacial/encephalotrigeminal.
      See Sturge-Weber syndrome
   choroidal, **6**:377, 377*f*
   racemose (Wyburn-Mason syndrome), **4**:296, 297*f*,
      5:339*t*, 345, 345*f*, **6**:342, 364*t*, 381, 381*f*, **12**:151
   retinal (retinae). *See* Retinal angiomatosis
   venous, **1**:97–98
Angiomatous tumors, **4**:291–296, 297*f*. *See also specific
   type and* Angiomas
Angioplasty, coronary
   for angina, **1**:108–110
   for ST-segment elevation acute coronary syndrome,
      1:112–113
   troponin levels in determining need for, **1**:105
Angiopoietin 1, nevus flammeus and, **8**:241
Angiotensin II receptor blockers
   for heart failure, **1**:118
   for hypertension, **1**:76*t*, 78*t*, 79*t*, 81

Angiotensin-converting enzyme (ACE), in sarcoidosis, 5:335, 7:32
Angiotensin-converting enzyme (ACE) inhibitors
  for heart failure, 1:118
  for hypertension, 1:76t, 78t, 79t, 81
  for ischemic heart disease, 1:109t
    non–ST-segment elevation acute coronary syndrome, 1:111
  ocular effects of, 1:129
  in perioperative setting, 1:305
Angle
  alpha (α), 3:106, 107f
  anterior chamber. See Anterior chamber angle
  basic principles of, 3:34–35, 35f
  Brewster, 3:12, 12f
  critical, 3:46–48, 48f
  of deviation, prisms producing, 3:84–85, 84f
    prism diopter and, 3:85, 85f, 86f
  of incidence, 3:12f, 43f, 44, 44f, 45f
    critical angle and, 3:46–48, 48f
    reflection and, 3:12, 12f
  kappa (κ) (positive and negative), 3:106, 107f, 236, 6:77, 78f
    in retinopathy of prematurity, 6:287, 287f
  of reflection, 3:43f, 44, 44f
  of refraction/transmission, 3:44, 45t
    critical angle and, 3:47–48, 48f
    wavelength and, 3:50, 51f
  in uveitis, 9:86t
Angle alpha (α), 3:106, 107f
Angle closure/angle-closure glaucoma, 10:4, 5t, 6f, 7t, 109–137. See also Glaucoma
  acute, 10:5t, 109, 114–116, 115f
  age and, 10:10, 113
  anisocoria and, 5:270
  aphakic, 10:124
    in children, 10:148–149
  aqueous misdirection and (malignant/ciliary block glaucoma), 10:30, 131–133, 132f
    cataract surgery and, 10:131, 11:153, 157–158
  central retinal vein occlusion and, 10:135, 12:129, 130
    neovascularization and, 10:127
  childhood (congenital/infantile/juvenile), 10:5t, 141t
    with iris bombé, 6:239–240
    topiramate causing, 6:239
  chronic, 10:5t, 109, 117–118
  classification of, 10:4, 5t, 6f, 7t
  combined-mechanism glaucoma and, 10:8
  cornea plana and, 8:255
  creeping, 10:117
  drug-induced, 10:136–137, 137f
  ectopia lentis and, 10:90t, 112, 121–122, 122f, 123f, 123t
  epithelial and fibrous ingrowth and, 10:133–134, 134f
  family history and, 10:10, 114
  flat anterior chamber and, 10:10, 30, 113, 136
    aqueous misdirection and, 10:30, 131, 132, 132f
  gender and, 10:10, 114
  genetic/hereditary factors in, 10:10
  gonioscopic identification of, 10:35, 73
  inflammatory, 10:130–131, 130f, 131f
  intermittent (subacute), 10:5t, 117
  iridocorneal endothelial (ICE) syndrome and, 4:105, 10:128–130, 128f, 129f

iris bombé and, 9:89, 296, 10:30, 130, 130f
  in children, 6:239–240
iris-induced, 6:238, 10:112, 142, 147
lens-induced, 10:90, 90t, 112, 120–124, 121f, 122f, 123f, 123t
management of
  medical, 10:160, 175
  surgical, 10:200–204, 201f
    cataract extraction, 10:204
    chamber deepening/goniosynechialysis, 10:204
    incisional procedures, 10:204. See also Incisional surgery
    laser gonioplasty/peripheral iridoplasty, 10:203
    laser iridotomy, 10:201, 201f, 202–203
    peripheral (surgical) iridectomy, 10:201, 201f, 204
microcornea and, 8:253
microspherophakia and, 10:122, 123f, 11:29
nanophthalmos and, 4:112, 113, 8:251, 252, 10:135–136
occludable/narrow chamber angle and, 10:118–119
ocular biometrics and, 10:113
ocular inflammation and, 10:130–131, 130f, 131f
in open-angle glaucoma, 10:73
outflow obstruction mechanisms in, 10:7t
pain caused by, 5:300
pars planitis and, 9:138
pathogenesis and pathophysiology of, 10:110–112, 111f, 111t
persistent fetal vasculature (persistent hyperplastic primary vitreous) and, 6:280, 10:136, 12:308
phacomorphic, 10:90t, 112, 120–121, 121f, 122f, 11:63, 64f
plateau iris and, 10:5t, 7t, 112, 119–120, 120f
primary, 10:5t, 10, 109, 110, 112–119
  acute, 10:114–116, 115f
  chronic, 10:117–118
  epidemiology of, 10:10
  with pupillary block, 10:5t, 7t, 110–111, 111f
    iridotomy/iridectomy for, 10:111, 201, 201f, 202–203, 204
  risk factors for, 10:112–114
  subacute/intermittent, 10:117
pseudophakic, 10:124
with pupillary block, 10:5t, 7t, 110–111, 111f, 120–124, 121f, 122f, 123f, 123t
  iridotomy/iridectomy for, 10:111, 201, 201f, 202–203, 204
without pupillary block, 10:5t, 7t, 111, 124–137
  surgery for, 10:201
race and, 10:10, 109, 112–113
refraction/refractive errors and, 10:10, 27, 114
retinal detachment and, 10:133
retinal surgery and, 10:135
retinal vascular disease and, 10:135
retinopathy of prematurity and, 12:163
risk factors for, 10:112–114
in sarcoidosis, 9:175
secondary, 10:5t, 110. See also specific cause
  in infants and children, 10:141t
  with pupillary block, 10:5t, 7t, 120–124
    iridotomy/iridectomy for, 10:201, 201f, 202–203, 204

microspherophakia and, **11**:29
phacomorphic glaucoma and, **11**:63, 64*f*
without pupillary block, **10**:5*t*, 7*t*, 111, 124–137
surgery for, **10**:201
uveitic, **9**:89, 295, 296, **10**:130*f*, 131
subacute/intermittent, **10**:5*t*, 117
trauma and, **4**:18, **10**:135
fibrous ingrowth and, **10**:134, 134*f*
tumors causing, **10**:93, 130
uveal effusions and, **10**:131, 133
uveitis and, **9**:89, 295, 296, **10**:130*f*, 131
Angle kappa (κ) (positive and negative), **3**:106, 107*f*,
236, **6**:77, 78*f*
in retinopathy of prematurity, **6**:287, 287*f*
Angle recession, traumatic, **4**:18, 19*f*, 109
glaucoma and, **4**:18, 109, **10**:38–39, 38*f*, 39*f*, 100–101,
100*f*
Angle-supported intraocular lenses, **13**:127*t*, 129
complications of, **13**:134–135
Angular artery, **5**:14*f*, 15*f*, 16, **7**:246
eyelids supplied by, **2**:29, **7**:143
orbit supplied by, **2**:37*f*
Angular magnification, **3**:36. *See also* Magnification;
Transverse magnification
Angular vein, **2**:40*f*, **5**:25, 25*f*, 26, **7**:246
eyelids drained by, **7**:143
Anhedonia, **1**:247
Anhidrosis, in Horner syndrome, **5**:266
Anhidrotic ectodermal dysplasia, **8**:75
Anidulafungin, **1**:65
Animal bites, eyelid injuries caused by, **7**:181
Aniridia, **2**:205–207, **4**:188, **6**:223–224, 224*f*, **10**:142,
147, **11**:29–30, 29*f*
cataract and, **6**:251*f*, **11**:29*f*, 30
surgery for removal of, **11**:200
glaucoma and (iris-induced angle closure), **10**:112,
142, 147
pediatric, **6**:238, **10**:142, 147
Axenfeld-Rieger syndrome differentiated from,
10:146*t*
mutation rate of, **2**:207
nystagmus and, **6**:223
pupil irregularity and, **5**:263
short arm 11 deletion syndrome/*PAX6* gene
mutations and, **2**:141, 166, 205, 206, 216, **4**:188,
6:223–224, **10**:142, **11**:29
Wilms tumor and, **4**:188, **6**:224, **10**:147, **11**:29
Aniseikonia, **3**:116
anisometropia correction causing, **3**:116
contact lenses for, **3**:171
contact lenses for management of, **3**:171–172
intraocular lenses and, **3**:223
meridional (meridional magnification). *See also*
Distortion
adaptation to distortion and, **3**:140, 320–321
astigmatic spectacle lenses causing, **3**:140, 310–311,
310*f*
avoidance of with contact lenses, **3**:174–176,
316–317
blurred retinal images and, **3**:312, 312*f*
conventional analysis of, **3**:311, 312*f*
minimizing, **3**:316–320, 318*f*, 319*f*

sources of, **3**:310–311, 310*f*
relative contributions from, **3**:315, 315*f*
uncorrected/inappropriately corrected astigmatism
and, **3**:314
monocular aphakia and, **3**:171–172
Anisocoria, **5**:264–273, 271*f*, 272*f*, 278, **6**:229–230. *See
also specific cause*
Adie tonic pupil and, **5**:265*f*, 270–271, 271*f*, 272*f*,
6:229
cocaine in testing for, **5**:264, 265*f*, 266, 267
equal in dim and bright light, **5**:264, 265*f*
flowchart for evaluation of, **5**:265*f*
greater in bright light, **5**:265*f*, 269–273, 271*f*, 272*f*
greater in dim light, **5**:264–269, 265*f*, 267*f*, 268*f*, 269*f*
history in, **5**:261
in Horner syndrome, **5**:265*f*, 266–269, 267*f*, 268*f*,
269*f*, **6**:230
iris disorders and, **5**:265*f*
mechanical, **5**:266
pharmacologic, **5**:266, 270
physiologic (simple/essential), **5**:264, 265*f*, **6**:229
posterior synechiae causing, **5**:266
third nerve (oculomotor) palsy in, **5**:265*f*, 271–273
Anisohyperopia, amblyopia in conjunction with, **3**:142
Anisometropia, **3**:116
amblyopia caused by. *See* Anisometropic amblyopia
aniseikonia caused by correction of, **3**:116
contact lenses for, **3**:171
anisophoria caused by correction of, **3**:116, 152–153.
See also Anisophoria, induced
asymmetric lens-induced myopia causing, **11**:70
in infants and children, **3**:116, 142, **6**:47–48, 61–62, 63
after penetrating keratoplasty, refractive surgery for,
13:169
prismatic effect of lenses in, **3**:87, 151, 152*f*, 153*f*
second-eye cataract surgery for, **11**:73
Anisometropic amblyopia, **3**:116, 142, **6**:63
refractive surgery and, **13**:178–179
visual development affected by, **6**:47–48, 61–62
Anisomyopia, amblyopia in conjunction with, **3**:142
Anisophoria, induced (anisometropia correction),
3:116, 152–153
calculating, **3**:153–154, 154*f*
compensating for, **3**:152–156, 154*f*, 155*f*, 156*f*
Ankyloblepharon, **6**:176, 176*f*, **7**:147, 148*f*, **8**:249, 249*f*
filiforme adnatum, **6**:176, 176*f*
Ankylosing spondylitis, **1**:163–164, **9**:119*f*, 121
cataract surgery in patients with, **11**:188, 189*f*
glaucoma and, **9**:296
HLA in, **1**:163–164, **9**:72, 121
juvenile, **1**:166, **6**:271
ANNA-1 (anti-Hu) antibody, paraneoplastic-induced
saccadic intrusions and, **5**:256
ANNA-2 (anti-Ri) antibody, paraneoplastic-induced
saccadic intrusions and, **5**:256
Annular (concentric) bifocal contact lenses, **3**:189, 189*f*
Annular gap, **12**:8
Annular keratopathy, traumatic, **8**:363
Annular zones, in multifocal intraocular lenses, **3**:227,
227*f*
Annulus of Zinn, **2**:10, 16*f*, 17*f*, 18, 19*t*, 91, **5**:10*f*, 31,
7:11, 12*f*

Anomalies, congenital. *See specific type and* Congenital anomalies

Anomaloscope, red-green color defects tested with, **12**:47, 50

Anomalous retinal correspondence, **6**:39, 51*f*, 52–53, 53*f*
  harmonious, **6**:55
  testing in, **6**:52, 53–59
  unharmonious, **6**:55

Anomalous trichromatism, **12**:213, 213–214

Anophthalmia, **7**:33

Anophthalmic ectropion, **7**:124–125

Anophthalmic ptosis, **7**:125

Anophthalmic socket, **7**:117–127. *See also specific aspect*
  complications and treatment of, **7**:122–125, 122*f*, 123*f*
  contracted, **7**:124, 124*f*
  enucleation and, **7**:117, 117–119
  evisceration and, **7**:117, 119–120
  exenteration and, **7**:117, 126–127, 126*f*
  implants and, **7**:119, 121–122, 121*f*

Ansa subclavia, **5**:63

Ansaid. *See* Flurbiprofen

ANSI (American Standards Institute), on corneal topography standards, **8**:43

Anspor. *See* Cephradine

Antagonist (drug), **2**:332

Antagonist (muscle), **6**:34

Antazoline, **2**:364

Antazoline/naphazoline, **2**:364, 365*t*

Anterior banded zone, of Descemet membrane, **2**:45, 46*f*, 251

Anterior basement membrane dystrophy. *See* Epithelial/subepithelial dystrophies, basement membrane

Anterior border/pigmented layer, of iris, **2**:58, 60*f*, **4**:185, 186*f*

Anterior capsule, management of in pediatric cataract surgery, **6**:255, 256*f*

Anterior capsule fibrosis and phimosis, **11**:171
  Nd:YAG laser capsulotomy for, **11**:171, 171–175, 172*f*, 199. *See also* Nd:YAG laser therapy, capsulotomy

Anterior capsule opacity, **11**:169, 170

Anterior capsulotomy. *See* Capsulotomy, anterior

Anterior cerebral artery, **2**:93, **5**:20–21
  cranial nerve relationship and, **5**:52*f*

Anterior chamber, **2**:41–42, 41*f*, 50–52, 51*f*, 52*f*. *See also* Anterior chamber angle; Anterior segment
  blunt trauma to, **10**:38–39, 38*f*, 39*f*, 96
  congenital anomalies of, **4**:102–103, 103*f*, 104*f*. *See also* Anterior segment, dysgenesis of
  degenerations of, **4**:104–109, 110*f*
  depth of, **2**:50, **4**:101
    angle closure and, **10**:10, 30, 113
    in IOL power determination/selection, **3**:217, 218, 218*f*, **11**:84. *See also* Estimated lens position
    phakic IOL implantation and, **13**:129
    refractive lens exchange/clear lens extraction and, **13**:139–140
  development of, **2**:135–136, 136*f*, **6**:169–170
  disorders of, **4**:101–109, 110*f*. *See also specific type*
  flat or shallow
    angle closure/angle-closure glaucoma and, **10**:10, 30, 113, 136
    aqueous misdirection and, **10**:30, 131, 132, 132*f*

cataract surgery and, **11**:152–154
  angle-closure glaucoma and, **10**:131, 136
  intraoperative complications and, **11**:152–153
  posterior fluid misdirection and, **11**:152–153
  postoperative complications and, **11**:153–154
  preoperative considerations/IOL power determination and, **11**:79, 84
glaucoma drainage device implantation and, **10**:207, 208*t*
penetrating keratoplasty and, **8**:421
refractive surgery and, **13**:35–36
gonioscopy/evaluation of, **10**:30, 30*f*, 31*f*, 31*t*, 32–40, 109
  assessment/documentation systems for, **10**:34–40, 36*f*, 37*f*, 38*f*, 39*f*
  before cataract surgery, **11**:79
  in glaucoma, **10**:30, 30*f*, 31*f*, 31*t*, 32–40, 109
immune response in, **9**:58*t*, 59–63
  corneal allograft immunity and, **9**:65
Onchocerca volvulus microfilariae in, **9**:242
in persistent fetal vasculature, **12**:308
phacoemulsification in, **11**:119
pigment dispersion affecting, **4**:109, 109*f*, 110*f*
topography of, **2**:41–42, 41*f*, **4**:101–102, 101*f*, 102*f*
in uveitis, **9**:78*t*, 79, 85–89, 86*f*, 86*t*, 87*f*, 88*t*. *See also* Anterior uveitis
vitreous prolapse in, **11**:162

Anterior chamber angle, **2**:41*f*, 49*f*, 50, 51*f*, 52*f*, 53*f*, **4**:101–102, 102*f*. *See also* Anterior chamber
  blood vessels in, **10**:37, 37*f*
  development of, **2**:135–136, 136*f*
    abnormalities of, glaucoma and, **10**:7*t*
  in glaucoma, **10**:30, 109. *See also* Angle closure/angle-closure glaucoma
  gonioscopy of, **4**:101–102, 102*f*, **10**:30, 30*f*, 31*f*, 31*t*, 32–40, 109
  in infant, **6**:236, 237*f*
  neovascularization of, **10**:30–31, 37, 37*f*, 124–128, 125*f*, 125*t*, 126*f*, 127*f*. *See also* Neovascular glaucoma
    in diabetes mellitus, **12**:108–109
  normal, **10**:30*f*, 31*f*
    in infants and children, **10**:151–152
  occludable/narrow, **10**:30, 31*f*, 31*t*, 118–119
  pigmentation in, in exfoliation syndrome/pseudoexfoliation, **10**:38, 86, 86*f*, 87*f*
  traumatic recession of, **4**:18, 19*f*, 109
    glaucoma and, **4**:18, 109, **10**:38–39, 38*f*, 39*f*, 100–101, 100*f*
  in uveitis, **9**:86*t*

Anterior chamber–associated immune deviation (ACAID), **9**:62
  corneal graft tolerance and, **8**:408
  immune privilege and, **9**:62
    corneal allograft immunity and, **9**:65

Anterior chamber cleavage syndrome (anterior segment dysgenesis), **4**:81–82, 81*f*, 102–103, 103*f*, 104*f*, **6**:212–214, 213*f*, **8**:255–263. *See also specific type and* Neurocristopathy
  glaucoma and, **6**:238, **10**:7*t*
  Peters anomaly and, **11**:27–28. *See also* Peters anomaly

Anterior chamber intraocular lenses. *See* Intraocular lenses
Anterior chamber/aqueous paracentesis
  in acute retinal necrosis, **9**:201
  in coccidioidomycosis, **9**:280
  in cysticercosis, **9**:238
  in endogenous endophthalmitis, **9**:272–273
  in uveitis, **9**:96–97
Anterior chamber tube shunt to an encircling band (ACTSEB), **10**:205
Anterior chiasmal syndrome, **5**:159–161, 160*f*
Anterior choroidal artery, **5**:19–20, 20*f*
Anterior ciliary arteries, **2**:21, 34, 36–38, 38, 38*f*, 39*f*, 62, 64, **5**:14*f*, 16–18, **6**:16–18
  anterior segment ischemia after strabismus surgery and, **6**:158–159
  development of, **2**:132
Anterior ciliary sclerotomy, for presbyopia, **13**:158
Anterior clinoid process, **2**:11*f*, **5**:7*f*, 9*f*, 7:7*f*
Anterior collateral vein, **5**:24*f*
Anterior communicating artery, **2**:93, **5**:20
  aneurysm of, **5**:350*f*, 351
  cranial nerve relationship and, **5**:52*f*
Anterior cortical gel, **12**:7
Anterior cranial fossa, **5**:6*f*, 7, 11*f*, **7**:7*f*
Anterior crocodile shagreen (mosaic degeneration), **8**:337
Anterior cyclitis, **9**:78*t*
Anterior ethmoidal artery, **5**:13*f*, 14*f*, 15–16, 18
Anterior ethmoidal foramen, **5**:12
Anterior facial vein, **5**:25*f*
Anterior focal length (AFL), **3**:78
Anterior focal plane, **3**:69, 70*f*
Anterior (primary) focal point, **3**:69, 70*f*
Anterior inferior cerebellar artery, **2**:104, **5**:21, 22*f*
  cranial nerve relationship and, **5**:52*f*
Anterior lacrimal crest, **2**:5, 6*f*, 27
Anterior lamella, **2**:25*f*
Anterior lenticonus/lentiglobus, **4**:121, **11**:26
Anterior limiting membrane dystrophy type 1. *See* Reis-Bücklers corneal dystrophy
Anterior limiting membrane dystrophy type 2. *See* Thiel-Behnke corneal dystrophy
Anterior megalophthalmos, **6**:211
Anterior microphthalmos, **8**:253
Anterior optic neuropathy
  CMV infection causing, **5**:359
  ischemic, **5**:125–129, 126*t*
    arteritic, **5**:125, 125–127, 126*f*, 126*t*, 319
    nonarteritic, **5**:125, 126*f*, 126*t*, 127–129, 128*f*
  with optic disc edema, **5**:116–132
  without optic disc edema, **5**:133–142
Anterior orbitotomy. *See also* Orbitotomy
  incisions for, **7**:108, 108*f*
Anterior pigmented layer. *See* Anterior border/pigmented layer
Anterior pituitary hormones, **1**:214
Anterior polar cataract (APC), **6**:247, 247*t*, 248*f*, 250*t*, **11**:30–31, 32*f*
Anterior pole, **11**:5, 6*f*
Anterior principal plane, **3**:75, 75*f*, 76, 77*f*
Anterior principal point, **3**:75
Anterior pupillary membrane, **11**:25, 25*f*

Anterior segment. *See also* specific structure and under Anterior chamber
  in coccidioidomycosis, **9**:279, 280
  development of, **8**:4
  disorders of
    cataract surgery complications causing, **11**:151–162. *See also* specific type
    developmental anomalies, **8**:249–253. *See also* Anterior segment, dysgenesis of
    in infants and children, **6**:211–221
    Th1 delayed hypersensitivity and, **9**:50*t*
    toxic keratoconjunctivitis from medications and, **8**:359–361, 359*t*, 361*f*
    traumatic, **8**:351–385. *See also* Anterior segment, trauma to
  dysgenesis of (anterior chamber cleavage syndrome), **4**:81–82, 81*f*, 102–103, 103*f*, 104*f*, **6**:212–214, 213*f*, **8**:255–263. *See also* specific type and Neurocristopathy
    glaucoma and, **6**:238, **10**:7*t*
    Peters anomaly and, **11**:27–28. *See also* Peters anomaly
  examination of. *See also* Slit-lamp biomicroscopy/examination
    fluorescein angiography in, **8**:33
    imaging in, **8**:33–35, 33*f*, 34*f*, 35*f*
    in penetrating trauma, **6**:408, 408*f*
    photography in, **8**:31–36, 32*f*, 33*f*, 34*f*, 35*f*, 36*f*
    in primary congenital glaucoma, **6**:236–237, 237*f*, **10**:150
    before refractive surgery, **13**:34, 35–36
  function of, **8**:3
  immune response in, **9**:58*t*, 59–63
  ischemia of, after strabismus surgery, **6**:158–159, 158*f*
  leukemic infiltration of, **6**:354
  metastatic disease of, **4**:317
  neovascularization of, **10**:124–128, 125*f*, 125*t*, 126*f*, 127*f*. *See also* Neovascular glaucoma
  in onchocerciasis, **9**:242
  pigmentation in, in exfoliation syndrome/pseudoexfoliation, **10**:38, 85–87, 86*f*, 87*f*
  surgery on
    posterior segment complications of, vitrectomy for, **12**:354–362
    pupil irregularity and, **5**:263
    topical anesthetics for, **2**:389–390
    traumatic injury and, **8**:382–385, 384*f*, **10**:101–102
  in syphilis, **9**:245
  in toxocariasis, **9**:235
  trauma to, **8**:351–385, **10**:38–39, 38*f*, 39*f*, 96–102, **11**:206
    animal and plant substances causing, **8**:361–362
    chemical injuries, **8**:353–359. *See also* Chemical injury
    concussive, **8**:362–369, 364*f*, 365*f*, 366*f*, 367*f*, 369*t*
    nonperforating mechanical, **8**:369–372, 370*f*, 371*f*
    perforating, **8**:373–382, 373*t*, 374*t*, 376*f*, 377*t*, 378*f*, 379*f*, 381*f*, 382*f*. *See also* Perforating injuries
    surgical, **8**:382–385, 384*f*, **10**:101–102
    temperature and radiation causing, **8**:351–353
  in uveitis, **9**:78*t*, 79, 85–89, 86*f*, 86*t*, 87*f*, 88*t*. *See also* Anterior uveitis

Anterior segment developmental anomalies (ASDA).
    See Anterior segment, dysgenesis of
Anterior segment optical coherence tomography. *See
    also* Optical coherence tomography
    in glaucoma, **10**:70
Anterior stromal micropuncture, for recurrent corneal
    erosions, **8**:84, 85*f*
Anterior sutures, **11**:9
Anterior synechiae
    in glaucoma
        angle closure and, **10**:109, 113, 117
            inflammation and, **10**:130, 131, 131*f*
        anterior segment/iris neovascularization and,
            10:37, 37*f*, 124, 125, 126*f*
        chamber deepening/goniosynechialysis in
            management of, **10**:204
        flat anterior chamber and, **10**:136
        gonioscopy in identification of, **10**:37, 37*f*
        inflammation and, **9**:296
        iridocorneal endothelial (ICE) syndrome and,
            4:105, 105*f*, **10**:128, 128*f*
        plateau iris and, **10**:120
        uveitis and, **9**:296
    in sarcoidosis, **9**:175
    in uveitis, **9**:85, 88
        glaucoma and, **9**:296
Anterior toric (plus cylinder) form/lenses, **3**:311, 316
Anterior uvea. *See* Uvea
Anterior uveitis, **9**:78*t*, 79, 85–89, 86*f*, 86*t*, 87*f*, 88*t*,
    118–134. *See also specific cause and* Iridocyclitis;
    Iritis; Uveitis
    acute, **9**:84, 119–128
    ankylosing spondylitis and, **9**:119*f*, 121
    in *Bartonella*-associated neuroretinitis, **9**:264
    in Behçet disease, **9**:193, 193*f*
    in children, **6**:267, 267–272, 270*f*, 271*t*
        differential diagnosis of, **6**:268*t*
        in juvenile idiopathic (chronic/rheumatoid) arthritis,
            6:268–271, 270*f*, 271*t*, **9**:128–132, 130*f*, 131*t*
        laboratory tests for, **6**:277*t*
        masquerade syndromes and, **6**:276*t*
        sarcoidosis and, **6**:271
        treatment of, **6**:276–278
        tubulointerstitial nephritis and, **6**:271–272
    chronic, **9**:84–85, 128–134
    CMV, **9**:207–208
    corticosteroids for, **9**:100–106, 101*t*, 102*f*, 103*f*,
        119–120, 120*f*
        route of administration of, **2**:360*t*
    drug-induced, **9**:128
    fibrin in, **9**:24, 85, 88, 119, 119*f*
    flowchart for evaluation of, **9**:80*t*
    glaucoma and, **10**:93–95
    herpetic disease and, **9**:197–199, 198*f*
    in HIV infection/AIDS, **9**:305
    HLA association and, **1**:163, 164, 165, 166, **6**:269, 271,
        9:71, 72*t*, 119*f*, 120–123, 122*f*, 123*f*
    in HTLV-1 infection, **9**:219
    incidence/prevalence of, **9**:91, 92*t*, 118
    in inflammatory bowel disease, **9**:123
    iris nodules in, **4**:270*t*, **9**:85, 87*f*
    juvenile idiopathic (chronic/rheumatoid) arthritis
        and, **6**:268–271, 270*f*, 271*t*, **9**:128–132, 130*f*, 131*t*

keratic precipitates in, **9**:85, 86*f*, 87–88
lens-associated, **9**:125–126, 125*f*
in leptospirosis, **9**:255
in Lyme disease, **9**:251
noninfectious (autoimmune), **9**:118–134
in onchocerciasis, **9**:242
postoperative
    infections and, **9**:126
    IOL-associated inflammation and, **9**:125*f*, 126–127,
        127*f*
    lens-associated, **9**:125, 125*f*
in psoriasis/psoriatic arthritis, **9**:123
in Rift Valley fever, **9**:217, 218
in sarcoidosis, **9**:174–175
    in children, **6**:271
signs of, **9**:85–89, 86*f*, 86*t*, 87*f*, 88*t*
in spondyloarthropathies/spondyloarthritis, **1**:163,
    164, 165, 166, **6**:271
SUN Working Group grading scheme for, **9**:88, 88*t*
symptoms of, **9**:84–85
Th1 delayed hypersensitivity and, **9**:50*t*
in toxoplasmosis, **9**:229
tubulointerstitial nephritis and, **6**:271–272
varicella-zoster infection and, **9**:197–199, 198*f*
in Vogt-Koyanagi-Harada (VKH) syndrome, **9**:184,
    185–187
in Whipple disease, **9**:265
Anterior vestibular artery, **5**:21
Anterior vitreous detachment, **12**:297
Anteriorization (extraocular muscle) and recession,
    6:148*t*
Anthracyclines, in cancer chemotherapy, **1**:239
Antiacetylcholine receptor antibodies, in myasthenia
    gravis, **5**:331, **6**:138, **7**:209
Antiangiogenic agents. *See also specific agent*
    for age-related macular degeneration, **12**:72–73
    in cancer therapy, **1**:243
    for retinal capillary hemangioblastoma, **4**:295
    for retinopathy of prematurity, **6**:281
Antianxiety drugs, **1**:253–254, 253*t*
    ocular effects of, **1**:301*t*
    preoperative, **1**:310–311
Antiarrhythmic drugs/therapy, **1**:123*t*
    with ICDs, **1**:127
    tear production affected by, **8**:66*t*
    for ventricular fibrillation, **1**:126–127
Antibacterial agents, **1**:44–64, 45–53*t*, **2**:368–378, 368*t*,
    372*t*, 373*t*. *See also specific agent and* Antibiotics
    resistance to, **1**:3, 44–56
Antibiotic-associated colitis, *Clostridium difficile*
    causing, **1**:8–9
Antibiotics, **1**:44–64, 45–53*t*, **2**:368–378, 368*t*, 372*t*,
    373*t*. *See also specific type and agent*
    for *Acanthamoeba* keratitis, **2**:385–386, **8**:169
    for acute purulent conjunctivitis, **8**:150–151
    for bacterial keratitis, **8**:161–163, 162*t*
    β-lactam, **1**:44, 56–59, **2**:368–371, 368*t*
    for blebitis, **12**:356–357
    in cancer chemotherapy, **1**:239, 241*t*
    for cat-scratch disease, **9**:264–265
    in combination preparations with anti-inflammatory
        agents, **2**:373*t*
    for corneal abrasion, **8**:372

for endophthalmitis, **12**:354
    after cataract surgery, **11**:181
for gonococcal conjunctivitis, **8**:152
intravenous administration of, **2**:329
intravitreal administration of, for postoperative
        endophthalmitis, **12**:354
after LASIK, **13**:85, 86
for Lyme disease, **9**:252–253, 253*t*
for meibomian gland dysfunction, **8**:68
new/new classes of, **1**:3, 53*t*, 63–64
ocular effects of, **1**:301*t*
ototoxicity of, mitochondrial DNA mutations and,
        2:176
for perforating injury, **8**:375, 380, 381
preoperative, **1**:303, 307
    photoablation and, **13**:74
prophylactic
    cataract surgery and, **11**:127–129, 128*f*, 180
        corneal melting and, **11**:150
    for endocarditis, **1**:7, 8*t*
        ocular surgery and, **1**:307
    for endophthalmitis, **11**:127–129, 128*f*, 180, **12**:329
    photoablation and, **13**:74
    for *Pneumocystis jiroveci (Pneumocystis carinii)*
        pneumonia, **1**:37
    for tuberculosis reactivation, **1**:19
pseudomembranous enterocolitis and, **1**:8–9
for recurrent corneal erosions, **8**:84
resistance to, **1**:3, 44–56, **2**:369, 371, 375, 377. *See also*
        specific agent and specific organism
    new drug classes and, **1**:63–64
for scleritis, **8**:171, **9**:267
for seborrheic blepharitis, **8**:72
for septic shock, **1**:294
for staphylococcal blepharitis/blepharoconjunctivitis,
        8:147
after surface ablation, **13**:85, 86
for tuberculosis, **9**:261–262
Antibodies, **9**:41, 43. *See also* Immunoglobulins
local production of, **9**:48
monoclonal, **9**:46. *See also* Monoclonal antibodies
primary versus secondary immune response and, **9**:44
structural and functional properties of, **9**:45–46, 45*f*, 47*t*
Antibody-dependent cellular cytotoxicity, **8**:180,
        9:51–55, 54*f*
Antibody isotypes, **9**:45, 46, 47*t*
Antibody-mediated immune effector responses,
        9:45–48, 45*f*, 47*t*, 48
B-cell tissue infiltration and local antibody
        production and, **9**:46–48
with cellular effector mechanisms, **9**:51–55, 54*f*
immunoglobulin structure and function and,
        9:45–46, 45*f*, 47*t*
in poison ivy, **9**:34
terminology associated with, **9**:46
in viral conjunctivitis, **9**:60
Anticardiolipin antibodies, in antiphospholipid
        antibody syndrome, **1**:170, 171
Anti-CCP antibodies, in rheumatoid arthritis, **1**:162
Anti-centromere antibodies, in scleroderma, **1**:173
Anticholinergic agents, **2**:260, 334, 340–342, 341*t*, 342
adverse effects of, **2**:342, 343*f*
Alzheimer disease and, **1**:268

angle closure caused by, **10**:119
dry eye caused by, **8**:66*t*
for extrapyramidal side effects of antipsychotics,
        1:252, 252*t*
for ocular deviation, **5**:213
for Parkinson disease, **1**:259
for pulmonary diseases, **1**:145, 145*t*
Anticholinesterase agents. *See* Cholinesterase/
    acetylcholinesterase inhibitors
Anticipation (genetic), **2**:148, 162, 208–209
Anticoagulant therapy, **1**:158–159. *See also specific agent*
for antiphospholipid antibody syndrome, **1**:172–173
for arterial dissections, **5**:354
for atrial fibrillation, **1**:125
cataract surgery and, **11**:74, 175–176, 189–190
in central retinal vein occlusion, **12**:131
cephalosporin interactions and, **1**:58
for cerebral ischemia/stroke, **1**:94
after coronary stenting, **1**:99
facial and eyelid surgery and, **7**:189
for non–ST-segment elevation acute coronary
        syndrome, **1**:111–112
in perioperative setting, **1**:306–307
tailoring dosages and, **1**:152
Anticonvulsant drugs, **1**:262–263, 263*t*
as mood stabilizers, **1**:257
ophthalmic side effects of, **1**:245, 264, 301*t*
in perioperative setting, **1**:306
Anticyclic citrullinated peptide antibodies, in
        rheumatoid arthritis, **1**:162
Anticytokine therapy, **1**:185–187
for rheumatoid arthritis, **1**:162
Antidepressants, **1**:254–256, 255*t*
apraclonidine/brimonidine interactions and, **2**:348,
        10:170
ocular effects of, **1**:255, 301*t*
    tear production and, **8**:66*t*
Antidiabetic agents. *See* Insulin therapy; Oral
    hypoglycemic agents
Antidiuretic hormone (vasopressin), **1**:214
Anti–double-stranded DNA (anti-dsDNA) antibodies,
    in systemic lupus erythematosus, **1**:169, **9**:140, 141*t*
Anti-elevation syndrome, **6**:115, 153
Antienolase antibodies, retinopathy associated with,
        12:256
Antiepileptic drugs, **1**:262–263, 263*t*
as mood stabilizers, **1**:257
ophthalmic side effects of, **1**:245, 264, 301*t*
in perioperative setting, **1**:306
Antifibrinolytic agents, **2**:394
for hyphema, **6**:410, **8**:368
Antifibrotic agents, **2**:366–368. *See also* Fluorouracil;
    Mitomycin/mytomycin C
in glaucoma drainage device implantation, **10**:207
toxic keratoconjunctivitis caused by, **8**:360
in trabeculectomy, **10**:186, 193–194, 195*f*
    bleb-related endophthalmitis and, **10**:196
Antifungal agents, **1**:20, 54–55*t*, 64–65, **2**:378–380, 379*t*.
    See also specific type
for endophthalmitis, **9**:271
    Aspergillus, **9**:278
    Candida, **9**:275–276
for keratitis, **8**:166–167

Antigen–antibody complexes. *See* Immune (antigen–antibody) complexes
Antigen-presenting cells, **9**:11, 37, 38*f*, 39*f*, 58*t*
  in conjunctiva, **8**:173, **9**:57, 58*t*, 59
  in cornea, **2**:43, **8**:174, **9**:58*t*, 63, 64
  dendritic cells as, **9**:11–12
  in external eye defense, **8**:96
  locations of, **9**:58*t*
  in poison ivy, **9**:34
Antigen receptors
  in adaptive immune response/immune response arc, **9**:36*f*, 38, 38*f*, 39*f*, 41, 47*t*, 51
  B-lymphocyte, **9**:41, 47*t*
  in innate immune response, **9**:12–13
  T-lymphocyte, **9**:38, 38*f*, 39*f*, 51
Antigenic surface variation, as microbial virulence factor, **1**:4
Antigens, **9**:36–37
  endogenous, **8**:407
  histocompatibility, **8**:407. *See also* Human leukocyte antigens
  homologous, **8**:407
  transplantation, **8**:407, **9**:65
Antiglaucoma agents, **10**:161–173, 162–165*t*. *See also* Glaucoma, management of
  administration of eyedrops and, **10**:175–176
    in children, **10**:156
    compliance and, **10**:177
  adrenergic agonists, **10**:163*t*, 168–170
    α-adrenergic agonists, **2**:264*t*, 346–347, **10**:157, 163*t*, 169–170, 169*f*
    β-adrenergic agonists, **2**:347*t*, 348–349
  for angle-closure glaucoma, **10**:160, 175
  for angle-recession glaucoma, **10**:101
  anisocoria caused by, **5**:270
  for aqueous misdirection (malignant/ciliary block glaucoma), **10**:132
  β-blockers, **2**:264*t*, 349–351, 350*t*, **10**:156, 162–163*t*, 167–168
  calcium channel blockers, **2**:261
  carbonic anhydrase inhibitors, **2**:255, 351–354, 352*t*, **10**:156–157, 163–164*t*, 170–171
  in children, **6**:242–243, **10**:156–157
  ciliary body as target for, **2**:254
  combined preparations, **2**:355, **10**:165*t*, 173
  conjunctiva affected by use of, **10**:29
  cornea affected by use of, **10**:29–30
  cycloplegics, **2**:341
  dry eye and, **8**:61
  in elderly patients, **10**:176–177
  for elevated episcleral venous pressure, **10**:96
  for Fuchs heterochromic iridocyclitis, **10**:95
  generic agents and, **10**:177
  for ghost cell glaucoma, **10**:100
  for hemolytic glaucoma, **10**:100
  hyperosmotic/osmotic agents, **2**:355–356, 356*t*, **10**:165*t*, 173
  for hyphema, **10**:98
  interrelationship between medical and surgical treatment and, **10**:104, 160
  for iridocorneal endothelial (ICE) syndrome, **10**:130
  latanoprost, **2**:354, 354*t*, **10**:162*t*, 166, 167*f*
  for lens particle glaucoma, **10**:92

  miotics, **2**:264*t*, 338, **10**:157, 164*t*, 171–172
  for neovascular glaucoma, **10**:127
  for normal-tension glaucoma, **10**:81–82
  for ocular hypertension, **10**:83, 84–85, 105–106
  for open-angle glaucoma, **10**:161–173, 162–165*t*
    general approach to use of, **10**:174–175
  parasympathomimetics, **10**:164*t*, 171–172
  for phacoantigenic glaucoma, **10**:92
  for pigmentary glaucoma, **10**:89
  for postoperative elevated intraocular pressure, **10**:101
  during pregnancy/lactation, **10**:176
  prostaglandin analogues, **2**:256–257, 264*t*, 354–355, 354*t*, **10**:157, 162*t*, 166, 167*f*
  receptors in mode of action of, **2**:264, 264*t*
  for uveitic glaucoma, **9**:297
  uveitis caused by, **9**:128
Antihelminthic therapy, for diffuse unilateral subacute neuroretinitis, **9**:241
Antihistamines, **1**:295, **2**:364, 365*t*. *See also specific agent*
  for allergic reactions, **1**:295
  for ocular allergies, **6**:198, 198*t*, 199*t*
    conjunctivitis, **8**:186
    vernal keratoconjunctivitis, **8**:188
  ocular effects of, **1**:301*t*
  refractive surgery in patient taking, **13**:31
  tear production affected by, **8**:66*t*
Anti-HIV antibody tests, **1**:31–32
Anti-Hu (ANNA-1) antibody, paraneoplastic-induced saccadic intrusions and, **5**:256
Antihypertensive drugs, **1**:69, 74, 76–77*t*, 78*t*, 79*f*, 79*t*, 80–84. *See also specific agent*
  for children and adolescents, **1**:87
  combination therapy and, **1**:78*t*, 83
  for hyphema, **8**:368
  new developments and, **1**:69
  in older patients, **1**:86
  parenteral, **1**:83
  in perioperative setting, **1**:305
  during pregnancy, **1**:86
  tear production affected by, **8**:66*t*
  withdrawal from, rebound hypertension and, **1**:87
Anti-idiotypic antibodies, **9**:46
Anti-infective agents, **2**:368–386. *See also specific type and* Antibiotics
Anti-inflammatory agents, **2**:356–368, 357*t*, 360*t*, 362*t*, 365*t*. *See also specific agent and* Corticosteroids; Nonsteroidal anti-inflammatory drugs
  arachidonic acid release affected by, **2**:358
  in combination preparations with antibiotics, **2**:373*t*
  for keratoconjunctivitis sicca, **2**:245
  ocular effects of, **1**:301*t*
  for pulmonary diseases, **1**:146
Anti-La (SSB) autoantibodies
  in aqueous tear deficiency, **8**:57
  in Sjögren syndrome, **1**:174, **8**:57, 64*t*
  in systemic lupus erythematosus, **9**:140
Antimetabolites, **2**:366–368, **9**:108*t*
  in cancer chemotherapy, **1**:240*t*
  for uveitis, **9**:108*t*, 109–111
    in children, **6**:277
Antimetropia
  amblyopia in conjunction with, **3**:142
  prismatic effect of bifocals in, **3**:151, 152*f*

Antimicrobial polypeptides, in neutrophil granules, 9:31
Antimicrobial prophylaxis
    cataract surgery and, 11:127–129, 128f
        corneal melting and, 11:150
    for CMV retinitis, 9:207
    for endocarditis, 1:7, 8t
        ocular surgery and, 1:307
    for endophthalmitis, 11:127–129, 128f, 12:329
    for photoablation, 13:74
    for Pneumocystis jiroveci (Pneumocystis carinii)
        pneumonia, 1:37
    for toxoplasmic retinochoroiditis, 9:234
    for tuberculosis reactivation, 1:19
Antimicrobial susceptibility testing, 1:56
Antimicrobial therapy, 1:44–68, 45–55t. See also specific
    agent and Antibiotics
Antimicrosomal (thyroid microsomal) antibody
    testing for, 1:210
    in thyroid eye disease, 7:48
Antimuscarinic agents, 2:340–342, 341t
    adverse effects of, 2:342, 343f
Anti-MuSK protein (anti–muscle-specific kinase)
    antibodies, in myasthenia gravis, 5:331, 6:138
Antineoplastic drugs. See Chemotherapy
Antinuclear (antineutrophil) antibodies
    in aqueous tear deficiency, 8:57
    in juvenile idiopathic (chronic/rheumatoid) arthritis,
        1:166, 6:269, 9:129
    in polyarteritis nodosa/microscopic polyangiitis, 9:144
    in scleroderma, 1:173
    in Sjögren syndrome, 8:57
    in systemic lupus erythematosus, 1:168–170, 169t,
        9:140, 141t
    testing for, 8:182t
    in Wegener granulomatosis, 1:179, 7:32, 57–58,
        9:145–146
Antioncogenes. See Tumor-suppressor genes
Antioxidants
    age-related macular degeneration and, 4:168,
        12:61–62
    in lens, 2:313–314, 314f
    in retina and retinal pigment epithelium, 2:315–316,
        316–318
    retinitis pigmentosa and, 12:231
    supplemental, 2:395
Anti-Parkinson agents, tear production affected by,
    8:66t
Antiphospholipid antibodies, systemic lupus
    erythematosus and, 9:140, 141t
    retinal vasculitis and, 9:142
Antiphospholipid antibody syndrome (phospholipid
    antibody syndrome), 1:13, 158, 170–173
    choroidal perfusion abnormalities and, 12:179
Antiplatelet antibodies, in idiopathic thrombocytopenic
    purpura, 1:154
Antiplatelet therapy. See also Aspirin
    for carotid artery disease, 5:182
    cataract surgery and, 11:175–176
    for central retinal vein occlusion, 12:131
    for cerebral ischemia/stroke, 1:94
    after coronary stenting, 1:99
    dual (DAT). See Dual antiplatelet therapy
    for ischemic heart disease, 1:107

for non–ST-segment elevation acute coronary
        syndrome, 1:111
    in perioperative setting, 1:306
Antipsychotic drugs, 1:251–252, 252t
    atypical, 1:251, 252t
    ocular side effects of, 1:252
    oculogyric crisis caused by, 5:212–213
Antirecoverin antibodies
    cancer-associated retinopathy and, 12:256, 257
    retinitis pigmentosa and, 12:257
Antireflection films, interference and, 3:8, 9f
Antiretroviral therapy, 1:33–37
    drug resistance and, 1:33, 34, 35, 36
    HAART, 1:35–37
        CMV retinitis and, 1:3, 9:206, 12:201
        immune recovery uveitis and, 1:41, 9:306,
            12:201
        immune reconstitution syndromes and, 1:40–41,
            9:306, 12:201
    prophylactic, 1:37
    recent developments in, 1:3
Anti-Ri (ANNA-2) antibody, paraneoplastic-induced
    saccadic intrusions and, 5:256
Anti-RNA polymerase antibodies, in scleroderma, 1:173
Anti-Ro (SSA) autoantibodies
    in aqueous tear deficiency, 8:57
    in Sjögren syndrome, 1:174, 8:57, 64t
    in systemic lupus erythematosus, 9:140
Anti–Scl-70, in scleroderma, 1:173
Antiself-antibodies. See Autoantibodies
Antisense DNA, 2:148
    in gene therapy, 2:188, 189f
Antisense oligonucleotides, in gene therapy, 2:188, 189f
Anti–single-stranded DNA (anti-ssDNA) antibodies, in
    systemic lupus erythematosus, 9:140
Anti-Smith (anti-Sm) antibodies, in systemic lupus
    erythematosus, 1:169, 9:140, 141t
Antispasmodics, tear production affected by, 8:66t
Anti–SS-A (anti-Ro) autoantibodies
    in aqueous tear deficiency, 8:57
    in Sjögren syndrome, 1:174, 8:57, 64t
    in systemic lupus erythematosus, 9:140
Anti–SS-B (anti-La) autoantibodies
    in aqueous tear deficiency, 8:57
    in Sjögren syndrome, 1:174, 8:57, 64t
    in systemic lupus erythematosus, 9:140
Antithrombin III, 1:151, 152
    deficiency of, 1:152, 157
Antithrombin therapy, for non–ST-segment elevation
    acute coronary syndrome, 1:111–112
Antithrombotic components, 1:151–152
Antithyroid antibodies
    in Hashimoto thyroiditis, 1:213
    testing for, 1:210
    in thyroid eye disease, 1:211, 7:48, 50
Antithyroid drugs, for hyperthyroidism, 7:52
Antithyroperoxidase antibody, 1:210
Anti–TNF-α agents
    anti-idiotype antibodies and, 9:46
    for iritis, 9:120
    for juvenile idiopathic (chronic/rheumatoid) arthritis,
        9:131
    for rheumatic disorders, 1:161, 186

for scleritis, 8:222
for uveitis, 9:114–115, 120
in children, 6:278
Antitopoisomerase I antibodies, in scleroderma, 1:173
Antitoxoplasma antibodies, 9:230
α₁-Antitrypsin, in aqueous humor, 2:269
Antitumor antibiotics, 1:239, 241t
Antiulcer agents, tear production affected by, 8:66t
Anti-VEGF agents
    for age-related macular degeneration/choroidal
        neovascularization, 12:72–79, 75f, 86–87, 87–88
        combination treatment and, 12:78
        photodynamic therapy and, 12:78, 79, 344
    for branch retinal vein occlusion, 12:127
    for central retinal vein occlusion, 12:131, 132f
    for diabetes mellitus, 1:189, 205
    for macular edema, 4:158–160, 169
        in diabetes mellitus, 12:100, 101f
    for neovascular glaucoma, 10:127, 127f
    for ocular histoplasmosis syndrome, 9:225
    for parafoveal (juxtafoveal) retinal telangiectasia, 12:147
    for proliferative diabetic retinopathy, 12:106
    for retinal capillary hemangioblastoma, 4:295
    for retinopathy of prematurity, 12:169
    uveitis caused by, 9:128
Anti-VEGF Antibody for the Treatment
    of Predominantly Classic Choroidal
    Neovascularization in AMD (ANCHOR) study,
    12:73–74, 75, 75f
Antiviral agents, 1:55t, 65–66, 2:380–385, 381t
    for Bell's palsy, 5:286
    for CMV retinitis, 9:206–207
    for herpetic eye disease, 2:380, 381t, 382–383, 8:109,
        109t, 9:202
        acute retinal necrosis, 9:202
        epitheliopathy caused by, 8:116–117
        herpes simplex epithelial keratitis, 8:111–113
        herpes zoster ophthalmicus, 8:121
        stromal keratitis, 8:108t, 115–116
        uveitis, 9:199
    for HIV infection/AIDS. See Antiretroviral therapy
    intravitreal administration of, 2:328
    laser skin resurfacing and, 7:230
    resistance to, 2:382
    systemic, 2:381t, 382–385
    topical, 2:380, 381t
Anton syndrome, 5:172, 195
Antoni A pattern/Antoni B pattern, in schwannomas,
    4:244–245, 245f, 7:76
Anwar big-bubble technique, 8:435–436
Anxiety, 1:249
    drugs for management of (antianxiety drugs/
        anxiolytics), 1:253–254, 253t
        ocular effects of, 1:301t
        preoperative, 1:310–311
Aortic arch, 5:13f, 21
Aortic arch (Takayasu) arteritis, 1:176–178, 177t
Aortic coarctation, hypertension in, 1:72, 72t
Aortic dissection, cerebral ischemia/stroke and, 1:92
Aortitis syndrome (Takayasu arteritis), 1:176–178, 177t
AOX. See Adult-onset xanthogranuloma
AP3B1 gene, in Hermansky-Pudlak syndrome, 12:258t
Apathetic thyrotoxicosis, 1:233

APC. See Activated protein C; Anterior polar cataract;
    Antigen-presenting cells
Apert syndrome (acrocephalosyndactyly), 6:388, 389f,
    391f, 7:35, 8:322t
Apex, cornea, 3:168, 195
APH. See American Printing House for the Blind
Aphakia, 3:113
    ametropia and, 3:171–172
    aniseikonia and, 3:171–172
    after cataract surgery, lensectomy technique and,
        6:255–256, 257f
    congenital, 4:121, 6:260, 11:26
    contact lenses for, 3:116, 171–172
        in children, 6:259
    epikeratoplasty (epikeratophakia) for, 13:55
    glaucoma and. See Aphakic glaucoma
    homoplastic corneal inlays for, 13:54
    intraocular lenses for, 3:206, 208f, 210, 11:132–141.
        See also Intraocular lenses
        in children, 6:258–259
        secondary anterior chamber IOL implantation and,
            11:140
    monocular/unilateral, 3:116
        aniseikonia and, contact lenses for, 3:171–172
    posterior vitreous detachment and, 12:275
    prophylactic treatment of retinal breaks and, 12:285
    spectacle lenses for, 3:118, 158. See also Aphakic
        spectacles
        in children, 6:258, 259
Aphakic (pseudophakic) bullous edema/keratopathy
    after cataract surgery, 4:89–91, 90f, 8:384–385,
        11:147, 147f, 167
    IOL design and, 11:167
Aphakic glaucoma, 6:239–240, 10:124
    in children, 10:148–149
    glaucoma drainage device implantation and, 10:206
    pediatric cataract surgery and, 6:239, 260
Aphakic spectacles, 3:118, 158
    for children, 6:258, 259
    refracting technique for, 3:158
Apical alignment fit, for rigid gas-permeable contact
    lenses, 3:184, 184–185, 184f
Apical bearing (flatter than K) fit, for rigid gas-
    permeable contact lenses, 3:184, 185
Apical clearance (steeper than K) fit, for rigid gas-
    permeable contact lenses, 3:184, 184–185
Apical zone (optic cap), 3:168, 195, 8:37
Apidra. See Glulisine insulin
Aplastic anemia
    carbonic anhydrase inhibitors causing, 2:354, 1
        0:171
    chloramphenicol causing, 1:63, 2:375
APMPPE. See Acute posterior multifocal placoid
    pigment epitheliopathy
Apo-B. See Apolipoprotein B
Apocrine cystadenoma (oncocytoma), 4:75, 75f, 8:233
Apocrine glands of eyelid, 2:23, 27t, 4:205, 207t, 7:160,
    8:4. See also Glands of Moll
    tumors arising in, 7:162, 162f
Apocrine hidrocystoma, 4:214, 214f, 7:162, 162f
Apodization, in AcrySof ReSTOR intraocular lens,
    3:228
Apolipoprotein, 1:132

Apolipoprotein B
  hypercholesterolemia management and, **1**:131
  risk assessment and, **1**:133
Apolipoprotein D, in aqueous humor, **2**:269
Apolipoprotein E
  in Alzheimer disease, **1**:266
  in hyperlipoproteinemia, **8**:308
Aponeurosis, levator. *See* Levator aponeurosis
Aponeurotic ptosis, **5**:280, 280*t*, **7**:206, 206*f*, 207*t*
Apoplexy, pituitary (Sheehan syndrome), **1**:216,
  5:162–164, 163*f*
Apoptosis, **2**:147, 148
  by cytotoxic T lymphocytes, **9**:51, 53*f*
  in DNA repair, **2**:170
  Fas ligand (CD95 ligand/FasL) in, **9**:51, 53*f*, 62
Apostilb, **3**:17, 18*t*
APP. *See* Amyloid precursor protein
APP gene, in Alzheimer disease, **1**:266
Apparent diffusion coefficient (ADC) mapping,
  conventional/catheter/contrast, **1**:93
Appendage neoplasms, **4**:221–224, 221*f*, 222*f*, 223*f*
Applanation tonometer/tonometry, **3**:256–258, 257*f*,
  258*f*, **10**:22–25, 23*f*, 24*f*
  in children, **6**:236
  corneal thickness affecting, **8**:30, **10**:24–25, 84, **13**:35,
    173, 194
  fluorescein for, **8**:17
  infection control and, **10**:26
  in normal-tension glaucoma, **10**:81
  portable electronic, **10**:26
  after refractive surgery, **13**:35
    LASIK, **13**:35, 97
    surface ablation, **13**:35, 97
Applanation ultrasonography, for axial length
  measurement in IOL power determination/
  selection, **3**:214, 214*f*, **11**:82
Appositional growth, in development of lamellae, **2**:135
Approximations, for analysis of optical system, **3**:55–62,
  56*f*, 57*f*, 58*f*, 61*f*, 62*f*. *See also specific type and* First-
  order optics
Apraclonidine, **2**:259*t*, 346, 347*t*, **10**:157, 163*t*, 169–170
  anisocoria diagnosis and, **5**:265*f*
  for childhood glaucoma, **6**:243, **10**:157
  Horner syndrome diagnosis and, **5**:265*f*, 266–267,
    267*f*, **6**:230
Apraxia
  of eyelid opening, **5**:281
  ocular motor, **5**:208, 209–210, **6**:141–142
    acquired, **5**:194, 210
    congenital, **5**:209–210, **6**:141
    parietal lobe lesions and, **5**:168
Apresazide. *See* Hydralazine
Apresoline. *See* Hydralazine
Apricitabine, **1**:34
APS. *See* Antiphospholipid antibody syndrome
Aptamers, in cancer chemotherapy, **1**:243
Aptivus. *See* Tipranavir
aPTT. *See* Activated partial thromboplastin time
AquaLase Liquefaction Device, **11**:127
Aquaporin 0 (major intrinsic protein/MIP), **2**:274, 277,
  11:12, 17
  in lens transport, **2**:277
Aquaporins (water channels), **11**:12, 17

Aqueous cellular reaction, in uveitis, **9**:85
Aqueous–cornea interface, reflection at, **3**:12
Aqueous drainage devices/shunts. *See* Glaucoma
  drainage devices
Aqueous flare, in uveitis, **9**:85, 86, 87*f*, 88*t*
Aqueous humor, **2**:50, 254, 265–272
  biochemistry and metabolism of, **2**:254–255, 265–272
  carbohydrates in, **2**:266*t*, 268
  carbon dioxide in, **2**:272
  composition of, **10**:14–15
  dynamics of, **2**:254–255, 265, **10**:3*f*, 13–19
  formation of, **10**:3*f*, 13–16, 15*f*
    rate of, **10**:16
    suppression of, **10**:15–16
      α2-agonists in, **10**:15, 169
      β-blockers in, **10**:15, 167
      carbonic anhydrase inhibitors in, **2**:351, 352,
        10:15, 170
  glutathione in, **2**:268
  growth modulatory factors in, **2**:270–271
  immunologic microenvironments and, **9**:61
  inorganic ions in, **2**:266*t*, 267
  intraocular pressure and, **2**:255, 265, **10**:3–4, 3*f*
  organic anions in, **2**:266*t*, 267
  outflow of, **10**:3*f*, 16–19, 17–18*f*
    facility of, **10**:16
      classification of glaucomas and, **10**:7*t*
      intraocular pressure and, **10**:13, 14*t*, 16
      tonography in measurement of, **10**:19
    prostaglandin analogues affecting, **10**:166
    trabecular, **10**:16–18, 17–18*f*
    uveoscleral, **10**:3*f*, 16, 19
  oxygen in, **2**:271–272
  proteins in, **2**:254, 255, 266, 268–270
  refractive index of, **3**:40*t*, 104*f*, 105*t*, **8**:38
  separation of from blood. *See* Blood–aqueous barrier
  sodium transport and, **2**:351
  urea in, **2**:268
  vascular endothelial growth factor (VEGF) in, **2**:270,
    271
Aqueous layer (component) of tear film, **2**:42, 237,
  238*f*
  deficiency of. *See* Aqueous tear deficiency
  secretion of, **2**:239–240, 239*f*
  tests of, **8**:53–54, 54*f*, 54*t*
Aqueous misdirection (malignant/ciliary block
  glaucoma; posterior aqueous diversion syndrome),
  10:30, 131–133, 132*f*
  cataract surgery and, **10**:131, **11**:153, 157–158
  in infants and children, **10**:142*t*
Aqueous/anterior chamber paracentesis
  in acute retinal necrosis, **9**:201
  in coccidioidomycosis, **9**:280
  in cysticercosis, **9**:238
  in endogenous endophthalmitis, **9**:272–273
  in uveitis, **9**:96–97
Aqueous shunt implantation. *See* Glaucoma drainage
  devices
Aqueous tear deficiency, **2**:244–245, **8**:49–50, 50*f*, 51,
  51*f*, 52, 55–65. *See also* Dry-eye syndrome
  blepharitis and, **8**:144*t*, 145
  clinical presentation of, **8**:55–56, 56*f*, 57*f*, 58*t*
  laboratory evaluation of, **8**:57, 59*f*, 59*t*

medications causing, **8**:55, 61, 66*t*
non–Sjögren syndrome, **8**:50, 51*f*, 52, 65
refractive surgery and, **13**:35, 36*f*
Sjögren syndrome, **8**:50, 51*f*, 52, 63–65, 64*t*
in staphylococcal blepharitis, **8**:144*t*, 145
systemic diseases associated with, **8**:59*t*
tear composition assays in, **8**:54–55
tests of, **8**:53–54, 54*f*, 54*t*
treatment of
medical management, **8**:57–61, 60*t*
surgical management, **8**:61–63, 61*f*, 62*f*
Aqueous veins, **2**:54, 57*f*
Ara-A. *See* Vidarabine
Ara-C. *See* Cytarabine
Arachidonic acid (arachidonate)
in eicosanoid synthesis, **2**:255, 256*f*, 257, **9**:25–27, 26*f*
nonsteroidal anti-inflammatory drug derivation and, **2**:361–362
release of, **2**:257
anti-inflammatory drugs affecting, **2**:358
in retinal pigment epithelium, **2**:305
in vitreous, **2**:286
Arachnodactyly, in Marfan syndrome, **6**:263, **11**:36, 36*f*
Arachnoid mater, optic nerve, **2**:91, 92*f*, 93*f*, **4**:249, 250*f*, **5**:19*f*, 30
Arachnoid villi, **5**:26
Arachnoidal gliomatosis, **6**:368
Aralen. *See* Chloroquine
Arava. *See* Leflunomide
ARBs. *See* Angiotensin II receptor blockers
ARC. *See* Anomalous retinal correspondence
Arc of contact, **6**:28
Arc minutes, for Snellen test letters, **3**:109, 109*f*
ARC-T trial, **13**:52
Arc welding, occupational light injury and, **12**:334
Arcade retinal arteries, inferior/superior, **5**:16
Arcade retinal vein, **5**:23
Archaeocerebellum, **5**:48
Arcuate fibers, visual field defects and, **5**:116, 119*f*
in glaucoma, **10**:41
Arcuate (tangential/linear) incisions, for keratorefractive surgery, **13**:21, 21*f*, 50
Arcuate keratotomy (AK), **13**:4*t*, 49, 50–52, 51*t*
complications of, **13**:52
instrumentation for, **13**:51
ocular surgery after, **13**:52
outcomes of, **13**:52
surgical technique for, **13**:51
Arcuate (Bjerrum) scotoma, **10**:68, 70*f*
Arcus (corneal), **8**:336–337, 338*f*
in dyslipoproteinemia/hyperlipoproteinemia, **1**:139, **8**:308, 309*t*, 336
juvenilis, **8**:266, 336
lipoides, in Schnyder corneal dystrophy, **8**:285, 285*f*
senilis, **8**:336–337, 338*f*
Arcus marginalis, **7**:10
Arden ratio, **12**:43
in Best disease, **12**:237
Area centralis, **2**:79, 80*f*, **12**:8, 9*f*, 9*t*. *See also* Macula
Area of Martegiani, **12**:7*f*, 8
in posterior vitreous detachment, **12**:274, 274*f*, 297
AREDS (Age-Related Eye Disease Study), **2**:314–315, **11**:66, **12**:61–63

Areolar atrophy of retinal pigment epithelium, central (geographic atrophy), **4**:169, 170*f*, **12**:58–59, 59*f*
patient education/follow-up and, **12**:60
Areolar choroidal dystrophy, central, **12**:245, 245*f*
ArF laser. *See* Argon-fluoride excimer laser
Arginine restriction, in gyrate atrophy, **12**:244
Argon-fluoride excimer laser, **3**:24, 25. *See also* Excimer laser; Lasers
for photoablation, **13**:23, 65, 65–69, 66–67*f*. *See also* Photoablation
Argon laser, **3**:24. *See also* Lasers
Argon laser therapy. *See also* Laser therapy; Photocoagulation
for age-related macular degeneration, ineffectiveness of, **12**:63
for branch retinal vein obstruction, **12**:124–125
for diabetic retinopathy/macular edema, **4**:167, 167*f*, **12**:101–103
for gonioplasty/iridoplasty, **10**:203
for plateau iris, **10**:120, 120*f*, 203
for iridotomy, **10**:201, 202
for iris bombé in uveitis, **9**:296
ocular damage (laser burns) caused by, **8**:385
for retinoblastoma, **4**:311
for trabeculoplasty, **10**:82, 107–108, 180, 181, 182*f*
for trichiasis, **7**:200
Argyll Robertson–like pupil, **5**:274
Argyll Robertson pupil, **5**:274
in syphilis, **9**:246
Argyriasis, corneal pigmentation in, **8**:337*t*, 349
Aricept. *See* Donepezil
Arion sling, for corneal exposure in facial palsy, **5**:288
Aristocort. *See* Triamcinolone
Arixtra. *See* Fondaparinux
Arlt line, **8**:154, 155
Arlt triangle, keratic precipitates in viral infection in, **9**:198
ARN. *See* Acute retinal necrosis
Arnold-Chiari malformation, downbeat nystagmus caused by, **5**:251, 252*f*
Arnott lens, **3**:209*f*
ARPE. *See* Acute retinal pigment epitheliitis
Array (microarray-based) comparative genomic hybridization (array CGH), **4**:39*t*
Array multifocal lens, **13**:154
Arrestin, **2**:293
in experimental autoimmune uveitis, **9**:69
mutations in, **2**:182, 295
Arrhythmias, **1**:121–127. *See also specific type*
drugs for management of, **1**:123*t*
heart failure and, **1**:120
sudden cardiac death and, **1**:103
ARRP. *See* Autosomal recessive retinitis pigmentosa
ARS. *See* Adjustable refractive surgery
Artane. *See* Trihexyphenidyl
Arterial circles, **2**:38, 39*f*, 57*f*, 58, **5**:14*f*, 18
development of, **2**:132, 138
Arterial occlusive disease
carotid. *See* Carotid occlusive disease
retinal. *See* Retinal artery occlusion
Arterial plexus, ciliary body, **2**:62
Arterial retrobulbar hemorrhage, cataract surgery and, **11**:176

Arteries, 5:12–23, 13–14*f*, 15*f*, 17*f*, 19*f*, 20*f*, 22*f*, 23*f*. *See also specific artery*
  dissections in, 5:353–354, 354*f*
  extraocular muscles supplied by, 6:16–18
    surgery and, 6:25
Arteriography. *See* Angiography/arteriography
Arteriohepatic dysplasia (Alagille syndrome)
  pigmentary retinopathy and, 12:250*t*
  posterior embryotoxon and, 6:212
Arteriolitis, Kyrieleis, 9:229
Arteriovenous anastomoses, retinal, in Takayasu arteritis, 1:178
Arteriovenous fistulas, 7:67–69, 68*f*
  glaucoma associated with, 10:28
  orbital, 7:67–69, 68*f*
Arteriovenous malformations, 5:354–356, 355*f*, 7:67
  cerebral ischemia caused by, 1:92
  congenital retinal, 4:296, 297*f*, 12:151
  dural, choroidal perfusion abnormalities and, 12:176
  headache caused by, 5:297, 297*f*, 356
  intracranial hemorrhage caused by, 1:97, 98
  neuroimaging in evaluation of, 5:82*t*, 355*f*, 356
  orbital, 7:67
    in children, 6:342
  in Wyburn-Mason syndrome, 5:345
Arteritic anterior ischemic optic neuropathy, 5:125, 125–127, 126*f*, 126*t*, 319
Arteritis
  cerebral ischemia/stroke and, 1:92
  giant cell (temporal), 1:177*t*, 5:319–320, 7:55–56
    anterior ischemic optic neuropathy and, 5:125, 125–127, 126*f*, 126*t*, 319–320
    central retinal artery occlusion and, 12:139
    choroidal perfusion abnormalities and, 12:177–179, 179*f*
    corticosteroid route of administration in, 2:360*t*
    facial pain associated with, 5:301
    headache in, 5:125, 294
    optic nerve affected in, 4:252, 252*f*, 5:125, 125–127, 126*f*, 126*t*, 319–320
    transient visual loss and, 5:183
  Takayasu (aortic arch arteritis/aortitis syndrome/pulseless disease), 1:176–178, 177*t*
Artery of Bernasconi-Cassinari, 5:16
Artery of Percheron, 5:23
Arthritis
  in ankylosing spondylitis, 1:164
  in Behçet disease, 1:180
  cataract surgery in patients with, 11:188
  enteropathic, 1:165
  juvenile idiopathic. *See* Juvenile idiopathic (chronic/rheumatoid) arthritis
  Lyme, 1:15, 9:250, 251, 251*f*, 253*t*
  mutilans, 1:166
  psoriatic, 1:165–166, 9:123, 123*f*
    in children, 6:269*t*, 270–271
  reactive/Reiter syndrome, 1:164–165, 8:209, 9:121–123, 122*f*
    HLA association in, 1:164, 9:72*t*, 121
  rheumatoid, 1:161–162
    cataract surgery in patients with, corneal melting/keratolysis and, 11:150

juvenile. *See* Juvenile idiopathic (chronic/rheumatoid) arthritis
  peripheral ulcerative keratitis and, 8:211, 212, 212*f*
  refractive surgery contraindicated in, 13:184
  scleritis/scleromalacia perforans and, 8:220, 220*f*, 222
  in systemic lupus erythematosus, 1:167, 169*t*, 9:140, 141*t*
  in Whipple disease, 9:265
Arthro-ophthalmopathy
  hereditary hyaloideoretinopathy with optically empty vitreous and, 12:309
  hereditary progressive. *See* Stickler syndrome
  pigmentary retinopathy and, 12:250*t*
Arthropods, 8:142–143, 142*f*
Arthrotec. *See* Diclofenac, with misoprostol
Arthus reaction, 8:180, 181
  chronic, 9:48
Artifacts, on automated perimetry, 10:56, 61–62, 62*f*, 63*f*
Artificial tears, 2:245, 390–391. *See also* Lubricants
  for allergic conjunctivitis, 8:186
  for corneal exposure in facial palsy, 5:288
  for dry eye, 2:245, 390–391, 8:57, 58, 60*t*
  for exposure keratopathy, 8:80
  for paralytic ectropion, 7:216
  for Stevens-Johnson syndrome, 6:201, 8:196
  for Thygeson superficial punctate keratitis, 8:206
Artisan (Worst "iris claw") lens, 3:207, 208*f*
Arubendol. *See* Terbutaline
ARV. *See* AIDS-related virus
Arylsulfatase A, defective, 2:213*t*
AS. *See* Ankylosing spondylitis
AS-OCT. *See* Anterior segment optical coherence tomography
Ascending optic atrophy, 4:253–254
Ascending tract of Deiters, 5:45*f*, 46–47
Ascertainment, 2:148
Ascorbate. *See* Ascorbic acid
Ascorbic acid (vitamin C)
  for age-related macular degeneration, 12:61–62
  antioxidant effect of, 2:317–318
    in lens, 2:314–315
    in retina and retinal pigment epithelium, 2:317–318
  in aqueous humor, 2:255, 266*t*
  for chemical injuries, 8:79, 358
  corneal wound healing and, 13:27
  deficiency of (scurvy), 1:153, 8:79
  oral supplements and, 2:314–315
  in tear film, 2:240
  in vitreous, 2:266*t*
ASCRS online post-refractive IOL power calculator, 13:188–189, 190*f*
ASDA (anterior segment developmental anomalies). *See* Anterior segment, dysgenesis of
Aseptic thrombosis
  cavernous sinus, 5:357
  lateral (transverse) sinus, 5:357
  superior sagittal sinus, 5:357–358
Ash-leaf spot (hypopigmented macule), in tuberous sclerosis, 5:341, 342*f*, 6:372, 372*f*, 10:28
Asian eyelid, 7:136
  epicanthus tarsalis and, 7:147

Asian Harmonization Working Party (AHWP), **13**:202
Asmaline. *See* Terbutaline
ASO. *See* Allele-specific oligonucleotides
Asparaginase, **1**:242*t*
Aspart insulin, **1**:196, 196*t*
Aspergilloma (fungus ball), **5**:364–365, 365*f*
  in endophthalmitis, **9**:277*f*
Aspergillus (aspergillosis), **5**:364–366, 365*f*, **7**:46
  allergic, **5**:364
    sinusitis and, **7**:46
  endophthalmitis caused by
    endogenous, **9**:273–274, 276–278, 277*f*,
      12:203–204, 205*f*
    postoperative, **9**:270
  flavus, **9**:270, 276
  fumigatus, **9**:276
  invasive, **5**:365
  keratitis caused by, **4**:84, **8**:166
  ocular infection caused by, **5**:364–366, 365*f*, **8**:139
  orbital infection caused by, **4**:234, 234*f*, **5**:364–365, **7**:46
Aspheric lenses, high-plus, in low vision/vision
  rehabilitation, **3**:297–298
Aspheric (multifocal) simultaneous vision contact
  lenses, **3**:190, 190*f*
Aspiration, in phacoemulsification, **11**:104, 108–109,
  108*f*, 109*f*, 110*f*
  strategies for, **11**:125–126
Aspiration biopsy. *See* Fine-needle aspiration biopsy
Aspiration flow rate, in phacoemulsification, **11**:104
  setting, **11**:119
  vacuum rise time and, **11**:109, 110*f*
Aspirin, **1**:183*t*, **2**:362–363, 362*t*. *See also* Dual
    antiplatelet therapy
  for antiphospholipid antibody syndrome, **1**:173
  cataract surgery in patient taking, **11**:189
  for cerebral ischemia/carotid occlusive disease, **1**:91,
    94, 95, **5**:182
  for diabetic retinopathy/macular edema, **12**:98
  discontinuing before surgery, **1**:306
  facial and eyelid surgery in patient taking, **7**:189
  for ischemic heart disease, **1**:107, 108, 109*t*, 111
  ocular effects of, **1**:301*t*
  platelet function affected by, **1**:155
  prostaglandin synthesis affected by, **2**:257
Aspirin-dipyridamole
  for carotid artery disease, **1**:95, **5**:182
  for cerebral ischemia/stroke, **1**:94
Assassination (cell), by cytotoxic T lymphocytes, **9**:51, 53*f*
Association (genetic), **2**:177, **6**:171
  allelic. *See* Linkage disequilibrium
Assortative mating, **2**:148
Astebron. *See* Terbutaline
Asteroid bodies, **4**:138–139, 139*f*
  in sarcoidosis, **4**:191, **9**:173
Asteroid hyalosis, **4**:138–139, 139*f*, **12**:311, 312*f*
Asthenopia
  corrective treatment of intermittent exotropia and,
    6:102
  strabismus surgery and, **6**:145
Asthma, **1**:142
  in Churg-Strauss syndrome, **1**:179
  drug treatment for, **1**:145, 145*t*, 146
    ocular effects of, **1**:301*t*

Asthmasian. *See* Terbutaline
Asthmo-Kranit Mono. *See* Terbutaline
Asthmoprotect. *See* Terbutaline
Astigmatic dial refraction, **3**:130–132, 131*f*
Astigmatic keratotomy, **13**:4*t*
  for astigmatism/refractive errors after penetrating
    keratoplasty, **8**:427
  cataract surgery and, **11**:130
  wound healing/repair and, **13**:26
Astigmatic lenses, **3**:93. *See also* Cylinders;
  Spherocylindrical lenses
Astigmatism, **3**:114–116, 115*f*
  against-the-rule, **3**:115
  amblyopia and, **6**:63, 64, 178
  angle-supported anterior chamber PIOLs and, **13**:129
  arcuate keratotomy for, **13**:49
  in cataract patient
    modification during surgery and, **11**:130–131
    toric intraocular lenses for, **11**:131, **13**:141–144,
      142*f*
  after cataract surgery, **11**:150, 213
  conductive keratoplasty for, **13**:120–123
  corneal topography in detection/management of,
    8:43, 43*f*, 44, **13**:12–14, 13*f*, 14*f*, 38–39, 38*f*
  after penetrating keratoplasty, **8**:426, 427*f*, **13**:20
  correction of. *See also* Astigmatism, surgical
    correction of
    with contact lenses, **3**:174–176
      distortion reduction and, **3**:174–176, 316–317
      scleral lenses for, **3**:193
      toric soft lenses for, **3**:186–188, 187*t*, 188*f*
    with cylindrical spectacle lenses, **3**:139–140. *See
      also* Cylinders; Spherocylindrical lenses
    distortion and, **3**:140, 309–310, 310*f*. *See also*
      Distortion
    prescribing guidelines for, **3**:140, 309–323
      common misconceptions and, **3**:314–316,
        315*f*, 316*f*
      revised, **3**:321–322
  hyperopic, **3**:114, 115*f*
    photoablation for, **13**:89
  inappropriately corrected, meridional magnification/
    distortion and, **3**:314
  irregular, **3**:93, 115–116. *See also* Wavefront
    aberrations
    after arcuate keratotomy, **13**:52
    causes of, **3**:240–241, 241*f*
    chalazia causing, **3**:164
    contact lens masking of, **3**:190
    corneal topography in detection/management of,
      8:43, 43*f*, 44, **13**:13–14, 14*f*, 16, 38–39, 38*f*
    keratorefractive/refractive surgery and, **3**:232,
      237–241, 239*f*, 241*f*, **13**:16, 38–39, 38*f*, 171
    cataract surgery outcome and, **11**:193, 193*f*
    after limbal relaxing incisions, **13**:52
    retinoscopy in detection of, **3**:129, **8**:45
    wavefront analysis and, **3**:237–240, 239*f*, **13**:9. *See
      also* Wavefront analysis
  in keratoconus, **8**:297
  LASIK for, **13**:89
  lenticular
    contact lenses and, **3**:175
    refractive surgery and, **13**:39, 73, 139, 143

light-adjustable IOLs for, **13**:146–147, 147*f*
limbal relaxing incisions for, **11**:130–131, **13**:49
mixed, **3**:114, 115*f*
  limbal relaxing incisions for, **13**:52
  photoablation for, **13**:89
myopic, **3**:114, 115*f*
oblique, **3**:115
after penetrating keratoplasty, management of,
  8:426–427, 427*f*
  corneal topography in, **8**:426, 427*f*, **13**:20
  refractive surgery in, **13**:169–172
postoperative, conductive keratoplasty for, **13**:122
PRK for, **13**:89
progressive addition lenses and, **3**:149, 150*f*
ptosis and, **6**:178
after radial keratotomy, **13**:45–46
refractive, contact lenses and, **3**:175–176
refractive lens exchange/clear lens extraction and,
  13:139
regular, **3**:93–97, 93*f*, 94*f*, 95*f*, 96*f*, 97*f*, 98, 98*f*, 115
  corneal topography in detection/management of,
    13:12–13, 13*f*
  retinoscopy of, **3**:125–129, 126*f*, 127*f*, 128*f*
  wavefront aberration produced by, **13**:6, 7*f*
residual, **3**:317, 318, 319*f*
retinoscopy in detection of, **3**:125–129, 126*f*, 127*f*,
  128*f*, **8**:45
secondary, wavefront aberration produced by, **13**:8
surgical correction of. *See also specific procedure*
  cataract surgery and, **11**:130–131
  incisional corneal surgery for, **13**:49–52, 49*f*, 50*f*, 51*t*
  limbal relaxing incisions for, **11**:130–131
  after penetrating keratoplasty, **8**:427
  preoperative patient preparation and, **13**:74
  re-treatment and, **13**:89
suture-induced, cataract surgery and, **11**:150,
  212–213
tonometry accuracy and, **10**:23
toric lenses for
  intraocular, **3**:225, **11**:131, **13**:141–144, 142*f*
  posterior (minus), **3**:316
  soft contact lenses, **3**:186–188, 187*t*, 188*f*
transverse keratotomy for, **13**:49
uncorrected, meridional magnification/distortion
  and, **3**:314
wavefront analysis and, **3**:237–240, 239*f*, **13**:6, 7*f*. *See
  also* Wavefront analysis
wavefront-guided laser ablation for, **13**:25
with-the-rule, **3**:115
Astrocytes
optic nerve, **2**:90, 91, 92*f*, **4**:249
retinal, **2**:77, 301, **5**:29
Astrocytoma (astrocytic hamartoma), **4**:257, 257*f*
malignant, **5**:153–154
optic. *See* Optic nerve (optic pathway/chiasm) glioma
retinal, **4**:305–306, 306*f*
  optic disc drusen differentiated from, **5**:136, 136*f*
  retinoblastoma differentiated from, **4**:305–306, 306*f*,
    6:358
  in tuberous sclerosis, **5**:341, 342*f*, **6**:372
Astronomical (Keplerian) telescope, **3**:81–83, 82*f*, 83*f*, 252
in operating microscope, **3**:262, 262*f*
in slit-lamp biomicroscope, **3**:82*f*, 252

Asymptomatic Carotid Atherosclerosis Study, **1**:95
AT. *See* Ataxia-telangiectasia
AT III. *See* Antithrombin III
Atacand. *See* Candesartan
Ataxia
  Friedreich, pigmentary retinopathy and, **12**:250*t*, 254
  intermittent, **2**:213*t*
  with neuropathy and retinitis pigmentosa, **2**:175–176,
    12:265
    mitochondrial DNA mutations and, **2**:174*f*, 175–176
  optic, **5**:194
Ataxia-telangiectasia (Louis-Bar syndrome), **5**:339*t*, 344,
  345*f*, **6**:364*t*, 378–379, 379*f*, **8**:77, 241
  ATM mutation in, **2**:170, **6**:379
Atazanavir, **1**:34
ATC. *See* Apricitabine
ATD. *See* Aqueous tear deficiency
Atenolol, **1**:76*t*, 78*t*, **2**:345*f*
Atheroma, transient visual loss and, **5**:177, 179*f*
Atherosclerosis
  central retinal artery occlusion and, **12**:139
  cerebral ischemia and, **1**:92
  coronary artery (coronary heart disease), **1**:99. *See
    also* Ischemic heart disease
    diabetes mellitus and, **1**:133*t*, 207
    hypercholesterolemia and, **1**:100, 131, 132, 132–
      133, 133*t*
    hypertension management and, **1**:79*t*, 84
    ophthalmic considerations and, **1**:128
    risk factors for, **1**:99, 100–101, 132–133, 133*t*
    screening for, **1**:271–272
  hypertension and, **1**:70
  ocular ischemic syndrome and, **12**:133
  ophthalmic considerations and, **1**:138
  transient visual loss and, **5**:177, 179*f*
Ativan. *See* Lorazepam
ATM gene, in ataxia telangiectasia, **2**:170, **6**:379
Atopic dermatitis, **8**:185
  cataracts associated with, **11**:62
  keratoconjunctivitis and, **8**:190–192, 191*f*
Atopic hypersensitivity (immediate/type I) reaction,
  8:178*f*, 179–180, 179*t*, **9**:44, 44*t*, 54–55. *See also*
  Allergic reactions/allergies
  allergic conjunctivitis and, **8**:185, **9**:55
  fluorescein angiography and, **12**:24
  topical medications/substances and, **8**:183, 184, 184*f*
Atopic keratoconjunctivitis, **6**:200, **8**:190–192, 191*f*, **9**:55
Atopy. *See under* Atopic
Atorvastatin, for hypercholesterolemia/heart disease
  prevention, **1**:136, 137*t*
Atovaquone
  for *Pneumocystis jiroveci (Pneumocystis carinii)*
    pneumonia, **1**:37
  for toxoplasmosis, **9**:233, 234
ATP binding cassette (ABC/ABCR) transporters, **2**:293
  mutations in, **2**:296
    in Stargardt disease, **2**:296, **4**:172, **6**:293, **12**:233, 234
ATP production
  in lens, **2**:278–279
  in rod outer segments, **2**:293
ATP reports. *See* Adult Treatment Panel (ATP) reports
ATPase-6 gene, in neuropathy with ataxia and retinitis
  pigmentosa, **2**:175

Atraline. *See* Terbutaline
Atrial complexes/contractions, premature (PACs),
    1:121, 122*t*
Atrial fibrillation, **1**:124–125, 124*t*
    heart failure and, **1**:119, 120
    stroke and, **1**:92, 94
Atrial flutter, **1**:124*t*, 125
Atrial natriuretic peptide, in aqueous humor, **2**:267
Atrioventricular block, **1**:121, 122*t*
Atrioventricular junction, **1**:121
Atrioventricular junctional rhythm, **1**:122*t*
Atrioventricular junctional tachycardia, **1**:124*t*
Atrophia bulbi
    with shrinkage, **4**:22
    without shrinkage, **4**:22
Atrophic retinal holes, 12:271
    lattice degeneration and, **4**:155, **12**:278, 278*f*
        treatment of, **12**:284–285, 284*t*
    treatment of, **12**:283, 284, 284*t*
Atrophy
    gyrate, **2**:213*t*, **12**:243–244, 244*f*
        ornithine aminotransferase defects causing, **2**:213*t*,
            298, **12**:243
        retinal pigment epithelium in, **2**:309, **12**:243–244,
            244*f*
    optic. *See* Optic atrophy
Atropine, **2**:259*t*, 260, 340–342, 341*t*
    accommodation affected by, **11**:19
    adverse effects of, **2**:343*f*
    for amblyopia, **6**:67
    for cholinergic stimulation in toxic overdose, **1**:299
    for cycloplegia/cycloplegic refraction, **3**:137*t*, 141,
        6:5, 88, 88*t*
    in Down syndrome, pharmacogenetics and, **2**:229
    for edrophonium adverse effects, **5**:329
    for medical emergencies, **1**:292*t*, 299
    for pulmonary diseases, **1**:145
    side effects of, **3**:137, **6**:88
    systemic absorption of, **2**:324
    for uveitis, **9**:99
Atropine-Care. *See* Atropine
Atropisol. *See* Atropine
Atrovent. *See* Ipratropium
Attachment, as microbial virulence factor, **1**:4
Atypia, cellular
    dysplastic nevi and, **4**:226
    primary acquired melanosis and, **4**:68*f*, 69, 70*f*, **8**:237,
        238
Atypical antipsychotic agents, **1**:251, 252*t*
Atypical fibroxanthoma (malignant fibrous
    histiocytoma), **4**:117–118, 240–242
Atypical granular corneal dystrophy. *See* Reis-Bücklers
    corneal dystrophy
Atypical lymphoid hyperplasia, of orbit, **4**:239
Atypical mole. *See also* Nevus, dysplastic
    melanoma arising from, **1**:277
Atypical mycobacteria, **1**:18, **8**:164
    in HIV infection/AIDS, **1**:18, 39, **5**:360
    keratitis after photoablation caused by, **13**:98, 99*f*
Auditory aids, for low vision patient, **3**:301–302
Auditory artery, internal, **5**:21
Auditory meatus, internal, **2**:105
Auditory nerve. *See* Cranial nerve VIII

Augmentin. *See* Amoxicillin, with clavulanic acid
Aura
    with headache (classic migraine), **5**:191, 295, 295*f*
    headache without (common migraine), **5**:296
    seizures and, **1**:261
    without headache (acephalgic migraine/migraine
        equivalent), **5**:296–297
Auricular chondritis, in relapsing polychondritis, **1**:175
Auscultation, in orbital disorders, **7**:25
Autism, MMR vaccine and, **1**:282
Autoantibodies. *See also specific type*
    in aqueous tear deficiency, **8**:57
    in diabetes mellitus, **1**:191, 192
    in juvenile idiopathic (chronic/rheumatoid) arthritis,
        1:166, 167, **6**:269, **9**:129
    in rheumatoid arthritis, **1**:162
    in scleroderma, **1**:173
    in Sjögren syndrome, **1**:174, **8**:57, 64*t*
    in systemic lupus erythematosus, **1**:168–170, 169*t*,
        9:140, 141*t*
        retinal vasculitis and, **9**:142
    in thyroid eye disease, **1**:211, **7**:48, 50
    in Wegener granulomatosis, **1**:179, **7**:32, 57–58
        scleritis/retinal vasculitis and, **9**:145–146
Autocrine action, of cytokines, **9**:27
Autofluorescence. *See also* Hyperfluorescence
    drusen demonstrating, **5**:135
    fundus, **12**:22
        in acute zonal occult outer retinopathy, **9**:171, 171*f*
        in birdshot retinochoroidopathy, **9**:153, 154*f*
        in central serous chorioretinopathy, **12**:173–174
        in multifocal choroiditis and panuveitis syndrome,
            9:163, 163*f*
        near-infrared, **12**:31
        in serpiginous choroiditis, **9**:160, 160*f*
        in uveitis, **9**:93
Autogenous fascia lata, for frontalis suspension, **6**:179,
    7:212
Autografts
    conjunctival, **8**:94, 392*f*, 393–395. *See also*
        Conjunctiva, transplantation of
        for chemical injuries, **8**:358
        indications for, **8**:387*t*, 395
        for wound closure after pterygium excision, **8**:392*f*,
            393, 393–395
    corneal, **8**:413, 431–432. *See also* Keratoplasty
    limbal, **8**:94, 389, 395–398, 396–397*f*
        for chemical injuries, **8**:94, 358
        indications for, **8**:387*t*
Autoimmune diseases. *See also specific type*
    birdshot retinochoroidopathy as, **9**:152
    Graves hyperthyroidism as, **1**:211
    Mooren ulcer as, **8**:213–216, 215*f*
    ocular inflammatory disease/uveitis, **4**:189–191,
        9:117–196. *See also* Noninfectious (autoimmune)
        ocular inflammatory disease
    peripheral keratitis as, **8**:211–213, 211*t*, 212*f*
    refractive surgery in patient with, **13**:184–185
    retinopathy in, **12**:256
    scleritis in, **8**:222
    systemic lupus erythematosus as, **1**:167, **9**:140
    type 1 diabetes mellitus as, **1**:191
    Vogt-Koyanagi-Harada (VKH) syndrome as, **9**:183

Autoimmune hemolytic anemia, **1**:150
Autoimmune regulator (AIRE) deficiency, uveitis in
  mice and, **9**:69–70
Autoimmune retinopathy, **12**:256
Autoimmune uveitis. *See* Noninfectious (autoimmune)
  uveitis
Automated DNA sequencing, **2**:184, 185*f*
Automated lamellar keratoplasty, **13**:68
Automated perimetry
  nonorganic ophthalmic disorder evaluation and,
    5:312, 313*f*
  short-wavelength (SWAP/blue-yellow), **10**:60–61
    in glaucoma suspect screening, **10**:82–83
  standard (SAP/achromatic), **10**:54, 73
  static, **5**:100–104, 101*f*, 102*f*, 103*f*, **10**:53–54, 54*f*, 55,
    56–58, 57*f*, 58*f*
    artifacts seen on, **10**:56, 61–62, 62*f*, 63*f*
    in glaucoma, **10**:53–54, 55, 56–58, 57*f*, 58*f*
    high false-negative rate in, **10**:61–62
    high false-positive rate in, **10**:61, 63*f*
    incorrect corrective lens used in, **10**:61
    learning effect and, **10**:64, 64*f*
    screening tests, **10**:58
Automated refraction, **3**:275–277, 276*f*
  in low vision/vision rehabilitation, **3**:294
Automated subjective refractors, **3**:277
Automatic lensmeters, **3**:271–272
Automatic objective refractors (automatic retinoscopes),
  3:276, 277
Automatisms, **1**:261
Autonomic cephalgias, trigeminal, **5**:299
Autonomic pathways
  cholinergic drug action and, **2**:334, 335*f*
  ocular, **5**:63–67
    parasympathetic, **5**:65–67, 65*f*, 66*f*
    sympathetic, **5**:63–65, 64*f*
Auto-oxidation, **2**:312–313
  in lens, **2**:313, 314*f*
  vitamin E affecting, **2**:312, 317
Autoregulation, vascular, disturbances of, in glaucoma,
  10:45
Autosomal dominant inheritance, **2**:216–217, 217*t*
  of pigmentary retinopathies, **12**:250*t*
    retinitis pigmentosa, **2**:217, **12**:228. *See also*
      Autosomal dominant retinitis pigmentosa
Autosomal dominant optic atrophy, **5**:139, 140*f*, **6**:310–311
Autosomal dominant retinitis pigmentosa, **2**:217, **12**:228
  oxygen-related protein mutations causing, **2**:296
  rhodopsin mutations causing, **2**:295
Autosomal recessive inheritance, **2**:212–216, 213*t*, 215*t*
  of pigmentary retinopathies, **12**:250–251*t*
    retinitis pigmentosa, **12**:228, 229. *See also*
      Autosomal recessive retinitis pigmentosa
Autosomal recessive retinitis pigmentosa, **12**:228
  retinal pigment epithelium defects in, **2**:308
  rhodopsin mutations causing, **2**:295
  rod cGMP-gated channel mutations causing, **2**:295
  rod cGMP phosphodiesterase mutations causing, **2**:295
Autosomes, **2**:148, 193
  aneuploidy of, **2**:199–203. *See also specific disorder*
AV block. *See* Atrioventricular block
AV junction. *See* Atrioventricular junction
Avalide. *See* Irbesartan

Avandamet. *See* Rosiglitazone, with metformin
Avandia. *See* Rosiglitazone
Avapro. *See* Irbesartan
Avastin. *See* Bevacizumab
Avellino (granular-lattice) corneal dystrophy, **4**:97, 97*t*,
  99*f*, **8**:268*t*, 270*t*, 278*t*, 282, 282*f*
  genetics of, **4**:97, **8**:269*t*, 282
  refractive surgery and, **13**:35
Avelox. *See* Moxifloxacin
Average effect, **1**:337
Avilamycin, **1**:53*t*, 64
AVMs. *See* Arteriovenous malformations
Avonex. *See* Interferons (IFNs), β
Awareness of vision, disorders of, **5**:195–196
Axenfeld anomaly/syndrome, **2**:141, **4**:104*f*, **6**:213,
  8:256, **10**:145. *See also* Axenfeld-Rieger syndrome
Axenfeld loop/Axenfeld nerve loop, **2**:48, **4**:112, 112*f*, **8**:9
Axenfeld-Rieger syndrome, **4**:102–103, 103, 104*f*,
  6:213–214, 213*f*, **8**:256, 257*f*, 261*t*, **10**:28, 29, 30, 142,
  145–146, 146*t*
  glaucoma associated with, **4**:102, **6**:213, 214, 238,
    10:28, 30, 142, 145–146, 146*t*
  posterior embryotoxon in, **4**:102–103, 103*f*, 104*f*,
    6:212, 212*f*, 213, **8**:256, **10**:30, 146
  pseudopolycoria in, **6**:231, 231*f*
Axes, **6**:11–12
  cylinder
    locating, **3**:126–127, 126*f*, 127*f*, 128*f*
    refinement of, cross-cylinder refraction and, **3**:132,
      133
    rotating, distortion reduction and, **3**:140, 317
      residual astigmatism and, **3**:317, 318, 319*f*
  of Fick, **6**:27, 27*f*
  optical, **3**:31, 31*f*, 32*f*, 106, 107*f*, **6**:12, **11**:5, 6*f*
  pupillary, **6**:12
  visual, **6**:12, 14*f*, 39
    accommodative convergence and, **6**:37
    muscle action/gaze position and, **6**:30
Axial ametropia, **3**:113
Axial curvature, **8**:40, 41*f*, **13**:11
Axial displacement of globe, in orbital disorders, **7**:23
Axial distance, **8**:40
Axial length, **6**:167–168, 167*f*, 167*t*
  angle closure and, **10**:113
  congenital glaucoma and, **6**:238
  extremes in, cataract surgery in patients with,
    11:200–201
  in IOL power determination, **3**:213–216, 214*f*, 215*f*,
    216*f*, **11**:82–83, 84, 84–85
    optical measurement of, **3**:214–216, 216*f*, **11**:83
    ultrasound measurement of, **3**:213–214, 214*f*, 215*f*,
      11:82–83, 83*f*, 84, 84–85
    unexpected refractive results after surgery and,
      11:168
  in primary congenital glaucoma, **10**:152
Axial (longitudinal) magnification, **3**:36. *See also*
  Magnification
Axial power, **13**:11, 12*f*
Axonal transport system, of optic nerve, **5**:29
AZA. *See* Azathioprine
Azactam. *See* Aztreonam
Azalides, **1**:50*t*, 61. *See also specific agent*
Azar 91Z anterior chamber IOL, **3**:210, 210*f*

Azasite. *See* Azithromycin
Azathioprine, 1:187, 9:108*t*, 109–110
  for Behçet disease, 1:180, 9:195
  for uveitis, 9:108*t*, 109–110
    in children, 6:277
AZD2563, 1:64
Azelastine, 2:364, 365*t*, 366
Azidodeoxythymidine. *See* Zidovudine
Azidothymidine. *See* Zidovudine
Azimilide, 1:123*t*
Azithromycin, 1:50*t*, 61, 2:372*t*, 377
  for chlamydial conjunctivitis, 8:157
  for endocarditis prophylaxis, 1:8*t*
  for toxoplasmosis, 9:233
  for trachoma, 8:156
Azlocillin, 1:57, 2:370
Azmacort. *See* Triamcinolone
AZOOR. *See* Acute zonal occult outer retinopathy
AZOOR complex, 9:172. *See also specific disorder and*
  White dot syndromes
Azopt. *See* Brinzolamide
AZT (azidothymidine). *See* Zidovudine
AZTEC. *See* Zidovudine
Aztreonam, 1:49*t*, 58
Azulfidine. *See* Sulfasalazine

B

B5 tissue fixative, 4:29*t*
B&B stain (Brown and Brenn stain), 4:31*t*
B&H stain (Brown and Hopps stain), 4:31*t*
B-cell lymphomas. *See also* Lymphomas
  conjunctival, 4:72–74, 73*f*, 8:244, 245*f*
  in HIV infection/AIDS, 1:40, 5:358
  intraocular (primary central nervous system), 1:244,
    4:140–142, 141*f*, 142*f*, 143*f*, 323–325, 323*f*, 325*f*,
    9:136, 281–284, 282*f*, 283*f*, 12:199, 199*f*
    central serous retinopathy differentiated from,
      12:174
    in HIV infection/AIDS, 9:314
    uveitis differentiated from, 9:91, 136, 281–283
      in children, 6:276*t*
  orbital, 4:239–240, 239*f*, 7:80
B cells (B lymphocytes), 4:9, 9:12
  activation of, 9:37–38, 40*f*, 41, 42
  in external eye, 8:174*t*
  in HIV infection/AIDS, 1:4
  infiltration of into tissues, in antibody-mediated
    immune response, 9:46–48
  monoclonal proliferation of, corneal deposits and,
    8:319–320
  in poison ivy, 9:34
  primary versus secondary immune response and,
    9:43–44
  in Sjögren syndrome, 8:63
  in tuberculosis, 9:35
B-lymphocyte antigen receptors, 9:41, 47*t*
B-scan ultrasonography/echography, 3:274–275, 274*f*.
  See also Ultrasonography
  anterior segment (ultrasound biomicroscopy), 2:50,
    52*f*, 8:33, 33*f*
  before corneal transplantation, 8:417

  in glaucoma, 10:70, 72*f*
    uveitic glaucoma and, 9:296
  in pars planitis, 9:136
  for axial length measurement in IOL power
    determination/selection, 3:213
  before cataract surgery, 11:80–81, 84, 84–85
  in choroidal/ciliary body melanoma, 4:276, 276*f*
  in choroidal hemangioma, 4:291*f*, 292
  in drusen versus papilledema differentiation,
    5:134–135, 135*f*
  in metastatic eye disease, 4:319
  in primary congenital glaucoma evaluation, 10:152
B-type natriuretic peptide (BNP)
  in aqueous humor, 2:267
  in heart failure, 1:114, 117–118
b-wave, of electroretinogram, 5:109, 12:34, 34*f*. *See also*
  Electroretinogram
  vascular disease and, 12:40, 41*f*
Babesia/babesiosis, 1:15
  Lyme disease coinfection and, 9:254
BAC (bacterial artificial chromosome), 2:149
Bacampicillin, 2:370
Bacille Calmette-Guérin (BCG) vaccination
  PPD test affected by, 1:19, 9:260
  uveitis associated with, 9:128
Bacillus, 8:135
  cereus, 8:135, 9:16, 12:328, 329
    endogenous bacterial endophthalmitis caused by,
      9:272, 12:202
  as normal ocular flora, 8:97*t*
  ocular infection caused by, 8:135, 9:16
    after ocular trauma, 8:375, 12:328–329
    traumatic endophthalmitis caused by, 12:328
Bacitracin, 2:368*t*, 372*t*, 378
  in combination preparations, 2:372*t*, 373*t*
Back toric contact lenses, 3:187
Back (posterior) vertex power, lensmeter in
  measurement of, 3:167, 270, 270*f*, 271
Background diabetic retinopathy. *See* Diabetic
  retinopathy, nonproliferative
Background luminance, perimetry variations and, 10:56
Background wavelength, perimetry variations and,
  10:56
Baclofen, for nystagmus, 5:257
Bacteria, 8:131–137, 132*t*. *See also specific organism or*
  type of infection
  classification of, 8:131, 132*t*
  conjunctivitis caused by, 4:53, 55*f*, 8:149–154, 150*t*
    in children, 6:189–190, 190*f*, 8:149–152
    classification of, 8:149, 150*t*
    in neonates, 6:187–188, 187*f*, 8:152–154
  corneal infection caused by, 4:82, 83*f*, 8:158–164,
    160*f*, 160*t*, 162*t*
  endophthalmitis caused by
    endogenous, 9:271–273, 272*f*, 12:202–203, 202*f*
    postoperative, 9:269–270, 270*f*
    vitreous affected in, 4:133, 134*f*
  eyelid margin and conjunctival infection caused by,
    8:143–148
  innate immunity triggered by, 9:14–17, 14*t*
  keratitis caused by, 4:82, 83*f*, 8:158–164, 160*f*, 160*t*,
    162*t*. *See also* Keratitis, bacterial
    contact lens wear and, 3:180, 8:159

as normal flora, **8**:96–97, 97*t*
ocular infection caused by, **8**:131–137, 132*t*, 143–164.
  See also specific type or structure involved
  adherence and, **8**:98, 159
  evasion and, **8**:98
  invasion and, **8**:98–99
  specimen collection/isolation techniques for
    diagnosis of, **8**:101*t*, 103
optic nerve infection caused by, **4**:251
orbital infection caused by, **4**:234
  cellulitis, **7**:39*t*, 40
  necrotizing fasciitis, **7**:44
scleritis caused by, **8**:171, 171*f*, **9**:266
treatment of infection caused by. *See* Antibiotics
uveitis caused by, **9**:15
Bacterial artificial chromosome (BAC), **2**:149
Bacterial cell wall, **8**:131–132
  innate immune response and, **9**:14–15, 14*t*, 15
Bacteriology, **8**:131–137, 132*t*. *See also* Bacteria
Bacteriophage, **2**:149
Bactrim. *See* Trimethoprim-sulfamethoxazole
Badal principle, **3**:80, 269, 270*f*
Baerveldt glaucoma implant, **10**:205, 205*t*
  for childhood glaucoma, **6**:241
  for uveitic glaucoma, **9**:298
Bagolini glasses, in sensory adaptation testing, **6**:56–57,
  56*f*
Bailey-Lovie visual acuity chart, **3**:110
BAL (British antilewisite), for Wilson disease, **2**:231
BAL9141, **1**:58
Balance lens, in low vision/vision rehabilitation, **3**:296,
  297
Balanced general anesthesia, **1**:310
Balanced salt solution (BSS)
  in ECCE, **11**:94
  in phacoemulsification, **11**:108
  in trabeculectomy, **10**:188
Balanitis, circinate, in reactive arthritis, **9**:122
Balint syndrome, **5**:194, 210
  in Alzheimer disease, **1**:268
Balloon angioplasty. *See* Percutaneous coronary
  intervention
Balloon catheters, in dacryocystorhinostomy, **7**:269
Balloon cells
  in choroidal/ciliary body melanoma, **4**:196
  in choroidal/ciliary body nevus, **4**:195
Balloon dacryoplasty (balloon catheter dilation), for
  congenital nasolacrimal duct obstruction, **6**:209,
  209*f*, **7**:253–255
Baltimore Eye Survey, **1**:331, 331*f*, **10**:75, 76, 77, **11**:67
BAM. *See* Benign acquired melanosis
Bamboo spine, in ankylosing spondylitis, **1**:164
Band atrophy, in optic tract syndrome, **5**:166
Band keratopathy
  calcific (calcium hydroxyapatite deposition), **4**:88,
    89*f*, **8**:328, 342–344, 343*f*
  in sarcoidosis, **8**:73
  in uveitis, **9**:85, 291
  in juvenile idiopathic (chronic/rheumatoid) arthritis,
    6:270, 270*f*, **9**:129, 130, 130*f*, 132
  in pars planitis, **9**:136
  in sarcoidosis, **9**:175
  surgery for, **6**:278
  in uveitis, **9**:85, 291

Bandage contact lenses, **3**:193–194, **8**:403
  for chemical injuries, **8**:358
  contraindications to, in exposure keratopathy, **8**:80
  for corneal abrasion, **8**:372
  for dry eye, **8**:60*t*, 61, 403
  for graft-vs-host disease, **8**:203
  for involutional entropion, **7**:196
  after LASIK, **13**:85, 194
    epithelial ingrowth prevention and, **13**:114, 194
    epithelial sloughing/defects and, **13**:104–105
    microkeratome complications and, **13**:103
    striae and, **13**:107–108
  for perforating injury, **8**:375
  for peripheral ulcerative keratitis, **8**:213
  for recurrent corneal erosions, **8**:84, 403
  after surface ablation, **13**:85, 86, 193
    sterile infiltrates and, **13**:100, 100*f*
  for Thygeson superficial punctate keratitis, **8**:206
Banked fascia lata, for frontalis suspension, **6**:179, **7**:212
Barbados Eye Study, **11**:67
Barbiturates, **1**:253*t*. *See also* Sedative-hypnotics/sedation
Bardet-Biedl syndrome, **12**:250*t*, 252–253, 252*f*
  pigmentary retinopathy and, **12**:250*t*, 252, 252*f*
  pleiotropism in, **2**:210
  renal disease and, **12**:254
Bare-metal stents, **1**:99, 108
Bare sclera, wound closure after pterygium excision
  and, **8**:391, 391*f*
Bariatric surgery, for obesity in type 2 diabetes mellitus,
  1:195
Barium enema, in cancer screening, **1**:276
Barkan membrane, **10**:143–144, 144*f*, 152
Baroreceptors, phenylephrine affecting, **2**:346
Barr body, **2**:149
Barraquer erysiphake, **11**:92, 92*f*
Barrett esophagus, **1**:275
Barrier devices, for basic life support, **1**:291
Bartonella (bartonellosis)
  cat-scratch disease caused by, **5**:130, **6**:190, **8**:136,
    9:262–265, 264*f*, **12**:206, 207*f*
  henselae (Rochalimaea henselae), **6**:190, **8**:136, 157,
    158, **9**:262–265, **12**:206
  neuroretinitis and, **5**:130, **6**:312, **9**:263–264
  ocular infection caused by, **6**:312, **8**:136, 157, 158,
    9:262–265, 264*f*, **12**:206, 207*f*
  quintana, **5**:130, **9**:262
Basal cell carcinoma, of eyelid, **4**:215*t*, 217–219, 218*f*,
  219*f*, **7**:168–172, 169*f*, 170*f*
  intraocular extension of, **4**:322
Basal cell nevus syndrome (Gorlin syndrome), eyelid
  manifestations of, **4**:215*t*, **7**:168
Basal ganglia, **5**:36, 40*f*, 41, 61
  in blepharospasm, **5**:289
  in Parkinson disease, **1**:258
Basal lamina (basal cell layer)
  of choriocapillaris, **2**:64, 65*f*
  ciliary body, **2**:62, 62*f*
  corneal, **2**:43, 44*f*, 45, 46*f*, 248. *See also* Descemet
    membrane/layer
  drusen of (cuticular drusen), **4**:169, **12**:60, 239–240
    age-related macular degeneration differentiated
      from, **12**:60, 69
    vitelliform exudative macular detachment and,
      12:238, 238*f*

lens. *See* Lens capsule
of retinal blood vessels, **2**:78
of retinal pigment epithelium, **2**:64, 65*f*
Basal laminar deposits, **4**:168, **12**:55, 56*f*, 57
Basal linear deposits, **4**:168, **12**:55, 56*f*, 57
Basal skull fracture, arteriovenous fistula caused by, **7**:67
Base curve, contact lens, **3**:167, 168*f*, 170
changing, **3**:169, 169*f*
power determination and, **3**:185
rigid gas-permeable contact lens fitting and, **3**:183–184, 184*t*
soft contact lens fitting and, **3**:182, 183*t*
Base-out prism effect, with bifocals, segment decentration and, **3**:157, 164
Base-out prism test
in nonorganic ophthalmic disorders, **5**:309
in sensory adaptation testing, **6**:57–58, 57*f*
Base pair, **2**:149
mutations in, **2**:171
conserved, **2**:171
Baseline probability of outcome, **1**:336–337
Basement membrane
corneal endothelial. *See* Descemet membrane/layer
corneal epithelial, **4**:77, 78*f*
Basement membrane dystrophies, epithelial (map-dot-fingerprint/Cogan microcystic/anterior basement membrane), **4**:95, 95*f*, **8**:268*t*, 270–272, 270*t*, 271*f*
cataract surgery in patients with, **11**:191, 192*f*
genetics of, **8**:269*t*, 270
recurrent corneal erosion and, **8**:83, 271, 272
refractive surgery in patients with, **13**:35, 37*f*, 67–68, 70, 71
Basement membrane zone, in cicatricial pemphigoid, **8**:198, 201, 202*f*
Basic (acquired) esotropia, **6**:95–96
Basic fibroblast growth factor, **2**:270, 348. *See also* Fibroblast growth factor
in aqueous humor, **2**:270
Basic life support, **1**:289–292, 292*t*
medications used in, **1**:292*t*
for ventricular fibrillation, **1**:289, 292
Basic secretion test/basic secretors, **2**:241, **8**:53–54, 54*t*
Basilar artery, **2**:109, **5**:12, 13*f*, 21, 22*f*
aneurysm of, **5**:350, 350*f*
cranial nerve relationship and, **5**:52*f*
dissection of, **5**:353, 354
median perforators of, **5**:21–23
Basilar plexus, **5**:27*f*
Basilar-type (complicated) migraine, **5**:185, 295–296. *See also* Migraine headache
Basilar vein of Rosenthal, **5**:26
Basophils, **4**:7, 8*f*, **9**:10
cytologic identification of, in immune-mediated keratoconjunctivitis, **8**:182*t*
Bassen-Kornzweig syndrome, MTP defects causing, **2**:298
Batson venous plexus, **2**:104
Batten disease, **12**:251*t*, 254, 259–260, 260*f*
pigmentary retinopathy in, **12**:251*t*, 254, 260, 260*f*
Battle sign, **5**:287
bax expression, in adenoid cystic carcinoma, **4**:236
BAX gene, in DNA repair, **2**:170
Bayes theorem, **1**:333

Baylisascaris procyonis (raccoon roundworm), diffuse unilateral subacute neuroretinitis caused by, **9**:239, **12**:210
BCG (Bacille Calmette-Guérin) vaccination
PPD test affected by, **1**:19, **9**:260
uveitis associated with, **9**:128
bcl-2 expression, in adenoid cystic carcinoma, **4**:236
BD. *See* Behçet disease
BD ProbeTec ET System, for tuberculosis screening, **1**:279
BDUMP. *See* Bilateral diffuse uveal melanocytic proliferation
Beaded filaments, **2**:277, **11**:12
Bear tracks (grouped pigmentation of retina), **4**:278, 279*f*, **12**:282
in children, **6**:352
BEAT-ROP (Bevacizumab Eliminates the Angiogenic Threat of Retinopathy of Prematurity) Cooperative Group, **12**:169
Beaver Dam Eye Study, **1**:326, **11**:67
BEB. *See* Benign essential blepharospasm
Beclomethasone, for pulmonary diseases, **1**:145*t*
Beclovent. *See* Beclomethasone
Bee stings, ocular injury caused by, **8**:361–362
Behavioral/psychiatric disorders, **1**:245–257. *See also specific type*
aging and, **1**:226–227
anxiety disorders, **1**:249
cataract surgery in patients with, **11**:187
hallucinations/illusions in, **5**:188*t*
mental disorders due to general medical condition, **1**:246
mood (affective) disorders, **1**:247–248
noncompliance and, **1**:257
ophthalmic considerations and, **1**:257
pharmacologic treatment of, **1**:251–257, 252*t*, 253*t*, 255*t*
ocular side effects and, **1**:257
recent developments and, **1**:245
recent developments in, **1**:245
schizophrenia, **1**:246–247
somatoform disorders, **1**:248–249
substance abuse disorders, **1**:250–251
Behçet disease, **1**:180–181, **9**:190–196, 190*f*, 191*t*, 192*f*, 193*f*, 194*f*, **12**:194–195
azathioprine for, **1**:180, **9**:195
diagnosis/differential diagnosis of, **9**:190–191, 191*t*, 194
HLA association in, **1**:180, **9**:72*t*, 194, **12**:194
hypopyon in, **1**:180, 181, **9**:193, 193*f*
nonocular systemic manifestations of, **9**:191–192, 192*f*
ocular manifestations of, **1**:181, **9**:192–193
pathogenesis of, **9**:194
prognosis for, **9**:195–196
treatment of, **1**:180, **9**:194–195
Behr optic atrophy, **6**:311
Belafilcon A contact lenses, **3**:177*t*
Bell phenomenon, in ptosis evaluation, **6**:179, **7**:203
Bell's palsy, **5**:286
Benadryl. *See* Diphenhydramine
Benazepril, **1**:76*t*, 78*t*
Bence Jones protein, corneal deposition of, **8**:319–320
Bendroflumethiazide, for hypertension, **1**:78*t*
Benedikt syndrome, **5**:226

Benicar. *See* Olmesartan
Benign acquired melanosis, 4:65*t*, 67, 67*f*, 8:234, 235*f*, 237
Benign episodic pupillary mydriasis, 5:274
Benign essential blepharospasm, 5:289–290, 289*t*, 290*f*, 7:218–220, 219*f*. *See also* Blepharospasm
Benign facial fasciculations, 5:292
Benign hereditary intraepithelial dyskeratosis, 8:226*t*
Benign lymphoid folliculosis, 4:71, 8:24, 24*f*
Benign lymphoid hyperplasia, 4:72, 72*f*. *See also* Lymphoid hyperplasia
Benign lymphoid pseudotumor/pseudolymphoma. *See* Lymphoid hyperplasia
Benign melanosis. *See* Benign acquired melanosis
Benign mixed tumor (pleomorphic adenoma)
  of eyelid, 7:162
  of lacrimal gland, 4:236, 237*f*, 7:86–87, 86*f*
Benign monoclonal gammopathy, corneal deposits in, 8:320
Benign paroxysmal positional vertigo, nystagmus and, 5:250
Benign prostatic hypertrophy, α-blockers for, intraoperative floppy iris syndrome and, 11:74, 154–155
Benign reactive lymphoid hyperplasia. *See* Lymphoid hyperplasia
Benign retinal vasculitis (papillophlebitis), 4:164, 5:131–132, 132*f*, 12:128
"Benjamin Franklin" bifocal, 3:147, 148*f*
Benoxinate, with fluorescein, 2:387*t*, 389
Benzalkonium
  absorption affected by, 2:327
  in artificial tears, 2:391
  toxic reactions to, 2:322, 8:359, 360, 10:169
Benzathine penicillin, 1:45*t*
Benzodiazepines, 1:253–254, 253*t*
  for seizures, 1:263*t*, 297
Benztropine, for Parkinson disease, 1:259
Benzylamines, 1:55*t*, 65
Berger space, 12:7
Bergmeister papilla, 2:85, 4:132, 133, 6:307, 12:307. *See also* Hyaloid artery/system, persistence/remnants of
Berlin edema (commotio retinae), 4:20, 12:319, 320*f*
Berlin nodules, in uveitis, 9:87*f*, 88
Bernasconi-Cassinari, artery of, 5:16
Bernheimer-Seitelberger disease (GM$_2$ gangliosidosis type III), 6:401*t*
Berry (saccular) aneurysm, 1:97, 5:350
Besifloxacin, 1:61
Best-corrected visual acuity, in low vision assessment, 5:92. *See also* Visual acuity
Best disease (vitelliform macular dystrophy/vitelliruptive macular degeneration), 4:174–175, 6:293–294, 294*f*, 12:236–237, 237*f*
  bestrophin defect causing, 2:297, 4:175, 6:294, 12:236
  electro-oculogram in, 6:293, 294, 12:44, 237
  identification of carriers for, 2:217
  retinal pigment epithelium in, 2:308–309
Best1 (*VMD2*/vitelliform macular dystrophy) gene, 4:174–175, 6:294, 10:11*t*, 12:236
Bestrophin, mutations in, 2:297, 4:175, 6:294, 12:236
Beta (β)-adrenergic agents, 2:347*t*, 348–351, 350*t*
  agonists, 2:347*t*, 348–349
    for pulmonary diseases, 1:144–145, 145*t*

antagonists, 2:349–351, 350*t*. *See also* Beta (β)-blockers
    for glaucoma, 2:264*t*, 347*t*, 348–349
Beta (β)-adrenergic receptors, 2:264*t*, 344, 345*f*, 347*t*, 348–349
  in iris–ciliary body, 2:259*t*, 262, 263
  signal transduction and, 2:262, 262*f*, 263, 264*t*
  in tear secretion, 2:243, 243*f*
Beta (β)-blockers, 2:349–351, 350*t*
  for angina, 1:108, 109*t*
  cholesterol levels affected by, 1:139
  dry eye and, 8:61
  elevated intraocular pressure masked by, 10:80
  for glaucoma, 2:264*t*, 349–351, 350*t*, 10:156, 162–163*t*, 167–168
    in children, 6:242, 10:156
    in combination preparations, 10:165*t*, 167, 173
    during pregnancy/lactation, 10:176
    side effects of, 10:156, 162–163*t*, 168
    suppression of aqueous formation and, 10:15, 167
  for heart failure, 1:118–119, 120
  for hemangiomas, 7:64
  for hypertension, 1:76*t*, 78*t*, 79*t*, 80–81
    with α-blockers, 1:77*t*, 82
  for hyperthyroidism, 1:211
  for hyphema, 8:368
  for ischemic heart disease, 1:109*t*
    non–ST-segment elevation acute coronary syndrome, 1:111
  ocular effects of, 1:128, 301*t*. *See also* Beta (β)-blockers, for glaucoma
  in perioperative setting, 1:303, 305, 307
  for postoperative elevated intraocular pressure, 10:101
Beta (β) carotene
  for age-related macular degeneration, 12:61–62
  antioxidant effect of, 2:315
  oral supplements and, 2:315
Beta (β) cells, pancreatic, in diabetes mellitus, 1:190
  injection of in management and, 1:202
Beta chemokines, 9:28*t*
Beta (β)-crystallins, 2:70, 276, 11:12
Beta (β)-galactosidase, defective, 2:213*t*
Beta (β)-hemolytic group A streptococci (*Streptococcus pyogenes*), 1:6, 8:133, 149
  orbital cellulitis in children caused by, 6:195
  orbital necrotizing fasciitis caused by, 7:44
Beta (β)-interferon, 1:243
  for multiple sclerosis, 5:327
Beta (β)-lactam antibiotics, 1:44, 56–59, 2:368–371, 368*t*. *See also specific agent*
Beta (β)-lactam ring, 1:56
Beta (β)-lactamase inhibitors, 1:59. *See also specific antibiotic combination*
Beta (β)-lactamases, 2:369
Beta (β)-lysin, in external eye defense, 8:95
Beta (β)-thalassemia, 1:148
  angioid streaks in, 12:84
  bone marrow transplantation for, 1:147, 148–149
Beta-zone peripapillary atrophy, 10:50
Betadine. *See* Povidone-iodine
Betagamma (β,γ)-crystallins, 2:276, 11:11*f*, 12
Betagan. *See* Levobunolol
Betaine, for homocystinuria, 6:399
Betamethasone, for uveitis, 9:101*t*

Betaseron. *See* Interferons (IFNs), β
Betaxolol, **1**:76*t*, **2**:259*t*, 350, 350*t*, 351, **10**:82, 106, 163*t*, 168
  for childhood glaucoma, **6**:242, **10**:156
Bethanechol, **2**:336*f*
Betimol. *See* Timolol
Betoptic. *See* Betaxolol
Better Hearing Institute, **6**:418*t*
Bevacizumab, **2**:333, 396
  for age-related macular degeneration/choroidal neovascularization, **2**:396, **12**:78, 86, 87
  for branch retinal vein occlusion, **12**:127
  for central retinal vein occlusion, **12**:131, 132*f*
  for macular edema, **4**:160, 169
    in diabetes mellitus, **12**:100
  for ocular histoplasmosis syndrome, **9**:225
  for proliferative diabetic retinopathy, **12**:106
  for retinopathy of prematurity, **12**:169
  for uveitic cystoid macular edema, **9**:301
  for uveitic neovascularization, **9**:303
Bevacizumab Eliminates the Angiogenic Threat of Retinopathy of Prematurity (BEAT-ROP) Cooperative Group, **12**:169
Bextra. *See* Valdecoxib
bFGF. *See* Basic fibroblast growth factor
BGI. *See* Baerveldt glaucoma implant
Biapenem, **1**:59
Bias (statistical)
  measurement, **1**:319
  recall, **1**:323–324
  selection, **1**:317
    in case-control studies, **1**:325
    in case series, **1**:322
Biaxin. *See* Clarithromycin
Biber-Haab-Dimmer (classic lattice) dystrophy, **4**:96–97, 97*t*, 99*f*, **8**:268*t*, 270*t*, 278–279, 279*f*
  genetics of, **4**:97, **8**:269*t*, 278
Bicanalicular stents, for canalicular trauma, **7**:272
Bicarbonate
  in aqueous humor, **2**:266*t*, 267
  in ciliary epithelium, **2**:351
  for malignant hyperthermia, **1**:313*t*
  for shock, **1**:294
  in tear film, **2**:238*t*, 240
  in vitreous, **2**:266*t*
Bicentric grinding (slab-off), for induced anisophoria, **3**:154, 155*f*
  reverse, **3**:154–155
Bichrome (red-green/duochrome/Worth 4-dot) test, **3**:135–136, **6**:55, 55*f*, 87
  in binocular sensory cooperation evaluation, **6**:87
  in nonorganic ophthalmic disorder evaluation
    monocular no light perception and, **5**:309–310
    monocular reduced vision and, **5**:311
  before refractive surgery, **13**:33
  in sensory adaptation testing, **6**:55, 55*f*
Bicillin. *See* Benzathine penicillin
Bick procedure, **7**:192
BiCNU. *See* Carmustine
Biconvex indirect lenses, for slit-lamp biomicroscopy, **12**:19–20
Biconvex optic, of intraocular lens, **3**:204*f*
Bielschowsky head-tilt test, **6**:85–86, 85*f*
  in superior oblique muscle paralysis, **6**:119

Bietti crystalline corneoretinal dystrophy/retinopathy, **8**:313, **12**:250*t*
Bietti nodular dystrophy, **8**:334–335, 335*f*. *See also* Spheroidal degeneration
Bifixation, in monofixation syndrome, **6**:57–58, 60
Bifocal add. *See also* Bifocal lenses
  power of
    determining, **3**:145–147
      with lensmeter, **3**:270–271, 271*f*
    occupation and, **3**:156–157
  selecting, **3**:146–147
Bifocal lenses. *See also* Bifocal add; Multifocal lenses
  for consecutive esotropia, **6**:103
  contact, **3**:176, 189–190, 189*f*, 190*f*
    alternating, **3**:176, 189, 189*f*
    simultaneous vision, **3**:176, 189–190, 190*f*
  for high accommodative convergence/accommodative esotropia, **6**:94, 95
  intraocular, **3**:226–227, 227*f*
  spectacle
    decentration and, **3**:157, 164
    design of, **3**:150–156, 151*f*, 152*f*, 153*f*, 154*f*, 155*f*, 156*f*
      occupation and, **3**:157
      Prentice rule and, **3**:150–156, 151*f*, 152*f*, 153*f*, 154*f*, 155*f*, 156*f*
    diplopia and, progressive addition lenses and, **3**:147
    fused, **3**:147, 148*f*
    image displacement and, **3**:150–151, 151*f*, 152*f*, 153*f*
    image jump and, **3**:151–152, 153*f*
      progressive addition lenses and, **3**:147
    induced anisophoria and, **3**:152–156, 154*f*, 155*f*, 156*f*
    in low vision/vision rehabilitation, **3**:296
    occupation and, **3**:156–157
    one-piece, **3**:147, 148*f*
    prismatic effects of, **3**:150–156, 151*f*, 152*f*, 153*f*, 154*f*, 155*f*, 156*f*
    progressive addition, **3**:147–150, 150*f*
    reading position and, **3**:150–151, 151*f*, 152*f*, 153*f*
    types of, **3**:147, 148*f*
Bifonazole, **1**:65
Big-H3 gene. *See* TGFBI gene
Biglycan, **8**:9
Biguanides, **1**:199*t*, 200–201
  for *Acanthamoeba* keratitis, **2**:385, **8**:169
Bilateral acoustic/central (type 2) neurofibromatosis, **5**:338, 339*t*, 340–341, **6**:363, 365, 371, **10**:148. *See also* Neurofibromas, acoustic
Bilateral diffuse uveal melanocytic proliferation, **9**:287, **12**:183, 183*f*
Bilateral no light perception, testing, **5**:307–308, 308*f*
Bilateral ptosis. *See* Ptosis
Bilateral vision/bilateral visual loss. *See* Binocular vision
Bile acid sequestrants, for hypercholesterolemia/heart disease prevention, **1**:137*t*
Bimatoprost, **2**:354, 354*t*, **10**:162*t*, 166
  for children, **6**:242–243
  in combination preparations, **10**:165*t*, 173
Binary fission, in bacterial replication, **8**:132
Binkhorst iris clip lens, **3**:207, 207*f*
Binkhorst prepupillary iridocapsular 2-loop lens, **3**:207, 207*f*
Binocular amplitude of accommodation, **3**:145
Binocular balance, in subjective refraction, **3**:136

Binocular blur, **5**:215

Binocular cells, in visual processing, **6**:43*f*, 44

Binocular diplopia, **5**:218

Binocular eye movements, **6**:34–37. *See also specific type*
  conjugate (versions), **6**:34, 35, 36*f*
    assessment of, **6**:81
  disconjugate (vergences), **5**:198–199, 198*t*, 204, **6**:34,
    35–37, 86–87, 413. *See also* Vergences/vergence
    system

Binocular indirect ophthalmoscope (BIO), in retinal
  examination, **12**:19. *See also* Ophthalmoscopy

Binocular observation, in indirect ophthalmoscopy,
  3:246–248, 248*f*, 249*f*

Binocular states of eyes, **3**:116

Binocular telescopes, **3**:300, 301*f*

Binocular transient visual loss, **5**:173, 185–186

Binocular viewing system
  for operating microscope, **3**:262, 262*f*
  for slit-lamp biomicroscope, **3**:253

Binocular vision
  abnormalities of, **6**:49–50, 50*f*. *See also specific type*
    abnormal visual experience and, **6**:46–49, 47*f*,
    48*f*
  assessment of, **6**:86–87
    low vision evaluation and, **5**:91
    nonorganic disorder evaluation and, **5**:311–314,
    313*f*, 314*f*, 315*f*
  physiology of, **6**:39–42, 40*f*, 41*t*
  single
    Panum's area of, **6**:40, 40*f*, 49
    testing field of, **6**:83, 84*f*
  transient loss and, **5**:173, 185–186

BIO. *See* Binocular indirect ophthalmoscope

Bio-Hep-B. *See* Hepatitis B vaccine

Biofilm, microbial, **8**:98, 132
  staphylococci forming, **8**:132–133
  virulence and, **1**:4

Biologic response modifiers/biological therapies, **9**:108*t*,
  114–115. *See also* Immunomodulatory therapy
  in cancer, **1**:235, 242*t*, 243–244
  in rheumatic disorders, **1**:161, 186
  for uveitis, **9**:108*t*, 114–115

Biomechanics of cornea, **8**:9, **13**:9–10

Biometry/biometrics
  before cataract surgery, **11**:82–83, 83*f*
  in IOL power determination/selection, **3**:213–219,
    214*f*, 215*f*, 216*f*, 217*f*, 218*f*, **11**:82–83, 83*f*, 84
    axial length, **3**:213–216, 214*f*, 215*f*, 216*f*, **11**:82–83,
      83*f*, 84
      unexpected refractive results after surgery and,
        11:168
    corneal power, **3**:216–217, 217*f*
    estimated lens position, **3**:217–219, 218*f*
    refractive lens exchange/clear lens extraction and,
      13:140–141
  primary angle closure and, **10**:113

Biomicroscopy
  slit-lamp. *See* Slit-lamp biomicroscopy/examination
  ultrasound, **2**:50, 52*f*, **8**:33, 33*f*
    before corneal transplantation, **8**:417
    in glaucoma, **10**:70, 72*f*
    in pars planitis, **9**:136
    in uveitic glaucoma, **9**:296

Bioptic telescope, for distance spectacles, **3**:300

Bioptics, **13**:125, 137

Bioterrorism, smallpox vaccination and, ocular
  complications of, **8**:128

Biotherapy. *See* Biologic response modifiers;
  Immunomodulatory therapy

Bipedicle (bucket handle) flap, **8**:400

Biphakic eye, ultrasound axial length measurement in,
  3:214

Bipolar cells, **2**:74, 75*f*, 298, 299*f*, **5**:16, 28, 29, **12**:12,
  14*f*
  cone, **2**:298, 299*f*
  differentiation of, **2**:126
  rod, **2**:298

Bipolar disorder, **1**:247
  lithium for, **1**:257

Birdshot retinochoroidopathy (vitiliginous
  chorioretinitis), **9**:148–150*t*, 152–155, 152*f*, 153*f*,
  154*f*, **12**:186*t*, 190–191, 190*f*
  HLA association in, **9**:72*t*, 73, 148*t*, 152, **12**:190

Birth defects. *See specific type and* Congenital anomalies

Birth trauma
  congenital facial palsy and, **5**:287
  corneal edema and, **8**:265–266, 266*f*
  infantile corneal opacities and, **6**:216*t*, 217
  nystagmus and, **6**:318

Birth weight, retinopathy and, **6**:281, **12**:157, 163, 164,
  166. *See also* Retinopathy, of prematurity

Bisoprolol
  for heart failure, **1**:118
  for hypertension, **1**:76*t*, 78*t*

Bisphosphonates
  for osteoporosis, **1**:230–231
  uveitis caused by, **9**:128

Bitemporal visual field loss, chiasmal lesions causing,
  5:159–162, 160*f*, 161*f*

Bites, eyelid injuries caused by, **7**:181

Bitôt spot, **8**:77, 78, 78*f*
  Corynebacterium xerosis and, **8**:134

Bivalirudin, for non–ST-segment elevation acute
  coronary syndrome, **1**:111–112

Bjerrum (arcuate) scotoma, **10**:68, 70*f*

"Black box" optical system, **3**:76, 77*f*

Black sunburst lesions, in sickle cell disease, **12**:118,
  119*f*

Bladder (Wedl) cells, **4**:125, 125*f*, **11**:44, 170

Blastocyst, **2**:118*f*

Blastula, **2**:117

Blau syndrome (familial juvenile systemic
  granulomatosis), **6**:274–275, **9**:176

Bleb, filtering. *See* Filtering bleb; Filtering procedures

Bleb-associated endophthalmitis, **10**:196, 197*f*, **12**:354,
  356–357, 357*f*

Blebitis, **12**:356–357
  after filtering surgery, **10**:196, 197*f*

Bleeding/blood loss. *See* Hemorrhages

Bleeding disorders. *See also* Coagulation, disorders of;
  Hemostasis, disorders of
  cataract surgery in patients with, **11**:189–190

Bleeding time, **1**:152

Blend zone, **13**:74

Bleomycin, **1**:239, 241*t*

Bleph-10/Bleph-30. *See* Sulfacetamide

Blepharitis, 8:144*t*
  α-agonists causing, 10:169, 169*f*
  cataract surgery in patients with, 11:77, 190
  corticosteroid route of administration in, 2:360*t*
  dry eye and, 8:53, 53*f*
  infectious, 8:101*t*, 143–149, 144*f*, 144*t*, 146*f*
    in children, 6:193–194
  meibomian gland dysfunction and, 8:68, 143, 144*t*
  refractive surgery in patients with, 13:35, 37*f*
  in rosacea, 8:69, 144*t*
  seborrheic, 8:71–72, 143, 144*t*
  staphylococcal, 8:143–148, 144*f*, 144*t*, 146*f*
    keratitis and, 8:145–146, 146*f*
    marginal infiltrates in, 8:145, 146*f*, 147
Blepharochalasis, 7:222
Blepharoconjunctivitis
  α-agonists causing, 10:169, 169*f*
  contact, 8:183–185, 184*f*
  herpes simplex virus causing, 8:106, 106*f*, 110
  marginal corneal infiltrates associated with, 8:145, 146*f*, 147, 210
  staphylococcal, 8:145, 150. *See also* Blepharitis, staphylococcal
Blepharodermatitis, α-agonists causing, 10:169, 169*f*
Blepharophimosis, 6:178, 179*f. See also*
    Blepharophimosis syndrome
Blepharophimosis syndrome, 6:178, 179*f*, 7:145, 146*f*, 204
  with congenital ectropion, 7:145, 146
  with epicanthus, 6:178, 179*f*, 7:145, 147
Blepharoplasty, 7:222–227
  complications of, 7:226
    eyelid retraction, 7:214, 215, 226
  functional indications for, 7:222
  infraciliary incision for, for orbitotomy, 7:108*f*, 110
  laser resurfacing as adjunct to, 7:230
  preoperative evaluation for, 7:223
  techniques for, 7:224–225
Blepharoptosis. *See* Ptosis
Blepharospasm
  botulinum toxin for, 5:290, 6:163–164, 7:218–220, 219*f*
  essential, 5:289–290, 289*t*, 290*f*, 7:218–220, 219*f*
  nonorganic, 5:317
  in primary congenital glaucoma, 6:234, 10:143
  reflex, 5:292
  transient visual loss and, 5:175
Blessig-Iwanoff cysts, 2:82, 83*f*
Blind spot, 5:27
  idiopathic enlargement of, 5:112–113, 12:190
Blindness, 3:285. *See also* Low vision; Visual loss/impairment
  age-related macular degeneration causing, 4:167
  bilateral, testing, 5:307–308, 308*f*
  after blepharoplasty, 7:226
  cataract causing, 11:65, 65*t*
  cerebral/cortical, 5:172, 195, 6:415–416
  color. *See* Color vision, defects in
  day (hemeralopia)
    in achromatopsia, 6:291
    in cone–rod dystrophies, 5:114, 12:232
  diabetic retinopathy causing, 4:165, 12:89, 90
  functional. *See* Nonorganic (functional/nonphysiologic) ophthalmic disorders

  in glaucoma, 10:8, 78, 109, 117
    in children, 6:243
    incisional surgery contraindicated in, 10:185
    newborn PCG and, 10:143
    race and, 10:76, 78, 109
  herpetic stromal keratitis causing, 8:113
  "hysterical." *See* Nonorganic (functional/nonphysiologic) ophthalmic disorders
  in inborn errors of metabolism, 6:401*t*
  legal, 3:284
    central visual field loss and, 3:287
    peripheral visual field loss and, 3:292
  monocular
    testing, 5:308–310, 309*f*, 310*f*
    transient. *See* Monocular transient visual loss
  near, 3:285
  night. *See* Night blindness
    in Norrie disease, 6:296
    ocular ischemic syndrome causing, 12:134
    persistent fetal vasculature causing, 12:308
    postmeasles, 9:212
    in retinitis pigmentosa, 12:229, 230, 231
    in retinopathy of prematurity, 6:287, 12:157
    river (onchocerciasis), 8:141, 9:241–242
    snow, 8:352
    trachoma causing, 8:154
  transient. *See* Transient visual loss
  in uveitis, 9:304
  xerophthalmia causing, 8:77
Blindsight, 5:196
Blinking (blink reflex)
  abnormal, illusions caused by, 5:188
  medication absorption and, 2:323, 324, 327
  in newborn, 6:413
  protective/defensive function of, 8:3, 95
  tear secretion and, 2:244
BLOC1S3 gene, in Hermansky-Pudlak syndrome, 12:258*t*
Blocadren. *See* Timolol
Bloch-Sulzberger syndrome (incontinentia pigmenti), 2:219, 220, 6:364*t*, 379–381, 380*f*, 12:251*t*, 255
  retinopathy and, 6:380, 380*f*, 381, 12:251*t*, 255
Blocked fluorescence, 12:22
Blood. *See also* Hemorrhages
  clotting pathways of, 1:151, 151*f. See also* Coagulation
  composition of, 1:147
  cornea stained by, 4:92–93, 94*f*, 8:337*t*, 366–367, 367*f*, 10:96, 97*f*
  in LASIK interface, 13:114, 114*f*
Blood–aqueous barrier, 2:254, 265
  clinical implications of breakdown of, 2:272
  medication administration and, 2:329
Blood cells, 1:147
  development of, 1:147
Blood clotting/coagulation. *See* Coagulation
Blood-derived macrophages, 9:11
Blood glucose. *See* Glucose, plasma levels of
Blood–ocular barrier, immune response and
  of anterior chamber/anterior uvea/vitreous, 9:61
  of retina/retinal pigment epithelium/choroid, 9:64, 66
Blood oxygenation level–dependent (BOLD) imaging, 5:69, 80
Blood-pool isotope scans, in ischemic heart disease, 1:106

Blood pressure. *See also* Hypertension
ambulatory monitoring of, **1**:70, 270
cardiovascular risk and, **1**:69, 73*t*, 133*t*
classification of, **1**:70–71, 70*t*
glaucoma risk and, **10**:77
normal, **1**:69, 70*t*
phenylephrine affecting, **2**:345–346
screening, **1**:270–271
Blood–retina barrier, **2**:72, 78, 254, **12**:249
breakdown of, medication administration and, **2**:329
immune response and, **9**:64, 66
ischemic damage to, hemorrhages and, **4**:160, 161*f*
Blood vessels. *See* Vascular system
Blowout fractures
diplopia after, **5**:238–239, **7**:100–101
of medial orbital wall, **7**:98, 99*f*
orbital cellulitis following, **7**:42–43
of orbital floor, **7**:100–104, 102*f*
in children, **6**:124–126, 125*f*, 411, **7**:101, 102*f*
vertical deviations and, **6**:124–126, 125*f*
surgery for, **7**:101, 102*f*, 103–104
indications for, **7**:102–103
Blue-blocking intraocular lenses, **11**:138
Blue-cone monochromatism/monochromacy/
achromatopsia, **12**:214, 214*t*, 215
in children, **6**:291
ERG patterns in, **12**:36*f*
gene defects causing, **2**:297
ocular findings in carriers of, **2**:222*t*
Blue cones, enhanced (enhanced S-cone syndrome),
12:218–219, 219*f*, 248. *See also* Goldmann-Favre
disease/syndrome
Blue-dot (cerulean) cataract, **6**:247*t*, **11**:33, 34*f*
Blue-light phototoxicity, **2**:316
Blue nevus, **4**:65, **7**:165, **8**:235
Blue sclera, **8**:252–253
in Ehlers-Danlos syndrome, **8**:252, 325
in keratoglobus, **8**:302
in Marfan syndrome, **8**:325
in osteogenesis imperfecta, **8**:252
Blue-yellow color vision defects, **12**:47, 213, 214*t*
in dominant optic atrophy, **5**:139
tests for, **12**:49
Blue-yellow (short-wavelength automated) perimetry,
10:60–61
in glaucoma suspect screening, **10**:82–83
Blunt trauma, **12**:318–323, 320*f*, 321–322*f*, 322*f*, 323*f*.
See also Trauma
anisocoria caused by, **5**:269–270
in children, **6**:409–411, 410*f*, 411*f*
abuse and, **6**:404
orbital fractures and, **6**:124, 411, 411*f*
commotio retinae and, **4**:20
corneal injury caused by, **8**:363
eyelid, **7**:178
glaucoma and, **4**:109, **10**:38–39, 38*f*, 39*f*, 96
hyphema caused by, **8**:365, 365*f*
in children, **6**:409–411, 410*f*
LASIK flap dislocation and, **13**:108
lens injury/cataract caused by, **11**:50–51, 50*f*
optic neuropathy caused by, **2**:93
posterior segment, **12**:318–323, 320*f*, 321–322*f*, 322*f*,
323*f*

pupil irregularity caused by, **5**:263
retinal breaks/detachment caused by, **12**:272
in young patients, **12**:272–273
Blur circles, **3**:37, 39
blurred retinal image and, **3**:312
pupil size affecting, **3**:107–108, 107*f*
Blurred retinal images, meridional magnification and,
3:312, 312*f*
Blurred vision/blurring. *See also* Visual loss/impairment
in central serous chorioretinopathy, **12**:171
ocular misalignment and, **5**:215
SSRIs causing, **1**:255
in uveitis, **9**:84, 84*t*, 85
vertebrobasilar insufficiency and, **5**:186, 347
in Vogt-Koyanagi-Harada (VKH) syndrome, **9**:184
BMI. *See* Body mass index
BMP. *See* Bone morphogenetic protein
BMS. *See* Bare-metal stents
BMZ. *See* Basement membrane zone
BNP. *See* B-type natriuretic peptide
Bobbing, ocular, **5**:210, 251*t*, 259
Body dysmorphic disorder, **1**:248
Body lice, ocular infection caused by, **8**:149. *See also* Lice
Body mass index (BMI), cataract risk and, **11**:67
BOLD (blood oxygenation level–dependent) imaging,
5:69, 80
Bone
brown tumor of, orbital involvement and, **6**:343
eosinophilic granuloma of, **6**:337, 338*f*, **7**:84
in osteoporosis, **1**:227–228
Paget disease of, angioid streaks in, **12**:84
physiology of, **1**:228
Bone cyst, aneurysmal, orbital involvement and, **6**:343
Bone density/bone mass, measurement of, **1**:229
Bone marrow transplantation, for thalassemia, **1**:147,
148–149
Bone morphogenetic protein, lens placode formation
and, **11**:21
Boniva. *See* Ibandronate
Bony orbit. *See* Orbit
Bony tumors of orbit, **4**:245–246, 246*f*
in children, **6**:342–343
Borderline neoplastic proliferations, **4**:10
Borrelia burgdorferi, **1**:14–16, **5**:363, **8**:137, **9**:250,
12:210. *See also* Lyme disease/Lyme borreliosis
Boston keratoprosthesis, **8**:432, 433*f*
Botox. *See* Botulinum toxin, type A
Botryoid rhabdomyosarcoma, **4**:243, **6**:335, **7**:78
Bottom-up acuity testing, in nonorganic ophthalmic
disorders, **5**:311. *See also* Visual acuity, testing
Botulinum toxin, **7**:218–220, 219*f*
type A, **2**:26, 390
for acute spastic entropion, **7**:194
for blepharospasm, **5**:290, **6**:163–164, **7**:218–220,
219*f*
complications of use of, **6**:164
for consecutive esotropia, **6**:103
for corneal exposure in facial palsy, **5**:288
cosmetic uses of, **7**:231–232
for hemifacial spasm, **5**:291, **7**:221
indications/techniques/results of, **6**:163–164
for infantile esotropia, **6**:92
for migraine headache, **5**:298

for nystagmus, 5:258
for paralytic ectropion, 7:216
periocular injection of, 2:327
pharmacology and mechanism of action of, 6:163
ptosis caused by, 6:164, 7:208
for residual exotropia, 6:103
for sixth nerve (abducens) paralysis, 6:134–135
for strabismus, 6:163–164
strabismus caused by, 6:143
as tarsorrhaphy alternative, 8:391
for thyroid eye disease, 7:55
type B, for blepharospasm, 7:218–219
Botulism poisoning, ptosis/facial paralysis caused by, 5:280
Bouin solution, as tissue fixative, 4:29t
Bourneville disease/syndrome (tuberous sclerosis), 5:339t, 341, 6:364t, 371–374, 372f, 373f
glaucoma associated with, 10:28
Bovine spongiform encephalopathy ("mad cow" disease), 5:368
Bow-tie atrophy, 5:30f, 166
Bow-tie pattern, in regular astigmatism, 13:12–13, 13f
Bow zone/region, 2:274, 274f
Bowen disease, 7:167
Bowman layer/membrane, 2:44, 44f, 247f, 249, 4:77, 78f, 8:7, 7f
anatomy of, 2:44, 44f, 247f
biochemistry and metabolism of, 2:249
development of, 2:135, 8:4
dystrophies involving, 8:268t, 275–278. See also Bowman layer corneal dystrophies
healing/repair of, 4:16
refractive surgery and, 2:249
preparation of, 13:75–77, 76f
Bowman layer corneal dystrophies, 8:268t, 275–278
Reis-Bücklers, 8:268t, 270t, 275–277, 275f
genetics of, 8:269t, 276
Bowman probe, 6:208, 7:251, 252f
Bowman's zone, development of, 2:135
Boxer's syndrome, 1:265
bp. See Base pair
BP 180. See Bullous pemphigoid antigen II
BPD. See Butterfly pattern dystrophy
BPPV. See Benign paroxysmal positional vertigo
Brachium conjunctivum, 5:20f, 46, 48
Brachycephaly, 6:383
Brachydactyly, in Saethre-Chotzen syndrome, 6:388, 390f
Brachytherapy
for choroidal hemangioma, 4:292–293
for melanoma, 4:283–284, 284f
of iris, 4:271
for metastatic eye disease, 4:322
for retinoblastoma, 4:312
retinopathy after, 12:151–153, 153f
Bradyarrhythmias, 1:121, 122t
heart failure and, 1:120
Bradykinetic movement disorders, 1:258. See also Parkinson disease
Bradykinin, 8:177t
Brain. See specific structure and under Cerebral
Brain lesions
in Sturge-Weber syndrome, 6:376, 376f
in tuberous sclerosis, 5:341, 342f, 6:372, 373f

Brain natriuretic peptide (BNP)
in aqueous humor, 2:267
in heart failure, 1:114, 117–118
Brain stones (calcified astrocytic hamartomas), in tuberous sclerosis, 5:341, 342f
Brainstem
lesions of
arteriovenous malformations, 5:356
coma caused by, eye movements and, 5:258–259
facial weakness/paralysis caused by, 5:285
gaze palsy caused by, 5:210, 211f
vestibular disorders and, 5:205
in ocular motility, 5:37, 42–49, 44f, 45f, 46f, 47f, 49f
Brainstem encephalitis
CMV infection causing, 5:359
saccadic intrusions and, 5:256
Brainstem neural network, 5:40
Brainstem pursuit generators, 5:42f
Brainstem saccade generators, 5:40, 40f
Branch chain decarboxylase, defective, 2:213t
Branch retinal artery occlusion, 4:163, 12:136–137, 136f, 137f
Branch retinal vein occlusion, 4:164, 12:121–127, 122f, 125f
evaluation/management of, 12:124–127, 125f
neovascularization in, 4:164, 12:123
risk factors for, 12:123
visual prognosis in, 12:123
Branch Retinal Vein Occlusion (BRAVO) study, 12:127
Branch Vein Occlusion Study (BVOS), 12:124–125, 125f
Branchial arch syndromes, 6:392–394
BRAO. See Branch retinal artery occlusion
BRAVO (Branch Retinal Vein Occlusion) study, 12:127
Brawny scleritis, 4:114, 114f, 115f
Break, in retinal reflex, axis determination and, 3:126, 126f
Breaks (retinal). See Retinal breaks
Breast cancer, 1:273–274
eye involvement and, 1:244, 4:200, 215t, 316f, 316t, 320, 320f, 321, 322, 7:91–92, 92f
numb chin associated with, 5:303
paraneoplastic-induced saccadic intrusions and, 5:256
screening for, 1:272t, 273–274
Breast examination, for cancer screening, 1:272t, 274
Breast feeding
fluorescein dye transmission to breast milk and, 12:25
glaucoma medication use during, 10:176
refractive surgery contraindicated during, 13:31
Breathing exercises, 1:144
Brethaire. See Terbutaline
Brethine. See Terbutaline
Brevibloc. See Esmolol
Brevital. See Methohexital
Brewster angle, 3:12, 12f
Bricanyl. See Terbutaline
Bridge flap, 8:400
Brief psychotic disorder, 1:247
Bright-flash electroretinogram, 12:35, 37
in hereditary retinal/choroidal dystrophies, 12:224t
Brightness (radiance), 3:18, 19. See also Intensity
as image characteristic, 3:19
for medical lasers, 3:18t, 21
as positive dysphotopsia, 3:223

Brightness acuity, Brightness Acuity Test (BAT) for evaluation of, **3**:278, 279f, 293
Brilliance of retinal reflex, **3**:124, 124f
axis determination and, **3**:126
Brimonidine, **2**:346–348, 347t, **10**:157, 163t, 169–170
in combination preparations, **2**:347t, 350t, 355, **10**:165t, 173
in infants and children, **6**:243, **10**:157, 170, 176
during pregnancy/lactation, **10**:176
Brinzolamide, **2**:352, 352t, **10**:156, 164t, 170
in children, **6**:242, **10**:156
in combination preparations, **10**:165t, 173
British antilewisite (BAL), for Wilson disease, **2**:231
Brivudine, **1**:66
Broad-beam illumination, for slit-lamp biomicroscopy, **8**:13
Broad-beam lasers, for photoablation, **13**:24–25, 25
Brodmann area 8, **5**:40
Brodmann area 17 (striate cortex), **5**:28f, 34, 35f, **6**:42. See also Visual (calcarine/occipital) cortex
development of, **6**:44, 45f
abnormal visual experience affecting, **6**:46–49, 47f, 48f
Brodmann area 18 (parastriate cortex), **5**:28f, 34, **6**:42. See also Visual (calcarine/occipital) cortex
Brodmann area 19, **6**:42
Bromfenac, **2**:357t, 363
for cystoid macular edema, **9**:100
Bromocriptine, for Parkinson disease, **1**:259
Bronchial lavage, **1**:143
Bronchiectasis, **1**:142
Bronchitis, **1**:142
Bronchodilators, **1**:144–145, 145t
Bronchogenic carcinoma. See also Lung cancer
eye involvement and, **7**:92
Bronchoscopy, **1**:143
in cancer screening, **1**:275
Brow and forehead lift, **7**:232, 233f
Brow lift, pretrichial approach, **7**:232
Brow ptosis, **7**:227–228, 227f
dermatochalasis and, **7**:222, 227
Brown and Brenn (B&B) stain, **4**:31t
Brown and Hopps (B&H) stain, **4**:31t
Brown-McLean syndrome, **11**:148
Brown syndrome, **5**:239–240, 240f, **6**:122t, 130–132, 131f
iatrogenic, tucking procedure causing, **6**:120
inferior oblique muscle paralysis compared with, **6**:122f, 122t
surgery for, **6**:131–132
Brown tumor of bone, orbital involvement and, **6**:343
Browpexy, **7**:228
Bruch membrane, **2**:64–66, 65f, 75f, **12**:16f, 17
age-related macular degeneration/choroidal neovascularization and, **4**:168, 168f, 169, 169f, **12**:55, 56f, 57, 63–64, 64–65f, 65, 66f, 87, 88t
development of, **2**:127, 132
drusen and, **12**:55, 56f, 57
in retinal healing/repair, **4**:17
rupture of, **4**:22, **12**:320
photocoagulation causing, **12**:341
Brücke muscle, **4**:186
Brückner test, for strabismus and amblyopia, **6**:77

Bruits
carotid, **1**:95, **5**:180. See also Carotid occlusive disease
in orbital disorders, **7**:25
Brunescent cataract, **4**:127, 128f, **11**:40. See also Cataract
lens proteins in, **11**:13
surgery for removal of, **11**:195–196
Bruns nystagmus, **5**:250
Brush marks, in meibomian gland dysfunction, **8**:67
Brushfield spots, **4**:270t, 272f, **6**:227
BRVO. See Branch retinal vein occlusion
BSS. See Balanced salt solution
BTX-B. See Botulinum toxin, type B
Buccal mucous membrane graft, **8**:401. See also Mucous membrane grafting
for cicatricial entropion, **7**:198
for contracted socket, **7**:124
for eyelid repair, **7**:180
for eyelid retraction, **7**:215
for symblepharon, **7**:200
Buccal nerve, **5**:61, **7**:133, 134f
Buccinator muscle, **7**:133, 133f
Bucket handle (bipedicle) flap, **8**:400
Bucrylate. See Cyanoacrylate adhesives
Budesonide, for pulmonary diseases, **1**:145t
Budge-Waller, ciliospinal nucleus of, **5**:63
Bulbar conjunctiva, **2**:29, 30f, 34, **4**:47, 48f, **8**:4, 6. See also Conjunctiva
in superior limbic keratoconjunctivitis, **8**:81, 82, 82f
Bulbar (limbal) vernal conjunctivitis/keratoconjunctivitis, **6**:199–200, **8**:187, 188f
Bulla
of cornea, **8**:21t
in keratopathy (bullous keratopathy), **4**:89–91, 90f
in ocular cicatricial pemphigoid, **4**:54, 55f
of eyelid, **8**:20t
"Bullet" bifocal intraocular lens, **3**:226–227, 227f
Bullous keratopathy, **4**:89–91, 90f
bandage contact lenses for, **8**:403
after cataract surgery, **4**:89–91, 90f, **8**:384–385, **11**:147, 147f, 167
IOL design and, **11**:167
disciform keratitis and, **8**:117
Bullous pemphigoid, **8**:205t
Bullous pemphigoid antigen II, in cicatricial pemphigoid, **8**:199
Bull's-eye maculopathy/depigmentation
chloroquine/hydroxychloroquine causing, **1**:185, **12**:266, 266f
in cone dystrophies, **5**:114, **12**:232, 233f
differential diagnosis of, **12**:235, 236t
in Stargardt disease, **12**:235
Bumetanide
for heart failure, **1**:118, 119
for hypertension, **1**:76t
Bumex. See Bumetanide
Bundle branch block, left or right, **1**:122t
Bundle of His, **1**:121
Buphthalmos (megaloglobus)
in neurofibromatosis, **6**:370
in primary congenital glaucoma, **6**:238, **10**:143, 143f, 150

Bupivacaine, **2:**387*t*, 388, 389
　for blepharoplasty, **7:**224
　maximum safe dose of, **1:**298*t*
　toxic reaction to, **1:**299
Bupropion, **1:**256
Burkitt lymphoma
　Epstein-Barr virus associated with, **1:**25, 237
　of orbit, in children, **6:**337
Burns
　chemical. *See* Chemical injury
　in children, accidental cigarette burns, **6:**407
　eyelid, **7:**181
　thermal, **8:**351–352
　　cataract surgery incision, **11:**149
　　in children, **6:**407
Burst cells, **5:**46, 46*f*
Burst-mode phacoemulsification, **11:**107
Busacca nodules
　in iridocyclitis, **4:**270*t*, 272*f*
　in sarcoidosis, **4:**190, 272*f*, **9:**87*f*, 175
　in uveitis, **9:**87*f*, 88
Butazolidin. *See* Phenylbutazone
Butenafine, **1:**55*t*, 65
Butoxamine, **2:**259*t*
Butterfly pattern dystrophy, **4:**175, **12:**240, 240*f*
Buttonhole flap, **13:**102–103, 103*f*
Butylcyanoacrylate tissue adhesive, **8:**403–404. *See also*
　Cyanoacrylate adhesives
BVOS (Branch Vein Occlusion Study), **12:**124–125, 125*f*
Byetta. *See* Exenatide
Bypass grafting, coronary artery, **1:**110
　troponin levels in determining need for, **1:**105

C

C3 complement, in age-related macular degeneration,
　12:56
C₃F₈
　for retinal detachment, **12:**367
　for submacular hemorrhage, **12:**350–351
C4 complement, in aqueous humor, **2:**269
C5a complement, **8:**177*t*
C5a peptidase, streptococcal production of, **8:**133
C (parafollicular) cells, **1:**208
　medullary carcinoma arising in, **1:**214
c-Kit, in immunohistochemistry, **4:**34
C-loop posterior chamber IOL, modified, **3:**209*f*
C-reactive protein
　in coronary artery disease, **1:**99
　in giant cell arteritis/AAION, **5:**126*t*, 320
　　central retinal artery occlusion and, **12:**139
　in immune-mediated disease, **8:**182*t*
　statins affecting, **1:**136
c-wave, of electroretinogram, **5:**109, **12:**37. *See also*
　Electroretinogram
CA-MRSA. *See* Community-associated MRSA
Ca²⁺/protein kinase C–dependent signal transduction,
　in tear secretion, **2:**242–243, 242*f*
CAB. *See* Cellulose acetate butyrate
CAB mnemonic, **1:**289
CABG. *See* Coronary artery bypass graft
CACD. *See* Central areolar choroidal dystrophy

CAD (coronary artery disease). *See* Coronary heart
　disease; Ischemic heart disease
CADASIL. *See* Cerebral autosomal dominant
　arteriopathy with subcortical infarcts and
　leukoencephalopathy
Café-au-lait spots
　in neurofibromatosis, **5:**338, 340*f*, **6:**365
　in tuberous sclerosis, **5:**341
　in von Hippel–Lindau disease, **6:**374
CAIs. *See* Carbonic anhydrase inhibitors
Cajal, interstitial nucleus of, **5:**38, 39*f*, 42–44, 44*f*, 203
　skew deviation and, **5:**222
Calan. *See* Verapamil
Calcarine artery, **5:**22*f*
Calcarine cortex. *See* Occipital (primary visual/
　calcarine/striate) cortex
Calcarine fissure, **5:**34, 35*f*
Calcific band keratopathy (calcium hydroxyapatite
　deposition), **4:**88, 89*f*, **8:**328, 342–344, 343*f*
　in sarcoidosis, **8:**73
　in uveitis, **9:**85, 291
Calcific (calcified) drusen, **4:**169
Calcific plaques, senile scleral, **4:**115, 116*f*, **8:**9, 345–346,
　346*f*
Calcifications, neuroimaging in evaluation of, **5:**82*t*, 87
Calcified astrocytic hamartomas (brain stones), in
　tuberous sclerosis, **5:**341, 342*f*
Calcinosis, in scleroderma, **1:**173
Calcitonin/calcitonin nasal spray, for osteoporosis, **1:**231
Calcitonin gene-related peptide
　in iris–ciliary body, **2:**259
　outflow facility affected by, **2:**50
　in signal transduction, **2:**264*t*
　in tear secretion, **2:**240
Calcium
　in aqueous humor, **2:**267
　for osteoporosis, **1:**230
　in signal transduction
　　in iris–ciliary body, **2:**261, 262–263, 263*f*
　　in tear secretion, **2:**242–243, 242*f*
　in tear film, **2:**238*t*
Calcium antagonists. *See* Calcium channel blockers
Calcium channel blockers, **2:**261
　for heart failure, **1:**119
　for hypertension, **1:**77*t*, 78*t*, 79*t*, 82
　for ischemic heart disease
　　angina, **1:**108
　　non–ST-segment elevation acute coronary
　　　syndrome, **1:**111
　ocular effects of, **1:**302*t*
Calcium channels, **2:**261
　L-type, **2:**261
　　mutations in, **2:**296
Calcium deposits, on intraocular lenses, **11:**169
Calcium embolus, transient visual loss and, **5:**177, 178*f*,
　179*t*
Calcium hydroxyapatite deposition. *See* Calcific band
　keratopathy
Calcium oxalate crystals, in nuclear cataract, **4:**127, 129*f*
Calcium (Ca²⁺)/protein kinase C–dependent signal
　transduction, in tear secretion, **2:**242–243, 242*f*
Caldwell-Luc procedure, for orbital decompression/
　thyroid eye disease, **5:**334, **7:**113

Callender classification, of uveal melanomas, 4:199
CALT. *See* Conjunctiva-associated lymphoid tissue
Calvarium, 6:383, 384*f*
   suture fusion and, 6:386
CAM. *See* Cell-adhesion molecules
cAMP
   in β-blocker mechanism of action, 10:167
   in signal transduction
      in iris–ciliary body, 2:262–263, 262*f*, 263*f*
      in tear secretion, 2:243, 243*f*
Campath. *See* Alemtuzumab
Can-opener capsulotomy
   for ECCE, 11:212
   for phacoemulsification, 11:115, 116*f*
Canal. *See specific type*
Canal of Dorello, 5:50
   sixth nerve (abducens) injury/palsy and, 5:235
Canalicular plugs, for dry eye, 7:271, 8:62. *See also*
      Lacrimal plugs
   canalicular obstruction and, 7:263–264, 271
   nasolacrimal duct obstruction and, 7:267
Canalicular stenting
   for canalicular obstruction, 7:264
   for canalicular trauma, 7:254*f*, 272–273
Canaliculi, lacrimal, 2:32*f*, 33, 34, 7:245, 245*f*
   agenesis/dysgenesis of, 7:250
   atresia/stenosis of, 6:203, 7:250
   development of, 7:243
   duplication of, 7:277
   infection of, 7:274, 274*f*. *See also* Canaliculitis
   obstruction of, 7:263–265
      irrigation/probing in evaluation of, 7:259–261,
         261*f*, 263
   reconstruction of, 7:186, 264–265
   trauma to, 7:179, 272–273
      obstruction caused by, 7:264
Canaliculitis, 7:274, 274*f*, 8:101*t*
   lacrimal plug migration causing, 7:271
   obstruction and, 7:264
Canaliculodacryocystorhinostomy, for canalicular
   obstruction, 7:265
Canaliculotomy, for canaliculitis, 7:274
Canaloplasty, 10:200, 211
Cancer, 1:235–244. *See also specific type or organ or
      structure affected and* Carcinoma; Intraocular
      tumors; Tumors
   chemicals associated with, 1:236
   chemotherapy and, 1:239–244, 240–242*t*
   classification/growth patterns and, 4:10*t*, 11*f*
   corneal nerve enlargement and, 8:328–329, 328*f*,
      329*t*
   DNA damage and, 2:169
   epidemiology of, 1:236
   etiology of, 1:235–237
   genetic and familial factors in, 1:236, 2:171–173, 172*f*
   in HIV infection/AIDS, 1:29, 40
   hypercoagulability and, 1:158
   incidence of, 1:235
   junk DNA and, 2:166
   loss of telomeric DNA and, 2:162, 166
   ophthalmic considerations and, 1:244
   radiation/radiation therapy and, 1:236, 237–239
   recent developments in, 1:235

   retinopathy associated with, 5:112, 114–115, 190,
      12:256–257, 256*f*
   screening for, 1:272–278, 272*t*
   vaccines against, 1:244
   viruses causing, 1:236–237
Cancer checkup, 1:272*t*
Cancer chemotherapy. *See* Chemotherapy
Cancer-cluster families, 1:237
Cancer genes, 2:171–173, 172*f*
Cancer vaccines, 1:244
Cancidas. *See* Caspofungin
Candela, 3:17, 18*t*
Candesartan
   diabetic retinopathy affected by, 1:205
   for heart failure, 1:118
   for hypertension, 1:76*t*, 78*t*
Candida (candidiasis), 8:139
   albicans, 1:20, 8:139, 139*f*, 9:274
      adherence in virulence of, 8:98
      chorioretinitis/retinitis caused by, 9:274–276, 275*f*
      dacryolith formation and, 7:266
      endophthalmitis caused by
         endogenous, 9:273–274, 274–276, 275*f*, 12:203
         postoperative, 9:126, 270
   glabrata, 9:274
   keratitis caused by, 4:83, 8:165, 166
   as normal ocular flora, 8:97, 97*t*, 139
   parapsilosis, 9:270
Candidate gene screening, 2:180–182
   positional, 2:182
Candle power (luminous intensity), 3:18*t*
Candlewax drippings, in sarcoidosis, 4:190, 9:175
Cannabis, intraocular pressure affected by, 1:251,
   10:21–22, 21*t*
Cannulas, for ECCE, 11:95–96, 95*f*
Canthal index, Farcas, 6:173
Canthal reconstruction, 7:179–180, 186–187. *See also*
   Eyelids, surgery/reconstruction of
Canthal soft tissues, trauma involving, 7:178–180
Canthal tendons, 7:141–142
   lateral, 7:137*f*, 139*f*, 142
   medial, 7:136, 137*f*, 141, 246
   trauma involving, 7:178–180
Canthaxanthine, crystalline maculopathy caused by,
   12:268*f*, 269
Cantholysis
   lateral, bulbar hemorrhage release and, 11:99
   for traumatic visual loss, 7:105
Canthoplasty, for persistent corneal epithelial defects, 8:87
Canthotomy, lateral
   for orbital decompression, 7:113, 113*f*
   for orbitotomy, 7:108*f*
   for traumatic visual loss, 7:105
CAP. *See* Chromosome arm painting
Capacitance, venous, increase in for heart failure, 1:119
Capillary-free zone (foveal avascular zone), 2:79*f*, 81,
   82*f*, 12:8
Capillary hemangioblastoma, retinal, 4:294–295, 294*f*,
   5:339*t*, 344, 344*f*, 6:364*t*, 374–375, 375*f*, 12:148–151,
   149*f*, 150*f*. *See also* Retinal angiomatosis
Capillary hemangiomas. *See also* Hemangiomas
   amblyopia and, 7:151
   of conjunctiva, 4:50, 8:240–241

of eyelid, 4:219–220, 220f, 7:24, 151–152, 8:240–241
of orbit, 4:240, 7:24, 63–64, 63f
of periorbital structures, 7:24
of retina. *See* Capillary hemangioblastoma; Retinal
    angiomatosis
and thrombocytopenia (Kasabach-Merritt
    syndrome), 6:339, 7:63
Capillary malformations, orbital, in children, 6:342,
    7:63–69
Capillary nonperfusion. *See* Retinal capillary
    nonperfusion
Capillary plexus
of ciliary process, 2:61
retinal, 12·12
Capillary retinal arteriole obstruction, 12:135–136, 135f.
    See also Cotton-wool spots
Capillary telangiectasias, 1:97
Capoten. *See* Captopril
Capozide. *See* Captopril
Capsaicin cream, for postherpetic neuralgia, 8:122
Capsid (viral), 8:104
Capsular block syndrome, 10:124, 11:166–167
Capsular cataracts, 11:33–34
Capsular fibrosis, 11:171
IOL decentration/dislocation and, 11:164
Nd:YAG laser capsulotomy for, 11:171, 171–175,
    172f, 199. *See also* Nd:YAG laser therapy,
    capsulotomy
Capsular hooks, 11:198, 198f, 199
Capsular opacification, 11:169–171
IOL design/material and, 11·170
multifocal IOLs and, 13:156
Nd:YAG laser capsulotomy for, 11:169, 171–175,
    174f. *See also* Nd:YAG laser therapy,
    capsulotomy
in uveitis, 9:294
Capsular phimosis, 11:171
in exfoliation syndrome, 11:199
Nd:YAG laser capsulotomy for, 11:171, 172f, 199. *See
    also* Nd:YAG laser therapy, capsulotomy
Capsular rupture, cataract surgery and, 11:144t,
    160–162
Capsular tension rings, for zonular incompetence,
    11:198, 199
Capsular theory (Helmholtz hypothesis) of
    accommodation, 11:19, 13:149–150, 150f
Capsule, lens. *See* Lens capsule
Capsule staining, for cataract surgery, 11:195, 195f
Capsulectomy/vitrectomy, for pediatric cataract
lensectomy without intraocular lens implantation
    and, 6:256, 257f
lensectomy with intraocular lens implantation and,
    6:258
Capsulopalpebral fascia, 7:135f, 140
Capsulopalpebral muscle, 2:28
Capsulorrhexis
advanced cataract and, 11:195
capsule staining for, 11:195, 195f
in children, 6:255, 256f
continuous curvilinear, 11:115–117, 116f
    capsule staining for, 11:195, 195f
    in children, 6:255, 256f
    for ECCE, 11:212

loose zonules and, 11:117
    in glaucoma, 11:202
    in uveitis, 9:292
for ECCE, 11:212
loose zonules and, 11:117
    in glaucoma, 11:202
for phacoemulsification, 11:115–117, 116f
Capsulotomy
anterior
    for ECCE, 11:211–212
    for phacoemulsification, 11:115, 116f
can-opener, 11:115, 116f
intraocular lens condensation and, 3:206
Nd:YAG laser, 11:171–175, 172f, 174f
    for anterior capsule fibrosis and phimosis, 11:171,
        171–175, 172f, 199
    for capsular block syndrome, 11:166–167
    for capsule opacification, 11:169, 171–175, 174f
    in uveitis, 9:294
    complications of, 11:173–175
    contraindications to, 11:172
    indications for, 11:171–172
    lens particle glaucoma and, 10:91–92, 11:63
    procedure for, 11:172–173, 174f
    retinal detachment and, 11:175, 184, 12:363
CAPT (Complications of Age-Related Macular
    Degeneration Prevention Trial), 12:63
Captopril
for heart failure, 1:118
for hypertension, 1:76t
for non–ST-segment elevation acute coronary
    syndrome, 1:111
ocular effects of, 1:302t
CAR. *See* Cancer, retinopathy associated with
CAR antigen (recoverin), 5:115, 12:256, 257
Carbacephems, 1:49t
Carbachol, 2:335–337, 336f, 338, 338t
Carbamazepine, 1:263t
as mood stabilizer, 1:257
ocular side effects of, 1:264
Carbapenems, 1:49–50t, 58–59. *See also specific agent*
Carbatrol. *See* Carbamazepine
Carbenicillin, 1:57, 2:368t, 370, 376
Carbidopa, for Parkinson disease, 1:259
Carbocaine. *See* Mepivacaine
Carbohydrate ("sugar") cataracts, 2:279–281
aldose reductase in development of, 2:280–281, 11:15
Carbohydrate sulfotransferase 6 (CHST6) gene, in
    macular dystrophy, 4:96, 8:269t, 283
Carbohydrates
in aqueous humor, 2:266t, 268
metabolism of
    in cornea, 2:248
        corneal changes in disorders of, 8:305–308, 306t
            mucolipidoses and, 8:312
    in lens, 2:279, 279–281, 280f, 11:13–15, 14f
    in retinal pigment epithelium, 2:304
Carbon, corneal pigmentation caused by, 8:337t
Carbon dioxide, in aqueous humor, 2:272
Carbon dioxide laser, 3:24. *See also* Laser therapy;
    Lasers
for hemangioma, 7:152
for skin resurfacing, 7:230

Carbonic anhydrase
in aqueous humor, 2:269
dynamics and, 2:255, 351, 10:15
in ciliary epithelium, 2:351, 352, 10:170
Carbonic anhydrase inhibitors, 2:255, 351–354, 352t
dry eye and, 8:61
for glaucoma, 2:255, 351–354, 352t, 10:156–157,
163–164t, 170–171
in children, 6:242, 243, 10:156–157
for intraocular pressure control in chemical injuries,
8:358
for postoperative elevated intraocular pressure,
10:101
in suppression of aqueous formation, 2:255, 351, 352,
10:15, 170
teratogenicity of, 10:176
Carboplatin, for retinoblastoma, 4:310, 311
Carboxypenicillins, 1:57
Carboxypeptidase E, in aqueous humor, 2:267, 270
Carcinogenesis, 1:235–237
loss of telomeric DNA and, 2:162, 166
Carcinoma, 4:10t, 11f. See also specific type or structure
affected and Adenocarcinoma; Carcinoma in situ
adenoid cystic (cylindroma)
of eyelid, 7:162
of lacrimal glands, 4:236–238, 237f, 7:87
basal cell. See Basal cell carcinoma
of conjunctiva, 8:226t, 231–232, 232f
intraocular extension and, 4:322
staging of, 4:332–333t
of eyelid, 4:217–219, 218f, 219f, 220f, 7:168–172, 169f,
170f, 172, 173f
intraocular extension of, 4:322
metastatic, 4:315–322. See also Metastatic eye disease
sebaceous, 4:215t, 221–224, 222f, 223f, 7:173–175,
174f, 8:233, 234f
squamous cell. See Squamous cell carcinoma
thyroid, 1:213–214
retinoblastoma associated with, 4:314t
Carcinoma in situ
of conjunctiva, 4:63–64, 64f, 8:228
of cornea, 4:100
of eyelid
Bowen disease, 7:167
keratoacanthoma, 4:215t, 216, 216f, 7:167–168, 167f
sebaceous, 4:222, 223f
Cardene. See Nicardipine
Cardiac arrest. See Cardiopulmonary arrest
Cardiac compressions, in CPR, 1:290, 291
Cardiac disease. See Heart disease
Cardiac emboli, transient visual loss and, 5:177–178,
179f
Cardiac enzymes, in ischemic heart disease, 1:104–105
Cardiac failure. See Congestive heart failure
Cardiac glycosides. See Digitalis/digitoxin/digoxin
Cardiac rhythm, disorders of, 1:121–127. See also
Arrhythmias
Cardiac-specific troponins (troponins T and I), in acute
coronary syndrome, 1:105
Cardiac transplantation, for heart failure, 1:120
Cardiff Acuity Test, 6:73
Cardinal points, 3:75
in schematic eye, 3:104f

Cardinal positions of gaze, 6:28, 28f, 80
extraocular muscle action and, 6:30–32, 30f, 31f, 32f,
33f, 34f
yoke muscles and, 6:28f, 35, 80
Cardiogenic shock, 1:103, 293. See also Shock
Cardiolite scintigraphy. See Technetium-99m sestamibi
scintigraphy
Cardiopulmonary arrest, 1:289–293, 292t
Cardiopulmonary resuscitation, 1:126, 289–293, 292t
medications used in, 1:292t
for ventricular fibrillation, 1:289, 292
Cardioselective β-blockers, 1:80
Cardiovascular disorders. See also specific type
central retinal artery occlusion and, 12:139
COX-2 inhibitors causing, 1:184
in Lyme disease, 1:15, 9:253t
ocular ischemic syndrome and, 12:134
risk factors for, 1:132–133, 133t
diabetes mellitus and, 1:203, 207
hypercholesterolemia and, 1:132, 132t
hypertension and, 1:69, 73t
smoking and, 1:99, 133t
screening for, 1:270–272
Cardiovascular drugs. See also Digitalis/digitoxin/
digoxin
ocular effects of, 1:301–302t
Cardioversion
for atrial fibrillation, 1:125
for ventricular fibrillation, 1:126
for ventricular tachycardia, 1:125
Cardioverter-defibrillators, implantable. See Implantable
cardioverter-defibrillators
Cardizem. See Diltiazem
Cardura. See Doxazosin
Carmustine, 1:242t
Carney complex, eyelid manifestations of, 4:213t
Carotenoids (xanthophylls)
absorption spectrum for, 12:337, 338f
cataract risk affected by, 11:58
in lens, 2:314–315, 314f
in macula, 4:147, 12:8
age-related macular degeneration and, 12:62
in retina, 2:81, 318, 318f
Carotid arteries
common, 5:13f
disorders of, 1:95–97. See also specific type and
Carotid occlusive disease
dissection of, 5:353, 354
neuroimaging in evaluation of, 5:82t, 354
pain caused by, 5:301, 302
external, 5:12, 13–15, 13f, 15f
eyelids supplied by, 7:143
internal, 2:107, 107f, 109, 5:11f, 12, 13f, 14f, 15, 15f,
16, 17f, 18f, 20f
aneurysm of, 5:164, 350, 350f, 351
chiasmal syndromes caused by, 5:164
third nerve (oculomotor) palsy and, 5:229, 273,
351
cranial nerve relationship and, 5:52f
dissection of, 5:353
Horner syndrome and, 5:267, 268, 269f, 302, 353
optic nerve supplied by, 2:93, 95
neuroimaging in evaluation of, 5:82t

orbit supplied by, 7:143
stenosis of. *See* Carotid stenosis
stenting of, 5:182–183
ultrasonography in evaluation of, 5:81, 180
Carotid bruits, 1:95, 5:180. *See also* Carotid occlusive
disease
Carotid cavernous fistula, 5:237–238, 237f, 7:67, 68f, 69
choroidal perfusion abnormalities and, 12:176
neuroimaging in evaluation of, 5:82t
Carotid endarterectomy
for carotid stenosis, 1:91, 95, 95–97, 5:181–182
for ocular ischemic syndrome, 9:288, 12:134–135
Carotid occlusive disease, 1:95–97
central retinal artery occlusion and, 12:139
clinical/laboratory evaluation of, 5:180
diabetic retinopathy and, 12:94
neuroimaging in evaluation of, 5:81, 82t, 180
ocular ischemic syndrome and, 9:287, 12:133–135,
134f
retinopathy of, 12:133–135, 134f
central retinal vein occlusion differentiated from,
12:130, 133
stroke risk and, 1:95, 5:181, 181t
transient visual loss caused by, 5:173, 174, 177–183,
179f, 183–184
treatment of, 5:181–183
Carotid plexus, 2:105, 106f, 107
Carotid siphon, cerebral ischemia/stroke and, 1:92
Carotid stenosis, 1:91, 95–96. *See also* Carotid occlusive
disease
neuroimaging in evaluation of, 5:81, 82t, 180
stroke risk and, 5:181, 181t
transient visual loss caused by, 5:173, 174, 177–183,
179f, 183–184
treatment of, 5:181–183
Carotid territory ischemia. *See* Carotid occlusive
disease; Carotid stenosis
Carotidynia, 5:302
Carpenter syndrome, 8:322t
Carrier (genetic), 2:149, 214–215, 220. *See also specific
disorder*
inborn errors of metabolism and, 6:397
ocular findings in, 2:221–222f, 222t
Carrier (infection), in HIV infection/AIDS, 1:31
Carrier zone, of lenticular contact lens, 3:169
Carteolol, 2:350, 350t, 10:162t, 168
in children, 6:242
cholesterol levels affected by, 1:139
Cartesian ellipsoid/conoid, 3:54, 54f
Cartrol. *See* Carteolol
Caruncle, 2:22f, 31, 4:47, 48f, 8:4
edema of, in thyroid eye disease, 7:49
glandular lesions involving, 4:75
hypertrophied, punctal obstruction/malposition and,
7:263
lymphocytic lesions involving, 4:71
nevi in, 4:65
Carvedilol
for heart failure, 1:118
for hypertension, 1:77t
CAS. *See* Carotid arteries, stenting of
Case-control studies, 1:321f, 323–325, 324f
Case reports, 1:321, 321f

Case series, 1:321f, 322–323
Caseating granulomas, 4:7, 9f
Caspofungin, 1:65
for *Aspergillus* endophthalmitis, 9:278
for *Candida* endophthalmitis, 9:275–276
Cat-scratch disease, 5:130, 6:190, 8:136, 157–158,
9:262–265, 264f, 12:206, 207f
neuroretinitis and, 5:130, 6:312, 9:263–264
Parinaud oculoglandular syndrome and, 6:190,
8:157–158, 9:263
Catabolism, glucose, 1:190
Cataflam. *See* Diclofenac
Catalase, 2:312f
in lens, 2:313, 11:16
in retina and retinal pigment epithelium, 2:317
Catapres. *See* Clonidine
Cataract, 4:124–127, 125f, 127f, 128f, 129f, 11:39–64. *See
also specific type*
advanced, surgery for extraction of, 11:195–196
age-related, 11:39–47. *See also* Age-related cataracts
epidemiology of, 11:65–68
genetic contributions to, 11:37–38
alcohol use/abuse and, 11:58–59
amblyopia and, 6:64, 65–66
anterior polar, 6:247, 247t, 248f, 250t, 11:30–31, 32f
anterior subcapsular. *See* Cataract, subcapsular,
anterior
antioxidants affecting risk of, 2:314–315
atopic dermatitis and, 11:62
brunescent, 4:127, 128f, 11:40
lens proteins in, 11:13
surgery for removal of, 11:195–196
capsular, 11:33–34
carbohydrate ("sugar"), 2:279–281
aldose reductase in development of, 2:280–281,
11:15
cerulean, 6:247t, 11:33, 34f
chemical injuries causing, 11:53
in children, 6:245–260, 11:30–35, 31t. *See also*
Cataract, congenital; Cataract, pediatric
genetic contributions to, 11:37–38
"Christmas tree," in myotonic dystrophy, 5:338
clinical studies of, 11:66–68
complete (total), 11:34
congenital, 6:245, 11:30–35, 31t. *See also* Cataract,
pediatric
amblyopia and, 6:64, 65–66, 246
aniridia and, 11:29f, 30
bilateral, 11:31t
genetic contributions to, 11:37–38
hereditary factors in, 6:247t
surgical management of. *See* Cataract surgery, in
children
unilateral, 11:31t
contrast sensitivity affected by, 3:112, 11:70, 76–77
contusion, 11:50, 50f
coronary, 11:33
cortical, 4:126–127, 127f, 128f, 11:41–42, 42f, 43f,
44f, 45f
uveitis and, 11:59, 60f
visual acuity and, 11:70t
in cytomegalic inclusion disease, 6:184
degenerative ocular disorders and, 11:64

diabetic, **11**:55, 56*f*
  carbohydrate ("sugar"), **2**:279–281
    aldose reductase in development of, **2**:280–281,
      11:15
  in children, **6**:247*t*, 297
  surgery for, **11**:188, **12**:111
    preoperative evaluation and, **11**:80
drug-induced, **11**:47–49
duplication, **4**:124, 125*f*
electrical injury causing, **11**:54, 55*f*
epidemiology of, **11**:65–68, 65*t*
ERG and, **12**:41
etiology of, **6**:245, 246*t*, **11**:31*t*
evaluation of, **11**:69–88, 70*t*
  in children, **6**:250–251, 253*f*, 254*t*
fundus evaluation in patients with, **11**:80–81
in galactosemia, **11**:56–57, 56*f*
glassblowers', **11**:52–53
glaucoma and, **4**:106–107, 107*f*, **9**:22, 126, **10**:90–91,
    91*f*, 120–121, 122*f*, **11**:63, 64*f*, 201–203, 202*f*
  in children, **10**:141*t*, 148
  management of, **10**:199–200, **11**:201–203, 202*f*
  preoperative evaluation/management and, **11**:75,
    201–202, 202*f*
glaucoma surgery and, **10**:179
graft-vs-host disease and, **8**:203–204
in herpes simplex infection, **6**:185
history in, **11**:69–71, 70*t*
  in children, **6**:251
  surgery evaluation and, **11**:73–75
hypermature, **11**:42, 45*f*
  phacolytic glaucoma and, **4**:106–107, 107*f*, **9**:22,
    126, **10**:90–91, 91*f*, **11**:63
hypocalcemia and, **11**:57
infantile, **11**:30–35, 31*t*. *See also* Cataract, congenital
intralenticular foreign-body causing, **11**:51
intraocular lens implantation and. *See* Cataract
  surgery
intumescent, **11**:42
  phacomorphic glaucoma and, **11**:63, 64*f*
  surgery for removal of, **11**:196
ischemia causing, **11**:64
in juvenile idiopathic (chronic/rheumatoid) arthritis,
  9:129, 130, 130*f*, 131–132, 293
after keratoplasty, **11**:193
lamellar (zonular), **6**:247*f*, 247*t*, 248, 248*f*, 250*t*, **11**:30,
  32*f*
lens proteins and, **11**:13
in Lowe syndrome, **6**:247*t*, 302
management of, **11**:71–88. *See also* Cataract surgery
  in glaucoma, **10**:199–200, **11**:201–203, 202*f*
  low vision aids in, **11**:71
  nonsurgical, **11**:71–72
  pharmacologic, **11**:71–72
mature, **11**:42, 44*f*
  phacolytic glaucoma and, **10**:90–91, 91*f*, **11**:63
membranous, **11**:34, 35*f*
metabolic, **11**:55–57, 56*f*
  in infants and children, **6**:253–254, 253*f*, 254*t*, 398
morgagnian, **4**:127, 128*f*, **11**:42, 46*f*
  phacolytic glaucoma and, **10**:91
in multifocal choroiditis and panuveitis syndrome,
  9:162

muscarinic therapy and, **2**:338, 340
in myotonic dystrophy, **11**:57
in neurofibromatosis type 2, **6**:371
nuclear, **4**:127, 128*f*, 129*f*, **11**:39–40, 41*f*
  in children/congenital, **6**:247–248, 248*f*, 250*t*,
    11:33, 34*f*
  genetic contributions to, **11**:37–38
  hyperbaric oxygen therapy and, **11**:60–61
  postvitrectomy, **12**:368
  visual acuity and, **11**:39, 70*t*
  vitrectomy and, **11**:16, 60, 205–206
nutritional disease and, **11**:57–58
oxidative damage and, **11**:16
in pars planitis, **9**:138
pathology of, **11**:39–64. *See also specific type of*
  cataract
pediatric, **6**:245–260, **11**:30–35, 31*t*. *See also* Cataract,
  congenital
  abuse and, **6**:404
  age at onset and, **6**:245–246
  amblyopia and, **6**:64, 65–66
  bilateral, **6**:246*t*, **11**:31*t*
  evaluation of, **6**:250–251, 253*f*, 254*t*
  hereditary factors in, **6**:246, 247*t*
  history in, **6**:251
  laterality and, **6**:246, 246*t*, **11**:31*t*
  morphologic types of, **6**:246–250, 246*t*, 248*f*, 249*f*,
    251*f*
  ocular examination and, **6**:252–253
  persistent fetal vasculature (persistent hyperplastic
    primary vitreous) and, **6**:250, 250*t*, 252*f*, 279,
    280, **11**:38
  surgery for, **6**:254–260, 256*f*, 257*f*. *See also* Cataract
    surgery, in children
  systemic implications of, **6**:245, 246*t*, 253–254,
    253*f*, 254*t*
  unilateral, **6**:246*t*, **11**:31*t*
  visual function and, **6**:252
  workup for, **6**:253–254, 253*f*, 254*t*
perforating/penetrating injuries causing, **11**:51, 51*f*,
  52*f*. *See also* Cataract, traumatic
perimetry interpretation and, **10**:65
persistent fetal vasculature (persistent hyperplastic
  primary vitreous) and, **4**:132, **6**:250, 250*t*, 252*f*,
  279, 280, **11**:38, **12**:308, 308*f*
phacolytic glaucoma and, **4**:106–107, 107*f*, 127, **9**:22,
  126, **10**:90–91, 91*f*, **11**:63
phacomorphic glaucoma and, **10**:91, 120–121, 122*f*,
  11:63, 64*f*
after phakic intraocular lens insertion, **13**:126, 133*t*
  iris-fixated PIOLs, **13**:135
  posterior chamber PIOLs, **13**:136
polar, **6**:247, 247*t*, 248*f*, 250*t*, **11**:30–31, 32*f*
  surgery for removal of, **11**:196–197
posterior lenticonus/lentiglobus and, **6**:249, 249*f*,
  250*t*, **11**:26
posterior polar, **6**:247*t*, **11**:31
  surgery for removal of, **11**:196–197
posterior subcapsular. *See* Cataract, subcapsular,
  posterior
postvitrectomy, **11**:16, 60, 205–206, **12**:368
quetiapine use and, **1**:252
radiation-induced, **1**:238, **11**:51–53

after refractive surgery, **11**:193–194, 193*f*
refractive surgery in patient with, **13**:36–37, 154–156, 154*f*, 155*f*
    international trends in use of, **13**:201
removal of. *See* Cataract surgery
in retinitis pigmentosa, **12**:225–226, 230
rosette, **11**:50, 50*f*
rubella, **6**:183, **9**:210, **11**:35
scleritis and, **8**:220
in siderosis bulbi, **11**:53, 54*f*
smoking/tobacco use and, **11**:58–59, 67–68
snowflake, **11**:55, 56*f*
socioeconomic impact of, **11**:66
starfish, **6**:251*f*
statin use and, **1**:139, **11**:49
steroid-induced, **11**:47–48, 203
    pediatric uveitis treatment and, **6**:276
subcapsular
    anterior (subcapsular fibrous plaques), **4**:124, 125*f*
    posterior, **4**:124–125, 125*f*, **11**:42–44, 47*f*
        in children, **6**:249, 250*t*
        corticosteroids causing, **11**:47–48
        ischemia causing, **11**:64
        in myotonic dystrophy, **11**:57
        retinoblastoma differentiated from, **4**:305*t*
        silicone oil use and, **11**:205
        uveitis and, **11**:59
        visual acuity and, **11**:43, 70, 70*t*
"sugar," **2**:279–281
    aldose reductase in development of, **2**:280–281, **11**:15
sunflower, in chalcosis/Wilson disease, **8**:327, **11**:54, 57, **12**:327
surgery for. *See* Cataract surgery
sutural (stellate), **11**:33, 33*f*
tetanic, **11**:57
total (complete), **11**:34
traumatic, **4**:20, **11**:50–54, 50*f*, 51*f*, 52*f*, 55*f*, 206–209, 207*f*. *See also specific type*
    in children, **6**:251*f*
    surgery for, **11**:206–209
treatment-induced, **11**:60. *See also* Cataract, drug-induced
uveitis and, **9**:125, 291–294, **11**:59, 60*f*, 203–204
visual acuity and, **11**:39, 43, 70, 70*t*
    preoperative evaluation and, **11**:75, 76
in Vogt-Koyanagi-Harada (VKH) syndrome, **9**:189
in Wilson disease, **8**:327, **11**:57, **12**:327
zonular (lamellar), **6**:247*f*, 247*t*, 248, 248*f*, 250*t*, **11**:30, 32*f*
Cataract surgery, **11**:89–142. *See also specific procedure and* Lensectomy; Phacoemulsification
in acne rosacea, **11**:77, 190
α-blocker use and, **11**:74, 154–155
ancient/medieval techniques for, **11**:89–90, 89*f*, 90*f*
anesthesia for, **11**:98–102, 99*f*, 100*f*, 101*f*
for angle-closure glaucoma, **10**:204
aniridia and, **11**:200
anterior capsule fibrosis and phimosis and, **11**:171, 172*f*
anticoagulant use and, **11**:74, 175–176, 189–190
antimicrobial prophylaxis for, **11**:127–129, 128*f*
    corneal melting and, **11**:150
aphakic glaucoma after, **10**:148–149

aqueous misdirection (malignant/ciliary block glaucoma) and, **10**:131, **11**:153, 157–158
arcuate keratotomy and, **13**:52
astigmatism and
    conductive keratoplasty for, **13**:122
    modification of preexisting, **11**:130–131
    suture-induced, **11**:150, 212–213
    toric IOLs for, **11**:131, **13**:141–144, 142*f*
axial length extremes and, **11**:200–201
biometry before, **11**:82–83, 83*f*
in bleeding diathesis, **11**:189–190
in blepharitis, **11**:190
Brown-McLean syndrome after, **11**:148
bullous keratopathy after, **4**:89–91, 90*f*, **8**:384–385, **11**:147, 147*f*, 167
    IOL design and, **11**:167
capsular block syndrome and, **10**:124, **11**:166–167
capsular opacification and contraction and, **11**:169–175, 172*f*, 174*f*
    Nd:YAG laser capsulotomy for, **11**:169, 171–175, 174*f*. *See also* Nd:YAG laser therapy, capsulotomy
capsular rupture and, **11**:144*t*, 160–162
capsule staining and, **11**:195, 195*f*
capsulorrhexis in, **11**:115–117, 116*f*
    capsule staining for, **11**:195, 195*f*
    in children, **6**:255, 256*f*
    loose zonules and, **11**:117
in children, **6**:254–260, 256*f*, 257*f*
    amblyopia and, **6**:65–66, 255, 259
    aphakia correction and, **6**:259
    complications of, **6**:260
    glaucoma after, **6**:239, 260, **10**:141*t*, 148
    after penetrating trauma, **6**:409
    uveitis and, **6**:278
choroidal hemorrhage and. *See* Cataract surgery, suprachoroidal hemorrhage/effusion and
chronic uveitis after, **11**:158–159
ciliary block (malignant) glaucoma and, **11**:153, 157–158
in claustrophobia, **11**:187
clear corneal incision for, **11**:113–115, 113*f*, 115*f*
    with filtering surgery, **10**:200
    glaucoma and, **11**:201–202
    in uveitis, **9**:292
communication with patient and, **11**:188
complications of, **11**:143–185, 144*t*. *See also specific type*
    anterior segment, **11**:151–162
    antimicrobial prophylaxis in prevention of, **11**:127–129, 128*f*, 180
    capsular opacification and contraction and, **11**:169–175, 172*f*, 174*f*
    in children, **6**:260
    corneal, **11**:146–150
    endophthalmitis, **4**:123, 123*f*, 124, **9**:126, 269–271, **11**:143, 144*t*, 179–181, 179*f*
    hemorrhage, **11**:175–179
    IOL implantation and, **11**:133, 144*t*, 162–169
    needle penetration/perforation of globe and, **11**:185, **12**:325
    retinal, **11**:181–185, 182*f*
    in uveitis, **9**:293–294

conjunctival evaluation before, **11**:78
corneal conditions and, **11**:191–194, 192*f*, 193*f*
corneal edema and, **11**:143, 144*t*, 146–148, 146*t*, 147*f*
corneal endothelial changes caused by, **8**:384–385
corneal evaluation before, **11**:78, 83–84
    pachymetry, **11**:84
    topography, **11**:83–84
corneal melting/keratolysis after, **11**:150
    in patient with dry eye, **11**:150, 191
cyclodialysis and, **11**:157
cystoid macular edema and, **11**:143, 144*t*, **12**:142,
    143, 360
    in glaucoma, **11**:202–203
    after Nd:YAG capsulotomy, **11**:175
    vitreous prolapse and, **11**:162
in dementia/mental disability, **11**:187
Descemet membrane detachment and, **11**:149
with Descemet stripping automated endothelial
    keratoplasty and intraocular lens insertion (triple
    procedure), **11**:141, 192
in diabetes mellitus, **11**:188, **12**:111
    preoperative evaluation and, **11**:80
diplopia after, **5**:239
economics of, **11**:66
elevated intraocular pressure after, **11**:154. *See also*
    Elevated intraocular pressure
    in glaucoma, **11**:202
endophthalmitis after, **4**:123, 123*f*, 124, **9**:126,
    269–271, **11**:143, 144*t*, 179–181, 179*f*. *See also*
    Postoperative endophthalmitis
    prevention of, **11**:127–129, 128*f*, 180
    Propionibacterium acnes causing, **4**:123, 123*f*, 124,
    9:126, 269–270
endothelial keratoplasty and, **11**:141, 192
epithelial downgrowth and, **11**:151
in exfoliation syndrome, **11**:199
external eye examination before, **11**:77–78
external ocular abnormalities and, **11**:190–191
extracapsular cataract extraction (ECCE), **11**:94–96,
    95*f*, 211–213. *See also* Extracapsular cataract
    extraction
    early techniques for, **11**:90–92, 91*f*
    modern procedure for, **11**:94–96, 95*f*, 211–213
    renaissance/rediscovery of, **11**:94
filtering bleb (inadvertent) after, **11**:148–149
filtering surgery and
    cataract surgery combined with, **10**:199–200
    cataract surgery following, **11**:203
flat or shallow anterior chamber and, **11**:152–154
    angle-closure glaucoma and, **10**:131, 136
    intraoperative complications and, **11**:152–153
    postoperative complications and, **11**:153–154
    preoperative considerations/IOL power
        determination and, **11**:79, 84
Fuchs heterochromic iridocyclitis/uveitis and, **9**:134,
    11:59
fundus evaluation before, **11**:80–81
glaucoma and, **10**:199–200, **11**:201–203, 202*f*
    filtering surgery before, **11**:203
    filtering surgery combined with, **10**:199–200
    preoperative evaluation and, **11**:75, 201–202, 202*f*
globe exposure for, **11**:110
hemorrhage and, **11**:175–179, 189–190

high hyperopia and, **11**:200–201
high myopia and, **11**:200
history of use of
    in recent past, **11**:93–96, 93*f*, 95*f*
    in remote past, **11**:89–92, 89*f*, 91*f*, 92*f*
hyphema after, **11**:167, 177
hypotony/flat anterior chamber after, **11**:153
in hypotony, **11**:201
illusions caused by, **5**:188
incisions for. *See also type of incision and type of
    surgery and* Incisions, for cataract surgery
    complications related to, **11**:148–149
    for ECCE, **11**:211
    glaucoma and, **11**:201–202
    for ICCE, **11**:214
    intraocular lens implantation and, **11**:138
    leaking, **11**:144*t*, 148–149
        flat anterior chamber and, **11**:153
    modification of preexisting astigmatism and,
        11:130
    for phacoemulsification
        clear corneal, **11**:113–115, 113*f*, 115*f*
        scleral tunnel, **11**:111–113, 111*f*, 112*f*
indications for, **11**:72–73
    in children, **6**:254–255
informed consent for, **11**:88
intracapsular cataract extraction (ICCE), **11**:93–94,
    93*f*, 213–215. *See also* Intracapsular cataract
    extraction
    early techniques for, **11**:92, 92*f*
    modern advances/procedure for, **11**:93–94, 93*f*,
        213–215
intraocular lens implantation and, **11**:132–141,
    13:154–156, 154*f*, 155*f*. *See also* Intraocular lenses
    in children, **6**:257–258, 258–259
    complications of, **11**:162–169
intraoperative floppy iris syndrome and, **11**:74,
    154–155, 156*f*
iridodialysis and, **11**:157
iris trauma and
    in patient with preexisting iris trauma, **11**:207–208,
        207*f*
    as surgical complication, **11**:144*t*, 157
juvenile idiopathic (chronic/rheumatoid) arthritis–
    associated iridocyclitis/uveitis and, **9**:131–132,
    293
in keratoconjunctivitis sicca, **11**:190–191
after keratoplasty, **11**:193
lens anatomy alterations and, **11**:195–200
lens–iris diaphragm retropulsion syndrome and,
    11:156
lens particle glaucoma and, **10**:91–92, 92*f*
lens visualization and, **11**:194–195, 194*f*, 195*f*
    trauma affecting, **11**:206
limbal relaxing incisions and, **11**:130–131, **13**:52
loose zonules and, **11**:117, 118
    in glaucoma, **11**:202
macular function evaluation before, **11**:82
    retinal disease and, **11**:204–205
manual small-incision, **11**:96
measurements taken before, **11**:82–84, 83*f*
in megalocornea, **8**:254
in nanophthalmos, **8**:252, **11**:200–201

nucleus removal in
femtosecond laser for, **11**:127
fluid-based phacolysis for, **11**:127
laser photolysis for, **11**:127
phacoemulsification for, **11**:102–126. *See also*
Phacoemulsification
ocular hypotension after, **11**:153
ophthalmic viscosurgical devices (viscoelastic
agents) in, **11**:96–98, 97*t. See also* Ophthalmic
viscosurgical devices
outcomes of, **11**:141–142
in children, **6**:260
improving, **11**:86
paracentesis for, **11**:110
pars plana lensectomy, **11**:132
in pars planitis, **9**:138
patient preparation for, **11**:88
in patient unable to communicate, **11**:188
in pemphigoid, **11**:191
with penetrating keratoplasty and intraocular lens
insertion (triple procedure), **11**:141, 192
persistent fetal vasculature and, **6**:280
phacoemulsification, **11**:102–126. *See also*
Phacoemulsification
for phacomorphic glaucoma, **10**:121
for plateau iris, **10**:119–120
posterior capsule opacification and, **11**:143, 169–171
Nd:YAG laser capsulotomy for, **11**:169, 171–175,
174*f. See also* Nd:YAG laser therapy,
capsulotomy
in uveitis, **9**:294
posterior capsule rupture and, **11**:144*t*, 160–162
posterior misdirection of irrigation fluid and,
11:152–153
postoperative care and
in children, **6**:259–260
after ECCE, **11**:213
after ICCE, **11**:215
potential acuity estimation before, **11**:81
preoperative evaluation/preparation for, **11**:73–75
pseudophakic/aphakic bullous keratopathy after,
4:89–91, 90*f*, **8**:384–385, **11**:147, 147*f*, 167
IOL design and, **11**:167
psychosocial considerations in, **11**:72, 75, 187–188
pupil expansion and, **11**:194, 194*f*
in uveitis, **11**:203–204
pupil irregularity caused by, **5**:263
pupillary capture and, **11**:166, 167*f*
IOL decentration and, **11**:163
after radial keratotomy, **13**:48
rate of, **11**:65
refraction before, **11**:76
refractive errors after, **11**:168
after refractive surgery, **11**:75, 78, 193–194
IOL power calculation and, **11**:86–88, 193, **13**:189
with refractive surgery, **11**:130–131, **13**:154–156,
154*f*, 155*f. See also* Cataract surgery, astigmatism
and
international trends in use of, **13**:201
retained foreign matter and, **11**:207
retained lens material and, **11**:143, 147, 159–160,
12:357–359, 358*t*, 359*f*
retinal complications and, **11**:181–185, 182*f*

retinal detachment after, **11**:143, 144*t*, 184–185,
12:314, 362–363, 363*f*, **13**:176–177
family history as risk factor and, **11**:75
Nd:YAG laser capsulotomy and, **11**:175, 184,
12:363
retained lens material and, **12**:357, 358
in retinal disease, **11**:75, 204–205
retinal light toxicity and, **11**:183–184, **12**:333, 334
in retinitis pigmentosa, **12**:230
retrobulbar hemorrhage and, **11**:144*t*, 176–177, 189
scleral tunnel incisions for, **11**:111–113, 111*f*, 112*f*
shallow anterior chamber and. *See* Cataract surgery,
flat or shallow anterior chamber and
slit-lamp examination before, **11**:78–80
specular microscopy before, **11**:84
stromal/epithelial edema after, **11**:146–148
suprachoroidal hemorrhage/effusion and, **11**:144*t*,
177–179, 189
delayed, **11**:178–179
expulsive, **11**:178
flat anterior chamber and, **11**:152
systemic conditions and, **11**:188–190, 189*f*
tamsulosin use and, **11**:74, 154, 155
toxic anterior segment syndrome and, **11**:151–152
after trauma, **11**:206–209, 207*f*
in triple procedure, **11**:141, 192
uveitis and, **9**:126–127, 127*f*, 291–294, **11**:75,
158–159, 203–204
in pediatric patient, **6**:278
visual function evaluation after, **11**:141
visual function evaluation before, **11**:71, 76–77
vitreal complications/vitreous abnormalities and,
11:162, **12**:314
with ICCE, **11**:214
posterior vitreous detachment, **11**:184, **12**:275,
297
prolapse, **11**:162
vitreocorneal adherence, **11**:148
wound closure
complications associated with, **11**:148–149
after ECCE, **11**:212–213
postoperative endophthalmitis and, **11**:180
for scleral tunnel incisions, **11**:112–113, 112*f*
wound dehiscence/rupture and, **11**:149
zonular abnormalities and, **11**:195–200
iris coloboma/corectopia and, **11**:196, 197*f*
zonular dehiscence/lens subluxation or dislocation
and, **11**:197–199, 198*f*
Catarrhal (marginal corneal) infiltrates, staphylococcal
blepharitis/blepharoconjunctivitis and, **8**:145, 146*f*,
147, 210
Catastrophic antiphospholipid antibody syndrome,
1:171
Catatonic stupor, in schizophrenia, **1**:247
Caterpillar hairs, ocular inflammation caused by, **8**:362
Cathepsin D, in aqueous humor, **2**:267, 269
Cathepsin O, in aqueous humor, **2**:267, 269
Catheter/conventional/contrast angiography, **5**:77, 79*f*
in aneurysm detection, **5**:229
Catheter-based reperfusion. *See* Percutaneous coronary
intervention
Cation balance, in lens, maintenance of, **11**:17–19, 18*f*
Cationic protein, **8**:179*t*

Cats
  Bartonella henselae transmitted by, **8:**136, 157, 158, **9:**262
  toxoplasmosis transmitted by, **8:**141
CATT (Comparison of Age-Related Macular Degeneration Treatments Trials), **12:**78
Causal risk factors, **1:**337. *See also* Risk factor
Cause-and-effect diagram, **1:**346, 347*f*
Cautery, thermal
  for involutional ectropion, **7:**190
  for involutional entropion, **7:**196
  for punctal occlusion, **7:**271, **8:**61, 61*f*, 62
Cavernous hemangioma, **1:**97, **4:**6, **8:**240–241. *See also* Vascular malformations
  cerebrofacial. *See* Sturge-Weber syndrome
  of orbit, **4:**6, 240, 241*f*, **7:**64–65, 65*f*
  of retina, **4:**295, 296*f*, **12:**151, 152*f*
Cavernous optic atrophy of Schnabel, **4:**254, 255*f*
Cavernous sinus, **2:**104–105, 107, 107*f*, **5:**6*f*, 10, 26, 26*f*, 27*f*
  abducens nerve in, **5:**50–51
  carotid artery fistulas and, **5:**82*t*, 237–238, 237*f*
  choroidal perfusion abnormalities and, **12:**176
  ophthalmoplegia caused by lesions of, **5:**236–238, 237*f*
Cavernous sinus syndrome, **5:**351
Cavernous sinus thrombosis, **5:**357
  orbital infection/cellulitis and, **6:**196, **7:**43
Cavitation, **11:**102, 105, 105*f*, 107
CBD. *See* Corneal dystrophies, of Bowman layer
CCAAT box, **2:**149
CCBs. *See* Calcium channel blockers
CCC. *See* Continuous curvilinear capsulorrhexis
CCDF. *See* Central cloudy dystrophy, of François
CCN1 gene, in neurofibromatosis, **4:**244
CCR5/CCR5 receptor, HIV infection/AIDS and, **1:**34
CCR5-delta32 gene, HIV infection/AIDS and, **1:**34
CCR5 receptor inhibitors, for HIV infection/AIDS, **1:**34, 35
CCT (central corneal thickness). *See* Central cornea, thickness of
CCTA. *See* Coronary CT angiography
CCTV. *See* Closed-circuit television
CD antigens. *See also specific type*
  in immunohistochemistry, **4:**34
CD4+ T cells. *See also* Helper T cells; T cells
  in anaphylactic/atopic (type I) reactions, **8:**179
  class II MHC molecules as antigen-presenting platform for, **9:**37, 39*f*
  CMV retinitis control and, **12:**200, 201
  in delayed hypersensitivity (type IV) reactions, **8:**180, **9:**42, 48–51, 49*f*
  sympathetic ophthalmia and, **9:**52
  differentiation of, **9:**39–41
  in external eye defense, **8:**96
  in herpetic stromal keratitis, **8:**114
  in HIV infection/AIDS, **1:**29, 29–30, 30*t*, 33, **8:**130, **9:**305
  in HTLV-1 infection, **9:**218
  in immune processing, **9:**38–39, 40*f*
  regulatory, **9:**40, 41
  in Sjögren syndrome, **8:**63
CD4+/CD8+ ratio, in HIV infection/AIDS, **1:**29

CD8+ T cells. *See also* T cells
  class I MHC molecules as antigen-presenting platform for, **9:**37, 38*f*
  cytotoxic, **9:**42*f*, 43, 51, 53*f*
    in viral conjunctivitis, **9:**60
  in external eye defense, **8:**96
  in herpetic stromal keratitis, **8:**114
  in immune processing, **9:**40*f*
  regulatory (suppressor), **9:**41. *See also* Regulatory (suppressor) T cells
  in sympathetic ophthalmia, **9:**52
  in Sjögren syndrome, **8:**63
  in viral conjunctivitis, **9:**60
CD15, in lymphoma, **4:**239
CD19, in lymphoma, **4:**240
CD20, in lymphoma, **4:**240
CD20/CD25 receptors, in nonspecific orbital inflammation, **4:**232
CD25+ T cells, regulatory, **9:**40, 41
CD30, in lymphoma, **4:**239
CD34, in hemangiopericytoma, **4:**242
CD40
  orbital fibroblast, thyroid eye disease and, **4:**232, **7:**50
  in Sjögren syndrome, **8:**63
CD40 ligand, in Sjögren syndrome, **8:**63
CD45
  in fibrous histiocytoma, **4:**240
  in lymphoma, **4:**239
CD68, in fibrous histiocytoma, **4:**240
CD95 ligand. *See* Fas ligand
CD154, orbital fibroblast, thyroid eye disease and, **4:**232
CDA. *See* Granular corneal dystrophy, type 2
CDB1 (corneal dystrophy of Bowman layer type 1). *See* Reis-Bücklers corneal dystrophy
CDB2 (corneal dystrophy of Bowman layer type 2). *See* Thiel-Behnke corneal dystrophy
CDCR. *See* Conjunctivodacryocystorhinostomy
CDGDL. *See* Gelatinous droplike corneal dystrophy
CDKs. *See* Cyclin-dependent kinases
CDL1. *See* Classic lattice corneal dystrophy
cDNA, **2:**150
  from ciliary body–encoding plasma proteins, **2:**269
  sequencing, **2:**184, 185*f*
cDNA clone, **2:**149
cDNA library, **2:**154, 182
CDRB. *See* Reis-Bücklers corneal dystrophy
CDS (Cornea Donor Study), **8:**411
CDTB. *See* Thiel-Behnke corneal dystrophy
CEA. *See* Carotid endarterectomy
Ceclor. *See* Cefaclor
Cedax. *See* Ceftibuten
CeeNU. *See* Lomustine
Cefaclor, **1:**47*t*
  ocular effects of, **1:**301*t*
Cefadroxil, **1:**47*t*, **2:**370
Cefamandole, **1:**47*t*, **2:**370
Cefamycins, **1:**49*t*
Cefazolin, **1:**47*t*, **2:**368*t*, 370
  for bacterial keratitis, **8:**162*t*
  for endocarditis prophylaxis, **1:**8*t*
Cefdinir, **1:**49*t*
Cefditoren, **1:**49*t*
Cefepime, **1:**49*t*, 58, **2:**371

Cefixime, 1:48*t*
Cefizox. *See* Ceftizoxime
Cefmetazole, 1:49*t*
Cefobid. *See* Cefoperazone
Cefonicid, 1:47*t*
Cefoperazone, 1:48*t*, 2:371
Cefotan. *See* Cefotetan
Cefotaxime, 1:48*t*, 2:371
Cefotetan, 1:48*t*
Cefoxitin, 1:47*t*, 2:370
Cefozopran, 1:58
Cefpirome, 1:49*t*, 58, 2:371
Cefpodoxime, 1:48*t*
Cefprozil, 1:48*t*
Ceftazidime, 1:48*t*, 58, 2:368*t*, 371
    for bacterial keratitis, 8:162*t*
    for endophthalmitis, 12:355
        after cataract surgery, 11:181
Ceftibuten, 1:49*t*
Ceftin. *See* Cefuroxime
Ceftizoxime, 1:48*t*, 2:371
Ceftobiprole, 1:58
Ceftriaxone, 1:48*t*, 2:371
    for bacterial keratitis, 8:162*t*
    for endocarditis prophylaxis, 1:8*t*
    for gonococcal conjunctivitis, 8:152
        in neonates, 8:153
    for Lyme disease, 9:253*t*
Cefuroxime, 1:48*t*, 2:370–371
    for Lyme disease, 9:253*t*
    ocular effects of, 1:301*t*
Cefzil. *See* Cefprozil
"Ceiling effect," 1:340
Celebrex. *See* Celecoxib
Celecoxib, 1:183*t*, 184, 2:258, 9:99
Celestone. *See* Betamethasone
Cell-adhesion molecules, 8:177*t*, 9:39
    in homing, 9:44
    in neutrophil recruitment and activation, 9:18
Cell death, programmed (PCD/apoptosis), 2:147, 148
    by cytotoxic T lymphocytes, 9:51, 53*f*
    in DNA repair, 2:170
    Fas ligand (CD95 ligand/FasL) in, 9:51, 53*f*, 62
Cell lysis, by cytotoxic lymphocytes, 9:51, 53*f*
Cell-mediated immunity. *See* Cellular immunity
Cell wall, bacterial, 8:131–132
    innate immune response and, 9:14–15, 14*t*, 15
CellCept. *See* Mycophenolate mofetil
Cellophane maculopathy, 12:300
Cellular atypia
    dysplastic nevi and, 4:226
    primary acquired melanosis and, 4:68*f*, 69, 70*f*, 8:237, 238
Cellular immunity (cell-mediated immunity), 1:4–5, 8:178*f*, 179*t*, 180. *See also* Lymphocyte-mediated immune effector responses
    in cicatricial pemphigoid, 8:199
    in conjunctiva, 8:181
    deficient, in HIV infection/AIDS, 1:29
Cellular retinaldehyde-binding protein/cytoplasmic retinal-binding protein (CRALBP)
    in aqueous humor, 2:267
    mutations in, 2:297

Cellulitis, 4:208, 209*f*, 7:39*t*, 40–44
    dacryocystitis and, 7:275, 275*f*
    orbital, 7:41–44, 42*f*, 42*t*, 43*f*
        in children, 6:195–197, 196*f*, 7:42
        fungal (mucormycosis), 6:197, 197*f*
        after strabismus surgery, 6:156, 156*f*
    preseptal, 4:208, 209*f*, 7:40–41
        in children, 6:194–195, 7:40
        Haemophilus causing, 6:195, 7:40, 8:150
        after strabismus surgery, 6:156
Cellulose acetate butyrate (CAB), 3:176
CEMAS (Committee for the Classification of Eye Movement Abnormalities and Strabismus), 6:317–318
Center of rotation, 6:27, 27*f*
Centers for Disease Control, 1:280, 286
Centimorgan, 2:149
Central areolar atrophy of retinal pigment epithelium (geographic atrophy), 4:169, 170*f*, 12:58–59, 59*f*
    patient education/follow-up and, 12:60
Central areolar choroidal dystrophy, 12:245, 245*f*
Central caudal nucleus, 5:53
Central cloudy dystrophy
    of François, 8:268*t*, 270*t*, 289–290, 289*f*
        genetics of, 8:269*t*, 289
    genetics of, 8:269*t*
Central cornea, 2:43, 44*f*, 3:264
    thickness of. *See also* Cornea, thickness/rigidity of
        glaucoma and, 10:25, 74, 80
            in infants and children, 6:236, 10:151
            normal-tension glaucoma and, 10:80
        ocular hypertension and, 10:74, 84, 84*f*, 105
        tonometry measurements affected by, 10:24–25, 84
Central corneal power
    in IOL power determination, 3:216–217, 217*f*
    measurement of, 3:263–265, 263*f*, 264*f*, 265*f*, 266*f*, 8:38–39, 13:3–4. *See also* Keratometry
Central (pupillary) cysts, 6:227
Central (interpalpebral) fit, for rigid gas-permeable contact lenses, 3:184–185
Central fusion, 6:41
Central fusional disruption (horror fusionis), 6:49–50, 104–105
Central islands, after photoablation, 13:94–95, 94*f*
Central nervous system
    disorders of. *See* Neurologic disorders
    lymphoma of (primary intraocular lymphoma), 1:244, 4:140–142, 141*f*, 142*f*, 143*f*, 323–325, 323*f*, 325*f*, 5:358, 9:136, 281–284, 282*f*, 283*f*, 12:199, 199*f*
        central serous retinopathy differentiated from, 12:174
        in HIV infection/AIDS, 9:314
        uveitis differentiated from, 9:91, 136, 281–283
            in children, 6:276*t*
    metabolic abnormalities of, retinal degeneration and, 12:259–264
    midline anomalies of, optic nerve hypoplasia and, 6:308, 309
    mucormycosis of, 5:366–367
Central (type 2) neurofibromatosis, 3:365, 5:338, 339*t*, 340–341, 6:363, 371, 10:148. *See also* Neurofibromas, acoustic

Central optical clear zone. *See also* Optical zone (corneal)
  arcuate keratotomy and, **13**:49, 50, 51, 52
  radial keratotomy and, **13**:43, 45, 45*f*
    IOL power calculations affected by, **13**:187
Central posterior keratoconus (posterior corneal depression), **6**:215
Central posterior surface. *See* Base curve
Central (chief) ray
  for lenses, **3**:69
  for mirrors, **3**:90, 91*f*
Central retinal artery, **2**:78, 90, 94, 95*f*, 96, **5**:13*f*, 14*f*, 15, 16, 31, **10**:42, 43*f*, 44, **12**:12, 135
  angiography and, **12**:21
  occlusion of, **4**:162–163, 163*f*, **12**:138–140, 138*f*, 139*f*
    ERG in evaluation of, **12**:40*f*
    in sickle cell hemoglobinopathies, **12**:119
  optic nerve supplied by, **10**:42, 43*f*, 44
Central retinal vein, **2**:40*f*, 90, 96, **5**:19*f*, 24, 24*f*, **10**:43*f*, 44
  occlusion of, **4**:163–164, 165*f*, **12**:127–133, 127*f*, 128*f*, 129*f*, 132*f*
    angle-closure glaucoma and, **10**:135, **12**:129, 130
    neovascularization and, **10**:127
    cilioretinal artery occlusion and, **12**:137–138
    ERG in, **12**:40, 41*f*, 128
    evaluation and management of, **12**:130–131
    iris neovascularization in, **12**:128–129
      photocoagulation for, **12**:132
    ischemic/nonperfused, **4**:164, 165*f*, **12**:127, 128, 129*f*
    nonischemic/perfused, **12**:127, 128, 128*f*
    open-angle glaucoma and, **10**:77, **12**:129
    papillophlebitis and, **4**:164, **12**:128
    risk factors for, **12**:129–130
    treatment of, **12**:131–133, 132*f*
  optic nerve drained by, **10**:43*f*, 44
Central Retinal Vein Occlusion (CRUISE) study, **12**:131
Central scotoma, in low vision, **3**:285, 286, 293
Central serous chorioretinopathy/retinopathy/choroidopathy, **12**:171–176, 173*f*
  age-related macular degeneration differentiated from, **12**:60, 70, 71*f*
  fluorescein angiography in, **12**:23, 24*f*, 172–173, 173*f*
  photocoagulation for, **12**:175, 176, 341
Central suppression, **6**:50
Central surgical space (intraconal fat/surgical space), **7**:10, 107*f*, 108
Central tangent screening, for central visual field assessment, **3**:292, 293
Central Vein Occlusion Study (CVOS), iris neovascularization in central retinal vein occlusion and, **12**:128
Central vestibular nystagmus, **5**:249*t*, 250–253, 251*t*, 252*f*
  instability (periodic alternating), **5**:251*t*, 252–253, **6**:322
Central vision loss. *See also* Visual loss/impairment
  in leukemia, **6**:298
Central visual field deficit, **3**:286–287, 287*f*, 292–293
Central zone, **2**:70, **8**:37, 37*f*
Centration, for photoablation, **13**:83–84, 84*f*
  decentered ablation and, **13**:95–96, 97*f*

Centromere, **2**:149
CEP290 gene, in Leber congenital amaurosis, **6**:290
Cephalexin, **1**:47*t*, **2**:370
  for endocarditis prophylaxis, **1**:8*t*
Cephalgias, trigeminal autonomic, **5**:299
Cephalosporins, **1**:47–49*t*, 57–58, **2**:368–369, 368*t*, 370–371. *See also specific agent*
  allergic reaction to, **2**:369
Cephalothin, **2**:370
Cephradine, **1**:47*t*, **2**:370
Ceramide trihexosidase, defective, **2**:213*t*
Ceramide trihexoside, in Fabry disease, **8**:310, **12**:262–263
  plasma infusions for, **2**:231
Cerebellar arteries
  anterior inferior, **2**:104, **5**:21, 22*f*
    cranial nerve relationship and, **5**:52*f*
  posterior inferior, **5**:21, 22*f*
  superior, **5**:20*f*, 22*f*, 23
    cranial nerve relationship and, **5**:52*f*
Cerebellar hemangioblastoma, with retinal angiomatosis (von Hippel–Lindau disease), **4**:294–295, **5**:339*t*, 344, **6**:364*t*, 374–375, 375*f*, **12**:150
Cerebellopontine angle, **2**:104, 105
  tumors of
    Bruns nystagmus and, **5**:250
    seventh nerve (facial) palsy and, **5**:286, 287*f*
    sixth nerve (abducens) palsy and, **5**:234
Cerebellum, **5**:48–49
  dysfunction of, in multiple sclerosis, **5**:323
Cerebral achromatopsia, **5**:194
Cerebral akinetopsia, in Alzheimer disease, **1**:268
Cerebral aneurysm, **5**:349–353, 350*f*, 351*f*, 352*f*
  neuroimaging in diagnosis of, **5**:77, 79*f*, 80, 82*t*
  ruptured, **1**:97, 98, **5**:351, 351*f*
  third nerve (oculomotor) palsy and, **5**:228, 228*f*, 273, 351
    aberrant regeneration and, **5**:232
    divisional palsy and, **5**:231
    pupil-involving palsy and, **5**:229, 229*f*, 273, 351
    pupil-sparing palsy and, **5**:230
    in younger patients, **5**:231
Cerebral (intracerebral) angiography/arteriography. *See* Angiography/arteriography
Cerebral artery
  aneurysms of, **5**:350*f*. *See also* Cerebral aneurysm
  anterior, **2**:93, **5**:20–21
    cranial nerve relationship and, **5**:52*f*
  middle, **5**:20, 20*f*, 21
    cranial nerve relationship and, **5**:52*f*
  posterior, **5**:12, 19, 20*f*, 22*f*
    cranial nerve relationship and, **5**:52*f*
Cerebral autosomal dominant arteriopathy with subcortical infarcts and leukoencephalopathy, migrainelike headache in, **5**:300
Cerebral/cortical blindness, **5**:172, 195, **6**:415–416
Cerebral diplopia, **5**:218
Cerebral ischemia, **1**:91–95. *See also* Stroke
Cerebral peduncles, **5**:20*f*
Cerebral ptosis, **5**:280
Cerebral venous thrombosis, **5**:356–358
Cerebral visual impairment, **6**:415–416. *See also* Cerebral/cortical blindness

Cerebrofacial (encephalofacial/encephalotrigeminal) angiomatosis/Sturge-Weber syndrome, 5:339*t*, 341–342, 343*f*, 6:342, 364*t*, 375–378, 376*f*, 377*f*, 10:28, 147–148
  choroidal hemangioma in, 4:200, 292, 6:377, 377*f*, 12:181
  glaucoma associated with, 5:341, 343*f*, 10:28, 147–148
  in children, 5:341, 343*f*, 6:238, 377, 378, 10:147–148
  port-wine stain (nevus flammeus) in, 5:341, 343*f*, 6:238, 342, 375, 376, 376*f*, 8:241, 10:28, 147
Cerebrohepatorenal (Zellweger) syndrome, 6:398, 12:251*t*, 254, 261
  pigmentary retinopathy and, 12:251*t*, 254, 261
Cerebroside α-galactosidase, defective, 2:213*t*
Cerebrospinal fluid
  in primary central nervous system lymphoma, 9:282
  in syphilitic serology, 5:361, 9:248
  in uveitis, 9:94*t*
Cerebrovascular accident. *See* Stroke
Cerebrovascular disease, 1:91–98, 5:347–358. *See also specific type and* Stroke
  in diabetes mellitus, 1:207
  fourth nerve (trochlear) palsy caused by, 5:234
  hypertension management and, 1:79*t*, 85, 94
  internuclear ophthalmoplegia caused by, 5:225
  neuroimaging in evaluation of, 5:82*t*
  neuro-ophthalmic signs of, 5:347–358
  recent developments and, 1:91
  sixth nerve (abducens) palsy caused by, 5:234, 235
  third nerve (oculomotor) palsy caused by, 5:230
  transient visual loss caused by, 5:173
Cerebyx. *See* Fosphenytoin
Ceroid lipofuscinosis, 6:398, 401*t*, 12:251*t*, 254, 259–260
  pigmentary retinopathy in, 12:251*t*, 254, 260
Certolizumab pegol, 1:186
Cerulean cataract, 6:247*t*, 11:33, 34*f*
Ceruloplasmin, in Wilson disease, 2:231, 8:327
Cervical cancer, 1:273
  screening for, 1:273
  viral carcinogenesis and, 1:27, 236, 269, 273
Cervical fascia, 7:133
Cervical ganglia, 5:63
  superior, 2:15, 60
    dilator muscle innervation and, 2:258
Cervical nerve, 7:133, 134*f*
Cervicofacial trunk, of cranial nerve VII (facial), 2:106, 5:61
Cetamide. *See* Sulfacetamide
Cethromycin, 1:61, 64
Cevimeline, for dry eye, 8:60
C₃F₈. *See* Perfluoropropane
CFEOM1 (congenital fibrosis of extraocular muscles type 1) syndrome, 5:240
CFH (complement factor H) gene
  in age-related macular degeneration, 1:17, 4:167, 12:56
  in basal laminar/cuticular drusen, 12:240
CGDD1. *See* Granular corneal dystrophy, type 1
CGH. *See* Comparative genomic hybridization
cGMP
  in cone phototransduction, 2:293
  mutations in, 2:181, 295
  in rod phototransduction, 2:292, 293

cGMP-gated channel
  cone, 2:293
    mutations in, 2:296
  rod, 2:292–293
    mutations in, 2:295
CGRP. *See* Calcitonin gene-related peptide
Chalasis, 8:20*t*
Chalazion, 4:210–211, 211*f*, 7:152–154, 153*f*, 8:72–73, 72*f*, 148
  in children, 6:350–351
  internal hordeolum and, 8:148
  irregular astigmatism/monocular diplopia caused by, 3:164
  in meibomian gland dysfunction, 8:67
  in rosacea, 8:69
  sebaceous carcinoma misdiagnosed as, 7:173–174
Chalcosis, 11:54, 12:327
  corneal pigmentation in, 8:337*t*
  glaucoma and, 10:97
Chamber angle. *See* Anterior chamber angle
Chamber deepening. *See also* Anterior chamber, flat or shallow
  for angle-closure glaucoma, 10:204
Chancre, syphilitic, 1:12, 9:244
Chandler syndrome, 4:104, 8:344, 10:128–129, 129*f*. *See also* Iridocorneal endothelial (ICE) syndrome
Channelopathy, migraine headache and, 5:296
Charcot-Marie-Tooth disease, pigmentary retinopathy and, 12:250*t*, 254
CHARGE association, 6:171, 306
Charged particle radiation
  for choroidal hemangioma, 4:292–293
  for melanoma, 4:284
  for retinal capillary hemangioblastoma, 4:295
Charles Bonnet syndrome, 5:191
Chart review, monitoring systems and, 1:341–342
Chatter, 11:103, 107
Checklist (system of care), 1:346, 347*f*
CHED/CHED1/CHED2. *See* Congenital hereditary endothelial dystrophy
Chédiak-Higashi syndrome, 6:300*t*, 302, 12:259
Cheek advancement/rotation flap (Mustardé flap), for eyelid repair, 7:185–186, 185*f*
Cheek elevation, in eyelid repair, 7:184
Chelation therapy
  for band keratopathy, 2:334, 8:343
  for Wilson disease, 2:231
Chemical conjunctivitis, in neonates, 6:188
Chemical exposure, cancer associated with, 1:236
Chemical injury (burns), 8:353–359
  acid burns, 8:355
    in children, 6:407
  alkali burns, 8:353–355, 353*t*, 354*f*
    in children, 6:407
  cataracts caused by, 11:53
  in children, 6:407
  glaucoma and, 10:97
  limbal transplantation for, 8:94, 358
  management of, 8:355–359, 356*t*, 357*f*
  mucous membrane grafting for, 8:401
Chemodenervation. *See also* Botulinum toxin
  for strabismus and blepharospasm, 6:163–164
Chemokines, 8:177, 177*t*, 9:27, 28*t*

Chemoreduction. *See also* Chemotherapy (cancer)
for retinoblastoma, **6**:358–359, 360*f*
Chemosis, **8**:20*t*, 21
extraocular surgery causing, **8**:385
ionizing radiation causing, **8**:352
in thyroid eye disease, **7**:47*f*, 49
Chemotaxis, in neutrophil recruitment and activation,
9:18, 19*f*
Chemotherapy (cancer), **1**:239–244, 240–242*t*. *See also*
specific agent
canalicular obstruction caused by, **7**:264
for lacrimal gland tumors, **7**:87
for lymphoma, **4**:74, 324
for melanoma, **4**:285
for metastatic eye disease, **4**:322
for optic nerve glioma, **5**:152, 153, **7**:72
recent developments in, **1**:235
for retinoblastoma, **4**:310–311, 311*f*, **6**:358–359, 360*f*
for rhabdomyosarcoma, **7**:78
Cherry-red spot, **6**:302–303, 400–401*t*
in central retinal artery occlusion, **4**:163, **12**:138, 138*f*
in gangliosidoses, **6**:303, 401*t*, **12**:262, 263*f*
in inborn errors of metabolism, **6**:400–401*t*
in lysosomal metabolism disorders, **12**:262, 263*f*
myoclonus and, **6**:400*t*, **12**:262
Cherry-red spot myoclonus syndrome, **6**:400*t*, **12**:262
Chest compressions, in CPR, **1**:290, 291
Chest pain, in angina pectoris/myocardial infarction,
1:101
Chest physiotherapy
postoperative, **1**:144
preoperative, **1**:308
Chest x-ray
in cancer screening, **1**:272*t*, 275
in congestive heart failure, **1**:116
in pulmonary diseases, **1**:143
CHF. *See* Congestive heart failure
Chi (χ)-square tests, **1**:320
Chiasm (optic), **2**:89*f*, 93, 96, **5**:28*f*, 31–32, 32*f*, 33*f*
gliomas involving, **5**:151, 164
in neurofibromatosis, **6**:367–369
lesions of, **5**:159–165
anterior chiasmal lesions and, **5**:159–161, 160*f*
bitemporal visual loss patterns and, **5**:159–162,
160*f*, 161*f*
mid-chiasmal lesions and, **5**:161, 161*f*
in multiple sclerosis, **5**:324
neuroimaging in evaluation of, **5**:82*t*, 84, 84*f*
parasellar lesions and, **5**:162–165, 163*f*
posterior chiasmal lesions and, **5**:161
ocular development and, **2**:128
Chibroxin. *See* Norfloxacin
Chickenpox. *See* Varicella
Chief (central) ray
for lenses, **3**:69, 71*f*
for mirrors, **3**:90, 91*f*
Chievitz, transient nerve fiber layer of, **2**:126
Chikungunya fever, **9**:220
CHILD (congenital hemidysplasia with ichthyosiform
erythroderma and limb defects) syndrome, **8**:74
Childhood glaucoma. *See* Glaucoma, childhood
Children. *See also specific topic*
absence seizures in, **1**:261

abuse of
cataract and, **6**:404
gonococcal conjunctivitis and, **6**:189
ocular trauma and, **6**:404–407, 405*f*, 406*f*,
12:330–331, 330*f*
ametropia correction in, **3**:141–142
anisometropia in, **3**:116, 142
amblyopia caused by. *See* Anisometropic amblyopia
astigmatic spectacle correction in, **3**:140
bacterial conjunctivitis in, **8**:149–152
cancer in, **1**:235
cataract in, **6**:245–260, **11**:30–35, 31*t*. *See also*
Cataract, congenital; Cataract, pediatric
genetic contributions to, **11**:37–38
cataract surgery in, **6**:254–260, 256*f*, 257*f*. *See also*
Cataract surgery, in children
clinical/cycloplegic refraction in, **3**:137, 137*t*,
141–142, **6**:87–88, 88*t*
Coats disease in, **4**:149, 150*f*, **6**:287–288, 288*f*,
12:143–145, 144*f*
retinoblastoma differentiated from, **4**:305, 305*t*,
306*f*, **6**:358
corneal transplantation in, **6**:219, **8**:430–431, 431*t*
decreased/low vision in, **3**:306–307, **6**:413–417,
417–418*t*
enucleation in, **7**:119
ERG in, **12**:40, 41*f*
examination of, **6**:3–5
glaucoma and, **10**:149–152, 149*f*
preparation for, **6**:3, 4*f*
rapport and, **6**:3–5
eye development in, **6**:167–171, 167*f*, 167*t*, 168*f*, 169*f*
abnormalities of, **6**:171. *See also specific type and*
Congenital anomalies
eyelid anomalies in, **7**:145–152
glaucoma in, **6**:216*t*, 233–244, **10**:5*t*, 139–158. *See also*
Glaucoma, childhood
hepatitis B immunization in, **1**:281
Hib vaccine in, **1**:285
Horner syndrome in, **5**:267–268, **6**:230
hyperopia in, **3**:117, 141–142, **6**:169, 169*f*
hypertension in, **1**:69, 86–87
idiopathic intracranial hypertension in, **5**:124–125,
6:312–313
immunization schedule for, **1**:269
influenza immunization in, **1**:282
intraocular lens implantation in, **3**:223, **6**:257–258,
258–259
iris heterochromia in, **6**:227–228, 228*f*, 228*t*
in leukemia, **6**:354
low vision in. *See* Children, decreased/low vision in
meningococcal vaccine in, **1**:285
mydriasis in epilepsy and, **1**:263
myopia in, **3**:118, 141, **6**:169
neuroimaging in, **5**:82*t*
nystagmus in, **5**:245–247, **6**:288–289, 289*t*, 317–330,
319*t*. *See also* Nystagmus
monocular, **5**:246–247, 251*t*, **6**:326
ocular infection in, **6**:181–197
ocular trauma in, **6**:403–411, **12**:272–273
abuse and, **6**:404–407, 405*f*, 406*f*, **12**:330–331, 330*f*
optic nerve sheath meningioma in, **5**:149, **6**:368
orbital cellulitis in, **6**:195–197, 196*f*, **7**:42

orbital fractures in, **6**:124–126, 125*f*, 411, 411*f*, **7**:98
orbital hemangiomas in, **6**:338–341, 339*f*, **7**:63–64, 63*f*
orbital metastatic disease in, **6**:333*t*, 336–338, 336*f*, 338*f*, **7**:90–91, 91*f*
orbital tuberculosis in, **7**:45
pars planitis in, **9**:135
pneumococcal vaccine for, **1**:284–285
preoperative assessment in, **1**:305
preseptal cellulitis in, **6**:194–195, **7**:40, **8**:150
proptosis in, **6**:173
refractive surgery in, **13**:180–181
retinal degeneration onset in, **12**:251–252
staphylomas in, **4**:116, **6**:310, 415
third nerve (oculomotor) palsy/paralysis in, **5**:231–232, **6**:132–134, 133*f*
Chin lift, for opening airway, **1**:290
Chlamydia, **1**:16–17, **8**:137
conjunctival lymphoma and, **4**:74
conjunctivitis caused by, **4**:54, 55*f*, **8**:154–157, 155*f*, 156*f*
in adults, **8**:156–157, 156*f*
in neonates, **6**:187–188, **8**:153–154
gonococcal coinfection and, **1**:11, **8**:152
ocular infection/inflammation caused by, **8**:154–157, 155*f*, 156*f*
HLA disease associations and, **9**:71
persistence and, **8**:99
pneumoniae, **4**:74
psittaci, **1**:17, **4**:74, **8**:154
specimen collection/isolation techniques for diagnosis of, **8**:101*t*, 103
trachoma caused by, **4**:54, **8**:154–156, 155*f*, 156*f*
trachomatis, **1**:11, 16–17, **4**:54, 74, **6**:187, **8**:154
Chloasma, **7**:164
Chlorambucil, **1**:186–187, 240*t*, **9**:108*t*, 113
for Behçet disease, **1**:180, **9**:195
in cancer chemotherapy, **1**:240*t*
for uveitis, **9**:108*t*, 112, 113
in children, **6**:278
Chloramphenicol, **1**:52*t*, 63, **2**:372*t*, 375
intravenous administration of, **2**:329
Chlorhexidine, for *Acanthamoeba* keratitis, **8**:169
Chloride
in aqueous humor, **2**:255, 266*t*, 267
in lens, **2**:278
in tear film, **2**:238*t*, 240
in vitreous, **2**:266*t*, 286
Chloroma (granulocytic sarcoma), **4**:328, **6**:337, **7**:90
Chloromycetin. *See* Chloramphenicol
Chloroprocaine, maximum safe dose of, **1**:298*t*
Chloroptic. *See* Chloramphenicol
Chloroquine, **1**:185
toxicity of, **12**:266–267, 266*f*
age-related macular degeneration differentiated from, **12**:60
cornea verticillata and, **8**:346
EOG in evaluation of, **12**:44
multifocal ERG tracing in, **12**:38*f*
Chlorothiazide, **1**:76*t*, 78*t*
Chlorpromazine, **1**:251
corneal pigmentation caused by, **8**:348–349
lens changes caused by, **11**:49
retinal degeneration caused by, **12**:267
retrobulbar injection of, for pain control, **7**:118

Chlorpropamide, **1**:199*t*
Chlortetracycline, **2**:374
Chlorthalidone, **1**:76*t*, 78*t*
CHM (Rab escort protein 1/*REP-1*) gene, mutation in, **2**:298
in choroideremia, **2**:298, **12**:242
Chocolate cyst, **8**:243
Choking, **1**:292, 294
Cholesterol crystals, vitreous hemorrhage and, **4**:138
Cholesterol emboli (Hollenhorst plaques)
in branch retinal artery occlusion, **4**:63, **12**:136, 137*f*
in central retinal artery occlusion, **12**:139
transient visual loss and, **5**:175*f*, 177, 179*t*
Cholesterol intake/metabolism, abnormal, in ischemic heart disease, **1**:100
Cholesterol levels, **1**:132, 132*t*
classification of, **1**:131, 132*t*
drugs for modification of. *See* Lipid-lowering therapy
elevated. *See* Hypercholesterolemia
goals for, hypercholesterolemia management and, **1**:134, 134*f*, 135*t*
risk assessment and, **1**:132–133, 133*t*
screening, **1**:271
total, **1**:132*t*
Cholesterolosis, vitreous involvement in, **12**:311–312
Cholestyramine, for hypercholesterolemia/heart disease prevention, **1**:137*t*
Choline magnesium trisalicylate, **1**:183*t*
Cholinergic agents, **2**:334–344, 335*f*, 336*f*, 337*f*, 339*f*, 343*f*. *See also specific agent and* Muscarinic agents; Nicotinic agents
adverse effects of, **2**:338, 339*f*
antagonists, **2**:334, 340–342, 341*t*, 344, 348
adverse effects of, **2**:342, 343*f*
as mydriatics, **2**:260, 340–342, 341*t*
direct-acting agonists, **2**:334, 335–339, 336*f*, 337*f*, 338*t*, 339*f*
for acute angle closure, **10**:115
for glaucoma, **10**:157, 164*t*
in children, **10**:157
indirect-acting agonists, **2**:334, 336*f*, 339–340, 342–343, 346–348, 347*f*
as miotics, **2**:259, 335–340, 337*f*, 338*f*, 339*f*
Cholinergic neurons, **2**:259
Cholinergic receptors, **2**:259, 259*t*
drugs affecting, **2**:334–344, 335*f*, 336*f*, 337*f*, 339*f*, 343*f*
in iris–ciliary body, **2**:259, 259*t*
locations of, **2**:334
signal transduction and, **2**:264*t*
Cholinesterase/acetylcholinesterase
in acetylcholine degradation, **2**:335, 337*f*
defective, succinylcholine effects and, **2**:229–230
Cholinesterase/acetylcholinesterase inhibitors (anticholinesterase agents), **2**:259, 334, 336*f*, 338*t*, 339–340, 342–343
angle closure caused by, **10**:119
in cataract surgery, traumatic cataract and, **11**:208
cataracts caused by, **11**:49
for glaucoma, **10**:164*t*, 171
for high accommodative convergence/accommodative esotropia, **6**:94, 95
miotic action of, **2**:259, 338*t*, 339–340
uveitis caused by, **9**:128

Chondritis, auricular or nasal, in relapsing
    polychondritis, **1**:175
Chondroitin sulfate
    in cornea, **2**:250
    in corneal storage medium, **2**:395
    as viscoelastic, **2**:393, **11**:96
        elevated intraocular pressure and, **10**:101
Chondroitinase, for enzymatic vitreolysis, **2**:289
Chondrosarcoma, of orbit, **7**:79
    in children, **6**:336
Chopping techniques, in phacoemulsification,
    11:122–124, 124*f*
    instrument settings for, **11**:118–119
Chord diameter, of contact lens, **3**:167, 168*f*, 170. *See
    also* Diameter
    rigid gas-permeable contact lens fitting and, **3**:184*t*,
        185
    soft contact lens fitting and, **3**:183*t*
Chorda tympani, **2**:106, **5**:61
Choriocapillaris, **2**:65*f*, 66, 66*f*, 67*f*, 74*f*, **4**:187, 187*f*,
    12:12, 17–18, 17*f*
    angiography and, **12**:21
    atrophy of (choroidal dystrophy), **12**:242–246, 243*f*,
        244*f*, 246*f*
    in choroideremia, **12**:242–243, 243*f*
    differentiation of, **2**:132
    in gyrate atrophy, **12**:244
    immune response in, **9**:64–67
    perfusion abnormalities and, **12**:171
Choriomeningitis, lymphocytic, **6**:186, **9**:211–212
Chorionic villus sampling, **2**:149, 229
Chorioretinal biopsy
    in tuberculosis, **9**:261
    in uveitis, **9**:97–98
Chorioretinal disruption, traumatic (sclopetaria), **4**:22,
    203, **12**:323, 323*f*
Chorioretinal edema, in photocoagulation, **12**:342
Chorioretinal inflammation. *See specific disorder and*
    Chorioretinitis; Chorioretinopathy
Chorioretinal scarring
    ocular histoplasmosis and, **9**:221, 222*f*, **12**:81, 82*f*
    prophylactic treatment of retinal breaks and,
        12:283
    toxoplasmic chorioretinitis and, **9**:229, 229*f*, **12**:207,
        208*f*
Chorioretinitis, **9**:78*t*, 82*t*
    Candida causing, **9**:274–276, 275*f*
    in coccidioidomycosis, **9**:279, 280
    Cryptococcus neoformans causing, **9**:278
    in endogenous fungal endophthalmitis, **9**:273, 273*f*
    fungal, **4**:152, 153*f. See also specific type*
    in ocular histoplasmosis syndrome, **9**:221–226, 222*f*,
        223*f*, 224*f*, 225*f*
    in onchocerciasis, **9**:242
    relentless placoid, **9**:157, 158*f*
    sclopetaria, **4**:22, 203, **12**:323, 323*f*
    in syphilis, **9**:243, 245, 245*f*, **12**:205–206, 207*f*
        HIV infection/AIDS and, **9**:309–310
        in infants and children, **6**:185
        posterior placoid, **9**:245, 246*f*, 309–310
    toxoplasmic, **1**:21, **12**:206–209, 208*f*, 208*t*
    with uveitis, **9**:78*t*, 82*t*, 83*t*. *See also* Posterior uveitis
        flowchart for evaluation of, **9**:81*t*

vitiliginous (birdshot retinochoroidopathy),
    9:148–150*t*, 152–155, 152*f*, 153*f*, 154*f*, **12**:186*t*,
        190–191, 190*f*
    HLA association in, **9**:72*t*, 73, 148*t*, 152, **12**:190
    in West Nile virus infection, **9**:215, 215*f*, 216*f*, **12**:211
Chorioretinopathy. *See also specific type and*
    Retinopathy
    central serous, **12**:171–176, 173*f*
        age-related macular degeneration differentiated
            from, **12**:60, 70, 71*f*
        fluorescein angiography in, **12**:23, 24*f*, 172–173, 173*f*
        photocoagulation for, **12**:175, 176, 341
    infectious, **12**:200–211
    inflammatory (white dot syndromes), **9**:147–172,
        148–150*t*, 151*t*, **12**:185–193, 186*t. See also specific
            disorder*
    noninfectious, **12**:185–199
Choristomas, **4**:6, 47–50, 49*f*, **5**:338, **8**:246–247, 247*f. See
    also* Dermoids
    complex, **4**:49*f*, 50, **8**:246–247, 247*f*
    conjunctival, **4**:47–50, 49*f*
    epibulbar, **8**:245–247, 246*f*, 247*f*
    neuroglial, **8**:247
    orbital, **6**:343, **7**:36. *See also specific type*
    osseous, **4**:49*f*, 50, **8**:247
    phakomatous (Zimmerman tumor), **4**:20*f*, 207, **8**:247
Choroid, **2**:41*f*, 64–66, **5**:28, **12**:17–18, 17*f*
    amelanotic masses of, **4**:266, 278, 278*t*
    anatomy of, **2**:41*f*, 64–66, 65*f*, 66*f*, 67*f*, **4**:186–187,
        187*f*, **5**:28, **12**:17–18, 17*f*
    coloboma of, retinoblastoma differentiated from, **4**:305*t*
    cryptococcosis affecting, **9**:278, 310–311
    dark, in Stargardt disease, **6**:293, **12**:234–235, 235*f*
    detachment of, **4**:203
        photocoagulation causing, **12**:342, 342*f*
    development of, **2**:132–133
    diseases of. *See also specific disorder and*
        Chorioretinitis; Chorioretinopathy; Choroiditis;
        Choroidopathy
        dystrophies, **12**:242–246, 243*f*, 244*f*, 245*f*
        inflammatory, **12**:185–211
            infectious, **12**:200–211
            noninfectious, **12**:185–199
            posttraumatic granulomatous, **4**:22, 22*f*
        noninflammatory, **12**:171–183
        Th1 delayed hypersensitivity and, **9**:50*t*
    in tuberculosis, **9**:258, 259*f*, **12**:204–205, 205*f*
    in endogenous fungal endophthalmitis, **9**:273, 273*f*
    gyrate atrophy of, **2**:213*t*, **12**:243–244, 244*f*
    healing/repair of, **4**:17
    hemangiomas of, **4**:200–202, 201*f*, 291–293, 291*f*,
        293*f*, **12**:180–182, 181*f*
        age-related macular degeneration differentiated
            from, **12**:70
        in children, **6**:354, 377, 377*f*
        in Sturge-Weber syndrome, **4**:200, 292, **6**:377, 377*f*,
            12:181
    in HIV infection/AIDS, **9**:311
    hypertension affecting, **12**:114–115, 115*f*, 116*f*,
        176–177, 178*f*
    immune response in, **9**:58*t*, 64–67
    ischemia of, **12**:176–180, 177*f*, 178*f*, 179*f*, 180*f*
    in leukemia, **4**:327, **6**:354

lymphoid proliferation in, 4:202, 202*f*
melanocytoma of, 4:195, 268
melanoma of, 4:195–200, 196*f*, 197*f*, 198*f*, 199*f*, 263, 273–288, 9:285–286. *See also* Choroidal/ciliary body melanoma
  age-related macular degeneration differentiated from, 4:278, 12:70
  in children, 6:353
  clinical presentation of, 4:273–274, 275*f*
  enucleation for, 7:118
  glaucoma caused by, 4:109, 109*f*, 198, 10:93, 130
  nevus differentiated from, 4:266–268, 278
  staging of, 4:337–341*t*
  transpupillary thermotherapy for, 4:285, 12:343
neovascularization of. *See* Choroidal neovascularization
in neurofibromatosis, 6:352, 366
nevus of, 4:195, 195*f*, 266–268, 267*f*
  in children, 6:352
  melanoma differentiated from, 4:266–268, 278
osteoma of, 4:202, 6:353
  melanoma differentiated from, 4:280, 280*f*
photocoagulation causing lesions/detachment of, 12:342, 342*f*
photocoagulation for disorders of, 12:71, 340
  complications of, 12:342, 342*f*
posttraumatic granulomatous inflammation of, focal, 4:22, 22*f*
rupture of, 4:22, 22*f*, 203, 12:320–321, 320*f*, 321–322*f*
stroma of, 4:187
  development of, 2:133
in Sturge-Weber syndrome, 4:200, 292, 6:377, 377*f*, 12:181
topography of, 4:186–187, 187*f*
tumors of, 4:195–200. *See also* Choroidal/ciliary body melanoma
  age-related macular degeneration differentiated from, 12:70
  in children, 6:352–355
  glaucoma caused by, 10:93, 130
  metastatic, 4:200, 201*f*, 315, 316*t*, 317*f*, 318*f*, 319*f*, 320*f*, 9:286
in uveitis, 9:78*t*, 82, 83*t*, 86*t*, 89–90, 140. *See also* Posterior uveitis
vasculature of, 2:64, 65*f*, 66, 66*f*, 67, 12:17–18, 17*f*
  development of, 2:132–133
  fluorescein angiography in study of, 12:21, 22–23, 23*f*
  indocyanine green angiography in study of, 12:26
  insufficiency of, central retinal artery occlusion and, 12:138, 139*f*
  perfusion abnormalities and, 12:176–180, 177*f*, 178*f*, 179*f*, 180*f*
  retina supplied by, 4:146
Choroidal artery
  anterior, 5:19–20, 20*f*
  lateral, 5:20*f*
  optic nerve supplied by, 2:94, 95*f*
  posterior, 5:22*f*
Choroidal/ciliary body melanoma (posterior uveal melanoma), 4:195–200, 196*f*, 197*f*, 198*f*, 199*f*, 263, 273–288, 9:285–286
  age-related macular degeneration differentiated from, 4:278, 12:70

in children, 6:353
  uveitis differentiated from, 6:276*t*
classification of, 4:199, 281
clinical presentation of, 4:273–274, 275*f*
diagnosis of, 4:274–277, 276*f*, 277*f*
  differential, 4:277–281, 278*t*, 279*f*, 280*f*, 281*f*
enucleation for, 7:118
epithelioid, 4:196, 199
glaucoma caused by, 4:109, 109*f*, 198, 10:93, 130
metastatic, 4:200
  evaluation of, 4:281–282, 282*t*
nevus differentiated from, 4:266–268, 278
ocular surface/conjunctival involvement and, 4:70, 71*f*
prognosis/prognostic factors for, 4:198–200, 286–288
spindle cell, 4:196, 196*f*, 199
spread of, 4:197–198, 197*f*, 198*f*, 200
staging of, 4:337–341*t*
transpupillary thermotherapy for, 4:285, 12:343
treatment of, 4:282–286, 284*f*
Choroidal effusion, after filtering surgery, 10:197–198
Choroidal fissure. *See* Embryonic fissure
Choroidal hemorrhage. *See* Choroidal/suprachoroidal hemorrhage
Choroidal neovascularization, 4:159, 168*f*, 12:23*f*, 63–64, 64–65*f*, 65–68, 66*f*, 67*f*, 80–88, 88*t*. *See also* Neovascularization
  in age-related macular degeneration, 4:169–170, 171*f*, 12:23*f*, 63–64, 64–65*f*, 65–68, 66*f*, 67*f*
    photocoagulation and, 12:63, 71, 340
  angioid streaks and, 12:84–85, 84*f*
  antiangiogenic agents in management of, 12:72–73
  central serous chorioretinopathy and, 12:174–175
  choroidal rupture and, 12:320–321, 321–322*f*
  classic, 12:23*f*, 66, 67, 67*f*, 68
  conditions associated with, 12:87, 88*t*
  fellow eye considerations and, 12:79
  fluorescein angiography in, 12:22, 23*f*, 65–68, 67*f*
  idiopathic, 12:83
  indocyanine green angiography in, 12:25–26
  in multifocal choroiditis and panuveitis syndrome, 9:162, 163*f*, 164
  in myopia, 12:86–87
  occult, 12:23*f*, 66, 67, 67*f*, 68
  in ocular histoplasmosis syndrome, 9:221, 223, 224*f*, 12:80–83, 82*f*, 351, 351*f*
    management of, 9:223–226, 224*f*, 225*f*, 12:81–83, 351, 351*f*
  pathologic (high/degenerative) myopia and, 12:86–87
  photocoagulation for, 12:71, 340
    complications of, 12:342, 342*f*
    wavelength selection and, 12:338
  photodynamic therapy for, 12:71–72, 78, 79, 343–344
  poorly defined/demarcated, 12:67*f*, 68
  in punctate inner choroiditis/choroidopathy, 9:165, 165*f*, 12:192
  in Sorsby macular dystrophy, 12:241, 242*f*
  subfoveal, 12:351, 351*f*
  in systemic lupus erythematosus, 9:142
  in toxoplasmosis, 9:230, 230*f*
  transpupillary therapy for, 12:79, 343
  treatment of, 12:71–80, 75*f*
    combination, 12:72, 78–79
  in uveitis, 9:303–304

vitrectomy for, **12**:351, 351*f*
in Vogt-Koyanagi-Harada (VKH) syndrome, **9**:189
well-defined/demarcated, **12**:68
Choroidal/suprachoroidal hemorrhage, **4**:18–19, 19*f*,
   12:360–361, 362*f*
angle-closure glaucoma and, **10**:133
cataract surgery and, **11**:144*t*, 177–179, 189
delayed, **11**:178–179
expulsive, **11**:178
flat or shallow anterior chamber and, **11**:152
expulsive, **4**:18–19, 19*f*
cataract surgery and, **11**:178
postoperative, **12**:360–361, 362*f*
Choroidal vasculopathy, polypoidal (posterior uveal
   bleeding syndrome), **4**:171, 172*f*, 173*f*
age-related macular degeneration differentiated from,
   12:69–70, 70*f*
central serous chorioretinopathy differentiated from,
   12:174, 175
Choroidal vein, **5**:24
Choroideremia, **12**:242–243, 243*f*
ERG in evaluation of, **12**:40
ocular findings in carriers of, **2**:221*f*, 222*t*
REP-1 (Rab escort protein 1/*CHM*) gene in, **2**:298,
   12:242
retinal pigment epithelium in, **2**:309, **12**:242–243, 243*f*
Choroiditis, **9**:78*t*, 82. *See also* Choroidopathy; Posterior
   uveitis
diffuse, **9**:78*t*
focal, **9**:78*t*
geographic. *See* Choroiditis, serpiginous
in HIV infection/AIDS
   Cryptococcus neoformans causing, **9**:310–311
   multifocal, **9**:311
   Pneumocystis jiroveci (Pneumocystis carinii)
     causing, **9**:310, 310*f*, 311*f*
multifocal, **9**:78*t*, 83*t*
in HIV infection/AIDS, **9**:311
in Lyme disease, **9**:251
and panuveitis (MCP), **9**:148–150*t*, 161–164, 162*f*,
   163*f*, **12**:186*t*, 191–192, 191*f*
   EBV infection and, **9**:164, 208
in systemic lupus erythematosus, **9**:142, 142*f*
West Nile infection causing, **12**:211
in ocular histoplasmosis syndrome, **9**:221, 223, 223*f*
punctate inner (PIC), **9**:148–150*t*, 161, 164–167, 165*f*,
   166*f*, **12**:186*t*, 192, 192*f*
serpiginous (geographic/helicoid), **9**:148–150*t*,
   158–161, 159*f*, 160*f*, **12**:186*t*, 188–189, 188*f*
tuberculosis and, **9**:258, 259*f*
solitary idiopathic, **12**:194
in sympathetic ophthalmia, **9**:178, 179*f*
tuberculous, **9**:258, 259*f*
in Vogt-Koyanagi-Harada (VKH) syndrome, **9**:184
Choroidopathy. *See also* Choroiditis
central serous, **12**:171–176, 173*f*
age-related macular degeneration differentiated
   from, **12**:60, 70, 71*f*
fluorescein angiography in, **12**:23, 24*f*, 172–173, 173*f*
photocoagulation for, **12**:175, 176, 341
hypertensive, **12**:114–115, 115*f*, 116*f*, 176–177, 178*f*
lupus, **9**:142, 142*f*, **12**:195
punctate inner (PIC), **9**:148–150*t*, 161, 164–167, 165*f*,
   166*f*, **12**:186*t*, 192, 192*f*

serpiginous (geographic/helicoid), **9**:148–150*t*,
   158–161, 159*f*, 160*f*, **12**:186*t*, 188–189, 188*f*
tuberculosis and, **9**:258, 259*f*
"Christmas tree" cataracts, in myotonic dystrophy, **5**:338
Chromatic aberrations, **3**:40, 41, 41*f*, 93, 100–102, 102*f*
duochrome test and, **3**:135–136
with polycarbonate lenses, **3**:162
prisms producing, **3**:88
sunglasses affecting, **3**:101–102
Chromatid, **2**:149
Chromatin, **2**:149
Chromogens, in immunohistochemistry, **4**:33, 35*f*
Chromogranin, in immunohistochemistry, **4**:34, 35*f*
Chromophores, ultraviolet, intraocular lenses with,
   11:138
Chromosomal aneuploidy, **2**:148. *See also specific*
   disorder
autosome, **2**:199–203
sex chromosome, **2**:199
Chromosome arm painting, **2**:199, 200*f*, 201*f*
Chromosomes, **2**:193–194. *See also* Autosomes
abnormalities of. *See also specific type*
congenital anomalies and, **2**:141, 197–198
etiology of, **2**:204–207, 205*t*
identification of, **2**:197–207, 198*t*, 200*f*, 201*f*. *See*
   also Cytogenetics
incidence of, **2**:197
acrocentric, **2**:147
analysis of, **2**:197–207, 198*t*, 200*f*, 201*f*. *See also*
   Cytogenetics
bacterial artificial (BAC), **2**:149
homologous, **2**:153, 193
morphologically variant (cytogenetic markers), **2**:177
sex, **2**:193, 194. *See also* X chromosome; Y
   chromosome
aneuploidy of, **2**:199
mosaicism and, **2**:204
translocation of, **2**:162
Down syndrome caused by, **2**:201–202
yeast artificial (YAC), **2**:163
Chromostereopsis, **3**:41, 41*f*
Chronic bronchitis, **1**:142
Chronic cyclitis. *See* Pars planitis
Chronic disease, anemia of, **1**:148
iron deficiency differentiated from, **1**:147
Chronic kidney disease. *See* Renal disease
Chronic lymphocytic lymphoma, of orbit, **7**:80
Chronic migraine, **5**:293. *See also* Migraine headache
Chronic obstructive pulmonary disease, **1**:142
corticosteroid use and, **1**:141
ocular surgery in patients with, **1**:308
Chronic progressive external ophthalmoplegia (CPEO),
   2:174–175, **5**:336–337, 336*f*, 337*f*, **6**:137, 139*t*,
   12:251*t*, 254, 265
mitochondrial DNA defects and, **2**:173, 174–175, 191,
   12:251*t*, 265
ptosis in, **5**:280, 336, 336*f*
Chronic progressive external ophthalmoplegia
   (CPEO)-plus syndromes, **2**:174–175
CHRPE. *See* Congenital hypertrophy of retinal pigment
   epithelium
Chrysiasis, corneal pigmentation in, **8**:337*t*
CHS. *See* Chédiak-Higashi syndrome
CHSD. *See* Congenital hereditary stromal dystrophy

CHST6 gene, in macular dystrophy, 4:96, 8:269*t*, 283
Churg-Strauss syndrome, 1:177*t*, 179–180
Chylomicrons, 1:132
Chymotrypsin (α-chymotrypsin), for ICCE, 11:93, 214
Cialis. *See* Tadalafil
Cicatricial ectropion, 7:191*f*, 193–194
    after blepharoplasty, 7:226
Cicatricial entropion, 7:197–199, 198*f*, 199*f*
Cicatricial (mucous membrane) pemphigoid, 4:54, 56*f*,
    8:180, 196*t*, 198–203, 199*f*, 200*f*, 201*f*, 202*f*, 205*t*
    cataract surgery in patients with, 11:191
    drug-induced (pseudopemphigoid), 8:199, 361
    mucous membrane grafting for, 8:401
CID. *See* Cytomegalic inclusion disease
Cidofovir, 1:55*t*, 66, 2:381*t*, 384
    for CMV retinitis, 1:24, 38, 66, 2:381*t*, 384
    for herpes simplex virus infection, 1:23
    uveitis caused by, 9:128
Cigarette burns of cornea, in children, 6:407
Cigarette smoking
    cancer and, 1:274, 275
    cataract development and, 11:58–59, 67–68
    cessation of, 1:107, 109*t*
    heart disease and, 1:99, 100, 107, 109*t*, 133*t*
    hypertension and, 1:74
    optic neuropathy and, 5:154
    pulmonary disease and, 1:143
    thyroid disease and, 1:211, 5:333, 6.135, 7:52
CIGTS (Collaborative Initial Glaucoma Treatment
    Study), 10:75, 78, 104, 160, 179
Cilastin, with imipenem, 1.49*t*, 59
Cilia (eyelashes), 4:205, 8:4, 5*f*
    accessory. *See* Distichiasis
    disorders of, 8:89
    lice infestation of, 8:142, 149
    misdirection of. *See* Trichiasis
    in staphylococcal blepharitis, 8:144*t*, 145
Ciliary arteries, 2:21, 34, 36–38, 37*f*, 38, 38*f*, 39*f*, 62,
    12:12, 17, 17*f*. *See also* Cilioretinal artery
    anterior, 2:21, 34, 36–38, 38, 38*f*, 39*f*, 62, 132, 5:14*f*,
        16–18, 6:16–18
        anterior segment ischemia after strabismus surgery
            and, 6:158–159
    choroid supplied by, 2:64
    development of, 2:132, 138
    extraocular muscles supplied by, 2:38, 38*f*, 6:16–18
    long, 5:13*f*, 14*f*, 18
    optic nerve supplied by, 2:94, 95, 95*f*, 10:42, 43, 43*f*,
        44
    posterior, 2:36–38, 37*f*, 38, 38*f*, 39*f*, 62, 132, 5:14*f*,
        18–19, 12:12, 17, 17*f*
    short, 5:13*f*, 14*f*, 18
Ciliary block, after cataract surgery, flat or shallow
    anterior chamber and, 11:153
Ciliary block glaucoma. *See* Aqueous misdirection
Ciliary body, 2:41*f*, 51*f*, 52*f*, 53*f*, 61–64, 253–264
    ablation of, 10:209–210, 209*f*
    anatomy of, 2:41*f*, 51*f*, 52*f*, 61–64, 62*f*, 63*f*, 4:186, 187*f*
    biochemistry and metabolism of, 2:253–264
    development of, 2:137
    epithelium of. *See* Ciliary epithelium
    healing/repair of, 4:17
    hyalinization of, 4:192
    immunologic microenvironment of, 9:61

injury of in cataract surgery, 11:144*t*
melanocytoma of, 4:195, 268
melanoma of, 4:195–200, 196*f*, 197*f*, 198*f*, 199*f*,
    263, 273–288. *See also* Choroidal/ciliary body
    melanoma
    clinical presentation of, 4:273, 274*f*
    glaucoma caused by, 4:109, 109*f*, 198, 10:93, 130
    staging of, 4:337–341*t*
neoplastic disorders of, 4:195–200. *See also*
    Choroidal/ciliary body melanoma
    in children, 6:351–352
    glaucoma and, 10:93, 130
    metastatic, 4:316
    nevus of, 4:195, 266
    protein types expressed in, 2:253
    signal transduction in, 2:258–261
    smooth muscle in, 2:253–254
    stroma of, 2:61–63
    tear in (angle recession), 4:18, 19*f*, 109
        glaucoma and, 4:18, 109, 10:38–39, 38*f*, 39*f*,
            100–101, 100*f*
    topography of, 2:41*f*, 4:186, 187*f*
    uveal portion of, 2:62–63
    in uveitis, 9:89
Ciliary epithelium, 2:61–63, 62*f*, 265
    aqueous humor formation and, 2:254, 265, 266–267,
        270, 10:3*f*, 13–14, 15*f*
    development of, 2:137
    nonpigmented, 2:62, 62*f*, 265
        benign adenomas of, 4:288
    pigmented, 2:62, 62*f*, 265
        acquired hyperplasia of, 4:288
        benign adenomas of, 4:288
Ciliary flush, 8:110
    in uveitis, 9:85, 88
Ciliary ganglion, 2:14–16, 15*f*, 5:59*f*, 66*f*
    branches of, 2:15–16
Ciliary margin, 7:142
Ciliary muscle, 2:63–64, 63*f*, 258, 259
    in accommodation, 2:68, 11:19, 19*t*, 13:149–152,
        150*f*, 151*f*
    development of, 2:137
    miotics affecting, 2:335, 339, 10:172
    muscarinic drugs affecting, 2:335, 339, 341–342
Ciliary muscle spasm (spasm of accommodation), 5:316
    accommodative excess caused by, 3:143
Ciliary nerves
    long, 2:36, 247, 7:17
    posterior, 2:36, 247
    short, 2:15*f*, 16, 36, 99, 7:11*f*, 17
        ciliary muscle supplied by, 2:64
        iris sphincter supplied by, 2:61
Ciliary processes, 2:52*f*, 61, 258, 10:13, 15*f*
    in aqueous humor formation, 10:3*f*, 13–14, 15*f*
    development of, 2:137
    plateau iris and, 10:119
Ciliobursal canal, 12:7*f*, 8
Cilioretinal artery, 2:78, 94, 95*f*, 5:18, 19*f*, 12:12, 15*f*, 135
    macular preservation in central retinal artery
        occlusion and, 12:138
    occlusion of, 12:137–138
Ciliospinal nucleus of Budge-Waller, 5:63
Cilium, photoreceptor, 2:73, 76*f*
Cilostazol, for carotid artery disease, 5:182

Ciloxan. *See* Ciprofloxacin
Cimzia. *See* Certolizumab pegol
CIN. *See* Conjunctival intraepithelial neoplasia
Cingulate gyrus, 5:63
Cipro. *See* Ciprofloxacin
Ciprofloxacin, 1:52*t*, 60–61, 2:371–373, 372*t*
   for bacterial keratitis, 8:163
    corneal deposits caused by, 8:348
   for gonococcal conjunctivitis, 8:152
   ocular effects of, 1:301*t*
Circinate balanitis, in reactive arthritis, 9:122
Circle of least confusion, 3:93–94
Circle of Willis, 2:93, 94*f*, 109, 109*f*, 5:20
Circle of Zinn-Haller (circle of Haller and Zinn), 2:94,
   5:19, 10:42, 43, 44
Circular venous plexus, 5:27*f*
Circularly polarized light, 3:10
Circulatory failure, in shock, 1:293
Circumscribed (localized) choroidal hemangioma,
   4:200, 291, 291*f*
Circumscribed iris nevus, 4:266
Cirrhosis
   from hepatitis B, 1:280
   from hepatitis C, 1:26
11-*cis*-retinaldehyde, 2:292, 305–306, 12:15
11-*cis*-retinol dehydrogenase, mutations in, 2:297
Cisapride, perioperative, 1:308, 309*t*
Cisplatin, 1:242*t*
Citrate, in tear film, 2:240
Citric acid/sodium citrate, for chemical injuries, 8:358
Citrobacter, 8:135
Citrullinated peptide antibodies, anticyclic, in
   rheumatoid arthritis, 1:162
CJD. *See* Creutzfeldt-Jakob disease
CK. *See* Conductive keratoplasty; Creatine kinase
CK-MB, in acute coronary syndrome, 1:105
Cl. *See* Chloride
Claforan. *See* Cefotaxime
Claravis. *See* Isotretinoin
Clarin-1, in Usher syndrome, 12:253
Clarithromycin, 1:50*t*, 61, 2:377
   for bacterial keratitis, 8:162*t*
   for endocarditis prophylaxis, 1:8*t*
Class I major histocompatibility complex molecules,
   9:37, 38*f*, 70
Class I medical devices, 13:204
Class II major histocompatibility complex molecules,
   9:37, 39*f*, 70
   primed macrophages as, 9:21–22
Class II medical devices, 13:204
Class III major histocompatibility complex molecules,
   9:70
Class III medical devices, 13:204
Classic lattice corneal dystrophy, 4:96–97, 97*t*, 99*f*,
   8:268*t*, 270*t*, 278–279, 279*f*
   genetics of, 4:97, 8:269*t*, 278
Classic migraine, 5:191, 295, 296*f*. *See also* Migraine
   headache
Claude syndrome, 5:226
Claudication, jaw
   in AAION, 5:125
   in giant cell arteritis, 5:319
Claustrophobia, cataract surgery in patient with, 11:187

Clavulanic acid, 1:59. *See also specific antibiotic
   combination*
"Claw" haptics, for iris-fixated phakic IOL, 13:129
Clear cell hidradenoma (eccrine acrospiroma), 7:162
Clear corneal incision, for cataract surgery, 11:113–115,
   113*f*, 115*f*
   with filtering surgery, 10:200
   in glaucoma, 11:201–202
   in uveitis, 9:292
Clear lens extraction (refractive lens exchange), 13:4*t*,
   41*t*, 138–141
   advantages of, 13:141
   complications of, 13:141
   disadvantages/limitations of, 13:41*t*, 141
   for hyperopia, 13:139, 140
   indications for, 13:138
   informed consent for, 13:138
   IOL calculations in, 13:140–141
   for myopia, 13:138, 139–140, 140, 141
   patient selection for, 13:138–139
   retinal detachment and, 13:138, 141, 177
   surgical planning/techniques for, 13:139–140
Cleft syndromes, 7:34–35, 34*f*, 35*f*. *See also* Craniofacial
   malformations
   nasolacrimal duct obstruction and, 7:278
Cleocin. *See* Clindamycin
Climatic droplet keratopathy, 8:334–335, 335*f*. *See also*
   Spheroidal degeneration
Climatotherapy, for vernal keratoconjunctivitis, 8:188
Clinafloxacin, 1:52*t*
Clindamycin, 1:50*t*, 61, 2:368*t*
   for endocarditis prophylaxis, 1:8*t*
   for endophthalmitis, 12:329
   for *Pneumocystis jiroveci (Pneumocystis carinii)*
    pneumonia, 1:37
   for toxoplasmosis, 9:232, 309
Clinical breast examination, for cancer screening,
   1:272*t*, 274
Clinical heterogeneity, 2:149, 193
"Clinical history method," for IOL power calculation
   after refractive surgery, 13:188. *See also* Historical
   methods
Clinical refraction. *See* Refraction, clinical
Clinical research/studies
   application to clinical practice and, 1:338–348
    data presentation and, 1:343–346, 344*f*, 345*f*, 346*f*
    measurement system design and, 1:339–340
    monitoring system implementation and, 1:340–342
    quality improvement and, 1:346, 347*f*
    results analysis and, 1:342–343
   designs for, 1:320–329, 321*f*. *See also specific type of
    study*
    case-control studies, 1:321*f*, 323–325, 324*f*
    case reports, 1:321, 321*f*
    case series, 1:321*f*, 322–323
    clinical trials, 1:327–328, 327*f*
     systematic reviews/meta-analyses of, 1:328–329
    cohort studies, 1:321*f*, 324*f*, 326–327
    cross-sectional studies, 1:325–326
   evaluation of, 1:315–320
    clinical relevance and, 1:319–320
    intervention issues and, 1:318
    outcome issues and, 1:318–319

participants and setting and, 1:316–317
sample size and, 1:317–318
validity and, 1:319, 339
interpreting results for patients and, 1:336–338
for medical device, 13:204, 206
test interpretation and, 1:329–336
Clinical trials (experimental/interventional studies),
    1:320, 321, 321f, 327–328, 327f. See also Clinical
    research
for medical device, 13:204, 206
for new drug, 2:333
systematic reviews/meta-analyses of, 1:328–329
Clinically significant diabetic macular edema, 12:90, 97,
    98, 99f
photocoagulation for, 12:97, 98, 99f, 101–103, 102t
Clinoid process
anterior, 2:11f, 5:7f, 9f, 7:7f
posterior, 2:104
Clinoril. See Sulindac
Clip-on lenses
for prism correction, 3:163–164
for refraction in aphakia, 3:158
Clivus, 2:104, 5:7
CLL lymphoma. See Chronic lymphocytic lymphoma
Clobetasol, for hemangiomas, 7:64, 152
in children, 6:340
Clobetasone, for atopic dermatitis, 8:185
Clofazimine, 1:39
corneal pigmentation caused by, 8:349
Clofibrate, for hypercholesterolemia/heart disease
    prevention, 1:137t
Clomid. See Clomiphene
Clomiphene, ocular effects of, 1:302t
Clonality, 9:46
Clonazepam
for benign essential blepharospasm, 7:220
for nystagmus, 5:257
Clone
cDNA, 2:149
genomic, 2:152
Clonidine
for heart failure, 1:119
for hypertension, 1:77t
in perioperative setting, 1:305
Cloning vector, 2:149–150
Clopidogrel. See also Dual antiplatelet therapy
for cerebral ischemia/carotid occlusive disease, 1:94,
    95, 5:182
for ischemic heart disease, 1:108, 109–110, 109t, 111
Cloquet (hyaloid) canal, 2:85, 4:132, 12:307
Closed-circuit television, 3:302–303, 302f
Closed-loop intraocular lenses, pseudophakic bullous
    keratopathy and, 11:167
Clostridium
botulinum, toxin derived from, 6:163, 7:218. See also
    Botulinum toxin
difficile, 1:8–9
Clotrimazole, 1:54t
Clotting. See Coagulation
Cloudy media, 3:286
"Clover-shaped" wavefront aberration, 3:240
Cloverleaf visual field, 10:61, 62f
Cloxacillin, 1:45t, 57, 2:369–370

Clozapine, 1:251, 252
Clozaril. See Clozapine
CLSLK. See Contact lens superior limbic
    keratoconjunctivitis
Clump cells, in iris, 4:185–186
Cluster headache, 5:299
Horner syndrome and, 5:268
Clusters A, B, and C personality disorders, 1:249
cM. See Centimorgan
CME. See Cystoid macular edema
CMV. See Cytomegalovirus
CN. See Congenital nystagmus
CNGA3 gene, in achromatopsia, 6:291, 12:215
CNGB3 gene, in achromatopsia, 6:291, 12:215
CNS. See Central nervous system
CNTGS (Collaborative Normal-Tension Glaucoma
    Study), 10:81
CNV. See Choroidal neovascularization
CO₂ laser. See Carbon dioxide laser
Coagulation, 1:151, 151f. See also Hemostasis
disorders of, 1:155–157. See also Hemostasis,
    disorders of; Hypercoagulable states
acquired, 1:156–157
cataract surgery in patient with, 11:189–190
hereditary, 1:155–156
transient visual loss and, 5:184–185
laboratory evaluation of, 1:152–153
before cataract surgery, 11:189–190
pathways of, 1:151, 151f
Coagulation factors, 1:151, 151f
abnormalities/deficiencies of, 1:155–156
vitamin K and, 1:156
Coarctation of aorta, hypertension in, 1:72, 72t
Coats disease, 4:149, 150f, 305, 306f, 6:287–288, 288f,
    12:143–145, 144f
in children, 6:287–288, 288f, 12:143–145, 144f
retinal detachment and, 12:143, 144, 144f
retinoblastoma differentiated from, 4:305, 305t, 306f,
    6:358
Coats reaction, 12:143, 144f
Coats white ring, 8:334, 335f
Coaxial illumination, for operating microscope, 3:263
Cobblestone (paving-stone) degeneration, 4:156, 156f,
    12:281–282, 281f
Cocaine
abuse of
choroidal perfusion abnormalities and, 12:176–177
during pregnancy, 1:250–251
anisocoria diagnosis and, 5:264, 265f, 266, 267
Horner syndrome diagnosis and, 5:265f, 266, 267, 6:230
norepinephrine uptake affected by, 2:260, 346
as topical anesthetic, 2:387t, 389
Coccidioides immitis (coccidioidomycosis)
endogenous endophthalmitis caused by, 9:273–274,
    279–280, 279f
optic nerve infection caused by, 4:251
Coche-Bonnet esthesiometer, 8:31
Cochlear artery, 5:21
Cochlear nerve, 5:48
Cochlin, in vitreous, 2:286
Cochrane Eyes and Vision Group, 1:328
Cochrane Library, 1:316
Cockayne syndrome, 8:322t

Coding strand of DNA (sense DNA), **2:**160
Codominance (codominant inheritance), **2:**150, 211
Codon, **2:**150
  amber, **2:**148
  initiator, **2:**154
  stop/termination, **2:**161
    frameshift mutation and, **2:**152
Coefficient of variation, specular photomicroscopy in
  evaluation of, **8:**32
Coenzyme Q$_{10}$, for Leber hereditary optic neuropathy,
  5:138
Cogan microcystic epithelial dystrophy. *See* Epithelial/
  subepithelial dystrophies, basement membrane
Cogan-Reese (iris nevus) syndrome, **4:**104, 105*f*, 270*t*,
  8:345, **10:**128, 129. *See also* Iridocorneal endothelial
  (ICE) syndrome
Cogan syndrome, **1:**178, **8:**209–210
Cogan twitch/Cogan lid-twitch sign, **5:**276–277, 328,
  6:137
Cogentin. *See* Benztropine
Cogwheel (saccadic) pursuit, **5:**213
Coherence, **3:**7–10, 8*f*, 9*f*
  applications of, **3:**8–10
  of laser light, **3:**8, 20
  spatial (lateral), **3:**8, 8*f*
  temporal (longitudinal), **3:**8, 8*f*
Coherence tomography, optical. *See* Optical coherence
  tomography/biometry
Cohesive ophthalmic viscosurgical devices, **11:**97, 97*t*.
  See also Ophthalmic viscosurgical devices
Cohort studies (follow-up studies), **1:**321*f*, 324*f*, 326–327
COL1A1/COL1A2 genes, in osteogenesis imperfecta,
  8:252
COL2A1 gene
  retinal tears/detachment and, **12:**310
  in Stickler syndrome, **12:**310
COL8A2 gene
  in Fuchs endothelial corneal dystrophy, **8:**269*t*, 291
  in posterior polymorphous corneal dystrophy, **8:**269*t*,
    293
Colchicine, for Behçet disease, **9:**195
Cold (temperature), anterior segment injuries caused by,
  8:351–352
Cold mirror, **3:**9
Colenbrander 1-m chart, **3:**290
Colesevelam, for hypercholesterolemia/heart disease
  prevention, **1:**137*t*
Colestipol, for hypercholesterolemia/heart disease
  prevention, **1:**137*t*
Colistimethate, **2:**368*t*
Colitis
  antibiotic-associated, **1:**8–9
  granulomatous (Crohn disease), **1:**165, **9:**123
  ulcerative, **1:**165, **9:**123
Collaborative Initial Glaucoma Treatment Study
  (CIGTS), **10:**75, 78, 104, 160, 179
Collaborative Normal-Tension Glaucoma Study
  (CNTGS), **10:**81
Collaborative Ocular Melanoma Study (COMS), **4:**263,
  281, 287–288
Collagen
  in choroid, **2:**66
  in ciliary muscle, **2:**64

corneal, **2:**44, 45, 134, 249, 249–250, **8:**7, 8, 9, **13:**9
  in Ehlers-Danlos syndrome, **8:**325
  in lens capsule, **2:**68, 273
  scleral, **2:**48, **8:**9, **12:**18
  stromal, **2:**44, 249–250, **8:**7, 8
    corneal haze after surface ablation and, **13:**101
  in vitreous, **2:**82–83, 83*f*, 130, 132, 283, 283–284, 284*f*,
    4:131, **12:**7, 297
  liquefaction and, **2:**286
Collagen cornea shields, for drug administration, **2:**331
Collagen crosslinking, **13:**4*t*, 123–124, 124*f*, 168
Collagen plugs, for dry eye, **7:**271, **8:**61–62. *See also*
  Lacrimal plugs
Collagen shrinkage, **13:**4*t*, 22, 22*f*, 119–123. *See also*
  specific procedure
  conductive keratoplasty for, **13:**4*t*, 22, 22*f*, 120–123,
    121*f*, 153–154
  history of, **13:**119–120
  thermokeratoplasty for, **13:**4*t*, 22, 22*f*, 119, 120
Collagen type VIII alpha *(COL8A2)* gene
  in Fuchs endothelial corneal dystrophy, **8:**269*t*, 291
  in posterior polymorphous corneal dystrophy, **8:**269*t*,
    293
Collagen-vascular diseases. *See also specific type and*
  Connective tissue disorders
  Purtscherlike retinopathy and, **12:**154, 155*t*
  refractive surgery in patient with, **13:**165
  uveitis in, **9:**140–146
Collagenase inhibitors, for peripheral ulcerative
  keratitis, **8:**212
Collagenases, **8:**177*t*, **9:**31
  in ocular infections, **8:**98
Collagenoma, in tuberous sclerosis, **6:**372
Collagenous layer, posterior (retrocorneal fibrous
  membrane), **2:**251, **4:**91, 92*f*, **8:**29
Collamer, for posterior chamber phakic IOLs, **13:**130, 130*f*
Collarette (iris), **2:**58, 59*f*, 137
Collateral vein, anterior, **5:**24*f*
Collateral vessels, retinochoroidal (optociliary shunt
  vessels), **5:**25, 149
  in optic nerve sheath meningioma, **5:**149, 150*f*
  in papilledema, **5:**121–122
Collector channels, **2:**54–55, 57*f*, **10:**3*f*
Colliculus
  facial, **2:**104, **5:**61
  superior, **5:**39*f*, 40*f*, 41, 61
Collier sign
  in convergence-retraction nystagmus, **5:**256
  in dorsal midbrain syndrome, **5:**211, 273, 281
Collimating keratoscope, **8:**39
Colloid bodies. *See* Optic disc (optic nerve head), drusen of
Colloidal iron stain, **4:**30, 31*t*
Colobomas, **2:**123, 125*f*, 166
  embryonic fissure closure and, **2:**123, 125*f*
  eyelid, **6:**175, 176*f*, **7:**150–151, 151*f*
    in Treacher Collins syndrome (mandibulofacial
      dysostosis), **4:**213*t*, **6:**394
  Fuchs (tilted disc syndrome), **5:**142–143, 142*f*, **6:**307,
    307*f*
  in Goldenhar syndrome, **6:**175, 393
  iris, **6:**224–225, 225*f*
    cataract surgery in patient with, **11:**196, 197*f*
  lens, **4:**121, **6:**260–261, 261*f*, **11:**26–27, 27*f*

optic nerve/optic disc, 2:141, 4:249–250, 251*f*, 5:143,
  6:306, 306*f*, 415
pupil irregularity and, 5:263
retinoblastoma differentiated from, 4:305*t*
uveal, 4:188
Colobomatous cyst (microphthalmia with cyst), 6:345,
  346*f*, 7:34
Colon cancer. *See* Colorectal cancer
Colonography, computed tomographic (CT) (virtual
  colonoscopy), 1:269, 272*t*, 276
Colonoscopy
  in cancer screening, 1:272*t*, 276
  virtual, 1:269, 272*t*, 276
  for polyp removal, 1:276
Colony-stimulating factors
  in cancer therapy, 1:243–244
  in cicatricial pemphigoid, 8:199
Color blindness. *See* Color vision, defects in
Color contrast, sunglasses affecting, 3:159, 160*f*
Color flow Doppler imaging. *See also* Doppler imaging
  in ischemic heart disease, 1:105–106
Color fringing, with polycarbonate lenses, 3:162
Color plate testing, pseudoisochromatic, 12:48, 48*f*
  in low vision evaluation, 5:104–105
Color vision, 2:294–295, 298, 12:46–50
  defects in, 12:47, 213–215, 214*t*. *See also specific type*
    achromatopsia (monochromatism), 6:291,
      12:214–215, 214*t*
      rod, 12:214*t*, 215
    acquired, 12:214, 214*t*, 231
    assessment of, 12:47, 48–50, 48*f*, 49*f*
    blue-cone monochromatism/monochromacy/
      achromatopsia, 2:222*t*, 297, 6:291, 12:36*f*, 214,
      214*t*, 215
    in cone dystrophies, 12:232
    congenital, 12:213–214, 214*t*
    cortical lesions and, 5:194
    in dominant optic atrophy, 5:139, 6:310
    genetic basis of, 2:294–295, 12:213–214, 214*t*
    low vision/vision rehabilitation and, 3:294
    nuclear cataract and, 11:40
    ocular findings in carriers of, 2:222*t*
    in optic neuritis, 5:144
    simultanagnosia and, 5:194
  retina as source of changes in, 5:189
  testing, 12:48–50, 48*f*, 49*f*
    in low vision evaluation, 5:104–105
  trivariant, 2:294–295
  wavelength affecting, 3:19
Colorectal cancer, 1:275–276
  incidence of, 1:275
  screening for, 1:276
Colvard pupillometer, 13:34
Coma
  eye movements in patients in, 5:258–259
  myxedema, 1:212
  nonketotic hyperglycemic-hyperosmolar, 1:204–205
Coma (wavefront aberration), 3:233*f*, 238–240, 239*f*,
  13:7, 8*f*
Combigan. *See* Brimonidine, in combination
  preparations
Combined granular-lattice corneal dystrophy. *See*
  Granular-lattice (Avellino) corneal dystrophy

Combined hamartoma of retina and retinal pigment
  epithelium, 4:184, 289, 289*f*, 6:352
Combined interrupted and continuous sutures, for
  penetrating keratoplasty, 8:419, 420*f*
Combined-mechanism glaucoma, 10:6
Combipres. *See* Clonidine
Combivent. *See* Albuterol, with ipratropium
Combivir. *See* Lamivudine (3TC), with zidovudine
Comitance, spread of, 5:219
  in superior oblique muscle paralysis, 6:120
Comitant (concomitant) deviations, 5:219, 6:10
  vertical, 6:113
    surgery for, 6:152
Comma sign, in sickle cell hemoglobinopathies, 12:120
Commissure, posterior, 5:38, 39*f*
Committee for the Classification of Eye Movement
  Abnormalities and Strabismus (CEMAS),
  6:317–318
Common carotid artery, 5:13*f*
Common cause factors, 1:345
Common migraine, 5:296. *See also* Migraine headache
Commotio retinae, 4:20, 12:319, 320*f*
Communicating arteries
  anterior, 2:93, 5:20
    aneurysm of, 5:350*f*, 351
    cranial nerve relationship and, 5:52*f*
  posterior, 5:19, 20*f*, 22*f*, 23
    aneurysm of, 5:350*f*, 351
      third nerve (oculomotor) palsy and, 5:228*f*, 229,
      229*f*, 273, 351
    cranial nerve relationship and, 5:52*f*
Communication
  between clinician and pathologist, 4:25–26
  between clinician and patient, cataract surgery and,
    11:188
Community-associated MRSA, preseptal cellulitis
  caused by, 7:41
Comparative genomic hybridization (CGH), 4:39*t*
  microarray-based (array CGH), 4:39*t*
Comparison of Age-Related Macular Degeneration
  Treatments Trials (CATT), 12:78
Compartment syndrome, visual loss after orbital trauma
  and, 7:101, 105
Complement, 8:177*t*, 9:23–24, 24*f*
  in aqueous humor, 2:269
  in conjunctiva, 9:59
  in external eye defense, 8:95
  in immune response, 9:23–24, 24*f*
  in paroxysmal nocturnal hemoglobinuria, 1:150
  Purtscher/Purtscherlike retinopathy and, 12:154
  receptors for, in phagocytosis, 9:19–20
Complement C3, in age-related macular degeneration,
  12:56
Complement C4, in aqueous humor, 2:269
Complement C5a, 8:177*t*
Complement C5a peptidase, streptococcal production
  of, 8:133
Complement factor B/complement component 2, in
  age-related macular degeneration, 12:56
Complement factor H (*CFH*) gene
  in age-related macular degeneration, 1:17, 4:167,
  12:56
  in basal laminar/cuticular drusen, 12:240

Complement inhibitors, for age-related macular degeneration, 12:63
Complementary DNA (cDNA), 2:150
  from ciliary body–encoding plasma proteins, 2:269
  sequencing, 2:184, 185f
Complementary DNA clone (cDNA clone), 2:149
Complementary DNA library (cDNA library), 2:154, 182
Complete blood count, in immune-mediated disease, 8:182t
Complete bundle branch blocks, 1:122t
Complete cataract, 11:34
Completed stroke, 1:92
Complex cells/neurons, 5:34
Complex choristomas, 4:49f, 50, 8:246–247, 247f
Complex partial seizures, 1:261
Compliance with therapy
  amblyopia and, 6:66–67, 68
  behavioral/psychiatric disorders and, 1:257
  glaucoma management and, 10:176–177, 177
    surgery and, 10:212
  in older patients, 1:222, 10:176–177
    glaucoma surgery and, 10:212
Complications of Age-Related Macular Degeneration Prevention Trial (CAPT), 12:63
Compound heterozygote, 2:150, 194–195, 216
Compound hyperopic astigmatism, 3:114, 115f
Compound myopic astigmatism, 3:114, 115f
Compound nevi, 7:164
  of conjunctiva, 4:65, 66f
    in children, 6:349
  of eyelid, 4:225, 225f, 7:164
Compression (dynamic) gonioscopy, 10:33f, 34
  in acute primary angle closure, 10:114–115
Compressive optic neuropathy
  intraorbital/intracanalicular, 5:149–154
    optic glioma causing, 5:151–154, 151f, 152t
    optic nerve sheath meningioma causing, 5:149–151, 150f, 150t
  in thyroid eye disease, 5:147–149, 148f, 333, 7:49, 51, 53–54
Compromised host. See Immunocompromised host
Computed tomographic angiography (CTA), 5:69, 78–80
  advantages/disadvantages/contraindications and, 5:86t
  in aneurysm detection, 5:229, 229f
  in carotid artery evaluation, 5:180
  in cerebral aneurysm, 5:352
  in cerebral ischemia/stroke, 1:93
  in ischemic heart disease, 1:107
  in orbital evaluation, 7:31
Computed tomographic (CT) colonography (virtual colonoscopy), 1:269, 272t, 276
Computed tomography (CT scan), 5:70–72, 71f
  advantages/disadvantages/contraindications and, 5:86–88, 86t
  in cerebral ischemia/stroke, 1:93
  in choroidal/ciliary body melanoma, 4:277
  corneal, 13:15–16, 15f, 16f
    postoperative, 13:17
  in foreign-body identification, 12:318, 325, 326f
  helical (spiral)
    low-dose chest, in cancer screening, 1:275
    in orbital evaluation, 7:26
  in intracranial hemorrhage, 1:98
  in ischemic heart disease, 1:107

keratorefractive surgery and, 13:15–16, 15f, 16f
  postoperative, 13:17
in lacrimal drainage evaluation, 7:262
in orbital evaluation, 5:70–72, 71f, 87, 87f, 7:25–26, 25f, 26f
  MRI compared with, 7:28–29, 28t, 30f
  tumor diagnosis and, 6:334
in pulmonary diseases, 1:143
in retinoblastoma, 4:303, 6:356, 356f
in Sturge-Weber syndrome, 6:376
Computerized corneal topography, 3:267, 267f, 268f, 8:40–45, 40f, 41f, 42f, 43f, 44f, 13:10–14, 11f, 12f, 13f, 14f, 38–39, 38f. See also Cornea, topography of
Computerized videokeratoscopy. See Videokeratoscopy
Computers, as low vision devices, 3:303–304
COMS (Collaborative Ocular Melanoma Study), 4:263, 281, 287–288
Comtan. See Entacapone
Concave (minus/negative) lenses, 3:72–73, 73f
  anophthalmic socket camouflage and, 7:125
  paraxial ray tracing through, 3:73–74, 73f, 74f
  prismatic effect of, 3:87
Concave mirror, 3:89
  retinoscopy settings and, 3:122, 122f
  vergence calculations for, 3:91–92
Concentric (annular) bifocal contact lenses, 3:189, 189f
Conchae (turbinates), nasal, 7:18, 245f, 246
  inferior, 7:18, 245f, 246
  infracture of, for congenital nasolacrimal duct obstruction, 6:208–209, 7:255
Concomitant deviations. See Comitant (concomitant) deviations
Concretions, conjunctival, 8:332–333
Concussive trauma. See also Trauma
  anterior segment, 8:362–369, 364f, 365f, 366f, 367f, 369t
Condensing lens
  in fundus camera, 3:248, 250f
  in indirect ophthalmoscopy, 3:245, 245f
    fundus illumination and, 3:245, 246, 246f
Conduction disturbances, 1:121, 122t
Conductive keratoplasty, 13:4t, 22, 22f, 120–123, 121f, 153–154
  corneal transplantation after, 13:192
  for presbyopia, 13:120–123, 153–154
Cone dystrophies/degenerations, 5:114, 12:232–233, 233f
  ERG in, 12:36f, 232
  visual field testing in, 12:232
Cone inner segments, 2:76f, 4:145, 146f, 12:10, 11f, 13f. See also Cones; Photoreceptor inner segments
Cone outer segments, 2:76f, 81, 4:145, 146f, 12:10, 11f, 13f. See also Cones; Photoreceptor outer segments
  differentiation of, 2:126
  shed, retinal pigment epithelium phagocytosis of, 2:306–307
Cone response, 2:294, 301f, 302
  single-flash (photopic/light-adapted electroretinogram), 12:34, 34f, 35, 36f
    in cone dystrophies, 12:232
    in hereditary retinal/choroidal dystrophies, 12:224t
Cone–rod dystrophies/degenerations, 12:233–234. See also Retinitis pigmentosa
  ERG in, 12:36f, 233
  Stargardt disease and, 6:293, 12:233, 235

visual field defects in, **12**:234
visual field testing in, **12**:223
Cone–rod homeobox-containing *(CRX)* gene, **12**:222
cone–rod dystrophy and, **12**:233
Cones, **2**:73, 74, 76*f*, 77*f*, **4**:145, 146*f*, 147, **5**:27–28, **12**:10, 12, 13*f*, 14*f*. *See also* Cone outer segments
abnormalities of, **12**:213–215, 214*t*. *See also* Color vision, defects in
amacrine cells for, **2**:300
bipolar cells for, **2**:298, 299*f*
development of, **2**:126
electrophysiologic responses of, **2**:301*f*, 302
extrafoveal, **2**:74
foveal, **2**:74, 81
gene defects in, **2**:296–297
horizontal cells for, **2**:299–300
phototransduction in, **2**:293–294
retinoblastoma and, **4**:178, 180
Confluent drusen, **12**:58
Confocal microscopy, **8**:35–36, 36*f*
in dry eye evaluation, **8**:55
Confocal scanning laser ophthalmoscopy, **12**:29–30
in fundus autofluorescence, **12**:30
in indocyanine green angiography, **12**:25
in optic disc evaluation, **10**:51, 52*f*
Confounding factor, **1**:325–326, 342–343
Confrontation testing, **5**:98
before cataract surgery, **11**:81–82
in nonorganic ophthalmic disorders, **5**:312–313
before refractive surgery, **13**:34
Confusion (mental), postoperative, in older patients, **1**:224
Confusion (visual), **6**:49, 50*f*
Confusion tests, in nonorganic ophthalmic disorder evaluation
monocular no light perception and, **5**:309–310, 310*f*
monocular reduced vision and, **5**:310–311
Congenital, definition of, **2**:150, 191–192. *See also* Genetics
Congenital anomalies, **2**:141–143, 142*f*, **4**:6, 7*f*, **6**:171. *See also specific type*
of anterior segment/chamber, **4**:102–103, 103*f*, 104*f*, **6**:212–214, 213*f*, **8**:253–266
chromosomal analysis and, **2**:198, 198*t*
of conjunctiva, **4**:47–50, 49*f*
of cornea, **4**:79–82, 79*f*, 80*f*, 81*f*, **6**:211–216, **8**:253–266, 261–262*t*
craniofacial malformations, **6**:383–395, **7**:34–35, 34*f*, 35*f*
of eyelid, **4**:207, 208*f*, **6**:175–180, **7**:145–152
genetic influences and, **2**:141, 197–198
glaucoma associated with, **4**:102, 103*f*, **6**:238, **10**:5*t*, 7*t*, 140*t*, 142, 145–148. *See also* Glaucoma, childhood
of globe, **8**:249–253
of lens, **4**:121, 122*f*, **6**:260–261, 261*f*, **11**:26–35. *See also* Cataract, congenital
nongenetic teratogens causing, **2**:141–143, 142*f*
of optic disc and nerve, **4**:249–250, 251*f*, **5**:141–143, 142*f*, 143*f*, **6**:305–310
of orbit, **4**:229–230, 230*f*, **6**:173–175, 174*f*, 175*f*, **7**:33–37, 34*f*, 35*f*, 36*f*, 37*f*
of retina and retinal pigment epithelium, **4**:148–151, 149*f*, 150*f*, **6**:352, 353*f*
of sclera, **4**:112–113, **8**:249–253

of trabecular meshwork, **4**:102–103, 103*f*, 104*f*
of uveal tract, **4**:188
of vitreous, **4**:132–133, 132*f*
Congenital aphakia, **4**:121, **6**:260, **11**:26. *See also* Aphakia
Congenital bilateral mydriasis, **6**:229
Congenital cataract, **6**:245, **11**:30–35, 31*t*. *See also specific type and* Cataract, congenital
genetic contributions to, **11**:37–38
Congenital epithelial melanosis, **8**:233
Congenital esotropia. *See* Infantile (congenital) esotropia
Congenital fibrosis (congenital cranial dysinnervation/agenesis) syndromes, **5**:240–241, 241*f*, 241*t*, **6**:127, 138–140, 171
type 1 (CFEOM1), **5**:240
Congenital glaucoma (primary congenital glaucoma), **4**:102, 103*f*, **6**:233–238, 234*f*, 235*t*, 236*f*, 237*f*, **8**:265, **10**:5*t*, 139, 140*t*, 143–145, 143*f*, 144*f*, 144*t*. *See also* Glaucoma, childhood
corneal opacities and, **6**:218, 234, 235*t*
differential diagnosis of, **10**:144–145, 144*t*
genetics of, **6**:233, **10**:142–143
treatment of, **10**:152–157
medical, **10**:156–157
surgical, **10**:145, 152–156, 153*f*, 154*f*
Congenital hemidysplasia with ichthyosiform erythroderma and limb defects (CHILD) syndrome, **8**:74
Congenital hereditary endothelial dystrophy, **4**:79–80, 79*f*, **6**:216*t*, 217, **8**:260–263, 268*t*, 270*t*, 295–296, 295*f*
CHED1, **8**:260, 268*t*, 270*t*, 295–296, 295*f*
CHED2, **8**:260, 268*t*, 270*t*, 296, 296*f*
genetics of, **8**:269*t*, 295, 296
Congenital hereditary stromal dystrophy, **6**:216*t*, 219, **8**:260, 286. *See also* Congenital stromal corneal dystrophy
Congenital hypertrophy of retinal pigment epithelium (CHRPE), **4**:149–151, 150*f*, **6**:352, 353*f*, **12**:255*f*, 282
melanoma differentiated from, **4**:150, 278, 279*f*
Congenital infection syndrome/TORCHES, **6**:181. *See also specific disorder*
lymphocytic choriomeningitis virus causing, **9**:211–212
Congenital iris ectropion syndrome, **6**:231
glaucoma in neurofibromatosis and, **6**:370
Congenital keratitis-ichthyosis-deafness (KID) syndrome, **8**:74
Congenital lacrimal fistula, **6**:204, **7**:277, 278, 278*f*
Congenital measles, **9**:212
Congenital miosis (microcoria), **6**:223, 228–229
Congenital mydriasis, **6**:229
Congenital myopia, **3**:141
Congenital nevocellular nevi of skin, **6**:349–350, 350*f*
Congenital night blindness
with normal fundi, **12**:215–217, 216*f*, 217*f*
with prominent fundus abnormality, **12**:217–219, 218*f*, 219*f*
stationary, **6**:291–292, **12**:215–217, 216*f*, 217*f*
ERG patterns in, **6**:291, **12**:36*f*, 216, 217, 217*f*
with myopia, ocular findings in carriers of, **2**:222*t*
Congenital nystagmus, **5**:243, 244*f*, 245–246, **6**:288–289, 289*t*, 321–323, 321*t*, 323*f*, 324*f*
latent (fusion maldevelopment), **5**:246, **6**:322–323, 323*f*, 324*f*
dissociated vertical deviation and, **6**:116, 117, 323

motor, **6**:321
  periodic alternating, **5**:251*t*, 252–253, **6**:322
  sensory, **6**:322, 414
Congenital ocular motor apraxia, **5**:209–210, **6**:141
Congenital ptosis. *See* Ptosis
Congenital retinal arteriovenous malformations, **4**:296,
    297*f*, **12**:151. *See also* Racemose angioma
Congenital rubella syndrome, **1**:283, **6**:183–184, 183*f*,
    8:130, **9**:209–210, 209*f*, 210*f*, 211
  aphakia and, **4**:121
  cataracts and, **6**:183, **9**:210, **11**:35
Congenital strabismus, **6**:11. *See also* Strabismus
Congenital stromal corneal dystrophy, **8**:268*t*, 270*t*,
    286–287, 286*f*. *See also* Congenital hereditary
    stromal dystrophy
  genetics of, **8**:269*t*, 286
Congenital syphilis, **1**:12, 279, **6**:185–186, 221,
    9:243–244, 244*f*, 247, 248*t*, 249
  corneal manifestations of/interstitial keratitis, **4**:87, 87*f*,
      6:185, 221, **8**:207–209, 208*f*, 264, **9**:243–244, 244*f*
Congenital tarsal kink, **6**:176–177
Congenital tilted disc syndrome (Fuchs coloboma),
    5:142–143, 142*f*, **6**:307, 307*f*
Congestive heart failure, **1**:99, 113–121
  atrial fibrillation and, **1**:119, 120
  clinical course of, **1**:117–118
  clinical signs of, **1**:114
  compensated, **1**:113
  decompensated, **1**:113
  diagnosis of, **1**:114–116
  epidemiology of, **1**:113
  etiology of, **1**:116
  high-output, **1**:116
  hypertension management and, **1**:79*t*, 84, 118
  incidence of, **1**:113
  ischemic heart disease causing, **1**:116, 120
  management of, **1**:115*f*
    invasive/surgical, **1**:120–121
    medical/nonsurgical, **1**:118–120
  after myocardial infarction, **1**:103
  pathophysiology of, **1**:117–118
  refractory, **1**:113–114
  at risk patients and, **1**:115*f*
  stages of, **1**:114, 115*f*
  symptoms of, **1**:114
Congo red stain, **4**:30, 31*t*
Congruous visual field defects, retrochiasmal lesions
    producing, **5**:165
Conidia, **8**:138
Conidiophores, **8**:138
Conjugacy/conjugate, **3**:28, 28–29, 29*f*, 30*f*
  in direct ophthalmoscopy, **3**:28–29, 30*f*
  emmetropia/infinity and, **3**:113, 113*f*
  in indirect ophthalmoscopy, **3**:246, 247*f*
  in retinoscopy, **3**:28, 29*f*
  saccadic system evaluation and, **5**:203, 209
Conjugate eye movements (versions), **5**:215, **6**:34, 35,
    36*f*. *See also specific type*
  assessment of, **6**:81
  development of, **6**:170
Conjugate points
  in geometric optics, **3**:28, 28–29, 29*f*, 30*f*
  nodal points and, **3**:33, 34*f*

Conjunctiva, **2**:29, 30*f*, 34–35, **4**:47–75, **7**:135*f*, 141. *See
    also under Conjunctival*
  age-related/involutional changes in, **8**:331
  amyloid deposits in, **4**:58–59, 60*f*, **8**:317*t*, 318, 318*f*.
    See also Amyloidosis/amyloid deposits
  anatomy of, **2**:29, 30*f*, 34–35, **8**:4–6
  biopsy of, **8**:389–390
    in cicatricial pemphigoid, **4**:54, **8**:201
    in granulomatous conjunctivitis, **4**:52
    in intraepithelial melanosis, **4**:67
    in lymphocytic lesions, **4**:71
    in mucopolysaccharidoses, **8**:307
    for ocular microbiology, **8**:102
    in pseudopemphigoid, **8**:361
    in squamous neoplasms, **4**:64
    in superior limbic keratoconjunctivitis, **8**:82
  blood under, **8**:75, 76, 76*t*, 362–363
  blood vessels of, **2**:34–35
  bulbar, **2**:29, 30*f*, 34, **4**:47, 48*f*, **8**:4, 6
  carcinoma of. *See also* Conjunctiva, tumors of
    intraocular extension and, **4**:322
    squamous cell, **8**:226*t*, 231–232, 232*f*
      in situ, **4**:63–64, 64*f*
      invasive, **4**:63*f*, 64, 64*f*
      staging of, **4**:332–333*t*
  caruncular, **4**:47, 48*f*. *See also* Caruncle
    lymphocytic lesions involving, **4**:71
  concretions of, **8**:332–333
  congenital anomalies of, **4**:47–50, 49*f*
  contact lenses causing injury to, **3**:200, **4**:50,
    8:193–195, 194*f*
  cysts of, **4**:59–60, 60*f*, **6**:348, **8**:225–226, 226*f*
    nevi and, **4**:65
    after strabismus surgery, **6**:157, 157*f*
  degenerations of, **4**:56–60, 58*f*, 59*f*, 60*f*, **8**:331–333
  development of, **8**:4
  discharge from, **8**:20*t*
  disorders of, **4**:47–75, **8**:20*t*. *See also specific type and*
    Conjunctivitis; Keratoconjunctivitis
    contact lenses causing, **3**:200, **4**:50, **8**:193–195, 194*f*
    in glaucoma, **10**:29
    immune-mediated, **8**:180–181, 185–204, 197*t*
    ionizing radiation causing, **8**:352–353
    neoplastic, **4**:61–75, **8**:225–247. *See also*
      Conjunctiva, tumors of
    Th1 delayed hypersensitivity and, **9**:50*t*
  drug absorption and, **2**:325
  dysplasia of (conjunctival intraepithelial neoplasia),
    4:62, 63*f*, 64*f*, **8**:226*t*, 228–229, 229*f*, 230*f*. *See also*
    Ocular surface squamous neoplasia
  epithelium of, **2**:35, 239*f*, **4**:47, 48*f*, **8**:5
    cysts of, **4**:59–60, 60*f*, **8**:225–226, 226*f*
    nevi and, **4**:65
    dysplasia of (conjunctival intraepithelial neoplasia),
      4:62, 63*f*, 64*f*, **8**:226*t*, 228–229, 229*f*, 230*f*. *See
      also* Ocular surface squamous neoplasia
    evaluation of in pseudoepiphora, **7**:257
    immunologic features of, **8**:173, 174*t*
    tear secretion and, **2**:239*f*, 240, 241
    tumors of, **8**:226–233, 226*t*
    wound healing/repair and, **8**:388
  erosions of, **8**:22*t*
    punctate epithelial, **8**:20*t*

examination of
before cataract surgery, 11:78
in glaucoma, 10:29
before refractive surgery, 13:35
in external eye defense, 8:96
extraocular surgery affecting, 8:385
eyelid, 2:29, 30f, 34–35, 7:135f, 141
follicles of, 8:20t, 24, 24f
foreign body on, 4:53, 53f, 8:370, 370f
forniceal, 2:29, 30f, 34, 4:47, 48f
lymphocytic lesions involving, 4:71
glaucoma/glaucoma therapy affecting, 10:29
goblet cells in. See Goblet cells
granuloma of, 8:20t, 22t, 241–242, 241f
foreign-body, 4:53, 53f
in Parinaud oculoglandular syndrome, 4:52, 8:157, 158
in sarcoidosis, 4:52, 53f, 8:73–74, 9:174, 174f
hemangiomas of, 4:50, 8:240–241
hemorrhage of, 8:76, 76t, 362–363
in child abuse, 6:404
in hereditary hemorrhagic telangiectasia, 8:76
immune response/immunologic features of, 8:173, 174t, 180–181, 9:57–59, 58t
infection/inflammation of, 4:50–56, 51f, 52f, 53f, 55f, 56f, 57f, 8:20t, 21–24, 22f, 22t, 23f, 24f, 143–148, 149–158, 150t. See also Conjunctivitis; Keratoconjunctivitis
intraepithelial neoplasia of (CIN), 4:62, 63f, 64f, 8:226t, 228–229, 229f, 230f. See also Ocular surface squamous neoplasia
laceration of, 8:369–370
in children, 6:409
lithiasis of, 8:333
lymphoid tissue associated with (CALT), 2:35, 4:47, 8:3, 5, 180–181, 9:59
lymphoma of, 4:72, 72–74, 72f, 73f, 8:244, 245f
mast cells in, 9:10–11
melanoma of, 4:69–70, 70f, 71f, 8:238–240, 238t, 239f
in children, 6:349
intraocular extension of, 4:322
primary acquired melanosis and, 4:67, 68f, 69, 70f, 8:239
staging of, 4:334–336t
membrane of, 8:20t, 22t
in epidemic keratoconjunctivitis, 8:124, 125, 125f
in ligneous conjunctivitis, 8:192, 192f
nevus of, 4:65–66, 65t, 66f, 8:236–237, 236f, 238t
in children, 6:349, 349f
normal flora of, 8:96–97, 97t
palpebral, 2:29, 30f, 34, 4:47, 48f, 205, 206f, 8:4, 6
papillae of, 8:20t, 21–22, 22f, 22t, 23f. See also Papillae, conjunctival
papillomas of, 4:61–62, 61f, 8:128, 129, 226–228, 226t, 227f
pH of, chemical injury management and, 8:355
pigmented lesions of, 8:238t
benign, 8:233–237, 234t
malignant, 8:234t, 238–240
preinvasive, 8:234t, 237–238
pseudomembrane of, 8:20t, 22t
in epidemic keratoconjunctivitis, 8:124

scarring of
glaucoma drainage device implantation and, 10:206
after strabismus surgery, 6:157, 157f
scrapings/swabbings from, 8:47
specimen collection from
for ocular cytology, 8:47–48
for ocular microbiology, 8:100–102, 101t
stem cells of, 8:92
stroma of (substantia propria), 4:47, 48f, 8:5–6, 9:57
age-related/involutional changes in, 8:331
in external eye defense, 8:96
immune and inflammatory cells in, 8:173, 174t, 9:59
in superior limbic keratoconjunctivitis, 8:81, 82, 82f
tarsal, 8:4
telangiectasia of, in ataxia-telangiectasia, 5:344, 345f, 6:378, 379f
topography of, 4:47, 48f
transplantation of, 8:94, 392f, 393–395
for chemical injuries, 8:358
indications for, 8:387t, 395
for wound closure after pterygium excision, 8:392f, 393, 393–395
tumors of, 4:61–75, 8:225–247
epithelial, 8:226–233, 226t
glandular, 4:75, 75f, 8:233
human papillomaviruses causing, 4:61–62, 61f, 8:128, 129, 226–227
inflammatory, 8:241–242, 241f, 241t
lymphocytic/lymphatic, 4:71–74, 72f, 73f, 8:242–244
malignant, 8:234t, 238–240
melanocytic, 4:65–70, 65t, 66f, 67f, 68f, 70f, 71f
metastatic, 8:245
neurogenic and smooth muscle, 8:240
pigmented, 8:238t
benign, 8:233–237, 234t
malignant, 8:234t, 238–240
preinvasive, 8:234t, 237–238
staging of, 4:332–336t
vascular and mesenchymal, 8:240–242, 241t
ulceration of, 8:22t
in uveitis, 9:86t
vascular anomalies of, noninflammatory, 8:75–77
wound healing/repair of, 8:388
Conjunctiva-associated lymphoid tissue (CALT/ conjunctival MALT), 2:35, 4:47, 8:3, 5, 180–181, 9:59
Conjunctival arteries, 5:14f
posterior, 2:34
Conjunctival autograft, 8:94. See also Conjunctiva, transplantation of
indications for, 8:387t, 395
for wound closure after pterygium excision, 8:392f, 393, 393–395
Conjunctival congestion. See Conjunctival hyperemia/ congestion
Conjunctival flaps, 8:398–401, 399f
cataract surgery and
for ICCE, 11:214
leak causing inadvertent filtering bleb and, 11:148–149
for postoperative corneal edema, 11:147–148
for neurotrophic keratopathy, 8:88–89
for symblepharon, 7:200

for trabeculectomy, **10**:187–188, 188*f*, 189*f*
closure of, **10**:191–192, 193*f*
management of, **10**:194
for trabeculotomy, in children, **10**:154
for wound closure after pterygium excision,
8:391–393, 392*f*
Conjunctival hyperemia/congestion, **8**:20*t*, 75
in glaucoma, **10**:29, 91, 91*f*
in leptospirosis, **9**:254, 255
prostaglandin analogues causing, **10**:166
Conjunctival inclusion cysts, **4**:59–60, 60*f*, **8**:225–226,
226*f*
in children, **6**:157, 157*f*, 348
nevi and, **4**:65
after strabismus surgery, **6**:157, 157*f*
Conjunctival intraepithelial neoplasia (CIN), **4**:62, 63*f*,
64*f*, **8**:226*t*, 228–229, 229*f*, 230*f*. *See also* Ocular
surface squamous neoplasia
Conjunctival sac, **2**:237, **8**:4
Conjunctivalization of cornea, **8**:355
Conjunctivitis, **4**:50–56, **8**:20*t*, 21–24, 22*f*, 22*t*, 23*f*, 24*f*,
101*t*. *See also* Keratoconjunctivitis
acute
hemorrhagic, **8**:130
purulent, **8**:149–151
adenoviral, **8**:124–127, 125*f*
in children, **6**:190–191
allergic, **8**:185–187, **9**:55
drugs for, **2**:364–366, 365*t*
perennial, **6**:198, **8**:185–187
seasonal, **6**:198, 198*t*, 199*t*, **8**:185–187
bacterial, **4**:53, 55*f*, **8**:149–154, 150*t*
in children, **6**:189–190, 190*f*, **8**:149–152
classification of, **8**:149, 150*t*
in neonates, **6**:187–188, 187*f*, **8**:152–154
blepharitis and, **8**:101*t*, 144*t*, 145. *See also*
Blepharoconjunctivitis
in children, **6**:193–194
chemical, in neonates, **6**:188
in children, **6**:188–193, 189*t*, **8**:149–152
preseptal cellulitis caused by, **6**:195, **8**:150
chlamydial, **4**:54, 55*f*, **8**:154–157, 155*f*, 156*f*
in adults, **8**:156–157, 156*f*
in neonates, **6**:187–188, **8**:153–154
cicatricial, **4**:54, 56*f*, **8**:196*t*, 198–203, 199*t*, 200*f*,
201*f*, 202*f*. *See also* Ocular cicatricial (mucous
membrane) pemphigoid
differential diagnosis of, **8**:199, 199*t*
contact lens–induced, **3**:200, **4**:50, **8**:193–195, 194*f*
corticosteroid route of administration in, **2**:360*t*
coxsackievirus, **8**:130
enterovirus, **8**:130
Epstein-Barr virus causing, **8**:122–123
follicular, **4**:51, 51*f*, 52*f*, **8**:22*t*, 24, 24*f*
in acute hemorrhagic conjunctivitis, **8**:130
adenoviral, **8**:124
in Lyme disease, **9**:251, **12**:210
in measles, **8**:129
medication toxicity causing, **8**:359*t*, 360, 361*f*
in mumps, **8**:129–130
RNA viruses causing, **8**:129
giant papillary (contact lens–induced), **3**:200, **4**:50,
8:23*f*, 194–195, 194*f*

gonococcal, **8**:134, 151–152, 151*f*
in children, **6**:189
in neonates, **6**:187, 187*f*, **8**:153
granulomatous, **4**:52–53, 53*f*
in HIV infection/AIDS, **9**:313–314
Haemophilus causing, **4**:53, **8**:150
in children, **6**:189
hay fever, **8**:185–187
hemorrhagic, **8**:130
herpes simplex virus causing
in children, **6**:191–192, 192*f*
in neonates, **6**:185, 188
herpes zoster causing, **6**:192–193, 193*f*, **8**:106, 106*f*
in HIV infection/AIDS, **9**:313–314
in infants, **6**:186–188, 187*f*, **8**:152–154. *See also*
Ophthalmia, neonatorum
infectious, **4**:53–54, 55*f*, **8**:101*t*. *See also specific type*
and causative agent
in children, **6**:188–193, 189*t*
in infectious mononucleosis, **6**:193
ligneous, **8**:192–193, 192*f*
in children, **6**:351
in Lyme disease, **9**:251, **12**:210
measles virus causing, **8**:129, **9**:212
medication toxicity causing, **8**:359–361, 359*t*, 361*f*
meningococcal, **6**:189
microsporidial, **8**:170
in molluscum contagiosum, **6**:193, 194*f*
mumps virus causing, **8**:129–130
in neonates, **6**:186–188, 187*f*, **8**:152–154. *See also*
Ophthalmia, neonatorum
noninfectious, **4**:54, 56*f*
papillary, **4**:50, 51*f*, **8**:22*t*, 23*f*
in Parinaud oculoglandular syndrome, **4**:52,
6:189–190, 190*f*, **8**:157–158, **9**:263, **12**:206
in pharyngoconjunctival fever, **6**:191
in reactive arthritis/Reiter syndrome, **1**:165, **8**:209,
9:123
RNA viruses causing, **8**:129
rubella, **9**:211
in sarcoidosis, **4**:52, 53*f*
seasonal allergic, **6**:198, 198*t*, 199*t*, **8**:185–187
staphylococcal/staphylococcal blepharitis and, **8**:101*t*,
144*t*, 145
in Stevens-Johnson syndrome, **6**:201, 201*f*, **8**:196
after strabismus surgery, **6**:156
streptococcal, **8**:101*t*, 149–150
in children, **6**:189
subconjunctival hemorrhage caused by, **8**:76*t*
toxic
contact lens solutions causing, **8**:92
medications causing, **8**:359–361, 359*t*, 361*f*
in trachoma, **6**:190
trachoma-inclusion, in neonates, **6**:187
varicella-zoster virus causing, **6**:192–193, 193*f*,
8:117–119
vernal, **8**:187–190, 188*f*, 189*f*
atopic keratoconjunctivitis differentiated from,
8:190, 191*f*
in children, **6**:198–200, 199*f*
viral, **4**:53–54, 55*f*
in children, **6**:190–193
immune response to, **9**:60–61

Conjunctivochalasis, **8**:21, 53, 53*f*, 333, 333*f*
  punctal obstruction/malposition and, **7**:263
Conjunctivodacryocystorhinostomy
  for canalicular obstruction, **7**:265
  after canthal repair, **7**:186
  for punctal disorders, **7**:250, 262
Connective tissue
  eyelid, **2**:23, **7**:141–142
  pericanalicular, **2**:54, 55*f*
Connective tissue disorders. *See also specific disorder*
  and Collagen-vascular diseases
  cataract surgery in patient with, **11**:188, 191
  corneal changes in, **8**:320–325, 322–324*t*
  mixed, **1**:174
  peripheral ulcerative keratitis in, **8**:211–213, 211*t*,
    212*f*
  refractive surgery in patient with, **13**:31, 184–185
  scleritis in, **8**:222
  uveitis in, **9**:140–146
  vasculitis associated with, **7**:58
Connective tissue mast cells, **9**:10
Connective tissue tumors, of orbit, in children, **6**:343
Conoid
  Cartesian, **3**:54, 54*f*
  of Sturm, **3**:93, 93*f*
    astigmatic dial refraction and, **3**:130
Conradi syndrome, ichthyosis in, **8**:74
Consanguinity, **2**:150, 215, 227
Consecutive anophthalmia, **7**:33
Consecutive (surgical) esodeviation, **6**:97–98
  management of, **6**:103
Consecutive exotropia, **6**:105
Consecutive hyperopia, **13**:93–94
Consensual response, in pupillary reaction to light, **5**:262
Consensus sequence, **2**:150
Consent, informed
  for cataract surgery, **11**:88
  older patients and, **1**:224
  for refractive surgery, **13**:30*t*, 41–42, 41*t*, 209–217
    LASIK and, **13**:213–217
    in patient with ocular or systemic disease,
      13:163–164
    phakic intraocular lens insertion and, **13**:128
    photorefractive keratectomy (PRK) and,
      13:209–212
    refractive lens exchange/clear lens extraction and,
      13:138
Conservation (genetic), **2**:150
Conserved base-pair mutations, **2**:171
CONSORT (Consolidated Standards of Reporting
  Trials) guidelines, **1**:328
Constant exotropia, **6**:103–104
Construct validity, **1**:339
Constructive interference, **3**:7, 8*f*
Consultand, **2**:225
Contact, arc of, **6**:28
Contact dermatitis/dermatoblepharitis/
  blepharoconjunctivitis, **8**:180, 183–185, 184*f*
Contact hypersensitivity, **9**:34, 35
  response to poison ivy as, **9**:34, 35
Contact inhibition, in corneal wound repair, **4**:13
Contact lens electrode, corneal, for electroretinogram,
  12:35

Contact lens method, for IOL power calculation after
  refractive surgery, **11**:87, **13**:188
Contact lens solutions, **3**:195–196, 195*t*
  allergic reactions to, **8**:92
  giant papillary conjunctivitis and, **8**:195
  for keratoglobus, **8**:303
  toxic conjunctivitis caused by, **8**:92
Contact lens superior limbic keratoconjunctivitis
  (CLSLK), **3**:198
Contact lenses, **3**:167–202, 168*f*. *See also specific*
  type and Soft (flexible) contact lenses; Rigid gas-
  permeable contact lenses
  Acanthamoeba keratitis associated with, **3**:196,
    4:84–85, **8**:167, 168
  accommodation and, **3**:144–145, 172–173
  alternating vision, **3**:176, 189, 189*f*
  aniseikonia and, **3**:171–172
  anisometropia and, **3**:171
  for aphakia, **3**:116, 171
    in children, **6**:259
  astigmatism correction and, **3**:174–176, 186–188,
    187*t*, 188*f*, 316–317
  bacterial keratitis associated with, **3**:180, **8**:159
    orthokeratology and, **13**:64
  bandage, **3**:193–194, **8**:403
    for chemical injuries, **8**:358
    contraindications to, in exposure keratopathy, **8**:80
    for corneal abrasion, **8**:372
    for dry eye, **8**:60*t*, 61, 403
    for graft-vs-host disease, **8**:203
    for involutional entropion, **7**:196
    after LASIK, **13**:85, 194
      epithelial ingrowth prevention and, **13**:114, 194
      epithelial sloughing/defects and, **13**:104–105
      microkeratome complications and, **13**:103
      striae and, **13**:107–108
    for perforating injury, **8**:375
    for peripheral ulcerative keratitis, **8**:213
    for recurrent corneal erosions, **8**:84, 403
    after surface ablation, **13**:85, 86, 193
      sterile infiltrates and, **13**:100, 100*f*
    for Thygeson superficial punctate keratitis, **8**:206
  base curve of, **3**:167, 168*f*, 170
  bifocal, **3**:176, 189–190, 189*f*, 190*f*
    alternating vision, **3**:176, 189, 189*f*
    simultaneous vision, **3**:176, 189–190, 190*f*
  care of, **3**:196–197, 196*t*
    teaching, **3**:182, 197
  clinically important features of optics of, **3**:170–176
  complications of. *See* Contact lenses, problems/
    complications with
  conjunctivitis caused by, **3**:200, **4**:50, **8**:193–195, 194*f*
  convergence and, **3**:144–145, 173
  corneal disorders caused by, **3**:197–199, 198*f*
  for corneal reshaping, **3**:194–195
  custom, **3**:195–196
  daily wear (DW), **3**:180
  damaged, red eye caused by, **3**:200
  deposits on, **3**:200
  diameter (chord diameter) of, **3**:167, 168*f*, 170
    rigid gas-permeable contact lens fitting and, **3**:184*t*,
      185
    soft contact lens fitting and, **3**:183*t*

discontinuing use of before refractive surgery, **13**:32
disposable, **3**:180
in dry-eye disorders, **8**:61
edge lift of, **3**:168
extended-wear (EW), **3**:180
　as bandage lenses, **3**:193–194
　materials for, **3**:178
federal regulations for, **3**:201–202
field of vision and, **3**:170
filtering bleb and, **10**:198
fitting, **3**:181–193. *See also* Fitting (contact lens)
flexible. *See* Soft (flexible) contact lenses
for fundus biomicroscopy, **3**:253–255, 254*f*, 255*f*, 256*f*
fungal keratitis associated with, **8**:165
glaucoma drainage device implantation and, **10**:206
glossary of terms related to, **3**:167–169
history of use of, refractive surgery evaluation and,
　13:31–32
HIV transmission and, **3**:201
hybrid, **3**:191
image size and, **3**:170–172
　anisometropia and, **3**:171
for induced anisophoria, **3**:156
keratitis associated with use of, **3**:180, 196, 198–199,
　201, **4**:84–85, **8**:159, 165, 167, 168
　orthokeratology and, **13**:64
for keratoconus, **3**:190–191, 191*f*, **8**:300
after LASIK, **13**:193–194, 193*f*
lenticular, **3**:169
manufacturing of, **3**:178–179
　custom lenses and, **3**:196
materials for, **3**:176–178, 177*t*
monovision and, **3**:176, 189
　as trial for surgery, **13**:153, 192
for myopia reduction (orthokeratology), **3**:194–195,
　13:63–64
optic zone of, **3**:168*f*, 169
optics of, clinically important features of, **3**:170–176
for orthokeratology, **3**:194–195, **13**:63–64
oxygen transmissibility of, **3**:168, 176–178, 177*t*. *See
　also* Gas-permeability constant
　corneal hypoxia and, **3**:200
　orthokeratology and, **3**:194
　rigid contact lenses and, **3**:176–178
　scleral contact lenses and, **3**:192
　soft (flexible) contact lenses and, **3**:178, 181*t*
parameters of, **3**:168*f*, 170, 180, 181*t*, 182, 182–185,
　184*t*
patient examination for, **3**:179–180
for pellucid marginal degeneration, **8**:302
after penetrating keratoplasty, **13**:169
peripheral curves of, **3**:168*f*, 169
power curve of, **3**:170
power of, **3**:167, 170, 183, 185
　lensmeters in measurement of, **3**:268–272, 269*f*,
　　270*f*, 271*f*
for presbyopia, **3**:176, 189–190, 189*f*, 190*f*. *See also*
　Contact lenses, bifocal
problems/complications with, **3**:180, 197–201, 198*f*
　ocular surface, **3**:197–199, 198*f*, **8**:91–92
after radial keratotomy, **13**:193, 193*f*
red eye caused by, **3**:199–201
after refractive/keratorefractive surgery, **3**:191,
　13:192–194, 193*f*

rigid (hard). *See* Rigid contact lenses; Rigid gas-
　permeable contact lenses
rotational movement of, **3**:195
sagittal depth (vault) of, **3**:169, 169*f*
scleral, **3**:179, 191–193, 192*f*
　in dry-eye disorders, **8**:61
　for graft-vs-host disease, **8**:204, 204*f*
　for keratoconus, **3**:191, 193
selection of type of, **3**:180–181, 181*t*
simultaneous vision, **3**:176, 189–190, 190*f*
for slit-lamp biomicroscopy, **12**:19
for slit-lamp delivery of photocoagulation, **12**:339, 340*t*
soft. *See* Soft (flexible) contact lenses
after surface ablation, **13**:193
tear (fluid) lens and, **3**:169, 173–174, 174*f*, 175
　fitting and, **3**:183, 185
therapeutic, **3**:193–194. *See also* Contact lenses,
　bandage
toric soft, **3**:186–188, 187*t*, 188*f*
for trial fitting
　disinfection of, **1**:41, **3**:201, **8**:46
　　for rigid gas-permeable contact lenses, **3**:182–186,
　　　184*f*, 184*t*, 186*f*, 187*f*
　　for soft (flexible) contact lenses, **3**:182, 183*t*
vault of, **3**:169, 169*f*
vertical movement of, **3**:195
wavefront technology and, **3**:195–196
wetting angle of, **3**:169, 170*f*
Contact specular microscopy/photomicroscopy, **3**:261,
　8:32–33, 32*f*
Contig, **2**:150
Contiguous gene deletion syndrome, **2**:206
Continuous curvilinear capsulorrhexis, **11**:115–117,
　116*f. See also* Capsulorrhexis
　capsule staining for, **11**:195, 195*f*
　in children, **6**:255, 256*f*
　for ECCE, **11**:212
　loose zonules and, **11**:117
　for manual small-incision cataract surgery, **11**:96
　for phacoemulsification, **11**:115–117, 116*f*
　in uveitis, **9**:292
Continuous outcome, in screening/diagnostic test,
　1:330–332, 331*f*, 332*f*
Continuous phacoemulsification, **11**:106–107
Continuous positive airway pressure (CPAP), **1**:144
Continuous quality improvement, **1**:344, 346, 347*f*
Continuous subcutaneous insulin infusion (CSII), **1**:197
Continuous sutures, for penetrating keratoplasty, **8**:419,
　420*f*
Contour interaction (crowding phenomenon), **6**:62, 65,
　65*f*
Contour interaction (crowding) bars, for amblyopia
　evaluation, **6**:65, 65*f*, 73
Contour stereopsis tests, **6**:87
Contraceptives, oral
　central retinal vein occlusion and, **12**:129
　hypercoagulability associated with, **1**:158
　hypertension and, **1**:86
　ocular effects of, **1**:302*t*
　tetracycline use and, **2**:374
　thyroxine levels affected by, **1**:208
　uveitis caused by, **9**:128
Contracted fornices, anophthalmic socket and, **7**:123
Contracted socket, **7**:124, 124*f*

Contractility, myocardial, **1**:117
  enhancement of in heart failure management, **1**:119
  reduction of in angina management, **1**:108
Contraction, wound, **4**:13, 14*f*
Contralateral corneal autograft, **8**:432
Contrast. *See also* Contrast sensitivity
  enhancing
    in low vision, **3**:291–292, 304
      sunglasses for, **3**:159, 160
  formula for measurement of, **3**:111
Contrast/catheter/conventional angiography, **5**:77, 79*f*
  in aneurysm detection, **5**:229
Contrast grating (modulation transfer function), **3**:111,
  278
Contrast sensitivity, **3**:111–113, 112*f*, **12**:50, 51*f*
  central visual field deficits and, **3**:287
  definition of, **3**:111
  in low vision/vision rehabilitation, **3**:285, 291–292, 304
  with multifocal IOLs, **13**:145, 155
  with phakic IOLs, **13**:134
  Snellen acuity and, **3**:111, 112
  sunglasses affecting, **3**:159
  testing, **5**:105–106, **12**:50–52, 51*f*
    cataracts and, **11**:70, 76–77
    in low vision evaluation, **3**:291–292, 292, 304,
      5:105–106
Contrast sensitivity curve, **3**:111, 112*f*
Contrast sensitivity function (CSF), **3**:111–112, 112*f*, **5**:105
Contrast threshold, **3**:111, **5**:105
Contrecoup mechanism, in blunt trauma, retinal breaks
  caused by, **12**:272
Control charts, **1**:344–345, 346*f*
Contusion cataract, **11**:50, 50*f*
Contusion injury. *See also* Blunt trauma; Trauma
  lens damage caused by, **11**:50–51, 50*f*
  retinal breaks caused by, **12**:272, 273*f*
Convergence, **5**:198, **6**:35
  accommodative, **6**:37
    assessment of, **6**:81
    in refractive accommodative esotropia, **6**:93
  assessment of, **5**:204, **6**:81–82
  development of, **6**:170
  disorders of, **5**:213–214
  fusional, **6**:37, 41, 41*t*, 82
  near point of, **6**:81
  near reflex and, **2**:99, **6**:37, 81
  proximal (instrument), **6**:37
  tonic, **6**:36
  voluntary, **6**:37
Convergence/convergent rays, **3**:62
  AC/A ratio and, **3**:143–144
  spectacle and contact lens correction affecting,
    3:144–145, 173
Convergence insufficiency, **5**:213, 222*t*, **6**:106
  intermittent exotropia and, **6**:101
Convergence paralysis, exotropia and, **6**:106
Convergence-retraction nystagmus (induced
  convergence-retraction), **5**:44, 251*t*, 256
  in children, **6**:325
Convergence spasm, **5**:214, 222*t*
Convergence tone, **6**:36
Convergent strabismus, **6**:9
Converging lens, **3**:139
Converse bobbing, **5**:259

Conversion disorders, **1**:248
Convex (plus/positive) lenses
  anophthalmic socket camouflage and, **7**:125
  paraxial ray tracing through, **3**:69–72, 71*f*
  prismatic effect of, **3**:87
Convex mirror, **3**:89
  vergence calculations for, **3**:92
Coombs and Gell type IV hypersensitivity. *See* Delayed
  hypersensitivity (type IV) reaction
Copaxone. *See* Glatiramer
COPD. *See* Chronic obstructive pulmonary disease
Copeland anterior chamber IOL, **3**:210, 210*f*
Copeland retinoscope, **3**:121, 121*f*, 122, 127
Copper
  in aqueous humor, **2**:267
  corneal deposition of, **6**:221, **8**:327–328, 327*f*, 337*t*,
    11:54, 57
    Kayser-Fleischer ring caused by, **6**:221, **8**:327, 327*f*,
      337*t*, **11**:57
  foreign body of, **11**:54, **12**:327
  in free-radical formation, **2**:311–312, 313
  sunflower cataract in chalcosis/Wilson disease and,
    8:327, **11**:54, 57, **12**:327
  in Wilson disease, **2**:231, **8**:327–328, 328*f*, **11**:57
Coppock-like cataract, **6**:247
Cordarone. *See* Amiodarone
Core therapy, for glaucoma, indications for surgery and,
  10:184
Corectopia, **5**:264, **6**:230
  cataract surgery in patient with, **11**:196
  in iridocorneal endothelial (ICE) syndrome, **10**:128,
    129*f*
Coreg. *See* Carvedilol
Corgard. *See* Nadolol
Cornea. *See also under* Corneal
  abrasions of, **4**:13–14, **8**:372
    in children, **6**:407
    contact lenses causing, **3**:198
    posttraumatic recurrent corneal erosion and,
      8:372
  age-related/involutional changes in, **8**:334
    stromal corneal degenerations and, **8**:336–338,
      338*f*, 339*f*
  amyloid deposits in. *See* Cornea, deposits in
  anatomy of, **2**:41*f*, 42, 43–47, 44*f*, 46*f*, 47*f*, **8**:6–9, 7*f*, 8*f*
  anesthesia of
    congenital, **8**:264–265
    herpes simplex epithelial keratitis and, **8**:110
    neurotrophic keratopathy/persistent corneal
      defects and, **8**:86, 87
  apex of, **3**:168, 195, **8**:37, 38*f*
  apical zone of, **3**:168, 195, **8**:37
  basal lamina of, **2**:43, 44*f*, 45, 46*f*
  biochemistry and metabolism of, **2**:247–251, 247*f*
  biomechanics of, **8**:9, **13**:9–10
  biopsy of, **8**:402–403
    for ocular microbiology, **8**:103
  blood staining of, **4**:92–93, 94*f*, **8**:337*t*, 366–367, 367*f*,
    10:96, 97*f*
  Bowman layer/membrane of, **2**:44, 44*f*, 247*f*, 249,
    4:77, 78*f*, **8**:7, 7*f*
    anatomy of, **2**:44, 44*f*, 247*f*
    biochemistry and metabolism of, **2**:249
    development of, **2**:135, **8**:4

dystrophy of, **8**:268*t*, 275–278. *See also* Bowman
  layer corneal dystrophies
 healing/repair of, **4**:16
 refractive surgery and, **2**:249
  preparation of, **13**:75–77, 76*f*
central, **2**:43, 44*f*, **3**:264. *See also* Central cornea
 healing in, **4**:15, 15*f*
childhood systemic diseases affecting, **6**:220–221, 220*f*
congenital/developmental anomalies of, **4**:79–82, 79*f*,
  80*f*, 81*f*, **6**:211–216, **8**:253–266, 261–262*t*. *See also*
  specific type
 central, **6**:214–216, 215*f*
 peripheral, **6**:212–214, 213*f*. *See also* Anterior
  segment, dysgenesis of
 secondary abnormalities causing, **8**:263–266
 of size and shape, **6**:211–212, 212*f*, **8**:253–255, 254*f*,
  261–262*t*
 of structure and/or clarity, **8**:255–263, 256*f*, 257*f*,
  259*f*, 260*f*, 261–262*t*, 263*f*
conjunctivalization of, **8**:355
contact lenses for abnormalities of, **3**:190–191, 191*f*
contrast sensitivity affected by disorders of, **3**:112
curvature of, **8**:37–38. *See also* Cornea, topography of
 axial, **8**:40, 41*f*, **13**:11
 in cornea plana, **8**:254
 in infants and children, **6**:167*t*, 168, 168*f*
 mean, **8**:41, 42*f*
 measurement of. *See also* Keratometry;
  Keratoscopy
  keratometry for, **3**:263–265, 263*f*, 264*f*, 265*f*,
   266*f*, **8**:38–39
  keratoscopy for, **3**:267, 267*f*, 268*f*, **8**:39, 39*f*
 power and, **8**:37–38, **13**:3–4, 11, 12*f*
 radius of, **8**:6, 39
  in cornea plana, **8**:254
  instantaneous (meridional/tangential power),
   8:40, 41*f*, **13**:11, 12*f*
  keratometry in measurement of, **3**:263–265,
   263*f*, 264*f*, 265*f*, 266*f*, **8**:38–39
  in schematic eye, **3**:105*t*
 refractive surgery affecting, **3**:232–234, **13**:4–5,
  20–22, 21*f*, 22*f*
  IOL power calculation and, **13**:187–189, 190*f*
degenerations/dystrophies of. *See specific type and*
  Corneal degenerations; Corneal dystrophies;
  Keratopathy
deposits in, **8**:321*t*
 amyloid, **8**:317*t*, 318–319, 318*f*. *See also*
  Amyloidosis/amyloid deposits
  in Avellino dystrophy, **4**:97, 99*f*
  in gelatinous droplike corneal dystrophy,
   8:274–275, 275*f*, 317*t*, 318, 318*f*
  in lattice dystrophy, **4**:96–97, 99*f*, 212, **8**:278, 280
 copper/Wilson disease causing, **6**:221, **8**:327–328,
  327*f*, 337*t*, **11**:54, 57
 differential diagnosis of, **8**:320, 321*t*
 drug-induced, **8**:346–349, 347*t*
 immunoglobulin synthesis disorders and,
  8:319–320
 nonpigmented, **8**:321*t*
 pigment, **4**:91–93, 94*f*, **8**:321*t*
  drug-induced, **8**:346–349, 347*t*
 refractile/crystalline, **8**:321*t*

Descemet membrane of. *See* Descemet membrane/
  layer
development of, **2**:133–135, 133*f*, 134*f*, **6**:167*t*, 168,
  168*f*, **8**:4
diameter of, in infants and children, **6**:167*f*, 168
 abnormalities of, **6**:211–212, 212*f*
 glaucoma and, **6**:234, 234*f*, **10**:143, 150
disorders of, **4**:77–100, **8**:20–21*t*. *See also specific type*
  and Keratitis; Keratoconjunctivitis; Keratopathy
 blunt trauma causing, **8**:363
 as cataract surgery complication, **11**:146–150
 cataract surgery in patient with, **11**:191–194, 192*f*,
  193*f*
 contact lens–related, **3**:197–199, 198*f*, **8**:91–92
 contrast sensitivity affected by, **3**:112
 decreased vision and, **5**:111
 degenerations/dystrophies. *See specific type and*
  Corneal degenerations; Corneal dystrophies;
  Keratopathy
 ectatic, **8**:296–303, 302*t*
 illusions caused by, **5**:188
 immune-mediated, **8**:181, 204–216
 in infants and children, **6**:211–221
 introduction to pathology of, **4**:78–79, 79*t*
 ionizing radiation causing, **8**:352–353
 metabolic disorders and, **6**:400–401*t*, **8**:305–329.
  See also specific disorder
 monocular diplopia and, **3**:164
 neoplastic, **4**:100, **8**:225–247. *See also specific tumor*
  type
 in rosacea, **8**:70, 70*f*
 scleritis and, **8**:220, 221, 221–222, 221*f*
 surgical approach to, **8**:413–414
 Th1 delayed hypersensitivity and, **9**:50*t*
 thermal burns causing, **8**:351–352
 ultraviolet radiation causing, **3**:19, **8**:352
donor. *See* Donor cornea
drug absorption and, **2**:325
dysplasia of (corneal intraepithelial neoplasia), **4**:100,
  8:226*t*, 229–231, 231*f*
dystrophies/degenerations of. *See specific type and*
  Corneal degenerations; Corneal dystrophies;
  Keratopathy
ectasia of. *See* Ectasia/ectatic disorders
edema of, **8**:29–30, 30*t*
 birth trauma causing, **8**:265–266, 266*f*
 after cataract surgery, **11**:143, 144*t*, 146–148, 146*t*,
  147*f*
  persistent, with vitreocorneal adherence, **11**:148
 cold-induced, **8**:351–352
 in Fuchs endothelial dystrophy, **8**:291, 292*f*
 intraocular surgery causing, **8**:383, 384
 in iridocorneal endothelial (ICE) syndrome, **10**:128
 in keratoconus, **8**:298–299, 300
 management of, **8**:403–405
 in primary congenital glaucoma, **6**:234, 235*t*, **10**:150
 after radial keratotomy, **13**:48
 refractive surgery contraindicated in, **13**:35
 tonometry accuracy and, **10**:23
endothelium of, **2**:46–47, 247*f*, 251, **4**:77–78, 78*f*, **8**:7*f*,
  8–9
 anatomy of, **2**:46–47, 46*f*, 47*f*, 247*f*, **8**:7*f*, 8–9
 biochemistry and metabolism of, **2**:251

development of, 2:133, 134f, 135, 8:4
dysfunction of, corneal edema and, 8:25
glucose metabolism in, 2:248
healing/repair of, 4:15–16, 15f
  keratorefractive surgery and, 13:26
intraocular surgery causing changes in, 8:383, 383–385
phakic IOLs affecting, 13:133t
  angle-supported PIOLs, 13:134–135
  iris-fixated PIOLs, 13:135
  posterior chamber PIOLs, 13:136
photoablation and, 13:97
pigmentation of, 8:349
in uveitis, 9:86t
enlargement of
  in glaucoma, 10:29
    primary congenital glaucoma and, 6:234, 234f, 235t, 10:143, 150
  in neurofibromatosis, 6:370
epithelium of, 2:43, 44f, 239f, 247f, 248–249, 4:77, 78f, 8:6, 7f
  anatomy of, 2:43, 44f, 247f, 8:6, 7f
  biochemistry and metabolism of, 2:248–249
  cysts of, 8:348
  debridement of for surface ablation, 13:75, 76f
  defects/persistent defects of, 8:21t, 85–87
    after cataract surgery, 11:150
    glaucoma medication toxicity and, 10:29
    after LASIK, 13:104–105
    ocular infection and, 8:99
    after penetrating keratoplasty, 8:422, 423f
    after surface ablation, 13:100
  development of, 2:133, 133f, 134f
  drug-induced deposits in, 8:346–348, 347t, 348f
  dysplasia of (corneal intraepithelial dysplasia), 4:100, 8:229–231, 231f
  evaluation of in pseudoepiphora, 7:257
  glucose metabolism in, 2:248
  healing/repair of, 4:13–16, 15f, 8:387–388
    keratorefractive surgery and, 13:26–27
    delayed, 13:86, 100
  intraocular surgery causing changes in, 8:382–383
  metabolic damage in contact lens overwear syndromes and, 8:91
  preparation of for refractive surgery, 13:75–87, 76f
  preservation techniques for
    in epi-LASIK, 13:76–77
    in LASEK, 13:75
  tear secretion and, 2:239f, 240, 241
  tumors of, 8:226–233, 226t
erosions of
  in epithelial basement membrane dystrophy, 8:83, 271, 272
  in herpetic keratitis, 8:117
  punctate epithelial, 8:20t, 25, 26f, 27t
    in vernal keratoconjunctivitis, 8:187
  recurrent, 8:83–85, 85f
    eye pain and, 5:300, 8:83
    posttraumatic, 8:372
  refractive surgery in patient with, 13:35, 36f
examination of, 8:11–46. See also Examination, ophthalmic
  before cataract surgery, 11:78, 83–84

in glaucoma, 10:29–30
  in children, 6:235, 236f, 10:150, 151
  before refractive surgery, 13:10–14, 11f, 12f, 13f, 14f, 38–39, 38f
exposure of
  in craniosynostosis-induced proptosis, 6:388–389
  in facial palsy, 5:288
in external eye defense, 8:96
extraocular surgery affecting, 8:385
farinata, 8:337–338, 338f
fetal, secondary abnormalities affecting, 8:263–266
flat (cornea plana), 8:254–255, 261t
  flap creation and, 13:39
  sclerocornea and, 4:82, 8:254, 255, 258
foreign body in, 8:371–372, 371f
  in children, 6:407–408
  plant/vegetation, 8:362, 371
function of, 8:3
glaucoma/glaucoma therapy affecting, 10:29–30
guttae/guttata, 8:30, 345
  age-related, 8:334
  Brown-McLean syndrome and, 11:148
  cataract surgery and, 11:78
  central, 2:45
  in Fuchs endothelial corneal dystrophy, 2:47f, 4:99, 100f, 8:291, 292f
  peripheral (Hassall-Henle bodies/warts), 2:45, 8:334, 345
  refractive surgery and, 13:35
healing/repair of, 4:13–16, 15f, 8:387–388
  keratorefractive surgery and, 13:26–27
  delays in, 13:86, 100
hydration of, 8:8
hypoxia of, in contact lens wearers, 3:200
imaging of. See also specific type and Cornea, topography of
  for keratorefractive surgery, 13:10–20, 38–39, 38f
    indications for, 13:16–17, 17f, 18f
    postoperative evaluation and, 13:17, 17f, 18f
immune response/immunologic features of, 8:174–175, 174f, 9:58t, 63–64, 63f, 64f, 65
infection/inflammation of, 4:82–87, 83f, 84f, 85f, 86f, 87f, 8:20–21t, 24–25, 26f, 27f, 27t, 28f, 158–171. See also Keratitis; Keratoconjunctivitis
  contact lens wear and, 3:197–201
innervation of, 2:247, 8:6. See also Corneal nerves
intraepithelial neoplasia of, 4:100, 8:226t, 229–231, 231f
irritation of, pseudoepiphora and, 7:257
keloids of, 8:341
  congenital, 8:264
lacerations of, 12:324. See also Corneoscleral laceration
  in children, 6:408
  Seidel test in identification of, 8:17, 19f
layers of, 2:247, 247f
marginal infiltrates of, staphylococcal blepharitis/blepharoconjunctivitis and, 8:145, 146f, 147, 210
melting of (keratolysis)
  cataract surgery and, 11:150
    in patient with dry eye, 11:150, 191
  gonococcal infection and, 8:134
  peripheral ulcerative keratitis and, 8:211, 212, 213
  refractive surgery and, 13:184

multifocal, retinoscopy in detection of, **8**:45
neovascularization/vascularization of
  in atopic keratoconjunctivitis, **8**:190, 191*f*
  contact lens wear causing, **3**:199, **8**:92
  inflammation and, **8**:25
  after lamellar keratoplasty, **8**:436
  after pediatric corneal transplantation, **8**:431
  in stem cell deficiency, **8**:93, 94
nonepithelial cells in, **2**:43
oblate shape of, **3**:232, **13**:10, 20
opacification of
  cataract/cataract surgery and, **11**:191–192
  chromosomal aberrations and, **8**:263
  in hereditary syndromes, **8**:263
  infantile/congenital, **6**:216–219, 216*t*, 218*f*,
    8:260–263
  inflammation causing, **8**:25
  after lamellar keratoplasty, **8**:436
  in Peters anomaly, **4**:81, 81*f*, **10**:146, **11**:27
  in primary congenital glaucoma, **10**:150
  in Schnyder corneal dystrophy, **8**:285, 285*f*
perforation of. *See also* Corneoscleral laceration;
  Perforating injuries
  in children, **6**:408
  foreign-body removal and, **8**:372
  LASIK and, **13**:104
  management of, **8**:403–405
    surgical repair in, **8**:377, 378*f*, 379*f*. *See also*
      Corneoscleral laceration, repair of
  radial keratotomy and, **13**:46, 46*f*
peripheral, **2**:43, 44*f*
  degenerations of, **8**:339–340, 340*f*
pigmentation/pigment deposits in, **4**:91–93, 94*f*,
  8:321*t*
  drug-induced, **8**:346–349, 347*t*
plana (flat cornea), **8**:254–255, 261*t*
  flap creation and, **13**:39
  sclerocornea and, **4**:82, **8**:254, 255, 258
posterior depression of (central posterior
  keratoconus), **6**:215
preparation of for refractive surgery, **13**:75–83, 76*f*,
  78*f*, 79*f*, 81*f*, 82*f*, 83*t*
prolate shape of, **13**:10, 20
refractive index of, **3**:40*t*, 104*f*, 105*t*, **8**:6, 38
refractive power of, **8**:37–38, **13**:3–4
  measurement of, **3**:263–265, 263*f*, 264*f*, 265*f*, 266*f*,
    8:38–39, **13**:3–4. *See also* Keratometry
    after refractive surgery, **13**:187
  in schematic eye, **3**:105*t*
reshaping, orthokeratology and, **3**:194–195,
  13:64–65
retention of, in evisceration, **7**:120
in schematic eye, **3**:105*t*
sensation in, **8**:6
  measurement of (esthesiometry), **8**:30–31
  reduction of
    in diabetes mellitus, **8**:308
    in herpes simplex epithelial keratitis, **8**:110
    in neurotrophic keratopathy, **8**:87
    after photoablation, **13**:97–98
shape of, **3**:231, 232*f*, **8**:6, 36–37, **13**:10, 20
  aspheric, **13**:10
  curvature and power and, **8**:36–37, **13**:3–4, 10, 11*f*

disorders of, **6**:211–212, 212*f*, **8**:253–255, 261–262*t*
  contact lenses causing, **3**:199
  orthokeratology and, **3**:194–195, **13**:63–64
  refractive surgery and, **3**:231–235, 232*f*, 233*f*, 234*f*,
    235*f*, **13**:10, 20
size of, disorders of, **6**:211–212, **8**:253–255, 254*f*,
  261–262*t*
specimen collection from, **8**:101*t*, 102–103, 102*f*
staphyloma of, congenital, **8**:258–260, 262*t*, 263*f*
steep, flap creation and, **13**:39
stem cells of, **8**:5, 6, 9, 92–93, 389
stroma of, **2**:45, 46*f*, 247*f*, 249–250, **4**:77, 78*f*, **8**:7–8,
  7*f*, 8*f*
  anatomy of, **2**:45, 46*f*, 247*f*, **8**:7–8, 7*f*, 8*f*
  biochemistry and metabolism of, **2**:249–250
  development of, **2**:133–135, 134*f*, **8**:4
  healing/repair of, **4**:14
  inflammation of, **8**:25, 27*f*, 27*t*
    in systemic infections, **8**:169–170
  neovascularization of, contact lenses causing, **8**:92
  pigmentation of, **8**:348–349
    drug-induced, **8**:347*t*
  refractive index of, **8**:38
  wound healing/repair and, **4**:14
subepithelial infiltrates of, **8**:21*t*
  in epidemic keratoconjunctivitis, **8**:124, 125*f*
surgery affecting
  extraocular procedures and, **8**:385
  intraocular procedures and, **8**:382–385, 384*f*
thickness/rigidity of, **4**:77, 78*f*, **8**:28
  glaucoma and, **10**:25, 74, 80
    in infants and children, **6**:236, **10**:151
    normal-tension glaucoma and, **10**:80
  intraocular pressure/pressure measurement and,
    8:8, 9, 30, **10**:24–25, 74, 84, **13**:35, 173, 194
  measurement of, **3**:259, 260*f*, **8**:28–30, 29*f*, 30*t*. *See*
    also Pachymetry/pachymeter
    before cataract surgery, **11**:78, 84
    minimum requirements for LASIK and,
      13:39–40, 71
      corneal perforation and, **13**:104
    before refractive surgery, **13**:39–40, 70–71, 71
  ocular hypertension and, **10**:74, 84, 84*f*, 105
  tonometry measurements affected by, **8**:30,
    10:24–25, 84, **13**:35, 173, 194
thinning of, over Intacs, **13**:60, 61*f*
tomography of, **13**:15–16, 15*f*, 16*f*
  postoperative, **13**:17
topography of, **2**:41*f*, 42, 43, **3**:265–268, 266*f*, 267*f*,
  268*f*, **4**:77–78, 78*f*, **8**:36–45, **9**:63, 63*f*, **13**:10–14,
  11*f*, 12*f*, 13*f*, 14*f*, 38–39, 38*f*
  astigmatism detection/management and, **8**:43, 43*f*,
    44, **13**:12–14, 14*f*, 38–39, 38*f*
  after penetrating keratoplasty, **8**:426, 427*f*,
    13:20
  cataract surgery and, **11**:83–84
  central islands after surface ablation and, **13**:94, 94*f*
  computerized, **8**:40–45, 40*f*, 41*f*, 42*f*, 43*f*, 44*f*,
    13:10–14, 11*f*, 12*f*, 13*f*, 14*f*, 38–39, 38*f*
  in contact lens fitting, **3**:195
  corneal thickness measurement and, **13**:39
  corneal zones and, **8**:36–37, 37*f*
  indications for, **8**:43–44, 43*f*, 44*f*

IOL power determination/selection and, 3:216–217, 217f, 11:86, 87
after refractive surgery, 3:220, 11:86, 87, 13:187
before LASIK, 13:71–72
limitations of, 8:44–45, 13:14
measurement of, 8:36–45
Placido-based, 3:265, 266f, 268f, 8:39, 40, 40f, 13:10, 11f, 13, 16
computerized, 8:40, 40f, 13:10, 11f
IOL power calculation after refractive surgery and, 13:187
in keratoconus, 8:43–44, 44f, 299, 300f
in pellucid marginal degeneration, 13:16
after radial keratotomy, 13:44
refractive/keratorefractive surgery and, 8:43–44, 44f, 13:10–14, 11f, 12f, 13f, 14f, 38–39, 38f, 70–71, 71, 167–168, 168f, 169f
clinical situations illustrating role of, 13:18–20, 19f
indications for, 13:16–17, 17f, 18f
postoperative, 13:17, 17f, 18f
refractive lens exchange/clear lens extraction and, 13:139
toric IOLs and, 13:143
scanning-slit, 8:34, 34f
transparency of, 8:8
transplantation of, 8:407–411, 413–445. See also Donor cornea; Keratoplasty
autograft procedures for, 8:413, 431–432
basic concepts of, 8:407–411
cataract/cataract surgery following, 11:193
for chemical injuries, 8:358
clinical approach to, 8:413–445
comparison of procedures for, 8:415–416t
donor selection and, 8:408–411, 410t
eye banking and, 8:408–411, 410t
histocompatibility antigens and, 8:407
immune privilege and, 8:175, 407–408
immunobiology of, 8:407–408
IOL power calculations after, 3:222
lamellar keratoplasty for, 8:413, 433–437, 434f
pediatric, 6:219, 8:430–431, 431t
penetrating keratoplasty for, 8:413, 415–416t, 417–430
preoperative evaluation/preparation and, 8:414–417
rabies virus transmission and, 8:130
after refractive surgery, 13:191–192
rejection and, 4:91, 92f, 8:407, 408, 427–430, 428f, 429f, 436, 9:63, 64, 64f, 65. See also Rejection
in triple procedure, 11:141, 192
tumors of, 4:100, 8:225–247. See also specific type
in uveitis, 9:86t
vertex of, 8:37, 38f
verticillata (vortex keratopathy), 8:310, 311f, 346–348, 347t, 348f, 360
in Fabry disease, 12:263, 264f
warpage of
contact lens wear causing, 3:199
refractive surgery and, 13:32, 38
topography in identification of, 13:38, 71
zones of, 8:36–37, 37f
Cornea–air interface, reflection at, 3:12
Cornea–aqueous interface, reflection at, 3:12

Cornea Donor Study, 8:411
Cornea shields, collagen, for drug administration, 2:331
Corneal allografts. See Corneal grafts
Corneal arcus, 8:336–337, 338f
in dyslipoproteinemia/hyperlipoproteinemia, 1:139, 8:308, 309t, 336
juvenilis, 8:266, 336
lipoides, in Schnyder corneal dystrophy, 8:285, 285f
senilis, 8:336–337, 338f
Corneal autografts. See Corneal grafts
Corneal buttons, 4:78
Corneal cap, 8:6
Corneal contact lens electrode, for electroretinogram, 12:35
Corneal contact lenses. See Contact lenses
Corneal degenerations, 4:87–93, 94f, 8:334–345. See also specific type and Keratopathy
dystrophies differentiated from, 8:334t
endothelial, 8:344–345, 344f
epithelial/subepithelial, 8:334–336, 335f
stromal
age-related/involutional changes and, 8:336–338, 338f, 339f
peripheral, 8:339–340, 340f
postinflammatory changes and, 8:340–344, 341f, 342f, 343f
Corneal dystrophies, 4:94–100, 8:267–268, 268–296, 268t, 269t, 270t. See also specific type
Bowman layer, 8:268t, 275–278. See also Bowman layer corneal dystrophies
cataract/cataract surgery in patient with, 11:191–192, 192f
classification of, 8:267–268, 268t, 269t, 270t
definition of, 8:267
degenerations differentiated from, 8:334t
Descemet membrane, 8:268t
endothelial, 4:98–100, 100f, 8:268t, 291–296. See also Endothelial dystrophies
cataract surgery in patient with, 11:192
epithelial/subepithelial, 4:95, 95f, 8:268t, 270–275. See also Epithelial/subepithelial dystrophies
genetics of, 8:269t
metabolic disorders and, 8:305–329
refractive surgery in patients with, 13:35, 37f, 67–68, 70, 71
stromal, 4:96–97, 97f, 97t, 98f, 99f, 8:268t, 278–290, 278t. See also Stromal corneal dystrophies
Corneal dystrophy of Bowman layer type 1. See Reis-Bücklers corneal dystrophy
Corneal dystrophy of Bowman layer type 2. See Thiel-Behnke corneal dystrophy
Corneal elastosis, 8:334–335, 335f. See also Spheroidal degeneration
Corneal endothelial rings, traumatic, 8:363
Corneal flap folds, after LASIK, 13:105–108, 106t, 107f. See also Striae
Corneal grafts. See also Cornea, transplantation of; Donor cornea; Keratoplasty
allografts, 8:413
autografts, 8:413, 431–432
disease recurrence in, 8:422, 423f
dislocation of, after Descemet stripping automated endothelial keratoplasty, 8:442, 443f

endothelial failure of, **4**:91, 92*f*
  late nonimmune, **8**:425–426
  primary, **8**:422, 422*f*
    after Descemet stripping automated endothelial
      keratoplasty, **8**:444–445
  inflammatory necrosis of, after lamellar keratoplasty,
    8:436–437
  rejection of, **4**:91, 92*f*, **8**:407, 408, 427–430, 428*f*, 429*f*,
    436, **9**:63, 64, 64*f*, 65. *See also* Rejection
Corneal haze. *See* Haze formation
Corneal hydrops, in keratoconus, **4**:91, 93*f*, **8**:299
  management of, **8**:300
Corneal hysteresis, **8**:9
Corneal incision, clear, for cataract surgery, **11**:113–115,
    113*f*, 115*f*
  filtering surgery and, **10**:200
  in glaucoma, **11**:201–202
  in uveitis, **9**:292
Corneal inlays, **13**:53–64
  alloplastic, **13**:54
  homoplastic, **13**:54
  in keratophakia, **13**:53–55
  for presbyopia, **13**:53, 54, 157, 200
Corneal intraepithelial neoplasia, **4**:100, **8**:226*t*, 229–
    231, 231*f*
Corneal light reflex
  corneal vertex and, **8**:37
  eyelid margin distance to (margin–reflex distance),
    5:276, 278*f*, **6**:179
    in ptosis, **6**:179, **7**:201–202, 202*f*, 205*f*
    tests of, **6**:76–78, 77*f*, 78*f*
Corneal melting (keratolysis)
  cataract surgery and, **11**:150
    in patient with dry eye, **11**:150, 191
  gonococcal infection and, **8**:134
  peripheral ulcerative keratitis and, **8**:211, 212, 213
  refractive surgery and, **13**:184
Corneal nerves, **2**:247, **8**:6
  damage to, in photoablation, **13**:97–98
  enlarged, **8**:328–329, 328*f*, 329*t*
    in *Acanthamoeba* keratitis, **8**:167
    in multiple endocrine neoplasia, **1**:216, 217*f*,
      8:328–329, 329*t*
Corneal nodules, Salzmann, **4**:88, 88*f*, **8**:340–341, 341*f*
Corneal onlays, **13**:53–64
Corneal optics, **13**:3–5
Corneal power
  in IOL power determination, **3**:216–217, 217*f*
    instrument error after refractive surgery and, **3**:220
  lenses for slit-lamp biomicroscopy and, **3**:253, 255*f*
Corneal power maps, **8**:40–43, 41*f*, 42*f*, **13**:11, 12*f*
  keratorefractive surgery and, **8**:44
Corneal refractive lens/therapy (orthokeratology),
    3:194–195, **13**:64–65
Corneal refractive surgery. *See* Keratorefractive surgery
Corneal ring segments, intrastromal, **13**:4*t*, 22, 22*f*, 41*t*,
    53, 55–63, 56*f*, 58*f*, 60*f*, 61*f*, 62*f*
  advantages of, **13**:56
  complications of, **13**:60–63, 61*f*, 62*f*
  corneal transplantation after, **13**:192
  instrumentation for, **13**:57
  international trends in use of, **13**:200–201
  for keratoconus, **13**:58–60, 60*f*, 62–63, 168

after LASIK, **13**:63
  limitations of, **13**:41*t*
  for myopia, **13**:55–56, 56*f*, 57, 58
    patient selection and, **13**:57
  outcomes of, **13**:58
  removal of, **13**:58
Corneal storage medium, **2**:394–395, **8**:408–409
Corneal tattoo, **8**:337*t*, 405
Corneal tomography, **13**:15–16, 15*f*, 16*f*
  postoperative, **13**:17
Corneal transplant. *See* Cornea, transplantation of;
    Donor cornea; Keratoplasty
Corneal ulcers, **8**:21*t*. *See also* Keratitis
  abrasions differentiated from, **8**:372
  contact lens wear and, **3**:198, 201
  in herpes simplex keratitis, **4**:82, 83, 84*f*, **8**:110, 117
  infantile corneal opacities and, **6**:219
  Mooren, **8**:213–216, 215*f*
  neurotrophic, herpetic keratitis and, **4**:83, 84*f*, **8**:87,
    88, 117
  in vernal conjunctivitis/keratoconjunctivitis, **6**:200,
    8:187, 189*f*
  in vitamin A deficiency, **8**:78
  von Hippel internal. *See* Internal ulcer of von Hippel
Corneal vacuum trephines, for penetrating keratoplasty,
    8:418
Corneoretinal dystrophy, Bietti crystalline, **8**:313,
    12:250*t*
Corneoscleral junction, **2**:49, 52*f*
Corneoscleral laceration. *See also* Anterior segment,
    trauma to; Perforating injuries
  repair of, **8**:375–381, 376*f*
    anesthesia for, **8**:376
    in children, **6**:408
    postoperative management and, **8**:381–382
    preoperative management and, **8**:374–375
    secondary repair measures and, **8**:380–381, 381*f*,
      382*f*
    steps in, **8**:376–380, 377*t*, 378*f*, 379*f*
  Seidel test in identification of, **8**:17, 19*f*
Corneoscleral meshwork, **2**:53, 54, 55*f*, **10**:16, 17*f*
Corona, lymphoid follicle, **4**:51, 52*f*, 71
Coronal scalp flap, for orbitotomy, **7**:109
Coronal suture, **5**:7
Coronary angiography/arteriography, **1**:103, 107. *See
    also* Angiography/arteriography
  computed tomographic, **1**:107
Coronary angioplasty
  for angina, **1**:108–110
  for ST-segment elevation acute coronary syndrome,
    1:112–113
  troponin levels in determining need for, **1**:105
Coronary artery bypass graft (CABG), **1**:110
  troponin levels in determining need for, **1**:105
Coronary artery stenosis, hemodynamically significant,
    1:107
Coronary cataract, **11**:33
Coronary CT angiography, **1**:107
Coronary heart disease (coronary artery
    atherosclerosis), **1**:99. *See also* Ischemic heart
    disease
  in diabetes mellitus, **1**:133*t*, 207
  hypercholesterolemia and, **1**:100, 131, 132–133, 133*t*

hypertension management and, 1:79*t*, 84
ophthalmic considerations and, 1:128
risk factors for, 1:99, 100–101, 132–133, 133*t*
  hypercholesterolemia management and, 1:134,
    134*f*, 135*t*
  screening for, 1:271–272
Coronary syndrome, acute. *See* Acute coronary
  syndrome; Myocardial infarction
Coronary vasospasm, angina pectoris caused by, 1:101
Coronary ventriculography, 1:107
Corpuscular theory of light, 3:3
Correcting lenses
  in direct ophthalmoscopy, 3:243–244, 244*f*
  in retinoscopy, 3:124–125, 125*f*
Correspondence. *See* Retinal correspondence
Corrugator muscle, 7:17, 131, 133*f*, 137*f*
Cortex
  lens, 2:70, 274–275, 274*f*, 4:120, 120*f*, 11:6*f*, 8–9
    degenerations of, 4:126–127, 127*f*, 128*f*
  occipital/visual. *See* Occipital (primary visual/
    calcarine/striate) cortex
  vitreous, 4:131
Cortical/cerebral blindness, 5:172, 195, 6:415–416
Cortical cataracts, 4:126–127, 127*f*, 128*f*, 11:41–42, 42*f*,
    43*f*, 44*f*, 45*f*
  uveitis and, 11:59, 60*f*
  visual acuity and, 11:70*t*
Cortical gel, anterior, 12:7
Cortical–nuclear barrier, in lens, 2:314
Cortical potentials, 12:44–45, 45*f*
  electrically evoked, 12:45
  visually evoked, 12:44–45, 45*f*. *See also* Visually
    evoked cortical potentials
Cortical spokes, 11:42, 43*f*
Cortical syndromes, 5:191–196, 192*t*
  recognition disorders and, 5:192–194, 192*t*, 193*f*
  vision/visual deficit awareness disorders and, 5:192*t*,
    195–196
  visual–spatial relationship disorders and, 5:192*t*,
    194–195, 195*f*
Cortical visual impairment, 6:415–416. *See also*
  Cortical/cerebral blindness
Corticosteroids (steroids), 1:181–183, 181*t*, 2:357–361,
    357*t*, 360*t*, 9:100–106, 101*t*, 102*f*, 103*f*
  Acanthamoeba keratitis treatment and, 8:168
  for acute retinal necrosis, 9:202
  for adenovirus infection, 8:125–126
  adverse effects of, 1:182, 2:358–359, 9:101*t*, 104
  for allergic eye disease, 2:364, 366, 6:198, 199*t*,
    8:184–185, 185, 187
    route of administration of, 2:360, 360*t*
  for anaphylaxis, 1:295
  anti-inflammatory effects/potency of, 2:359–360,
    360*t*, 364, 366
  for atopic dermatitis, 8:185
  for bacterial keratitis, 8:163–164
  for Behçet disease, 1:180, 9:194
  for Bell's palsy, 5:286
  for birdshot retinochoroidopathy, 9:155
  for blowout fractures, 7:101
  for branch retinal vein occlusion, 12:126
  after cataract surgery in children, 6:259
  cataracts caused by, 11:47–48, 203

for central retinal vein occlusion, 12:131
in central serous chorioretinopathy, 12:172
for chalazion, 8:73
for chemical injuries, 8:355
for Cogan syndrome, 8:210
for contact dermatoblepharitis, 8:184–185
for corneal graft rejection, 8:429–430
for cystoid macular edema, 12:143, 360
  after cataract surgery, 11:183
  in uveitis, 9:300
for diabetic macular edema, 12:100
for diffuse unilateral subacute neuroretinitis, 9:240
for dry eye, 2:245, 246*f*, 8:60, 60*t*
for epidemic keratoconjunctivitis, 8:125–126
after filtering surgery, 10:194–195
fungal keratitis associated with use of, 8:165
for giant cell arteritis/AAION, 5:126–127, 126*t*, 320
  central retinal artery occlusion and, 12:139
for giant papillary conjunctivitis, 8:195
glaucoma caused by, 10:103–104
  in infants and children, 10:141*t*
  refractive surgery and, 13:35, 173–174, 173*f*, 194, 195
for hemangiomas, 7:64, 151–152
  in children, 6:340
herpes simplex keratitis and, 8:113, 115–116
for herpes zoster, 8:121
for hyphema, 6:410, 8:367–368, 10:98
for idiopathic intracranial hypertension, 5:124
intraocular pressure affected by, 2:359–360, 360*t*, 361,
    10:103–104
  inflammatory glaucoma treatment and, 10:94, 131
  optic nerve damage and, 10:81, 103
  after refractive surgery, 13:35, 96–97, 173–174,
    173*f*, 194, 195
  in uveitis, 9:103, 105, 295, 297, 10:103
for iritis, 9:119–120
for juvenile idiopathic (chronic/rheumatoid) arthritis,
    9:130, 293
for Lyme disease, 9:253
for meibomian gland dysfunction, 8:68
for multifocal choroiditis and panuveitis syndrome,
    9:164, 12:191
for multiple sclerosis, 5:327
for nonspecific (idiopathic) orbital inflammation
  diagnosis and, 7:59
  treatment and, 7:61
for ocular allergies/inflammation, 2:364, 366, 6:198,
    199*t*, 8:184–185, 185, 187
  route of administration of, 2:360, 360*t*
for ocular histoplasmosis syndrome, 9:223, 225
for ocular hypertension, 9:295
ocular hypertension caused by, 9:103, 105, 295, 297
ocular side effects of, 1:182, 301*t*
for optic neuritis, 5:146
for pars planitis, 9:137
in perioperative setting, 1:306
for peripheral ulcerative keratitis, 8:213
after photoablation
  complications associated with, 13:96–97
    pressure-induced stromal keratitis (PISK),
      13:112, 112*f*
  corneal haze reduction and, 13:86, 101
  for diffuse lamellar keratitis, 13:109–110

elevated IOP/glaucoma and, **13**:35, 96–97,
173–174, 173*f*, 194, 195
LASIK, **13**:85, 86–87, 97
regression in overcorrection and, **13**:93
regression in undercorrection and, **13**:94
surface ablation, **13**:85, 86, 96–97
with photodynamic therapy, **12**:344
ptosis caused by eyedrops containing, **5**:280
for pulmonary diseases, **1**:141, 145*t*, 146
for punctate inner choroiditis/choroidopathy,
9:165–166, **12**:192
for recurrent corneal erosions, **8**:84
after refractive surgery, elevated IOP/glaucoma and,
13:35, 96–97, 173–174, 173*f*, 194, 195
for rheumatic disorders, **1**:181–183, 181*t*
for Rift Valley fever ocular infection, **9**:218
for rosacea, **8**:70
for sarcoidosis, **9**:177
for scleritis, **8**:222, 223, **9**:117–118, 267
for seborrheic blepharitis, **8**:72
for serpiginous choroiditis, **9**:160, 161
for shock, **1**:294
for staphylococcal blepharitis/blepharoconjunctivitis,
8:147
for Stevens-Johnson syndrome, **6**:201, **8**:197
for stromal keratitis, **8**:108*t*, 115–116
for sympathetic ophthalmia, **9**:182–183
route of administration of, **2**:360*t*
in tear secretion, **2**:244
for Thygeson superficial punctate keratitis, **8**:206
for thyroid eye disease, **5**:148–149, 333–334, 334,
7:53–54
for toxocariasis, **6**:274, **12**:209–210
for toxoplasmosis, **9**:232, 233*f*, 309, **12**:208–209, 208*t*
for traumatic iritis, **8**:363
for traumatic visual loss, **5**:156–157, **7**:106
for tuberculous ocular disease, **9**:261, 262*f*
for uveal lymphoid infiltration, **4**:326
for uveitic glaucoma, **9**:296
for uveitic neovascularization, **9**:303
for uveitis, **9**:100–106, 101*t*, 102*f*, 103*f*, 119–120, 120*f*,
300
before cataract surgery, **9**:291, 292, 292–293
in children, **6**:276–277
herpetic, **9**:199
intraocular pressure elevation and, **9**:103, 105, 295,
297, **10**:103
syphilitic, **9**:249
for vernal keratoconjunctivitis, **8**:189
for Vogt-Koyanagi-Harada (VKH) syndrome, **9**:189,
12:198
for Wegener granulomatosis, **1**:179
withdrawal from, **1**:182
wound healing affected by, **8**:391, **13**:27, 31
Corticotroph adenomas, **1**:215
Corticotropin-releasing hormone, **1**:214*t*
Cortisol, **1**:181*t*
deficiency of, **1**:216
Cortisone, **1**:181*t*
Corvert. *See* Ibutilide
Corynebacterium, **8**:134
diphtheriae, **8**:134
endophthalmitis caused by, **9**:269

as normal ocular flora, **8**:97*t*, 134
ocular infection caused by, **8**:134
xerosis, **8**:77, 134
Corzide. *See* Nadolol
Cosmetic facial surgery, **7**:228–229. *See also specific
procedure and* Facial surgery
Cosmetic optics, for anophthalmic socket, **7**:125
Cosmid vector, **2**:150
Cosopt, **2**:350*t*, 352–353, 352*t*, 355
in children, **6**:242
Costimulatory molecules, **9**:39
Cottage cheese pattern, in treated retinoblastoma, **6**:360
Cotton-wool spots, **4**:157, **12**:135–136, 135*f*
in AAION, **5**:125–126
in branch retinal vein occlusion, **4**:164
in capillary retinal arteriole obstruction, **12**:135–136,
135*f*
in central retinal vein occlusion, **4**:164, **12**:128, 128*f*
in diabetic retinopathy, **4**:166, **12**:104
in HIV retinopathy, **9**:305, 306*f*
in hypertensive retinopathy, **12**:113, 114*f*
in leukemia, **4**:326
in Purtscher retinopathy, **12**:154, 154*f*
in systemic lupus erythematosus, **1**:170, **9**:141, 141*f*,
12:195
Couching, **11**:89–90, 89*f*, 90*f*
Cough, **1**:141
cataract surgery in patient with, **11**:188
Coumadin. *See* Warfarin
Counseling
genetic. *See* Genetic testing/counseling
in low vision/vision rehabilitation, **3**:305
Coup mechanism, in blunt trauma, retinal breaks
caused by, **12**:272
Coupling, **13**:21, 49–50, 49*f*
arcuate keratotomy and limbal relaxing incisions and,
13:50
astigmatic keratotomy and, **11**:130
Cover tests, **6**:74–76, 75*f*, 76*f*
ARC testing and, **6**:53
for intermittent exotropia evaluation, **6**:100
Cover-uncover test, **6**:74, 75*f*
Covera. *See* Verapamil
Coviracil. *See* Emtricitabine
Cowden disease, eyelid manifestations of, **4**:215*t*
COX-1/COX-2. *See* Cyclooxygenase
COX-2 inhibitors, **1**:183*t*, 184, **2**:257–258, **9**:99
for cystoid macular edema, **9**:25–26
Coxsackievirus conjunctivitis, **8**:130
Cozaar. *See* Losartan
CP. *See* Cicatricial pemphigoid
CPAP. *See* Continuous positive airway pressure
CPC. *See* Cyclophotocoagulation/cycloablation
CPEO. *See* Chronic progressive external ophthalmoplegia
CPEO-plus syndromes, **2**:174–175
CPR. *See* Cardiopulmonary resuscitation
CQI. *See* Continuous quality improvement
CR-39, **3**:162. *See also* Plastic spectacle lenses
CRA. *See* Central retinal artery
Crab louse (*Phthirus pubis*), **8**:142, 142*f*
ocular infection caused by, **8**:142, 149
cholinesterase inhibitors for, **2**:340
Crack cocaine abuse, **1**:251. *See also* Cocaine

CRALBP. *See* Cellular retinaldehyde-binding protein/
cytoplasmic retinal-binding protein
Cranial dysinnervation, congenital (congenital fibrosis/
agenesis syndromes), **5**:240–241, 241*f*, 241*t*, **6**:127,
138–140, 171
type 1 (CFEOM1), **5**:240
Cranial fossae
anterior, **5**:6*f*, 7, 11*f*, **7**:7*f*
middle, **5**:6*f*, 8, 11*f*
neuroimaging in evaluation of, **5**:82*t*
posterior, **5**:6*f*
neuroimaging in evaluation of, **5**:82*t*, 85, 88
Cranial nerve I (olfactory nerve), **2**:87, 88*f*, 89*f*
Cranial nerve II (optic nerve). *See* Optic nerve
Cranial nerve III (oculomotor nerve), **2**:88*f*, 97–99, 97*f*,
98*f*, **5**:10*f*, 39, 39*f*, 50*f*, 51*f*, 52*f*, 53–55, 53*f*, 59*f*, 66*f*,
7:11*f*, 12*f*
aberrant regeneration of, **5**:232, 232*f*, **6**:132
pupillary reactivity disorders and, **5**:273*t*
synkinesis in, **7**:203, 207
in accommodation, **11**:19
anatomy of, **2**:88*f*, 97–99, 97*f*, 98*f*, **5**:10*f*, 39, 39*f*, 50*f*,
51*f*, 52*f*, 53–55, 53*f*, 59*f*, 66*f*
aneurysms affecting, **2**:98
diplopia associated with lesions of, **5**:223, 227
aberrant regeneration and, **5**:232, 232*f*
extraocular muscles innervated by, **2**:21, 97–99, 97*f*,
6:13, **7**:11
horizontal gaze and, **5**:45*f*
levator muscle innervated by, **7**:139
motor root of, **2**:14, 15*f*
palsy/paralysis of. *See* Third nerve (oculomotor)
palsy/paralysis
saccadic system and, **5**:40
Cranial nerve IV (trochlear nerve), **2**:88*f*, 99–100, **5**:10*f*,
39, 39*f*, 50*f*, 51–53, 51*f*, 52*f*, 53*f*, 59*f*, **7**:12*f*
aberrant regeneration of, superior oblique myokymia
and, **6**:142
anatomy of, **2**:88*f*, 99–100, **5**:10*f*, 39, 39*f*, 50*f*, 51*f*, 52*f*,
53*f*, 59*f*
diplopia caused by lesions of, **5**:223, 226–227
extraocular muscles innervated by, **2**:21, **6**:13, **7**:11
palsy/paralysis of. *See* Fourth nerve (trochlear) palsy/
paralysis
saccadic system and, **5**:40
Cranial nerve V (trigeminal nerve), **2**:88*f*, 100–104,
101*f*, 102*f*, **5**:53*f*, 57–60, 57*f*, 58*f*, 59*f*
anatomy of, **2**:88*f*, 100–104, 101*f*, 102*f*, **5**:53*f*, 57–60,
57*f*, 58*f*, 59*f*
divisions of, **2**:100, 102*f*, 103–104
facial innervation and, **7**:134
facial pain caused by lesions of, **5**:303
in herpes simplex infection, **8**:106
in herpes zoster, **8**:118, 119–120
neurotrophic keratopathy caused by damage to, **8**:87
V₁ (ophthalmic nerve), **2**:88*f*, 101, 101*f*, 102*f*, 103,
5:53*f*, 59, 59*f*, **7**:13
in reflex tear arc, **7**:244
sensory root of, **2**:14, 15*f*
V₂ (maxillary nerve), **2**:88*f*, 101, 101*f*, 102*f*, 103, **5**:53*f*,
59*f*, 60, **7**:13
V₃ (mandibular nerve), **2**:88*f*, 101, 101*f*, 102*f*, 104,
5:53*f*, 59*f*, 60, 61

Cranial nerve VI (abducens nerve), **2**:88*f*, 104–105,
104*f*, **5**:10*f*, 39, 39*f*, 50–51, 50*f*, 51*f*, 52*f*, 53*f*, 59*f*, **7**:12*f*
anatomy of, **2**:88*f*, 104–105, 104*f*, **5**:10*f*, 39, 39*f*,
50–51, 50*f*, 51*f*, 52*f*, 53*f*, 59*f*
diplopia caused by lesions of, **5**:227, 233–234
extraocular muscles innervated by, **2**:21, **6**:13, **7**:11
horizontal gaze and, **5**:44–46, 45*f*, 210
palsy/paralysis of. *See* Sixth nerve (abducens) palsy/
paralysis
saccadic system and, **5**:40
Cranial nerve VII (facial nerve), **2**:105–107, 106*f*, **5**:51*f*,
52*f*, 60–61, 62*f*, **7**:17, 133, 134*f*
aberrant regeneration of, synkinesis in, **5**:284, 284*f*,
7:203, 221
anatomy of, **2**:105–107, 106*f*, **5**:51*f*, 52*f*, 60–61, 62*f*
autonomic function of, testing, **5**:282–283
brainstem lesions involving, **5**:285
cervicofacial division of, **2**:106
diplopia and, **5**:227
distribution of, **5**:283*f*
evaluation of, **5**:282–284, 283*f*
facial movement abnormalities caused by disorders
of, **5**:277, 282–292
overactivity and, **5**:288–292, 289*t*, 290*f*, 291*f*
underactivity and, **5**:284–288, 284*f*, 285*t*, 287*f*
fixed, dilated pupil caused by damage to, **5**:316
hemifacial spasm and, **7**:221
labyrinthine segment of, **2**:105
mastoid segment of, **2**:106
palsy/paralysis/weakness of. *See* Facial paralysis/
weakness
peripheral lesions involving, **5**:285–288, 287*f*
in reflex tear arc, **7**:244
sarcoidosis involving, **5**:287, 288, 335
supranuclear lesions involving, **5**:284–285
surgical ablation of, for essential blepharospasm,
5:290, **7**:220
synkinesis caused by lesions of, **5**:284*f*, 286
temporofacial division of, **2**:106
tumors involving, **5**:286, 287*f*
tympanic segment of, **2**:105
Cranial nerve VIII (auditory nerve), **5**:39, 45*f*, 48
anatomy of, **5**:39, 45*f*, 48
Cranial nerves, **2**:13, 87–109, 88*f*, **5**:38, 50–55, 51*f*,
52–53*f*. *See also specific nerve*
anatomy of, **2**:13, 87–109, 88*f*, **5**:38, 50–55, 51*f*, 52–53*f*
extraocular muscles supplied by, **2**:21, **5**:50–55, 51*f*,
52–53*f*, **6**:13–16, 17*t*, **7**:11
ocular motor, **5**:38, 50–55, 51*f*, 52–53*f*, **6**:13
extraocular muscle surgery and, **6**:24
orbit supplied by, **7**:13–17, 16*f*
palsy/paralysis of
isolated. *See specific type*
in Lyme disease, **5**:364
microvascular, **5**:301
multiple, diplopia caused by, **5**:236
in multiple sclerosis, **5**:325
neuroimaging in evaluation of, **5**:85, 85*f*
Cranial sutures
normal, **6**:384*f*, 385*f*
premature closure of in craniosynostosis, **6**:383, 385*f*,
7:35
Craniofacial bones, **5**:5, 7–8*f*

Craniofacial cleft syndromes, 7:34–35, 34f, 35f. See also
    specific type and Craniofacial malformations
nasolacrimal duct obstruction and, 7:278
Craniofacial dysostosis (Crouzon syndrome), 2:216,
    6:387–388, 387f, 7:35, 35f, 8:322t
Craniofacial malformations, 6:383–395, 7:34–35, 34f,
    35f. See also specific type
    Apert syndrome (acrocephalosyndactyly), 6:388,
        389f, 391f, 7:35, 8:322t
    branchial arch syndromes, 6:392–394
    craniosynostosis, 6:383–387, 385f, 386f, 7:35, 35f
    craniosynostosis syndromes, 6:387–388, 387f, 389f,
        390f
    Crouzon syndrome, 2:216, 6:387–388, 387f, 7:35, 35f,
        8:322t
    in fetal alcohol syndrome, 6:394–395, 395f
    Goldenhar syndrome/oculoauricular dysplasia, 6:393,
        393f, 7:34, 150
    infantile exotropia and, 6:104
    management of, 6:392
    mandibulofacial dysostosis. See Craniofacial
        malformations, Treacher Collins/Treacher
        Collins–Franceschetti syndrome
    nonsynostotic, 6:392–395, 393f, 394f, 395f
    ocular complications of, 6:388–392, 391f
    oculoauriculovertebral (OAV) spectrum/sequence,
        6:392–393, 8:323t
    Pfeiffer syndrome, 6:388
    Pierre Robin sequence (anomaly/deformity), 6:394,
        8:324t
    Saethre-Chotzen syndrome, 6:388, 390f
    Treacher Collins/Treacher Collins–Franceschetti
        syndrome (mandibulofacial dysostosis),
        6:393–394, 394f, 7:34, 34f, 8:324t
        eyelid manifestations of, 4:213t
        palpebral fissure slanting in, 6:178, 393–394, 394f
    V-pattern deviations associated with, 6:110
Craniopharyngiomas, 5:163f, 164
    nystagmus caused by, 5:254, 6:325
Craniosynostosis, 6:383–387, 385f, 386f, 7:35, 35f
    etiology of, 6:386–387
    ocular complications of, 6:388–392, 391f
    pulley system pathology and, 6:23
    syndromes associated with, 6:386–387, 387–388, 387f,
        389f, 390f. See also specific type
CRAO. See Central retinal artery, occlusion of
Crawford stent, for nasolacrimal intubation, 7:253, 254f
CRB1 gene, in Leber congenital amaurosis, 6:290
Creases (eyelid). See Eyelids, creases of
Creatine kinase (CK)/creatine kinase isoenzymes, in
    acute coronary syndrome, 1:105
Credé (silver nitrate) prophylaxis, 6:188
    chemical conjunctivitis caused by, 6:188
Creeping angle closure, 10:117. See also Angle closure/
    angle-closure glaucoma
"Crescent moon sign," in internal carotid artery
    aneurysm, 5:269f, 354
Crest cells. See Neural crest cells
CREST syndrome, 1:173
Cretinism, 1:208
Creutzfeldt-Jakob disease, 5:368
    corneal transplant in transmission of, 8:143
Cribriform plate, 2:92f. See also Lamina cribrosa

Cricothyrotomy, 1:292
    for anaphylaxis, 1:295
Crigler-Najjar syndrome, 2:213t
Critical angle, 3:46–48, 48f
Crixivan. See Indinavir
CRN. See Convergence-retraction nystagmus
Crocodile shagreen, 8:337
Crocodile tears, 5:285
Croconazole, 1:54t, 65
Crohn disease (granulomatous ileocolitis), 1:165, 9:123
Crolom. See Cromolyn
Cromolyn, 2:365, 365t
    for allergic conjunctivitis, 8:186
    for giant papillary conjunctivitis, 8:195
    for pulmonary diseases, 1:145t, 146
Cross-cylinder refraction, 3:132–135, 133f, 134f
Cross-fixation, in infantile esotropia, 6:90
Cross-over test, alternating, 5:216
Cross-sectional studies, 1:325–326
Crossed diplopia, 6:54, 54f
Crossing over (genetic), 2:150, 197. See also
    Recombination
    unequal, 2:162
        color vision defects and, 2:295
Crouzon syndrome (craniofacial dysostosis), 2:216,
    6:387–388, 387f, 7:35, 35f, 8:322t
Crowding (contour interaction) bars, for amblyopia
    evaluation, 6:65, 65f, 73
Crowding phenomenon (contour interaction), 6:62, 65,
    65f
CRP. See C-reactive protein
CRS. See Congenital rubella syndrome
CRT contact lens. See Corneal refractive lens
CRUISE (Central Retinal Vein Occlusion) study, 12:131
CRV. See Central retinal vein
CRVO. See Central retinal vein, occlusion of
CRX gene, 12:222
    cone–rod dystrophy and, 12:233
CRYO-ROP (Cryotherapy for Retinopathy of
    Prematurity) study, 6:282, 283, 285–286, 286f,
    12:166–167
Cryoglobulin precipitation, ophthalmic findings and,
    8:320
Cryoglobulinemic vasculitis, essential, 1:177t
Cryoprobe, for lens extraction, 11:93, 93f
Cryoretinopexy, for retinal detachment in uveitis, 9:302
Cryotherapy
    for basal cell carcinoma of eyelid, 7:172
    for Coats disease, 12:145
    for conjunctival intraepithelial neoplasia, 8:229, 230f
    for conjunctival papillomas, 8:228
    for corneal intraepithelial neoplasia, 8:230–231
    for ligneous conjunctivitis, 8:193
    for melanoma, 4:285
    for neovascular glaucoma, 10:127
    for pars planitis, 9:137–138
    for retinal angiomas/hemangiomas, 4:295, 6:375, 12:150
    for retinal breaks, 12:283
    for retinoblastoma, 4:312
    for retinopathy of prematurity, 6:285–286, 286f,
        12:166–167, 167–168, 169f
    for squamous cell carcinoma of conjunctiva, 8:231
    for trichiasis, 7:200, 8:89

Cryotherapy for Retinopathy of Prematurity
Cooperative Group, **12**:164
Cryotherapy for Retinopathy of Prematurity (CRYO-
ROP) study, **6**:282, 283, 285–286, 286f, **12**:166–167
Cryptococcus neoformans (cryptococcosis), **5**:367, **8**:139,
9:278–279
endophthalmitis caused by, **9**:278–279
in HIV infection/AIDS, **5**:367, **9**:310–311, 313–314
optic nerve infection caused by, **4**:251, 251f, **5**:367
Cryptophthalmos, **6**:175, 175f, **7**:152, 152f, **8**:249–250,
249f
Cryptophthalmos-syndactyly (Fraser syndrome), eyelid
manifestations of, **4**:213t
Cryptosporidium parvum (cryptosporidiosis), in HIV
infection/AIDS, **1**:38
Crystal violet stain, **4**:31t
Crystalens, for refractive errors/presbyopia, **13**:146,
159–160, 159f
Crystalline corneal dystrophy, Schnyder, **8**:268t, 270t,
284–285, 285f
genetics of, **8**:269t, 284
Crystalline corneoretinal dystrophy, Bietti, **8**:313,
12:250t
Crystalline keratopathy, infectious, **4**:85–86, 86f, **8**:159,
160f
after penetrating keratoplasty, **4**:85, **8**:425, 425f
Crystalline lens. *See* Lens
Crystalline maculopathy/retinopathy, **12**:268–269, 268f,
269t
Bietti, **8**:313, **12**:250t
drug toxicity causing, **12**:268–269, 268f, 269t
Crystallins, **2**:70, 130, 273, **11**:11–12, 11f. *See also* Lens
proteins
aging affecting, **11**:39
α, **2**:70, 276, **11**:11–12, 11f
β, **2**:70, 276, **11**:12
β,γ, **2**:276, **11**:11f, 12
development of, **2**:130
ε, **2**:276
γ, **2**:70, 276, **11**:12
taxon-specific, **2**:276
zeta (ξ), **2**:115
Crystalloids, for shock, **1**:294
CS. *See* Cockayne syndrome
CSC/CSCR. *See* Central serous chorioretinopathy
CSCD. *See* Congenital stromal corneal dystrophy
CSD. *See* Cat-scratch disease
CSDME. *See* Clinically significant diabetic macular
edema
CSF. *See* Cerebrospinal fluid; Contrast sensitivity
function
CSII. *See* Continuous subcutaneous insulin infusion
CSM method, for visual acuity assessment in children,
6:72
CSNB. *See* Congenital night blindness, stationary
CSR (central serous retinopathy). *See* Central serous
chorioretinopathy
CSS. *See* Churg-Strauss syndrome
CST. *See* Cavernous sinus thrombosis
CT/CT scan. *See* Computed tomography
CTA. *See* Computed tomographic angiography
CTLs. *See* Cytotoxic T lymphocytes
CTNS gene, in cystinosis, **8**:313, 314t

CTRs. *See* Capsular tension rings
Cu-Zn SOD, **2**:317
Cultured epithelial stem cells, for transplantation, **8**:389,
398. *See also* Limbal transplantation
Cuneiform opacities, **11**:42, 43f
Cup, optic disc. *See* Cupping of optic disc; Optic cup
Cup–disc ratio
in glaucoma evaluation, **10**:46, 47, 50
in infants and children, **6**:237, **10**:152
in megalopapilla, **6**:307
Cupping of optic disc, **2**:90
asymmetry of, **10**:47, 47f, 47t
glaucomatous, **10**:44, 46–48, 47f, 47t, 48f
in infants and children, **6**:235t, 237, 237f, **10**:44
visual field changes correlated with, **10**:66–67, 75
in megalopapilla, **6**:307
physiologic, **10**:46–47, 47t, 50
vertical elongation and, **10**:48, 48f
Curly fibers corneal dystrophy. *See* Thiel-Behnke
corneal dystrophy
Curvature
corneal, **8**:37–38. *See also* Cornea, topography of
axial, **8**:40, 41f, **13**:11
in cornea plana, **8**:254
in infants and children, **6**:167t, 168, 168f
keratometry in measurement of, **3**:263–265, 263f,
264f, 265f, 266f, **8**:38–39
keratoscopy in measurement of, **3**:267, 267f, 268f,
8:39, 39f
mean, **8**:41, 42f
power and, **8**:37–38, **13**:3–4, 11, 12f
radius of, **8**:6, 39
in cornea plana, **8**:254
instantaneous (meridional/tangential power),
8:40, 41f, **13**:11, 12f
keratometry in measurement of, **3**:263–265,
263f, 264f, 265f, 266f, **8**:38–39
in schematic eye, **3**:105t
refractive surgery affecting, **3**:232–234, **13**:4–5,
20–22, 21f, 22f
IOL power calculation and, **13**:187–189, 190f
rigid gas-permeable contact lens fitting and, **3**:184
radius of, of mirror, **3**:90
Curvature maps, **13**:11, 12f
Curvularia, **8**:139
Cushing syndrome
central serous chorioretinopathy and, **12**:172
corticotroph adenoma causing, **1**:215
elevated intraocular pressure in, **10**:103
hypertension in, **1**:72, 72t
Custom ablation, **13**:40, 69. *See also* Wavefront-guided
laser ablation
for presbyopia, **13**:156–157, 157f
Cutaneous horn, **4**:217, **7**:158
Cutaneous leishmaniasis, **8**:141
Cutaneous leukocytoclastic angiitis, **1**:177t
Cuticular (basal laminar) drusen, **4**:169, **12**:60, 239–240
age-related macular degeneration differentiated from,
12:60, 69
vitelliform exudative macular detachment and,
12:238, 238f
Cutler-Beard procedure, **7**:183f, 184
Cutting head, of microkeratome, **13**:77, 78f

CVOS (Central Vein Occlusion Study), iris
    neovascularization in central retinal vein occlusion
    and, **12**:128
CVS. *See* Chorionic villus sampling
CXCR4 receptor antagonists, for HIV infection/AIDS,
    1:35
Cyanoacrylate adhesives, **8**:403–404
    for corneal perforation/corneoscleral laceration,
        8:377, 404
    for peripheral ulcerative keratitis, **8**:213
    as tarsorrhaphy alternative, **8**:391
Cyclic adenosine monophosphate (cAMP)
    in β-blocker mechanism of action, **10**:167
    in signal transduction
        in iris–ciliary body, **2**:262–263, 262*f*, 263*f*
        in tear secretion, **2**:243, 243*f*
Cyclic esotropia, **6**:96
Cyclic guanosine monophosphate (cGMP)
    in cone phototransduction, **2**:293
    mutations in, **2**:181
    in rod phototransduction, **2**:292, 293
Cyclic guanosine monophosphate (cGMP)-gated
        channel
    cone, **2**:293
        mutations in, **2**:296
    rod, **2**:292–293
        mutations in, **2**:295
Cyclin-dependent kinases, in cancer, **1**:236
Cyclitic membrane formation, after penetrating injury,
    12:324
Cyclitis
    anterior, **9**:78*t*
    chronic. *See* Intermediate uveitis; Pars planitis
    posterior, **9**:78*t*
Cycloablation. *See* Cyclophotocoagulation/cycloablation
Cyclocryotherapy, **10**:209, 209*f*, 210
    for childhood glaucoma, **6**:241, **10**:155–156
Cyclodeviations, double Maddox rod test for evaluation
    of, **6**:79, 79*f*
Cyclodialysis, **4**:18, 19*f*, 109, **8**:364, 364*f*
    after cataract surgery, **11**:157
Cyclogyl. *See* Cyclopentolate
Cyclomydril. *See* Cyclopentolate
Cyclooxygenase (COX-1/COX-2), **1**:184, **9**:25–26, 26*f*, 99
    aspirin affecting, **2**:257, 362
    in eicosanoid synthesis, **2**:256*f*, 257, **9**:25–26, 26*f*
    nonsteroidal anti-inflammatory drugs and, **1**:184,
        2:362, **9**:99. *See also* Cyclooxygenase-2 (COX-2)
        inhibitors
    in prostaglandin synthesis, **2**:256*f*, 257, **9**:25, 26*f*
Cyclooxygenase-2 (COX-2) inhibitors, **1**:183*t*, 184,
    2:257–258, **9**:99
    for cystoid macular edema, **9**:25–26
Cyclopentolate, **2**:260, 341*t*
    for cycloplegia/cycloplegic refraction, **3**:137*t*, **6**:87–
        88, 88*t*
        in premature infant, **6**:285
        in uveitis, **9**:99, 120
Cyclophosphamide, **1**:186–187, 240*t*, **9**:108*t*, 112–113
    for Behçet disease, **1**:180, **9**:195
    in cancer chemotherapy, **1**:240*t*
    for cicatricial pemphigoid, **8**:202
    for peripheral ulcerative keratitis, **8**:213

for rheumatoid arthritis, **1**:162
for scleritis, **8**:223
for uveitis, **9**:108*t*, 112, 112–113
    in children, **6**:278
for Wegener granulomatosis, **1**:179
Cyclophotocoagulation/cycloablation, **10**:209, 209*f*, 210
    for childhood glaucoma, **6**:241, 241*f*, **10**:153, 155–156
        endoscopic, **6**:241, 242*f*
    for uveitic glaucoma, **9**:298
Cyclopia, sonic hedgehog mutations causing, **2**:141
Cycloplegia/cycloplegics, **2**:260, 341*t*, **3**:137, 137*t*, **11**:19
    for amblyopia, **6**:67
    anticholinergic agents/muscarinic antagonists and,
        2:260, 341–342, 341*t*
    binocular balance testing and, **3**:136
    for chemical injuries, **8**:358
    for corneal abrasions, **8**:372
    for herpes zoster, **8**:121
    for hyphema, **6**:410, **8**:367, **10**:98
    intraocular pressure affected by, **10**:104
    for recurrent corneal erosions, **8**:84
    refraction with. *See* Cycloplegic refraction
    for sarcoidosis, **9**:177
    side effects of, **3**:137, **6**:88
    for thermal burns, **8**:351
    for traumatic iritis, **8**:363
    for uveitis, **9**:99, 120
    for Vogt-Koyanagi-Harada (VKH) syndrome, **9**:189
Cycloplegic refraction, **3**:137, 137*t*. *See also* Refraction,
    clinical
    in children, **3**:137, 137*t*, 141–142, **6**:87–88, 88*t*
    instilling eyedrops for, **6**:5
    before refractive surgery, **13**:33, 73
Cyclospora cayatanensis (cyclosporiasis), in HIV
    infection/AIDS, **1**:38
Cyclosporine/cyclosporine A, **1**:187, **2**:334, **9**:108*t*,
    111–112
    for allergic conjunctivitis, **8**:186
    for atopic keratoconjunctivitis, **8**:191
    for Behçet disease, **1**:180, **9**:195
    for birdshot retinochoroidopathy, **9**:155
    for corneal graft rejection, **8**:430
    for dry eye, **2**:245, 246*f*, 391, **8**:60, 60*t*
    for graft-vs-host disease, **8**:203
    for peripheral ulcerative keratitis, **8**:212
    for rheumatoid arthritis, **1**:162
    for scleritis, **8**:223
    for serpiginous choroiditis, **9**:161
    for Thygeson superficial punctate keratitis, **8**:206
    topical, **2**:245, 246*f*, 334, **8**:60, 60*t*
    for uveitis, **9**:108*t*, 111–112
        in children, **6**:277–278
    for vernal keratoconjunctivitis, **8**:189–190
Cyclothymic disorder, **1**:247
Cyclovertical muscle palsies, 3-step test in, **6**:83–86, 85*f*
Cyclovertical strabismus, surgery planning and, **6**:146
Cyklokapron. *See* Tranexamic acid
Cylate. *See* Cyclopentolate
Cylinder axis
    locating, **3**:126–127, 126*f*, 127*f*, 128*f*
    refinement of, cross-cylinder refraction and, **3**:132, 133
    rotating, distortion reduction and, **3**:140, 317
        residual astigmatism and, **3**:317, 318, 319*f*

Cylinder power, 3:97, 98f
  combined lenses and, 3:99
  finding, 3:127–129
  optimal value for, 3:319
  reducing, distortion reduction and, 3:140, 317
    residual astigmatism and, 3:318, 319f
  refinement of, cross-cylinder refraction for, 3:132,
    133–134, 133f, 134f
Cylinders (cylindrical lenses). See also Spherocylindrical
    lenses
  combining at oblique axes, 3:99
  correcting, 3:139–140
  distortion and, 3:140, 309–310, 310f. See also
    Meridional magnification
    adaptation to, 3:140, 320–321
    altering astigmatic correction and, 3:317–320, 318f,
      319f
    blurred retinal images and, 3:312, 312f
    contact lenses for reduction/elimination of,
      3:316–317
    conventional analysis and, 3:311, 312f
    lens–entrance pupil distance and, 3:311
    location effect and, 3:313–314, 313f
    minimizing, 3:140, 316–320, 318f, 319f
    minimizing vertex distance and, 3:316–317
    minus cylinder (posterior toric) spectacle lenses
      and, 3:316
    photographic simulation of, 3:315–316, 316f
      altering astigmatic correction and, 3:317, 318f
    "shape factor" of spectacle lens and, 3:311
    sources of, 3:310–311, 310f
      relative contributions from, 3:315, 315f
    with uncorrected/inappropriately corrected
      astigmatism, 3:314
  power of. See Cylinder power
  prescribing guidelines for, 3:140, 309–323
    common misconceptions and, 3:314–316, 315f, 316f
    revised, 3:321–322
Cylindroma (adenoid cystic carcinoma)
  of eyelid, 7:162
  of lacrimal glands, 4:236–238, 237f, 7:87
Cymbalta. See Duloxetine
CYP1B1 gene
  in glaucoma, 6:233, 10:11t, 142
  in Peters anomaly, 8:258, 10:142
Cyst. See specific type
Cystadenoma, apocrine/oxyphilic/eosinophilic
    (oncocytoma), 4:75, 75f, 8:233
Cystathionine β-synthase, abnormality of in
    homocystinuria, 2:213t, 6:263, 399
Cysteamine, for cystinosis, 6:220, 399, 8:313, 314, 12:265
Cysteine-rich proteins, in neurofibromatosis, 4:244
Cystic carcinoma, adenoid (cylindroma)
  of eyelid, 7:162
  of lacrimal glands, 4:236–238, 237f, 7:87
Cystic fibrosis, 1:142
Cystic Fibrosis Foundation, 6:418t
Cystic retinal tufts, 12:278, 279f
Cysticercus cellulosae (cysticercosis), 8:142, 9:237–239,
    238f
  orbital involvement and, 4:235, 7:47
Cystine accumulation/crystals, in cystinosis, 8:313, 314,
    314t, 315f, 12:264

Cystinosis, 6:220, 398, 399, 401t, 8:314–315, 314t, 315f,
    12:264–265
  corneal changes in, 6:220, 220f, 401t, 8:314–315, 314t,
    315f
  cysteamine for, 6:220, 8:313, 314, 12:265
  renal transplant for, 2:231
  retinal degeneration in, 12:264–265
Cystitome, for ECCE, 11:95
Cystoid degeneration, peripheral, 4:154, 154f, 12:282
  reticular, 4:154, 154f, 12:282, 293
  typical, 4:154, 154f, 12:282, 292
Cystoid macular edema, 12:142–143, 142f
  angiographic, 12:143
    after cataract surgery, 11:182
  corticosteroids for, 12:143, 360
    after cataract surgery, 11:183
    route of administration of, 2:360t
    in uveitis, 9:300
  in HTLV-1 infection, 9:219
  in multifocal choroiditis and panuveitis syndrome,
    9:162
  in pars planitis, 9:135, 137, 138, 12:196
  postoperative, 12:360, 360f
    cataract surgery and, 11:143, 144t, 181–183, 182f,
      12:142, 143, 360
    in glaucoma, 11:202–203
    after Nd:YAG capsulotomy, 11:175
    vitreous prolapse and, 11:162
  prostaglandins and, 9:25–26
  in retinitis pigmentosa, 9:287, 12:225, 230, 230f
  in sarcoidosis, 8:74, 9:175
  in uveitis, 9:300–301
    cataract surgery and, 9:293
  vitrectomy for, 12:360, 360f
Cytarabine, 1:240t
  epithelial cysts caused by, 8:348
  for primary central nervous system lymphoma, 9:283
Cytobrush, 8:47
Cytochrome-b gene, in Leber hereditary optic
    neuropathy, 2:175
Cytogenetics, 2:197–207, 198t, 200f, 201f
  indications for, 2:198, 198t
  markers in, 2:177
  preparation for, 2:198–199
Cytoid bodies, 4:157, 158f
Cytokeratins, in immunohistochemistry, 4:33
Cytokines, 8:177, 177t, 9:27–30, 28–29t. See also specific
    type
  in cancer therapy, 1:243
  in delayed hypersensitivity, 9:49f, 50
  in external eye defense, 8:95, 96
  in immune processing, 9:39
  in inflammation/rheumatic disorders, 1:185–186
  macrophage synthesis of, 9:22
  in neutrophil recruitment and activation, 9:18
  in Sjögren syndrome, 8:63
  in tear film, 2:241
  in uveitic cystoid macular edema, 9:300
Cytology (ocular), 8:47–48. See also specific cell type
  in immune-mediated keratoconjunctivitis, 8:182t
  impression, 8:47–48
    in Sjögren syndrome diagnosis, 8:57
    in stem cell deficiency, 8:94

interpretation of, **8**:48
specimen collection for, **8**:47–48
Cytolysin, enterococci producing, **8**:134
Cytomegalic inclusion disease (congenital CMV
infection), **6**:184–185, 184*f*, **9**:204, 205, 206
Cytomegalovirus, **1**:24, **9**:204–208
cancer association and, **1**:237
congenital infection caused by, **1**:24, **6**:184–185, 184*f*,
9:204, 205, 206
Fuchs heterochromic iridocyclitis/uveitis associated
with, **9**:134
in HIV infection/AIDS, **1**:3, 24, 37–38, **4**:151, **5**:359,
360*f*, **9**:204, 205, 206, 306–307
treatment of, **1**:37–38
infection in children caused by, **6**:184–185, 184*f*
retinitis caused by, **1**:3, 24, 37–38, **4**:151, 152*f*, **5**:359,
9:204–207, 205*f*, 206*f*, 306–307, **12**:200–201, 200*f*
acute retinal necrosis, **9**:202
cidofovir for, **1**:24, 38, 66, **2**:381*t*, 384
congenital (cytomegalic inclusion disease),
6:184–185, 184*f*, **9**:204, 205, 206
fomivirsen for, **1**:24, 38
foscarnet for, **1**:24, 38, 66, **2**:381*t*, 384, **9**:207,
12:200
ganciclovir for, **1**:24, 37–38, 66, **2**:381*t*, 383–384,
9:207, **12**:200
in HIV infection/AIDS, **1**:3, 24, **4**:151, **5**:359, **9**:204,
205, 206, 306–307
immune recovery uveitis and, **1**:41, **9**:306, **12**:201
retinal detachment and, **9**:302, 307
Cytoplasmic retinal-binding protein/cellular
retinaldehyde-binding protein (CRALBP)
in aqueous humor, **2**:267
mutations in, **2**:297
Cytoskeletal (urea-soluble) lens proteins, **2**:277, **11**:11*f*,
12
Cytotoxic drugs, for Wegener granulomatosis, **1**:179
Cytotoxic hypersensitivity (type II) reaction,
8:178*f*, 179*t*, 180, **9**:44, 44*t*. *See also* Cytotoxic
T lymphocytes
Cytotoxic T lymphocytes, **9**:42*f*, 43, 51, 53*f*
in external eye defense, **8**:96
in viral conjunctivitis, **9**:60
Cytotoxicity, antibody-dependent, **8**:180, **9**:51–55, 54*f*
Cytovene. *See* Ganciclovir
Cytoxan. *See* Cyclophosphamide

D

d4T. *See* Stavudine
D-15 test, **3**:294, **12**:48–50, 49*f*
in anomalous trichromatism, **12**:214
in low vision evaluation, **5**:105
D-penicillamine, for Wilson disease, **2**:231, **8**:327–328
Daclizumab, **1**:186, **9**:108*t*, 115
for uveitis, **9**:108*t*, 115
in children, **6**:278
Dacryoadenitis, **4**:231, **7**:273–274, **8**:101*t*
Epstein-Barr virus causing, **7**:273–274, **8**:122–123
lacrimal gland masses and, **7**:85
mumps virus causing, **8**:129
nonspecific orbital inflammation and, **7**:59

Dacryocele/dacryocystocele, **6**:204–205, 204*f*, 205*f*,
7:255–256, 256*f*
in dacryocystitis, **7**:275
Dacryocystectomy, for lacrimal sac tumors, **7**:277
Dacryocystitis, **7**:274–276, 275*f*, **8**:101*t*
dacryocele progressing to, **6**:205
in nasolacrimal duct obstruction, **7**:251, 274–275, 276
tumor associated with, **7**:276
Dacryocystocele/dacryocele, **6**:204–205, 204*f*, 205*f*,
7:255–256, 256*f*
in dacryocystitis, **7**:275
Dacryocystography
for lacrimal drainage evaluation, **7**:261–262
for lacrimal sac tumor evaluation, **7**:276
Dacryocystorhinostomy, **7**:267–270, 269*f*, 270*f*
for acquired nasolacrimal duct obstruction,
7:267–270, 269*f*, 270*f*
for congenital nasolacrimal duct obstruction, **6**:210,
7:255
Dacryoliths, **7**:266
Dacryoplasty, balloon (balloon catheter dilation), for
congenital nasolacrimal duct obstruction, **6**:209,
209*f*, **7**:253–255
Dacryops, **4**:214
Dacryoscintigraphy, for lacrimal drainage evaluation,
7:261–262
Dactinomycin, **1**:239
DAG. *See* Diacylglycerol
Daily-wear contact lenses, **3**:180
Dalen-Fuchs nodules/spots
in sympathetic ophthalmia, **4**:189, 190*f*, **9**:178, 179,
180
in Vogt-Koyanagi-Harada (VKH) syndrome, **9**:184,
186*f*, **12**:197
Dalfopristin/quinupristin, **1**:53*t*, 63–64
DALK. *See* Deep anterior lamellar keratoplasty
Danazol, ocular effects of, **1**:302*t*
Danocrine. *See* Danazol
Dantrolene, for malignant hyperthermia, **1**:313*t*
Dapiprazole, **2**:259*t*, 260, 348
angle closure prevention and, **10**:119
Dapsone
for cicatricial pemphigoid, **8**:202
for *Pneumocystis jiroveci* (*Pneumocystis carinii*)
pneumonia, **1**:37
Daptomycin, **1**:53*t*, 64
Daranide. *See* Dichlorphenamide
Daraprim. *See* Pyrimethamine
Dark adaptation
sunglasses affecting, **3**:159
testing, **12**:46, 47*f*
in congenital stationary night blindness, **12**:215,
216*f*
Dark-adapted electroretinogram, **12**:33, 34*f*, 35, 36*f*. *See
also* Dark adaptation, testing; Electroretinogram
in hereditary retinal/choroidal dystrophies, **12**:224*t*
Dark choroid, in Stargardt disease, **6**:293, **12**:234–235,
235*f*
Dark-field illumination, for *Treponema pallidum*
visualization, **8**:137
Darkroom prone-position test, for occludable/narrow
chamber angle, **10**:118
Darkschewitsch, nucleus of, **5**:39*f*, 42

Darunavir, 1:34
DASH (Dietary Approaches to Stop Hypertension) eating plan, 1:74, 75t
Data presentation, 1:343–346, 344f, 345f, 346f
Database
  monitoring systems and, 1:340–342
  searching, 1:316
Dawn phenomenon, 1:197
Day blindness (hemeralopia)
  in achromatopsia, 6:291
  in cone/cone–rod dystrophies, 5:114, 12:232
Daypro. See Oxaprozin
dB. See Decibel
DCCT (Diabetes Control and Complications Trial), 1:197, 202, 203, 203f, 12:91, 92, 94f
DCN gene, in congenital stromal corneal dystrophy, 8:286
DCR. See Dacryocystorhinostomy
DCs. See Dendritic cells
DCT. See Dynamic contour tonometer/tonometry
ddI. See Didanosine
DDT. See Dye disappearance test
de Morsier syndrome (septo-optic dysplasia), 5:141, 6:308
Deafness (hearing loss)
  cataract surgery in patient with, 11:188
  gene for, synteny and, 2:176
  mitochondrial DNA mutations and, 2:173, 174f, 176
  pigmentary retinopathy and, 12:251t, 253. See also Usher syndrome
  vestibular nystagmus and, 5:248, 249t, 250
Death, sudden, 1:102–103, 103–104
Debridement
  for Acanthamoeba keratitis, 8:169
  for chemical injuries, 8:358
  for fungal keratitis, 8:166
  for herpes simplex epithelial keratitis, 8:112
  for recurrent corneal erosions, 8:84–85
  for surface ablation, 13:75, 76f
  for thermal burns, 8:351
Decadron. See Dexamethasone
Decamethonium, 2:344
Decentered ablation, 13:95–96, 97f
Decentration, bifocal segment, 3:157, 164
  for prism correction, 3:87, 164
Decentration/dislocation (intraocular lens), 11:143, 144t, 162–166, 163f, 164f, 165f
  laser capsulotomy and, 11:173
  multifocal IOLs and, 3:226, 11:163
  phakic IOLs and, 13:135, 145
Decibel, 5:100, 10:55
Decompression
  optic canal, for traumatic visual loss, 7:106
  orbital, 7:113–115, 113f, 114f
    complications of, 7:116
    for thyroid eye disease, 5:149, 334, 7:53, 54, 113–115, 114f
    for traumatic visual loss, 7:105, 106
Decongestants
  ocular, 2:392
  tear production affected by, 8:66t
Decorin, 8:7, 9
  in congenital stromal corneal dystrophy, 8:269t, 286

Decreased vision. See Low vision; Visual loss/impairment
Deep anterior lamellar keratoplasty (DALK), 4:78, 8:300, 413, 415–416t, 435–436
  advantages of, 8:416t
  in children, 8:431
  complications of
    intraoperative, 8:415t
    postoperative, 8:415t
  disadvantages of, 8:416t
  indications for, 8:415t
  for keratoconus, 8:300
  penetrating/selective keratoplasty compared with, 8:415–416t
  surgical technique for, 8:435–436
Deep-brain stimulation, for Parkinson disease, 1:259–260
Deep mimetic muscles, 7:131–133, 133f
Deep petrosal nerve, 2:107
Deep-plane rhytidectomy, 7:236, 237f
Deep superior sulcus deformity, anophthalmic socket and, 7:122, 122f
Deep temporal artery, 5:15f
Deep temporal fascia, 7:132f, 134
Deep venous thrombosis. See also Thrombosis/thrombotic disorders
  anticoagulation therapy in prevention of, 1:152
  in antiphospholipid antibody syndrome, 1:171
Defense mechanisms, host
  of external eye, 8:95–96, 99–100
  impaired, 8:100. See also Immunocompromised host
Defensins, in tear film, 2:240
Defibrillator-cardioverters, implantable. See Implantable cardioverter-defibrillators
Defibrillators, portable, public availability of, 1:289, 292
Defocus aberrations, positive and negative, 3:238, 239f, 13:6, 6f
Deformable intraocular lenses, 13:160
Defy. See Tobramycin
Degeneracy, of genetic code, 2:150
Degenerated epithelial cells. See Keratinization (keratinized/degenerated epithelial cells)
Degenerations, 4:9–10, 12t
  anterior chamber/trabecular meshwork, 4:104–109, 110f
  cataracts associated with, 11:64
  choroidal
    diffuse, 12:242–244, 243f, 244f
    regional and central, 12:244–246, 245f
  conjunctival, 4:56–60, 58f, 59f, 60f, 8:331–333
  corneal, 4:87–93, 94f, 8:334–345
  definition of, 4:9–10, 8:331
  dystrophies differentiated from, 8:334t
  elastotic (elastosis)
    corneal, 8:334–335, 335f. See also Spheroidal degeneration
    in pinguecula/pterygium, 4:56, 58, 58f, 59f
    solar, of eyelid, 4:217, 218f
  eyelid, 4:211–212, 211f, 212f, 213t
  lens, 4:124–127, 125f, 126f, 127f, 128f, 129f. See also Cataract
  macular. See Macular degeneration
  optic nerve, 4:253–255, 253f, 254f, 255f

orbital, 4:235
peripheral cystoid, 4:154, 154*f*, 12:282
  reticular, 4:154, 154*f*, 12:282, 293
  typical, 4:154, 154*f*, 12:282, 292
retinal, 4:154–177, 12:249–270, 250–251*t*. *See also*
  specific type and Retinal degenerations; Retinal
  dystrophies
retinal pigment epithelium, 12:58
scleral, 4:115–116, 116*f*, 8:345–346, 346*f*
uveal tract, 4:192–193, 192*t*, 193*f*
vitreous, 4:134–140
Degenerative myopia. *See* High (pathologic/
  degenerative) myopia
Degenerative retinoschisis, typical and reticular, 4:154,
  12:293–294, 293*f*
Degradation, optical, for amblyopia, 6:67
Dehydration, preoperative fasting and, 1:308
Deiters, ascending tract of, 5:45*f*, 46–47
Delayed hypersensitivity (type IV) reaction, 8:178*f*,
  179*t*, 180, 9:42–43, 42*f*, 44, 44*t*, 48–51, 49*f*, 50*t*
  contact dermatitis/dermatoblepharitis as, 8:180, 183,
    184–185, 184*f*
  contact lens solutions and, 8:92
  in graft rejection, 8:408
  response to poison ivy as, 9:35
  in sympathetic ophthalmia, 9:52–53
  topical medications/substances and, 8:183, 184–185,
    184*f*
  in *Toxocara* granuloma, 9:52
  tuberculin form of, 9:35
Delayed hypersensitivity (DH) T lymphocytes, 9:42–43,
  42*f*, 48–51, 49*f*, 50*t*. *See also* T cells
Delayed suprachoroidal hemorrhage, after cataract
  surgery, 11:178–179
Deletion mapping, 2:177
Deletions, mitochondrial DNA, disorders caused by,
  2:173, 191
Delirium, 1:264–265
  hallucinations and, 5:187
  postoperative, in older patient, 1:224
Delivery (birth), difficult. *See also* Obstetric history
  corneal edema caused by, 8:265–266, 266*f*
  infantile corneal opacities and, 6:216*t*, 217
  nystagmus and, 6:318
Dellen, 8:90–91
  after strabismus surgery, 6:158, 158*f*
Delta hepatitis, 1:26
Delusions, 1:247
DEM. *See* Diagnostic electron microscopy
Demadex. *See* Torsemide
Demecarium, 2:340
Demeclocycline, 2:374
Dementia, 1:227, 264–268
  AIDS-associated (HIV encephalopathy), 1:29,
    5:359–360. *See also* HIV infection/AIDS
  Alzheimer, 1:227, 264–268
  cataract surgery in patient with, 11:187
  depression and (pseudodementia), 1:227
  hallucinations and, 5:187
  hypertension and, 1:86
  Lewy body, 1:265
  mixed, 1:265
  multi-infarct, 1:227, 265

in older patients, 1:227, 264, 265
  screening for, 1:220
pugilistica, 1:265
toxic, 1:265
treatment of, 1:267–268
  recent developments in, 1:245
vascular, 1:227, 265
vitamin B$_{12}$ deficiency and, 1:149, 232
Demi-Regroton. *See* Reserpine
Demodex, 8:142, 148
  brevis, 8:97, 142, 148
  folliculorum, 8:97, 142, 148
  as normal ocular flora, 8:97, 97*t*, 142, 148
  ocular infection caused by, 8:148
de Morsier syndrome (septo-optic dysplasia), 5:141, 6:308
Demulcents, 2:390–391, 8:58–60
Demyelination/demyelinating disease
  internuclear ophthalmoplegia caused by, 5:225
  multiple sclerosis, 5:321–322, 322*f*. *See also* Multiple
    sclerosis
  neuroimaging in evaluation of, 5:82*t*
  optic neuritis and, 5:144, 145*f*
    illusions and, 5:189
DENALI study, 12:79
Denaturing gradient gel electrophoresis, 2:183–184
Dendrites/dendritic keratitis, 4:82, 84*f*, 8:21*t*
  amebic infection and, 8:167
  contact lens wear and, 3:198–199
  herpes simplex, 4:82, 84*f*, 8:107, 110, 111, 111*f*
  herpes zoster, 8:120
Dendritic cells, 8:173, 174, 174*f*, 174*t*, 9:11–12
  in choroidal/ciliary body nevus, 4:195
Denervation
  with botulinum toxin, 6:163–164
  and extirpation, 6:148*t*
Dengue fever, 9:219–220
Dental procedures, endocarditis prophylaxis and, 1:8*t*
Dentate nucleus, 5:48
Dentate processes, 12:8, 10*f*
  enclosed ora bays and, 12:8
  meridional folds and, 12:280, 281*f*
Deorsumduction/deorsumversion. *See* Depression of eye
Deoxyribonucleic acid. *See* DNA
Depacon. *See* Valproate/valproic acid
Depakote. *See* Valproate/valproic acid
Dependence (drug), 1:250
Depigmentation, bull's-eye, in cone dystrophy, 5:114.
  See also Maculopathies, bull's-eye
Depo-Medrol. *See* Methylprednisolone
Depolarizing neuromuscular blocking agents, 2:344
Depot injections, corticosteroid
  for pars planitis, 9:137
  for uveitis, 9:102
Deprenyl. *See* Selegiline
Depression of eye (downgaze), 6:33, 35
  disorders/limitation of, 5:210–211
    in blowout fractures, 6:125, 7:100–101
      surgery and, 7:102
    in premature newborn, 5:212
  extraocular muscles controlling, 5:55–56, 56*f*
    inferior rectus, 5:55, 56*f*, 6:14, 17*t*, 29*t*
    superior oblique, 5:55, 56*f*, 6:15, 17*t*, 29, 29*t*, 31, 33*f*
    3-step test in evaluation of, 6:83–86, 85*f*

ptosis exacerbation in, 7:201
ptotic eyelid position in, 7:203
Depression (mood disorder), 1:247, 248
 drugs for (antidepressants), 1:254–256, 255t
  ocular effects of, 1:255, 301t
 masked, 1:226
 in older patients, 1:226, 248
  pseudodementia and, 1:227
  screening for, 1:220
Depression (perimetry), 10:55
 generalized, in glaucoma, 10:68
Depressor anguli oris muscle, 7:133, 133f
Depressor labii inferioris muscle, 7:133, 133f
Deprivation amblyopia, 6:64
 eye trauma and, 6:403
 visual development affected by, 6:46–47, 47f, 61–62
Depth of field, 3:37
Depth of focus, 3:36–37
Depth perception
 stereoacuity testing of, 6:87
 stereopsis differentiated from, 6:42
Dermal melanocytosis, 4:66, 7:166, 166f. See also
   Oculodermal melanocytosis
 glaucoma associated with, 10:28
Dermal nevus, 7:164
Dermal orbital melanocytosis, 4:66
Dermatan sulfate
 in cornea, 2:250, 8:7
 in mucopolysaccharidoses, 8:305
Dermatan sulfate–proteoglycan, in cornea, macular
   dystrophy and, 8:283
Dermatitis. See also Dermatoblepharitis
 α-agonists causing, 10:169, 169f
 atopic, 8:185
  cataracts associated with, 11:62
  keratoconjunctivitis and, 8:190–192, 191f
 contact, 8:180
 herpetiformis, 8:205t
 zoster, 8:119–120
Dermatoblepharitis, 8:101t
 contact, 8:183–185, 184f
 herpes simplex virus causing, 8:106, 106f, 110
 varicella-zoster virus causing, 8:117–119
Dermatochalasis, 7:221–222, 221f
 brow ptosis and, 7:222, 227
 pseudoptosis and, 7:210, 211f
Dermatographism, in Behçet disease, 1:180
Dermatologic disorders. See Skin, disorders of
Dermatomyositis, 1:175, 175f
 eyelid manifestations of, 4:213t
Dermis, eyelid, 4:205, 206f
 neoplasms of, 4:219–220, 220f
Dermis-fat grafts
 after enucleation in children, 7:119
 for exposure and extrusion of orbital implant, 7:123
 for superior sulcus deformity, 7:122
Dermoids (dermoid cysts/tumors), 4:6, 48, 8:245,
   246f
 conjunctival, 4:48, 49f
 corneal, 4:81, 6:218, 218f
  infantile opacities and, 6:216t, 218, 218f
 epibulbar, 6:348, 8:245–246, 245f
 of eyelid, 4:207, 213

Goldenhar syndrome and, 4:48, 6:218, 349f, 393, 393f,
   8:246
 limbal, 4:48, 49f, 6:218, 218f, 348
  Goldenhar syndrome and, 6:218, 349f, 393, 393f,
   8:246
 orbital, 4:229–230, 230f, 7:36–37, 36f
  in children, 6:343–344, 344f
Dermolipomas (lipodermoids), 4:49f, 50, 8:246
 in children, 6:348–349, 349f
 Goldenhar syndrome and, 4:50, 6:349, 349f, 393, 393f
 of orbit, 7:37, 37f
Dermopathy
 in hyperthyroidism (pretibial myxedema), 1:211, 7:51
 nephrogenic fibrosing, gadolinium causing, 5:72
Derry disease (GM$_1$ gangliosidosis type II), 6:401t
DES. See Drug-eluting stents
Desaturated 15-hue test, Lanthony, in low vision
   evaluation, 5:105
Descemet membrane/layer, 2:45, 46f, 247f, 251, 4:77,
   78f, 8:7f, 9
 age-related/involutional changes in, 8:334
 anatomy of, 2:45, 46f, 247f, 8:7f, 9
 biochemistry and metabolism of, 2:251
 detachment of
  after cataract surgery, 11:149
  during intraocular surgery, 8:383, 383f
 development of, 2:134f, 135
 guttae in, 2:45
  in Fuchs dystrophy, 2:47f
 healing/repair of, 4:15f, 16
 injuries to, infantile corneal opacities and, 6:216t, 217
 intraocular surgery causing changes in, 8:383, 383f
 pigmentation of, 8:348–349
 retained, penetrating keratoplasty and, 8:421
 rupture of, 4:18, 18f
  birth trauma and, 8:265, 266f
  infantile corneal opacities and, 6:216t, 217
  in keratoconus, 4:18, 18f, 91, 93f, 8:298–299
Descemet membrane dystrophies, 8:268t
Descemet membrane endothelial keratoplasty (DMEK),
   8:445
Descemet stripping/Descemet stripping automated
   endothelial keratoplasty (DSEK/DSAEK), 4:79,
   8:413, 415–416t, 437–445
 advantages of, 8:416t, 438
 complications of
  intraoperative, 8:415t, 441, 441f
  postoperative, 8:415t, 442–445, 442f, 443f, 444f
 disadvantages of, 8:416t, 438
 indications for, 8:415t, 437
 penetrating/selective keratoplasty compared with,
   8:415–416t
 precut tissue for, 8:409, 438
 surgical procedure for, 8:438–441, 440f
 in triple procedure, 11:141
Descemetocele, management of, 8:403–405
 lamellar keratoplasty for, 8:434f
Descemetorhexis, in Descemet stripping automated
   endothelial keratoplasty, 8:437
Descending optic atrophy, 4:254
Desferrioxamine, retinopathy caused by, 12:269
Desmin, in immunohistochemistry, 4:33
Desmoid tumors, of orbit, 6:343

Desmosomes, in corneal epithelium, 2:43
Desquamating skin conditions, ocular surface involved in, 8:74
Destructive interference, 3:7, 8f
Desyrel. See Trazodone
Detemir insulin, 1:196, 196t
Deutan defects (deuteranopia), 12:47, 49, 50
  ocular findings in carriers of, 2:222t
Deuteranomalous dichromatism, 12:214t
Deuteranomalous trichromatism, 12:213, 214t
Developmental defects. See also specific type and Congenital anomalies
  of lens, 11:35–38
Developmental glaucomas, 10:145–148. See also Glaucoma, childhood
Developmental hyperopia, 3:119
Developmental myopia, 3:118–119, 141
Deviations, 5:211–213. See also specific type and Esodeviations; Exodeviations; Horizontal deviations; Strabismus; Vertical deviations
  in comatose patients, 5:258
  comitant (concomitant), 5:219, 6:10
    vertical, 6:113
      surgery for, 6:152
  extraocular muscle field of action and, 6:29
  incomitant (noncomitant), 5:219, 220f, 6:10
    esodeviations, 6:90t, 98
      strabismus surgery planning and, 6:146
    vertical, 6:113
      strabismus surgery planning and, 6:146
  primary, 6:35
  prisms producing, 3:84–85, 84f
    prism diopter and, 3:85, 85f, 86f
  secondary, 6:35
  seizure activity and, 1:263, 5:211–212
  skew. See Skew deviation
  strabismic amblyopia and, 6:62
  strabismus classification and, 6:11
  terminology in description of, 6:9–11
  tonic, 5:211–213
Devic syndrome (neuromyelitis optica), 5:147
Dexamethasone, 1:181t, 2:357t, 359
  anti-inflammatory potency of, 1:181t, 2:360t
  in combination preparations, 2:373t
  for corneal graft rejection, 8:429
  for endophthalmitis, 12:354
  intravenous administration of, 2:329
  for nonspecific orbital inflammation, 7:61
  after photoablation, elevated IOP associated with, 13:97
  pressure-elevating potency of, 2:360t
  for uveitis, 9:101t, 106
    cystoid macular edema and, 9:301
  for vernal keratoconjunctivitis, 8:189
Dexamethasone implant
  for branch or central retinal vein occlusion, 12:126
  for uveitis, 9:106
Dextran
  in corneal storage medium, 2:395
  in demulcents, 2:390
Dextrocycloversion, 6:35
Dextroversion (right gaze), 6:35
DFP. See Diisopropyl phosphorofluoridate
DGGE. See Denaturing gradient gel electrophoresis

DH. See Delayed hypersensitivity (type IV) reaction
DHA. See Docosahexaenoic acid
DHD. See Dissociated horizontal deviation
DHPG. See Ganciclovir
DiaBeta. See Glyburide
Diabetes Control and Complications Trial (DCCT), 1:197, 202, 203, 203f, 12:91, 92, 94f
Diabetes mellitus, 1:189–208. See also under Diabetic
  aqueous humor growth factors and, 2:271
  cataracts associated with, 2:279–281, 11:55, 56f
    carbohydrate ("sugar"), 2:279–281
      aldose reductase in development of, 2:280–281, 11:15
    in children, 6:247t, 297
    surgery for, 11:188, 12:111
      preoperative evaluation and, 11:80
  in children, 6:296–297
  classification of, 1:190–193
  clinical presentation of, 1:193
  complications of
    acute, 1:204–205
    glucose control affecting, 1:202–203, 203f. See also Diabetes mellitus, glucose surveillance (glycemic control) and
    long-term, 1:205–207
    ocular, 1:207. See also Diabetes mellitus, cataracts associated with; Diabetic macular edema; Diabetic retinopathy
  corneal changes in, 4:166, 8:307–308
    neurotrophic keratopathy/persistent corneal defects and, 8:87
  definition of, 1:190, 191t
  diagnosis of, 1:190, 191t, 193, 194t
  diet in prevention/management of, 1:194, 194–195
  exercise in management of, 1:189, 195
  gestational, 1:191t, 192
  glaucoma and, 10:76–77
  glucose metabolism and, 1:189–190
  glucose surveillance (glycemic control) and, 1:189, 204
    importance of, 1:202–203, 203f, 207
    retinopathy incidence and progression affected by, 1:202–203, 203f, 207, 12:91–94
      Diabetes Control and Complications Trial, 1:202, 203f, 12:91, 92, 94f
      United Kingdom Prospective Diabetes Study, 1:203, 12:91, 92, 93
    type 2 diabetes and, 1:203
  hypertension/hypertension management and, 1:79t, 84–85, 205–206, 206
  impaired glucose tolerance/impaired fasting glucose and, 1:191t, 192–193
  insulin therapy for, 1:195–198, 196t
  latent autoimmune in adults (LADA), 1:192
  management of, 1:194–202
    recent developments in, 1:189
  metabolic syndrome and, 1:193
  ophthalmic considerations and, 1:207. See also Diabetes mellitus, cataracts associated with; Diabetic macular edema; Diabetic retinopathy
  ophthalmic examination timetables and, 12:111–112, 112t
  oral agents for, 1:198–201, 199t, 200f
  pancreatic transplantation for, 1:202

prediabetic disorders and, 1:192–193
prevention of, 1:193–194
refractive surgery in patient with, 13:31, 183–184
retinopathy of. See Diabetic retinopathy
screening for, 1:193, 194t
surgical considerations in patients with, 1:305, 307–308
terminology used in, 12:89
type 1 (insulin-dependent/IDDM/juvenile-onset),
    1:191, 6:296–297, 12:89
type 2 (non–insulin-dependent/NIDDM/adult-onset),
    1:192, 12:89
    approach to treatment of, 1:200f, 201
    mitochondrial DNA mutations and, 2:173
Diabetic ketoacidosis, 1:204–205
Diabetic macular edema, 12:95–103, 96f, 97f, 99f, 101f
    cataract surgery and, 11:205
    clinically significant, 12:90, 97, 98, 99f
    treatment of, 12:98, 98–103, 101f, 102t
        pharmacologic treatment, 12:100–101, 101f
        photocoagulation/laser treatment, 12:97, 98, 99f,
            101–103, 102t
        surgical treatment, 12:101–103, 102t, 353
Diabetic macular ischemia, 12:103
Diabetic nephropathy, 1:206
    glycemic control/diabetic retinopathy and, 1:202–203,
        12:94
Diabetic neuropathy, 1:206
    glycemic control affecting, 1:202–203
    neurotrophic keratopathy/persistent corneal defects
        and, 8:87
Diabetic papillopathy, 5:130–131, 131f
Diabetic retinopathy, 1:207, 4:165–167, 166f, 167f,
    12:89–112
    anterior chamber angle neovascularization and,
        12:108–109
    background. See Diabetic retinopathy,
        nonproliferative
    cataract surgery and, 12:111
    in children, 6:296–297
    classification of, 12:89–90
    conditions associated with vision loss from, 12:95
    cotton-wool spots in, 12:104
    epidemiology of, 12:90
    glycemic control affecting, 1:202–203, 203f, 207,
        12:91–94
        Diabetes Control and Complications Trial, 1:202,
            203f, 12:91, 92, 94f
        United Kingdom Prospective Diabetes Study,
            1:203, 12:91, 92, 93
    iris neovascularization and, 4:166, 166f, 12:108–109
    macular edema and, 12:95–103, 96f, 97f, 99f, 101f,
        102t, 353
    medical management of, 12:91–94
    neurotrophic keratopathy/persistent corneal epithelial
        defect and, 8:87
    nonproliferative (background), 12:89–90, 95–104,
        105f. See also Diabetic macular edema; Diabetic
        macular ischemia
        in children, 6:297
    severe, 12:104, 104f, 105f
    ophthalmic examination timetables and, 12:111–112,
        112t
    pathogenesis of, 12:90–91, 91f

photocoagulation for, 4:167
    in nonproliferative retinopathy/macular edema,
        12:97, 98, 99f, 101–103, 102t
    in proliferative retinopathy, 12:106–108, 108f, 109f,
        340
    preproliferative, 12:104
    proliferative, 12:90, 91f, 105–111, 106f, 108f, 109f
        nonsurgical management of, 12:106
        surgical management of, 12:106–109, 108f, 109f
        vitrectomy surgery for complications of,
            12:109–111, 352–353, 353f
    retinal detachment and, 12:110–111, 291
        vitrectomy for, 12:110–111, 352–353, 353f
    stages/progression of, 12:90, 91
    terminology used in, 12:89–90
    vitrectomy for, 12:109–111, 352–353, 353f
    vitreous detachment in, 12:110
    vitreous hemorrhage in, 12:105, 106f, 313
        vitrectomy for, 12:110, 352
Diabetic Retinopathy Clinical Research Network
    (DRCR.net), 12:100, 103
Diabetic Retinopathy Study (DRS), 12:105, 107–108, 109f
Diabetic Retinopathy Vitrectomy Study (DRVS), 12:110
Diabinese. See Chlorpropamide
Diacylglycerol (DAG), in signal transduction, in tear
    secretion, 2:242f, 243
Diagnostic agents, 2:392–393
Diagnostic electron microscopy, 4:34t, 43
Diagnostic positions of gaze, 6:80, 80f
Diagnostic tests. See Screening/diagnostic tests
Diagnostic ultrasonography. See Ultrasonography
Dialing, for posterior chamber IOL implantation, 11:139
Dialyses, 4:20, 12:271, 272, 273f
    treatment of, 12:284t
Diameter, contact lens, 3:167, 168f, 170
    rigid gas-permeable contact lens fitting and, 3:184t,
        185
    soft contact lens fitting and, 3:183t
Diamidines, for Acanthamoeba keratitis, 8:169
Diamox. See Acetazolamide
Diaphragm pump, for phacoemulsification aspiration,
    11:109, 109f
    vacuum rise time for, 11:109, 110f
Diarrhea
    antibiotic-associated, 1:8–9
    in HIV infection/AIDS, 1:38
Diastole (diastolic phase), 1:117
Diastolic dysfunction, 1:117–118
    causes of, 1:116
    management of, 1:119
Diathermy
    for conductive keratoplasty, 13:22
    for hyphema, 8:368
    for recurrent corneal erosions, 8:84
    for retinal capillary hemangioblastoma, 4:295
    transscleral, contraindications to, 4:285
Diazepam, 1:253–254
    for medical emergencies, 1:292t, 297
    perioperative, 1:309t, 310
    for seizures, 1:297
Diazoxide, for hypertensive emergency, 1:83
Dibenamine, 2:260
DIC. See Disseminated intravascular coagulation

Dichlorphenamide, **2**:353, **10**:171
Dichromatism/dichromacy, **12**:213, 214*t*
Diclofenac, **1**:183*t*, **2**:257, 357*t*
    with misoprostol, **1**:183*t*
Dicloxacillin, **1**:45*t*, **2**:369–370
Didanosine, **1**:33
DIDMOAD syndrome
    in children, **6**:297
    pleiotropism in, **2**:210
Diet/diet therapy
    cancer and, **1**:276
    cardiovascular disease risk modification and, **1**:133*t*, 135*t*
    in diabetes mellitus prevention/management, **1**:194, 194–195
        surgery and, **1**:195
    heart disease and, **1**:100, 133*t*, 135*t*
    in hypercholesterolemia management, **1**:134*f*, 135, 135*t*
    in hypertension management, **1**:74
    in inborn errors of metabolism, **2**:231
    osteoporosis and, **1**:229
Dietary Approaches to Stop Hypertension (DASH) eating plan, **1**:74, 75*t*
Diethylcarbamazine
    for loiasis, **8**:170
    uveitis caused by, **9**:128
Difference map, after keratorefractive surgery, **13**:17, 17*f*
Differential membrane filtration (rheopheresis), for nonneovascular age-related macular degeneration, ineffectiveness of, **12**:63
Diffraction, **3**:13–16, 14*f*, 15*f*
    applications of, **3**:14–16, 14*f*, 15*f*
    law of rectilinear propagation and, **3**:41
Diffractive multifocal intraocular lenses, **3**:227–228, 227*f*, 228*f*
Diffractive simultaneous vision contact lenses, **3**:190
Diffuse anterior scleritis, **8**:28, 218, 218*f*, 218*t*
Diffuse choroidal hemangioma, **4**:200, 292, 293*f*
Diffuse drusen, **4**:168, 168*f*
Diffuse (simple) episcleritis, **4**:113, 113*f*, **8**:28, 216
Diffuse illumination, for slit-lamp biomicroscopy, **8**:12
Diffuse iris nevus, **4**:266
Diffuse lamellar (interface) keratitis (DLK), after LASIK, **13**:108–111, 109*f*, 109*t*, 110*t*, 111*f*
    glaucoma/IOP elevation and, **13**:97, 174, 195
    infectious keratitis differentiated from, **13**:110–111, 110*t*, 111*f*
Diffuse neonatal hemangiomatosis, **6**:340
Diffuse reflection, at rough optical interfaces, **3**:42, 43*f*
Diffuse soft-tissue histiocytosis. *See* Histiocytosis
Diffuse toxic goiter, **1**:211. *See also* Thyroid eye disease
Diffuse transmission, at rough optical interfaces, **3**:42, 43*f*
Diffuse unilateral subacute neuroretinitis (DUSN), **9**:239–241, 240*f*, 241*f*, **12**:210–211
Diffuse uveitis. *See* Panuveitis
Diffusion
    in aqueous humor dynamics/formation, **2**:254, **10**:14
    glucose transport into lens and, **11**:13
Diffusion-weighted magnetic resonance imaging (DWI), **5**:69, 73, 78*f*
    in cerebral ischemia/stroke, **1**:93
Diflucan. *See* Fluconazole

Diflunisal, **1**:183*t*
Difluprednate, for uveitis, **9**:100, 101*t*
Digenic inheritance, **2**:150
Digital eversion test, for cicatricial entropion, **7**:198
Digital pressure, for intraocular pressure estimation, **10**:26
Digital rectal exam, in cancer screening, **1**:272*t*, 276
Digital subtraction angiography, **5**:77
Digitalis/digitoxin/digoxin
    for heart failure, **1**:119
    ocular effects of, **1**:128–129, 302*t*
    in perioperative setting, **1**:305
    retinopathy caused by, **12**:269
    visual changes caused by, **5**:189
Dihydropyridines, for hypertension, **1**:77*t*
Dihydroxy propoxymethyl guanine. *See* Ganciclovir
Diisopropyl phosphorofluoridate, **2**:259, 339–340
Diktyoma (medulloepithelioma), **4**:183–184, 183*f*, 307, 307*f*, **6**:352
    retinoblastoma differentiated from, **4**:307, 307*f*
    teratoid, **4**:184
Dilacor. *See* Diltiazem
Dilantin. *See* Phenytoin
Dilated fundus examination, before refractive surgery, **13**:38
    refractive lens exchange/clear lens extraction, **13**:139
Dilator muscle, **2**:58*f*, 59*f*, 60*f*, 258, 259, **4**:186, 186*f*
    α-adrenergic agents affecting, **2**:345, 346, 348
    development of, **2**:60, 137
    miotics affecting, **2**:259*t*, 260
    mydriatics affecting, **2**:259*t*, 260, 345
    tadpole pupil caused by spasm of, **5**:263
Diltiazem
    for arrhythmias, **1**:123*t*
    for heart failure, mortality increases and, **1**:119
    for hypertension, **1**:77*t*
    for ischemic heart disease
        angina, **1**:108
        non–ST-segment elevation acute coronary syndrome, **1**:111
Dimorphic fungi, **8**:138
Dinucleotide repeats, **2**:155
Diode laser, **3**:25, **12**:338. *See also* Lasers
    for cycloablation/cyclophotocoagulation, **10**:210
        in childhood glaucoma, **6**:241, **10**:155
    for hyperthermia
        in melanoma, **4**:285
        in retinoblastoma, **4**:311
    for trabeculoplasty, **10**:180, 181
Diopter, **3**:62, **8**:37
    prism, **3**:85, 85*f*, 86*f*
Dioptric mean, **3**:93
Dioptric power, **3**:145. *See also* Power (optical)
    of bifocal segment, occupation and, **3**:156–157
Diovan. *See* Valsartan
Dipeptidyl peptidase IV (DPP-IV) inhibitors, for diabetes mellitus, **1**:202
Diphenhydramine, for allergic reactions/medical emergencies, **1**:292*t*, 295
Diphtheria, immunization against, **1**:284
Diphtheria-tetanus-pertussis vaccine (DTP), replacement of with diphtheria and tetanus toxoid with acellular pertussis vaccine (DTaP), **1**:269, 284

Diphtheria and tetanus toxoid with acellular pertussis
vaccine (DTaP), 1:269, 284
in combination vaccines, 1:285
Diphtheroids, 8:134
as normal ocular flora, 8:96, 97t, 134
Dipivefrin (dipivalyl epinephrine), 2:330, 347t
for glaucoma, 10:168–169
in children, 6:243
Diploid/diploid number, 2:151
Diplopia, 5:215–241
in aphakia/aniseikonia, contact lenses for, 3:171–172
binocular, 5:218
after blepharoplasty, 7:226
in blowout fractures, 5:238–239, 7:100–101
surgery and, 7:102
in Brown syndrome, 5:239–240, 240f
after cataract surgery, 5:239
cavernous sinus/superior orbital fissure lesions
causing, 5:236–238, 237f
cerebral, 5:218
in children, 6:39, 40, 40f, 49–50
comitant deviations and, 5:219
in congenital fibrosis syndrome, 5:240–241, 241f
crossed, 6:54, 54f
divergence insufficiency and, 5:222t, 234
fourth nerve (trochlear) palsy causing, 5:232–234,
234f
heteronymous, 6:54, 54f
history in, 5:215
homonymous, 6:54, 54f
incomitant deviations and, 5:219, 220f
infranuclear causes of, 5:226–238, 228f, 229f, 232f,
234f, 237f
internuclear causes of, 5:224–226, 224f, 225f, 226f
after LASIK, 13:116
in amblyopia patient, 13:179
localization of lesions causing, 5:220, 221f
monocular, 3:164–165, 5:188, 218
in cataracts, 11:40, 41, 43, 70
multifocal IOLs and, 3:226
pinhole imaging in identification of, 3:108, 164
with multifocal lenses
intraocular lenses and, 3:226
prismatic effects of bifocal lenses and, 3:150–151
progressive addition lenses and, 3:147
multiple cranial nerve palsies causing, 5:236
in multiple sclerosis, 5:324–325
in myasthenia gravis, 5:238, 329
myopathic/restrictive/orbital causes of, 5:238–241,
240f, 241f
neuroimaging in evaluation of, 5:84
neuromuscular junction causes of, 5:238
neuromyotonia causing, 5:235, 369
nuclear causes of, 5:223–224
one-and-a-half syndrome and, 5:225–226, 226f
orbital myositis causing, 5:239
orbital neoplasia causing, 5:239
Panum's area and, 6:40, 40f, 49
paradoxical, 6:52, 53f
paretic syndromes causing, 5:226–235, 228f, 229f,
232f, 234f, 236
restrictive syndromes differentiated from, 5:218,
219f
physical examination in, 5:215–218, 216f, 217f
restrictive syndromes causing, 5:238–241, 240f, 241f
paretic syndromes differentiated from, 5:218,
219f
posttraumatic, 5:238–239
sixth nerve (abducens) palsy causing, 5:234–235
skew deviation and, 5:222–223, 222t
after strabismus surgery, 6:155
supranuclear causes of, 5:220–223, 222t
testing for (red-glass test), 6:53–55, 54f
thalamic esodeviation and, 5:222t, 223
third nerve (oculomotor) palsy/paralysis or aberrant
regeneration causing, 5:228–232, 228f, 229f, 232f,
6:132
surgery and, 6:133
in thyroid eye disease, 5:238, 333, 334, 6:135, 139t,
7:51, 54
uncrossed, 6:54, 54t
vergence dysfunction causing. See Vergences/
vergence system
Dipping, ocular, 5:259
Diprivan. See Propofol
Dipyridamole, for carotid artery disease, 5:182
Direct ophthalmoscopy. See Ophthalmoscopy
Direct renin inhibitors, for hypertension, 1:77t, 83
Direct response, in pupillary reaction to light, 5:262
Direct sequencing, 2:184, 185f
Direct traumatic optic neuropathy, 5:156, 156f
Directionality, of laser light, 3:20
Dirithromycin, 1:50t, 61
Disability, visual, 3:283, 284f. See also Low vision
Disalcid. See Salsalate
Disc edema. See Optic disc (optic nerve head),
edema of
Disc sign, in sickle cell hemoglobinopathies, 12:120
Disciform keratitis, herpes simplex virus causing,
4:82–83, 8:114, 114f
persistent bullous keratopathy and, 8:117
Disciform scar, in choroidal neovascularization, 12:64,
64–65f, 66, 68, 83
Discoid systemic lupus erythematosus, 1:167, 169t,
9:140, 141t
Disconjugate/disjunctive nystagmus, 5:244
Disconjugate eye movements (vergences), 5:198–199,
198t, 204, 6:34, 35–37. See also specific type
assessment of, 5:204, 6:86–87
disorders of, 5:213–214
fusional, 6:41, 41t, 82–83
assessment of, 6:82
in infants, 6:413
supranuclear control systems in, 6:37
Disconnection syndromes, 5:192
"Discontinuation syndrome," with SSRIs, 1:256
Discontinuity, zone of, 2:70
DisCoVisc, 11:98
Disease-modifying (slow-acting) antirheumatic drugs,
1:162, 186
Dislocated lens, 11:35. See also Ectopia lentis
cataract surgery in patient with, 11:197–199, 198f
in children, 6:261–265, 261f, 262f, 262t, 264f
abuse and, 6:404
traumatic, 11:36, 50–51, 50f
child abuse and, 6:404

Dislocation/decentration (intraocular lens), **11**:143, 144*t*, 162–166, 163*f*, 164*f*, 165*f*
  laser capsulotomy and, **11**:173
  multifocal IOLs and, **3**:226, **11**:163
  phakic IOLs and, **13**:135, 145
Disodium ethylenediaminetetraacetic acid (EDTA)
  in artificial tears, **2**:391
  for band keratopathy, **2**:334, **8**:343
  in irrigating solutions, **2**:392
Disomy, uniparental, **2**:162, 169
Disopyramide, **1**:123*t*
Dispase, for enzymatic vitreolysis, **2**:289
Dispersion, **3**:40, 49–51, 51*f*
  chromatic aberration and, **3**:40, 41, 41*f*, 100–102, 102*f*
Dispersive ophthalmic viscosurgical devices, **11**:97, 97*t*.
  See also Ophthalmic viscosurgical devices
  elevated intraocular pressure and, **10**:101
Disposable contact lenses, **3**:180
Dissection, gross, for pathologic examination, **4**:27–28, 28*f*
Dissections (arterial), **5**:353–354, 354*f*. *See also specific type or artery affected*
Disseminated intravascular coagulation, **1**:156–157
  cancer and, **1**:158
  choroidal perfusion abnormalities and, **12**:179
  pregnancy and, **1**:158
Dissimilar image tests, **6**:78–79, 79*f*
Dissimilar segments, for induced anisophoria, **3**:155, 156*f*
Dissimilar target tests, **6**:79–80
Dissociated horizontal deviation, **6**:105–106, 105*f*, 117
Dissociated nystagmus, **5**:244, 254, **6**:326
Dissociated vertical deviation, **6**:105, 105*f*, 116–118, 117*f*
  surgery for, **6**:117, 153
Distaclor. *See* Cefaclor
Distance-near incomitance, strabismus surgery planning and, **6**:146
Distance spectacles, low vision/vision rehabilitation and, **3**:295
Distance visual acuity
  in low vision
    magnification for (telescopes), **3**:299–300, 301*f*
    testing, **3**:289–290, **5**:92
  testing
    in children, **6**:71–73, 72*t*
      nystagmus and, **6**:73, 319
    in low vision, **3**:289–290, **5**:92
    Snellen testing for, **3**:109–110, 109*f*, 110*t*, 289–290
      in children, **6**:72*t*, 73
Distichiasis, **2**:29, **4**:207, **6**:177, 177*f*, **8**:89
  acquired, **7**:143
  congenital, **4**:207, **6**:177, 177*f*, **7**:143, 150, 151*f*
Distortion, cylinders in spectacle lenses causing, **3**:140, 309–310, 310*f*. *See also* Meridional magnification
  adaptation to, **3**:140, 320–321
  altering astigmatic correction and, **3**:317–320, 318*f*, 319*f*
  blurred retinal images and, **3**:312, 312*f*
  contact lenses for reduction/elimination of, **3**:316–317
  conventional analysis and, **3**:311, 312*f*
  lens–entrance pupil distance and, **3**:311
  location effect and, **3**:313–314, 313*f*
  minimizing, **3**:140, 316–320, 318*f*, 319*f*
  minimizing vertex distance and, **3**:316–317
  minus cylinder (posterior toric) spectacle lenses and, **3**:316
  monocular, **3**:309–310, 310–311, 310*f*
  photographic simulation of, **3**:315–316, 316*f*
    altering astigmatic correction and, **3**:317, 318*f*
  prescribing guidelines and, **3**:140, 309–323
    common misconceptions and, **3**:314–316, 315*f*
    revised, **3**:321–322
  "shape factor" of spectacle lens and, **3**:311
  sources of, **3**:310–311, 310*f*
    relative contributions from, **3**:315, 315*f*
  with uncorrected/inappropriately corrected astigmatism, **3**:314
Distraction test, **7**:195
Distribution, normal, clinical relevance of research and, **1**:320
Distributive shock, **1**:293. *See also* Shock
Disuse anopsia. *See* Deprivation amblyopia
Diupres. *See* Reserpine
Diuretics
  central retinal vein occlusion and, **12**:129
  for heart failure, **1**:118, 119
  for hypertension, **1**:69, 75, 76*t*, 78*t*, 79*t*, 80
    in combination, **1**:78*t*, 83
  ocular effects of, **1**:302*t*
  in perioperative setting, **1**:306
Diuril. *See* Chlorothiazide
Diurnal variation
  in intraocular pressure, **10**:22, 74
  in vision, after radial keratotomy, **13**:44–45
Divergence, **5**:198, **6**:35
  fusional, **6**:37, 41*t*, 82
    in refractive accommodative esotropia, **6**:93
Divergence excess exotropia, **6**:101
Divergence insufficiency/paralysis, **5**:214, 222*t*, 234, **6**:97
  esodeviation and, **6**:97
Divergent strabismus, **6**:9
Diverging lens, **3**:138, 139*f*
Divisional third nerve palsy, **5**:231
Dix-Hallpike maneuver, **5**:250
Dk (gas-permeability constant), **3**:168, 176, 177*t*, 200
  corneal hypoxia and, **3**:200
  for hybrid contact lenses, **3**:191
  orthokeratology and, **3**:194
  for rigid contact lenses, **3**:176–178, 180, 191
  for soft (flexible) contact lenses, **3**:178, 180
  for therapeutic (bandage) contact lenses, **3**:193
Dk/L, of contact lens, **3**:168
DKA. *See* Diabetic ketoacidosis
DLK. *See* Diffuse lamellar (interface) keratitis
DLPN. *See* Dorsolateral pontine nuclei
DM. *See* Diabetes mellitus
DMARDs. *See* Disease-modifying (slow-acting) antirheumatic drugs
DME. *See* Diabetic macular edema
DMEK. *See* Descemet membrane endothelial keratoplasty
DNA, **2**:151
  amplification of, in polymerase chain reaction, **2**:158, **4**:40, 40*f*
  antisense, **2**:148
    in gene therapy, **2**:188, 189*f*

complementary (cDNA), 2:150
 from ciliary body–encoding plasma proteins, 2:269
 clone, 2:149
 sequencing, 2:184, 185f
 damage to, 2:169–170
 fecal, testing in cancer screening, 1:272t, 276
 junk, 2:165–166
 methylation of, 2:168
 mitochondrial
  diseases associated with deletions/mutations of,
   2:173–176, 174f, 191, 208
  galtonian inheritance of, 2:208
  Leber hereditary optic neuropathy, 2:174f, 175,
   5:138, 6:311
  maternal inheritance/transmission and, 2:208,
   220
  retinal degeneration and, 12:251t, 265, 265f
  in replicative segregation, 2:160, 173
 plasmid, 8:131
 recombinant, 2:159
 repair of, 2:169–170. See also Mutation
 replication of, 2:159
  origin, 2:157
  segregation and, 2:160, 196
  slippage, 2:160
 satellite, 2:160, 166, 180
 sense, 2:160
 sequencing of, 2:184, 185f
 telomeric (telomeres), 2:162, 166
 virus, 8:104
DNA libraries, 2:182, 183f
 cDNA, 2:154, 182
 genomic, 2:154, 182, 183f
DNA probes, 4:41
 in infection diagnosis, 1:3
 in microarray, 4:41
 multiplex ligation-dependent amplification of
  (MLPA), 4:38t, 41
DNA viruses
 adenoviruses, 8:123–127
 cancer association of, 1:236
 herpesviruses, 8:105–123
 papovaviruses, 8:128–129
 poxviruses, 8:127–128
Do not resuscitate orders, surgery in older patients and,
 1:224–225
Dobutamine, for heart failure, 1:119
Dobutrex. See Dobutamine
Docosahexaenoic acid
 in retinal pigment epithelium, 2:305
 supplementary, in retinitis pigmentosa, 12:231
Dofetilide, 1:123t
Dog bites, eyelid injuries caused by, 7:181
Dog hookworm (Ancylostoma caninum), diffuse
 unilateral subacute neuroretinitis caused by, 9:239,
 12:210
Dog tapeworm (Echinococcus granulosus), orbital
 infection caused by, 4:235, 7:47
Dolichocephaly, 6:383
Dolichoectasia, intracavernous carotid aneurysm as,
 5:351
Doll's head maneuver/phenomenon, 5:208
Dolobid. See Diflunisal

Domains, immunoglobulin, 9:45f, 46
Dominance, ocular, determining, 13:33
Dominance columns, ocular, 5:34
Dominant allele, 2:151, 211, 216
Dominant (familial) drusen, 12:239–240, 239f
Dominant eye, in low vision assessment, contrast
 sensitivity and, 3:291
Dominant inheritance (dominant gene/trait), 2:151,
 211–212
 autosomal, 2:216–217, 217t
 disorders associated with, 2:151, 212
  gene therapy for, 2:188, 189f
  X linked, 2:219–220
 X-linked, 2:219, 219t
Dominant negative mutation, 2:151
 gene therapy for disorders caused by, 2:188, 189f
Dominant optic atrophy, 5:139, 140f, 6:310–311
Donepezil, for Alzheimer disease, 1:267–268
Donor cornea, 8:408–411. See also Keratoplasty
 disease transmission and, 8:409–411, 410t
 dislocation of, after Descemet stripping automated
  endothelial keratoplasty, 8:442, 443f
 endothelial failure of, 4:91, 92f
  late nonimmune, 8:425–426
  primary, 8:422, 422f
   after Descemet stripping automated endothelial
    keratoplasty, 8:444–445
 for epikeratoplasty (epikeratophakia), 13:55
 for homoplastic corneal inlay, 13:53
 preparation of
  for Descemet stripping automated endothelial
   keratoplasty, 8:438
  for penetrating keratoplasty, 8:417–418
 prior LASIK affecting, 8:410, 13:191–192
 rejection of, 4:91, 92f, 8:407, 408, 427–430, 428f, 429f,
  436, 9:63, 64, 64f, 65. See also Rejection
 selection/screening of, 8:409–411, 410t
  HIV infection transmission and, 1:41
 storage of, 2:394–395, 8:408–409
Donor splice site, 2:151
L-Dopa, for Parkinson disease, 1:258–259
Dopamine
 antipsychotic mechanism of action and, 1:251
 for heart failure, 1:119
 outer-segment disc shedding and, 2:306–307
 in Parkinson disease, 1:258
 for shock, 1:294
Dopamine-β-hydroxylase, defective, 2:213t
Dopamine neurons, transplantation of, for Parkinson
 disease, 1:260
Dopamine-norepinephrine reuptake inhibitors, 1:255t
Doppler imaging. See also Ultrasonography/ultrasound
 carotid, 5:81
  in cerebral ischemia/stroke, 1:93, 94
  in ischemic heart disease, 1:105–106
  in ocular ischemic syndrome, 9:288
  in orbital evaluation, 7:30
Dorello canal, 2:104, 5:50
 sixth nerve (abducens) injury/palsy and, 5:235
Doripenem, 1:59
Dorsal light reflex, dissociated vertical deviation and,
 6:116
Dorsal meningeal artery, 5:16

Dorsal midbrain (Parinaud) syndrome, 5:44, 211, 212*f*
eyelid retraction in, 5:211, 273, 281, 7:214
nystagmus in, 6:325
Dorsal subnucleus, of cranial nerve VII (facial), 5:61
Dorsal vermis, 5:43*f*, 48–49
Dorsal visual processing stream, 5:204
Dorsolateral pontine nuclei, 5:38, 41, 43*f*
Dorzolamide, 2:352, 352*t*, 10:156, 164*t*, 170
in children, 6:242, 10:156
in combination preparations, 2:350*t*, 352–353, 352*t*,
355, 10:165*t*, 173
Dot-and-blot hemorrhages, 5:183, 184, 184*f*
ischemia causing, 4:160, 161*f*
Dot-and-flame hemorrhages, in central retinal vein
occlusion, 12:128
Double convexity deformity, 7:229, 233
Double elevator palsy (monocular elevation deficiency),
6:123–124, 123*f*, 7:205
Double freeze–thaw technique, for trichiasis, 7:200
Double heterozygotes, 2:195
"Double hump" sign, in plateau iris, 10:119
Double-K method, for IOL power calculation in
postkeratorefractive eye, 3:221
Double Maddox rod testing, 5:216–218, 217*f*, 6:79, 79*f*
in superior oblique muscle paralysis, 6:118
Double-ring sign, in optic nerve hypoplasia, 5:141, 141*f*,
6:308
Double simultaneous stimulation, in confrontation
testing, 5:98
Double vision. *See* Diplopia
Doubling principle, 3:264
"Dowager's hump," 1:229
Down syndrome (trisomy 21/trisomy G syndrome),
2:201–203, 202*t*
Brushfield spots in, 4:270*t*, 272*f*, 6:227
congenital ectropion and, 7:146
mosaicism in, 2:204
pharmacogenetics and, 2:229
pseudopapilledema in, 6:314
Downbeat nystagmus, 5:49, 251–252, 251*t*, 252*f*
in children, 6:325–326
Downgaze. *See* Depression of eye
Doxazosin
for heart failure, 1:119
for hypertension, 1:77*t*
intraoperative floppy iris syndrome and, 11:74, 155
Doxorubicin, 1:239, 241*t*
Doxycycline, 1:51*t*, 2:334, 374
for chalazia and hordeola in children, 6:351
for chlamydial conjunctivitis, 8:157
for leptospirosis, 9:256
for Lyme disease, 9:253*t*
for meibomian gland dysfunction, 8:68
ocular effects of, 1:301*t*
for onchocerciasis, 9:242
for recurrent corneal erosions, 8:84
for rosacea, 2:334, 8:70
for seborrheic blepharitis, 8:72
Doyne honeycombed dystrophy, 12:239. *See also* Drusen
EFEMP1 defects causing, 2:297, 12:239
DPE. *See* Dipivefrin
DPP-IV inhibitors. *See* Dipeptidyl peptidase IV
(DPP-IV) inhibitors

Drance hemorrhage, in glaucoma, 10:48*f*
DRCR.net (Diabetic Retinopathy Clinical Research
Network), 12:100, 103
Dressler (post-MI) syndrome, 1:103
DRIs. *See* Direct renin inhibitors
Drop attacks, 5:347
Drotrecogin alfa, for septic shock, 1:294
DRS (Diabetic Retinopathy Study), 12:105, 107–108, 109*f*
Drug addiction, 1:250
Drug dependence, 1:250
Drug-eluting stents, 1:99, 108–109
Drug resistance. *See also specific agent and specific
organism*
antibiotic, 1:3, 44–56, 2:369, 371, 375, 377
new drug classes and, 1:63–64
antiretroviral, 1:33, 34, 35, 36
antiviral, 2:382
in tuberculosis, 1:19–20, 39, 9:261
Drug tolerance, 1:250
Drugs. *See also specific drug or drug group*
allergic reaction to. *See specific drug and* Allergic
reactions
antibiotic, 1:44–64, 45–53*t*, 2:368–378, 368*t*, 372*t*, 373*t*
canalicular obstruction caused by, 7:264
diabetes mellitus associated with, 1:191
dry eye caused by, 8:50, 65, 66*t*
fixed, dilated pupil caused by, 5:316
genetics affecting (pharmacogenetics), 2:157, 229–230
glaucoma caused by
angle closure/angle-closure glaucoma and,
10:136–137, 137*f*
open-angle glaucoma and, 10:103–104
hallucinations/illusions caused by, 5:188*t*
lens changes caused by, 11:47–49
medication use in older patients and, 1:222
ocular. *See also specific agent*
absorption of, 2:322, 323–327, 324*f*, 325*f*
adrenergic, 2:344–351, 345*f*
age/aging and, 1:222
antibiotic, 2:368–378, 368*t*, 372*t*, 373*t*
antifibrinolytic, 2:394
antifungal, 2:378–380, 379*t*
anti-inflammatory, 2:356–368, 357*t*, 360*t*, 362*t*, 365*t*
antioxidant/vitamin supplements, 2:395
antiviral, 2:380–385, 381*t*
carbonic anhydrase inhibitors, 2:351–354, 352*t*
cholinergic, 2:334–344, 335*f*, 336*f*, 337*f*, 339*f*, 343*f*
cicatricial pemphigoid (pseudopemphigoid) caused
by, 8:199, 361
combined agents, 2:355
concentration of, absorption affected by, 2:326
contact dermatoblepharitis caused by, 8:183–185,
184*f*
corneal deposits and pigmentation caused by,
8:346–349, 347*t*
for corneal storage medium, 2:394–395
decongestants, 2:392
diagnostic agents, 2:392–393
for dry eye, 2:245, 246*f*, 390–391
in eyedrops, 2:323–327, 324*f*, 325*f*
fibrinolytic, 2:393
growth factors, 2:395–397
hyperosmolar, 2:391

interferons, **2**:395
intraocular injection of, **2**:328
intraocular pressure affected by. *See* Antiglaucoma
    agents
intravenous administration of, **2**:329
investigational/clinical testing of, **2**:333
for irrigation, **2**:392
legal aspects of use of, **2**:333–334
local administration of, **2**:327–328
local anesthetics, **2**:386–390, 387*t*
mechanisms of action of, **2**:322, 331–332
methods of design and delivery of, **2**:330–331
new
    future research areas and, **2**:321
    investigational/clinical testing of, **2**:333
off-label usage of, **2**:333–334
in ointments, **2**:327
oral preparations of, sustained-release, **2**:329
osmotic agents, **2**:355–356, 356*t*
partition coefficients of, **2**:326
periocular injection of, **2**:327
persistent corneal epithelial defects caused by, **8**:86
pharmacodynamics of, **2**:322, 331–332
pharmacokinetics of, **2**:322, 323–331
pharmacologic principles and, **2**:321–332
pharmacotherapeutics of, **2**:322
prostaglandin analogues, **2**:354–355, 354*t*
purified neurotoxin complex, **2**:390
receptor interactions and, **2**:331–332
solubility of, absorption affected by, **2**:326
systemic absorption of, **2**:322, 324–325, 325*f*
systemic administration and, **2**:328–330
thrombin, **2**:393–394
tissue binding of, **2**:327
topical, **2**:323–327, 324*f*, 325*f*. *See also* Eyedrops
    sustained-release devices for, **2**:330–331
toxicity of, **2**:321, 322–323
    aging and, **2**:323
    conjunctivitis/keratoconjunctivitis and,
        8:359–361, 359*t*, 361*f*
    tissue binding and, **2**:327
    ulcerative keratopathy and, **8**:86
viscoelastics, **2**:393. *See also* Ophthalmic
    viscosurgical devices
viscosity of, absorption affected by, **2**:326
vitamin/antioxidant supplements, **2**:395
ocular toxicity and, **1**:300–302, 301–302*t*
    age-related macular degeneration differentiated
        from, **12**:60
    ERG in evaluation of, **12**:41
    optic neuropathy caused by, **5**:154
    retinal degenerations caused by, **12**:266–270, 266*f*,
        268*f*, 269*t*
platelet dysfunction caused by, **1**:154, 155
restrictive lung disease and, **1**:142
thrombocytopenia caused by, **1**:154
uveitis caused by, **9**:128
Drusen, **2**:73
    in age-related macular degeneration, **4**:168–169, 168*f*,
        169*f*, **12**:57–58, 57*f*
    calcific (calcified), **4**:169
    in children, **6**:314–315, 315*f*
    classification of, **12**:58

confluent, **12**:58
cuticular (basal laminar), **4**:169, **12**:60, 239–240
    age-related macular degeneration differentiated
        from, **12**:60, 69
    vitelliform exudative macular detachment and,
        12:238, 238*f*
diffuse, **4**:168, 168*f*
familial (dominant), **12**:239–240, 239*f*
giant, **4**:306, **5**:136, 136*f*
    retinoblastoma differentiated from, **4**:306
    in tuberous sclerosis, **4**:306, **6**:373
hard, **4**:168, 168*f*, **12**:58
optic disc/nerve, **4**:255, 255*f*, 306, **5**:133–136, 134*f*,
        135*f*, 136*f*
    astrocytic hamartoma differentiated from, **5**:136,
        136*f*
    extruded, **5**:133
    papilledema/pseudopapilledema and, **4**:255, **5**:120,
        120*f*, 134–136, 135*f*
    in children, **6**:314–315, 315*f*
refractile, **12**:59
regressed, **12**:59
soft, **4**:169, 169*f*, **12**:57, 57*f*, 58
    drusenoid RPE detachment and, **12**:57, 238, 239*f*
Drusenoid retinal pigment epithelial detachment, **12**:57,
        238, 239*f*
DRVS (Diabetic Retinopathy Vitrectomy Study),
        12:110
Dry-eye syndrome, **8**:48–55, 50*f*, 51*f*. *See also specific
    causative factor and* Ocular surface, disorders of
    aqueous tear deficiency causing, **8**:49–50, 50*f*, 51, 51*f*,
        52, 55–65. *See also* Aqueous tear deficiency
    β-blockers causing, **1**:128
    blepharitis and, **8**:144*t*, 145
    in blepharospasm, **7**:218, 220
    cataract surgery in patient with, **11**:190–191
        corneal melting/keratolysis and, **11**:150, 191
    classification of, **8**:51–52, 51*f*
    clinical presentation of, **8**:55–56, 56*f*, 57*f*, 58*t*
    contact lens wear and, **3**:200–201
    evaporative tear dysfunction causing, **8**:51, 51*f*, 52,
        65–75
    glaucoma and, **8**:61
    in graft-vs-host disease, **8**:203
    imaging in evaluation of, **8**:55
    keratoprosthesis use and, **8**:432
    laboratory evaluation in, **8**:57, 59*f*, 59*t*
    lacrimal plugs for, **7**:271, **8**:60*t*, 61–62, 62*f*
        canalicular obstruction and, **7**:263–264, 271
        extrusion/migration of, **7**:271
        nasolacrimal duct obstruction and, **7**:267
    after LASIK, **8**:50, 65, **13**:71, 97–98, 164–165
    LASIK in patient with, **13**:71, 164–165
    lymphocytic lacrimal infiltrates and, **7**:88
    mechanisms of, **8**:49–51, 50*f*
    medications causing, **8**:50, 65, 66*t*
    non–Sjögren syndrome, **8**:50, 51*f*, 52, 65
    ocular infection and, **8**:99
    pain and, **5**:300
    after photoablation, **13**:97–98, 164–165
    after photorefractive keratectomy, **8**:65
    radiation causing, **1**:239
    refractive surgery and, **8**:50, 50*f*, 65, **13**:35, 164–165

rose bengal in diagnosis of, 8:17
sarcoidosis and, 8:73, 9:174
severity of, 8:56, 58t
Sjögren syndrome, 1:174, 8:50, 51f, 52, 63–65, 64t
after surface ablation, 13:97–98, 164–165
epithelial defect and, 13:100
surface inflammation and, 2:245, 245f, 246f
systemic diseases associated with, 8:59t
tear-film abnormalities and, 2:244, 246f
tear-film evaluation in, 8:52–55, 53f, 54f, 54t
treatment of
medical management, 2:245, 246f, 390–391,
8:57–61, 60t
surgical management, 8:61–63, 61f, 62f
DSA. See Digital subtraction angiography
DSAEK/DSEK. See Descemet stripping/Descemet
stripping automated endothelial keratoplasty
DTacP-IPV-Hib vaccine, 1:285
DTacP-IPV vaccine, 1:285
DTaP (diphtheria and tetanus toxoid with acellular
pertussis) vaccine, 1:284
in combination vaccines, 1:285
DTNBP1 gene, in Hermansky-Pudlak syndrome,
12:258t
DTP (diphtheria-tetanus-pertussis) vaccine,
replacement of with DTaP (diphtheria and tetanus
toxoid with acellular pertussis) vaccine, 1:284
DTPa-HBV-IPV/Hib vaccine, 1:285
Dual antiplatelet therapy (DAT), 1:99
for ischemic heart disease, 1:99, 109–110, 109t
cataract surgery and, 1:303
non–ST-segment elevation acute coronary
syndrome, 1:111
stable angina, 1:109–110, 109t
Dual-energy radiographic absorptiometry, for bone
density measurement, 1:229
Dual-optic intraocular lenses, 13:146, 160
DualChip low-density microarray, 4:41
Duane/Duane retraction syndrome, 5:235, 240–241,
241f, 241t, 6:127–130, 128f
esotropic, 6:128, 128f, 129
exotropic, 6:105, 128, 128f, 129
Goldenhar syndrome and, 6:127, 393
sixth nerve (abducens) paralysis differentiated from,
6:134
synkinesis in, 7:203, 207
Duchenne muscular dystrophy
mutation rate of, 2:207
pigmentary retinopathy and, 12:254
Ductal cysts of eyelid, 4:213–214, 214f
Ductions, 5:215, 6:33–34. See also specific type
forced. See Forced ductions
Dulcitol (galactitol)
in cataract formation, 2:281, 11:56
in lens glucose/carbohydrate metabolism, 2:280f
Duloxetine, 1:256
Duochrome (red-green/bichrome/Worth 4-dot) test,
3:135–136, 6:55, 55f, 87
in binocular sensory cooperation evaluation, 6:87
in nonorganic ophthalmic disorder evaluation
monocular no light perception and, 5:309–310
monocular reduced vision and, 5:311
before refractive surgery, 13:33
in sensory adaptation testing, 6:55, 55f

Duplex ultrasonography. See also Ultrasonography
in carotid artery evaluation, 5:81, 180
in cerebral ischemia/stroke, 1:93, 94
Duplication, cataract, 4:124, 125f
Duplication mapping, 2:177
Dura mater, optic nerve, 2:91, 92f, 93f, 4:249, 250f
Duracef. See Cefadroxil
Dural arteriovenous/arterial malformation, 5:356
choroidal perfusion abnormalities and, 12:176
Dural cavernous fistula, 7:67–68, 69
Dural rings, 5:16, 18f
Dural sheath, optic nerve, 5:30, 31
Dural sinus thrombosis, 5:356–358
Dural tail, 5:85f
DUSN. See Diffuse unilateral subacute neuroretinitis
Duty cycle, in phacoemulsification, 11:103
DVD. See Dissociated vertical deviation
DW. See Daily-wear contact lenses
DWI. See Diffusion-weighted magnetic resonance
imaging
DXA. See Dual-energy radiographic absorptiometry
Dyazide. See Triamterene
Dye disappearance test, 7:258, 259f, 8:17
Dye laser, 3:23, 24. See also Lasers
Dynabac. See Dirithromycin
Dynacin. See Minocycline
DynaCirc. See Isradipine
Dynamic contour tonometer/tonometry, 3:258–259,
259f, 10:25
Dynamic gonioscopy, 10:33f, 34
in acute primary angle closure, 10:114–115
Dynamic visual acuity, vestibular ocular reflex and, 5:201
Dynapen. See Dicloxacillin
Dyrenium. See Triamterene
Dysautonomia, familial (Riley-Day syndrome), 2:213t,
6:221
congenital corneal anesthesia and, 8:264
neurotrophic keratopathy in, 8:87
racial and ethnic concentration of, 2:211
Dyschromatopsia. See Color vision, defects in
Dyscoria, 6:223
Dysgenesis, mesodermal, 8:255–263. See also Anterior
segment, dysgenesis of; Axenfeld-Rieger syndrome
Dysgeusia, Horner syndrome and, 5:268
Dyskeratosis
in actinic keratosis, 4:217, 217f
benign hereditary intraepithelial, 8:226t
definition of, 4:206
Dyskinesia, tardive
blepharospasm and, 5:289
facial movements and, 5:292
Dyslexia, surface, in Alzheimer disease, 1:268
Dyslipoproteinemia/dyslipidemia, 1:271. See also
Hypercholesterolemia; Hyperlipoproteinemia
screening for, 1:271
Dysmorphic sialidosis, 8:312
Dysphotopsias, 3:223–225, 224f
intraocular lenses and, 11:168
Dysplasia
of bony orbit, 4:245–246, 246f, 6:342
of conjunctiva (conjunctival intraepithelial
neoplasia), 4:62, 63f, 64f, 8:226t, 228–229, 229f,
230f. See also Ocular surface squamous neoplasia
squamous, 8:228

of cornea (corneal intraepithelial neoplasia), 4:100,
8:226t, 229–231, 231f
ectodermal, 8:74–75
retinal, retinoblastoma differentiated from, 4:305t
Dysplastic nevus, 4:226
melanoma arising from, 1:277, 4:226
Dyspnea, 1:141
in heart failure, 1:114
Dysport (abobotulinumtoxinA). See Botulinum toxin,
type A
Dysraphia, 6:171
Dysthymic disorder, 1:247
Dysthyroid ophthalmopathy/orbitopathy. See Thyroid
eye disease
Dystonia, facial, 7:218–221, 219f
Dystopia canthorum, 6:175, 175f
Dystrophies, 4:9–10, 12t. See also specific type
choroidal, 12:242–246, 243f, 244f, 245f. See also
specific type
corneal, 4:94–100, 8:267–268, 268–296, 268t,
269t, 270t. See also specific type and Corneal
dystrophies
cataract/cataract surgery in patient with,
11:191–192, 192f
refractive surgery in patients with, 13:35, 37f,
67–68, 70, 71
definition of, 4:10, 8:267
degenerations differentiated from, 8:334t
foveomacular, 4:175, 176f, 12:237–238, 238f
hereditary, 12:221–248. See also specific type
macular, 4:96, 97f, 97t, 172–175, 8:268t, 270t, 278t,
283–284, 284f, 12:234–242. See also specific type
and Macular dystrophies
pattern, 4:175, 176f, 12:240–241, 240f, 241f
adult-onset foveomacular vitelliform, 4:175, 176f,
12:237–238, 238f
age-related macular degeneration differentiated
from, 12:60, 69
butterfly, 4:175, 12:240, 240f
retinal. See also specific type and Retinal
degenerations
ERG in evaluation of, 12:39–41, 40f, 41f
hereditary, 12:221–248. See also specific type and
Hereditary dystrophies
diagnostic and prognostic testing in, 12:223,
224t
inner, 12:246–248
photoreceptor (diffuse), 4:175–177, 12:223–234
stromal, 4:96–97, 97f, 97t, 98f, 99f
vitreoretinal, 12:246–248
Goldmann-Favre, 6:296, 12:219, 248
Dystrophin, mutations in gene for, in Duchenne
muscular dystrophy, 12:254

E

E coli. See Escherichia coli
E-game, for visual acuity testing in children, 6:72t, 73
E-selectin, in neutrophil rolling, 9:18
Eagle Vision drainage device, 10:205t
Eales disease, 9:258, 260f, 12:141
Early latent syphilis, 1:12–13, 9:244, 248t
Early Manifest Glaucoma Trial (EMGT), 10:78, 82, 86, 106

Early-onset Alzheimer disease, 1:266
Early-onset (childhood) nystagmus, 5:245–247,
6:288–289, 289t, 317–330, 319t. See also
Nystagmus
monocular, 5:246–247, 251t, 6:326
Early receptor potentials, 12:37, 37f
Early Treatment Diabetic Retinopathy Study (ETDRS),
12:97, 98, 101–102, 104. See also ETDRS visual
acuity chart
scatter laser treatment and, 12:98, 102, 107, 108f
Early Treatment for Retinopathy of Prematurity
(ETROP) study, 6:281, 283–285, 286, 12:160,
166–167
EAU. See Experimental uveitis, autoimmune
EB. See Elementary body
EBAA. See Eye Bank Association of America
Eberconazole, 1:65
EBMD. See Epithelial/subepithelial dystrophies,
basement membrane
EBV. See Epstein-Barr virus
EBV-associated hemophagocytic lymphohistiocytosis/
syndrome (EBV-HLH), 1:25
ECA. See External carotid artery
ECCE. See Extracapsular cataract extraction
Eccentric fixation, 3:293, 6:53, 63
ARC testing and, 6:53
Eccentric gaze, 5:47
Ecchymoses, 1:153. See also Purpura
periorbital
in blowout fractures, 7:100
in child abuse, 6:404
in neuroblastoma, 6:336, 336f
Eccrine hidrocystoma, 4:214, 7:161
Eccrine sweat glands of eyelid, 4:205, 207t, 7:160, 8:4
tumors arising in, 7:161–162, 161f
ECD. See Erdheim-Chester disease
ECG. See Electrocardiography
Echinocandins, 1:65
Echinococcus granulosus (echinococcosis), orbital
infection caused by, 4:235, 7:47
Echocardiography
in cerebral ischemia/stroke, 1:94, 5:180
in congestive heart failure, 1:116
exercise (stress), 1:106
in ischemic heart disease, 1:105–106
transesophageal Doppler, in cerebral ischemia/stroke,
1:94
Echography. See Ultrasonography
Echothiophate, 2:259, 338t, 339–340, 10:164t, 171
cataract and, 11:49
in Down syndrome patients, pharmacogenetics and,
2:229
for glaucoma, 10:164t
in children, 6:243
for high accommodative convergence/
accommodative esotropia, 6:94
succinylcholine and, 1:306
Eclampsia, 1:86. See also Preeclampsia
choroidal perfusion abnormalities and, 12:176,
178f
transient visual loss and, 5:173
Eclipse (solar) retinopathy, 12:332–333
Econopred. See Prednisolone
ECP. See Endoscopic cyclophotocoagulation

Ectasia/ectatic disorders
  corneal, **8**:296–303, 302*t. See also specific type*
    after LASIK, **13**:72, 114–116
      collagen crosslinking for, **13**:123–124, 168
      intrastromal corneal ring segments for, **13**:63
      refractive surgery contraindicated in, corneal
        topography and, **13**:16–17, 18–19, 19*f*, 167
    parafoveal (juxtafoveal), **12**:145–147, 145*f*, 146*f*
    retinal, **12**:143–145, 144*f. See also* Coats disease;
      Retinal telangiectasia
      arterial macroaneurysms, **12**:147–148, 147*f*
Ectodactyly-ectodermal dysplasial–clefting (EEC)
  syndrome, **8**:75
Ectoderm, **2**:117, 119*f*, 120*f*
  ocular structures derived from, **2**:116*t*, **8**:4
    cornea, **2**:133, 134*f*
    lens, **2**:128–129, 129*f*, **11**:21, 22*f*
Ectodermal dysplasia, **8**:74–75
  anhidrotic, **8**:75
Ectopia lentis, **10**:121–122, 122*f*, 123*f*, 123*t*, **11**:35–37,
  36*f*
  angle-closure glaucoma and, **10**:90*t*, 112, 121–122,
    122*f*, 123*f*, 123*t*
  cataract surgery in patient with, **11**:197–199, 198*f*
  in children, **6**:261
    abuse and, **6**:404
  et pupillae, **6**:229, 230, 262, 262*f*, **11**:38
    Axenfeld-Rieger syndrome differentiated from,
      10:146*t*
  in homocystinuria, **6**:263, 264*f*, **11**:37
  in hyperlysinemia, **11**:37
  in Marfan syndrome, **6**:263, **11**:36–37, 36*f*
  simple, **6**:262, **11**:36
  in sulfite oxidase deficiency, **6**:264
  traumatic, **11**:36, 50–51, 50*f*
    child abuse and, **6**:404
  treatment of, **6**:264–265
  in Weill-Marchesani syndrome, **6**:264
Ectopic lacrimal gland, **6**:345, **8**:246
Ectopic tissue masses, orbital, in children, **6**:343–346
Ectropion, **2**:60, **7**:190–194, 191*f*
  anophthalmic, **7**:124–125
  cicatricial, **7**:191*f*
    after blepharoplasty, **7**:226
  congenital, **6**:176, **7**:146, 147*f*
    in blepharophimosis syndrome, **7**:145, 146
    iris, **6**:231
      glaucoma in neurofibromatosis and, **6**:370
  involutional, **7**:190–193, 191*f*, 192*f*
  mechanical, **7**:191*f*, 194
  paralytic, **7**:191*f*, 216, 217*f*
  tarsal, **7**:193
  uveae, **2**:60, **4**:192, **6**:231, **10**:148
Eczema, of eyelid, **8**:20*t*
Edema
  corneal. *See* Cornea, edema of
  epithelial, **8**:20*t*
    cataract surgery and, **11**:146–148
    central (Sattler veil), **8**:91
    intraocular surgery causing, **8**:383
  eyelid, **7**:154
    in blowout fractures, **7**:100
  in heart failure, **1**:114
  in hypothyroidism, **1**:212
  macular. *See* Macular edema
  optic disc. *See* Optic disc (optic nerve head), edema of
  pulmonary. *See* Pulmonary edema
  retinal, **4**:158–160, 159*f*, 160*f*
    in branch retinal artery occlusion, **12**:136
    in central retinal artery occlusion, **12**:138, 138*f*
    in central retinal vein occlusion, **12**:128, 129*f*
    in clinically significant diabetic macular edema,
      12:97, 99*f*
    in cystoid macular edema, **12**:142–143, 142*f*
  stromal, **8**:29
    cataract surgery and, **11**:146–148
Edetate disodium, for band keratopathy, **2**:334, **8**:343
Edge lift, of contact lens, **3**:168
EDI. *See* Enhanced depth imaging
Edinger-Westphal nucleus, **2**:61, 97*f*, 98, 99, **5**:53–54,
  65, 66*f*
Edrophonium, **2**:336*f*, 342–343
  in myasthenia gravis diagnosis, **2**:329, 342–343,
    5:329–330, **6**:138, 138*f*, 139*t*, **7**:209
  toxic reaction/side effects of, **1**:299, **5**:329
EDS. *See* Ehlers-Danlos syndrome
EDTA
  in artificial tears, **2**:391
  for band keratopathy, **2**:334, **8**:343
  in irrigating solutions, **2**:392
EEC (ectodactyly-ectodermal dysplasial–clefting)
  syndrome, **8**:75
EEG. *See* Electroencephalography
EF. *See* Ejection fraction
Efavirenz, **1**:34
EFEMP1 gene, **12**:239
EFEMP1 protein (EGF-containing fibrillinlike
  extracellular matrix protein) mutations, **2**:297, **12**:239
Effector blockade, **9**:62
Effector cells, **9**:42–43, 42*f*
  basophils and mast cells as, **9**:10
  dendritic cells and Langerhans cells as, **9**:11–12
  eosinophils as, **9**:10
  locations of, **9**:58*t*
  lymphocytes as, **9**:12, 42–43, 42*f*, 48–51, 49*f*, 50*t*,
    52–53, 53*f*
  monocytes and macrophages as, **9**:11, 20
  neutrophils as, **9**:9, 17
Effector phase of immune response arc, **9**:33–36, 36*f*,
  42–43, 42*f*
  adaptive immunity and, **9**:42–43, 42*f*, 44–55, 44*t*
  in anterior chamber–associated immune deviation,
    9:62
  antibody-mediated, **9**:45–48, 45*f*, 47*t*, 48
  cells in. *See* Effector cells
  combined antibody and cellular, **9**:51–55, 54*f*
  innate immunity and, **9**:14–23, 14*t*, 23*t*
  lymphocyte-mediated, **9**:42–43, 42*f*, 48–51, 49*f*, 50*t*,
    52–53, 53*f*
  mediator systems and, **9**:23–31, 23*t*
  response to poison ivy and, **9**:34, 35
  response to tuberculosis and, **9**:35
  in viral conjunctivitis, **9**:60–61
Efference copy information, **5**:48
Efferent fibers, visceral, **2**:105
Efferent lymphatic channels, **9**:33, 34

Efferent pupillary pathway, 2:99
Efferent visual pathways/efferent visual system, 5:37–56, 197. *See also* Ocular motility, control of; Ocular motor pathways
Effexor. *See* Venlafaxine
Efficient threshold strategies, 10:57–58
Effusion
suprachoroidal
cataract surgery and, 11:177–178
flat or shallow anterior chamber and, 11:152
after filtering surgery, 10:197–198
uveal, angle-closure glaucoma and, 10:131, 133
Eflone. *See* Fluorometholone
EGF-containing fibrillinlike extracellular matrix protein (EFEMP1) mutations, 2:297, 12:239
EGPS (European Glaucoma Prevention Study), 10:86, 159
Ehlers-Danlos syndrome, 1:153, 2:213t, 8:252, 320–325, 322t
angioid streaks in, 12:84
blue sclera in, 8:252, 325
keratoglobus in, 6:211, 8:302, 325
Ehrlichiosis, human granulocytic (human granulocytic anaplasmosis), 1:15
Lyme disease coinfection and, 9:254
Eicosanoids, 2:255–258, 256f, 8:177t, 9:25, 25–27, 26f
Eight-and-a-half syndrome, 5:226
"Eight ball" hyphema, 8:365, 366f
Eighth nerve tumors. *See also* Neurofibromas, acoustic in neurofibromatosis type 2, 6:371
EIU. *See* Experimental uveitis, immune
Ejection fraction, in congestive heart failure, 1:116
EK. *See* Keratoplasty, endothelial
EKC. *See* Epidemic keratoconjunctivitis
Elastases, in ocular infections, 8:98–99
Elastin, 8:9
in exfoliation syndrome, 10:85, 86
Elastotic degeneration/elastosis
corneal, 8:334–335, 335f. *See also* Spheroidal degeneration
in pinguecula/pterygium, 4:56, 58, 58f, 59f
solar, of eyelid, 4:217, 218f
Eldepryl. *See* Selegiline
Elder abuse, 1:223–224
Elderly patients. *See* Age/aging; Geriatrics
Electric field, of light wave, 3:3, 4, 4f, 5f
Electrical injury, lens damage/cataracts caused by, 11:54, 55f
Electrically evoked potentials, 12:45
Electrocardiography (ECG)
in congestive heart failure, 1:116
exercise, 1:106
in ischemic heart disease, 1:104, 106
in stroke evaluation, 1:94
Electroencephalography (EEG), in epilepsy diagnosis, 1:262
Electrolysis, for trichiasis, 7:200, 8:89
Electrolytes
in lens, maintenance of balance of, 11:17–19, 18f
in tear film, 2:238t, 240
Electromagnetic wave spectrum, 3:4, 6f
Electromyography, 6:32
in myasthenia gravis, 5:331, 6:138

Electron beam CT, in ischemic heart disease, 1:107
Electron microscopy, diagnostic, 4:34t, 43
Electronic magnification, in low vision/vision rehabilitation, 3:302–303, 302f
Electronystagmography, in latent/latent manifest (fusion maldevelopment) nystagmus, 6:323, 324f
Electro-oculogram, 12:42–44, 42f, 43f. *See also specific disorder*
trans-RPE potential as basis for, 2:307
Electrophoresis
denaturing gradient gel, 2:183–184
hemoglobin, in sickling disorders, 6:409, 12:116
Electrophysiologic testing
cardiac, in ventricular tachycardia, 1:123
of retina, 2:301–302, 301f, 12:33–45. *See also specific test*
in inflammatory chorioretinopathies, 9:150t
in Leber congenital amaurosis, 12:229
in low vision evaluation, 5:108–110, 110f
in nonorganic ophthalmic disorders, 5:308
Electroretinogram, 2:301, 5:109–110, 110f, 12:33, 33–41
in achromatopsia, 6:291, 12:36f, 214
aging affecting, 12:36
applications and cautions for, 12:39–41, 40f, 41f
in birdshot retinochoroidopathy, 9:150t, 153, 12:190
in blue-cone monochromatism, 12:36f, 214
bright-flash, 12:35, 37
in hereditary retinal/choroidal dystrophies, 12:224t
c-wave, 12:37
in choroideremia, 12:40
in cone dystrophies, 12:36f, 232
in cone–rod dystrophies, 12:36f, 233
in congenital stationary night blindness, 6:291, 12:36f, 216, 217, 217f
dark-adapted. *See* Electroretinogram, scotopic
in Duchenne muscular dystrophy, 12:254
early receptor potential, 12:37, 37f
focal, 12:37
foveal, 12:37
in fundus albipunctatus, 12:218
in glaucoma evaluation, 12:39
in hereditary retinal and choroidal dystrophies, 12:223, 224t
in infants/children, 6:415, 12:40, 41f
interpretation of, 12:35–36, 36f
in Leber congenital amaurosis, 6:290, 12:229
light-adapted. *See* Electroretinogram, photopic
in low vision evaluation, 5:109–110, 110f
in infant, 6:415
in macular disorders, 12:39, 40f
multifocal, 12:37, 38f
in multiple evanescent white dot syndrome, 5:114, 9:168, 12:190
negative
in congenital stationary night blindness, 12:216, 217f
in hereditary retinal/choroidal dystrophies, 12:224t
in ocular ischemic syndrome, 12:133
in older patients, 12:36
pattern, 12:38–39, 39f
pediatric, 6:415, 12:40, 41f
photopic/light-adapted, 12:34, 34f, 35, 36f
in cone dystrophies, 12:232
in hereditary retinal/choroidal dystrophies, 12:224t

recording, **12**:33–35, 34*f*
in retinal disease, **12**:33–41
in retinitis pigmentosa, **12**:40*f*, 226
scotopic/dark-adapted, **12**:33, 34*f*, 35, 36*f*. *See also*
    Dark adaptation, testing
    in hereditary retinal/choroidal dystrophies,
        12:224*t*
    in siderosis, **12**:328
specialized types of, **12**:37–39, 37*f*, 38*f*, 39*f*
in uveitis, **9**:95
in X-linked retinoschisis, **6**:295, **12**:36*f*, 247
Elementary body, *Chlamydia*, **8**:137
Elestat. *See* Epinastine
Elevated intracranial pressure. *See* Intracranial
    hypertension
Elevated intraocular pressure, **10**:3–4, 74
    aqueous humor dynamics and, **10**:3*f*, 13, 14*t*
    cataract surgery and, **11**:154
        epithelial downgrowth and, **11**:151
        expulsive suprachoroidal hemorrhage and, **11**:178
        flat or shallow anterior chamber and, **11**:152,
            153–154, 154
        in glaucoma, **11**:75, 201, 202
        retrobulbar hemorrhage and, **11**:176
        stromal/epithelial corneal edema and, **11**:147
    central retinal artery occlusion and, **12**:140
    central retinal vein occlusion and, **10**:77, **12**:129, 130
    in chemical injury, management and, **8**:358
    in children, **10**:143, 150–151
    cholesterol levels and, **1**:139
    conjunctiva affected by, **10**:29
    corneal blood staining and, **4**:92–93
    corticosteroids causing, **2**:359–360, 360*t*, 361,
        10:103–104
        optic nerve damage and, **10**:81, 103
        after refractive surgery, **13**:35, 96–97, 173–174,
            173*f*, 194, 195
        uveitis and, **9**:103, 105, 295, 297, **10**:103
    cycloplegics causing, **2**:341
    diurnal variation in, **10**:22, 74, 80
    drugs for. *See specific agent and* Antiglaucoma agents
    episcleral venous pressure and, **10**:13, 14*t*, 19–20,
        95–96
    in exfoliation syndrome, **10**:85–86
    factors causing, **10**:21–22, 21*t*
    frequency of, **10**:20, 20*f*
    in glaucoma, **10**:3–4
        angle closure/angle-closure glaucoma, **10**:110
            acute, **10**:5*t*, 114–116
            chronic, **10**:5*t*, 117
            subacute/intermittent, **10**:117
        angle-recession glaucoma, **10**:101
        cataract surgery and, **11**:75, 201, 202
        childhood glaucoma and, **6**:234, 235, 236, 243–244,
            10:143, 150–151
        combined-mechanism, **10**:6
        corticosteroids after refractive surgery and, **13**:35,
            173–174, 173*f*, 194, 195
        ghost cell glaucoma, **10**:99–100
        glaucoma risk and, **10**:9, 20–21, 73, 74
        glaucomatocyclitic crisis (Posner-Schlossman
            syndrome) and, **10**:94
        hemolytic glaucoma, **10**:99–100

indications for surgery and, **10**:184–185
optic neuropathy and, **10**:44–45
phacolytic glaucoma and, **9**:126, **11**:63
pigmentary glaucoma, **10**:89
postoperative, **10**:101–102
uveitis and, **9**:294, 295, **10**:93, 94
glaucoma without, **10**:4, 5*t*, 78–82, 80*t*. *See also*
    Glaucoma, normal-tension
in glaucomatocyclitic crisis (Posner-Schlossman
    syndrome), **10**:94
in hyphema, **8**:366, 367
    in children, **6**:409, 410
    surgery and, **8**:368, 369*t*
hyphema causing, **10**:97–99
indications for surgery and, **10**:184–185
after laser trabeculoplasty, **10**:101, 182–183
after LASIK, **13**:97, 112, 172–175, 194–195
    pressure-induced stromal keratitis and (PISK),
        13:112, 112*f*
lens epithelium affected by, **4**:124
nasal CPAP affecting, **1**:144
Nd:YAG laser capsulotomy and, **11**:173–175
in ocular ischemic syndrome, **12**:133
optic neuropathy and, **10**:44–45
after penetrating keratoplasty, **8**:421
after phakic intraocular lens insertion, **13**:133*t*
    angle-supported PIOLs, **13**:134–135
    iris-fixated PIOLs, **13**:135
    posterior chamber PIOLs, **13**:136
after photoablation, **13**:96–97
postoperative, **10**:101–102
    after combined cataract and filtering surgery,
        10:199
    after glaucoma drainage device implantation,
        10:207
refractive surgery and, **13**:35, 172–175, 173*f*, 194–195
retinal detachment and, **10**:102–103
in sickle cell hemoglobinopathies, **10**:98–99
after surface ablation, **13**:96–97, 194–195
in Terson syndrome, **12**:155
trauma and, **7**:105, **10**:96–102
in uveitis, **9**:294, 295
    corticosteroid-induced, **9**:103, 105, 295, 297,
        10:103
    glaucoma and, **9**:294, 295, **10**:93, 94
    herpetic infection and, **9**:199
in Valsalva retinopathy, **12**:153
Elevation-based tomography, **13**:15–16, 15*f*, 16*f*
    postoperative, **13**:17
Elevation of eye (upgaze), **6**:33, 35
    disorders/limitation of, **5**:210–211
        in blowout fractures, **6**:125, **7**:100–101
            surgery and, **7**:102
        in Brown syndrome, **5**:239–240, 240*f*, **6**:130, 131,
            131*f*
        in inferior oblique muscle paralysis, **6**:122
        monocular deficiency (double elevator palsy) and,
            6:123–124, 123*f*, **7**:205
        in newborns, **5**:212
    extraocular muscles controlling, **5**:55–56, 56*f*
        inferior oblique, **5**:56, 56*f*, **6**:15, 17*t*, 29, 29*t*, 32, 34*f*
        superior rectus, **5**:55, 56*f*, **6**:14, 17*t*, 29*t*, 31, 31*f*
    3-step test in evaluation of, **6**:83–86, 85*f*

11p13 syndrome (short arm 11 deletion syndrome), 2:205–207
in aniridia, 4:188
ELISA. *See* Enzyme-linked immunosorbent assay
Ellipsoid
Cartesian, 3:54, 54*f*
photoreceptor, 12:10
of cone, 2:74, 76*f*
of rod, 2:73, 76*f*
Elliptically polarized light, 3:10
ELM. *See* External limiting membrane
ELOV4/ELOVL4 gene, in Stargardt disease, 4:172, 12:234
ELP. *See* Estimated lens position
Elschnig pearls, 4:125–126, 126*f*, 11:170
Elschnig ring, 10:42
Elschnig spots, 12:114, 115*f*, 177
in polyarteritis nodosa/microscopic polyangiitis, 9:143
Elspar. *See* Asparaginase
Emadine. *See* Emedastine
Emboli
branch retinal artery occlusion and, 12:136, 137
central retinal artery occlusion and, 12:139
cholesterol (Hollenhorst plaques)
in branch retinal artery occlusion, 4:163, 12:136, 137*f*
in central retinal artery occlusion, 12:139
transient visual loss and, 5:175*f*, 177, 179*t*
choroidal perfusion abnormalities and, 12:179
Purtscherlike retinopathy and, 12:154, 155*t*
retinal vasculitis and, 12:141
stroke caused by, 1:92
transient visual loss caused by, 5:175*f*, 176*t*, 177–183, 178*f*, 179*f*, 179*t*, 181*t*
clinical/laboratory evaluation of carotid artery disease and, 5:180–181
prognosis/stroke risk and, 5:181, 181*t*
treatment of carotid artery disease and, 5:181–183
Embryogenesis, 2:117–120, 118*f*, 119*f*, 121*f*, 122*t*. *See also* Eye, development of
Embryology. *See* Congenital anomalies; Eye, development of
Embryonal rhabdomyosarcoma, 4:243, 243*f*, 6:335, 7:77
Embryonic fissure, 2:121, 123, 124*f*
closure of, 2:123, 125*f*
colobomas and, 2:123, 125*f*
persistence of, in fetal alcohol syndrome, 2:143
Embryonic lens nucleus, 2:130, 4:120, 11:9, 22–23, 23*f*
opacification of (congenital nuclear cataract), 11:33, 34*f*
Embryotoxon, posterior, 2:141, 4:102–103, 103*f*, 104*f*, 6:212, 212*f*, 8:255, 256*f*, 261*t*. *See also* Anterior segment, dysgenesis of; Neurocristopathy
in Axenfeld-Rieger syndrome, 4:102–103, 103*f*, 104*f*, 6:212, 212*f*, 213, 8:256, 10:30, 146
isolated, Axenfeld-Rieger syndrome differentiated from, 10:146*t*
Emedastine, 2:364, 365*t*
Emergencies, 1:289–302. *See also specific type*
cardiopulmonary arrest, 1:289–293, 292*t*
medications used in, 1:292*t*
ocular side effects of systemic medications, 1:201–202*t*, 300–302

recent developments and, 1:289
seizures/status epilepticus, 1:297–298
shock, 1:293–296
toxic overdose, 1:298–299, 298*t*
Emergency kit, personal, 1:296
Emergency Medical Service (EMS) system, 1:290
EMGT (Early Manifest Glaucoma Trial), 10:78, 82, 86, 106
Emissaria/emissarial channels, 2:48, 4:111*f*, 112, 112*f*
melanoma spread via, 4:198, 198*f*
Emission, spontaneous and stimulated, in lasers, 3:21, 21–23, 23*f*
Emmetropia, 3:113, 113*f*
Emmetropization, 3:117, 6:169
Emollients, ocular, 2:390, 391
Emphysema, 1:142
Emphysema (ocular), of orbit and eyelids, in blowout fractures, 7:101
Empirical horopter, 6:39–40, 40*f*
EMS (Emergency Medical Service) system, 1:290
Emtricitabine, 1:34
Emtriva. *See* Emtricitabine
Emulsification. *See also* Phacoemulsification
locations of, 11:119–120, 120*f*, 121*f*
En grappe nerve endings, for tonic (slow twitch) fibers, 2:21, 5:55
En plaque nerve endings, for fast twitch fibers, 2:21, 5:55
Enalapril/enalaprilat
for heart failure, 1:118, 119
for hypertension, 1:76*t*, 78*t*, 83
for non–ST-segment elevation acute coronary syndrome, 1:111
ocular effects of, 1:302*t*
Enantiomorphism, in keratoconus, 8:297
Enbrel. *See* Etanercept
Encapsulation, polysaccharide, as microbial virulence factor, 1:4
Encephalitis
brainstem
CMV infection causing, 5:359
saccadic intrusions and, 5:256
herpes, 1:22, 5:359, 360*f*
acute retinal necrosis and, 9:202
Encephalitozoon, 8:141
keratoconjunctivitis caused by, 8:170
Encephaloceles, 7:35
orbital region, 6:346, 7:35
Encephalofacial/encephalotrigeminal angiomatosis (Sturge-Weber syndrome), 5:339*t*, 341–342, 343*f*, 6:342, 364*t*, 375–378, 376*f*, 377*f*, 10:28, 147–148
choroidal hemangioma in, 4:200, 292, 6:377, 377*f*, 12:181
glaucoma associated with, 5:341, 343*f*, 10:28, 147–148
in children, 5:341, 343*f*, 6:238, 377, 378, 10:147–148
port-wine stain (nevus flammeus) in, 5:341, 343*f*, 6:238, 342, 375, 376, 376*f*, 8:241, 10:28, 147
Encephalomyelitis, acute disseminated, optic nerve involvement and, 4:252
Encephalopathy
HIV, 1:29, 5:359–360
inherited, migrainelike headache and, 5:300

Leigh necrotizing (Leigh syndrome), **2**:176, 213*t*
  mitochondrial DNA mutation and, **2**:174*f*, 176
  posterior reversible, **5**:346, 346*f*
  transmissible spongiform, **5**:368
Encephalotrigeminal angiomatosis. *See* Encephalofacial/
  encephalotrigeminal angiomatosis
Enchondromas, in Maffucci syndrome, **6**:340
Enclavation, **13**:129
Encopred. *See* Prednisolone
End-stopped cells/neurons, **5**:34
Endarterectomy, carotid
  for carotid stenosis, **1**:91, 95, 95–97, **5**:181–182
  for ocular ischemic syndrome, **9**:288, **12**:134–135
Endarteritis, in syphilis, **1**:13
Endemic Kaposi sarcoma, **9**:312
Endocarditis/endocarditis prophylaxis, **1**:6, 7, 8*t*
  ocular surgery and, **1**:307
Endocrine action, of cytokines, **9**:27
Endocrine disorders, **1**:189–217. *See also specific type*
  diabetes mellitus, **1**:189–208
  hypothalamic-pituitary axis and, **1**:214–216
  multiple endocrine neoplasia syndromes, **1**:216–217
  recent developments in, **1**:189
  thyroid disease, **1**:208–214
Endocrinopathies. *See* Endocrine disorders
Endoderm, **2**:117, 119*f*, 120*f*
Endoepithelial corneal dystrophy. *See* Fuchs endothelial
  corneal dystrophy
Endoflagella, of spirochetes, **8**:137
Endogenous antigens, **8**:407. *See also* Human leukocyte
  antigens
Endogenous endophthalmitis, **9**:269, 271–280. *See also*
  Endophthalmitis
Endogenous infection, uveal, **4**:188
Endokeratoplasty, **4**:79. *See also* Descemet stripping/
  Descemet stripping automated endothelial
  keratoplasty
Endometrial tissue sampling, for cancer screening, **1**:272*t*
Endonasal dacryocystorhinostomy, **7**:268–270, 270*f*
Endonucleases, **2**:151. *See also* Restriction
  endonucleases
Endophthalmitis, **9**:269–280
  bacterial, **12**:202–203, 202*f*
    endogenous, **9**:271–273, 272*f*
    postoperative, **9**:269–270, 270*f*
    toxins affecting severity of, **9**:16
    vitreous affected in, **4**:133, 134*f*
  bleb-associated, **10**:196, 197*f*, **12**:354, 356–357, 357*f*
  corticosteroid route of administration in, **2**:360*t*
  endogenous, **9**:269, 271–280
    Aspergillus/molds causing, **9**:273–274, 276–278,
      277*f*, **12**:203–204, 205*f*
    bacterial, **9**:271–273, 272*f*, **12**:202–203, 202*f*
    Candida/yeasts causing, **9**:273–274, 274–276, 275*f*,
      12:203, 204*f*
    in coccidioidomycosis, **9**:273–274, 279–280, 279*f*
    in cryptococcosis, **9**:278–279
    fungal, **9**:273–280, 273*f*, 275*f*, 277*f*, 279*f*,
      12:203–204, 204*f*
  evisceration for, **7**:120
  fungal, **12**:203–204, 204*f*
    endogenous, **9**:273–280, 273*f*, 275*f*, 277*f*, 279*f*,
      12:203–204, 204*f*

iris nodule in, **4**:270*t*
  postoperative, **9**:270
  infectious, **4**:133, 134*f*, **9**:126. *See also specific type and
    causative agent*
  intraocular specimens for diagnosis of, **9**:270–271,
    272–273
  after penetrating keratoplasty, **8**:422
  after perforating injury, **8**:375
  phacoanaphylactic/lens-induced granulomatous
    (phacoantigenic/lens-associated uveitis), **4**:122,
      122*f*, 123*f*, **9**:125–126, 125*f*, **11**:62
  sympathetic ophthalmia and, **9**:182
  postoperative, **9**:126, 269–271, 270*f*, **12**:354–357,
    355*f*, 356*f*, 357*f*
    acute-onset, **9**:269, **12**:354, 354–356, 355*f*
    bleb-associated, **10**:196, 197*f*, **12**:354, 356–357, 357*f*
    after cataract surgery, **4**:123, 123*f*, 124, **9**:269–271,
      11:143, 144*t*, 179–181, 179*f*
      prevention of, **11**:127–129, 128*f*, 180
    chronic (delayed-onset), **9**:269–271, 270*f*, **12**:355,
      356, 356*f*
      bacterial, **9**:269–270, 270*f*
      fungal, **9**:270
    prophylaxis of, **11**:127–129, 128*f*, 180
    Propionibacterium acnes causing, **9**:126, 269–270,
      270*f*
  after strabismus surgery, **6**:156
  after vitrectomy, **12**:368
  vitrectomy for, **12**:354–357, 355*f*, 356*f*, 357*f*
  posttraumatic, **12**:328–329
    Propionibacterium acnes causing, **4**:123, 123*f*, 124,
      9:126, **12**:354, 356
  sterile, **9**:269
  in toxocariasis, **9**:235, 236*t*
Endophthalmitis Vitrectomy Study (EVS), **11**:179, 180,
  12:354, 355
Endoscopic brow and forehead lift, **7**:232, 233*f*
Endoscopic brow lift, pretrichial approach, **7**:232
Endoscopic cyclophotocoagulation/endoscopic laser
  delivery, **10**:210. *See also* Cyclophotocoagulation/
  cycloablation
  for childhood glaucoma, **6**:241, 242*f*, **10**:155–156
Endoscopic dacryocystorhinostomy, **7**:269
Endoscopic subperiosteal midface lift, **7**:234, 235*f*
Endoscopy, nasal, for lacrimal drainage evaluation,
  7:261
Endothelial cell density, specular photomicroscopy in
  evaluation of, **8**:32, 32*f*
Endothelial degenerations, **8**:344–345, 344*f*
Endothelial dystrophies, **4**:98–100, 100*f*, **8**:268*t*, 291–296
  cataract surgery in patient with, **11**:192
  congenital hereditary, **4**:79–80, 79*f*, **6**:216*t*, 217,
    8:260–263, 268*t*, 270*t*, 295–296, 295*f*
    CHED1, **8**:260, 268*t*, 270*t*, 295–296, 295*f*
    CHED2, **8**:260, 268*t*, 270*t*, 296, 296*f*
    genetics of, **8**:269*t*, 295, 296
  Fuchs, **2**:47, 47*f*, **4**:98–100, 100*f*, **8**:268*t*, 270*t*, 291–293,
    292*f*
    genetics of, **8**:269*t*, 291
    refractive surgery and, **13**:35
  posterior polymorphous, **4**:80, 80*f*, **8**:268*t*, 270*t*,
    293–295, 294*f*
    genetics of, **4**:80, **8**:269*t*, 293

Endothelial failure
after Descemet stripping automated endothelial keratoplasty, primary, 8:444–445
after penetrating keratoplasty, 4:91, 92f
late nonimmune, 8:425–426
primary, 8:422, 422f
Endothelial graft rejection, 8:429, 429f. *See also* Rejection
Endothelial keratoplasty. *See* Keratoplasty, endothelial
Endothelial meshwork, 2:54
Endothelial pump
corneal edema and, 8:29
corneal hydration and, 8:8
Endothelial rings, corneal, traumatic, 8:363
Endotheliitis (disciform keratitis), herpes simplex virus causing, 4:83, 8:114, 114f
persistent bullous keratopathy and, 8:117
Endothelin receptors, in signal transduction, 2:264t
Endothelium
corneal, 2:46–47, 247f, 251, 4:77–78, 78f, 8:7f, 8–9
anatomy of, 2:46–47, 46f, 47f, 247f, 8:7f, 8–9
biochemistry and metabolism of, 2:251
development of, 2:133, 134f, 135, 8:4
dysfunction of, corneal edema and, 8:25
glucose metabolism in, 2:248
healing/repair of, 4:15–16, 15f
keratorefractive surgery and, 13:26
intraocular surgery causing changes in, 8:383, 383–385
phakic IOLs affecting, 13:133t
angle-supported PIOLs, 13:134–135
iris-fixated PIOLs, 13:135
posterior chamber PIOLs, 13:136
photoablation and, 13:97
pigmentation of, 8:349
in uveitis, 9:86t
retinal blood vessel, 2:78
Endotoxins, microbial, 8:132
endophthalmitis severity and, 9:16
in innate immune response, 9:14–15, 14t
virulence and, 1:4
Energy
for medical lasers, 3:18t, 21
phaco, 11:103, 126. *See also* Power
advances in, 11:126
Energy production
in lens, 2:278–279
in retinal pigment epithelium, 2:304
in rods, 2:293
Enfuvirtide, 1:34
Engerix-B. *See* Hepatitis B vaccine
Enhanced depth imaging, in central serous chorioretinopathy, 12:173
Enhanced S-cone/blue-cone syndrome, 12:218–219, 219f, 248. *See also* Goldmann-Favre disease/syndrome
Enhancer, 2:151
Enlon. *See* Edrophonium
Enolase antibodies, retinopathy associated with, 12:256
Enophthalmos, 5:278, 7:22
in blowout fractures, 6:126, 7:98–100, 101
surgery and, 7:102, 103
cataract surgery in patient with, 11:77
orbital varices and, 7:66–67

Enoxacin, 1:52t, 61
Enoxaparin, for non–ST-segment elevation acute coronary syndrome, 1:111–112
Entacapone, for Parkinson disease, 1:259
Enteritis, regional (Crohn disease), 1:165, 9:123
Enterobacter/Enterobacteriaceae, 8:135
Enterococcus, 8:133–134
faecalis, 8:133–134
postoperative endophthalmitis caused by, 11:180
vancomycin-resistant, 1:3, 5, 60
Enterocolitis, pseudomembranous, *Clostridium difficile* causing, 1:8–9
Enterocytozoon, 8:141
Enteropancreatic tumors, in multiple endocrine neoplasia, 1:216
Enteropathic arthritis, 1:165
Enteroviruses, 8:129
conjunctivitis caused by, 8:130
Enthesitis
in juvenile idiopathic (chronic/rheumatoid) arthritis, 6:269t, 271
in spondyloarthropathies/spondyloarthritis, 1:163, 6:271
Entrance pupil, 3:108
blurred retinal images and, 3:312, 312f
location effect of cylindrical lenses and, 3:313–314, 313f
spectacle lens distance from, distortion and, 3:311
Entropion, 7:194–199
acute spastic, 7:194, 195f
cicatricial, 7:197–199, 198f, 199f
congenital, 6:176, 7:149–150, 150f
involutional, 7:194–196, 195f, 197f
lash margin, in anophthalmic socket, 7:125
Enucleation, 7:117, 117–119
in childhood, 7:119
guidelines for, 7:118–119
intraoperative complications of, 7:119
for melanoma, 4:283, 7:118
ocular prostheses after, 7:122
orbital implants after, 7:121–122
ptosis/extraocular muscle damage and, 7:119
removal of wrong eye and, 7:119
for retinoblastoma, 4:310, 6:358, 7:118
rubeosis iridis and, 4:192, 193f
for sympathetic ophthalmia prevention, 4:189, 7:117, 118, 8:376, 9:182, 12:198–199, 329
for uveal lymphoid infiltration, 4:326
Envelope (virus)/enveloped viruses, 8:104, 105
Environment/environmental factors
in dry-eye syndrome, 8:51–52, 51f
in glaucoma, 10:12
Enzymatic method, for DNA sequencing, 2:184, 185f
Enzymatic vitreolysis, 2:289
Enzyme defects, disorders associated with, 2:212–214, 213t, 6:397, 398, 400–401t
management of, 2:231–232, 6:399–402
recessive inheritance of, 2:212–214, 213t
Enzyme-linked immunosorbent assay (ELISA)
in cysticercosis, 9:238
in HIV infection/AIDS, 1:31
in leptospirosis, 9:255
in Lyme disease, 1:16, 9:252
in meningococcal infection, 1:10

in syphilis, 9:248
in toxocariasis, 9:236, 237
in toxoplasmosis, 9:230
in tuberculosis, 9:261
Enzymes, in aqueous humor, 2:269–270
EOG. *See* Electro-oculogram
EOMs. *See* Extraocular muscles
Eosinophil chemotactic factor, 8:179*t*
Eosinophilic (oxyphilic) cystadenoma (oncocytoma), 4:75, 75*f*, 8:233
Eosinophilic granuloma of bone, 7:84. *See also* Histiocytosis
    orbital, 7:84
        in children, 6:337, 338*f*
Eosinophils, 4:7, 8*f*, 9:10
    cytologic identification of, in immune-mediated keratoconjunctivitis, 8:182*t*
    in external eye, 8:174*t*
    mediators released by, 8:179*t*
Eotaxin, 8:179*t*
Eperezolid, 1:53*t*, 64
EPHA2 gene, in age-related cataracts, 11:37
Ephelis, 4:224. *See also* Freckle
    conjunctival, 8:233
    of eyelid, 7:164–165
Epi-LASIK. *See* Epipolis-LASIK
Epiblast, 2:117, 118*f*
Epiblepharon, 6:176, 7:148, 148*f*, 149*f*
Epibulbar tumors
    in children, 6:333*t*, 347–351
    choristomas, 8:245–247, 246*f*, 247*f*
    dermoids, 6:348, 8:245–246, 245*f*
        Goldenhar syndrome and, 6:218, 349*f*, 393, 393*f*, 8:246
Epicanthus, 6:177–178, 178*f*, 7:147–148, 148*f*, 149*f*
    inversus, 6:177, 7:147
        in blepharophimosis syndrome, 6:178, 179*f*, 7:145, 147
    palpebralis, 6:177, 178*f*, 7:147
    supraciliaris, 6:177, 7:147
    tarsalis, 6:177, 178*f*, 7:147
Epicapsular star, 11:27, 28*f*
Epidemic Kaposi sarcoma, 9:312
Epidemic keratoconjunctivitis, 8:124, 125, 125*f*, 126*f*
    in children, 6:191
        preseptal cellulitis caused by, 6:195
Epidermal/epidermoid cysts
    of eyelid, 4:213, 213*f*, 7:158–159, 159*f*
    of orbit, 4:229–230, 6:343, 7:36
Epidermal growth factor, 2:395–396
    in tear film, 2:241
Epidermal growth factor–containing fibrillinlike extracellular matrix protein (EFEMP1) mutations, 2:297, 12:239
Epidermal necrolysis, toxic, 8:196, 196*t*
Epidermis, eyelid, 4:205, 206*f*, 8:4
    neoplasms of, 4:214–219, 214*f*, 215*f*, 215*t*, 216*f*, 217*f*, 218*f*, 219*f*, 220*f*, 7:155. *See also* Eyelids, tumors of
        benign, 7:158–160, 159*f*, 160*f*
        premalignant, 7:166, 167*f*
Epidermoid/epidermal cysts
    of eyelid, 4:213, 213*f*, 7:158–159, 159*f*
    of orbit, 4:229–230, 6:343, 7:36
Epidermolysis bullosa acquisita, 8:205*t*

Epifrin. *See* Epinephrine
Epigastric thrusts, 1:292
Epikeratoplasty (epikeratophakia), 13:4*t*, 21, 53, 55, 55*f*
Epilation, for trichiasis, 7:200, 8:89
Epilepsy, 1:260–264. *See also* Seizures
    hallucinations and, 5:190
    transient visual loss and, 5:186
Epilepsy Information Line, 6:418*t*
Epimerase deficiency, galactosemia/cataract formation and, 11:57
Epimyoepithelial islands, 7:88
Epinastine, 2:365*t*, 366
Epinephrine, 2:347*t*
    adrenergic agents/receptor response and, 2:344–351, 345*f*
    adrenochrome deposition caused by, 8:337*t*, 348, 348*f*
    for anaphylaxis, 1:292*t*, 295, 296
    dipivalyl. *See* Dipivefrin
    for glaucoma, 10:168–169
        in children, 6:243
    with local anesthetic, 1:298*t*, 299, 2:388
        for blepharoplasty, 7:224
        for dacryocystorhinostomy, 7:268
        maximum safe dosage and, 1:298*t*
        toxic reaction to, 1:299
    for medical emergencies, 1:292*t*, 295, 296
    in personal emergency kits, 1:296
    for pulmonary diseases, 1:145
"Epipapillary vessels," 10:42–43
EpiPen/EpiPen Jr, 1:296
Epiphora, 7:256, 257. *See also* Tearing
Epipolis LASIK (epi-LASIK), 13:4*t*, 65. *See also* Surface ablation
    complications/side effects of, 13:102
    corneal preparation for, 13:76–77
    epithelial debridement for, 13:75, 76*f*
    epithelial preservation techniques for, 13:76–77
    glaucoma/ocular hypertension and, 13:172–175, 173*f*
    immediate postablation measures for, 13:85
    international trends in use of, 13:199
Epiretinal membrane, 12:298–301, 302*f*, 346, 347*f*, 348*f*
    in birdshot retinochoroidopathy, 9:152
    in multifocal choroiditis and panuveitis syndrome, 9:162
    vitrectomy for, 12:301, 346, 347*f*, 348*f*
Episclera, 2:48, 4:111, 111*f*
    disorders of. *See also specific type and* Episcleritis
        immune-mediated, 8:216–217, 217*f*
    in glaucoma, 10:29
    melanosis of, 8:235–236, 235*f*
    nodular fasciitis causing tumor of, 4:118, 118*f*
Episcleral artery, 5:14*f*
Episcleral plexus, 2:62, 5:24
Episcleral (sub-Tenon) surgical space, 7:107*f*, 108
Episcleral venous plexus, 10:3*f*
Episcleral venous pressure, 10:19–20
    elevated, 10:95–96, 95*t*, 96*f*
        adnexal signs of, 10:28
        in infants and children, 10:142*t*
        intraocular pressure and, 10:13, 14*t*, 19–20, 95–96
        open-angle glaucoma caused by, 10:95–96, 95*t*, 96*f*
            Sturge-Weber syndrome and, 10:147
    normal, 10:95

Episcleritis, 4:113, 113f, 8:21t, 28, 216–217, 217f
  in Chikungunya fever, 9:220
  corticosteroid route of administration in, 2:360t
  in herpes zoster, 8:120
  immune-mediated, 8:216–217, 217f
  in Lyme disease, 9:251, 253
  nodular, 4:113, 8:28, 216, 217f
    in children, 6:351
  in reactive arthritis/Reiter syndrome, 8:209
  simple (diffuse), 4:113, 113f, 8:28, 216
  in Stevens-Johnson syndrome, 8:196
Epithelial cells. See also Epithelium
  keratinization of (keratinized/degenerated), 8:21
    cytologic identification of, in immune-mediated
        keratoconjunctivitis, 8:182t
    in meibomian gland dysfunction, 8:65
    in vitamin A deficiency, 8:77, 78, 78f
Epithelial cysts. See also Epithelial inclusion cysts
  of cornea, drug-induced, 8:348
  of eyelids, benign, 7:158–159, 159f
  of orbit, 4:229–230, 6:343, 7:36
Epithelial debridement. See Debridement
Epithelial defects
  conjunctival, 8:20t
  corneal/persistent corneal, 8:21t, 85–87
    after cataract surgery, 11:150
    glaucoma medication toxicity and, 10:29
    after LASIK, 13:104–105
      in diabetes mellitus, 13:183–184
    ocular infection and, 8:99
    after penetrating keratoplasty, 8:422, 423f
    refractive surgery in patients with, 13:35, 36f
    after surface ablation, 13:100
    in toxic keratoconjunctivitis, 8:360
Epithelial degenerations, 8:334–336, 335f
Epithelial downgrowth. See Epithelial ingrowth
    (downgrowth)
Epithelial/subepithelial dystrophies, 4:95, 95f, 8:268t,
    270–275
  basement membrane (map-dot-fingerprint/Cogan
      microcystic/anterior basement membrane), 4:95,
      95f, 8:268t, 270–272, 270t, 271f
    cataract surgery in patient with, 11:191, 192f
    genetics of, 8:269t, 270
    recurrent corneal erosion and, 8:83, 271, 272
    refractive surgery in patients with, 13:35, 37f,
        67–68, 70, 71
  Lisch, 8:268t, 270t, 273–274, 274f
    genetics of, 8:269t, 273
  Meesmann (juvenile hereditary epithelial), 8:268t,
      270t, 272–273, 273f
    genetics of, 8:269t, 272
Epithelial edema, 8:20t. See also Cornea, edema of
  central (Sattler veil), 8:91
  intraocular surgery causing, 8:383
Epithelial erosions
  herpetic keratitis and, 8:117
  punctate
    of conjunctiva, 8:20t
    of cornea, 8:20t, 25, 26f, 27t
      vernal keratoconjunctivitis and, 8:187
    refractive surgery in patient with, 13:35, 36f
Epithelial graft rejection, 8:428, 428f, 436. See also
    Rejection

Epithelial hyperplasias, of eyelids, 7:157–158, 157f,
    158f
Epithelial inclusion cysts, conjunctival, 4:59–60, 60f,
    8:225–226, 226f
  in children, 6:157, 157f, 348
  nevi and, 4:65
  after strabismus surgery, 6:157, 157f
Epithelial ingrowth (downgrowth)
  angle-closure glaucoma and, 10:133–134, 134f
  cataract surgery and, 11:151
  corneal graft failure and, 4:91, 92f
  after Descemet stripping automated endothelial
      keratoplasty, 8:444, 444f
  after LASIK, 13:112–114, 113f
    in diabetes mellitus, 13:183–184
Epithelial invasion of iris, 4:270t
Epithelial keratitis/keratopathy
  adenoviral, 8:124, 126f
  dry eye and, 8:55, 56, 56f
  herpes simplex virus causing, 8:110–113, 111f, 112f
  in herpes zoster ophthalmicus, 8:120
  measles virus causing, 8:129, 9:212
  punctate, 8:20t, 25, 26f, 27t
    exposure causing, 8:80
    herpes simplex virus causing, 8:110
    microsporidial, 8:170
    staphylococcal blepharitis/blepharoconjunctivitis
        and, 8:145, 146f, 147
    superficial Thygeson, 8:204–207, 206f
Epithelial melanosis, congenital, 8:233
Epithelial slough/slide, LASIK and, 13:104
Epithelial tumors, 4:10t, 11f, 8:226–233, 226t
  benign, 8:226–228, 226t, 227f
  of conjunctiva, 8:226–233, 226t
  of cornea, 8:226–233, 226t
  of eyelids
    benign, 7:157–160, 157f, 158f, 159f, 160f
    in situ, 7:167–168, 167f
  of lacrimal glands, 7:86–88, 86f
    exenteration for, 7:87, 126
  malignant, 8:226t, 231–233, 232f
  pigmented, of uvea and retina, 4:288–289, 289f
  preinvasive, 8:226t, 228–231, 229f, 230f, 231f
    pigmented, 8:234t, 237–238
Epithelial ulcer, geographic, in herpes simplex keratitis,
    8:110, 112f
Epitheliitis, acute retinal pigment (ARPE/Krill disease),
    9:148–150t, 170, 170f, 12:193–194
Epithelioid (Leber) cells, 9:11, 22. See also Macrophages
  in choroidal/ciliary body melanoma, 4:196, 199
  in sarcoidosis, 9:173
Epithelioid histiocytes, 4:7, 8f
Epitheliopathy
  acute posterior multifocal placoid pigment
      (APMPPE), 9:148–150t, 155–158, 156f, 157f, 158f,
      12:185–187, 186t, 187f
  in herpetic keratitis, 8:116–117
  microcystic, 8:91
  in toxic keratoconjunctivitis, 8:360
Epithelium. See also under Epithelial and Ocular surface
  ciliary, 2:61–63, 62f, 265
    aqueous humor formation and, 2:254, 265, 266–267,
        270
    development of, 2:137

nonpigmented, **2:**62, 62*f*, 265
  benign adenomas of, **4:**288
pigmented, **2:**62, 62*f*, 265
  acquired hyperplasia of, **4:**288
  benign adenomas of, **4:**288
conjunctival, **2:**35, 239*f*, **4:**47, 48*f*, **8:**5
  cysts of, **4:**59–60, 60*f*, **8:**225–226, 226*f*
  nevi and, **4:**65
  dysplasia of (conjunctival intraepithelial
    neoplasia), **4:**62, 63*f*, 64*f*, **8:**226*t*, 228–229,
    229*f*, 230*f*. *See also* Ocular surface squamous
    neoplasia
  evaluation of in pseudoepiphora, **7:**257
  immunologic features of, **8:**173, 174*t*
  tear secretion and, **2:**239*f*, 240, 241
  tumors of, **8:**226–233, 226*t*
  wound healing/repair and, **8:**388
corneal. *See* Cornea, epithelium of
development of, **8:**4
in external eye defense, **8:**96
eyelid
  benign lesions of, **7:**157–160, 157*f*, 158*f*, 159*f*, 160*f*
  hyperplasia of, **7:**157–158, 157*f*, 158*f*
  in situ carcinoma of, **7:**167–168, 167*f*
  immune and inflammatory cells in, **8:**174*t*
  iris pigment. *See* Iris pigment epithelium
  lens, **2:**68, 68*f*, 69*f*, 70, 274, 274*f*, **4:**119–120, 120*f*,
    11:6*f*, 8, 8*f*
    active transport and, **11:**17–18
    degenerations of, **4:**124–126, 125*f*, 126*f*. *See also*
      Cataract
    development of, **11:**23, 23*f*
    opacification of (capsular cataract), **11:**33–34
  retinal pigment. *See* Retinal pigment epithelium
  tumors of. *See* Epithelial tumors
Epitopes, **9:**36–37, 46
  in adaptive immunity, **1:**4, **9:**36–37, 46
Epivir. *See* Lamivudine
Eplerenone, **1:**76*t*
Epley procedure, for BPPV, **5:**250
Eprosartan, **1:**76*t*, 78*t*
Epsilon (ε)-crystallins, **2:**276
Epstein-Barr virus, **1:**24–25, **9:**208–209, 208*f*
  cancer association and, **1:**237
  dacryoadenitis caused by, **7:**273–274, **8:**122–123
  in multifocal choroiditis and panuveitis syndrome,
    9:164, 208
  ocular infection caused by, **6:**193, **8:**122–123, 123*f*,
    9:208–209, 208*f*
  Sjögren-like syndromes caused by, **8:**63
Epstein prepupillary intraocular lens, **3:**207, 208*f*
Eptifibatide, for ischemic heart disease, **1:**109, 109*t*
  non–ST-segment elevation acute coronary syndrome,
    1:112
Equator (lens), **2:**274, 274*f*, **4:**120, 120*f*, **11:**5, 6*f*
Equatorial lens bow, **4:**120, 120*f*
Equatorial retina, **12:**8
Equatorial streaks, in ocular histoplasmosis syndrome,
  9:221, 222*f*
Equine recurrent uveitis, **9:**69
Eraxis. *See* Anidulafungin
Erbium:YAG (Er:YAG) laser. *See also* Laser therapy
  for skin resurfacing, **7:**230

Erdheim-Chester disease (ECD), **7:**85
  eyelid manifestations of, **4:**213*t*
Erectile dysfunction, ocular effects of drugs for,
  1:302*t*
ERG. *See* Electroretinogram
ERM. *See* Epiretinal membrane
Erosions
  conjunctival, **8:**22*t*
    punctate epithelial, **8:**20*t*
  corneal
    epithelial
      punctate, **8:**20*t*, 25, 26*f*, 27*t*
        vernal keratoconjunctivitis and, **8:**187
        refractive surgery in patient with, **13:**35, 36*f*
      in herpetic keratitis, **8:**117
      recurrent, **8:**83–85, 85*f*
        eye pain in, **5:**300, **8:**83
        posttraumatic, **8:**372
  eyelid, **8:**20*t*
ERP. *See* Early receptor potentials
Ertapenem, **1:**50*t*, 59
Erysiphakes, **11:**92, 92*f*
Erythema, in thyroid eye disease, **7:**48*f*, 49
Erythema migrans/erythema chronicum migrans, in
  Lyme disease, **1:**15, **5:**363, 363*f*, **9:**250, 250*f*, 253*t*,
  12:210
Erythema multiforme, **8:**196
  major (Stevens-Johnson syndrome), **8:**195–198, 196*t*,
    197*f*, 198*f*
    in children, **6:**200–201, 201*f*
    mucous membrane grafting for, **8:**198, 401
  minor, **8:**196
Erythrocyte sedimentation rate
  in giant cell arteritis/AAION, **5:**126*t*, 320
    central retinal artery occlusion and, **12:**139
  in immune-mediated disease, **8:**182*t*
  in NAION, **5:**126*t*
Erythrocytes, **1:**147
  development of, **1:**147
  in hemolytic anemia, **1:**149
Erythromycin, **1:**50*t*, 61, **2:**368*t*, 372*t*, 377
  for chlamydial conjunctivitis, **8:**157
    in neonates, **6:**188, **8:**154
  intravenous administration of, **2:**329
  for meibomian gland dysfunction, **8:**68
  for ophthalmia neonatorum prophylaxis, **6:**188
  for trachoma, **8:**156
Erythropoiesis, **1:**147
Erythropoietin, **1:**147
  for HIV infection/AIDS, **1:**36
Escherichia coli (E coli), **8:**135
  endogenous endophthalmitis caused by, **9:**272
  as normal ocular flora, **8:**96
  ocular infection caused by, **8:**135
ESCS. *See* Enhanced S-cone/blue-cone syndrome
Eserine. *See* Physostigmine
Esidrix. *See* Hydrochlorothiazide
Esimil. *See* Guanethidine
Eskalith. *See* Lithium
Esmolol
  for arrhythmias, **1:**123*t*
  for hypertensive emergency, **1:**83
Eso- (prefix), **6:**9

Esodeviations, **6**:89–98, 90*t*. *See also specific type and*
  Esotropia
  divergence insufficiency/paralysis, **6**:97
  incomitant, **6**:90*t*, 98
  medial rectus muscle restriction causing, **6**:98
  negative angle kappa and, **6**:77, 78*f*
  sensory deprivation, **6**:96–97
  sixth nerve (abducens) paralysis causing, **6**:98
  strabismic amblyopia and, **6**:62
  surgery for, **6**:150–151, 150*t*
  thalamic, **5**:222*t*, 223
Esophageal cancer, screening for, **1**:275
Esophageal dysmotility, in scleroderma, **1**:173
Esophoria, **6**:89
  juvenile-onset myopia and, **3**:118
  prisms for, **3**:163
Esotropia, **6**:89. *See also* Esodeviations
  A-pattern, **6**:107–112, 109*f*
    treatment of, **6**:112
  accommodative, **6**:90*t*, 93–95
    muscarinic agents for management of, **2**:339
    refractive surgery and, **13**:181
  acute, **6**:96
  basic (acquired), **6**:95–96
  cyclic, **6**:96
  divergence insufficiency/paralysis, **6**:97
  in Duane syndrome, **6**:128, 128*f*, 129
  exotropia following surgery for (consecutive
    exotropia), **6**:105
  false appearance of (pseudoesotropia), **6**:89, 90*t*
  with high myopia, **6**:141
  hyperopia in children and, **3**:142
  incomitant, **6**:90*t*, 98
  infantile (congenital), **6**:89–92, 90*t*, 91*f*
  intermittent, **6**:89
  latent nystagmus and, **5**:246
  management of, **6**:103
  medial rectus muscle restriction causing, **6**:98
  in Möbius syndrome, **6**:140
  myopia in children and, **3**:141
  nonaccommodative acquired, **6**:90*t*, 95–98
  with nystagmus, **6**:90*t*, 92, 321. *See also* Nystagmus
  red-glass (diplopia) testing and, **6**:54
  sensory deprivation, **6**:96–97
  sixth nerve (abducens) paralysis causing, **6**:98, 134, 134*f*
  spasm of near synkinetic reflex and, **6**:97
  surgical (consecutive), **6**:97–98
    management of, **6**:103
  thalamic, convergence spasm and, **5**:214
  V-pattern, **6**:107–112, 108*f*
    treatment of, **6**:112
Essential (physiologic/simple) anisocoria, **5**:264, 265*f*,
  6:229
Essential blepharospasm, **5**:289–290, 289*t*, 290*f*,
  7:218–220, 219*f*
Essential cryoglobulinemic vasculitis, **1**:177*t*
Essential (primary) hypertension, **1**:71, 71*f*
Essential/progressive iris atrophy, **4**:104, 105*f*, **10**:128,
  129, 129*f*. *See also* Iridocorneal endothelial (ICE)
  syndrome
EST. *See* Expressed sequence tags
Estazolam, **1**:254
Esterase D, retinoblastoma and, **2**:177

Esthesiometry, **8**:30–31
Estimated lens position
  in IOL power determination, **3**:211–212, 217–219,
    218*f*
    formula errors after corneal refractive surgery and,
      3:221
Estradiol, ocular effects of, **1**:302*t*
Estrogen/hormone replacement therapy
  breast cancer risk and, **1**:273–274
  osteoporosis and, **1**:230
  refractive surgery in patient taking, **13**:31
Eszopiclone, **1**:254
ET/HRT. *See* Estrogen/hormone replacement therapy
Etafilcon, for contact lenses, **3**.177*t*
Etanercept, **1**:161, 186, **9**:114
  for cicatricial pemphigoid, **8**:202
  for uveitis, **9**:114
    in children, **6**:278
ETD. *See* Evaporative tear dysfunction
ETDRS (Early Treatment Diabetic Retinopathy Study),
  12:97, 98, 101–102, 104
  scatter laser treatment and, **12**:98, 102, 107, 108*f*
ETDRS visual acuity chart, **3**:110, 110*f*, **12**:102
  in branch retinal vein occlusion, **12**:127
  in central retinal vein occlusion, **12**:131
  in low vision, **3**:290
Ethambutol, **1**:19, 39
Ethanol. *See* Alcohol
Ethmoid/ethmoidal air cells/sinuses, **2**:7*f*, 8*f*, 12, 13*f*, 14*f*,
  5:7, 11*f*, **7**:18–19, 18*f*
Ethmoid/ethmoidal bone (lamina papyracea), **2**:7, **5**:5,
  7, 7*f*, 8*f*, 9, 9*f*, **7**:6*f*, 7*f*, 8, 246
Ethmoidal arteries, **2**:37*f*, 39*f*, **5**:12, 13*f*, 14*f*, 15–16, 18
Ethmoidal complex, **5**:7, 12
Ethmoidal foramina, anterior/posterior, **2**:8*f*, 10, **5**:12,
  7:6*f*, 7*f*, 8–9
Ethmoidal suture, frontal, **5**:7
Ethmoidectomy, for thyroid eye disease, **5**:334
Ethnic background. *See also* Race
  genetic disorders and, **2**:210–211
  hypertension and, **1**:87
  osteoporosis risk and, **1**:228
  spasmus nutans and, **5**:247
Ethosuximide, **1**:263*t*
Ethylene glycol
  crystalline maculopathy caused by, **12**:269
  optic neuropathy caused by, **5**:154
Ethylenediaminetetraacetic acid (EDTA)
  in artificial tears, **2**:391
  for band keratopathy, **2**:334, **8**:343
  in irrigating solutions, **2**:392
Etodolac, **1**:183*t*
Etoposide, **1**:239, 241*t*
Etravirine, **1**:34
ETROP (Early Treatment for Retinopathy of Prematurity)
  study, **6**:281, 283–285, 286, **12**:160, 166–167
Eukaryotes/eukaryotic cells, **2**:151, **8**:131
EULAR. *See* European League of Associations of
  Rheumatology
Eulexin. *See* Flutamide
European Carotid Surgery Trial, **1**:96
European Glaucoma Prevention Study (EGPS), **10**:86,
  159

European League of Associations of Rheumatology (EULAR), chronic childhood arthritis nomenclature and, 6:267–268, 269*t*

Euryblepharon, 6:177, 7:146–147, 148*f*, 149*f*

Evaporative tear dysfunction, 8:51, 51*f*, 52
   chalazion and, 8:72–73, 72*f*
   desquamating skin conditions and, 8:74
   ectodermal dysplasia and, 8:74–75
   ichthyosis and, 8:74
   meibomian gland dysfunction and, 8:65–69, 67*f*
   rosacea and, 8:69–71, 70*f*, 71*f*
   sarcoidosis and, 8:73–74
   seborrheic blepharitis and, 8:71–72
   xeroderma pigmentosum and, 8:75

Evasion, as microbial virulence factor, 8:98

Evernimicin, 1:53*t*, 64

Everninomicins, 1:53*t*, 64

Evisceration, 7:117, 119–120
   ocular prostheses after, 7:122
   sympathetic ophthalmia and, 7:120, 9:182, 12:329

Evista. *See* Raloxifene

Evoked cortical potentials, 12:44–45, 45*f*
   electrical, 12:45
   visual, 12:44–45, 45*f. See also* Visually evoked cortical potentials

Evolving stroke, 1:93

EVR1/EVR2/EVR4 genes, in familial exudative vitreoretinopathy, 12:310–311

EVS (Endophthalmitis Vitrectomy Study), 11:179, 180, 12:354, 355

EW. *See* Edinger-Westphal nucleus; Extended-wear contact lenses

Ewing sarcoma
   of orbit, 6:337
   retinoblastoma associated with, 4:314*t*

Exact ray tracing, 3:55, 55*f. See also* Ray tracing

Examination, ophthalmic, 8:11–46. *See also specific method used and* Refraction, clinical
   age-related macular degeneration follow-up and, 12:60
   under anesthesia
      in childhood glaucoma, 10:149, 149*t*
         for gonioscopy, 10:151–152
         for retinoblastoma, 4:301–302, 302*f*
   anterior segment photography in, 8:31–36, 32*f*, 33*f*, 34*f*, 35*f*, 36*f*
   before cataract surgery, 11:77–78, 78–80
   in children, 6:3–5
   for chloroquine/hydroxychloroquine toxicity, 12:267
   in contact lens selection, 3:179–180
   corneal pachymetry/pachometry in, 8:28–30, 29*f*, 30*t. See also* Pachymetry/pachymeter
   corneal topography measurement in, 8:36–45
   before corneal transplantation, 8:414–417
   in diabetes mellitus, timetables for, 12:111–112, 112*t*
   in diplopia, 5:215–218, 216*f*, 217*f*
   in dry eye, 8:52–53, 53*f*
   esthesiometry in, 8:30–31
   in glaucoma, 10:27–32
      in infants and children, 6:234–238, 236*f*, 237*f*, 10:149–152, 149*f*
   HIV infection precautions and, 9:314
   infection prevention and, 8:45–46

   in inflammatory chorioretinopathies, 9:149*t*
   in inflammatory disorders, 8:19–28, 20–21*t*, 22*t*, 27*t*
   in juvenile idiopathic (chronic/rheumatoid) arthritis, 6:270, 271*t*, 9:130, 131*f*
   in low vision evaluation, 5:92–110. *See also* Low vision, assessment of
   for nystagmus, 6:318–320, 320*t*
   in perforating injury, 8:373–374, 374*t*
   physical examination in, 8:11–12
   in primary congenital glaucoma, 6:234–238, 236*f*, 237*f*, 10:149–152, 149*f*
   before refractive surgery, 13:30*t*, 33–38, 36*f*, 37*f*
      ancillary tests and, 13:38–40, 38*f*
   in retinitis pigmentosa, 12:230
   for retinoblastoma, 4:301–302, 302*f*
   for retinopathy of prematurity, 6:285, 286*t*, 12:164–165
   slit-lamp. *See* Slit-lamp biomicroscopy/examination
   stains used in, 8:17, 18*f*, 19*f*
   for Sturge-Weber syndrome, 6:377–378
   in transient visual loss evaluation, 5:174–175, 175*f*
   vision testing, 8:11

Excavated optic disc
   congenital anomalies and, 5:143
   in glaucoma, 5:139–140, 141*f*

Excimer laser, 3:24, 24–25, 13:4*t*, 65–69. *See also* Lasers
   international trends in use of, 13:199
   for photoablation, 13:4*t*, 23, 23–24, 25, 25–26, 40, 41*t*, 65, 65–69, 66–67*f. See also specific procedure and* Photoablation
      ablation technique and, 13:73–87
      application of treatment and, 13:83–84, 84*f*
      calibration of, 13:73
      herpes simplex virus keratitis and, 13:166–167
      preoperative programming of, 13:73–74
      for presbyopia, 13:156–157, 157*f*
      tracking/centration/ablation and, 13:83–84, 84*f*
   for phototherapeutic keratectomy (PTK), 8:402–403
      for recurrent corneal erosions, 8:85
   for radial keratotomy, 13:43

Excision repair, 2:169

Excisional biopsy, 7:170, 170*f*, 8:390

Excitation filter, 3:9

EXCITE study, 12:76

Exciting eye, 9:178, 180, 182. *See also* Sympathetic ophthalmia

Exclusion criteria, 1:339–340
   clinical trial interpretation and, 1:328

Excretory lacrimal system, 2:27*f*, 33–34, 34*f*, 7:244–246, 245*f. See also* Lacrimal drainage system
   anatomy of, 7:244–246, 245*f*
   development of, 7:243
      abnormalities of, 7:277–278, 278*f*
   disorders of, 7:249–278

Excyclo- (prefix), 6:10

Excycloduction. *See* Extorsion

Excyclotorsion
   extraocular muscles in, 5:55–56, 56*f*
   in superior oblique muscle paralysis, 6:119

Excyclovergence, 6:35–36

Executive function deficit, 1:246

Exenatide, for diabetes mellitus, 1:202

Exenteration, 7:117, 126–127, 126*f*
    for lacrimal system tumors, 7:87, 126, 277
    for melanoma, 4:286, 7:126, 8:240
Exercise/activity
    diabetes mellitus prevention/management and, 1:189,
        194, 195
    hypercholesterolemia management and, 1:133*t*, 134,
        134*f*
    hypertension management and, 1:74, 75*t*
    osteoporosis and, 1:229
Exercise stress tests, in ischemic heart disease, 1:106
    echocardiography, 1:106
Exfoliation, true. *See also* Exfoliation syndrome
    infrared radiation/heat causing, 4:106, 11:52–53
Exfoliation glaucoma, 10:11*t*, 85, 87
Exfoliation syndrome (pseudoexfoliation), 4:106, 106*f*,
        107*f*, 10:11*t*, 38, 85–87, 86*f*, 87*f*, 122, 123*f*, 11:61–62,
        61*f*
    cataract surgery in patient with, 11:199
    glaucoma and, 10:11*t*, 85, 87, 122, 123*f*
    postoperative hyphema and, 11:177
    zonular incompetence and, 10:122, 123*f*, 11:197, 198*f*,
        199
Exo- (prefix), 6:9
Exodeviations, 6:99–106. *See also specific type and*
    Exotropia
    esodeviation following surgery for (surgical/
        consecutive esodeviation), 6:97–98
        management of, 6:103
    overcorrection in, value of, 6:103, 151
    positive angle kappa and, 6:77, 78*f*
    surgery for, 6:150–151, 150*t*
Exogenous infection, uveal, 4:188
Exon, 2:151, 165
Exon shuffling, 2:165
Exophoria, 6:99
Exophthalmometry, 7:23, 23*f*
Exophthalmos, 7:22. *See also* Proptosis
    thyrotoxic. *See* Thyroid eye disease
Exorbitism, 6:173, 7:22. *See also* Proptosis
Exotoxins, microbial, 8:98
    in innate immune response, 9:14*t*, 16–17
    virulence and, 1:4
Exotropia
    A-pattern, 6:107–112, 109*f*
        treatment of, 6:112
    consecutive, 6:105
    constant, 6:103–105
    convergence insufficiency and, 6:101, 106
    convergence paralysis and, 6:106
    in craniosynostosis, 6:390–391, 391*f*
    dissociated horizontal deviation and, 6:105–106, 105*f*
    in Duane syndrome, 6:105, 128, 128*f*, 129
    false appearance of (pseudoexotropia), 6:99
        in retinopathy of prematurity, 6:287, 287*f*
    infantile, 6:104, 104*f*
    intermittent, 6:99–103
    neuromuscular abnormalities causing, 6:105
    red-glass (diplopia) testing and, 6:54
    residual, management of, 6:103
    sensory, 6:104–105
    V-pattern, 6:107–112, 108*f*
        treatment of, 6:112

Expansile dot pattern, in central serous
    chorioretinopathy, 12:172, 173*f*
Experimental (interventional) studies (clinical trials),
    1:320, 321, 321*f*, 327–328, 327*f*. *See also* Clinical
    research
    for medical device, 13:204, 206
    for new drug, 2:333
    systematic reviews/meta-analyses of, 1:328–329
Experimental uveitis
    autoimmune, 9:69
    immune, 9:15, 69
Exposure keratitis/keratopathy, 8:80
    in craniosynostosis-induced proptosis, 6:388–389
Exposure staining, 8:56, 56*f*
Expressed sequence tags, 2:151, 182, 253
Expression, of genes. *See* Transcription (gene)
Expressivity (genetic), 2:151, 209–210
Expulsive choroidal/suprachoroidal hemorrhage,
    4:18–19, 19*f*
    cataract surgery and, 11:178
Extended-wear contact lenses, 3:180
    as bandage lenses, 3:193–194
    materials for, 3:178
    stromal neovascularization and, 8:92
External adnexa. *See* Ocular adnexa
External-beam radiation
    for choroidal hemangioma, 4:292–293
    for lymphoma, 4:324
    for melanoma, 4:285
    for metastatic eye disease, 4:322
    for retinal capillary hemangioblastoma, 4:295
    for retinoblastoma, 4:312, 6:358
        secondary tumors and, 4:312, 313–314, 314*t*
    retinopathy after, 12:151–153
    for uveal lymphoid infiltration, 4:326
External carotid artery, 5:12, 13–15, 13*f*, 15*f*
External dacryocystorhinostomy, 7:268, 269*f*
External (outer) eye, 8:3. *See also specific structure*
    anatomy of, 8:4–9, 5*f*, 7*f*, 8*f*
    cataract surgery in patient with abnormalities of,
        11:190–191
    defense mechanisms of, 8:95–96
        compromise of, 8:100
    development of, 8:4
    examination of, 8:11–46. *See also* Examination,
        ophthalmic
        before cataract surgery, 11:77–78
        in primary congenital glaucoma, 10:150
    function of, 8:3
    HIV infection/AIDS affecting, 9:311–314
    infections of. *See* Infection (ocular)
    photography in evaluation of, 8:31
External hordeolum (stye), 4:208, 7:154, 8:148
External jugular vein, 5:26
External limiting membrane, 2:75*f*, 76*f*, 78, 80*f*, 4:145,
        12:10, 11*f*, 12, 13*f*, 14*f*
    development of, 2:126
Extinction, parietal lobe lesions causing, 5:98
Extirpation and denervation, 6:148*t*
Extorsion (excycloduction), 6:10, 33
    extraocular muscles in
        inferior oblique, 6:15, 17*t*, 29*t*, 32, 34*f*
        inferior rectus, 6:14, 17*t*, 29, 29*t*, 31, 32*f*

Extorsional strabismus, 6:10
Extracapsular cataract extraction (ECCE), 11:94–96,
    95f, 211–213. See also Cataract surgery
  for advanced cataract, 11:196
  advantages of, 11:95
  anterior capsulotomy in, 11:211–212
  in anticoagulated patient, 11:189
  capsular opacification and, 11:169–171
    Nd:YAG laser capsulotomy for, 11:169, 171–175,
      174f. See also Nd:YAG laser therapy, capsulotomy
  cystoid macular edema and, 11:182, 12:143
  early techniques for, 11:90–92, 91f
  equipment for, 11:95–96, 95f
  flat or shallow anterior chamber and, 11:152–154
    intraoperative complications, 11:152–153
    postoperative complications, 11:153–154
  incisions for, 11:211
  intraocular lenses for, 11:133, 133–136, 136f, 212
  lens particle glaucoma and, 11:63
  manual small-incision cataract surgery and, 11:96
  nucleus removal in, 11:95, 212
  ocular trauma affecting visualization and, 11:206
  patient preparation for, 11:211
  posterior vitreous detachment and, 12:275
  postoperative course and, 11:213
  procedure for, 11:94–96, 95f, 211–213
  renaissance/rediscovery of, 11:94
  retained lens fragments after, 11:159
  retinal detachment and, 11:184
    after vitrectomy, 11:206
  vitreocorneal adherence/persistent corneal edema
    and, 11:148
  wound closure and, 11:212–213
Extracapsular IOL dislocation, 11:162, 163f
Extraconal fat/surgical space (peripheral surgical space),
    7:10, 107, 107f
Extracranial trunk, of cranial nerve VII (facial), 5:61
Extrafoveal cones, 2:74
Extranodal marginal zone lymphoma (MALToma),
    4:72–73, 73f, 74
  of orbit, 7:80
Extraocular muscle surgery, 6:145–162. See also specific
    type or disorder
  for A-pattern deviations, 6:110–111, 111f, 112
  acuity considerations and, 6:145–146
  adjustable sutures used in, 6:148–149
  anatomical considerations and, 6:23f, 24–25
  anesthesia for, 6:160–162
  complications of, 6:154–160
  for constant exotropia, 6:103
  cyclovertical strabismus and, 6:146–147
  for dissociated vertical deviation, 6:117, 153
  for Duane syndrome, 6:129
  esodeviation after, 6:97–98
    management of, 6:103
  for esodeviations and exodeviations, 6:150–151, 150t
  exotropia after, 6:105
  guidelines for, 6:149–154, 150t
  for high accommodative convergence/
    accommodative esotropia, 6:94
  for hypo- and hypertropia, 6:152–153
  incisions for, 6:154
  incomitance and, 6:146
  indications for, 6:145

  for infantile esotropia, 6:91–92
  infections after, 6:156, 156f
  for inferior oblique muscle paralysis, 6:122
  for intermittent exotropia, 6:101–102, 102–103
  for monocular elevation deficiency (double elevator
    palsy), 6:124
  monocular recession-resection procedures, 6:150–151,
    150t
  for nystagmus, 5:258, 6:328–329, 328f, 329t
  oblique muscle procedures and, 6:148t, 151–152
  for partially accommodative esotropia, 6:95
  planning, 6:145–147
  posterior fixation in, 6:148t, 149
  prior surgery and, 6:147
  pull-over (stay) sutures used in, 6:149
  rectus muscle procedures and, 6:152–154
  for refractive accommodative esotropia, 6:93
  for residual exotropia, 6:103
  for sensory deprivation esodeviation, 6:96–97
  for sixth nerve (abducens) paralysis, 6:135
  strengthening procedures in, 6:147–148, 152
  for superior oblique muscle paralysis, 6:120–121
  for superior oblique myokymia, 6:142–143
  symmetric, 6:150, 150t
  techniques for, 6:147–149, 148t
  for third nerve (oculomotor) paralysis, 6:132–134
  in thyroid eye disease, 6:135–136
  transposition procedures in, 6:149, 153
  for V-pattern deviations, 6:110–111, 111f, 112
  weakening procedures in, 6:147, 148t, 151–152. See
    also Weakening procedures
Extraocular muscles, 2:16–22, 16f, 17f, 18f, 19f, 19t, 20f,
    21t, 5:38, 55–56, 56f, 6:13–25, 14f, 16f, 17t, 7:10–11,
    11f. See also specific muscle and Ocular motility
  actions of, 6:13–16, 17t, 28–32, 29t, 30f, 31f, 32f
    field of, 6:29
    gaze position and, 6:30–32, 30f, 31f, 32f, 33f, 34f
    primary/secondary/tertiary, 6:13, 28–29, 29t
  anatomy of, 2:21–22, 21t, 5:55–56, 56f, 6:13–25, 14f,
    16f, 17t, 170
    growth/development and, 2:139, 6:170
    surgery and, 6:23f, 24–25
  approaches to, in surgery, 6:154
  arc of contact of, 6:28
  blood supply/arterial system of, 2:18–21, 19t, 38, 38f,
    6:16–18
    surgery and, 6:25
  congenital fibrosis of, 5:240–241, 241f, 241t, 6:127,
    138–140, 171
  damage to
    during blepharoplasty, 7:226
    in blowout fractures, 7:100–101
    during enucleation, 7:119
  development of, 2:139, 6:170
  fascial relationships of, 6:19–24, 20f
  fiber types in, 2:21, 21t, 6:18–19
  field of action of, 6:29
  innervation of, 2:21, 5:50–55, 51f, 52–53f, 6:13–16,
    17t, 7:11. See also Cranial nerves
    surgery and, 6:24
  insertions of, 2:16–17, 18f, 19t, 6:13–16, 17t
    advancing, as strengthening procedure, 6:147–148
  lost, during surgery, 6:24, 159–160
    esodeviations and, 6:97–98

metastatic disease of, 7:91
nonspecific orbital inflammation involving, 7:59, 60f
orbital implants and, 7:121
orbital relationships of, 6:19–24, 20f
origins of, 2:18, 19t, 6:13–16, 17t
paralysis/paresis of
    in myasthenia gravis, 6:137, 139t
    3-step test in evaluation of, 6:83–86, 85f
physiology of, 6:170
in ptosis, 7:203–204
slipped, surgery and, 6:24, 160, 160f
    esodeviations and, 6:97–98
structure of, 6:18 19
surgery of. See Extraocular muscle surgery;
    Strabismus surgery
in thyroid eye disease, 4:232, 233f, 7:49, 49f, 51
    optic neuropathy and, 5:147–149, 148f, 333
venous system of, 6:18
within orbit, 2:18, 19f, 20f
Extraocular myopathy. See also specific disorder
neuro-ophthalmic signs of, 5:336–338, 336f, 337f
in thyroid eye disease, 4:232, 233f, 5:332f, 333, 6:135,
    7:49, 49f, 51
Extrinsic pathway (coagulation), 1:151, 151f
Extruded drusen, 5:133
Exuberant hyperkeratosis (cutaneous horn), 7:158
Exudates
hard, 4:158, 159f
    in diabetic macular edema, 12:96, 97f, 99f
    in leukemia, 4:326
soft. See Cotton-wool spots
Exudative retinal detachment. See Retinal detachment
Exudative retinopathy, retinopathy of prematurity and,
    12:164
Exudative vitreoretinopathy, familial, 6:296, 12:310–311,
    310f
Eye
aging affecting, 1:221, 227
anatomy of, 2:41–85. See also specific structure
antipsychotic drugs affecting, 1:252
axes of, 3:106, 107f, 6:11–12
axial length of
    angle closure and, 10:113
    extremes of, cataract surgery in patient with,
        11:200–201
    in infants and children, 6:167–168, 167f, 167t
        in congenital glaucoma, 6:238, 10:152
    in IOL power determination, 3:213–216, 214f, 215f,
        216f, 11:82–83, 83f, 84, 84–85, 168
    unexpected refractive results after surgery and,
        11:168
color of, age affecting, 6:169
congenital anomalies of, 2:141–143, 142f, 4:6, 7f,
    6:171. See also specific type and Congenital
    anomalies
    glaucoma associated with, 6:238, 10:5t, 7t, 140t,
        142, 145–148
depression of (downgaze). See Depression of eye
development of, 2:113–143, 6:167–171, 167f, 167t,
    168f, 169f, 8:4. See also specific structure
    abnormalities of, 2:117, 141–143, 142f, 4:6, 7f, 6:171.
        See also specific type and Congenital anomalies
    glaucoma associated with, 6:238, 10:5t, 7t. See
        also Glaucoma, childhood

chronology of, 2:122t
    embryogenesis, 2:117–120, 118f, 119f, 121f
    growth factors in, 2:113–114
    homeobox genes and, 2:114–115
    neural crest cells and, 2:115–117, 116t, 120f, 121f
    organogenesis, 2:120–140, 122t
dimensions of, 6:167–168, 167f, 167t, 168f
dominant, in low vision assessment, contrast
    sensitivity and, 3:291
dry. See Dry-eye syndrome
elevation of (upgaze). See Elevation of eye
examination of. See Examination
external. See External (outer) eye
fellow. See Fellow eye
glands of, 2:27t
infection of. See Infection (ocular)
information about position of (efference copy
    information), 5:48
injury to. See Trauma
normal flora of, 8:96–97, 97t
optics of, 3:103–120, 105t
    accommodation/presbyopia and, 3:116–117, 117f,
        142, 143t
    axes of eye and, 3:106, 107f, 6:11–12
    binocular states and, 3:116
    contrast sensitivity/contrast sensitivity function
        and, 3:111–113, 112f
    power prediction formulas for IOLs based on,
        3:212–213, 212f
    pupil size/resolution and, 3:107–108, 107f
    refractive states and, 3:113–116, 113f, 114f, 115f.
        See also under Refractive
        developmental hyperopia and, 3:119
        developmental myopia and, 3:118–119
        epidemiology of refractive errors and,
            3:117–118
        prevention of refractive errors and, 3:119–120
        treatment of refractive errors and, 3:120
    schematic eye and, 3:103–104, 104f, 105t, 106f. See
        also Schematic eye
    visual acuity and, 3:108–111, 109f, 110f, 110t
phthisical (phthisis bulbi), 4:22, 23f
    after penetrating injury, 12:324
    retained foreign body and, 12:327
    retinoblastoma regression and, 6:356
    sympathetic ophthalmia and, 9:182
physical examination of, 8:11–12. See also
    Examination, ophthalmic
    in children, 6:3–5
preparation of
    for Descemet stripping automated endothelial
        keratoplasty, 8:439–441, 440f
    for penetrating keratoplasty, 8:418
radiation affecting, 1:238, 244
refractive states of, 3:113–116, 113f, 114f, 115f. See
    also Eye, optics of, refractive states and
removal of. See Anophthalmic socket; Enucleation;
    Evisceration; Exenteration
schematic, 3:103–104, 104f, 105t, 106f
    optical constants of, 3:104f, 105t
    reduced, 3:103–104, 106f
systemic drugs affecting, 1:300–302, 301–302t
in systemic malignancies, 1:244, 4:315–328
traumatic injury of. See Trauma

tumors of. *See* Intraocular tumors
    vascular system of, development of, **2**:137–138, 139*f*
Eye Bank Association of America (EBAA), **8**:409
Eye banking, **8**:408–411, 410*t. See also* Cornea,
    transplantation of
    screening for prior LASIK and, **13**:192
Eye Disease Case-Control Study
    in branch retinal vein occlusion, **12**:123
    in central retinal vein occlusion, **12**:129
Eye drops. *See* Eyedrops
Eye examination. *See* Examination
Eye fields, frontal, **5**:40, 40*f*, 202, 204
    ocular deviations caused by lesion of, **5**:211–212
Eye movements. *See specific type and* Ocular motility
Eye muscles. *See* Extraocular muscles
Eye pain. *See* Pain
Eye patches. *See* Patching
Eye protection, lens materials for, **3**:162
Eye socket. *See* Socket
"Eye strain," pain and, **5**:300
Eyeball. *See* Globe
Eyebrows
    direct elevation of, **7**:228
    drooping of (brow ptosis), **7**:227–228, 227*f*
        dermatochalasis and, **7**:222, 227
Eyedrops
    administration of, **10**:175–176
        in children, **10**:156
        compliance and, **10**:177
    for glaucoma. *See also* Antiglaucoma agents
        administration of, **10**:175–176
            in children, **10**:156
            compliance and, **10**:177
Eyedrops (topical medications), **2**:323–327, 324*f*, 325*f*
    administration of, in children, **6**:5
    for allergic eye disease, **6**:198, 199*t*
    after cataract surgery, **11**:129
        corneal melting and, **11**:150, 191
    corticosteroid. *See also* Corticosteroids
        ptosis caused by, **5**:280
        for uveitis, **9**:100–102, 101*t*, 119
    for glaucoma, in children, **6**:242–243
    sustained-release devices for, **2**:330–331
Eyeglasses. *See* Spectacle lenses (spectacles)
Eyelashes (cilia), **2**:23, 23*f*, 29, **4**:205, **7**:143, **8**:4, 5*f*
    accessory. *See* Distichiasis
    disorders of, **8**:89
    entropion/ptosis of. *See also* Trichiasis
        in anophthalmic socket, **7**:125
    in epiblepharon, **7**:148, 148*f*, 149*f*
    follicles of, **7**:142*f*
        tumors arising in, **7**:162–164, 163*f*
    lice infestation of, **8**:142, 149
    misdirection of. *See* Trichiasis
    in staphylococcal blepharitis, **8**:144*t*, 145
Eyelid crutches, for benign essential blepharospasm,
    7:218
Eyelid droop. *See* Ptosis
Eyelid–globe incongruity, in tear deficiency, **2**:244
Eyelid hygiene
    in blepharitis/meibomian gland dysfunction, **8**:68,
        72, 147
    for chalazia and hordeola in children, **6**:351
    in staphylococcal eye infection, **8**:147

Eyelid imbrication syndrome, **7**:155
Eyelid myokymia, **5**:289*t*, 292
Eyelid retractor/speculum
    for examination in chemical injury, **8**:355, 357*f*
    for examination in conjunctival foreign body, **8**:370
Eyelid-sharing techniques, in eyelid repair, **7**:185
Eyelid splints, as tarsorrhaphy alternative, **8**:391
Eyelid springs
    for corneal exposure in facial palsy, **5**:288
    for paralytic lagophthalmos, **7**:217
Eyelid taping
    for exposure keratopathy, **8**:80
    for floppy eyelid syndrome, **8**:81
Eyelid weights
    for corneal exposure in facial palsy, **5**:288
    for exposure keratopathy, **8**:80
    for paralytic ectropion, **7**:216
    for paralytic lagophthalmos, **7**:216–217
Eyelids, **2**:22–31, 22*f*, **5**:61–62, **7**:134–143, **8**:4, 5*f*
    absence of (ablepharon), **8**:249
    accessory structures of, **2**:31
    aging affecting, **1**:221
        orbital septum changes and, **7**:137
        skin changes and, **7**:135
        SOOF and, **7**:141
    amyloid deposits in, **4**:211–212, 212*f*, 213*t*
    anatomy of, **2**:22–29, 22*f*, 23*f*, 24*f*, 25*f*, 26*f*, 27*f*, 29*f*,
        4:205–206, 205*f*, **5**:61–62, **7**:134–143, 135*f*, 137*f*,
        139*f*, 140*f*, 142*f*, **8**:4, 5*f*
    anterior fascial support system of, **2**:36*f*
    apraxia of opening of, **5**:281
    in atopic dermatitis, **8**:185
    basal cell carcinoma of, **4**:215*t*, 217–219, 218*f*, 219*f*,
        7:168–172, 169*f*, 170*f*
        intraocular extension of, **4**:322
    biopsy of, **7**:170, 170*f*
        for basal cell carcinoma, **7**:170, 170*f*
        for melanoma, **7**:176
        for sebaceous carcinoma, **7**:174
    canthal tendons and, **7**:137*f*, 141–142
    coloboma of, **6**:175, 176*f*, **7**:150–151, 151*f*
        in Goldenhar syndrome, **6**:175, 393
        in Treacher Collins syndrome (mandibulofacial
            dysostosis), **4**:213*t*, **6**:394
    congenital anomalies of, **4**:207, 208*f*, **6**:175–180,
        7:145–152
        lesions, **7**:151–152, 152*f*
    conjunctiva of, **2**:29, 30*f*, 34–35, **7**:135*f*, 141. *See also*
        Conjunctiva
    connective tissue structures of, **2**:23, **7**:141–142
    in contact dermatoblepharitis, **8**:183–185, 184*f*
    creases of, **5**:62, **7**:135*f*, 136, 139
        for orbitotomy incision, **7**:108–109, 108*f*, 110, 110*f*,
            112
        in ptosis, **7**:202, 202*f*
    cysts of, **4**:213–214, 213*f*, 214*f*
        dermoid, **4**:207, 213
        ductal, **4**:213–214, 214*f*
        epidermoid/epidermal, **4**:213, 213*f*, **7**:158–159,
            159*f*
        inclusion/sebaceous, **4**:213, 213*f*, **7**:158–159,
            159*f*
    degenerations of, **4**:211–212, 211*f*, 212*f*, 213*t*
    development of, **2**:139–140, 140*f*, **8**:4

disorders of, **4:**205–227, **5:**275–282, **7:**24, 145–187, **8:**20*t. See also specific disorder*
acquired, **7:**152–155
congenital, **4:**207, 208*f,* **6:**175–180, **7:**145–152
evaluation of, **5:**275–278, 276*f,* 277*f,* 278*f*
immune-mediated, **8:**183–185, 184*f*
lice infestation, **8:**149
neoplastic, **4:**214–227, **7:**155–177. *See also* Eyelids, tumors of
nonorganic, **5:**316–317
in Parkinson disease, **1:**260
in thyroid eye disease, **4:**232, 233*f,* **5:**332, 332*f,* **7:**24. *See also* Thyroid eye disease
traumatic, **7:**177–181. *See also* Eyelids, trauma to
drooping. *See* Ptosis
ectropion of, **7:**190–194, 191*f. See also* Ectropion
congenital, **6:**176, **7:**146, 147*f*
edema of, **7:**154
in blowout fractures, **7:**100
in orbital cellulitis, **6:**195, 196*f*
in preseptal cellulitis, **6:**194
in thyroid eye disease, **7:**49
emphysema of, in blowout fractures, **7:**101
entropion of, **7:**194–199. *See also* Entropion
congenital, **6:**176, **7:**149–150, 150*f*
epithelium of
benign lesions of, **7:**157–160, 158*f,* 159*f,* 160*f*
hyperplasia of, **7:**157–158, 157*f,* 158*f*
in situ carcinoma of, **7:**167–168, 167*f*
eversion of. *See* Ectropion
examination of, **5:**275–278, 276*f,* 277*f,* 278*f,* **8:**11
before refractive surgery, **13:**35, 37*f*
excursion of, **5:**275–276, 277*f*
in external eye defense, **8:**95
floppy, **7:**154–155, 154*f,* **8:**53, 81, 81*f*
folds of, **7:**136, 139
fusion of (ankyloblepharon), **6:**176, 176*f,* **7:**147, 148*f,* **8:**249, 249*f*
glands of, **4:**205, **8:**4. *See also specific type*
tumors of
benign, **7:**160–164, 161*f,* 162*f,* 163*f*
malignant, **7:**173–175, 174*f*
healing/repair of, **4:**17–18
in herpes simplex dermatoblepharitis, **8:**106, 106*f,* 107, 110
in herpes zoster ophthalmicus, **8:**120
horizontal shortening/tightening of
for cicatricial ectropion, **7:**193
for exposure keratopathy, **8:**80
for involutional ectropion, **7:**190, 192–193, 192*f*
for involutional entropion, **7:**196
infection/inflammation of, **4:**208–211, 209*f,* 210*f,* 211*f,* **8:**19–21, 20*t,* 143–149, 144*f,* 144*t,* 146*f. See also* Blepharitis
in children, **6:**350–351
fungal and parasitic, **8:**148–149
staphylococcal, **8:**143–148, 144*f,* 144*t,* 146*f*
inversion of. *See* Entropion
keratosis of, **8:**20*t*
actinic, **4:**216–217, 217*f,* 218*f,* **7:**166, 167*f*
seborrheic, **4:**214–215, 214*f,* 215*f,* **7:**157–158, 157*f*
lacerations of
canthal tissue involved in, **7:**178–180
lid margin involved in, **7:**178, 179*f*

lid margin not involved in, **7:**178
ptosis caused by, **7:**210
repair of, **7:**178, 179–180, 179*f. See also* Eyelids, surgery/reconstruction of
in children, **6:**409
secondary, **7:**180–181
lower
anatomy of, **2:**22, 26*f*
blepharoplasty on, **7:**222–223, 223, 225
laser resurfacing as adjunct to, **7:**230
visual loss after, **7:**226
crease of, **7:**136
for orbitotomy incision, **7:**110, 110*f*
development of, **2:**110, 140*f*
horizontal laxity of
in involutional ectropion, **7:**190
in involutional entropion, **7:**194–195
reconstruction of, **7:**182, 184–186, 185*f*
retractors of, **7:**135*f,* 140
in involutional ectropion, repair of, **7:**193
in involutional entropion, **7:**194–195, 196*f*
repair of, **7:**196, 197*f*
reverse ptosis of, **7:**207
vertical elevation of, for paralytic ectropion, **7:**216
lymphatics of, **2:**30–31, 31*f*
malpositions of, **7:**190–227. *See also specific type*
in nonorganic disorders, **5:**316–317
margin of, **2:**23, 26*f,* **7:**142, 142*f*
distance from corneal reflex and, **5:**276, 278*f,* **6:**179
in ptosis, **6:**179, **7:**201–202, 202*f,* 205*f*
distance from upper eyelid crease and, **5:**276, 278*f*
eversion of. *See* Ectropion
infections of, **8:**143–149, 144*f,* 144*t,* 146*f*
inversion of. *See* Entropion
lacerations of, **7:**178, 179*f*
nevus involving, **7:**164, 165*f*
repair of, **7:**178, 179*f,* 183–186, 183*f,* 185*f*
sebaceous carcinoma arising in, **7:**174
vascular and mesenchymal tumors of, **8:**240–242, 241*t*
in molluscum contagiosum, **8:**128, 128*f*
in children, **6:**193, 194*f*
movement of, in tear film renewal and distribution, **2:**244
muscles of, **5:**61–62
normal flora, **8:**96–97, 97*t*
orbital fat and, **2:**27, **7:**135*f,* 138
orbital septum and, **2:**25*f,* 27–28, **7:**135*f,* 137–138
orbital tumors originating in, **7:**88
plexiform neurofibroma involving, **5:**275, 276*f,* 339–340, **6:**367, 367*f,* **7:**24, **10:**28
protractors of, **7:**136, 137*f*
spasms of, **7:**218–220, 219*f. See also* Blepharospasm
reconstruction of. *See* Eyelids, surgery/reconstruction of
retraction of, **5:**281–282, 282*t,* **7:**213–216
after blepharoplasty, **7:**214, 215, 226
in convergence-retraction nystagmus, **5:**256
in dorsal midbrain (Parinaud) syndrome, **5:**211, 273, 281, **7:**214
ptosis and, **5:**275
seizures causing, **1:**263–264

in thyroid eye disease, **4:**232, 233*f*, **5:**276, 278*f*, 281, 332, 332*f*, **7:**47*f*, 49, 51, 54, 213–214, 214*f*, 215
  management and, **5:**334
  proptosis differentiated from, **7:**213–214
  treatment of, **7:**215–216
retractors of, **7:**135*f*, 138–140, 139*f*
  in involutional ectropion, repair of, **7:**193
  in involutional entropion, **7:**194–195, 196*f*
    repair of, **7:**196, 197*f*
in scleroderma, **1:**174, **4:**213*t*
skin of, **2:**22–23, **4:**205, 206*f*, **7:**135*f*, 136, **8:**4
  excessive removal of, in blepharoplasty, **7:**226
  melanoma arising in, **4:**226–227, 227*f*, **7:**175–176, 176*f*
  preoperative assessment of, **7:**229
  redundancy of. *See* Dermatochalasis
  tumors of, **4:**219–220, 220*f*. *See also* Eyelids, tumors of
specimen collection from, **8:**100, 101*t*
squamous cell carcinoma of, **4:**219, 220*f*, **7:**172, 173*f*
  actinic keratosis and, **4:**216–217, 217*f*, 218*f*, **7:**166, 172
  Bowen disease, **7:**167
  well-differentiated keratinizing (keratoacanthoma), **4:**215*t*, 216, 216*f*, **7:**167–168, 167*f*
strabismus surgery affecting position of, **6:**159, 159*f*
in Sturge-Weber syndrome, **6:**376, 376*f*
subcutaneous tissue of, **2:**23, **7:**135*f*, 136
suborbicularis fat pads and, **7:**135*f*, 141
  midface rejuvenation surgery and (SOOF lift), **7:**233, 234*f*
surgery/reconstruction of, **7:**181–187
  for basal cell carcinoma, **7:**171
  for blepharophimosis syndrome, **7:**145
  blepharoplasty, **7:**222–227
  for cicatricial pemphigoid, **8:**203
  for cryptophthalmos/pseudocryptophthalmos, **8:**250
  for defects involving eyelid margin, **7:**183–186, 183*f*, 185*f*
  for defects not involving eyelid margin, **7:**182
  for epicanthus, **7:**148
  for euryblepharon, **7:**147
  for eyelid retraction, **7:**215–216
  history and examination in patient considering, **7:**189–190
  laceration/trauma repair and, **7:**177, 178–180, 179*f*, 180–181, 181–187
  lateral canthal defects and, **7:**186
  medial canthal defects and, **7:**186–187
  after Mohs micrographic surgery, **7:**171
  preoperative considerations and, **7:**189–190, 229
  principles of, **7:**182
  priorities in, **7:**181–182
  for ptosis repair, **6:**179, **7:**210–213, 212*f*
    in blepharophimosis syndrome, **7:**145
    in children, **6:**179
  for Stevens-Johnson syndrome, **8:**198
  for thyroid eye disease, **7:**53, 54
symblepharon and, **7:**199–200
systemic diseases manifesting in, **4:**211–212, 213*t*
in systemic lupus erythematosus, **1:**170, **4:**213*t*
tarsus of, **2:**25*f*, **7:**135*f*, 140–141, 140*f*

topography of, **4:**205–206, 206*f*, 207*t*
trauma to, **7:**177–181
  bite wounds (dog and human), **7:**181
  blunt, **7:**178
  burns, **7:**181
  penetrating, **7:**178–180, 179*f*
  ptosis caused by, **7:**181, 210
  repair of, **7:**177, 178–180, 179*f*, 180–181, 181–187. *See also* Eyelids, surgery/reconstruction of
    secondary, **7:**180–181
tumors of, **4:**214–227, **7:**155–177
  appendage neoplasms, **4:**221–224, 221*f*, 222*f*, 223*f*
  basal cell carcinoma, **4:**215*t*, 217–219, 218*f*, 219*f*
    intraocular extension of, **4:**322
  benign, **4:**214–215, 214*f*, 215*f*, 219–220, 220*f*, 221, 221*f*, 224–226, 224*f*, 225*f*, 226*f*, **7:**157–166
    adnexal lesions, **7:**160–164, 161*f*, 162*f*, 163*f*
    epithelial hyperplasias, **7:**157–158, 157*f*, 158*f*
    epithelial lesions, **7:**158–160, 159*f*, 160*f*
    melanocytic, **4:**224–226, 224*f*, 225*f*, 226*f*, **7:**164–166, 165*f*, 166*f*
  biopsy in evaluation of, **7:**170, 170*f*
  in children, **6:**333*t*, 347–351
  clinical evaluation/diagnostic approaches to, **7:**155–156
  dermal, **4:**219–220, 220*f*
  epidermal, **4:**214–219, 214*f*, 215*f*, 215*t*, 216*f*, 217*f*, 218*f*, 219*f*, 220*f*, **7:**155
    benign, **7:**158–160, 159*f*, 160*f*
    premalignant, **7:**166, 167*f*
  epithelial
    benign lesions, **7:**157–160, 157*f*, 158*f*, 159*f*, 160*f*
    hyperplasias, **7:**157–158, 157*f*, 158*f*
    in situ malignancies, **7:**167–168, 167*f*
  frozen section/Mohs surgery for, **4:**45
  malignant, **4:**217–219, 218*f*, 219*f*, 220*f*, 221–224, 222*f*, 223*f*, **7:**155–156, 168–177
    basal cell carcinoma, **4:**215*t*, 217–219, 218*f*, 219*f*, **7:**168–172, 169*f*, 170*f*
      intraocular extension of, **4:**322
    in situ epithelial, **7:**167–168, 167*f*
    intraocular extension of, **4:**322
    Kaposi sarcoma, **7:**176–177, 177*f*
    melanocytic (melanoma), **4:**226–227, 227*f*, **7:**175–176, 176*f*
    Merkel cell carcinoma, **7:**177
    predisposing factors and, **7:**155–156
    sebaceous gland carcinoma, **4:**215*t*, 221–224, 222*f*, 223*f*, **7:**173–175, 174*f*
    squamous cell carcinoma, **4:**219, 220*f*, **7:**172, 173*f*
      actinic keratosis and, **4:**216–217, 217*f*, 218*f*, **7:**166, 172
      Bowen disease, **7:**167
      well-differentiated keratinizing (keratoacanthoma), **4:**215*t*, 216, 216*f*, **7:**167–168, 167*f*
    staging of, **4:**329–331*t*
  mechanical ptosis caused by, **7:**210
  melanocytic, **4:**224–227, 224*f*, 225*f*, 226*f*
    benign, **7:**164–166, 165*f*, 166*f*
    malignant (melanoma), **4:**226–227, 227*f*, **7:**175–176, 176*f*
    premalignant, **7:**168

in multiple endocrine neoplasia, 1:216, 217*f*
papillomas, in children, 6:348
premalignant
   epidermal, 4:216–217, 217*f*, 218*f*, 7:166, 167*f*
   melanocytic, 7:168
sebaceous gland carcinoma, 4:215*t*, 221–224, 222*f*,
   223*f*, 8:233, 234*f*
signs suggesting, 7:156
squamous cell carcinoma, 4:219, 220*f*
   actinic keratosis and, 4:216–217, 217*f*
   Bowen disease, 7:167
   well-differentiated keratinizing
      (keratoacanthoma), 4:215*t*, 216, 216*f*,
      7:167–168, 167*f*
systemic malignancies and, 4:215, 215*t*
vascular and mesenchymal, 8:240–242, 241*t*
upper
   anatomy of, 2:22, 22–29, 22*f*, 23*f*, 24*f*, 25*f*, 26*f*, 27*f*, 29*f*
   blepharoplasty on, 7:222, 223, 224–225
   crease of, 7:135*f*, 136, 139
      distance of from lid margin and, 5:276, 278*f*
      for orbitotomy incision, 7:108–109, 108*f*, 112
      in ptosis, 7:202, 202*f*
   development of, 2:139–140, 140*f*
   drooping of. See Ptosis
   fold of, 7:136, 139
   reconstruction of, 7:182, 183–184, 183*f*
   retractors of, 7:138–140, 139*f*
in uveitis, 9:86*t*
vascular supply of, 2:29–30, 30*f*, 5:15, 7:143
venous drainage of, 2:30, 5:26
vertical splitting of, for orbitotomy, 7:108*f*, 109
Eyepiece (ocular), of telescope, 3:81, 81*f*, 82, 82*f*
   for operating microscope, 3:262*f*
   for slit-lamp biomicroscope, 3:251*f*, 252

F

F₃. See Trifluridine
FA. See Fluorescein angiography
Fab region (antibody molecule), 9:37, 45*f*, 46
Fabry disease (angiokeratoma corporis diffusum),
   2:213*t*, 6:399, 400*t*, 8:310, 311, 12:262–263, 264*f*
cataract and, 6:247*t*
ocular findings in carriers of, 2:222*t*
plasma infusions in management of, 2:231
retinal degeneration and, 12:262–263, 264*f*
Face. See also under Facial
aging affecting
   cosmetic/rejuvenation surgery and, 7:228–229. See
      also specific procedure and Facial surgery
   facial ligaments and, 7:131
   forehead rejuvenation and, 7:232, 233*f*
   lower face and neck rejuvenation and, 7:234–238,
      237*f*, 238*f*
   midface rejuvenation and, 7:233–234, 234*f*, 235*f*
   pathogenesis of, 7:228–229
   physical examination and, 7:229
anatomy of, 7:131–134, 132*f*, 133*f*, 134*f*
sensory and motor components and, 5:56–62
Face-lift, 7:235–236, 237*f*
   SMAS and, 7:131, 236, 237*f*

Facial angiofibromas, in tuberous sclerosis, 5:341, 342*f*,
   6:372, 372*f*
Facial artery, 5:12, 14*f*, 15, 15*f*, 16
   eyelids supplied by, 2:29, 30*f*
   orbit supplied by, 2:37*f*
Facial clefts, 7:34–35, 34*f*, 35*f*. See also Craniofacial
   malformations
   nasolacrimal duct obstruction and, 7:278
Facial colliculus, 2:105, 5:61
Facial contracture, spastic paretic, 5:291–292
Facial defects. See Craniofacial malformations
Facial diplegia, in Guillain-Barré syndrome, 5:287
Facial dystonia, 7:218–221, 219*f*
Facial fasciculation, benign, 5:292
Facial genu, 5:227
Facial grimacing, blepharospasm associated with,
   5:289–290, 290*f*
Facial hemiatrophy, progressive, 8:324*t*
Facial motor pathways, 5:60–62, 62*f*. See also Cranial
   nerve VII
Facial movement abnormalities, 5:282–292
   cranial nerve VII (facial) disorders causing,
      5:282–292
         overactivity and, 5:288–292, 289*t*, 290*f*, 291*f*
         underactivity and, 5:284–288, 284*f*, 285*t*, 287*f*
   evaluation of, 5:277–278
Facial muscles, 7:131–133, 133*f*
   innervation of, 5:51*f*, 52*f*, 60–61, 62*f*. See also Cranial
      nerve VII
Facial myokymia, 5:289*t*, 292
Facial nerve. See Cranial nerve VII
Facial nerve block, for cataract surgery, 11:101, 101*f*
Facial neurectomy, for benign essential blepharospasm,
   7:220
Facial numbness, pain associated with, 5:303
Facial pain, 5:301–303. See also Headache; Pain
   atypical, 5:301
Facial paralysis/weakness, 5:62*f*, 282–284, 283*f*, 284–288,
   284*f*, 7:216–218
   bilateral, 5:288
   brainstem lesions causing, 5:285
   diplopia and, 5:227
   ectropion and, 7:191*f*, 216, 216*f*
   in HIV infection/AIDS, 5:359
   lagophthalmos and, 7:216–217
   Möbius syndrome/sequence and, 6:140
   peripheral lesions causing, 5:285–288, 287*f*
   progressive, 5:288
   recurrent, 5:288
   in sarcoidosis, 5:287, 288, 335
   seventh nerve lesions causing, 5:284–288, 284*f*, 285*t*,
      287*f*
   supranuclear lesions causing, 5:284–285
   treatment of, 5:288
Facial surgery, 7:228–238. See also specific procedure and
   Eyelids, surgery/reconstruction of
   aging face and, 7:228–229
   anatomy and, 7:131–134, 132*f*, 133*f*, 134*f*
   communication and, 7:228, 239
   cosmetic surgery, 7:228–229
   history and examination in patient considering,
      7:189–190
   preoperative considerations and, 7:189

rejuvenation surgery, 7:230–238
   botulinum toxin, 7:231–232
   forehead rejuvenation, 7:232, 233*f*
   laser skin resurfacing, 7:230–231
   lower face and neck rejuvenation, 7:234–238, 237*f*, 238*f*
   midface rejuvenation, 7:233–234, 234*f*, 235*f*
Facial synkinesis, 5:284*f*, 286
Facial tic (habit spasm), 5:292
Facial vein, 2:40*f*, 5:25, 25*f*, 26
   eyelids drained by, 5:26, 7:143
Facial venous system, 5:26
Facilitated diffusion, glucose transport into lens and, 11:13
FACT (Functional Acuity Contrast Test), 3:292
Factitious disorders, 1:249
   ocular surface, 8:89–90
Factive. *See* Gemifloxacin
Factor V Leiden, 1:147, 157
Factor VIII deficiency (hemophilia A/classic hemophilia), 1:155
Factor VIII transfusions, 1:155
Factor Xa inhibitor, for non–ST-segment elevation acute coronary syndrome, 1:111–112
Factor Q, 3:231–232
Facultative suppression, 6:51
Fadenoperation (posterior fixation suture), 6:148*t*
   for dissociated vertical deviation, 6:153
FAF. *See* Fundus autofluorescence
Falciform ligament, 5:31
Fallopian canal, 2:105, 5:61
Falls, in older patients, 1:231–232
False-negative responses, in perimetry, 5:104, 10:61–62
False passage, probing of nasolacrimal duct obstruction and, 6:208
False-positive responses, in perimetry, 5:104, 10:61–62
Famciclovir, 1:55*t*, 66, 2:329, 381*t*, 383
   for acute retinal necrosis/herpetic retinitis, 9:202, 12:201
   for herpes simplex virus infections, 1:23, 66, 8:109*t*, 9:202, 12:201
   for herpes zoster virus infections, 1:23, 66, 2:381*t*, 383, 8:121, 9:202, 12:201
Familial, definition of, 2:191. *See also* Family history/familial factors; Genetics
Familial adenomatous polyposis (Gardner syndrome), retinal manifestations of, 4:150–151, 12:255, 255*f*
   in children, 6:352
Familial Alzheimer disease, 1:266
Familial amyloidosis
   Finnish-type (amyloidosis IV/gelsolin-type lattice corneal dystrophy), 4:212, 8:268*t*, 270*t*, 280, 280*f*, 317*t*, 319
      genetics of, 4:212, 8:269*t*, 280, 317*t*
   primary of cornea (subepithelial amyloidosis/gelatinous droplike dystrophy), 8:268*t*, 270*t*, 274–275, 275*f*, 317*t*, 318, 318*f*
      genetics of, 8:269*t*, 274, 317*t*
   vitreous opacification in, 12:312–313, 313*f*
Familial amyloidotic polyneuropathy
   types I and II, 4:140, 141*f*, 212
   type IV (gelsolin-type lattice corneal dystrophy), 4:212, 8:268*t*, 270*t*, 280, 280*f*, 317*t*, 319
      genetics of, 4:212, 8:269*t*, 280, 317*t*
   vitreous involvement in, 4:140, 141*f*

Familial (dominant) drusen, 12:239–240, 239*f*
Familial dysautonomia (Riley-Day syndrome), 2:213*t*, 6:221
   congenital corneal anesthesia and, 8:264
   neurotrophic keratopathy in, 8:87
   racial and ethnic concentration of, 2:211
Familial exudative vitreoretinopathy, 6:296, 12:310–311, 310*f*
Familial glaucoma iridogoniodysplasia, 6:213. *See also* Axenfeld-Rieger syndrome
Familial iridoplegia (congenital mydriasis), 6:229
Familial juvenile nephronophthisis, retinal degeneration and, 12:254
Familial juvenile systemic granulomatosis (Blau syndrome), 6:274–275, 9:176
Familial oculorenal syndromes, 6:302
Familial penetrance, 2:216
Family history/familial factors. *See also under Genetic*
   in cancer, 1:237
   in genetic counseling, 2:225–226, 226*f*, 227
   in glaucoma, 10:10, 76, 114
      angle closure/angle-closure glaucoma and, 10:10, 114
      open-angle glaucoma and, 10:76
   in hereditary dystrophies, 12:221, 221–222
   in nystagmus, 6:318, 319*t*
   in ocular hypertension, 10:84
   osteoporosis risk and, 1:228
   in pediatric cataract, 6:253–254, 253*f*, 254*t*
   pedigree analysis and, 2:225–226, 226*f*
   in uveitis, 9:315
Family Support America, 6:417*t*
Famotidine, preoperative, 1:308
Famvir. *See* Famciclovir
Fanconi syndrome, 6:220
   tetracyclines causing, 2:375
FAP. *See* Familial adenomatous polyposis; Familial amyloidotic polyneuropathy; Flatter add plus (FAP) rule
Far points/far point concept, 3:113
   cylindrical correcting lenses and, 3:139–140
   spherical correcting lenses and, 3:138–139, 139*f*
Farcas canthal index, 6:173
Farnsworth-Munsell 100-hue test, 12:48
   in low vision evaluation, 5:105
Farnsworth Panel D-15 test (Farnsworth Dichotomous Test for Color Blindness), 3:294, 12:48–50, 49*f*
   in anomalous trichromatism, 12:214
   in low vision evaluation, 5:105
Faropenem, 1:50*t*, 59
FAS. *See* Fetal alcohol syndrome
Fas ligand (CD95 ligand/FasL), 9:51, 53*f*
   in apoptosis (programmed cell death), 9:51, 53*f*, 62
   in corneal allograft immunity, 9:65
   in effector blockade, 9:62
Fasanella-Servat procedure (tarsoconjunctival müllerectomy), for ptosis correction, 7:212
Fascia bulbi. *See* Tenon capsule
Fascia lata, autogenous and banked, for frontalis suspension, 6:179, 7:212
Fascia lata sling, for paralytic ectropion, 7:216
Fascicles
   cranial nerve III (oculomotor), 5:54, 66
   cranial nerve IV (trochlear), 2:99, 5:51
   cranial nerve V (trigeminal), 5:59

cranial nerve VII (facial), 5:61, 66, 67
optic nerve, 2:90, 92*f*
Fascicular blocks (cardiology), 1:122*t*
Fascicular ocular motor nerve palsies, 5:226
Fasciculations, benign facial, 5:292
Fasciitis
necrotizing, of orbit, 7:44
nodular, 4:118, 118*f*, 8:242
episcleral tumor caused by, 4:118, 118*f*
FasL. *See* Fas ligand
Fast hemoglobin (glycosylated hemoglobin/HbA$_1$/
HbA$_{1c}$), in glucose control/surveillance, 1:203, 203*f*,
204, 12:92, 94*f*
Fast twitch fibers, 2:21, 21*t*, 5:55, 6:18–19
Fastigial nucleus, 5:48, 49
Fasting, preoperative, 1:308
Fasting glucose
in diabetes mellitus diagnosis/screening, 1:193
impaired, 1:191*t*, 192–193
Fat
orbital, 2:27, 6:19, 20*f*, 7:10–11, 135*f*, 138
retro-orbicularis oculi (ROOF), 7:141
sub-brow, 7:135*f*, 141
suborbicularis oculi (SOOF/suborbicularis fat pads),
7:135*f*, 141
midface rejuvenation surgery and (SOOF lift),
7:233, 234*f*
Fat embolism, Purtscherlike retinopathy and, 12:154, 155*t*
Fat-suppression techniques, in MRI, 5:73, 76*f*, 76*t*, 7:27*f*,
28
Fatty acid supplements, for meibomian gland
dysfunction, 8:68
Fatty acids
peroxidation of, 2:311, 312–313
in retina, 2:315
in retinal pigment epithelium, 2:305
in vitreous, 2:286
Fatty streak, 1:100
FAZ. *See* Foveal avascular zone
Fc portion (immunoglobulin)/Fc receptors, 9:45*f*, 46
in antibody-dependent cellular cytotoxicity, 9:51–54
mast cells and, 9:10
phagocytosis and, 9:19–20
FCD. *See* Fleck corneal dystrophy
FD. *See* Familial dysautonomia
FDA. *See* Food and Drug Administration
FDT perimetry. *See* Frequency-doubling technology
(FDT) perimetry
Fecal DNA testing, in cancer screening, 1:272*t*, 276
Fecal occult blood tests, in cancer screening, 1:272*t*,
276
FECD/FECD1. *See* Fuchs endothelial corneal dystrophy
Federal Fairness to Contact Lens Consumers Act,
3:201–202
Feedback, optical, in lasers, 3:21, 23–24, 24*f*
FEFs. *See* Frontal eye fields
Fehr spotted dystrophy (macular corneal dystrophy),
8:268*t*, 270*t*, 278*t*, 283–284, 284*f*
genetics of, 8:269*t*, 283
Feiz and Mannis formula, for IOL power determination/
selection, 11:87
Felbamate, 1:263*t*
Felbatol. *See* Felbamate
Feldene. *See* Piroxicam

Felderstruktur muscle fibers, 2:21, 21*t*
Fellow eye. *See also* Sympathetic ophthalmia
in patient with acute angle closure, 10:116
in patient with choroidal neovascularization
age-related macular degeneration and, 12:79
ocular histoplasmosis and, 12:82–83
in patient with exfoliation syndrome, 10:87
in patient with macular hole, 12:305
in patient with retinal detachment, 12:285
in patient with traumatic/angle-recession glaucoma,
10:100–101
in preoperative evaluation for incisional surgery,
10:185
Felodipine, 1:77*t*, 78*t*
Felty syndrome, 1:162
Femto-LASIK. *See* Femtosecond laser, for LASIK flap
creation
Femtosecond laser
for cataract extraction, 11:127
for incision for intrastromal corneal ring segment
placement, 13:57
for LASIK flap creation, 13:4*t*, 23, 80–83, 81*f*, 82*f*,
83*t*
aberrations and, 13:95
advantages/disadvantages of, 13:83*t*
international trends in use of, 13:199
re-treatment and, 13:90, 90*f*
steep or flat corneas and, 13:39
visual disturbances related to, 13:116
for penetrating keratoplasty, 8:417, 418
for photodisruption, 13:23
for presbyopia treatment, 13:199–200
for superficial anterior lamellar keratoplasty, 8:435
FENDrix. *See* Hepatitis B vaccine
Fenofibrate
diabetic retinopathy affected by, 1:205
for hypercholesterolemia/heart disease prevention,
1:137*t*
Fenoprofen, 1:183*t*, 2:362*t*
Fenoterol, 1:144
with ipratropium, 1:145*t*
Fentanyl, perioperative, 1:309*t*, 311
Fenton reaction, 12:328
Fermat principle, 3:51–53, 52*f*, 53*f*
wavefront analysis and, 3:238, 239*f*
Ferrara rings, 13:53, 55, 56, 201. *See also* Intrastromal
corneal ring segments
Ferritin levels, in iron deficiency anemia, 1:148
Ferry lines, 8:337*t*
Fetal alcohol syndrome, 1:250, 2:142–143, 142*f*,
6:394–395, 395*f*
craniofacial malformations and, 6:394–395, 395*f*
Fetal banded zone, 2:135
Fetal fissure. *See* Embryonic fissure
Fetal hydantoin syndrome, 1:264
Fetal lens nucleus, 4:120, 11:9, 23*f*, 24–25, 24*f*
opacification of (congenital nuclear cataract), 11:33,
34*f*
Fetal radiation, effects/ocular manifestations of, 1:238
Fetal vasculature, persistent. *See* Persistent fetal
vasculature
FEV$_1$ (forced expiratory volume in 1 second), 1:143
FEVR. *See* Familial exudative vitreoretinopathy
FGF. *See* Fibroblast growth factor

FGFR genes, **6**:387
   in Apert syndrome, **6**:388
   in Crouzon syndrome, **2**:216, **6**:387
   in Pfeiffer syndrome, **6**:388
FHI. *See* Fuchs heterochromic iridocyclitis
FHS. *See* Fetal hydantoin syndrome
Fiber layer of Henle, **2**:78, 79, 79*f*, **4**:147, 147*f*, **5**:29. *See also* Nerve fiber layer
Fiber optics
   operating microscope illumination and, **3**:263
   total reflection in, **3**:12
Fibric acid derivatives, for hypercholesterolemia/heart disease prevention, **1**:137*t*
Fibril-associated proteins, in vitreous, **2**:285–286
Fibrillar opacities, **2**:286
Fibrillation
   atrial, **1**:124–125, 124*t*
      heart failure and, **1**:119, 120
      stroke and, **1**:92, 94
   ventricular, **1**:125, 126–127, 126*t*, 289, 292
Fibrillenstruktur muscle fibers, **2**:21, 21*t*
Fibrillin, **2**:286
   defects in, in Marfan syndrome, **6**:263, **8**:325, **11**:36
Fibrin, **8**:177*t*, **9**:24
   in uveitis, **9**:24, 85, 88, 119, 119*f*
Fibrin clots, after penetrating trauma in children, **6**:408–409
Fibrin tissue adhesive, for corneal autograft fixation, **8**:394
Fibrinogen, **9**:24
Fibrinolytic agents, **2**:393
Fibrinolytic system, **1**:152
Fibroblast growth factor (FGF), **2**:114, 395–396
   in aqueous humor, **2**:270
   homeobox gene expression affected by, **2**:115
   in ocular development, **2**:114
   in tear film, **2**:241
Fibroblast growth factor receptor *(FGFR)* genes, **6**:387
   in Apert syndrome, **6**:388
   in Crouzon syndrome, **2**:216, **6**:387
   in Pfeiffer syndrome, **6**:388
Fibroblasts, orbital, in thyroid eye disease, **4**:232, **7**:50
Fibrocellular proliferation, intraocular, **4**:20, 21*f*
Fibrohistiocytic tumor. *See* Fibrous histiocytoma
Fibroma/fibromatosis
   juvenile, of orbit, **4**:246, 246*f*, **6**:343
   molluscum, **6**:366
   ossifying, of orbit, **4**:246, 246*f*, **6**:343
   in tuberous sclerosis, **5**:341, 342*f*, **6**:372
Fibronectin, **8**:9
   in vitreous, **2**:283
Fibro-osseous dysplasia (juvenile ossifying fibroma), of orbit, **4**:246, 246*f*, **6**:343
Fibroplasia, retrolental. *See* Retinopathy, of prematurity
Fibrosarcoma
   of orbit, **7**:79
      in children, **6**:336
   retinoblastoma associated with, **4**:314*t*, **6**:336
Fibrosis, congenital, **5**:240–241, 241*f*, 241*t*, **6**:138–140, 171
Fibrotic pulmonary disease, **1**:142
Fibrous astrocytes, **2**:77
Fibrous downgrowth. *See* Fibrous ingrowth (downgrowth)

Fibrous dysplasia, of orbit, **4**:245–246, 246*f*, **6**:342, **7**:78, 79*f*
   secondary, **7**:89
Fibrous histiocytoma (fibroxanthoma), **8**:242
   malignant (atypical fibroxanthoma), **4**:117–118, 240–242
   orbital, **4**:240–242, 242*f*, **7**:78
   scleral, **4**:117–118, 117*f*
Fibrous ingrowth (downgrowth)
   angle-closure glaucoma and, **10**:133, 134, 134*f*
   corneal graft failure and, **4**:91, 92*f*
Fibrous tumor, solitary, of orbit, **7**:78
Fibrovascular pigment epithelial detachment, **12**:66–67
Fibrovascular plaque, anterior, in persistent fetal vasculature, **4**:132, 132*f*
Fibroxanthoma. *See* Fibrous histiocytoma
Fibulin-1, in vitreous, **2**:283
Fick, axes of, **6**:27, 27*f*
Field of action, **6**:29
Field defects. *See* Visual field defects
Field depth, **3**:37
Field (standard) lens, in lensmeter, **3**:269, 269*f*
Field of vision. *See also* Visual field
   with contact lenses, **3**:170
15-hue test, Lanthony desaturated, in low vision evaluation, **5**:105
Fifth cranial nerve. *See* Cranial nerve V
Filamentary keratopathy, **8**:56, 57*f*, 60–61
   bandage contact lenses for, **8**:403
Filamentous fungi, **8**:138, 138*f*, 139, 140, 238*t*
   keratitis caused by, **8**:164–167, 165*f*
   as normal ocular flora, **8**:97*t*
   ocular infection caused by, **8**:139, 140
Filaments, corneal, **8**:21*t*
   in dry-eye states, **8**:56, 57*f*
Filariae
   loa loa, **8**:170–171
      orbital involvement and, **4**:235
   onchocercal, **8**:141
      in anterior chamber, **9**:242
Filensin, **2**:277, **11**:12
Filling defect, vascular, **12**:22
Filtering bleb
   endophthalmitis associated with, **10**:196, 197*f*, **12**:354, 356–357, 357*f*
   evaluation for, before glaucoma surgery, **10**:29
   inadvertent, after cataract surgery, **11**:148–149
   postoperative complications and, **10**:196–198, 197*f*
Filtering procedures, **10**:183–198
   antifibrotic agents used with, **10**:186, 193–194, 195*f*
   bleb-related endophthalmitis and, **10**:196
   cataract surgery after, **11**:203
   cataract surgery combined with, **10**:199–200
   complications of, **10**:196–198, 196*t*, 197*f*
   conjunctival evaluation before, **10**:29
   contraindications to, **10**:185
   flap management in, **10**:194
   flat or shallow anterior chamber and, angle-closure glaucoma and, **10**:136
   indications for, **10**:184–185
   LASIK and, **13**:174–175
   in neovascular glaucoma, **10**:127
   for pigmentary glaucoma, **10**:89
   postoperative considerations in, **10**:194–195

preoperative evaluation for, **10**:185–186
trabeculectomy technique in, **10**:186–193. *See also*
Trabeculectomy
for uveitic glaucoma, **9**:298
Fimbriae, bacterial, **8**:132
Finasteride, ocular effects of, **1**:301*t*
Fine-needle aspiration biopsy (FNAB), **4**:34*t*, 43–44,
44*f*, 263
in metastatic eye disease, **4**:263, 319
of orbit, **4**:44, **7**:115
in rhabdomyosarcoma diagnosis, **6**:335
of thyroid gland, **1**:210
in uveal lymphoid infiltration, **4**:326
Fingerprint lines, in epithelial basement membrane
dystrophy, **8**:271
Finnish Twin Cohort Study, **10**:12, 76
Finnish-type amyloidosis (gelsolin-type lattice corneal
dystrophy), **4**:212, **8**:268*t*, 270*t*, 280, 280*f*, 317*t*, 319
genetics of, **4**:212, **8**:269*t*, 280, 317*t*
FIPTs. *See* Focal intraretinal periarteriolar transudates
First cranial nerve. *See* Cranial nerve I
First-degree atrioventricular block, **1**:122*t*
First-degree relatives, **2**:159
First-order aberrations, **13**:7
First-order approximation, **3**:59. *See also* Paraxial rays,
approximation/tracing of
First-order neuron
dilator muscle innervation and, **2**:60
Horner syndrome caused by lesions of, **5**:267
First-order optics, **3**:55–62, 55*f*
exact ray tracing in, **3**:55, 55*f*
first approximation in, **3**:59
image quality and, **3**:56
lensmaker's equation (LME) in, **3**:60–62, 61*f*
ophthalmic lenses and, **3**:62–83. *See also* Ophthalmic
lenses
paraxial approximation in, **3**:56–57, 56*f*, 57*f*, 58*f*
small-angle approximation in, **3**:57–60, 57*f*, 58*f*
FISH. *See* Fluorescence in situ hybridization
Fish eye disease, **8**:310
Fish flesh pattern, in treated retinoblastoma, **6**:360
Fishbone diagram, **1**:346, 347*f*
Fissures
calcarine, **5**:34, 35*f*
embryonic, **2**:121, 123, 124*f*
closure of, **2**:123, 125*f*
colobomas and, **2**:123, 125*f*
persistence of, in fetal alcohol syndrome, **2**:143
orbital, **2**:10–12, 12*f*, **5**:10, **7**:6*f*, 7*f*, 9
inferior, **2**:8*f*, 9*f*, 10–12, **5**:7*f*, 8, 8*f*, 9*f*, 12, **7**:6*f*, 7*f*, 9
superior, **2**:7*f*, 10, 11*f*, 12*f*, **5**:6, 6*f*, 7*f*, 9*f*, 10, **7**:6*f*,
7*f*, 9
ophthalmoplegia caused by lesions of, **5**:236–238
palpebral, **2**:22, 22*f*, 29*f*, **7**:142
in infants and children, **6**:169
congenital widening of (euryblepharon), **6**:177,
7:146–147, 148*f*, 149*f*
slanting of, **6**:178
A- and V-pattern deviations and, **6**:110, 110*f*
in Treacher Collins syndrome, **6**:178, 393–394,
394*f*
surgery affecting, **6**:24–25
vertical height of, **5**:275, 276*f*
in ptosis, **6**:179, **7**:202, 202*f*

Fistulas
arteriovenous
glaucoma associated with, **10**:28
of orbit, **7**:67–69, 68*f*
carotid cavernous sinus, **5**:237–238, 237*f*, **7**:67, 68*f*,
69
choroidal perfusion abnormalities and, **12**:176
neuroimaging in evaluation of, **5**:82*t*
dural cavernous, **7**:67–68, 69
lacrimal–cutaneous, **7**:277, 278, 278*f*
lacrimal gland, **6**:204, **7**:277
Fistulizing procedures, **10**:183–198. *See also* Filtering
procedures
Fitting (contact lens), **3**:181–193
disinfection of trial lenses and, **3**:201
for keratoconus/abnormal cornea, **3**:190–191, 191*f*
lens selection and, **3**:180–181, 181*f*
patient examination and, **3**:179–180
for presbyopia (bifocal contact lenses), **3**:189–190,
189*f*, 190*f*
after refractive surgery, **13**:192, 193
rigid gas-permeable contact lenses, **3**:182–186, 184*f*,
184*t*, 186*f*, 187*f*
scleral gas-permeable contact lenses, **3**:191–193, 192*f*
soft (flexible) contact lenses, **3**:182, 183*t*
toric soft lenses, **3**:188, 188*f*
therapeutic (bandage) contact lenses, **3**:194
trial, disinfection and, **1**:41, **8**:46
Fitzpatrick skin type, **7**:229
5 minutes of arc, for Snellen test letters, **3**:109, 109*f*
510(k) (premarket notification) application, **13**:205
Fixation (visual), **5**:198, 198*t*, 199
alternating, **6**:11
assessment of, **5**:199–200
disorders of, **5**:204–205
distance acuity assessment in children and, **6**:72, 72*t*
eccentric, **6**:53, 63
ARC testing and, **6**:53
monocular, **6**:11
nystagmus affected by, **5**:249, 249*t*
pediatric cataract and, **6**:252
perimetry variations and, **10**:55
recruitment during, **6**:33
for retinoscopy, **3**:122
spasm of. *See* Ocular motor apraxia
strabismus classification and, **6**:11
VOR suppression and, **5**:206–207, 207*f*
Fixation duress, for orbital floor fracture, **6**:126
Fixation loss, in perimetry, **5**:104
Fixation target, moving (heterophoria method), for
AC/A ratio measurement, **3**:144, **6**:81–82
Fixatives, for tissue preparation, **4**:28–29, 29*t*
Fixed, dilated pupil, **5**:316
FK506. *See* Tacrolimus
FKHL7 gene. *See* *FOXC1* gene
Flagella, bacterial, **8**:132
of spirochetes, **8**:137
Flagyl/Flagyl IV. *See* Metronidazole
FLAIR (fluid-attenuated inversion recovery) technique,
5:69, 73, 73*f*, 73*t*, 76*t*, 77*f*, 78*f*, **7**:28
in multiple sclerosis, **5**:322*f*, 325
Flame hemorrhages
ischemia causing, **4**:160, 161*f*
in leukemia, **6**:297

Flap folds, after LASIK, 13:105–108, 106t, 107f. See also
    Striae
Flap tears (horseshoe tears), 12:271, 272, 273f
    treatment of, 12:283, 284, 284t
Flaps
    advancement, 8:400
    bipedicle (bucket handle), 8:400
    for canthal repair, 7:186
    conjunctival, 8:398–401, 399f
        cataract surgery and
            for ICCE, 11:214
            leak causing inadvertent filtering bleb and,
                11:148–149
            for postoperative corneal edema, 11:147–148
        for neurotrophic keratopathy, 8:88–89
        for symblepharon, 7:200
        for trabeculectomy, 10:187–188, 188f, 189f
            closure of, 10:191–192, 193f
            management of, 10:194
        for trabeculotomy, in children, 10:154
        for wound closure after pterygium excision,
            8:391–393, 392f
    coronal scalp, for orbitotomy, 7:109
    for eyelid repair, 7:180, 182
        in burn patients, 7:181
    Gundersen, 8:399–400, 399f, 11:147–148
    lamellar, for superficial anterior lamellar keratoplasty,
        8:435
    LASIK, 13:24, 77–83, 78f, 79f, 81f, 82f, 83t
        aberrations associated with creation of, 13:95, 96f
        buttonhole, 13:102–103, 103f
        dislocation/subluxation of, 13:107–108, 108
            striae and, 13:107–108
        femtosecond, 13:4t, 23, 80–83, 81f, 82f, 83t
            aberrations and, 13:95
            advantages/disadvantages of, 13:83t
            international trends in use of, 13:199
            re-treatment and, 13:90, 90f
            steep or flat corneas and, 13:39
            visual disturbances related to, 13:116
        haze formation and, 13:27
        immediate postablation care of, 13:85
        infected, 13:99, 99f, 111
            diffuse lamellar keratitis (DLK) differentiated
                from, 13:110–111, 110t, 111f
        microkeratome creation of, 13:77–80, 78f, 79f
            aberrations and, 13:95
            complications associated with, 13:102–104, 103f
            international trends in use of, 13:199
        penetrating keratoplasty and, 13:171–172
        re-treatment and, 13:90, 90f
        retinal detachment repair and, 13:189–191
        steep or flat corneas and, 13:39
        striae in, 13:107–108
    partial (bridge), 8:400
    scleral, for trabeculectomy, 10:186, 188, 190f
        closure of, 10:191, 192f
        management of, 10:194
    single-pedicle (racquet), 8:400
    for symblepharon, 7:200
    for wound closure after pterygium excision, 8:391–393,
        392f
Flarex. See Fluorometholone

Flashing lights. See also Photopsias
    optic neuritis causing, 5:190, 323
    retinal disease causing, 5:189–190
Flashing lights. See Photopsias
Flat anterior chamber. See Anterior chamber, flat or
    shallow
Flattening, in myopia surgery, 13:20
Flatter add plus (FAP) rule, 3:174, 175, 185
Flatter than K (apical bearing) fit, for rigid gas-
    permeable contact lenses, 3:184, 185
Flecainide, 1:123t
    ocular effects of, 1:302t
Fleck corneal dystrophy, 8:268t, 270t, 287, 287f
    genetics of, 8:269t, 287
Fleck retina of Kandori, 12:218
Fleischer ring/line, in keratoconus, 4:91, 93f, 8:298, 299f,
    335–336, 337t
Fleurettes
    in retinoblastoma, 4:180, 181f, 6:358
    in retinocytoma, 4:181
Flexible contact lenses. See Soft (flexible) contact lenses
Flexible-loop anterior chamber intraocular lenses,
    11:133, 135f
Flexivue corneal inlay, 13:200
Flexner-Wintersteiner rosettes, in retinoblastoma, 4:180,
    181f, 6:358
Flicker fusion frequency, 2:294
Flicker response
    30-Hz, 12:34, 34f, 35, 36f
    vascular disease and, 12:40, 41f
Floaters
    in posterior vitreous detachment, 12:275
    in rhegmatogenous retinal detachment, 12:286
    in spontaneous vitreous hemorrhages, 12:313
    in uveitis/pars planitis, 9:79, 84t, 85, 135
Flocculonodular lobe, 5:48
Flomax. See Tamsulosin
"Floor effect," 1:340
Floppy eyelid syndrome, 7:154–155, 154f, 8:53, 81, 81f
Floppy iris syndrome, intraoperative, 11:74, 154–155,
    156f
Flovent. See Fluticasone
Flow cytometry, 4:34t, 36–37, 36f, 37f
    in paroxysmal nocturnal hemoglobinuria screening,
        1:147, 150
Flowchart (system of care), 1:346, 347f
Floxacillin, 2:369–370
Floxin. See Ofloxacin
Flu. See Influenza
Flucaine. See also Fluorescein, with proparacaine
Fluconazole, 1:54t, 64–65, 2:379t, 380
    for Candida endophthalmitis, 9:275, 12:203
    for coccidioidomycosis, 9:280
    for yeast keratitis, 8:166
Flucytosine/5-fluorocytosine, 1:54t, 2:379t, 380
Fluid-attenuated inversion recovery (FLAIR) technique,
    5:69, 73, 73f, 73t, 76t, 77f, 78f, 7:28
    in multiple sclerosis, 5:322f, 325
Fluid-based phacolysis, 11:127
Fluid (tear) lens, contact lenses and, 3:169, 173–174,
    174f, 175
    fitting and, 3:183, 185
Fluid-ventilated scleral lenses, 3:192, 193

Flumadine. *See* Rimantadine
Flumazenil, for benzodiazepine reversal, 1:310
FluMist. *See* Intranasal influenza vaccine
Flunisolide, for pulmonary diseases, 1:145*t*
Fluocinolone implant, 2:328, 331, 361, 9:105
  for birdshot retinochoroidopathy, 9:155, 12:191
  for branch retinal vein occlusion, 12:126
  for diabetic macular edema, 12:100
  for multifocal choroiditis and panuveitis syndrome, 9:164
  for sarcoidosis, 9:177
  for uveitic cystoid macular edema, 9:300–301
  for uveitis, 9:103
  for Vogt-Koyanagi-Harada (VKH) syndrome, 9:189
Fluor-Op. *See* Fluorometholone
Fluoracaine. *See* Fluorescein, with proparacaine
Fluorescein, 2:392, 8:17, 18*f*, 19*f*, 12:20–21
  for acquired nasolacrimal duct obstruction evaluation, 7:257–261, 259*f*
  allergic reactions to, 1:295, 12:24–25
  angiography with. *See* Fluorescein angiography
  for applanation tonometry, 8:17
  for aqueous deficiency diagnosis, 8:56
  with benoxinate, 2:387*t*, 389
  for congenital nasolacrimal duct obstruction evaluation, 6:206
  for conjunctival foreign-body identification, 8:370
  for contact lens fitting, 3:168, 186, 186*f*, 187*f*
  for dye disappearance test, 7:258, 8:17
  for fluorophotometry, 10:16
  intravenous administration of, 2:329. *See also* Fluorescein angiography
  photon (particle) aspects of light and, 3:7
  with proparacaine, 2:387*t*
  for pseudoepiphora evaluation, 7:257–261, 259*f*
  punctate staining patterns and, 8:17, 18*f*
  for tear breakup time testing, 7:257, 8:17, 52–53
  tonometry accuracy and, 10:23
Fluorescein angiography, 2:392, 5:107, 107*f*, 12:20–25, 23*f*, 24*f*
  in AAION, 5:126, 126*t*
  in acute posterior multifocal placoid pigment epitheliopathy (APMPPE), 9:149*t*, 156, 156*f*, 12:187, 187*f*
  in acute retinal pigment epitheliitis, 9:149*t*, 170, 170*f*, 12:194
  in acute zonal occult outer retinopathy, 9:149*t*, 170*f*, 171
  adverse effects of, 12:24–25
  in age-related macular degeneration, 12:59–60, 64
  allergic reactions to, 1:295–296
  anterior segment, 8:33
  in Behçet disease, 9:194
  in birdshot retinochoroidopathy, 9:149*t*, 152–153, 153*f*, 12:190
  in branch retinal vein occlusion, 12:122*f*, 123, 125*f*
  in capillary hemangioblastoma, 4:294
  in cataract surgery evaluation, 11:82
  in cavernous hemangioma, 4:295, 12:151, 152*f*
  in central retinal vein occlusion, 12:128, 128*f*, 129*f*
  in central serous chorioretinopathy, 12:23, 24*f*, 172–173, 173*f*
  in choroidal/ciliary body melanoma, 4:277

in choroidal hemangioma, 4:292
in choroidal neovascularization, 12:22, 23*f*, 65–68, 67*f*
in choroidal perfusion abnormalities, 12:176, 177*f*, 180*f*
in Coats disease, 12:143, 144*f*
before corneal transplantation, 8:417
in cystoid macular edema, 12:142, 142*f*
in dengue fever, 9:219–220
in diabetic macular edema, 12:95–96, 97*f*
in diabetic retinopathy, 12:90, 91*f*
in drusen versus papilledema differentiation, 5:135, 135*f*
extravasation of dye and, 12:25
in HTLV-1–associated uveitis, 9:219
in hypertensive choroidopathy, 12:115, 116*f*
in inflammatory chorioretinopathies, 9:149*t*
in iris melanoma, 4:269
in juxtafoveal/parafoveal retinal telangiectasia, 12:145*f*, 146*f*, 147
in low vision evaluation, 5:107, 107*f*
in lymphoma, 4:323–324, 9:282
in macular holes, 12:305
in metastatic eye disease, 4:318
in multifocal choroiditis and panuveitis syndrome, 9:149*t*, 162–163, 162*f*
in multiple evanescent white dot syndrome, 5:113, 9:149*t*, 168, 169*f*, 12:189, 189*f*
in NAION, 5:126*t*, 128, 128*t*
in ocular histoplasmosis syndrome, 9:223, 224*f*
in ocular ischemic syndrome, 9:287–288, 12:134
in optic neuritis, 5:128*t*
in pars planitis, 9:136, 12:196
in punctate inner choroiditis, 9:149*t*, 165, 165*f*, 166*f*
in radiation retinopathy, 12:152–153, 153*f*
in retinal disease, 12:20–25, 23*f*, 24*f*. *See also specific disease*
  capillary hemangioblastoma, 4:294, 12:150, 150*f*
  cavernous hemangioma, 4:295
in Rift Valley fever, 9:217
in serpiginous choroiditis, 9:149*t*, 159, 159*f*
in solitary idiopathic choroiditis, 12:194
in Stargardt disease, 12:234, 235*f*
in subretinal fibrosis and uveitis syndrome (SFU), 9:149*t*, 167
in Susac (SICRET) syndrome, 9:147, 147*f*
in sympathetic ophthalmia, 9:179, 180*f*
in tuberculous choroiditis, 9:258
in uveal effusion syndrome, 12:182, 182*f*
in uveitis, 9:93, 96*f*
in Vogt-Koyanagi-Harada (VKH) syndrome, 9:188, 188*f*, 12:198, 198*f*
in West Nile virus chorioretinitis, 9:215, 215*f*, 216*f*, 12:211
Fluorescein patterns, in contact lens fitting, 3:168, 186, 186*f*, 187*f*
Fluorescence in situ hybridization (FISH), 2:199, 200*f*, 4:38*t*
Fluorescent bronchoscopy, in cancer screening, 1:275
Fluorescent treponemal antibody absorption (FTA-ABS) test, 1:13, 279, 9:247, 248
  in syphilitic chorioretinitis, 12:205–206
Fluorexon, 8:17
5-Fluorocytosine. *See* Flucytosine

Fluorometholone, 2:357*t*, 359
  anti-inflammatory/pressure-elevating potency of,
    2:360*t*
  after photoablation, elevated IOP associated with,
    13:97
  for recurrent corneal erosions, 8:84
  for uveitis, 9:101*t*, 102
Fluorophotometry, 10:16
Fluoropolymer, for contact lenses, 3:178
Fluoroquinolones, 1:60–61, 2:371–373, 372*t*. *See also*
    Quinolones
  for bacterial keratitis, 8:162*t*, 163
  for gonococcal conjunctivitis, 8:152
Fluorouracil, 1:240*t*, 2:334, 366–367, 385
  for conjunctival intraepithelial neoplasia, 8:229, 230*f*
  for corneal intraepithelial neoplasia, 8:231
  in trabeculectomy, 10:186, 193, 193–194
Fluoxetine, ocular effects of, 1:301*t*
Fluphenazine, 1:251
  oculogyric crisis caused by, 5:212
Flurbiprofen, 1:183*t*, 2:257, 357*t*, 363
Fluress. *See* Fluorescein, with benoxinate
Flurox. *See* Fluorescein, with benoxinate
Flutamide, 1:242*t*
Fluticasone, 1:145*t*
  with salmeterol, 1:145*t*
Flutrimazole, 1:65
Flutter
  atrial, 1:124*t*, 125
  ocular, 5:251*t*, 255–256, 255*f*
  ventricular, 1:125, 126*t*
Fluvastatin, for hypercholesterolemia/heart disease
    prevention, 1:137*t*
Flux, luminous, 3:18*t*
Fly larvae, ocular infection caused by, 8:143
Flying spot lasers, for photoablation, 13:25
FML. *See* Fluorometholone
fMRI. *See* Functional magnetic resonance imaging
FNAB. *See* Fine-needle aspiration biopsy
Foam cells, 1:100
Focal electroretinogram, 5:109, 12:37
Focal intraretinal periarteriolar transudates (FIPTs),
    12:113, 114*f*
Focal length, 3:78–79
  of mirror, 3:90
  for operating microscope, 3:262
Focal lines, in astigmatism, 3:114, 115*f*
Focal planes, 3:69, 70*f*
Focal points, 3:69, 70*f*, 76, 77*f*
  refractive states of eye and, 3:113
Focimeter. *See* Lensmeters
Focus, depth of, 3:36–37
Focus Night & Day contact lenses, 3:177*t*
Fogging
  for astigmatic dial refraction, 3:130, 131*f*
  for binocular balance testing, 3:136
  for duochrome test, 3:136
  for nonorganic ophthalmic disorder evaluation
    monocular no light perception and, 5:309
    monocular reduced vision and, 5:310–311
  for retinoscopy, 3:122
  for subjective refraction, 3:136

Folate/folic acid
  antagonists of, in cancer chemotherapy, 1:240*t*
  deficiency of, 1:149
    optic neuropathy caused by, 5:154
  supplementary, for homocystinuria management,
    6:399
Foldable intraocular lenses, 3:205, 11:135–136, 136*f*
  in children, 6:257, 259
  implantation procedure for, 11:138, 139
  light-adjustable, 13:146–147, 147*f*
  multifocal, 13:155
  posterior chamber phakic, 13:130–131, 130*f*, 131*f*
  toric, 13:142, 142*f*
  in uveitis patient, 9:127
Folic acid. *See* Folate/folic acid
Folinic acid, 2:374
  for toxoplasmosis, 12:208–209, 208*t*
Follicle-stimulating hormone, pituitary adenoma
    producing, 1:215
Follicles
  conjunctival, 8:20*t*, 24, 24*f*
  lash, 7:142*f*
    tumors arising in, 7:162–164, 163*f*
Follicular carcinoma, of thyroid gland, 1:213–214
Follicular conjunctivitis, 4:51, 51*f*, 52*f*, 8:22*t*, 24, 24*f*
  in acute hemorrhagic conjunctivitis, 8:130
  adenoviral, 4:53, 8:124
  Epstein-Barr virus causing, 8:122–123
  in Lyme disease, 9:251, 12:210
  in measles, 8:129
  medication toxicity causing, 8:359*t*, 360, 361*f*
  in mumps, 8:129–130
  RNA viruses causing, 8:129
  varicella-zoster virus causing, 8:118
Follicular keratosis, inverted, 4:215, 215*f*
Follicular lymphoma/follicular center lymphoma
  of conjunctiva, 4:73
  of orbit, 7:81
Folliculosis, benign lymphoid, 4:71, 8:24, 24*f*
Follow-up, in case series, 1:322–323
Follow-up studies (cohort studies), 1:321*f*, 324*f*,
    326–327
Followability, in phacoemulsification, 11:104
Fomivirsen, for CMV retinitis, 1:24, 38
Fondaparinux, for non–ST-segment elevation acute
    coronary syndrome, 1:111–112
Food and Drug Administration (FDA), 2:333, 13:203–208
  adverse event reporting to, 13:207–208
  delays in device approval by, 13:207
  LASIK and, 13:91, 117
  medical device classification by, 13:203–204
  medical device pathways to market and, 13:205
  Ophthalmic Devices Panel of, 13:205–207
Food, Drug, and Cosmetic Act, 13:203
Foot-candle, 3:18*t*
Foot-lambert, 3:18*t*
Foot-pedal controls, phaco machine, 11:104–105
Foradil. *See* Formoterol
Foramen (foramina)
  ethmoidal, anterior/posterior, 2:8*f*, 10, 5:12, 7:6*f*, 7*f*,
    8–9
  infraorbital, 2:9

magnum, 5:7
oculomotor, 7:11, 12f
optic, 2:7f, 8f, 10, 11f, 5:9f, 7:9
orbital, 2:10, 11f
ovale, 5:6f
rotundum, 5:8, 7:6f
spinosum, 5:6f
supraorbital, 2:5, 6f, 7f, 10, 5:12, 7:6, 6f
zygomatic, 2:10
zygomaticofacial, 7:6f
zygomaticotemporal, 5:12
Forced ductions, 6:83
in blowout fractures, 7:101
surgery and, 7:102
in Brown syndrome, 6:122t, 130
in diplopia, 5:218, 219f
in sixth nerve (abducens) paralysis, 6:134
in thyroid eye disease, 6:135, 139t
Forced expiratory volume in 1 second (FEV₁), 1:143
Forced vital capacity (FVC), 1:143
Forceps injury, during delivery, infantile corneal
    opacities and, 6:216t, 217
Forehead
    drooping of (brow ptosis), 7:227–228, 227f
        dermatochalasis and, 7:222, 227
    surgical rejuvenation of, 7:232, 233f
Forehead flap
    for canthal repair, 7:186–187
    for eyelid repair, 7:183f
Forehead rejuvenation, 7:232, 233f
Foreheadplasty, 7:232, 233f
Foreign bodies
    intralenticular, 11:51
    intraocular, 9:288, 12:325–328, 326f, 328t
        anesthesia for removal of in children, 6:5
        conjunctival, 4:53, 53f, 8:370, 370f
        corneal, 8:371–372, 371f
            in children, 6:407–408
            iron, 8:337t, 371–372, 371f
            plant/vegetation, 8:362, 371
        endophthalmitis and, 8:375, 12:328
        of iris, 4:270t
        retained, 9:288, 12:327–328
            cataract surgery and, 11:207
            endophthalmitis caused by, 8:375
            glaucoma and, 10:97
            siderosis and, 4:124, 11:53, 54f, 12:328, 328f
            surgical techniques for removal of, 12:326–327
        uveitis differentiated from, in children, 6:276t
    intraorbital, 7:104
    neuroimaging in evaluation of, 5:82t
Foreign body giant cells, 4:7, 9f
Foreign-body granuloma, after strabismus surgery,
    6:156, 156f
Foreign-body sensation
    in corneal abrasion, 8:372
    in dry eye, 8:55, 65
    fluorescein in investigation of, 8:370
Forkhead genes/forkhead transcription factor
    Axenfeld-Rieger syndrome and, 8:256, 10:142
    glaucoma and, 10:142
Formalin, as tissue fixative, 4:28–29, 29t

Forme fruste. See also Keratoconus
    ectasia after LASIK and, 13:115
    refractive surgery contraindicated in, 13:16–17, 168
        topography in detection and, 8:43–44, 44f,
            13:16–17, 71, 168, 168f
Formed elements, 1:147. See also Blood cells
Formed hallucinations, 5:172, 189, 190. See also
    Hallucinations
Formoterol, 1:145, 145t
Fornices, 2:29, 30f, 34, 4:47, 48f, 8:4
    contracture of, anophthalmic socket and, 7:123
    lymphocytic lesions involving, 4:71
    reconstruction of
        for cicatricial pemphigoid, 8:203
        conjunctival graft for, 8:395
        for pseudocryptophthalmos, 8:250
    sterilization of during cataract surgery, 11:128
Fornix-based conjunctival flap, for trabeculectomy,
    10:187, 188f
    closure of, 10:191–192, 193f
Fornix incision, for extraocular muscle surgery, 6:154
Forster-Fuchs spots, 12:86
Fortaz. See Ceftazidime
Forteo. See Teriparatide
Fortical. See Calcitonin/calcitonin nasal spray
Fortification spectrum, in migraine, 5:295, 295f
Fortovase. See Saquinavir
Fosamax/Fosamax Plus D. See Alendronate
Fosamprenavir, 1:34
Foscarnet, 1:55t, 66, 2:381t, 384
    for acute retinal necrosis, 9:202, 12:201
    for CMV retinitis, 1:24, 38, 66, 2:381t, 384, 9:207,
        12:200
Foscavir. See Foscarnet
Fosinopril, 1:76t
Fosphenytoin, 1:263t, 297
Fossae
    anterior cranial, 5:6f, 7, 11f, 7:7f
    lacrimal, 2:7, 7f, 8f, 5:8f, 9f, 7:5, 6f
    middle cranial, 5:6f, 8, 11f
    posterior cranial, 5:6f
        neuroimaging in evaluation of, 5:82t, 85, 88
    pterygopalatine, 7:7f, 9
    temporal, 5:7, 11f
    for trochlea of superior oblique tendon, 7:5–6
Foster Kennedy syndrome/pseudo–Foster Kennedy
    syndrome, 5:127, 128f
4:2:1 rule, 12:104
4Δ base-out prism test, in sensory adaptation testing,
    6:57–58, 57f
4-mirror goniolens, Zeiss, for slit-lamp biomicroscopy,
    3:253, 255f
Fourier reconstruction, in wavefront analysis, 13:6
Fourier transform infrared (FTIR) spectroscopy, in
    cervical cancer screening, 1:273
Fourth cranial nerve. See Cranial nerve IV
Fourth nerve (trochlear) palsy/paralysis, 5:232–234, 234f
    bilateral, 5:233
    congenital, 5:233, 234f
    diplopia and, 5:223, 226–227, 232–234, 234f
    superior oblique muscle paralysis and, 6:118–121,
        119f

Fovea (fovea centralis), **2:**71, 74*f*, 79, 79*f*, 80*f*, 81, 82*f*,
 4:146, **5:**28, **12:**8, 9*f*, 9*t*, 10
 in albinism, **12:**258, 259*f*
 development of, **2:**126–127, **6:**44–45
 hypoplasia of, **6:**292, 320, 415
Fovea externa, **2:**80*f*, 81
Foveal avascular zone, **2:**79*f*, 81, 82*f*, **12:**8
Foveal burns, photocoagulation causing, **12:**341
Foveal cones, **2:**74, 81
Foveal electroretinogram, **12:**37
Foveal fibers, **2:**90
Foveal pit, **2:**127
Foveal pseudocyst, **12:**304, 305*f*
Foveal retinoschisis, **6:**294, **12:**246, 246*f*
Foveation, **5:**199, 204
Foveola, **2:**79, 80*f*, 81, **4:**146, 147*f*, **12:**8, 9*f*, 9*t*
Foveomacular retinitis (solar retinopathy/retinitis),
 12:332–333
Foveomacular vitelliform dystrophy, adult-onset, **4:**175,
 176*f*, **12:**237–238, 238*f*
 age-related macular degeneration differentiated from,
 12:69, 69*f*
Foville syndrome, **5:**227
FOXC1 (FKHL7) gene
 in Axenfeld-Rieger syndrome, **6:**214, 233, **10:**142
 in glaucoma, **10:**11*t*, 142
 in Peters anomaly, **8:**258, **11:**28, **10:**142
FOXP1 gene, in extranodal marginal zone lymphoma,
 4:73
Foxp3⁺ T cells, regulatory, **9:**40, 41
FPG (fasting plasma glucose test). *See* Fasting glucose
Fractures. *See also specific type or structure affected*
 osteoporosis-related, **1:**228
Fragile site/fragility, chromosomal, **2:**151–152
Fragile X syndrome, **2:**152
Frames (spectacle), anophthalmic socket camouflage
 and, **7:**125
Frameshift mutation (framing error/frameshift), **2:**141,
 152
François, central cloudy dystrophy of, **8:**268*t*, 270*t*,
 289–290, 289*f*
 genetics of, **8:**269*t*, 289
François-Neetens speckled corneal dystrophy (Fleck
 corneal dystrophy), **8:**268*t*, 270*t*, 287, 287*f*
 genetics of, **8:**269*t*, 287
FRAS1 gene, **8:**250
Fraser syndrome, **6:**175, **8:**249–250
 eyelid manifestations of, **4:**213*t*
Freckle, **4:**224
 conjunctival, **8:**233
 of eyelid, **7:**164–165
 Hutchinson melanotic (lentigo maligna/precancerous
 melanosis), **7:**168
 iris, **4:**270*t*, 272*f*, **6:**351
Fredrickson classification, of hyperlipoproteinemias,
 8:308, 309*t*
Free cap formation, in LASIK, **13:**103–104, 103*f*
Free-living amebae, **8:**140
Free radicals (oxygen radicals), **2:**311–318, **3:**160
 in Alzheimer disease, **1:**266
 cellular sources of, **2:**311–312, 312*f*
 as inflammatory mediators, **9:**30–31

 in lens, **2:**313–315, 314*f*, **11:**16–17
 lipid peroxidation and, **2:**311, 312–313
 in retina, **2:**315–316
Free T₄, **1:**208, 209
Freezing, anterior segment injuries caused by, **8:**351–352
Frenzel goggles, in nystagmus assessment, **5:**201, 244
Frequency, in phacoemulsification, **11:**103
Frequency doubling, **10:**61
Frequency-doubling technology (FDT) perimetry, **10:**61
 in glaucoma suspect screening, **10:**82–83
Frequency-encoding analysis, **5:**69
Frequency of light wave, **3:**4
 relationship to wavelength, **3:**4, 7
Frequency response, modulation transfer function and,
 3:111
Fresnel prisms, **3:**88–89, 89*f*. *See also* Prisms
 for consecutive esotropia, **6:**103
 for esotropia in sixth nerve (abducens) paralysis, **6:**98
 for nystagmus, **6:**326
 temporary, **3:**89, 164
 for thyroid eye disease, **5:**334
 for vertical heterophorias, **3:**163
Friedewald formula, **1:**133
Friedreich ataxia, pigmentary retinopathy and, **12:**250*t*,
 254
Front toric contact lenses, **3:**187
Frontal artery, **5:**14*f*, 18
Frontal bone, **5:**5, 7, 7*f*, 8*f*, 9, 9*f*, **7:**6*f*, 7*f*
Frontal ethmoidal suture, **5:**7
Frontal eye fields, **5:**40, 40*f*, 202, 204
 ocular deviations caused by lesion of, **5:**211–212
Frontal lobe, **5:**28*f*
Frontal/temporal nerve, **2:**103, **5:**10*f*, 59, 59–60, 59*f*,
 7:12*f*, 13, 133–134, 133*f*
Frontal sinuses, **2:**9*f*, 12, 13*f*, 14*f*, **5:**7, 11*f*, **7:**7*f*, 18, 18*f*
Frontalis muscle, **7:**17, 131, 132*f*, 133*f*, 135*f*, 137*f*
Frontalis sling, for blepharophimosis syndrome
 correction, **7:**145
Frontalis suspension, for ptosis correction, **6:**179,
 7:212–213, 212*f*
Frontoethmoidal incision, for orbitotomy, **7:**108*f*,
 110–111
Frontoethmoidal suture, **5:**8*f*, **7:**7
Frontosphenoid suture, **5:**7*f*
Frontozygomatic suture, **5:**7*f*, **7:**6, 6*f*
Frozen section, for pathologic examination, **4:**34*t*,
 44–45
FTA-ABS (fluorescent treponemal antibody absorption)
 test, **1:**13, 279, **9:**247, 248
 in syphilitic chorioretinitis, **12:**205–206
FTC. *See* Emtricitabine
FTIR spectroscopy. *See* Fourier transform infrared
 (FTIR) spectroscopy
5-FU. *See* Fluorouracil
Fuchs adenoma (pseudoadenomatous hyperplasia),
 4:184, 288
Fuchs coloboma (tilted disc syndrome), **5:**142–143,
 142*f*, **6:**307, 307*f*
Fuchs endothelial corneal dystrophy, **2:**47, 47*f*, **4:**98–100,
 100*f*, **8:**268*t*, 270*t*, 291–293, 292*f*
 genetics of, **8:**269*t*, 291
 refractive surgery and, **13:**35

Fuchs heterochromic iridocyclitis (Fuchs uveitis syndrome), 9:132–134, 133f
cataracts/cataract surgery in, 9:133, 134, 11:59, 60f
glaucoma and, 9:133, 134, 10:94–95, 95f
rubella reactivation and, 9:48, 134, 211
Fuchs superficial marginal keratitis, 8:340
Fucosidosis, 6:400t, 8:312, 12:263
Full-field electroretinography, 5:109
Full-thickness eyelid biopsy, 7:170f
Full-thickness pentagonal resection, for trichiasis, 7:200
Full-threshold testing algorithms (perimetry), 10:57, 57f, 58
Fumagillin, for microsporidial keratoconjunctivitis, 8:170
Functional Acuity Contrast Test (FACT), 3:292
Functional disorders
in older patients, 1:226–227
assessment of, 1:219–220
treatment of, 1:227
ophthalmic considerations and, 1:227. See also Nonorganic (functional/nonphysiologic) ophthalmic disorders
Functional history, in low vision assessment, 3:288
Functional imaging, 5:80
Functional magnetic resonance imaging (fMRI), 5:69, 80
Functional visual loss. See Nonorganic (functional/nonphysiologic) ophthalmic disorders
Fundus
in acute posterior multifocal placoid pigment epitheliopathy (APMPPE), 9:156, 156f
in albinism, 12:258, 259f
albipunctatus, 6:292, 12:218, 218f
11-cis-retinol dehydrogenase defects causing, 2:297
in birdshot retinochoroidopathy, 9:152, 152f, 154f
in congenital night blindness
abnormalities of, 12:217–219, 218f, 219f
normal, 12:215–217, 216f, 217f
evaluation of. See also Fundus photography; Ophthalmoscopy; Slit-lamp biomicroscopy/examination
before cataract surgery, 11:80–81
in choroidal/ciliary body melanoma, 4:275–276, 277
in glaucoma, 10:32
in infants and children, 10:152
in low vision evaluation, 5:95–97, 96f, 97f
in nystagmus, 6:320, 320t
in penetrating trauma, 6:408, 408f
in premature infants, 6:285, 286t
before refractive surgery, 13:38
refractive lens exchange/clear lens extraction, 13:139
in transient visual loss evaluation, 5:175, 175f
flavimaculatus (Stargardt disease/juvenile macular degeneration), 4:172, 174f, 6:292–293, 293f, 12:234–236, 235f, 236t
ABC/ABCR transporter mutations causing, 2:296, 4:172, 6:293, 12:233, 234
cone–rod dystrophy and, 6:293, 12:233, 235
gene for, 12:222, 233, 234
retinal pigment epithelium in, 2:309, 12:234, 235f

illumination of
in direct ophthalmoscopy, 3:244
in indirect ophthalmoscopy, 3:245, 246, 246f, 248f
in Leber hereditary optic neuropathy, 5:137–138, 137f
in multiple evanescent white dot syndrome, 9:168, 168f
in multiple sclerosis, 5:324
in ocular histoplasmosis syndrome, 9:221
oculi, 2:71
pulverulentus, 12:240
in retinitis pigmentosa, 12:225, 225f
salt-and-pepper
in rubella, 6:183, 183f, 9:210, 210f
in syphilis, 9:243
in infants and children, 6:185
in serpiginous choroiditis, 9:159, 159f, 160f
in solitary idiopathic choroiditis, 12:194
sunset-glow, in Vogt-Koyanagi-Harada (VKH) syndrome, 9:184, 185, 186f, 12:197
in sympathetic ophthalmia, 9:180f
tomato ketchup, 4:292, 293f
xerophthalmic, 8:78
Fundus autofluorescence, 12:22
in acute zonal occult outer retinopathy, 9:171, 171f
in birdshot retinochoroidopathy, 9:153, 154f
in central serous chorioretinopathy, 12:173–174
in multifocal choroiditis and panuveitis syndrome, 9:163, 163f
near-infrared, 12:31
in serpiginous choroiditis, 9:160, 160f
in uveitis, 9:93
Fundus biomicroscopy. See Slit-lamp biomicroscopy/examination
Fundus lenses, slit-lamp, 3:251–255, 251f, 253f, 254f, 255f, 256f
Fundus near-infrared autofluorescence, 12:31
Fundus photography
camera for, 3:248–251, 250f
in choroidal/ciliary body melanoma, 4:277
Funduscopic lenses, for slit-lamp biomicroscopy, 3:253, 255f
Fungi, 1:20–21, 8:138–140, 138t. See also specific organism or type of infection
allergic sinusitis caused by, orbital involvement and, 4:234
chorioretinitis caused by, 4:152, 153f
disseminated infection in HIV infection/AIDS and, 1:20, 40
drugs for infection caused by. See Antifungal agents
endophthalmitis caused by, 12:203–204, 204f
endogenous, 9:273–280, 273f, 275f, 277f, 279f, 12:203–204, 204f
iris nodule in, 4:270t
postoperative, 9:270
eyelid infections caused by, 8:148–149
isolation techniques for identification of, 8:103
keratitis caused by, 4:83–84, 85f, 8:164–167, 165f
after photoablation, 13:98
plant sources of, 8:362
as normal ocular flora, 8:97t
ocular infection caused by, 8:138–140
neuro-ophthalmic signs of, 5:364–367, 365f, 366f

optic nerve infection caused by, 4:251, 251*f*
orbital infection caused by, 4:234, 234*f*
aspergillosis, 4:234, 234*f*, 7:46
exenteration in management of, 7:126
mucormycosis/zygomycosis/phycomycosis, 4:234,
6:197, 197*f*, 7:45–46
exenteration in management of, 7:45, 126
retinal infection caused by, 4:152–153, 153*f*
scleritis caused by, 8:171
stains and culture media for identification of, 8:103*t*
uveitis caused by, 9:221–226
Fungizone. *See* Amphotericin B
Fungus ball (aspergilloma), 5:364–365, 365*f*
in endophthalmitis, 9:277*f*
Furazolidone, 1:64
Furosemide
for heart failure, 1:118, 119
for hypertension, 1:76*t*
for idiopathic intracranial hypertension, 5:124
Furoxone. *See* Furazolidone
Furrow degeneration, senile, 8:339
Fusarium, 8:139
keratitis caused by, 4:83, 85*f*, 8:139, 165*f*, 166
contact lens solutions and, 3:196
oxysporum, 8:139
solani, 8:138*f*, 139, 165*f*
Fused bifocals, 3:147, 148*f*
Fusion, 6:41–42, 41*t*
peripheral, in monofixation syndrome, 6:60
strabismus classification and, 6:10
tenacious proximal, in intermittent exotropia,
6:100–101
Fusion (HIV) inhibitors, 1:34
Fusion maldevelopment nystagmus syndrome (latent
nystagmus), 5:246, 6:322–323, 323*f*, 324*f*
dissociated vertical deviation and, 6:116, 117, 323
Fusional amplitudes, 6:41, 41*t*
therapeutic use of prisms and, 3:163
Fusional convergence, 6:37, 41, 41*t*, 82
Fusional divergence, 6:37, 41*t*, 82
in refractive accommodative esotropia, 6:93
Fusional vergence, 6:41, 41*t*, 82–83
assessment of, 6:82
Fuzeon. *See* Enfuvirtide
FVC (forced vital capacity), 1:143
Fyodorov Sputnik intraocular lens, 3:207, 208*f*

G

G6P. *See* Glucose-6-phosphate
G6PD deficiency. *See* Glucose-6-phosphate
dehydrogenase deficiency
G38D mutation, 2:295
G protein α-subunit, uveal melanoma and, 4:200
G-protein–coupled receptors, 2:262
prostaglandin, 2:258
in tear secretion, 2:242, 242*f*, 243, 243*f*
G proteins
in cone phototransduction, 2:294
in signal transduction, 2:262–263, 262*f*, 263*f*
in tear secretion, 2:242, 242*f*

GABA
in cone phototransduction, 2:294
horizontal cell release of, 2:299, 300
GABA agonists, for nystagmus, 5:257–258
Gabapentin, 1:263*t*
for nystagmus, 5:258
Gabitril. *See* Tiagabine
GAD. *See* Generalized anxiety disorder
Gadolinium, 5:69, 72, 77, 7:28
in multiple sclerosis imaging, 5:325
GAGs. *See* Glycosaminoglycans
Gain/gain adjustment (eye movement), 5:48
pursuit system and, 5:204, 213
vestibular ocular reflex, 5:201
Gain of function mutations, 2:171
Galactitol (dulcitol)
in cataract formation, 2:281, 11:56
in lens glucose/carbohydrate metabolism, 2:280*f*
Galactokinase
defective/deficiency of, 2:213*t*, 6:398
galactosemia/cataract formation and, 2:280, 6:398,
11:56, 57
Galactose
in cataract formation, 2:281, 11:56
in lens glucose/carbohydrate metabolism, 2:280*f*
Galactose 1-phosphate uridyltransferase (Gal-1-PUT),
galactosemia caused by defects in, 2:213*t*, 280, 11:56
Galactose-free diet, 2:231
Galactosemia, 2:213*t*, 6:398, 401*t*, 11:56–57, 56*f*
cataracts in, 2:280, 281, 6:398, 11:56–57, 56*f*
dietary therapy for, 2:231, 11:56
Galactosialidoses, 6:401*t*
cherry-red spot in, 6:401*t*, 12:262
α-Galactosidase, defective, 2:213*t*
α-Galactosidase A, in Fabry disease, 8:310, 311
β-Galactosidase, defective/deficiency of, 2:213*t*
in gangliosidoses, 6:303, 401*t*, 8:310
Galanin, in aqueous humor, 2:267, 270
Galen, vein of, 5:26
Galilean telescope, 3:81–83, 81*f*, 83*f*, 252. *See also*
Telescopes
contact lens correction of aphakia and, 3:171, 171–172
in operating microscope, 3:262, 262*f*
reverse
contact lens correction of aphakia and, 3:171–172
in slit-lamp biomicroscopy, 3:252
in slit-lamp biomicroscopy, 3:81, 81*f*, 251*f*, 252
zoom, in operating microscope, 3:262, 263
Galilei device, for corneal power measurement, in IOL
power determination, 3:217, 217*f*
Gallamine, 2:344
adverse effects of, 2:343*f*
Galtonian inheritance, of mitochondrial DNA diseases,
2:208
Galyfilcon A contact lenses, 3:177*t*
Gametes, 2:195
Gamma (γ)-aminobutyric acid (GABA)
in cone phototransduction, 2:294
horizontal cell release of, 2:299, 300
Gamma (γ)-aminobutyric acid (GABA) agonists, for
nystagmus, 5:257–258
Gamma (γ)-crystallins, 2:70, 276, 11:12

Gamma (γ)-interferon, 1:243, 9:29t
  in delayed hypersensitivity, 9:49f, 50
Gamma knife technique, 5:368
Gammopathy, benign monoclonal, corneal deposits in,
  8:320
Ganciclovir, 1:55t, 66, 2:330–331, 381t, 383–384
  for acute retinal necrosis/herpetic retinitis, 9:202,
    12:201
  for CMV retinitis, 1:24, 37–38, 66, 2:381t, 383–384,
    9:207, 12:200
Ganciclovir sustained-release intraocular device/
  implant, 2:328, 330–331, 381t, 384
  for CMV retinitis, 12:200
Ganglion cells, retinal, 2:74f, 75, 75f, 78, 79f, 299f, 300,
  4:145, 146f, 5:28, 29, 30f, 12:8, 10, 11f, 12, 14f
  development/differentiation of, 2:126, 6:44
  K system originating in, 6:44
  M system originating in (parasol), 6:42, 43f
  in optic nerve, 10:40–41
    degeneration of, in glaucomatous optic neuropathy,
      10:44–45
  P system originating in (midget), 6:43, 43f
  ratio of to photoreceptors, 5:29
Ganglioneuromas, in multiple endocrine neoplasia, 1:216
Ganglionic blocking agents, adverse effects of, 2:343f
Ganglionic neurons, dilator muscle innervation and, 2:60
Gangliosidoses, 6:303–304, 401t, 8:310. See also specific
  type under GM
  retinal degeneration and, 12:262–264, 263f, 264f
Gantrisin. See Sulfisoxazole
Ganzfield stimulus, electroretinogram evoked by, 12:35
Gap junctions, in lens, 2:278, 11:17
GAPP. See Good acuity, postoperative photophobia
Garamycin. See Gentamicin
Gardner syndrome (familial adenomatous polyposis),
  retinal manifestations of, 4:150–151, 12:255, 255f
  in children, 6:352
Garenoxacin, 1:61
Gargoyle cells, in mucopolysaccharidoses, 8:307
Gas laser, 3:23, 24–25. See also specific type and Lasers
Gas-permeability constant (Dk), 3:168, 176, 177t, 200
  corneal hypoxia and, 3:200
  for hybrid contact lenses, 3:191
  orthokeratology and, 3:194
  for rigid contact lenses, 3:176–178, 180, 191
  for soft (flexible) contact lenses, 3:178, 180
  for therapeutic (bandage) contact lenses, 3:193
Gas-permeable contact lenses. See Rigid gas-permeable
  contact lenses; Scleral contact lenses; Soft (flexible)
  contact lenses
Gas retinal tamponade, in retinal detachment, 12:290,
  345, 364–365, 365f, 366–367
Gasserian ganglion (semilunar/trigeminal ganglion),
  2:101, 101–102, 101f, 5:59, 59f
Gastric bypass surgery, for weight loss
  in idiopathic intracranial hypertension, 5:124
  in type 2 diabetes mellitus, 1:195
Gastric cancer, 1:275
Gastrinomas, in multiple endocrine neoplasia, 1:216
Gastroesophageal reflux disease (GERD)
  cancer and, 1:275
  scleroderma and, 1:173

Gastrointestinal carcinoma, metastatic eye disease and,
  4:316t
Gastrointestinal disease
  in Behçet disease, 9:192
  cancer screening and, 1:275
  in HIV infection/AIDS, 1:38
  in polyarteritis nodosa/microscopic polyangiitis,
    9:143
  retinal degeneration associated with, 12:255, 255f
  in scleroderma, 1:173
  in Whipple disease, 9:265
Gastrula, 2:117
Gastrulation, 2:117, 118f, 119f
Gatifloxacin, 1:52t, 61, 2:371–373, 372t
  for bacterial keratitis, 8:162t, 163
Gaucher disease, 6:398, 400t, 12:262
  corneal changes in, 8:311
  racial and ethnic concentration of, 2:211
  retinal degeneration/cherry-red spot in, 12:262
Gaussian reduction, 3:79
  IOL power selection and, 3:212
Gaze. See also Ocular motility
  horizontal, 5:44–46, 45f
  positions of, 6:27–28, 80
    assessment of, 6:80, 80f
    cardinal, 6:28, 28f, 80
      extraocular muscle action and, 6:30–32, 30f, 31f,
        32f, 33f, 34f
      yoke muscles and, 6:28f, 35, 80
    diagnostic, 6:80, 80f
    extraocular muscle action affected by, 5:55, 6:30–32,
      30f, 31f, 32f, 33f, 34f
    midline, 6:80
    nystagmus affected by, 5:244, 247–248, 6:317
    primary, 6:13, 27, 80, 80f
    secondary, 6:27
    strabismus and, 6:80, 80f
    tertiary, 6:28
    variation of deviation with, 6:10
  psychic paralysis of. See Ocular motor apraxia
  vertical, 5:42–44, 44f
Gaze deviation
  periodic alternating, in comatose patients, 5:259
  seizure activity and, 1:263, 5:211–212
Gaze-evoked nystagmus, 5:244f, 247–248
  in internuclear ophthalmoplegia, 5:224–225
Gaze palsy/preference, 5:210–211, 211f, 212f
  in ataxia-telangiectasia, 5:344
  in comatose patient, 5:258
  ipsilateral, 5:50
  nonorganic, 5:315
  psychic. See Ocular motor apraxia
GB virus C, 1:26
GCA (giant cell/temporal arteritis). See Arteritis, giant
  cell
GCAPs. See Guanylate cyclase assisting proteins
GCD1. See Granular corneal dystrophy, type 1
GCD2. See Granular corneal dystrophy, type 2
GCL (ganglion cell layer). See Ganglion cells, retinal
GCP. See Glaucoma Change Probability
GDLD. See Gelatinous droplike corneal dystrophy
GDM. See Gestational diabetes mellitus

GDx nerve fiber analysis, 5:81
Gel electrophoresis, denaturing gradient, 2:183–184
Gel phenomenon, in rheumatoid arthritis, 1:161
Gelatinase (MMP-2)
  in recurrent corneal erosion, 8:83
  in Sjögren syndrome, 8:63
  in vitreous, 2:283
Gelatinous droplike corneal dystrophy (primary familial
    amyloidosis), 8:268t, 270t, 274–275, 275f, 317t, 318,
    318f
  genetics of, 8:269t, 274, 317t
Gelsolin gene mutation
  amyloidosis/amyloid deposits and, 4:212, 8:317t
  lattice corneal dystrophy and, 4:212, 8:269t, 280,
    317t
Gelsolin-type lattice corneal dystrophy, 4:212, 8:268t,
    270t, 280, 280f, 317t, 319
  genetics of, 4:212, 8:269t, 280, 317t
Gemfibrozil, for hypercholesterolemia/heart disease
    prevention, 1:137t
Gemifloxacin, 1:52t, 61
Gender
  in glaucoma, 10:10, 114
  osteoporosis risk and, 1:228
Gene, 2:152, 165, 193–194. See also Genetic/hereditary
    factors; Genetics
  cancer, 2:171–173, 172f
  candidate, 2:180–182
  defective copy of (pseudogene), 2:159
  expression of. See Gene transcription
  structure of, 2:165
Gene dosage, 2:177
Gene duplication. See DNA, replication of
Gene expression profile, 4:41
Gene mapping, 2:178, 193
Gene replacement therapy, 2:187–188, 231
Gene therapy, 2:184–189, 189f
  for HIV infection/AIDS, 1:34
  for inborn errors of metabolism, 6:399–402
  for Leber congenital amaurosis, 6:290
  retinal, 9:66
  for retinoblastoma, 4:313
Gene transcription, 2:162, 166–169, 167f
  reverse, 2:160
Gene translation, 2:162, 166
  gene product changes/modification after
    (posttranslational modification), 2:158
  of lens proteins, 2:277
General anesthesia. See Anesthesia
Generalizability
  of clinical research study, 1:317
  of screening/diagnostic test, 1:335
Generalized anxiety disorder (GAD), 1:249. See also
    Anxiety
Generalized gangliosidosis (GM₁ gangliosidosis type I),
    2:213t, 6:303, 401t, 8:310
  cherry-red spot in, 6:401t, 12:262
Generalized seizures, 1:261
Generic drugs, antiglaucoma, 10:177
Genetic, definition of, 2:152, 191
Genetic code, degeneracy of, 2:150
Genetic counseling. See Genetic testing/counseling

Genetic/hereditary factors. See also Family history/
    familial factors; Genetics, clinical; Inborn errors of
    metabolism
  in age-related cataracts, 11:37–38
  in age-related macular degeneration, 12:56–57
  in Alzheimer disease, 1:266
  in cancer, 1:236
  in choroidal melanoma, 4:263
  in diabetes, mellitus, 1:191, 192
  in epilepsy, 1:261
  eye involvement in hereditary diseases and, 6:397
  in glaucoma, 6:233, 10:10, 10–12, 11t
    in infants and children, 6:233, 10:11t, 142–143
  in myopia, 3:118–119
  in Parkinson disease, 1:258
  in pediatric cataract, 6:246, 247t
  in retinitis pigmentosa, 12:228–229, 230
  in retinoblastoma, 2:204–205, 4:178, 263, 299–301,
    300f, 6:356–357, 357f
Genetic heterogeneity, 2:153, 192, 193
Genetic imprinting, 2:154, 169
Genetic mapping/genetic map, 2:178, 193
Genetic profiling of tumors, 1:235, 244
Genetic testing/counseling, 2:226–229
  autosomal dominant disorders and, 2:217
  family history/pedigree analysis and, 2:225–226, 226f
  in glaucoma, 10:12, 142
  issues in, 2:227–228
  in Leber congenital amaurosis, 6:290
  in multiple endocrine neoplasia, 1:217
  polygenic and multifactorial inheritance and, 2:224–225
  prenatal diagnosis and, 2:228–229
  in retinitis pigmentosa, 12:230
  in retinoblastoma, 4:299–301, 300f, 6:356–357, 357f
  in sickle cell disease, 1:147, 150
  support group referral and, 2:232
Genetic therapy. See Gene therapy
Genetics
  clinical, 2:191–232. See also specific disorder and
    Family history/familial factors; Genetic/
    hereditary factors
    alleles and, 2:194–195
    chromosomal analysis and, 2:197–207, 198t, 200f,
      201f
    congenital anomalies and, 2:141
    counseling and. See Genetic testing/counseling
    disease management and, 2:230–232
    genes and chromosomes and, 2:193–194
    independent assortment and, 2:196–197
    inheritance patterns and, 2:211–220
    linkage and, 2:193, 197
    Lyonization (X chromosome inactivation) and,
      2:220–224
    meiosis and, 2:195–196, 196f
    mitosis and, 2:195
    mutations and, 2:207–210
    pedigree analysis in, 2:225–226, 226f
    pharmacogenetics and, 2:229–230
    polygenic and multifactorial inheritance and,
      2:224–225
    racial and ethnic concentration of disorders and,
      2:210–211

segregation and, **2:**193, 196
terminology used in, **2:**191–193
molecular, **2:**165–189
correlation of genes with specific diseases and, **2:**176–182, 179*f*, 181*f*
DNA damage/repair and, **2:**169–170
gene structure and, **2:**165
gene therapy and, **2:**184–189, 189*f*
junk DNA and, **2:**165–166
Lyonization (X chromosome inactivation) and, **2:**168–169
mitochondrial disease and, **2:**173–176, 174*f*
mutations/disease and, 2:170–173, 172*f*
screening and, 2:182–184, 183*f*, 185*f*, 186–187*f*
transcription (expression) and, **2:**166–169, 167*f*
translation and, **2:**166
terms used in, **2:**147–163
Geniculate body/nucleus/ganglion, **2:**105
lateral, **2:**92, 94*f*, 96, **5:**19–20, 20*f*, 28*f*, 33, **6:**42
development of, **6:**44
abnormal visual experience affecting, **6:**46
lesions of, **5:**167–168, 167*f*
medial, **5:**20*f*
Geniculocalcarine pathways (optic radiations), **2:**93, 94*f*, 96, **5:**20*f*, 21, 28*f*, 34
lesions of, **5:**165–172
Genital ulcers, in Behçet disease, **1:**180, **9:**192, **12:**194
Gennari, line of, **5:**34
Genocopy, **2:**152
Genome, **2:**113, 152, 191, 208
Genomic clone, **2:**152
Genomic DNA library, **2:**154, 182, 183*f*
Genoptic. *See* Gentamicin
Genotype, **2:**152, 194, 208
Gentacidin. *See* Gentamicin
Gentak. *See* Gentamicin
Gentamicin, **1:**51*t*, 61–62, **2:**368*t*, 372*t*, 375–376
in combination preparations, **2:**373*t*
ototoxicity of, mitochondrial DNA mutations and, **2:**176
Gentasol. *See* Gentamicin
Geographic atrophy, of retinal pigment epithelium, **4:**169, 170*f*, **12:**58–59, 59*f*
patient education/follow-up and, **12:**60
Geographic choroiditis/choroidopathy (serpiginous/helicoid), **9:**148–150*t*, 158–161, 159*f*, 160*f*, **12:**186*t*, 188–189, 188*f*
tuberculosis and, **9:**258, 259*f*
Geographic corneal dystrophy. *See* Reis-Bücklers corneal dystrophy
Geographic epithelial ulcer, in herpes simplex keratitis, **8:**110, 112*f*
Geographic map lines, in epithelial basement membrane dystrophy, **8:**271, 271*f*
Geometric optics, **3:**3, 27–102. *See also specific aspect*
aberrations and, **3:**93–102
definition of, **3:**3
first-order optics and, **3:**55–62, 55*f*. *See also* First-order optics
image characteristics and, **3:**31–39
intraocular lenses and, **11:**136
lenses and, **3:**62–83
imaging with, **3:**30–31, 31*f*
light propagation and, **3:**39–55
mirrors and, **3:**89–92
imaging with, **3:**30–31, 32*f*
object characteristics and, **3:**31
pinhole imaging and, **3:**27–30, 27*f*, 29*f*, 30*f*
power prediction formulas for IOLs based on, **3:**212–213, 212*f*
prisms and, **3:**83–89
Geometric wavefront, **3:**238
Geranylgeranyl transferase Rab escort protein, in choroideremia, **12:**242
GERD. *See* Gastroesophageal reflux disease
Geriatrics, **1:**219–233. *See also* Age/aging
elder abuse and, **1:**223–224
falls and, **1:**231–232
medication use and, **1:**222
osteoporosis and, **1:**227–231
outpatient visits and, **1:**222–223
physiologic/pathologic eye changes and, **1:**221, 227
psychology/psychopathology of aging and, **1:**225–227
psychosocial assessment of older person and, **1:**219–220
surgical considerations and, **1:**224–225
systemic disease incidence and, **1:**232–233
Germ layer theory, **2:**113
German measles. *See* Rubella
Germinal center, lymphoid follicle, **4:**51, 52*f*, 71
Germinal mosaicism, **2:**152
Germinative zone, **2:**70, **11:**8
Gerstmann syndrome, **5:**168, 194
Gestational age, retinopathy and, **6:**281, **12:**157, 162, 164, 166. *See also* Retinopathy, of prematurity
Gestational diabetes mellitus, **1:**191*t*, 192
Gestational pemphigoid, **8:**205*t*
Ghost cell glaucoma, **4:**108, 108*f*, 138, **10:**99–100, 99*f*
Ghost cells, **2:**288, **4:**108, 108*f*, 138, **10:**99, 99*f*
Ghost dendrites, in herpes simplex keratitis, **8:**110, 112*f*
Ghost images
with multifocal IOLs, **13:**145
after photoablation, **13:**95
GHT. *See* Glaucoma hemifield test
GHTF (Global Harmonization Task Force), **13:**202
Giant aneurysm, **5:**350, 352
Giant cell (temporal) arteritis. *See* Arteritis, giant cell
Giant cells, **9:**11, 22
foreign body, **4:**7, 9*f*
Langhans, **4:**7, 9*f*
multinucleated, **4:**7, 9*f*
in sarcoidosis, **4:**191, 191*f*
Touton, **4:**7, 9*f*
in juvenile xanthogranuloma, **4:**191, 191*f*, **6:**351, **9:**286
Giant congenital melanocytic nevi, **4:**224
Giant drusen, **4:**306, **5:**136, 136*f*
retinoblastoma differentiated from, **4:**306
in tuberous sclerosis, **4:**306, **6:**373
Giant papillary (contact lens–induced) conjunctivitis, **3:**200, **4:**50, **8:**23*f*, 194–195, 194*f*
Giant retinal tear, **12:**271
retained lens fragments after phacoemulsification and, **12:**358
Giant vacuoles, in Schlemm canal, **2:**54, 55*f*, 56*f*

Gigantism, **1**:215
  regional, **6**:367
Gillespie syndrome (MIM 206700), aniridia in, **2**:206,
  10:147
GIOD. *See* Ganciclovir sustained-release intraocular
  device
Glabellar flap, for canthal repair, **7**:186–187
Glands of Krause, **2**:23*f*, 26*f*, 27*t*, 33, 239–240, **4**:205,
  207*t*, **7**:135*f*, 141, 244
Glands of Moll, **2**:23, 23*f*, 26*f*, 27*t*, **4**:205, 207*t*, **7**:142*f*,
  160, **8**:4, 5*f*. *See also* Apocrine glands of eyelid
  hidrocystoma arising in, **7**:162, 162*f*
Glands of Wolfring, **2**:23*f*, 26*f*, 27*t*, 33, 240, **4**:205, 207*t*,
  7:135*f*, 141, 244
Glands of Zeis, **2**:23, 23*f*, 26*f*, 27*t*, **4**:205, **7**:142*f*, 160,
  8:4, 5*f*
  chalazion caused by obstruction of, **4**:210–211, 211*f*,
    8:72
  hordeolum caused by infection of, **4**:208, **7**:154
  sebaceous adenocarcinoma arising in, **4**:221–222,
    7:173
  in tear-film lipids/tear production, **2**:237
Glare
  cataracts and, **11**:41, 43, 70, 70*t*, 76
  with intraocular lenses, **11**:168
    multifocal IOLs, **13**:145, 156
    phakic IOLs, **13**:133*t*
      angle-supported PIOLs, **13**:134–135
      iris-fixated PIOLs, **13**:135
      posterior chamber PIOLs, **13**:136
  in low vision/vision rehabilitation, **3**:293, 304
  after photoablation, **13**:95
  as positive dysphotopsia, **3**:224, 224*f*, **11**:168
  pupil size and, **13**:34
  after radial keratotomy, **13**:45–46
  rainbow, after LASIK with femtosecond flap creation,
    13:116
  scattering causing, **3**:16
  sunglasses affecting sensitivity to, **3**:159, 304
    polarizing lenses and, **3**:11, 12, 12*f*, 159, 304
Glare testing, **3**:278–279, 279*f*
  in cataract evaluation, **11**:70, 76
  in vision rehabilitation, **3**:293
Glargine insulin, **1**:196, 196*t*
Glass, refractive index of, **3**:40, 40*t*, 162
Glass–air interface, reflection at, **3**:12
Glass foreign body, **8**:371
Glass lenses
  hi-index, **3**:162–163
  standard, **3**:162
Glass prism, calibration of, **3**:84*f*, 85, 86*f*
Glassblowers' cataract, **11**:52–53
Glasses. *See* Spectacle lenses (spectacles)
Glatiramer, for multiple sclerosis, **5**:327
Glaucoma, **10**:3–12, 87–90, 88*f*, 89*f*, 90*f*. *See also*
  Angle closure/angle-closure glaucoma; Elevated
  intraocular pressure; Open-angle glaucoma;
  Uveitis-glaucoma-hyphema (UGH) syndrome
  age affecting development of
    angle closure/angle-closure glaucoma and, **10**:10, 113
    open-angle glaucoma and, **10**:8, 75
  angle-closure. *See* Angle closure/angle-closure
    glaucoma

angle-recession, **4**:18, 109, **10**:38–39, 38*f*, 39*f*, 100–101,
  100*f*
aniridia and, **10**:112, 142, 147
anterior chamber evaluation in, **10**:30, 30*f*, 31*f*, 31*t*,
  32–40, 109. *See also* Gonioscopy
aphakic, **10**:124, 148–149
  glaucoma drainage device implantation and,
    10:206
aqueous misdirection and, **10**:30, 131–133, 132*f*
Axenfeld-Rieger syndrome and, **4**:102, **6**:213, 214,
  238, **10**:28, 30, 142, 145–146, 146*t*
biomicroscopy in evaluation of
  slit-lamp, **10**:29–32, 46
  ultrasound, **10**:70, 72*f*
cataracts and, **4**:106–107, 107*f*, **9**:22, 126, **10**:90–91,
  91*f*, 120–121, 122*f*, **11**:63, 64*f*, 201–203, 202*f*
  management of, **10**:199–200, **11**:201–203, 202*f*. *See
    also* Cataract surgery, glaucoma and
  preoperative evaluation/management and, **11**:75,
    201–202, 202*f*
central retinal vein occlusion and, **12**:129, 130
childhood (congenital/infantile/juvenile), **4**:102, 103*f*,
  6:216*t*, 233–244, **8**:265, **10**:5*t*, 139–158
  aniridia and, **6**:238, **10**:142, 147
  anomalies associated with, **6**:238, **10**:5*t*, 7*t*, 140*t*,
    142, 145–148
  anterior segment examination in, **10**:150
  aphakic, **6**:239–240, **10**:148–149
    cataract surgery and, **6**:239, 260
  Axenfeld-Rieger syndrome and, **4**:102, **6**:213, 214,
    238, **10**:28, 30, 142, 145–146, 146*t*
  axial length measurements in, **10**:152
  cataract surgery associated with, **6**:239, 260,
    10:141*t*, 148
  central corneal thickness in, **10**:151
  classification of, **10**:5*t*, 139, 140*t*, 141–142*t*
  clinical features of, **6**:234–238, 234*f*, 235*t*, 236*f*,
    237*f*
  corneal enlargement and, **6**:234, 234*f*, 235*t*, **10**:29,
    143, 150
  corneal opacities and, **6**:218, 234, 235*t*
  corticosteroid-induced, pediatric uveitis treatment
    and, **6**:276
  developmental, **10**:145–148
  diagnosis/differential diagnosis of, **6**:235–238, 235*t*,
    236*f*, 237*f*, **10**:144, 144*t*, 149–152, 149*t*
  examination/evaluation in, **6**:234–238, 236*f*, 237*f*,
    10:149–152, 149*t*
  follow-up care and, **6**:243–244, **10**:158
  genetic/hereditary factors in, **6**:233, **10**:11*t*,
    142–143
  gonioscopy in, **10**:151–152
  history in, **10**:149–150
  juvenile open-angle, **6**:234, **10**:5*t*, 145
  leukemia and, **6**:354
  Lowe syndrome and, **6**:239, 302
  medical therapy for, **6**:242–243, **10**:156–157
  natural history of, **6**:238
  neurofibromatosis and, **5**:340, **6**:238, 367, 370,
    10:148
  optic nerve/fundus evaluation in, **10**:152
  pathophysiology of, **6**:234
  Peters anomaly and, **6**:238, **10**:142, 146

primary, **10**:5*t*, 139, 140*t*
  congenital/infantile, **4**:102, 103*f*, **6**:233–238,
    234*f*, 235*t*, 236*f*, 237*f*, **8**:265, **10**:5*t*, 139, 140*t*,
    143–145, 143*f*, 144*f*, 144*t*. *See also* Primary
    congenital glaucoma
  genetics of, **6**:233, **10**:142–143
  juvenile, **6**:234, **10**:5*t*, 139, 140*t*, 145
  prognosis for, **6**:243–244, **10**:157–158
  pseudophakic, **6**:239
  retinopathy of prematurity and, **12**:163
  secondary, **6**:238–240, **10**:5*t*, 139, 141–142*t*,
    148–149
    mechanical, **6**:239
  Sturge-Weber syndrome and, **5**:341, 343*f*, **6**:238,
    377, 378, **10**:147–148
  surgery for, **6**:240–242, 240*f*, 242*f*, **10**:145, 152–156,
    153*f*, 154*f*
  uveitis and, **6**:278
  systemic disease and, **6**:238–239
  tearing/epiphora in, **6**:203, 234, 235*t*
  tonometry in, **10**:150–151
  traumatic hyphema and, **6**:411
  treatment of, **6**:240–243, 240*f*, 242*f*, **10**:152–157
    medical, **6**:242–243, **10**:156–157
    surgical, **6**:240–242, 240*f*, 242*f*, **10**:145, 152–156,
      153*f*, 154*f*
    uveitis and, **6**:278
  tumors causing, **10**:93, 141*t*
  visual acuity and, **10**:150
cholesterol levels and, **1**:139
ciliary block. *See* Aqueous misdirection
classification of, **10**:4–6, 5*t*, 6*f*, 7*t*
  in children, **10**:5*t*, 139, 140*t*, 141–142*t*
clinical evaluation of, **1**:330–335, 331*f*, 332*f*, 333*f*,
  10:27–72. *See also specific type*
  in children, **6**:234–238, 234*f*, 235*t*, 236*f*, 237*f*,
    10:149–152, 149*t*
  gonioscopy in, **10**:30, 30*f*, 31*f*, 31*t*, 32–40, 73
  history and general examination in, **10**:27–32
    in children, **10**:149–150
  optic nerve and, **10**:40–44
    in infants and children, **6**:237, 237*f*, **10**:152
  optic neuropathy and, **10**:44–52, 45*f*, 47*t*
  visual field examination in, **10**:53–68. *See also*
    Perimetry; Visual field testing; Visual field
    testing, in glaucoma
combined-mechanism, **10**:6
congenital, **4**:102, 103*f*, **6**:233–238, 234*f*, 235*t*, 236*f*,
  237*f*, **8**:265, **10**:5*t*, 139, 140*t*, 143–145, 143*f*, 144*f*,
  144*t*. *See also* Glaucoma, childhood; Primary
  congenital glaucoma
conjunctiva affected in, **10**:29
contrast sensitivity affected in, **3**:112–113
cornea affected in, **10**:29–30
  cornea plana and, **8**:255
corticosteroid-induced, **2**:358, 359, 360, **10**:103–104
  pediatric uveitis treatment and, **6**:276
  refractive surgery and, **13**:35, 173–174, 173*f*, 194,
    195
definitions and, **10**:3–4
developmental, **10**:145–148. *See also* Glaucoma,
  childhood
diabetes mellitus as risk factor for, **10**:76–77

drug-induced
  angle-closure glaucoma and, **10**:136–137, 137*f*
  open-angle glaucoma and, **10**:103–104
drugs for, **10**:161–173, 162–165*t*. *See also*
  Antiglaucoma agents
dry eye disorders and, **8**:61
environmental factors in, **10**:12
epidemiology of, **10**:8–10, 9*t*
episclera affected in, **10**:29
exfoliation syndrome/pseudoexfoliation and, **4**:106,
  106*f*, 107*f*, **10**:11*t*, 38, 85–87, 86*f*, 87*f*, 122, 123*f*
external adnexae affected in, **10**:27–28
Fuchs heterochromic iridocyclitis/uveitis and, **9**:133,
  134, **10**:94–95, 95*f*
fundus examination in, **10**:32
gender affecting risk of, **10**:10, 114
genetic/hereditary factors in, **6**:233, **10**:10, 10–12, 11*t*
ghost cell, **4**:108, 108*f*, 138, **10**:99–100, 99*f*
hemolytic, **4**:108, 108*f*, **10**:99–100
hemorrhage/hyphema and, **4**:108–109, 108*f*, **10**:48–49,
  48*f*, 79, 97–99, 97*f*, 102. *See also* Uveitis-glaucoma-
  hyphema (UGH) syndrome
  in children, **6**:411
hemosiderin in, **4**:108–109, 108*f*
incidence of, **10**:8, 9
infantile, **4**:102, 103*f*, **6**:216*t*, 233–238, 234*f*, 235*t*, 236*f*,
  237*f*, **10**:139, 140*t*. *See also* Glaucoma, childhood
inflammatory
  angle closure/angle-closure glaucoma and,
    10:130–131, 130*f*, 131*f*
  open-angle glaucoma and, **10**:93–95
inheritance patterns in, **10**:10. *See also* Glaucoma,
  genetic/hereditary factors in
intraocular pressure in, **10**:3–4, 3*f*, 20–21, 74. *See also*
  Elevated intraocular pressure
  childhood glaucoma and, **6**:234, 235, 236, 243–244
  uveitis and, **9**:294, 295
iridocorneal endothelial (ICE) syndrome and, **4**:105,
  8:345, **10**:128–130, 128*f*, 129*f*
iridocyclitis and, **9**:296
iris bombé and, **9**:89, 296, **10**:30, 130, 130*f*
  in children, **6**:239–240
juvenile, **6**:234, **10**:5*t*, 139, 140*t*, 145. *See also*
  Glaucoma, childhood
juvenile idiopathic (chronic/rheumatoid) arthritis–
  associated iridocyclitis and, **9**:132
Leber congenital amaurosis and, **6**:290
lens evaluation in, **10**:32
lens-induced, **4**:106–107, 107*f*, **9**:22, 126, **10**:90,
  90–92, 90*t*, 91*f*, 92*f*, 112, 120–124, 121*f*, 122*f*, 123*f*,
  123*t*, **11**:63–64, 64*f*
  angle-closure glaucoma and, **10**:90, 90*t*, 112,
    120–124, 121*f*, 122*f*, 123*f*, 123*t*
  in infants and children, **6**:239, **10**:141*t*
  open-angle glaucoma and, **10**:90–92, 90*t*, 91*f*, 92*f*
lens particle, **10**:90*t*, 91–92, 92*f*, **11**:63
low-tension, **10**:4, 5*t*, 78–82, 80*t*. *See also* Glaucoma,
  normal-tension
malignant. *See* Aqueous misdirection
management of
  in children, **6**:240–243, 240*f*, 242*f*, **10**:145, 152–156,
    153*f*, 154*f* 156–157
  clinical trials in evaluation of, **10**:78, 104–108, 159

goals of, **10**:159–160
interrelationship between medical and surgical
treatment and, **10**:104, 160
medical, **10**:159–177
agents used in, **10**:161–173, 162–165*t. See also
specific drug and* Antiglaucoma agents
in children, **6**:242–243, **10**:156–157
ciliary body as target of, **2**:254
compliance and, **10**:176–177, 177
general approach to, **10**:174–177
during pregnancy/lactation, **10**:176
prognosis and, **10**:78
risk–benefit assessment in, **10**:159
surgical, **10**:179–212. *See also specific procedure and*
Glaucoma surgery
cataract surgery and, **10**:199–200, **11**:201–203, 202*f*
in children, **6**:240–242, 240*f*, 242*f*, **10**:145,
152–156, 153*f*, 154*f*
compliance and, **10**:212
megalocornea and, **8**:254
melanocytoma and, **4**:109, 268
melanomalytic, **4**:109, 109*f*, 198
microcornea and, **8**:253
microspherophakia and, **10**:122, 123*f*, **11**:29
nanophthalmos and, **4**:112, 113, **8**:251, 252,
10:135–136
neovascular, **10**:124–128, 125*f*, 125*t*, 126*f*, 127*f*
central retinal vein occlusion and, **12**:130
glaucoma drainage device implantation and, **10**:206
incisional surgery and, **10**:185
iris examination in, **10**:30–31
rubeosis iridis and, **4**:192
nerve fibers/nerve fiber layer in, **10**:49–50, 49*f*
diffuse/focal loss and, **10**:49, 49*f*
evaluation of, **10**:41–42, 41*f*
patterns of loss and, **10**:68, 69*f*, 70*f*, 71*f*, 72*f*
neurofibromatosis and, **5**:340, **10**:28, 148
in children, **6**:238, 367, 370, **10**:148
normal-tension, **5**:140, **10**:4, 5*t*, 78–82, 80*t*
clinical features of, **10**:79
diagnostic evaluation of, **10**:80–81
differential diagnosis of, **10**:79–80, 80*t*
disc hemorrhages in, **10**:48, 79
genetic/hereditary factors in, **10**:11*t*
prevalence of, **10**:80–81
prognosis/therapy of, **10**:81–82
ocular receptors and, **2**:264, 264*t*
open-angle. *See* Open-angle glaucoma
ophthalmoscopic signs of, **10**:46, 47*t*
optic neuropathy/optic nerve changes in, **5**:139–140,
141*f*, **10**:3–4, 44–52, 45*f*, 47*t*
in infants and children, **6**:237, 237*f*
optic disc evaluation and, **10**:32, 40, 45*f*, 46–52, 47*f*,
47*t*, 48*f*, 49*f*, 52–53*f*, 75
in infants and children, **6**:237, 237*f*
normal-tension glaucoma and, **10**:81
perimetry changes correlated with, **10**:66–67
quantitative measurement and, **10**:46, 51–52,
52–53*f*
recording findings and, **10**:50–51
optic nerve evaluation and, **10**:40–44, 41*f*, 43*f*
in infants and children, **6**:237, 237*f*
patterns of nerve loss and, **10**:68, 69*f*, 70*f*, 71*f*, 72*f*

outflow facility in, **10**:16
intraocular pressure and, **10**:13, 14*t*, 16
outflow obstruction mechanisms in, **10**:7*t*
pain caused by, **5**:300
pars planitis and, **9**:138
pattern electroretinogram in identification of, **12**:39
pediatric. *See* Glaucoma, childhood
penetrating keratoplasty and, **8**:421, **10**:102
peripapillary atrophy in, **10**:50
persistent fetal vasculature (persistent hyperplastic
primary vitreous) and, **6**:250, 280, **10**:136, **12**:308
phacoantigenic, **10**:90*t*, 92
phacolytic, **4**:106–107, 107*f*, 127, **9**:22, 126, **10**:90–91,
90*t*, 91*f*, **11**:63
phacomorphic, **10**:90*t*, 112, 120–121, 121*f*, 122*f*,
11:63, 64*f*
pigmentary/pigment dispersion syndrome and,
4:91–92, 94*f*, 109, 109*f*, 110*f*, **10**:87–90, 88*f*, 89*f*,
90*f*
posterior polymorphous corneal dystrophy and, **8**:295
preperimetric, **10**:4
prevalence of, **10**:8
primary, **10**:4, 5*t*, 8–10, 9*t. See also* Angle closure/
angle-closure glaucoma, primary; Open-angle
glaucoma, primary
congenital, **4**:102, 103*f*, **6**:233–238, 234*f*, 235*t*,
236*f*, 237*f*, **8**:265, **10**:5*t*, 139, 140*t*, 143–145,
143*f*, 144*f*, 144*t. See also* Primary congenital
glaucoma
juvenile, **6**:234, **10**:5*t*, 139, 140*t*, 145
management of. *See also* Antiglaucoma agents;
Glaucoma surgery
medical, **10**:159–177
surgical, **10**:179, 180–200
in infants and children, **10**:145, 152–156, 153*f*,
154*f*
pseudophakic, **10**:124
in children, **6**:239
pupils affected in, **10**:28–29
race affecting risk of, **10**:8, 10, 76, 84, 109, 112–113
in angle-closure glaucoma, **10**:10, 109, 112–113
in open-angle glaucoma, **10**:8, 76
refraction/refractive errors in, **10**:10, 27, 56, 76, 114
refractive surgery and, **13**:35, 172–175, 173*f*,
194–195
retained lens fragments after phacoemulsification
and, **12**:357
retinoblastoma and, **4**:303
retinopathy of prematurity and, **12**:163
risk factors for
in angle closure, **10**:112–114
in open-angle glaucoma, **10**:9, 9*t*
rubella (congenital) and, **9**:210
sarcoidosis and, **9**:175
scleral involvement/scleritis and, **8**:220, **10**:29
screening perimetry in, **10**:58
secondary, **10**:4, 5*t. See also* Angle closure/
angle-closure glaucoma, secondary; Open-angle
glaucoma, secondary
in infants and children, **6**:238–240, **10**:5*t*, 139,
141–142*t*, 148–149
mechanical, **6**:239
leukemia and, **4**:327

management of, **10**:160. *See also* Antiglaucoma
    agents; Glaucoma surgery
with material in trabecular meshwork, **4**:106–109,
    110*f*
melanomalytic, **4**:109, 109*f*, 198
rubeosis iridis and, **4**:192
uveal lymphoid infiltration and, **4**:325
uveitis and, **9**:294–299, 295*t*
slit-lamp biomicroscopy in evaluation of, **10**:29–32, 46
Sturge-Weber syndrome and, **5**:341, 343*f*, **6**:238, 377,
    378, **10**:28
surgery for, **10**:179–212. *See also specific procedure*
    and Glaucoma surgery
sympathetic ophthalmia and, **9**:296
tests for, **1**:330–335, 331*f*, 332*f*, 333*f*, **10**:27–72. *See*
    also Glaucoma, clinical evaluation of
topiramate causing, **1**:245, 264
    in children, **6**:239
trauma and, **4**:107–109, 108*f*, **10**:38–39, 38*f*, 39*f*,
    100–101, 100*f*, 135
    in infants and children, **10**:141*t*
tumors causing, **4**:109, 110*f*, **10**:92–93, 130
    in infants and children, **10**:93, 141*t*
ultrasound biomicroscopy in evaluation of, **10**:70,
    72*f*
uveal effusion syndrome and, **12**:182
uveitis and, **9**:17, 84, 294–299, 295*t*, **10**:93–95, 130*f*,
    131. *See also* Uveitis-glaucoma-hyphema (UGH)
    syndrome
    in infants and children, **10**:141*t*
visual field changes in, **10**:68, 69*f*, 70*f*, 71*f*, 72*f*, 73, 75,
    79. *See also* Visual field defects
    evaluation of, **10**:53–68. *See also* Perimetry; Visual
        field testing
      serial fields and, **10**:62–68, 64*f*, 65*f*, 66*f*, 67*f*
      single field and, **10**:59–62, 60*f*, 62*f*, 63*f*
      patterns of nerve loss and, **10**:68, 69*f*, 70*f*, 71*f*, 72*f*
      progression of, **10**:65–66, 65*f*, 66*f*, 67*f*
vitrectomy and, **10**:135, **12**:368
vitreous injury and, **2**:288
Vogt-Koyanagi-Harada (VKH) syndrome and,
    9:189
Glaucoma Change Probability (GCP), **10**:66, 67*f*
Glaucoma drainage devices, **10**:204–209, 205*t*, 208*t*
cataract surgery and, **10**:200
in childhood glaucoma, **10**:153, 155
in neovascular glaucoma, **10**:127
strabismus and, **6**:143
in Sturge-Weber syndrome, **6**:378
for uveitic glaucoma, **9**:298
Glaucoma genes, **6**:233, **10**:10–11, 11*t*, 12
Glaucoma Hemifield Test (GHT), **10**:60–61, 60*f*
Glaucoma Laser Trial (GLT), **10**:160, 180
Glaucoma surgery, **10**:179–212. *See also specific*
    procedure
for angle-closure glaucoma, **10**:179, 200–204, 201*f*
cataract surgery and, **10**:199–200, **11**:203
chamber deepening/goniosynechialysis, **10**:204
in children, **6**:240–242, 240*f*, 242*f*, **10**:145, 152–156,
    153*f*, 154*f*
ciliary body ablation procedures, **10**:209–210, 209*f*
deep sclerectomy, **10**:210–211
drainage devices, **10**:204–209, 205*t*, 208*t*

in elderly patients, **10**:211–212
filtering procedures, **10**:183–198. *See also* Filtering
    procedures
goniotomy, **6**:240, 240*f*, **10**:152–153, 153*f*, 155
incisional. *See also* Filtering procedures; Incisional
    surgery
    for angle closure, **10**:204
    for open-angle glaucoma, **10**:107–108, 183–198
interrelationship between medical and surgical
    treatment and, **10**:104, 160
laser gonioplasty, **10**:203
laser iridotomy, **10**:201, 201*f*, 202–203
laser trabeculoplasty, **10**:180–183, 182*f*
nonpenetrating, **10**:210–211
for open-angle glaucoma, **10**:179, 180–200
peripheral (surgical) iridectomy, **10**:201, 201*f*, 204
peripheral iridoplasty, **10**:203
trabeculotomy, **10**:107–108, 183–198
    in children, **10**:152–153, 154, 154*f*, 155
viscocanalostomy, **10**:211
Glaucoma suspect, **10**:5*t*, 82–83
screening tests for, **1**:334, **10**:58, 82–83
Glaucomatocyclitic crisis (Posner-Schlossman
    syndrome), **9**:124–125, **10**:94
Glaucomatous cupping. *See* Cupping of optic disc,
    glaucomatous
Glauctabs. *See* Methazolamide
Glaukomflecken, **4**:124, **10**:115, **11**:64
GLC1A gene, **10**:11*t*
    in pediatric glaucoma, **6**:233
GLC1B gene, **10**:11*t*
GLC1C gene, **10**:11*t*
GLC1D gene, **10**:11*t*
GLC1E gene, **10**:11*t*
GLC1F gene, **10**:11*t*
GLC1G gene, **10**:11*t*
GLC1I gene, **10**:11*t*
GLC1J gene, **10**:11*t*
GLC1K gene, **10**:11*t*
GLC3A gene, **10**:11*t*, 142
GLC3B gene, **10**:11*t*, 142
    in pediatric glaucoma, **6**:233
GLC3C gene, **10**:11*t*, 142
    in pediatric glaucoma, **6**:233
Glial cells
optic nerve, **4**:249, 250*f*
retinal, **2**:77, 300–301, **5**:28–29
    differentiation/development of, **2**:126
    in healing/repair, **4**:17
    lesions originating in, in neurofibromatosis,
        6:366–367, 367*f*, 368*f*
    in retinal ischemia, **4**:157
Glimepiride, **1**:199, 199*t*
Glioblastoma/glioblastoma multiforme, optic nerve
    (malignant optic gliomas), **4**:257, **5**:153–154, **7**:69
Gliomas, optic nerve/pathway/chiasm, **4**:257, 257*f*,
    5:151–154, 151*f*, 152*t*, 164, **7**:69–72, 70*f*
    in children (juvenile), **4**:257, **6**:343, 367–369, 368*f*
    malignant (glioblastomas), **4**:257, **5**:153–154, **7**:69
    in neurofibromatosis, **5**:152, 153, 340, **6**:343, 367–369,
        368*f*, **7**:69, 71, 73
    nystagmus caused by, **5**:153
    orbital involvement in, **6**:343

Gliomatosis, arachnoidal, **6**:368
Gliosis, retinal, **4**:164, 165
  of peripapillary nerve fiber layer, **5**:121, 121*f*
Gliotic (sclerotic) lesions, in multiple sclerosis, **5**:322
Glipizide, **1**:199, 199*t*
  with metformin, **1**:201
Glistenings, intraocular lens, **11**:169
Global Harmonization Task Force (GHTF), **13**:202
Global Initiative for Chronic Obstructive Lung Disease
    (GOLD), **1**:141
Global layer, of extraocular muscle, **6**:18
Globe
  blunt injury to
    mydriasis/miosis caused by, **8**:363
    rupture caused by, **12**:323
  developmental anomalies of, **8**:249–253
  displacement of, **4**:229
    in craniosynostosis, **6**:389–390
    in orbital disorders, **7**:22–23
    after orbital surgery, **7**:116
  embryologic/perinatal realignment of, **2**:140
  evaluation of injury to, **12**:318
  exposure of for phacoemulsification, **11**:110
  gross dissection of, for pathologic examination,
    4:27–28, 28*f*
  in infant, **8**:4
  open injury of, **12**:318
  orbital tumors originating in, **7**:88
  orientation of, pathologic examination and, **4**:26,
    26*f*
  penetrating and perforating injuries of, **12**:324, 325
    needle penetration/perforation and, **11**:185,
      12:325, 362, 363*f*
  ptosis of, in blowout fractures, **7**:101
  rupture of, **12**:323
    repair and, **8**:375–381. *See also* Corneoscleral
      laceration, repair of
  stabilization of, for clear corneal incision, **11**:113
  topographic features of, **2**:41–42, 41*f*
Globus pallidus, in Parkinson disease, **1**:259
Glomerulonephritis
  retinal degeneration and, **12**:254
  in Wegener granulomatosis, **9**:145
Glossopharyngeal nerve, **5**:66*f*
Glossopharyngeal neuralgia, **5**:302
GLT (Glaucoma Laser Trial), **10**:160, 180
Glucocorticoids/glucocorticosteroids, **1**:181–183, 181*t*,
    2:357–361, 357*t*, 360*t*. *See also* Corticosteroids
Glucophage/Glucophage XR. *See* Metformin
Glucose
  in aqueous humor, **2**:255, 266*t*, 268
  in cataract formation, **2**:279–281, **11**:15, 55. *See also*
    Diabetes mellitus
  for medical emergencies, **1**:292*t*
  metabolism of, **1**:189–190
    in cornea, **2**:248
    in lens, **2**:279, 279–281, 280*f*, **11**:13–15, 14*f*
    in retinal pigment epithelium, **2**:304
  plasma levels of
    in diabetes mellitus
      diagnosis/screening and, **1**:191*t*, 193, 194*t*
      self-monitoring of, **1**:204

surgery and, **1**:307–308
  surveillance of (glycemic control), **1**:189, 204.
    See also Glycemic control
    importance of, **1**:2–3*f*, 202–203, 207
  normal, **1**:191*t*
  in tear film, **2**:240
  in vitreous, **2**:266*t*
Glucose control. *See* Glycemic control
Glucose-6-phosphate, in lens glucose/carbohydrate
    metabolism, **2**:279, **11**:13, 14*f*
Glucose-6-phosphate dehydrogenase deficiency,
    1:150
  dapsone use in cicatricial pemphigoid and, **8**:202
  pharmacogenetics and, **2**:229
Glucose tolerance/intolerance
  in gestational diabetes mellitus, **1**:191*t*, 192
  impaired, **1**:191*t*, 192–193
  screening for, **1**:193
Glucose tolerance test, **1**:192
Glucose toxicity, **1**:192
Glucose transport inhibitors, for diabetes mellitus,
    1:202
α-Glucosidase inhibitors, **1**:199*t*, 201
Glucotrol/Glucotrol XL. *See* Glipizide
Glucovance. *See* Glyburide, with metformin
Glucuronide transferase, defective, **2**:213*t*
Glulisine insulin, **1**:196, 196*t*
Glutaraldehyde, as tissue fixative, **4**:29, 29*t*
Glutathione, **2**:314*f*
  in aqueous humor, **2**:268
  in lens, **2**:313, 314
    oxidative changes and, **2**:314, **11**:13, 16
  in retina and retinal pigment epithelium, **2**:316–317
Glutathione peroxidase, **2**:314*f*
  in lens, **2**:313, **11**:16
  in retina and retinal pigment epithelium, **2**:316–317
Glutathione redox cycle, **2**:314
Glutathione-S-transferase, in retina and retinal pigment
    epithelium, **2**:316–317
Glyburide, **1**:199, 199*t*
  with metformin, **1**:201
Glycation cross-link breakers, for hypertension, **1**:84
Glycemic control (glucose surveillance), **1**:189, 204
  importance of, **1**:202–203, 203*f*, 207
  retinopathy incidence and progression affected by,
    1:202–203, 203*f*, 207, **12**:91–94
    Diabetes Control and Complications Trial, **1**:202,
      203*f*, **12**:91, 92, 94*f*
    United Kingdom Prospective Diabetes Study,
      1:203, **12**:91, 92, 93
  surgery and, **1**:307–308
Glycerin, **2**:356, 356*t*
  for dry eye, **2**:390
Glycerol, for glaucoma, **10**:165*t*, 173
Glycine cell transport, defective, **2**:213*t*
Glycocalyx, corneal epithelium, **2**:42, 248
Glycolysis, in glucose/carbohydrate metabolism
  in cornea, **2**:248–249
  in lens, **2**:278, **11**:13–15, 14*f*
Glycopeptide antibiotics, **1**:44, 50–51*t*, 59–60
Glycopeptide-intermediate *S aureus,* **1**:5
Glycoprotein IIb/IIIa receptor, **1**:112

Glycoprotein IIb/IIIa receptor antagonists, 1:112
  for ischemic heart disease, 1:109t
    myocardial infarction, 1:103, 109t, 112
    non–ST-segment elevation acute coronary
      syndrome, 1:112
  after stent placement, 1:109
Glycoproteins
  corneal, 2:248, 249
  scleral, 8:9
  viral envelope, 8:104
  in vitreous, 2:283, 285, 4:131
Glycosaminoglycans
  corneal haze after surface ablation and, 13:101
  in macular corneal dystrophy, 8:283
  in mucopolysaccharidoses, 8:305, 307
  stromal, 2:45, 250
  in thyroid eye disease, 4:232, 7:50
  in vitreous, 4:131
Glycosylated hemoglobin (fast hemoglobin/HbA$_1$/
  HbA$_{1c}$), in glucose control/surveillance, 1:203, 203f,
  204, 12:92, 94f
Glycylcycline antibiotics, 1:64
Glynase. See Glyburide
Glyrol. See Glycerin
Glyset. See Miglitol
GM$_1$ gangliosidosis type I (generalized), 2:213t, 6:303,
  401t, 8:310
  cherry-red spot in, 6:401t, 12:262
GM$_1$ gangliosidosis type II (Derry disease), 6:401t
GM$_1$ gangliosidosis type III (adult), 6:401t
GM$_1$ gangliosidosis type IV (Goldberg-Cotlier
  syndrome), retinal degeneration and, 12:262
GM$_2$ gangliosidosis type I (Tay-Sachs disease), 2:213t,
  6:303, 398, 401t, 8:310, 12:262, 263f
  racial and ethnic concentration of, 2:210–211
  retinal degeneration and, 12:262, 263f
GM$_2$ gangliosidosis type II (Sandhoff disease), 2:213t,
  6:303, 401t
  cherry-red spot in, 6:401t, 12:262
GM$_2$ gangliosidosis type III (Bernheimer-Seitelberger
  disease), 6:401t
GMS. See Gomori methenamine silver stain
GNAQ. See G protein α-subunit
GNAQ gene, in nevus of Ota, 4:66
GNAT2 gene, in achromatopsia, 6:291, 12:215
Goblet cells, 2:26f, 27t, 34, 239f, 4:47, 48f, 207t, 7:141,
  8:5
  mucin tear secretion by, 2:42, 239f, 241, 7:244
Goiter. See also Hyperthyroidism; Thyroid eye disease
  diffuse toxic, 1:211
  nodular toxic, 1:212
GOLD (Global Initiative for Chronic Obstructive Lung
  Disease), 1:141
Gold compounds/salts, 1:185
  corneal pigmentation caused by, 8:337t, 349
Gold eyelid weights, 5:288
  for exposure keratopathy, 8:80
  for paralytic ectropion, 7:216
  for paralytic lagophthalmos, 7:216–217
Gold standard, 1:339
Goldberg-Cotlier syndrome (GM$_1$ gangliosidosis type
  IV), retinal degeneration and, 12:262

Goldberg syndrome, 8:312
"Golden ring" sign, 11:118
Goldenhar-Gorlin syndrome, 8:323t
Goldenhar syndrome, 4:48, 6:393, 393f, 7:34, 150
  colobomas and, 6:175, 393
  dermoids/dermolipomas/lipodermoids and, 4:48, 50,
    6:218, 349, 349f, 393, 393f, 8:246
  Duane syndrome and, 6:127, 393
Goldmann applanation tonometry, 3:256–258, 257f,
  258f, 10:22–23, 23f, 24f. See also Applanation
  tonometer/tonometry
  in children, 6:236
  corneal thickness affecting, 8:30, 13:35, 173, 194
  infection control and, 10:26
  after refractive surgery, 13:35
    LASIK, 13:35, 97
    surface ablation, 13:35, 97
Goldmann equation, 10:13
Goldmann-Favre disease/syndrome, 6:296, 12:219, 248
Goldmann lenses
  for gonioscopy, 10:34
  for slit-lamp biomicroscopy
    fundus contact lens, 3:253, 254f
    3-mirror contact lens, 3:253, 254f
Goldmann perimetry, 5:99–100
  for central visual field assessment, 3:292
  in hereditary retinal/choroidal degenerations, 12:223
  in nonorganic ophthalmic disorders, 5:313, 314f
  in peripheral visual field assessment, 3:292
  in photoreceptor dystrophies, 12:223, 225f
  in strabismus/amblyopia evaluation, 6:83
Goldmann-Weekers adaptometer, 12:46, 47f
Goldmann-Witmer coefficient, 9:48
  in acute retinal necrosis, 9:201
  in toxocariasis, 9:237
  in toxoplasmosis, 9:231
Golimumab, 1:186
Gomori methenamine silver stain, 4:30, 31t
Gonadotroph adenomas, 1:215
Gonadotropin-releasing hormone, 1:214t
Gonadotropins, pituitary adenoma producing, 1:215
Goniolenses, 10:32–34, 33f. See also Gonioscopy
Gonioplasty, laser, for angle-closure glaucoma, 10:203
Gonioscopy, 10:30, 30f, 31f, 31t, 32–40
  assessment/documentation systems for, 10:34–40,
    36f, 37f, 38f, 39f
  before cataract surgery, 11:79
  in central retinal vein occlusion, 12:130
  chamber angle, 4:101–102, 102f, 10:30, 30f, 31f, 31t,
    32–40, 109
    in traumatic/angle-recession glaucoma, 10:100, 100f
  in choroidal/ciliary body melanoma, 4:275
  direct, 10:32, 32–33, 33f
  dynamic (compression/indentation), 10:33f, 34
  in elevated episcleral venous pressure, 10:96
  in Fuchs heterochromic iridocyclitis (Fuchs uveitis
    syndrome), 10:94–95, 95f
  in glaucoma, 10:30, 30f, 31f, 31t, 32–40, 73
    angle-closure, 10:109, 114–115, 115f
    in children, 6:236–237, 237f, 10:151–152
    inflammatory, 10:94
    neovascular, 10:126, 127

normal-tension, **10**:81
primary open-angle, **10**:73
indirect, **10**:32, 32–34, 33*f*
in iris nevus, **4**:266
Koeppe-type lenses in, **10**:33
normal angle landmarks in, **10**:34
in pigment dispersion syndrome, **10**:38, 88, 88*f*
in pupillary examination, **5**:262
total internal reflection and, **3**:49–50, 50*f*
in trauma evaluation, **10**:38–39, 38*f*, 39*f*, **11**:206
Goniosynechialysis
for angle-closure glaucoma, **10**:204
with cataract extraction, **10**:204
for subacute/intermittent angle closure, **10**:117
Goniotomy, **6**:240, 240*f*, **10**:152–153, 153*f*, 155
uveitis and, **6**:278, **9**:298
Gonococcus (*Neisseria gonorrhoeae*/gonorrhea), **1**:10–11,
  8:134, 134*f*, 149
conjunctivitis caused by, **8**:134, 151–152, 151*f*
in children, **6**:189
in neonates, **6**:187, 187*f*, **8**:152, 153
resistant strains of, **1**:11, **8**:152, 153
Good acuity, postoperative photophobia, after LASIK
  with femtosecond flap creation, **13**:116
Gorlin syndrome (basal cell nevus syndrome), eyelid
  manifestations of, **4**:215*t*, **7**:168
Gottron sign, in dermatomyositis, **1**:175
Gout, **8**:325–326
gp120/gp160 glycoproteins, HIV vaccine development
  and, **1**:36
GPC. *See* Giant papillary (contact lens–induced)
  conjunctivitis
GPDS1 genes, **10**:11*t*
GPR143 gene, in ocular albinism, **12**:258*t*
Graded-density sunglasses, for glare reduction, **3**:159
Gradenigo syndrome, **5**:235, 357
Gradient echo MR sequences, **7**:28
Gradient method, for AC/A ratio measurement, **3**:144,
  6:81
Graft-vs-host disease, **8**:196*t*, 203–204, 204*f*
Grafts
for canthal repair, **7**:186
for cicatricial ectropion, **7**:193–194
for cicatricial entropion, **7**:198, 199
conjunctival, **8**:94. *See also* Conjunctiva,
  transplantation of
indications for, **8**:387*t*, 395
for wound closure after pterygium excision, **8**:392*f*,
  393, 393–395
corneal. *See also* Cornea, transplantation of; Donor
  cornea; Keratoplasty
allografts, **8**:413
autografts, **8**:413, 431–432
disease recurrence in, **8**:422, 423*f*
dislocation of after Descemet stripping automated
  endothelial keratoplasty, **8**:442, 443*f*
endothelial failure of, **4**:91, 92*f*
late nonimmune, **8**:425–426
primary, **8**:422, 422*f*
after Descemet stripping automated
  endothelial keratoplasty, **8**:444–445
inflammatory necrosis of, after lamellar
  keratoplasty, **8**:436–437

rejection of, **4**:91, 92*f*, **8**:407, 408, 427–430, 428*f*,
  429*f*, 436, **9**:63, 64, 64*f*, 65. *See also* Rejection
after penetrating keratoplasty, **9**:65
dermis-fat
after enucleation in children, **7**:119
for exposure and extrusion of orbital implant, **7**:123
for superior sulcus deformity, **7**:122
for eyelid repair, **7**:180, 182, 183*f*
in burn patients, **7**:181, **8**:351
for eyelid retraction, **7**:215
HLA/transplantation antigens and, **8**:407
limbal, **8**:94, 389, 395–398, 396–397*f*. *See also* Limbal
  transplantation
for chemical injuries, **8**:94, 358
indications for, **8**:387*t*
mucous membrane, **8**:389, 401–402
for cicatricial entropion, **7**:198
for contracted socket, **7**:124
for eyelid repair, **7**:180
for eyelid retraction, **7**:215
indications for, **8**:387*t*, 401–402
for symblepharon, **7**:200
rejection of, **8**:407, 408, 427–430, 428*f*, 429*f*, 436. *See
  also* Rejection
HLA/transplantation antigens and, **8**:407, **9**:65
retinal/retinal pigment epithelium, **9**:66
scleral patch, for exposure and extrusion of orbital
  implant, **7**:123
for symblepharon, **7**:200
tarsoconjunctival
for cicatricial entropion, **7**:199
for eyelid repair, **7**:180, 183*f*, 184, 185*f*, 186
transplantation antigens and, **9**:65
Gram-negative bacteria, **8**:131, 132*t*
cocci, **8**:132*t*, 134, 134*f*
as normal ocular flora, **8**:97*t*
rods, **8**:132*t*, 135–136, 136*f*
Gram-positive bacteria, **8**:131, 132, 132*t*
cocci, **8**:132–134, 132*t*, 133*f*
filaments, **8**:132*t*, 136–137
rods, **8**:132*t*, 134–135, 135*f*
Gram stain, **4**:30, 31*t*, **8**:131, 132*t*
Gramicidin, with polymyxin B and neomycin, **2**:372*t*
Grand mal (tonic-clonic) seizures, **1**:261
Granular corneal dystrophy, **8**:268*t*, 278*t*. *See also
  specific type*
genetics of, **4**:96, **8**:269*t*, 276, 281
refractive surgery and, **13**:35
type 1 (classic/GCD1), **4**:96, 97*t*, 98*f*, **8**:268*t*, 270*t*,
  280–281, 281*f*
type 2 (granular-lattice/GCD2), **4**:97, 97*t*, 99*f*, **8**:268*t*,
  269*t*, 270*t*, 278*t*, 282, 282*f*, **13**:35
type 3 (Reis-Bücklers), **8**:268*t*, 269*t*, 270*t*, 275–277,
  276*f*
Granular-lattice (Avellino) corneal dystrophy, **4**:97, 97*t*,
  99*f*, **8**:268*t*, 270*t*, 278*t*, 282, 282*f*
genetics of, **4**:97, **8**:269*t*, 282
refractive surgery and, **13**:35
Granulocytes
basophils and mast cells, **9**:10–11
eosinophils, **9**:10
neutrophils, **9**:9–10
Granulocytic sarcoma (chloroma), **4**:328, **6**:337, **7**:90

Granulomas, **4**:7, 8*f*, 9*f*. *See also* Granulomatosis;
  Granulomatous disease
    chalazia, **8**:72–73, 72*f*
    in coccidioidomycosis, **9**:279, 279*f*, 280
    conjunctival, **8**:20*t*, 22*t*, 241–242, 241*f*
      foreign-body, **4**:53, 53*f*
      in Parinaud oculoglandular syndrome, **4**:52, **8**:157,
        158
      pyogenic, **4**:56, 57*f*, **8**:241–242, 241*f*
    in sarcoidosis, **4**:52, 53*f*, **8**:73–74, **9**:174, 174*f*
    eosinophilic, orbital, **6**:337, 338*f*, **7**:84
      in children, **6**:337, 338*f*
    foreign-body, after strabismus surgery, **6**:156, 156*f*
    necrobiotic, in scleritis, **4**.114, 115*f*
    pyogenic, **4**:56, 57*f*, **8**:241–242, 241*f*
      in children, **6**:351
    in sarcoidosis, **4**:52, 53*f*, 191, 191*f*, **5**:335, **8**:73–74,
      9:84, 173, 174, 174*f*, 175, 176*f*
    in toxocariasis, **6**:273, 273*f*, **9**:52, 136, 235, 236*f*, 236*t*,
      12:209, 209*f*
    in tuberculosis, **12**:205, 205*f*
    zonal, **4**:122
Granulomatosis. *See also* Granulomas; Granulomatous
  disease
    allergic, and angiitis (Churg-Strauss syndrome),
      1:177*t*, 179–180
    familial juvenile systemic (Blau syndrome), **6**:274–275,
      9:176
    larval *(Toxocara)*, retinoblastoma differentiated from,
      4:305, 305*t*
    Wegener, **1**:177*t*, 179, **7**:32, 56–58, 57*f*, **9**:145–146, 146*f*
      choroidal perfusion abnormalities and, **12**:179, 180*f*
      cyclid manifestations of, **4**:213*t*
      scleritis/retinal vasculitis and, **7**:56, **9**:145, 146*f*
Granulomatous conjunctivitis, **4**:52–53, 53*f*
    in HIV infection/AIDS, **9**:313–314
Granulomatous delayed hypersensitivity, **9**:51
Granulomatous disease. *See also* Granulomas;
  Granulomatosis
    ileocolitis (Crohn disease), **1**:165, **9**:123
    optic nerve involvement and, **5**:144
    pulmonary, **1**:142
    subacute thyroiditis, **1**:212–213
    uveitis, **9**:84
      lens-associated, **9**:126
      tuberculous, **9**:257–258, 258*f*
Granulomatous inflammation, **4**:6
    conjunctivitis, **4**:52–53, 53*f*
      in HIV infection/AIDS, **9**:313–314
    focal posttraumatic choroidal, **4**:22, 22*f*
Granulomatous inflammatory infiltrate, necrobiotic, in
  episcleritis, **4**:113, 113*f*
Graphical image analysis, **3**:76, 77*f*
Grating acuity
    contrast sensitivity and, **3**:111, 112*f*, **5**:105
    in strabismic amblyopia, **6**:62
Graves hyperthyroidism/ophthalmology/eye disease,
  1:210, 211, **7**:47, 48, 51. *See also* Thyroid eye disease
Gray (Gy), radiation dose measurement, **1**:237
Gray line (intermarginal sulcus), **2**:23, 26*f*, 237, **7**:137, 142
Grayscale map, **5**:100–101, 102*f*, 103*f*
Greater (major) arterial circle, **2**:38, 39*f*, 58, **5**:14*f*, 18
    development of, **2**:138

Greater superficial petrosal nerve, **2**:106, 107, **5**:16, 61
Green lasers, **12**:338
Grid pattern photocoagulation, in central retinal vein
  occlusion, **12**:131
Groenouw dystrophy type I (granular corneal
  dystrophy, type 1), **8**:268*t*, 270*t*, 280–281, 281*f*
Groenouw dystrophy type II (macular corneal
  dystrophy), **8**:268*t*, 270*t*, 278*t*, 283–284, 284*f*
Grönblad-Strandberg syndrome. *See* Pseudoxanthoma
  elasticum
Gross dissection, for pathologic examination, **4**:27–28, 28*f*
Group A β-hemolytic streptococci (*Streptococcus
  pyogenes),* **1**:6, **8**:133, 149
    orbital cellulitis in children caused by, **6**:195
    orbital necrotizing fasciitis caused by, **7**:44
Grouped pigmentation of retina (bear tracks), **4**:278,
  279*f*, **12**:282
    in children, **6**:352
Growth factors, **2**:113, 395–397, **9**:27, 29*t*
    in aqueous humor, **2**:270–271
    homeobox gene expression affected by, **2**:115
    as inflammatory mediators, **8**:177*t*
    in ocular development, **2**:113–114
    in retinopathy of prematurity, **12**:157
    in tear film, **2**:241
Growth hormone, pituitary adenoma producing, **1**:215
Growth hormone-releasing hormone, **1**:214*t*
Gruber (petroclinoid) ligament, **2**:104, **5**:50
GSH. *See* Glutathione
GSN gene, lattice corneal dystrophy and, **8**:269*t*, 280
Guaiac stool test, in cancer screening, **1**.272*t*, 276
Guanethidine, **2**:260
Guanfacine, **1**:77*t*
Guanylate cyclase
    mutations in, **2**:296
    in rod phototransduction, **2**:293
Guanylate cyclase activator 1A, in cone dystrophies,
  12:232
Guanylate cyclase activators, for hypertension, **1**:84
Guanylate cyclase-assisting proteins (GCAPs), **2**:293
GUCA1A gene, in cone dystrophies, **12**:232
GUCY2D gene
    in cone dystrophies, **12**:232
    in cone–rod dystrophies, **12**:233
    in Leber congenital amaurosis, **6**:290
Guérin (Le Fort I) fracture, **7**:95, 96*f*
Guillain-Barré syndrome
    facial diplegia in, **5**:287
    immunization and, **1**:280
    Miller Fisher variant of, **5**:280, 287
Guillain-Mollaret triangle lesion, oculopalatal
  myoclonus and, **5**:253
Gullstrand schematic eye, **3**:103, 104*f*, 105*t*
    IOL power prediction formulas based on, **3**:212–213,
      212*f*
Gummas, syphilitic, **1**:13, **9**:244
GUN syndrome, in primary central nervous system
  lymphoma, **9**:282
Gundersen flap, **8**:399–400, 399*f*, **11**:147–148
Gustatory nucleus, **2**:105
Guyton-Minkowski Potential Acuity Meter (PAM),
  3:277–278, 278*f*
GVHD. *See* Graft-vs-host disease

GW coefficient. *See* Goldmann-Witmer coefficient
Gyne-Lotrimin. *See* Clotrimazole
Gyrate atrophy, 2:213*t*, 12:243–244, 244*f*
ornithine aminotransferase defects causing, 2:213*t*,
298, 12:243
retinal pigment epithelium in, 2:309, 12:243–244, 244*f*
Gyrus
cingulate, 5:63
precentral, 5:60
rectus, 2:87, 89*f*, 5:31

H

H&E (hematoxylin and eosin) stain, 4:30, 30*f*, 31*t*
H_1-receptor blockers. *See also* Antihistamines
for ocular allergy, 6:198, 199*t*
H_2-receptor blockers
corticosteroid treatment in uveitis and, 9:104
preoperative, 1:308
Haab striae, 6:234, 235, 236*f*, 8:265, 10:29, 143, 143*f*, 150
HAART. *See* Highly active antiretroviral therapy
Habenular complex, 5:39*f*
Habit spasm, 5:292
Haemophilus/Haemophilus influenzae, 1:9–10, 8:136
biotype III *(H aegyptius)*, conjunctivitis caused by,
8:150
bleb-associated endophthalmitis caused by, 12:354,
357
conjunctivitis caused by, 4:53, 8:150
in children, 6:189
endogenous endophthalmitis caused by, 9:272
immunization against, 1:9–10, 285
as normal ocular flora, 8:97*t*
orbital cellulitis caused by, 7:42
preseptal cellulitis caused by, 6:195, 7:40, 8:150
resistant strains of, 1:9
type B (Hib), 1:9–10, 8:136
Haemophilus influenzae type B (Hib) vaccine, 1:9–10, 285
in combination vaccines, 1:285
Hagberg-Santavuori disease, 6:401*t*
Haidinger brushes, 3:10, 11*f*
Haigis formula, for IOL power determination/selection,
3:212–213, 217, 219, 11:85
refractive lens exchange/clear lens extraction and,
13:140
Hair cells, 5:47, 47*f*, 48
Hair follicles, of eyelid (lash follicles), 7:142*f*
tumors arising in, 7:162–164, 163*f*
Halberg trial clips, for overrefraction, 3:138
Halcion. *See* Triazolam
Haldol. *See* Haloperidol
Half-eye glasses, high-plus prismatic, in low vision/
vision rehabilitation, 3:297, 298*f*
Haller layer, 12:17
Haller and Zinn, circle of, 2:94, 5:19, 10:42, 43, 44
Hallermann-Streiff-François syndrome, 8:323*t*
Hallucinations, 1:247, 5:187, 188*t*, 189–191
cortical origin of, 5:172, 190–191
nonvisual causes of, 5:188*t*
ocular origin of, 5:189–190
optic nerve origin of, 5:190
Hallucinatory palinopsia, 5:191

Haloperidol, 1:251
oculogyric crisis caused by, 5:212
Halos
with intraocular lenses
multifocal IOLs, 13:145, 156
phakic IOLs, 13:133*t*
angle-supported PIOLs, 13:134–135
iris-fixated PIOLs, 13:135
posterior chamber PIOLs, 13:136
macular, in Niemann-Pick disease, 12:262, 263*f*
after photoablation, 13:95
scattering causing, 3:16
spherical aberrations causing, 13:7
Haltia-Santavuori syndrome, pigmentary retinopathy
in, 12:251*t*, 260
Hamartias, 5:338
Hamartin, 5:341
Hamartomas, 4:6, 50, 5:338
astrocytic (astrocytomas), 4:257, 257*f*
juvenile pilocytic, 4:257
malignant, 5:153–154
optic. *See* Optic nerve (optic pathway/chiasm)
glioma
pilocytic. *See* Optic nerve (optic pathway/chiasm)
glioma
retinal, 4:305–306, 306*f*
optic disc drusen differentiated from, 5:136, 136*f*
retinoblastoma differentiated from, 4:305–306,
306*f*, 6:358
in tuberous sclerosis, 5:341, 342*f*, 6:372
combined, of retina and retinal pigment epithelium,
4:184, 289, 289*f*, 6:352
of conjunctiva, 4:50, 8:241*t*
of eyelid, 8:241*t*
in neurofibromatosis, 6:363
of orbit, 7:35–36
in phakomatoses, 6:363
of retinal pigment epithelium
combined, 4:184, 289, 289*f*, 6:352
in Gardner syndrome, 4:151
Hand-Schüller-Christian disease/syndrome. *See also*
Histiocytosis
orbital involvement in, 7:84
in children, 6:337
Hand washing, in infection control, 8:46
HIV transmission prevention and, 1:41
Handheld magnifiers, 3:298–299
Handicap, visual, 3:283, 284*f*. *See also* Low vision
Handpiece, phaco, 11:105–106, 105*f*, 106*f*, 107*f*
"Hang-back" recession, 6:147
for dissociated vertical deviation, 6:153
Hanna trephine
for arcuate keratotomy, 13:51
for penetrating keratoplasty, 8:418
Haploid/haploid number, 2:152, 195
Haploid insufficiency (haploinsufficiency), 2:152, 206
in aniridia/*PAX6* gene disorders, 2:206
gene therapy for disorders caused by, 2:188
Haplotype, 2:152, 9:70
Hapten, poison ivy toxin and, 9:34
Haptic
of intraocular lens, 3:205
anterior chamber lens, 3:210, 211

insertion of lens with, **11**:139
    posterior chamber lens, **3**:209
    of scleral contact lens, **3**:192, 192*f*
Harada disease, **12**:197, 198*f*
Harada-Ito procedure, **6**:121, 148
HARBOR study, **12**:77
Hard contact lens method, for IOL power calculation
    after refractive surgery, **11**:87, **13**:188
Hard contact lenses. *See* Rigid contact lenses; Rigid
    gas-permeable contact lenses
Hard (hyaline) drusen, **4**:168, 168*f*, **12**:58
Hard exudates, **4**:158, 159*f*
    in diabetic macular edema, **12**:96, 97*f*, 99*f*
    in leukemia, **4**:326
Hard palate composite grafts
    for eyelid repair, **7**:180
    for eyelid retraction, **7**:215
Hard resin, **3**:162. *See also* Plastic spectacle lenses
"Hard" tubercles, **4**:7, 8*f*. *See also* Tubercles
Hardy-Rand-Rittler color plates, **5**:105, **12**:48
Harmonin gene, in Usher syndrome, **12**:253
Harmonious anomalous retinal correspondence, **6**:55
Hartmann-Shack wavefront sensor/aberrometry,
    3:279–281, 280*f*, **13**:5–6, 5*f*
Hashimoto thyroiditis, **1**:212, 213
    hypothyroidism caused by, **1**:212, 213
    thyroid eye disease and, **7**:47, 48, 51
Hasner, valve of, **7**:245*f*, 246
    nasolacrimal duct obstruction and, **7**:243, 246, 250
Hassall-Henle bodies/warts (peripheral corneal guttae),
    2:45, **8**:334, 345
"Hatchet face," in myotonic dystrophy, **5**:338
HATTS (hemagglutination treponemal test for syphilis),
    1:13, 279
HAV. *See* Hepatitis, type A
Havrix. *See* Hepatitis A vaccine
Hay fever conjunctivitis, **8**:185–187
Haze formation
    after LASIK, **13**:27
        diffuse lamellar keratitis and, **13**:109
        surface ablation re-treatment and, **13**:90
    pupil size and, **13**:34
    scattering and, **3**:16
    after surface ablation, **13**:101, 101*f*
        corticosteroids in reduction of, **13**:86, 101
        mitomycin C in reduction of, **13**:84–85, 86
    wound healing and, **13**:27, 101
Hb. *See* Hemoglobin
HbA₁/HbA₁c. *See* Fast hemoglobin
HBID. *See* Hereditary benign intraepithelial
    dyskeratosis
HBV. *See* Hepatitis, type B
HCO₃. *See* Bicarbonate
HCV. *See* Hepatitis, type C
HDE. *See* Humanitarian Device Exemption
HDL cholesterol. *See* High-density-lipoprotein cholesterol
Head
    bony anatomy of, **5**:5–7, 6*f*, 7–8*f*, 9–10*f*
    vascular anatomy of, **5**:12–27
        arterial, **5**:12–23, 13–14*f*, 15*f*, 17*f*, 19*f*, 20*f*, 22*f*, 23*f*
        venous, **5**:23–27, 24–25*f*, 27*f*
Head lice. *See also* Lice
    ocular infection caused by, **8**:149

Head movements, abnormal, spasmus nutans and, **5**:247
Head-shaking nystagmus, **5**:200–201
Head thrust maneuver, VOR gain evaluation and, **5**:201
Head thrusts, in ocular motor apraxia patients, **5**:209
Head-tilt, chin-lift maneuver, for opening airway, **1**:290
Head-tilt test, Bielschowsky, **6**:85–86, 85*f*
    in superior oblique muscle paralysis, **6**:119
Head trauma. *See also* Trauma
    anisocoria caused by, **5**:269–270
    convergence insufficiency caused by, **5**:213
    fourth nerve (trochlear) palsy caused by, **5**:234
    optic nerve damage caused by, **5**:156–157, 156*f*
    pupil irregularity caused by, **5**:263
    Purtscher retinopathy and, **12**:154, 154*f*, 155*t*
    retinal breaks and, **12**:272–274, 273*f*
    seventh nerve (facial) palsy caused by, **5**:287
Headache, **5**:293–300, 293*t*
    in AAION, **5**:125
    analgesic rebound, **5**:298
    cerebral aneurysms causing, **5**:351
    classification of, **5**:293–294
    cluster, **5**:299
        Horner syndrome and, **5**:268
    evaluation of, **5**:293–294, 293*t*
    in giant cell (temporal) arteritis, **5**:125, 294, 319
    history in, **5**:293*t*
    in Horner syndrome, **5**:268
    idiopathic stabbing, **5**:299
    intracranial hemorrhage causing, **1**:98, **5**:351
    intracranial hypertension causing, **5**:294
        idiopathic, **5**:123, 124, 294
    migraine. *See* Migraine headache
    primary, **5**:293
    secondary, **5**:293
    tension-type, **5**:298, 299
    with visual loss, **5**:92. *See also* Migraine headache
        transient, **5**:174
Healing, ophthalmic wound. *See* Wound healing/repair
Healon 5, **11**:98
Health counseling, in cancer prevention, **1**:272*t*
Hearing loss (deafness)
    cataract surgery in patient with, **11**:188
    gene for, synteny and, **2**:176
    mitochondrial DNA mutations and, **2**:173, 174*f*, 176
    pigmentary retinopathy and, **12**:251*t*, 253. *See also*
        Usher syndrome
    vestibular nystagmus and, **5**:248, 249*t*, 250
Heart block, **1**:121, 122*t*
Heart disease, **1**:99–129
    congestive failure, **1**:113–121. *See also* Congestive
        heart failure
    in diabetes mellitus, **1**:133*t*, 207
    endocarditis prophylaxis recommendations and, **1**:7, 8*t*
    hypertension management and, **1**:79*t*, 84
    hypertension and risk of, **1**:69, 73*t*
    ischemic, **1**:99–113
    in Lyme disease, **1**:15
    ophthalmic considerations and, **1**:128–129
    recent developments in, **1**:99
    rhythm disturbances, **1**:121–127
    in scleroderma, **1**:173
    screening for, **1**:271–272
    in systemic lupus erythematosus, **1**:168

Heart failure. *See* Congestive heart failure
Heart rate, reduction of in angina management, 1:108
Heart transplantation, for heart failure, 1:120
Heat, anterior segment injuries caused by, 8:351
Heavy chain disease, corneal deposits in, 8:319–320
Heavy chains, immunoglobulin, 9:45, 45*f*
  isotype classification and, 9:46, 47*t*
"Heavy eye syndrome," 6:23
HEDS (Herpetic Eye Disease Study), 8:107, 108*t*, 109, 115–116
Heerfordt syndrome, 8:73, 9:174
Heidelberg retina tomography, 5:81
Height maps, 13:15–16, 16*f*
Heimann-Bielschowsky phenomenon, 5:247
Heimlich maneuver, 1:292, 294
Heinz bodies, 1:150
Helical (spiral) computed tomography
  chest, in cancer screening, 1:275
  in orbital evaluation, 7:26
Helicases, 2:169
Helicobacter pylori infection
  cancer screening and, 1:275
  conjunctival lymphoma and, 4:74
Helicoid choroidopathy (serpiginous/geographic), 9:148–150*t*, 158–161, 159*f*, 160*f*, 12:186*t*, 188–189, 188*f*
  tuberculosis and, 9:258, 259*f*
Heliotrope rash, in dermatomyositis, 1:175, 175*f*
Helix-loop-helix motif, 2:166, 167*f*
Helix-turn-helix motif, 2:166, 167*f*
HELLP syndrome, choroidal perfusion abnormalities and, 12:178*f*
Helmholtz hypothesis (capsular theory) of accommodation, 11:19, 13:149–150, 150*f*
Helminths, 8:141–142
  uveitis caused by, 9:235–242
Helper T cells. *See also specific type under* T helper and CD4⁺ T cells; T cells
  in anaphylactic/atopic (type I) reactions, 8:179
  class II MHC molecules as antigen-presenting platform for, 9:37, 39*f*
  in delayed hypersensitivity (type IV) reactions, 8:180, 9:42–43, 42*f*, 48–51, 49*f*, 50*t*
    sympathetic ophthalmia and, 9:52–53
    Toxocara granuloma and, 9:52
  differentiation of, 9:39–41
  in external eye, 8:174*t*
  in HIV infection/AIDS, 1:29, 9:305
  in immune processing, 9:38–39, 40*f*
  in Vogt-Koyanagi-Harada (VKH) syndrome, 9:183
HEMA. *See* Hydroxyethylmethacrylate
Hemagglutination treponemal test for syphilis (HATTS), 1:13, 279
Hemangioblastomas
  cerebellar, with retinal angiomatosis (von Hippel–Lindau disease), 4:294–295, 5:339*t*, 344, 6:364*t*, 374–375, 375*f*, 12:150
  retinal, 4:294–295, 294*f*, 5:339*t*, 344, 344*f*, 6:364*t*, 374–375, 375*f*, 12:148–151, 149*f*, 150*f*. *See also* Retinal angiomatosis
    retinoblastoma differentiated from, 6:358
Hemangiomas (hemangiomatosis), 4:291–295. *See also* Angiomas (angiomatosis)
  capillary, 4:219–220, 220*f*, 8:240–241
  cavernous, 1:97, 4:6, 8:240–241
  of choroid, 4:200–202, 201*f*, 291–293, 291*f*, 293*f*, 12:180–182, 181*f*
    age-related macular degeneration differentiated from, 12:70
    in children, 6:354, 377, 377*f*
    in Sturge-Weber syndrome, 4:200, 292, 6:377, 377*f*, 12:181
  classification of, 6:339, 339*f*
  of conjunctiva, 4:50, 8:240–241
  definition of, 6:338
  diffuse neonatal, 6:340
  of eyelid, 4:219–220, 220*f*, 7:24, 151–152, 8:240–241
  of orbit, 4:240, 241*f*
    capillary, 4:240, 7:24, 63–64, 63*f*
    cavernous, 4:6, 240, 241*f*, 7:64–65, 65*f*
    in children, 6:338–341, 339*f*, 7:63–64, 63*f*
    transient visual loss and, 5:177
  racemose (Wyburn-Mason syndrome), 4:296, 297*f*, 5:339*t*, 345, 345*f*, 6:342, 364*t*, 381, 381*f*, 12:151
  of retina
    capillary (retinal capillary hemangioblastoma/angiomatosis retinae). *See* Capillary hemangioblastoma; Retinal angiomatosis
    cavernous, 4:295, 296*f*, 12:151, 152*f*
  systemic disease associated with, 6:339–340, 339*f*
Hemangiopericytoma, of orbit, 4:242, 242*f*, 7:65
  in children, 6:342
Hematologic disorders, 1:147–159. *See also specific type*
  anemia, 1:148–150
  blood composition and, 1:147
  erythropoiesis and, 1:147
  hemostasis disorders, 1:151–159, 151*f*
  recent developments in, 1:147
  in systemic lupus erythematosus, 1:168, 169*t*
Hematologic tests, in uveitis, 9:94*t*
Hematopoietic growth factors
  in cancer therapy, 1:243–244
  for HIV infection/AIDS, 1:36
Hematopoietic stem cells, 1:147
Hematopoietic tissue, tumors arising in, 4:10*t*, 11*f*
Hematoxylin and eosin (H&E) stain, 4:30, 30*f*, 31*t*
Hemeralopia (day blindness)
  in achromatopsia, 6:291
  in cone/cone–rod dystrophies, 5:114, 12:232
Hemianopia
  bitemporal, chiasmal lesions causing, 5:159–162, 160*f*, 161*f*
  homonymous, 5:84, 91
    arteriovenous malformations causing, 5:355*f*, 356
    cortical injury causing, 5:29, 34
    hallucinations within, 5:191
    lateral geniculate body lesions causing, 5:167–168, 167*f*
    low vision evaluation and, 5:91
    occipital lobe lesions causing, 5:169–172, 170*f*, 171*f*, 172*f*
    OKN testing in evaluation of, 5:208
    optic tract lesions causing, 5:165–167, 166*f*
    parietal lobe lesions causing, 5:168–169
    partial prism for, 3:300–301
    temporal lobe lesions causing, 5:168, 169*f*
    in vertebrobasilar disease, 5:348
Hemiatrophy, progressive facial, 8:324*t*

Hemicrania, paroxysmal, 5:299
Hemidesmosomes, 2:43, 44f
Hemifacial microsomia, 6:392–393, 393f, 8:323t
Hemifacial spasm, 5:289t, 291, 291f, 7:221
Hemispatial neglect, 5:196
Hemispheric (hemicentral) retinal vein occlusion, 12:127, 127f
Hemizygote/hemizygous alleles, 2:152–153, 195, 218
Hemoccult slides. See Stool guaiac slide test
Hemochromatosis, 8:328
Hemoglobin
  absorption spectrum for, 12:337, 338f
  in anemia, 1:148
  glycosylated (fast hemoglobin/HbA$_1$/HbA$_{1c}$), in glucose control/surveillance, 1:203, 203f, 204, 12:92, 94f
  sickle cell, 2:207
  in thalassemia, 1:148
Hemoglobin A$_1$/hemoglobin A$_{1c}$. See Hemoglobin, glycosylated
Hemoglobin AS (sickle cell trait), 12:116, 117t
Hemoglobin C, mutant, 12:115, 116
Hemoglobin C trait (hemoglobin AC), 12:117t
Hemoglobin CC, 12:117t
Hemoglobin electrophoresis, in sickling disorders, 6:409, 12:116
Hemoglobin S, 1:150
  mutant, 12:115, 116
Hemoglobin SC disease, 12:116, 117t
Hemoglobin spherules, 4:138, 139f
Hemoglobin SS, 12:116, 117t
Hemoglobinopathies, sickle cell. See Sickle cell disease; Sickle cell retinopathy
Hemoglobinuria, paroxysmal nocturnal, 1:150
  hypercoagulability and, 1:158
  screening test for, 1:147
Hemolytic anemia, 1:149–150
  autoimmune, 1:150
Hemolytic glaucoma, 4:108, 108f, 10:99–100
Hemophilia A (classic hemophilia/factor VIII deficiency), 1:155
Hemorrhages. See also Hyphema
  cataract surgery and, 11:144t, 175–179, 189–190
    flat anterior chamber and, 11:152
    patient receiving anticoagulation therapy and, 11:74, 175–176, 189–190
  choroidal. See Hemorrhages, suprachoroidal/choroidal
  coagulation disorders and, 1:155–157
  conjunctival, 8:76, 76t, 362–363
    in child abuse, 6:404
    in dengue fever, 9:219
    in hereditary hemorrhagic telangiectasia, 8:76
  after Descemet stripping automated endothelial keratoplasty, 8:441f
  dot-and-blot, 5:183, 184, 184f
    ischemia causing, 4:160, 161f
  flame
    ischemia causing, 4:160, 161f
    in leukemia, 6:297
  glaucoma and, 4:108–109, 108f, 10:48–49, 48f, 79
  in hemophilia, 1:155
  hemostatic derangement and, 1:153
  histologic sequelae of, 4:20

intracranial, 1:97–98
  arteriovenous malformations causing, 1:97, 98, 5:354, 356
  headache caused by, 1:98, 5:294
  ruptured aneurysm causing, 1:97, 98, 5:351
  in shaking injury, 6:404
  Terson syndrome caused by, 12:155
iron deficiency anemia and, 1:148
nerve fiber layer, in glaucoma, 10:48–49, 48f
neuroimaging in evaluation of, 5:82t, 88
orbital, 7:69, 104
  after blepharoplasty, visual loss and, 7:226
  in blowout fractures, 7:101
  from orbital lymphatic malformation, 7:65, 66
  postoperative, 7:116
platelet disorders and, 1:152, 153–155
retinal. See also specific type
  in arterial macroaneurysms, 12:147–148
  in branch retinal vein occlusion, 12:123
  in central retinal vein occlusion, 12:128, 128f, 129f
  in dengue fever, 9:219
  in diabetic retinopathy, 12:104, 104f
  in glaucoma, 10:48–49, 48f
  ischemia causing, 4:160, 161f, 164, 165f
  in leukemia, 4:326, 327f, 6:297
  in Rift Valley fever, 9:217
  in shaking injury, 6:405, 405f, 406, 12:330, 330f, 331
  in systemic lupus erythematosus, 9:141
  in Terson syndrome, 12:155
retrobulbar
  after blepharoplasty, visual loss and, 7:226
  cataract surgery and, 11:144t, 176–177, 189
salmon patch
  in sickle cell disease, 12:118, 118f, 119f
  syphilitic keratitis and, 6:221, 8:208, 208f
subarachnoid, 1:97, 98
  arteriovenous malformations causing, 5:354
  with ocular hemorrhage, 5:351
subconjunctival, 8:76, 76t, 362–363
  in child abuse, 6:404
submacular, 12:349–351, 350f
suprachoroidal/choroidal, 4:18–19, 19f, 12:360–361, 362f
  angle-closure glaucoma and, 10:133
  cataract surgery and, 11:144t, 177–179, 189
    delayed, 11:178–179
    expulsive, 11:178
    flat anterior chamber and, 11:152
  expulsive, 4:18–19, 19f
    cataract surgery and, 11:178
  postoperative, 12:360–361, 362f
vascular disorders and, 1:153
vitreous, 2:288, 4:137–138, 139f, 12:313–314, 319
  blunt trauma causing, 12:319
  in branch retinal vein occlusion, 12:123, 125, 126
  in diabetic retinopathy, 12:105, 106f, 310, 313, 352
  hemolytic/ghost cell glaucoma and, 10:99–100
  in pars planitis, 12:196
  in posterior vitreous detachment, 12:275, 313
  retinal cavernous hemangioma causing, 12:151
  retinoblastoma differentiated from, 4:305t
  in shaking injury, 6:405, 407
  spontaneous, 12:313–314

in systemic lupus erythematosus, 9:141
vitrectomy for, in diabetes mellitus, 12:110, 352
Hemorrhagic conjunctivitis, acute, 8:130
Hemorrhagic disease of newborn, 1:156
Hemorrhagic retinopathy (severe/ischemic CRVO),
    12:127, 128, 129f
Hemorrhagic stroke, 1:91. See also Stroke
Hemorrhagic suprachoroidal detachment, melanoma
    differentiated from, 4:279–280
Hemorrhagic telangiectasia, hereditary (Osler-Weber-
    Rendu disease), 1:153, 8:76
Hemosiderin, in glaucoma, 4:108–109, 108f
Hemosiderosis oculi, 4:109
Hemostasis, 1:151–152, 151f
    disorders of, 1:151–159
        cataract surgery in patient with, 11:189–190
        clinical manifestations of/hemorrhage, 1:153
        coagulation disorders and, 1:155–157
        hypercoagulable states and, 1:157–159
        platelet disorders and, 1:153–155
        vascular disorders and, 1:153
    laboratory evaluation of, 1:152–153
Henderson-Patterson bodies, 8:127
Henle fiber layer/Henle layer, 2:78, 79, 79f, 4:147, 147f,
    5:29. See also Nerve fiber layer
Henoch-Schönlein purpura, 1:177t
HEP. See Hepatoerythropoietic porphyria
Hepacare. See Hepatitis B vaccine
Heparan sulfate
    in microbial adherence, 8:98
    in mucopolysaccharidoses, 8:305
        retinal dystrophy and, 12:262
Heparan sulfate sulfatase, defective, 2:213t
Heparin
    as inflammatory mediator, 8:179t
    in mast cells, 9:10
Heparin therapy, 1:91, 158
    for antiphospholipid antibody syndrome, 1:172–173
    cataract surgery and, 11:189
    for cerebral ischemia/stroke, 1:94
    for deep venous thrombosis prophylaxis in stroke
        patients, 1:91
    for ischemic heart disease, 1:109, 109t
        non–ST-segment elevation acute coronary
            syndrome, 1:111–112
    in perioperative setting, 1:306–307
Hepatic disease. See Hepatitis; Liver disease
Hepatitis, 1:25–27
    delta, 1:26
    HIV coinfection and, 1:39–40
    transfusion-transmitted virus causing, 1:26
    type A, 1:25
        immunization against, 1:25, 281
            travel and, 1:286
    type B, 1:280–281
        cancer and, 1:237, 280
        in HIV infection/AIDS, 1:39–40
        immunization against, 1:280–281
            travel and, 1:286
        in polyarteritis nodosa/microscopic polyangiitis,
            9:143
    type C, 1:25–26
        in HIV infection/AIDS, 1:39–40

type E, 1:26
type G, 1:26
Hepatitis A vaccine, 1:25, 281
    travel and, 1:286
Hepatitis B immune globulin, 1:281
Hepatitis B vaccine, 1:280–281
    in combination vaccines, 1:285
    travel and, 1:286
Hepatitis D virus, 1:26
Hepatitis E virus, 1:26
Hepatitis G virus, 1:26
Hepatocellular carcinoma, viral carcinogenesis and,
    1:237, 275, 280
Hepatoerythropoietic porphyria (HEP), 8:326
Hepatolenticular degeneration (Wilson disease), 2:231,
    6:220–221, 398, 8:327–328, 327f, 11:57
    cataracts associated with, 6:247t, 8:327, 11:57
    oculogyric crisis in, 5:212–213
    penicillamine for, 2:231, 8:327–328
HepB. See Hepatitis B vaccine
Her2Neu, in immunohistochemistry, 4:34
Herbal supplements, cessation of before surgery,
    7:189–190
Herbert pits, 8:154, 155f
Hereditary, definition of, 2:153, 191. See also Genetics
Hereditary benign intraepithelial dyskeratosis, 8:226t
Hereditary dystrophies, 12:221–248. See also specific
    type
    choroidal, 12:242–246, 243f, 244f, 245f
    diagnostic/prognostic testing in, 12:223, 224t
    endothelial, congenital, 4:79–80, 79f, 6:216t, 217,
        8:260–263, 268t, 270t, 295–296, 295f
        CHED1, 8:260, 268t, 270t, 295–296, 295f
        CHED2, 8:260, 268t, 270t, 296, 296f
        genetics of, 8:269t, 295, 296
    inner retinal, 12:246–248
    macular, 12:234–242
        in children, 6:292–294
    photoreceptor (diffuse), 4:175–177, 12:223–234
    retinal, 12:221–242
        diagnostic and prognostic testing in, 12:223, 224t
        inner, 12:246–248
        photoreceptor (diffuse), 4:175–177, 12:223–234
    stromal, congenital, 6:216t, 219, 8:260, 268t, 270t,
        286–287, 286f
    vitreoretinal, 12:246–248
        in children, 6:294–296
Hereditary factors. See Genetic/hereditary factors
Hereditary hemorrhagic telangiectasia (Osler-Weber-
    Rendu disease), 1:153, 8:76
Hereditary hyaloideoretinopathies with optically empty
    vitreous, 12:309–310, 309f
Hereditary optic neuropathy, Leber, 5:137–139, 137f,
    6:311
        mitochondrial DNA mutations and, 2:174f, 5:138,
            6:311
Hereditary progressive arthro-ophthalmopathy. See
    Stickler syndrome
Hereditary sensory and autonomic neuropathy, type 3.
    See Familial dysautonomia
Hereditary spherocytosis, 1:149–150
Hering's law of motor correspondence, 6:35, 36f
    eyelid retraction and, 5:281, 7:214

Heritable, definition of, 2:153
Hermansky-Pudlak syndrome, 6:300t, 302, 12:258t, 259
  racial and ethnic concentration of, 2:211
Herpes simplex virus, 1:22–23, 6:185, 8:105–117
  acute retinal necrosis/progressive outer retinal necrosis/nonnecrotizing herpetic retinitis caused by, 4:151, 5:359, 9:199–204, 200t, 201f, 203f, 307–308, 308f, 12:201–202, 202f
  acyclovir for infection caused by, 1:22–23, 65, 2:381t, 382–383, 8:108t, 109t, 113, 115
  anterior uveitis caused by, 9:197–199, 198f
  antiviral agents for, 2:380, 381t, 382–384, 8:109, 109t, 111–113
  blepharoconjunctivitis caused by, 8:106, 106f, 110
  cancer association and, 1:237
  congenital infection caused by, 6:185
  conjunctivitis caused by, 4:53
    in children, 6:191–192, 192f
    in neonates, 6:185, 188
  famciclovir for infection caused by, 1:23, 66, 8:109t, 9:202, 12:201
  Fuchs heterochromic iridocyclitis/uveitis and, 9:134
  in HIV infection/AIDS, 5:359, 361f, 9:307–308, 313–314, 313f
  iridocyclitis caused by, 8:114, 116–117
  keratitis caused by, 4:82–83, 84f, 8:109, 110–116, 111f, 112f, 114f, 115f, 9:197
    Acanthamoeba keratitis differentiated from, 8:168–169
    disciform, 4:83, 8:114, 114f
      persistent bullous keratopathy and, 8:117
    epithelial, 8:110–113, 111f, 112f
    in HIV infection/AIDS, 9:313–314, 313f
    in infants and children, 6:185
    interstitial, 4:82–83, 84f, 87, 8:113, 114f
    necrotizing, 8:115, 115f, 116
    neurotrophic keratopathy/ulcers and, 4:83, 8:87, 88, 117
    in newborn, 6:185
    penetrating keratoplasty for, 4:83, 8:117
    refractive surgery and, 13:166–167
    stromal, 4:82, 84f, 8:108t, 113–116, 114f, 115f
    topical antiviral agents for, 2:380, 381t, 382–383
  in multifocal choroiditis and panuveitis syndrome, 9:164
  ocular infection/inflammation caused by, 1:22, 8:105–117
    adenovirus infection differentiated from, 8:107
    complications of, 8:116–117
    evasion and, 8:98
    in infants and children, 6:185, 188, 191–192, 192f
    iridocorneal endothelial syndrome and, 8:344
    pathogenesis of, 8:105–106
    primary infection, 8:106, 106–109, 106f, 107f, 108t, 109t
    recurrent infection, 8:109–117, 111f, 112f, 114f, 115f
    refractive surgery and, 13:166–167
    treatment of, 8:108t
    varicella-zoster virus infection differentiated from, 8:118t
  perinatal infection caused by, 1:22, 6:185, 8:106

retinitis caused by
  necrotizing, 4:151, 151f, 9:200, 307–308, 308f, 12:201–202, 202f. See also Acute retinal necrosis; Progressive outer retinal necrosis
  nonnecrotizing (nonnecrotizing posterior uveitis), 9:203–204
  skin infection after laser resurfacing caused by, 7:231
  type 1, 1:22, 237, 6:185, 191, 8:105
  type 2, 1:22, 237, 6:185, 191–192, 8:105
  valacyclovir for infection caused by, 1:23, 8:109t, 113, 115, 9:199, 12:201
Herpes zoster, 1:23–24, 8:118, 119–122. See also Varicella-zoster virus
  acute retinal necrosis/progressive outer retinal necrosis/nonnecrotizing herpetic retinitis caused by, 4:151, 5:359, 9:199–204, 200t, 201f, 203f, 12:201–202, 202f
  acyclovir for, 1:23, 65–66, 8:121
  conjunctivitis and, 4:53, 6:192–193, 193f, 8:106, 106f
  cranial nerve VII (facial) involvement and, 5:286, 287
  famciclovir for, 1:23, 66, 2:381t, 383, 8:121
  in HIV infection/AIDS, 5:359, 9:307–308, 308f, 313
  in older patients, 1:233
  ophthalmic manifestations in, 5:302–303, 303f, 359, 8:119–122, 119f, 120f, 121f
    refractive surgery and, 13:166
  scleritis and, 8:120, 9:266
  valacyclovir for, 1:23, 2:381t, 383, 8:121
  varicella vaccine in prevention of, 8:121
  without vesicles (zoster sine herpete), 5:302, 9:197
Herpes zoster ophthalmicus, 5:302–303, 303f, 359, 8:119–122, 119f, 120f, 121f
  acyclovir for, 1:23, 65–66, 8:121
  neurotrophic keratopathy in, 8:87, 122
  in older patients, 1:233
  refractive surgery and, 13:166
Herpesviruses (Herpesviridae)/herpesvirus infection, 1:22–25, 8:105–123. See also specific virus
  cancer association and, 1:237
  refractive surgery and, 13:166–167
  uveitis, 9:197–209
Herpetic Eye Disease Study (HEDS), 8:107, 108t, 109, 115–116
Herpex. See Idoxuridine
Herrick Lacrimal Plug, canalicular obstruction and, 7:263
Hertel exophthalmometer, 7:23, 23f
Hess screen test, 6:80
  in superior oblique muscle paralysis, 6:119
Heterochromia (heterochromia iridis)
  in Fuchs heterochromic iridocyclitis/uveitis, 9:133, 133f, 10:94
  in Horner syndrome, 5:266
  pediatric, 6:227–228, 228f, 228t
    in leukemia, 6:354
  in siderosis bulbi, 11:54f
Heterocyclic antidepressants, 1:255t, 256
Heterogeneity, 2:193–194
  allelic, 2:148, 192–193, 193
  clinical, 2:149, 193
  genetic, 2:153, 192, 193
  locus, 2:155, 192, 193
Heteronuclear (heterogeneous nuclear) RNA (hnRNA), 2:153, 161

Heteronymous diplopia, **6**:54, 54*f*
Heterophoria method, for AC/A ratio measurement, **3**:144, **6**:81–82
Heterophorias/phorias, **6**:9, 10
    cover tests in assessment of, **6**:74–76, 75*f*
    prismatic effects of bifocal lenses and, **3**:151, 151*f*, 152*f*, 153*f*
        decentration and, **3**:157
    prisms for, **3**:163
    refractive surgery and, **13**:34, 181
    strabismus classification and, **6**:10
Heteroplasmy, **2**:153, 173
Heterotopy, of rectus pulleys, **6**:23
Heterotropias/tropias, **6**:9, 10
    A- and V-pattern deviations and, **6**:110
    alternating, **6**:74
    cover tests in assessment of, **6**:74–76, 75*f*
    induced, testing visual acuity and, **6**:72–73
    intermittent, **6**:10
        esotropia, **6**:89
        exotropia, **6**:99–103
    refractive surgery and, **13**:34
    strabismic amblyopia and, **6**:62
Heterozygosity, loss of, **2**:173
Heterozygote/heterozygous alleles, **2**:153, 194
    carrier, **2**:149, 214–215. *See also* Carrier (genetic)
    compound, **2**:150, 194, 216
    double, **2**:195
Hex K. *See* Hexagonal keratotomy
Hexagonal cells, specular photomicroscopy in evaluation of percentage of, **8**:32–33
Hexagonal keratotomy, **13**:4*t*
Hexokinase, in lens glucose/carbohydrate metabolism, **2**:279, **11**:13, 14*f*, 15
Hexosaminidase, defective/deficiency of, **2**:213*t*
    in gangliosidoses, **6**:303, **8**:310, **12**:262
Hexose monophosphate shunt, in glucose/carbohydrate metabolism
    in cornea, **2**:248
    in lens, **2**:279, **11**:14*f*, 15
Hexosidase, defective, **2**:213*t*
HFS. *See* Hemifacial spasm
Hi-index spectacle lenses, **3**:162–163
Hib (*Haemophilus influenzae* type B), **1**:9–10, **8**:136
Hib (*Haemophilus influenzae* type B) vaccine, **1**:9–10, 285
    in combination vaccines, **1**:285
Hib-DTaP vaccine, **1**:285
Hib-MenC-TT vaccine, **1**:285
Hidradenoma, clear cell (eccrine acrospiroma), **7**:162
Hidrocystoma
    apocrine, **4**:214, 214*f*, **7**:162, 162*f*
    eccrine, **4**:214, **7**:161
High accommodative convergence/accommodation ratio
    accommodative (nonrefractive) esotropia and, **6**:82, 94–95
    intermittent exotropia and, **6**:100–101
High accommodative convergence/accommodative esotropia, **6**:82, 94–95
High-density-lipoprotein cholesterol, **1**:132, 132*t*. *See also* Cholesterol
    β-blockers affecting, **1**:139
    drugs affecting metabolism of, **1**:137*t*

ischemic heart disease risk and, **1**:100, 132–133, 132*t*, 133*t*
    risk assessment and, **1**:132–133, 133*t*
    screening, **1**:271
High-grade lymphoma, of orbit, **7**:81
High hyperopia, cataract surgery in patient with, **11**:200–201
High-impact plastic lenses, **3**:162
High (pathologic/degenerative) myopia, **12**:85–87, 86*f*
    cataract surgery in patient with, **11**:200
    choroidal neovascularization and, **12**:86–87
    correction of
        bioptics for, **13**:137
        phakic IOLs for, **13**:128
        refractive lens exchange/clear lens extraction for, **13**:138, 139–140, 140, 141
        retinal detachment and, **13**:138, 141, 175–176, 176–177
    esotropia and, **6**:141
    glaucoma and, **10**:76
    in inborn errors of metabolism, **6**:401*t*
    in infants and children, **3**:141, **6**:141, 401*t*
High-output failure, causes of, **1**:116
High-plus aspheric lenses, in low vision/vision rehabilitation, **3**:297–298
High-plus-power lenses
    for slit-lamp biomicroscopy, **12**:19–20
    for slit-lamp delivery of photocoagulation, **12**:339
High-plus prismatic half-eye glasses, in low vision/ vision rehabilitation, **3**:297, 298*f*
High-resolution ultrasonography, in corneal imaging, **8**:29
Higher-order aberrations, **3**:93, 115–116, 240, **13**:7–8, 8*f*, 9*f*. *See also specific type and* Irregular astigmatism
    contact lens masking of, **3**:190
    custom contact lenses for, **3**:195–196
    after LASIK, **13**:7, 95, 96*f*
    after surface ablation, **13**:7, 95
    wavefront-guided/wavefront-optimized ablation and, **13**:7, 8, 25, 69, 95
Highly active antiretroviral therapy (HAART), **1**:35–37
    CMV retinitis and, **1**:3, **9**:206, **12**:201
        immune recovery uveitis and, **1**:41, **9**:306, **12**:201
    immune reconstitution syndromes and, **1**:40–41, **9**:306, **12**:201
    mycobacterial infections and, **1**:39
Hilafilcon, for contact lenses, **3**:177*t*
Hip fracture, osteoporosis-related, **1**:228
Hirschberg test, **6**:76–77, 77*f*
Hirudin, for non–ST-segment elevation acute coronary syndrome, **1**:111–112
His bundle, **1**:121
Histamine, **2**:364, **8**:177*t*, 179*t*, **9**:10, 25
    allergic conjunctivitis and, **8**:185
Histiocytes, **4**:7
    epithelioid, **4**:7, 8*f*
Histiocytic (large) cell lymphoma. *See* Intraocular tumors, lymphoma
Histiocytoma, fibrous (fibroxanthoma), **8**:242
    malignant (atypical fibroxanthoma), **4**:117–118, 240–242
    orbital, **4**:240–242, 242*f*, **7**:78
    scleral, **4**:117–118, 117*f*

Histiocytosis (Langerhans cell histiocytosis/histiocytosis X/diffuse soft tissue histiocytosis), orbital involvement in, 7:84
in children, 6:332t, 337–338, 338f
Histo spots, 9:221, 222f, 223, 12:81
maculopathy development and, 9:223
Histocompatibility antigens, 8:407. See also Human leukocyte antigens
Histocryl. See Cyanoacrylate adhesives
Histogram, 1:344, 344f
for flow cytometry results, 4:37, 37f
Histoplasma capsulatum (histoplasmosis), ocular, 9:221–226, 222f, 223f, 224f, 225f, 12:80–83, 82f
management of, 9:223–226, 224f, 225f, 12:81–83, 351, 351f
Historical methods, for IOL power calculation after refractive surgery, 11:87–88, 13:188
History
in amblyopia, 6:71
in cataract, 11:69–71, 70t
evaluation for surgery and, 11:73–75
pediatric, 6:251
in child abuse, 6:404
contact lens selection and, 3:179
in diplopia, 5:215
family. See also under Genetic
cancer and, 1:237
in genetic counseling, 2:225–226, 226f, 227
in glaucoma, 10:10, 76, 114
angle closure/angle-closure glaucoma and, 10:10, 114
open-angle glaucoma and, 10:76
in hereditary dystrophies, 12:221, 221–222
in nystagmus, 6:318, 319t
in ocular hypertension, 10:84
in pediatric cataract, 6:253–254, 253f, 254t
pedigree analysis and, 2:225–226, 226f
in uveitis, 9:315
glaucoma evaluation and, 10:27
in children, 10:149–150
in headache, 5:293t
in hereditary dystrophies, 12:221–222
in infant with decreased vision, 6:414
in intraocular foreign body, 12:325
in low vision assessment, 3:288–289, 5:91–92
in nystagmus, 6:318, 319t
in pediatric cataract, 6:251
in penetrating/perforating injury, 8:373, 373t
preoperative assessment and, 1:304t
in pulmonary disease, 1:143
refractive surgery evaluation and, 13:29–33, 30t
in strabismus, 6:71
in trauma, 8:373, 373t, 12:317
in uveitis, 9:90, 90t, 315–319
family, 9:315
personal medical, 9:316–319
social, 9:315
HIV (human immunodeficiency virus), 1:27–28, 28–29, 8:130, 9:305–314. See also HIV infection/AIDS
drug resistance and, 1:33, 34, 35, 36
superinfection and, 1:33
testing for antibody to, 1:31–32
in syphilis patients, 9:247

vaccine development and, 1:36
viability of after excimer laser ablation, 13:182–183
HIV-1, 1:28. See also HIV infection/AIDS
superinfection and, 1:33
HIV-1 delta4 vaccine, 1:36
HIV-2, 1:28. See also HIV infection/AIDS
HIV infection/AIDS, 1:27–44, 5:358–362, 360f, 361f, 362f, 8:130, 9:305–314
acute retinal necrosis in, 9:199–200
atypical mycobacterial infections and, 1:18, 39, 5:360
CDC definition of, 1:29–30, 30t, 31t
choroiditis in
Cryptococcus neoformans, 9:310–311
multifocal, 9:311
Pneumocystis jiroveci (Pneumocystis carinii), 9:310, 310f, 311f
clinical syndrome of, 1:29–31, 30t, 31t
CMV infection in, 1:3, 24, 5:359, 360f
retinitis, 4:151, 5:359, 9:204, 205, 206, 306–307, 12:200–201
in children, 6:184
conjunctival intraepithelial neoplasia in, 8:228
cryptococcosis in, 5:367, 9:278, 310–311, 313–314
diagnosis of, 1:31–32
encephalopathy in, 1:29, 5:359–360
endophthalmitis in, 9:271
etiology of, 1:28–29
herpes simplex keratitis in, 9:313–314, 313f
herpes zoster in, 9:313
herpesvirus infection in, 5:359, 361f, 8:109, 9:307–308, 313, 313–314, 313f
incidence of, 1:28
influenza vaccine in patients with, 1:33, 282
Kaposi sarcoma in, 1:29, 40, 7:176–177, 177f, 8:242, 9:312, 312f
lymphoma in, 1:40, 5:358, 9:314
malignancies associated with, 1:29, 40
management of, 1:33–41
drug resistance and, 1:33, 34, 35, 36
HAART in, 1:3, 35–37
CMV retinitis and, 9:206, 306, 12:201
immune reconstitution syndromes/immune recovery uveitis and, 1:40–41, 9:306, 12:201
recent developments in, 1:3
microsporidiosis in, 1:38, 8:170, 9:313, 313f
conjunctival involvement and, 4:54
molluscum contagiosum in, 7:159, 8:128, 129f, 9:312–313
natural immunity to, 1:34
nephropathy associated with, 1:29
neuro-ophthalmic signs of, 5:359–360
occupational exposure to, precautions in health care setting and, 9:314
ocular infection/manifestations and, 1:41, 8:100, 130, 9:305–314
in children, 6:304
external eye manifestations, 9:311–314
ophthalmic manifestations, 9:305–311
ocular surface squamous neoplasia in, 4:62
opportunistic infections associated with, 1:3, 29–31, 30t, 31t, 37–40, 9:311
pathogenesis of, 1:28–29

Pneumocystis jiroveci (Pneumocystis carinii) infections
   and, 1:37, **9**:310, 310*f*, 311*f*
  primary, 1:30–31
  prognosis for, 1:32–33
  progressive multifocal leukoencephalopathy in, **5**:361,
   362*f*
  progressive outer retinal necrosis in, **5**:359, **9**:203,
   307–308, 308*f*, **12**:201
  refractive surgery in patients with, **13**:31, 182–183
  retinitis in, **4**:151, **9**:204, 205, 206, 306–307, 307–308,
   308*f*, **12**:200–201
  retinopathy associated with, **9**:305, 306*f*
  seroepidemiology of, 1:31–32
  seventh nerve (facial) palsy in, **5**:287
  spore-forming intestinal protozoal infection and, 1:38
  superinfection and, 1:33
  syphilis/syphilitic chorioretinitis in, 1:14, **5**:361,
   9:246, 247, 248, 249, 309–310
  Toxoplasma retinochoroiditis/toxoplasmosis in,
   5:362, **9**:228, 232, 233–234, 308–309, 309*f*,
   12:208
  transmission of, 1:32, 41
   disinfection of trial contact lenses and, **3**:201
  tuberculosis and, 1:19, 39, **5**:360, **9**:256–257, 257, 258,
   313–314, **12**:205
  uveitis in, **9**:305
  vaccine development and, 1:36
HIV p24 antigen testing, 1:31–32
HIV RNA, 1:31–32, 33
  therapy and, 1:35
HIV vaccine, development of, 1:36
Hives (urticaria), from fluorescein angiography, **12**:24,
  25
HLA. *See* Human leukocyte antigens
HLA system. *See* Human leukocyte antigen (HLA)
  system
HLH. *See* Helix-loop-helix motif
HMB-45, in immunohistochemistry, **4**:33
HMG-CoA (3-hydroxy-3-methylglutaryl coenzyme-A)
  reductase inhibitors. *See also* Statins
  Alzheimer disease prevention and, 1:267
  cataracts and, 1:139, **11**:49
  hypercholesterolemia/heart disease prevention and,
   1:137*t*
HMGA2 gene mutation, in pleomorphic adenoma,
  4:236
HMP shunt. *See* Hexose monophosphate shunt
HMR 3467. *See* Telithromycin
hnRNA. *See* Heteronuclear (heterogeneous nuclear)
  RNA
Ho:YAG laser. *See* Holmium:YAG (Ho:YAG) laser
Hodgkin disease
  in HIV infection/AIDS, 1:40
  orbital, lymphoma and, **4**:239, **7**:80
  transfusion-transmitted virus (TTV) associated with,
   1:26
Hoffer Q formula, for IOL power determination/
  selection, **3**:212–213, 217, 219, **11**:85, 87
  refractive lens exchange/clear lens extraction and,
   13:140
Hoffer split bifocal, **3**:226, 227*f*
Holandric inheritance/trait, **2**:218

Holes
  macular, **4**:136–137, 138*f*, **12**:304–306, 305–306*f*, 349,
   350*f*
   idiopathic, **12**:304–306, 305–306*f*, 349, 350*f*
    vitrectomy for, **12**:305–306, 349, 350*f*
   impending, **12**:304, 305*f*
   posterior vitreous detachment and, **12**:298,
    304–306, 305–306*f*
   posttraumatic, **12**:321–322, 322*f*
   treatment of, **12**:305–306, 349, 350*f*
   vitreous in formation of, **2**:288
  optic (optic pits, optic nerve/disc pits), **2**:120, 121,
   5:143, **12**:294–295, 295*f*
   acquired, **10**:48
   central serous chorioretinopathy differentiated
    from, **12**:174
   in children, **6**:310, 310*f*
  retinal
   atrophic, **12**:271
    lattice degeneration and, **4**:155, **12**:278, 278*f*
     treatment of, **12**:284–285, 284*t*
    treatment of, **12**:283, 284, 284*t*
   lattice degeneration and, **4**:155, **12**:276, 277*f*, 278,
    278*f*
   operculated, **12**:271
    treatment of, **12**:283, 284*t*
   photocoagulation causing, **12**:342
   retinal breaks and, **12**:271
Holladay formulas, for IOL power determination/
  selection, **3**:212–213, 217, 219, **11**:85
  refractive lens exchange/clear lens extraction and,
   13:140
Hollenhorst plaques (cholesterol emboli)
  in branch retinal artery occlusion, **4**:163, **12**:136, 137*f*
  in central retinal artery occlusion, **12**:139
  transient visual loss and, **5**:175*f*, 177, 179*t*
Holmes-Adie syndrome, **5**:270. *See also* Adie tonic pupil
Holmium:YAG (Ho:YAG) laser, **3**:24. *See also* Lasers
  photothermal effects of, **13**:23
  for thermokeratoplasty, **13**:120
Holmium-YLF laser, **3**:24. *See also* Lasers
Holoprosencephaly, sonic hedgehog mutation causing,
  2:141
Holter monitoring, 1:94, 96
Homatropine, **2**:260, 341*t*
  for amblyopia, **6**:67
  for cycloplegia/cycloplegic refraction, **3**:137*t*, **6**:88, 88*t*
Homeobox, **2**:114, 153. *See also* Homeobox genes
Homeobox genes/homeotic selector genes, **2**:114, 147,
  153
  congenital anomalies associated with mutations in,
   2:141, 142
  growth factors affecting expression of, **2**:115
  in ocular development, **2**:114–115
  in retinal dystrophies, **12**:222, 233
Homeodomain, **2**:114
Homeotic genes/homeotic selector genes. *See*
  Homeobox genes
Homer Wright rosettes, in retinoblastoma, **4**:180, 181*f*,
  6:358
Homing, **9**:44, 61
  MALT and, **9**:59

Homocysteine
  carotid artery disease and, 1:97
  hypercoagulability and, 1:158
Homocystinuria, 2:213t, 6:263–264, 398, 401t, 11:37
  ectopia lentis in, 6:263, 264f, 11:37
  pigmentary retinopathy and, 12:250t
  treatment of, 6:399
  vitamin B$_6$ replacement therapy for, 2:232, 11:37
Homogentisate 1,2-dioxygenase, in alkaptonuria, 8:315
Homogentisic acid/homogentisic acid oxidase,
    alkaptonuria and, 2:212, 213t, 8:315
Homologous antigens, 8:407. See also Human leukocyte
    antigens
Homologous chromosomes, 2:153, 193
Homonymous diplopia, 6:54, 54f
Homonymous hemianopia, 5:84, 91
  arteriovenous malformations causing, 5:355f, 356
  cortical injury causing, 5:29, 34
  hallucinations within, 5:191
  lateral geniculate body lesions causing, 5:167–168, 167f
  low vision evaluation and, 5:91
  occipital lobe lesions causing, 5:169–172, 170f, 171f,
    172f
  OKN testing in evaluation of, 5:208
  optic tract lesions causing, 5:165–167, 166f
  parietal lobe lesions causing, 5:168–169
  partial prism for, 3:300–301
  temporal lobe lesions causing, 5:168, 169f
  in vertebrobasilar disease, 5:348
Homoplasmy, 2:153, 173
Homoplastic corneal inlays, in keratophakia, 13:54
Homotropaire. See Homatropine
Homozygote/homozygous alleles, 2:153, 194
Honeycomb-shaped corneal dystrophy. See Thiel-
    Behnke corneal dystrophy
Hookworm, dog (Ancylostoma caninum), diffuse
    unilateral subacute neuroretinitis caused by, 9:239,
    12:210
Hordeolum, 7:154, 8:148
  in children, 6:350–351
  external (stye), 4:208, 7:154, 8:148
  internal, 7:152, 154, 8:148. See also Chalazion
HORIZON study, 12:77
Horizontal cells, 2:74, 75f, 299–300, 299f, 5:28, 12:12, 14f
  in cone phototransduction, 2:294
Horizontal deviations, 6:11
  A-pattern and V-pattern, 6:107–112, 108f, 109f. See
    also A-pattern deviations; V-pattern deviations
  in craniosynostosis, 6:390–391, 391f
  dissociated, 6:105–106, 105f, 117
  in internuclear ophthalmoplegia, 6:141
  strabismus surgery planning and, 6:146
Horizontal eyelid shortening/tightening
  for cicatricial ectropion, 7:193
  for exposure keratopathy, 8:80
  for involutional ectropion, 7:190, 192–193, 192f
  for involutional entropion, 7:196
Horizontal gaze, 5:44–46, 45f
Horizontal gaze palsy, 5:210, 211f
Horizontal heterophoria/phoria
  prismatic effects of bifocal lenses and, 3:151, 152f
  prisms for, 3:163

Horizontal incomitance, strabismus surgery planning
    and, 6:146
Horizontal phaco chop techniques, 11:122–123, 124f
Horizontal rectus muscles, 6:13, 14f. See also Lateral
    rectus muscles; Medial rectus muscles
  A-pattern deviations associated with dysfunction of,
    6:107–108
  action of, 6:13, 28, 29t
    gaze position and, 6:30, 30f
  anatomy of, 6:13, 14f
  surgery of
    for A- and V-pattern deviations, 6:110, 111, 111f,
      112
    for nystagmus, 6:328, 329
    for third nerve (oculomotor) paralysis, 6:133
  V-pattern deviations associated with dysfunction of,
    6:107–108
Horizontal strabismus. See Horizontal deviations
Hormone replacement therapy. See Estrogen/hormone
    replacement therapy
Hormones
  in aqueous humor, 2:267
  in cancer chemotherapy, 1:242t
    for metastatic eye disease, 4:322
  cytokines as, 9:27
  ocular effects of, 1:302t
  pituitary adenoma producing, 1:214–216
Horner muscle, 2:27, 7:136, 246
Horner syndrome, 5:265f, 266–269, 267f, 268f, 269f,
    302, 6:230, 7:17, 204, 204f
  carotid artery dissection causing, 5:267, 268, 269f,
    302, 353
  congenital, 5:266, 267, 7:207
  dilator muscle and, 2:60
  localization of lesions causing, 5:267, 268f, 269f
  in neuroblastoma, 6:230, 336, 336f, 7:91
  neuroimaging in evaluation of, 5:86
  pharmacologic testing for, 5:265f, 266–267, 267f, 268f,
    7:204, 204f
  ptosis and, 7:204, 204f, 207
Horner-Trantas dots, 4:50, 6:200, 8:187, 188f
Horopter, empirical, 6:39–40, 40f
Horror fusionis (central fusional disruption), 6:49–50,
    104–105
Horseshoe tears (flap tears), 12:271, 272, 273f
  treatment of, 12:283, 284, 284t
Host cell, 2:153–154
Host defenses
  impaired, 8:100. See also Immunocompromised host
  of outer eye, 8:95–96, 99–100
Hot spots, focal, in indocyanine angiography, 12:25–26
HOTV test, in children, 6:72t, 73
Hounsfield unit, 5:69
Houseplants, ocular injuries caused by, 8:362
HOX genes, 2:115, 147, 153
HOX7.1 gene, 2:115
HOX8.1 gene, 2:115
HPMC. See Hydroxypropyl methylcellulose
HPMPC. See Cidofovir
HPS. See Hermansky-Pudlak syndrome
HPS1/HPS3/HPS4/HPS5/HPS6 genes, in Hermansky-
    Pudlak syndrome, 6:300t, 12:258t

HPV. *See* Human papillomaviruses
HPV vaccine, **1**:27, 237, 273
HRT. *See* Estrogen/hormone replacement therapy;
    Heidelberg retina tomography
Hruby lens, for slit-lamp biomicroscopy, **3**:253, 254*f*,
    12:20
HSV. *See* Herpes simplex virus
HTH. *See* Helix-turn-helix motif
HTLV-1. *See* Human T-lymphotropic virus type 1
HTLV-1–related chronic interstitial keratitis, **9**:219
HTLV-2. *See* Human T-lymphotropic virus type 2
HTLV-3. *See* Human T-lymphotropic virus type 3
HTRA1 gene, in age-related macular degeneration,
    12:56
HU. *See* Human T-lymphotropic virus type 1 (HTLV-1),
    uveitis caused by
Hudson-Stähli line, **8**:336, 337*t*
Hughes/modified Hughes procedure, in eyelid repair,
    7:185, 185*f*
Humalog. *See* Lispro insulin
Human bites, eyelid injuries caused by, **7**:181
Human gene mapping, **2**:178, 193
Human Genome Project, **2**:178
Human granulocytic anaplasmosis/ehrlichiosis, **1**:15
    Lyme disease coinfection and, **9**:254
Human herpes virus 8, Kaposi sarcoma caused by, **1**:22,
    8:129, 242, **9**:312
Human herpesviruses, **1**:22–25. *See also specific type*
    cancer association of, **1**:237
Human immunodeficiency virus (HIV), **1**:27–28, 28–
    29, **8**:130, **9**:305–314. *See also* HIV infection/AIDS
    drug resistance and, **1**:33, 34, 35, 36
    superinfection and, **1**:33
    testing for antibody to, **1**:31–32
        in syphilis patients, **9**:247
    vaccine development and, **1**:36
    viability of after excimer laser ablation, **13**:182
Human leukocyte antigen (HLA) system, **8**:407. *See also*
    Human leukocyte antigens
Human leukocyte antigens (HLA), **8**:407, **9**:37, 70–73,
    72*t*, 120. *See also* Major histocompatibility complex
    in acute posterior multifocal placoid pigment
        epitheliopathy (APMPPE), **9**:155
    in acute retinal necrosis, **9**:200
    allelic variations and, **9**:70–71
    in ankylosing spondylitis, **1**:163–164, **9**:72, 121
    in anterior uveitis, **1**:163, 164, 165, 166, **6**:269, 271,
        9:71, 72*t*, 119*f*, 120–123, 122*f*, 123*f*
    in Behçet disease, **1**:180, **9**:72*t*, 194, **12**:194
    in birdshot retinochoroidopathy, **9**:72*t*, 73, 148*t*, 152,
        12:190
    in cicatricial pemphigoid, **8**:199
    detection and classification of, **9**:71–72
    in diabetes mellitus, **1**:191
    disease associations of, **9**:72–73, 72*t*, 120–123, 122*f*,
        123*f*
    in glaucomatocyclitic crisis (Posner-Schlossman
        syndrome), **9**:125
    in inflammatory bowel disease, **1**:165, **9**:123
    in intermediate uveitis/pars planitis, **9**:72*t*
    in juvenile idiopathic (chronic/rheumatoid) arthritis,
        6:269, **9**:72*t*, 129
    in Lyme disease, **9**:251

in multiple sclerosis, **5**:321, **9**:72*t*, 139
    normal function of, **9**:70
    in ocular histoplasmosis syndrome, **9**:222–223
    in psoriatic arthritis, **1**:166
    in reactive arthritis/Reiter syndrome, **1**:164, **9**:72*t*,
        121
    in retinal vasculitis, **9**:72*t*
    in rheumatoid arthritis, **1**:162
    in sarcoidosis, **9**:72*t*, 173
    in serpiginous choroiditis, **9**:148*t*, 158
    in Sjögren syndrome, **8**:63
    in spondyloarthropathies/spondyloarthritis, **1**:163
    in sympathetic ophthalmia, **9**:72*t*, 181
    in systemic lupus erythematosus, **1**:167, **9**:140
    transplantation and, **8**:407
    in tubulointerstitial nephritis and uveitis, **9**:72*t*, 124
    in Vogt-Koyanagi-Harada (VKH) syndrome, **9**:72*t*,
        184, **12**:197
Human papillomaviruses, **1**:27, **8**:128–129, 226–227
    cancer association of, **1**:27, 237, 269, 273
        conjunctival intraepithelial neoplasia, **8**:228
    conjunctival papillomas caused by, **4**:61–62, 61*f*
    eyelid infections caused by, **4**:209, 209*f*, **7**:158, 158*f*
    ocular infection/papillomas caused by, **4**:61–62, 61*f*,
        209, 209*f*, **8**:128–129, 226–227
    ocular surface squamous neoplasia and, **4**:62
    screening for, **1**:273
    vaccine against, **1**:27, 237, 273
Human T-lymphotropic virus type 1 (HTLV-1), **1**:29,
    9:218
    uveitis caused by, **9**:218–219
Human T-lymphotropic virus type 2 (HTLV-2), **1**:29
Human T-lymphotropic virus type 3 (HTLV-3), **1**:28.
    See also Human immunodeficiency virus
Humanitarian Device Exemption (HDE), **13**:205
    for Intacs use in keratoconus, **13**:58–59
Humira. *See* Adalimumab
Humoral immunity, **1**:4, **8**:180. *See also* Antibody-
    mediated immune effector responses
    in conjunctiva, **8**:180
Humorsol. *See* Demecarium
Humphrey Field Analyzers (HFA), **10**:57, 57*f*, 58, 58*f*
Humphrey STATPAC 2 program, **10**:59, 60, 60*f*, 63
Humphrey Visual Field Analyzer
    for central visual field assessment, **3**:292
    for peripheral visual field assessment, **3**:292
Hunter syndrome, **2**:213*t*, **6**:400*t*, **8**:305, 306*t*, 307,
    12:251*t*, 262
    pigmentary retinopathy and, **12**:251*t*, 262
Hurler-Scheie syndrome, **8**:305
Hurler syndrome, **2**:213*t*, **6**:398*f*, 400*t*, **8**:305, 306*t*,
    12:250*t*, 262
    congenital/infantile corneal opacities and, **6**:217,
        8:263
    pigmentary retinopathy and, **12**:250*t*, 262
Hurricane (vortex) keratopathy (cornea verticillata),
    8:310, 311*f*, 346–348, 347*t*, 348*f*, 360
    in Fabry disease, **12**:263, 264*f*
Hutchinson melanotic freckle (lentigo maligna/
    precancerous melanosis), **7**:168
Hutchinson sign, **5**:59, **9**:198*f*
Hutchinson teeth, **9**:243, 244
Hutchinson triad, **6**:185, **9**:244

Hyaline bodies. *See* Optic disc (optic nerve head), drusen of
Hyaline deposits, corneal, in Avellino dystrophy, 4:97, 99*f*
Hyaline (hard) drusen, 4:168, 168*f*, 12:58
Hyalitis, 9:78*t*
Hyalocytes, 2:83–84, 130, 4:132
Hyaloid artery/system
    development of, 2:123, 124*f*, 131*f*, 138
    persistence/remnants of, 2:85, 85*f*, 131*f*, 138, 139*f*, 4:132–133, 132*f*, 133, 6:250, 252*f*, 279, 307, 12:307, 308. *See also* Persistent fetal vasculature
        disc edema differentiated from, 5:120
        tunica vasculosa lentis development and, 11:25, 25*f*
Hyaloid (Cloquet) canal, 2:85, 4:132, 12:307
Hyaloid corpuscle (Mittendorf dot), 2:85, 85*f*, 4:133, 6:307, 11:25, 27, 12:307
Hyaloid face, of vitreous, 4:131
Hyaloideocapsular ligament, 4:131
Hyaloideoretinopathies, hereditary, with optically empty vitreous, 12:309–310, 309*f*
Hyalosis, asteroid, 4:138–139, 139*f*, 12:311, 312*f*
Hyaluronan/hyaluronic acid
    in corneal development, 2:134
    in thyroid eye disease, 4:232, 7:50
    in vitreous, 2:83*f*, 130–132, 283, 284–285, 12:7, 297
Hyaluronate/sodium hyaluronate, as viscoelastic, 2:393, 11:96
    elevated intraocular pressure and, 10:101
Hyaluronidase
    in aqueous humor, 2:269
    for enzymatic vitreolysis, 2:289
    streptococcal production of, 8:133
    in vitreous, 2:283
Hybrid contact lenses
    for keratoconus, 3:191
    after LASIK, 13:194
    after radial keratotomy, 13:193
Hybridization, 2:154
    comparative genomic (CGH), 4:39*t*
        microarray-based (array CGH), 4:39*t*
    fluorescence in situ (FISH), 2:199, 200*f*, 4:38*t*
    in lymphoma diagnosis, 7:83
    oligonucleotide, in mutation screening, 2:184, 186*f*
Hybridomas, 1:244
Hydatid cyst, orbital infection caused by, 4:235, 7:47
Hydralazine
    for heart failure, 1:119
    for hypertension, 1:77*t*, 82, 83
Hydrocephalus, otitic, 5:357
Hydrochlorothiazide, 1:76*t*, 78*t*
Hydrocortisone
    for anaphylaxis, 1:295
    anti-inflammatory/pressure-elevating potency of, 2:360*t*
    in combination preparations, 2:373*t*
    for medical emergencies, 1:292*t*
    perioperative, 1:306
Hydrocortisone sodium succinate
    for medical emergencies, 1:292*t*
    for uveitis, 9:101*t*
Hydrodelineation, in phacoemulsification, 11:118

for advanced cataract, 11:195
Hydrodissection, in phacoemulsification, 11:117–118
    for advanced cataract, 11:195
HydroDIURIL. *See* Hydrochlorothiazide
Hydrogel polymers
    for contact lenses, 3:167, 177*t*, 178
    for corneal inlays, 13:53, 54, 200
    for intraocular lenses, 3:203
        capsular opacification and, 11:170
Hydrogen peroxide, 2:311, 311–312, 312*f*, 313, 317, 9:30. *See also* Free radicals
    as inflammatory mediator, 8:177*t*, 9:30
Hydroperoxides, 2:313
Hydrophobic interaction, 3:178
Hydropres. *See* Reserpine
Hydrops, in keratoconus, 4:91, 93*f*, 8:299
    management of, 8:300
3-Hydroxy-3-methylglutaryl coenzyme-A (HMG-CoA) reductase inhibitors. *See also* Statins
    Alzheimer disease prevention and, 1:267
    cataracts and, 1:139, 11:49
    hypercholesterolemia/heart disease prevention and, 1:137*t*
Hydroxyamphetamine, 2:260, 341*t*
    in Horner syndrome diagnosis, 5:265*f*, 267, 268*f*
    for pupillary testing, 2:346
Hydroxyapatite deposition (calcific band keratopathy), 4:88, 89*f*, 8:328, 342–344, 343*f*
    in sarcoidosis, 8:73
    in uveitis, 9:85, 291
Hydroxyapatite orbital implants, 7:121. *See also* Orbital implants
Hydroxychloroquine, 1:162, 185
    cornea verticillata caused by, 8:346
    ocular effects/retinal toxicity of, 1:185, 301*t*, 12:266–267, 266*f*
        EOG in evaluation of, 12:44
        multifocal ERG tracing in, 12:38*f*
Hydroxyethylmethacrylate (HEMA), contact lenses made from, 3:177*t*, 178
Hydroxyl radicals, 2:313, 9:30. *See also* Free radicals
Hydroxypropyl methylcellulose (HPMC)
    for dry eye, 2:390
    as viscoelastic, 2:393, 11:97
Hyfrecator, for punctal occlusion, 8:62
Hyper- (prefix), 6:10
Hyperaldosteronism, hypertension in, 1:72, 72*t*
Hyperbaric oxygen therapy, oxidative lens damage/cataracts and, 11:16, 60–61
Hypercalcemia, corneal changes in, 8:328, 342. *See also* Band keratopathy
Hypercholesterolemia, 1:131–139. *See also* Hyperlipoproteinemias
    coronary heart disease and, 1:100, 131, 132–133, 133*t*
    management of, 1:134–136, 134*f*, 135*t*, 136*f*, 137*t*. *See also* Lipid-lowering therapy
    statin treatment and, 1:136–138, 137*t*
    metabolic syndrome and, 1:138
    ophthalmic considerations and, 1:138–139
    recent developments in, 1:131
    risk assessment and, 1:132–133, 133*t*
    in Schnyder corneal dystrophy, 8:285, 309
    screening for, 1:271

Hypercoagulable states (hypercoagulability), 1:157–159.
    See also Thrombophilia; Thrombosis/thrombotic
    disorders
    fetal loss/preeclampsia and, 1:147, 158
    primary, 1:157–158
    secondary, 1:158–159
    transient visual loss and, 5:184–185
Hyperemia, conjunctival, 8:20t, 75
    in glaucoma, 10:29, 91, 91f
    in leptospirosis, 9:254, 255
    prostaglandin analogues causing, 10:166
Hyperfluorescence, angiographic, 12:22–23, 23f, 24f
    in age-related macular degeneration/choroidal
        neovascularization, 12:23f, 59, 66, 67, 67f
    in angioid streaks, 12:84
    in central serous chorioretinopathy, 12:23, 24f, 172, 173f
    in multiple evanescent white dot syndrome, 5:113,
        9:168, 169f, 12:189
Hyperglobus, 7:22
Hyperglycemia, 1:190. *See also* Diabetes mellitus;
        Glycemic control
    acute diabetes mellitus complications and, 1:204–205
    cataract formation and. *See* Diabetes mellitus,
        cataracts associated with
    diabetic retinopathy incidence and progression and,
        1:202–203, 203f, 12:90
        Diabetes Control and Complications Trial, 1:202,
            203f, 12:91, 92, 94f
        United Kingdom Prospective Diabetes Study,
            1:203, 12:91, 92, 93
    long-term diabetes mellitus complications and,
        1:205–206
    obesity and, 1:190
    rebound, 1:196–197
Hyperglycinemia, 2:213t
Hyperhomocysteinemia, 1:147, 158
    carotid artery disease and, 1:97
Hyperimmunoglobulin, 1:286
Hyperkeratosis
    in actinic keratosis, 4:217
    definition of, 4:206
    exuberant (cutaneous horn), 7:158
Hyperlipoproteinemias, 8:308–309, 309t. *See also*
        Hypercholesterolemia
    Schnyder corneal dystrophy and, 8:309
    xanthelasma associated with, 4:211, 211f, 213t, 7:160,
        160f
Hyperlysinemia, 11:37
Hypermature cataract, 11:42, 45f
    lens-associated uveitis and, 9:125
    phacolytic glaucoma and, 4:106–107, 107f, 9:22, 126,
        10:90–91, 91f, 11:63
Hypermetabolism, in hyperthyroidism, 1:210
Hypermetric saccades, 5:203, 209
Hyperopia, 3:113, 114, 114f
    amblyopia and, 6:63, 64
    angle closure/angle-closure glaucoma and, 10:10, 27,
        114
    after cataract surgery, prior refractive surgery and,
        11:193–194
    cataract surgery in patient with, 11:200–201
    consecutive, 13:93–94
    contact lens–corrected aphakia and, 3:172

converging lens for correction of, 3:139
    cornea plana and, 8:255
    developmental, 3:119, 141–142
    diabetic retinopathy and, 6:297
    epidemiology of, 3:119
    glaucoma and, 10:10, 27
    high, cataract surgery in patient with, 11:200–201
    high accommodative convergence/accommodative
        esotropia and, 6:94, 95
    refractive surgery and, 13:181
    in infants and children, 3:117, 141–142, 6:169, 169f
    intermittent exotropia and, 6:102
    microcornea and, 8:253
    myopia overcorrection and, 13:93–94
        conductive keratoplasty for, 13:122
    nanophthalmos and, 8:251, 252
    prismatic effect of bifocals in, 3:151, 151f, 152, 152f
    after radial keratotomy, 13:44, 45, 47, 48
    refractive accommodative esotropia and, 6:93
    retinal reflex in, 3:123
    surgical correction of
        conductive keratoplasty for, 13:120–123, 121f,
            153–154
        examination before, 13:33
        keratophakia for, 13:53–55
        LASIK for, 3:235, 235f
        light-adjustable IOLs for, 13:146–147, 147f
        monovision for, 13:152–153
        multifocal IOLs for, 13:154–156, 154f, 155f
        phakic IOLs for, 13:126, 128
        photoablation for, 13:24
            outcomes of, 13:88
            re-treatment and, 13:89
        photothermal therapy for, 13:23
        refractive lens exchange/clear lens extraction for,
            13:139, 140
        wavefront-guided laser ablation for, 13:25
            outcomes of, 13:88–89
    uveal effusion syndrome and, 12:182, 183
    wavefront aberration produced by (negative defocus),
        3:238, 13:6
Hyperopic astigmatism, 3:114, 115f
    photoablation for, outcomes of, 13:88
Hyperosmolar agents, 2:391
Hyperosmolarity, tear, dry eye and, 8:49–50, 50f
Hyperosmotic/osmotic agents, 2:355–356, 356t, 10:165t,
        173
Hyperparathyroidism, in multiple endocrine neoplasia,
        1:216
Hyperpigmentation
    after laser skin resurfacing, 7:230
    of retinal pigment epithelium, in age-related macular
        degeneration, 12:58
Hyperplasia, 4:10t, 6:171
    epithelial
        ciliary pigmented, 4:288
        of eyelid, 7:157–158, 157f, 158f
    lymphoid
        conjunctival, 4:71, 72f, 8:243, 244f
        of orbit, 4:239, 7:79–84, 81f, 82f. *See also*
            Lymphomas, orbital; Lymphoproliferative lesions
        of uveal tract (uveal lymphoid infiltration), 4:202,
            325–326

pseudoadenomatous (Fuchs adenoma), **4**:184, 288
pseudoepitheliomatous, **7**:158, **8**:226*t*
reactive. *See* Hyperplasia, lymphoid
of retinal pigment epithelium, **12**:282
sebaceous, **4**:221, 221*f*, **7**:160–161
Hyperprolactinemia, pituitary adenoma causing, **1**:215
Hypersensitivity reactions, **8**:178–180, 178*f*, 179*t*,
   9:44–45, 44*t*. *See also* Allergic reactions/allergies
anaphylactic or atopic (immediate/type I), **8**:178*f*,
      179–180, 179*t*, **9**:44, 44*t*, 54–55
   allergic conjunctivitis and, **8**:185, **9**:55
   fluorescein angiography and, **12**:24
   topical medications/substances and, **8**:183, 184,
      184*f*
contact, **9**:34, 35
   response to poison ivy as, **9**:34, 35
to cycloplegics, **6**:88
cytotoxic (type II), **8**:178*f*, 179*t*, 180, **9**:44, 44*t*
delayed (type IV), **8**:178*f*, 179*t*, 180, **9**:42–43, 42*f*, 44,
      44*t*, 48–51, 49*f*, 50*t*
   contact dermatoblepharitis as, **8**:180, 183, 184–185,
      184*f*
   contact lens solutions and, **8**:92
   in graft rejection, **8**:408
   response to poison ivy as, **9**:35
   in sympathetic ophthalmia, **9**:52–53
   topical medications/substances and, **8**:183,
      184–185, 184*f*
   in *Toxocara* granuloma, **9**:52
   tuberculin form of, **9**:35
granulomatous, **9**:51
immediate (type I/anaphylactic/atopic). *See*
   Hypersensitivity reactions, anaphylactic or atopic
immune-complex (type III), **8**:178*f*, 179*t*, 180,
   9:44, 44*t*. *See also* Immune (antigen–antibody)
   complexes
ocular allergy and, **6**:197–198
stimulatory (type V), **9**:44, 44*t*
Hyperstat. *See* Diazoxide
Hypertelorism (telorbitism), **6**:173, 384, **7**:22
in craniosynostosis, **7**:35
Hypertension, **1**:69–89, **12**:113
cardiovascular risk and, **1**:69, 73*t*, 133*t*
in children and adolescents, **1**:69, 86–87
choroidal perfusion abnormalities and, **12**:114–115,
   115*f*, 116*f*, 176–177, 178*f*
in diabetes mellitus, **1**:192, 207
   diabetic retinopathy and, **12**:94
      United Kingdom Prospective Diabetes Study,
         12:92
diagnosis/definition of, **1**:70–71, 70*t*, 270
etiology and pathogenesis of, **1**:71–72, 71*f*, 72*t*
evaluation of, **1**:73–74, 73*t*
glaucoma and, **10**:77
incidence and prevalence of, **1**:69–70
intracranial. *See* Intracranial hypertension
intracranial hemorrhage and, **1**:98
left ventricular hypertrophy and, **1**:85
MAO inhibitor interactions and, **1**:87, 256
masked, **1**:69, 70–71
metabolic syndrome and, **1**:85
minority populations and, **1**:70, 87
obesity and, **1**:85

ocular, **10**:5*t*, 83–85, 84*f*, 105–106. *See also* Elevated
   intraocular pressure
   cholesterol levels and, **1**:139
   corneal thickness and, **10**:74, 84, 84*f*
   glaucoma risk and, **10**:9, 83
   glaucoma suspect and, **10**:83
   nasal CPAP affecting, **1**:144
   refractive surgery and, **13**:172–175, 173*f*, 194–195
   uveitic, **9**:294, 295
in older patients, **1**:86
ophthalmic considerations and, **1**:88, 88*t*
orthostatic hypotension and, **1**:85–86
peripheral arterial disease and, **1**:85
phenylephrine causing, **2**:345–346
in polyarteritis nodosa/microscopic polyangiitis, **9**:143
during pregnancy, **1**:86
primary (essential), **1**:71, 71*f*
rebound, **1**:87
recent developments in, **1**:69
resistant, **1**:72
retinal arterial macroaneurysms and, **12**:148
retinal disease associated with, **1**:88, 88*t*, **12**:113–115,
   114*f*, 116*f*, 117*f*
screening for, **1**:270–271
secondary, **1**:72, 72*t*
sleep disorders and, **1**:75*t*, 85
treatment of, **1**:74–87
   cerebrovascular disease and, **1**:79*t*, 85, 94
   chronic renal disease and, **1**:79*t*, 85
   diabetes mellitus and, **1**:79*t*, 84–85, 205–206, 206
   future therapies/targets and, **1**:83–84
   heart failure and, **1**:79*t*, 84, 118
   ischemic heart disease and, **1**:79*t*, 84
   lifestyle modifications and, **1**:74, 75*t*, 79*f*
   obesity and, **1**:85
   pharmacologic, **1**:74, 76–77*t*, 78*t*, 79*f*, 79*t*, 80–84.
      See also Antihypertensive drugs
   special considerations in, **1**:84–87
white coat, **1**:70
withdrawal syndromes and, **1**:87
in women, **1**:86
Hypertensive choroidopathy, **12**:114–115, 115*f*, 116*f*,
   176–177, 178*f*
Hypertensive crisis, **1**:87
   MAO inhibitor interactions and, **1**:87, 256
   parenteral antihypertensive agents for, **1**:83
Hypertensive optic neuropathy, **12**:115, 117*f*
Hypertensive retinopathy, **1**:88, 88*t*, **12**:113–114, 114*f*,
   117*f*
in polyarteritis nodosa/microscopic polyangiitis, **9**:143
Hyperthermia
malignant, **1**:312–313, 313*t*, **6**:161–162
therapeutic
   for melanoma, **4**:285
   for retinoblastoma, **4**:311
Hyperthyroidism, **1**:210–212
Graves, **1**:210, 211, **7**:47, 48, 51. *See also* Thyroid eye
   disease
in older patients, **1**:233
orbitopathy/ophthalmopathy and. *See* Thyroid eye
   disease
toxic nodular goiter, **1**:212
treatment of, **7**:52–53, 53*t*

Hypertonic medications, for recurrent corneal erosions, **8**:84
Hypertrichosis, prostaglandin analogues/latanoprost causing, **10**:162*t*, 166, 167*f*
Hypertropia, **6**:113
vertical rectus muscle surgery for, **6**:152–153
Hypertyrosinemia, **8**:315
Hyperuricemia, **8**:325–326
Hypervariable region, immunoglobulin, **9**:46
Hyperviscosity
retinopathy and, central retinal vein occlusion differentiated from, **12**:129–130
transient visual loss and, **5**:184–185
Hyphae, **8**:138, 138*f*
Hyphema
after cataract surgery, **11**:167, 177
corneal blood staining and, **4**:92–93, 94*f*
after Descemet stripping automated endothelial keratoplasty, **8**:441*f*
glaucoma/elevated intraocular pressure and, **4**:92–93, 108, 108*f*, **10**:97–99, 97*f*. *See also* Uveitis-glaucoma-hyphema (UGH) syndrome
in infants and children, **6**:409–411, 410*f*
abuse and, **6**:404
iris-fixated phakic IOL insertion and, **13**:135
microscopic, **8**:365
sickle cell disease and, **6**:409, **8**:369, **10**:98–99, **12**:120
elevated intraocular pressure and, **10**:98–99
spontaneous, **8**:365
traumatic, **8**:365–369, 365*f*, 366*f*, 367*f*, 369*t*
in infants and children, **6**:409–411, 410*f*
medical management of, **8**:367–368
rebleeding after, **8**:365–367, 367*f*, **10**:97–98
sickle cell disease and, **6**:409, **8**:369, **10**:98–99, **12**:120
elevated intraocular pressure and, **10**:98–99
surgery for, **8**:368, 369*t*, **10**:98–99
Hypnotic drugs, **1**:253–254, 253*t*
Hypo- (prefix), **6**:10
Hypoblast, **2**:117, 118*f*
Hypocalcemia, cataracts associated with, **11**:57
Hypochondriasis, **1**:248
in older patients, **1**:227
Hypoesthesia
corneal
in diabetes mellitus, **8**:308
in herpes simplex epithelial keratitis, **8**:110
in neurotrophic keratopathy, **8**:87
in infraorbital nerve distribution
in blowout fractures, **6**:125, **7**:9, 19, 101
after orbital surgery, **7**:116
Hypofluorescence, angiographic, **12**:22
in age-related macular degeneration, **12**:59
in multiple evanescent white dot syndrome, **5**:113–114, **9**:168, 169*f*, **12**:189–190
in serpiginous choroiditis/choroidopathy, **9**:160, **12**:188, 188*f*
in uveal effusion syndrome, **12**:182, 182*f*
in uveitis, **9**:93–95
Hypoglobus, **7**:22
Hypoglycemia
insulin therapy causing, **1**:198, 203
sulfonylurea-induced, **1**:199

Hypoglycemia unawareness, **1**:198, 204
Hypoglycemic agents. *See* Insulin therapy; Oral hypoglycemic agents
Hypokalemia, carbonic anhydrase inhibitors causing, **2**:353, **10**:171
Hypolipoproteinemias, corneal changes in, **8**:309–310
Hypomania, **1**:247
Hypometabolism, in hypothyroidism, **1**:212
Hypometric saccades, **5**:203, 209
Hypoparathyroidism, childhood cataracts associated with, **6**:247*t*
Hypoperfusion. *See also* Ischemia
systemic, scotomata caused by, **5**:172, 183
transient visual loss caused by, **5**:176*t*, 183–184
Hypophosphatasia, **8**:323*t*
Hypophyseal artery, inferior, of tentorium, **5**:16
Hypophysitis, lymphocytic, **5**:346–347
Hypopigmented macule (ash-leaf spot), in tuberous sclerosis, **5**:341, 342*f*, **6**:372, 372*f*, **10**:28
Hypoplasia, **6**:171. *See also specific structure affected*
Hypoplasminogenemia, in ligneous conjunctivitis, **8**:192
Hypopyon
in Behçet disease, **1**:180, 181, **9**:193, 193*f*, **12**:194
after cataract surgery, **11**:158
in endophthalmitis, **9**:272
Aspergillus, **9**:276, 277, 277*f*
in leptospirosis, **9**:255
in uveitis, **9**:85, 119, 119*f*
Hypotelorism, **6**:173
Hypotension
glaucoma and, **10**:77, 81
ocular. *See* Hypotony
orthostatic, **1**:85–86
Hypotensive lipids. *See* Prostaglandin analogues
Hypothalamic hormones, **1**:214, 214*t*
Hypothalamic-pituitary axis, **1**:214–216, 214*t*
Hypothalamus, **1**:214, **5**:63
Hypothyroidism, **1**:212
congenital, **1**:208
thyroid eye disease and, **7**:51. *See also* Thyroid eye disease
Hypotony
cataract surgery in patient with, **11**:201
cycloplegics causing, **6**:88
during/after surgery
filtering surgery and, **10**:196–197
flat anterior chamber and, **11**:153
angle-closure glaucoma and, **10**:136
glaucoma drainage device implantation and, **10**:207
suprachoroidal hemorrhage and, **12**:361
in uveitis, **9**:299–300
Hypotony maculopathy, **10**:197
antifibrotic use and, **10**:193
Hypotropia, **6**:113
in monocular elevation deficiency (double elevator palsy), **6**:123, 123*f*
ptosis and, **5**:275, 276*f*
vertical rectus muscle surgery for, **6**:152–153
Hypovitaminosis A, **8**:77–79, 77*t*, 78*f*
Hypovolemic shock, **1**:293. *See also* Shock
Hypoxia, corneal, contact lens use causing, **3**:200
Hysteresis, corneal, **8**:9
Hysteria, **5**:305

"Hysterical blindness." *See* Nonorganic (functional/nonphysiologic) ophthalmic disorders
Hytrin. *See* Terazosin
Hyzaar. *See* Losartan
HZO. *See* Herpes zoster ophthalmicus

I

I-cell (inclusion-cell) disease, 6:400*t*, 8:312
I–S number, 13:18
    after intrastromal corneal ring segment implantation, 13:59
IADL. *See* Instrumental activities of daily living
IAPB (International Agency for the Prevention of Blindness), 11:65
Iatrogenic abnormalities, choroidal ischemia caused by, 12:180
Iatrogenic amblyopia, 6:67–68
Ibandronate, for osteoporosis, 1:230–231
IBU. *See* Ibuprofen
Ibuprofen, 1:183*t*, 2:362*t*
    ocular effects of, 1:301*t*
    for scleritis, 8:222
Ibutilide, 1:123*t*
    for cardioversion, 1:125
IC3D classification of corneal dystrophies, 4:96, 8:267–268, 268*t*, 269*t*, 270*t*
ICA. *See* Internal carotid artery
ICAM-1, 8:177*t*
    in neutrophil rolling, 9:18
    in Sjögren syndrome, 8:63
ICAM-2, in neutrophil rolling, 9:18
ICCE. *See* Intracapsular cataract extraction
ICDs. *See* Implantable cardioverter-defibrillators
Ice-pack test, for myasthenia gravis, 5:330, 330*f*, 7:209
ICE syndrome. *See* Iridocorneal endothelial (ICE) syndrome
Icepick pain, 5:299
ICG. *See* Indocyanine green
ICG angiography. *See* Indocyanine green angiography
Ichthyosis, 8:74
    congenital ectropion and, 7:146
    retinal degeneration and, 12:255
    vulgaris, 8:74
ICK. *See* Infectious crystalline keratopathy
Iclaprim, 1:64
ICROP (International Classification of ROP), 6:282, 282*t*, 283*f*, 284*f*, 285*t*, 12:157, 158*t*
ICRS. *See* Intrastromal corneal ring segments
ICSB (International Committee for Systemic Bacteriology), 8:131
IDDM (insulin-dependent diabetes mellitus). *See* Diabetes mellitus, type 1
IDE. *See* Investigational device exemption
Idiopathic autoantibody, 1:280
Idiopathic choroidal neovascularization, 12:83
Idiopathic enlargement of blind spot syndrome (IEBSS), 5:112–113, 12:190
Idiopathic intracranial hypertension (pseudotumor cerebri), 5:123–125, 123*t*
    in children, 5:124–125, 6:312–313
    headache in, 5:123, 124, 294

Idiopathic macular hole, 12:304–306, 305–306*f*, 349, 350*f*
    posterior vitreous detachment and, 12:298, 304–306, 305–306*f*
    vitrectomy for, 12:305–306, 349, 350*f*
Idiopathic multiple cranial neuropathy syndrome, 5:236
Idiopathic orbital inflammation/inflammatory syndrome. *See* Nonspecific orbital inflammation
Idiopathic polypoidal choroidal vasculopathy. *See* Polypoidal choroidal vasculopathy
Idiopathic retinal vasculitis/aneurysms/neuroretinitis (IRVAN), 12:141
Idiopathic stellate maculopathy. *See* Leber idiopathic stellate neuroretinitis
Idiopathic thrombocytopenic purpura, 1:154
Idiotopes, 9:46
Idiotypes, 9:46
Idoxuridine, 2:380, 381*t*
α-L-Iduronidase
    defective, 2:213*t*
    in mucopolysaccharidoses, 8:305
IEBSS. *See* Idiopathic enlargement of blind spot syndrome
IEK. *See* Intralase-enabled keratoplasty
Ifex. *See* Ifosfamide
IFG. *See* Impaired fasting glucose
IFIS. *See* Intraoperative floppy iris syndrome
IFNs. *See* Interferons
Ifosfamide, 1:240*t*
Ig. *See under* Immunoglobulin
IgA dermatosis, linear, 8:199, 205*t*
IgA pemphigus, 8:205*t*
IgA protease, as microbial virulence factor, 1:4
IGF–I. *See* Insulinlike growth factor I
IGFBPs. *See* Insulinlike growth factor binding proteins
IGT. *See* Impaired glucose tolerance
IHD. *See* Ischemic heart disease
IIH. *See* Idiopathic intracranial hypertension
IK. *See* Interstitial keratitis
IL. *See under* Interleukin
ILAR (International League of Associations of Rheumatology), chronic childhood arthritis nomenclature and, 6:268, 269*t*
Ileocolitis, granulomatous (Crohn disease), 1:165, 9:123
Illiterate E chart (E-game), for visual acuity testing in children, 6:72*t*, 73
Illuminance, 3:17, 18*t*
    retinal, 3:18*t*
Illumination, 3:16–19, 17*f*, 18*t*
    for fundus camera, 3:248–249
    improving, for low vision patients, 3:304
    for operating microscope, 3:262, 263
    for ophthalmoscope
        direct, 3:244
        indirect, 3:245, 246, 246*f*, 248*f*
    for optical coherence tomography, 3:281, 282*f*
    for retinoscopy, 3:121, 121*f*
    for slit-lamp biomicroscope, 3:252–253, 252*f*
        direct, 8:12–14, 13*f*, 14*f*
        indirect, 8:14–15, 15*f*, 16*f*

Illusions, **5**:187, 187–189, 188*t*
  cortical origin of, **5**:189
  nonvisual causes of, **5**:188*t*
  ocular origin of, **5**:187–189
  optic nerve origin of, **5**:189
ILM. *See* Internal limiting membrane
Ilotycin. *See* Erythromycin
Image displacement, bifocal design and, **3**:150–151,
  151*f*, 152*f*, 153*f*
Image jump, with multifocal lenses, **3**:151–152, 153*f*
  progressive addition lenses and, **3**:147
Image size
  calculation of, **3**:103–104, 106*f*
  contact lenses and, **3**:170–172
Image space, reversal of by mirrors, **3**:90
Images
  aerial, **3**:245, 246*f*
  characteristics of, **3**:31–39. *See also specific type*
    depth of focus, **3**:36–37
    graphical analysis of, **3**:76, 77*f*
    irradiance, **3**:19
    location, **3**:36
    magnification, **3**:32–36, 33*f*, 34*f*
    quality, **3**:37–39, 38*f*, 39*f*
  displacement of by prisms, **3**:86–87, 86*f*
    bifocal design and, **3**:150–151, 151*f*, 152*f*, 153*f*
  at infinity, **3**:74
  magnification of, **3**:32–36, 33*f*, 34*f*. *See also*
    Magnification
    with intraocular lenses, **3**:223
  stigmatic, **3**:37, 39, 39*f*. *See also* Imaging, stigmatic
  virtual, **3**:67–68, 67*f*, 69*f*
    displacement of by prisms, **3**:86–87, 86*f*
Imaging
  with lenses, **3**:30–31, 31*f*
    image quality and, **3**:37–39, 39*f*
  with mirrors, **3**:30–31, 32*f*
    image quality and, **3**:37–39, 39*f*
  pinhole, **3**:27–30, 27*f*, 29*f*, 30*f*, 107–108, 107*f*
    image quality and, **3**:37, 38*f*
    with lenses and mirrors, **3**:30–31, 31*f*, 32*f*
    visual resolution and, **3**:107–108, 107*f*
  radiographic. *See specific modality and* Neuroimaging
  stigmatic, **3**:37, 39, 39*f*
    single refractive surface and, **3**:53–55, 54*f*
    wavefront analysis and, **3**:238
Imbert-Fick principle, **10**:22
Imbibition pressure, **8**:8
Imidazoles, **1**:20, 54*t*, 64–65, **2**:379*t*, 380
  for *Acanthamoeba* keratitis, **8**:169
Imigran. *See* Sumatriptan
Imipenem-cilastin, **1**:49*t*, 59, **2**:368*t*
Imipramine, ocular effects of, **1**:301*t*
Imitrex. *See* Sumatriptan
Immediate hypersensitivity (type I) reaction, **8**:178*f*,
  179–180, 179*t*, **9**:44, 44*t*, 54–55. *See also* Allergic
  reactions/allergies
  allergic conjunctivitis and, **8**:185, **9**:55
  fluorescein angiography and, **12**:24
  topical medications/substances and, **8**:183, 184, 184*f*
Immersion ultrasonography, for axial length
  measurement, in IOL power determination/
  selection, **3**:214, 215*f*, **11**:82, 83*f*

Immune-complex hypersensitivity (type III) reaction,
  8:178*f*, 179*t*, 180, **9**:44, 44*t*. *See also* Immune
  (antigen–antibody) complexes
Immune (antigen–antibody) complexes, **9**:23, 24*f*
  in type III hypersensitivity reaction, **8**:178*f*, 179*t*, 180,
    9:44, 44*t*
Immune hypersensitivity reactions. *See* Hypersensitivity
  reactions
Immune privilege, **8**:407–408, **9**:62
  in anterior chamber/anterior uvea/vitreous, **9**:62
    corneal allograft immunity and, **9**:65
  corneal, **8**:174–175, 407–408, **9**:64, 65
  in retina/retinal pigment epithelium/choriocapillaris/
    choroid, **9**:66
Immune processing, **9**:33, 36*f*, 37–41, 40*f*
  response to poison ivy and, **9**:34, 35
  response to tuberculosis and, **9**:35
Immune reconstitution syndromes (IRS), **1**:40–41
Immune recovery uveitis, **1**:41, **9**:306, **12**:201
Immune response (immunity), **9**:13. *See also* Immune
  response arc; Immunology
  adaptive, **1**:4, **9**:9, 33–55. *See also* Adaptive immune
    response
  cellular, **1**:4–5, **8**:178*f*, 179*t*, 180. *See also* Lymphocyte-
    mediated immune effector responses
  definition of, **9**:9
  disorders of. *See also specific structure affected*
    in HIV infection/AIDS, **1**:29. *See also* HIV
      infection/AIDS
    neuro-ophthalmic signs of, **5**:319–336
    in systemic lupus erythematosus, **1**:169*t*
  glucocorticoids affecting, **2**:358
  humoral, **1**:4, **8**:180. *See also* Antibody-mediated
    immune effector responses
  inflammation and, **9**:13
  innate, **1**:3, **9**:9, 12–13, 14–23. *See also* Innate immune
    response
  mediator systems in, **9**:23–31, 23*t*
  ocular, **8**:173–182, **9**:57–67
    of anterior chamber/anterior uvea/vitreous, **9**:58*t*,
      59–63
      corneal allograft immunity and, **9**:65
    cellular elements of, **8**:173–175, 174*f*, 174*t*
    of conjunctiva, **8**:173, 174*t*, 180–181, **9**:57–59,
      58*t*
    of cornea/sclera, **8**:174–175, 174*f*, 181, **9**:58*t*,
      63–64, 63*f*, 64*f*, 65
    disorders of. *See also specific type*
      clinical approach to, **8**:183–223
      diagnostic approach to, **8**:181–182, 182*t*
      infection and, **8**:100
      patterns of, **8**:180–181
    hypersensitivity reactions and, **8**:178–180, 178*f*,
      179*t*, **9**:44–45, 44*t*
    of retina/retinal pigment epithelium/
      choriocapillaris/choroid, **9**:58*t*, 64–67
    soluble mediators of, **8**:175, 176*f*, 177*f*, 179*t*
    tear film and, **8**:175–177, 177*t*
  population-wide, **9**:70–71
  primary, **9**:43–44
    secondary response differentiated from, **9**:43–44
  regional, **9**:57, 58*t*. *See also* Immunologic
    microenvironments

secondary, **9**:43–44
  primary response differentiated from, **9**:43–44
Immune response arc, **9**:33–55, 36*f. See also* Immune
    response
  clinical examples of, **9**:34–35
  overview of, **9**:33–36, 36*f*
  phases of, **9**:36–43, 36*f*
    afferent, **9**:33, 36–37, 36*f*, 38*f*, 39*f*
      response to poison ivy and, **9**:34, 35
      response to tuberculosis and, **9**:35
    effector, **9**:33–36, 36*f*, 42–43, 42*f. See also* Effector
      phase of immune response arc
      response to poison ivy and, **9**:34, 35
      response to tuberculosis and, **9**:35
    processing, **9**:33, 36*f*, 37–41, 40*f*
      response to poison ivy and, **9**:34, 35
      response to tuberculosis and, **9**:35
  primary versus secondary, **9**:43–44
  regional immunity and, **9**:57, 58*t*
Immune system, **1**:3–5. *See also* Immune response;
    Immune response arc
  components of, **9**:9–12
Immunization, **1**:279–287. *See also specific disease*
  active, **1**:280
  adaptive immunity and, **9**:33–55. *See also* Immune
    response arc
  childhood, recommendations for, **1**:269
  in immunocompromised host/HIV infection/AIDS,
    1:33
  new developments in, **1**:269
  passive, **1**:280
  for travel, **1**:286
Immunocompromised host. *See also* HIV infection/AIDS
  acute retinal necrosis in, **9**:199–200
  CMV retinitis in, **1**:24, 37–38, **4**:151, **6**:184, **9**:204, 205
  cryptococcosis in, **9**:278, 310–311, 313–314
  endophthalmitis in, **9**:271
    endogenous mold *(Aspergillus)*, **12**:203
  herpes zoster in, **8**:120
  immunization in, **1**:280, 282
  ocular infection in, **8**:100
  progressive outer retinal necrosis in, **9**:203, **12**:201
  refractive surgery and, **13**:31
  syphilis in, **9**:246
  toxoplasmic chorioretinitis in, **12**:208
Immunofluorescence assay
  in HIV infection/AIDS, **1**:31
  in Lyme disease, **1**:16
Immunoglobulin A (IgA)
  secretory, **8**:173
    in tear film, **2**:240
    in external eye defense, **8**:95
  structural and functional properties of, **9**:47*t*
  in tear film, **2**:240, **9**:59
    viral conjunctivitis and, **9**:60–61
  in toxoplasmosis, **9**:230–231
Immunoglobulin A (IgA) dermatosis, linear, **8**:199, 205*t*
Immunoglobulin A (IgA) pemphigus, **8**:205*t*
Immunoglobulin A (IgA) protease, as microbial
    virulence factor, **1**:4
Immunoglobulin D (IgD), **9**:41
  structural and functional properties of, **9**:47*t*
  in tear film, **2**:240

Immunoglobulin E (IgE)
  Fc receptors for
    on mast cells, **9**:10
    in phagocytosis, **9**:19–20
  mast-cell degranulation mediated by, **9**:10, 54–55, 54*f*
  structural and functional properties of, **9**:47*t*
  in tear film, **2**:240
  in type I hypersensitivity/anaphylactic reactions,
    1:295, **2**:264, **8**:179, 183, **9**:10
Immunoglobulin G (IgG)
  in neuromyelitis optica, **5**:147
  structural and functional properties of, **9**:47*t*
  in tear film, **2**:240
  in thyroid eye disease, **4**:232, **7**:50
  in toxoplasmosis, **9**:230
Immunoglobulin G4-positive infiltrates, in nonspecific
    orbital inflammation, **4**:232
Immunoglobulin M (IgM), **9**:41
  structural and functional properties of, **9**:47*t*
  in tear film, **2**:240
  in toxoplasmosis, **9**:230
Immunoglobulin superfamily molecules, in neutrophil
    rolling, **9**:18
Immunoglobulins, **9**:43. *See also specific type and*
    Antibodies
  classes of, **9**:45, 47*t*
  disorders of synthesis of, **8**:319–320
  in external eye defense, **8**:95
  isotypes of, **9**:45, 46, 47*t*
  structural and functional properties of, **9**:45–46, 45*f*,
    47*t*
Immunohistochemistry, **4**:33–36, 35*f*
Immunologic competence, ocular infection and, **8**:100
Immunologic memory, **9**:43–44
  response to poison ivy and, **9**:35
  response to tuberculosis and, **9**:35
Immunologic microenvironments, **9**:57, 58*t*
  of anterior chamber/anterior uvea/vitreous, **9**:58*t*,
    59–61
  of conjunctiva, **9**:57–59, 58*t*
  of cornea/sclera, **9**:58*t*, 63, 63*f*, 64*f*
  of retina/retinal pigment epithelium/choriocapillaris/
    choroid, **9**:58*t*, 64–65
Immunologic tolerance
  corneal transplantation and, **8**:175, 408
  T regulatory cells in, **9**:40, 41
Immunology (ocular), **9**:5–73. *See also* Immune
    response; Immune response arc
  basic concepts in, **9**:9–31
Immunomodulatory therapy/immunotherapy/
    immunosuppression, **1**:185–187
  for allergic conjunctivitis, **8**:186
  for atopic keratoconjunctivitis, **8**:191
  for Behçet disease, **1**:180, **9**:195
  for birdshot retinochoroidopathy, **9**:155, **12**:190–191
  for cancer, **1**:235, 242*t*, 243–244
  cataract surgery/IOLs in uveitis and, **9**:291, 292,
    292–293
    juvenile idiopathic (chronic/rheumatoid) arthritis
      and, **9**:131–132, 293
  for cicatricial pemphigoid, **8**:202
  for corneal graft rejection, **8**:430
  for cystoid macular edema, **9**:300–301

diabetes mellitus affected by, 1:191
for graft-vs-host disease, 8:203
in HIV infection/AIDS, 1:36
for melanoma, 4:285–286
for multifocal choroiditis and panuveitis syndrome, 9:164, 12:191
for multiple sclerosis, 5:146, 327
for pars planitis, 9:138
for peripheral ulcerative keratitis, 8:213
for pulmonary diseases, 1:146
for rheumatic disorders, 1:185–187
for rheumatoid arthritis, 1:162
for sarcoidosis, 9:177
for scleritis, 8:223, 9:118
for serpiginous choroiditis/choroidopathy, 9:161, 12:188–189
for Stevens-Johnson syndrome, 8:198
for sympathetic ophthalmia, 9:182
for uveitic neovascularization, 9:303
for uveitis, 9:106–116, 108t, 300–301
cataracts/cataract surgery and, 9:291, 292, 292–293, 293
in children, 6:277, 278
corticosteroid therapy and, 9:104, 106, 107, 297
for vernal keratoconjunctivitis, 8:189
for Vogt-Koyanagi-Harada (VKH) syndrome, 9:189, 12:198
Immunoregulation/immunoregulatory systems, 9:58t
for anterior chamber/anterior uvea/vitreous, 9:58t, 62–63
corneal allograft immunity and, 9:65
for conjunctiva, 9:58t, 59
for cornea/sclera, 9:58t, 64, 65
for retina/retinal pigment epithelium/choriocapillaris/choroid, 9:58t, 66–67
Immunosuppression. See Immunomodulatory therapy
Immunotherapy. See Immunomodulatory therapy
Impact resistance, lens materials and, 3:161–162, 162–163
Impaired fasting glucose, 1:191t, 192–193
Impaired glucose tolerance, 1:191t, 192–193
Impairment, visual, 3:283, 285f. See also Low vision; Visual loss/impairment
Impending macular holes, 12:304, 305f
Implant, orbital, 7:119, 121–122, 121f
for blowout fractures, 7:103
in children, 7:119
exposure and extrusion of, 7:123, 123f
for superior sulcus deformity, 7:122
Implant (Intacs) extrusion, 13:60, 61f
Implant surgery, for childhood glaucoma, 6:241
Implantable cardioverter-defibrillators (ICDs), 1:99, 104, 127
for heart failure, 1:99, 120
laser surgery in patient with, 13:31
after MI, 1:104
for tachyarrhythmias, 1:99, 126, 127
Implantable insulin pumps, 1:197
Implantation membrane, of iris, 4:270t
Implicit time (τ), in electroretinogram, 12:34, 34f
Impotence, ocular effects of drugs for, 1:302t
Impression cytology, 8:47–48
in Sjögren syndrome diagnosis, 8:57
in stem cell deficiency, 8:94
in superior limbic keratoconjunctivitis, 8:82

Imprinting (genetic), 2:154, 169
IMT. See Immunomodulatory therapy
Imuran. See Azathioprine
In situ hybridization, fluorescence, 2:199, 200f, 4:38t
In situ keratomileusis, 13:68. See also LASIK
Inactivated poliovirus vaccine (IPV/Salk vaccine), 1:283
in combination vaccines, 1:285
Inborn errors of metabolism, 6:397–402, 400–401t
dietary therapy in, 2:231
enzyme defect in, 2:212, 213t, 214, 6:397, 398, 400–401t
inheritance of, 6:397, 400–401t
ocular findings in, 2:213t, 6:397–398, 398f, 400–401t
treatment of, 6:399–402
INC. See Interstitial nucleus of Cajal
Incision leaks, after cataract surgery, 11:144t, 148–149
flat anterior chamber and, 11:153
angle-closure glaucoma and, 10:136
Incisional biopsy, 7:170, 170f
Incisional surgery
for angle-closure glaucoma, 10:204
corneal (keratorefractive), 13:4t, 20–21, 21f. See also specific procedure
for astigmatism, 13:49–52, 49f, 50f, 51t
for myopia, 13:43–48, 45f, 46f, 47f
for open-angle glaucoma, 10:107–108, 183–198
antifibrotic agents used with, 10:186, 193–194, 195f
bleb-related endophthalmitis and, 10:196
complications of, 10:196–198, 196t, 197f
contraindications to, 10:185
flap management in, 10:194
indications for, 10:184–185
postoperative considerations in, 10:194–195
preoperative evaluation for, 10:185–186
trabeculectomy technique in, 10:186–193. See also Trabeculectomy
Incisions. See also Incisional surgery
for arcuate keratotomy, 13:50, 50f, 51t
for cataract surgery. See also type of incision and type of surgery
clear corneal, 11:113–115, 113f, 115f
closure of
complications associated with, 11:148–149
after ECCE, 11:212–213
postoperative endophthalmitis and, 11:180
scleral tunnel incisions and, 11:112–113, 112f
complications associated with, 11:148–149
flat or shallow anterior chamber, 11:152
dehiscence/rupture of, 11:149
for ECCE, 11:211
wound closure and, 11:212–213
glaucoma and, 11:201–202
for ICCE, 11:214
problems associated with, 11:94
induced astigmatism and, 11:150, 213
intraocular lens implantation and, 11:138
modification of preexisting astigmatism and, 11:130
for phacoemulsification
clear corneal, 11:113–115, 113f, 115f
scleral tunnel, 11:111–113, 111f, 112f
postoperative leaking and, 11:144t, 148–149
flat anterior chamber and, 11:153
angle-closure glaucoma and, 10:136

after radial keratotomy, 13:48
scleral tunnel, 11:111–113, 111*f*, 112*f*
  wound closure and, 11:112–113, 112*f*
self-sealing
  beveled/biplanar, clear corneal incisions and, 11:114, 115*f*
  scleral tunnel incisions and, 11:112, 113
thermal wounds of, 11:149
for extraocular muscle surgery, 6:154
for intrastromal corneal ring segment placement, 13:57
for keratorefractive surgery, 13:20–21, 21*f*
limbal relaxing, 13:50, 50*f*, 51*t*
for orbital surgery, 7:108, 108*f*
for radial keratotomy, 13:44, 45*f*, 46*f*
  traumatic rupture of, 13:47, 47*f*
for trabeculectomy, 10:187–188, 188*f*, 189*f*
Inclusion-cell (I-cell) disease, 6:400*t*, 8:312
Inclusion conjunctivitis, trachoma (TRIC), 6:187
Inclusion criteria, 1:339–340
Inclusion cysts
epidermal, of eyelid, 4:213, 213*f*, 7:158–159, 159*f*
epithelial, conjunctival, 4:59–60, 60*f*, 8:225–226, 226*f*
  in children, 6:157, 157*f*, 348
  nevi and, 4:65
  after strabismus surgery, 6:157, 157*f*
IncobotulinumtoxinA. *See* Botulinum toxin, type A
Incomitant (noncomitant) deviations, 5:219, 220*f*, 6:10
esodeviations, 6:90*t*, 98
strabismus surgery planning and, 6:146
vertical, 6:113
  strabismus surgery planning and, 6:146
Incomplete achromatopsia, 6:291
Incomplete penetrance (skipped generation), 2:209, 217
Incongruous visual field defects, retrochiasmal lesions producing, 5:165
Incontinentia pigmenti (Bloch-Sulzberger syndrome), 2:219, 220, 6:364*t*, 379–381, 380*f*, 12:251*t*, 255
retinopathy and, 6:380, 380*f*, 381, 12:251*t*, 255
Incorrect corrective lens artifact, in perimetry, 10:61
Increased intracranial pressure. *See* Intracranial hypertension
Increased intraocular pressure. *See* Elevated intraocular pressure; Ocular hypertension
Incretins, for diabetes mellitus, 1:202
Incyclo- (prefix), 6:10
Incycloduction. *See* Intorsion
Incyclotorsion, extraocular muscles in, 5:55–56, 56*f*
Incyclovergence, 6:35
Indapamide, 1:76*t*
Indentation (dynamic) gonioscopy, 10:33*f*, 34
in acute primary angle closure, 10:114–115
Indentation (Schiøtz) tonometry, 10:19, 26
Independent assortment, 2:196–197
Inderal/Inderal LA. *See* Propranolol
Inderide. *See* Propranolol
Index case (proband), 2:158, 225
Index features, in diagnosis, 4:11
Index of refraction. *See* Refractive index
Indinavir, 1:34, 40
Indirect ophthalmoscopy. *See* Ophthalmoscopy
Indirect traumatic optic neuropathy, 2:93, 5:156

Individual effect, 1:337
Indocin. *See* Indomethacin
Indocyanine green, 2:392, 12:25
allergic reactions to, 12:26
angiography with. *See* Indocyanine green angiography
phototoxicity and, 12:333
Indocyanine green angiography, 2:392, 12:25–26
in acute posterior multifocal placoid pigment epitheliopathy (APMPPE), 9:150*t*, 156, 157*f*
adverse effects of, 12:26
in age-related macular degeneration, 12:64
in birdshot retinochoroidopathy, 9:150*t*, 153, 154*f*
in central serous chorioretinopathy, 12:174
in choroidal hemangioma, 12:181, 181*f*
in choroidal neovascularization, 12:25–26
in choroidal perfusion abnormalities, 12:176, 177*f*
in dengue fever, 9:220
in inflammatory chorioretinopathies, 9:150*t*
in low vision evaluation, 5:107
in multifocal choroiditis and panuveitis syndrome, 9:150*t*, 163
in multiple evanescent white dot syndrome, 5:113–114, 9:150*t*, 168, 169*f*, 12:189–190, 189*f*
in punctate inner choroiditis, 9:150*t*, 165, 166*f*
in serpiginous choroiditis, 9:150*t*, 160
in sympathetic ophthalmia, 9:179, 180*f*
in tuberculous choroiditis, 9:258
in uveitis, 9:93–95
in Vogt-Koyanagi-Harada (VKH) syndrome, 9:188
in West Nile virus chorioretinitis, 9:215
Indoles, 2:362. *See also* Nonsteroidal anti-inflammatory drugs
Indomethacin, 1:183*t*, 2:362*t*, 363
cornea verticillata caused by, 8:346
prostaglandin synthesis affected by, 2:257
Induced convergence-retraction (convergence-retraction nystagmus), 5:44, 251*t*, 256
in children, 6:325
Induced tropia test, 6:72–73
Induction, in ocular development, 2:113
Infantile cataract. *See* Cataract, congenital
Infantile (congenital) esotropia, 6:89–92, 90*t*, 91*f*
Infantile exotropia, 6:104, 104*f*
Infantile glaucoma, 4:102, 103*f*, 6:216*t*, 233–238, 234*f*, 235*t*, 236*f*, 237*f*, 10:139, 140*t*. *See also* Glaucoma, childhood; Primary congenital glaucoma
corneal opacities and, 6:218, 234, 235*t*
genetics of, 6:233, 10:142
Infantile nystagmus syndrome, 5:244*f*, 245–246, 6:288–289, 289*t*, 321–323, 321*t*, 323*f*, 324*f*. *See also* Congenital nystagmus
Infantile primary congenital glaucoma. *See* Infantile glaucoma
Infantile Refsum disease, 2:213*t*, 6:401*t*, 12:261
gene defects causing, 2:213*t*, 298
Infantile strabismus, 6:11. *See also* Strabismus
Infants. *See also under Infantile and* Children
conjunctivitis in, 6:186–188, 187*f*, 8:152–154. *See also* Ophthalmia, neonatorum
corneal transplantation in, 6:219, 8:430–431, 431*f*
cystinosis in, 6:220, 220*f*, 8:313
decreased/low vision in, 3:306, 6:413–417, 417–418*t*
ERG in, 6:415, 12:36, 40, 41*f*

hemorrhagic disease of newborn in, **1**:156
hepatitis B immunization in, **1**:281
herpes simplex infection in, **1**:22, **6**:185, 188, **8**:106
hyperopia in, **3**:117
intraocular lens use in, **6**:255, 258
monocular nystagmus in, **5**:247
normal ocular flora in, **8**:96
ocular deviations in, **5**:212
ocular infections in, **6**:181–186, **8**:152–154. *See also specific type*
ophthalmia neonatorum in, **6**:186–188, 187*f*, **8**:152–154. *See also* Ophthalmia, neonatorum
pneumococcal vaccine for, **1**:285
retinal degeneration onset in, **12**:251–252
  peroxisomal disorders/Refsum disease and, **12**:254, 261
screening eye examinations in, **6**:250–251
shaking injury and, **6**:404–407, 405*f*, 406*f*, **12**:330–331, 330*f*
visually evoked cortical potentials in, **6**:72*t*, 171, 413
Infarction. *See also specific type/tissue or organ involved*
neuroimaging in evaluation of, **5**:82*t*
Infection (ocular). *See also specific type, structure affected, causative agent and under Infectious*
bacterial/bacteriology, **8**:131–137, 132*t*
  cornea and scleral involvement and, **8**:158–164
  eyelid margin and conjunctival involvement and, **8**:143–148, 149–158, 150*t*
basic concepts of, **8**:95–103
canalicular obstruction caused by, **7**:264
childhood glaucoma and, **10**:142*t*
cytology in, **8**:47–48
defense mechanisms and, **8**:95–96, 99–100
diagnostic laboratory techniques in, **8**:100–103, 101*t*, 102*f*, 103*t*
eyelid, **4**:208–210, 209*f*, 210*f*
fungal/mycology, **8**:138–140, 138*t*
  cornea and scleral involvement and, **8**:164–167
  eyelid margin and conjunctival involvement and, **8**:148–149
in infants and children, **6**:181–197
  conjunctivitis, **6**:188–193, 189*t*
  intrauterine and perinatal, **6**:181–186
    corneal anomalies and, **8**:263–264
  ophthalmia neonatorum, **6**:186–188, 187*f*, **8**:152–154
  orbital and adnexal, **6**:194–197, 196*f*
inoculum and, **8**:99
lacrimal system, **7**:273–276, 274*f*, 275*f*
microbiology of, **8**:100, 101*t*
neuroimaging in evaluation of, **5**:82*t*
normal flora and, **8**:96–97, 97*t*
parasitic/parasitology, **8**:140–143
  cornea and scleral involvement and, **8**:167–169
  eyelid margin and conjunctival involvement and, **8**:148–149
pathogenesis of, **8**:97–100
prevention of, **8**:45–46
prions causing, **8**:143
public health ophthalmology and, **8**:104
retinal and choroidal, **12**:200–211
in Stevens-Johnson syndrome, **8**:196, 197
after strabismus surgery, **6**:156

systemic infections associated with, **8**:169–170
uveal tract, **4**:188–189
viral/virology, **8**:104–130
virulence factors in, **8**:98–99
Infection control, **8**:45–46
in clinical tonometry, **8**:46, **10**:26
Infectious chorioretinopathies, **12**:200–211
Infectious conjunctivitis, **4**:53–54, 55*f*, **8**:101*t*. *See also specific type and causative agent*
Infectious crystalline keratopathy, **4**:85–86, 86*f*, **8**:159, 160*f*
after penetrating keratoplasty, **4**:85, **8**:425, 425*f*
Infectious disease, **1**:1–68. *See also specific organism and disorder and* Infection
antibiotic therapy and, **1**:44–68, 45–55*t*
immunization in prevention of, **1**:279–287
microbiologic principles and, **1**:3–5
neuro-ophthalmic signs of, **5**:358–368
ocular inflammatory. *See* Infectious ocular inflammatory disease
recent developments in, **1**:3
screening for, **1**:278–279
seventh nerve pathology caused by, **5**:287
Infectious keratitis, **4**:82–87, **8**:101*t*, 158–171, 160*f*, 160*t*, 162*t*, 168*f*. *See also specific type and causative agent*
clinical presentation of, **8**:159
contact lens wear and, **3**:180, 196, 198, 201, **8**:159, 165, 167, 168
  for orthokeratology, **13**:64
intrauterine, **8**:263–264
laboratory evaluation/causes of, **8**:159–161, 160*t*
management of, **8**:161–164, 162*t*
orthokeratology and, **13**:64
pathogenesis of, **8**:159
after penetrating keratoplasty, **8**:425, 425*f*
after photoablation, **13**:98–99, 99*f*
  diffuse lamellar keratitis differentiated from, **13**:110–111, 110*t*, 111*f*
stains and culture in identification of, **8**:103*t*
Infectious mononucleosis
Epstein-Barr virus causing, **1**:24–25
ocular involvement in, **6**:193, **8**:122–123, 123*f*
Infectious ocular inflammatory disease, **9**:197–267. *See also specific type and specific causative agent*
bacterial uveitis, **9**:242–266
endophthalmitis, **4**:133, 134*f*, **9**:126
fungal uveitis, **9**:221–226
helminthic uveitis, **9**:235–242
as masquerade syndrome, **9**:289
protozoal uveitis, **9**:226–235
scleritis, **9**:266–267
viral uveitis, **9**:197–220
Inferior hypophyseal artery of tentorium, **5**:16
Inferior marginal arcade, **5**:14*f*
Inferior meatus, **2**:7, 10, 34*f*, **5**:12, **7**:245*f*, 246. *See also* Inferior turbinate
Inferior muscular artery, **5**:18
Inferior oblique muscles, **2**:9, 16*f*, 17*f*, 18, 19*t*, 38*f*, 39*f*, 40*f*, **5**:55, 55–56, 56*f*, **6**:14–15, 14*f*, 16*f*, 17*t*, 18*f*, **7**:10, 135*f*
action of, **6**:15, 17*t*, 29, 29*t*
  gaze position and, **6**:32, 34*f*
  3-step test in evaluation of, **6**:83–86, 85*f*

anatomy of, **2:**9, 16*f*, 17*f*, 18, 19*t*, 38*f*, 39*f*, 40*f*, **5:**55, 55–56, 56*f*, **6:**14–15, 14*f*, 16*f*, 17*t*, 18*f*
  surgery and, **6:**24
field of action of, **6:**29
insertion relationships of, **2:**17, 18*f*, 19*t*
nerves supplying, **2:**21, **7:**11
overaction of, **6:**113–115, 114*f*
  in infantile esotropia, **6:**92
  V-pattern deviations associated with, **6:**107, 108*f*
  vertical deviations caused by, **6:**113, 113–115, 114*f*
paralysis of, **6:**121–122, 122*f*, 122*t*
pulley system of, **6:**22, 22*f*, 23
surgery of, **6:**151–152, 152
  for dissociated vertical deviation, **6:**117, 153
  for infantile esotropia, **6:**92
  for superior oblique muscle paralysis, **6:**120–121
  for V-pattern deviations, **6:**110, 112
  for vertical deviations, **6:**114–115
Inferior oblique subnucleus, **5:**54
Inferior ophthalmic vein, **5:**10*f*, 24*f*, 25, 27*f*
Inferior orbital fissure, **2:**8*f*, 9*f*, 10–12, **5:**7*f*, 8, 8*f*, 9*f*, 12, **7:**6*f*, 7*f*, 9
Inferior orbital vein, **6:**18
Inferior palpebral vein, **5:**25*f*
Inferior petrosal nerve, **2:**106
Inferior petrosal sinus, **2:**108*f*, **5:**26, 27*f*, 50
Inferior punctum, **2:**23, 33
Inferior rectus muscles, **2:**16*f*, 17*f*, 19*t*, 20*f*, 37*f*, 38, 38*f*, 39*f*, 40*f*, **5:**10*f*, 55, 56*f*, **6:**14, 14*f*, 16*f*, 17*t*, 18*f*, **7:**10, 135*f*
  action of, **6:**14, 17*t*, 29*t*
    gaze position and, **6:**31, 32*f*
    3-step test in evaluation of, **6:**83–86, 85*f*
  anatomy of, **2:**16*f*, 17*f*, 19*t*, 20*f*, 37*f*, 38, 38*f*, 39*f*, 40*f*, **5:**10*f*, 55, 56*f*, **6:**14, 14*f*, 16*f*, 17*t*, 18*f*
    surgery and, **6:**24
  injury of in orbital floor fractures, **6:**125, 126, **7:**100–101
  insertion relationships of, **2:**16, 18*f*, 19*t*
  nerves supplying, **2:**21, **7:**11
  surgery of
    for dissociated vertical deviation, **6:**153
    eyelid position changes after, **6:**159, 159*f*
    for monocular elevation deficiency (double elevator palsy), **6:**124
    for nystagmus, **6:**329
    for orbital floor fracture, **6:**126, **7:**101, 102*f*
    for superior oblique muscle paralysis, **6:**120, 121
    for V-pattern deviation, **6:**111
Inferior rectus subnucleus, **5:**54
Inferior–superior (I–S) values, **13:**18
  after intrastromal corneal ring segment implantation, **13:**59
Inferior tarsal muscle, **7:**140
Inferior turbinate, **7:**18, 245*f*, 246
  infracture of, for congenital nasolacrimal duct obstruction, **6:**208–209, **7:**255
Inferolateral displacement of globe, in orbital disorders, **7:**23
Inferolateral trunk, **5:**16
Inferomedial displacement of globe, in orbital disorders, **7:**23
Inferonasal crescent, in congenital tilted disc syndrome, **5:**142

Infiltrative dermopathy (pretibial myxedema), in hyperthyroidism, **1:**211, **7:**51
Infiltrative lesions, orbital, **5:**132, 133*f*, 158–159
Infiltrative optic neuropathy, **5:**132, 133*f*, 158–159
Infinity
  focal planes and focal points at, **3:**69, 70*f*
  objects and images at, **3:**74
Inflamase Forte/Inflamase Mild. *See* Prednisolone
Inflammation (ocular), **4:**6–9, 8*f*, 9*f*, 12*t*. *See also specific type or structure affected and* Endophthalmitis; Inflammatory response; Uveitis
  acute, **4:**6, 13
  age-related macular degeneration differentiated from, **12:**70
  angle-closure glaucoma and, **10:**130–131, 130*f*, 131*f*
  canalicular obstruction caused by, **7:**264
  cataracts/cataract surgery and, **11:**59, 60*f*, 75, 158, 188
    postoperative, **11:**158–159
    trauma and, **11:**206–207
  in chemical injury, management and, **8:**357
  in children, **6:**350–351
    orbital, **6:**272, 346–347, 347*f*
  choroidal, **12:**185–211. *See also* Chorioretinitis; Chorioretinopathy; Choroidopathy
    posttraumatic, **4:**22, 22*f*
  chronic, **4:**6
  clinical evaluation of, **8:**19–28, 20–21*t*, 22*t*, 27*t*
  conjunctival, **4:**50–56, 51*f*, 52*f*, 53*f*, 55*f*, 56*f*, 57*f*, **8:**20*t*, 21–24, 22*f*, 22*t*, 23*f*, 24*f*
  corneal, **4:**82–87, 83*f*, 84*f*, 85*f*, 86*f*, 87*f*, **8:**20–21*t*, 24–25, 26*f*, 27*f*, 27*t*, 28*f*
  cytology in, **8:**47–48
  dry eye caused by, **8:**48–49, 50
  eyelid, **4:**208–211, 209*f*, 210*f*, 211*f*, **8:**19–21, 20*t*
  glaucoma and, **10:**93–95, 130–131, 130*f*, 131*f*
  granulomatous, **4:**6
    focal posttraumatic choroidal, **4:**22, 22*f*
  lens-related, **4:**122–123, 122*f*, 123*f*, 124*f*
  nasolacrimal duct obstruction caused by, **7:**267
  nongranulomatous, **4:**6
  nonsteroidal anti-inflammatory agents for, **1:**184
  open-angle glaucoma and, **10:**93–95
  optic nerve, **4:**251–253, 251*f*, 252*f*, 253*f*
  orbital, **4:**230–235, 231*f*, 233*f*, 234*f*, **5:**300–301, **7:**39, 39*t*, 47–61. *See also* Nonspecific orbital inflammation
    in children, **6:**272, 346–347, 347*f*
  pupil irregularity and, **5:**263
  retinal, **4:**151–153, 151*f*, 152*f*, 153*f*, 154*f*, **12:**185–211
  in retinoblastoma, **4:**301, 301*t*, **9:**286
  scleral, **4:**113–114, 113*f*, 114*f*, 115*f*, **8:**21*t*, 28
  soluble mediators of. *See* Mediators
  treatment of. *See* Anti-inflammatory agents
  uveal tract, **4:**188–191, 189*f*, 190*f*, 191*f*, **9:**77–116. *See also* Uveitis
  vitreal, **2:**288, **4:**133, 134*f*
Inflammatory bowel disease, **1:**165, **9:**123
Inflammatory infiltrate, necrobiotic granulomatous, in episcleritis, **4:**113, 113*f*
Inflammatory (stimulated) macrophages, **9:**20, 21*f*, 22–23
Inflammatory mediators. *See* Mediators
Inflammatory optic neuropathy, pain in, **5:**301
Inflammatory pseudoguttae, **8:**25, 30

Inflammatory pseudotumor. *See* Nonspecific orbital inflammation
Inflammatory response, 9:13. *See also* Inflammation
  immunity and, 9:13
  local antibody production and, 9:48
Inflammatory vascular tumors, 8:241–242, 241*f*, 241*t*
Inflammatory vasculitis, 12:194–196. *See also* Vasculitis
Infliximab, 1:161, 186, 9:46, 108*t*, 114
  for Behçet disease, 1:180, 9:195
  for sarcoidosis, 9:177
  for scleritis, 8:222
  for uveitis, 9:108*t*, 114
    in children, 6:278
Inflow, in phacoemulsification, 11:103
Influenza virus, 8:129
  antiviral agents for infection caused by, 1:66
  vaccination against, 1:281–282
    uveitis associated with, 9:128
Informed consent
  for cataract surgery, 11:88
  older patients and, 1:224
  for refractive surgery, 13:30*t*, 41–42, 41*t*, 209–217
    LASIK and, 13:213–217
    in patient with ocular or systemic disease, 13:163–164
    phakic intraocular lens insertion and, 13:128
    photorefractive keratectomy (PRK) and, 13:209–212
    refractive lens exchange/clear lens extraction and, 13:138
Infraciliary blepharoplasty incision, for orbitotomy, 7:108*f*, 110
Infracture of turbinates, for congenital nasolacrimal duct obstruction, 6:208–209, 7:255
Infraduction. *See* Depression of eye
Infranuclear pathways, 5:38, 50–55, 51*f*, 52–53*f*, 197
  disorders of, 5:226–238, 228*f*, 229*f*, 232*f*, 234*f*, 237*f*. *See also* Diplopia
Infraorbital artery, 5:14*f*, 15*f*, 16, 19
  extraocular muscles supplied by, 2:18, 6:16
  orbit supplied by, 2:37*f*
Infraorbital canal, 2:10, 5:8, 7:8
Infraorbital foramen, 2:9, 7:6*f*
Infraorbital groove, 2:8*f*, 9, 7:8
Infraorbital nerve, 2:14*f*, 103, 5:59*f*, 60, 61, 7:9, 11*f*, 19
  hypoesthesia in distribution of
    in blowout fractures, 6:125, 7:9, 19, 101
    after orbital surgery, 7:116
Infraorbital vein, 2:40*f*, 5:24*f*
Infrared lasers, 12:338
  for SD-OCT, 12:30–31, 31*f*
  for transpupillary thermotherapy, 12:343
Infrared light, for fundus photography, 3:249
Infrared pupillometer, 13:34
Infrared radiation. *See also* Radiation
  lens affected by, 11:52–53
Infrared reflectance imaging, 12:30–31, 31*f*
Infrared spectroscopy, in cervical cancer screening, 1:273
Infratrochlear artery, 5:14*f*, 16
Inhaled corticosteroids, for pulmonary diseases, 1:141, 146
Inhaled insulin, 1:202

Inhalers, metered-dose, β₂-adrenergics for pulmonary disease and, 1:144
Inheritance. *See also specific disorder and* Genetics
  codominant, 2:150, 211
  digenic, 2:150
  dominant, 2:151, 211–212
    autosomal, 2:216–217, 217*t*
      disorders associated with, 2:151, 212
        gene therapy for, 2:188, 189*f*
        X-linked, 2:219–220
    X-linked, 2:219, 219*t*
  galtonian, of mitochondrial DNA diseases, 2:208
  holandric, 2:218
  maternal, 2:173, 208, 220
  multifactorial, 2:156, 224–225
  patterns of, 2:211–220
  polygenic, 2:158, 224–225
  recessive, 2:211–212
    autosomal, 2:212–216, 213*t*, 215*t*
      disorders associated with, 2:159, 212–216, 213*t*, 215*t*
        gene therapy for, 2:187–188
        X-linked, 2:218–219, 219*t*
    sex-linked, 2:160, 218
    X-linked, 2:163, 185
      disorders associated with, 2:219–220
        gene therapy for, 2:187–188
  Y-linked, 2:163
Inherited disorders
  migrainelike headache and, 5:300
  neuro-ophthalmic signs of, 5:336–345. *See also specific disorder*
Inhibitors, 2:332
Initiator codon, 2:154
Initiator tRNA, 2:154
Injection drug use. *See also* Substance abuse disorders
  endogenous mold (*Aspergillus*) endophthalmitis and, 12:203
INL. *See* Inner nuclear layer
Inlays, corneal, 13:53–64
  alloplastic, 13:54
  homoplastic, 13:54
  in keratophakia, 13:53–55
  for presbyopia, 13:53, 54, 157, 200
Innate immune response, 1:3, 9:9, 12–13, 14–23
  bacteria-derived molecules in, 9:14–17, 14*t*
  complement and, 9:23–24, 24*f*
  effector reactivities of, 9:14–23, 14*t*, 23*t*
  inflammation and, 9:13
  macrophage recruitment and activation and, 9:14*t*, 20–23, 21*f*
  mediator systems in, 9:23–31, 23*t*
  neutrophil recruitment and activation and, 9:14*t*, 17–20, 19*f*
  receptors in, 9:12–13
  triggers of, 9:14–23, 14*t*, 23*t*
  in viral conjunctivitis, 9:60
Inner cell mass, 2:117, 118*f*
Inner ischemic retinal atrophy, 4:157, 157*f*
  in retinal arterial and venous occlusions, 4:157*f*, 163, 164
Inner marginal zone, 2:124
Inner neuroblastic layer, 2:126

Inner nuclear layer, 2:2, 74*f*, 75*f*, 78, 79*f*, 298–301, 299*f*, 300*f*, 4:145, 146*f*, 12:10, 11*f*
Inner plexiform layer, 2:74*f*, 75*f*, 78, 79*f*, 4:145, 146*f*, 12:10, 11*f*, 12
  development of, 2:126
Inner segments, photoreceptor, 2:73, 74*f*, 76*f*, 12:10, 11*f*, 13*f*. *See also* Cone inner segments; Photoreceptors; Rod inner segments
Innominate artery, 5:12
INO. *See* Internuclear ophthalmoplegia
Inoculum, 8:99
Inositol-1,4,5-triphosphate (IP₃), in signal transduction
  in iris–ciliary body, 2:263, 263*f*
  in tear secretion, 2:242*f*, 243
Inotropic agents, for heart failure, 1:119
INR. *See* International normalized ratio
Insect hairs/stings, ocular injury/infection caused by, 8:361–362
Insertions, mitochondrial DNA, disorders caused by, 2:173
Insomnia, benzodiazepines for, 1:254
Inspection, in orbital disorders, 7:22–24, 23*f*, 24*f*
Inspra. *See* Eplerenone
Instantaneous radius of curvature (meridional/ tangential power), 8:40, 41*f*, 13:11, 12*f*
Instrument (proximal) convergence, 6:37
Instrument error, IOL power calculations and, 3:220
Instrument myopia, in automated refraction, 3:276
Instrumental activities of daily living (IADL). *See also* Activities of daily living
  visual loss and, 1:224
Instrumentation. *See* Ophthalmic instrumentation; Surgical instruments
Insulin. *See also* Insulin therapy
  in glucose metabolism/diabetes mellitus, 1:189–190
Insulin-dependent diabetes mellitus (IDDM). *See* Diabetes mellitus, type 1
Insulin-like growth factor I. *See* Insulinlike growth factor I
Insulin-like growth factor binding proteins. *See* Insulinlike growth factor binding proteins
Insulin-neutralizing antibodies, 1:198
Insulin pumps, 1:197
  surgery and, 1:308
Insulin resistance
  immunologic, insulin therapy and, 1:198
  metabolic syndrome and, 1:138, 193
Insulin therapy, 1:195–198, 196*t*
  allergic reactions and, 1:198
  complications of, 1:198
  importance of, 1:202–203, 203*f*
  inhaled, 1:202
  intensive (tight control), 1:196. *See also* Glycemic control
  recent developments in, 1:189
  surgery and, 1:307–308
  in type 2 diabetes mellitus, 1:189, 196
  types of insulin for, 1:196, 196*t*
Insulinlike growth factor I, 2:114, 396
  in aqueous humor, 2:270
  in ocular development, 2:114
  in retinopathy of prematurity, 6:281, 12:166
  in thyroid eye disease, 4:232, 7:50

Insulinlike growth factor binding proteins, in aqueous humor, 2:270
Insulinoma, in multiple endocrine neoplasia, 1:216
Intacs, 13:55–63, 56*f*, 58*f*, 60*f*, 61*f*, 62*f*. *See also* Intrastromal corneal ring segments
  international trends in use of, 13:200
Intal. *See* Cromolyn
Integrase inhibitors, for HIV infection/AIDS, 1:35
Integrilin. *See* Eptifibatide
Integrins, 8:98
  in neutrophil rolling, 9:18
Intelence. *See* Etravirine
Intensity. *See also* Brightness
  of laser light, 3:21
  luminous (candle power), 3:18*t*
  radiant, for medical lasers, 3:18*t*
  of retinal reflex, in axis determination, 3:126
Intention-to-treat analysis, 1:328
Intercellular adhesion molecules. *See also* Cell-adhesion molecules
  in neutrophil rolling, 9:18
Intercrines. *See* Chemokines
Interface debris, after LASIK, 13:114, 114*f*
Interface keratitis
  diffuse (diffuse lamellar keratitis/sands of the Sahara), after LASIK, 13:108–111, 109*f*, 109*t*, 110*t*, 111*f*
  glaucoma/IOP elevation and, 13:97, 174, 195
  infectious, 13:98–99, 99*f*, 110–111, 110*t*, 111*f*
  pressure-induced, 13:112, 112*f*
Interfaces, optical, 3:42
  light propagation at, 3:42, 42*f*, 43*f*
  reflection at, 3:12–13, 12*f*, 42, 42*f*, 43*f*
Interference, 3:7–10, 8*f*, 9*f*
  applications of, 3:8–10, 9*f*
  constructive, 3:7, 8*f*
  destructive, 3:7, 8*f*
Interference filters, 3:8, 9, 9*f*
Interferometry/interferometer
  laser, 3:8, 277
  before cataract surgery, 11:81
Interferons (IFNs), 1:243, 2:395, 9:27, 29*t*
  α, 1:243, 9:29*t*
    for Behçet disease, 1:180, 9:195
    for cancer therapy, 1:242*t*, 243
    for delta hepatitis, 1:26
    for hemangiomas, 7:64, 152
    in children, 6:340
    for hepatitis B, 1:281
    for hepatitis C, 1:26
    for uveitis, 9:115
  β, 1:243
    for multiple sclerosis, 5:327
  for conjunctival intraepithelial neoplasia, 8:229, 230*f*
  for corneal intraepithelial neoplasia, 8:231
  γ, 1:243, 9:29*t*
    in delayed hypersensitivity, 9:49*f*, 50
  ocular effects of, 1:301*t*
  in tear film, 2:240
Intergroup Rhabdomyosarcoma Study Group, 6:335
Interlenticular membranes, piggyback IOLs and, 13:140
Interlenticular opacifications, IOL, 11:169
Interleukin-1, 8:177, 177*t*
  in external eye defense, 8:96

Interleukin-1α, **9:**28*t*
 in Sjögren syndrome, **8:**63
 in tear film, **2:**241
Interleukin-1β
 in Sjögren syndrome, **8:**63
 in tear film, **2:**241
Interleukin-2, **9:**28*t*
 in immune processing, **9:**39
Interleukin-4, **9:**28*t*
 atopy and, **8:**179
 in delayed hypersensitivity, **9:**49*f*, 50
Interleukin-5, **9:**28*t*
 in delayed hypersensitivity, **9:**49*f*, 50
 in eosinophil activation, **9:**10
Interleukin-6, **9:**28*t*
 in primary central nervous system lymphoma,
  9:283
 in Sjögren syndrome, **8:**63
 thyroid eye disease and, **4:**232, **7:**50
Interleukin-8, **9:**28*t*
 in Sjögren syndrome, **8:**63
 thyroid eye disease and, **4:**232, **7:**50
Interleukin-10, in primary central nervous system
  lymphoma, **9:**283
Interleukin-17, T cells producing (Th17 cells), **9:**40
Interleukins, **9:**27, 28*t*
 in cancer therapy, **1:**243
 in delayed hypersensitivity, **9:**49*f*, 50
 in external eye defense, **8:**96
 for HIV infection/AIDS, **1:**36
 in Sjögren syndrome, **8:**63
 thyroid eye disease and, **4:**232, **7:**50
Intermarginal sulcus (gray line), **2:**23, 26*f*, 237, **7:**136,
  142
Intermediate uveitis, **9:**78*t*, 79, 89, 134–140, **12:**196. *See
  also specific cause and* Pars planitis; Uveitis
 in children, **6:**267, 272, 273*f*
  differential diagnosis of, **6:**268*t*
  laboratory tests for, **6:**277*t*
 flowchart for evaluation of, **9:**80*t*
 HLA association in, **9:**72*t*
 HTLV-1 causing, **9:**218–219
 in Lyme disease, **9:**251
 multiple sclerosis and, **9:**136, 139
 noninfectious (autoimmune), **9:**134–140
 prevalence of, **9:**92, 92*t*
 signs of, **9:**89
 symptoms of, **9:**85
Intermediate zone, **2:**70
Intermittent ataxia, **2:**213*t*
Intermittent tropias, **6:**10
 esotropia, **6:**89
 exotropia, **6:**99–103
Intermuscular septum, **2:**35, **6:**22, **7:**10
 surgery and, **6:**24
Internal auditory artery, **5:**21
Internal auditory meatus, **2:**105
Internal carotid artery, **2:**107, 107*f*, 109, **5:**11*f*, 12, 13*f*,
  14*f*, 15, 15*f*, 16, 17*f*, 18*f*, 20*f*
 aneurysm of, **5:**164, 350, 350*f*, 351
  chiasmal syndromes caused by, **5:**164
  third nerve (oculomotor) palsy and, **5:**229, 273, 351
  cranial nerve relationship and, **5:**52*f*

 dissection of, **5:**353
  Horner syndrome caused by, **5:**267, 268, 269*f*, 302,
   353
 optic nerve supplied by, **2:**93, 95
Internal dacryocystorhinostomy, **7:**268, 269
Internal hordeolum, **7:**152, 154, **8:**148. *See also*
  Chalazion
Internal jugular vein, **5:**26
Internal limiting membrane, **2:**74*f*, 75*f*, 79, 80*f*, **4:**145,
  146*f*, **12:**10, 11*f*, 12, 14*f*
 optic disc, **2:**90, 92*f*
 in retinal healing/repair, **4:**17
 in Valsalva retinopathy, **12:**153–154
 vitreous detachment and, **2:**286–287, **4:**135
Internal reflection, total (TIR), **3:**12, 13
 anterior chamber examination and, **3:**49, 50*f*
Internal scleral sulcus, **2:**50, **4:**102
Internal ulcer of von Hippel, **4:**81, 81*f*
 intrauterine inflammation and, **8:**263–264
International Agency for the Prevention of Blindness
  (IAPB), **11:**65
International Classification of ROP (ICROP), **6:**282,
  282*t*, 283*f*, 284*f*, 285*t*, **12:**157, 158*t*
International Classification System for Intraocular
  Retinoblastoma, **4:**307–308, 308*t*, **6:**358
International Committee for the Classification of Corneal
  Dystrophies, **4:**96, **8:**267–268, 268*t*, 269*t*, 270*t*
International Committee for Systemic Bacteriology
  (ICSB), **8:**131
International Harmonized System for medical devices
  control, **13:**202
International League of Associations of Rheumatology
  (ILAR), chronic childhood arthritis nomenclature
  and, **6:**268, 269*t*
International normalized ratio (INR), **1:**152
Internuclear lesions, diplopia caused by, **5:**224–226,
  224*f*, 225*f*, 226*f*
Internuclear ophthalmoplegia, **5:**46, 224–226, 224*f*, 225*f*,
  226*f*, **6:**141
 dissociated nystagmus and, **5:**254
 in multiple sclerosis, **5:**325
 nystagmus in, **5:**224–225, **6:**141
 pursuit dysfunction in, **5:**213
 wall-eyed bilateral, **5:**225, 225*f*
Interocular distance, abnormal, **6:**173–175, 175*f*
Interpalpebral fissure, vertical, height of, **5:**275, 276*f*
 in ptosis, **6:**179, **7:**202, 202*f*
Interpalpebral (central) fit, for rigid gas-permeable
  contact lenses, **3:**184–185
Interphotoreceptor matrix (IPM), **2:**72, 74*f*
 development of, **2:**123
 retinal pigment epithelium in maintenance of, **2:**308
Interphotoreceptor retinoid-binding protein, **2:**306, **4:**178
 in AIRE-deficient mice, **9:**70
 in sympathetic ophthalmia, **9:**181
Interphotoreceptor retinoid-binding protein–derived
  proteins, in experimental autoimmune uveitis, **9:**69
Interplexiform cells, **5:**28
Interpulse time (TI), **5:**70
Interpupillary distance
 bifocal segment decentration and, **3:**157
 binocular observation in indirect ophthalmoscopy
  and, **3:**247–248, 248*f*, 249*f*

Interrater reliability, **1**:339
Interrupted sutures
  "clover-shaped" aberration caused by, **3**:240
  for penetrating keratoplasty, **8**:418–419, 419*f*, 420*f*
Intersex, **2**:204
Interstitial growth, in development of lamellae, **2**:134
Interstitial keratitis, **4**:86–87, 87*f*
  glaucoma and, **10**:131
  herpetic, **4**:82–83, 84*f*, 87, **8**:113, 114*f*
  HTLV-1–related, **9**:219
  in infectious disease, **8**:207–209, 208*f*
  syphilitic, **4**:87, 87*f*, **6**:186, 221, **8**:207–209, 208*f*,
    9:243, 244*f*
    intrauterine infection and, **4**:87, **8**:264
Interstitial nucleus of Cajal, **5**:38, 39*f*, 42–44, 44*f*, 203
  skew deviation and, **5**:222
Interstitial nucleus of medial longitudinal fasciculus,
    rostral, **5**:38, 39*f*, 42, 44*f*, 46*f*, 199, 199–200
Intervening sequence. *See* Intron
Intervention, in clinical research, **1**:318
Interventional (experimental) studies (clinical trials),
    1:320, 321, 321*f*, 327–328, 327*f*. *See also* Clinical
    research
  for medical device, **13**:204, 206
  for new drug, **2**:333
  systematic reviews/meta-analyses of, **1**:328–329
Intorsion (incycloduction), **6**:10, 29, 33
  extraocular muscles in
    superior oblique, **6**:15, 17*t*, 29*t*, 31, 33*f*
    superior rectus, **6**:14, 17*t*, 29, 29*t*, 31, 31*f*
Intorsional strabismus, **6**:10
Intra-axial ocular motor nerve palsies, **5**:226
Intracameral injections, **2**:328
  acetylcholine, **2**:337
  carbachol, **2**:337
  lidocaine, **2**:389
    for cataract surgery, **11**:99–100
Intracanalicular region of optic nerve, **2**:87, 89*t*, 93,
    4:249
  blood supply of, **2**:93, 95
  compressive lesions of, **5**:149
Intracapsular cataract extraction (ICCE), **11**:93–94, 93*f*,
    213–215. *See also* Cataract surgery
  advantages of, **11**:93
  in anticoagulated patient, **11**:189
  contraindications to, **11**:94
  cystoid macular edema and, **11**:182, **12**:143
  disadvantages of, **11**:94
  early techniques for, **11**:92, 92*f*
  intraocular lenses for, **11**:94, 133, 135*f*
    limitations and, **11**:94
  modern advances in, **11**:93–94, 93*f*
  patient preparation for, **11**:213
  postoperative course for, **11**:215
  postoperative flat or shallow anterior chamber and,
    11:153–154
  procedure for, **11**:213
  retinal detachment and, **11**:184
  vitreocorneal adherence/persistent corneal edema
    and, **11**:148
  vitreous changes/detachment and, **12**:275
Intracapsular IOL dislocation, **11**:163, 163*f*
Intracavernous carotid aneurysms, **5**:351

Intracerebral hemorrhage, **1**:97. *See also* Intracranial
    hemorrhage
Intraconal fat/surgical space (central surgical space),
    7:10, 107*f*, 108
Intracranial hemorrhage, **1**:97–98
  arteriovenous malformations causing, **1**:97, 98, **5**:354,
    356
  headache caused by, **1**:98, **5**:294
  ruptured aneurysm causing, **1**:97, 98, **5**:351
  in shaking injury, **6**:405
  Terson syndrome caused by, **12**:155
Intracranial hypertension (increased intracranial
    pressure)
  in craniosynostosis, optic nerve abnormalities and,
    6:391
  headache caused by, **5**:294
  idiopathic (pseudotumor cerebri), **5**:123–125, 123*t*
    in children, **5**:124–125, **6**:312–313
    headache and, **5**:123, 124, 294
  optic disc edema in. *See* Papilledema
  ruptured aneurysms causing, **5**:351
  symptoms associated with, **5**:117
Intracranial region of optic nerve, **2**:87, 89*t*, 93, 94*f*,
    4:249, **5**:31
  blood supply of, **2**:95
Intradermal nevus, **4**:225, 226*f*
Intradiploic epidermoid cyst, **7**:36
Intraepithelial dyskeratosis, benign hereditary, **8**:226*t*
Intraepithelial melanosis, **4**:67–69, 67*f*, 68*f*
Intraepithelial neoplasia
  conjunctival (CIN), **4**:62, 63*f*, 64*f*, **8**:226*t*, 228–229,
    229*f*, 230*f*. *See also* Ocular surface squamous
    neoplasia
  corneal, **4**:100, **8**:226*t*, 229–231, 231*f*
Intralase-enabled keratoplasty (IEK), precut tissue for,
    8:409
Intralenticular foreign bodies, **11**:51
Intramuscular agents, in ocular pharmacology, **2**:330
Intramuscular circle of the iris, **2**:38, 39*f*
Intramuscular plexus, ciliary body, **2**:62
Intranasal influenza vaccine, **1**:282
Intraocular chemotherapy, for lymphoma, **4**:324
Intraocular culture
  in endogenous endophthalmitis, **9**:272–273
  in postoperative endophthalmitis, **9**:270–271
Intraocular fine-needle aspiration biopsy (FNAB), **4**:34*t*,
    43–44, 44*f*
Intraocular fluid analysis, in uveitis, **9**:94–95*t*
Intraocular foreign bodies. *See* Foreign bodies
Intraocular inflammation. *See* Inflammation (ocular)
Intraocular lenses (IOLs), **3**:203–230, **11**:132–141. *See
    also* Cataract surgery
  accommodating/accommodative, **3**:229, **11**:137,
    13:4*t*, 146, 159–160
    complications associated with, **11**:169
  anterior chamber, **3**:204*f*, 210–211, 210*f*, 211*f*, **11**:133,
    135*f*
    after capsular rupture, **11**:161
    closed-loop, pseudophakic bullous keratopathy
      and, **11**:167
    complications associated with, **11**:133
    contraindications to, **11**:140–141
    flexible-loop, **11**:133, 135*f*

history of development of, **11**:133, 135*f*
after ICCE, **11**:94, 133, 134*f*, 214
implantation procedure for
  primary, **11**:139–140
  secondary, **11**:140
phakic, **13**:4*t. See also* Phakic intraocular lenses
preoperative gonioscopy and, **11**:79
pupillary block and, **10**:124
bifocal, **3**:226–227, 227*f*
biometry in power calculation/selection of,
  3:213–219, 214*f*, 215*f*, 216*f*, 217*f*, 218*f*, **11**:82–83,
  83*f*, 84
  axial length, **3**:213–216, 214*f*, 215*f*, 216*f*, **11**:82–83,
    84, 84–85
    unexpected refractive results after surgery and,
      11:168
  corneal power, **3**:216–217, 217*f*
  estimated lens position, **3**:217–219, 218*f*
  refractive lens exchange/clear lens extraction and,
    13:140–141
blue-blocking, **11**:138
capsular block syndrome and, **10**:124, **11**:166–167
in children, **3**:223
classification of, **3**:203–204, 204*f*
closed-loop, pseudophakic bullous keratopathy and,
  11:167
complications of, **11**:133, 144*t*, 162–169
contraindications to, **11**:140–141
corneal disease and, **11**:191
corneal endothelial changes caused by, **8**:385
cystoid macular edema and, **11**:183, **12**:143, 360
decentration and dislocation of, **11**:143, 144*t*,
  162–166, 163*f*, 164*f*, 165*f*, **12**:359–360
  laser capsulotomy and, **11**:173
  multifocal IOLs and, **3**:226, **11**:163
  phakic IOLs and, **13**:135, 145
  vitrectomy for, **12**:359–360
deformable, **13**:160
design considerations for, **3**:203–211
  innovations in, **13**:160–161
diffractive multifocal, **3**:227–228, 227*f*, 228*f*
flexible-loop, **11**:133, 135*f*
foldable, **3**:205, **11**:135–136, 136*f*
  for children, **6**:257, 259
  implantation procedure for, **11**:138, 139
  in uveitis, **9**:127
Fuchs heterochromic iridocyclitis/uveitis and, **9**:134
glare and, **11**:168
glaucoma and, **10**:102
history of, **3**:204–207, 205*f*, 206*f*, 207*f*, 208*f*,
  11:132–133, 132*f*, 134*f*, 135*f*
image magnification and, **3**:223
implantation of, **11**:132–141
  anterior chamber, **11**:139–140
  after capsular rupture, **11**:161
  complications of, **11**:133, 144*t*, 162–169
  contraindications to, **11**:140–141
  after ECCE, **11**:133, 133–136, 136*f*, 212
  after ICCE, **11**:94, 133, 214
    limitations and, **11**:94
  posterior chamber, **11**:138–139
  procedure for, **11**:138–140
    in children, **6**:257–258, 258–259

secondary, **11**:140
  in children, **6**:259
  techniques of, **11**:138
in infants and children, **6**:257–258, 258–259
  visual outcomes and, **6**:260
juvenile idiopathic (chronic/rheumatoid) arthritis–
  associated iridocyclitis/uveitis and, **9**:131–132,
  293
light-adjustable, **13**:146–147, 147*f*, 161
materials for, **3**:205, 206
  in infants and children, **6**:259
multifocal, **3**:225–229, **11**:136–137, **13**:4*t*, 144–146,
  154–156, 154*f*, 155*f*
  bifocal, **3**:226–227, 227*f*
  clinical results of, **3**:228–229
  complications associated with, **11**:169
  diffractive, **3**:227–228, 227*f*, 228*f*
  multiple-zone, **3**:227, 227*f*
  for presbyopia, **13**:154–156, 154*f*, 155*f*
multiple-zone, **3**:227, 227*f*
nonspherical optics and, **3**:225
after ocular trauma, **11**:208–209
opacification of, **11**:168–169
optical considerations for, **3**:211–220
in pars planitis, **9**:138
with penetrating/Descemet membrane–stripping
  keratoplasty and cataract surgery (triple
  procedure), **11**:141, 192
after penetrating keratoplasty, **13**:169
phakic, **13**:4*t*, 41*t*, 125, 125–136, 127*t*, 130*f*, 131*f*,
  132*t*, 133*t. See also* Phakic intraocular lenses
  advantages/disadvantages/limitations of, **13**:41*t*, 126
  in children, **13**:180–181
  with LASIK (bioptics), **13**:125, 137
  retinal detachment and, **13**:135, 136
piggyback, **3**:206–207, 219–220
  refractive lens exchange/clear lens extraction and,
    13:140
plano, **3**:206
posterior chamber, **3**:204*f*, 208–209, 209*f*, **11**:133–136,
  136*f*
  capsular block syndrome and, **10**:124, **11**:166–167
  after capsular rupture, **11**:161
  contraindications to, **11**:140–141
  dislocated, **12**:359–360
  after ECCE, **11**:133, 133–136, 136*f*, 212
  history of development of, **11**:133
  implantation procedure for, **11**:138–139
  after keratoplasty, **11**:193
  light-adjustable, **13**:146–147, 147*f*, 161
  phakic, **13**:4*t*, 126, 130–131, 130*f*, 131*f. See also*
    Phakic intraocular lenses
    with LASIK (bioptics), **13**:125, 137
  pupillary capture caused by anterior displacement
    of, **11**:166, 167*f*
in retinal disease, **11**:205
sutured, **11**:139
power determination for, **3**:211–219, **11**:84–88
  biometry in, **3**:213–219, 214*f*, 215*f*, 216*f*, 217*f*,
    218*f*, **11**:82–83, 83*f*, 84. *See also* Intraocular
    lenses (IOLs), biometry in power calculation/
    selection of
  in children, **3**:223, **6**:258

contact lens method for, 11:87, 13:188
corneal transplantation and, 3:222
formulas for, 3:212–213, 212f, 217–219, 11:85, 87
   biometric requirements and, 3:213–219, 214f,
      215f, 216f, 217f, 218f
   choice of, 3:219
   errors in, 3:221
   for postkeratorefractive eye, 3:221–222
      refractive lens exchange/clear lens extraction
         and, 13:140–141
   regression formulas, 3:212, 218, 11:85, 87
historical methods for, 11:87, 13:188
improving outcomes of surgery and, 11:86
incorrect, 11:168
online post-refractive calculator for (ASCRS),
   13:188–189, 190f
preventing errors in, 11:84–85
after radial keratotomy, 13:48
refraction and, 11:76
refractive lens exchange/clear lens extraction and,
   13:140–141
refractive surgery and, 3:220–222, 11:86–88, 193,
   13:187–189
regression formulas for, 11:85, 87
silicone oil placement and, 3:222–223
topographical method for, 11:87
   after refractive surgery, 13:187
triple procedure and, 11:192
unexpected refractive results after surgery and,
   11:168
prepupillary, 3:204f, 207, 207f, 208f
pseudoaccommodative, 11:137
pseudophakic bullous keratopathy and, 11:167
pupil evaluation and, 11:78
pupillary block and, 10:124
pupillary capture of, 11:166, 167f
for refractive errors. See also specific type
accommodating, 3:229, 13:4t, 146, 159–160
   with clear lens extraction, 13:4t, 41t, 138–141. See
      also Refractive lens exchange
   piggybacking and, 13:140
deformable, 13:160
dual-optic, 13:146, 160
innovations in, 13:160–161
light-adjustable, 13:146–147, 147f, 161
multifocal, 13:4t, 144–146, 154–156, 154f, 155f
   for presbyopia, 13:154–156, 154f, 155f
phakic, 13:4t, 41t, 125, 125–136, 127t, 130f, 131f,
   132t, 133t. See also Phakic intraocular lenses
   advantages/disadvantages/limitations of, 13:41t,
      126
   anterior chamber, 13:4t
   with LASIK (bioptics), 13:125, 137
   retinal detachment and, 13:135, 136
power determination of
   refractive lens exchange/clear lens extraction
      and, 13:140–141
   after refractive surgery, 13:187–189
   after radial keratotomy, 13:48
single-optic, 13:146. See also Crystalens
toric, 13:4t, 126, 141–144, 142f
in retinal disease, 11:205
in retinitis pigmentosa, 12:230

silicone oil use and, 3:222–223
standards for, 3:229–230
toric, 3:225, 11:131, 13:4t, 126, 141–144, 142f
   complications associated with, 11:169
traumatic cataract and, 11:208–209
with UV chromophores, 11:138
in uveitis, 9:127, 291, 292–293, 294, 11:204
   postoperative inflammation and, 9:126–127, 127f,
      294
uveitis-glaucoma-hyphema (UGH) syndrome and,
   3:210, 9:17, 126–127, 11:167
   decentration and, 11:163
visual disturbances related to, 3:223–225, 224f
Intraocular lymphoma. See Intraocular tumors,
   lymphoma
Intraocular medications, 2:328. See also specific drug
   for uveitis, 9:101t
Intraocular pressure, 10:20–26, 20f, 73–75
age affecting, 10:20, 22, 75
aqueous humor dynamics and, 2:255, 265, 10:3f, 13,
   14t
in central retinal artery occlusion, 12:140
in central retinal vein occlusion, 12:129, 130
in chemical injury, management and, 8:358
corneal thickness/rigidity and, 8:8, 9, 30, 10:24–25,
   74, 80, 84, 13:35, 173, 194
   in infants and children, 10:151
corticosteroids affecting, 2:359–360, 360t, 361,
   10:103–104
   optic nerve damage and, 10:81, 103
   after refractive surgery, 13:35, 96–97, 112, 173 174,
      173f, 194, 195
   in uveitis, 9:103, 105, 295, 297, 10:103
cycloplegics affecting, 2:341
decreased
   after cataract surgery, flat anterior chamber and,
      11:153
   factors causing, 10:21–22, 21t
digital pressure in estimation of, 10:26
distribution in population and, 10:20–21, 20f
diurnal variation in, 10:22, 74, 80
drugs for lowering. See Antiglaucoma agents
elevated/increased. See Elevated intraocular pressure
episcleral venous pressure and, 10:13, 14t, 19–20,
   95–96
factors affecting, 10:21–22, 21t
flap creation affected by, 13:78
in glaucoma, 10:3–4, 20–21, 73–75. See also Elevated
   intraocular pressure
   in infants and children, 6:234, 235, 236, 243–244
   target range for, 10:160
   uveitis and, 9:294, 295
in hyphema, 8:366, 367
   in children, 6:409, 410
   surgery and, 8:368, 369t
lowering of, in glaucoma management, 10:159–161,
   204–211. See also Antiglaucoma agents
   clinical trials in study of, 10:78, 104–108, 159
   before incisional surgery, 10:186
measurement of, 10:22–26, 23f, 24f, 24t. See also
   Tonometry
   artifact in, normal-tension glaucoma and, 10:4, 80
   in infants and children, 6:236, 10:150–151

before refractive surgery, **13**:35
  after refractive surgery, **13**:97, 112, 172–175, 173*f*, 194, 195
    pressure-induced stromal keratitis after LASIK and, **13**:112, 112*f*
  during refractive surgery, suction ring placement and, **13**:78–79
  as screening tool, **1**:330–332, 331*f*, 332*f*
  normal range for, **10**:20, 73–74
  in infants and children, **6**:170, 236, **10**:151
  in ocular ischemic syndrome, **12**:133
  in ocular trauma, **12**:318
  in rhegmatogenous retinal detachment, **12**:286
  target range for, in glaucoma treatment, **10**:160
  in uveitis, **9**:86*t*, 89, 294, 295
    corticosteroids affecting, **9**:103, 105, 295, 297, **10**:103
Intraocular region of optic nerve, **2**:87, 89, 89–91, 89*t*, **4**:249
Intraocular specimens, for endophthalmitis diagnosis, **9**:270–271, 272–273, **12**:354
Intraocular surgery. *See* Ocular (intraocular) surgery
Intraocular tumors. *See also specific type of tumor and structure affected*
  angiomatous, **4**:291–296, 297*f*
  canalicular obstruction and, **7**:264
  in children, **6**:351–361
    choroidal and retinal pigment epithelial lesions, **6**:352–354, 353*f*
    iris and ciliary body lesions, **6**:351–352, 352*f*
    leukemic infiltrates, **6**:354. *See also* Leukemia
    retinoblastoma, **6**:354–361. *See also* Retinoblastoma
  enucleation for, **7**:117–118
  exenteration for, **7**:117, 126–127, 126*f*
  glaucoma caused by, **4**:109, 110*f*, **10**:92–93, 130
    in infants and children, **10**:93, 141*t*
  leukemia and. *See* Leukemia
  lymphoma (primary central nervous system lymphoma), **1**:244, **4**:140–142, 141*f*, 142*f*, 143*f*, 323–325, 323*f*, 325*f*, **9**:136, 281–284, 282*f*, 283*f*, **12**:199, 199*f*
    central serous retinopathy differentiated from, **12**:174
    in HIV infection/AIDS, **9**:314
    uveitis differentiated from, **9**:91, 136, 281–283
      in children, **6**:276*t*
  melanocytic, **4**:265–289
  metastatic, **1**:244. *See also* Metastatic eye disease
  nasolacrimal duct obstruction and, **7**:267
  retinoblastoma, **4**:178–181, 263, 299–314, **6**:354–361, **9**:286. *See also* Retinoblastoma
  staging of, **4**:329–352*t*
  in systemic malignancies, **4**:315–328. *See also* Metastatic eye disease
    direct extension from extraocular tumors and, **4**:322
    leukemia and, **4**:326–328, 327*f*
    lymphomatous, **4**:140–142, 141*f*, 142*f*, 143*f*, 323–326, 323*f*, 325*f*
    secondary, **4**:315–322
  transillumination in identification of, **4**:26–27, 27*f*
Intraoperative complications of ocular surgery, **1**:310–313, 313*t*
Intraoperative floppy iris syndrome, **11**:74, 154–155, 156*f*

Intraorbital foreign bodies, **7**:104
Intraorbital pressure, in traumatic optic neuropathy, **7**:105
Intraorbital region of optic nerve, **2**:87, 89, 89*t*, **4**:249, **5**:30–31, **7**:5, 10, **10**:40
  blood supply of, **2**:94, 95*f*
  compressive lesions of, **5**:149–154. *See also specific lesion*
  length of, **7**:5*t*, 10
Intrarater reliability, **1**:339
Intraretinal microvascular abnormalities (IRMAs), **4**:160, 161*f*
  in diabetic retinopathy, **4**:166, **12**:104, 105*f*
  photocoagulation for, **12**:340
Intraretinal periarteriolar transudates, focal (FIPTs), **12**:113, 114*f*
Intrastromal corneal ring segments, **13**:4*t*, 22, 22*f*, 41*t*, 53, 55–63, 56*f*, 58*f*, 60*f*, 61*f*, 62*f*
  advantages of, **13**:56
  complications of, **13**:60–63, 61*f*, 62*f*
  corneal transplantation after, **13**:192
  instrumentation for, **13**:57
  international trends in use of, **13**:200–201
  for keratoconus, **13**:58–60, 60*f*, 62–63, 168
  after LASIK, **13**:63
  limitations of, **13**:41*t*
  for myopia, **13**:55–56, 56*f*, 57, 58
    patient selection and, **13**:57
  outcomes of, **13**:58
  removal of, **13**:58
Intrauterine ocular infection, **6**:181–186. *See also specific type*
  corneal anomalies and, **8**:263–264
    keratectasia, **8**:259
Intravascular ultrasound, in ischemic heart disease, **1**:107
Intravenous drug administration, in ocular pharmacology, **2**:329
Intravenous drug use. *See also* Substance abuse disorders
  endogenous mold *(Aspergillus)* endophthalmitis and, **12**:203
Intraventricular hemorrhage, **1**:97. *See also* Intracranial hemorrhage
Intravitreal medications, **2**:328
  for acute retinal necrosis, **9**:202
  for birdshot retinochoroidopathy, **9**:155, **12**:190–191
  for branch retinal vein occlusion, **12**:126, 127
  for central retinal vein occlusion, **12**:131
  for CMV retinitis, **1**:24, 37–38, **9**:207
  corticosteroids
    for branch retinal vein occlusion, **12**:126
    after cataract surgery, **11**:183
    for central retinal vein occlusion, **12**:131
    for cystoid macular edema, **9**:301, **11**:183
    elevated intraocular pressure and, **10**:103–104
    for macular edema, **12**:143, 360
    for pars planitis, **9**:137
    with photodynamic therapy, **12**:344
    for uveitis, **9**:105–106, 301
  for endophthalmitis
    endogenous *Aspergillus,* **9**:278
    endogenous *Candida,* **9**:275
    postoperative, **12**:354

for macular edema, **12**:143, 360
for multifocal choroiditis and panuveitis (MCP), **9**:164
for ocular histoplasmosis syndrome, **9**:225
with photodynamic therapy, **12**:344
for sarcoidosis, **9**:177
for uveitic neovascularization, **9**:303
for Vogt-Koyanagi-Harada (VKH) syndrome, **9**:189
Intravitreal triamcinolone acetonide (IVTA). *See* Triamcinolone
Intrinsic factor, in vitamin B$_{12}$ absorption, **1**:149
Intrinsic pathway (coagulation), **1**:151, 151*f*
Intrinsic sympathomimetic activity, β-blockers with, **1**:76*t*, 80–81
Intrinsically photosensitive retinal ganglion cells, **5**:28, 32
Intron, **2**:154, 165
excision of, **2**:168. *See also* Splicing
Intron-A. *See* Interferons (IFNs), α
Intropin. *See* Dopamine
Intrusions, saccadic, **5**:200, 204–205, 208, 243, 244, 254–256, 255*f*
with normal intersaccadic intervals, **5**:254–255, 255*f*
without normal intersaccadic intervals, **5**:255–256, 255*f*
Intubation, lacrimal
for acquired nasolacrimal obstruction, **7**:267
for canalicular obstruction, **7**:264
for canalicular trauma, **7**:272–273
for congenital lacrimal drainage obstruction, **6**:209–210, **7**:252–253, 254*f*
Intumescent cortical cataract, **11**:42
phacomorphic glaucoma and, **11**:63, 64*f*
surgery for removal of, **11**:196
Invasion, as microbial virulence factor, **8**:98–99
Inverse bobbing, **5**:259
Inversion recovery (IR) imaging, **5**:69
Inverted follicular keratosis, **4**:215, 215*f*
Inverting prism
in operating microscope, **3**:262, 262*f*
in slit-lamp biomicroscope, **3**:251*f*, 252
Investigational device exemption (IDE), **13**:204
Invirase. *See* Saquinavir
Involutional ectropion, **7**:190–193, 191*f*, 192*f*
Involutional entropion, **7**:194–196, 195*f*, 197*f*
Involutional stenosis, nasolacrimal obstruction caused by, **7**:266
IO. *See* Inferior oblique muscles
Iodine, radioactive
for hyperthyroidism, **1**:211, **7**:52–53
orbital disease exacerbation and, **5**:333
nasolacrimal duct obstruction and, **7**:267
for thyroid scanning, **1**:210
thyroid uptake of, **1**:209
for uveal melanoma, **4**:284
Iodine 123, for thyroid scanning, **1**:210
Iodine 125, for uveal melanoma, **4**:284
Iodine 131, for hyperthyroidism, **1**:211
IOI (idiopathic orbital inflammation). *See* Nonspecific orbital inflammation
IOL power calculator, online post-refractive (ASCRS), **13**:188–189, 190*f*
IOLMaster, **3**:214–216, 216*f*, 218

IOLs. *See* Intraocular lenses
Ionic charge, of ocular medication, absorption affected by, **2**:326
Ionizing radiation. *See also* Radiation
anterior segment injury caused by, **8**:352–353
cataracts caused by, **11**:51–52
DNA repair after, **2**:170
in free-radical generation, **2**:312
Iontophoresis, for drug delivery, **2**:331
IOP. *See* Intraocular pressure
Iopidine. *See* Apraclonidine
IP. *See* Incontinentia pigmenti
IP$_3$. *See* Inositol-1,4,5-triphosphate
IPL. *See* Inner plexiform layer
IPM. *See* Interphotoreceptor matrix
Ipratropium, **1**:145, 145*t*
in combination agents, **1**:145*t*
iPRGCs. *See* Intrinsically photosensitive retinal ganglion cells
Ipsilateral gaze palsy, **5**:50
IPV (inactivated poliovirus vaccine/Salk vaccine), **1**:283
in combination vaccines, **1**:285
IR. *See* Inferior rectus muscles
IR (index of refraction). *See* Refractive index
IR (inversion recovery) imaging, **5**:69
Irbesartan, **1**:76*t*, 78*t*
IRBP. *See* Interphotoreceptor retinoid-binding protein
IRID1 gene, **10**:11*t*
Iridectomy
for angle-closure glaucoma, **10**:111, 201, 201*f*, 204
acute angle closure and, **10**:115, 116
chronic angle closure and, **10**:117–118
for bacterial keratitis, **8**:164
cataract surgery on inflamed eye and, **11**:207
for ICCE, **11**:214
for iris bombé in uveitis, **9**:296
with penetrating keratoplasty, **8**:420
in trabeculectomy, **10**:189–190, 191*f*
Irides. *See* Iris
Iridocapsular 2-loop intraocular lens, **3**:207, 207*f*
Iridocorneal endothelial (ICE) syndrome, **4**:104–105, 105*f*, **8**:344–345, 344*f*, **10**:128–130, 129*f*
Axenfeld-Rieger syndrome differentiated from, **10**:146*t*
glaucoma and, **4**:105, **10**:128–130, 129*f*
posterior polymorphous corneal dystrophy differentiated from, **8**:293
Iridocyclitis, **9**:78*t*, 79. *See also specific cause and* Anterior uveitis; Iritis
acute, **9**:84, 119–128, 119*f*, 120*f*
in ankylosing spondylitis, **1**:164, **9**:119*f*, 121
in Behçet disease, **1**:181
in Chikungunya fever, **9**:220
chronic, **9**:84–85, 128–134
in coccidioidomycosis, **9**:279
EBV infection and, **9**:208
Fuchs heterochromic (Fuchs uveitis syndrome), **9**:132–134, 133*f*
cataracts/cataract surgery in, **9**:133, 134, **11**:59, 60*f*
glaucoma and, **9**:133, 134, **10**:94–95, 95*f*
rubella reactivation and, **9**:48, 134, 211
glaucoma and, **9**:296
herpetic, **8**:114, 116–117, **9**:197, 198*f*

HLA-associated diseases and, **1**:165, **9**:120–121
  idiopathic, **9**:134
  iris nodules in, **4**:270*t*, 272*f*
  in juvenile idiopathic (chronic/rheumatoid) arthritis,
      1:166, **9**:128–132, 130*f*, 131*t*
  in Lyme disease, **12**:210
  in multiple sclerosis, **9**:136
  muscarinic antagonists for, **2**:341, 342
  in nocardiosis, **9**:256
  in sarcoidosis, **9**:174, 175*f*
  symptoms of, **9**:84–85
  in syphilis, **9**:245
  varicella-zoster infection and, **9**:197, 198*f*
Iridodialysis, **4**:19–20, 20*f*, 109, **8**:364, 364*f*, **10**:39*f*
  during cataract surgery, **11**:157
  cataract surgery in patient with, **11**:207–208, 207*f*
  pupil irregularity and, **5**:263
  repair of, **8**:381, 382*f*
Iridodonesis
  cataract surgery and, **11**:79, 197
  in dislocated lens in children, **6**:261
  in exfoliation syndrome/pseudoexfoliation, **10**:86–87
Iridogoniodysgenesis anomaly and syndrome, **6**:213,
      213*f*, **8**:255–263. *See also specific disorder and*
      Axenfeld-Rieger syndrome
Iridogoniodysplasia, familial glaucoma, **6**:213. *See also*
      Axenfeld-Rieger syndrome
Iridoplasty
  for angle-closure glaucoma, **10**:203
  for plateau iris, **10**:120, 120*f*, 203
Iridoplegia, familial (congenital mydriasis), **6**:229
Iridoschisis, **4**:102
  Axenfeld-Rieger syndrome differentiated from,
      10:146*t*
Iridotomy
  for acute angle closure, **10**:115, 116
  for angle-closure glaucoma, **10**:201, 201*f*, 202–203
      cataract extraction after, **10**:204
  for aqueous misdirection (malignant/ciliary block
      glaucoma), **10**:132
  for ectopia lentis, **10**:122
  for iris bombé in uveitis, **9**:296
  for occludable/narrow chamber angle, **10**:118
  for phacomorphic glaucoma, **10**:120–121, 121*f*
  for phakic IOL insertion, **13**:129
  for pigmentary glaucoma, **10**:89
  for plateau iris, **10**:119–120, 202
  for subacute/intermittent angle closure, **10**:117
Iris, **2**:41*f*, 51*f*, 52*f*, 56–61, 253
  abnormalities of
      anisocoria and, **5**:265*f*, 269–270, **6**:229–230
      in infants and children, **6**:223–231
      nystagmus and, **6**:223, 320
      pupil irregularity caused by, **5**:263
  absence of (aniridia), **2**:205–207, **4**:188, **6**:223–224,
      224*f*, **10**:142, 147, **11**:29–30, 29*f*
      cataract and, **6**:251*f*, **11**:29*f*, 30
          surgery for removal of, **11**:200
      glaucoma and (iris-induced angle closure), **10**:112,
          142, 147
          pediatric, **6**:238, **10**:142, 147
              Axenfeld-Rieger syndrome differentiated
              from, **10**:146*t*

mutation rate of, **2**:207
      nystagmus and, **6**:223, 320
      pupil irregularity and, **5**:263
      short arm 11 deletion syndrome/*PAX6* gene
          mutations and, **2**:141, 166, 205, 206, 216, **4**:188,
          6:223–224, **10**:142, **11**:29
      Wilms tumor and, **4**:188, **6**:224, **10**:147, **11**:29
  anatomy of, **2**:41*f*, 51*f*, 52*f*, 56–61, 58*f*, 59*f*, 60*f*,
      4:185–186, 186*f*
  angle closure and, **10**:110, 111*f*, 112
  anterior border/pigmented layer of, **2**:58, 60*f*, **4**:185,
      186*f*
  atrophy of, **4**:104, 105*f*, **8**:344, 344*f*, **10**:128, 129, 129*f*.
      See also Iridocorneal endothelial (ICE) syndrome
      in acute angle closure, **10**:115
      in Fuchs heterochromic iridocyclitis/uveitis, **9**:132,
          133, 133*f*
      in herpetic inflammation, **9**:198*f*, 199
  in Axenfeld-Rieger syndrome, **6**:213, 214
  biochemistry and metabolism of, **2**:253–264
  bowing of
      in pupillary block, **10**:110, 111*f*
      with reverse pupillary block, in pigmentary
          glaucoma, **10**:89, 90*f*
  collarette of, **2**:58, 59*f*
  coloboma of, **6**:224–225, 225*f*
      cataract surgery in patient with, **11**:196, 197*f*
  color of, in infants, **6**:169
  cysts of, **4**:270*t*, 272*f*
      muscarinic therapy and, **2**:338, 340
      primary, **6**:226–227, 226*f*
      secondary, **6**:227
  development of, **2**:137
  dyscoria and, **6**:223
  ectropion of, congenital, **6**:231
      glaucoma in neurofibromatosis and, **6**:370
  epithelial invasion of, **4**:270*t*
  evaluation of
      before cataract surgery, **11**:79
      in glaucoma, **10**:30–31
          in children, **6**:237
      in pupillary examination, **5**:262
  healing/repair of, **4**:16–17
  heterochromia of (heterochromia iridis)
      in Fuchs heterochromic iridocyclitis/uveitis, **9**:133,
          133*f*, **10**:94
      in Horner syndrome, **5**:266
      pediatric, **6**:227–228, 228*f*, 228*t*
          in leukemia, **6**:354
      in siderosis bulbi, **11**:54*f*
  hypoplasia of, **6**:213, 214. *See also* Axenfeld-Rieger
      syndrome
  immunologic microenvironment of, **9**:61
  incarceration of, after penetrating keratoplasty, **8**:421
  innervation of, **2**:58
  intramuscular circle of, **2**:38, 39*f*
  juvenile xanthogranuloma affecting, **4**:191, 270*t*,
      6:226, 351, 352*f*, **9**:286
  in leukemia, **4**:271*t*, 272*f*, 327, **6**:351, 354
  melanocytoma of, **4**:268
  melanoma of, **4**:193–194, 194*f*, 268–271, 269*f*, 271*t*,
      273*f*
  metastatic disease of, **4**:271*t*, 316, 316*f*, 317*f*

neoplastic disorders of, **4:**193–194, 194*f*
  in children, **6:**351–352, 352*f*
neovascularization of (rubeosis iridis), **4:**192, 192*t*, 193*f*
  in branch retinal vein occlusion, **12:**124
  in central retinal artery occlusion, **12:**140
  in central retinal vein occlusion, **12:**128–129
    photocoagulation for, **12:**132
  in diabetes mellitus, **4:**166, 166*f*, **12:**108–109
  glaucoma and, **4:**192, **10:**30–31, 37, 125, 125*f*, 125*t*,
    126*f*, 201. *See also* Neovascular glaucoma
    incisional surgery contraindicated in, **10:**185
  in infants and children, **10:**141*t*
    laser iridotomy contraindicated in, **10:**202
  in ocular ischemic syndrome, **12:**133, 134, 134*f*
  in retinoblastoma, **4:**179, 180*f*, 303
nodules of. *See* Iris nodules
persistent pupillary membranes and, **6:**228, 229*f*
pigment epithelium of. *See* Iris pigment epithelium
pigmentation of, **2:**56
  development of, **2:**137, **6:**169
  exfoliation syndrome/glaucoma and, **10:**87
  in pigment dispersion syndrome/pigmentary
    glaucoma, **10:**88, 88*f*
  prostaglandin analogues/latanoprost affecting,
    2:354, **10:**162*t*, 166
plateau, **10:**5*t*, 7*t*, 112, 119–120, 120*f*
  laser iridotomy in diagnosis of, **10:**202
posterior pigmented layer of, **2:**58–60, 58*f*
  development of, **2:**137
posterior synechiae and, **6:**231
pupillary abnormalities and, **5:**263, **6:**228–231, 231*f*
repair of defects in, with penetrating keratoplasty,
  8:420
rubella (congenital) and, **9:**210
in sarcoidosis, **9:**87*f*, 175, 175*f*
segmental palsy of, anisocoria and, **5:**265*f*
signal transduction in, **2:**258–261
smooth muscle in, **2:**253–254
stroma of, **2:**56, 60*f*, **4:**185–186
  cysts of, **6:**227
topography of, **2:**41*f*, **4:**185–186, 186*f*
transillumination of, **6:**231
  in albinism, **4:**149*f*, **6:**231, 298, 301*f*
  in pigment dispersion syndrome, **10:**87, 88, 88*f*
traumatic damage to
  anisocoria and, **5:**265*f*, 269–270
  during cataract surgery, **11:**144*t*, 157
  cataract surgery in patient with, **11:**207–208, 207*f*
  iridodialysis, **4:**19–20, 20*f*, 109
    cataract surgery and, **11:**157, 207–208, 207*f*
  pupil irregularity and, **5:**263
  repair of, **4:**16–17, **8:**380–381, 381*f*
  tumors of, **4:**193–194, 194*f*
    in children, **6:**351–352, 352*f*
  in uveitis, **9:**86*t*, 88. *See also* Iridocyclitis; Iritis
  vessels of, **2:**58, 59*f*
    development of, **2:**138
Iris bombé
  glaucoma and, **9:**89, 296, **10:**30, 130, 130*f*
    in children, **6:**239–240
  uveitis and, **9:**89, 296
    angle closure/angle-closure glaucoma and, **9:**89,
      296

Iris–ciliary body smooth muscle, **2:**253–254
"Iris claw" (Worst/Artisan) lens, **3:**207, 208*f*
Iris clip intraocular lenses, **3:**207, 207*f*
  pseudophakic bullous keratopathy and, **11:**167
Iris diaphragm/iris diaphragm pattern, **2:**56, **5:**183
Iris dilator. *See* Dilator muscle
Iris-fixated (iris-supported) phakic intraocular lenses,
  13:4*t*, 126, 127*t*, 129–130, 130*f*. *See also* Phakic
    intraocular lenses
  complications of, **13:**135
  results with, **13:**132*t*
  sizing, **13:**130, 130*f*
Iris freckle, **4:**270*t*, 272*f*, **6:**351
Iris hooks
  for pupil expansion, **11:**194, 194*f*
  for zonular incompetence, **11:**199
Iris hypoplasia, **6:**213, 214. *See also* Axenfeld-Rieger
    syndrome
Iris-induced angle closure, **6:**238, **10:**112, 142, 147
Iris mamillations, **6:**226, 226*f*
Iris nevus, **4:**193, 265–266, 265*f*, 270*t*
  in children, **6:**351
Iris nevus syndrome (Cogan-Reese syndrome), **4:**104,
    105*f*, 270*t*, **8:**345, **10:**128, 129. *See also* Iridocorneal
      endothelial (ICE) syndrome
Iris nodosa, in syphilis, **9:**245
Iris nodules, **4:**270–271*t*, 272*f*. *See also* Lisch nodules
  in children, **6:**225–226, 225*f*, 226*f*
  differential diagnosis of, **4:**270–271*t*
  in leukemia, **4:**271*t*, 272*f*, 327
  in metastatic disease, **4:**271*t*
  in neurofibromatosis, **5:**340, 340*f*, **6:**225, 225*f*,
    365–366, 366*f*
  in retinoblastoma, **4:**271*t*, 303
  in sarcoidosis, **4:**190, 272*f*, **9:**87*f*, 175, 175*f*
  in syphilis, **9:**245
  in uveitis, **9:**85, 87*f*, 88
Iris papulosa, in syphilis, **9:**245
Iris pigment epithelium, **2:**58*f*, **4:**186, 186*f*
  cysts of, **4:**270*t*, 272*f*, **6:**226, 226*f*
    at pupillary border (central/pupillary cysts),
      6:227
  development of, **2:**137
  in diabetic retinopathy, **4:**166, 166*f*
  in healing/repair, **4:**16
  in pigment dispersion syndrome, **10:**88, 88*f*
  proliferation of, **4:**270*t*
Iris plane, phacoemulsification at, **11:**119–120, 120*f*
Iris processes, **2:**51*f*
Iris retractor, for intraoperative floppy iris syndrome,
  11:155
Iris roseola, in syphilis, **9:**245
Iris sphincter. *See* Sphincter muscle
Iris suture fixation, peripheral, for intraocular lens
    decentration, **11:**163–164, 164*f*
Iritis, **9:**78*t*, 79. *See also specific cause and* Anterior
      uveitis; Iridocyclitis
  acute/nongranulomatous, **9:**84, 119–128, 119*f*, 120*f*
  in ankylosing spondylitis, **9:**119*f*, 121
  in Behçet disease, **12:**194
  chronic, **9:**120
  glaucoma and, **10:**94
    incisional surgery contraindicated in, **10:**185

in glaucomatocyclitic crisis (Posner-Schlossman
    syndrome), 9:124–125, **10**:94
herpetic, **8**:108*t*, **9**:197
HLA-associated diseases and, **9**:120–121
in inflammatory bowel disease, **9**:123
after laser trabeculoplasty, **10**:183
muscarinic antagonists for, **2**:341, 342
mydriasis in treatment of, **2**:341
after phakic intraocular lens insertion, **13**:133*t*
    iris-fixated PIOLs, **13**:135
in psoriasis/psoriatic arthritis, **9**:123
in reactive arthritis/Reiter syndrome, **8**:209, **9**:121, 123
traumatic, **8**:363
tubulointerstitial nephritis and, **9**:119, 124
varicella-zoster infection and, **9**:197
viral, **9**:220
IRMAs. *See* Intraretinal microvascular abnormalities
Iron
    in aqueous humor, **2**:267
    colloidal, for tissue staining, **4**:30, 31*t*
    corneal deposits of, **8**:335–336, 336*f*, 337*t*
        in keratoconus, **4**:91, 93*f*, **8**:298, 299*f*, 335–336
    foreign body of, **8**:337*t*, 371–372, 371*f*, **12**:328
        siderosis caused by, **4**:124, **11**:53, 54*f*, **12**:328, 328*t*
    in free-radical formation, **2**:311–312, 314
    in hemosiderosis oculi, glaucoma and, **4**:108–109, 108*f*
Iron deficiency anemia, **1**:147, 148
    anemia of chronic disease differentiated from, **1**:147
Iron lines, **8**:336, 336*f*
    in pterygium, **8**:332
Irradiance, **3**:16, 18
    as image characteristic, **3**:19
    for medical lasers, **3**:18*t*, 21
Irregular astigmatism, **3**:93, 115–116, 164. *See also*
    Higher-order aberrations; Wavefront aberrations
    after arcuate keratotomy, **13**:52
    causes of, **3**:240–241, 241*f*
    chalazia causing, **3**:164
    contact lens masking of, **3**:190
    corneal topography in detection/management of,
        8:43, 43*f*, 44, **13**:13–14, 14*f*, 38–39, 38*f*
    keratorefractive/refractive surgery and, **3**:232,
        237–241, 239*f*, 241*f*, **13**:16, 38–39, 38*f*, 171
    after limbal relaxing incisions, **13**:52
    monocular diplopia and, **3**:164
    retinoscopy of, **3**:129, **8**:45
    scleral lenses for, **3**:193
    wavefront analysis and, **3**:237–240, 239*f*, **13**:9. *See also*
        Wavefront analysis
Irrigation. *See also* Ophthalmic irrigants
    for chemical injuries, **8**:355
    for conjunctival foreign body, **8**:370
    for hyphema, **8**:368
    of lacrimal drainage system
        for acquired obstruction, **7**:259, 260*f*
        for canalicular obstruction, **7**:259–261, 261*f*, 263
        for canalicular trauma, **7**:272
        for congenital obstruction, **7**:251–252, 253*f*
    in phacoemulsification, **11**:108
        posterior fluid misdirection and, **11**:152–153
        strategies for, **11**:125–126
        with toxic solutions, corneal edema caused by,
            11:147, 151–152

for plant materials, **8**:362
solutions for, **2**:392
    endothelial changes caused by, **8**:384–385
IRS. *See* Immune reconstitution syndromes
IRSG. *See* Intergroup Rhabdomyosarcoma Study Group
IRU. *See* Immune recovery uveitis
IRVAN. *See* Idiopathic retinal vasculitis/aneurysms/
    neuroretinitis
Irvine-Gass syndrome, **11**:162, 181, **12**:142, 314. *See also*
    Cystoid macular edema
ISA. *See* Intrinsic sympathomimetic activity
Ischemia, **1**:100
    cardiac. *See* Ischemic heart disease
    carotid territory. *See also* Carotid occlusive disease
        transient visual loss and, **5**:173, 174, 177–183, 179*f*,
            183–184
    cataracts caused by, **11**:64
    cerebral, **1**:91–95. *See also* Stroke
    choroidal, **12**:176–180, 177*f*, 178*f*, 179*f*, 180*f*
    facial pain associated with, **5**:301
    IOP-induced, in acute angle closure, **10**:115
    macular, in diabetes mellitus, **12**:103
    occipital, transient visual loss caused by, **5**:185–186
    ocular (ocular ischemic syndrome), **5**:183–184, 184*f*,
        9:287–288, **12**:94, 133–135, 134*f*
    retinal, **4**:156–164. *See also* Retinal ischemia
    time course of visual loss and, **5**:91
Ischemic/nonperfused central retinal vein occlusion,
    4:164, 165*f*, **12**:127, 128, 129*f*
Ischemic heart disease, **1**:99–113. *See also* Acute
    coronary syndrome; Angina pectoris
    asymptomatic patients with, **1**:101, 102, 104
    clinical syndromes in, **1**:101–104
    in diabetes mellitus, **1**:133*t*, 207
    diagnosis of
        invasive procedures for, **1**:107
        noninvasive procedures for, **1**:104–107
    heart failure and, **1**:116, 120
    hypercholesterolemia and, **1**:100, 131, 132–133, 133*t*
    hypertension management in, **1**:79*t*, 84
    incidence of, **1**:99
    management of, **1**:107–113, 109*t*
    ophthalmic considerations and, **1**:128
    pathophysiology of, **1**:100
    risk factors for, **1**:99, 100–101, 132–133, 133*t*
        hypercholesterolemia management and, **1**:134,
            134*f*, 135*t*
    screening for, **1**:271–272
Ischemic optic neuropathy
    anterior, **5**:125–129, 126*t*
        arteritic, **5**:125, 125–127, 126*f*, 126*t*, 316
        nonarteritic, **5**:125, 126*f*, 126*t*, 127–129, 128*f*
        in giant cell arteritis/AAION, **5**:125, 125–127, 126*f*,
            126*t*, 319–320
    posterior, **5**:157–158
Ischemic stroke, **1**:91, 92, 94. *See also* Stroke
    emergency transport and, **1**:289, 291
Ischemic uveitis, **5**:184
Iseikonic lenses/spectacles, **3**:140, 321
Isentress. *See* Raltegravir
Ishihara color plates, **12**:48
    in anomalous trichromatism, **12**:213
Island of vision, in perimetry, **5**:99

Islet cell injection, for diabetes mellitus, **1**:202
Ismelin. *See* Guanethidine
Ismotic. *See* Isosorbide
ISNT rule, **10**:47–48
Isoantibody production, posttransfusion, **1**:154
Isochromosomes, **2**:154
Isoetharine, **1**:145
Isoflurophate, **2**:336*f*
Isoforms, **2**:168
Isolated (simplex) case/genetic disease, **2**:161, 192
Isolated stromal rejection, **8**:429. *See also* Rejection
Isolation techniques, in ocular microbiology, **8**:103
Isoniazid, **1**:19, 39
     pharmacogenetics of, **2**:229
Isophane insulin suspension (NPH insulin), **1**:196, 196*t*
Isoproterenol, **2**:259*t*
Isopter, **5**:99, **10**:55
Isoptin. *See* Verapamil
Isopto Atropine. *See* Atropine
Isopto Carbachol. *See* Carbachol
Isopto Carpine. *See* Pilocarpine
Isopto Cetamide. *See* Sulfacetamide
Isopto Eserine. *See* Physostigmine
Isopto Homatropine. *See* Homatropine
Isopto Hyoscine. *See* Scopolamine
Isosorbide, **2**:356
Isospora belli (isosporiasis), in HIV infection/AIDS, **1**:38
Isotretinoin
     corneal pigmentation caused by, **8**:349
     laser skin resurfacing contraindicated in patients
          taking, **7**:231
     ocular effects of, **1**:301*t*
     refractive surgery in patient taking, **13**:31, 70
     retinopathy caused by, **12**:269
Isotypes, **9**:45, 46, 47*t*
Isradipine, **1**:77*t*
Istalol. *See* Timolol
ITP. *See* Idiopathic thrombocytopenic purpura
Itraconazole, **1**:20, 54*t*, 64–65, **2**:379*t*, 380
     for fungal keratitis, **8**:166
IU. *See* Intermediate uveitis
Ivermectin
     for loiasis, **8**:171
     for onchocerciasis, **9**:242
IVTA (intravitreal triamcinolone acetonide). *See*
     Triamcinolone
Ixodes ticks, Lyme disease transmitted by, **1**:14–15,
     9:250

J

J-loop posterior chamber IOL, **3**:209*f*
Jabs and jolts syndrome, **5**:299
Jackson cross cylinder
     optimal cylinder power and, **3**:319
     for refraction, **3**:130, 132
          in monocular diplopia, **3**:164
Jaeger numbers, **3**:290
Jansky-Bielschowsky disease/syndrome, **6**:401*t*
     pigmentary retinopathy in, **12**:251*t*, 260
Januvia. *See* Sitagliptin
Japanese encephalitis vaccine, **1**:286

Jarisch-Herxheimer reaction
     in Lyme disease treatment, **1**:16, **9**:253
     in syphilis treatment, **9**:249
Javal-Schiøtz keratometers, **3**:264, 266*f*
Jaw claudication
     in AAION, **5**:125
     in giant cell arteritis, **5**:319
Jaw thrust/modified jaw thrust, for opening airway,
     1:290
Jaw-winking ptosis/syndrome
     Marcus Gunn, **5**:279, 279*f*, 284, **6**:180, **7**:203, 207, 208*f*
          synkinesis in, **6**:180, **7**:203, 207, 208*f*
JC virus, in progressive multifocal leukoencephalopathy,
     5:361
Jerk nystagmus, **5**:243, 244, **6**:317, 318*f*, 321, 322 323,
     324*f*, 325. *See also* Nystagmus
     in multiple sclerosis, **5**:325
JIA. *See* Juvenile idiopathic (chronic/rheumatoid)
     arthritis
JOAG. *See* Juvenile open-angle glaucoma
Joint Commission on Accreditation of Healthcare
     Organizations, Universal Protocol of, **1**:303,
     306–310
Jones I and Jones II tests, **7**:259
Jones tubes, **7**:186, 265
Josamycin, **1**:50*t*, 61
Joule, laser energy reading in, **3**:18*t*, 21
JRA (juvenile rheumatoid arthritis). *See* Juvenile
     idiopathic (chronic/rheumatoid) arthritis
Jugular bulb, **5**:26
Jugular veins, external/internal, **5**:26
Junctional complexes
     in corneal endothelium, **2**:47
     in retinal pigment epithelium, **2**:72
Junctional complexes (cardiac arrhythmia), premature
     (PJCs), **1**:121, 122*t*
Junctional nevus, **7**:164
     of conjunctiva, **4**:65, **8**:236
          in children, **6**:349
     of eyelid, **4**:224–225, 225*f*, **7**:164
Junctional rhythm, atrioventricular, **1**:122*t*
"Junctional syndrome," **5**:160, 160*f*
Junctional tachycardia, **1**:124*t*
Junk DNA, **2**:165–166
Juvenile ankylosing spondylitis, **1**:166, **6**:271
Juvenile chronic arthritis. *See* Juvenile idiopathic
     (chronic/rheumatoid) arthritis
Juvenile fibroma/fibromatosis, of orbit, **6**:343
Juvenile glaucoma. *See* Glaucoma, childhood; Juvenile
     open-angle glaucoma
Juvenile hereditary epithelial (Meesmann) dystrophy,
     8:268*t*, 270*t*, 272–273, 273*f*
     genetics of, **8**:269*t*
Juvenile idiopathic (chronic/rheumatoid) arthritis,
     1:166–167, **6**:267–271, 269*t*, 271*t*, **9**:128–132, 130*f*,
     131*t*
     cataract and, **9**:129, 130, 130*f*, 131–132, 293
     classification of, **1**:167, **9**:129–130
     criteria for, **6**:267–268, 269*t*
     eye examination schedule for children with, **6**:270,
          271*t*, **9**:130, 131*t*
     glaucoma and, **9**:132
     HLA association in, **6**:269, **9**:72*t*, 129

iridocyclitis in, **9**:128–132, 130*f*, 131*t*
  management of, **9**:130–132
  nomenclature for, **6**:267–268, 269*t*
  pauciarticular (oligoarticular/oligoarthritis), **1**:166,
    6:269, 269*t*, **9**:129
  polyarticular (polyarthritis), **1**:166, **6**:269, 269*t*, **9**:129
  prognosis for, **9**:129–130
  systemic-onset (Still disease), **1**:167, **9**:129
  uveitis in, **6**:268–271, 270*f*, 271*t*, **9**:84–85, 128–132,
    130*f*, 131*t*
    cataracts and, **9**:129, 130, 130*f*, 131–132, 293
Juvenile macular degeneration (Stargardt disease/
    fundus flavimaculatus), **4**:172, 174*f*, **6**:292–293, 293*f*,
    12:234–236, 235*f*, 236*t*
  ABC/ABCR transporter mutations causing, **2**:296,
    4:172, **6**:293, **12**:233, 234
  cone–rod dystrophy and, **6**:293, **12**:233, 235
  gene for, **12**:222, 233, 234
  retinal pigment epithelium in, **2**:309, **12**:234, 235*f*
Juvenile nephronophthisis, retinal degeneration and,
    12:254
Juvenile-onset diabetes mellitus. *See* Diabetes mellitus,
    type 1
Juvenile-onset myopia, **3**:118
Juvenile-onset vitelliform macular dystrophy. *See* Best
    disease
Juvenile open-angle glaucoma, **6**:234, **10**:5*t*, 139, 140*t*,
    145. *See also* Glaucoma, childhood
  genetics of, **10**:142, 145
Juvenile ossifying fibroma (fibro-osseous dysplasia), of
    orbit, **4**:246, 246*f*, **6**:343
Juvenile pilocytic astrocytoma, **4**:257
Juvenile retinoschisis. *See* Retinoschisis, X-linked
Juvenile rheumatoid arthritis. *See* Juvenile idiopathic
    (chronic/rheumatoid) arthritis
Juvenile spondyloarthropathy, **1**:166
Juvenile systemic granulomatosis, familial (Blau
    syndrome), **6**:274–275, **9**:176
Juvenile xanthogranuloma, **6**:226, 351, 352*f*, **7**:85, **8**:242,
    9:286
  glaucoma associated with, **6**:351, **10**:28
  of iris, **4**:191, 270*t*, **6**:226, 351, 352*f*
  of uveal tract, **4**:191, 191*f*
  uveitis in children differentiated from, **6**:276*t*
Juxtacanalicular meshwork/tissue, **2**:53, **10**:16, 17*f*
  development of, **2**:136
Juxtafoveal/parafoveal retinal telangiectasia, **12**:145–147,
    145*f*, 146*f*
JXG. *See* Juvenile xanthogranuloma

K

K. *See* Potassium
K_m (Michaelis/affinity constant), "sugar" cataract
    development and, **11**:15
K (keratometry) readings, **3**:168. *See also* Keratometry
  simulated (SIM K), **3**:267
K system (koniocellular system), **6**:42, 44, **10**:40–41
  development of, **6**:44
Kaletra. *See* Lopinavir/ritonavir
Kalt forceps, **11**:92, 92*f*
Kamra Inlay, **13**:54, 200

Kanamycin, **1**:61–62, **2**:368*t*, 375–376
  ototoxicity of, mitochondrial DNA mutations and,
    2:176
Kandori, fleck retina of, **12**:218
Kaposi sarcoma, **1**:29, 40, **7**:176–177, 177*f*, **8**:242, 243*f*
  human herpes virus 8 causing, **1**:22, **8**:129, 242, **9**:312
  ocular adnexal, **7**:176–177, 177*f*, **9**:312, 312*f*
  treatment of, **1**:40
Kaposi sarcoma–associated herpesvirus/human herpes
    virus 8, **1**:22, **8**:129, 242, **9**:312
Kappa (κ) statistic, **1**:339
Kartagener syndrome, **1**:142
Karyotype/karyotyping, **2**:154, 198–199, 200*f*
Kasabach-Merritt syndrome, **6**:339, **7**:63
Kawasaki disease (mucocutaneous lymph node
    syndrome), **1**:177*t*, **6**:201–202
Kayser-Fleischer ring, **6**:221, **8**:327, 327*f*, 337*t*, **11**:57
kb. *See* Kilobase
KC. *See* Keratoconus
KCS (keratoconjunctivitis sicca). *See* Dry-eye syndrome
Kearns-Sayre syndrome, **2**:174–175, **5**:337, 337*f*, **6**:137,
    398, **12**:251*t*, 265, 265*f*
  mitochondrial DNA deletions and, **2**:173, 174–175,
    6:398
  pigmentary retinopathy and, **12**:251*t*, 265, 265*f*
Keflex. *See* Cephalexin
Kefurox. *See* Cefuroxime
Kefzol. *See* Cefazolin
Kelman phaco tip, **11**:105, 105*f*
Kelman tripod ("Pregnant 7") anterior chamber IOL,
    3:211, 211*f*
Keloids
  corneal, **8**:341
    congenital, **8**:264
  refractive surgery in patient with history of, **13**:70
Kenalog. *See* Triamcinolone
Kennedy disease, **2**:209
Keplerian (astronomical) telescope, **3**:81–83, 82*f*, 83*f*,
    252
  in operating microscope, **3**:262, 262*f*
  in slit-lamp biomicroscope, **3**:82*f*, 252
Keppra. *See* Levetiracetam
KERA gene, in cornea plana, **8**:254–255
Keratan sulfate
  in cornea, **2**:250, **8**:7
  cornea plana and, **8**:254–255
  macular corneal dystrophy and, **4**:96, **8**:283
  mucopolysaccharidoses and, **8**:305
Keratectasia, **8**:258–260, 262*t*
  after LASIK, **13**:115
Keratectomy, **8**:402–403
  mechanical, **8**:402
  multizone, **13**:24, 24*f*
  photorefractive (PRK). *See* Photorefractive
    keratectomy
  phototherapeutic (PTK), **8**:402–403, 413
    for calcific band keratopathy, **8**:344
    for corneal/epithelial erosions
      after LASIK, **13**:105
      recurrent, **8**:85
    for corneal haze after surface ablation, **13**:101
    for epithelial basement membrane dystrophy,
      8:272

herpes simplex virus keratitis and, **13**:166, 167
  for striae in LASIK flaps, **13**:108
  superficial, **8**:402–403
Keratectomy/sclerostomy, in trabeculectomy, **10**:189,
  191*f*
Keratic precipitates, **8**:25, **9**:85, 86*f*, 87–88
  in Fuchs heterochromic iridocyclitis/uveitis, **9**:132, 133*f*
  in glaucomatocyclitic crisis (Posner-Schlossman
    syndrome), **10**:94
  in herpetic ocular infection, **9**:197–198
  in inflammatory glaucoma, **10**:94
  in phacoantigenic glaucoma, **10**:92
  in sarcoidosis, 9:174, 9:86f 175 175f
  in sympathetic ophthalmia, **4**:189, **9**:178
  in uveitis, **9**:85, 86*f*, 87–88, 119
Keratin, in adenoid cystic carcinoma, **4**:236
Keratin gene mutation, in Meesmann corneal dystrophy,
  8:268, 269*t*, 272
Keratinization (keratinized/degenerated epithelial cells),
  8:21
  in immune-mediated keratoconjunctivitis, **8**:182*t*
  in meibomian gland dysfunction, **8**:65
  in superior limbic keratoconjunctivitis, **8**:82
  in vitamin A deficiency, **8**:77, 78, 78*f*
Keratinizing squamous cell carcinoma, well-
  differentiated (keratoacanthoma), eyelid, **4**:215*t*,
  216, 216*f*, **7**:167–168, 167*f*
Keratinoid degeneration, **8**:334–335, 335*f*. *See also*
  Spheroidal degeneration
Keratitis, **8**:20–21*t*, 24–25, 26*f*, 27*f*, 27*t*, 28*f*, 101*t*
  Acanthamoeba, **4**:54, 84–85, 86*f*, **8**:167–169, 168*f*
    contact lens wear and, **3**:196, **4**:84–85, **8**:167, 168
    herpes simplex keratitis differentiated from,
      8:168–169
    isolation techniques for diagnosis of, **4**:85, **8**:103
    stains and culture media for identification of, **8**:103*t*
    treatment of, **2**:385–386, **8**:168–169
  bacterial, **4**:82, 83*f*, **8**:158–164, 160*f*, 160*t*, 162*t*. *See
    also* Keratitis, infectious/microbial
    clinical presentation of, **8**:159
    contact lens wear and, **3**:180, **8**:159
      for orthokeratology, **13**:64
    intrauterine, **8**:263–264
    laboratory evaluation/causes of, **8**:159–161, 160*t*
    management of, **8**:161–164, 162*t*
    pathogenesis of, **8**:159
    stains and culture media for identification of,
      8:103*t*
  blepharitis and, **8**:144*t*, 145–146, 146*f*
  Candida causing, **8**:165
  in Cogan syndrome, **8**:209, 210
  contact lens wear and, **3**:180, 196, 198–199, 198*f*, 201,
    4:84–85, **8**:159, 165, 167, 168
    for orthokeratology, **13**:64
  corticosteroid route of administration in, **2**:360*t*
  dendritic
    contact lens wear and, **3**:198–199
    herpes simplex virus causing, **4**:82, 84*f*, **8**:107, 110,
      111, 111*f*
    herpes zoster causing, **8**:120
  diffuse lamellar/interface (DLK), after LASIK,
    13:108–111, 109*f*, 109*t*, 110*t*, 111*f*
    glaucoma/IOP elevation and, **13**:97, 174, 195

infectious keratitis differentiated from, **13**:110–111,
  110*t*, 111*f*
disciform, herpes simplex virus causing, **4**:82–83,
  8:114, 114*f*
  persistent bullous keratopathy and, **8**:117
epithelial
  adenovirus causing, **8**:124, 126*f*
  herpes simplex virus causing, **8**:110–113, 111*f*, 112*f*
  measles virus causing, **8**:129, **9**:212
  varicella-zoster virus causing, **8**:117–119
Epstein-Barr virus causing, **8**:122–123, 123*f*
exposure, **8**:80
  in craniosynostosis-induced proptosis, **6**:388–389
Fuchs superficial marginal, 8:340
fungal, **4**:83–84, 85*f*, **8**:164–167, 165*f*
  plant sources of, **8**:362
gonococcal conjunctivitis and, **8**:152
herpes simplex, **4**:82–83, 84*f*, **8**:109, 110–116, 111*f*,
  112*f*, 114*f*, 115*f*, **9**:197. *See also* Herpes simplex
  virus, keratitis caused by
  Acanthamoeba keratitis differentiated from,
    8:168–169
  in HIV infection/AIDS, **9**:313–314, 313*f*
  in infants and children, **6**:185
  neurotrophic keratopathy/ulcers caused by, **4**:83,
    8:87, 117
  refractive surgery and, **13**:166–167
  topical antiviral agents for, **2**:380, 381*t*, 382–383
herpes zoster, **8**:120
in HIV infection/AIDS, **9**:313–314, 313*f*
  after LASIK, **13**:182
infectious/microbial, **4**:82–87, **8**:101*t*, 158–171, 160*f*,
  160*t*, 162*t*, 168*f*. *See also specific infectious agent*
  clinical presentation of, **8**:159
  contact lens wear and, **3**:180, 196, 198, 201, **8**:159,
    165, 167, 168
    for orthokeratology, **13**:64
  intrauterine, **8**:263–264
  laboratory evaluation/causes of, **8**:159–161, 160*t*
  management of, **8**:161–164, 162*t*
  orthokeratology and, **13**:64
  pathogenesis of, **8**:159
  after penetrating keratoplasty, **8**:425, 425*f*
  after photoablation, **13**:97–99, 98–99, 99*f*, 110–111,
    110*t*, 111*f*
  stains and culture in identification of, **8**:103*t*
interstitial, **4**:86–87, 87*f*
  glaucoma and, **10**:131
  herpetic, **4**:82–83, 84*f*, 87, **8**:113, 114*f*
  HTLV-1–related, **9**:219
  in infectious disease, **8**:207–209, 208*f*
  syphilitic, **4**:87, 87*f*, **6**:186, 221, **8**:207–209, 208*f*,
    9:243, 244*f*
    intrauterine infection and, **4**:87, **8**:264
intrauterine, **8**:263–264
  keratectasia caused by, **8**:259
in Lyme disease, **5**:364, **9**:252
measles virus causing, **8**:129, **9**:212
Microsporida causing, **8**:170, **9**:313, 313*f*
necrotizing, **8**:25
  herpes simplex causing, **8**:115, 115*f*, 116
  noninfectious, **4**:87
  nonnecrotizing, **8**:27*f*

in onchocerciasis, 8:141
pain caused by, 5:300
peripheral, 8:27t
  scleritis and, 8:220
  ulcerative, 8:211–213, 211t, 212f, 339
    differential diagnosis of, 8:211t
    in polyarteritis nodosa/microscopic polyangiitis,
      1:179, 9:143
    in systemic immune-mediated diseases,
      8:211–213, 211t, 212f
    in Wegener granulomatosis, 1:179
punctate, 8:20t, 25, 26f, 27t
  contact lens wear and, 3:198
in reactive arthritis/Reiter syndrome, 8:209, 9:123
in rosacea, 8:70, 70f
rubella, 9:211
scleritis and, 8:220, 221, 221–222, 221f
sicca. See Dry-eye syndrome
staphylococcal, 8:145–146, 146f
stromal, 8:21t, 25, 27f, 27t
  in Cogan syndrome, 8:209, 210
  Epstein-Barr virus causing, 8:122–123, 123f
  herpes simplex virus causing, 4:82, 84f, 8:108t,
    113–116, 114f, 115f
    penetrating keratoplasty for, 8:117
  in herpes zoster ophthalmicus, 8:120
  microsporidial, 8:170
  necrotizing, 8:25
  nonnecrotizing, 8:27f
  nonsuppurative, 8:21t, 25, 27f, 27t
    systemic infections and, 8:169–170
  pressure-induced (PISK), after LASIK, 13:112, 112f
  scleritis and, 8:221
  suppurative, 8:21t, 25, 27f, 27t
  syphilitic, 8:207, 208
syphilitic, 4:87, 87f, 6:185, 186, 221, 8:207–209, 208f,
  9:243, 244f
  intrauterine, 8:263–264
Thygeson superficial punctate, 8:204–207, 206f
toxic, 8:360. See also Toxic conjunctivitis/
    keratoconjunctivitis
ulcerative, 8:211–213, 211t, 212f, 339
  differential diagnosis of, 8:211t
  in rosacea, 8:70
  in systemic immune-mediated diseases, 8:211–213,
    211t, 212f
varicella-zoster virus causing, 8:117–119
in vitamin A deficiency, 8:78
yeast, 8:166
Keratoacanthoma, eyelid, 4:215t, 216, 216f, 7:167–168,
  167f
Keratocan, mutation in gene for, in cornea plana, 8:255
Keratoconjunctivitis. See also Conjunctivitis
  adenoviral, 8:124, 125, 125f, 126f
  atopic, 6:200, 8:190–192, 191f, 9:55
  chlamydial, 8:154
  contact lens superior limbic (CLSLK), 3:198
  epidemic, 8:124, 125, 125f, 126f
    in children, 6:191
      preseptal cellulitis caused by, 6:195
  immune-mediated, ocular surface cytology in,
    8:182t
  microsporidial, 8:170

phlyctenular, in children, 6:351
plants causing, 8:362
sicca. See Dry-eye syndrome
superior limbic, 8:81–82, 82f
toxic
  contact lens solutions causing, 8:92
  medications causing, 8:359–361, 359t, 361f
vernal, 8:187–190, 188f, 189f
  atopic keratoconjunctivitis differentiated from,
    8:190, 191f
  in children, 6:198–200, 199f
Keratoconjunctivitis sicca
  cataract surgery in patient with, 11:190–191
  corneal melting/keratolysis and, 11:150, 191
Keratoconus, 4:91, 93f, 5:111, 6:212, 8:296–300, 297f,
  298f, 299f, 300f, 302t, 303f
  collagen crosslinking for, 13:123–124, 123f, 168
  contact lenses for, 3:190–191, 191f
  Descemet membrane rupture and, 4:18, 18f, 91, 93f
  ectasia after LASIK and, 13:115
  Fleischer ring in, 4:91, 93f, 8:298, 299f, 335–336, 337t
  in floppy eyelid syndrome, 8:81
  intrastromal corneal ring segments for, 13:58–60, 60f,
    62–63, 168
  Marfan syndrome and, 8:325
  posterior, 4:102
    central (posterior corneal depression), 6:215
    circumscribed, 8:258, 259f, 262t
  refractive surgery contraindicated in, 8:300, 13:16–17,
    18, 35, 38, 167–168
    corneal topography and, 8:43–44, 44f, 13:16–17,
      18–19, 19f, 38, 38f, 71, 167–168, 168f, 169f,
      170f
  scleral lenses for, 3:191, 193
  thermokeratoplasty for, 13:119
Keratocytes, 2:45, 249, 8:7
  differentiation of, 2:134
  stromal, corneal haze after surface ablation and,
    13:101
Keratoderma blennorrhagicum, in reactive arthritis,
  9:122, 122f
Keratoepithelin
  gene for, amyloidosis and, 8:317t
  transforming growth factor β–induced, in Reis-
    Bücklers corneal dystrophy, 8:276
Keratoglobus, 6:211, 8:302–303, 302t, 303f
Keratolimbal allograft, 8:398. See also Limbal
    transplantation
Keratolysis (corneal melting)
  cataract surgery and, 11:150
    in patient with dry eye, 11:150, 191
  gonococcal infection and, 8:134
  peripheral ulcerative keratitis and, 8:211, 212, 213
  refractive surgery and, 13:184
Keratomalacia, in vitamin A deficiency, 8:78, 79
Keratometry, 3:263–265, 263f, 264f, 265f, 266f, 8:38–39
  in contact lens fitting, 3:168
  in IOL power determination/selection, 3:216–217,
    217f, 11:84
  corneal irregularities and, 11:191
  refractive surgery and, 11:86, 13:187, 188
  unexpected refractive results after surgery and,
    11:168

in low vision/vision rehabilitation, 3:294
refractive surgery and, 3:232–235, 13:38
  IOL power calculation and, 11:86, 13:187, 188
  postoperative estimation of, 13:39
  toric IOLs, 13:143
values for, in infants and children, 6:168, 168f
Keratometry (K) readings, 3:168. *See also* Keratometry
  simulated (SIM K), 3:267
Keratomileusis, 13:21, 68. *See also* LASEK; LASIK
Keratoneuritis, radial, in *Acanthamoeba* keratitis,
  4:85
Keratopathy
  actinic (Labrador keratopathy/spheroidal
    degeneration), 4:88–89, 90f, 8:334–335, 335f
  annular, traumatic, 8:363
  band
    calcific (calcium hydroxyapatite deposition), 4:88,
      89f, 8:328, 342–344, 343f
    in sarcoidosis, 8:73
    in uveitis, 9:85, 291
    in juvenile idiopathic (chronic/rheumatoid)
      arthritis, 6:270, 270f, 9:129, 130, 130f, 132
    in pars planitis, 9:136
    in sarcoidosis, 9:175
    surgery for, 6:278
    in uveitis, 9:85, 291
  bullous, 4:89–91, 90f
    bandage contact lenses for, 8:403
    after cataract surgery, 4:89–91, 90f, 8:384–385,
      11:147, 147f, 167
    IOL design and, 11:167
    disciform keratitis and, 8:117
  climatic droplet, 8:334–335, 335f. *See also* Spheroidal
    degeneration
  exposure, 8:80
    in craniosynostosis-induced proptosis,
      6:388–389
  filamentary, 8:56, 57f, 60–61
    bandage contact lenses for, 8:403
  infectious crystalline, 4:85–86, 86f, 8:159, 160f
    after penetrating keratoplasty, 4:85, 8:425, 425f
  Labrador, 4:88–89, 90f, 8:334–335, 335f
  lipid, 8:342, 342f
    in herpes zoster ophthalmicus, 8:120, 121f
  measles, 8:129
  medications causing, 8:359–361, 359t, 361f
  neurotrophic, 8:87–89, 88f
    diabetic neuropathy and, 8:87
    esthesiometry in evaluation of, 8:30–31
    herpetic eye disease and, 8:87, 88, 117, 122
    postherpetic, 4:83, 84f
  punctate epithelial, 8:20t, 25, 26f, 27t
    exposure causing, 8:80
    microsporidial, 8:170
    staphylococcal blepharitis/blepharoconjunctivitis
      and, 8:145, 146f, 147
    topical anesthetic abuse causing, 8:90
  striate, intraocular surgery causing, 8:383
  toxic ulcerative, 8:86, 88
  vortex (hurricane/cornea verticillata), 8:310, 311f,
    346–348, 347t, 348f, 360
    in Fabry disease, 12:263, 264f
Keratophakia, 13:21, 53–55

Keratoplasty
  conductive, 13:4t, 22, 22f, 120–123, 121f, 153–154
    corneal transplantation after, 13:192
    for presbyopia, 13:120–123, 153–154
  for corneal edema after cataract surgery, 11:147
  endothelial, 8:413
    cataract surgery and, 11:141, 192
    in children, 8:413
    for corneal edema after cataract surgery, 11:147
    Descemet membrane (DMEK), 8:445
    Descemet stripping automated (DSAEK/DSEK),
      4:79, 8:413, 415–416t, 437–445
      advantages of, 8:416t, 438
      complications of
        intraoperative, 8:415t, 441, 441f
        postoperative, 8:415t, 442–445, 442f, 443f,
          444f
      disadvantages of, 8:416t, 438
      donor cornea preparation in, 8:438
      indications for, 8:415t, 437
      penetrating/selective keratoplasty compared
        with, 8:415–416t
      precut tissue for, 8:409, 438
      recipient eye preparation and, 8:439–441, 440f
      in triple procedure, 11:141
  indications for, 4:78–79, 79t
  for infantile corneal opacities, 6:219
  Intralase-enabled (IEK), precut tissue for, 8:409
  lamellar, 8:433–437
    advantages of, 8:434–435
    anterior, 8:433–435, 434f
    automated, 13:68
    deep anterior (DALK), 4:78, 8:300, 413, 415–416t,
      435–436
      advantages of, 8:416t
      in children, 8:431
      complications of
        intraoperative, 8:415t
        postoperative, 8:415t
      disadvantages of, 8:416t
      indications for, 8:415t
      for keratoconus, 8:300
      penetrating/selective keratoplasty compared
        with, 8:415–416t
      surgical technique for, 8:435–436
    disadvantages of, 8:435
    indications for, 8:413, 414t
    postoperative care and complications and,
      8:436–437
    rejection and, 8:436
    superficial anterior (SALK), 8:413, 415–416t,
      435
      advantages of, 8:416t
      complications of
        intraoperative, 8:415t
        postoperative, 8:415t
      disadvantages of, 8:416t
      indications for, 8:415t
      penetrating/selective keratoplasty compared
        with, 8:415–416t
      surgical technique for, 8:435
    surgical technique for, 8:435–436
    wound healing/repair and, 13:26

penetrating (PK), **8**:413, 415–416*t*, 417–430
    for *Acanthamoeba* keratitis, **8**:169
    advantages of, **8**:416*t*
    after arcuate keratotomy, **13**:52
    astigmatism after, control of, **8**:426–427, 427*f*
        corneal topography and, **8**:44, 426, 427*f*, **13**:20
        refractive surgery for, **13**:169–172
    for bacterial keratitis, **4**:82, 83*f*, **8**:164
    cataract/cataract surgery following, **11**:193
    cataract surgery and IOL implantation combined
        with (triple procedure), **11**:141, 192
    for chemical injuries, **8**:358
    in children, **8**:430–431, 431*t*
    for cicatricial pemphigoid, **8**:203
    complications of
        in children, **8**:430–431
        intraoperative, **8**:415*t*, 421
        postoperative, **8**:415*t*, 421–426
    conjunctival flap removal and, **8**:401
    for corneal changes in mucopolysaccharidoses,
        8:307
    for corneal edema after cataract surgery, **11**:147
    corneal topography after, **13**:20
    disadvantages of, **8**:416*t*
    disease recurrence in graft and, **8**:422, 423*f*
    donor cornea preparation in, **8**:417–418
    endophthalmitis after, **8**:422
    glaucoma after, **8**:421, **10**:102
    graft rejection and, **4**:91, 92*f*, **8**:427–430, 428*f*, 429*f*,
        9:65. *See also* Rejection
    for herpetic eye disease complications, **8**:117
    indications for, **8**:413, 414*t*, 415*t*
    IOL power calculations after, **3**:222
    for keratoconus, **8**:300
    for keratoglobus, **8**:303
    for neurotrophic keratopathy, **8**:88
    pathology specimens from, **4**:78, 83*f*
    for pellucid marginal degeneration, **8**:302
    for peripheral ulcerative keratitis, **8**:213
    postoperative care and, **8**:421–426
        in children, **8**:431–432
    procedures combined with, **8**:419–420
    after radial keratotomy, **13**:48
    recipient eye preparation and, **8**:418
    refractive error after, control of, **8**:426–427, 427*f*
    after refractive surgery, **13**:191–192
    refractive surgery after, **13**:169–172
    in rosacea patients, **8**:70
    selective keratoplasty compared with, **8**:415–416*t*
    in Stevens-Johnson syndrome, **8**:198
    surgical technique for, **8**:417–419, 419*f*
    suture techniques for, **8**:418–419, 419*f*, 420*f*
        postoperative problems and, **8**:423–425, 424*f*
        removal in children and, **8**:431, 431*t*
    tectonic
        for herpetic eye disease complications, **8**:117
        for peripheral ulcerative keratitis, **8**:213
Keratoprosthesis, **8**:413, 432–433, 433*f*
    for chemical injuries, **8**:358–359
    for children, **8**:431
    for cicatricial pemphigoid, **8**:203
    for Stevens-Johnson syndrome, **8**:198

Keratorefractive surgery (KRS), **13**:3, 4*t*, 41*t*. *See also*
        specific procedure and Refractive surgery
    adjustable refractive surgery (ARS) and, **13**:137. *See*
        also Bioptics
    amblyopia and, **13**:178–181
    astigmatism and, **3**:232, 237–241, 239*f*, 241*f*
        corneal topography in detection/management of,
            8:44, **13**:12–14, 13*f*, 14*f*, 20, 38–39, 38*f*
        penetrating keratoplasty and, **13**:169–172
    in autoimmune disease, **13**:184–185
    cataract/cataract surgery and, **11**:130–131, 193–194,
        193*f*, **13**:36–37, 154–156, 154*f*, 155*f*
        international trends in use of, **13**:201
        IOL power calculation and, **11**:86–88, 193,
            13:189
        preoperative evaluation/planning and, **11**:75, 78
    in children, **13**:180–181
    collagen crosslinking, **13**:4*t*, 123–124, 124*f*, 168
    collagen shrinkage, **13**:4*t*, 22, 22*f*
    in connective tissue diseases, **13**:31, 184–185
    contact lens use after, **3**:191, **13**:192–194, 193*f*
    corneal biomechanics affected by, **13**:9–10
    corneal effects of, **13**:4–5, 20–22, 21*f*, 22*f*
    corneal imaging for, **13**:10–20, 38–39, 38*f*. *See also*
        specific type and Cornea, topography of
        indications for, **13**:16–17, 17*f*, 18*f*
        postoperative evaluation and, **13**:17, 17*f*, 18*f*
    corneal optics and, **13**:3–5
    corneal shape and, **3**:231–235, 232*f*, 233*f*, 234*f*, 235*f*,
        13:10, 20
    corneal topography and, **8**:43–44, 44*f*, **13**:10–14, 11*f*,
        12*f*, 13*f*, 14*f*, 38–39, 38*f*, 70–71. *See also* Cornea,
        topography of
        indications for, **13**:16–17, 17*f*, 18*f*
        postoperative, **13**:17, 17*f*, 18*f*
    corneal transplant after, **13**:191–192
    corneal wound healing and, **13**:26–27
    in diabetes mellitus, **13**:31, 183–184
    excimer laser, **13**:4*t*
    glaucoma/ocular hypertension and, **13**:35, 172–175,
        173*f*, 194–195
    global estimates of, **13**:197–198, 198*f*
    in HIV infection/AIDS, **13**:31, 182–183
    incisional, **13**:4*t*, 20–21, 21*f*
        for astigmatism, **13**:49–52, 49*f*, 50*f*, 51*t*
        for myopia, **13**:43–48, 45*f*, 46*f*, 47*f*
    indications for, **13**:163–164
    informed consent for, **13**:30*t*, 41–42, 41*t*, 209–217
    international perspectives in, **13**:197–202
        global estimates of surgery procedures and,
            13:197–198, 198*f*
        regulation of practices and devices and,
            13:201–202
        trends in surgery and, **13**:199–201
    IOL power calculations after, **3**:220–222, **13**:187–189,
        190*f*
    iron lines associated with, **8**:336
    irregular astigmatism and, **3**:232, 237–241, 239*f*, 241*f*,
        13:16, 38–39, 38*f*, 171
    laser biophysics and, **13**:23–26, 24*f*
    laser–tissue interactions and, **13**:23
    limitations of, **13**:41*t*

medical history and, **13**:31
monovision and, **13**:32–33, 152–153
nonlaser lamellar, **13**:4*t*
ocular history and, **13**:31–32
in ocular and systemic disease, **13**:163–185. *See also specific disorder*
optical considerations in, **3**:231–241
  angle kappa (κ), **3**:236
  corneal shape, **3**:231–235, 232*f*, 233*f*, 234*f*, 235*f*
  irregular astigmatism, **3**:237–241, 239*f*, 241*f*
  pupil size, **3**:236–237
optical principles and, **13**:5–9, 5*f*, 6*f*, 7*f*, 8*f*, 9*f*
patient age and, **13**:32–33
patient evaluation for, **13**:29–42, 30*t*. *See also* Keratorefractive surgery (KRS), preoperative evaluation for
patient expectations and, **13**:29–30, 30*t*
after penetrating keratoplasty, **13**:169–172
penetrating keratoplasty after, **13**:191–192
postoperative considerations and, **13**:187–195
preoperative evaluation for, **13**:29–42, 30*t*
  ancillary tests in, **13**:38–40, 38*f*
  corneal imaging in, **13**:10–20, 38–39, 38*f*. *See also specific type and* Cornea, topography of
  discussion of findings/informed consent and, **13**:30*t*, 41–42, 41*t*, 209–217
  examination in, **13**:30*t*, 33–38, 36*f*, 37*f*
  history in, **13**:29–33, 30*t*
  in presbyopia patient, **13**:32–33
  retinal disease and, **13**:175–178
  social history/occupation and, **13**:30–31
spherical aberration after, **3**:99–100, 232, 233*f*
strabismus and, **13**:34–35, 178–181
wavefront aberrations/analysis and, **3**:140, **13**:5–9, 5*f*, 6*f*, 7*f*, 8*f*, 9*f*, 40, 72, 74
wavefront-guided/wavefront-optimized, **13**:25, 26, 40, 69, 72. *See also* Wavefront-guided laser ablation; Wavefront-optimized laser ablation
Keratoscopy, **8**:39, 39*f*, **13**:10
  computerized, **3**:267, 267*f*, 268*f*, **8**:40–45, 40*f*, 41*f*, 42*f*, 43*f*, 44*f*
  photographic, **3**:267, **8**:39
Keratosis, **8**:20*t*
  actinic, **4**:216–217, 217*f*, 218*f*, **7**:166, 167*f*
  inverted follicular, **4**:215, 215*f*
  seborrheic, **4**:214–215, 214*f*, 215*f*, **7**:157–158, 157*f*
Keratotomy
  arcuate, **13**:4*t*, 49, 50–52, 51*t*
    complications of, **13**:52
    instrumentation for, **13**:51
    ocular surgery after, **13**:52
    outcomes of, **13**:52
    surgical technique for, **13**:51
  astigmatic, **13**:4*t*
    for astigmatism/refractive errors after penetrating keratoplasty, **8**:427
    cataract surgery and, **11**:130
    wound healing/repair and, **13**:26
  hexagonal, **13**:4*t*
  radial. *See* Radial keratotomy
  transverse, **13**:49

Keratouveitis, **9**:79
  in herpetic disease, **9**:197
  syphilitic, **9**:243–244
  varicella, **8**:118, 121
Kerlone. *See* Betaxolol
Kestenbaum-Anderson procedure, **5**:258, **6**:328–329, 329*t*
Kestenbaum rule, **3**:295
Ketek. *See* Telithromycin
Ketoacidosis, diabetic, **1**:204–205
Ketoconazole, **1**:54*t*, **2**:379*t*, 380
  for fungal keratitis, **8**:166
Ketolides, **1**:50*t*, 61, 64
Ketoprofen, **1**:183*t*, **2**:362*t*
Ketorolac, **2**:257, 357*t*, 363, 364, 365*t*
  for cystoid macular edema, **9**:100, 301
    after cataract surgery, **11**:183
  perioperative, **1**:309*t*, 310
  for recurrent corneal erosions, **8**:84
Ketotifen, **2**:365*t*, 366
Keyboards (computer), large-key, in low vision/vision rehabilitation, **3**:303
Keywords, in online searching, **1**:316
Khodadoust line, **8**:429, 429*f*, **9**:63, 64*f*
Ki-67, in pingueculae/pterygia, **4**:57
KID (congenital keratitis-ichthyosis-deafness) syndrome, **8**:74
Killer cells, **8**:180
  in antibody-dependent cellular cytotoxicity, **9**:54
  natural, **9**:51
    in viral conjunctivitis, **9**:60
Kilobase, **2**:154
Kindergarten children, low vision in, **3**:307
Kineret. *See* Anakinra
Kinetic perimetry, **5**:99, **10**:54*f*, 55. *See also* Visual field testing
  for central visual field assessment, **3**:292
  in hereditary retinal/choroidal degenerations, **12**:223
  for peripheral visual field assessment, **3**:292
  in photoreceptor dystrophies, **12**:223, 225*f*
Kinins, **8**:177*t*
"Kissing" nevi, **4**:224, 224*f*
c-Kit, in immunohistochemistry, **4**:34
Klebsiella, **8**:135
  endogenous endophthalmitis caused by, **9**:272
Kleeblattschädel, **6**:383
Klippel-Trénaunay-Weber syndrome, **5**:342, **6**:376
  glaucoma associated with, **10**:28
Klonopin. *See* Clonazepam
KM. *See* Keratomileusis
K_m (Michaelis/affinity constant), "sugar" cataract development and, **11**:15
Knapp procedure
  inverse, for orbital floor fracture, **6**:126
  for monocular elevation deficiency (double elevator palsy), **6**:124
Knapp's law, **3**:79–80, 80*f*
  aniseikonia and, **3**:171
Knolle lens, **3**:209*f*
Koeppe lens/Koeppe-type lenses, for gonioscopy/funduscopy, **10**:33

Koeppe nodules
  in iridocyclitis, 4:270*t*, 272*f*
  in sarcoidosis, 4:190, 272*f*, 9:87*f*, 175
  in uveitis, 9:87*f*, 88
Koganei, clump cells of, 4:186
Koniocellular (K) system, 6:42, 44, 10:40–41
  development of, 6:44
KP. *See* Keratic precipitates
KPro. *See* Boston keratoprosthesis
Krabbe disease/leukodystrophy, 2:213*t*, 6:400*t*
Kratz-Sinskey IOL, 3:209*f*
Krause, glands of, 2:23*f*, 26*f*, 27*t*, 33, 239–240, 4:205,
  207*t*, 7:135*f*, 141, 244
Krill disease (acute retinal pigment epitheliitis/ARPE),
  9:148–150*t*, 170, 170*f*, 12:193–194
Krimsky test, 6:77, 77*f*
  in infantile exotropia, 6:104*f*
KRS. *See* Keratorefractive surgery
KRT3/KRT12 mutations, in Meesmann corneal
  dystrophy, 8:268, 269*t*, 272
Krukenberg spindles, 4:91–92, 94*f*, 109, 8:337*t*, 345,
  10:87, 88, 88*f*. *See also* Pigment/pigmentary
  dispersion syndrome
Krypton fluoride excimer laser, 3:25. *See also* Lasers
Krypton laser, 3:24. *See also* Lasers
KSHV. *See* Kaposi sarcoma–associated herpesvirus
Kufs disease, 6:401*t*
Kuglen hook, for pupil expansion, 11:194
Kyphosis, in osteoporosis, 1:229
Kyrieleis arteriolitis, 9:229

L

L-cone opsin genes, 2:294–295
  mutations in, 2:297
L cones, 2:294
  absent/defective
    in achromatopsia, 12:214
    in dichromacy, 12:213
  bipolar cells for, 2:298
  gene for, on X chromosome, 2:294–295
  horizontal cells for, 2:299
  retinal ganglion cells for, 2:299*f*, 300
L-Dopa, for Parkinson disease, 1:258–259
L1 repeat element/sequence, 2:166
L-selectin, in neutrophil rolling, 9:18
L-type calcium channels, 2:261
  mutations in, 2:296
Labbé, vein of, 5:26
Labetalol, 1:77*t*
  for hypertensive emergency, 1:83
  intraoperative floppy iris syndrome and, 11:155
Labial gland biopsy, in Sjögren syndrome, 8:57, 59*f*
Labrador (actinic) keratopathy, 4:88–89, 90*f*, 8:334–335,
  335*f*
Labyrinth, 5:47*f*, 48
Labyrinthine reflex system, 6:37
Labyrinthine segment of cranial nerve VII (facial),
  2:105, 5:61
Lacerations. *See also* Trauma
  canalicular, 7:179, 272–273
  conjunctival, 8:369–370
    in children, 6:409

corneoscleral. *See also* Anterior segment, trauma to;
  Perforating injuries
  repair of, 8:375–381, 376*f*
    anesthesia for, 8:376
    in children, 6:408
    postoperative management and, 8:381–382
    preoperative management and, 8:374–375
    secondary repair measures and, 8:380–381, 381*f*,
      382*f*
    steps in, 8:376–380, 377*t*, 378*f*, 379*f*
    Seidel test in identification of, 8:17, 19*f*
eyelid
  canthal tissue involved in, 7:178–180
  lid margin involved in, 7:178, 179*f*
  lid margin not involved in, 7:178
  ptosis caused by, 7:210
  repair of, 7:178, 179–180, 179*f*. *See also* Eyelids,
    surgery/reconstruction of
    in children, 6:409
    secondary, 7:180–181
  iris, repair of, 8:380–381, 381*f*
  lacrimal sac/nasolacrimal duct, 7:273
  posterior segment, 12:324
Lacquer cracks, in pathologic myopia, 12:84, 86, 86*f*
Lacrimal artery, 2:32, 37*f*, 38, 39*f*, 5:13*f*, 14*f*, 15*f*, 16–18,
  7:11*f*
  extraocular muscles supplied by, 2:18, 38, 39*f*, 6:16,
    7:11*f*
  eyelids supplied by, 7:143
Lacrimal bone, 5:5, 8*f*, 9, 9*f*, 7:6*f*, 7*f*
Lacrimal canaliculi. *See* Canaliculi
Lacrimal crests, anterior and posterior, 2:5, 6*f*, 27
Lacrimal–cutaneous fistula, 7:277, 278*f*
Lacrimal drainage system, 2:27*f*, 33–34, 34*f*, 6:203–210,
  7:244–246, 245*f*. *See also* Nasolacrimal duct
  anatomy of, 2:27*f*, 33–34, 34*f*, 7:244–246, 245*f*
  in children, 6:203–210
  development of, 7:243
    abnormalities of, 6:203–204, 7:277–278, 278*f*
  diagnostic tests for evaluation of, 7:258–262, 259*f*,
    260*f*, 261*f*
  disorders of, 7:249–278. *See also* Tearing
    infectious, 7:274–276, 274*f*, 275*f*
    neoplastic, 7:276–277
      canalicular obstruction and, 7:264
      nasolacrimal duct obstruction and, 7:267
    traumatic, 7:272–273
  duplications in, 7:277
  irrigation of
    for acquired lacrimal drainage evaluation, 7:259,
      260*f*
    for canalicular obstruction, 7:259–261, 261*f*, 263
    for canalicular trauma, 7:272
    for congenital lacrimal drainage management,
      7:251–252, 253*f*
  obstruction of. *See also* Tearing
    acquired, 7:256–270
      evaluation of, 7:256–262, 259*f*, 260*f*, 261*f*
      neoplastic causes of, 7:264
    in canalicular disorders
      acquired, 7:263–265
      congenital, 7:250
    congenital, 7:249–256
      evaluation of, 7:249

dacryocystocele and, 7:255–256, 256f
diagnostic tests for evaluation of, 7:258–262, 259f, 260f, 261f
examination in patient with, 7:257–258
history in patient with, 7:256–257
lacrimal outflow evaluation in patient with, 7:258
nasolacrimal duct obstruction
    acquired, 7:266–270, 269f, 270f
    congenital, 7:250–255, 252f, 253f, 254f
pseudoepiphora evaluation and, 7:257–258
in punctal disorders
    acquired, 7:262–263
    congenital, 7:250
reconstruction of, 7:186
after medial canthal basal cell carcinoma removal, 7:171
therapeutic closure of, 7:271
Lacrimal ducts, 2:32, 32f, 7:244. See also Lacrimal drainage system
development of, 2:140
Lacrimal fossa, 2:7, 7f, 8f, 5:8f, 9f, 7:5, 6f
Lacrimal functional unit, 8:48, 49f, 173
Lacrimal gland fistula, 6:204, 7:277
Lacrimal glands, 2:26f, 27t, 32–33, 32f, 33f, 239–240, 239f, 4:229, 7:17, 243–244. See also Lacrimal system
accessory, 2:26f, 27t, 33, 239–240, 239f, 4:205, 207t, 7:135f, 141, 244
anatomy of, 2:26f, 27t, 32–33, 32f, 33f, 239–240, 239f, 7:243–244
aqueous component/tears produced by, 2:239–240, 239f
biopsy/histologic features of, in Sjögren syndrome, 8:57, 63
development of, 2:140, 7:243
    abnormalities of, 7:277
dysfunction of
    non–Sjögren syndrome, 8:50, 51f, 52, 65
    in sarcoidosis, 8:73
    in Sjögren syndrome, 8:50, 51f, 63
    tear composition assays in, 8:54–55
ectopic, 6:345, 8:246
Epstein-Barr virus infection and, 8:122–123
in external eye defense, 8:95
immune response/immunologic features of, 8:176f
infection of. See Dacryoadenitis
inflammatory damage to, dry eye and, 8:50
nonspecific orbital inflammation involving, 7:59, 61
orbital, 2:32, 32f, 239
palpebral, 2:32, 32f, 239
parasympathetic innervation of, 5:66
sarcoidosis involving, 7:58–59, 8:73
in tear secretion, 2:239–240, 239f
tumors of, 4:235–238, 237f, 7:85–88
    in children, 6:333t
    epithelial, 4:236–238, 237f, 7:86–88, 86f
    exenteration for, 7:87, 126
    nonepithelial, 7:88
    staging of, 4:345–347t
Lacrimal intubation
for acquired nasolacrimal obstruction, 7:267
for canalicular obstruction, 7:264
for canalicular trauma, 7:272–273
for congenital lacrimal drainage obstruction, 6:209–210, 7:252–253, 254f

Lacrimal nerve, 2:103, 5:10f, 59, 59f, 60, 67, 7:12f, 13
in reflex tear arc, 7:244
Lacrimal nucleus, 2:106
Lacrimal outflow evaluation, 7:258
Lacrimal papillae, 2:33
Lacrimal plugs, for dry eye, 7:271, 8:60t, 61–62, 62f
canalicular obstruction and, 7:263–264, 271
extrusion/migration of, 7:271
nasolacrimal duct obstruction and, 7:267
Lacrimal probing
for acquired nasolacrimal duct/canalicular obstruction, 7:261
for canalicular trauma, 7:272
for congenital dacryocele, 6:205
for congenital nasolacrimal duct obstruction, 6:207, 207–208, 208f, 7:250–251, 251–252, 252f, 253f
Lacrimal pump, 7:136, 246, 247f
evaluation of function of, 7:258
ocular medication absorption affected by, 2:324
Lacrimal puncta. See Puncta
Lacrimal sac (tear sac), 2:27f, 32f, 33, 34, 7:245f, 246
cast formation in (dacryoliths), 7:266
development of, 7:243
distension of, 7:249
    in dacryocystitis, 7:275, 275f, 276
    in dacryocystocele, 7:255, 256f
    in dacryolith, 7:266
    in nasolacrimal duct obstruction, 7:258, 261, 266, 267
    neoplasm causing, 7:267
evaluation of, 7:258
inflammation of, 7:274–276, 275f. See also Dacryocystitis
trauma to, 7:273
tumors of, 4:235, 7:275–277
Lacrimal sac massage
for congenital dacryocele, 6:205, 205f
for congenital nasolacrimal duct obstruction, 6:206
Lacrimal scintigraphy, for lacrimal drainage evaluation, 7:261–262
Lacrimal system. See also specific structure
anatomy of, 7:243–246, 245f
development of, 7:243
    abnormalities of, 7:277–278, 278f
disorders of, 7:249–278. See also Tearing
    acquired, 7:256–270
    congenital, 7:249–256
    developmental abnormalities, 7:277–278
    infection, 7:273–276, 274f, 275f
    neoplastic, 7:85–88, 276–277
    therapeutic closure of drainage system for, 7:271
    traumatic, 7:272–273
excretory apparatus of, 2:27f, 33–34, 34f, 7:243, 244–246, 245f. See also Lacrimal drainage system
healing/repair of, 4:17–18
intubation of
    for acquired nasolacrimal obstruction, 7:267
    for canalicular obstruction, 7:264
    for canalicular trauma, 7:272–273
    for congenital lacrimal drainage obstruction, 6:209–210, 7:252–253, 254f
physiology of, 7:246, 247f

secretory apparatus/function of, **2**:26*f*, 32–33, 32*f*, 33*f*, 241–244, 242*f*, 243*f*, **7**:243, 243–244. *See also* Lacrimal glands
tumors of, **7**:85–88, 276–277
  canalicular obstruction and, **7**:264
  nasolacrimal duct obstruction and, **7**:267
Lacrimal vein, **5**:24*f*, **7**:11*f*
Lacrimation, **7**:256. *See also* Tearing
Lactate
  in aqueous humor, **2**:266*t*, 267
  in tear film, **2**:240
  in vitreous, **2**:266*t*
Lactation
  fluorescein dye transmission to breast milk and, **12**:25
  glaucoma medication use during, **10**:176
  refractive surgery contraindicated during, **13**:31
Lactoferrin, in tear film, **2**:240, **8**:54–55
  in external eye defense, **8**:95
Lactotroph adenomas (prolactinomas), **1**:215
LADA. *See* Latent autoimmune diabetes in adults
Lagophthalmos
  assessment for, **5**:277
  after blepharoplasty, **7**:226
  causes of, **8**:80
  exposure keratopathy and, **8**:80
  paralytic, **7**:216–217
    gold weight loading for, **7**:216–217
  in paralytic ectropion, **7**:216
  in ptosis, **7**:202
    after repair, **7**:213
  in thyroid eye disease, **5**:334
Lake-Cavanagh disease, pigmentary retinopathy in, **12**:251*t*, 260
LAL. *See* Light-adjustable intraocular lenses
Lambdoid suture, **5**:7
Lamellae
  corneal, **2**:45, 249, **8**:7–8
    development of, **2**:134–135
  eyelid, **2**:25*f*
  zonular, **11**:7
Lamellar bodies, in sarcoidosis, **9**:173
Lamellar (zonular) cataracts, **6**:247*f*, 247*t*, 248, 248*f*, 250*t*, **11**:30, 32*f*
  pulverulent, **6**:247*t*
Lamellar channels, for intrastromal corneal ring segment placement, **13**:57, 58*f*
  deposits in, **13**:62, 62*f*
Lamellar deficiency, surgery for eyelid retraction and, **7**:215
Lamellar flaps
  LASIK, **13**:24, 77–83, 78*f*, 79*f*, 81*f*, 82*f*, 83*t*. *See also* Flaps, LASIK
  for superficial anterior lamellar keratoplasty, **8**:435
Lamellar surgery, **13**:4*t*. *See also specific type and* LASIK
  corneal wound healing and, **13**:26
  keratectomy, **8**:402
  keratoplasty. *See* Keratoplasty
  nonlaser, **13**:4*t*
Lamellar tectonic graft, for keratoglobus, **8**:303
Lamictal. *See* Lamotrigine
Lamina cribrosa, **2**:42, 90, 92*f*, **4**:111, 249, 250*f*, **5**:19*f*, 29*f*, **10**:42, 43–44, 43*f*
  blood supply of, **2**:94

Lamina densa, **2**:135
Lamina fusca, **2**:48, **4**:112, 186
Lamina granularis interna, **5**:34
Lamina lucida, **2**:135
Lamina papyracea (ethmoid/ethmoidal bone), **2**:7, **5**:5, 7, 7*f*, 7:6*f*, 7*f*, 8, 246
Laminar area of optic nerve, **2**:90, **10**:42, 44
Laminar dots, **10**:42
Laminin, **2**:68
Lamisil. *See* Terbinafine
Lamivudine (3TC)
  for delta hepatitis, **1**:26
  for hepatitis B, **1**:281
  for HIV infection/AIDS, **1**:33
  with zidovudine, **1**:33
Lamotrigine, **1**:263*t*
Lancaster red-green test, **6**:80
Lancefield groups, **8**:133
Lang stereopsis tests, **6**:87
Langerhans cell histiocytosis (histiocytosis X), orbital involvement in, **7**:84
  in children, **6**:332*t*, 337–338, 338*f*
Langerhans cells, **2**:43, **8**:173, 174*f*, **9**:12
  in external eye defense, **8**:96
  in poison ivy, **9**:34, 35
Langhans giant cells, **4**:7, 9*f*
Lanoconazole, **1**:65
Lanthony desaturated 15-hue test, in low vision evaluation, **5**:105
Lanthony tritan plates, in low vision evaluation, **5**:105
Lantibiotics, staphylococci producing, **8**:133
Lantus. *See* Glargine insulin
Large cell lymphoma (primary intraocular/central nervous system lymphoma), **1**:244, **4**:140–142, 141*f*, 142*f*, 143*f*, 323–325, 323*f*, 325*f*, **9**:136, 281–284, 282*f*, 283*f*, **12**:199, 199*f*
  central serous retinopathy differentiated from, **12**:174
  in HIV infection/AIDS, **9**:314
  uveitis differentiated from, **9**:91, 136, 281–283
    in children, **6**:276*t*
Large-key keyboards, in low vision/vision rehabilitation, **3**:303
Large-print materials, **3**:301
Large-print publications, sources of, **6**:418*t*
Larval/larvae migrans. *See also Toxocara* (toxocariasis)
  neural, **9**:240
  ocular, **8**:142
  visceral, **6**:273, **8**:142, **9**:235
LASEK (laser subepithelial keratomileusis), **13**:4*t*, 65. *See also* Keratorefractive surgery; Photorefractive keratectomy; Surface ablation
  Bowman layer and, **2**:249
  in children, **13**:180–181
  complications/side effects of, **13**:102
  corneal preparation for, **13**:75
  epithelial preservation techniques for, **13**:75
  glaucoma/ocular hypertension and, **13**:175
  immediate postablation measures, **13**:85
  international trends in use of, **13**:199, 201
  IOL power calculations after, **3**:220–222
  after retinal detachment surgery, **13**:177
Laser burns, corneal endothelial damage caused by, **8**:385

Laser capsulotomy (Nd:YAG), **11**:171–175, 172*f*, 174*f*
  for anterior capsule fibrosis and phimosis, **11**:171,
    171–175, 172*f*, 199
  for capsular block syndrome, **11**:166–167
  for capsule opacification, **11**:169, 171–175, 174*f*
    in uveitis, **9**:294
  complications of, **11**:173–175
  contraindications to, **11**:172
  indications for, **11**:171–172
  lens particle glaucoma and, **10**:91–92, **11**:63
  procedure for, **11**:172–173, 174*f*
  retinal detachment and, **11**:175, 184, **12**:363
Laser gonioplasty, for angle-closure glaucoma, **10**:203
Laser in situ keratomileusis. *See* LASIK
Laser interferometry/interferometer, **3**:8, 277
  before cataract surgery, **11**:81
Laser iridotomy, **10**:202–203. *See also* Iridotomy
  for acute angle closure, **10**:115, 116
  for angle-closure glaucoma, **10**:201, 201*f*, 202–203
    cataract extraction after, **10**:204
  for aqueous misdirection (malignant/ciliary block
    glaucoma), **10**:133
  for ectopia lentis, **10**:122
  for phacomorphic glaucoma, **10**:120–121, 121*f*
  for phakic IOL insertion, **13**:129
  for pigmentary glaucoma, **10**:89
  for subacute/intermittent angle closure, **10**:117
Laser ophthalmoscopy, **3**:251, **12**:29–30
  in fundus autofluorescence, **12**:30
  in indocyanine green angiography, **12**:25
  in optic disc evaluation, **10**:51, 52*f*
Laser photoablation. *See* Photoablation
Laser photolysis, **11**:127
Laser pointers, retinal injury caused by, **12**:334
Laser pupilloplasty, for cataracts, **11**:71
Laser scanning confocal microscope, **8**:36. *See also*
    Confocal microscopy
Laser speckle, **3**:20
Laser subepithelial keratomileusis. *See* LASEK
Laser suture lysis, **10**:186, 191
  scleral flap closure and, **10**:191, 194
Laser therapy (laser surgery). *See also specific*
    procedure and Photocoagulation; Photodynamic
    therapy
  aqueous misdirection (malignant/ciliary block
    glaucoma) and, **10**:131
  for childhood glaucoma, **6**:241
  for choroidal hemangioma, **4**:292
  for dacryocystorhinostomy, **7**:269
  for diabetic retinopathy, **4**:167, 167*f*
  for hemangiomas, **7**:64, 152
    in children, **6**:340
  for iris bombé in uveitis, **9**:296
  for keratoconus, **8**:300
  for melanoma, **4**:285
  for multifocal choroiditis and panuveitis syndrome,
    9:164
  ocular damage after (laser burns), **8**:385
  for pars planitis, **9**:137, 138
  for posterior segment disease, **12**:337–344
  for punctal occlusion, **7**:271
  for retinal angioma, **6**:375
  for retinoblastoma, **4**:311, 311*f*
  for retinopathy of prematurity, **6**:286, **12**:167–168,
    168*f*
  for skin resurfacing, **7**:230–231
  for trichiasis, **7**:200
  for uveitic glaucoma, **9**:296, 298
Laser thermokeratoplasty, **13**:4*t*, 22, 22*f*, 120
  corneal transplantation after, **13**:192
Laser trabeculoplasty, **10**:17–18, 180–183, 182*f*
  for exfoliation glaucoma, **10**:87
  for open-angle glaucoma, **10**:82, 107–108, 180–183,
    182*f*
  for pigmentary glaucoma, **10**:89
  selective, **10**:180, 181–182
Lasers, **3**:19, 26, 22*f*, 23*f*, 24*f*, 26*f*. *See also specific type*
    and Laser therapy
  absorption and, **3**:21, 23*f*
  active medium of, **3**:19, 21, 23, 24*f*
  biophysics of, **13**:23–26, 24*f*
  elements of, **3**:21–24, 23*f*
  emission by, **3**:21, 21–23, 23*f*
  fundamentals of, **3**:19–26, 22*f*, 23*f*, 24*f*, 26*f*
  interference and coherence and, **3**:8, 20
  occupational light injury and, **12**:334
  optical feedback in, **3**:21, 23–24, 24*f*
  photic damage in therapeutic mechanism of, **12**:332,
    337
  population inversion and, **3**:23
  power readings on, **3**:18*t*, 21
  properties of light from, **3**:20–21, 22*f*
  pumping in, **3**:21, 23, 24*f*
  sources for, **3**:24–25
  tissue interactions and, **3**:25–26, 26*f*, **13**:23
  visual pigment absorption spectra and, **12**:337,
    338*f*
  wavefront-guided, **13**:25, 74. *See also* Wavefront-
    guided laser ablation
  wavelengths used in, **3**:20, 26*f*
    for photocoagulation, **12**:337–339
Lash follicles, **7**:142*f*
  tumors arising in, **7**:162–164, 163*f*
Lash margin entropion, in anophthalmic socket, **7**:125
Lashes. *See* Eyelashes
LASIK (laser in situ keratomileusis), **13**:4*t*, 24, 41*t*,
    65, 68–69. *See also* Keratorefractive surgery;
    Photoablation
  aberrations after, **13**:7, 95, 96*f*
  for accommodative esotropia, **13**:181
  for amblyopia/anisometropic amblyopia, **13**:179
  application of laser treatment and, **13**:83–84, 84*f*
  arcuate keratotomy and, **13**:52
  in astigmatism, **3**:235, **13**:89
    after penetrating keratoplasty, **13**:171–172
  bandage contact lenses after, **13**:85, 104–105
    epithelial ingrowth prevention and, **13**:114, 194
    epithelial sloughing/defects and, **13**:104–105
    microkeratome complications and, **13**:103
    striae and, **13**:107–108
  Bowman layer and, **2**:249
  calibration of excimer laser for, **13**:73
  cataract surgery after, **11**:194
    IOL power calculation and, **11**:86
  central islands and, **13**:94–95, 94*f*
  in children, **13**:180–181

complications/side effects of, **13**:93–99, 102–117. *See also specific type*
 in diabetes mellitus, **13**:183–184
 femtosecond flap creation and, **13**:116
 rare, **13**:116
in connective tissue/autoimmune diseases, **13**:184–185
contact lens use after, **13**:193–194, 193*f*
corneal preparation for, **13**:77–83, 78*f*, 79*f*, 81*f*, 82*f*, 83*t*
corneal sensation affected by, **13**:97–98
corneal thickness and, **13**:39–40, 71–72
corneal transplantation after, **13**:191–192
corticosteroids after, **13**:85, 86–87
 complications associated with, **13**:96–97
decentered ablation and, **13**:95–96, 97*f*
in diabetes mellitus, **13**:183–184
diffuse lamellar/interface keratitis (DLK) after, **13**:108–111, 109*f*, 109*t*, 110*t*, 111*f*, 195
 glaucoma/IOP elevation and, **13**:97, 174, 195
 infectious keratitis differentiated from, **13**:110–111, 110*t*, 111*f*
dry eye after, **8**:50, 65, **13**:71, 97–98, 164–165
in dry eye disorders, **13**:71, 164–165
ectasia/keratoconus and, **13**:72, 114–116, 167–168, 168*f*
 intrastromal corneal ring segment placement and, **13**:63, 168
endothelial effects of, **13**:97
epipolis. *See* Epipolis-LASIK
epithelial ingrowth after, **13**:112–114, 113*f*
epithelial sloughing/defects and, **13**:104–105
FDA concerns/guidelines and, **13**:91, 117
filtering surgery and, **13**:174–175
flap creation for, **13**:77–83, 78*f*, 79*f*, 81*f*, 82*f*, 83*t*. *See also* Flaps, LASIK
 aberrations and, **13**:95, 96*f*
 femtosecond laser, **13**:4*t*, 23, 80–83, 81*f*, 82*f*, 83*t*
  aberrations and, **13**:95
  advantages/disadvantages of, **13**:83*t*
  international trends in use of, **13**:199
  re-treatment and, **13**:90, 90*f*
  steep or flat corneas and, **13**:39
  visual disturbances related to, **13**:116
 infection and, **13**:99, 99*f*, 111
  diffuse lamellar keratitis (DLK) differentiated from, **13**:110–111, 110*t*, 111*f*
 microkeratome, **13**:77–80, 78*f*, 79*f*
  aberrations and, **13**:95
  complications associated with, **13**:102–104, 103*f*
  international trends in use of, **13**:199
flap dislocation and, **13**:107–108, 108
glaucoma/ocular hypertension and, **13**:172–175, 173*f*, 194–195
haze formation and, **13**:27
herpes simplex virus keratitis and, **13**:166, 167
in HIV infection/AIDS, **13**:182
for hyperopia, **3**:235, 235*f*, **13**:88
infectious keratitis after, **13**:98–99, 99*f*
 diffuse lamellar keratitis differentiated from, **13**:110–111, 110*t*, 111*f*
informed consent for, **13**:213–217
interface debris after, **13**:114, 114*f*

international trends in use of, **13**:199, 201
intraocular lens power calculations after, **3**:220–222
intraocular pressure elevations after, **13**:97, 112, 172–175, 194–195
intraocular pressure measurements after, **10**:24
intrastromal corneal ring segment placement and, **13**:63
keratitis after
 atypical mycobacteria causing, **8**:164
 diffuse lamellar/interface (DLK), **13**:108–111, 109*f*, 109*t*, 110*t*, 111*f*
  glaucoma/IOP elevation and, **13**:97, 174, 195
  infectious keratitis differentiated from, **13**:110–111, 110*t*, 111*f*
 herpes simplex, **13**:166, 167
 infectious, **13**:98–99, 99*f*
  diffuse lamellar keratitis differentiated from, **13**:110–111, 110*t*, 111*f*
 pressure-induced, **13**:112, 112*f*
in keratoconus patients, **8**:300
 corneal topography and, **8**:43–44, 44*f*
limbal relaxing incisions and, **13**:52
limitations of, **13**:41*t*, 117
microkeratome for, **13**:77–80, 78*f*, 79*f*
 aberrations and, **13**:95
 complications associated with, **13**:102–104, 103*f*
 international trends in use of, **13**:199
for mixed astigmatism, **13**:89
for myopia, **3**:235, 235*f*
 spherical aberrations after, **13**:7
outcomes of, **13**:87–89
overcorrection and, **13**:93–94
 conductive keratoplasty for, **13**:122
patient selection for, **13**:71–73
after penetrating keratoplasty, **13**:171–172
with phakic IOL insertion (bioptics), **13**:125, 137
postoperative care for, **13**:86–87
 immediate postablation measures, **13**:85
preoperative patient evaluation and, **13**:71–73
preoperative patient preparation for, **13**:74–75
preoperative planning/laser programming for, **13**:73–74
pressure-induced stromal keratitis (PISK) after, **13**:112, 112*f*
after radial keratotomy, **13**:47–48
re-treatment (enhancements) and, **13**:89–91, 90*f*
 corneal perforation and, **13**:104
residual myopia after, intrastromal corneal ring segments for, **13**:63
residual stromal bed thickness and, **13**:40, 71–72
 corneal perforation and, **13**:104
 ectasia and, **13**:72, 114–116
retinal detachment/retinal detachment repair and, **13**:176, 177–178, 189–191
spherical aberration after, **3**:100, 101*f*
striae and, **13**:105–108, 106*t*, 107*f*
surface ablation for enhancement of, **13**:90–91
surgical technique for, **13**:73–87
tracking/centration/ablation and, **13**:83–84, 84*f*
undercorrection and, **13**:94
wavefront aberrations after, **13**:7, 95
wavefront-guided. *See* Wavefront-guided laser ablation

Lasix. *See* Furosemide
Latanoprost, **2:**330, 354, 354*t*, **10:**162*t*, 166, 167*f*
 for childhood glaucoma, **6:**242–243
 in combination preparations, **10:**165*t*, 167, 173
Late-diagnosed primary congenital glaucoma, **10:**139, 140*t*. *See also* Glaucoma, childhood
Late latent syphilis, **1:**13, **9:**244, 248*t*
Late-onset Alzheimer disease, **1:**266
Late-onset corneal haze, **13:**101
Latency (viral), herpesvirus infection and, **1:**22, 23, **8:**99, 105, 109, 117–118, 119
Latency (visual reaction time)
 perimetry variations and, **10:**56
 saccadic system evaluation and, **5:**203, 208
Latent autoimmune diabetes in adults (LADA), **1:**192
Latent/manifest latent (fusion maldevelopment) nystagmus, **5:**246, **6:**322–323, 323*f*, 324*f*
 dissociated vertical deviation and, **6:**116, 117, 323
Latent syphilis, **1:**12–13, **9:**244, 248*t*
Lateral canthal defects, repair of, **7:**186
Lateral canthal tendon, **7:**137*f*, 139*f*, 142
 trauma involving, **7:**178–180
Lateral cantholysis, bulbar hemorrhage release and, **11:**99
Lateral canthotomy. *See* Canthotomy
Lateral choroidal artery, **5:**20*f*
Lateral (spatial) coherence, **3:**8, 8*f*
Lateral flare, in thyroid-related eyelid retraction, **7:**214, 215
Lateral gaze, alternating skew deviation on, **5:**222, 222*t*
Lateral geniculate body/nucleus, **2:**93, 94*f*, 96, **5:**19–20, 20*f*, 28*f*, 33, **6:**42
 development of, **6:**44
  abnormal visual experience affecting, **6:**46
 lesions of, **5:**167–168, 167*f*
Lateral incomitance, strabismus surgery planning and, **6:**146
Lateral long posterior ciliary arteries, **5:**18
Lateral medullary syndrome of Wallenberg (Wallenberg syndrome), **5:**21, 195, 205–206
Lateral muscular branch of ophthalmic artery, extraocular muscles supplied by, **6:**16
Lateral ophthalmic vein, **5:**10*f*
Lateral orbital tubercle of Whitnall, **2:**9, **7:**6, 6*f*, 7*f*
Lateral orbital wall, **2:**9, 9*f*, **5:**7*f*, 9, **7:**6–7
Lateral orbitotomy, **7:**112–113. *See also* Orbitotomy
 incisions for, **7:**108, 108*f*
Lateral palpebral artery, **5:**14*f*
Lateral pontine cistern, **2:**105
Lateral rectus muscles, **2:**17*f*, 18, 19*t*, 20*f*, 38, 38*f*, 39*f*, **5:**10*f*, 56, 56*f*, **6:**13, 14*f*, 16*f*, 17*t*, 18*f*, **7:**10, 11*f*
 A-pattern deviations associated with dysfunction of, **6:**107–108
 action of, **6:**13, 17*t*, 29, 29*t*
  gaze position and, **6:**30, 30*f*
 anatomy of, **5:**10*f*, **6:**13, 14*f*, 16*f*, 17*t*, 18*f*
 field of action of, **6:**29
 insertion relationships of, **2:**16, 18*f*, 19*t*
 nerves supplying, **2:**21, **7:**11
 paralysis of, incomitant esotropia and, **6:**98
 surgery of
  for A- and V-pattern deviations, **6:**111, 111*f*
  for consecutive esotropia, **6:**103

 for constant exotropia, **6:**103
 for Duane syndrome, **6:**129
 for intermittent exotropia, **6:**102–103
 for monocular elevation deficiency (double elevator palsy), **6:**124
 for nystagmus, **6:**328, 329, 329*t*
 for sixth nerve (abducens) paralysis, **6:**135
 for third nerve (oculomotor) paralysis, **6:**133
 V-pattern deviations associated with dysfunction of, **6:**107–108
Lateral (transverse) sinus thrombosis, **5:**357
Lateral subnucleus, of cranial nerve VII (facial), **5:**61
Lateral tarsal strip operation
 for cicatricial ectropion, **7:**193
 for involutional ectropion, **7:**190, 192*f*
 for involutional entropion, **7:**196
Lateropulsion, ocular, in Wallenberg syndrome, **5:**206
Latex allergy, **1:**308–309
Lattice corneal dystrophy, **4:**96–97, 97*t*, 99*f*, **8:**268*t*, 278*t*
 classic (*TGFBI*-type/LCD1), **4:**96–97, 97*t*, 99*f*, **8:**268*t*, 270*t*, 278–279, 279*f*
  genetics of, **4:**97, **8:**269*t*, 278
 gelsolin-type (LCD2), **4:**212, **8:**268*t*, 270*t*, 280, 280*f*, 317*t*, 319
  genetics of, **4:**212, **8:**269*t*, 280, 317*t*
Lattice degeneration, **4:**155–156, 155*f*, **12:**276–278, 277*f*, 278*f*
 in hereditary hyaloideoretinopathies with optically empty vitreous, **12:**309, 309*f*
 radial perivascular, **4:**155–156
 treatment of, **12:**283, 284–285, 284*t*
Lattice lines, **8:**279, 279*f*, 280, 280*f*
LAV. *See* Lymphadenopathy-associated virus
Lavage, bronchial, **1:**143
Law of motor correspondence, Hering's, **6:**35, 36*f*
 eyelid retraction and, **5:**281, **7:**214
Law of reciprocal innervation, Sherrington's, **6:**34
Law of rectilinear propagation, **3:**41, 42*f*
Law of reflection, **3:**42–44, 43*f*, 44*f*, 45
Law of refraction (Snell's law), **3:**44–46, 45*f*, 46*f*, 47, 47*f*, **8:**38
 contact lens power and, **3:**167
 critical angle calculation and, **3:**47, 48
 Fermat principle and, **3:**52–53, 52*f*
 small-angle approximation and, **3:**58–60
Lazy-T procedure, for involutional ectropion, **7:**192–193
LBBB. *See* Left bundle branch block
LBD. *See* Lewy body dementia
LCA. *See* Leber congenital amaurosis
LCAT deficiency. *See* Lecithin–cholesterol acyltransferase (LCAT) deficiency
LCD. *See* Lattice corneal dystrophy
LCD1. *See* Lattice corneal dystrophy, classic
LCD2. *See* Lattice corneal dystrophy, gelsolin-type
LCMV. *See* Lymphocytic choriomeningitis virus
LCs. *See* Langerhans cells
LD. *See* Lyme disease
LDL cholesterol. *See* Low-density-lipoprotein cholesterol
Le Fort fractures, **7:**95, 96*f*
LEA Low-Contrast Test, **3:**292
LEA symbols, for visual acuity testing in children, **6:**73

Leakage, fluorescein, **12**:22–23, 23*f*, 24*f*. *See also* Hyperfluorescence
   in central serous chorioretinopathy, **12**:24*f*, 172–173, 173*f*
   in choroidal neovascularization/age-related macular edema, **12**:23*f*, 67, 67*f*
   in cystoid macular edema, **12**:142, 142*f*
   in diabetic macular edema, **12**:95–96, 97*f*
   in hypertensive choroidopathy, **12**:115, 116*f*
Leão, spreading depression in, **5**:191
Learning effect, in automated perimetry, **10**:64, 64*f*
Leber (epithelioid) cells, **9**:11. *See also* Macrophages
   in choroidal/ciliary body melanoma, **4**:196, 196*f*, 199
   in sarcoidosis, **9**:173
Leber congenital amaurosis (Leber amaurosis congenita; congenital/infantile/childhood retinitis pigmentosa), **6**:289–291, 290*f*, **12**:229, 251–252
   gene therapy for, **9**:66
   guanylate cyclase mutations causing, **2**:296
   pleiotropism and, **2**:210
   RPE65 gene defects causing, **2**:297, **6**:290
Leber hereditary optic neuropathy, **2**:175, **5**:137–139, 137*f*, **6**:311
   mitochondrial DNA mutations and, **2**:174*f*, 175, **5**:138, **6**:311
Leber idiopathic stellate neuroretinitis, **9**:263
Leber miliary aneurysm, **12**:146
LECD. *See* Lisch epithelial corneal dystrophy
Lecithin–cholesterol acyltransferase (LCAT) deficiency, **8**:309–310
Leflunomide, **1**:186
   for CMV retinitis, **1**:24
   for uveitis in children, **6**:277
Left anterior and posterior fascicular blocks, **1**:122*t*
Left bundle branch block, **1**:122*t*
Left gaze (levoversion), **6**:35
Left ventricular hypertrophy, hypertension and, **1**:85
Legal blindness, **3**:284
   central visual field loss and, **3**:287
   peripheral visual field loss and, **3**:292
Leigh syndrome (Leigh necrotizing encephalopathy), **2**:176, 213*t*
   mitochondrial DNA mutations and, **2**:174*f*, 176
Leiomyoma
   of ciliary body, **4**:203
   of iris, **4**:270*t*
   of orbit, **4**:244
Leiomyosarcoma
   conjunctival, **8**:240
   of orbit, **4**:244
Leishmania (leishmaniasis), **8**:141
Lens (crystalline), **2**:67–70, 273–281, **11**:5–9, 11–17
   absence of, **4**:121, **6**:260, **11**:26. *See also* Aphakia
   aging changes in, **11**:7, 20, 39–47, 40*f*. *See also* Age-related cataracts
     presbyopia and, **3**:117, 142, 143*t*
   alcohol use/abuse and, **11**:58–59
   anatomy of, **2**:41*f*, 53*f*, 67–70, 68*f*, 69*f*, 71*f*, 273–275, 274*f*, **11**:5–9, 5*f*, 6*f*, 7*f*, 8*f*
     altered, cataract surgery and, **11**:195–200
   antioxidants in, **2**:313–314, 314*f*
   biochemistry and metabolism of, **2**:273–281, **11**:11–17
   carbohydrate ("sugar") cataracts and, **2**:279–281

   capsule of. *See* Lens capsule
   carbohydrate metabolism in, **2**:279–281, 280*f*, **11**:13–15, 14*f*
   changing shape of. *See* Accommodation
   chemical composition of, **2**:275–277
   chemical injuries affecting, **11**:53
   in children, **6**:168, 168*f*
     disorders of, **6**:245–265. *See also specific type*
   colobomas of, **4**:121, **6**:260–261, 261*f*, **11**:26–27, 27*f*
   coloration change in, **4**:126, **11**:39, 40*f*
   congenital anomalies and abnormalities of, **4**:121, 122*f*, **6**:260–261, 261*f*, **11**:26–35
   cortex of, **2**:70, 274–275, 274*f*, **4**:120, 120*f*, **11**:6*f*, 8–9
   degenerations of, **4**:126–127, 127*f*, 128*f*
   degenerations of, **4**:124–127, 125*f*, 126*f*, 127*f*, 128*f*, 129*f*. *See also* Cataract
   degenerative ocular disorders and, **11**:64
   development/embryology of, **2**:69*f*, 128–130, 129*f*, **6**:168, 168*f*, **11**:21–38
     cataract development and. *See* Cataract, congenital
     congenital anomalies and abnormalities and, **4**:121, 122*f*, **6**:260–261, 261*f*, **11**:26–35
     developmental defects and, **11**:35–38
     normal, **11**:21–25, 22–23*f*, 24*f*, 25*f*
   diabetes mellitus affecting, **11**:55, 56*f*. *See also* Cataract, diabetic
   dislocated, **11**:35. *See also* Ectopia lentis
     cataract surgery in patient with, **11**:197–199, 198*f*
     in children, **6**:261–265, 261*f*, 262*f*, 262*t*, 264*f*
     abuse and, **6**:404
     traumatic, **11**:36, 50–51, 50*f*
     child abuse and, **6**:404
   disorders of, **4**:119–129, **11**:39–64. *See also specific disorder and* Cataract
     in children, **6**:245–265
     contrast sensitivity affected by, **3**:112
     illusions caused by, **5**:188
     monocular diplopia and, **3**:164
     systemic disorders and, **4**:129
     ultraviolet light causing, **3**:19, 160–161
   drug-induced changes in, **11**:47–49
   ectopic. *See* Ectopia lentis
   electrical injury of, **11**:54, 55*f*
   energy production in, **2**:278–279
   epithelium of, **2**:68, 68*f*, 69*f*, 70, 274, 274*f*, **4**:119–120, 120*f*, **11**:6*f*, 8, 8*f*
     active transport and, **11**:17–18
     degenerations of, **4**:124–126, 125*f*, 126*f*
     development of, **11**:23, 23*f*
     opacification of (capsular cataract), **11**:33–34
   evaluation of
     before cataract surgery, **11**:79
     in glaucoma, **10**:32. *See also* Lens-induced glaucoma; Lens particle glaucoma
     before refractive surgery, **13**:36–37
   exfoliation syndrome/pseudoexfoliation and, **11**:61–62, 61*f*
   focal opacifications and, **4**:126, 126–127, 127*f*
   foreign body in, **11**:51
   free radicals affecting, **2**:313–315, 314*f*, **11**:16–17
   generalized discoloration with loss of transparency and, **4**:126

glaucoma and. *See* Lens-induced glaucoma; Lens particle glaucoma
healing/repair of, 4:17
in homocystinuria, 6:263, 264*f*, 11:37
in hyperlysinemia, 11:37
infection/inflammation of, 4:122–123, 122*f*, 123*f*, 124*f*. *See also* Lens (crystalline), uveitis and
intumescent, phacomorphic glaucoma and, 10:120, 121*f*
ionic current flow around/through, 2:278, 279*f*
ischemic damage to, 11:64
luxed/luxated, 6:261, 261*f*, 11:35. *See also* Ectopia lentis
cataract surgery in patient with, 11:197–199, 198*f*
in children, 6:261, 261*f*
traumatic, 11:36, 50–51, 50*f*
in Marfan syndrome, 6:263, 11:36–37, 36*f*
membranes of, 2:275, 277
metabolic diseases affecting, 11:55–57, 56*f*
molecular biology of, 11:11–13, 11*f*
nucleus of, 2:70, 274–275, 275*f*, 4:120, 120*f*, 11:6*f*, 8–9
congenital cataract of, 11:33, 34*f*
degenerations of, 4:127, 128*f*, 129*f*
embryonic, 2:69*f*, 11:9, 22–23, 23*f*
opacification of (congenital nuclear cataract), 11:33, 34*f*
emulsification of. *See* Phacoemulsification
fetal, 11:9, 23*f*, 24–25, 24*f*
opacification of (congenital nuclear cataract), 11:33, 34*f*
opacification of. *See* Nuclear cataract
removal/disassembly of. *See also* Cataract surgery; Lensectomy; Phacoemulsification
in ECCE, 11:95, 212
femtosecond laser for, 11:127
fluid-based phacolysis for, 11:127
laser photolysis for, 11:127
in manual small-incision cataract surgery, 11:96
in phacoemulsification
locations for, 11:119–120, 120*f*, 121*f*
techniques of, 11:121–125, 122*f*, 123*f*, 124*f*, 125*f*
rotation of in phacoemulsification, 11:118, 125*f*
nutritional diseases affecting, 11:57–58
opacification of. *See* Cataract
oxidative damage to, 2:313–315, 314*f*, 11:16–17
perforating and penetrating injury of, 11:51, 51*f*, 52*f*
glaucoma and, 11:63
physiology of, 2:277–278, 279*f*, 11:17–19, 19*f*
radiation affecting, 1:238, 11:51–53
removal of. *See also* Cataract surgery; Lensectomy; Phacoemulsification
in early cataract surgery, 11:91–92, 91*f*, 92, 92*f*
retained, cataract surgery and, 11:143, 147, 159–160, 12:357–359, 358*t*, 359*f*
rubella (congenital) and, 9:210
in schematic eye, 3:105*t*
size of, 2:67, 11:7
smoking/tobacco use and, 11:58–59, 67–68
spherophakic, 6:260, 260*f*
subluxed/subluxated, 6:261, 262*t*, 11:35, 36*f*. *See also* Ectopia lentis
angle closure and, 10:90*t*, 112
cataract surgery in patient with, 11:197–199, 198*f*

in children, 6:261, 262*t*
traumatic, 11:36, 50–51, 50*f*
in sulfite oxidase deficiency, 6:264
sutures of, 2:69*f*, 70, 11:9
development of, 2:130, 11:23*f*, 24–25, 24*f*
opacification of (sutural/stellate cataract), 11:33, 33*f*
topography of, 2:41*f*, 4:119–120, 119*f*, 120*f*
transport functions in, 2:277–278, 11:17–19, 18*f*
traumatic damage to, 11:50–54, 50*f*, 51*f*, 52*f*, 54*f*, 55*f*, 206–209, 207*f*
child abuse and, 6:404
glaucoma and, 10:91–92, 11:63
phacoantigenic uveitis and, 4:122, 11:62
surgery and, 11:206–209, 207*f*
uveitis and, 4:122, 122*f*, 123*f*, 9:125–126, 125*f*, 11:59, 60*f*. *See also* Phacoantigenic (lens-associated) uveitis
water and cation balance in, maintenance of, 11:17–19, 18*f*
in Weill-Marchesani syndrome, 6:264
zonular fibers/zonules of, 2:41*f*, 51*f*, 52*f*, 61, 69*f*, 70, 273, 286, 4:120, 120*f*, 11:5, 6*f*, 7–8
absent/abnormal
cataract surgery and, 11:117, 118
in glaucoma, 11:202
iris coloboma/corectopia and, 11:196, 197*f*
in glaucoma, 10:112
in accommodation, 13:149–152, 150*f*, 151*f*
development of, 2:129*f*, 130, 11:25
evaluation of, before cataract surgery, 11:79
tertiary vitreous, 2:132, 4:132
Lens-associated (phacoantigenic) uveitis (lens-induced granulomatous/phacoanaphylactic endophthalmitis), 4:122, 122*f*, 123*f*, 9:125–126, 125*f*, 11:62
sympathetic ophthalmia and, 9:182
Lens block, 10:112
Lens capsule, 2:41*f*, 68, 68*f*, 69*f*, 273, 274*f*, 4:119, 120*f*, 11:6*f*, 7, 7*f*. *See also* Capsulorrhexis; Capsulotomy
anatomy of, 2:41*f*, 68, 69*f*, 273, 274*f*, 4:119, 120*f*
degenerations of, 4:124
development of, 2:129–130, 129*f*, 11:21, 22*f*, 23, 23*f*
healing/repair of, 4:17
rupture of
cataract formation and, 4:20. *See also* Cataract, traumatic
cataract surgery and, 11:144*t*, 160–162
staining, in cataract surgery, 11:195, 195*f*
topography of, 4:119, 120*f*
Lens clips. *See* Trial lens clips
Lens crystallins, 2:70, 130, 273, 275–276, 11:11–12, 11*f*. *See also* Crystallins
Lens edge barrier theory, posterior capsular opacification and, 3:205–206, 205*f*, 206*f*
Lens-fiber plasma membranes, 2:275, 277
Lens fibers, 2:68*f*, 69*f*, 70, 71*f*, 274–275, 274*f*, 4:120, 120*f*
accommodation and, 11:19
development of, 2:129*f*, 130, 11:8, 8*f*
primary fibers, 11:22, 23*f*
secondary fibers, 11:23–24, 23*f*
microspherophakia and, 11:29
opacities of, 4:126–127, 127*f*, 128*f*

zonular (zonules of Zinn), **2**:41*f*, 51*f*, 52*f*, 61, 69*f*, 70, 273, 286, **4**:120, 120*f*, **11**:5, 6*f*, 7–8
  absent/abnormal
    cataract surgery and, **11**:117, 118
      in glaucoma, **10**:112, **11**:202
        iris coloboma/corectopia and, **11**:196, 197*f*
      in glaucoma, **10**:112
  in accommodation, **13**:149–152, 150*f*, 151*f*
  development of, **2**:129*f*, 130, **11**:25
  evaluation of, before cataract surgery, **11**:79
  tertiary vitreous, **2**:132, **4**:132
Lens-induced glaucoma, **4**:106–107, 107*f*, **9**:22, 126, **10**:90, 90–92, 90*t*, 91*f*, 92*f*, 112, 120–124, 121*f*, 122*f*, 123*f*, 123*t*, **11**:63–64, 64*f*
  angle-closure, **10**:90, 90*t*, 112, 120–124, 121*f*, 122*f*, 123*f*, 123*t*
  in children, **6**:239
  in infants and children, **10**:141*t*
  open-angle, **10**:90–92, 90*t*, 91*f*, 92*f*
Lens-induced granulomatous endophthalmitis. *See* Lens-associated (phacoantigenic) uveitis
Lens–iris diaphragm retropulsion syndrome, **11**:156
Lens–iris interface, angle closure/angle-closure glaucoma and, **10**:110, 111*f*
Lens Opacities Classification System III (LOCS III), **11**:67
Lens particle glaucoma, **10**:90*t*, 91–92, 92*f*, **11**:63
Lens pit, **11**:21
Lens placode, **2**:121, 129, **11**:21, 22*f*
Lens proteins, **2**:275–277, **11**:11–12, 11*f*. *See also specific type*
  aging affecting, **11**:13, 39
  crystallins, **2**:70, 130, 273, 275–276, **11**:11–12, 11*f*. *See also* Crystallins
  cytoskeletal and membrane, **2**:277, **11**:11*f*, 12
  in phacoantigenic glaucoma, **10**:92
  in phacoantigenic uveitis/endophthalmitis, **4**:122, **9**:125–126, 125*f*, **11**:62
  in phacolytic glaucoma, **4**:107, 127, **9**:22, 126, **10**:90–91, 91*f*, **11**:63
  posttranslational modification of, **2**:277
  urea-insoluble (membrane structural), **2**:277, **11**:11*f*, 12
  urea-soluble (cytoskeletal), **2**:277, **11**:11*f*, 12
  in uveitis, **4**:122, **9**:125–126, 125*f*, **11**:62
  water-insoluble, **11**:11, 11*f*, 12
    age affecting, **11**:13
  water-soluble, **11**:11, 11*f*. *See also* Crystallins
    conversion of to water-insoluble, **11**:13
Lens rim artifact, in perimetry, **10**:56, 61, 62*f*
Lens vesicle, formation of, **2**:121, 129, 129*f*, **11**:21, 22*f*
Lensectomy. *See also* Cataract surgery
  for acute angle closure, **10**:115, 116
  in children
    with intraocular lens, **6**:257–258
    without intraocular lens, **6**:255–256, 257*f*
    for rubella, **6**:183
    for subluxed lenses, **6**:265
  for ectopia lentis, **10**:122
  in Marfan syndrome, **11**:37
  pars plana, **11**:132
    for uveitis, **9**:293
      juvenile idiopathic (chronic/rheumatoid) arthritis and, **9**:131
  for plateau iris, **10**:119–120

refractive. *See* Refractive lens exchange
  for subacute/intermittent angle closure, **10**:117
Lenses, **3**:62–83. *See also* Bifocal lenses; Contact lenses; Intraocular lenses; Ophthalmic lenses
  afocal systems and, **3**:80–83, 81*f*, 82*f*, 83*f*
  anophthalmic socket camouflage and, **7**:125
  aphakic. *See* Aphakic spectacles
  astigmatic, **3**:93. *See also* Cylinders; Spherocylindrical lenses
  Badal principle and, **3**:80, 269, 270*f*
  combinations of, **3**:66–67
    negative and positive, **3**:72–73, 72*f*
    spherocylindrical lenses at oblique axes and, **3**:99
  concave (minus/negative), **3**:72–73, 73*f*
    anophthalmic socket camouflage and, **7**:125
    paraxial ray tracing through, **3**:73–74, 73*f*, 74*f*
    prismatic effect of, **3**:87
  contact. *See* Contact lenses
  convex (plus/positive)
    anophthalmic socket camouflage and, **7**:125
    paraxial ray tracing through, **3**:69–72, 71*f*
    prismatic effect of, **3**:87
  correcting, in retinoscopy, **3**:124–125, 125*f*
  cylindrical. *See* Cylinders
  focal lengths of, **3**:78–79
  focal planes/points and, **3**:69, 70*f*
  Gaussian reduction and, **3**:79
  graphical image analysis and, **3**:76, 77*f*
  imaging with, **3**:30–31, 31*f*
    image quality and, **3**:37–39, 39*f*
  index of refraction and, **3**:6–7
  intraocular. *See* Intraocular lenses
  Knapp's law and, **3**:79–80, 80*f*
  lensmeters and, **3**:80, 268–271, 269*f*, 270*f*, 271*f*
  modeling unknown system and, **3**:76, 77*f*
  objects/images at infinity and, **3**:74
  principal planes/points and, **3**:75, 75*f*
  prismatic effect of (Prentice rule), **3**:87, 87*f*
    bifocal design and, **3**:150–156, 151*f*, 152*f*, 153*f*, 154*f*, 155*f*, 156*f*
  for slit-lamp biomicroscopy, **3**:251–255, 251*f*, 253*f*, 254*f*, 255*f*, 256*f*, **12**:19–20
  special materials used for, **3**:161–163
  spectacle. *See* Spectacle lenses
  spherocylindrical. *See* Cylinders; Spherocylindrical lenses
  standard (field), in lensmeter, **3**:269, 269*f*, 270*f*
  of telescope, **3**:81, 81*f*
  thick, **3**:76–78, 78*f*
  thin, **3**:66
    negative, **3**:72*f*, 73
  transverse magnification for single spherical refracting surface and, **3**:64–65, 65*f*
  vergence/reduced vergence and, **3**:62–64, 63*f*, 65
  virtual images/objects and, **3**:67–68, 67*f*, 69*f*
Lensmaker's equation (LME), **3**:59–60, 60–62, 61*f*
  reduced vergence and, **3**:63–64, 65
  thin-lens approximation and, **3**:66
  transverse magnification and, **3**:64–65, 65*f*
Lensmeters
  automatic, **3**:271–272
  manual, **3**:268–271, 269*f*, 270*f*, 271*f*
    Badal principle and, **3**:80, 269, 270*f*
    bifocal add measured with, **3**:270–271, 271*f*

Lensometers. *See* Lensmeters
Lente insulin, 1:196
Lenticonus/lentiglobus, 11:26, 26f
  anterior, 4:121, 11:26
  posterior, 4:121, 122f, 6:249, 249f, 250t, 11:26, 26f
Lenticular astigmatism
  contact lenses and, 3:175
  refractive surgery and, 13:39, 73, 139, 143
Lenticular contact lens, 3:169
Lenticular irregularities, decreased vision and, 5:111
Lenticular myopia (myopic shift), 11:39, 70
Lenticular refractive procedures, 3:231. *See also specific procedure and* Intraocular lenses (IOLs), for refractive errors
Lenticules, 13:53
  in epikeratoplasty, 13:53, 55, 55f
  in keratophakia, 13:53
  in LASIK, 13:68
Lentiglobus. *See* Lenticonus/lentiglobus
Lentigo (lentigines)
  senile, 7:165
  simplex (simple lentigines), 7:165
  solar, 7:165
Lentigo maligna (Hutchinson melanotic freckle/ precancerous melanosis), 7:168
Lentigo maligna melanoma, 4:69, 226, 227f, 7:168, 175
Leopard spot fluorescence pattern
  in primary central nervous system lymphoma, 9:282
  in uveal effusion syndrome, 12:182, 182f
"Leopard spotting," in posterior pole tumor, 4:317, 320f
Leptospirosis *(Leptospira interrogans)*, 9:254–256
Lescol. *See* Fluvastatin
Leser-Trélat sign, 4:215
Lesionectomy, for seizures, 1:262–263
Lesser (minor) arterial circle, 2:58, 59f, 5:14f, 18
  development of, 2:138
Lester hooks, for pupil expansion, 11:194
Letter chart visual acuity. *See* Visual acuity
Letterer-Siwe disease/syndrome. *See also* Histiocytosis
  orbital involvement in, 7:84
  in children, 6:338
Leucine zipper motif, 2:166, 167f
Leukemia, 4:10t, 11f, 6:297–298, 298f, 354
  neoplastic masquerade syndromes secondary to, 9:285
  ocular involvement in, 1:244, 4:326–328, 327f, 6:297–298, 298f
    choroid, 4:327, 6:354
    iris, 4:271t, 272f, 327, 6:351, 354
    optic disc/optic nerve, 4:327–328, 327f, 6:298, 298f, 354
    orbit, 4:328, 6:337, 7:90–91
    retina, 4:326, 327, 327f, 6:297
    uvea, 4:326–327
    uveitis differentiated from, 6:276t
    vitreous, 4:326
Leukemic retinopathy, 4:326, 327f
Leukeran. *See* Chlorambucil
Leukocoria, 5:263. *See also specific cause*
  in Coats disease, 4:150f, 12:144
  in persistent fetal vasculature (persistent hyperplastic primary vitreous), 12:308
  in retinoblastoma, 4:301, 301t, 302f, 5:263, 6:354, 355f
    differential diagnosis and, 6:358, 359t
  in toxocariasis, 9:235, 236f

Leukocyte common antigen, in immunohistochemistry, 4:34
Leukocyte function–associated antigen 1 (LFA-1), in neutrophil rolling, 9:18
Leukocyte oxidants, as inflammatory mediators, 8:177t
Leukocytes, 1:147, 9:9–12. *See also specific type*
  in inflammation, 4:6–7, 8f
Leukodystrophy
  Krabbe, 2:213t, 6:400t
  metachromatic, 2:213t, 6:400t
Leukoencephalopathy
  with cerebral autosomal dominant arteriopathy and subcortical infarcts, migrainelike headache in, 5:300
  progressive multifocal, in HIV infection/AIDS, 5:361, 362f
Leukomalacia, periventricular, 6:309
Leukomas, in Peters anomaly, 10:146, 11:27
Leukotriene modifiers, for pulmonary diseases, 1:145t, 146
Leukotrienes, 2:255, 256f, 258, 8:177t, 179t, 9:26f, 27
Leuprolide, ocular effects of, 1:302t
Levaquin. *See* Levofloxacin
Levatol. *See* Penbutolol
Levator anguli oris muscle, 7:133, 133f
Levator aponeurosis, 2:23, 25f, 27, 28, 239, 7:135f, 138–139, 139f
  eyelid retraction and, 5:281
  horns of, 7:138, 139f
  laceration of, 7:178
  ptosis and, 5:280, 280t, 7:206, 206f, 207t, 210
  repair of, for ptosis correction, 6:179, 7:211
Levator labii superioris alaeque nasi muscle, 7:133, 133f
Levator labii superioris muscle, 7:133, 133f
Levator muscle (levator palpebrae superioris), 2:17f, 20f, 25f, 26f, 28, 4:205, 5:10f, 62, 6:13, 15–16, 16f, 17t, 7:10, 135f, 138, 139
  anatomy of, 5:10f, 6:15–16, 16f, 17t
  congenital ptosis caused by dystrophic development of, 5:278–279
  disinsertion of, 2:27
  evaluation of function of, 5:275–276, 277f, 278f
    in ptosis, 6:179, 7:202, 202f, 203f
  external (transcutaneous) advancement of, for ptosis correction, 7:211
  innervation of, 2:21, 7:11, 139
  laceration of, 7:178
  in myasthenia gravis/myogenic ptosis, 6:137, 139t, 7:205
  in traumatic ptosis, 7:210
Levemir. *See* Detemir insulin
Levetiracetam, 1:263t
Levobunolol, 2:350, 350t, 10:162t, 168
  for childhood glaucoma, 6:242, 10:156
Levocabastine, 2:364, 365t
Levocycloversion, 6:35
Levodopa (L-dopa), for Parkinson disease, 1:258–259
Levodopa/carbidopa, for Parkinson disease, 1:259
Levofloxacin, 1:52t, 61, 2:371–373, 372t
  for bacterial keratitis, 8:163
Levothyroxine, for hypothyroidism, 1:212
Levoversion (left gaze), 6:35
Lewis antigens, transplant rejection and, 8:407
Lewy bodies, in Parkinson disease, 1:258

Lewy body dementia (LBD), **1**:265
Lexan lenses. *See* Polycarbonate spectacle lenses
Lexiva. *See* Fosamprenavir
Lexxel. *See* Felodipine
LFA-1. *See* Leukocyte function–associated antigen 1
LFU. *See* Lacrimal functional unit
LGB. *See* Lateral geniculate body/nucleus
Lhermitte sign, in multiple sclerosis, **5**:323
LHON. *See* Leber hereditary optic neuropathy
Liability, in inheritance, **2**:154
Library, DNA, **2**:154, 182, 183*f*
    cDNA, **2**:154, 182
    genomic, **2**:154, 182, 183*f*
Library for the Blind and Physically Handicapped,
    6:418*t*
Lice, ocular infection caused by, **8**:142, 142*f*, 149
    cholinesterase inhibitors for, **2**:340
Lid, Lids. *See* Eyelids
Lid lag, in thyroid eye disease, **7**:51
Lid margin. *See* Eyelids, margin of
Lid-twitch sign, Cogan, **5**:276–277, 328, **6**:137
Lidocaine, **1**:123*t*, **2**:387*t*, 388
    for blepharoplasty, **7**:224
    for cardioversion, **1**:125
    for cataract surgery, **11**:99–101, 101*f*
    for dacryocystorhinostomy, **7**:268
    intraocular, **2**:389
    maximum safe dose of, **1**:298*t*, 312
    for medical emergencies, **1**:292*t*
    toxic reaction to, **1**:299, 312
LIDRS. *See* Lens–iris diaphragm retropulsion syndrome
Lifestyle modification
    in age-related macular degeneration, **12**:63
    in coronary artery disease prevention, **1**:99, 133*t*
    in diabetes mellitus prevention/management, **1**:194,
        194–195
    in hypercholesterolemia management, **1**:131, 133*t*,
        134, 134*f*, 135*t*
    in hypertension management, **1**:74, 75*t*, 79*f*
Ligaments. *See specific ligament*
Ligand-gated channels, in signal transduction, **2**:261
Ligands, **2**:261, 262
Light. *See also specific aspect and* Light waves
    absorption of, **3**:13
        lasers and, **3**:21, 23*f*
    cone opsin changes caused by, **2**:293
    corneal reflex to
        corneal vertex and, **8**:37
        eyelid margin distance to (margin–reflex distance),
            5:276, 278*f*, **6**:179
        in ptosis, **6**:179, **7**:201–202, 202*f*, 205*f*
        tests of, **6**:76–78, 77*f*, 78*f*
    corpuscular theory of, **3**:3
    eye injury caused by exposure to, **2**:313, 315, 316,
        3:19, 160–161, 206, **12**:332–334. *See also* Light
        toxicity/photic damage/phototoxicity
    laser, properties of, **3**:20–21, 22*f*
    measurement of, **3**:16–19, 16*f*, 18*t*
    photon (particle) aspects of, **3**:3, 7
    photo-oxidative processes triggered by, **2**:313
        in retina, **2**:315
    point source of, in geometric optics, **3**:27–28

polarization of, **3**:10–12, 11*f*
propagation of, **3**:39–55. *See also* Propagation of light
pupillary response to. *See* Pupillary light reflex
reflection of, **3**:12–13, 12*f*. *See also* Reflection
retinal changes caused by, **2**:315, 316
retinal pigment epithelial transport systems affected
    by, **2**:307
rhodopsin changes caused by, **2**:291–293, 292*f*
scattering of, **3**:16
speed of, **3**:4, 40
transmission of, **3**:13. *See also* Transmission
as visible portion of electromagnetic spectrum, **3**:4,
    6*f*
wave theory of, **3**:3–7, 4*f*, 5*f*, 6*f*
Light adaptation, **2**:294
Light-adapted electroretinogram, **12**:34, 34*f*, 35, 36*f*. *See*
    also Electroretinogram
    in hereditary retinal/choroidal degenerations, **12**:224*t*
Light-adjustable intraocular lenses (Light Adjustable
    Lens), **13**:146–147, 147*f*, 161
Light amplification by stimulated emission of radiation,
    3:19. *See also* Lasers
Light chains, immunoglobulin, **9**:45, 45*f*
Light–dark (Arden) ratio, **12**:43
    in Best disease, **12**:237
Light–near dissociation, **2**:99, **5**:273–274, 274*t*
Light rays. *See* Rays
Light reflex. *See* Pupillary light reflex
Light response, of standing potential, **12**:42–43, 43*f*
Light-ROP study, **6**:281
Light toxicity/photic damage/phototoxicity, **2**:313, 316,
    3:19, 160–161, 206, **12**:332–334
    age-related macular degeneration and, **12**:63
    ambient exposure to ultraviolet or visible light and,
        12:334
    cataract surgery and, **11**:183–184, **12**:333, 334
    free-radical damage and, **2**:313, 315–316
    occupational, **12**:334
    ophthalmic instrumentation causing, **12**:333–334
        cataract surgery and, **11**:183–184, **12**:333, 334
    retinal, **2**:315, 316, **3**:19, 160–161, 206, **12**:332–334
    in retinitis pigmentosa, **12**:231
    retinopathy of prematurity and, **6**:281
    solar retinopathy and, **12**:332–333
Light waves. *See also* Light
    characteristics of, **3**:3–4, 4*f*, 5*f*
    coherence of, **3**:7–10, 8*f*, 9*f*
    diffraction of, **3**:13–16, 14*f*, 15*f*
    interference and, **3**:7–10, 8*f*, 9*f*
    theory of, **3**:3–7, 4*f*, 5*f*, 6*f*
Lighthouse for the Blind, **6**:417*t*
Lighthouse Continuous Text Cards, **3**:290
Lighthouse Distance Visual Acuity Test, **3**:290
Lighting, in low vision/vision rehabilitation, **3**:304
    contrast sensitivity and, **3**:291
Lightning streaks of Moore, **5**:189
Ligneous conjunctivitis, **8**:192–193, 192*f*
    in children, **6**:351
Lignocaine. *See* Lidocaine
Likelihood ratio, **1**:333–334, **2**:180
    combining screening tests and, **1**:334–335
    log of (LOD score), **2**:155, 180

Limbal dermoids, 4:48, 49f, 6:218, 218f, 348, 8:245–246, 246f
  Goldenhar syndrome and, 6:218, 349f, 393, 393f, 8:246
Limbal groove, for ECCE, 11:211
Limbal incision, for extraocular muscle surgery, 6:154
Limbal papillae, 4:50
Limbal relaxing incisions, 13:4t, 21f, 49, 50–52, 50f, 51t
  cataract surgery and, 11:130–131
    manual small-incision, 11:96
  instrumentation for, 13:51
  ocular surgery after, 13:52
  outcomes of, 13:52
  technique for, 13:51
Limbal stem cells, 8:6, 92–93
  in corneal epithelium maintenance, 2:43, 8:6, 92–93
  deficiency of, 8:92–94, 93t, 94f, 395–398. See also Limbal transplantation
    in aniridia, 10:147
    toxic insults/toxic keratoconjunctivitis from medications and, 8:87, 360
  transplantation of. See Limbal transplantation
Limbal transplantation (limbal autograft/allograft/stem cell transplantation), 8:94, 389, 395–398, 396–397f
  for chemical injuries, 8:94, 358
  indications for, 8:387t
Limbal (bulbar) vernal conjunctivitis/keratoconjunctivitis, 6:199–200, 8:187, 188f
Limbic system (cingulate gyrus), 5:63
Limbitis, in onchocerciasis, 9:242
Limbus, 2:48–49, 49f, 8:5, 37, 37f. See also under Limbal
  healing/repair in, 4:16
  immune response and, 9:63, 63f, 64
  marginal corneal infiltrates in blepharoconjunctivitis and, 8:210
  squamous cell carcinoma of, 8:231–232, 232f
Limbus-based conjunctival flap, for trabeculectomy, 10:187, 189f
  closure of, 10:192
Limiting membrane
  external, 2:75f, 76f, 78, 80f, 4:145, 12:10, 11f, 12, 13f, 14f
    development of, 2:126
  internal, 2:74f, 75f, 79, 80f, 4:145, 146f, 12:10, 11f, 12, 14f
    optic disc, 2:90, 92f
    in retinal healing/repair, 4:17
    in Valsalva retinopathy, 12:153–154
    vitreous detachment and, 2:286–287, 4:135
  middle, 12:10, 11f, 12, 14f
Lincoff rules, 12:286, 288f, 289f
Line of Gennari, 5:34
Line of vision, principal, 3:106
Linear IgA dermatosis, 8:199, 205t
Linear incisions (tangential/arcuate incisions), for keratorefractive surgery, 13:21, 21f
Linear staining, 8:56
Linearly polarized (plane-polarized) light, 3:10
LINEs. See Long interspersed elements

Linezolid, 1:53t, 64
Lingua plicata, in Melkersson-Rosenthal syndrome, 5:287
Lingual nerve, 5:66f
Link protein, in vitreous, 2:283
Linkage (gene), 2:154–155, 177–180, 179f, 181f, 193, 197
Linkage disequilibrium (allelic association), 2:155
  HLA-associated diseases and, 9:73
Lipid A, lipopolysaccharide-induced inflammation and, 9:14
Lipid keratopathy, 8:342, 342f
  in herpes zoster ophthalmicus, 8:120, 121f
Lipid layer of tear film, 2:42, 237–239, 238f, 238t, 239f
  in external eye defense, 8:95
Lipid-lowering therapy, 1:134–136, 134f, 135t, 136f, 137t. See also specific agent
  for ischemic heart disease, 1:107, 109t
  statins in, 1:136–138, 137t
Lipid peroxidation, 2:311, 312–313
  in lens opacification, 11:16
  retinal vulnerability and, 2:315
Lipid strip, 2:239
Lipidoses. See Lipids, disorders of metabolism and storage of
Lipids
  disorders of metabolism and storage of (lipidoses), 6:400t, 8:308–313, 309t
    corneal changes in, 8:308–313, 309t
      in Schnyder corneal dystrophy, 8:284, 309
    mucolipidoses and, 8.312
  as inflammatory mediators, 9:25–27, 26f
  as ocular hypotensive agents. See Prostaglandin analogues
  in retinal pigment epithelium, 2:305
  solubility of, medication absorption affected by, 2:326, 329
  in tear film. See Lipid layer of tear film
  in vitreous, 2:286
Lipitor. See Atorvastatin
Lipoatrophy, at insulin injection site, 1:198
Lipocalins, in tear film, 2:240
Lipodermoids (dermolipomas), 4:49f, 50, 8:246
  in children, 6:348–349, 349f
    Goldenhar syndrome and, 4:50, 6:349, 349f, 393, 393f
  of orbit, 7:37, 37f
Lipofuscin granules (wear-and-tear pigment), 2:72
  accumulation of, in Best disease, 12:236
Lipofuscinlike material, in Stargardt disease, 12:235, 235f
Lipofuscinosis, neuronal ceroid, 6:398, 401t, 12:251t, 254, 259–260
  pigmentary retinopathy in, 12:251t, 254, 260
Lipohypertrophy, at insulin injection site, 1:198
Lipomas, of orbit, 4:245
Lipopeptide antibiotics, 1:53t, 64
Lipopolysaccharide, bacterial, 8:132. See also Endotoxins
  endophthalmitis severity and, 9:16
  in innate immune response, 9:14–15, 14t, 15
  uveitis caused by, 9:15, 71
    animal model of (experimental immune uveitis), 9:69

Lipoproteins, **1**:132, 132*t*
    risk assessment and (lipoprotein analysis), **1**:132–133,
        133*t*
Liposarcomas, of orbit, **4**:245, **7**:79
Liposomes
    for drug delivery, **2**:331
    for gene therapy, **2**:187–188
Liposuction, neck, **7**:236–238
Lipoxygenase
    in eicosanoid synthesis, **2**:256*f*, 257, **9**:25, 26–27, 26*f*
    in leukotriene synthesis, **2**:256*f*, 258
Lisch epithelial corneal dystrophy, **8**:268*t*, 270*t*, 273–274,
    274*f*
    genetics of, **8**:269*t*, 273
Lisch nodules, **4**:271*t*, 272*f*, **5**:340, 340*f*, **6**:225, 225*f*,
    365–366, 366*f*
    in neurofibromatosis, **6**:225, 225*f*, 365–366, 366*f*, 370
Lisinopril
    for heart failure, **1**:118
    for hypertension, **1**:76*t*, 78*t*
    for non–ST-segment elevation acute coronary
        syndrome, **1**:111
Lispro insulin, **1**:196, 196*t*
Lissamine green, **2**:392, **8**:17
    in ocular surface evaluation, **8**:17
    in tear-film evaluation, **8**:17, 56
Listing's equatorial plane, **6**:27, 27*f*
Lithiasis, conjunctival, **8**:333
Lithium, **1**:257
Lithonate. *See* Lithium
Liver disease
    hemostatic abnormalities and, **1**:156
    hepatitis C and, **1**:26
    metastatic uveal melanoma causing, **4**:281–282, 282*t*
    viral carcinogenesis and, **1**:237, 275, 280
Living will, surgery in older patients and, **1**:224–225
Livostin. *See* Levocabastine
LK (lamellar keratoplasty). *See* Keratoplasty, lamellar
LME. *See* Lensmaker's equation
LMs. *See* Lymphatic malformations
LMWHs (low-molecular-weight heparins). *See* Heparin
    therapy
LMX1B gene, **10**:11*t*
LN. *See* Latent/manifest latent (fusion maldevelopment)
    nystagmus
Loa loa (loiasis), **8**:141, 170–171
    orbital involvement and, **4**:235
Load, in phacoemulsification, **11**:103
Lobectomy, for seizures, **1**:262–263
"Lobster claw" (Worst/Artisan) lens, **3**:207, 208*f*
LOC387715 (Ala69Ser) gene, in age-related macular
    degeneration, **12**:56
Local anesthesia. *See* Anesthesia (anesthetics), local
Localized (circumscribed) choroidal hemangioma,
    4:200, 291, 291*f*
Location, image, **3**:36
Location effect, of cylindrical lenses, **3**:313–314, 313*f*
Lockwood, suspensory ligament of (Lockwood
    ligament), **2**:35, 36*f*, **6**:22, 23*f*, **7**:138, 140
LOCS III (Lens Opacities Classification System III),
    11:67
Locus (gene), **2**:155, 193. *See also* Gene
Locus heterogeneity, **2**:155, 192, 193

LOD score, **2**:155, 180
Lodine. *See* Etodolac
Lodosyn. *See* Carbidopa
Lodoxamide, **2**:365, 365*t*
    for allergic conjunctivitis, **8**:186
Lofgren/Löfgren syndrome, **8**:73, **9**:174
Log of the likelihood ratio (LOD score), **2**:155, 180
LogMAR, **3**:109, 110*t*, **6**:73
    cystoid macular edema after cataract surgery and,
        11:182
Lomefloxacin, **1**:52*t*, 61
Lomustine, **1**:242*t*
Long (q) arm, **2**:159
Long arm 13 deletion (13q14) syndrome, **2**:204–205, 205*t*
Long-chain polyunsaturated fatty acids, age-related
    macular degeneration and, **12**:62
Long ciliary arteries, **5**:13*f*, 14*f*, 18
Long ciliary nerves, **2**:36, 247
Long interspersed elements, **2**:166
Longitudinal (temporal) coherence, **3**:8, 8*f*
Longitudinal fasciculus, medial, **2**:104, 104*f*, **5**:38, 39*f*,
    42, 44*f*, 45*f*, 46
    diplopia caused by disruption of, **5**:224–226, 224*f*,
        225*f*, 226*f*
    dissociated nystagmus caused by lesions of, **5**:254
    internuclear ophthalmoplegia caused by lesions of,
        6:141
    rostral interstitial nucleus of, **5**:38, 39*f*, 42, 44*f*, 46*f*,
        199, 199–200
Longitudinal (axial) magnification, **3**:36. *See also*
    Magnification
Longitudinal/spin-lattice relaxation time (T1), **5**:70, 72,
    7:26–27
Longitudinal Study of Cataract, **11**:67
Loniten. *See* Minoxidil
Loop diuretics
    for heart failure, **1**:118, 119
    for hypertension, **1**:76*t*, 80
Loop of Meyer, **2**:94*f*, 96, **5**:34
Lopinavir/ritonavir, **1**:34
Lopressor. *See* Metoprolol
Lorabid. *See* Loracarbef
Loracarbef, **1**:49*t*, 59
Lorazepam
    for benign essential blepharospasm, **7**:220
    for seizures, **1**:297
Losartan, **1**:76*t*, 78*t*
Loss, as issue for older patient, **1**:225
Loss of heterozygosity, **2**:173
Lost muscle, surgery and, **6**:24, 159–160
    esodeviations and, **6**:97–98
Lotemax. *See* Loteprednol
Lotensin. *See* Benazepril
Loteprednol, **2**:357*t*, 361, 365*t*, 366
    with tobramycin, **2**:373*t*
    for uveitis, **9**:101*t*, 102
Lotrafilcon A contact lenses, **3**:177*t*
Lotrel. *See* Amlodipine
Lotrimin. *See* Clotrimazole
Louis-Bar syndrome (ataxia-telangiectasia), **5**:339*t*, 344,
    345*f*, **6**:364*t*, 378–379, 379*f*, **8**:77, 241
    ATM mutation in, **2**:170, **6**:379
Louse. *See* Lice

Lovastatin
  cataracts and, **1**:139
  for hypercholesterolemia/heart disease prevention,
    1:137*t*
Lovenox. *See* Enoxaparin
Low birth weight, retinopathy and, **6**:281, **12**:157, 163,
  164, 166. *See also* Retinopathy, of prematurity
Low-density-lipoprotein cholesterol, **1**:131, 132, 132*t*.
  See also Cholesterol
  β-blockers affecting, **1**:139
  drugs affecting metabolism of, **1**:137*t*
  ischemic heart disease risk and, **1**:100, 131, 132–133,
    132*t*, 133*t*
  reducing levels of, **1**:131, 137*t*. *See also* Lipid-lowering
    therapy
    goals for, hypercholesterolemia management and,
      1:134, 134*f*, 135*t*
  risk assessment and, **1**:132–133, 133*t*
  screening, **1**:271
Low-dose helical chest CT, in cancer screening, **1**:275
Low-molecular-weight heparins. *See* Heparin therapy
Low-tension glaucoma, **10**:4, 5*t*, 78–82, 80*t*. *See also*
  Glaucoma, normal-tension
Low vision, **3**:283, 284*f*, 285. *See also* Blindness; Vision
  rehabilitation; Visual loss/impairment
  assessment of, **3**:288–294, **5**:91–110
    adjunctive testing in, **5**:104–110
    Amsler grid testing in, **5**:98–99
    associated symptoms and, **5**:91–92
    best-corrected visual acuity and, **5**:92
    in children, **6**:414
    color vision and, **3**:294, **5**:104–105
    confrontation testing in, **5**:98
    contrast sensitivity and, **3**:291–292, 292, **5**:105–106
    distance visual acuity and, **3**:289–290, **5**:92
    electrophysiologic testing in, **5**:108–110, 110*f*
    electroretinography in, **5**:109–110, 110*f*
      in infant, **6**:415
    fluorescein angiography in, **5**:107, 107*f*
    functional history in, **3**:288–289
    fundus examination in, **5**:95–97, 96*f*, 97*f*
    glare and, **3**:293
    history in, **5**:91–92
    near visual acuity and, **3**:290–291, **5**:92
    neuroimaging in, **5**:83
    nonorganic disorders and, **5**:310–314, 311*t*, 313*f*,
      314*f*, 315*f*
    optical coherence tomography in, **5**:108
    patient well-being and, **3**:289
    perimetry in, **5**:99–104, 101*f*, 102*f*, 103*f*
    photostress recovery testing in, **5**:106
    potential acuity meter testing in, **5**:106
    pupillary testing and, **5**:92–95, 94*f*
    refraction in, **3**:294, **5**:92
    time course and, **5**:91
    visual evoked potential testing in, **5**:108–109
    visual field testing in, **5**:97–104, 101*f*, 102*f*, 103*f*.
      See also Visual field testing
      central visual field testing and, **3**:292–293
      peripheral visual field testing and, **3**:292
    visual function measurement and, **3**:289–294
  bilateral/binocular, **5**:91
    nonorganic disorders and, **5**:311–314, 313*f*, 314*f*, 315*f*

central visual field deficit causing, **3**:286–287, 287*f*
  assessment of, **3**:292–293
classification of, **3**:286–288, **5**:111–172. *See also*
  specific causative factor
cloudy media causing, **3**:286
counseling/support groups and, **3**:305
definition of, **3**:285
in infants and children, **3**:306–307, **6**:413–417,
  417–418*t*
  achromatopsia and, **6**:291
  albinism and, **6**:298
  approach to infant with, **6**:414–416
  cataracts and, **6**:252
  craniosynostosis and, **6**:390
  delayed visual maturation and, **6**:416
  in glaucoma, **6**:233, 243
  Leber congenital amaurosis and, **6**:289
  management of, **6**:416–417
  nystagmus and, **6**:330
  optic atrophy and, **6**:310, 415
  optic nerve hypoplasia and, **6**:414–415
  pregeniculate visual loss and, **6**:414–415
  retrogeniculate visual loss/cortical visual
    impairment and, **6**:415–416
  sources of information on, **6**:417–418*t*
management of, **3**:283, 294–304, **5**:111–172.
  See also Low vision aids; Vision
    rehabilitation
  levels of services and, **3**:305–306
  nonoptical aids in, **3**:301–304, 302*f*
  optical devices in, **3**:295–301
  professionals providing, **3**:305
moderate impairment, **3**:285
near-total vision loss, **3**:285
peripheral visual field deficit causing, **3**:288
  assessment of, **3**:292
profound impairment, **3**:285
severe impairment, **3**:285
socioeconomic consequences of, **3**:283, 284*f*
sources of information on, **6**:417–418*t*
terminology used in, **3**:284–286
total blindness, **3**:285
unilateral/monocular, **5**:91
  nonorganic disorders and, **5**:310–311, 311*t*
Low vision aids, **3**:294–304. *See also* Vision
  rehabilitation
  afocal systems for, **3**:81–83, 81*f*, 82*f*, 83*f*
  in age-related macular degeneration, **12**:79
  for cataract, **11**:71
  in cone dystrophies, **12**:232
  contrast sensitivity affecting use of, **3**:291
  nonoptical, **3**:301–304, 302*f*
  optical, **3**:295–301
    contrast sensitivity affecting use of, **3**:291
    magnifiers, **3**:298–299, 300*f*
    prisms as, **3**:300–301
    spectacles, **3**:295–298, 298*f*
    telescopes, **3**:299–300, 301*f*
  in retinitis pigmentosa, **12**:230
Lowe disease/syndrome (oculocerebrorenal syndrome),
  4:121, **6**:302
  childhood glaucoma and, **6**:239, 302
  congenital corneal keloids in, **8**:264

ocular findings in carriers of, 2:222t, 223
pediatric cataract and, 6:247t, 302
Lower eyelid. See Eyelids, lower
Lower eyelid reverse ptosis, 7:207
Lower face and neck rejuvenation, 7:234–238, 237f, 238f
Lower-order aberrations, 13:6, 6f, 7f
LOXL1 gene, 10:11t, 85
in exfoliation/pseudoexfoliation, 4:106, 10:85
Lozol. See Indapamide
LPS. See Lipopolysaccharide
LPS (levator palpebrae superioris). See Levator muscle
LR. See Lateral rectus muscles
LRI. See Limbal relaxing incisions
LSC (Longitudinal Study of Cataract), 11:67
LSCM. See Laser scanning confocal microscope
LSL. See Laser suture lysis
LTBP2 gene, in glaucoma, 10:11t, 142
LTK. See Laser thermokeratoplasty
LTP. See Laser trabeculoplasty
Lubricants. See also Artificial tears
for chemical injuries, 8:358
for craniosynostosis-induced corneal exposure, 6:389
for dry eye, 8:57, 60t
for paralytic ectropion, 7:216
for peripheral ulcerative keratitis, 8:212
for persistent corneal epithelial defects, 8:87
for recurrent corneal erosions, 8:84
for Stevens-Johnson syndrome, 6:201, 8:196–197
Lucentis. See Ranibizumab
Luliconazole, 1:65
Lumbar puncture
in cerebral ischemia/stroke, 1:94
in subarachnoid hemorrhage, 1:98
in syphilis, 1:14, 9:248
Lumboperitoneal shunting, for idiopathic intracranial hypertension, 5:124
Lumens, 3:17, 18t
Lumican, 8:7
mutation in gene for, in cornea plana, 8:255
Lumigan. See Bimatoprost
Luminance, 3:17, 18t
background, perimetry variations and, 10:56
contrast sensitivity function testing and, 3:112
stimulus, perimetry variations and, 10:56
Luminous flux, 3:18t
Luminous intensity (candle power), 3:18t
Luminous object, 3:31
Lunesta. See Eszopiclone
Lung cancer, 1:274–275
eye involvement and, 1:244, 4:200, 201f, 316t, 321f, 7:92
paraneoplastic-induced saccadic intrusions and, 5:256
screening for, 1:274
Lung diseases. See Pulmonary diseases
Lupron. See Leuprolide
Lupus anticoagulant
in antiphospholipid antibody syndrome, 1:170, 171–172
retinal vasculitis and, 9:142
Lupus choroidopathy, 9:142, 142f, 12:195

Lupus erythematosus, systemic, 1:167–170, 168f, 169t, 9:140–143, 141f, 141t, 142f
choroidal perfusion abnormalities and, 12:179
eyelid manifestations of, 4:213t
HLA association in, 1:167, 9:140
optic nerve involvement and, 5:144
refractive surgery contraindicated in, 13:184
retinal manifestations of, 9:141–142, 141f, 142f, 12:195–196, 195f
Lupus nephritis, 1:167
Lupus retinopathy, 9:141–142, 141f, 142f, 12:195–196, 195f
Lupus vasculitis, 9:141–142, 141f, 142f, 12:195–196, 195f
choroidal perfusion abnormalities and, 12:179
Lutein, 2:81
antioxidant effect of, 2:316
cataract risk affected by, 11:58
in macula, 12:8
age-related macular degeneration and, 12:62
Luteinizing hormone, pituitary adenoma producing, 1:215
Lux, 3:18t
Luxed/luxated globe, in craniosynostosis, 6:389–390
Luxed/luxated lens, 11:35. See also Ectopia lentis
cataract surgery in patient with, 11:197–199, 198f
in children, 6:261, 261f
traumatic, 11:36, 50–51, 50f
Lyme disease/Lyme borreliosis, 1:14–16, 5:363–364, 363f, 8:137, 9:250–254, 250f, 251f, 252f, 253t, 12:210
ocular manifestations of, 5:363–364, 9:136, 251–252, 252f, 12:210
Lymecycline, 1:62
Lymph node biopsy
in eyelid melanoma, 7:176
in sebaceous adenocarcinoma, 7:174–175
Lymphadenopathy, in HIV infection/AIDS, 1:31
Lymphadenopathy-associated virus (LAV), 1:28. See also Human immunodeficiency virus
Lymphangiectasia, 8:76–77, 243
Lymphangiomas. See Lymphatic malformations
Lymphatic malformations (lymphangiomas), 7:65–66, 66f, 8:243. See also Vascular malformations
orbital, 4:240, 241f, 6:341–342, 341f, 7:65–66, 66f
Lymphatic/lymphocytic tumors. See also specific type and Lymphoproliferative lesions
conjunctival, 4:71–74, 72f, 73f, 8:242–244
Lymphatics (afferent lymphatic channels), 9:12, 22, 33, 34, 37
conjunctival, 8:173
eyelid, 2:30–31, 31f, 7:143
Lymphocyte-mediated immune effector responses, 9:42–43, 42f, 48–51, 49f, 50t, 52–53, 53f
with antibody effector mechanisms, 9:51–55, 54f
cytotoxic lymphocytes and, 9:42f, 43
delayed hypersensitivity T lymphocytes and, 9:42–43, 42f, 48–51, 49f, 50t
Lymphocytes, 4:7–9, 8f, 9:12, 42–43, 42f. See also B cells; T cells
activation of, 9:37–38, 40f, 42
cytologic identification of, in immune-mediated keratoconjunctivitis, 8:182t
effector, 9:42–43, 42f, 48–51, 49f, 50t, 52–53, 53f

Lymphocytic choriomeningitis virus (LCMV), 6:186, 9:211–212
Lymphocytic hypophysitis, 5:346–347
Lymphocytic thyroiditis, subacute ("painless"), 1:213
Lymphocytic/lymphatic tumors. *See also specific type and* Lymphoproliferative lesions
  conjunctival, 4:71–74, 72*f*, 73*f*, 8:242–244
Lymphohistiocytosis, EBV-associated hemophagocytic (EBV-HLH), 1:25
Lymphoid follicle, 4:51, 52*f*, 71
Lymphoid folliculosis, benign, 4:71, 8:24, 24*f*
Lymphoid hyperplasia (lymphoid infiltration/reactive lymphoid hyperplasia/benign lymphoid pseudotumor/pseudolymphoma). *See also* Lymphoproliferative lesions
  of conjunctiva, 4:71–72, 72*f*, 8:243, 244*f*
  of orbit, 4:239, 7:79–84, 81*f*, 82*f*. *See also* Lymphomas, orbital
    atypical, 4:239
  of uveal tract (uveal lymphoid infiltration), 4:202, 325–326
Lymphoid proliferation, uveal tract involvement and, 4:202, 202*f*
  masquerade syndromes secondary to, 9:285
Lymphoid pseudotumor/pseudolymphoma, benign. *See* Lymphoid hyperplasia
Lymphoid stem cells, 1:147
Lymphoid tissues, mucosa-associated (MALT), 4:47, 8:173, 9:59
  in allergic reactions, 9:55
  of conjunctiva (conjunctiva-associated/CALT), 2:35, 4:47, 8:3, 5, 180–181, 9:59
  lymphoma of (extranodal marginal zone lymphoma/MALToma), 4:72–73, 73*f*, 74, 7:80
Lymphokines, 9:27
Lymphomas, 4:10*t*, 11*f*
  Burkitt
    Epstein-Barr virus associated with, 1:25, 237
    of orbit, in children, 6:337
  Chlamydia psittaci and, 1:17
  conjunctival, 4:72, 72–74, 72*f*, 73*f*, 8:244, 245*f*
  extranodal marginal zone (mucosa-associated/MALT), 4:72–73, 73*f*, 74, 7:80
  in HIV infection/AIDS, 1:40, 5:358, 9:314
  intraocular (primary central nervous system/large cell/vitreoretinal/retinal/histiocytic/non-Hodgkin of CNS/reticulum cell sarcoma), 1:244, 4:140–142, 141*f*, 142*f*, 143*f*, 323–325, 323*f*, 325*f*, 9:136, 281–284, 282*f*, 283*f*, 12:199, 199*f*
    central serous retinopathy differentiated from, 12:174
    in HIV infection/AIDS, 9:314
    uveitis differentiated from, 9:91, 136, 281–283
    in children, 6:276*t*
  mucosa-associated (MALToma/extranodal marginal zone), 4:72–73, 73*f*, 74, 7:80
  numb chin associated with, 5:303
  ocular adnexa, staging of, 4:350–352*t*
  ocular involvement in, 1:244
  orbital, 4:239–240, 239*f*, 7:79–84, 81*f*, 82*f*
    in children, 6:337
    in HIV infection/AIDS, 9:314
    lacrimal gland origin and, 7:82, 83
    mucosa-associated (MALT), 7:80
    orbital inflammatory syndrome differentiated from, 4:232
  systemic, neoplastic masquerade syndromes secondary to, 9:284–285
  transfusion-transmitted virus (TTV) associated with, 1:26
  of uveal tract, 4:202, 202*f*
  of vitreous, 4:140–142, 141*f*, 142*f*, 143*f*, 323*f*
Lymphoproliferative lesions/lymphomatous tumors. *See also specific type and* Lymphoid hyperplasia; Lymphomas
  Epstein-Barr virus and, 1:25
  of lacrimal glands, 7:88
  of orbit, 4:238–240, 239*f*, 7:79–85
    histiocytic disorders, 7:84
    lymphoid hyperplasia/lymphomas, 4:239, 7:79–84, 81*f*, 82*f*
    plasma cell tumors, 7:84
    xanthogranuloma, 7:85
Lynch incision, for orbitotomy, 7:108*f*, 110–111
Lyonization (X chromosome inactivation/Barr body), 2:149, 155, 168–169, 220–224
  ocular findings in carrier states and, 2:220–224, 221–222*f*, 222*t*
Lysin, β, in external eye defense, 8:95
Lysis, cell, by cytotoxic lymphocytes, 9:51, 53*f*
Lysosomal fusion, blocking, as microbial virulence factor, 1:4
Lysosomal storage disorders, 6:398, 8:305–307, 306*t*. *See also* Mucopolysaccharidoses
  GM₁ gangliosidosis type I and, 6:303
  retinal degeneration and, 12:262–264, 263*f*, 264*f*
    mucopolysaccharidoses, 12:250*t*, 251*t*, 262
Lysosomes, in outer segment phagocytosis, 12:15
Lysozyme
  in aqueous humor, 2:270
  in tear film, 2:240, 8:54–55
  in external eye defense, 8:95
LYST gene, in Chédiak-Higashi syndrome, 6:300*t*, 12:258*t*
Lysyl hydroxylase, defects in gene for, in Ehlers Danlos syndrome, 2:213*t*, 8:252, 325
Lysyl oxidase–like (LOXL1) gene, 10:11*t*, 85
  in exfoliation/pseudoexfoliation, 4:106, 10:85

M

M1S1 gene, in amyloidosis, 8:317*t*
M cells (magnocellular neurons/system), 5:28, 33, 6:42–43, 43*f*, 10:40
  development of, 6:42, 43*f*, 44
    abnormal visual experience affecting, 6:46
M-cone opsin genes, 2:294–295
  mutations in, 2:297
M cones, 2:294
  absent/defective
    in achromatopsia, 12:214
    in dichromacy, 12:213
  bipolar cells for, 2:298

gene for, on X chromosome, 2:294–295
horizontal cells for, 2:299
retinal ganglion cells for, 2:299f, 300
M proteins
overproduction of, corneal deposits and, 8:319
streptococcal, 8:133
M-like proteins, streptococcal, 8:133
M unit, 3:290
MAC. *See* Membrane attack complex
MAC (*Mycobacterium avium* complex) infections, in
HIV infection/AIDS, 1:39, 5:360, 9:128
Mac-1. *See* Macrophage-1 antigen
Macroadenoma, pituitary, 1:214
Macroaneurysms, retinal arterial, 12:147–148, 147f
age-related macular degeneration differentiated from,
12:68–69, 69f
Macrocytic anemia, 1:148
Macroglia, retinal, 2:301
α₂-Macroglobulin, in aqueous humor, 2:269
Macroglobulinemia, Waldenström, corneal deposits in,
8:320
Macrolides, 1:44, 50t, 61, 2:377. *See also specific agent*
polyene, 2:378–380, 379t
Macromers, for light-adjustable IOLs, 13:146, 161
Macrophage-1 antigen (Mac-1), in neutrophil rolling, 9:18
Macrophage-activating factor, in delayed
hypersensitivity, 9:49f, 50
Macrophage chemotactic protein-1, 9:28t
Macrophage colony-stimulating factor, in cicatricial
pemphigoid, 8:199
Macrophages, 4:7, 9:11
activation and recruitment of, 9:11, 14t, 20–23, 21f
Macropsia, 5:189
migraine and, 5:191
Macrosaccadic oscillations, 5:255, 255f
Macrosquare-wave jerks, 5:205, 254, 255f
Macrostriae, in LASIK flaps, 13:105–108, 107t. *See also*
Striae
Macugen. *See* Pegaptanib
Macula/macula lutea, 2:71, 73f, 79–81, 4:146, 147f, 12:8,
9f, 9t. *See also under Macular*
age-related changes in, 12:55–56, 56f. *See also*
Age-related macular degeneration
anatomy of, 2:71, 73f, 79–81, 80f, 82f, 12:8, 9f, 9t
antioxidants in, 2:318f
choroidal neovascularization in. *See* Age-related
macular degeneration
detachment of, visual acuity after reattachment
surgery and, 12:291
development of, 6:170
diseases of. *See also specific type*
decreased vision and, 5:112
ERG in evaluation of, 12:39, 40f
illusions and, 5:188
transient visual loss and, 5:175, 176
vitrectomy for, 12:346–352
evaluation of, 3:277–278, 278f
before cataract surgery, 11:80, 82
retinal pigment epithelium in, 4:148
vitreous attachment to, 12:7f, 8
posterior vitreous detachment and, 12:298,
302–304, 303f

Macular atrophy
chloroquine/hydroxychloroquine causing, 12:266,
266f
in cone dystrophies, 12:232, 233f
in Stargardt disease, 12:235, 235f
Macular corneal dystrophy. *See* Macular dystrophies
Macular degeneration
age-related. *See* Age-related macular degeneration
cataract surgery in patient with, 11:80
juvenile (Stargardt disease/fundus flavimaculatus),
4:172, 174f, 6:292–293, 293f, 12:234–236, 235f,
236t
ABC/ABCR transporter mutations causing, 2:296,
4:172, 6:293, 12:233, 234
cone–rod dystrophy and, 6:293, 12:233, 235
gene for, 12:222, 233, 234
retinal pigment epithelium in, 2:309, 12:234,
235f
vitelliform
adult-onset, 4:175, 176f, 12:237–238, 238f
age-related macular degeneration differentiated
from, 12:69, 69f
Best disease/vitelliruptive macular degeneration,
4:174–175, 6:293–294, 294f, 12:236–237,
237f
bestrophin defect causing, 2:297, 4:175, 6:294,
12:236
electro-oculogram in, 6:293, 294, 12:44, 237
identification of carriers for, 2:217
retinal pigment epithelium in, 2:308–309
Macular detachment
optic pits and, 12:295, 295f
vitelliform exudative, 12:238, 238f
Macular dystrophies, 4:96, 97f, 97t, 172–175, 8:268t,
270t, 278t, 283–284, 284f, 12:234–242. *See also
specific type*
corneal, 4:96, 97f, 97t, 8:268t, 270t, 278t, 283–284,
284f
genetics of, 8:269t, 283
hereditary, 12:234–242. *See also specific type*
in children, 6:292–294
North Carolina, 12:245–246, 245f
Sorsby, 12:241–242, 242f
retinal pigment epithelium in, 2:308
TIMP3 defects causing, 2:182, 297, 12:241
vitelliform. *See* Macular degeneration, vitelliform
Macular edema, 4:158–160, 159f, 160f
in branch retinal vein occlusion, 12:123
photocoagulation for, 12:124, 125f
in central retinal vein occlusion, 12:128
grid pattern photocoagulation for, 12:131
cystoid, 12:142–143, 142f
angiographic, 12:143
after cataract surgery, 11:182
corticosteroids for, 12:143, 360
after cataract surgery, 11:183
route of administration of, 2:360t
in uveitis, 9:300
in HTLV-1 infection, 9:219
in multifocal choroiditis and panuveitis syndrome,
9:162
in pars planitis, 9:135, 137, 138, 12:196

postoperative, **12**:360, 360*f*
  cataract surgery and, **11**:143, 144*t*, 181–183,
    182*f*, **12**:142, 143, 360
  in glaucoma, **11**:202–203
  after Nd:YAG capsulotomy, **11**:175
  vitreous prolapse and, **11**:162
  prostaglandins and, **9**:25–26
  in retinitis pigmentosa, **9**:287, **12**:225, 230, 230*f*
  in sarcoidosis, **8**:74, **9**:175
  in uveitis, **9**:300–301
    cataract surgery and, **9**:293
  diabetic, **12**:95–103, 96*f*, 97*f*, 99*f*, 101*f*, 102*t*
    cataract surgery and, **11**:205
    clinically significant, **12**:90, 97, 98, 99*f*
    treatment of, **12**:98, 98–103, 101*f*, 102*t*
      corticosteroids for, route of administration of,
        2:360*t*
      pharmacologic treatment, **12**:100–101, 101*f*
      photocoagulation/laser treatment, **12**:97, 98, 99*f*,
        101–103, 102*t*
      surgical treatment, **12**:101–103, 102*t*, 353
  diffuse, **12**:96, 97*f*
  focal, **12**:95–96, 97*f*
  in multifocal choroiditis and panuveitis syndrome,
    9:162
Macular electroretinogram, **5**:109. *See also*
  Electroretinogram
Macular epiretinal membrane. *See* Epiretinal membrane
Macular fibers/projections, **2**:90, 96
Macular fibrosis, preretinal, **12**:300
Macular function testing, **3**:277–278, 278*f*, **11**:82
  before cataract surgery, **11**:82
  retinal disease and, **11**:204–205
Macular halo, in Niemann-Pick disease, **12**:262, 263*f*
Macular holes, **4**:136–137, 138*f*, **12**:304–306, 305–306*f*,
  349, 350*f*
  idiopathic, **12**:304–306, 305–306*f*, 349, 350*f*
    vitrectomy for, **12**:305–306, 349, 350*f*
  impending, **12**:304, 305*f*
  posterior vitreous detachment and, **12**:298, 304–306,
    305–306*f*
  posttraumatic, **12**:321–322, 322*f*
  treatment of, **12**:305–306, 349, 350*f*
  vitreous in formation of, **2**:288
Macular ischemia, diabetic, **12**:103
Macular neuroretinopathy, acute, **9**:169, **12**:193
Macular Photocoagulation Study (MPS), **9**:223–224,
  224*f*, **12**:71, 81, 85, 86
Macular pits, trauma causing, **12**:322
Macular pucker, **12**:300
Macular star, **5**:130, 130*f*
  inflammatory disc edema with (neuroretinitis), **6**:312,
    313*f*
  in toxoplasmic optic neuritis, **5**:362
Macular translocation procedures
  for age-related macular degeneration/choroidal
    neovascularization, **12**:79
  strabismus and, **6**:143
Macule
  of eyelid, **8**:20*t*
  hypopigmented (ash-leaf spot), in tuberous sclerosis,
    5:341, 342*f*, **6**:372, 372*f*, **10**:28

Maculopathies, **5**:112–115. *See also specific type*
  acute idiopathic, **12**:193
  age-related. *See* Age-related macular degeneration
  bull's-eye
    chloroquine/hydroxychloroquine causing, **1**:185,
      12:266, 266*f*
    in cone dystrophies, **5**:114, **12**:232, 233*f*
    differential diagnosis of, **12**:235, 236*t*
    in Stargardt disease, **12**:235
  cellophane, **12**:300
  crystalline, drug toxicity causing, **12**:268–269, 268*f*,
    269*t*
  in dengue fever, **9**:219–220
  hypotony, **10**:197
    antifibrotic use and, **10**:193
  idiopathic stellate. *See* Leber idiopathic stellate
    neuroretinitis
  in ocular histoplasmosis, **9**:221, 223
  optic pit, **12**:294–295, 295*f*
    central serous chorioretinopathy differentiated
      from, **12**:174
  in subacute sclerosing panencephalitis, **9**:213, 214*f*
"Mad cow" disease (bovine spongiform
  encephalopathy), **5**:368
Madarosis, in staphylococcal blepharitis, **8**:144*t*, 145
Maddox rod/Maddox rod testing, **3**:95, 96*f*, **5**:216, 216*f*,
  6:78
  double, **5**:216–218, 217*f*, **6**:79, 79*f*
    in superior oblique muscle paralysis, **6**:118
Maffucci syndrome, **6**:340
Maggots (fly larvae), ocular infection caused by,
  8:143
Magnesium
  in aqueous humor, **2**:267
  in tear film, **2**:238*t*
Magnetic field, of light wave, **3**:4, 5*f*
Magnetic resonance angiography (MRA), **5**:69, 77–78,
  79*f*
  advantages/disadvantages/contraindications and,
    5:86–88, 86*t*
  in aneurysm detection, **5**:229
  in carotid artery evaluation, **5**:180
  in cerebral aneurysm, **5**:352, 352*f*
  in cerebral ischemia/stroke, **1**:93
  in orbital evaluation, **7**:31
Magnetic resonance imaging (MRI), **5**:72–74, 73*f*, 74*f*,
  75*f*, 76*t*, 77*f*, 78*f*
  advantages/disadvantages/contraindications and,
    5:86*t*
  in Alzheimer disease, **1**:267
  in arterial dissections, **5**:354, 354*f*
  in cerebral aneurysm, **5**:352, 352*f*
  in cerebral ischemia/stroke, **1**:93
  in choroidal/ciliary body melanoma, **4**:277
  in foreign-body identification, **12**:318, 326
  functional (fMRI), **5**:69, 80
  in ischemic heart disease, **1**:104, 107
  in lacrimal drainage evaluation, **7**:262
  in multiple sclerosis, **5**:322*f*, 325
  in NAION, **5**:128*t*
  in neurofibromatosis screening, **6**:370
  in optic neuritis, **5**:83–84, 128*t*, 144, 145*f*

in orbital evaluation, 5:73, 76f, 87–88, 7:26–28, 27f
  CT scanning compared with, 7:28–29, 28t, 30f
  hemangioma diagnosis and, 6:340
  tumor diagnosis and, 6:334
in primary central nervous system lymphoma, 9:282
in retinoblastoma, 4:303–304, 309, 6:356
in Sturge-Weber syndrome, 6:376, 376f
in Susac (SICRET) syndrome, 9:147
T1- and T2-weighted images in, 5:72–73, 73f, 73t, 74f,
  75f, 76f, 76t, 77f, 78f, 7:26–28, 27f
Magnetic resonance spectroscopy (MRS), 5:69, 80
Magnetic resonance venography (MRV), 5:77–78, 79f
  in idiopathic intracranial hypertension, 5:123
Magnetic source imaging (MSI), in epilepsy diagnosis,
  1:262
Magnetoencephalography (MEG), in epilepsy diagnosis,
  1:262
Magnification
  angular, 3:36
  axial (longitudinal), 3:36
  electronic, in low vision/vision rehabilitation,
    3:302–303, 302f
  with intraocular lenses, 3:223
  in low vision
    contrast sensitivity affecting, 3:291
    for distance vision (telescopes), 3:299–300, 301f
    electronic, 3:302–303, 302f
    for reading, 3:295–296, 297
  meridional (meridional aniseikonia). See also
    Distortion
    adaptation to distortion and, 3:140, 320–321
    astigmatic spectacle lenses causing, 3:140, 310–311,
      310f
      avoidance of with contact lenses, 3:174–176,
        316–317
    blurred retinal images and, 3:312, 312f
    conventional analysis of, 3:311, 312f
    minimizing, 3:316–320, 318f, 319f
    sources of, 3:310–311, 310f
      relative contributions from, 3:315, 315f
    uncorrected/inappropriately corrected astigmatism
      and, 3:314
  of operating microscope, 3:263
  transverse, 3:32–36, 33f, 34f, 64–65, 65f
    in afocal system, 3:80, 82
    calculation of, 3:32, 64–65, 65f
  unit, planes of (principal planes), 3:75, 75f
Magnifiers, 3:298–299, 300f. See also Vision
  rehabilitation
  electronic, 3:302–303, 302f
  handheld, 3:298–299
  stand, 3:299, 300f
Magnocellular neurons (M cells/system), 5:28, 33,
  6:42–43, 43f, 10:40
  development of, 6:42, 43f, 44
    abnormal visual experience affecting, 6:46
Magnocellular nevus. See Melanocytoma
MAI (Mycobacterium avium-intracellulare complex)
  infections, in HIV infection/AIDS, 1:39, 5:360, 9:128
Main sensory nucleus, of cranial nerve V (trigeminal),
  2:100, 101f, 5:57, 57f
Main sequence, 5:202
Major amblyoscope testing, 6:58–59, 59f, 78, 80

Major (greater) arterial circle, 2:38, 39f, 58, 62–63, 5:14f,
  18
  development of, 2:138
Major basic protein, 8:179t
Major depressive disorder, 1:247. See also Depression
  drugs for (antidepressants), 1:254–256, 255t
    ocular effects of, 1:255, 301t
  in older patients, 1:226
Major histocompatibility complex (MHC), 8:174, 407,
  9:70. See also Human leukocyte antigens
  class I molecules of, 9:37, 38f, 70
  class II molecules of, 9:37, 39f, 70
    primed macrophages as, 9:21–22
  class III molecules of, 9:70
Major intrinsic protein (MIP/aquaporin 0), 2:274, 277,
  11:12, 17
  in lens transport, 2:277
Major tranquilizers. See Antipsychotic drugs
Malar rash, in systemic lupus erythematosus, 1:167,
  169t, 9:140, 141t
Malaria prevention, 1:286
Malassezia furfur
  as normal ocular flora, 8:97, 97t
  ocular infection caused by, 8:148
Malattia Leventinese. See also Drusen
  EFEMP1/EFEMP1 gene defects causing, 2:297,
    12:239
  retinal pigment epithelium in, 2:309
Malformation, 6:171. See also specific type and
  Congenital anomalies
Malignancy. See Cancer
Malignant fibrous histiocytoma (atypical
  fibroxanthoma), 4:117–118, 240–242
Malignant glaucoma. See Aqueous misdirection
Malignant hypertension, choroidal perfusion
  abnormalities and, 12:116f, 176
Malignant hyperthermia, 1:312–313, 313f, 6:161–162
Malignant Hyperthermia Association of the United
  States (MHAUS), 1:313, 313t
Malignant lymphomas. See Lymphomas
Malignant melanomas. See Melanomas
Malignant mixed tumor, lacrimal gland, 7:87
Malignant myopia. See High (pathologic/degenerative)
  myopia
Malingering, 1:249, 257, 5:305
Malondialdehyde (MDA), oxidative lens damage and,
  11:16
Malpositioning, of rectus pulleys, 6:23
MALT. See Mucosa-associated lymphoid tissue
MALT lymphoma/MALToma. See Mucosa-associated
  lymphoid tissue (MALT) lymphoma
Malyugin ring, for pupil expansion, 11:194f
Mamillations, iris, 6:226, 226f
Mammography, for cancer screening, 1:272t, 274
Mandibular nerve. See Cranial nerve V (trigeminal
  nerve), V₃
Mandibulofacial dysostosis (Treacher Collins/Treacher
  Collins–Franceschetti syndrome), 6:393–394, 394f,
  7:34, 34f, 8:324t
  eyelid manifestations of, 4:213t
  palpebral fissure slanting in, 6:178, 393–394, 394f
Mandol. See Cefamandole
Mania, 1:247

Manic depression. *See* Bipolar disorder
Manifest latent nystagmus, 5:246, 6:323, 324f
Manifest (noncycloplegic) refraction, 3:137. *See also* Refraction, clinical
  after penetrating keratoplasty, 8:426, 427f
  before refractive surgery, 13:33, 73
Manifest strabismus, 6:9
  cover tests in assessment of, 6:74
Mannitol, 2:356, 356t, 10:165t, 173
α-Mannosidase, defective, 2:213t
Mannosidosis, 2:213t, 6:401t, 8:312
  pediatric cataracts in, 6:247t
  pigmentary retinopathy and, 12:250t
Mantle cell lymphoma, conjunctival, 4:73
Mantle zone, 4:71
Manual lensmeters, 3:268–271, 269f, 270f, 271f
  Badal principle and, 3:80, 269, 270f
  bifocal add measured with, 3:270–271, 271f
Manual objective refractors, 3:276, 277
Manual perimetry, 10:68
Manual small-incision cataract surgery, 11:96
MAO inhibitors. *See* Monoamine oxidase inhibitors
Map-dot-fingerprint dystrophy. *See* Epithelial/subepithelial dystrophies, basement membrane
Map lines, in epithelial basement membrane dystrophy, 8:271, 271f
Maple syrup urine disease, 2:213t
MAR. *See* Melanoma-associated retinopathy
MAR (minimum angle of resolution/recognition), 3:109, 110t
  logarithm of (logMAR), 3:109, 110t
    cystoid macular edema after cataract surgery and, 11:182
Maraviroc, 1:34
Marax. *See* Theophylline
Marcaine. *See* Bupivacaine
Marcus Gunn jaw-winking ptosis/syndrome, 5:279, 279f, 284, 6:180, 7:207, 208f, 210
  synkinesis in, 6:180, 7:203, 207, 208f
Marcus Gunn pupil (relative afferent pupillary defect)
  cataract surgery on patient with, 11:77
  in multiple evanescent white dot syndrome, 5:113, 113f
  in optic tract syndrome, 5:167
  testing for, 5:92–95, 94f
    in glaucoma evaluation, 10:28, 29
    in nonorganic ophthalmic disorders, 5:308
Marfan syndrome, 1:153, 6:263, 8:323t, 325, 11:36–37, 36f
  lens defects/ectopia lentis and, 6:263, 11:36–37, 36f
  megalocornea and, 8:254, 325
  pleiotropism and, 2:210
Margin
  ciliary, 7:142
  lid. *See* Eyelids, margin of
Margin–reflex distance (MRD$_1$ and MRD$_2$), 5:276, 278f, 6:179
  in ptosis, 6:179, 7:201–202, 202f, 205f
Marginal arterial arcades, 2:23f, 29–30, 34, 5:14f, 15
  eyelids supplied by, 7:135f, 143
Marginal corneal infiltrates, staphylococcal blepharitis/blepharoconjunctivitis and, 8:145, 146f, 147, 210

Marginal degeneration
  pellucid, 4:91, 8:301–302, 301f, 302t, 303f
    refractive surgery contraindicated in, 8:44, 13:18, 38, 167–168
    corneal topography and, 13:18–19, 19f, 38, 38f, 71, 167–168, 169f
  Terrien, 8:339–340, 340f
Marginal keratitis, Fuchs superficial, 8:340
Marginal mandibular nerve, 7:133, 134f
Marginal myotomy, 6:148t
Marginal rotation, for cicatricial entropion, 7:198–199, 199f
Marginal tear strip (tear meniscus), 2:237
  inspection of, 8:52
  in pseudoepiphora evaluation, 7:257
Marginal zone, 4:71
  extranodal lymphoma (MALToma) involving, 4:72–73, 73f, 74, 7:80
Marijuana, intraocular pressure affected by, 1:251, 10:21–22, 21t
MARINA (Minimally Classic/Occult Trial of the Anti-VEGF Antibody Ranibizumab in the Treatment of Neovascular AMD), 12:73, 74, 75f
Mark VIII anterior chamber IOL, 3:210, 210f
Marker site, 2:179
Markers (gene). *See also specific type*
  cytogenetic, 2:177
  microsatellites/minisatellites/satellites, 2:155, 156, 166, 180, 181f
  restriction fragment length polymorphisms, 2:160, 178–180, 179f
Maroteaux-Lamy syndrome, 6:398f, 400t, 8:306t
Mars Letter Contrast Sensitivity Test, 3:292
Marshall syndrome, vitreous collapse in, 2:288
Martegiani, area of, 12:7f, 8
  in posterior vitreous detachment, 12:274, 274f, 297
Masked bilateral superior oblique muscle paralysis, 6:120
Masked depression, in older patients, 1:226
Masked hypertension, 1:69, 70–71
Masquerade syndromes, 9:281–289, 12:199, 199f
  in children, 6:275, 276t
  neoplastic, 9:281–287, 282f, 283f, 12:199, 199f
  nonneoplastic, 9:287–289
    endogenous fungal endophthalmitis as, 9:273–274
    retinal vasculitis and, 12:141
Masseter muscle, 7:132f, 133
Masson trichrome stain, 4:30, 31t
Mast-cell stabilizers, 2:364–366, 365t. *See also specific agent*
  for giant papillary conjunctivitis, 8:195
  for ocular allergy, 6:198, 199t, 8:186
  for pulmonary diseases, 1:145t
  for vernal keratoconjunctivitis, 8:188
Mast cells, 2:364, 4:7, 9:10–11
  cytologic identification of, in immune-mediated keratoconjunctivitis, 8:182t
  degranulation of, acute IgE-mediated, 9:10, 54–55, 54f
  in external eye, 8:174t, 181
  mediators released by, 8:179t, 181
Mastoid segment of cranial nerve VII (facial), 2:106, 5:61

MAT. *See* Microagglutination test
Maternal age, Down syndrome incidence and, 2:201, 202
Maternal drug/alcohol use, malformations associated
    with, 1:250, 2:142–143, 142f, 6:394–395, 395f
Maternal infection transmission, 6:181–186. *See also
    specific infection*
Maternal inheritance, 2:173, 208, 220. *See also*
    Mitochondrial DNA
Mating, assortative, 2:148
MATP gene, in OCA4, 6:299t, 301
Matrix metalloproteinases. *See also specific type under
    MMP*
    in cornea, 2:250
    in ligneous conjunctivitis, 8:192
    in ocular infection, 8:99
    in Sjögren syndrome, 8:63
    in Sorsby dystrophy, 12:241
    in vitreous, 2:283
Matrix perimeter, 10:61
Mature cataract, 11:42, 44f
    lens-associated uveitis and, 9:125
    phacolytic glaucoma and, 10:90–91, 91f, 11:63
Mavik. *See* Trandolapril
Maxair. *See* Pirbuterol
Maxaquin. *See* Lomefloxacin
Maxide. *See* Triamterene
Maxidex. *See* Dexamethasone
Maxilla/maxillary bone, 5:5, 7, 7f, 8f, 7:6f, 7f, 8
    fracture of, 7:8
Maxillary artery, 2:37f, 5:12, 15f
    internal, orbit supplied by, 7:12
Maxillary nerve. *See* Cranial nerve V (trigeminal nerve),
    V₂
Maxillary osteomyelitis, 6:197
Maxillary sinuses, 2:12, 13f, 14f, 5:7, 7f, 11f, 7:7f, 18f, 19
Maximal combined response, in electroretinogram,
    12:33, 34f, 35, 36f
Maxipime. *See* Cefepime
Maxzide. *See* Triamterene
Maze procedure, 1:125
Mazzocco foldable intraocular lens, 11:135, 136f
MB isoenzyme, in acute coronary syndrome, 1:105
McCannel sutures, for intraocular lens decentration,
    11:163–164, 164f
McCannel technique
    for iridodialysis repair, 8:381, 382f
    for iris laceration repair, 8:380–381, 381f
McCarey-Kaufman tissue transport medium, for donor
    corneas, 8:408–409
MCD. *See* Macular dystrophies, corneal
McDonald criteria, for multiple sclerosis, 5:326t, 327
MCP. *See* Multifocal choroiditis and panuveitis
    syndrome
MCP-1. *See* Macrophage chemotactic protein-1
MCTD. *See* Mixed connective tissue disease
MCV vaccine, 1:285
MDA. *See* Malondialdehyde
MDRTB. *See* Multidrug-resistant tuberculosis
Mean curvature/mean curvature map, 8:41, 42f
Mean performance, 1:342
Mean of the ten largest melanoma cell nuclei (MLN),
    4:199

Measles-mumps-rubella (MMR) vaccine, 1:282, 286
Measles retinopathy, 9:212, 213
Measles (rubeola) virus, 8:129, 9:212
    immunization against, 1:282
    ocular infection caused by, 8:129, 9:212–214, 214f
Measurement bias/error, in clinical research, 1:319
Measurement system, designing, 1:339–340
Mecamylamine, adverse effects of, 2:343f
MECD. *See* Meesmann corneal (juvenile hereditary
    epithelial) dystrophy
Mechanical anisocoria, 5:266
Mechanical ectropion, 7:191f, 194
Mechanical glaucomas, secondary, 6:239
Mechanical ptosis/blepharoptosis, 7:210, 8:21
Mechlorethamine (nitrogen mustard), 1:240t
Meckel cave, 2:103
Meclofenamate, 1:183t
Meclomen. *See* Meclofenamate
Medallion prepupillary intraocular lens, 3:207, 208f
Media, ocular/optical. *See* Optical medium
Medial canthal defects, repair of, 7:186–187
Medial canthal tendon, 7:136, 137f, 141, 246
    trauma involving, 7:178–180
Medial canthal tumors
    basal cell carcinoma, 7:171
    canalicular obstruction and, 7:264
    reconstructive surgery after removal of, 7:186
Medial complex, 5:54
Medial geniculate nucleus, 5:20f
Medial long posterior ciliary arteries, 5:18
Medial longitudinal fasciculus, 2:104, 104f, 5:38, 39f, 42,
    44f, 45f, 46
    diplopia caused by disruption of, 5:224–226, 224f,
        225f, 226f
    dissociated nystagmus caused by lesions of, 5:254
    internuclear ophthalmoplegia caused by lesions of,
        6:141
    rostral interstitial nucleus of, 5:38, 39f, 42, 44f, 46f,
        199, 199–200
Medial muscular branch, of ophthalmic artery,
    extraocular muscles supplied by, 6:16
Medial notochordal process, 2:117
Medial orbital fractures, 7:98–100, 99f
Medial orbital wall, 2:7, 8f, 5:8f, 9, 10, 7:5, 5t, 7–8
Medial rectus muscles, 2:16f, 17f, 19t, 20f, 37f, 38, 38f,
    39f, 5:10f, 55, 56f, 6:13, 14f, 16f, 17t, 18f, 7:10, 11f
    A-pattern deviations associated with dysfunction of,
        6:107–108
    action of, 6:13, 17t, 29, 29t
        gaze position and, 6:30, 30f
    anatomy of, 5:10f, 6:13, 14f, 16f, 17t, 18f
    field of action of, 6:29
    insertion relationships of, 2:16, 18f, 19t
    laceration of during pterygium removal/sinus
        surgery, 6:143
    nerves supplying, 2:21, 7:11
    restriction of, incomitant esotropia and, 6:98
    surgery of, 6:150, 150t
        for A- and V-pattern deviations, 6:111, 111f
        for consecutive esotropia, 6:103
        for constant exotropia, 6:103
        for convergence insufficiency, 6:106

for Duane syndrome, 6:129
for infantile esotropia, 6:92
lost/slipped muscle and, 6:159–160, 160*f*
for monocular elevation deficiency (double
    elevator palsy), 6:124
for nystagmus, 6:328, 329, 329*t*
for sixth nerve (abducens) paralysis, 6:135
V-pattern deviations associated with dysfunction of,
    6:107–108
Medial spindle procedure, for involutional ectropion,
    7:190, 192*f*
Medial superior temporal area, 5:41, 42*f*, 204
Medial temporal area, 5:41, 42*f*, 204
Median forehead flap, for eyelid repair, 7:183*f*
Median perforators, of basilar artery, 5:21–23
Mediators, 2:364, 8:175, 176*f*, 177*t*, 179*t*, 9:23–31, 23*t*.
    See also specific type
    allergic conjunctivitis and, 8:185
    cytokines, 8:177, 177*t*, 9:27–30, 28–29*t*
    lipid, 9:25–27, 26*f*
    macrophage synthesis of, 9:22–23
    neutrophil-derived granule products, 9:31
    plasma-derived enzyme systems, 9:23–25, 24*f*
    reactive nitrogen products, 9:31
    reactive oxygen intermediates, 9:30–31
    in Sjögren syndrome, 8:63
    in uveitis, 9:85
Medical Device Amendments, to Food, Drug, and
    Cosmetic Act, 13:203
Medical devices
    adverse event reporting and, 13:207–208
    FDA approval of
        clinical data required for, 13:204, 206
        delays in, 13:207
        premarket, 13:204, 205
    FDA classification of, 13:203–204
    international regulation of, 13:201–202
    labeling, 13:206–207
    pathways to market for, 13:205
Medical emergencies. *See* Emergencies
Medical history. *See also* History
    cataract surgery evaluation and, 11:73–74, 188,
        189*f*
    glaucoma evaluation and, 10:27
    in hereditary dystrophies, 12:221–222
    refractive surgery evaluation and, 13:30*t*, 31
Medicare Improvement Act, 1:245, 246
Medications. *See* Drugs
Medium, ocular/optical. *See* Optical medium
Medline/PubMed, 1:316
MedRF. *See* Medullary reticular formation
Medroxyprogesterone
    for chemical injuries, 8:358
    for neurotrophic keratopathy, 8:88
Medrysone, 2:359
    anti-inflammatory/pressure-elevating potency of,
        2:360*t*
Medullary carcinoma of thyroid gland, 1:214
    in multiple endocrine neoplasia, 1:216
Medullary epithelium, medulloepithelioma (diktyoma)
    arising from, 4:183, 183*f*, 307
Medullary reticular formation, 5:39, 39*f*

Medullated (myelinated) retinal nerve fibers, 4:148,
    6:306, 306*f*
Medulloepithelioma (diktyoma), 4:183–184, 183*f*, 307,
    307*f*, 6:352
    retinoblastoma differentiated from, 4:307, 307*f*
    teratoid, 4:184
Meesmann corneal (juvenile hereditary epithelial)
    dystrophy, 8:268*t*, 270*t*, 272–273, 273*f*
    genetics of, 8:269*t*, 272
Mefenamic acid, 1:183*t*
Mefoxin. *See* Cefoxitin
MEG. *See* Magnetoencephalography
Megaloblastic anemia, 1:148, 149
Megalocornea, 6:211, 8:253–254, 254*f*, 261*t*
    Marfan syndrome and, 8:254, 325
Megaloglobus (buphthalmos)
    in neurofibromatosis, 6:370
    in primary congenital glaucoma, 6:238, 10:143, 143*f*,
        150
Megalopapilla, 6:307–308
Megalophthalmos, anterior, 6:211
Meglitinides, 1:199*t*, 201
Meibomian glands, 2:23, 23*f*, 26*f*, 27*t*, 28, 29*f*, 239*f*,
    4:205, 206*f*, 7:135*f*, 142*f*, 143, 152, 160, 8:4, 5*f*
    chalazion/hordeolum caused by infection of, 4:208,
        210–211, 211*f*, 6:350, 7:152, 154, 8:72
    dysfunction of, 2:244, 8:50, 50*f*, 65–69, 67*f*, 143,
        144*t*
        blepharitis in, 8:68, 143, 144*t*
        cataract surgery and, 11:190
        dry eye and, 8:50, 50*f*, 65–69, 67*f*
        refractive surgery and, 13:35
    in external eye defense, 8:95
    immune response/immunologic features of, 8:175,
        176*f*
    sebaceous adenocarcinoma arising in, 4:221, 7:173
    in tear-film lipids/tear production, 2:42, 237, 239*f*,
        7:244
Meige syndrome, 5:289, 290*f*, 7:220
Meiosis, 2:155, 195–196, 196*f*
    nondisjunction during, 2:196*f*. *See also*
        Nondisjunction
Melan A, in immunohistochemistry, 4:33
Melanin
    absorption spectrum for, 12:337, 338*f*
    corneal pigmentation caused by, 8:337*t*, 345
    defective synthesis of, in albinism, 2:308, 12:257
    photoprotective function of, 2:308, 315–316
    in retinal pigment epithelium, 2:304, 307–308,
        315–316
        albinism and, 4:148, 149*f*
        hypertrophy and, 4:150, 150*f*, 12:282
Melanin-associated antigens
    sympathetic ophthalmia and, 9:181
    Vogt-Koyanagi-Harada (VKH) syndrome and,
        9:183
Melanin-like pigment, corneal pigmentation caused
    by, 8:337*t*, 348, 348*f*
α-Melanocyte-stimulating hormone (α-MSH), 8:177*t*
    in tear secretion, 2:244
Melanocyte-stimulating hormone-releasing factor,
    1:214*t*

Melanocytes, 7:164
  choroidal, 2:65f, 66, 133
  in iris stroma, 2:56
  tumors arising from. *See* Melanocytic tumors;
    Pigmented lesions
Melanocytic nevus
  of anterior chamber/trabecular meshwork, 4:109, 110f
  congenital, 4:224, 224f
  conjunctival, 4:65–66, 65t, 66f
  of eyelid, 4:224–226, 224f, 225f, 226f, 7:164, 165f
  glaucoma and, 4:109
Melanocytic proliferation, bilateral diffuse uveal, 9:287,
    12:183, 183f
Melanocytic tumors, 4:265–289, 8:233, 234t. *See also*
    specific type and Nevus
  of anterior chamber/trabecular meshwork, 4:109,
    110f
  of conjunctiva, 4:65–70, 65t, 66f, 67f, 68f, 70f, 71f
  of eyelid, 4:224–227, 224f, 225f, 226f
    benign, 7:164–166, 165f, 166f
    malignant (melanoma), 4:226–227, 227f, 7:175–176,
      176f
    nevi, 7:164, 165f
    premalignant, 7:168
  in neurofibromatosis, 6:355–356, 366f
  of ocular surface, 4:65–70, 65t, 66f, 67f, 68f, 70f, 71f
Melanocytoma
  in children, 6:353, 353f
  glaucoma and, 4:109, 268
  of iris/ciliary body/choroid, 4:195, 268
  of optic disc/optic nerve, 4:256, 256f
    melanoma differentiated from, 4:278–279, 280f
Melanocytosis
  dermal, 4:66, 7:166, 166f
  dermal orbital, 4:66
  ocular (melanosis oculi/racial), 4:65–66, 65t, 66f,
    8:235–236, 235f, 238t
    in children, 6:350, 350f
    of iris, 4:271t
  oculodermal (nevus of Ota), 4:65t, 66, 7:166, 166f,
    8:235–236, 238t
    in children, 6:350
    glaucoma associated with, 10:28
    of iris, 4:271t
Melanogenesis, 2:127, 133, 308
  latanoprost and, 2:354
Melanokeratosis, striate, 4:67, 8:234
Melanoma-associated retinopathy, 5:112, 115, 12:256,
  257
Melanomalytic glaucoma, 4:109, 109f, 198, 10:93, 130
Melanomas, 1:276–277, 7:175–176, 176f
  acral-lentiginous, 4:226, 227f
  amelanotic, 4:69, 274f, 278, 278t
  of anterior chamber/trabecular meshwork, 4:109,
    110f
  choroidal/ciliary body (uveal), 4:195–200, 196f, 197f,
    198f, 199f, 263, 273–288, 9:285–286. *See also*
    Choroidal/ciliary body melanoma
    age-related macular degeneration differentiated
      from, 4:278, 12:70
    in children, 6:353
    uveitis differentiated from, 6:276t

  classification of, 4:199, 281
  diagnosis of, 4:274–277, 276f, 277f
    differential, 4:277–281, 278t, 279f, 280f, 281f
  enucleation for, 7:118
  epithelioid cell, 4:196, 199
  glaucoma caused by, 4:109, 109f, 198, 10:93, 130
  metastatic, 4:200
    evaluation of, 4:281–282, 282t
  nevus differentiated from, 4:266–268, 278
  ocular surface/conjunctival involvement and, 4:70,
    71f
  prognosis/prognostic factors for, 4:198–200,
    286–288
  spindle cell, 4:196, 196f, 199
  spread of, 4:197–198, 197f, 198f, 200
  staging of, 4:337–341t
  transpupillary thermotherapy for, 4:285, 12:343
  treatment of, 4:282–286, 284f
congenital hypertrophy of RPE differentiated from,
    4:150, 278, 279f
conjunctival, 4:69–70, 70f, 71f, 8:238–240, 238t,
    239f
  in children, 6:349
  intraocular extension of, 4:322
  primary acquired melanosis and, 4:67, 68f, 69, 70f,
    8:239
  staging of, 4:334–336t
exenteration for, 4:286, 7:126, 8:240
of eyelid, 4:226–227, 227f, 7:175–176, 176f
glaucoma and, 4:109, 109f, 198, 10:93, 130
incidence of, 1:276–277
in situ, 4:69
of iris, 4:193–194, 194f, 268–271, 269f, 271t, 273f
lentigo maligna, 4:69, 226, 227f, 7:168, 175
metastatic, 4:200, 9:286–287
nodular, 4:226, 227f, 7:175, 176f
ocular melanocytosis and, 8:239
retinoblastoma associated with, 4:314, 314t
retinopathy associated with, 5:112, 115, 12:256, 257
ring, 4:197, 197f, 200
screening for, 1:277
superficial spreading, 4:226, 227f
tapioca, 4:271t
uveal. *See* Melanomas, choroidal/ciliary body
Melanosis, 8:233, 238t
  benign acquired, 4:65t, 67, 67f, 8:234, 235f, 237
  congenital epithelial, 8:233
  intraepithelial, 4:67–69, 67f, 68f
  oculi (ocular melanocytosis/racial), 4:65–66, 65t, 66f,
    8:235–236, 235f, 238t
    in children, 6:350, 350f
    of iris, 4:271t
  precancerous (lentigo maligna/Hutchinson melanotic
    freckle), 7:168
  primary acquired, 4:65t, 67–69, 68f, 8:237–238, 237f,
    238t
    melanoma and, 4:67, 68f, 69, 70f, 8:239
Melanosomes
  in choroid, 2:66, 133
  in ciliary body epithelium, 2:62
  in iris dilator muscle, 2:60
  in retinal pigment epithelium, 2:72, 12:15

MELAS (mitochondrial myopathy with encephalopathy/lactic acidosis/strokelike episodes) syndrome, 12:265
migrainelike headache and, 5:300
mitochondrial DNA mutation and, 2:173, 174f, 12:265
Melasma, 7:164
Melkersson-Rosenthal syndrome, 5:287
Melphalan, 1:240t
for retinoblastoma, 6:359
MEM. See Minimum essential medium
Memantine, for Alzheimer disease, 1:267–268
Membrane-associated transporter protein (MATP) gene, in OCA4, 6:299t, 301
Membrane attack complex, 9:23, 24, 24f
Membrane sacs, in rods, 2:291
Membrane structural (urea-insoluble) lens proteins, 2:277, 11:11f, 12
Membrane-type frizzled protein (MFRP) gene
in glaucoma, 10:11t
in nanophthalmos, 8:251, 10:11t
Membranes
conjunctival, 8:20t, 22t
in epidemic keratoconjunctivitis, 8:124, 125, 125f
in ligneous conjunctivitis, 8:192, 192f
Descemet. See Descemet membrane
implantation, of iris, 4:270t
retrocorneal fibrous (posterior collagenous layer), 2:251, 4:91, 92f, 8:29
Membranous cataract, 11:34, 35f
Memenatine, for nystagmus, 5:258
Memory, immunologic, 9:43–44
response to poison ivy and, 9:35
response to tuberculosis and, 9:35
MEN. See Multiple endocrine neoplasia
Mendelian disorder (single-gene disorder), 2:155, 208
Mendelian Inheritance in Man (MIM) abbreviations/ numbers, for corneal dystrophies, 8:270t
Ménière disease, nystagmus in, 5:250
Meningeal artery
dorsal, 5:16
middle, 5:12–13
recurrent, 5:14f, 15f
Meningeal nerve, middle, 5:60
Meninges
neuroimaging in evaluation of, 5:82t
optic nerve, 2:91, 92f, 93f, 4:249, 250f
Meningiomas, 7:73–76, 74f, 75f
cerebellopontine angle
Bruns nystagmus and, 5:250
seventh nerve (facial) palsy and, 5:286
malignant, 7:75
MR imaging of, 5:85, 85f
optic nerve sheath, 4:258, 258f, 259f, 5:149–151, 150f, 150t, 7:74–75, 75–76, 75f
optic glioma differentiated from, 6:368
orbital, 4:258, 7:73–76, 74f, 75f
in children, 6:343
transient visual loss and, 5:177
parasellar, 5:164
sphenoid wing, 7:73, 74, 74f, 75

Meningitis
cryptococcal, 5:367, 9:278
Haemophilus influenzae causing, 1:9
immunization against, 1:285
meningococcal, 1:10
immunization against, 1:10, 285
tuberculous, neuro-ophthalmic signs of, 5:360
Meningoceles, 7:35
orbital, 6:346, 7:35
Meningococcal vaccine, 1:10, 285
Meningococcus (Neisseria meningitidis), 1:10, 8:134, 149
conjunctivitis in children caused by, 6:189
endogenous endophthalmitis caused by, 9:272, 272f
immunization against, 1:10, 285
combination vaccines and, 1:285
Meningoencephaloceles, 7:35
Meningohypophyseal trunk, 5:16
Meningothelial optic meningioma, 4:258, 258f
Meningovascular syphilis, 5:361
Meniscus optic, of intraocular lens, 3:204f
Mental acuity disturbances, in multiple sclerosis, 5:323
Mental disorders due to general medical condition (organic mental syndromes), 1:246. See also Alzheimer disease; Behavioral/psychiatric disorders in older patients, 1:227
Mental Health Parity Act, 1:245, 246
Mental nerve neuropathy, 5:303
Mentalis muscle, 7:133, 133f
Mentax. See Butenafine
Meperidine, perioperative, 1:310
Mepivacaine, 2:387t, 388
maximum safe dose of, 1:298t
Mepron. See Atovaquone
6-Mercaptopurine, 1:240t
Merci Retriever, for cerebral ischemia/stroke, 1:95
Meretoja syndrome (gelsolin-type lattice corneal dystrophy), 4:212, 8:268t, 270t, 280, 280f, 317t, 319
genetics of, 4:212, 8:269t, 280, 317t
Meridians, 11:5
alignment of, combination of spherocylindrical lenses and, 3:99
of astigmatic surface or lens, 3:97, 97f
locating axes of, in retinoscopy, 3:126–127, 126f, 127f, 128f
reordering of, adaptation to distortion and, 3:320–321
Meridional amblyopia, 6:64
Meridional complex, 12:8, 10f, 281f
Meridional folds, 12:8, 10f, 280, 281f
Meridional magnification (meridional aniseikonia). See also Distortion
adaptation to distortion and, 3:140, 320–321
astigmatic spectacle lenses causing, 3:140, 310–311, 310f
avoidance of with contact lenses, 3:174–176, 316–317
blurred retinal images and, 3:312, 312f
conventional analysis of, 3:311, 312f
minimizing, 3:316–320, 318f, 319f
sources of, 3:310–311, 310f
relative contributions from, 3:315, 315f
uncorrected/inappropriately corrected astigmatism and, 3:314

Meridional power (instantaneous radius of curvature), **8**:40, 41*f*, **13**:11, 12*f*
Merkel cells/Merkel cell carcinoma, **7**:177
Meropenem, **1**:50*t*, 59
Merrem. *See* Meropenem
MERRF. *See* Myoclonic epilepsy with ragged red fibers
Mesectodermal dysgenesis. *See* Anterior segment, dysgenesis of
Mesectodermal leiomyoma, **4**:203
Mesencephalic nucleus, of cranial nerve V (trigeminal), **2**:100, 101*f*, **5**:57, 57*f*
Mesencephalon, cranial nerve III (oculomotor) arising from, **2**:97
Mesenchymal cells, in ocular development, **8**:4
Mesenchymal dysgenesis. *See* Anterior segment, dysgenesis of
Mesenchymal tumors
  of eyelid and conjunctiva, **8**:240–242, 241*t*
  orbital, **7**:76–79
Mesoderm, **2**:117, 118*f*, 119*f*, 120*f*
  ocular structures derived from, **2**:116*t*
Mesodermal dysgenesis, **8**:255–263. *See also specific disorder and* Anterior segment, dysgenesis of; Axenfeld-Rieger syndrome
Messenger RNA (mRNA), precursor, **2**:161
Meta-analyses, of clinical trials, **1**:328–329
Metabolic acidosis, carbonic anhydrase IOP lowering and, **2**:353
Metabolic disorders. *See also specific type and* Inborn errors of metabolism
  cataracts and, **11**:55–57, 56*f*
    in infants and children, **6**:253–254, 253*f*, 254*t*, 398
  corneal changes and, **6**:398, 400–401*t*, **8**:305–329
  enzyme defects/ocular signs in, **2**:213*t*
  retinal manifestations of, **6**:302–303, 398, 400–401*t*, **12**:257–265
Metabolic imaging, **5**:80
Metabolic syndrome, **1**:85, 138, 193
Metabolism, thyroid hormone in regulation of, **1**:208
Metachromatic leukodystrophy, **2**:213*t*, **6**:400*t*
Metaglip. *See* Glipizide, with metformin
Metaherpetic ulcer, **8**:117
Metallic reflection, **3**:13
Metalloproteinases, matrix. *See also specific type under MMP*
  in cornea, **2**:250
  in ligneous conjunctivitis, **8**:192
  in ocular infection, **8**:99
  in Sjögren syndrome, **8**:63
  in Sorsby dystrophy, **12**:241
  in vitreous, **2**:283
Metallosis, lens damage/cataracts caused by, **11**:53–54, 54*f*
Metamorphopsia, **5**:99, 188–189
  in age-related macular degeneration, **12**:64
  in central serous chorioretinopathy, **12**:171, 175
  in epiretinal membrane, **12**:301, 346
  in macular holes, **12**:304
  in uveitis, **9**:85
Metarhodopsin II, **2**:292

Metastatic eye disease, **1**:244, **9**:286–287. *See also specific type and structure affected*
  carcinoma, **4**:315–322
    ancillary tests in evaluation of, **4**:318–320
    clinical features of, **4**:316–318, 316*f*, 317*f*, 318*f*, 319*f*, 320*f*
    diagnostic factors in, **4**:320–321, 321*f*
    direct intraocular extension and, **4**:322
    mechanisms of intraocular metastasis and, **4**:315–316
    primary sites and, **4**:315, 316*t*
    prognosis for, **4**:321–322
    treatment of, **4**:322
  of choroid, **4**:200, 201*f*, 315, 316*t*, 317*f*, 318*f*, **9**:286
  of conjunctiva, **8**:245
  of iris, **4**:271*t*, 316, 316*f*, 317*f*
  of optic disc/nerve, **4**:315–316, 320
  of orbit, **4**:247, **7**:90–93
    in adults, **7**:91–92, 92*f*
    in children, **6**:333*t*, 336–338, 336*f*, 338*f*, **7**:90–91, 91*f*
    management of, **7**:93
  of retina, **4**:315–316, 320, 321*f*, **9**:286–287
  retinoblastoma and, **4**:304
  of uvea, **4**:200, 201*f*, 316–317, 316*f*, 317*f*, **9**:286
Metered-dose inhalers, β₂-adrenergics for pulmonary disease and, **1**:144
Metformin, **1**:199*t*, 200–201
  in combination agents, **1**:201
Methanol, as tissue fixative, **4**:29, 29*t*
Methanol toxicity, optic neuropathy caused by, **5**:154
Methazolamide, **2**:351, 352*t*, 353, **10**:156–157, 164*t*, 171
  for childhood glaucoma, **6**:243, **10**:156–157
Methenamine silver stain, Gomori, **4**:30, 31*t*
Methicillin, **1**:56, **2**:368*t*, 369–370
Methicillin-resistant *S aureus*, **1**:5, 58
  keratitis after photoablation caused by, **13**:98
  preseptal cellulitis caused by, **7**:41
Methimazole, for Graves hyperthyroidism, **1**:211
Methionine, in homocystinuria, **11**:37
  dietary restriction in management of, **6**:399, **11**:37
Methohexital, perioperative, **1**:309*t*, 311
Methotrexate, **1**:184, 240*t*, **9**:108*t*, 110
  in cancer chemotherapy, **1**:240*t*
  for intraocular (primary central nervous system) lymphoma, **4**:324, **9**:283, 283–284
  for juvenile idiopathic (chronic/rheumatoid) arthritis, **9**:130–131
  for peripheral ulcerative keratitis, **8**:213
  for rheumatoid arthritis, **1**:162
  for scleritis, **8**:223
  for uveitis, **9**:108*t*, 110
    in children, **6**:277
    cystoid macular edema and, **9**:301
  for Wegener granulomatosis, **1**:179
Methoxyflurane, crystalline maculopathy caused by, **12**:269
Methylation, DNA, **2**:168
Methylcellulose
  hydroxypropyl (HPMC)
    for dry eye, **2**:390
    as viscoelastic, **2**:393, **11**:97
  as viscoelastic, **11**:97

Methyldopa, 1:77*t*, 78*t*, 82
Methylmalonic aciduria, 6:398
Methylprednisolone
    for corneal graft rejection, 8:430
    for giant cell arteritis/AAION, 5:126, 320
    for optic neuritis, 5:146
    for pars planitis, 9:137
    for thyroid eye disease, 7:54
    for traumatic visual loss, 7:106
    for uveitis, 9:101*t*, 102, 104
    for Vogt-Koyanagi-Harada (VKH) syndrome, 9:189
Metipranolol, 2:350, 350*t*, 10:162*t*, 168
    for childhood glaucoma, 6:242
    uveitis caused by, 9:128
Metoclopramide, perioperative, 1:308, 309*t*
Metolazone, 1:76*t*
Metoprolol, 2:345*f*
    for arrhythmias, 1:123*t*
    for heart failure, 1:118
    for hypertension, 1:76*t*, 78*t*
Metrogel. *See* Metronidazole
Metronidazole, 1:52*t*, 63
    for *C difficile* colitis, 1:8, 9
    for rosacea, 8:70
Mevacor. *See* Lovastatin
MEWDS. *See* Multiple evanescent white dot syndrome
Mexilitine, 1:123*t*
Meyer loop, 2:94*f*, 96, 5:34, 168
    lesions affecting, 5:168
Mezlin. *See* Mezlocillin
Mezlocillin, 1:46*t*, 57, 2:370
MFRP (membrane-type frizzled protein) gene
    in glaucoma, 10:11*t*
    in nanophthalmos, 8:251, 10:11*t*
mfVEP. *See* Multifocal VEP
MG. *See* Myasthenia gravis
MGD. *See* Meibomian glands, dysfunction of
MH. *See* Malignant hyperthermia
MHA-TP (microhemagglutination assay for *T pallidum*), 1:13, 279, 9:247
MHAUS (Malignant Hyperthermia Association of the United States), 1:313, 313*t*
MHC. *See* Major histocompatibility complex
MI. *See* Myocardial infarction
Miacalcin. *See* Calcitonin/calcitonin nasal spray
MIB-1 marker, in conjunctival lymphoma, 4:74
MIC. *See* Minimal inhibitory concentration
Micafungin, 1:65
    for *Candida* endophthalmitis, 9:276
Micardis. *See* Telmisartan
Micatin. *See* Miconazole
Michaelis constant (K_m), "sugar" cataract development and, 11:15
Michel medium, as tissue fixative, 4:29, 29*t*
Michelson interferometer, optical coherence tomography and, 3:281
Miconazole, 1:54*t*, 2:379*t*, 380
Microadenoma, pituitary, 1:214
Microagglutination test, in leptospirosis, 9:255
Microaneurysms, retinal, 4:160–162, 162*f*, 164
    in diabetes mellitus, 4:166
        in children, 6:297

    in diabetic macular ischemia, 12:103
    in nonproliferative diabetic retinopathy, 12:104, 104*f*
Microarray-based comparative genomic hybridization (array CGH), 4:39*t*
Microarrays, 4:41, 42*f*
    clinical use of, 4:42–43
    SNP oligonucleotide (SOMA), 4:38*t*
    tissue, 4:41, 42*f*
Microbial keratitis. *See* Keratitis, infectious/microbial
Microbiology, 8:100, 101*t*, 131–171. *See also specific organism*
    bacteriology, 8:131–137, 132*t*
    cytologic identification of organisms and, 8:47–48
    diagnostic laboratory techniques in, 8:100–103, 101*t*, 102*f*, 103*t*
    mycology, 8:138–140, 138*t*
    parasitology, 8:140–143
    principles of, 1:3–5
    prions, 8:143
    virology, 8:104–130
    virulence factors and, 8:98–99
Microcirculatory failure, in shock, 1:293
Micrococcus, as normal ocular flora, 8:97*t*
Microcoria (congenital miosis), 6:223, 228–229
Microcornea, 6:212, 212*f*, 8:253, 261*t*
    cornea plana and, 8:255
Microcystic dystrophy, Cogan. *See* Epithelial/subepithelial dystrophies, basement membrane
Microcystic epitheliopathy, 8:91
Microcysts
    in epithelial basement membrane dystrophy, 8:270, 271, 271*f*
    in Meesmann corneal dystrophy, 8:272
Microcytic anemia, 1:148
Microenvironments, immunologic. *See* Immunologic microenvironments
Microfilariae
    loa loa, 8:170–171
    onchocercal, 8:141
        in anterior chamber, 9:242
Microglial cells, 2:77, 301
    optic nerve, 4:249, 250*f*
    retinal ischemia affecting, 4:158
Micrographic surgery, Mohs
    for canthal tumors, 7:186, 187
    for neoplastic disorders of eyelid, 4:45
        basal cell carcinoma, 4:45, 219, 7:171
        sebaceous adenocarcinoma, 4:224, 7:174
        squamous cell carcinoma, 4:45, 219, 7:172
Microhemagglutination assay for *T pallidum* (MHA-TP), 1:13, 279, 9:247
Microkeratomes, for LASIK, 13:77–80, 78*f*, 79*f*
    aberrations and, 13:95
    complications associated with, 13:102–104, 103*f*
    international trends in use of, 13:199
Micronase. *See* Glyburide
Micronutrients. *See also specific type*
    in age-related macular degeneration management, 12:61–63
Micropannus. *See* Pannus
Microperoxisomes, in retinal pigment epithelium, 2:304
Microphakia, in fetal alcohol syndrome, 2:143

Microphthalmia (microphthalmos), 7:33–34, 8:250–251, 250f, 253
  anterior, 8:253
  in congenital CMV infection, 6:184
  in congenital rubella, 6:183
  with cyst (colobomatous cyst), 6:345, 346f, 7:34
  in fetal alcohol syndrome, 2:143
  with linear skin defects, 6:216
  persistent fetal vasculature associated with, 4:133, 304, 12:308
Microplicae, in corneal epithelium, 2:43, 44f, 248
Micropsia, 5:189
  in central serous chorioretinopathy, 12:171
  migraine and, 5:191
Micropuncture, anterior stromal, for recurrent corneal erosions, 8:84, 85f
Microsaccadic refixation movements, 5:199
Microsatellites, 2:155, 166, 180
Microscope
  confocal, 8:35–36, 36f
  operating, 3:262–263, 262f
    phototoxicity and, 11:183–184, 12:333
  slit-lamp. See Slit-lamp biomicroscopy/examination
  specular, 3:260–261, 261f, 8:14, 31–33, 32f
    examination before cataract surgery and, 11:84
    examination before phakic intraocular lens insertion and, 13:129
    in optical focusing technique for pachymetry, 3:259
Microscopic polyangiitis (microscopic polyarteritis), 1:177t, 179, 9:143–145, 144f
Microsomal triglyceride transfer protein (MTP) mutations, 2:298
Microsomia, hemifacial, 6:392–393, 393f, 8:323t
Microspherophakia, 11:28–29, 28f
  pupillary block/angle-closure glaucoma caused by, 10:122, 123f, 11:29
  in Weill-Marchesani syndrome, 6:264, 11:29
Microsporida (microsporidiosis), 8:141, 170
  conjunctivitis/keratitis/keratoconjunctivitis caused by, 4:54, 8:170, 9:313, 313f
  in HIV infection/AIDS, 1:38, 8:170, 9:313, 313f
Microstriae, in LASIK flaps, 13:107f, 107t, 108. See also Striae
Microtrauma, ocular infection and, 8:99
Microvascular abnormalities, intraretinal (IRMAs), 4:160, 161f
  in diabetic retinopathy, 12:104, 105f
  photocoagulation for, 12:340
Microvascular cranial nerve palsy, pain associated with, 5:301
Microvascular decompression surgery, for hemifacial spasm, 5:291
Microvascular disease, diabetic. See Diabetic retinopathy
Microvilli, in corneal epithelium, 2:43, 44f, 248
Microwave radiation, cataract development and, 11:53
Microzide. See Hydrochlorothiazide
MICS. See Manual small-incision cataract surgery
Midamor. See Amiloride
Midazolam, 1:254
  perioperative, 1:309t, 310
  for seizures, 1:297

Midbrain
  lesions of
    convergence insufficiency caused by, 5:213
    corectopia caused by, 5:264
    nystagmus and, 6:325
    pupillary reactivity disorders and, 5:273–274, 273t
    vertical eye movements and, 5:42–44, 44f
Midbrain corectopia, 5:264
Middle cerebral artery, 5:20, 20f, 21
  cranial nerve relationship and, 5:52f
Middle cranial fossa, 5:6f, 8, 11f
  neuroimaging in evaluation of, 5:82t, 88
Middle limiting membrane, 12:10, 11f, 12, 14f
Middle meatus, 7:245f, 246
Middle meningeal artery, 5:12–13
Middle meningeal nerve, 5:60
Midface hypoplasia, 6:386, 386f
Midface rejuvenation/lift, 7:233–234, 234f, 235f
Midfacial fractures, 7:95, 96f
Midget bipolar cell, 12:12
Midget retinal ganglion cells, 6:43, 43f
Midline positions of gaze, 6:80
Miglitol, 1:199t, 201
Migraine equivalent (acephalgic migraine), 5:296–297. See also Migraine headache
Migraine headache, 5:294–298
  acephalgic, 5:296–297
  with aura (classic migraine), 5:191, 295, 296f
  without aura (common migraine), 5:296
  basilar-type (complicated migraine), 5:185, 295–296
  branch retinal artery occlusion and, 12:136
  chronic, 5:293
  evaluation of, 5:297–298, 297f
  hallucinations and, 5:191
  inherited encephalopathies resembling, 5:300
  ophthalmoplegic, 5:231
  retinal/ocular, 5:184–185, 190, 297
  transient visual loss caused by, 5:174, 184–185, 185
  treatment of, 5:298–299
  visual phenomena of, 5:191
Migration inhibitory factor, in cicatricial pemphigoid, 8:199
Mikulicz syndrome, 7:88, 8:73
Milia, 7:159
Miliary aneurysm, Leber, 12:146
Miliary tuberculosis, 9:257
Millard-Gubler syndrome, 5:227
Miller Fisher syndrome, 5:280, 287
Miller-Nadler Glare Tester, 3:293
Milrinone, for heart failure, 1:119
MIM (Mendelian Inheritance in Man) abbreviations/numbers, for corneal dystrophies, 8:270t
Mimecan, mutation in gene for, in cornea plana, 8:255
Mimetic muscles, 7:131–133, 133f
  facial nerve supplying, 7:133, 134f
Mimicry, molecular
  HLA disease associations and, 9:71, 73
  in sympathetic ophthalmia, 9:181
Mineral metabolism, disorders of, corneal changes in, 8:327–328, 327f
"Mini-monovision," 13:32–33
Minimal inhibitory concentration (MIC), 1:56

Minimal lethal concentration (MLC), 1:56
Minimally Classic/Occult Trial of the Anti-VEGF
    Antibody Ranibizumab in the Treatment of
    Neovascular AMD (MARINA), 12:73, 74, 75f
Minimum angle of resolution/recognition (MAR),
    3:109, 110t
    logarithm of (logMAR), 3:109, 110t
        cystoid macular edema after cataract surgery and,
        11:182
Minimum essential medium, 2:394
Minimum legible threshold, 3:108
Minimum separable threshold, 3:108
Minimum visible threshold, 3:108
Minipress. See Prazosin
Minisatellites, 2:156, 166, 180
Minizide. See Prazosin
Minnesota Low Vision Reading Test, 3:290
Minocin. See Minocycline
Minocycline, 1:51t, 2:374
    for meibomian gland dysfunction, 8:68
    ocular effects of, 1:301t
    for rosacea, 8:70
Minor (lesser) arterial circle, 2:58, 59f, 5:14f, 18
    development of, 2:138
Minoxidil, 1:77t, 82
Minus cylinder (posterior toric) form/lenses
    contact lenses, 3:174, 175
    spectacle lenses, distortion and, 3:316
Minus cylinder refraction, 3:130–132, 131f
Minus lenses. See also Concave (minus/negative) lenses
    anophthalmic socket camouflage and, 7:125
    prismatic effect of, 3:87
Miochol. See Acetylcholine
Miosis/miotic agents, 2:259–260, 338t
    for acute angle closure, 10:115–116
    adrenergic antagonists, 2:260, 348
    adverse effects of, 2:338, 339f
    angle closure caused by, 10:119
    cataracts caused by, 11:49
    cholinergic/muscarinic agonists, 2:259, 335–340,
        337f, 338t, 339f
    cholinesterase inhibitors, 2:334, 336f, 338t, 339–340
    congenital (microcoria), 6:223, 228–229
    for consecutive esotropia, 6:103
    dry eye and, 8:61
    for glaucoma, 2:264t, 338, 10:157, 164t, 171–172
        cataract/cataract surgery and, 11:49, 202
        in children, 6:243, 10:157, 172
    toxic keratoconjunctivitis and, 8:360
    traumatic injury and, 8:363
Miostat. See Carbachol
MIP. See Major intrinsic protein
Mirapex. See Pramipexole
Mirror test, in nonorganic ophthalmic disorders, 5:307,
    308f
Mirrors, 3:89–92
    central ray for, 3:90, 91f
    cold, 3:9
    image space reversal and, 3:90
    imaging with, 3:30–31, 32f
        image quality and, 3:37–39, 39f
    in lasers, 3:24, 24f

metallic reflection and, 3:13
reflecting power of, 3:89–90
in retinoscope, 3:121, 121f
vergence calculations for, 3:90–92, 92f
Misdirection, in nonorganic ophthalmic disorder
    evaluation, 5:306
Mismatch repair, 2:169
Missense mutation, 2:156, 171
Mitochondrial DNA
    diseases associated with deletions/mutations of,
        2:173–176, 174f, 191, 208
        chronic progressive external ophthalmoplegia and,
            5:336, 12:251t, 265
        galtonian inheritance of, 2:208
        Leber hereditary optic neuropathy and, 2:174f, 175,
            5:138, 6:311
        maternal inheritance/transmission and, 2:208, 220
        pigmentary retinopathy and, 12:251t, 265, 265f
        retinal degeneration and, 12:251t, 265
    in replicative segregation, 2:160, 173
Mitochondrial myopathy, 12:251t, 265, 265f
    with encephalopathy/lactic acidosis/strokelike
        episodes (MELAS), 12:265
        migrainelike headache and, 5:300
        mitochondrial DNA mutation and, 2:173, 174f,
            12:265
    neuro-ophthalmic signs of, 5:336–338, 336f, 337f
Mitomycin/mitomycin C, 1:239, 241t, 2:334, 367
    for corneal intraepithelial neoplasia, 8:231
    in dacryocystorhinostomy, 7:270
    enhancement of LASIK flaps and, 13:91
    for ocular surface squamous neoplasia/conjunctival
        intraepithelial neoplasia, 4:64, 8:229, 230f
    in ocular surgery after radial keratotomy, 13:47
    in phototherapeutic keratectomy, 8:403
    for primary acquired melanosis, 4:67
    in pterygium surgery, 8:394–395
    in surface ablation, 13:84–85
        corneal haze prevention/corneal wound healing
            and, 13:27, 68, 84–85, 86, 101
        international trends in use of, 13:199
        for undercorrection, 13:94
    toxic keratoconjunctivitis caused by, 8:360
    in trabeculectomy, 10:186, 193, 194, 195f
        in children, 6:241, 10:155
        scleral flap closure and, 10:191, 192f
    for uveitic glaucoma, 9:298
Mitosis, 2:156, 195
    nondisjunction during, 2:203. See also
        Nondisjunction
Mitoxantrone, for multiple sclerosis, 5:327
Mitten deformity, 6:389f
Mittendorf dot, 2:85, 85f, 4:132, 6:307, 11:25, 27, 12:307
Mixed astigmatism, 3:114, 115f
    outcomes of photoablation for, 13:89
Mixed connective tissue disease, 1:174
Mixed dementia, 1:265
Mixed tumor
    benign (pleomorphic adenoma)
        of eyelid, 7:162
        of lacrimal gland, 4:236, 237f, 7:86–87, 86f
    malignant, of lacrimal gland, 7:87

Mizuo-Nakamura phenomenon, **12**:218, 219*f*, 233
ML I. *See* Dysmorphic sialidosis
ML II. *See* Inclusion-cell (I-cell) disease
ML III. *See* Pseudo-Hurler polydystrophy
ML IV, **8**:312
MLC. *See* Minimal lethal concentration
MLF. *See* Medial longitudinal fasciculus
MLM. *See* Middle limiting membrane
MLN. *See* Manifest latent nystagmus; Mean of the ten
  largest melanoma cell nuclei
MLPA. *See* Multiplex ligation-dependent probe
  amplification
MLs. *See* Mucolipidoses
MLS. *See* Microphthalmia (microphthalmos), with
  linear skin defects
MMC. *See* Mitomycin/mitomycin C
MMP. *See* Matrix metalloproteinases; Mucous
  membrane (ocular cicatricial) pemphigoid
MMP-2 (gelatinase)
  in recurrent corneal erosion, **8**:83
  in Sjögren syndrome, **8**:63
  in vitreous, **2**:283
MMP-2 proenzyme, in cornea, **2**:250
MMP-3, in Sjögren syndrome, **8**:63
MMP-9
  in ligneous conjunctivitis, **8**:192
  in recurrent corneal erosion, **8**:83
  in Sjögren syndrome, **8**:63
MMP-13, in Sjögren syndrome, **8**:63
MMR vaccine, **1**:282, 286
Mn SOD, **2**:317
MNRead, **3**:290
MOABs. *See* Monoclonal antibodies
Mobitz II atrioventricular block, **1**:122*t*
Möbius syndrome/sequence, **5**:210, 241, 285, **6**:140–141,
  140*f*
Modified monovision, **13**:152–153
Modulation transfer function, **3**:111, 278
Moduretic. *See* Amiloride
Moebius syndrome. *See* Möbius syndrome/sequence
Moexipril, **1**:76*t*, 78*t*
Mohs micrographic surgery
  for canthal tumors, **7**:186, 187
  for neoplastic disorders of eyelid, **4**:45
    basal cell carcinoma, **4**:45, 219, **7**:171
    sebaceous adenocarcinoma, **4**:224, **7**:174
    squamous cell carcinoma, **4**:45, 219, **7**:172
Molds, **5**:364, **8**:138, 138*t*
  endogenous endophthalmitis caused by, **9**:273–274,
    276–278, 277*f*, **12**:203–204, 205*f*
Molecular biologic techniques/molecular genetics. *See*
  Genetics, molecular
Molecular mimicry
  HLA disease associations and, **9**:71, 73
  in sympathetic ophthalmia, **9**:181
Molecular motifs, in innate immune response, **9**:12
Molecular pathology techniques, **4**:34*t*, 37–43, 38–39*t*,
  40*f*, 42*f*
Moles. *See also* Nevus
  atypical, melanoma arising from, **1**:277
Moll, glands of, **2**:23, 23*f*, 26*f*, 27*t*, **4**:205, 207*t*, **7**:142*f*,
  160, **8**:4, 5*f*. *See also* Apocrine glands of eyelid
  hidrocystoma arising in, **7**:162, 162*f*

Molluscum contagiosum, **6**:193, 194*f*, **8**:127, 128*f*,
  129*f*
  conjunctivitis in children and, **6**:193, 194*f*
  of eyelid, **4**:210, 210*f*, **7**:159–160, 159*f*
    in children, **6**:193, 194*f*
  in HIV infection/AIDS, **9**:312–313
Molteno implant, **9**:298, **10**:205, 205*t*
  for childhood glaucoma, **6**:241
Molybdenum cofactor deficiency. *See* Sulfite oxidase
  deficiency
Monistat. *See* Miconazole
Monitoring system, **1**:340–342
Monoamine oxidase inhibitors, **1**:255*t*, 256
  discontinuing before surgery, **1**:306
  drug interactions and, **1**:256
    apraclonidine/brimonidine interactions, **2**:348,
    10:170
    hypertension and, **1**:87
Monobactams, **1**:49*t*, 58
Monocanalicular stents
  for lacrimal trauma, **7**:254*f*, 272–273
  for nasolacrimal intubation, **7**:253, 254*f*
Monochromatic aberrations, **3**:93
Monochromaticity, of laser light, **3**:20
Monochromatism/monochromacy/achromatopsia,
  12:214–215, 214*t*
  blue-cone, **12**:214, 214*t*, 215
    in children, **6**:291
    ERG patterns in, **12**:36*f*
    gene defects causing, **2**:297
    ocular findings in carriers of, **2**:222*t*
  rod, **12**:214*t*, 215
    in children, **6**:291
  Sloan test for, **12**:50
Monocid. *See* Cefonicid
Monoclonal antibodies, **9**:46
  for age-related macular degeneration/choroidal
    neovascularization, **12**:78
  in cancer therapy, **1**:244
  for fungal infection, **1**:20
  for primary central nervous system lymphoma, **9**:284
  for rheumatic disorders, **1**:186
Monoclonal gammopathy, benign, corneal deposits in,
  8:320
Monocular aphakia, aniseikonia and, contact lenses for,
  3:171–172
Monocular cells, in visual processing, **6**:43*f*, 44
Monocular cover-uncover test, **6**:74, 75*f*
Monocular diplopia, **3**:164–165, **5**:188, 218
  in cataracts, **11**:40, 41, 43, 70
  multifocal IOLs and, **3**:226
  pinhole imaging in identification of, **3**:108, 164
Monocular distortion. *See also* Distortion
  adaptation to, **3**:140, 320–321
  binocular spatial perception and, **3**:309–310
  minimizing, **3**:316–320, 318*f*, 319*f*
  sources of, **3**:310–311, 310*f*
    relative contributions from, **3**:315, 315*f*
Monocular elevation deficiency (double elevator palsy),
  6:123–124, 123*f*, **7**:205
Monocular eye movements (ductions), **5**:215, **6**:33–34.
  See also specific type
  forced. *See* Forced ductions

Monocular fixation, 6:11
Monocular no light perception, testing, 5:308–310, 309f, 310f
Monocular nystagmus of childhood, 5:246–247, 251t, 6:326
Monocular recession-resection procedures, 6:150–151, 150t
Monocular reduced vision, 5:91
   in nonorganic disorders, 5:310–311, 311t
Monocular telescopes, 3:299–300
Monocular transient visual loss, 5:173, 175–185, 176t. See also Transient visual loss
   carotid artery disease and, 1:96, 5:173, 174, 177–183, 179f, 183–184
   embolic causes of, 5:175f, 176t, 177–183, 178f, 179f, 179t, 181t
      clinical/laboratory evaluation of carotid artery disease and, 5:180–181
      prognosis/stroke risk and, 5:181, 181t
      treatment of carotid artery disease and, 5:181–183
   hypoperfusion causing, 5:176t, 183–184
   ocular pathology causing, 5:175–177, 176t
   optic nerve disorders causing, 5:176t
   orbital causes of, 5:176t, 177
   systemic causes of, 5:177–184
   vasculitis causing, 5:176t, 183
   vasospasm/hyperviscosity/hypercoagulability causing, 5:174, 176t, 184–185
Monocytes, 4:7, 8f, 9:11. See also Macrophages
   cytologic identification of, in immune-mediated keratoconjunctivitis, 8:182t
Monofixation syndrome, 6:59–60
   Bagolini glasses in evaluation of, 6:56f, 57
   4Δ base-out prism test in evaluation of, 6:57–58, 57f
   simultaneous prism and cover test in evaluation of, 6:75–76
   Worth 4-dot test in evaluation of, 6:55
Monogenic (mendelian) disorder, 2:155, 208
Monokines, 9:27
Mononucleosis, infectious
   Epstein-Barr virus causing, 1:24–25
   ocular involvement in, 6:193, 8:122–123, 123f
Monopril. See Fosinopril
Monosomy, 2:199
Monovision, 3:176, 189, 13:32–33, 152–153
   modified, 13:152–153
Montelukast, 1:145t
Mood disorders (affective disorders), 1:247–248
   drugs for treatment of, 1:257
Moore, lightning streaks of, 5:189
Mooren ulcer, 8:213–216, 215f
Moraxella
   blepharoconjunctivitis caused by, 8:145
   conjunctivitis in children caused by, 6:189
   lacunata, 8:145
   as normal ocular flora, 8:97t
   orbital cellulitis caused by, 7:42
Morgagnian cataract, 4:127, 128f, 11:42, 46f
   phacolytic glaucoma and, 10:91
Morgagnian globules, 4:127, 127f, 128f, 129f, 11:42
Moricizine, 1:123t
Morning glory disc anomaly, 5:143, 6:305, 305f, 415

Morpheaform basal cell carcinoma, 4:218, 219, 219f, 7:169, 169f. See also Basal cell carcinoma
Morphine
   for heart failure, 1:119
   for non–ST-segment elevation acute coronary syndrome, 1:111
   perioperative, 1:310
Morquio syndrome, 6:400t, 8:306t
   congenital/infantile corneal opacities and, 6:217
Morula, 2:117, 118f
Mosaic degeneration (anterior crocodile shagreen), 8:337
Mosaicism (mosaic), 2:156, 203–204
   germinal, 2:152
   sex chromosome, 2:204
   trisomy 21, 2:204
Mossy fiber input, 5:48
Motifs, in innate immune response, 9:12
Motility, ocular. See Ocular motility
Motility disorders. See Ocular motility, disorders of
Motility examination. See Ocular motility, assessment of
Motor apraxia, ocular. See Ocular motor apraxia
Motor correspondence, Hering's law of, 6:35, 36f
   eyelid retraction and, 5:281, 7:214
Motor fusion, 6:41, 41t
Motor nucleus
   of cranial nerve V (trigeminal), 2:101f, 102–103, 5:59
   of cranial nerve VII (facial), 2:105
Motor nystagmus, congenital, 6:321
Motor pathways, facial, 5.60–62, 62f. See also Cranial nerve VII
Motor physiology, 6:27–37
   basic principles and terms related to, 6:27–32
   eye movements and, 6:32–37
   strabismus and, 6:27–37
Motor root
   of cranial nerve III (oculomotor), 2:14, 15f
   of cranial nerve V (trigeminal), 2:102
   of cranial nerve VII (facial), 2:105
Motor system disorders. See Movement disorders; Parkinson disease
Motor tests, in strabismus/amblyopia evaluation, 6:83
Motor units, 6:32–33
Motrin. See Ibuprofen
MOTSA. See Multiple overlapping thin-slab acquisition
Movement disorders. See also Parkinson disease
   bradykinetic, 1:258
   in schizophrenia, 1:247
Moxifloxacin, 1:52t, 61, 2:371–373, 372t
   for bacterial keratitis, 8:162t, 163
   ocular effects of, 1:301t
Moxisylyte. See Thymoxamine
Moyamoya disease, morning glory disc anomaly in, 6:305
6-MP. See 6-Mercaptopurine
MPS (Macular Photocoagulation Study), 9:223–224, 224f, 12:71, 81, 85, 86
MPS I H. See Hurler syndrome
MPS I H/S. See Hurler-Scheie syndrome
MPS I S. See Scheie syndrome
MPS II. See Hunter syndrome
MPS III. See Sanfilippo syndrome

MPS IV. *See* Morquio syndrome
MPS VI. *See* Maroteaux-Lamy syndrome
MPS VII. *See* Sly syndrome
MPSs. *See* Mucopolysaccharidoses
MPSV vaccine, 1:285
MR. *See* Medial rectus muscles
MRA. *See* Magnetic resonance angiography
MRD₁/MRD₂. *See* Margin–reflex distance
MRI. *See* Magnetic resonance imaging
MRKAd5 HIV vaccine, 1:36
mRNA. *See* Messenger RNA
MRS. *See* Magnetic resonance spectroscopy
MRSA. *See* Methicillin-resistant *S aureus*
MS. *See* Multiple sclerosis
α-MSH (α-melanocyte-stimulating hormone), 8:177*t*
    in tear secretion, 2:244
MSI. *See* Magnetic source imaging
MST area. *See* Medial superior temporal area
MT area. *See* Medial temporal area
mtDNA. *See* Mitochondrial DNA
MTF. *See* Modulation transfer function
MTP (microsomal triglyceride transfer protein)
    mutations, 2:298
MTX. *See* Methotrexate
Mucins/mucin layer, tear film, 2:42, 238*f*, 241, 248, 8:3
    deficiency of, 2:241, 244
    in dry-eye syndrome, 8:49, 50*f*
    in external eye defense, 8:95
    secretion of, 2:241
Mucoceles, 2:12–13
    congenital
        in lacrimal sac. *See* Dacryocystocele/dacryocele
        nasal, 6:204–205, 205
    dacryocystitis and, 7:275
    orbital invasion by, 6:346, 7:89, 89*f*
Mucocutaneous junction, eyelid, 7:142, 142*f*
Mucocutaneous lymph node syndrome (Kawasaki
    disease), 1:177*t*, 6:201–202
Mucoepidermoid carcinoma, 4:64, 8:226*t*, 232–233
Mucolipidoses, 6:400*t*, 8:312
    corneal changes in, 8:312
        congenital/infantile opacities and, 6:216*t*, 217,
        400*t*, 8:263
    retinal degeneration and, 12:262
Mucomyst. *See* Acetylcysteine
Mucopolysaccharidoses, 6:398, 400*t*, 8:305–307, 306*t*,
    12:250*t*, 251*t*, 262. *See also specific type*
    corneal changes in, 8:305–307, 306*t*
        congenital/infantile opacities and, 6:216*t*, 217,
        400*t*, 8:263
    pigmentary retinopathy and, 12:250*t*, 251*t*, 262
Mucopyoceles, orbital invasion by, 7:89
Mucor (mucormycosis/zygomycosis/phycomycosis),
    5:366–367, 366*f*, 8:140
    cornea involved in (keratitis), 4:83
    optic nerve involved in, 4:251
    orbit involved in, 4:234, 6:197, 197*f*, 7:45–46
        exenteration in management of, 7:45, 126
Mucosa-associated lymphoid tissue (MALT), 4:47,
    8:173, 9:59
    in allergic reactions, 9:55
    of conjunctiva (conjunctiva-associated/CALT), 2:35,
        4:47, 8:3, 5, 180–181, 9:59

Mucosa-associated lymphoid tissue (MALT) lymphoma
    (MALToma/extranodal marginal zone lymphoma),
    4:72–73, 73*f*, 74
    of orbit, 7:80
Mucosal mast cells, 9:10
Mucous membrane grafting (transplantation), 8:389,
    401–402
    for cicatricial entropion, 7:198
    for contracted socket, 7:124
    for eyelid repair, 7:180
    for eyelid retraction, 7:215
    indications for, 8:387*t*, 401–402
    for symblepharon, 7:200
Mucous membrane (ocular cicatricial) pemphigoid,
    4:54, 56*f*, 8:180, 196*t*, 198–203, 199*t*, 200*f*, 201*f*, 202*f*,
    205*t*
    cataract surgery in patient with, 11:191
    drug-induced (pseudopemphigoid), 8:199, 361
    mucous membrane grafting for, 8:401
Mucus excess, conjunctival, 8:20*t*
Mucus-fishing syndrome, 8:90
MUGA. *See* Multiple gated acquisition
Muir-Torre syndrome, 7:161
    eyelid manifestations of, 4:215*t*, 221
Mulberry lesions (astrocytic hamartomas), 5:136, 136*f*
Müller cells/fibers
    optic nerve, 2:92*f*
    retinal, 2:75*f*, 77, 300–301, 5:29, 12:12, 14*f*
        development/differentiation of, 2:126
        in healing/repair, 4:17
Müller muscle (superior tarsal muscle), 2:23*f*, 25*f*, 28,
    4:186, 205, 5:63, 64, 64*f*, 7:135*f*, 138, 139–140
    in Horner syndrome, 5:266, 7:207
    internal (transconjunctival) resection of, for ptosis
        correction, 7:212
Müllerectomy
    Putterman, for ptosis correction, 7:212
    tarsoconjunctival (Fasanella-Servat procedure), for
        ptosis correction, 7:212
Multicentric basal cell carcinoma, 4:218, 7:169. *See also*
    Basal cell carcinoma
Multidrug-resistant tuberculosis (MDRTB), 1:19–20,
    39, 9:261
Multifactorial inheritance, 2:156, 224–225
Multiflex II anterior chamber IOL, 3:211, 211*f*
Multifocal ablation, for presbyopia, 13:156–157, 157*f*
Multifocal choroiditis, 9:78*t*, 83*t*
    in HIV infection/AIDS, 9:311
    in Lyme disease, 9:251
    in systemic lupus erythematosus, 9:142, 142*f*
    West Nile infection causing, 12:211
Multifocal choroiditis and panuveitis syndrome (MCP),
    9:148–150*t*, 161–164, 162*f*, 163*f*, 12:186*t*, 191–192,
    191*f*
    EBV infection and, 9:164, 208
Multifocal cornea, retinoscopy in detection of, 8:45
Multifocal electroretinogram, 5:110, 110*f*, 12:37, 38*f*
Multifocal eosinophilic granuloma of bone, 7:84
Multifocal lenses, 3:145–157. *See also* Bifocal lenses
    contact (aspheric simultaneous vision contact lenses),
        3:190
    design of, Prentice rule and, 3:150–156, 151*f*, 152*f*,
        153*f*, 154*f*, 155*f*, 156*f*

intraocular, 3:225–229, 11:136–137, 13:4t, 144–146, 154–156, 154f, 155f
  bifocal, 3:226–227, 227f
  clinical results of, 3:228–229
  complications associated with, 11:169
  diffractive, 3:227–228, 227f, 228f
  multiple-zone, 3:227, 227f
  for presbyopia, 13:154–156, 154f, 155f
  occupation and, 3:156–157
  power of add for, 3:145–147
  types of
    bifocal types, 3:147, 148f
    progressive addition types, 3:147–150, 150f
    trifocal types, 3:147, 149
Multifocal VEP, 5:109
Multi-infarct dementia, 1:227, 265
Multinucleated giant cells, 4:7, 9f
  in sarcoidosis, 4:191, 191f
Multiplanar incisions, clear corneal, 11:113–114, 114f
Multiple endocrine neoplasia, 1:216–217, 217f, 237
  conjunctival neurogenic/smooth muscle tumors in, 8:240
  corneal nerve enlargement in, 8:328–329, 329t
Multiple evanescent white dot syndrome (MEWDS), 5:113–114, 113f, 9:148–150t, 168–170, 168f, 169f, 12:186t, 189–190, 189f
Multiple gated acquisition (MUGA), in ischemic heart disease, 1:107
Multiple overlapping thin-slab acquisition (MOTSA), for magnetic resonance angiography, 5:77
Multiple sclerosis, 5:320–328
  chiasmal/retrochiasmal abnormalities in, 5:324
  diagnostic criteria for, 5:326t, 327
  epidemiology and genetics of, 5:321
  funduscopic abnormalities in, 5:324
  HLA association in, 5:321, 9:72t, 139
  laboratory evaluation in, 5:325, 326t
  neuroimaging in, 5:82t, 322f, 325–326
  nonocular symptoms of, 5:323
  ocular flutter caused by, 5:256
  ocular motility disturbances in, 5:324–325
  optic nerve involvement and, 4:252, 252f, 5:144–146, 145f, 323–324
    in children, 6:312
  pathology of, 5:321–322, 322f
  presentation of, 5:323
  prognosis for, 5:321
  treatment of, 5:327–328
  uveitis in, 9:136, 139–140
    differential diagnosis in children and, 6:276t
Multiple sulfatase deficiency, 8:310
Multiple-zone intraocular lenses, 3:227, 227f
Multiplex ligation-dependent probe amplification (MLPA), 4:38t, 41
Multizone keratectomies, 13:24, 24f
Mumps virus, 8:129–130
  immunization against, 1:283
  ocular infection caused by, 8:129–130
Munchausen syndrome, 5:305
Munchausen syndrome by proxy, ocular trauma and, 6:404
Munnerlyn formula, 3:234, 13:23
Munson sign, in keratoconus, 8:298, 298f

Mural cells, retinal blood vessel, 2:78
Muro 128. See Sodium chloride
Muscarine, 2:259t
Muscarinic agents, 2:334, 335–342, 338t, 339f, 341t
  adverse effects of, 2:338, 339f
  antagonists, 2:340–342, 341t
    adverse effects of, 2:342, 343f
  direct-acting agonists, 2:334, 335–339, 337f, 338t, 339f
  indirect-acting agonists, 2:339–340
Muscarinic receptors
  in iris–ciliary body, 2:259, 259t, 262, 263
  signal transduction and, 2:262, 262f, 263, 263f, 264t
  in tear secretion, 2:242, 242f
Muscle capsule, of rectus muscles, 6:19–20
  surgery and, 6:24
Muscle cone, 6:19, 20f
Muscle relaxants
  for benign essential blepharospasm, 7:220
  tear production affected by, 8:66t
Muscle of Riolan, 2:23, 23f, 27, 7:137, 142, 142f
Muscle-specific kinase (MuSK) antibodies, in myasthenia gravis, 5:331, 6:138
Muscle-weakening procedures. See Weakening procedures
Muscles. See specific muscle and Extraocular muscles
Muscular arteries, inferior/superior, 5:14f, 15f, 18
Muscular dystrophy, Duchenne
  mutation rate of, 2:207
  pigmentary retinopathy and, 12:254
MuSK antibodies. See Muscle-specific kinase (MuSK) antibodies
Mustardé flap, for eyelid repair, 7:185–186, 185f
Mutagens, 2:169
Mutamycin. See Mitomycin/mitomycin C
Mutation, 2:156, 169, 207–210. See also specific type
  base pair, 2:171
    conserved, 2:171
  cancer and, 1:236
  carrier of, 2:149
  disease-producing, 2:170
  dominant negative, 2:151
  frameshift (framing error/frameshift), 2:141, 152
  gain of function and, 2:171
  missense, 2:156, 171
  nonsense, 2:156, 171
  null, 2:171
  point, 2:207
    mitochondrial DNA, 2:174f
    screening for, 2:184, 186–187f
  repair and, 2:169–170
  screening for, 2:182–184, 183f, 185f, 186–187f
  transcription factor, 2:166
Mutton-fat keratic precipitates, 8:25, 9:86f, 87–88. See also Keratic precipitates
  in sarcoidosis, 8:74, 9:86f, 175, 175f
  in sympathetic ophthalmia, 4:189, 9:178
  in uveitis, 9:86f, 87–88
Myasthenia gravis, 2:342, 5:328–331, 6:137–138, 138f, 139t, 7:209
  clinical presentation of, 5:328–329, 6:137–138, 138f, 139t
  diagnosis of, 5:329–331, 330f, 6:138, 138f
    edrophonium in, 2:329, 342–343, 5:329–330, 6:138, 138f, 139t, 7:209

diplopia in, 5:238, 329
extraocular motor dysfunction in, 5:227, 6:137, 139*t*
neuro-ophthalmic signs of, 5:328–331
pseudo-INO caused by, 5:225
ptosis in, 5:276–277, 277*f*, 280, 328, 6:137, 138*f*, 139*t*,
7:204–205, 209
strabismus in, 6:137–138, 138*f*, 139*t*
thyroid eye disease and, 7:51, 209
treatment of, 5:331, 6:138
Myasthenia Gravis Foundation of America, Inc, 6:137
Mycamine. *See* Micafungin
Mycelex. *See* Clotrimazole
Mycelium, 8:138
Mycobacterium (mycobacteria), 1:18–20, 8:136–137
avium/avium-intracellulare, 1:39, 5:360, 9:128
chelonei, 8:137, 13:99*f*
fortuitum, 8:137
in HIV infection/AIDS, 1:18, 39, 5:360
kansasii, 1:39
keratitis after photoablation caused by, 13:98
leprae, 8:136
nontuberculous (atypical) infection caused by, 1:18,
8:164
ocular infection/inflammation caused by, 8:136–137,
164
stains and culture media for identification of, 8:103*t*
tuberculosis, 1:18, 18–20, 39, 5:360, 8:136, 9:257,
12:204–205. *See also* Tuberculosis
immune response to, 9:35
screening/testing for, 1:19, 279–280, 9:259–261
Mycograb, 1:20
Mycology, 8:138–140, 138*t. See also* Fungi
Mycophenolate mofetil, 1:187, 9:108*t*, 110
for Behçet disease, 9:195
for uveitis, 9:108*t*, 110
in children, 6:277
Mycoplasma pneumoniae, 1:17–18
Mycostatin. *See* Nystatin
Mycotic (fungal) keratitis, 4:83–84, 85*f*, 8:164–167, 165*f*
plant sources of, 8:362
Mydfrin. *See* Phenylephrine
Mydral. *See* Tropicamide
Mydriacyl. *See* Tropicamide
Mydriasis/mydriatics, 2:260
adrenergic agents, 2:260, 345–346
angle closure caused by, 10:118–119
anisocoria and, 5:265*f*, 270
iris damage and, 5:269–270
benign episodic, 5:274
cholinergic agents, 2:260, 340–342, 341*t*
congenital, 6:229
cycloplegia/cycloplegic agents and, 3:137
multifocal IOLs and, 13:145
for pupillary capture, 11:166
for retinal examination, 12:19
seizures and, 1:263
SSRIs causing, 1:255
traumatic injury and, 8:363
for uveitis, 9:99, 120
for Vogt-Koyanagi-Harada (VKH) syndrome, 9:189
Myectomy, 6:148*t*
for benign essential blepharospasm, 7:220

Myelinated (medullated) retinal nerve fibers, 4:148,
6:306, 306*f*
Myelination, of nerve fiber layer, optic disc edema
differentiated from, 5:120–121, 121*f*
Myelitis, optic nerve involvement and, 4:252, 5:147
Myeloid stem cells, 1:147
Myeloproliferative disorders, hypercoagulability and,
1:158
Myiasis, 8:143
Mykrox. *See* Metolazone
MYO7A gene, 2:176
Myobloc. *See* Botulinum toxin, type B
MYOC gene. *See* TIGR/myocilin (TIGR/MYOC) gene
Myocardial contractility, 1:117
enhancement of in heart failure management, 1:119
reduction of in angina management, 1:108
Myocardial infarction, 1:101–102. *See also* Acute
coronary syndrome; Ischemic heart disease
in diabetes mellitus, 1:207
ECG changes in, 1:102, 104
heart failure and, 1:103
hypertension management and, 1:79*t*, 84
management of, 1:109*t*, 111–113
cardiac-specific troponins and, 1:105
percutaneous coronary intervention for, 1:99
ophthalmic considerations and, 1:128
painless/asymptomatic, 1:102, 104
pericarditis after (post-MI/Dressler syndrome),
1:103
stroke and, 1:92
Myocardial oxygen requirements, reducing
for acute coronary syndrome, 1:111
for angina, 1:108
Myocardial scintigraphy, thallium-201, 1:106
Myocilin, gene for. *See* TIGR/myocilin (TIGR/MYOC)
gene
Myoclonic epilepsy with ragged red fibers (MERRF),
mitochondrial DNA mutations and, 2:173, 174*f*
Myoclonus
cherry-red spot in, 6:400*t*, 12:262
oculopalatal, pendular nystagmus and, 5:253
Myoepithelial cells
iris, 2:60*f*
differentiation of, 2:137
lacrimal gland, 2:32, 33*f*
Myofibromas, of orbit, 6:343
Myogenic ptosis, 5:280*t*, 7:205, 205*f*, 207*t*
Myoglobin
in immunohistochemistry, 4:33
serum, in acute coronary syndrome, 1:105
Myoid, photoreceptor, 12:10
of cone, 2:74, 76*f*
of rod, 2:73, 76*f*
Myo-inositol, in aqueous humor, 2:255
Myokymia
eyelid, 5:289*t*, 292
facial, 5:289*t*, 292
superior oblique, 5:256–257, 6:142–143
Myopathies
diplopia caused by, 5:238–241, 240*f*, 241*f*
extraocular, in thyroid eye disease, 4:232, 5:332*f*, 333,
6:135, 7:49, 49*f*, 51

mitochondrial, **12**:251*t*, 265, 265*f*
    with encephalopathy/lactic acidosis/strokelike
        episodes (MELAS), **12**:265
    migrainelike headache and, **5**:300
    mitochondrial DNA mutation and, **2**:173, 174*f*,
        12:265
    neuro-ophthalmic signs of, **5**:336–338, 336*f*, 337*f*
Myopia, **3**:113–114, 114*f*
    with achromatopsia, racial and ethnic concentration
        of, **2**:211
    adult-onset, **3**:118
    age of onset and, **3**:118, **6**:169
    amblyopia and, **6**:63, 64, 69
    cataract causing, **11**:55, 70
    cataract surgery in patient with, **11**:200
    choroidal neovascularization in, **12**:86–87
    congenital, **3**:141
    congenital stationary night blindness with, ocular
        findings in carriers of, **2**:222*t*
    contact lenses for, **3**:171–172, 173
        orthokeratology and, **3**:194–195, **13**:63–64
    degenerative. *See* High (pathologic/degenerative)
        myopia
    developmental, **3**:118–119, 141
    diabetic retinopathy and, **6**:297
    diverging lens for correction of, **3**:138, 139*f*
    etiology of, **3**:118–119
    glaucoma and, **10**:27, 76, 80, 114
    high. *See* High (pathologic/degenerative) myopia
    hyperopia overcorrection and, **13**:93–94
        conductive keratoplasty for, **13**:122
    in inborn errors of metabolism, **6**:401*t*
    in infants and children, **3**:118, 141, **6**:169
    instrument, in automated refraction, **3**:275
    intermittent exotropia and, **6**:102
    juvenile-onset, **3**:118
    lattice degeneration and, **12**:276, 278
    lenticular (myopic shift), **11**:39, 70
    muscarinic agents causing, **2**:338
    night, spherical aberration causing, **3**:99, 100
    orthokeratology for correction of, **3**:194–195,
        13:63–64
    pathologic. *See* High (pathologic/degenerative)
        myopia
    prevalence of, **3**:117, 118–119
    prismatic effect of bifocals in, **3**:151, 151*f*, 152
    residual
        after intrastromal corneal ring segment placement,
            13:58
        after LASIK, intrastromal corneal ring segments
            for, **13**:63
    retinal reflex in, **3**:122–123, 123*f*
    retinopathy of prematurity and, **6**:286
    in Stickler syndrome, **6**:295
    surgical correction of. *See also specific procedure*
        bioptics for, **13**:137
        examination before, **13**:33
        hyperopia after (consecutive hyperopia), **13**:93–94
        incisional corneal surgery for, **13**:43–48, 45*f*, 46*f*,
            47*f*
        intrastromal corneal ring segments for, **13**:55–56,
            56*f*, 57, 58

LASIK for, **3**:235, 235*f*. *See also* LASIK
light-adjustable IOLs for, **13**:146–147, 147*f*
monovision for, **13**:153
nonlaser, **13**:4*t*
phakic IOLs for, **13**:126, 128, 130
photoablation for, **13**:23–24
    outcomes of, **13**:87–88
PRK for, outcomes of, **13**:87
radial keratotomy for, **13**:43–48, 45*f*, 46*f*, 47*f*. *See
    also* Radial keratotomy
refractive lens exchange/clear lens extraction for,
    13:138, 139–140, 140, 141
retinal detachment/retinal detachment repair and,
    13:138, 141, 175–178
wavefront-guided laser ablation for, **13**:23
    outcomes of, **13**:88–89
vitreous changes associated with, **2**:286, 287
wavefront aberration produced by (positive defocus),
    3:238, **13**:6, 6*f*
Myopic astigmatism, simple, **3**:114, 115*f*
Myopic keratomileusis, **13**:21
    laser, **13**:4*t*. *See also* LASIK
    nonlamellar, **13**:4*t*
Myopic shift, in cataracts (lenticular myopia), **11**:39, 70
Myorhythmia, oculomasticatory, **5**:257
Myosin gene mutations, in Usher syndrome, **12**:253
Myosin VIIA gene, mutations in, **2**:176, 296
Myositis, orbital, **4**:231, 231*f*, **5**:239, **6**:347
    nonspecific orbital inflammation and, **4**:231, 231*f*,
        7:59, 60*f*
Myotomy, **6**:140*t*
    marginal, **6**:148*t*
Myotonic dystrophy, **5**:337–338
    lens disorders/cataracts in, **11**:57, 58*f*
        in children, **6**:247*t*
    pigmentary retinopathy and, **12**:250*t*, 254
    ptosis in, **5**:280, 338
Mysoline, **1**:263*t*
Myxedema, **1**:211, 212
    pretibial (infiltrative dermopathy), in
        hyperthyroidism/thyroid eye disease, **1**:211, **7**:51
Myxedema coma, **1**:212
Myxedema madness, **1**:212
MZM. *See* Methazolamide

N

Na. *See* Sodium
Na$^+$,K$^+$-ATPase (sodium-potassium pump)
    in aqueous humor secretion/suppression, **2**:351, **10**:15
    corneal hydration and, **8**:8
    in Fuchs endothelial corneal dystrophy, **8**:291
    in lens active transport, **11**:18
        pump–leak theory and, **11**:18–19, 18*f*
    in lens ionic balance, **2**:278
    in retinal pigment epithelium, **2**:304, 307
    in rods, **2**:292
Na$^+$,K$^+$-Ca exchanger (sodium-potassium-calcium
    exchanger), in rods, **2**:292
NAAT (nucleic acid amplification test). *See* Polymerase
    chain reaction

Nabumetone, 1:183*t*
Nadbath block, adverse reactions to, 1:312
Nadifloxacin, 1:61
Nadolol, 1:76*t*, 78*t*
NADP, in lens glucose/carbohydrate metabolism, 11:14*f*, 15
NADPH
  in free-radical generation, 2:312
  in lens glucose/carbohydrate metabolism, 2:279, 280*f*, 11:14*f*, 15
    glutathione redox cycle and, 2:314
Nafcillin, 1:45*t*, 56, 2:369–370
Nagel anomaloscope, 12:50
Nail-patella syndrome, 8:323*t*
NAION. *See* Nonarteritic anterior ischemic optic neuropathy
Nalfon. *See* Fenoprofen
Nalidixic acid, 1:60
Naloxone, for narcotic reversal, 1:311
Namenda. *See* Memantine
Naming-meshing system, for uveitis differential diagnosis, 9:91
Nanophthalmos, 4:112–113, 8:251–252, 253
  angle-closure glaucoma and, 4:112, 113, 10:135–136
  cataract surgery in patient with, 11:200–201
Naphazoline, 2:364, 365*t*, 392
Naphazoline/antazoline, 2:364, 365*t*
Naphazoline/pheniramine, 2:364, 365*t*
Naphcon-A. *See* Naphazoline/pheniramine
Naprelan. *See* Naproxen
Naprosyn. *See* Naproxen
Naproxen, 1:183*t*, 2:362*t*
  ocular effects of, 1:301*t*
  for uveitis in children, 6:277
NAPVI (National Association of Parents of Children With Visual Impairments), 6:417*t*
NARP (neuropathy [neurogenic muscle weakness]/ataxia/retinitis pigmentosa) syndrome, 2:175–176, 12:265
  mitochondrial DNA mutations and, 2:174*f*, 175–176
Narrow complex tachycardias, 1:123
Nasal artery, 5:14*f*
Nasal bone, 7:6*f*
Nasal cavity, 7:18
Nasal chondritis, in relapsing polychondritis, 1:175
Nasal conchae (turbinates), 7:18, 245*f*, 246
  inferior, 7:18, 245*f*, 246
  infracture of, for congenital nasolacrimal duct obstruction, 6:208–209, 7:255
Nasal CPAP, 1:144
Nasal endoscopy, for lacrimal drainage evaluation, 7:261
Nasal mucoceles, congenital, 6:204–205, 205
Nasal radiating fibers, 5:29, 30*f*
  visual field defects and, 5:116
Nasal retina, 5:28*f*, 31
Nasal septum, 7:18
Nasal step, in glaucoma, 10:65*f*, 68, 71*f*
NASCET (North American Symptomatic Carotid Endarterectomy Trial), 1:95–96, 5:181–182, 183
Nasociliary nerve, 2:103, 5:10*f*, 59, 59*f*, 60, 7:11*f*, 12*f*, 17
Nasofrontal vein, 2:40*f*

Nasolacrimal canal, 7:9
  balloon catheter dilation of, for congenital nasolacrimal duct obstruction, 6:209, 209*f*, 7:253–255
Nasolacrimal duct, 2:10, 33, 34, 5:12, 7:245*f*, 246. *See also* Lacrimal drainage system
  development of, 6:169, 7:243
  irrigation of
    for acquired obstruction evaluation, 7:259, 260*f*
    for congenital obstruction management, 7:251–252, 253*f*
  obstruction of. *See also* Tearing
    acquired, 7:266–270, 269*f*, 270*f*
      dacryocystorhinostomy for, 7:267–270, 269*f*, 270*f*
      intubation and stenting for, 7:267
      irrigation in evaluation of, 7:259, 259–261, 260*f*
      probing in evaluation of, 7:261
    congenital, 6:169, 205–210, 206*f*, 7:243, 250–255, 252*f*, 253*f*, 254*f*, 278
      balloon catheter dilation (balloon dacryoplasty) for, 6:209, 209*f*, 7:253–255
      dacryocystorhinostomy for, 7:255
      differential diagnosis of, 6:206
      intubation for, 6:209–210, 7:252–253, 254*f*
      irrigation for, 7:251–252, 253*f*
      lacrimal sac massage for, 6:206
      nonsurgical management of, 6:206
      probing for, 6:207, 207–208, 208*f*, 7:250–251, 251–252, 252*f*, 253*f*
      surgical management of, 6:206–210, 208*f*, 209*f*
      turbinate infracture for, 6:208–209, 7:255
    dacryocystitis and, 7:251, 274–275, 276
    functional, 7:261
    primary congenital glaucoma differentiated from, 10:144, 144*t*
  occlusion of, 2:34
    ocular medication absorption and, 2:324, 324*f*, 325*f*, 10:175
      in children, 10:156
  stenosis of, 7:261
    involutional, 7:266
  trauma to, 7:266–267, 273
Nasolacrimal procedures, endocarditis prophylaxis and, 1:8*t*
Naso-orbital-ethmoidal fractures, 7:98, 99*f*
  nasolacrimal duct obstruction and, 7:266
Nasopharyngeal carcinoma, Epstein-Barr virus associated with, 1:25, 237
Natacyn. *See* Natamycin
Natalizumab, for multiple sclerosis, 5:327
Natamycin, 2:378–379, 379*t*
  for fungal keratitis, 8:166
Nateglinide, 1:199*t*, 201
National Association of Parents of Children With Visual Impairments, 6:417*t*
National Association for the Visually Handicapped, 6:417*t*
National Cholesterol Education Program (NCEP), 1:131
National Dissemination Center for Children with Disabilities, 6:417*t*
National Down Syndrome Society, 6:418*t*
National Easter Seal Society, 6:418*t*

National Eye Institute, on nystagmus terminology, 6:317–318
National Eye Institute Visual Function Questionnaire (NEI-VFQ), 11:71
National Fragile X Foundation, 6:418t
National Health Information Center, 6:418t
National Health and Nutrition Examination Survey III, 12:90
National Institutes of Health Consensus Development Conference, 1:219–220
National Institutes of Health Stroke Scale, 1:93
National Library Service for the Blind and Physically Handicapped, 6:417t
National Organization for Albinism and Hypopigmentation, 6:417t
National Osteoporosis Foundation, 1:230
National Registry of Drug-Induced Ocular Side Effects (NRDIOSE), 1:300
Natriuretic peptides
    in aqueous humor, 2:267, 270
    in heart failure, 1:114, 117–118
Natural (innate) immunity, 9:9. See also Innate immune response
Natural killer cells, 9:51
    in viral conjunctivitis, 9:60
Nausea and vomiting, postoperative
    management of, 1:310
    after strabismus surgery, 6:161
NAVH (National Association for the Visually Handicapped), 6:417t
NBX. See Necrobiotic xanthogranuloma
NCEP (US National Cholesterol Education Program), 1:131
NCL. See Neuronal ceroid lipofuscinosis
ND-1/ND-4/ND-6 genes, in Leber hereditary optic neuropathy, 2:174f, 175
NDP gene, in Norrie disease, 2:193, 6:296
Nd:YAG laser, 3:24. See also Lasers
    mechanical light damage caused by, 12:332
Nd:YAG laser therapy
    capsulotomy, 11:171–175, 172f, 174f
        for anterior capsule fibrosis and phimosis, 11:171, 171–175, 172f, 199
        for capsular block syndrome, 11:166–167
        for capsule opacification, 11:169, 171–175, 174f
            in uveitis, 9:294
        complications of, 11:173–175
        contraindications to, 11:172
        indications for, 11:171–172
        lens particle glaucoma and, 10:91–92, 11:63
        procedure for, 11:172–173, 174f
        retinal detachment and, 11:175, 184, 12:363
    cycloablation/cyclophotocoagulation, 10:210
        for childhood glaucoma, 6:241, 10:155
    for cystoid macular edema, 12:143
    for epithelial basement membrane dystrophy, 8:272
    iridotomy, 10:201, 202–203
    for iris bombé in uveitis, 9:296
    photolysis, 11:127
    trabeculoplasty (selective), 10:181–182
    vitreolysis, for vitreous prolapse in anterior chamber, 11:162

Near blindness, 3:285. See also Low vision; Visual loss/ impairment
"Near clear" incision, for cataract surgery, 11:114
Near-infrared fundus autofluorescence, 12:31
Near-infrared reflectance imaging, 12:30–31, 31f
Near periphery, 12:8
Near point of accommodation, 3:117, 117f
    measuring, 3:145–146
Near point of convergence, 6:81
Near reflex
    accommodative convergence and, 2:99, 6:37
    assessment of, 6:81
    pathways for, 2:99
    spasm of, 3:143, 5:315
        esotropia and, 6:97
    voluntary application of, 6:37
Near response, in pupillary examination, 5:262
    light–near dissociation and, 5:273–274, 273t
Near (reading) spectacles
    for low vision/vision rehabilitation, 3:295–296, 297
    for presbyopia, with contact lenses, 3:176, 189
    single-vision
        for induced anisophoria, 3:156
        for low vision/vision rehabilitation, 3:296
Near visual acuity
    age-related loss of, 2:67, 3:117, 142, 143t, 11:20, 13:149. See also Presbyopia
    in low vision
        magnification for, 3:295–296, 297
        testing, 3:290–291, 5:92
    testing
        in children, 6:74
            nystagmus and, 6:319
        in low vision, 3:290–291, 5:92
Nebcin. See Tobramycin
NebuPent. See Pentamidine
Neck
    age-related changes in, 7:229
    cosmetic/rejuvenation surgery on, 7:234–238, 237f, 238f
        liposuction, 7:236–238
Neck lift, for opening airway, 1:290
Necrobiotic granuloma, in scleritis, 4:114, 115f
Necrobiotic granulomatous inflammatory infiltrate, in episcleritis, 4:113, 113f
Necrobiotic xanthogranuloma (NBX), 7:85, 8:242
Necrotizing encephalopathy, Leigh (Leigh syndrome), 2:176, 213t
    mitochondrial DNA mutations and, 2:174f, 176
Necrotizing fasciitis, of orbit, 7:44
Necrotizing keratitis, 8:25
    herpes simplex causing, 8:115, 115f, 116
Necrotizing retinitis/retinopathy, herpetic, 4:151, 151f, 9:200, 307–308, 308f, 12:201–202, 202f. See also Acute retinal necrosis; Progressive outer retinal necrosis
Necrotizing scleritis, 4:114, 114f, 115f, 8:21t, 28, 218–220, 218t, 219f, 220f, 222, 223, 9:267f
    with inflammation, 8:218t, 219, 219f
    without inflammation (scleromalacia perforans), 4:114, 8:218t, 220, 220f
Nedocromil, 1:145t, 2:365t, 366

Needle penetration/perforation of globe, **11**:185, **12**:325, 362, 363*f*
Needle sticks
  HIV transmission by, **1**:32
    chemoprophylaxis for, **1**:37
  prevention of, **8**:46
Nefazodone, **1**:256
Negative angle kappa, **6**:77, 78*f*
Negative defocus, **3**:238, **13**:6
Negative dysphotopsias, intraocular lenses and, **11**:168
Negative lenses. *See* Concave (minus/negative) lenses
Negative predictive value (NPV), of screening/diagnostic test, **1**:330
Negative staining (fluorescein), **8**:17
Neglect, elder, **1**:223–224
NEI (National Eye Institute), on nystagmus terminology, **6**:317–318
NEI-VFQ (National Eye Institute Visual Function Questionnaire), **11**:71
Neisseria, **1**:10–11, **8**:134, 134*f*
  gonorrhoeae (gonococcus), **1**:10–11, **8**:134, 134*f*, 149
    conjunctivitis caused by, **8**:134, 151–152, 151*f*
      in children, **6**:189
      in neonates, **6**:187, 187*f*, **8**:152, 153
      resistant strains of, **1**:11, **8**:152, 153
  meningitidis (meningococcus), **1**:10, **8**:134, 149
    conjunctivitis in children caused by, **6**:189
    endogenous endophthalmitis caused by, **9**:272, 272*f*
    immunization against, **1**:10, 285
Nelfilcon, for contact lenses, **3**:177*t*
Nelfinavir, **1**:34
Nematodes, diffuse unilateral subacute neuroretinitis caused by, **9**:239, **12**:210
NEMO (NF-kB essential modulator) gene, in incontinentia pigmenti, **6**:379
Neo-Synephrine. *See* Phenylephrine
Neocerebellum, **5**:48
Neodymium:yttrium-aluminum-garnet laser. *See* Nd:YAG laser
Neofrin. *See* Phenylephrine
Neomycin, **2**:368*t*, 376
  in combination preparations, **2**:372*t*, 373*t*
  ototoxicity of, mitochondrial DNA mutations and, **2**:176
Neonatal adrenoleukodystrophy, **6**:398, **12**:250*t*, 254, 261, 261*f*
  pigmentary retinopathy in, **12**:250*t*, 254, 261, 261*f*
Neonatal hemangiomatosis, diffuse, **6**:340
Neonatal ophthalmia. *See* Ophthalmia, neonatorum
Neonates. *See also* Infants
  conjunctivitis in, **6**:186–188, 187*f*, **8**:152–154. *See also* Ophthalmia, neonatorum
  corneal transplantation in, **8**:430–431, 431*t*
  ERG in, **12**:36
  hemorrhagic disease of newborn in, **1**:156
  herpes simplex infection in, **1**:22, **8**:106
  normal ocular flora in, **8**:96
  ocular deviations in, **5**:212
  ocular infections in, **6**:181–186, **8**:152–154. *See also specific type*
  ophthalmia neonatorum in, **6**:186–188, 187*f*, **8**:152–154. *See also* Ophthalmia, neonatorum
  screening eye examinations in, **6**:250–251

Neoplasia, **4**:10, 10*t*, 11*f*, 12*t*. *See also specific type or structure involved and* Cancer; Intraocular tumors; Tumors
  classification of, **4**:10*t*
  definition of, **4**:10
  diplopia caused by, **5**:239
  facial pain associated with, **5**:303
  masquerade syndromes and, **9**:281–287, 282*f*, 283*f*, **12**:199, 199*f*
  neuroimaging in evaluation of, **5**:82*t*
  ocular flutter caused by, **5**:255–256
  ocular surface, **8**:225–247
    of epithelial origin, **8**:226–233, 226*t*
    of neuroectodermal origin, **8**:233–240, 234*t*
Neoral. *See* Cyclosporine/cyclosporine A
Neosporin, **2**:372*t*
Neostigmine, **2**:259, 336*f*, 342
  for myasthenia gravis diagnosis, **5**:330, **6**:138
Neo-Synephrine. *See* Phenylephrine
Neovascular glaucoma, **4**:192, **10**:37, 37*f*, 124–128, 125*f*, 125*t*, 126*f*, 127*f*
  central retinal vein occlusion and, **12**:130
  glaucoma drainage device implantation and, **10**:206
  incisional surgery and, **10**:185
  iris examination in, **10**:30–31
Neovascular membrane, subretinal. *See also* Neovascularization
  in age-related macular degeneration, **4**:169–170, 171*f*
Neovascularization
  of anterior chamber angle
    in diabetes mellitus, **12**:108–109
    in glaucoma, **10**:30–31, 37, 37*f*, 124–128, 125*f*, 125*t*, 126*f*, 127*f*. *See also* Neovascular glaucoma
  in Behçet disease, **9**:193
  in branch retinal vein occlusion, **4**:164, **12**:123
    photocoagulation for, **12**:124–126, 125*f*
  in central retinal artery occlusion, **12**:140
  in central retinal vein occlusion, **4**:164, **12**:128, 130
    photocoagulation for, **12**:132
  choroidal. *See* Choroidal neovascularization
  corneal
    contact lenses causing, **3**:199, **8**:92
    inflammation and, **8**:25
    after lamellar keratoplasty, **8**:436
    medications causing, **8**:360
    after pediatric corneal transplantation, **8**:431
    stem cell deficiency and, **8**:93, 94
  in diabetes mellitus, **4**:166, **12**:105, 106*f*, 108–109. *See also* Diabetic retinopathy, proliferative
  in Eales disease/tuberculosis, **9**:258, 260*f*, 303
  in glaucoma, **4**:192, **10**:30–31, 37, 37*f*, 124–128, 125*f*, 125*t*, 126*f*, 127*f*. *See also* Neovascular glaucoma
    glaucoma drainage device implantation and, **10**:206
    incisional surgery contraindicated in, **10**:185
    laser iridotomy contraindicated in, **10**:202
  of iris (rubeosis iridis), **4**:192, 192*t*, 193*f*
    in branch retinal vein occlusion, **12**:124
    in central retinal artery occlusion, **12**:140
    in central retinal vein occlusion, **12**:128–129
      photocoagulation for, **12**:132
    in diabetes mellitus, **4**:166, 166*f*, **12**:108–109

glaucoma and, **4:**192, **10:**30–31, 37, 125, 125*f*, 125*t*, 126*f*, 201. *See also* Neovascular glaucoma
incisional surgery contraindicated in, **10:**185
in infants and children, **10:**141*t*
laser iridotomy contraindicated in, **10:**202
in ocular ischemic syndrome, **12:**133, 134, 134*f*
in retinoblastoma, **4:**179, 180*f*, 303
in multifocal choroiditis and panuveitis syndrome, **9:**162, 163*f*, 164
in ocular histoplasmosis syndrome, **9:**221, 223, 224*f*, **12:**80–83, 82*f*, 351, 351*f*
management of, **9:**223–226, 224*f*, 225*f*, **12:**81–83, 351, 351*f*
in ocular ischemic syndrome, **9:**287, **12:**133, 134, 134*f*
optic disc (NVD), in diabetic retinopathy, **12:**105, 106*f*
in pars planitis, **9:**135–136, 138–139, 303, **12:**196
peripheral retinal, **12:**121, 122*t*
vitreous hemorrhage and, **12:**313, 314
in punctate inner choroiditis/choroidopathy, **9:**165, 165*f*, **12:**192
pupillary reactivity and, **5:**263
in radiation retinopathy, **12:**153, 153*f*
retinal. *See also* Retinal disease, vascular
in age-related macular degeneration, **4:**169–170, 171*f*
ischemia causing, **4:**162, 162*f*, 163, 164
in retinopathy of prematurity, **4:**167, **6:**280–287, **12:**157, 163
screening for, **6:**285, 286*t*
sea fan, in sickle cell disease, **12:**119, 119*f*
stromal, contact lenses causing, **8:**92
in systemic lupus erythematosus, **9:**141, 142, 142*f*
in toxoplasmosis, **9:**230, 230*f*
in uveitis, **9:**303–304
in Vogt-Koyanagi-Harada (VKH) syndrome, **9:**189
Nepafenac, **2:**357*t*, 363
for cystoid macular edema, **9:**100, 301
Nephritis
lupus, **1:**167
tubulointerstitial, uveitis and, **6:**271–272, **9:**72*t*, 119, 124
Nephroblastoma. *See* Wilms tumor
Nephrogenic fibrosing dermopathy, gadolinium causing, **5:**72
Nephronophthisis, juvenile, retinal degeneration and, **12:**254
Nephropathic (infantile) cystinosis, **8:**313
Nephropathy
diabetic, **1:**206
glycemic control/diabetic retinopathy and, **1:**202–203, **12:**94
HIV-associated, **1:**29
Nephrotic syndrome, diabetes mellitus and, **1:**206
Nephrotoxicity, of aminoglycosides, **1:**62
Neptazane. *See* Methazolamide
Nerve block
facial, for cataract surgery, **11:**101, 101*f*
local anesthetics for, **2:**386–390, 387*t*
Nerve endings
en grappe, **2:**21, **5:**55
en plaque, **2:**21, **5:**55
in scleral spur, **2:**51–52

Nerve fiber layer, **2:**74*f*, 75, 75*f*, 78, 79*f*, **4:**145, 146*f*, 147, **5:**30*f*, **10:**41–42, 41*f*, 43*f*, **12:**10, 11*f*, 12
defects of, **5:**29
in optic atrophy, **5:**95–96, 96*f*, 166
in glaucoma, **10:**49–50, 49*f*
diffuse/focal loss and, **10:**49, 49*f*
hemorrhages in, **10:**48–49, 48*f*
patterns of loss and, **10:**68, 69*f*, 70*f*, 71*f*, 72*f*
imaging of, **5:**81
infarcts of. *See* Cotton-wool spots
in multiple sclerosis, **5:**324
myelination of, optic disc edema differentiated from, **5:**120–121, 121*f*
optic nerve, **2:**90, **10:**41–42, 41*f*
blood supply of, **2:**94, 95*f*
peripapillary
assessment of, **5:**96, 96*f*
atrophy of, in glaucoma, **10:**50
gliosis of, **5:**121, 121*f*
quantitative measurement of, **10:**51–52, 52–53*f*
transient, of Chievitz, **2:**126
Nerve fibers. *See also* Nerve fiber layer
distribution of, **10:**41–42, 41*f*
medullated (myelinated), **4:**148, **6:**306, 306*f*
quantitative measurement of, **10:**51–52, 52–53*f*
Nerve loops, **2:**48
Nerve of pterygoid canal, **2:**107
Nerve (neural) sheath tumors
of orbit, **4:**244–245, 244*f*, 245*f*
of uveal tract, **4:**203
Nerves, cranial. *See specific nerve and* Cranial nerves
Nervus intermedius, **2:**105, **5:**61, 66–67, 66*f*
NES. *See* Nonepileptic seizures
Netilmicin, **1:**51*t*, 61–62
Netromycin. *See* Netilmicin
Nettleship-Falls X-linked ocular albinism, **6:**298, 300*t*, 301, **12:**258
ocular findings in carriers of, **2:**222*f*, 223, **12:**258
Neural crest cells, **2:**115–117, 116*t*, 120*f*, 121*f*, **8:**4
ocular structures derived from, **2:**116*t*, **8:**4
corneal endothelium, **2:**46
Neural folds, **2:**115, 119*f*, 120
Neural integrator, **5:**38, 42, 47
in gaze-evoked nystagmus, **5:**248
in peripheral vestibular nystagmus, **5:**249
Neural larvae migrans, **9:**240
Neural plate, **2:**117, 118, 118*f*, 120*f*
Neural reflex arc, immune response arc compared with, **9:**33, 36*f*
Neural (neuroretinal) rim, **10:**46
changes in, in glaucoma, **10:**47–48, 49
Neural tube, **2:**118*f*, 119*f*, 120, 124*f*
Neural/neurogenic tumors. *See also specific type*
conjunctival, **8:**240
orbital, **7:**69–76
in children, **6:**333*t*, 343
Neuralgia
glossopharyngeal, **5:**302
occipital, **5:**302
postherpetic, **1:**23, **5:**303, **8:**121–122
trigeminal (tic douloureux), **5:**59, 301–302
Neuraminidase inhibitors, **1:**66

Neurectomy, facial, for benign essential blepharospasm, 7:220
Neurilemoma (neurinoma/schwannoma)
 conjunctival, 8:240
 of orbit, 4:244–245, 245*f*, 7:76
  in children, 6:343
 of uveal tract, 4:203
Neuritis
 optic. *See* Optic neuritis
 perioptic, 5:147
Neuroblastic layers, inner and outer, 2:126
Neuroblastoma
 in children, 6:336–337, 336*f*
  Horner syndrome in, 6:230, 336, 336*f*
  paraneoplastic-induced saccadic intrusions caused by, 5:255–256
 of orbit, 6:336–337, 336*f*, 7:90, 91*f*
Neurocristopathy, 2:117, 4:102–103, 103*f*, 104*f*, 6:212–214, 213*f*, 8:255–263. *See also* Anterior segment, dysgenesis of; Axenfeld-Rieger syndrome
Neurocutaneous syndromes (phakomatoses), 5:338–345, 339*t*, 12:148–151, 149*f*, 150*f*, 152*f*. *See also specific type*
 in children, 6:363–381, 364*t*
Neuroectoderm, 2:115, 118, 8:4
 ocular structures derived from, 2:115, 116*t*, 8:4
 tumors arising in, 8:233–240, 234*t*
Neuroendocrine peptides, in aqueous humor, 2:270
Neurofibrillary tangles, in Alzheimer disease, 1:266
Neurofibromas. *See also* Neurofibromatosis
 acoustic, 5:338, 340–341, 6:371, 10:148. *See also* Neurofibromatosis, bilateral acoustic
  Bruns nystagmus and, 5:250
  seventh nerve (facial) palsy and, 5:286, 287*f*
 conjunctival, 8:240
 discrete, 7:72
 eyelid involvement and, 5:275, 276*f*, 339–340, 6:367, 367*f*, 7:24
 nodular cutaneous and subcutaneous, 6:366
 of orbit, 4:244, 244*f*, 7:72, 72*f*, 73*f*
 plexiform, 6:343, 366–367, 367*f*, 7:24, 72, 72*f*, 73*f*, 10:28
  eyelid involvement and, 5:275, 276*f*, 339–340, 6:367, 367*f*, 7:24, 10:28
  glaucoma and, 6:367, 370, 10:28
  of orbit, 4:244, 244*f*, 6:343, 367, 7:24, 72, 72*f*, 73*f*
 of uveal tract, 4:203
Neurofibromatosis, 6:363–371
 bilateral acoustic/central (type 2), 3:365, 5:338, 339*t*, 340–341, 6:363, 371, 10:148. *See also* Neurofibromas, acoustic
 eyelid abnormalities caused by, 5:275, 276*f*
 von Recklinghausen (type 1), 5:338–340, 339*t*, 340*f*, 6:363–365, 364*t*, 365–371, 7:73, 10:28, 148
  choroidal lesions in, 6:352, 366
  diagnostic criteria for, 6:365
  expressivity in, 2:210
  glaucoma and, 5:340, 6:238, 367, 370, 10:28, 148
  glial cell lesions in, 6:366–367, 367*f*, 368*f*
  iris mamillations associated with, 6:226
  Lisch nodules associated with, 4:271*t*, 272*f*, 6:225, 225*f*, 365–366, 366*f*, 370

 melanocytic lesions in, 6:355–356, 366*f*
 miscellaneous manifestations of, 6:369–371
 mutation rate of, 2:207
 nodular neurofibromas in, 6:366
 optic nerve meningiomas and, 4:258, 5:149
 optic pathway/optic nerve gliomas and, 4:257, 5:53, 152, 340, 6:343, 367–369, 368*f*, 7:69, 71, 73
 orbital involvement in, 4:244, 244*f*, 7:73
 plexiform neurofibromas in, 6:343, 366–367, 367*f*
  eyelid involvement and, 5:275, 276*f*, 6:367, 367*f*, 7:24, 10:28
  glaucoma and, 6:367, 370, 10:28
  orbital involvement and, 6:343, 367
Neurofibromin, 6:365
Neurofibrosarcoma, 6:367
Neurogenic muscle weakness/ataxia/retinitis pigmentosa (NARP) syndrome, 2:175–176, 12:265
 mitochondrial DNA mutations and, 2:174*f*, 175–176
Neurogenic ptosis, 5:279–280, 280*t*, 7:206–209, 208*f*
Neurogenic/neural tumors. *See also specific type*
 conjunctival, 8:240
 orbital, 7:69–76
  in children, 6:333*t*, 343
Neuroglial lesions
 choristoma, 8:247
 in neurofibromatosis, 6:366–367, 367*f*, 368*f*
Neuroimaging, 5:69–90. *See also specific modality*
 in Alzheimer disease, 1:267
 in aneurysm detection, 5:229
 in cerebral ischemia/stroke, 1:93
 clinical principals and, 5:83–88
  how to order studies and, 5:88
  what studies to order and, 5:81, 82*t*, 86–88, 86*t*, 87*f*
  when to order studies and, 5:83–86, 84*f*, 85*f*
 computed tomography, 5:70–72, 71*f*
 in cortical visual impairment, 6:416
 in cranial nerve palsy/paralysis, 5:85, 85*f*
 in drusen versus papilledema differentiation, 5:135*f*, 136
 in epilepsy, 1:262
 in hyphema, 6:409
 localization concepts and, 5:81, 82*t*
 magnetic resonance imaging, 5:72–74, 73*f*, 74*f*, 75*f*, 76*t*, 77*f*, 78*f*
 metabolic and functional, 5:80
 in migraine headache, 5:297–298, 297*f*
 in multiple sclerosis, 5:82*t*, 322*f*, 325–326
 negative studies and, 5:85–86, 88, 89*f*, 90*f*
 in optic nerve hypoplasia, 6:415
 in optic neuritis, 5:82*t*, 83–84, 144, 145*f*
 in orbital tumors, 6:334
  hemangiomas, 6:340
 in retinoblastoma, 4:303–304, 309, 6:356, 356*f*
 selecting modality for, 5:81, 82*t*, 86–88, 86*t*, 87*f*
 in Sturge-Weber syndrome, 6:376, 376*f*
 terminology used in, 5:69–70
 in tuberous sclerosis, 6:372, 373*f*
 vascular, 5:74–81, 79*f*
 in vertebrobasilar insufficiency, 5:349
 in visual field defects, 5:84, 84*f*
Neuroleptic malignant syndrome (NMS), 1:251–252

Neuroleptics (antipsychotic drugs), 1:251–252, 252*t*
    atypical, 1:251, 252*t*
    ocular side effects of, 1:252
    oculogyric crisis caused by, 5:212–213
Neurologic disorders, 1:258–268. *See also specific type*
    Alzheimer disease/dementia, 1:264–268
    in Behçet disease, 1:180, 9:192
    cerebrovascular disease, 1:91–98
    epilepsy, 1:260–264, 263*t*
    in Lyme disease, 1:15, 9:251, 252–253, 253*t*
    optic nerve hypoplasia and, 6:308, 309
    Parkinson disease, 1:258–260
    in primary central nervous system lymphoma, 9:282
    recent developments in, 1:245
    stroke, 1:91. *See also* Stroke
    in syphilis. *See* Neurosyphilis
    in systemic lupus erythematosus, 1:168, 169*t*, 9:140, 141*t*
    in Vogt-Koyanagi-Harada (VKH) syndrome, 9:184
    in Whipple disease, 9:265
Neuroma. *See also* Neurofibromas
    acoustic, 5:338, 340–341, 6:371, 10:148
        Bruns nystagmus and, 5:250
        in neurofibromatosis type 2, 6:371
        seventh nerve (facial) palsy and, 5:286, 287*f*
    conjunctival, 8:240
Neurometabolic disorders. *See also* Metabolic disorders
    retinal findings in, 6:302–303
Neuromuscular blocking agents, 2:344
    adverse effects of, 2:343*f*
Neuromuscular disorders. *See also specific type*
    constant exotropia and, 6:105
    pigmentary retinopathy and, 12:254
Neuromuscular junction disease, diplopia in, 5:238
Neuromuscular ptosis, 5:280*t*
Neuromyelitis optica (Devic syndrome), 5:147
Neuromyotonia, 5:235, 369
Neuronal ceroid lipofuscinosis, 6:398, 401*t*, 12:251*t*, 254, 259–260
    pigmentary retinopathy in, 12:251*t*, 254, 260
Neurons, retinal, 2:73–77, 74*f*, 75*f*, 76*f*, 77*f*
    ischemia affecting, 4:156–157, 157*f*, 158*f*
Neurontin. *See* Gabapentin
Neuro-ophthalmology
    anatomy and, 5:5–67
        afferent visual pathways and, 5:27–37
        autonomic pathways and, 5:63–67
        bony anatomy and, 5:5–12
        efferent visual (ocular motor) pathways and, 5:37–56
        sensory and facial motor pathways and, 5:56–62
        vascular anatomy and, 5:12–27
    neuroimaging in, 5:69–90. *See also* Neuroimaging
    pregnancy and, 5:162, 164, 345–347, 346*f*
    radiation therapy complications and, 5:368–369
    systemic conditions and, 5:319–369
        cerebrovascular disorders, 5:347–358
        immunologic disorders, 5:319–336
        infectious disorders, 5:358–368
        inherited disorders, 5:336–345
Neuropathy
    with ataxia and retinitis pigmentosa (NARP), 2:175–176, 12:265
    mitochondrial DNA mutations and, 2:174*f*, 175–176

    diabetic, 1:206
        glycemic control affecting, 1:202–203
        neurotrophic keratopathy/persistent corneal defects and, 8:87
    hereditary sensory and autonomic. *See* Familial dysautonomia
    mental nerve, 5:303
    optic. *See* Optic neuropathy
Neuropeptide-processing enzymes, in aqueous humor, 2:267, 270
Neuropeptide Y, in tear secretion, 2:237, 240
Neuropeptides, 8:177*t*, 9:29*t*
    for neurotrophic keratopathy, 8:88
Neuroretinal (neural) rim, 10:46
    changes in, in glaucoma, 10:47–48, 49
Neuroretinitis, 5:130, 130*f*, 6:312, 313*f*, 9:78*t*
    cat-scratch disease causing (*Bartonella*-associated), 5:130, 6:312, 9:263–264
    causes of, 9:263*t*
    diffuse unilateral subacute (DUSN), 9:239–241, 240*f*, 241*f*, 12:210–211
    idiopathic retinal vasculitis/aneurysms and (IRVAN), 12:141
    Leber idiopathic stellate, 9:263
    in sarcoidosis, 5:335
Neuroretinopathy, acute macular, 9:169, 12:193
Neurosarcoidosis, 5:334–336. *See also* Sarcoidosis
Neurosensory retina, 2:41*f*, 73–79, 291–298, 4:145, 145–147, 146*f*, 147*f*, 12:8–13, 9*f*, 9*t*, 10*f*, 11*f*, 13*f*, 14*f*, 15*f*. *See also* Retina
    anatomy of, 2:41*f*, 73–79, 74*f*, 75*f*, 76*f*, 77*f*, 79*f*, 12:8–13, 9*f*, 9*t*, 10*f*, 11*f*, 13*f*, 14*f*, 15*f*
    biochemistry and metabolism of, 2:291–298
    development of, 2:121, 124–126, 125*f*
    glial elements of, 2:74*f*, 77
    neuronal elements of, 2:73–77, 74*f*, 75*f*, 76*f*, 77*f*
        ischemia affecting, 4:156–157, 157*f*, 158*f*
    stratification of, 2:74*f*, 78–79, 79*f*
    vascular elements of, 2:74*f*, 78, 12:12, 15*f*. *See also* Retinal blood vessels
Neurosyphilis, 9:244
    tests for, 1:13, 5:361, 9:248
    treatment of, 1:14*t*, 9:248–249, 248*t*
Neurotensin, in aqueous humor, 2:267, 270
Neurotomy, radial optic, for central retinal vein occlusion, 12:133
Neurotoxin complex, purified, 2:390
Neurotransmitters
    in cornea, 8:6
    in iris–ciliary body, 2:258–261
    in tear secretion, 2:240, 242
Neurotrophic factor
    ciliary, for age-related macular degeneration, 12:63
    infusion of, for Parkinson disease, 1:260
Neurotrophic keratopathy, 8:87–89, 88*f*
    diabetic neuropathy and, 8:87
    esthesiometry in evaluation of, 8:30–31
    herpetic eye disease and, 8:87, 88, 117, 122
    postherpetic, 4:83, 84*f*
Neurotrophic proteins, 2:267, 270
Neurotrophic ulcers, herpetic keratitis and, 4:83, 84*f*, 8:87, 88, 117
Neurotrophins, for neurotrophic keratopathy, 8:88

Neutral-density filter effect, **6**:62
Neutral zone. *See also* Null point
　in congenital motor nystagmus, **6**:321
Neutrality, **3**:123*f*, 124
　with correcting lens, **3**:124–125, 125*f*
　finding, **3**:125, 126*f*
Neutrophil chemotactic factor, **8**:179*t*
Neutrophil elastase inhibitor, in vitreous, **2**:285
Neutrophil rolling, **9**:18, 19*f*
Neutrophils, **4**:7, 8*f*, **9**:9–10
　in chemical injuries, **8**:357, 358
　cytologic identification of, in immune-mediated
　　keratoconjunctivitis, **8**:182*t*
　in external eye, **8**:174*t*
　in inflammation, **4**:7, 8*f*, **9**:10
　　granule products of, **9**:31
　recruitment and activation of, **9**:14*t*, 17–20, 19*f*
Nevanac. *See* Nepafenac
Nevi. *See* Nevus
Nevirapine, **1**:34
Nevus, **7**:164, 165*f*
　anterior chamber/trabecular meshwork affected by,
　　4:109, 110*f*
　blue, **4**:65, **7**:165, **8**:235
　of choroid, **4**:195, 195*f*, 266–268, 267*f*
　　in children, **6**:352
　　melanoma differentiated from, **4**:266–268, 278
　of ciliary body, **4**:195, 266
　compound, **7**:164
　　of conjunctiva, **4**:65, 66*f*
　　of eyelid, **4**:225, 225*f*, **7**:164
　congenital, **4**:224, 224*f*
　conjunctival, **4**:65–66, 65*t*, 66*f*, **8**:236–237, 236*f*,
　　238*t*
　　in children, **6**:349, 349*f*
　dermal, **7**:164
　dysplastic, **4**:226
　　melanoma arising from, **1**:277, **4**:226
　of eyelid, **4**:224–226, 224*f*, 225*f*, 226*f*, **7**:164, 165*f*
　flammeus (port-wine stain), **6**:342, **8**:241. *See also*
　　Vascular malformations
　　increased episcleral venous pressure and, **10**:28
　　of orbit, **6**:342
　　in Sturge-Weber syndrome, **5**:341, 343*f*, **6**:238, 342,
　　　375, 376, 376*f*, **8**:241, **10**:28, 147
　　in von Hippel–Lindau disease, **6**:374
　intradermal, **4**:225, 226*f*
　iris, **4**:193, 265–266, 265*f*, 270*t*
　　in children, **6**:351
　junctional, **6**:349, **7**:164, **8**:236
　　of conjunctiva, **4**:65
　　of eyelid, **4**:224–225, 225*f*
　"kissing," **4**:224, 224*f*
　macular, **4**:224–225, 225*f*
　magnocellular. *See* Melanocytoma
　melanocytic
　　of anterior chamber/trabecular meshwork, **4**:109,
　　　110*f*
　　congenital, **4**:224, 224*f*
　　conjunctival, **4**:65–66, 65*t*, 66*f*
　　of eyelid, **4**:224–226, 224*f*, 225*f*, 226*f*, **7**:164, 165*f*
　　glaucoma and, **4**:109

　nevocellular, congenital, **6**:349–350, 350*f*
　of Ota (dermal/oculodermal melanocytosis), **4**:65*t*,
　　66, **7**:166, 166*f*, **8**:235–236, 238*t*
　　in children, **6**:350
　　glaucoma associated with, **10**:28
　　of iris, **4**:271*t*
　Spitz, **4**:226
　stromal, **4**:65
　subepithelial, **4**:65
Nevus cells, **4**:224, 225, 225*f*, 226*f*, **7**:164
　tumors arising from, **4**:224, **7**:164, 165*f*, **8**:233, 234*t*.
　　See also Nevus; Pigmented lesions
New York Times Large-Print Weekly, **6**:418*t*
Newborn primary congenital glaucoma, **10**:139, 140*t*,
　143. *See also* Glaucoma, childhood
Newborns. *See also* Infants
　conjunctivitis in, **6**:186–188, 187*f*, **8**:152–154. *See also*
　　Ophthalmia, neonatorum
　corneal transplantation in, **8**:430–431, 431*t*
　ectropion in, **7**:146, 147*f*
　ERG in, **12**:36
　hemorrhagic disease of, **1**:156
　herpes simplex infection in, **1**:22, **8**:106
　milia in, **7**:159
　normal ocular flora in, **8**:96
　ocular deviations in, **5**:212
　ocular infections in, **6**:181–186, 187*f*, **8**:152–154. *See
　　also specific type*
　ophthalmia neonatorum in, **6**:186–188, 187*f*,
　　8:152–154. *See also* Ophthalmia, neonatorum
　screening eye examinations in, **6**:250–251
Newcastle Control Score, in intermittent exotropia,
　6:100
NF. *See* Neurofibromatosis
NF-kB essential modulator *(NEMO)* gene, in
　incontinentia pigmenti, **6**:379
NF1. *See* Neurofibromatosis, von Recklinghausen
　(type 1)
NF1 gene, **6**:363–365
NF2 gene, **6**:365
NFL. *See* Nerve fiber layer
NFT. *See* Neurofibrillary tangles
NIA imaging. *See* Near-infrared fundus
　autofluorescence
Niacin (nicotinic acid)
　discontinuing before surgery, **1**:306
　for hypercholesterolemia/heart disease prevention,
　　1:137*t*
Niaspan. *See* Nicotinic acid
Nicardipine
　for angina, **1**:108
　for hypertension, **1**:77*t*, 83
NICHCY (National Dissemination Center for Children
　with Disabilities), **6**:417*t*
Nicotinamide adenine dinucleotide phosphate
　(NADPH)
　in free-radical generation, **2**:312
　in lens glucose/carbohydrate metabolism, **2**:279, 280*f*,
　　11:14*f*, 15
　glutathione redox cycle and, **2**:313
Nicotine, **2**:259*t*, 334. *See also* Nicotinic agents
　adverse effects of, **2**:343*f*

Nicotinic acid (niacin)
  discontinuing before surgery, 1:306
  for hypercholesterolemia/heart disease prevention,
    1:137t
Nicotinic agents, 2:334, 342–344
Nicotinic receptors, in iris–ciliary body, 2:259t
NIDDM (non–insulin-dependent diabetes mellitus). See
  Diabetes mellitus, type 2
Nidogen-1, in vitreous, 2:283
Niemann-Pick disease, 2:213t, 6:400t, 12:262, 263f
  racial and ethnic concentration of, 2:211
  retinal degeneration and, 12:262, 263f
Nifedipine
  for angina, 1:108
  contraindications to, in non–ST-segment elevation
    acute coronary syndrome, 1:111
  for hypertension, 1:77t
Night blindness
  in choroideremia, 12:242, 243
  congenital
    with normal fundi, 12:215–217, 216f, 217f
    with prominent fundus abnormality, 12:217–219,
      218f, 219f
    stationary, 6:291–292, 12:215–217, 216f, 217f
      ERG patterns in, 6:291, 12:36f, 216, 217, 217f
      with myopia, ocular findings in carriers of,
        2:222t
  dark adaptometry in evaluation of, 12:46, 47f
  in gyrate atrophy, 12:244
  in hypovitaminosis A, 8:78
Night myopia, spherical aberration causing, 3:99, 100
Night-vision abnormalities, 12:215–219. See also Night
  blindness
  after refractive surgery
    phakic IOLs
      angle-supported PIOLs, 13:134–135
      iris-fixated PIOLs, 13:135
      posterior chamber PIOLs, 13:136
    photoablation, 13:95
    pupil size and, 3:236
    radial keratotomy, 13:46
NIR reflectance imaging. See Near-infrared reflectance
  imaging
Nisin, 1:64
Nisoldipine, 1:77t
Nitrates
  for angina, 1:108
  for heart failure, 1:119
  for non–ST-segment elevation acute coronary
    syndrome, 1:111
Nitric oxide, 9:31
Nitric oxide synthase, 9:31
Nitrogen bases, 2:156
Nitrogen mustard (mechlorethamine), 1:240t
Nitrogen radicals, as inflammatory mediators, 9:31
Nitroglycerin
  for angina, 1:108
  for heart failure, 1:119
  for hypertensive emergency, 1:83
  for non–ST-segment elevation acute coronary
    syndrome, 1:111
Nitropress. See Nitroprusside

Nitroprusside
  for heart failure, 1:119
  for hypertensive emergency, 1:83
Nitrosureas, in cancer chemotherapy, 1:242t
Nizoral. See Ketoconazole
NK cells. See Natural killer cells
NKHHC. See Nonketotic hyperglycemic-hyperosmolar
  coma
NLD. See Nasolacrimal duct
NLS (National Library Service for the Blind and
  Physically Handicapped), 6:417t
NMO. See Neuromyelitis optica
NMO-IgG antibody, 5:147
NMS. See Neuroleptic malignant syndrome
NNO1 gene, 10:11t
NNRTIs. See Nonnucleoside reverse transcriptase
  inhibitors
NO. See Nitric oxide
No light perception (NLP). See also Blindness
  testing
    bilateral, 5:307–308, 308f
    monocular, 5:308–310, 309f, 310f
NOAH (National Organization for Albinism and
  Hypopigmentation), 6:417t
Nocardia/Nocardia asteroides (nocardiosis), 8:137,
  9:256
    keratitis after photoablation caused by, 13:98
    scleritis caused by, 9:266, 267f
Nodal points, 3:33, 34f, 76, 77f
  for calculation of retinal image size, 3:103–104, 106f
Nodular anterior scleritis, 8:28, 218, 218t, 219f
Nodular basal cell carcinoma, 4:218, 218f, 7:169, 169f.
  See also Basal cell carcinoma
Nodular episcleritis, 4:113, 8:28, 216, 217f
  in children, 6:351
Nodular fasciitis, 4:118, 118f, 8:242
  episcleral tumor caused by, 4:118, 118f
Nodular melanoma, 4:226, 227f, 7:175, 176f. See also
  Melanomas
Nodular neurofibromas, cutaneous and subcutaneous,
  in neurofibromatosis, 6:366
Nodules. See specific type
Nodulus, 5:48
Nolvadex. See Tamoxifen
Nonaccidental trauma. See Abuse; Trauma, in children
Nonaccommodative acquired esotropia, 6:90t, 95–98
Nonalternating suppression, 6:50–51
Nonarteritic anterior ischemic optic neuropathy
  (NAION), 5:125, 126f, 126t, 127–129, 128f
Nonaxial displacement of globe, in orbital disorders,
  7:23
Noncaseating granulomas, 4:8, 11–12
  in granulomatous conjunctivitis, 4:52, 53f
  in sarcoidosis, 4:52, 53f, 191, 191f, 9:173, 174, 174f,
    175, 176f
Noncoding strand of DNA (antisense DNA), 2:148
Noncomitant deviations. See Incomitant (noncomitant)
  deviations
Noncompliance with therapy
  behavioral/psychiatric disorders and, 1:257
  in older patients, 1:222, 10:176–177
Noncontact corneal esthesiometry, 8:31

Non–contact lenses, for slit-lamp biomicroscopy, 12:19–20
Noncontact specular microscopy/photomicroscopy, 8:32
Noncontact (air-puff) tonometers, 10:25
    infection control and, 10:26
Noncycloplegic (manifest) refraction, 3:137. *See also* Refraction, clinical
    after penetrating keratoplasty, 8:426, 427*f*
    before refractive surgery, 13:33, 73
Noncystic retinal tufts, 12:278, 279*f*
Nondepolarizing neuromuscular blocking agents, 2:344
Nondihydropyridines, for hypertension, 1:77*t*
Nondisjunction, 2:156, 196*f*, 199, 203
    aneuploidy and, 2:199, 203
    in Down syndrome, 2:202
    in mosaicism, 2:203
Nonenveloped viruses, 8:105
Nonepileptic seizures, 1:262
Nonexperimental (observational) studies, 1:320
Non-field testing, in nonorganic ophthalmic disorders, 5:312
Nongeographic atrophy (degeneration), of retinal pigment epithelium, 12:58
Nongranulomatous inflammation, 4:6
Nongranulomatous uveitis, 9:84
Non–high-density lipoprotein cholesterol, hypercholesterolemia management and, 1:131
Non–Hodgkin lymphomas. *See also* Lymphomas
    of CNS (primary intraocular lymphoma), 1:244, 4:140–142, 141*f*, 142*f*, 143*f*, 323–325, 323*f*, 325*f*, 5:358, 9:136, 281–284, 282*f*, 283*f*, 12:199, 199*f*
        central serous retinopathy differentiated from, 12:174
        in HIV infection/AIDS, 9:314
        uveitis differentiated from, 9:91, 136, 281–283
            in children, 6:276*t*
    conjunctival, 8:244, 245*f*
    orbital, 4:239, 7:79–84
Nonhomologous chromosomes, independent assortment and, 2:196–197
Noninfectious conjunctivitis, 4:54, 56*f*
Noninfectious (sterile) endophthalmitis, 9:269
Noninfectious keratitis, 4:87
Noninfectious (autoimmune) ocular inflammatory disease, 4:189–191, 9:117–196. *See also specific type and specific cause*
    anterior uveitis, 9:118–134
    endophthalmitis, 9:269
    intermediate uveitis, 9:134–140
    panuveitis, 9:172–196
    posterior uveitis, 9:140–172
    scleritis, 9:117–118
    uveitis, , 4:189–191
Noninfectious scleritis, 9:117–118
Noninfectious (autoimmune) uveitis, 4:189–191. *See also specific cause*
    anterior uveitis, 9:118–134
    intermediate uveitis, 9:134–140
    panuveitis, 9:172–196
    posterior uveitis, 9:140–172
    vitreous infiltrate in, 4:133
Non–insulin-dependent diabetes mellitus (NIDDM). *See* Diabetes mellitus, type 2

Noninvasive pressure support ventilation, 1:144
Nonischemic/perfused central retinal vein occlusion, 12:127, 128, 128*f*
Nonketotic hyperglycemic-hyperosmolar coma, 1:204–205
Nonlaser lamellar keratorefractive surgery, 13:4*t*
Nonnecrotizing herpetic retinitis (nonnecrotizing posterior uveitis), 9:203–204
Nonnecrotizing keratitis, 8:27*f*
Nonnecrotizing scleritis, 4:114, 8:21*t*, 28, 9:117–118
Nonnucleoside reverse transcriptase inhibitors (NNRTIs), 1:34
Nonoptic reflex systems, 6:37
Nonoptical visual aids, 3:301–304, 302*f*
Nonorganic (functional/nonphysiologic) ophthalmic disorders, 1:248, 257, 5:305–317
    afferent visual pathways and, 5:307–314, 308*f*, 309*f*, 310*f*, 311*t*, 313*f*, 314*f*, 315*f*
    categories of, 5:305
    examination in, 5:307–317, 308*f*, 309*f*, 310*f*, 311*t*, 313*f*, 314*f*, 315*f*
    eyelid position/function and, 5:316–317
    management of, 5:317
    ocular motility/alignment and, 5:314–315
    pupils/accommodation and, 5:316
Nonorganic overlay, 5:305, 317
Nonpenetrant gene, 2:209
Nonpenetrating glaucoma surgery, 10:210–211
Nonperfused/ischemic central retinal vein occlusion, 4:164, 165*f*, 12:127, 128, 129*f*
Nonperfusion, capillary. *See* Retinal capillary nonperfusion
Nonphysiologic ophthalmic disorders. *See* Nonorganic (functional/nonphysiologic) ophthalmic disorders
Nonpigmented epithelium, ciliary body, 2:62, 62*f*, 265
Nonproliferative diabetic retinopathy (NPDR). *See* Diabetic retinopathy, nonproliferative
Nonproliferative sickle cell retinopathy (NPSR). *See* Sickle cell retinopathy, nonproliferative
Non–Q-wave infarction, 1:102. *See also* Acute coronary syndrome
Nonrefractive accommodative esotropia (high accommodative convergence/accommodative esotropia), 6:82, 94–95
Nonrhegmatogenous retinal detachment. *See* Retinal detachment
Nonsense mutation, 2:156, 171
Nonseptate filamentous fungi, 8:138*t*, 140. *See also* Fungi
Non–Sjögren syndrome dry eye, 8:50, 51*f*, 52, 65
Nonspecific orbital inflammation (NSOI/orbital pseudotumor/idiopathic orbital inflammation/orbital inflammatory syndrome), 4:230–232, 231*f*, 5:300–301, 7:39, 39*t*, 59–61, 60*f*
    in children, 6:272, 346–347, 347*f*
    lacrimal gland masses and, 7:85
    orbital lymphoma differentiated from, 4:232
    plasma cell–rich, 7:84
    in Wegener granulomatosis, 1:179
Nonspherical optics, for intraocular lenses, 3:225
Non–ST-segment elevation MI (NSTEMI), 1:102. *See also* Acute coronary syndrome
    management of, 1:111–112

Nonsteroidal anti-inflammatory drugs (NSAIDs), 1:183–184, 183t, 2:357t, 361–366, 362t, 365t, 9:99–100
  Alzheimer disease and, 1:267
  for ankylosing spondylitis, 9:121
  corneal melting after cataract surgery associated with, 11:150, 191
  COX-1/COX-2 inhibition by, 1:184, 2:257, 362, 9:99
  for cystoid macular edema, 9:26, 12:143
  for episcleritis, 9:26
  hypertension and, 1:72, 72t
  after LASIK, 13:85
  for ocular allergy, 6:198, 199t
    allergic conjunctivitis, 8:187
  ocular side effects of, 1:184
  perioperative use of, 1:306
  platelet function affected by, 1:155
  prostaglandins affected by, 2:257
  for rheumatic disorders, 1:183–184, 183t
  for rheumatoid arthritis, 1:162
  for scleritis, 8:222, 9:26, 117
  after surface ablation, 13:85, 86
    delayed re-epithelialization and, 13:86, 100
  for uveitis, 9:99–100
    in children, 6:277t
Nontranslated strand of DNA (sense DNA), 2:160
Nontreponemal tests, for syphilis, 1:13, 279, 9:247–248
Nontuberculous (atypical) mycobacteria, 1:18, 8:164
  in HIV infection/AIDS, 1:18, 39, 5:360
Nonvalved glaucoma drainage devices, 10:205, 205t, 207
Nonvisual assistance, for low vision patient, 3:301–302
Nonvisual tasks, in nonorganic ophthalmic disorder evaluation, 5:307
Norepinephrine, 2:259t
  adrenergic agents/receptor response and, 2:344–351, 345f, 347f
  dilator muscle affected by, 2:258, 260
  in iris–ciliary body, 2:258, 259f, 260
  in tear secretion, 2:240, 242, 242f, 243, 243f
Norflex. See Orphenadrine
Norfloxacin, 1:52t, 60–61
Noritate. See Metronidazole
Normal distribution, clinical relevance of research and, 1:320
Normal flora, ocular, 8:96–97, 97t
Normal incidence, 3:46
Normal retinal correspondence, 6:39
Normal-tension glaucoma. See Glaucoma, normal-tension
Normodyne. See Labetalol
Noroxin. See Norfloxacin
Norrie disease, 6:296
  gene for, 2:193, 6:296
    X-linked familial exudative retinopathy and, 12:311
Norrin protein, in Norrie disease, 6:296
North American Symptomatic Carotid Endarterectomy Trial (NASCET), 1:95–96, 5:181–182
North Carolina macular dystrophy, 12:245–246, 245f
Northern blot analysis, 2:156
Norvasc. See Amlodipine
Norvir. See Ritonavir
NOS. See Nitric oxide synthase

Nose, 7:17–19. See also under Nasal
  inferior meatus of, 2:7, 10, 34f, 5:12, 7:245f, 246
  middle meatus of, 7:245f, 246
  orbital tumors originating in, 7:88–89
Nosema, 8:141
  stromal keratitis caused by, 8:170
NOTCH3 gene, mutation of, in cerebral autosomal dominant arteriopathy with subcortical infarcts and leukoencephalopathy (CADASIL), 5:300
Nothnagel syndrome, 5:226
Notochord, 2:117, 118f, 120f
Notochordal process, medial, 2:117
Nougaret disease, rod transducin mutation causing, 2:295
Novantrone. See Mitoxantrone
Novocain. See Procaine
Novolog. See Aspart insulin
Nozik technique, for periocular corticosteroid injection, 9:102–103, 102f
NPDR. See Diabetic retinopathy, nonproliferative
NPH. See Nucleus prepositus hypoglossi
NPH insulin, 1:196, 196t
NPS gene, 10:11t
NPSR. See Sickle cell retinopathy, nonproliferative
NPV. See Negative predictive value
NPY. See Neuropeptide Y
NR2E3 gene, in enhanced S-cone/blue-cone and Goldmann-Favre syndromes, 12:219, 248
NRC. See Normal retinal correspondence
NRDIOSE (National Registry of Drug-Induced Ocular Side Effects), 1:300
NRTIs. See Nucleoside reverse transcriptase inhibitors
NRTP. See Nucleus reticularis tegmenti pontis
NSAIDs. See Nonsteroidal anti-inflammatory drugs
NSOI. See Nonspecific orbital inflammation
NSSDE. See Non–Sjögren syndrome dry eye
NSTEMI. See Non–ST-segment elevation MI
nt. See Nucleotides
NtRTIs. See Nucleotide reverse transcriptase inhibitors
Nuclear cataracts, 4:127, 128f, 129f, 11:39–40, 41f
  congenital, 6:247–248, 248f, 250t, 11:33, 34f
  genetic contributions to, 11:37–38
  hyperbaric oxygen therapy and, 11:60–61
  postvitrectomy, 12:368
  visual acuity and, 11:39, 70t
  vitrectomy and, 11:16, 60, 205–206
Nuclear disassembly techniques, 11:121–125, 122f, 123f, 124f, 125f. See also Phacoemulsification
  chopping techniques, 11:122–124, 124f
  one-handed, 11:124–125, 125f
  phaco fracture, 11:121–122, 122f, 123f
Nuclear layer
  inner, 2:74f, 75f, 78, 79f, 298–301, 299f, 300f, 4:145, 146f, 12:10, 11f
  outer, 2:74f, 75f, 76f, 79f, 4:145, 146f, 12:10, 11f
Nuclear lesions, diplopia caused by, 5:223–224. See also specific nerve
Nuclear sclerosis, 11:39
Nucleic acid amplification test. See Polymerase chain reaction
Nucleic acids, 2:157. See also DNA; RNA
  in retinal pigment epithelium, 2:305
  viral, 8:104
Nucleoside, 2:156

Nucleoside analogues, 1:66
  for HIV infection/AIDS, 1:33
    in HAART, 1:35
Nucleoside reverse transcriptase inhibitors, 1:33
    in HAART, 1:35
Nucleosome, 2:156
Nucleotide reverse transcriptase inhibitors (NtRTIs),
    1:33–34
Nucleotides, 2:156–157
  corneal changes in disorders of metabolism of,
    8:325–326
Nucleus (lens). *See* Lens (crystalline), nucleus of
Nucleus of Darkschewitsch, 5:39f, 42
Nucleus prepositus hypoglossi, 5:38, 39f, 45f, 202
Nucleus raphe interpositus, 5:38, 44f, 46f
Nucleus reticularis tegmenti pontis, 5:38, 39f, 41
NuLens Accommodating IOL, 13:161
Null allele, gene therapy and, 2:187–188
Null-cell adenomas, 1:215–216
Null hypothesis, 1:318
Null mutations, 2:171
Null point, 6:317
  in congenital motor nystagmus, 6:321
  in downbeat nystagmus, 6:325–326
  in latent nystagmus, 6:323
  nystagmus surgery and, 6:328, 328f, 329
Numb chin syndrome, 5:303
Numbness, facial pain and, 5:303
Nursing (breast feeding)
  fluorescein dye transmission to breast milk and,
    12:25
  glaucoma medication use during, 10:176
  refractive surgery contraindicated during, 13:31
Nutritional deficiency
  cataract formation and, 11:57–58
  ocular surface disorders and, 8:77–79
  optic neuropathy and, 5:154–156, 155f
Nutritional supplements. *See also specific type*
  in age-related macular degeneration management,
    12:61–63
  cessation of before surgery, 7:189–190
  in retinitis pigmentosa management, 12:231
NVD. *See* Optic disc (optic nerve head),
    neovascularization of
NVG. *See* Neovascular glaucoma
Nyctalopia. *See also* Night blindness
  in hypovitaminosis A, 8:78
  rod-specific mutations causing, 2:295, 296
  in uveitis, 9:85
Nyctalopin, in congenital stationary night blindness,
    12:216
Nystagmus, 5:243–259, 244f
  acquired, 5:243, 244f
    in children, 6:324–326
    pendular, 5:244f, 253
  in albinism, 6:298, 12:258
  Alexander's law and, 5:248
  amplitude of, gaze position affecting, 5:244,
    247–248
  in aniridia, 6:223
  antiepileptic drugs causing, 1:264
  assessment of, 5:243–244, 244f
  Bruns, 5:250

childhood (early-onset), 5:245–247, 6:288–289, 289t,
    317–330, 319t
  differential diagnosis of, 6:326, 327f
  monocular, 5:246–247, 251t, 6:326
  treatment of, 6:326–330, 328f, 329t
  types of, 6:320–326
  in color blindness, 12:215
  congenital, 5:243, 244f, 245–246, 6:288–289, 289t,
    321–323, 321t, 323f, 324f
  convergence-retraction (induced convergence-
    retraction), 5:44, 251t, 256
    in children, 6:325
  in decreased vision, 6:414, 415
  disconjugate/disjunctive, 5:244
  dissociated, 5:244, 254, 6:326
  downbeat, 5:49, 251–252, 251t, 252f
    in children, 6:325–326
  with esotropia, 6:90t, 92, 321
  evaluation of, 6:318–320, 319t, 320t
  funduscopic assessment in, 6:320, 320t
  gaze-evoked, 5:244f, 247–248
    in internuclear ophthalmoplegia, 5:224–225
  gaze positions affecting, 5:244, 247–248, 6:317,
    318f
  head-shaking, 5:200–201
  in hereditary retinal disorders, 6:288–289, 289t
  history in, 6:318, 319t
  infantile, 6:288–289, 289t, 321–323, 321t, 323f, 324f
  in internuclear ophthalmoplegia, 5:224–225, 6:141
  jerk, 5:243, 244, 6:317
    in multiple sclerosis, 5:325
  latent/manifest latent (fusion maldevelopment),
    5:246, 6:322–323, 323f, 324f
    dissociated vertical deviation and, 6:116, 117, 323
  monocular, of childhood, 5:246–247, 251t, 6:326
  motor (congenital), 6:321
  in multiple sclerosis, 5:325
  nomenclature associated with, 6:317–318
  ocular examination in, 6:318–320, 320t
  ocular motility testing in, 6:320
  oculopalatal myoclonus/tremor and, 5:253
  opsoclonus and, 6:325
  optic nerve gliomas causing, 5:153
  in optic nerve hypoplasia, 6:308, 320, 415
  optokinetic (OKN), 5:198–199, 198t, 201, 6:319, 413
    assessment of, 5:201–202, 6:319, 413
    in congenital motor nystagmus, 6:321
    dysfunction of, 5:207–208
      in congenital nystagmus, 6:245
      parietal lobe lesions and, 5:168–169
    nonorganic ophthalmic disorder and, 5:307
  optokinetic after (OKAN), 5:202
  pediatric cataracts and, 6:252
  pendular, 5:243, 244, 244f, 6:317
    acquired, 5:244f, 253
    in multiple sclerosis, 5:325
  periodic alternating, 5:251t, 252–253, 6:322
  prisms for, in children, 6:326–328
  pupil assessment in, 6:319–320, 320t
  rebound, 5:248
  see-saw (vision loss), 5:251t, 253–254
    in children, 6:325
  seizures causing, 1:263

sensory (congenital), **6**:322, 414
spasmus nutans, **5**:247, **6**:324–325
spontaneous
fixation and, **5**:200
vestibular imbalance and, **5**:200–201, 205
with strabismus, surgery for, **6**:329
substance use/abuse and, **1**:250
surgery for, **6**:328–329, 328*f*, 329*t*
torsional, **5**:252
transient, **6**:320
treatment of, **5**:257–258
in children, **6**:326–330, 328*f*, 329*t*
upbeat, **5**:251*t*, 252
vestibular, **5**:200–201, 205, 244*f*, 248–253, 249*t*
central, **5**:249*t*, 250–253, 251*t*, 252*f*
peripheral, **5**:248–250, 249*t*
visual acuity testing in, **6**:73, 318–319
voluntary, **5**:256, 314–315
Nystagmus blockage syndrome, **6**:321
surgery for, **6**:329
Nystatin, **1**:54*t*, 65
NYX gene, in congenital stationary night blindness,
12:216

O

O&M (orientation and mobility) specialist, **3**:305
OA1 (albinism), **6**:300*t*, 301, **12**:258*t*. *See also* Ocular
albinism
OA1 gene, **6**:300*t*, 301
OAT (ornithine aminotransferase) gene, mutations/
defects of, **2**:298
in gyrate atrophy, **2**:213*t*, 298, **12**:243
OAV. *See* Oculoauriculovertebral (OAV) spectrum/
sequence
Obesity
cataract risk and, **11**:67
in diabetes mellitus type 2, **1**:192
weight reduction and, **1**:189, 194, 195
floppy eyelid syndrome and, **8**:81
hypertension and, **1**:85
insulin secretion affected by, **1**:190
ischemic heart disease and, **1**:100
Object agnosia, **5**:192
Object beam, in optical coherence tomography, **3**:281,
282*f*
Objective lens
of operating microscope, **3**:262, 262*f*
of slit-lamp biomicroscope, **3**:251*f*, 252
of telescope, **3**:81, 81*f*
Objective refraction, **3**:121–130, 121*f*, 122*f*. *See also*
Retinoscopy
automatic, **3**:276, 277
in children, **3**:141–142
manual, **3**:276, 277
Objects (optics)
characteristics of, **3**:31
at infinity, **3**:74
luminous, **3**:31
virtual, **3**:67–68, 67*f*, 69*f*
Oblate cornea, **3**:232, **13**:10, 20
Obligatory suppression, **6**:51

Oblique astigmatism, **3**:115
Oblique axes, combining cylinders at, **3**:99
Oblique muscles, **2**:9, 16*f*, 17*f*, 18, 19*t*, 20*f*, 38*f*, 39*f*, 40*f*,
5:55–56, 56*f*, **6**:13, 14–15, 14*f*, 15*f*, 16*f*, 17*t*, 18*f*, **7**:10,
11*f*, 135*f*. *See also* Inferior oblique muscles; Superior
oblique muscles
action of, **6**:14–15, 29, 29*t*
gaze position and, **6**:31–32, 33*f*, 34*f*
3-step test in evaluation of, **6**:83–86, 85*f*
anatomy of, **5**:55–56, 56*f*, **6**:14–15, 14*f*, 15*f*, 16*f*, 17*t*, 18*f*
surgery and, **6**:24
field of action of, **6**:29
insertion relationships of, **2**:17, 18*f*, 19*t*
myokymia affecting, **5**:256–257, **6**:142–143
nerves supplying, **2**:21, **5**:54, **7**:11
origins of, **2**:18, 19*t*
overaction of, **6**:113–116, 114*f*, 115*f*
A-pattern deviations associated with, **6**:107, 109*f*
apparent (pseudo-overaction), **6**:116
in infantile esotropia, **6**:92
V-pattern deviations associated with, **6**:107, 108*f*
vertical deviations caused by, **6**:113–116, 114*f*, 115*f*
paralysis of, **6**:118–121, 119*f*
pseudo-overaction of, **6**:116
pulley system of, **6**:22, 22*f*, 23
A- and V-pattern deviations and, **6**:109–110, 110*f*
strengthening procedures for, **6**:152
weakening procedures for, **6**:147, 148*t*, 151–152
for A- and V-pattern deviations, **6**:110, 111, 112
for infantile esotropia, **6**:92
for inferior oblique muscle paralysis, **6**:122
for superior oblique muscle paralysis, **6**:120–121
for vertical deviations, **6**:114–115, 116
Oblique subnucleus, inferior, **5**:54
Oblique tenotomy
for Brown syndrome, **6**:131–132
for third nerve (oculomotor) paralysis, **6**:133
Observational studies, **1**:320, 321
Obstetric history
in infant with decreased vision, **6**:414
infantile corneal opacities and, **6**:217
nystagmus and, **6**:318
strabismus/amblyopia and, **6**:71
Obstructive pulmonary disease, **1**:141–142
ocular surgery in patients with, **1**:308
Obstructive shock, **1**:293. *See also* Shock
Obstructive sleep apnea. *See* Sleep apnea
OCA1 (albinism), **2**:308, **6**:298, **12**:258*t*
OCA1A (albinism), **6**:298, 299*t*
OCA1B (albinism), **6**:298, 299*t*
OCA2 (albinism), **2**:308, **6**:299*t*, 301, 301*f*, **12**:258*t*
OCA2 gene (*P* gene), in albinism, **2**:195, **6**:299*t*, 301,
12:258*t*
OCA3 (albinism), **6**:299*t*, 301, **12**:258*t*
OCA4 (albinism), **6**:299*t*, 301, **12**:258*t*
Occipital artery, **5**:12
Occipital association cortex, near reflex initiated in, **2**:99
Occipital bone, **5**:7
Occipital (primary visual/calcarine/striate) cortex, **2**:97,
5:34–37, 35*f*, 36*f*, **6**:42
development of, **6**:44, 45*f*
abnormal visual experience affecting, **6**:46–49,
47*f*, 48*f*

disorders of, 5:191–196, 192*t*
hallucinations and, 5:172, 190–191
illusions and, 5:189
recognition disorders and, 5:192–194, 192*t*, 193*f*
vision/visual deficit awareness disorders and,
5:192*t*, 195–196
visual–spatial relationship disorders and, 5:192*t*,
194–195, 195*f*
eye movement control and, 5:37, 38–41, 38*f*, 39*f*, 40*f*,
42*f*, 43*f*
Occipital ischemia, transient visual loss and, 5:185–186
Occipital lobe, 5:28*f*
lesions of, 5:169–172, 170*f*, 171*f*, 172*f*
hallucinations and, 5:190–191
transient visual loss and, 5:174, 185
Occipital neuralgia, 5:302
Occipital seizures, transient visual loss and, 5:186
Occipitoparietal pathway, 5:36, 36*f*
Occipitotemporal pathway, 5:36, 36*f*
Occluding zonules, corneal, 2:43
Occlusion, in phacoemulsification, 11:104
Occlusion amblyopia, 6:64, 67–68
eye trauma and, 6:403
Occlusion therapy. *See also* Patching
for amblyopia, 6:66–67
cataract surgery and, 6:259
compliance issues and, 6:66–67, 68
complications of, 6:67–68
Occlusive retinal disease
arterial, 12:135–140. *See also* Retinal artery occlusion
branch retinal artery occlusion, 4:163, 12:136–137,
136*f*, 137*f*
capillary retinal arteriole occlusion, 12:135–136,
135*f*
central retinal artery occlusion, 4:162–163, 163*f*,
12:138–140, 138*f*, 139*f*
in systemic lupus erythematosus, 9:141–142, 142*f*
ocular ischemic syndrome/retinopathy of carotid
occlusive disease and, 12:133–135, 134*f*
venous, 12:121–133. *See also* Retinal vein occlusion
branch retinal vein occlusion, 4:164, 12:121–127,
122*f*, 125*f*
central retinal vein occlusion, 4:163–164, 165*f*,
12:127–133, 127*f*, 128*f*, 129*f*, 132*f*
angle-closure glaucoma and, 10:135
neovascularization and, 10:127
open-angle glaucoma and, 10:77
in sarcoidosis, 9:175
in systemic lupus erythematosus, 9:141–142, 142*f*
Occupation
bifocal segment and, 3:156–157
light toxicity and, 12:334
refractive surgery selection and, 13:30–31, 30*t*
Ochronosis, 2:214, 8:314*t*, 316, 337*t*
OCP. *See* Ocular cicatricial (mucous membrane)
pemphigoid
OCT. *See* Optical coherence tomography/biometry
Octopus Delta program, 10:63
Octopus perimeters, 10:57, 58
Ocu-Chlor. *See* Chloramphenicol
Ocufen. *See* Flurbiprofen
Ocufilcon D, for contact lenses, 3:177*t*
Ocuflox. *See* Ofloxacin

Ocular (eyepiece), of telescope, 3:81, 81*f*, 82, 82*f*
for operating microscope, 3:262*f*
for slit-lamp biomicroscope, 3:251*f*, 252
Ocular adnexa. *See also specific structure*
anatomy of, 2:5–13
benign lesions of, 7:160–164, 161*f*, 162*f*, 163*f*
in craniosynostosis syndromes, 6:391–392
development of, 6:169
in external eye defense, 8:95
glands of, 2:27*t*
in glaucoma evaluation, 10:27–28
infections of in children, 6:194–197, 196*f*
Kaposi sarcoma of, 9:312, 312*f*
lymphoma of, staging of, 4:350–352*t*
lymphoproliferative lesions of, 7:79–84
radiation affecting, 1:244
in systemic malignancies, 1:244
Ocular albinism, 2:308, 4:148, 6:298, 300*t*, 301, 12:258,
258*t*
autosomal recessive, 6:301
ocular findings in carriers of, 2:222*f*, 222*t*, 12:258
X-linked (Nettleship-Falls), 6:298, 300*t*, 301, 12:258
ocular findings in carriers of, 2:222*f*, 223, 12:258
Ocular alignment
disorders of/unsatisfactory. *See also* Diplopia
in infant with decreased vision, 6:414
nonorganic, 5:314–315
after strabismus surgery, 6:155
refractive surgery and, 13:34–35
tests of, 5:215–218, 216*f*, 217*f*. *See also specific type*
in children, 6:74–80
Vernier acuity and, 3:109
Ocular allergy. *See also* Allergic reactions/allergies
in children, 6:197–200
contact lens–induced red eye and, 3:200
Ocular autonomic pathways, 5:63–67
parasympathetic, 5:65–67, 65*f*, 66*f*
sympathetic, 5:65–67, 65*f*, 66*f*
Ocular biometrics. *See* Biometry/biometrics
Ocular bobbing, 5:210, 251*t*, 259
Ocular cicatricial (mucous membrane) pemphigoid,
4:54, 56*f*, 8:180, 196*t*, 198–203, 199*t*, 200*f*, 201*f*, 202*f*,
205*t*
cataract surgery in patient with, 11:191
drug-induced (pseudopemphigoid), 8:199, 361
mucous membrane grafting for, 8:401
Ocular cytology. *See* Cytology
Ocular development. *See* Eye, development of
Ocular deviations. *See* Deviations
Ocular dipping, 5:259
Ocular dominance, determining, 13:33
Ocular dominance columns, 5:34, 6:43*f*, 44
visual development and, 6:44, 45*f*
abnormal visual experiences affecting, 6:46, 47,
47*f*
Ocular examination. *See* Examination
Ocular flutter, 5:251*t*, 255–256, 255*f*
Ocular graft-vs-host disease, 8:196*t*, 203–204, 204*f*
Ocular hemorrhage. *See* Hemorrhages
Ocular histoplasmosis syndrome, 9:221–226, 222*f*, 223*f*,
224*f*, 225*f*, 12:80–83, 82*f*
choroidal neovascularization in, management of,
12:81–83, 351, 351*f*

management of, **9**:223–226, 224*f*, 225*f*, **12**:81–83, 351, 351*f*
photocoagulation for, **12**:340
Ocular history. *See also* History
in cataract, **11**:69–71, 70*t*
evaluation for surgery and, **11**:75
glaucoma evaluation and, **10**:27
in low vision assessment, **3**:288
refractive surgery evaluation and, **13**:30*t*, 31–32
Ocular hypertelorism, **6**:173, 384
Ocular hypertension, **10**:5*t*, 83–85, 84*f*, 105–106. *See also* Elevated intraocular pressure
cholesterol levels and, **1**:139
corneal thickness and, **10**:74, 84, 84*f*, 105
glaucoma risk and, **10**:9, 83, 105–106
glaucoma suspect and, **10**:83
nasal CPAP affecting, **1**:144
refractive surgery and, **13**:172–175, 173*f*, 194–195
uveitic, **9**:294, 295
Ocular Hypertension Treatment Study (OHTS), **10**:25, 75, 83–85, 84*f*, 105–106, 159
Ocular hypotension. *See* Hypotony
Ocular immunology/immune response. *See* Immune response; Immunology
Ocular infection. *See* Infection
Ocular inflammation. *See specific organ or structure affected and* Inflammation; Uveitis
Ocular injury/trauma. *See* Perforating injuries; Trauma
Ocular ischemia (ocular ischemic syndrome), **5**:183–184, 184*f*, **9**:287–288, **12**:94, 133–135, 134*f*
Ocular larval migrans, **8**:142. *See also* Toxocara (toxocariasis)
Ocular lateropulsion, in Wallenberg syndrome, **5**:206
Ocular media. *See* Optical (ocular) medium/media
Ocular melanocytosis (melanosis oculi/racial melanosis), **4**:65–66, 65*f*, 66*f*, **8**:235–236, 235*f*, 238*t*
in children, **6**:350, 350*f*
of iris, **4**:271*t*
Ocular microbiology. *See* Microbiology
Ocular migraine, **5**:184–185. *See also* Migraine headache
Ocular motility, **6**:32–37. *See also specific type of eye movement*
assessment of, **5**:199–204, **6**:81–83
before cataract surgery, **11**:77
in infants and children, **6**:81–83
convergence and, **6**:81–82
fusional vergence and, **6**:82–83
motor tests in, **6**:83
ocular rotations and, **6**:81
prism adaptation test in, **6**:86
3-step test in, **6**:83–86, 85*f*
in nonorganic disorders, **5**:314–315
optokinetic nystagmus and, **5**:201–202, **6**:319, 413
pursuit system and, **5**:204
before refractive surgery, **13**:34–35
saccadic system and, **5**:202–203, 203*f*
stability and, **5**:199–200
vergences and, **5**:204, **6**:86–87
vestibular ocular reflex and, **5**:200–201
binocular eye movements and, **6**:34–37
conjugate (versions), **6**:34, 35, 36*f*
assessment of, **6**:81

disconjugate (vergences), **5**:198–199, 198*t*, 204, 213–214, **6**:34, 35–37, 86–87, 413. *See also* Vergences/vergence system
control of, **5**:37–56, 197–199, 198*t*. *See also* Ocular motor pathways
brainstem in, **5**:37, 42–49, 44*f*, 45*f*, 46*f*, 47*f*, 49*f*
cortical/supranuclear pathways in, **5**:37, 38–41, 38*f*, 39*f*, 40*f*, 42*f*, 43*f*, **6**:37. *See also* Supranuclear (cortical) pathways
disorders of, **5**:197–214
cranial nerves/infranuclear pathways in, **5**:38, 50–55, 51*f*, 52–53*f*, 197
disorders of, **5**:226–238, 228*f*, 229*f*, 232*f*, 234*f*, 237*f*. *See also* Diplopia
extraocular muscles in, **2**:21, **5**:55–56, 56*f*, **7**:10–11
disorders of, **5**:204–214, **7**:23–24. *See also specific disorder*
in ataxia-telangiectasia, **5**:344, **6**:378
in blowout fractures, **7**:100–101
surgery and, **7**:102
in comatose patients, **5**:258–259
diplopia, **5**:215–241. *See also* Diplopia
history/presenting complaint in, **6**:71
in inborn errors of metabolism, **6**:400–401*t*
localization of lesions causing, **5**:220, 221*f*
in multiple sclerosis, **5**:324–325
nonorganic, **5**:314–315
nystagmus/spontaneous, **5**:243–259, **6**:320. *See also* Nystagmus
ocular bobbing, **5**:210, 251*t*, 259
optokinetic nystagmus dysfunction and, **5**:207–208
after orbital surgery, **7**:116
in Parkinson disease, **1**:260
pursuit dysfunction and, **5**:213
saccadic dysfunction and, **5**:208–213, 211*f*, 212*f*
gaze palsy/preference/tonic deviations and, **5**:210–213, 211*f*, 212*f*
intrusions, **5**:200, 204–205, 208, 243, 244, 254–256, 255*f*
ocular motor apraxia and, **5**:194, 208, 209–210, **6**:141–142
seizure activity and, **1**:263, **5**:211–212
stability dysfunction and, **5**:204–205
supranuclear, **5**:197–214. *See also* Supranuclear (cortical) pathways, disorders of
in thyroid eye disease, **4**:232, **7**:23–24
treatment of, **5**:257–258
vergence disorders and, **5**:213–214
in vertebrobasilar insufficiency, **5**:348
vestibular dysfunction and, **5**:205–207, 206*f*, 207*f*
efferent visual system and, **5**:37–56, 197. *See also* Ocular motility, control of; Ocular motor pathways
after evisceration, **7**:120
growth/development and, **6**:170
monocular eye movements (ductions) and, **5**:215, **6**:33–34
motor units and, **6**:32–33
orbital implants and, **7**:121
in ptosis, **7**:203–204
vergences and, **5**:198–199, 198*t*, 204, 213–214, **6**:34, 35–37, 86–87, 413. *See also* Vergences/vergence system

Ocular motor apraxia, 5:208, 209–210
acquired, 5:194, 210
congenital, 5:209–210, 6:141, 141–142
Ocular motor pathways, 5:37–56, 197–199, 198t. See also Ocular motility
brainstem and, 5:42–49, 44f, 45f, 46f, 47f, 49f
cortical input and, 5:38–41, 38f, 39f, 40f, 42f, 43f
cranial nerves and, 5:50–55, 50f, 51f, 52–53f. See also specific nerve
disorders of, 5:204–214
diplopia and, 5:226–227
extraocular muscles and, 5:55–56, 56f
Ocular myasthenia gravis, 7:209. See also Myasthenia gravis
Ocular neuromyotonia, 5:235, 369
Ocular pain. See Pain
Ocular perfusion pressure, glaucoma and, 10:77
Ocular pharmacology. See also specific agent and Drugs, ocular
age/aging and, 1:222
future research areas and, 2:321
legal aspects of, 2:333–334
principles of, 2:321–332
Ocular prostheses, 7:122
Ocular receptors. See Receptors
Ocular rotations
assessing, 6:81
in myasthenia gravis, 6:137
Ocular-scoliotic–type Ehlers-Danlos syndrome, 8:325
Ocular sensory pathways, 5:57–60, 57f, 58f, 59f, 197
Ocular stability, 5:199
assessment of, 5:199–200
dysfunction of, 5:204–205
Ocular surface. See also Conjunctiva; Cornea; Epithelium
definition of, 8:387
development of, 8:4
disorders of
aqueous tear deficiency, 8:55–65
contact lens wear and, 8:91–92
diagnostic approach to, 8:47–94, 181–182, 182t. See also specific disorder
ocular cytology in, 8:47–48
tear-film evaluation and, 8:52–55, 53f, 54f, 54t
dry-eye syndrome, 8:48–52. See also Dry-eye syndrome
evaporative tear dysfunction, 8:51, 51f, 52, 65–75
factitious, 8:89–90
immune-mediated, 8:183–223, 196t. See also specific disorder
clinical approach to, 8:183–223, 196t
diagnostic approach to, 8:181–182, 182t
patterns of, 8:180–181
infectious. See Infection
limbal stem cell deficiency and, 8:92–94, 93t, 94f, 395–398
neoplastic, 8:225–247. See also Ocular surface, tumors of
noninflammatory vascular conjunctival anomalies, 8:75–77
nutritional/physiologic disorders, 8:77–79
scleral contact lenses in management of, 3:193
structural/exogenous, 8:80–92

hypersensitivity reactions of, 8:178–180, 178f, 179t
immunologic features of, 8:173–175, 174f, 174t
inflammatory conditions in children affecting, 6:350–351
maintenance of, 8:388–389
surgery of, 8:387–405. See also specific procedure
indications for, 8:387t
tumors of, 8:225–247
epithelial origin of, 8:226–233, 226t
melanocytic, 4:65–70, 65t, 66f, 67f, 68f, 70f, 71f
neuroectodermal origin of, 8:233–240, 234t
squamous neoplasia, 4:62–64, 63f, 64f
wound healing/repair and, 8:387–388. See also Wound healing/repair
response to, 8:388–389
Ocular Surface Disease Index (OSDI), 8:56
Ocular surface squamous neoplasia (OSSN), 4:62–64, 63f, 64f. See also under Squamous and Conjunctival intraepithelial neoplasia
Ocular (intraocular) surgery. See also specific procedure
anisocoria diagnosis and, 5:270
anterior segment trauma caused by, 8:382–385, 384f
aqueous misdirection (malignant/ciliary block glaucoma) and, 10:131
after arcuate keratotomy, 13:52
corneal endothelial changes caused by, 8:383, 383–385
corneal epithelial changes caused by, 8:382–383
cystoid macular edema after, 12:360, 360f
Descemet membrane changes during, 8:383, 384f
endophthalmitis after, 9:126, 269–271, 270f, 12:354–357, 355f, 356f, 357f. See also Postoperative endophthalmitis
acute-onset, 12:354, 354–356, 355f
bleb-associated, 12:354, 356–357, 357f
chronic (delayed-onset), 12:355, 356, 356f
epithelial and fibrous ingrowth after, 10:133
after limbal relaxing incisions, 13:52
for melanoma, 4:285
needle penetration/perforation of globe and, 11:185, 12:325, 362, 363f
ocular surface, 8:387–405, 387t
in older patients, 1:224–225
perioperative management for, 1:303–313
intraoperative complications and, 1:310–313, 313t
medication management and, 1:305–307, 309t
preoperative assessment/management and, 1:303–310, 304t. See also Preoperative assessment/preparation for ocular surgery
after radial keratotomy, 13:47–48
refractive, 13:3, 4t, 41t, 125–147. See also specific procedure
accommodating intraocular lenses, 13:4t, 146, 159–160
bioptics, 13:125, 137
lens exchange/clear lens extraction/pseudophakic, 13:4t, 41t, 138–141
light-adjustable intraocular lenses, 13:146–147, 147f, 161
limitations of, 13:41t
multifocal intraocular lenses, 13:4t, 144–146, 154–156, 154f, 155f

phakic intraocular lenses, 13:4t, 41t, 125, 125–136,
127t, 130f, 131f, 132t, 133t
toric intraocular lenses, 13:4t, 126, 141–144, 142f
retinal detachment after, 12:314, 362–363, 363f
suprachoroidal hemorrhage and, 11:177–179,
12:360–361, 362f
sympathetic ophthalmia and, 4:189, 189f, 190f, 9:178,
182t, 12:198
for uveitis, 6:278, 9:116
vitrectomy for complications of, 12:354–362
Ocular tilt reaction, 5:205, 206f, 222–223, 222t
Ocular toxocariasis. See Toxocara (toxocariasis)
Ocular toxoplasmosis. See Toxoplasma (toxoplasmosis)
Ocular trauma. See Trauma
Ocular tumors. See Intraocular tumors; Tumors
Oculinum. See Botulinum toxin
Oculoauricular/oculoauriculovertebral dysplasia/
dysgenesis. See Goldenhar syndrome
Oculoauriculovertebral (OAV) spectrum/sequence,
6:392–393, 8:323t. See also Goldenhar syndrome
Oculocardiac reflex, 6:161
atropine affecting, 2:342
Oculocerebrorenal syndrome (Lowe disease/syndrome),
4:121, 6:302
childhood glaucoma and, 6:239, 302
congenital corneal keloids in, 8:264
ocular findings in carriers of, 2:222t, 223
pediatric cataract and, 6:247t, 302
Oculocutaneous albinism, 2:195, 308, 4:148, 6:298–301,
299t, 12:257–258, 258t, 259f
racial and ethnic concentration of, 2.211
Oculodentodigital dysplasia/syndrome
Axenfeld-Rieger syndrome differentiated from, 10:146t
pigmentary retinopathy and, 12:250t
Oculodentoosseous dysplasia, 8:323t
Oculodermal melanocytosis (nevus of Ota), 4:65t, 66,
7:166, 166f, 8:235–236, 238t
in children, 6:350
glaucoma associated with, 10:28
of iris, 4:271t
Oculodigital reflex, 6:413
in Leber congenital amaurosis, 12:229
Oculoglandular syndrome, Parinaud, 4:52, 8:157–158,
9:263, 12:206. See also Cat-scratch disease
in children, 6:189–190, 190f
Oculogyric crisis, 5:212–213
Oculomandibulodyscephaly, 8:323t
Oculomasticatory myorhythmia, 5:257
Oculomotor foramen, 7:11, 12f
Oculomotor nerve. See Cranial nerve III
Oculomotor nerve palsy/paralysis. See Third nerve
(oculomotor) palsy/paralysis
Oculomycosis, trauma and, 8:139
Oculopalatal myoclonus/tremor, pendular nystagmus
and, 5:253
Oculopharyngeal dystrophy, 5:337
Oculorenal syndromes, 2:141, 6:302
Ocupress. See Carteolol
Ocusert Delivery System, 2:330. See also Pilocarpine
for childhood glaucoma, 6:243
OD. See Optical density
ODD. See Optic disc (optic nerve head), drusen of
Odds ratio, 1:337

Off-bipolars, 2:298, 299f
Off-label uses
of drug, 2:333–334
of ophthalmic device, 13:206–207
Off retinal ganglion cells, 2:299f, 300
"Off-the-pump bypass surgery," 1:110
Office Record Review module, 1:341
Ofloxacin, 1:52t, 61, 2:371–373, 372t
for bacterial keratitis, 8:163
for gonococcal conjunctivitis, 8:152
OGTT. See Oral glucose tolerance test
Oguchi disease, 6:292, 12:218, 219f
arrestin mutation causing, 2:182, 295
racial and ethnic concentration of, 2:211
rhodopsin kinase mutations causing, 2:295
OHS. See Ocular histoplasmosis syndrome
OHT. See Ocular hypertension
OHTS (Ocular Hypertension Treatment Study), 10:25,
75, 83–85, 84f, 105–106, 159
OID. See Orbital inflammatory disease
Oil droplet appearance
in galactosemia, 11:56, 56f
in lenticonus/lentiglobus, 6:249, 11:26
visual acuity and, 11:70
Oil glands of eyelid, 7:160
tumors/lesions of, 7:160–161. See also under
Sebaceous
Oil red O stain, 4:30
Ointments, ocular, 2:327. See also Lubricants
OIS (orbital inflammatory syndrome). See Nonspecific
orbital inflammation
OKAN. See Optokinetic after nystagmus
OKN. See Optokinetic nystagmus
Olanzapine, 1:251, 252
Older patients. See Age/aging; Geriatrics
Oleate, in vitreous, 2:286
Olfactory bulb, 2:87, 89f
Olfactory nerve. See Cranial nerve I
Olfactory pits, 2:119f
Olfactory tract, 2:87, 89f
Oligemic shock, 1:293. See also Shock
Oligoarticular (pauciarticular)-onset juvenile idiopathic
(chronic/rheumatoid) arthritis (oligoarthritis),
1:166, 6:269, 269t, 9:129. See also Juvenile idiopathic
(chronic/rheumatoid) arthritis
eye examination schedule for children with, 6:271t,
9:131t
uveitis in, 6:269, 9:129–130, 130f
Oligodendrocytes, 2:92f, 4:249
Oligodendroglia, retinal, 2:301
Oligonucleotide hybridization, in mutation screening,
2:184, 186f
Oligonucleotide microarray analysis, SNP (SOMA),
4:38t
Oligonucleotides
allele-specific, 2:148
in mutation screening, 2:184
antisense, in gene therapy, 2:188, 189f
Oligosaccharide antibiotics, 1:64
Olivopontocerebellar atrophy, pigmentary retinopathy
and, 12:250t, 254
Olmesartan, 1:76t
Olopatadine, 2:365t, 366

Omega-3 fatty acid supplements
  age-related macular degeneration and, **12**:62
  for meibomian gland dysfunction, **8**:68
  retinitis pigmentosa management and, **12**:231
OMIM (Online Mendelian Inheritance in Man), **2**:178,
  12:221, 249
Omnicef. *See* Cefdinir
Omniflox. *See* Temafloxacin
Omnipause cells/neurons, **5**:38, 40, 46, 46*f*
On-bipolars, **2**:298, 299*f*
On retinal ganglion cells, **2**:299*f*, 300
OnabotulinumtoxinA. *See* Botulinum toxin, type A
Onchocerca/Onchocerca volvulus (onchocerciasis),
  8:141, **9**:241–242
Oncocytoma, **4**:75, 75*f*, **8**:233
Oncogenes/oncogenesis, **1**:235–236, **2**:157, 171, 172*f*
Oncologist, ophthalmic, **4**:43
Oncovin. *See* Vincristine
Ondansetron, perioperative, **1**:309*t*, 310
One-and-a-half syndrome, **5**:225–226, 226*f*
One-handed nucleus disassembly, **11**:124–125, 125*f*
100-hue test (Farnsworth-Munsell), **12**:48
  in low vision evaluation, **5**:105
One-piece bifocals, **3**:147, 148*f*
One toy, one look rule, for pediatric examination, **6**:3
ONH. *See* Optic nerve (cranial nerve II), hypoplasia of
ONL. *See* Outer nuclear layer
Onlays, corneal, **13**:53–64
Online Mendelian Inheritance in Man (OMIM), **2**:178,
  12:221, 249
Online post-refractive IOL power calculator (ASCRS),
  13:188–189, 190*f*
Online search, **1**:316
ONSM. *See* Optic nerve sheath meningioma
Onychoosteodysplasia, **8**:323*t*
OOKP. *See* Osteo-odonto-keratoprosthesis
OPA1 gene, in autosomal dominant optic atrophy, **5**:139
Opacities
  corneal. *See* Cornea, opacification of
  fundus evaluation with, **11**:80–81
  intraocular lens, **11**:168–169
  lens. *See* Cataract
  vitreous, **12**:311–314
    amyloidosis causing, **4**:140, **12**:312–313, 313*f*
    in asteroid hyalosis, **12**:311, 312*f*
    in cholesterolosis, **12**:311–312
    fibrillar, **2**:286
    hemorrhage causing, **12**:313–314
    pigment granules and, **12**:314
    in uveitis, **9**:302
Opcon-A. *See* Naphazoline/pheniramine
Open-angle glaucoma, **10**:4, 5*t*, 6*f*, 7*t*, 73–108. *See also*
  Glaucoma
  age and, **10**:8, 75
  central retinal vein occlusion and, **10**:77, **12**:129
  childhood (congenital/infantile/juvenile), **10**:5*t*,
    139–158. *See also* Glaucoma, childhood
    clinical manifestations and diagnosis of, **6**:234–238,
      234*f*, 235*t*, 236*f*, 237*f*
    genetics of, **6**:233, **10**:142–143
    natural history of, **6**:238
    pathophysiology of, **6**:234

primary
  congenital, **4**:102, 103*f*, **6**:233–238, 234*f*, 235*t*,
    236*f*, 237*f*, **10**:5*t*, 139, 140*t*, 143–145, 143*f*,
    144*f*, 144*t*. *See also* Primary congenital
    glaucoma
    genetics of, **6**:233, **10**:142–143
    juvenile, **6**:234, **10**:5*t*, 145
  secondary, **6**:238–240
  treatment of, **6**:240–243, 240*f*, 242*f*
classification of, **10**:4, 5*t*, 6*f*, 7*t*
combined-mechanism, **10**:6
cornea plana and, **8**:255
corneal thickness and, **10**:74
corticosteroids causing, **10**:103–104
cycloplegic use in, **2**:341
diabetes mellitus and, **10**:76–77
drug-induced, **10**:103–104
without elevated intraocular pressure, **10**:5*t*, 78–82,
  80*t*. *See also* Glaucoma, normal-tension
episcleral venous pressure elevation and, **10**:95–96,
  95*t*, 96*f*
exfoliation syndrome/pseudoexfoliation and, **10**:86, 87
family history and, **10**:76
Fuchs heterochromic iridocyclitis/uveitis and,
  10:94–95, 95*f*
genetic/hereditary factors in, **10**:11, 11*t*
glaucomatocyclitic crisis (Posner-Schlossman
  syndrome) and, **10**:94
hyphema and, **10**:97–99, 97*f*
intraocular pressure in, **10**:73–75
intraocular tumors and, **10**:92–93
lens-induced, **10**:90–92, 90*t*, 91*f*, 92*f*
management of
  clinical trials in evaluation of, **10**:78, 104–108, 159
  medical, **10**:159–177
    agents used in, **10**:161–173, 162–165*t*. *See also*
      specific drug and Antiglaucoma agents
    general approach to, **10**:174–175
  surgical, **10**:179, 180–200. *See also specific*
    procedure
    cataract and filtering surgery combined,
      10:199–200
    incisional, **10**:107–108, 183–198. *See also*
      Filtering procedures
    laser trabeculoplasty, **10**:82, 107–108
microcornea and, **8**:253
myopia and, **10**:76
normal-tension. *See* Glaucoma, normal-tension
ocular inflammation and, **10**:93–95
optic disc appearance in, **5**:139–140, **10**:75
outflow obstruction mechanisms in, **10**:7*t*
pars planitis and, **9**:138
penetrating keratoplasty and, **8**:421, **10**:102
pigmentary/pigment dispersion syndrome and,
  4:91–92, 94*f*, 109, 109*f*, 110*f*, **10**:87–90, 88*f*, 89*f*, 90*f*
posterior polymorphous corneal dystrophy and, **8**:295
primary, **10**:4, 5*t*, 6*f*, 8–10, 9*t*, 73–78
  clinical features of, **10**:73–75
  clinical trials in, **10**:104–108, 159. *See also specific*
    study
  congenital, **4**:102, 103*f*, **6**:233–238, 234*f*, 235*t*, 236*f*,
    237*f*

disorders associated with, 10:76–78
without elevated IOP, 10:78–82, 80t. *See also*
Glaucoma, normal-tension
epidemiology of, 10:8–10, 9t
genetic/hereditary factors in, 10:11, 11t
incidence of, 10:8, 9
juvenile, 6:234, 10:5t, 145
management of
medical, 10:159–177. *See also* Antiglaucoma
agents
surgical, 10:179, 180–200. *See also specific*
procedure
prevalence of, 10:8
prognosis for, 10:78
risk factors for, 10:9, 9t, 73, 74, 75–76, 104, 105–106
race and, 10:8, 76
refractive surgery and, 13:172–175, 173f, 194–195
risk factors for, 10:9, 9t, 73, 74, 75–76, 104, 105–106
Schwartz (Schwartz-Matsuo) syndrome and,
10:102–103
secondary, 10:4, 5t, 85–104. *See also specific cause*
in children, 6:238–240
trauma causing, 4:107–109, 108f, 10:38–39, 38f, 39f
uveitic, 9:296–297
in Sturge-Weber syndrome, 5:341, 343f
trauma causing, 4:107–109, 108f, 10:38–39, 38f, 39f
uveitic, 9:296–297
visual field loss in, 10:73, 75
vitrectomy and, 12:368
Open-loop trackers, 13:83
Open reading frame, 2:157, 165
Operating microscope, 3:262–263, 262f
phototoxicity and, 11:183–184, 12:333
Operculated holes, 12:271
treatment of, 12:283, 284t
Ophthacet. *See* Sulfacetamide
Ophthaine. *See* Proparacaine
Ophthalmia
neonatorum, 6:186–188, 187f, 8:152–154
chemical, 6:188
chlamydial, 6:187–188, 8:153–154
gonococcal, 6:187, 187f, 8:153
herpes simplex causing, 6:188. *See also*
Conjunctivitis, herpes simplex virus causing
prophylaxis for, 6:186, 188
nodosum, 8:372
sympathetic, 4:189, 189f, 190f, 9:52–53, 178–183,
179f, 180f, 181f, 182t, 12:198–199, 329–330
corticosteroids for, 9:182–183
route of administration of, 2:360t
enucleation in prevention of, 4:189, 7:117, 118,
8:376, 9:182, 12:198–199, 329
evisceration and, 7:120, 9:182, 12:329
experimental autoimmune uveitis as model for,
9:69
glaucoma and, 9:296
glaucoma surgery and, 10:185
histologic/histopathologic features of, 4:189, 189f,
190f, 9:180, 181f
HLA association in, 9:72t, 181
surgical procedures/injuries leading to, 4:189, 189f,
190f, 9:178, 182t, 12:198

Ophthalmic artery, 2:37f, 38, 39f, 5:10f, 12, 13f, 14f, 15f,
16, 18, 7:11f, 12, 12f, 13f
aneurysm of, 5:350–351
development of, 2:138
extraocular muscles supplied by, 2:18, 38, 6:16
eyelids supplied by, 2:29, 7:143
occlusion of, 12:140
chronic, ocular ischemic syndrome and, 12:133
optic nerve supplied by, 2:94, 94f, 95, 10:42
orbit supplied by, 7:12, 13f
terminal, 5:18–19
Ophthalmic Devices Panel, 13:205–206
Ophthalmic echography. *See* Ultrasonography
Ophthalmic examination. *See* Examination
Ophthalmic instrumentation. *See also specific type*
phototoxicity from, 12:333–334
cataract surgery and, 11:183–184, 12:333
Ophthalmic irrigants, 2:392. *See also* Irrigation
endothelial changes caused by, 8:384–385
Ophthalmic lenses, 3:62–83. *See also* Lenses
afocal systems and, 3:80–83, 81f, 82f, 83f
anophthalmic socket camouflage and, 7:125
Badal principle and, 3:80, 269, 270f
combinations of, 3:66–67
negative and positive, 3:72–73, 72f
spherocylindrical lenses at oblique axes and,
3:99
concave (minus/negative), 3:72–73, 73f
anophthalmic socket camouflage and, 7:125
paraxial ray tracing through, 3:73–74, 73f, 74f
prismatic effect of, 3:87
convex (plus/positive)
anophthalmic socket camouflage and, 7:125
paraxial ray tracing through, 3:69–72, 71f
prismatic effect of, 3:87
focal lengths of, 3:78–79
focal planes/points and, 3:69, 70f
Gaussian reduction and, 3:79
graphical image analysis and, 3:76, 77f
Knapp's law and, 3:79–80, 80f
lensmeters and, 3:80, 268–271, 269f, 270f, 271f
modeling unknown system and, 3:76, 77f
objects/images at infinity and, 3:74
principal planes/points and, 3:75, 75f
thick, 3:76–78, 78f
thin, 3:66
negative, 3:72f, 73
transverse magnification for single spherical
refracting surface and, 3:64–65, 65f
vergence/reduced vergence and, 3:62–64, 63f, 65
virtual images/objects and, 3:67–68, 67f, 69f
Ophthalmic nerve. *See* Cranial nerve V (trigeminal
nerve), V₁
Ophthalmic oncologist, 4:43
Ophthalmic pathology. *See also specific structure and*
specific disorder
of anterior chamber/trabecular meshwork, 4:101–109,
110f
checklist for requesting, 4:34t
communication among health care team members
and, 4:25–26
congenital anomalies and, 4:6, 7f, 12t

of conjunctiva, 4:47–75
of cornea, 4:77–100
degeneration and dystrophy and, 4:9–10, 12*t*
diagnosis/differential diagnosis and, 4:11–12, 12*t*
diagnostic electron microscopy in, 4:34*t*, 43
of eyelids, 4:205–227
fine-needle aspiration biopsy for, 4:34*t*, 43–44, 44*f*, 263
flow cytometry in, 4:34*t*, 36–37, 36*f*, 37*f*
frozen section for, 4:34*t*, 44–45
immunohistochemistry in, 4:33–36, 35*f*
inflammation and, 4:6–9, 8*f*, 9*f*, 12*t*
of lens, 4:119–129
molecular pathologic techniques in, 4:34*t*, 37–43, 38–39*t*, 40*f*, 42*f*
neoplasia and, 4:10, 10*t*, 11*f*, 12*t*
of optic nerve, 4:249–259
of orbit, 4:229–247, 7:31–32
organizational paradigm for, 4:5–12, 12*t*
of retina, 4:145–184
of sclera, 4:111–118
special procedures in, 4:33–45, 34*t*
specimen collection/handling for, 4:25–30, 31*t*
topography and, 4:6, 12*t*
of uveal tract, 4:185–203
of vitreous, 4:131–143
wound repair and, 4:13–23
Ophthalmic prisms. *See* Prisms
Ophthalmic surgery. *See* Ocular (intraocular) surgery
Ophthalmic ultrasonography. *See* Ultrasonography
Ophthalmic vein, 2:40*f*, 5:10*f*, 7:11*f*, 12*f*, 13, 14*f*, 15*f*, 12:18
    inferior, 5:10*f*, 24*f*, 25, 27*f*
    orbit drained by, 5:10, 24–25, 27*f*, 7:13, 14*f*, 15*f*
    superior, 5:10*f*, 24–25, 24*f*, 27*f*
Ophthalmic viscosurgical devices (viscoelastic agents), 2:393, 11:96–98, 97*t*
    for cataract surgery, 11:96–98, 97*t*
        advanced cataract extraction and, 11:196
        aniridia and, 11:200
        capsular rupture and, 11:160, 161
        ECCE, 11:94, 212
        high hyperopia and, 11:200–201
        inflamed eye and, 9:292, 11:207
        intraoperative floppy iris syndrome and, 11:155
        intumescent cataract extraction and, 11:196
        IOL implantation and, 11:138, 139, 140, 141, 13:129, 130
        phacoemulsification, 11:102, 110, 117, 126
        pupil expansion and, 11:98, 194
        traumatic cataract and, 11:208
        uveitis and, 9:292, 11:207
    characteristics of, 11:98
    elevated intraocular pressure and, 10:101, 11:154
    for goniotomy and trabeculotomy, in children, 10:155
    for penetrating keratoplasty, 8:418
    physical properties of, 11:97–98, 97*t*
Ophthalmic wound healing/repair. *See* Wound healing/ repair
Ophthalmometry. *See* Keratometry
Ophthalmomyiasis, 8:143

Ophthalmopathy, thyroid (Graves/dysthyroid). *See* Thyroid eye disease
Ophthalmoplegia
    in ataxia-telangiectasia, 5:344
    internuclear, 5:46, 224–226, 224*f*, 225*f*, 226*f*, 6:141
        in multiple sclerosis, 5:325
        myasthenia gravis and, 5:225, 329
        nystagmus in, 5:224–225, 6:141
            dissociated, 5:254
        pursuit dysfunction in, 5:213
        wall-eyed bilateral, 5:225, 225*f*
    progressive (chronic progressive) external, 2:174–175, 5:336–337, 336*f*, 337*f*, 6:137, 139*t*, 12:254
        mitochondrial DNA defects and, 2:173, 174–175, 191, 12:251*t*, 265
        ptosis in, 5:280, 336, 336*f*
Ophthalmoplegic migraine, 5:231. *See also* Migraine headache
Ophthalmoscopy
    before cataract surgery, 11:80
    direct, 3:243–245, 243*f*, 244*f*
        conjugacy/conjugate points and, 3:28–29, 30*f*
        fundus illumination in, 3:244
        in low vision evaluation, 5:95
        in optic disc evaluation, 10:46
        in retinal examination, 12:19
    in glaucoma evaluation, 10:46, 47*t*
        in infants and children, 10:152
    indirect, 3:245–248, 245*f*, 246*f*, 247*f*, 248*f*, 249*f*
        aerial image in, 3:245, 246*f*
        binocular observation and, 3:246–248, 248*f*, 249*f*
        in choroidal/ciliary body melanoma, 4:274
        fundus illumination in, 3:245, 246, 246*f*, 248*f*
        in ocular trauma, 12:318
        in optic disc evaluation, 10:46
        optics of image formation and, 3:245, 246*f*
        in posterior vitreous detachment, 12:276
        pupil conjugacy and, 3:246, 247*f*
        in retinal examination, 12:19
        in retinopathy of prematurity, 12:164
    laser, 3:251, 12:29–30
        in fundus autofluorescence, 12:30
        in indocyanine green angiography, 12:25
        in optic disc evaluation, 10:51, 52*f*
    video, 3:251
Ophthetic. *See* Proparacaine
OPL. *See* Optical path length; Outer plexiform layer
Opportunistic infections, 8:100. *See also specific type*
    CMV retinitis, 4:151, 152*f*, 9:306–307
    cryptococcosis, 9:278, 310–311, 313–314
    in HIV infection/AIDS, 1:3, 29–31, 30*t*, 31*t*, 37–40, 9:311
        treatment of, 1:37–40
Opsins
    cone, 2:293, 294
        genes for, 2:294–295
    rod. *See* Rhodopsin
Opsoclonus (saccadomania), 5:251*t*, 255–256
    in children, 6:325
        neuroblastoma and, 6:336

Opsoclonus-myoclonus syndrome, 5:256
Optic
  of intraocular lens, 3:204*f*, 205
    anterior chamber lens, 3:210, 211
    posterior chamber lens, 3:209
  of scleral contact lens, 3:192, 192*f*
Optic ataxia, 5:194
Optic atrophy, 4:253–254, 253*f*, 254*f*, 255*f*, 5:95–96, 96*f*,
    159, 6:310–311, 311*t*, 415
  ascending, 4:253–254
  autosomal dominant, 5:139, 140*f*, 6:310–311
  Behr, 6:311
  cavernous, of Schnabel, 4:254, 255*f*
  in children, 6:310–311, 311*t*, 415
  in cone dystrophies, 12:232
  in craniosynostosis, 6:391
  descending, 4:254
  dominant, 5:139, 140*f*, 6:310–311
  in inborn errors of metabolism, 6:400–401*t*
  Leber hereditary optic neuropathy and, 6:311
  in onchocerciasis, 9:242
  in optic tract syndrome, 5:166
  in Rift Valley fever, 9:218
Optic (optical) axis, 3:31, 31*f*, 32*f*, 106, 107*f*, 6:12, 11:5, 6*f*
Optic canal, 2:11*f*, 93, 5:6, 6*f*, 8, 9*f*, 11*f*, 12, 31, 7:6*f*, 7*f*, 9
  decompression of for traumatic visual loss, 5:156–157,
    7:106
Optic cap (apical zone), 3:168, 195, 8:37
Optic chiasm. *See* Chiasm
Optic chiasmal glioma, 5:151, 164
Optic cup, 2:89, 92*f*, 10:46
  asymmetry of, 10:47, 47*f*, 47*t*
  choroidal development and, 2:132
  development of, 2:121–122, 123, 123*f*, 124*f*, 8:4, 11:21
  enlargement of, 2:90, 10:44, 47, 47*t*. *See also* Cupping
    of optic disc
  ratio of, to optic disc
    in glaucoma evaluation, 10:46, 47, 50
      in infants and children, 6:237, 10:152
      in megalopapilla, 6:307
  retinal development and, 2:125–126, 125*f*
  vertical elongation of, 10:48, 48*f*
Optic disc (optic nerve head), 2:41*f*, 71, 89–92, 92*f*, 5:29.
    See also Optic nerve
  anatomy of, 2:41*f*, 71, 89–92, 92*f*, 5:29
  aplasia of, 6:309
  atrophy of. *See* Optic atrophy
  avulsion of, 12:331–332, 331*f*
  blood supply of, 2:94, 95*f*
  cavernous hemangioma of, 12:151
  coloboma of, 2:141, 4:249–250, 251*f*, 6:306, 306*f*, 415
    retinoblastoma differentiated from, 4:305*t*
  congenital/developmental abnormalities of, 5:141–143,
    142*f*, 143*f*, 6:305–310
  cupping of. *See* Cupping of optic disc
  differentiation of, 2:128
  disorders of in children, 6:305–315
  drusen of, 4:255, 255*f*, 306, 5:133–136, 134*f*, 135*f*,
    136*f*
    astrocytic hamartoma differentiated from, 5:136,
      136*f*
    in children, 6:314–315, 315*f*

papilledema/pseudopapilledema and, 4:255, 306,
    5:120, 120*f*, 134–136, 135*f*
  in children, 6:314–315, 315*f*
  dysplastic, 5:143
  edema of, 5:96–97, 97*f*. *See also* Papilledema;
    Pseudopapilledema
  in anterior optic neuropathy, 5:125, 126*t*, 127, 128,
    128*t*
  anterior orbital lesions causing, 5:132, 133*f*
  in central retinal vein occlusion, 12:128
  in children, 6:314*t*
    in craniosynostosis, 6:391
    in leukemia, 6:298, 298*f*, 354
    papilledema and, 6:312
    pseudopapilledema and, 6:313–315, 314*t*, 315*f*
  in cystoid macular edema, 12:142
  in diabetic papillopathy, 5:130–131, 131*f*
  in neuroretinitis, 5:130
  in optic atrophy, 4:253, 253*f*
  in papillitis, 5:129
  in papillophlebitis, 5:131–132, 132*f*
  examination of
    in glaucoma evaluation, 10:32, 40, 45*f*, 46–52, 47*f*,
      47*t*, 48*f*, 49*f*, 52–53*f*
    in low vision evaluation, 5:95–97, 96*f*, 97*f*
  excavation of
    congenital anomalies and, 5:143
    in glaucoma, 5:139–140, 141*f*
  in Foster Kennedy syndrome, 5:127, 128*f*
  in glaucoma, 10:3–4, 32, 40, 75
    evaluation of, 10:32, 40, 45*f*, 46–52, 47*f*, 47*t*, 48*f*,
      49*f*, 52–53*f*, 75
      in infants and children, 6:237, 237*f*
      normal-tension glaucoma and, 10:81
      perimetry changes correlated with, 10:66–67
      quantitative measurement and, 10:46, 51–52,
        52–53*f*
      recording findings and, 10:50–51
    in infants and children, 6:237, 237*f*
    open-angle glaucoma and, 10:75
    visual field changes and, 10:66–67, 75
  hemorrhage of, in glaucoma, 10:48–49, 48*f*, 79
  in HTLV-1 infection, 9:219
  hypoplasia of, 5:141–142, 141*f*, 6:308–309, 308*f*, 320,
    414–415
  in leukemia, 6:298, 298*f*, 354
  in megalopapilla, 6:307–308
  melanocytoma (magnocellular nevus) of, 4:256, 256*f*
    melanoma differentiated from, 4:278–279, 280*f*
  metastatic disease of, 4:315–316, 320
  morning glory, 5:143, 6:305, 305*f*, 415
  neovascularization of (NVD), in diabetic retinopathy,
    12:105, 106*f*
  nerve fibers entering, distribution of, 10:41–42, 41*f*
  in neuroretinitis, 9:264
  tilted (Fuchs coloboma), 5:142–143, 142*f*, 6:307, 307*f*
  tumors of, 4:256–258, 256*f*, 257*f*, 258*f*, 259*f*
  vasculitis of (papillophlebitis), 4:164, 5:131–132, 132*f*,
    12:128
  in Whipple disease, 9:265
Optic disc pit, acquired, 10:48
Optic disc topography, 10:50

Optic foramen, **2:**7*f*, *8f*, 10, 11*f*, **5:**9*f*, **7:**9
Optic gliomas. *See* Optic nerve (optic pathway/chiasm) glioma
Optic nerve (cranial nerve II). *See also* Optic disc
 anatomy of, **2:**41*f*, 75, 87–97, 88*f*, 89*f*, 94*f*, **5:**10*f*, 11*f*, 28*f*, 29–31, 53*f*, **10:**40–44, 41*f*, 43*f*
 anterior/anterior zone of, **10:**40, 41–44, 43*f*
 aplasia of, **6:**309
 atrophy of. *See* Optic atrophy
 avulsion of, **12:**331–332, 331*f*
 in Behçet disease, **9:**193
 blood supply of, **2:**93, 94–96, 95*f*, **5:**31, **10:**42–44, 43*f*
 coloboma of, **2:**141, **4:**249–250, 251*f*, **6:**306, 306*f*, 415
 congenital abnormalities of, **4:**249–250, 251*f*, **6:**305–310
 in fetal alcohol syndrome, **2:**142
 degenerations of, **4:**253–255, 253*f*, 254*f*, 255*f*
 development of, **2:**125*f*, 128
 disorders of, **4:**249–259. *See also specific type*
 in children, **6:**305–315
 in craniosynostosis, **6:**391
 hallucinations and, **5:**190
 illusions and, **5:**189
 neoplastic, **4:**256–258, 256*f*, 257*f*, 258*f*, 259*f*
 radiation causing, **1:**238–239, **5:**369, 369*f*
 relative afferent pupillary defect in, **5:**92, 95
 dysplastic, **5:**143
 evaluation of
 before cataract surgery, **11:**80
 in glaucoma, **10:**40–44, 41*f*, 43*f*
 in infants and children, **6:**237, 237*f*, **10:**152
 normal-tension glaucoma and, **10:**81
 in nystagmus, **6:**320
 in glaucoma, **10:**3–4
 examination of, **10:**40–44, 41*f*, 43*f*
 in infants and children, **10:**152
 normal-tension glaucoma and, **10:**81
 in infants and children, **6:**237, 237*f*
 glioma of. *See* Optic nerve (optic pathway/chiasm) glioma
 hypoplasia of, **5:**141–142, 141*f*, **6:**308–309, 308*f*, 320, 414–415
 in fetal alcohol syndrome, **2:**142
 infection/inflammation of, **4:**251–253, 251*f*, 252*f*, 253*f*
 intracanalicular region of, **2:**87, 89*t*, 93, **4:**249
 blood supply of, **2:**93, 95
 compressive lesions of, **5:**149
 intracranial region of, **2:**87, 89*t*, 93, 94*f*, **4:**249, **5:**31
 blood supply of, **2:**95
 intraocular region of, **2:**87, 89, 89–91, 89*t*, **4:**249
 intraorbital region of, **2:**87, 89, 89*t*, **4:**249, **5:**30–31, **7:**5, 10, **10:**40
 blood supply of, **2:**94, 95*f*
 compressive lesions of, **5:**149–154
 length of, **7:**5*t*, 10
 laminar area of, **2:**90, **10:**42, 44
 in leukemia, **6:**298, 298*f*
 in Lyme disease, **9:**252
 metastatic disease of, **4:**315–316, 320
 posterior, **10:**42, 43–44, 43*f*
 prelaminar area of, **2:**90, **10:**42, 43–44, 43*f*. *See also* Optic disc
 blood supply of, **2:**94, 95*f*

 regional differences in, **2:**87, 89*t*
 retinal ganglion cells in, **10:**40–41
 degeneration of, in glaucomatous optic neuropathy, **10:**44–45
 retinoblastoma involving, **4:**180, 182*f*
 retrolaminar area of, **2:**91, **10:**42, 43*f*, 44
 blood supply of, **2:**94, 95*f*
 in Rift Valley fever, **9:**217, 218
 in thyroid eye disease, **4:**232, **5:**147–149, 148*f*, **7:**49, 51, 53–54
 topography of, **4:**249, 250*f*
 trauma to, **5:**156–157, 156*f*, **7:**105, **12:**331–332, 331*f*
 tumors of, **4:**256–258, 256*f*, 257*f*, 258*f*, 259*f*. *See also specific type*
 in uveitis, **9:**86*t*
 in Wegener granulomatosis, **9:**145
Optic nerve glioblastoma (malignant optic glioma), **4:**257, **5:**153–154, **7:**69
Optic nerve (optic pathway/chiasm) glioma (pilocytic astrocytoma), **4:**257, 257*f*, **5:**151–154, 151*f*, 152*t*, 164, **7:**69–72, 70*f*
 in children (juvenile), **4:**257, **6:**343, 367–369, 368*f*
 malignant (glioblastoma), **4:**257, **5:**153–154, **7:**69
 in neurofibromatosis, **5:**152, 153, 340, **6:**343, 367–369, 368*f*, **7:**69, 71, 73
 nystagmus caused by, **5:**153
 orbital involvement in, **6:**343, **7:**69–72, 70*f*
Optic nerve head. *See* Optic disc
Optic nerve pits. *See* Optic pits
Optic nerve sheath, **5:**10*f*, 30
Optic nerve sheath decompression/fenestration, for idiopathic intracranial hypertension, **5:**124
Optic nerve sheath meningioma, **4:**258, 258*f*, 259*f*, **5:**149–151, 150*f*, 150*t*, **7:**74–75, 75–76, 75*f*
 optic glioma differentiated from, **6:**368
Optic neuritis, **5:**128*t*, 144–146, 145*f*, 323–324, **6:**311–312
 in children, **6:**311–312
 CMV infection causing, **5:**359, 360*f*
 contrast sensitivity affected by, **3:**113
 corticosteroids for, **5:**146
 route of administration of, **2:**360*t*
 cryptococcal, **5:**367
 hallucinations and, **5:**190
 illusions and, **5:**189
 in multiple sclerosis, **5:**144, 323–324
 NAION differentiated from, **5:**128, 128*t*
 neuroimaging in evaluation of, **5:**82*t*, 83–84, 144, 145*f*
 retrobulbar, **5:**144–146, 145*f*
 contrast sensitivity affected by, **3:**113
 in cryptococcosis, **5:**367
 toxoplasmic, **5:**362
Optic neuropathy, **5:**116–159
 anterior
 ischemic, **5:**125–129, 126*t*
 arteritic, **5:**125, 125–127, 126*f*, 126*t*, 316
 nonarteritic, **5:**125, 126*f*, 126*t*, 127–129, 128*f*
 with optic disc edema, **5:**116–132
 without optic disc edema, **5:**133–142
 autosomal dominant, **5:**139, 140*f*
 CMV infection causing, **5:**359
 compressive orbital lesions and, **5:**132, 133*f*, 149–154
 congenital disc anomalies and, **5:**141–143, 141*f*, 142*f*

diabetic papillopathy and, 5:130–131, 131*f*
drusen and, 5:133–136, 134*f*, 135*f*, 136*f*. *See also* Drusen
in giant cell arteritis, 5:125, 125–127, 126*f*, 126*t*, 319–320
in glaucoma, 5:139–140, 141*f*, 10:3–4, 44–52, 45*f*, 47*t*
  indications for surgery and, 10:184–185
  optic disc evaluation/cup changes and
    normal-tension glaucoma and, 10:81
     perimetry changes correlated with, 10:66–67
     quantitative measurement and, 10:46, 51–52, 52–53*f*
     recording findings and, 10:50–51
  optic nerve evaluation and, 10:40–44, 41*f*, 43*f*
  patterns of nerve loss and, 10:68, 69*f*, 70*f*, 71*f*, 72*f*
hallucinations and, 5:190
hypertensive, 5:123–125, 123*t*, 12:115, 117*f*
of increased intracranial pressure. *See* Papilledema
infiltrative lesions and, 5:132, 133*f*, 158–159
inflammatory, pain in, 5:301
intracanalicular lesions and, 5:149–154
Leber hereditary, 2:175, 5:137–139, 137*f*, 6:311
  mitochondrial DNA mutations and, 2:174*f*, 175, 5:138, 6:311
neuroimaging in evaluation of, 5:83
neuromyelitis optica (Devic syndrome) and, 5:147
neuroretinitis and, 5:130, 130*f*
nutritional, 5:154–156, 155*f*
optic atrophy and, 5:139, 140*f*, 169
optic glioma and, 5:151–154, 151*f*, 152*t*
optic nerve sheath meningioma and, 5:149–151, 150*f*, 150*t*
optic perineuritis and, 5:147
orbital lesions and, 5:132, 133*f*, 149
papillitis and, 5:129
papillophlebitis and, 5:131–132, 132*f*
posterior, 5:144–159
  ischemic, 5:157–158
pseudotumor cerebri and, 5:123–125, 123*t*
radiation-induced, 1:238–239, 5:369, 369*f*
retrobulbar optic neuritis and, 5:144–146, 145*f*
in sarcoidosis, 5:133*f*, 144, 335
thyroid eye disease and, 5:147–149, 148*f*, 333, 7:49, 51, 53–54
toxic, 1:250, 5:154–156
traumatic, 2:93, 5:156–157, 156*f*, 7:105–106
visual field patterns in, 5:116, 117*f*, 118*t*, 119*f*
Optic neurotomy, radial, for central retinal vein occlusion, 12:133
Optic perineuritis, 5:147
Optic pits (optic nerve/disc pits, optic holes), 2:120, 121, 5:143, 12:294–295, 295*f*
  acquired, 10:48
  central serous chorioretinopathy differentiated from, 12:174
  in children, 6:310, 310*f*
Optic radiations (geniculocalcarine pathways), 2:93, 94*f*, 96, 5:20*f*, 21, 28*f*, 34
  lesions of, 5:165–172
Optic stalks, 2:128
Optic strut, 5:9, 31, 7:6*f*, 9
Optic tract, 2:94*f*, 96, 5:28*f*, 32–33, 6:43*f*, 44
  lesions of, 5:165–167, 166*t*

Optic tract syndrome, 5:19–20, 166–167
Optic ventricle, 2:123
Optic vesicle, 2:121, 121*f*, 123*f*, 124*f*, 8:4
  lens development and, 2:128–129, 11:21, 22*f*
Optic zone (contact lens), 3:168*f*, 169
Optic zone (corneal). *See* Optical zone (corneal)
Optical aberrations. *See* Aberrations
Optical aids
  contrast sensitivity affecting use of, 3:291
  for magnification, 3:295–301
    magnifiers, 3:298–299, 300*f*
    spectacles, 3:295–298, 298*f*
    telescopes, 3:299–300, 301*f*
  prisms as, 3:300–301
Optical (optic) axis, 3:31, 31*f*, 32*f*, 106, 107*f*, 6:12
Optical clarity, of ophthalmic viscosurgical device, 11:98
Optical coherence tomography/biometry, 3:10, 281–282, 282*f*, 5:81, 108, 8:29, 34, 35*f*, 12:26–29, 27*f*, 28*f*
  anterior segment, in glaucoma, 10:70
  before cataract surgery, 11:82, 84
  in central serous chorioretinopathy, 12:173, 173*f*
  before corneal transplantation, 8:417
  in cystoid macular edema, 12:142
    in uveitis, 9:300
  in dengue fever, 9:220
  in epiretinal membrane, 12:300
  in idiopathic macular hole, 4:136–137, 138*f*, 12:304, 305, 305–306*f*
  in IOL power determination, 11:84
  in low vision assessment, 5:108
  in posterior vitreous detachment, 12:298, 299*f*
  ranibizumab therapy for AMD guided by, 12:74–76
  in retinal disease, 12:26–29, 27*f*, 28*f*
  in retinal nerve fiber evaluation, 10:51–52, 53*f*
  in uveitis, 9:95–96, 96*f*, 300
  in vitreomacular traction syndrome, 12:302, 346, 348*f*
  in Vogt-Koyanagi-Harada (VKH) syndrome, 9:188
Optical conjugacy. *See* Conjugacy/conjugate
Optical constants, of schematic eye, 3:104*f*, 105*t*
Optical degradation, for amblyopia, 6:67
Optical density, 3:13
Optical doubling, in pachymetry, 3:259, 260*f*
Optical feedback, in lasers, 3:21, 23–24, 24*f*
Optical focusing, in pachymetry, 3:259
Optical interfaces, 3:42
  light propagation at, 3:42, 42*f*, 43*f*
  reflection at, 3:12–13, 12*f*, 42, 42*f*, 43*f*
Optical (ocular) medium/media, 3:39
  abnormalities of, 5:111–112
    transient visual loss and, 5:175–176
  boundaries between. *See* Optical interfaces
  clear, traumatic visual loss with, 7:104–106
  cloudy, 3:286
  opaque. *See* Cataract; Opacities
  refractive index of, 3:6, 40, 40*t*, 104*f*, 105*t*. *See also* Refractive index
    light propagation and, 3:40–41, 40*t*
Optical pachometry, 8:28. *See also* Pachymetry/pachymeter
Optical path length (OPL), 3:53, 53*f*
Optical performance, IOL, standards for, 3:230
Optical pocket, for endoscopic brow and forehead lift, 7:232

Optical system
  afocal, **3:**80–83, 81*f*, 82*f*, 83*f*. *See also* Optics, of
    human eye
  approximation for analysis of, **3:**55–62, 56*f*, 57*f*, 58*f*,
    61*f*, 62*f*. *See also specific type and* First-order optics
  eye as, **3:**103
  Gaussian reduction and, **3:**79
  unknown, modeling, **3:**76, 77*f*
Optical zone (contact lens) , **3:**168*f*, 169
Optical zone (corneal), **8:**37
  arcuate keratotomy and, **13:**49, 50, 51, 52
  in photoablation, preoperative laser programming
    and, **13:**74
  pupil size and, **13:**34
  radial keratotomy and, **13:**43, 45, 45*f*
    IOL power calculations affected by, **13:**187
Opticin, in vitreous, **2:**283, 285
Opticrom. *See* Cromolyn
Optics
  of contact lenses, **3:**170–176
  cosmetic, for anophthalmic socket, **7:**125
  geometric, **3:**3, 27–102. *See also* Geometric optics
  of human eye, **3:**103–120
    accommodation/presbyopia and, **3:**116–117, 117*f*,
      142, 143*t*
    axes of eye and, **3:**106, 107*f*
    binocular states and, **3:**116
    contrast sensitivity/contrast sensitivity function
      and, **3:**111–113, 112*f*
    illusions and, **5:**188
    power prediction formulas for IOLs based on,
      3:212–213, 212*f*
    pupil size/resolution and, **3:**107–108, 107*f*
    refractive states and, **3:**113–116, 113*f*, 114*f*, 115*f*,
      13:3–5. *See also under* Refractive
      developmental hyperopia and, **3:**119
      developmental myopia and, **3:**118–119
      epidemiology of refractive errors and, **3:**117–118
      prevention of refractive errors and, **3:**119–120
      treatment of refractive errors and, **3:**120
    schematic eye and, **3:**103–104, 104*f*, 105*t*, 106*f*. *See*
      also Schematic eye
    visual acuity and, **3:**108–111, 109*f*, 110*f*, 110*t*
    wavefront analysis and, **13:**5–9, 5*f*, 6*f*, 7*f*, 8*f*, 9*f*
  physical, **3:**3–26. *See also* Physical optics
  quantum, **3:**3
OptiPranolol. *See* Metipranolol
Optisol GS, for donor cornea preservation, **8:**409
Optivar. *See* Azelastine
OPTN gene, **10:**11*t*
Optociliary shunt vessels (retinochoroidal collaterals),
  5:25, 149
  in optic nerve sheath meningioma, **5:**149, 150*f*
  in papilledema, **5:**121–122
Optokinetic nystagmus (OKN), **5:**198–199, 198*t*, 201,
  6:319, 413
  assessment of, **5:**201–202, **6:**319, 413
  in congenital motor nystagmus, **6:**321
  dysfunction of, **5:**207–208
    in congenital nystagmus, **5:**245
    parietal lobe lesions and, **5:**168–169
  nonorganic ophthalmic disorder and, **5:**307
Optokinetic after nystagmus (OKAN), **5:**202

Optometer principle, **3:**80
  in automated refraction, **3:**275
  in manual lensmeter operation, **3:**80
Optotypes
  for computer-based acuity devices, **3:**110
  for contrast sensitivity testing, **3:**111, **12:**51–52, 51*f*
  evaluation of visual acuity in children and, **6:**4, 73
    crowding bars and, **6:**65, 65*f*, 73
  for low vision testing, **3:**290
  for nonorganic ophthalmic disorder evaluation, **5:**312
  Snellen letters, **3:**109, 109*f*
OPV (oral polio vaccine/Sabin vaccine), **1:**283
OR. *See* Odds ratio
Ora bays, **12:**8, 10*f*
  enclosed, **12:**8, 280, 281*f*
Ora serrata, **2:**41*f*, 71, 82, 83*f*, **12:**8, 10*f*
  muscle insertion relationships and, **2:**16
Oral contraceptives
  central retinal vein occlusion and, **12:**129
  hypercoagulability associated with, **1:**158
  hypertension and, **1:**86
  ocular effects of, **1:**302*t*
  tetracycline use and, **2:**374
  thyroxine levels affected by, **1:**208
  uveitis caused by, **9:**128
Oral facial dyskinesias, **5:**292
Oral glucose tolerance test, **1:**192, 193
Oral hypoglycemic agents, **1:**198–201, 199*t*, 200*f*. *See*
  also specific type
  early intervention with, **1:**194
  surgery and, **1:**307
Oral medication, sustained-release preparations of,
  2:329
Oral polio vaccine (OCV/Sabin vaccine), **1:**283
Oral ulcers
  in Behçet disease, **1:**180, **9:**191, 192*f*, **12:**194
  in systemic lupus erythematosus, **1:**167, 169*t*
Orbicularis oculi muscle, **2:**23, 23*f*, 24–27, 24*f*, 27*f*,
  4:205, 206*f*, **5:**62, 7:17, 131, 133*f*, 135*f*, 136, 137*f*
  blepharospasm and, **5:**289, 290*f*
  hemifacial spasm and, **5:**291
  spastic paretic facial contracture and, **5:**291
  tear flow pumped by, **7:**136, 246, 247*f*
  weakness of, in myasthenia gravis, **5:**329
Orbicularis oris muscle, **7:**133, 133*f*
Orbit. *See also under* Orbital
  abscesses of, **7:**43, 43*f*
  amyloid deposits in, **4:**235
  anatomy of, **2:**5–13, **5:**7–12, 9–10*f*, 11*f*, **7:**5–19
    assessment of before refractive surgery, **13:**35
    sensory and motor components, **5:**56–62
    vascular, **7:**12–13, 13*f*, 14*f*, 15*f*
      arterial supply, **2:**36–38, 37*f*, 38*f*, 39*f*, **5:**13–14*f*,
        15–18
      venous drainage, **2:**38–40, 40*f*, **5:**10, 24–25*f*
  angiography/arteriography in evaluation of, **7:**31
  anophthalmic socket and, **7:**117–127
  apertures in walls of, **7:**6*f*, 7*f*, 8–9, 8*f*
  basal cell cancer involving, **7:**171
  biopsy of, **7:**31–32
    fine-needle aspiration, **4:**44, **7:**115
    in lymphoproliferative lesions, **4:**238–239
    in nonspecific orbital inflammation, **7:**61

bony, **2:**5, 6f, 8f, **4:**229, **5:**7–12, 9–10f, 11f
    neuroimaging in evaluation of, **5:**82t, 87–88, 87f
canals in, **5:**10–11
cellulitis affecting. *See* Orbital cellulitis
computed tomography in evaluation of, **5:**70–72, 71f,
    87, 87f, **7:**25–26, 25f, 26f
    MRI compared with, **7:**28–29, 28t, 30f
congenital disorders of, **4:**229–230, 230f, **6:**173–175,
    174f, 175f, **7:**33–37, 34f, 35f, 36f, 37f
connective tissues of, **2:**35, 35f
cysts of, **4:**229–230, 230f, **6:**332t, 343–344, 344f
    aneurysmal bone, **6:**343
    dermoid, **4:**229–230, 230f, **6:**343–344, 344f,
        7:36–37, 36f
    epithelial/epidermoid, **4:**229–230, **6:**343, **7:**36
    with microphthalmia (colobomatous cyst), **6:**345,
        346f, **7:**34
degenerations of, **4:**235
development of, **2:**139, **6:**169
dimensions of, **7:**5, 5t
disorders of, **4:**229–247. *See also specific type*
    autoimmune, **7:**39t. *See also* Thyroid eye disease
    in children
        congenital anomalies, **4:**229–230, 230f, **6:**173–175,
            174f, 175f, **7:**33–37, 34f, 35f, 36f, 37f
        cysts, **6:**332t, 343–344, 344f
        fractures, **6:**124–126, 125f, 411, 411f
        infection/inflammation, **6:**194–197
        tumors, **6:**331–347, 332–333t
    compressive, **5:**132. *See also* Orbital decompression
    congenital anomalies, **6:**173–175, 174f, 175f,
        7:33–37, 34f, 35f, 36f, 37f
    evaluation of, **7:**21–32
        biopsy in, **7:**31–32
        history in, **7:**21, 22t
        imaging studies in, **7:**25–30, 25f, 27f, 28t, 30f
            selecting, **5:**82t, 84, 87–88, 87f
        inspection in, **7:**22–24, 23f, 24f
        laboratory studies in, **7:**32
        physical examination in, **7:**22–25, 23f, 24f
        secondary imaging studies in, **7:**30–31
    globe displacement and, **7:**22–23
    granulomatous, **7:**39t
    infections, **4:**234–235, 234f, **7:**39t, 40–47. *See also*
        Orbit, infection/inflammation of
        in children, **6:**194–197
    infiltrative, **5:**132, 133f, 158–159
    inflammations, **4:**230–235, 231f, 233f, 234f,
        7:39, 39t, 47–61. *See also* Nonspecific orbital
        inflammation; Orbit, infection/inflammation of
        in children, **6:**194–197
    neoplastic, **4:**235–247, **7:**63–93. *See also* Orbit,
        tumors of
        in children, **6:**331–347, 332–333t
    pain and, **7:**21. *See also* Pain
    periorbital changes and, **7:**21, 22t
    pulsation and, **7:**25
    rate of progression of, **7:**21
    Th1 delayed hypersensitivity and, **9:**50t
    transient visual loss and, **5:**177
    vasculitic, **7:**39t, 55–58, 57f
    in Wegener granulomatosis, **9:**145
dysmorphic, **6:**173–175, 174f, 175f

emphysema of, in blowout fractures, **7:**101
in external eye defense, **8:**95
fascial system of, **6:**19–24, 20f
fibrous dysplasia of, **4:**245–246, 246f
fissures in. *See* Orbital fissures
floor of, **2:**7–9, 8f, **5:**8f, **7:**8
    fractures of, **7:**100–104, 102f
        in children, **6:**124–126, 125f, 411
            vertical deviations and, **6:**124–126, 125f
foramina in, **2:**10, 11f
foreign bodies in, **7:**104
fractures of, **7:**95–104, 97f, 99f, 102f
    in children, **6:**124–126, 125f, 411, 411f
        vertical deviations and, **6:**124–126, 125f
    diplopia after, **5:**238
    midfacial (Le Fort) fractures and, **7:**95, 96f
    healing/repair of, **4:**17–18
hemorrhages in, **7:**69, 104
    after blepharoplasty, visual loss and, **7:**226
    blowout fractures and, **7:**101
    from orbital lymphatic malformation, **7:**65, 66
    after surgery, **7:**116
hypoplasia of, in microphthalmia, **7:**33, 34
infection/inflammation of, **4:**230–235, 231f, 233f,
    234f, **5:**300–301, **7:**39–61, 39t
    in children, **6:**194–197
    idiopathic. *See* Nonspecific orbital inflammation
lacrimal gland neoplasia and, **4:**235–238, 237f,
    7:85–88
lacrimal sac neoplasia and, **4:**235
lateral wall of, **2:**9, 9f, **5:**7f, 9, **7:**6–7
lateralization of (orbital hypertelorism), **6:**173,
    384
leukemic infiltration of, **4:**328, **6:**337, **7:**90–91
lipodermoids of, **7:**37, 37f
lymphoproliferative lesions of, **4:**238–240, 239f,
    7:79–85
magnetic resonance imaging in evaluation of, **5:**73,
    76f, 87–88, **7:**26–28, 27f
    CT scanning compared with, **7:**28–29, 28t, 30f
margin of, **2:**5, 6f
measurement of, **6:**173, 174f
medial wall of, **2:**7, 8f, **5:**8f, 9, 10, **7:**5, 5t, 7–8
    fracture of, **7:**98–100, 99f
myositis affecting, **4:**231, 231f, **5:**239, **6:**347
    nonspecific orbital inflammation and, **4:**231, 231f,
        7:59, 60f
nerves of, **7:**13–17, 16f
optic nerve in, **2:**87, 89, 89t, **7:**5, 10
    blood supply of, **2:**94, 95f
    length of, **7:**5t, 10
paranasal sinuses and, **7:**5, 17–19, 18f
periorbital structures and, **7:**10, 17–19, 18f. *See also*
    Periorbita
retinoblastoma affecting, **4:**304, 304f
roof of, **2:**5–7, 7f, **5:**7f, **7:**5–6
    fractures of, **7:**98
        in children, **6:**411, 411f
sebaceous carcinoma involving, **7:**174
septum of, **2:**23f, 25f, 27–28, **7:**5, 135f, 137–138
    lacerations of, **7:**178
soft tissues of, **4:**229, **7:**10–17
    tumors arising in, **4:**240

surgery of, 7:107–116. *See also specific procedure*
  for blowout fractures, 7:101, 102*f*, 103–104
    indications for, 7:102–103
  complications of, 7:116
  decompression, 7:113–115, 113*f*, 114*f*. *See also*
    Orbital decompression
  incisions for, 7:108, 108*f*
  orbitotomy, 7:108–113, 108*f*, 110*f*, 111*f*, 113*f*. *See
    also* Orbitotomy
  postoperative care and, 7:115
  special techniques in, 7:115–116
  surgical spaces and, 7:107–108, 107*f*
  for volume expansion in craniosynostosis,
    6:392
teratomas of, 7:37
in thyroid eye disease, 4:232, 233*f*, 7:47–55, 47*f*, 48*f*,
    52*t*, 53*t*
tight, 7:105
topography of, 4:229, 7:5–8, 6*f*, 7*f*, 8*f*
trauma to, 7:95–106
  foreign bodies, 7:104
  fractures, 7:95–104, 97*f*, 99*f*, 102*f*
    midfacial (Le Fort) fractures, 7:95, 96*f*
  hemorrhages, 7:69, 104
  sclopetaria and, 12:323, 323*f*
  visual loss with clear media and, 7:104–106
tuberculosis affecting, 7:45
tumors of, 4:235–247, 7:63–93. *See also specific type*
  adipose, 4:245
  bony, 4:245–246, 246*f*
    in children, 6:342–343
  in children, 6:331–347, 332–333*t*
    benign, 6:338–343
    congenital, 7:35–37, 36*f*, 37*f*
    differential diagnosis of, 6:331–334
    ectopic tissue masses, 6:343–346
    inflammatory disorders simulating, 6:332*t*,
      346–347, 347*f*
    metastatic, 6:333*t*, 336–338, 336*f*, 338*f*, 7:90–91,
      91*f*
    primary malignant, 6:334–336, 335*f*
  congenital, 7:35–37, 36*f*, 37*f*
  connective tissue, in children, 6:343
  cystic, 6:332*t*, 343–344, 344*f*
  diplopia caused by, 5:239
  ectopic tissue masses, 6:343–346
  enucleation for, 7:117–118
  exenteration for, 7:117, 126–127, 126*f*
  with fibrous differentiation, 4:240–242, 242*f*
  hematopoietic, in children, 6:332*t*
  histiocytic, in children, 6:332*t*, 337–338, 338*f*
  lacrimal sac/gland, 4:235–238, 237*f*
  lymphoproliferative, 4:238–240, 239*f*, 7:79–85
    in children, 6:332*t*
  mesenchymal, 7:76–79
  mesodermal, in children, 6:332–333*t*
  metastatic, 4:247, 7:90–93
    in adults, 7:91–92, 92*f*
    in children, 6:333*t*, 336–338, 336*f*, 338*f*, 7:90–91,
      91*f*
    management of, 7:93
  MR imaging of, 5:75*f*, 87*f*

  with muscle differentiation, 4:242–244, 243*f*
  nerve sheath, 4:244–245, 244*f*, 245*f*
  neural/neurogenic, 7:69–76
    in children, 6:333*t*, 343
  pathologic examination of, 7:31–32
  primary malignant, in children, 6:334–336, 335*f*
  secondary, 4:247, 7:88–89, 89*f*, 90*f*
    eyelid carcinoma and, 7:171
  soft tissue, 4:240
  staging of, 4:348–349*t*
  vascular (vascular tumors/malformations/fistulas),
    4:240, 241*f*, 7:63–69
    in children, 6:332*t*, 338–342, 339*f*, 341*f*
ultrasonography in evaluation of, 5:81, 7:29–30
vascular system of, 7:12–13, 13*f*, 14*f*, 15*f*
  anatomy of, 2:36–40, 37*f*, 38*f*, 39*f*, 40*f*, 5:10, 13–14*f*,
    15–18, 24–25*f*, 7:12–13, 13*f*, 14*f*, 15*f*
  development of, 2:138
venography in evaluation of, 7:31
volume of, 2:5, 4:229, 5:9, 7:5*t*
  loss of in anophthalmic socket, 7:119
walls of
  apertures in, 7:6*f*, 7*f*, 8–9, 8*f*
  lateral, 2:9, 9*f*, 5:7*f*, 9, 7:6–7
  medial, 2:7, 8*f*, 5:8*f*, 9, 10, 7:5, 5*t*, 7–8
    fracture of, 7:98–100, 99*f*
Orbital apex fractures, 7:97–98
Orbital apex syndrome, 5:236
  in zygomycosis, 7:45
Orbital cellulitis, 7:41–44, 42*f*, 42*t*, 43*f*
  in children, 6:195–197, 196*f*, 7:42
  fungal (mucormycosis), 6:197, 197*f*
  after strabismus surgery, 6:156, 156*f*
Orbital decompression, 7:113–115, 113*f*, 114*f*
  complications of, 7:116
  for thyroid eye disease, 5:149, 334, 7:53, 54, 113–115,
    114*f*
  for traumatic visual loss, 7:105, 106
Orbital fat, 2:27, 7:10–11, 135*f*, 138
  dermatochalasis and, 7:221
  eyelid lacerations and, 7:178
Orbital fibroblasts, in thyroid eye disease, 4:232, 7:50
Orbital fissures, 2:10–12, 12*f*, 5:10, 7:6*f*, 7*f*, 9
  inferior, 2:8*f*, 9*f*, 10–12, 5:7*f*, 8, 8*f*, 9*f*, 12, 7:6*f*, 7*f*, 9
  superior, 2:7*f*, 10, 11*f*, 12*f*, 5:6, 6*f*, 7*f*, 9*f*, 10, 7:6*f*, 7*f*, 9
    ophthalmoplegia caused by lesions of, 5:236–238
Orbital hypertelorism, 6:173, 384
Orbital implants, 7:119, 121–122, 121*f*
  for blowout fractures, 7:103
  in children, 7:119
  exposure and extrusion of, 7:123, 123*f*
  for superior sulcus deformity, 7:122
Orbital inflammatory disease (OID), 4:230–235, 231*f*,
    233*f*, 234*f*. *See also specific type or cause*
Orbital inflammatory syndrome. *See* Nonspecific orbital
    inflammation
Orbital lacrimal gland, 2:32, 32*f*, 239
Orbital layer, of extraocular muscle, 6:18
  pulley system and, 6:18, 21, 22, 22*f*, 23
Orbital orbicularis muscles, 7:136, 137*f*
Orbital pseudotumor. *See* Nonspecific orbital
    inflammation

Orbital rim, 5:9
Orbital varices, 7:66–67
    in children, 6:342
    glaucoma associated with, 10:28
Orbital veins, 6:18
    eyelids drained by, 7:143
Orbitalis muscle, 5:10f
Orbitectomy, for lacrimal gland tumors, 7:87
Orbititis, sclerosing. See Nonspecific orbital
    inflammation
Orbitopathy, thyroid/thyroid-associated/Graves. See
    Thyroid eye disease
Orbitotomy, 7:108–113, 108f, 110f, 111f, 113f
    incisions for, 7:108, 108f
    inferior approach for, 7:109–110, 110f, 111f
    lateral approach for, 7:112–113
    medial approach for, 7:110–112
    superior approach for, 7:108–109
ORC. See Origin replication complex
Orencia. See Abatacept
ORF. See Open reading frame
Organ culture storage techniques, for donor cornea,
    8:409
Organ transplantation. See Transplantation
"Organic amblyopia," 6:64
Organic mental syndromes. See Mental disorders due to
    general medical condition
Organogenesis, in eye, 2:120–140, 122t. See also specific
    structure
Orientation and mobility specialist, in vision
    rehabilitation, 3:305
Origin of replication, 2:157
Origin replication complex, 2:157
Orinase. See Tolbutamide
Ornithine, elevated serum levels of, in gyrate atrophy,
    12:243, 244
Ornithine aminotransferase (OAT) gene, mutations/
    defects of, 2:298
    in gyrate atrophy, 2:213t, 298, 12:243
Ornithine transcarbamylase deficiency, 6:398
Orphenadrine, for benign essential blepharospasm, 7:220
Orthokeratology, 3:194–195, 13:63–64
Orthomyxoviruses, 8:129
Orthophoria/orthotropia, 6:9
Orthoptics
    for convergence insufficiency, 6:106
    fusional vergences and, 6:82
    for intermittent exotropia, 6:102
    for residual exotropia, 6:103
    for suppression, 6:52
Orthostatic hypotension, 1:85–86
Orudis. See Ketoprofen
Oruvail. See Ketoprofen
Oscillations. See Saccadic intrusions/oscillations
Oscillatory potentials, 12:34, 34f, 35
    vascular disease and, 12:40, 41f
Oscillopsia, 5:243
    in superior oblique myokymia, 5:257
OSDI (Ocular Surface Disease Index), 8:56
Oseltamivir, 1:55t, 66, 282
Osler-Weber-Rendu disease (hereditary hemorrhagic
    telangiectasia), 1:153, 8:76

Osmitrol. See Mannitol
Osmoglyn. See Glycerin
Osmolarity, tear film, 2:238t, 8:54
    dysfunctions and, 2:244
Osmotic/hyperosmotic agents, 2:355–356, 356t, 10:165t,
    173
Osmotic force, transendothelial, 8:8
Osmotic hypothesis, of carbohydrate ("sugar") cataract
    formation, 2:280
Osseous choristoma, 4:49f, 50, 8:247
Ossifying fibroma, of orbit, 4:246, 246f, 6:343
OSSN. See Ocular surface squamous neoplasia
Osteocutaneous ligaments, 7:131
Osteodystrophy, Albright hereditary, 8:322t
Osteogenesis imperfecta, 8:252, 323t
    bleeding disorders in, 1:153
    blue sclera in, 8:252
Osteoma
    choroidal, 4:202, 6:353
        melanoma differentiated from, 4:280, 280f
    orbital, 4:246, 7:79
    secondary, 7:89
Osteomyelitis, maxillary, 6:197
Osteo-odonto-keratoprosthesis, 8:432
Osteoporosis, 1:227–231
    bone physiology and, 1:228
    clinical features of, 1:229
    corticosteroid use and, 1:182, 9:104–105
    diagnosis of, 1:229
    evaluation of, 1:229
    risk factors for, 1:228–229
    testing for, 1:229
    treatment of, 1:229–231
Osteosarcoma
    of orbit, 7:79
        in children, 6:336
    retinoblastoma associated with, 4:312, 314t,
        6:336
Osteotomy, for dacryocystorhinostomy, 7:268
Ota, nevus of. See Nevus, of Ota
Otic ganglion, 5:66f
Otitic hydrocephalus, 5:357
Otoliths, 5:48
    ocular motor disorders and, 5:205, 222
    peripheral vestibular nystagmus and, 5:249
Ototoxicity
    of aminoglycosides, 1:62, 5:250
    mitochondrial DNA mutations and, 2:176
    peripheral vestibular dysfunction and, 5:250
Outcome/outcome measures, 1:318–319, 338
    baseline probability and, 1:336–337
    in clinical research, 1:318–319
        case series and, 1:323
    monitoring system and, 1:340–342
Outer cell mass, 2:117
Outer eye. See External (outer) eye
Outer ischemic retinal atrophy, 4:157, 157f
Outer neuroblastic layer, 2:126
Outer nuclear layer, 2:74f, 75f, 76f, 79f, 4:145, 146f,
    12:10, 11f
Outer plexiform layer, 2:74f, 75f, 76f, 78, 79f, 4:145, 146f,
    12:10, 11f, 12

Outer segments, photoreceptor, **2:**73, 74*f*, 76*f*, 79*f*,
    12:10, 11*f*, 12, 13*f*. *See also* Cone outer segments;
    Photoreceptors; Rod outer segments
  shed, retinal pigment epithelium phagocytosis of,
    12:12, 15
Outflow facility, **10:**16
  classification of glaucomas and, **10:**7*t*
  intraocular pressure and, **10:**13, 14*t*, 16
  tonography in measurement of, **10:**19
Outpatient visits, geriatric patient and, **1:**222–223
Ovarian cancer, paraneoplastic-induced saccadic
    intrusions and, **5:**256
OVDs. *See* Ophthalmic viscosurgical devices
Overcorrection
  in exodeviation, value of, **6:**103, 151
  with photoablation, **13:**93–94
Overdepression in adduction, **6:**115
Overelevation in adduction, **6:**114
Overlap syndromes (mixed connective tissue disease),
    1:174
Overrefraction, **3:**138
  acuity testing in corneal abnormalities and, **8:**11
  in aphakia, **3:**158
  with automated refractors, **3:**277
  cataract surgery evaluation and, **11:**76
  in rigid gas-permeable contact lens fitting, **3:**183, 185
  in soft contact lens fitting, **3:**182
Overwear syndromes (contact lens), metabolic epithelial
    damage in, **8:**91
Ovoid bodies, in neurofibromatosis, **6:**369
Ovum, **2:**196
Ox eye (buphthalmos/megaloglobus)
  in neurofibromatosis, **6:**370
  in primary congenital glaucoma, **6:**238, **10:**143, 143*f*,
    150
Oxacillin, **1:**56, **2:**369–370
  protein binding of, **2:**329
Oxaprozin, **1:**183*t*
Oxazolidinones, **1:**53*t*, 64
Oxcarbazepine, **1:**263*t*
Oxidoreductases, taxon-specific crystallins as, **2:**276
Oxitropium, **1:**145, 145*t*
Oxivent. *See* Oxitropium
Oxy radicals, **2:**313. *See also* Free radicals
Oxycephaly, **6:**383
Oxychloro complex, as ocular medication preservative,
    2:322–323
Oxygen
  in aqueous humor, **2:**271–272
  corneal supply of, contact lenses and, **3:**200
  reduction of myocardial requirements for
    for acute coronary syndrome, **1:**111
    for angina, **1:**108
  singlet, **2:**311, 312, 313, 314, 315
  vitrectomy affecting movement of, **2:**287–288
Oxygen radicals. *See* Free radicals
Oxygen-regulated protein, mutations in, **2:**296
Oxygen tension
  in lens, energy production and, **2:**279
  in retina, free-radical reactions and, **2:**315
Oxygen therapy
  for acute coronary syndrome, **1:**111
  for anaphylaxis, **1:**295
  in CPR, **1:**291

  hyperbaric, oxidative lens damage and, **11:**16, 60–61
  for pulmonary diseases, **1:**144
  retinopathy of prematurity and, **6:**281, **12:**165–166
  for shock, **1:**294
Oxygen transmissibility, **3:**168, 176–178, 177*t*. *See also*
    Gas-permeability constant
  corneal hypoxia and, **3:**200
  orthokeratology and, **3:**194
  of rigid contact lenses, **3:**176–178
  of scleral contact lenses, **3:**192
  of soft (flexible) contact lenses, **3:**178, 181*t*
Oxymetazoline, **2:**392
Oxyphilic (eosinophilic) cystadenoma (oncocytoma),
    4:75, 75*f*, **8:**233
Oxytetracycline, **2:**374
  with polymyxin B, **2:**372*t*, 374
Oxytocin, **1:**214

P

p7 nucleocapsid zinc finger inhibitors, for HIV
    infection/AIDS, **1:**35
p17 antigen, HIV vaccine development and, **1:**36
p21, in cancer, **1:**236
p23H rhodopsin mutation, **2:**295
p24 antigen, HIV vaccine development and, **1:**36
p24 antigen testing, in HIV infection/AIDS, **1:**31–32
p53 gene
  in adenoid cystic carcinoma, **4:**236–238
  in cancer, **1:**236, 244
  in conjunctival lymphoma, **4:**74
  in DNA repair, **2:**170
  in keratoacanthoma, **4:**216
  in ocular surface squamous neoplasia, **4:**62
  in pingueculae/pterygia, **4:**57
p63 gene, in pingueculae/pterygia, **4:**57
p arm, **2:**157
P cells (parvocellular neurons/system), **5:**28, 33, **6:**43,
    43*f*, 44, **10:**40
  development of, **6:**43, 43*f*, 44
    abnormal visual experience affecting, **6:**46, 48
P gene (*OCA2* gene), in albinism, **2:**195, **6:**299*t*, 301,
    12:258*t*
P-selectin, in neutrophil rolling, **9:**18
P value, **1:**320
PA. *See* Polyacrylamide
PABPN1 gene, mutation of in oculopharyngeal
    dystrophy, **5:**337
PAC. *See* Angle closure/angle-closure glaucoma, acute;
    Premature atrial complexes/contractions
Pacchionian granulations, **5:**26
pACD. *See* ACD prediction formula, personalized
PACD. *See* Posterior amorphous corneal dystrophy
Pacemakers
  for heart failure, **1:**120
  laser surgery in patient with, **13:**31
Pacerone. *See* Amiodarone
PACG. *See* Angle closure/angle-closure glaucoma,
    primary
Pachymetry/pachymeter (pachometry/pachometer),
    3:259, 260*f*, **8:**28–30, 29*f*, 30*t*
  for ACD or ELP measurement, **3:**218, 218*f*
  before cataract surgery, **11:**84

in children, **6:**236
in Fuchs endothelial dystrophy, **8:**293
infection control and, **8:**46
for intrastromal corneal ring segment placement, **13:**57
in keratoconus, **8:**299, 300*f*
before LASIK, **13:**71–72
corneal perforation and, **13:**104
before phakic intraocular lens insertion, **13:**129
before refractive surgery, **13:**39–40, 70–71, 71–72, 167, 168
Paclitaxel, **1:**239, 241*t*
PACs. *See* Premature atrial complexes/contractions
Paecilomyces/Paecilomyces lilacinus, **8:**139
endophthalmitis caused by, **9:**270
PAF. *See* Platelet-activating factors
Paget disease of bone, angioid streaks in, **12:**84
Pagetoid spread
of melanoma, **4:**227, 227*f*
in primary acquired melanosis, **4:**69
of sebaceous carcinoma, **4:**222, 223*f*, **7:**173, 174
PAHX gene, Refsum disease caused by mutations in, **2:**298
Pain. *See also specific type*
cerebral aneurysms causing, **5:**351
corneal abrasion causing, **8:**372
in endophthalmitis, **9:**272, 276
enucleation/evisceration for, **7:**118
facial, **5:**301–303
atypical, **5:**301
headache causing, **5:**293–300. *See also* Headache
in Horner syndrome, **5:**268–269, 302
icepick, **5:**299
neuroimaging in evaluation of, **5:**85–86
ocular causes of, **5:**300–301
in ocular ischemic syndrome, **5:**183
orbital, **5:**300–301, **7:**21
in blowout fractures, **7:**100
in myositis, **5:**239
in nonspecific orbital inflammation, **4:**231, **7:**59
after surgery, **7:**116
in thyroid eye disease, **7:**51
periorbital, **5:**301
in optic neuritis, **5:**91–92, 144
in recurrent corneal erosion, **5:**300, **8:**83
in scleritis, **5:**300, **8:**217–218, 219, **9:**118, 266
somatoform, **1:**248
after surface ablation, **13:**86
third nerve (oculomotor) palsy and, **5:**231
in Tolosa-Hunt syndrome, **5:**237, 301
in traumatic hyphema, **8:**367
in uveitis, **9:**84, 84*t*, 119
with visual loss, assessment and, **5:**91–92
"Painless" (subacute lymphocytic) thyroiditis, **1:**213
Palatal myoclonus/tremor, pendular nystagmus and, **5:**253
Palatine air cells, **2:**12
Palatine bone, **5:**5, 7*f*, 9–10, **7:**7*f*
Paleocerebellum, **5:**48
Palinopsia, **5:**191
Palisades of Vogt, **8:**5
Pallidotomy, for Parkinson disease, **1:**259–260
Palmitate/palmitic acid
in retinal pigment epithelium, **2:**206, 305
in vitreous, **2:**286

Palpation, orbital, **7:**24–25
Palpebral arteries, medial/lateral, **2:**37*f*, **5:**14*f*, 15*f*
Palpebral conjunctiva, **2:**29, 30*f*, 34, **4:**47, 48*f*, 205, 206*f*, **8:**4, 6. *See also* Conjunctiva
Palpebral fissures, **2:**22, 22*f*, 29*f*, **7:**143
in infants and children, **6:**169
congenital widening of (euryblepharon), **6:**177, **7:**146–147, 148*f*, 149*f*
slanting of, **6:**178
A- and V-pattern deviations and, **6:**110, 110*f*
in Treacher Collins syndrome, **6:**178, 393–394, 394*f*
surgery affecting, **6:**24–25
vertical height of, **5:**275, 276*f*
in ptosis, **6:**179, **7:**202, 202*f*
Palpebral lacrimal gland, **2:**32, 32*f*, 239
Palpebral muscles, **5:**61–62
Palpebral vein, inferior/superior, **5:**25*f*
Palpebral vernal conjunctivitis/keratoconjunctivitis, **6:**198–199, 199*f*, **8:**187, 188*f*
PALS. *See* Pediatric advanced life support; Progressive addition lenses
Palsy. *See specific type or structure affected and* Paralysis
PAM. *See* Potential acuity meter; Primary acquired melanosis
2-PAM. *See* Pralidoxime
PAMPs (pathogen-associated molecular patterns), **1:**3
PAN. *See* Periodic alternating nystagmus; Polyarteritis nodosa
Pan American Health Organization, **1:**283
Pancoast syndrome, **5:**267
Pancreas
β cells in, in diabetes mellitus, **1:**190
injection of in management and, **1:**202
cancer of, **1:**275
transplantation of, for diabetes mellitus, **1:**202
Pancreatitis, Purtscherlike retinopathy and, **12:**154, 155*t*
Pancuronium, **2:**344
adverse effects of, **2:**343*f*
Panel control ultrasound, for phacoemulsification, **11:**106
Panel D-15 (Farnsworth) test, **3:**294, **12:**48–50, 49*f*
in anomalous trichromatism, **12:**214
in low vision evaluation, **5:**105
Panel tests of color vision, **12:**48–50, 49*f*
in anomalous trichromatism, **12:**213–214
Panencephalitis, subacute sclerosing, **8:**129, **9:**213–214, 214*f*
Panfundoscope contact lens, **3:**255, 256*f*
Panic disorder, **1:**249
Panipenem, **1:**59
Pannus/micropannus, **4:**89, 90*f*, **8:**25, 28*f*
contact lens wear causing, **8:**92
bandage contact lenses and, **8:**403
in trachoma/chlamydial conjunctivitis, **8:**155, 156*f*, 157
in vernal keratoconjunctivitis, **8:**187
Panophthalmitis
in nocardiosis, **9:**256
tuberculous, **12:**204
Panretinal photocoagulation. *See also* Photocoagulation; Scatter laser treatment
angle-closure glaucoma after, **10:**135
for branch retinal vein occlusion, **12:**124–125, 125*f*
for central retinal artery occlusion, **12:**140

for central retinal vein occlusion, **12**:132
for diabetic retinopathy, **12**:106–108, 108*f*, 109*f*
    DRS/ETDRS, **12**:107–108, 108*f*, 109*f*
indications for, **12**:340
lenses for, **12**:339, 340*t*
for lupus vasculitis, **12**:195
for neovascular glaucoma, **10**:127
for ocular ischemic syndrome, **12**:134
Panum's area of single binocular vision, **6**:40, 40*f*, 49
Panuveitis, **9**:78*t*, 90, 172–196, **12**:196–199. *See also specific cause and* Uveitis
in acute retinal necrosis, **9**:200
in Behçet disease, **9**:190–196, 190*f*, 191*t*, 192*f*, 193*f*, 194*f*
in children, **6**:267, 268*t*, 274–275, 274*f*
    familial juvenile systemic granulomatosis (Blau syndrome) and, **6**:274–275
    sarcoidosis and, **6**:274, 274*f*
    Vogt-Koyanagi-Harada (VKH) syndrome and, **6**:275
in leptospirosis, **9**:255
in Lyme disease, **9**:251
multifocal choroiditis and (MCP), **9**:148–150*t*, 161–164, 162*f*, 163*f*, **12**:186*t*, 191–192, 191*f*
    EBV infection and, **9**:164, 208
multiple sclerosis and, **9**:139
neovascularization in, **9**:303
noninfectious (autoimmune), **9**:172–196
prevalence of, **9**:91, 92*t*
retinal detachment and, **9**:302
sarcoid, **9**:172–177, 174*f*, 175*f*, 176*f*, **12**:196–197, 197*f*
    in children, **6**:274, 274*f*
in subretinal fibrosis and uveitis syndrome (SFU), **9**:148–150*t*, 161, 167–168, 167*f*
sympathetic ophthalmia and, **4**:189, 189*f*, 190*f*, **9**:52–53, 178–183, 179*f*, 180*f*, 181*f*, 182*t*, **12**:198–199
in Vogt-Koyanagi-Harada (VKH) syndrome, **9**:183–190, 185*f*, 186*f*, 187*t*, 188*f*, **12**:197–198, 198*f*
    in children, **6**:275
in Whipple disease, **9**:265
Papanicolaou test (Pap smear), for cancer screening, **1**:272*t*, 273
in HIV infection/AIDS, **1**:33
Papillae
Bergmeister, **2**:85, **4**:132, 133, **6**:307, **12**:307
conjunctival, **8**:20*t*, 21–22, 22*f*, 22*t*, 23*f*
    in atopic keratoconjunctivitis, **8**:190, 191*f*
    in floppy eyelid syndrome, **8**:81, 81*f*
    in giant papillary (contact lens–induced) conjunctivitis, **8**:23*f*, 193, 194, 194*f*
    in palpebral vernal keratoconjunctivitis, **8**:187, 188*f*
    limbal, **4**:50
Papillary carcinoma of thyroid gland, **1**:213
Papillary conjunctivitis, **4**:50, 51*f*, **8**:22*t*, 23*f*
giant (contact lens–induced), **3**:200, **4**:50, **8**:23*f*, 194–195, 194*f*
in reactive arthritis/Reiter syndrome, **8**:209
Papillary muscle rupture, after myocardial infarction, **1**:103
Papilledema, **5**:116–117. *See also* Optic disc (optic nerve head), edema of
acute, **5**:116–121, 120*f*, 121*f*
in children, **6**:312

chronic, **5**:121–123, 121*f*, 122*f*
in craniosynostosis, **6**:391
in cryptococcal meningitis, **5**:367
drusen differentiated from, **5**:120, 120*f*, 134–136, 135*f*
in leukemia, **6**:298
pseudopapilledema and, **5**:118–120, 120*f*, **6**:313–315, 314*t*, 315*f*
pseudotumor cerebri and, **5**:123–125, 123*t*, **6**:312, 313
transient visual loss and, **5**:176
Papillitis, **5**:129
in acute posterior multifocal placoid pigment epitheliopathy (APMPPE), **9**:156
Papillomacular bundle/fibers, **2**:72, 73*f*, 75, **5**:29, 30*f*, 31
visual field defects and, **5**:116, 119*f*
Papillomas, **8**:129
conjunctival, **4**:61–62, 61*f*, **8**:128, 129, 226–228, 226*t*, 227*f*
eyelid, **4**:209, 209*f*, **7**:157–158, 157*f*, 158*f*
    in children, **6**:348
lacrimal sac, **7**:276–277
Papillomatosis, definition of, **4**:206
Papillomaviruses. *See* Human papillomaviruses
Papillopathy, diabetic, **5**:130–131, 131*f*
Papillophlebitis, **4**:164, **5**:131–132, 132*f*, **12**:128
Papillorenal syndrome, dysplastic optic nerve and, **5**:143
Papovaviruses/papovavirus infection, **8**:128–129
Papule, of eyelid, **8**:20*t*
Para-aminoclonidine. *See* Apraclonidine
Paracentesis
anterior chamber/aqueous
    in acute retinal necrosis, **9**:201
    in coccidioidomycosis, **9**:280
    in cysticercosis, **9**:238
    in endogenous endophthalmitis, **9**:272–273
    for hyphema, **8**:368
    in uveitis, **9**:96–97
in phacoemulsification, **11**:110
in trabeculectomy, **10**:188, 190*f*
Paracentral scotoma, **10**:68, 69*f*, 79
in age-related macular degeneration, **12**:64, 79
in central serous chorioretinopathy, **12**:171
in low vision, **3**:285, 286, 293
Paracentral zone, **8**:37, 37*f*
Paracrine actions, of cytokines, **9**:27
Paradoxical diplopia, **6**:52, 53*f*
Paradoxical pupillary phenomena, **5**:274, **6**:319, 319*t*, 414
Paraflocculus, **5**:48, 204
Parafollicular (C) cells, **1**:208
medullary carcinoma arising in, **1**:214
Parafovea, **2**:80*f*, 81, **4**:146, **12**:8, 9*f*, 9*t*
Parafoveal/juxtafoveal retinal telangiectasia, **12**:145–147, 145*f*, 146*f*
Parakeratosis
in actinic keratosis, **4**:217, 217*f*
definition of, **4**:206
Parallax, **13**:96, 96*f*
Paralysis (paresis/paretic syndromes). *See also specific type or structure affected*
diplopia caused by, **5**:226–235, 228*f*, 229*f*, 232*f*, 234*f*, 236
    restrictive syndromes differentiated from, **5**:218, 219*f*
in multiple sclerosis, **5**:323

Paralysis of accommodation, for refraction in infants and children, 3:141
Paralysis of gaze, psychic. *See* Ocular motor apraxia
Paralytic ectropion, 7:191*f*, 216, 217*f*
Paralytic lagophthalmos, 7:216–217
Paralytic strabismus, Hering's law and, 6:35
Paramedian pontine reticular formation, 2:104, 104*f*, 5:39, 39*f*, 42, 46*f*, 199
Paramedian tracts, 5:39
Paramyxoviruses, 8:129
Paranasal sinuses, 2:12–13, 13*f*, 14*f*, 5:7, 7:5, 17–19, 18*f*
  Aspergillus causing infection of, 7:46
  nasolacrimal duct obstruction caused by disorders of, 7:266
  neuroimaging in evaluation of disorders of, 5:82*t*
  orbital cellulitis caused by infection of, 6:195, 196, 196*f*, 7:40, 41, 42, 42*t*
  orbital tumors originating in, 7:88–89, 89*f*, 90*f*
  preseptal cellulitis caused by infection of, 6:195, 7:40, 41
  silent sinus syndrome caused by infection of, 7:89
  tuberculous infection of, orbital involvement and, 7:45
  in Wegener granulomatosis, 9:145
Paraneoplastic disorders
  bilateral diffuse uveal melanocytic proliferation, 12:183, 183*f*
  pemphigus, 8:205*t*
  retinopathies, 5:114–115, 12:256–257, 256*f*
  saccadic intrusions caused by, 5:255–256
Paranoia, in older patients, 1:226–227
Paraprotein, corneal deposition of, 8:319–320
Parasellar region, 5:6–7
  lesions of
    chiasm affected by, 5:162–165, 163*f*
    meningiomas, 5:164
    nystagmus caused by, 5:254
  neuroimaging in evaluation of, 5:82*t*, 85, 88
Parasellar (sphenocavernous) syndrome, 5:236
Parasites, ocular infection caused by, 8:140–143. *See also specific organism or type of infection*
  cornea and scleral involvement and, 8:167–169
  eyelid margin involvement and, 8:148–149
  Mooren ulcer and, 8:214, 215
  orbital involvement and, 4:235, 7:47
Parasitology, 8:140–143. *See also* Parasites
Parasol retinal ganglion cells, 6:42, 43*f*
Parastriate cortex (Brodmann area 18), 5:34, 6:42. *See also* Visual (calcarine/occipital) cortex
Parasympathetic ganglia/nerves/pathway, 5:65–67, 65*f*, 66*f*
  cholinergic drug action and, 2:334, 335*f*
  in ciliary ganglion, 2:14, 15*f*
  ciliary muscle innervation and, 2:64
  cranial nerve III (oculomotor) and, 2:98–99
  cranial nerve VII (facial) and, 2:106, 107
  dilator muscle innervation and, 2:60
  orbit supplied by, 7:17
  in reflex tear arc, 7:244
  sphincter muscle innervation and, 2:61, 258
  in tear secretion, 2:237, 240, 242, 242*f*, 243, 243*f*
Parasympatholytic agents, accommodation affected by, 11:19

Parasympathomimetic agents
  accommodation affected by, 11:19
  for glaucoma, 10:164*t*, 171–172
Parathyroid hormone (PTH), recombinant, for osteoporosis, 1:231
Paratopes, 9:37
Paratrigeminal syndrome, Raeder, 5:268–269
Paraxial rays, 3:56–57, 62*f*
  approximation/tracing of, 3:56–57, 57*f*, 58*f*
    small-angle approximation and, 3:57–60, 57*f*, 58*f*
    through concave lenses, 3:73–74, 73*f*, 74*f*
    through convex lenses, 3:69–72, 71*f*
  lens combination analysis and, 3:66–67
  power and, 3:61–62, 62*f*
Parcaine. *See* Proparacaine
Paredrine. *See* Hydroxyamphetamine
Paremyd. *See* Hydroxyamphetamine
Parental age, chromosomal aberrations in Down syndrome and, 2:201, 202
Paresis. *See specific type and* Paralysis
Pareto chart, 1:344, 345*f*
Parietal bone, 5:7
Parietal cortex, posterior, 5:36*f*, 40*f*, 41
Parietal lobe lesions, 5:168–169
  hallucinations and, 5:190–191
Parieto-occipital artery, 5:22*f*, 23, 23*f*
Parinaud oculoglandular syndrome, 4:52, 8:157–158, 9:263, 12:206. *See also* Cat-scratch disease
  in children, 6:189–190, 190*f*
Parinaud (dorsal midbrain) syndrome, 5:44, 211, 212*f*
  eyelid retraction in, 5:211, 273, 281, 7:214
  nystagmus in, 6:325
Parkinson disease/parkinsonism, 1:258–260
  convergence insufficiency in, 5:213
  with dementia, 1:265
  facial weakness/paralysis in, 5:285
  medications for, tear production affected by, 8:66*t*
  ophthalmic considerations in, 1:260
  postencephalitis, oculogyric crisis in, 5:212
  pursuit disorders in, 5:213
Parks-Bielschowsky 3-step test. *See* 3-step test
Parlodel. *See* Bromocriptine
Parotidomasseteric fascia, 7:133
Paroxetine, mydriasis caused by, 1:255
Paroxysmal hemicrania, 5:299
Paroxysmal nocturnal hemoglobinuria, 1:150
  hypercoagulability and, 1:158
  screening test for, 1:147
Paroxysmal supraventricular tachycardia, 1:124*t*
Parry-Romberg syndrome, 8:324*t*
Pars plana, 2:61, 4:186, 187*f*
  cryoablation of, for pars planitis, 9:137–138
  in uveitis, 9:79, 86*t*. *See also* Pars planitis
Pars plana lensectomy, 11:132
  for uveitis, 9:292, 293
    juvenile idiopathic (chronic/rheumatoid) arthritis and, 9:131
Pars plana magnet extraction, of foreign body, 12:327
Pars plana vitrectomy, 12:345–346. *See also* Vitrectomy
  angle-closure glaucoma after, 10:135
  for aqueous misdirection (malignant/ciliary block glaucoma), 10:133
  for branch retinal vein occlusion, 12:126

for capsular rupture during cataract surgery,
11:160–161
cataract/cataract surgery after, 11:205–206
for choroidal neovascularization, 12:351, 351f
uveitic, 9:303
for CMV retinitis, 12:201
for coccidioidomycosis, 9:280
complications of, 12:368, 368t
for cystoid macular edema, 12:143
postoperative, 12:360, 360f
in uveitis, 9:301
for diabetic retinopathy complications, 12:109–111,
352–353, 353f
macular edema, 12:103, 353
tractional retinal detachment, 12:110–111,
352–353, 353f
vitreous hemorrhage, 12:110, 352
for endophthalmitis
Aspergillus/mold, 9:277, 278f, 12:204
Candida/yeast, 9:275, 12:203
postoperative, 9:271, 11:181, 12:354–357, 355f,
356f, 357f
acute-onset, 12:354, 354–356, 355f
bleb-associated, 12:354, 356–357, 357f
chronic (delayed-onset), 12:355, 356, 356f
endophthalmitis after, 12:368
for epiretinal membranes, 12:301, 346, 347f, 348f
for foreign-body removal, 12:327
for Fuchs heterochromic iridocyclitis/uveitis, 9:134
for hemolytic/ghost cell glaucoma, 10:100
for idiopathic macular hole, 12:305–306, 349, 350f
for intraocular lymphoma diagnosis, 4:142, 324
for macular diseases, 12:346–352
open-angle glaucoma after, 12:368
pars plana lensectomy and, 11:132
for pars planitis, 9:138, 12:196
with phacoemulsification, in uveitis, 9:293
for postoperative endophthalmitis, 12:354–357, 355f,
356f, 357f
in primary central nervous system lymphoma, 9:282,
283
for retained lens fragments after phacoemulsification,
11:159–160, 12:357–359, 358t, 359f
for retinal detachment, 12:290
in CMV retinitis, 9:307
complex detachment, 12:367
in diabetes mellitus, 12:110–111, 352–353, 353f
in uveitis, 9:302
for subfoveal choroidal neovascularization, 12:351, 351f
for submacular hemorrhage, 12:349–351, 350f
for suprachoroidal hemorrhage, 12:360–361, 362f
sympathetic ophthalmia and, 9:178
for uveal lymphoid infiltration diagnosis, 4:326
for uveitic neovascularization, 9:303
for uveitis, 9:292, 293, 301
juvenile idiopathic (chronic/rheumatoid) arthritis–
associated, 9:131
vitreous biopsy and, 9:97
for vitreous opacification/vitritis, 9:302
Pars planitis, 9:78t, 79, 135–139, 135f, 12:196. See also
Intermediate uveitis; Uveitis
in children, 6:272, 273f
diagnosis of, 6:268t
clinical characteristics of, 9:135–136, 135f

complications of, 9:138–139
cystoid macular edema and, 9:135, 137, 138
diagnosis/differential diagnosis of, 6:268t, 9:136
HLA association in, 9:72t, 135
multiple sclerosis and, 9:136, 139
neovascularization in, 9:135–136, 138–139, 303
prognosis for, 9:136–137
retinal detachment and, 9:302
in toxocariasis, 9:136, 235
treatment of, 9:137–138
vitreous opacification and, 9:302
Pars plicata, 2:59f, 61, 4:186, 187f, 10:17f
Partial (bridge) conjunctival flap, 8:400
Partial polarization, 3:10
metallic reflection and, 3:13
Partial seizures, 1:261
Partial third nerve palsy, 5:230
Partial thromboplastin time, activated (aPTT), 1:152
Partially accommodative esotropia, 6:95
Particle characteristics of light, 3:3, 7
Particle–wave duality, 3:7
Partition coefficient, drug lipid solubility and, 2:326
Parvocellular neurons (P cells/system), 5:28, 33, 6:43,
43f, 44, 10:40
development of, 6:43, 43f, 44
abnormal visual experience affecting, 6:46, 48
PAS. See Peripheral anterior synechiae
PAS (periodic acid–Schiff) stain, 4:30, 31t
Passive immunization, 1:280
Passive transport, in aqueous humor dynamics, 2:254,
254–255
Pataday. See Olopatadine
Patanol. See Olopatadine
Patching
acute esotropia caused by, 6:96
for amblyopia, 6:66–67
after cataract surgery, 6:259
compliance issues and, 6:66–67, 68
for consecutive esotropia, 6:103
for corneal abrasion, 8:372
in children, 6:407
for dissociated vertical deviation, 6:117
for esotropia in sixth nerve (abducens) paralysis, 6:98
for hyphema, 10:98
for intermittent exotropia, 6:102
occlusion amblyopia caused by, 6:64, 67–68
orbital surgery and, 7:115
for perforating injury, 8:375
for residual exotropia, 6:103
Patellar fossa, 12:7
Path, optical, length of, 3:53, 53f
Pathergy, in Behçet disease, 1:180, 9:192
Pathogen-associated molecular patterns (PAMPs), 1:3
Pathologic myopia. See High (pathologic/degenerative)
myopia
Pathology, ophthalmic. See Ophthalmic pathology
Patient, perimetry variations and, 10:55, 56
Patient database, monitoring systems and, 1:340–342
Patient education
in age-related macular degeneration, 12:60
for medication instillation, 10:175–176
in children, 10:156
compliance and, 10:177
in vision rehabilitation, 3:304–305

Patient examination. *See* Examination
Patient selection/preparation. *See also* Preoperative
assessment/preparation for ocular surgery
for conductive keratoplasty, 13:120–122
for intrastromal corneal ring segments for myopia,
13:57
for LASIK, 13:71–73
for monovision, 13:153
for multifocal IOLs, 3:229, 13:145
for phakic IOLs, 13:128–129
for photoablation, 13:70–73, 71*t*
for refractive lens exchange/clear lens extraction,
13:138–139
for surface ablation, 13:70–71
for toric IOLs, 13:142–143
Pattern-deviation plot, 5:101
Pattern dystrophies, 4:175, 176*f*, 12:240–241, 240*f*,
241*f*
adult-onset foveomacular vitelliform, 4:175, 176*f*,
12:237–238, 238*f*
age-related macular degeneration differentiated from,
12:60, 69
butterfly, 4:175, 12:240, 240*f*
Pattern electroretinogram, 5:110, 12:38–39, 39*f*
Pattern scanners, for photocoagulation, 12:340
Pattern standard deviation, 10:59
Pauciarticular (oligoarticular)-onset juvenile
idiopathic (chronic/rheumatoid) arthritis
(oligoarthritis), 1:166, 6:269, 269*t*, 9:129. *See
also* Juvenile idiopathic (chronic/rheumatoid)
arthritis
eye examination schedule for children with, 6:271*t*,
9:131*t*
uveitis in, 6:269, 9:129–130, 130*f*
Paving-stone (cobblestone) degeneration, 4:156, 156*f*,
12:281–282, 281*f*
PAX genes, 2:115, 142, 147, 153, 206. *See also specific
type*
in aniridia, 2:141, 166, 205, 206, 216, 4:188, 6:223–224,
233, 10:142, 11:29
PAX2 gene, mutation in, 2:141, 166
optic nerve dysplasia and, 5:143
PAX3 gene, mutation in, 2:166, 216
PAX6 gene, 2:115, 205, 206
mutation in, 2:141, 166, 206
in aniridia, 2:141, 166, 206, 216, 4:188, 6:223–224,
233, 10:142, 11:29
in congenital aphakia, 4:121
in foveal hypoplasia, 6:292
in Peters anomaly, 8:258, 10:142, 11:28
Paxil. *See* Paroxetine
PC. *See* Posterior commissure
PCA. *See* Posterior cerebral artery
PCD. *See* Programmed cell death
PCG. *See* Primary congenital glaucoma
PCI. *See* Percutaneous coronary intervention
PCIOLs (posterior chamber intraocular lenses). *See*
Intraocular lenses (IOLs), posterior chamber
PCNSL. *See* Primary intraocular/central nervous system
lymphomas
PCO. *See* Posterior capsular opacification
PCoA. *See* Posterior communicating artery
PCP. *See Pneumocystis jiroveci (Pneumocystis carinii)*
infections, pneumonia

PCPIOL (posterior chamber phakic intraocular lenses).
See Phakic intraocular lenses, posterior chamber
PCR. *See* Polymerase chain reaction
PCV. *See* Polypoidal choroidal vasculopathy
PCV (pneumococcal vaccine), 1:7, 284–285
PDCD. *See* Pre-Descemet corneal dystrophy
PDE. *See* Phosphodiesterase
PDGF. *See* Platelet-derived growth factors
PDR. *See* Diabetic retinopathy, proliferative
PDT. *See* Photodynamic therapy
Pearl cyst, of iris, 4:270*t*
Pearson marrow-pancreas syndrome, 2:175
mitochondrial DNA deletions and, 2:173, 175
Peau d'orange, in pseudoxanthoma elasticum, 12:84,
84*f*
"Peculiar substance," in Meesmann corneal dystrophy,
8:272
PED (pigment epithelial detachment). *See* Retinal
pigment epithelium (RPE), detachment of
Pediatric advanced life support (PALS), 1:289, 293
Pediatric cataract. *See* Cataract, pediatric
Pediatric corneal transplantation, 6:219, 8:430–431,
431*t*
Pediatric electroretinogram, 6:415, 12:40, 41*f*
Pediatric glaucoma. *See* Glaucoma, childhood
Pedicle, of cone, 2:74, 77*f*
Pedicle flap, 7:182
for canthal repair, 7:186
Pediculus (pediculosis/lice)
humanus capitis, 8:149
humanus corporis, 8:149
ocular infection caused by, 8:142, 142*f*, 149
cholinesterase inhibitors for, 2:340
Pedigree analysis, 2:225–226, 226*f*
Pedunculated papillomas, conjunctival, 4:61, 61*f*
PEG-400, in demulcents, 2:390
Pegaptanib, 2:396
for age-related macular degeneration/choroidal
neovascularization, 12:73
for macular edema, 4:160, 169
in diabetes mellitus, 12:100
for ocular histoplasmosis syndrome, 9:225
Peginterferon-α$_{2a}$. *See also* Interferons
for hepatitis C, 1:26
Pelizaeus-Merzbacher disease, pigmentary retinopathy
and, 12:251*t*
Pelli-Robson chart/test, 3:111, 292, 5:105, 12:51–52, 51*f*
Pellucid marginal degeneration, 4:91, 8:301–302, 301*f*,
302*t*, 303*f*
refractive surgery contraindicated in, 8:44, 13:18, 38,
167–168
corneal topography and, 13:18–19, 19*f*, 38, 38*f*, 71,
167–168, 169*f*
Pelopsia, 5:189
Pelvic examination, for cancer screening, 1:272*t*
Pemirolast, 2:365, 365*t*, 366
Pemphigoid
bullous, 8:205*t*
cicatricial (mucous membrane), 4:54, 56*f*, 8:180, 196*t*,
198–203, 199*t*, 200*f*, 201*f*, 202*f*, 205*t*
cataract surgery in patient with, 11:191
drug-induced (pseudopemphigoid), 8:199, 361
mucous membrane grafting for, 8:401
gestational, 8:205*t*

Pemphigus
  foliaceus, **8**:205*t*
  IgA, **8**:205*t*
  paraneoplastic, **8**:205*t*
  vulgaris, **8**:200, 205*t*
Pen-Vee K. *See* Penicillin V
Penalization
  for amblyopia, **6**:67
  for dissociated vertical deviation, **6**:117
Penbutolol, **1**:76*t*
Penciclovir, **2**:383
  for herpes simplex virus infections, **8**:109*t*
Pencil of light, **3**:28, 41
Pendular nystagmus, **5**:243, 244, 244*f*, **6**:317
  acquired, **5**:244*f*, 253
  in multiple sclerosis, **5**:325
Penetrance/penetrant gene, **2**:157, 209
  familial, **2**:216
  incomplete (skipped generation), **2**:209, 217
Penetrating injuries, **12**:324. *See also* Perforating
    injuries; Trauma
  canthal soft tissue, **7**:178–180
  in children, **6**:408–409, 408*f*
  definition of, **8**:373
  endophthalmitis after, **12**:328–329
  eyelid, **7**:178–180, 179*f*. *See also* Lacerations, eyelid
  fibrocellular proliferation and, **4**:20
  fibrous ingrowth/angle-closure glaucoma and,
    10:134, 134*f*
  lens damage caused by, **11**:51, 51*f*, 52*f*
    glaucoma and, **11**:63
  needle penetration/perforation and, **12**:362, 363*f*
  retinal breaks caused by, **12**:272
  sympathetic ophthalmia and, **9**:52–53, 178, 180, 181,
    182*t*, **12**:198, 329–330
  tractional retinal detachment and, **12**:291, 324
Penetrating keratoplasty. *See* Keratoplasty, penetrating
Penetrex. *See* Enoxacin
Penicillamine, for Wilson disease, **2**:231, **8**:327–328
Penicillin G, **1**:45*t*, 56, **2**:368*t*, 369
Penicillin-resistant *N gonorrhoeae*, **8**:152, 153
Penicillin V (phenoxymethyl penicillin), **1**:45*t*, 56, **2**:369
Penicillinase, **2**:369
Penicillinase-resistant penicillins, **1**:56–57, **2**:369–370
Penicillins, **1**:45–47*t*, 56–57, **2**:368–369, 368*t*, 369–370.
  See also specific agent
  allergic reaction to, **1**:57, **2**:369
  broad-spectrum, **2**:370
  for leptospirosis, **9**:256
  penicillinase-resistant, **1**:56–57, **2**:369–370
  semisynthetic, **1**:45–47*t*
  for syphilis, **1**:14, 14*t*, **5**:361, **9**:248–249, 248*t*
    in HIV infection/AIDS, **9**:310
    in infants and children, **6**:186
Pentacam, for corneal power measurement, in IOL
    power determination, **3**:217, 217*f*
Pentagonal resection, for trichiasis, **7**:200
Pentam 300. *See* Pentamidine
Pentamidine, **1**:53*t*
  for *Pneumocystis jiroveci (Pneumocystis carinii)*
    pneumonia, **1**:37
Pentavac. *See* DTacP-IPV-Hib vaccine

Pentolair. *See* Cyclopentolate
Pentose phosphate pathway (hexose monophosphate
    shunt), in glucose/carbohydrate metabolism
  in cornea, **2**:248
  in lens, **2**:279, **11**:14*f*, 15
Penumbra, **1**:92
Pen-Vee K. *See* Penicillin V
Pepper Visual Skills for Reading test, **3**:290
Peptide fusion inhibitors, for HIV infection/AIDS, **1**:34
Peptide hormones
  in aqueous humor, **2**:267, 270
  in tear secretion, **2**:244
Peptidoglycan, in bacterial cell wall, **8**:132
Peptidyl-glycine-α-amidating monooxygenase, in
    aqueous humor, **2**:267, 270
"Percent agreement," **1**:339
Perception, age-related changes in, **1**:225
Perceptual completion, **3**:286
Perceptual distortion. *See* Metamorphopsia
Percheron, artery of, **5**:23
Percutaneous coronary intervention (PCI), **1**:99, 102,
    108–110, 112–113
  troponin levels in determining need for, **1**:105
Perennial allergic conjunctivitis, **6**:198, **8**:185–187
Perfluoropropane (C_3F_8)
  for retinal detachment, **12**:367
  for submacular hemorrhage, **12**:350–351
Perforating injuries. *See also* Penetrating injuries;
    Trauma
  anterior segment, **8**:373–382, 373*t*, 374*t*, 376*f*, 377*t*,
    378*f*, 379*f*, 381*f*, 382*f*
    ancillary tests in, **8**:374*t*
    evaluation of, **8**:373–374, 373*t*, 374*t*
    examination in, **8**:373–374, 374*t*
    history in, **8**:373, 373*t*
    management of, **8**:374–382
      nonsurgical, **8**:375
      postoperative, **8**:381–382
      preoperative, **8**:374–375
      surgical, **8**:375–381, 377*t*, 378*f*, 379*f*, 381*f*, 382*f*
    ocular signs of, **8**:374*t*
  definition of, **8**:373
  lens damage caused by, **11**:51, 51*f*, 52*f*
    glaucoma and, **11**:63
  needle penetration/perforation and, **12**:325, 362, 363*f*
  penetrating injury differentiated from, **8**:373
  posterior segment, **12**:325
    retinal breaks caused by, **12**:272
Perforators
  of basilar artery, **5**:21–23
  of posterior cerebral arteries, **5**:23
Perforin, **9**:51, 53*f*
Perforomist. *See* Formoterol
Perfused/nonischemic central retinal vein occlusion,
    12:127, 128, 128*f*
Perfusion pressure, ocular, glaucoma and, **10**:77
Perfusion-weighted magnetic resonance imaging, in
    cerebral ischemia/stroke, **1**:93
PERG. *See* Pattern electroretinogram
Pergolide, for Parkinson disease, **1**:259
Periarteriolar transudates, focal intraretinal (FIPTs),
    12:113, 114*f*

Peribulbar anesthesia, 1:312
  for cataract surgery, 11:99, 100f
  for extraocular muscle surgery, 6:160
  for phakic IOL insertion, 13:129
Pericanalicular connective tissue, 2:54, 55f
Pericarditis, after myocardial infarction, 1:103
Pericytes, retinal blood vessel, 2:78
Perifovea, 2:80f, 81, 4:146, 12:8, 9f, 9t
Perifoveal telangiectasia (type 2 parafoveal retinal
  telangiectasia), 12:14, 146f
Perifoveal vitreous detachment, posterior, 12:298
Perimacular folds, in shaking injury, 6:405
Perimetrist, perimetry variations and, 10:55
Perimetry, 5:99–104, 101f, 102f, 103f, 10:53–68. See also
  Visual field testing
  automated
    nonorganic ophthalmic disorder evaluation and,
      5:312, 313f
    short-wavelength (SWAP), 10:60–61
      in glaucoma suspect screening, 10:82–83
    standard (SAP/achromatic), 10:54, 73
    static, 5:100–104, 101f, 102f, 103f, 10:53–54, 54f,
      55, 56–58, 57f, 58f
      artifacts seen on, 10:56, 61–62, 62f, 63f
      in glaucoma, 10:53–54, 55, 56–58, 57f, 58f
      high false-negative rate in, 10:61–62
      high false-positive rate in, 10:61–62
      incorrect corrective lens used in, 10:61
      learning effect and, 10:64, 64f
      screening tests, 10:58
  blue-yellow, 10:60–61
    in glaucoma suspect screening, 10:82–83
  for central visual field assessment, 3:292
  clinical, 10:54–55
  definitions of terms used in, 10:54–55
  frequency-doubling technology (FDT), 10:61
    in glaucoma suspect screening, 10:82–83
  full-threshold, 10:57, 57f, 58
  in glaucoma, 10:53–68
    preperimetric glaucoma and, 10:4
  in glaucoma suspect screening, 10:82–83
  Goldmann, 5:99–100
    for central visual field assessment, 3:292
    in hereditary retinal/choroidal degenerations, 12:223
    in nonorganic ophthalmic disorders, 5:313, 314f
    in peripheral visual field assessment, 3:292
    in photoreceptor dystrophies, 12:223, 225f
    in strabismus/amblyopia evaluation, 6:83
  interpretation in
    artifacts and, 10:56, 61–62, 62f, 63f
    comparison of techniques and, 10:59–61
    normality versus abnormality of field and, 10:59, 60f
    optic disc changes and, 10:66–67
    progression of defect and, 10:65–66, 65f, 66f, 67f
    quality of field and, 10:59
    serial fields, 10:62–68, 64f, 65f, 66f, 67f
    single field, 10:59–62, 60f, 62f, 63f
  kinetic, 5:99, 10:54f, 55
    for central visual field assessment, 3:292
    in hereditary retinal/choroidal degenerations, 12:223
    for peripheral visual field assessment, 3:292
    in photoreceptor dystrophies, 12:223, 225f

  in optic neuropathy, 5:118t
  patterns of nerve loss and, 10:68, 69f, 70f, 71f, 72f
  for peripheral visual field assessment, 3:292
  preperimetric glaucoma and, 10:4
  screening, 10:58
  static, 5:99, 99–100, 10:54f, 55
    automated. See Perimetry, automated, static
    for central visual field assessment, 3:292
    for peripheral visual field assessment, 3:292
  suprathreshold, 10:54
  Swedish interactive thresholding algorithm, 5:101,
    10:57, 58
  tangent screen in, 5:99. See also Tangent screen
  tendency-oriented algorithm (TOP), 10:57
  threshold, 10:54, 57, 58, 58f
  variables in, 10:55–56
Perinatal ocular infection, 6:181–186. See also specific
  type
Perindopril, 1:76t
Perineural invasion, pain caused by, 5:303
Perineuritis
  optic (perioptic neuritis), 5:147
  radial, Acanthamoeba keratitis and, 8:167
Periocular drug administration, 2:327
  for pars planitis, 9:137
  for uveitis, 9:101t, 102–103, 102f
Periocular tissues
  development of, 2:139–140
  malpositions/involutional changes and, 7:189–239.
    See also specific type
    blepharochalasis, 7:222
    blepharoplasty and, 7:222–227
    blepharoptosis (ptosis), 7:201–213
    brow ptosis, 7:227–228
    dermatochalasis, 7:221–222
    ectropion, 7:190–194
    entropion, 7:194–199
    eyelid retraction, 7:213–216
    facial dystonia, 7:218–221
    facial paralysis, 7:216–218
    facial surgery and
      cosmetic surgery, 7:228–229
      rejuvenation surgery, 7:230–238
    history/examination/preoperative considerations
      and, 7:189–190
    pathogenesis of aging face and, 7:228–229
    symblepharon, 7:199–200
    trichiasis, 7:200
  prostaglandin analogues affecting pigmentation of,
    10:162t, 166
Periodic acid–Schiff (PAS) stain, 4:30, 31t
Periodic alternating gaze deviation, in comatose
  patients, 5:259
Periodic alternating nystagmus, 5:251t, 252–253,
  6:322
Periodic alternating skew deviation, 5:223
Perioperative management in ocular surgery
  intraoperative complications and, 1:310–313, 313t
  preoperative assessment and, 1:303–310, 304t
  recent developments and, 1:303
Perioperative medications, 1:309t
Perioptic neuritis, 5:147

Periorbita (periorbital structures), 7:10, 17–19, 18f. See
    also specific structure
  capillary hemangiomas involving, 7:24
  cellulitis affecting, 7:39t, 40–44. See also Orbital
    cellulitis; Preseptal cellulitis
  ecchymosis of
    in blowout fractures, 7:100
    in child abuse, 6:404
    in neuroblastoma, 6:336, 336f
  innervation of, 7:13–17, 16f
  involutional changes in, 7:221–222, 221f
  orbital diseases causing changes in, 7:21, 22t
Periorbital pain, 5:301
  in optic neuritis, 5:91–92, 144
Periorbital sinuses, 2:12–13, 13f, 14f
Peripapillary atrophy, in glaucoma, 10:50
Peripapillary fibers, 2:90
  assessment of, 5:96, 96f
  gliosis of, 5:121, 121f
Peripapillary staphyloma, 6:310, 415
Peripheral airway disease, 1:142
Peripheral anterior synechiae (PAS), in glaucoma
  angle closure and, 10:109, 113, 117
    inflammation and, 10:130, 131, 131f
  anterior segment/iris neovascularization and, 10:37,
    37f, 124, 125, 126f
  chamber deepening/goniosynechialysis in
    management of, 10:204
  flat anterior chamber and, 10:136
  gonioscopy in identification of, 10:37, 37f
  iridocorneal endothelial (ICE) syndrome and, 4:105,
    105f, 10:128, 128f
  plateau iris and, 10:120
  uveitis and, 9:296
Peripheral arterial arcade, 2:23f, 25f, 30, 34
  eyelids supplied by, 7:135f, 143
  superior, 5:14f
Peripheral arterial/peripheral vascular disease
  in diabetes mellitus, 1:207
  hypertension and, 1:85
Peripheral corneal guttae (Hassall-Henle bodies/warts),
    2:45, 8:334, 345
Peripheral curve, of contact lens, 3:168f, 169
  rigid gas-permeable contact lens fitting and, 3:184t,
    185
Peripheral cystoid degeneration, 4:154, 154f, 12:282
  reticular, 4:154, 154f, 12:282, 293
  typical, 4:154, 154f, 12:282, 292
Peripheral fusion, 6:41
  in monofixation syndrome, 6:60
Peripheral (surgical) iridectomy. See also Iridectomy
  for angle-closure glaucoma, 10:201, 201f, 203, 204
  for bacterial keratitis, 8:164
  with penetrating keratoplasty, 8:420
Peripheral iridoplasty, for plateau iris, 10:120, 120f, 203
Peripheral iris suture fixation, for intraocular lens
    decentration, 11:163–164, 164f
Peripheral keratitis, 8:27t
  scleritis and, 8:220
  ulcerative, 8:211–213, 211t, 212f, 339
    differential diagnosis of, 8:211t
    in polyarteritis nodosa/microscopic polyangiitis,
      1:179, 9:143

  in systemic immune-mediated diseases, 8:211–213,
    211t, 212f
  in Wegener granulomatosis, 1:179
Peripheral nervous system disorders, Sjögren syndrome
    and, 8:63
Peripheral neurofibromatosis, 10:148. See also
    Neurofibromatosis, von Recklinghausen
Peripheral resistance, reduction of in heart failure
    management, 1:118–119
Peripheral retina, 12:8
  excavations of, 12:280
  neovascularization of, 12:121, 122t
    vitreous hemorrhage and, 12:313, 314
Peripheral retinal tufts, 12:278, 279f, 280f
Peripheral (anterior) retina
  abnormalities affecting. See also specific disorder and
    Retinal detachment
  neovascularization of. See also Neovascularization
Peripheral suppression, 6:50
Peripheral surgical space (extraconal fat/surgical space),
    7:10, 107, 107f
Peripheral ulcerative keratitis. See Peripheral keratitis,
    ulcerative
Peripheral uveitis. See Intermediate uveitis; Pars planitis
Peripheral vestibular nystagmus, 5:248–250, 249t
Peripheral visual field deficit, 3:288, 292. See also Visual
    field defects
  in glaucoma, 10:68, 72f
Peripheral zone, 8:37, 37f
Peripherin, 2:293, 12:228
Peripherin/RDS gene mutations, 2:296, 12:222
  in adult-onset vitelliform lesions, 12:237
  in central areolar choroidal dystrophy, 12:245
  in pattern dystrophies, 4:175, 12:240
  in retinitis pigmentosa, 12:226, 228
  in Stargardt disease, 4:172, 12:234
Periphlebitis
  in multiple sclerosis, 9:139
  in sarcoidosis, 4:190, 8:74, 9:175, 176f
  in tuberculosis, 9:258
Peristaltic pump, for phacoemulsification aspiration,
    11:108, 108f
  vacuum rise time for, 11:108, 110f
Peritomy incision
  for extraocular muscle surgery, 6:154
  for Gundersen flap, 8:399f, 400
Periungal fibroma, in tuberous sclerosis, 5:341, 342f
Periventricular leukomalacia, 6:309
PERK (Prospective Evaluation of Radial Keratotomy)
    study, 13:43–44
Perkins tonometer, 10:23
  in infants and children, 6:236, 10:151
  infection control and, 10:26
Perls Prussian blue stain, 4:31t
Permax. See Pergolide
Pernicious anemia, 1:149
Peroxidase, 2:312f, 317, 8:179t
Peroxidation, lipid, 2:311, 312–313
  in lens opacification, 11:16
Peroxisomal disorders, 12:261–262
  pigmentary retinopathy in, 12:254, 261–262
  retinal degeneration in, 6:398
Peroxy radicals, 2:311, 312, 313. See also Free radicals

Persantine. *See* Dipyridamole
Persistence, as microbial virulence factor, 8:99
Persistent corneal epithelial defects, 8:85–89, 88*f*
    after cataract surgery, 11:150
    glaucoma medication toxicity and, 10:29
    after LASIK, 13:104–105
    ocular infection and, 8:99
    after penetrating keratoplasty, 8:422, 423*f*
    after surface ablation, 13:100
Persistent fetal vasculature (persistent hyperplastic
        primary vitreous), 4:132–133, 132*f*, 304–305,
        305*t*, 6:250, 250*t*, 252*f*, 279–280, 279*f*, 307, 11:38,
        12:307–309, 308*f*
    Bergmeister papilla and. *See* Bergmeister papilla
    cataract and, 4:132, 6:250, 250*t*, 252*f*, 279, 280, 11:38,
        12:308, 308*f*
    glaucoma and, 6:250, 280, 10:136, 12:308
    lensectomy and, 6:256
    microcornea and, 6:212
    retinoblastoma differentiated from, 4:304–305, 305*t*,
        12:308
Persistent hyaloid artery/system, 4:132–133, 132*f*, 133,
        12:307, 308. *See also* Persistent fetal vasculature
Persistent pupillary membranes, 2:139*f*, 6:228, 229*f*
Personal emergency kits, 1:296
Personality/personality disorders, 1:249
    in central serous chorioretinopathy, 12:172
Pes anscrinus, 2:106
PET. *See* Positron emission tomography
Petechiae, 1:153
Peters anomaly, 2:141, 166, 4:81–82, 81*f*, 102, 6:215–216,
        215*f*, 8:256–258, 257*f*, 261*t*, 10:142, 146, 11:27–28.
        See also Axenfeld-Rieger syndrome
    Axenfeld-Rieger syndrome differentiated from,
        10:146*t*
    glaucoma and, 6:238, 10:142, 146
Petit mal (absence) seizures, 1:261
Petroclinoid (Gruber) ligament, 2:104, 5:50
Petrosal nerve
    deep, 2:107
    greater superficial, 2:106, 107, 5:16, 61
    inferior, 2:106
Petrosal sinuses, inferior/superior, 2:108, 108*f*, 5:26, 26*f*,
        27*f*, 50
Petrous bone, 5:7
    inflammation of, sixth nerve (abducens) palsy and,
        5:234–235
PEX syndrome. *See* Pseudoexfoliation
PEX1 gene, Refsum disease caused by mutations in,
        2:298
Pfeiffer syndrome, 6:388
PFL. *See* Posterior focal length
PFV. *See* Persistent fetal vasculature
PG. *See* Prostaglandins; Proteoglycans
PG analogues. *See* Prostaglandin analogues
PG/PGH synthetase (prostaglandin synthetase/
        prostaglandin G/H synthetase). *See* Cyclooxygenase
PGI$_2$. *See* Prostacyclin
pH, of ocular medication, absorption affected by, 2:326
PHACE(S) syndrome, 6:339, 339*f*
Phaco burn, 8:384
Phaco chop technique, 11:122–124, 124*f*
Phaco fracture technique, 11:121–122, 122*f*, 123*f*

Phaco handpiece, 11:105–106, 105*f*, 106*f*, 107*f*
Phaco tip, 11:105–106, 105*f*, 106*f*, 107*f*
Phacoanaphylactic endophthalmitis/uveitis, 9:125,
        11:62. *See also* Phacoantigenic (lens-associated)
        uveitis
Phacoanaphylaxis. *See* Phacoantigenic glaucoma
Phacoantigenic glaucoma, 10:90*t*, 92
Phacoantigenic (lens-associated) uveitis (lens-
        induced granulomatous/phacoanaphylactic
        endophthalmitis), 4:122, 122*f*, 123*f*, 9:125–126, 125*f*,
        11:62
    sympathetic ophthalmia and, 9:182
Phacodonesis, cataract surgery and, 11:197
    in glaucoma, 11:202
    in exfoliation syndrome/pseudoexfoliation, 10:86–87
Phacoemulsification, 11:102–126. *See also* Cataract
        surgery
    for advanced cataract, 11:195–196
    anterior capsulotomy for, 11:115, 116*f*
    in anterior chamber, 11:119
    in anticoagulated patient, 11:189
    aspiration system for, 11:108–109, 108*f*, 109*f*, 110*f*
        strategies for use of, 11:125–126
    burst-mode, 11:107
    capsular opacification and, 11:169–171
        Nd:YAG laser capsulotomy for, 11:169, 171–175,
            174*f*. *See also* Nd:YAG laser therapy, capsulotomy
    capsular rupture during, 11:144*t*, 160–162
    capsulorrhexis in, 11:115–117, 116*f*
        loose zonules and, 11:117
    clear corneal incision for, 11:113–115, 113*f*, 115*f*
        in uveitis, 9:292
    continuous, 11:106–107
    corneal complications of, 8:384
    cystoid macular edema after, 11:182
    flat or shallow anterior chamber and, 11:152–154
        intraoperative complications, 11:152–153
        postoperative complications, 11:153–154
    foldable intraocular lenses for, 11:135–136, 136*f*. *See
        also* Foldable intraocular lenses
    in glaucoma, 11:201–203
        combined with filtering surgery, 10:200
        after filtering surgery, 11:203
        intraocular pressure lowered by, 11:201
    globe exposure for, 11:110
    high myopia and, 11:200
    hydrodelineation in, 11:118
    hydrodissection in, 11:117–118
    incisions for. *See also* Incisions, for cataract surgery
        clear corneal incisions, 11:113–115, 113*f*, 115*f*
        scleral tunnel incisions, 11:111–113, 111*f*, 112*f*
    instrumentation for, 11:104–106, 105*f*, 106*f*, 107*f*
        settings for, 11:118–119
    for intumescent cataract extraction, 11:196
    at iris plane, 11:119–120, 120*f*
    irrigation in, 11:108
        posterior fluid misdirection and, 11:152–153
        strategies for, 11:125–126
        toxic solutions exposure and, corneal edema
            caused by, 11:147, 151–152
    lens particle glaucoma and, 11:63
    linear ultrasound and, 11:106
    locations of, 11:119–120, 120*f*, 121*f*

nuclear rotation in, **11**:118, 125*f*
nucleus disassembly/removal in
    locations for emulsification and, **11**:119–120, 120*f*, 121*f*
        techniques of, **11**:121–125, 122*f*, 123*f*, 124*f*, 125*f*
            chopping techniques, **11**:122–124, 124*f*
            one-handed, **11**:124–125, 125*f*
            phaco fracture, **11**:121–122, 122*f*, 123*f*
    ocular trauma affecting visualization and, **11**:206
    panel control ultrasound and, **11**:106
    paracentesis for, **11**:110
    after pars plana vitrectomy, **11**:205–206
    in posterior chamber, **11**:120, 121*f*
    for posterior polar cataract, **11**:196–197
    power delivery and, **11**:106–108
        advances in, **11**:126
    procedure for, **11**:110–126
    pulsed, **11**:107
    retained lens fragments after, **11**:143, 147, 159–160, **12**:357–359, 358*t*, 359*f*
    retinal detachment and, **11**:143, 144*t*, 184
    scleral tunnel incisions for, **11**:111–113, 111*f*, 112*f*
    supracapsular, **11**:121
    suprachoroidal effusion/hemorrhage risk and, **11**:177
    in triple procedure, **11**:141
    ultrasonics terminology and, **11**:102–104
    in uveitis, **9**:291, 292–293
        with pars plana vitrectomy, **9**:293
    vacuum terminology and, **11**:104
    after vitrectomy, **11**:205–206
    vitreocorneal adherence/persistent corneal edema and, **11**:148
    in zonular dehiscence/lens subluxation or dislocation, **11**:197–199, 198*f*
Phacolysis, fluid-based, **11**:127
Phacolytic glaucoma, **4**:106–107, 107*f*, 127, **9**:22, 126, **10**:90–91, 90*t*, 91*f*, **11**:63
Phacomorphic glaucoma, **10**:90*t*, 112, 120–121, 121*f*, 122*f*, **11**:63, 64*f*
Phacotoxic uveitis, **9**:125. *See also* Uveitis, lens-associated/phacoantigenic
Phagocytes, **9**:9, 20
Phagocytosis, **9**:19–20
    by retinal pigment epithelium, **2**:306–307, **12**:12, 15
Phagolysosomes/phagosomes, **9**:20
    in retinal pigment epithelium, **2**:72, 304, 306, **12**:15
Phakic intraocular lenses, **13**:4*t*, 41*t*, 125, 125–136, 127*t*, 130*f*, 131*f*, 132*t*, 133*t*
    advantages of, **13**:126
    for amblyopia, **13**:178
    ancillary preoperative tests for, **13**:129
    anterior chamber, **13**:4*t*
        angle-supported, **13**:127*t*, 129
            complications of, **13**:134–135
    background of, **13**:125–126
    in children, **13**:180–181
    complications of, **13**:133*t*, 134–136
    contraindications to, **13**:128
    decentration of, **13**:135, 145
    disadvantages/limitations of, **13**:41*t*, 126
    indications for, **13**:128

informed consent for, **13**:128
international trends in use of, **13**:200, 201
iris-fixated (iris-supported), **13**:4*t*, 126, 127*t*, 129–130, 130*f*
    complications of, **13**:135
    results of, **13**:132*t*
    sizing, **13**:130, 130*f*
    with LASIK (bioptics), **13**:125, 137
    outcomes of, **13**:131–134, 132*t*, 133*t*
    patient selection/evaluation for, **13**:128–129
    posterior chamber, **13**:4*t*, 126, 130–131, 130*f*, 131*f*
        complications of, **13**:136
        results with, **13**:132*t*
    retinal detachment and, **13**:135, 136
    sulcus-supported, **13**:127*t*
    surgical technique for insertion of, **13**:129–131, 130*f*, 131*f*
Phakinin, **2**:277, **11**:12
Phakoma/phakomatoses (neurocutaneous syndromes), **5**:338–345, 339*f*, **12**:148–151, 149*f*, 150*f*, 152*f*. *See also specific type*
    in children, **6**:363–381, 364*t*
    retinal. *See* Retina, phakomas of
Phakomatous choristoma (Zimmerman tumor), **4**:20*f*, 207, **8**:247
Pharmacodynamics, **2**:322, 331–332
Pharmacogenetics, **2**:157, 229–230
Pharmacokinetics, **2**:322, 323–331
    age-related changes in, **1**:222, **2**:323
Pharmacologic anisocoria, **5**:266, 270
Pharmacologic penalization, for amblyopia, **6**:67
Pharmacology, ocular. *See also specific agent and* Drugs, ocular
    age/aging and, **1**:222
    future research areas and, **2**:321
    legal aspects of, **2**:333–334
    principles of, **2**:321–332
Pharmacotherapeutics, **2**:322. *See also specific agent and* Drugs, ocular
    future research areas and, **2**:321
    principles of, **2**:321–332
Pharyngoconjunctival fever, **6**:191, **8**:124
Phasic cells, **2**:298, 300, 300*f*
Phenethicillin, **2**:369
Pheniramine, **2**:364
Pheniramine/naphazoline, **2**:364, 365*t*
Phenobarbital, for seizures, **1**:263*t*, 297
Phenocopy, **2**:157, 208
Phenol red–impregnated cotton thread test, of tear secretion, **8**:54
Phenothiazines
    corneal pigmentation caused by, **8**:346, 348–349
    lens changes caused by, **11**:48–49, 48*f*
    retinal degeneration caused by, **12**:267–268, 268*f*
Phenotype, **2**:157, 208
    alleles and, **2**:194–195
Phenoxybenzamine, **2**:259*t*, 260
Phenoxymethyl penicillin. *See* Penicillin V
Phentolamine, **2**:259*t*, 260
    for hypertension, **1**:83
Phenylalanine, in phenylketonuria, **2**:214
    dietary restriction and, **2**:231

Phenylalkanoic acids, **2**:362. *See also* Nonsteroidal anti-inflammatory drugs
Phenylbutazone, **1**:183*t*
Phenylephrine, **2**:259*t*, 260, 341*t*, 345–346, 392
    drug interactions and, **2**:345
    for fundus examination in premature infant, **6**:285
    Horner syndrome diagnosis and, **5**:266
    for uveitis, **9**:120
Phenylketonuria, enzyme defect in, **2**:214
Phenytoin, **1**:123*t*, 263*t*, 297
    ocular side effects of, **1**:264
Pheochromocytoma
    hypertension in, **1**:72, 72*t*
    in multiple endocrine neoplasia, **1**:216
    in von Hippel–Lindau disease, **6**:374
Phialophora, **8**:139
Philadelphia practical classification, for retinoblastoma, **6**:358
Phleboliths, orbital varices and, **7**:67
Phlyctenular keratoconjunctivitis, in children, **6**:351
Phlyctenules/phlyctenulosis, **8**:20*t*, 145–146, 146*f*, 147
PHMB. *See* Polyhexamethylene biguanide
PHN. *See* Postherpetic neuralgia
"Phone first principle, in emergencies, **1**:290
-phoria (suffix), **6**:10
Phorias, **6**:10. *See also* Heterophorias
    refractive surgery and, **13**:34, 181
Phoropters, for overrefraction, **3**:138
Phosphate, in aqueous humor, **2**:267
Phosphatidylcholine, in retinal pigment epithelium, **2**:305
Phosphatidylethanolamine, in retinal pigment epithelium, **2**:305
Phosphatidylinositol-3-phosphate/phosphatidylinositol 5-kinase type III *(PIP5K3)*, in Fleck corneal dystrophy, **8**:269*t*, 287
Phosphatidyl-inositol-4,5-bisphosphate (PIP_2), in signal transduction in iris–ciliary body, **2**:263, 263*f*
Phosphenes
    in electrically evoked cortical potential, **12**:45
    optic neuritis causing, **5**:190, 323
    retinal vasospasm (migraine) causing, **5**:190
Phosphodiesterase
    receptor–effector coupling and, **2**:262, 262*f*
    rod (rod PDE), **2**:293
        mutations in, **2**:295
Phosphodiesterase inhibitors, for heart failure, **1**:119
Phosphofructokinase, in lens glucose/carbohydrate metabolism, **11**:13, 14*f*
Phospholine. *See* Echothiophate
Phospholipase A_2, **9**:25, 26*f*, 27
    in eicosanoid synthesis, **2**:255, 256*f*
    nonsteroidal anti-inflammatory drug derivation and, **2**:361–362
    receptor–effector coupling and, **2**:262
    in tear film, **2**:240
Phospholipase C
    receptor–effector coupling and, **2**:262, 263*f*
    in tear secretion, **2**:242*f*, 243
Phospholipid antibody syndrome (antiphospholipid antibody syndrome), **1**:13, 158, 170–173. *See also* Antiphospholipid antibodies
    choroidal perfusion abnormalities and, **12**:179

Phospholipids. *See also* Lipids
    in retinal pigment epithelium, **2**:305
    in tear film, **2**:239. *See also* Lipid layer of tear film
Phosphonoformic acid. *See* Foscarnet
Photic damage/phototoxicity/light toxicity, **2**:313, 316, **3**:19, 160–161, 206, **12**:332–334
    age-related macular degeneration and, **12**:63
    ambient exposure to ultraviolet or visible light and, **12**:334
    cataract surgery and, **11**:183–184, **12**:333, 334
    free-radical damage and, **2**:313, 315–316
    occupational, **12**:334
    ophthalmic instrumentation causing, **12**:333–334
        cataract surgery and, **11**:183–184, **12**:333, 334
    retinal, **2**:315, 316, **3**:19, 160–161, 206, **12**:332–334
    in retinitis pigmentosa, **12**:231
    retinopathy of prematurity and, **6**:281
    solar retinopathy and, **12**:332–333
Photisms, in optic neuritis, **5**:190, 323
Photo-ROP Cooperative Group, **12**:165
Photoablation, **3**:25, **13**:23, 65–91, 66–67*f*. *See also* LASEK; LASIK; Surface ablation; Wavefront-guided laser ablation; Wavefront-optimized laser ablation
    application of laser treatment for, **13**:83–84, 84*f*
    Bowman layer/stromal bed preparation for, **13**:75–83, 76*f*, 78*f*, 79*f*, 81*f*, 82*f*, 83*t*
    central islands and, **13**:94–95, 94*f*
    complications/side effects of, **13**:93–117. *See also* specific type
    corneal curvatures affected by, **13**:187
    corneal sensation affected by, **13**:97–98
    corticosteroids after, **13**:85, 86, 86–87
        complications associated with, **13**:96–97
    custom, **13**:40, 69. *See also* Wavefront-guided laser ablation
    for presbyopia, **13**:156–157, 157*f*
    decentered ablation and, **13**:95–96, 97*f*
    dry eye after, **13**:97–98, 164–165
    endothelial effects of, **13**:97
    FDA concerns/guidelines and, **13**:91
    herpes simplex virus keratitis and, **13**:166–167
    infectious keratitis after, **13**:98–99, 99*f*
        diffuse lamellar keratitis (DLK) differentiated from, **13**:110–111, 110*t*, 111*f*
    for melanoma, **4**:285
    outcomes of, **13**:87–89
    overcorrection and, **13**:93–94
    postoperative care for, **13**:86–87
        immediate postablation measures, **13**:84–85
    preoperative patient preparation for, **13**:74–75
    preoperative patient selection/potential contraindications for, **13**:70–73, 71*t*
    preoperative planning/laser programming for, **13**:47–48
    re-treatment (enhancements) and, **13**:89–91, 90*f*
        for overcorrection, **13**:93–94
        for undercorrection, **13**:94
    surgical technique for, **13**:73–87
    tracking/centration/ablation and, **13**:83–84, 84*f*
    types of lasers for, **13**:24–26
    undercorrection and, **13**:94

Photochemical injury, **12**:332
  laser effects/photocoagulation and, **12**:339
  occupational light toxicity and, **12**:334
  ophthalmic instrumentation causing, **12**:333–334
  in photodynamic therapy, **12**:344
  in solar retinopathy, **12**:332–333
Photochromic lenses, **3**:159–160
Photocoagulation, **3**:25, **12**:337–343
  for age-related macular degeneration, **12**:71
    ineffectiveness of, **12**:63
  anesthesia for, **12**:339
  for angioid streaks, **12**:85
  angle-closure glaucoma after, **10**:135
  for branch retinal vein occlusion, **12**:124–126, 125*f*
  for central retinal artery occlusion, **12**:140
  for central retinal vein occlusion, **12**:131–132
  for central serous chorioretinopathy, **12**:175, 176, 341
  for choroidal hemangioma, **4**:292
  choroidal lesions caused by, **12**:342
  for choroidal neovascularization
    in age-related macular degeneration, **12**:63, 71, 340
    in myopia, **12**:86
    in ocular histoplasmosis, **9**:223, 223–224, 224*f*, **12**:81–82
  choroidal perfusion abnormalities caused by, **12**:180
  for clinically significant diabetic macular edema, **12**:97, 98, 99*f*, 101–103, 102*t*
  for Coats disease, **12**:145
  complications of, **12**:341–343
  for diabetic retinopathy, **4**:167, 167*f*
    in nonproliferative retinopathy/macular edema, **12**:97, 98, 99*f*, 101–103, 102*t*
    in proliferative retinopathy, **12**:106–108, 108*f*, 109*f*
  for diffuse unilateral subacute neuroretinitis, **9**:240, 241*f*, **12**:210
  indications for, **12**:340–341
  laser wavelengths used in, **12**:337–339
  lenses for, **12**:339, 340*t*
  for lupus vasculitis, **12**:195
  for macroaneurysms, **12**:148
  for melanoma, **4**:285
  for metastatic eye disease, **4**:322
  for neovascular glaucoma, **10**:127
  for ocular histoplasmosis, **9**:223, 223–224, 224*f*, **12**:81–82
  for ocular ischemic syndrome, **12**:134
  for parafoveal (juxtafoveal) retinal telangiectasia, **12**:147
  parameter settings for, **12**:339
  for pars planitis, **9**:137, 138
  practical aspects of, **12**:339–340, 340*t*
  principles of, **12**:337–343
  prophylactic, in acute retinal necrosis, **9**:202, **12**:202
  for retinal angiomas, **4**:295, **6**:375, **12**:150
  for retinal breaks, **12**:283
  retinal/choroidal detachment caused by, **12**:342, 342*f*
  for retinoblastoma, **4**:311
  for retinopathy of prematurity, **6**:286, **12**:167–168, 168*f*
  for sickle cell retinopathy, **12**:120–121

  thermal light injury caused by, **12**:332, 337
  for uveitic neovascularization, **9**:303
Photodisruption, **3**:25, **13**:23
Photodynamic therapy, **12**:343–344
  for central serous chorioretinopathy, **12**:175
  for choroidal hemangioma, **4**:292, **12**:182
  for choroidal neovascularization, **12**:71–72, 78, 79, 343–344
    in age-related macular degeneration, **12**:71–72, 78, 79, 344
    angioid streaks and, **12**:85
    combination treatment and, **12**:72, 78, 79
    complications of, **12**:344
    in myopia, **12**:86, 343
    in ocular histoplasmosis syndrome, **9**:223, 224
  choroidal perfusion abnormalities caused by, **12**:180
  for retinal hemangioblastoma, **4**:295, **12**:150
Photographic keratoscope/photokeratoscopy, **3**:267, **8**:39
Photographic simulation of distortion, **3**:315–316, 316*f*
  altering astigmatic correction and, **3**:317, 318*f*
Photography, for recording optic disc evaluation, **10**:51, 75
Photolysis, laser, **11**:127
Photometry, **3**:17
  terms used in, **3**:18*t*
Photomicroscopy, specular, **3**:260–261, 261*f*, **8**:14, 31–33, 32*f*
  before cataract surgery, **11**:84
  in optical focusing technique for pachymetry, **3**:259
  before phakic intraocular lens insertion, **13**:129
Photomydriasis, multifocal IOLs and, **13**:145
Photon characteristics of light, **3**:3, 7
Photons, **3**:3, 7
Photo-oxidation, **2**:313
  in retina, **2**:315
Photophobia, **5**:301
  in achromatopsia, **6**:291
  in albinism, **12**:258
  in cone dystrophies, **5**:114, **12**:232
  postoperative, with good acuity, after LASIK with femtosecond flap creation, **13**:116
  in primary congenital glaucoma, **6**:234, **10**:143
  in uveitis, **9**:84, 84*t*, 119
Photopic/light-adapted electroretinogram, **12**:34, 34*f*, 35, 36*f. See also* Electroretinogram
  in cone dystrophies, **12**:232
  in hereditary retinal/choroidal dystrophies, **12**:224*t*
Photopsias, **5**:189, 347
  in posterior vitreous detachment, **12**:275
  retinal disease causing, **5**:189–190
  in rhegmatogenous retinal detachment, **12**:286
  in uveitis, **9**:85
Photoreceptor dystrophies, diffuse, **4**:175–177, **12**:223–234. *See also* Cone dystrophies/ degenerations; Cone–rod dystrophies/ degenerations; Retinitis pigmentosa
Photoreceptor inner segments, **2**:73, 74*f*, 76*f*, **12**:10, 11*f*, 13*f. See also* Cone inner segments; Photoreceptors; Rod inner segments

Photoreceptor outer segments, 2:73, 74f, 76f, 79f,
12:10, 11f, 12, 13f. See also Cone outer segments;
Photoreceptors; Rod outer segments
shed, retinal pigment epithelium phagocytosis of,
2:306–307, 12:12, 15
Photoreceptors, 2:73–74, 74f, 75f, 76f, 77f, 291–298,
4:145, 146f, 12:10–12, 11f. See also Cones; Rods
age-related changes in, 12:55
atrophy of, in macular degeneration, 4:169
biochemistry and metabolism of, 2:291–298
density/distribution of, 6:44–45, 12:10
development of, 2:126, 6:44–45
in macular degeneration/choroidal
neovascularization, 4:169, 12:57, 58, 64f, 66f
oxidative damage to, 2:315–316
ratio of to ganglion cells, 5:29
Photorefractive keratectomy (PRK), 13:4t, 65, 67–68.
See also Keratorefractive surgery; Surface ablation
for accommodative esotropia, 13:181
Bowman layer and, 2:249
cataract surgery after, 11:194
IOL power calculation and, 11:86
in children, 13:180–181
complications/side effects of, 13:102
corneal haze after, 13:101, 101f
corneal wound healing/repair and, 13:26
corticosteroids after, 13:86
dry eye and, 8:65
glaucoma/ocular hypertension and, 13:174, 175
herpes simplex virus keratitis and, 13:166
infectious keratitis after, 13:98–99
informed consent form for, 13:209–212
international trends in use of, 13:199, 201
intraocular lens power calculations after, 3:220–222
intraocular pressure measurements after, 10:24
mixed astigmatic, 13:89
myopic, 13:87
conductive keratoplasty for overcorrection in,
13:122
after penetrating keratoplasty, 13:169–171
after retinal detachment surgery, 13:177
spherical aberration after, 3:100
Photosensitive retinal ganglion cells, 5:28, 32
Photosensitivity. See also Photic damage/phototoxicity/
light toxicity
photodynamic therapy and, 12:344
in systemic lupus erythematosus, 1:167, 169t
Photostress recovery test, 5:106
transient visual loss and, 5:175, 176
Phototherapeutic keratectomy (PTK), 8:402–403, 413
for calcific band keratopathy, 8:344
for corneal/epithelial erosions, 11:147
after LASIK, 13:105
recurrent, 8:85
for corneal haze after surface ablation, 13:101
for epithelial basement membrane dystrophy,
8:272
herpes simplex virus keratitis and, 13:166, 167
for striae in LASIK flaps, 13:108
Photothermal laser therapy, 13:23
Phototoxicity. See Photic damage/phototoxicity/light
toxicity

Phototransduction, 5:27
cone, 2:293–294, 5:27
rod, 2:291–293, 292f, 5:27
PHPV (persistent hyperplastic primary vitreous). See
Persistent fetal vasculature
Phthiriasis palpebrum (Phthirus pubis infection), 8:142,
149
cholinesterase inhibitors for, 2:340
Phthirus pubis (crab/pubic louse), 8:142, 142f
ocular infection (phthiriasis palpebrum) caused by,
8:142, 149
cholinesterase inhibitors for, 2:340
Phthisis bulbi (phthisical eye), 4:22, 23f
after penetrating injury, 12:324
retained foreign body and, 12:327
retinoblastoma regression and, 6:356
sympathetic ophthalmia and, 9:182
Phycomycetes (phycomycosis/mucormycosis/
zygomycosis), 5:366–367, 366f, 8:140
cornea involved in (keratitis), 4:83
optic nerve involved in, 4:251
orbit involved in, 4:234, 6:197, 197f, 7:45–46
exenteration in management of, 7:45, 126
Physical activity. See Exercise
Physical drug dependence, 1:250
Physical examination. See also Examination, ophthalmic
preoperative assessment and, 1:304t
Physical optics, 3:3–26
absorption and, 3:13
coherence and, 3:7–10, 8f, 9f
definition of, 3:3
diffraction and, 3:13–16, 14f, 15f
illumination and, 3:16–19, 17f, 18t
interference and, 3:7–10, 8f, 9f
laser fundamentals and, 3:19–26, 22f, 23f, 24f, 26f
light hazards and, 3:19
photon (particle) aspects of light and, 3:3, 7
polarization and, 3:10–12, 11f
reflection and, 3:12–13, 12f
scattering and, 3:16
transmission and, 3:13
wave theory and, 3:3–7, 4f, 5f, 6f
Physician Quality Reporting Initiative (PQRI), 1:347
Physiologic (simple/essential) anisocoria, 5:264, 265f,
6:229
Physiologic cup/physiologic cupping, 2:89, 90, 92f,
10:46–47, 47t, 50. See also Cupping of optic disc;
Optic cup
Physostigmine, 2:259, 336f, 338t, 339, 340
for atropine intoxication, 6:88
for muscarinic antagonist side effects, 2:342
Phytanic acid oxidase, defective, 2:213t. See also Refsum
disease/syndrome
Phytanic acid storage disease. See Refsum disease/
syndrome
Pia mater, optic nerve, 2:91, 92f, 93f, 4:249, 250f
Pial arteries, optic nerve supplied by, 10:44
PIC. See Punctate inner choroiditis/choroidopathy
PICA. See Posterior inferior cerebellar artery
Picornaviruses, 8:129
Pie in the sky defect, 2:96, 5:168, 169f
PIER study, 12:74, 75f

Pierre Robin sequence (anomaly/deformity), 6:171, 394, 8:324*t*
  Stickler syndrome and, 12:310
Piezoelectric crystal, in phacoemulsification handpiece, 11:103
PIGF. *See* Placental-like growth factor
Piggybacking
  with contact lenses, for keratoconus, 3:191
  with intraocular lenses, 3:206–207, 219–220
    refractive lens exchange/clear lens extraction and, 13:140
Pigment, visual. *See* Pigments, visual
Pigment/pigmentary dispersion syndrome, 4:109, 109*f*, 110*f*, 9:85, 289, 10:11*t*, 38, 87–90, 88*f*, 89*f*
  anterior chamber and trabecular meshwork affected in, 4:109, 109*f*, 110*f*
  cornea affected in, 4:91–92, 94*f*
  glaucoma and, 4:91–92, 94*f*, 109, 109*f*, 110*f*, 10:11*t*, 87–90, 88*f*, 89*f*, 90*f*
  phakic intraocular lenses and, 13:133*t*, 136
Pigment epithelial detachment. *See* Retinal pigment epithelium (RPE), detachment of
Pigment epithelium. *See* Ciliary epithelium, pigmented; Iris pigment epithelium; Retinal pigment epithelium
Pigment epithelium–derived factor
  in aqueous humor, 2:267
  in vitreous, 2:287
Pigment granules
  in retinal pigment epithelium, 2:307–308
  in vitreous ("tobacco dust"/Shafer sign), 12:286, 314
Pigment spot of sclera, 8:233
Pigmentary glaucoma, 4:91–92, 94*f*, 109, 109*f*, 110*f*, 10:87–90, 88*f*, 89*f*, 90*f*
Pigmentary retinopathy, 12:223–224, 249. *See also* Retinitis pigmentosa
  in Bardet-Biedl syndrome, 12:250*t*, 252
  in congenital rubella syndrome, 9:210, 210*f*
  hearing loss and, 12:251*t*, 253. *See also* Usher syndrome
  in measles, 9:212, 213
  in neuromuscular disorders, 12:254
  secondary/systemic disease and, 12:224, 249, 250–251*t*
  X-linked, 12:251*t*
Pigmentations/pigment deposits. *See also* Pigmented lesions
  choroidal, 2:66
  conjunctival, 8:233–240
  corneal, 4:91–93, 94*f*, 8:321*t*
    drug-induced, 8:346–349, 347*t*
  iris, 2:56
    development of, 2:137
    prostaglandin analogues/latanoprost and, 2:354, 10:162*t*, 166
    after laser skin resurfacing, 7:230
  lens
    aging and, 11:39, 40*f*
    drugs causing, 11:48, 48*f*, 49
  retinal/retinal pigment epithelium, 2:307–308, 12:249. *See also* Pigmentary retinopathy
    in age-related macular degeneration, 12:58

trabecular meshwork, 4:109, 109*f*, 110*f*, 10:17, 37–38
  in exfoliation syndrome/pseudoexfoliation, 10:38, 86
  in pigmentary glaucoma, 10:87, 88, 88*f*, 89
Pigmented basal cell carcinoma, 7:169*f*. *See also* Basal cell carcinoma
Pigmented lesions, 8:233–240, 234*t*. *See also specific type and* Melanocytic tumors
  benign, 8:233–237, 234*t*
  malignant, 8:234*t*, 238–240
  preinvasive, 8:234*t*, 237–238
Pigments, visual, 12:15
  absorption spectra of, 12:337, 338*f*
  regeneration of, retinal pigment epithelium in, 2:305–306
Pilagan. *See* Pilocarpine
Pilar (trichilemmal) cyst, 7:159
Pili, bacterial, 8:132
Pilocar. *See* Pilocarpine
Pilocarpine, 2:260, 336*f*, 338, 338*t*, 10:164*t*, 172
  accommodation affected by, 11:19
  for acute angle closure, 10:115
  in Adie tonic pupil diagnosis, 5:270–271, 272*f*, 316
  anisocoria caused by, 5:266, 270
  cataracts caused by, 11:49
  for childhood glaucoma, 6:243
  for dry eye, 8:60
  in fixed, dilated pupil evaluation, 5:316
  sustained-release gel for administration of, 2:330, 338, 338*t*
  systemic side effects of, 2:338, 339*f*
Pilocytic astrocytoma, optic. *See* Optic nerve (optic pathway/chiasm) glioma
Pilomatricoma (pilomatrixoma), 7:163–164, 163*f*
Pilopine/Pilopine gel. *See* Pilocarpine
Piloptic. *See* Pilocarpine
Pilostat. *See* Pilocarpine
Pindolol, 1:76*t*
Pineal gland, 5:28*f*
Pinealoblastoma/pinealoma, retinoblastoma and, 4:309, 314, 314*t*
"Ping-Pong" gaze, 5:259
Pinguecula, 4:56, 57–58, 58*f*, 8:331–332
  conjunctival graft for, 8:395
  subconjunctival hemorrhage caused by, 8:76*t*
Pinhole imaging, 3:27–30, 27*f*, 29*f*, 30*f*, 107–108, 107*f*
  image quality and, 3:37, 38*f*
  with lenses and mirrors, 3:30–31, 31*f*, 32*f*
  visual resolution and, 3:107–108, 107*f*
Pinhole visual acuity, 3:108
Pioglitazone, 1:199*t*, 201
PIOL. *See* Phakic intraocular lenses; Primary intraocular/central nervous system lymphomas
PION (posterior ischemic optic neuropathy). *See* Posterior optic neuropathy, ischemic
PIP₂. *See* Phosphatidyl-inositol-4,5-bisphosphate
PIP5K3 (phosphatidylinositol-3-phosphate/ phosphatidylinositol 5-kinase type III), in Fleck corneal dystrophy, 8:269*t*, 287
Piperacillin, 1:46*t*, 57, 2:370
  with tazobactam, 1:47*t*, 59
Pipracil. *See* Piperacillin
Pirbuterol, 1:145*t*

Piroxicam, **1**:183*t*, **2**:362*t*
PISK. *See* Pressure-induced stromal keratitis
Piston, wavefront aberrations and, **13**:7
Pits
  foveal, **2**:127
  lens, **11**:21, 22*f*
  optic (optic nerve/disc pits, optic holes), **2**:120, 121,
    5:143, **12**:294–295, 295*f*
    acquired, **10**:48
    central serous chorioretinopathy differentiated
      from, **12**:174
    in children, **6**:310, 310*f*
Pituitary adenoma, **1**:214–216
  chiasmal syndromes caused by, **5**:161*f*, 162–163,
    163*f*
  neuroimaging in evaluation of, **1**:216, **5**:82*t*
  in pregnancy, **5**:162
Pituitary apoplexy (Sheehan syndrome), **1**:216,
  5:162–164, 163*f*
Pituitary autoimmune inflammation (lymphocytic
  hypophysitis), **5**:346–347
Pituitary gland disorders, optic nerve hypoplasia and,
  6:308–309, 415
Pituitary hormones, hypothalamic hormones and,
  1:214, 214*t*
PITX2 gene, **2**:141, **10**:11*t*
  in Axenfeld-Rieger syndrome, **6**:214, 233, **10**:11*t*,
    142
  in glaucoma, **10**:11*t*
  in Peters anomaly, **8**:258, **10**:142, **11**:28
Pixel, **5**:70
PJCs. *See* Premature junctional complexes/contractions
PK/PKP (penetrating keratoplasty). *See* Keratoplasty,
  penetrating
PKC. *See* Protein kinase C
PL. *See* Preferential looking
PLA₂. *See* Phospholipase A₂
Placental-like growth factor, in VEGF Trap mechanism
  of action, **12**:77
Placido-based topography/Placido disk, **3**:265, 266*f*,
  268*f*, **8**:39, 40, 40*f*, **13**:10, 11*f*, 13
  computerized, **8**:40, 40*f*, **13**:10, 11*f*
  IOL power calculation after refractive surgery and,
    13:187
  in keratoconus, **8**:43–44, 44*f*, 299, 300*f*
  in pellucid marginal degeneration, **13**:16
Placode, lens, **2**:121, 129, **11**:21, 22*f*
Placoid chorioretinitis
  relentless, **9**:157, 158*f*
  syphilitic posterior, **9**:245, 246*f*, 309–310
Plagiocephaly, **6**:383, 385*f*
  deformational, **6**:386
  in Saethre-Chotzen syndrome, **6**:388
Planck constant, **3**:7
Plane of incidence and reflection, **3**:43*f*, 44
Plane of incidence and transmission, **3**:44, 45*f*
Plane (plano) mirror, **3**:89
  retinoscopy settings and, **3**:121, 121*f*, 122
  vergence calculations for, **3**:90–91, 92*f*
Plane parallel plate, **3**:83–84, 84*f*
Plane-polarized (linearly polarized) light, **3**:10
Planes of unit magnification (principal planes), **3**:75, 75*f*

Plano intraocular lenses, **3**:206
Planoconcave lenses
  for slit-lamp biomicroscopy, **12**:20
  for slit-lamp delivery of photocoagulation, **12**:339
Planoconvex optic, of intraocular lens, **3**:204*f*
Planocylindrical lenses, **3**:95, 95*f*
Plant alkaloids, in cancer chemotherapy, **1**:241*t*
Plants/vegetation, ocular injuries caused by, **8**:362
  corneal foreign body, **8**:371
Plaque radiotherapy. *See* Radioactive plaque therapy
Plaquenil. *See* Hydroxychloroquine
Plaques
  atherosclerotic, **1**:100
    rupture of in acute coronary syndrome, **1**:101, 102
  demyelinating, in multiple sclerosis, **5**:322, 322*f*
  Hollenhorst (cholesterol emboli)
    in branch retinal artery occlusion, **4**:163, **12**:136, 137*f*
    in central retinal artery occlusion, **12**:139
    transient visual loss and, **5**:175*f*, 177, 179*t*
  in indocyanine green angiography, **12**:25
  optic nerve, **4**:252
  senile scleral, **4**:115, 116*f*, **8**:9, 345–346, 346*f*
Plasma, **1**:147
Plasma (ions/electrons), mechanical light injury and,
  12:332
Plasma cell–rich pseudotumors, **7**:84
Plasma cell tumors, of orbit, **7**:84
Plasma cells, **4**:9
  in external eye, **8**:174*t*
  monoclonal proliferation of, corneal deposits and,
    8:319–320
Plasma proteins. *See also* Proteins
  in aqueous humor, **2**:254, 255, 265, 266, 268–270
  drug-binding by, systemic administration and, **2**:329
Plasmacytoma, of orbit, **7**:84
Plasmid resistance, **1**:44–56
Plasmids, **2**:157, **8**:131, 132
  for gene therapy, **2**:187–188
Plasmin, **9**:24
  for enzymatic vitreolysis, **2**:289
Plasminogen, **9**:24
  antifibrinolytic agents affecting, **2**:394
  in aqueous humor, **2**:269
  in ligneous conjunctivitis, **8**:192, 193
Plasminogen activator
  in aqueous humor, **2**:269
  tissue. *See* Tissue plasminogen activator
Plastic spectacle lenses
  bifocal, **3**:147
    reverse slab-off and, **3**:155
  hi-index, **3**:162–163
  high-impact, **3**:162
  prism calibration for, **3**:85, 86*f*
  standard, **3**:162
Plate-haptic IOLs, implantation of, **11**:139
Plateau iris/plateau iris syndrome, **10**:5*t*, 7*t*, 112,
  119–120, 120*f*
  laser iridotomy in diagnosis of, **10**:202
Platelet-activating factors, **8**:179*t*, **9**:25, 26*f*, 27
  in neutrophil recruitment and activation, **9**:18
Platelet count, **1**:152
Platelet-derived growth factors, **2**:396, **9**:29*t*

Platelet-fibrin embolus, transient visual loss and, 5:177, 178f, 179f

Platelet glycoprotein IIb/IIIa receptor antagonists. *See* Glycoprotein IIb/IIIa receptor antagonists

Platelets, 1:147
aspirin affecting, 2:362
disorders of, 1:153–155
drugs causing, 1:154, 155
in hemostasis, 1:151

Platina prepupillary intraocular lens, 3:207, 208f

Platinol. *See* Cisplatin

Platinum eyelid weights, for exposure keratopathy, 8:80

Platysma muscle, 7:131, 132f, 133

Platysmaplasty, 7:238, 238f

Plavix. *See* Clopidogrel

Pleiotropism, 2:158, 177, 210

Pleistophora, 8:141

Plendil. *See* Felodipine

Pleomorphic adenoma (benign mixed tumor)
of eyelid, 7:162
of lacrimal gland, 4:236, 237f, 7:86–87, 86f

Pleomorphic rhabdomyosarcoma, 4:243, 6:335, 7:77–78

Pleomorphism, specular photomicroscopy in evaluation of, 8:32–33
before cataract surgery, 11:84

Pletal. *See* Cilostazol

Plexiform layer
inner, 2:74f, 75f, 78, 79f, 4:145, 146f, 12:10, 11f, 12
development of, 2:126
outer, 2:74f, 75f, 76f, 78, 79f, 4:145, 146f, 12:10, 11f, 12

Plexiform neurofibromas
in children, 6:343, 366–367, 367f
eyelid involvement and, 5:275, 276f, 339–340, 6:367, 367f, 7:24, 10:28
glaucoma and, 6:367, 370, 10:28
of orbit, 4:244, 244f, 6:343, 367, 7:24, 72, 72f, 73f

PLGA1 gene mutation, in pleomorphic adenoma, 4:236

Plica semilunaris, 2:22f, 31, 4:47
incorporation of during strabismus surgery, 6:157, 157f

Plurihormonal adenomas, 1:215

Pluripotential stem cells, 1:147

Plus cylinder (anterior toric) form/lenses, 3:311, 316

Plus cylinder refraction, 3:132

Plus disease, retinopathy of prematurity and, 4:167, 6:282t, 283, 284f, 12:160, 161f

Plus lenses. *See also* Convex (plus/positive) lenses
anophthalmic socket camouflage and, 7:125
prismatic effect of, 3:87

Plus-power lenses
for slit-lamp biomicroscopy, 12:19–20
for slit-lamp delivery of photocoagulation, 12:339

PMA. *See* Premarket approval

PMD. *See* Pellucid marginal degeneration

PML. *See* Progressive multifocal leukoencephalopathy

PMMA. *See* Polymethylmethacrylate

PMNs. *See* Polymorphonuclear leukocytes

PMPA. *See* Tenofovir

PMTs. *See* Paramedian tracts

Pneumatic retinopexy, for retinal detachment, 12:290, 364–365, 365f

Pneumatic tonometer (pneumotonometer/ pneumotonometry), 10:26
in infants and children, 10:151
for IOP measurement after refractive surgery, 13:97, 112, 174, 194

Pneumocandins, 1:65

Pneumococcal vaccine, 1:7, 284

Pneumococcus. *See Streptococcus, pneumoniae*

Pneumocystis jiroveci (Pneumocystis carinii) infections, 1:37, 8:140
choroiditis, 9:310, 310f, 311f
pneumonia, 1:37, 9:310
prophylaxis of, 9:109, 113

Pneumolysin, 8:133

Pneumonia
in HIV infection/AIDS, 1:37, 9:310
pneumococcal, 1:7
immunization against, 1:284–285

Pneumotonometry/pneumotonometer, 10:26
in infants and children, 10:151
for IOP measurement after refractive surgery, 13:97, 112, 174, 194

PO (pupil–optic nerve) section, 4:27–28, 28f

POAG. *See* Open-angle glaucoma, primary

Podophyllin/podophyllotoxins, in cancer chemotherapy, 1:239, 241t

POHS (presumed ocular histoplasmosis syndrome). *See* Ocular histoplasmosis syndrome

Point-by-point analysis, in perimetry, 10:63

Point mutations, 2:207. *See also* Mutation
mitochondrial DNA, 2:174f
screening for, 2:184, 186–187f

Point source of light, in geometric optics, 3:27–28

Point spread function (PSF), 3:15f, 39, 39f
keratorefractive surgery and, 3:232, 233f

Poison ivy toxin, immune response to, 9:34–35

Poker spine, in ankylosing spondylitis, 1:164

Poland syndrome, Möbius syndrome and, 6:140

Polar cataracts, 6:247, 247f, 248f, 250t, 11:30–31, 32f
surgery for removal of, 11:196–197

Polarimetry, scanning laser, in retinal nerve fiber evaluation, 10:51, 53f

Polarization, 3:10–12, 11f. *See also* Polarizing sunglasses
applications of, 3:10–12, 11f
of laser light, 3:21
reflection and, 3:12, 12f

Polarizing filter, 3:10

Polarizing projection charts, 3:11–12

Polarizing sunglasses (polarized/Polaroid lenses), 3:11, 12, 12f, 159, 304

Polaroid slide test, in nonorganic ophthalmic disorder evaluation
monocular no light perception and, 5:310, 310f
monocular reduced vision and, 5:311

Polio, immunization against, 1:283

Poliosis, in staphylococcal blepharitis, 8:144t, 145

Polyacrylamide, as viscoelastic, 2:393

Polyallelism, 2:194

Polyangiitis, microscopic, 1:177t, 179, 9:143–145, 144f

Polyarteritis nodosa, **1**:177*t*, 178, **7**:58, **9**:143–145, 144*f*
  choroidal perfusion abnormalities and, **12**:179
  eyelid manifestations of, **4**:213*t*
  refractive surgery contraindicated in, **13**:184
Polyarthritis. *See also* Arthritis
  in Behçet disease, **1**:180
  juvenile. *See* Polyarticular-onset juvenile idiopathic (chronic/rheumatoid) arthritis
  in systemic lupus erythematosus, **1**:167, 169*t*
Polyarticular-onset juvenile idiopathic (chronic/rheumatoid) arthritis (polyarthritis), **1**:166, **6**:269*t*, **9**:129. *See also* Juvenile idiopathic (chronic/rheumatoid) arthritis
  eye examination schedule for children with, **6**:271*t*, **9**:131*t*
  rheumatoid factor (RF)-negative, **6**:269, 269*t*
  uveitis in, **6**:269, **9**:129–130, 130*f*
Polycarbonate spectacle lenses, **3**:162
Polycarbophil, for dry eye, **2**:390
Polychondritis, relapsing, **1**:175–176
  eyelid manifestations of, **4**:213*t*
Polycillin. *See* Ampicillin
Polycin-B. *See* Polymyxin B, in combination preparations
Polyclonal response, **9**:46
Polycoria, **6**:230
Polycystic kidney disease, hypertension in, **1**:72
Polydactyly, in Bardet-Biedl syndrome, **12**:252, 252*f*
Polydystrophy, pseudo–Hurler, **6**:400*t*, **8**:312
Polyenes, **2**:378–380, 379*f*
Polyethylene orbital implants, **7**:121, 121*f*. *See also* Orbital implants
Polygenic inheritance, **2**:158, 224–225
Polyhedral cells, in choroidal/ciliary body nevus, **4**:195
Polyhexamethylene biguanide, for *Acanthamoeba* infection, **2**:385, **8**:169
Polymacon, for contact lenses, **3**:177*t*
Polymegethism, specular photomicroscopy in evaluation of, **8**:32
  before cataract surgery, **11**:84
Polymerase chain reaction (PCR), **1**:3, **2**:158, **4**:38*t*, 40–41, 40*f*
  in acute retinal necrosis, **9**:201–202
  in chlamydial infection, **1**:11
  clinical use of, **4**:42–43
  in clostridial infection, **1**:8
  in CMV infection, **1**:24
  in *Haemophilus influenzae* infection, **1**:9
  in infection diagnosis, **1**:3
  in Lyme disease, **1**:16, **9**:252
  in meningococcal infection, **1**:10
  in mutation screening, **2**:184, 186–187*f*
  in postoperative endophthalmitis, **9**:270, 271
  real-time quantitative, **4**:39*t*
  reverse, **4**:39*t*
  in syphilis, **1**:14, **9**:248
  in toxoplasmosis, **1**:21, **9**:231
  in tuberculosis, **1**:19
  in uveitis, **9**:95*t*, 97
Polymethylmethacrylate (PMMA), **3**:169
  contact lenses made from, **3**:169, 176, 180
  scleral lenses, **3**:192

  intraocular lenses made from, **3**:203, 205, **11**:132–133, 133*f*
  capsular opacification and, **11**:170
  for children, **6**:249
  implantation procedure for, **11**:138
  instrumentation for handling, **11**:138
  phakic IOLs, **13**:126
  intrastromal corneal ring segments made from, **13**:55
  refractive index of, **3**:40*t*, 45
Polymorphic amyloid degeneration, **8**:338, 339*f*
Polymorphisms, **2**:158, 171, 207–208
  denaturing gradient gel electrophoresis in identification of, **2**:184–185
  restriction fragment length (RFLP), **2**:160, 178–180, 179*f*
  single-stranded conformational, **2**:182
Polymorphonuclear leukocytes, **4**:7, 8*f*, **9**:9, 10. *See also* Basophils; Eosinophils; Neutrophils
  in inflammation, **4**:7, 8*f*
Polymorphous dystrophy, posterior, **4**:80, 80*f*, **8**:268*t*, 270*t*, 293–295, 294*f*
  genetics of, **4**:80, **8**:269*t*, 293
Polymyositis, **1**:175
Polymyxin B, **2**:368*t*, 377–378
  in combination preparations, **2**:372*t*, 373*t*, 374
Polymyxins, **1**:44
Polyneuropathy
  in diabetes mellitus, **1**:206
  familial amyloidotic
    types I and II, **4**:140, 141*f*, 212
    type IV (gelsolin-type lattice corneal dystrophy), **4**:212, **8**:268*t*, 270*t*, 280, 280*f*, 317*t*, 319
    genetics of, **4**:212, **8**:269*t*, 280, 317*t*
    vitreous involvement in, **4**:140, 141*f*
Polyol (sorbitol) pathway
  in cataract formation, **2**:280, 281, **11**:15
  diabetic retinopathy and, **2**:301
  in lens glucose/carbohydrate metabolism, **2**:280, 280*f*, **11**:14*f*, 15
Polyopia, **5**:216
  in cataracts, **11**:70
Polyphosphoinositide turnover, **2**:262–263, 262*f*, 263*f*
Polyploidy, **2**:199
Polypoidal choroidal vasculopathy (posterior uveal bleeding syndrome), **4**:171, 172*f*, 173*f*
  age-related macular degeneration differentiated from, **12**:69–70, 70*f*
  central serous chorioretinopathy differentiated from, **12**:174, 175
Polyposis, familial adenomatous (Gardner syndrome), retinal manifestations of, **4**:150–151, **12**:255, 255*f*
  in children, **6**:352
Polyps, colorectal cancer and, **1**:276
Polysaccharide encapsulation, as microbial virulence factor, **1**:4
Polysorbate, in demulcents, **2**:390, 391
Polysporin. *See* Polymyxin B
Polysulfone, for corneal inlays, **13**:54
Polythiazide, **1**:76*t*
Polytrim. *See* Trimethoprim-polymyxin B
Polyvinyl alcohol, for dry eye, **2**:390
Pons, horizontal eye movements and, **5**:42

Ponstel. *See* Mefenamic acid
Pontine cistern, lateral, 2:105
Pontine lesions
　facial myokymia caused by, 5:292
　facial weakness/paralysis caused by, 5:285, 285*t*
　ocular motility affected by, 5:210, 258
　spastic paretic facial contraction caused by, 5:292
Pontine nuclei, dorsolateral, 5:38
Pontine reticular formation, paramedian, 2:104, 104*f*,
　5:39, 39*f*, 42, 46*f*, 199
Pontocaine. *See* Tetracaine
Pontomedullary junction, 2:105
Pooling, fluorescein, 12:23, 24*f*. *See also*
　Hyperfluorescence
　in central serous chorioretinopathy, 12:23, 24*f*, 172,
　173*f*
　in cystoid macular edema, 12:142, 142*f*
Population, measurement systems and, 1:339–340
Population inversion, 3:23
Population-wide immunity, 9:70–71
Pork tapeworm *(Taenia solium)*, 8:142, 9:237
　orbital infection caused by, 4:235, 7:47
PORN. *See* Progressive outer retinal necrosis
Porous polyethylene orbital implants, 7:121, 121*f*. *See
　also* Orbital implants
Porphyria/porphyria cutanea tarda, 8:326
Porro-Abbe prism
　in operating microscope, 3:262*f*
　in slit-lamp biomicroscope, 3:251*f*, 252
PORT. *See* Punctate outer retinal toxoplasmosis
Port-wine stain (nevus flammeus), 6:342, 8:241. *See also*
　Vascular malformations
　increased episcleral venous pressure and, 10:28
　of orbit, 6:342
　in Sturge-Weber syndrome, 5:341, 343*f*, 6:238, 342,
　375, 376, 376*f*, 8:241, 10:28, 147
　in von Hippel–Lindau disease, 6:374
Portable electronic applanation devices, 10:26
　infection control and, 10:26
POS. *See* Parinaud oculoglandular syndrome
Posaconazole, 1:65
　for fungal keratitis, 8:166
Position, in schematic eye, 3:105*t*
Positional candidate gene screening, 2:182
Positions of gaze. *See* Gaze, positions of
Positive angle kappa, 6:77, 78*f*
　in retinopathy of prematurity, 6:287, 287*f*
Positive defocus, 3:238, 13:6, 6*f*
Positive dysphotopsias, intraocular lenses and, 11:168
Positive lenses. *See* Convex (plus/positive) lenses
Positive predictive value (PPV), of screening/diagnostic
　test, 1:330
Positive staining (fluorescein), 8:17
"Positive vitreous pressure," flat or shallow anterior
　chamber and, 11:152
Positron emission tomography (PET), 5:80
　in Alzheimer disease, 1:267
　in ischemic heart disease, 1:104, 106–107
Posner goniolens, 10:34
Posner-Schlossman syndrome (glaucomatocyclitic
　crisis), 9:124–125, 10:94
Post–cataract extraction restriction, diplopia caused by,
　5:239

Posterior alveolar nerve, 5:60
Posterior amorphous corneal dystrophy, 8:268*t*, 270*t*,
　288–289, 288*f*
　genetics of, 8:269*t*, 288
Posterior aqueous diversion syndrome. *See* Aqueous
　misdirection
Posterior capsular opacification (PCO)
　cataract surgery and, 11:143, 169–171
　IOLs and, 3:205
　Nd:YAG laser capsulotomy for, 11:169, 171–175,
　174*f*. *See also* Nd:YAG laser therapy,
　capsulotomy
　in uveitis, 9:294
Posterior capsular rupture, cataract surgery and,
　11:144*t*, 160–162
Posterior capsule, lensectomy with intraocular lens
　implantation and, 6:257
Posterior cerebral artery, 5:12, 19, 20*f*, 22*f*
　cranial nerve relationship and, 5:52*f*
Posterior chamber, 2:41*f*, 42, 52*f*. *See also* Posterior
　segment
　phacoemulsification in, 11:120, 121*f*
　in uveitis, 9:86*t*. *See also* Posterior uveitis
Posterior chamber intraocular lenses. *See* Intraocular
　lenses
Posterior choroidal artery, 5:22*f*
Posterior ciliary arteries, 2:36–38, 37*f*, 38, 38*f*, 39*f*, 62,
　64, 5:14*f*, 18–19, 12:12, 17, 17*f*
　development of, 2:132
　optic nerve supplied by, 10:42, 43, 43*f*, 44
Posterior ciliary nerves, 2:36, 247
Posterior clinoid process, 2:104
Posterior collagenous layer (retrocorneal fibrous
　membrane), 2:251, 4:91, 92*f*, 8:29
Posterior commissure, 5:38, 39*f*
Posterior communicating artery, 5:19, 20*f*, 22*f*, 23
　aneurysm of, 5:350*f*, 351
　　third nerve (oculomotor) palsy and, 5:228*f*, 229,
　　229*f*, 273, 351
　cranial nerve relationship and, 5:52*f*
Posterior conjunctival arteries, 2:34
Posterior corneal defects/depression. *See* Peters
　anomaly; Posterior keratoconus
Posterior cranial fossa, 5:6*f*
　neuroimaging in evaluation of, 5:82*t*, 85, 88
Posterior cyclitis, 9:78*t*
Posterior embryotoxon, 2:141, 4:102–103, 103*f*, 104*f*,
　6:212, 212*f*, 8:255, 256*f*, 261*t*. *See also* Anterior
　segment, dysgenesis of; Neurocristopathy
　in Axenfeld-Rieger syndrome, 4:102–103, 103*f*, 104*f*,
　6:212, 212*f*, 213, 8:256, 10:30, 146
　isolated, Axenfeld-Rieger syndrome differentiated
　from, 10:146*t*
Posterior ethmoidal artery, 5:13*f*, 14*f*, 15–16, 18
Posterior ethmoidal foramen, 5:12
Posterior fixation suture (fadenoperation), 6:148*t*
　for dissociated vertical deviation, 6:153
Posterior fluid misdirection, flat or shallow anterior
　chamber and, 11:152–153
Posterior focal length (PFL), 3:78
Posterior focal plane, 3:69, 70*f*
Posterior (secondary) focal point, 3:69, 70*f*
Posterior inferior cerebellar artery, 5:21, 22*f*

Posterior keratoconus, 4:102
   central (posterior corneal depression), 6:215
   circumscribed, 8:258, 259f, 262t
Posterior lacrimal crest, 2:5, 6f, 27
Posterior lamella, 2:25f
Posterior lenticonus/lentiglobus, 4:121, 122f, 6:249,
   249f, 250t, 11:26, 26f
Posterior nonbanded zone, of Descemet membrane,
   2:45, 46f, 135, 251
Posterior optic neuropathy, 5:144–159
   CMV infection causing, 5:359
   infiltrative, 5:158–159
   intraorbital/intracanalicular compressive lesions and,
      5:149–154, 150f, 150t, 151f, 152t
   ischemic, 5:157–158
   neuromyelitis optica and, 5:147
   optic glioma and, 5:151–154, 151f, 152t
   optic nerve sheath meningioma and, 5:149–151, 150f,
      150t
   optic perineuritis and, 5:147
   retrobulbar optic neuritis and, 5:144–146, 145f
   thyroid eye disease and, 5:147–149, 148f, 333
   toxic/nutritional, 5:154–156, 155f
   traumatic, 5:156–157, 156f
Posterior parietal cortex, 5:36f, 40f, 41
Posterior pigmented layer of iris, 2:58–60, 58f, 60f
   development of, 2:137
Posterior pituitary hormones, 1:214
Posterior polar cataract, 6:247t, 11:31
   surgery for removal of, 11:196–197
Posterior pole, 2:79, 11:5, 6f, 12:9f, 9t. See also Macula
   in uveal effusion syndrome, 12:182
Posterior polymorphous corneal dystrophy, 4:80, 80f,
   8:268t, 270t, 293–295, 294f
   genetics of, 4:80, 8:269t, 293
Posterior principal plane, 3:75, 75f, 76, 77f
Posterior principal point, 3:75
Posterior reversible encephalopathy syndrome, 5:326f,
   346
Posterior segment
   assessment of, before refractive surgery, 13:38
   in Bartonella-associated neuroretinitis, 9:264
   in Behçet disease, 9:193, 193f
   childhood glaucoma associated with abnormalities
      of, 6:239
   in coccidioidomycosis, 9:279
   complications of anterior segment surgery and,
      vitrectomy for, 12:354–362
   in cysticercosis, 9:238
   EBV infection and, 9:208, 208f
   hereditary dystrophies of, 12:221–248. See also
      Hereditary dystrophies
   metastatic tumors of, 4:317–318, 317f, 318f, 319f, 320f
   in Rift Valley fever, 9:217–218
   in sarcoidosis, 9:175, 176f
   in sympathetic ophthalmia, 9:178–179
   in syphilis, 9:245, 245f, 246f
   in toxocariasis, 9:235
   trauma to, 12:317–334. See also Trauma
      blunt trauma, 12:318–323, 320f, 321–322f, 322f,
         323f
      child abuse and, 12:330–331, 330f
      endophthalmitis and, 12:328–329

   foreign bodies, 12:325–328, 326f, 328t
   lacerating and penetrating injuries, 12:324
   optic disc avulsion and, 12:331–332, 331f
   patient evaluation after, 12:317–318
   perforating injuries, 12:325
   photic damage and, 12:332–334
   shaken baby syndrome and, 12:330–331, 330f
   sympathetic ophthalmia and, 12:329–330
   in uveitis, 9:86t, 89–90. See also Posterior uveitis
Posterior subcapsular cataract, 4:124–125, 125f,
   11:42–44, 47f
   in children, 6:249, 250t
   corticosteroids causing, 11:47–48
   ischemia causing, 11:64
   in myotonic dystrophy, 11:57
   retinoblastoma differentiated from, 4:305t
   silicone oil use and, 11:205
   uveitis and, 11:59
   visual acuity and, 11:43, 70, 70t
Posterior superior alveolar vein, 5:24f
Posterior sutures, 11:9
Posterior synechiae
   anisocoria and, 5:266
   in children, 6:231
   in glaucoma
      inflammation and, 10:130, 130f
      pupillary block/angle closure and, 10:110–111
      uveitis and, 9:296
   mydriasis in prevention of, 2:341
   in pars planitis, 9:136
   in sarcoidosis, 9:87f, 175
   in sympathetic ophthalmia, 9:178, 179f
   in uveitis, 9:85, 87f, 88
      glaucoma and, 9:296
      lens changes/cataract and, 11:59
Posterior temporal artery, 5:22f
Posterior toric (minus cylinder) form/lenses
   contact lenses, 3:174, 175
   spectacle lenses, distortion and, 3:316
Posterior uveal bleeding syndrome (polypoidal
   choroidal vasculopathy), 4:171, 172f, 173f
   age-related macular degeneration differentiated from,
      12:69–70, 70f
   central serous chorioretinopathy differentiated from,
      12:174, 175
Posterior uveal melanoma, 4:195–200, 196f, 197f, 198f,
   199f, 263, 273–288, 9:285–286. See also Choroidal/
   ciliary body melanoma
Posterior uveitis, 9:78t, 82, 82t, 83t, 89–90, 140–172. See
   also specific cause and Choroiditis; Retinitis; Uveitis
   in children, 6:267, 272–274, 273f, 275
      differential diagnosis of, 6:268t
      laboratory tests for, 6:277t
      masquerade syndromes and, 6:276t
      toxocariasis and, 6:273–274, 273f
      toxoplasmosis and, 6:272
   chorioretinal lesions in, 9:82t, 83t
   in collagen vascular diseases, 9:140–146
   corticosteroid route of administration in, 2:360t
   differential diagnosis of, 6:268t
   diffuse unilateral subacute neuroretinitis and,
      9:239–241, 240f, 241f
   flowchart for evaluation of, 9:81t

glaucoma and, **10**:131
inflammatory chorioretinopathies (white dot
    syndromes) and, **9**:147–172, 148–150*t*, 151*t*
in Lyme disease, **9**:251
neovascularization in, **9**:303
noninfectious (autoimmune), **9**:140–172
nonnecrotizing (nonnecrotizing herpetic retinitis),
    9:203–204
prevalence of, **9**:92, 92*t*
retinal detachment and, **9**:302
signs of, **9**:89–90
symptoms of, **9**:85
Posterior (back) vertex power, lensmeter in
    measurement of, **3**:167, 270, 270*f*, 271
Posterior vestibular artery, **5**:21
Posterior vitreous detachment, **2**:84, 84*f*, 85*f*, 286–287,
    4:134–135, 135*f*, **12**:200*f*, 274–276, 274*f*, 275*f*,
    297–306, 299*f*, 301*f*, 362
in diabetic retinopathy, **12**:110
    epiretinal membranes and, **12**:298–301, 302*f*
    macular holes and, **12**:298, 304–306, 305–306*f*
    perifoveal, **12**:298
    retinal detachment after cataract surgery and, **11**:184
    vitreomacular traction syndrome and, **12**:298,
        302–304, 303*f*
    vitreous hemorrhage and, **12**:275, 313
Postexposure prophylaxis
    hepatitis B, **1**:281
    measles, **1**:282
Postganglionic Horner syndrome, **5**:267, 268–269
Postganglionic nerves, **2**:98, 103, 107
    cholinergic drug action and, **2**:234, 235*f*
    iris sphincter supplied by, **2**:61
Postherpetic neuralgia, **1**:23, **5**:303, **8**:121–122
Postictal paresis (Todd paralysis), **1**:262, **5**:292
Postictal period, **1**:262
Postmeasles blindness, **9**:212
Post-MI (Dressler) syndrome, **1**:103
Postoperative care of ophthalmic surgery patient
    cataract surgery and
        in children, **6**:259–260
        after ECCE, **11**:213
        after ICCE, **11**:215
    corneoscleral laceration repair and, **8**:381–382
    Descemet stripping automated endothelial
        keratoplasty and, **8**:415*t*, 442–445, 442*f*, 443*f*, 444*f*
    filtering surgery and, **10**:194–195
    lamellar keratoplasty and, **8**:436–437
    orbital surgery and, **7**:115
    penetrating keratoplasty and, **8**:421–426
        in children, **8**:430–431
    refractive surgery and, **13**:187–195
        immediate postablation measures, **13**:84–85
        LASIK and, **13**:85, 86–87
        surface ablation and
            immediate postablation measures and, **13**:84–85
            subsequent postoperative care and, **13**:86
Postoperative chest physiotherapy, **1**:144
Postoperative endophthalmitis, **9**:126, 269–271, 270*f*,
    12:354–357, 355*f*, 356*f*, 357*f*. *See also* Uveitis,
    postoperative
    acute-onset, **9**:269, **12**:354, 354–356, 355*f*
    bleb-associated, **10**:196, 197*f*, **12**:354, 356–357, 357*f*

after cataract surgery, **4**:123, 123*f*, 124, **9**:269–271,
    11:143, 144*t*, 179–181, 179*f*
    prevention of, **11**:127–129, 128*f*, 180
    Propionibacterium acnes causing, **4**:123, 123*f*, 124,
        9:126, 269–270
    chronic (delayed-onset), **9**:269–271, 270*f*, **12**:355,
        356, 356*f*
        bacterial, **9**:269–270, 270*f*
        fungal, **9**:270
        Propionibacterium acnes causing, **4**:123, 123*f*, 124,
            9:126, 269–270, 270*f*
    after strabismus surgery, **6**:156
    after vitrectomy, **12**:368
    vitrectomy for, **12**:354–357, 355*f*, 356*f*, 357*f*
Postoperative state, hypercoagulability and, **1**:158
Postpartum thyroiditis, **1**:213
Poststroke dementia, **1**:265
Posttarsal venous drainage, of eyelid, **7**:143
Posttest odds of disease/posttest probability, **1**:333, 334
Posttransfusion hepatitis, transfusion-transmitted virus
    (TTV) causing, **1**:26
Posttransfusion isoantibody production, **1**:154
Posttranslational modification, **2**:158
    of lens proteins, **2**:277
Posttraumatic angle recession, **4**:18, 19*f*, 109
    glaucoma and, **4**:18, 109, **10**:38–39, 38*f*, 39*f*, 100–101,
        100*f*
Posttraumatic endophthalmitis, **12**:328–329
Posttraumatic macular hole, **12**:321–322, 322*f*
Post-traumatic stress disorder (PTSD), **1**:249
Postural hypotension, **1**:85–86
Postviral optic neuritis, **5**:144
Postvitrectomy cataract, **11**:16, 60, 205–206, **12**:368
Potassium
    in aqueous humor, **2**:255, 266*t*, 267
    in lens, **2**:278, **11**:18–19, 18*f*
    in tear film, **2**:238*t*, 240
    transport of, **2**:307
    in vitreous, **2**:266*t*, 286
Potassium balance, in lens, pump–leak theory of
    maintenance of, **11**:18–19, 18*f*
Potassium channels, in lens, **2**:278
Potassium-sparing diuretics
    for heart failure, **1**:118
    for hypertension, **1**:76*t*, 80
Potential acuity meter (PAM), **3**:277–278, 278*f*, **5**:106
    in cataract surgery evaluation, **11**:81
Potentials, cortical, **12**:44–45, 45*f*
    electrically evoked, **12**:45
    visually evoked, **12**:44–45, 45*f*. *See also* Visually
        evoked cortical potentials
Povidone-iodine, **2**:378
    for ophthalmia neonatorum prophylaxis, **6**:188
Power
    for medical lasers, **3**:18*t*, 21
    in phacoemulsification, **11**:103
        delivery of, **11**:106–108
        advances in, **11**:126
Power (optical). *See also* Transverse magnification
    of bifocal add
        determining, **3**:145–147
            with lensmeter, **3**:270–271, 271*f*
            occupation and, **3**:156–157

candle (luminous intensity), 3:18*t*
contact lens, 3:167, 170, 183, 185
  lensmeters in measurement of, 3:268–272, 269*f*,
    270*f*, 271*f*
corneal, in IOL power determination, 3:216–217,
  217*f*
cylinder, 3:97, 98*f*
  combined lenses and, 3:99
  finding, 3:127–129
  optimal value for, 3:319
  reducing, distortion reduction and, 3:140, 317
    residual astigmatism and, 3:318, 319*f*
  refinement of, cross-cylinder refraction and, 3:132,
    133–134, 133*f*, 134*f*
definition of, 3:33
of fluid lens. *See* Power (optical), of tear lens
intraocular lens, determination of, 3:211–219, 11:84–88
  biometry in, 11:82–83, 83*f*, 84
  in children, 3:223, 6:258
  contact lens method for, 11:87, 13:188
  corneal transplantation and, 3:222
  formulas for, 3:212–213, 212*f*, 217–219, 11:85, 87
    biometric requirements and, 3:213–219, 214*f*,
      215*f*, 216*f*, 217*f*, 218*f*
    choice of, 3:219
    errors in, 3:221
    for postkeratorefractive eye, 3:221–222
    refractive lens exchange/clear lens extraction
      and, 13:140–141
    regression formulas, 3:212, 218, 11:85, 87
  historical methods for, 11:87, 13:188
  improving outcomes of surgery and, 11:86
  incorrect, 11:168
  online post-refractive calculator for (ASCRS),
    13:188–189, 190*f*
  preventing errors in, 11:84–85
  after radial keratotomy, 13:48
  refraction and, 11:76
  refractive lens exchange/clear lens extraction and,
    13:140–141
  refractive surgery and, 3:220–222, 11:86–88, 193,
    13:187–189
  regression formulas for, 11:85, 87
  silicone oil placement and, 3:222–223
  topographical method for, 11:87
    after refractive surgery, 13:187
  triple procedure and, 11:192
  unexpected refractive results after surgery and,
    11:168
ophthalmic lens, 3:61–62
  for thick lenses, 3:76–78, 78*f*
  for thin lenses, 3:66
prism, Prentice rule and, 3:87, 87*f*
reflecting, of mirrors, 3:89–90
refractive, 3:61–62
  of cornea, 8:37–38, 13:3–4
    measurement of, 3:263–265, 263*f*, 264*f*, 265*f*,
      266*f*, 8:38–39, 13:3–4. *See also* Keratometry
    after refractive surgery, 13:187–189
  of schematic eye, 3:105*t*
sphere
  fogging in determination of, 3:136
  optimal value for, 3:320

of tear lens, 3:173–174, 174*f*, 175
  contact lens fitting and, 3:183, 185
Power cross, 3:97, 98, 98*f*. *See also* Cylinder power
Power curve, contact lens, 3:170
Power factor magnification, 3:311
Power maps, 8:40–43, 41*f*, 42*f*, 13:11, 12*f*
  keratorefractive surgery and, 8:44
Power prediction formulas, for IOLs, 3:212–213, 212*f*,
  217–219, 11:85, 87
  biometric requirements and, 3:213–219, 214*f*, 215*f*,
    216*f*, 217*f*, 218*f*
  choice of, 3:219
  errors in, 3:221
  for postkeratorefractive eye, 3:221–222
  refractive lens exchange/clear lens extraction and,
    13:140–141
  regression formulas, 3:212, 218, 11:85, 87
Power readings, on lasers, 3:18*t*, 21
Poxviruses/poxvirus infection, 8:127–128
pp65 antigen, CMV infection and, 1:24
PPC. *See* Posterior parietal cortex
PPCD/PPCD1. *See* Posterior polymorphous corneal
  dystrophy
PPD test. *See* Purified protein derivative (PPD) test
PPMD. *See* Posterior polymorphous corneal dystrophy
PPRF. *See* Paramedian pontine reticular formation
PPV. *See* Positive predictive value
PQRI (Physician Quality Reporting Initiative), 1:347
Prader-Willi syndrome, imprinting abnormalities
  causing, 2:154, 169
Pralidoxime, 2:336*f*, 340
Pramipexole, for Parkinson disease, 1:259
Pramlintide, for diabetes mellitus, 1:202
Prandin. *See* Repaglinide
Pravachol. *See* Pravastatin
Pravastatin, for hypercholesterolemia/heart disease
  prevention, 1:137*t*
Prazosin, 2:259*t*
  for heart failure, 1:119
  for hypertension, 1:77*t*
  intraoperative floppy iris syndrome and, 11:74, 155
pRB protein, retinoblastoma and, 6:356
Preadolescents, low vision in, 3:307
Prealbumin. *See* Transthyretin
Precancerous eyelid lesions
  epidermal, 7:166, 167*f*
  melanocytic, 7:168
Precancerous melanosis (lentigo maligna/Hutchinson
  melanotic freckle), 7:168
Precentral gyrus, 5:60
  facial weakness/paralysis caused by lesion of,
    5:284–285
Precorneal tear film, 2:42, 237. *See also* Tear film (tears)
Precortical vitreous pocket, 12:7*f*, 8
Precose. *See* Acarbose
Precursor cytotoxic T lymphocytes, 9:51, 53*f*
Precursor messenger RNA, 2:161
Pred Forte/Pred Mild. *See* Prednisolone
Pre-Descemet corneal dystrophy, 8:268*t*, 270*t*, 290,
  290*f*
  genetics of, 8:269*t*, 290
Prediabetic disorders, 1:192–193
Prednisol. *See* Prednisolone

Prednisolone, 1:181*t*, 2:357*t*
  anti-inflammatory potency of, 1:181*t*, 2:360*t*
  in combination preparations, 2:373*t*
  for corneal graft rejection, 8:429
  for hyphema, 6:410
  pressure-elevating potency of, 2:360*t*
  for sarcoidosis, 9:177
  for stromal keratitis, 8:115–116
  for uveitis, 9:101*t*
Prednisone, 1:181*t*
  for acute retinal necrosis, 9:202
  for Behçet disease, 9:194
  for giant cell arteritis/AAION, 5:126, 320
  for hyphema, 8:368
  for nonspecific orbital inflammation, 7:61
  for optic neuritis, 5:146
  for paroxysmal nocturnal hemoglobinuria, 1:150
  for rheumatoid arthritis, 1:162
  for Stevens-Johnson syndrome, 8:197
  for thyroid eye disease, 5:333–334, 7:53–54
  for toxoplasmosis, 9:232, 12:208–209, 208*t*
  for uveitis, 9:101*t*, 104
  for Vogt-Koyanagi-Harada (VKH) syndrome, 9:189
Preeclampsia, 1:86. *See also* Eclampsia
  choroidal perfusion abnormalities and, 12:178*f*
Preferential looking, for visual acuity testing in children,
    6:62, 63*f*, 72*t*, 73, 170–171, 413
Preferred Practice Patterns, 1:343
Preferred retinal locus (PRL), 3:286, 293
Preganglionic autonomic nerves, cholinergic drug
    action and, 2:334, 335*f*
Preganglionic Horner syndrome, 5:267
Pregeniculate visual loss, 6:414–415
Pregnancy. *See also under* Congenital
  alcohol use during (fetal alcohol syndrome), 1:250,
    2:142–143, 142*f*, 6:394–395, 395*f*
    craniofacial malformations and, 6:394–395, 395*f*
  antiphospholipid antibody syndrome and, 1:170, 171,
    172–173
  carbonic anhydrase use during, 2:354
  CMV infection during, 1:24, 6:184, 9:205
  cocaine abuse during, 1:250–251
  diabetes during (gestational diabetes mellitus), 1:191*t*,
    192
  diabetic retinopathy affected by, 12:94
    timetable for ophthalmic examination and, 12:111,
      112*t*
  fluorescein angiography during, 12:25
  glaucoma medication use during, 2:354, 10:176
  gonococcal infection during, ophthalmia neonatorum
    and, 8:153
  herpes simplex virus infection during, 1:22, 6:185, 8:106
  history of
    in infant with decreased vision, 6:414
    infantile corneal opacities and, 6:217
    nystagmus and, 6:318
    strabismus/amblyopia and, 6:71
  hypercoagulability associated with, 1:158
  hypertension/hypertension management and, 1:86
    methyldopa in, 1:82
  immunization during, 1:280
  lymphocytic choriomeningitis virus infection during,
    6:186, 9:211–212
  maternally transmitted eye infection and, 6:181–186
    ophthalmia neonatorum and, 6:186–188, 187*f*,
      8:152–154
  measles during, 9:212
  neuro-ophthalmic disorders associated with, 5:162,
    164, 345–347, 346*f*
  pemphigoid during, 8:205*t*
  phenytoin use during, 1:264
  radiation exposure during, 1:238
  refractive surgery contraindicated during, 13:31
  rubella during, 1:283, 6:183, 8:130, 9:209–211, 209*f*,
    210*f*
  syphilis during, 1:12, 279, 6:185, 221, 9:243, 243–244,
    244*f*, 249
  thyroiditis after, 1:213
  thyroxine levels affected by, 1:208
  toxemia of. *See* Eclampsia; Preeclampsia
  toxoplasmosis during, 1:21, 6:182, 9:228, 233,
    12:206–207
Pregnancy tests, preoperative, 1:305
"Pregnant 7" (Kelman tripod) anterior chamber IOL,
    3:211, 211*f*
Prehypertension, 1:69, 70, 70*t*, 270, 12:113
  in children and adolescents, 1:86–87
Prelaminar nerve/prelaminar area of optic nerve, 2:90,
    10:42, 43–44, 43*f*. *See also* Optic disc
  blood supply of, 2:94, 95*f*
Preload, 1:117
  reduction of for heart failure, 1:119
Premacular bursa, 12:7*f*, 8
Premacular hole, 12:304
Premalignant eyelid lesions
  epidermal, 7:166, 167*f*
  melanocytic, 7:168
Premarket approval (PMA), 13:204, 205
  delays in, 13:207
Premarket Notification 510(k) application, 13:205
Premature atrial complexes/contractions, 1:121, 122*t*
Premature contractions, 1:121–123, 122*t*
Premature junctional complexes/contractions, 1:121, 122*t*
"Premature presbyopia" (accommodative insufficiency),
    3:142–143
Premature ventricular complexes/contractions, 1:121,
    122*t*, 123
Prematurity
  ocular deviations and, 5:212
  retinopathy of. *See* Retinopathy, of prematurity
Premelanosomes, in retinal pigment epithelium, 2:72, 127
Premotor neurons, 5:40
Prenatal diagnosis, 2:198*t*, 228–229
Prentice position, glass prism calibration and, 3:84*f*, 85,
    86*f*
Prentice rule, 3:87, 87*f*
  bifocal design and, 3:150–156, 151*f*, 152*f*, 153*f*, 154*f*,
    155*f*, 156*f*
  calculating induced anisophoria and, 3:153–154, 154*f*
Preocular tear film, 2:237
  tear dysfunction and, 2:244
Preoperative assessment/preparation for ocular surgery,
    1:303–310, 304*t*
  cataract surgery, 11:73–88
    antimicrobial prophylaxis and, 11:127–128
    in diabetes mellitus, 11:80

ECCE, 11:211
ICCE, 11:213
ocular trauma and, 11:206
corneal transplantation, 8:414–417
diabetes mellitus and, 1:305, 307–308
eyelid surgery, 7:189–190, 229
fasting and, 1:308
incisional glaucoma surgery, 10:185–186
latex allergy and, 1:308–309
medication management and, 1:303, 305–307, 309t
in older patients, 1:224
in pediatric patients, 1:305
perforating injury repair, 8:374–375
photocoagulation, 12:341
recent developments and, 1:303
refractive surgery, 13:29–42, 30t
LASIK, 13:71–73
phakic intraocular lens insertion, 13:128–129
wavefront-guided laser ablation, 13:40, 72
respiratory diseases and, 1:308
testing recommendations and, 1:303, 303–304
Universal Protocol and, 1:303, 306–310
Prepapillary vascular loops, 4:133, 12:307, 307f
Preperimetric glaucoma, 10:4
Preperiosteal approach, for midface lift, 7:233, 234f
Pre-plus disease, retinopathy of prematurity and, 6:283
Prepupillary intraocular lens, 3:204f, 207, 207f, 208f
Preretinal macular fibrosis, 12:300
Preretinal tract, 12:8
PRES. See Posterior reversible encephalopathy
syndrome
PresbyLens, 13:200
Presbyopia, 2:63, 3:117, 142, 143t, 11:20, 13:149–161
contact lenses for, 3:176, 189–190, 189f, 190f. See also
Contact lenses, bifocal
Helmholtz hypothesis (capsular theory) of
accommodation and, 11:19, 13:149–150, 150f
perimetry variations and, 10:56
"premature" (accommodative insufficiency),
3:142–143
refractive surgery and, 13:32–33
Schachar theory of accommodation and, 13:150–152,
151f, 152f
surgical correction of, 13:149–161
accommodative, 13:157–160
conductive keratoplasty for, 13:120–123, 153–154
corneal inlays for, 13:53, 54, 157, 200
custom/multifocal ablations for, 13:156–157, 157f
international trends in use of, 13:199–200
intraocular lenses for
accommodating IOLs, 13:159–160, 159f
experimental IOLs, 13:160–161
multifocal IOLs, 13:154–156, 154f, 155f
keratophakia for, 13:53–55
monovision and, 13:152–153
nonaccommodative, 13:152–157
refractive lens exchange/clear lens extraction for,
13:139
scleral surgery for, 13:157–159, 158f
Preschool children. See also Children
low vision in, 3:306
Presentation time, in perimetry, variations associated
with, 10:56

Preseptal cellulitis, 4:208, 209f, 7:40–41
in children, 6:194–195, 7:40
Haemophilus causing, 6:195, 7:40, 8:150
after strabismus surgery, 6:156
Preseptal orbicularis muscles, 7:135f, 136, 137f
Preseptal palpebral muscles, 5:61–62
Preseptal tissues, 7:136
Preservatives
in contact lens solutions
allergic/sensitivity reactions and, 8:92
giant papillary conjunctivitis and, 8:195
in ocular medications
allergic/adverse reactions to, 2:322, 8:183, 10:169
demulcents, 2:391, 8:58–59
irrigating solutions, 2:392
persistent corneal defects caused by (toxic
ulcerative keratopathy), 8:86
toxic keratoconjunctivitis caused by, 8:359, 360
Press-On prism, 3:89, 164
for consecutive esotropia, 6:103
for esotropia in sixth nerve (abducens) paralysis, 6:98
for induced anisophoria, 3:154
for nystagmus, 6:326
for thyroid eye disease, 5:334
Pressure-independent (uveoscleral) outflow, 10:3f, 16,
19
Pressure-induced stromal keratitis (PISK), after LASIK,
13:112, 112f
Presumed ocular histoplasmosis syndrome. See Ocular
histoplasmosis syndrome
Pretarsal orbicularis muscles, 7:135f, 136, 137f
Pretarsal palpebral muscles, 5:61–62
Pretarsal space, 2:25f
Pretarsal tissues, 7:136
venous drainage of, 7:143
Pretectal (Parinaud/dorsal midbrain) syndrome, 5:44,
211, 212f
eyelid retraction in, 5:211, 273, 281, 7:214
nystagmus in, 6:325
Pretectum/pretectal nuclei, 2:99, 5:32, 33, 65, 65f
convergence insufficiency caused by damage to,
5:213
vertical gaze palsy caused by damage to, 5:210–211,
212f
Pretest probability, 1:333–334, 334t
Prethreshold disease, in retinopathy of prematurity,
6:285, 285t
oxygen therapy for, 6:281
treatment criteria and, 6:286
Pretibial myxedema (infiltrative dermopathy), in
hyperthyroidism/thyroid eye disease, 1:211, 7:51
Pretrichial brow lift, 7:232
Prevent Blindness America, 6:417t
Preventive medicine, 1:269–287
immunization in, 1:279–286
ophthalmology practices and, 8:45–46
recent developments in, 1:269
screening procedures in, 1:269–279. See also
Screening/diagnostic tests
Preveon. See Adefovir
Prevnar. See Pneumococcal vaccine
Prezista. See Darunavir
Primacor. See Milrinone

Primaquine, for *Pneumocystis jiroveci (Pneumocystis carinii)* pneumonia, 1:37
Primary acquired melanosis (PAM), 4:65*t*, 67–69, 68*f*, 8:237–238, 237*f*, 238*t*
  melanoma arising from, 4:67, 68*f*, 69, 70*f*, 8:239
Primary angle-closure glaucoma. *See* Angle closure/angle-closure glaucoma, primary
Primary anophthalmia, 7:33
Primary antiphospholipid antibody syndrome, 1:171
Primary aphakia, 4:121, 11:26. *See also* Aphakia
Primary central nervous system lymphomas. *See* Primary intraocular/central nervous system lymphomas
Primary coloboma, 11:26. *See also* Coloboma
  lens. *See also* Coloboma
Primary congenital glaucoma, 4:102, 103*f*, 6:233–238, 234*f*, 235*t*, 236*f*, 237*f*, 8:265, 10:5*t*, 139, 140*t*, 143–145, 143*f*, 144*f*, 144*t*. *See also* Glaucoma, childhood
  corneal opacities and, 6:218, 234, 235*t*
  differential diagnosis of, 10:144, 144*t*
  genetics of, 6:233, 10:142–143
  treatment of, 10:152–157
    medical, 10:156–157
    surgical, 10:145, 152–156, 153*f*, 154*f*
Primary deviation, 6:35
Primary dye test (Jones I test), 7:259
Primary endothelial failure, 8:422, 422*f*
  after Descemet stripping automated endothelial keratoplasty, 8:444–445
Primary (anterior) focal point, 3:69, 70*f*
Primary glaucoma. *See* Angle closure/angle-closure glaucoma; Glaucoma; Open-angle glaucoma
Primary HIV infection, 1:30–31
Primary (essential) hypertension, 1:71, 71*f*
Primary intraocular/central nervous system lymphomas, 1:244, 4:140–142, 141*f*, 142*f*, 143*f*, 323–325, 323*f*, 325*f*, 9:136, 281–284, 282*f*, 283*f*, 12:199, 199*f*
  central serous retinopathy differentiated from, 12:174
  in HIV infection/AIDS, 9:314
  uveitis differentiated from, 9:91, 136, 281–283
    in children, 6:276*t*
Primary lens fibers, development of, 2:130, 11:22, 23*f*
Primary open-angle glaucoma (POAG). *See* Open-angle glaucoma, primary
Primary position of gaze, 6:13, 27, 80, 80*f*
  extraocular muscle action and, 6:30, 30*f*
Primary visual (striate/occipital) cortex, 5:28*f*, 34, 35*f*, 6:42. *See also* Visual (calcarine/occipital) cortex
  development of, 6:44, 45*f*
    abnormal visual experience affecting, 6:46–49, 47*f*, 48*f*
Primary vitreous, 2:130, 131*f*, 4:132
  persistent hyperplasia of. *See* Persistent fetal vasculature
Primaxin. *See* Imipenem-cilastin
Primed macrophages, 9:20, 21–22, 21*f*
Primers, in polymerase chain reaction, 2:158, 4:40*f*, 41
Priming, of effector lymphocytes, 9:37–38, 40*f*, 42
Primitive node, 2:117
Primitive streak, 2:117, 118*f*
Primitive zone, 2:124

Prince rule, 3:146
Principal line of vision, 3:106
Principal meridians
  alignment of, combination of spherocylindrical lenses and, 3:99
  of astigmatic surface or lens, 3:97, 97*f*
  locating axes of, in retinoscopy, 3:126–127, 126*f*, 127*f*, 128*f*
Principal planes, 3:75, 75*f*
Principal points, 3:36, 75, 75*f*, 76, 77*f*
Prinivil. *See* Lisinopril
Prinzide. *See* Lisinopril
Prinzmetal (variant) angina, 1:101
Prions/prion diseases, 5:368, 8:143
Prism adaptation test, 6:86
Prism and cover test
  alternate (alternate cover test), 6:74–75, 76*f*
    for intermittent exotropia evaluation, 6:100
  simultaneous, 6:75–76
Prism diopter, 3:85, 85*f*, 86*f*
Prism dissociation
  for binocular balance testing, 3:136
  for nonorganic ophthalmic disorder evaluation, 5:309, 309*f*
Prism power. *See also* Transverse magnification
  Prentice rule and, 3:87, 87*f*
Prismatic half-eye glasses, high-plus, in low vision/vision rehabilitation, 3:297, 298*f*
Prisms, 3:83–89, 84*f*
  aberrations of, 3:88
  for acute esotropia, 6:96
  angle of deviation and, 3:84–85, 84*f*
    prism diopter and, 3:85, 85*f*, 86*f*
  anophthalmic socket camouflage and, 7:125
  for basic (acquired) esotropia, 6:96
  for consecutive esotropia, 6:103
  for convergence insufficiency, 6:106
  for convergence paralysis, 6:106
  Fresnel. *See* Fresnel prisms
  in high-plus half-eye glasses, 3:297, 298*f*
  for homonymous hemianopia, 3:300–301
  image displacement and, 3:86–87, 86*f*
    bifocal design and, 3:150–151, 151*f*, 152*f*, 153*f*
  for induced tropia test, 6:72–73
  for intermittent exotropia, 6:102
  inverting
    in operating microscope, 3:262, 262*f*
    in slit-lamp biomicroscope, 3:251*f*, 252
  lens as. *See* Prisms, Prentice rule and
  for low vision/vision rehabilitation, 3:293, 300–301
  methods of correction with, 3:300
  for monofixation syndrome evaluation, 6:57–58, 57*f*
  for nystagmus, 6:326–328
  plane parallel plate, 3:83–84, 84*f*
  Porro-Abbe, 3:252
  for postoperative diplopia, 6:155
  Prentice rule and, 3:87, 87*f*
    bifocal design and, 3:150–156, 151*f*, 152*f*, 153*f*, 154*f*, 155*f*, 156*f*
  for residual exotropia, 6:103
  rotary (Risley), 3:88
  in slit-lamp biomicroscope, 3:251*f*, 252
  in spectacle lenses, 3:83, 87, 164

for superior oblique muscle paralysis, 6:120
therapeutic use of, 3:163–164
for thyroid eye disease, 5:334, 6:135–136
vector addition of, 3:88, 88f
wavefront aberrations and, 13:6
PRK. See Photorefractive keratectomy
PRL. See Preferred retinal locus
PRNG. See Penicillin-resistant N gonorrhoeae
ProAir HFA. See Albuterol
Probability of outcome, baseline, 1:336–337
Proband, 2:158, 225
Probe amplification, multiplex ligation-dependent
(MLPA), 4:38t, 41
Probes, DNA. See DNA probes
Probing of lacrimal system
for acquired nasolacrimal duct/canalicular
obstruction, 7:261
for canalicular trauma, 7:272
for congenital dacryocele, 6:205
for congenital nasolacrimal duct obstruction, 6:207,
207–208, 208f, 7:250–251, 251–252, 252f, 253f
Procainamide, 1:123t
for cardioversion, 1:125
Procaine, 2:387t
in patients taking cholinesterase inhibitors, 2:340
Procaine penicillin, 1:45t
Procardia. See Nifedipine
Procerus muscle, 7:17, 131, 133f, 137f
Process (content of care), 1:338
monitoring system and, 1:340–342
Processing phase of immune response arc, 9:33, 36f,
37–41, 40f
primary versus secondary, 9:43–44
response to poison ivy and, 9:34, 35
response to tuberculosis and, 9:35
Prodrugs, 2:330
Profenal. See Suprofen
Prograf. See Tacrolimus
Programmed cell death (PCD/apoptosis), 2:147, 148
by cytotoxic T lymphocytes, 9:51, 53f
in DNA repair, 2:170
Fas ligand (CD95 ligand/FasL) in, 9:51, 53f, 62
Progressive addition lenses, 3:147–150, 150f
in low vision/vision rehabilitation, 3:296
Progressive (chronic progressive) external
ophthalmoplegia, 2:174–175, 5:336–337, 336f, 337f,
6:137, 139f, 12:254
mitochondrial DNA defects and, 2:173, 174–175, 191,
12:251t, 265
ptosis in, 5:280, 336, 336f
Progressive facial hemiatrophy, 8:324t
Progressive multifocal leukoencephalopathy, in HIV
infection/AIDS, 5:361, 362f
Progressive myopia. See High (pathologic/degenerative)
myopia
Progressive outer retinal necrosis (PORN), 9:203, 203f,
307–308, 308f, 12:201
Progressive supranuclear palsy
convergence insufficiency in, 5:213
facial weakness/paralysis in, 5:285
pursuit dysfunction in, 5:213
saccadic dysfunction in, 5:208
intrusions, 5:200

Progressive systemic sclerosis (scleroderma), 1:173–174
eyelid manifestations of, 4:213t
Project-O-Chart, 6:87
Projection charts
polarizing, 3:11–12
standard, distance acuity and, 3:290
Prokaryotes/prokaryotic cells, 2:158, 8:131. See also
Bacteria
Prolactin-inhibiting factors, 1:214t
Prolactin-releasing factors, 1:214t
Prolactinomas (lactotroph adenomas), 1:215
Prolate cornea, 13:10, 20
Proliferative diabetic retinopathy (PDR). See Diabetic
retinopathy, proliferative
Proliferative sickle cell retinopathy (PSR). See Sickle cell
retinopathy, proliferative
Proliferative vitreoretinopathy. See Vitreoretinopathies,
proliferative
Prolixin. See Fluphenazine
Promoter, 2:158
in alternative splicing, 2:168
Prone-position test, for occludable/narrow chamber
angle, 10:118
PrONTO study, 12:76–77
Propafenone, 1:123t
Propagation of light, 3:39–55
curved surfaces and, 3:51, 52f
dispersion and, 3:49–51, 51f
Fermat principle and, 3:51–53, 52f, 53f
law of reflection and, 3:42–44, 43f, 44f, 45
law of refraction and, 3:44–46, 45f, 46f, 47, 47f
normal incidence and, 3:46
optical interfaces and, 3:42, 42f, 43f
optical media and, 3:39–41, 40t
rectilinear, law of, 3:41, 42f
refractive index and, 3:39–41, 40t
specular reflection and, 3:42–44, 43f, 44f, 45
specular transmission and, 3:44–46, 45f, 46f, 47, 47f
stigmatic imaging and, 3:53–55, 54f
total internal reflection and, 3:46–49, 48f, 49–50, 50f
Propamidine, for Acanthamoeba keratitis, 8:169
Proparacaine, 2:387t, 388–389, 389
for cataract surgery, 11:99
with fluorescein, 2:387t
Propine. See Dipivefrin
Propionibacterium/Propionibacterium acnes, 8:134–135,
135f
chronic uveitis after cataract surgery caused by,
11:158
endophthalmitis caused by, 4:123, 123f, 124, 9:126,
269–270, 270f, 12:354, 356
as normal ocular flora, 8:97, 97t, 134
ocular infection caused by, 8:135
Propofol, perioperative, 1:309t, 311
Proposita/propositus, 2:158, 225
Propranolol, 2:259t, 345t
for arrhythmias, 1:123t
for hemangiomas, in children, 6:340
for hypertension, 1:76t, 78t
Proptosis (exophthalmos/exorbitism), 4:229, 6:173, 7:22
bilateral, 7:23
in craniosynostosis, 6:388, 7:35
exposure keratopathy and, 8:80, 385

in idiopathic orbital inflammatory disease, 6:346, 347f
in neuroblastoma, 6:336
in orbital cellulitis, 6:195, 196f
in orbital lymphangioma, 4:240, 6:341
in orbital zygomycosis, 7:45
in retinoblastoma, 4:304, 304f
in rhabdomyosarcoma, 4:242, 243f, 6:335, 7:76, 77f
in teratoma, 6:344, 345f
in thyroid eye disease, 4:232, 233f, 5:332, 332f, 7:23,
    47f, 49, 51. See also Thyroid eye disease
    in children/adolescents, 6:135, 136, 136f, 346, 347f
    eyelid retraction differentiated from, 7:213–214
    unilateral, 7:23
in uveal lymphoid infiltration, 4:326
Propulsid. See Cisapride
Propylene glycol, for dry eye, 2:390
Propylthiouracil, for Graves hyperthyroidism, 1:211
Proscar. See Finasteride
Prosom. See Estazolam
Prosopagnosia, 5:193
Prospective Evaluation of Radial Keratotomy (PERK)
    study, 13:43–44
Prostacyclin, 2:255–256
Prostaglandin analogues, 2:256–257, 264t, 354–355,
    354t, 10:157, 162t, 166, 167f
    cystoid macular edema and, 12:143
    for elevated episcleral venous pressure, 10:96
    for glaucoma, 2:256–257, 264t, 354–355, 354t, 10:157,
        162t, 166, 167f
        adnexal changes associated with, 10:28, 162t, 166,
            167f
        childhood glaucoma and, 6:242–243, 10:157
        cystoid macular edema after cataract surgery and,
            11:202–203
        inflammatory glaucoma and, 10:94
        during pregnancy/lactation, 10:176
        uveitic glaucoma and, 9:297
    uveitis caused by, 9:128
Prostaglandin E₂, thyroid eye disease and, 4:232, 7:50
Prostaglandin G/H synthase. See Cyclooxygenase
Prostaglandins, 2:255, 256–257, 8:179t, 9:25–26, 26f
    cystoid macular edema after cataract surgery and,
        11:202–203
    modes of action of, 2:264t
    nonsteroidal anti-inflammatory drugs and, 2:257
    receptors for, 2:258
        in signal transduction, 2:264t
    synthesis of, 2:256f, 257, 9:25, 26f
        anti-inflammatory drugs affecting, 2:257
        by mast cells, 9:10
Prostamides. See Bimatoprost; Prostaglandin analogues
Prostate cancer, 1:274
    eye/orbital metastases and, 4:316t, 7:92, 92f
    screening for, 1:274
Prostate-specific antigen, in cancer screening, 1:274
Prostheses, ocular, 7:122
Prostigmin. See Neostigmine
Protan defects (protanopia), 12:47, 49, 49f, 50, 213
    ocular findings in carriers of, 2:222t
Protanomalous dichromatism, 12:214t
Protanomalous trichromatism, 12:213, 214t
Protease inhibitors, 1:34
    in HAART, 1:35

Protease-sparing regimen, in HAART, 1:35
Proteases
    corneal, as inflammatory mediators, 8:177t
    microbial, in ocular infections, 8:99
Protective eyewear, lens materials for, 3:162
Protein AF, 8:316
Protein AP, 8:316
Protein C/activated protein C, 1:151, 152
    deficiency of, 1:152, 157
    resistance to, 1:157
Protein kinase C, diabetes mellitus complications and,
    1:205
Protein kinase C/Ca²⁺–dependent signal transduction,
    in tear secretion, 2:242–243, 242f
Protein kinase C inhibitors, in diabetes mellitus
    management, 1:189, 205
Protein S, 1:151, 152
    deficiency of, 1:152, 157
Proteinaceous degeneration, 8:334–335, 335f. See also
    Spheroidal degeneration
Proteinase-3, scleritis/retinal vasculitis in Wegener
    granulomatosis and, 1:179, 9:146
Proteinase inhibitors
    in aqueous humor, 2:267, 269
    in cornea, 2:250
Proteinases, in aqueous humor, 2:269
Proteins
    in aqueous humor, 2:265, 266, 268–270
        breakdown of blood–aqueous barrier and, 2:272
        dynamics and, 2:254, 255, 268–269
    ciliary body expression of, 2:253
    disorders of metabolism of, corneal changes in,
        8:316–319
    drug-binding by, systemic administration and, 2:329
    lens. See Lens proteins
    in retinal pigment epithelium, 2:304
    in rod outer segments ("rim" proteins), 2:293
        mutations of, 4:172
    in tear film, 2:240
    vitreous, 2:283, 285–286, 4:131
Proteoglycans
    corneal, 2:45, 249, 250, 8:7
    scleral, 8:9
Proteus, 8:135
Prothrombin
    cephalosporins affecting, 1:58
    mutation in gene for, 1:147, 158
Prothrombin time (PT), 1:152
    international normalized ratio and, 1:152
Proton density, 7:26
Proton density MRI, 5:73, 73t, 74f, 75f, 76t, 7:26
Proton pump inhibitors, corticosteroid treatment in
    uveitis and, 9:104
Proto-oncogene, 2:158, 171
Protoplasmic astrocytes, 2:77
Protozoa/protozoal infection. See also specific causative
        organism
    gastrointestinal, in HIV infection/AIDS, 1:38
    ocular, 8:140–141, 9:226–235
        Acanthamoeba keratitis, 4:54, 84–85, 86f,
            8:167–169, 168f
Protractors, eyelid, 7:136, 137f
    spasms of, 7:218–220, 219f. See also Blepharospasm

Proventil. *See* Albuterol

Provera. *See* Medroxyprogesterone

Proximal (instrument) convergence, 6:37

Proximal fusion, tenacious, in intermittent exotropia, 6:100–101

Proximal illumination, for slit-lamp biomicroscopy, 8:14

Prozac. *See* Fluoxetine

PRP. *See* Panretinal photocoagulation

PrP^C, 5:368

Prulifloxacin, 1:61

Prussian blue stain, Perls, 4:31*t*

PSA. *See* Prostate-specific antigen

Psammoma bodies, in optic nerve meningioma, 4:258

PSC. *See* Posterior subcapsular cataract

Pseudoaccommodative intraocular lenses, 11:137

Pseudoadenomatous hyperplasia (Fuchs adenoma), 4:184, 288

Pseudo-Brown syndrome, 6:130

Pseudocholinesterase. *See also* Cholinesterase
  defective, succinylcholine effects and, 2:230

Pseudocolobomas, in Treacher Collins syndrome, 6:394

Pseudocryptophthalmos, 8:249, 250

Pseudocyst, foveal, 12:304, 305*f*

Pseudodementia, in older patients, 1:227

Pseudodominance, 2:159, 215

Pseudoepiphora, evaluation of, 7:257–258

Pseudoepitheliomatous hyperplasia, 7:158, 8:226*t*

Pseudoesotropia, 6:89, 90*t*

Pseudoexfoliation (exfoliation syndrome), 4:106, 106*f*, 107*f*, 10:11*t*, 38, 85–87, 86*f*, 87*f*, 122, 123*f*, 11:61–62, 61*f*
  cataract surgery in patient with, 11:199
  glaucoma and, 10:11*t*, 85, 87, 122, 123*f*
  postoperative hyphema and, 11:177
  zonular incompetence and, 10:122, 123*f*, 11:197, 198*f*, 199

Pseudoexotropia, 6:99
  in retinopathy of prematurity, 6:287, 287*f*

Pseudo-Foster Kennedy syndrome, 5:127

Pseudogene, 2:159

Pseudogliomas, 4:178
  in incontinentia pigmenti, 6:380

Pseudoguttae, inflammatory, 8:25, 30

Pseudohermaphrodites, 2:204

Pseudohorn cysts, 4:214, 214*f*

Pseudo-Hurler polydystrophy, 6:400*t*, 8:312

Pseudohypopyon
  in leukemia, 4:327
  in retinoblastoma, 4:303, 303*f*, 6:354, 9:286

Pseudo-internuclear ophthalmoplegia, myasthenic, 5:225

Pseudoisochromatic plates, 12:48, 48*f*
  in low vision evaluation, 5:104–105

Pseudolymphoma. *See* Lymphoid hyperplasia

Pseudomembrane, 8:20*t*, 22*t*
  in epidemic keratoconjunctivitis, 8:124
  in ligneous conjunctivitis, 8:192, 192*f*

Pseudomembranous enterocolitis, *Clostridium difficile* causing, 1:8–9

Pseudomonas
  aeruginosa, 1:11–12, 8:135, 136*f*
    resistant strains of, 1:11, 12
  keratitis caused by, 8:159, 160*f*

Pseudo-overaction, oblique muscle, 6:116

Pseudopapilledema, 5:118–120, 120*f*
  in children, 6:313–315, 314*t*, 315*f*
  drusen and, 4:255, 5:120, 120*f*, 134–136, 135*f*
    in children, 6:314–315, 315*f*

Pseudopemphigoid, 8:199, 361

Pseudophakia
  prophylactic treatment of retinal breaks and, 12:285
  surgically-induced, accommodating IOLs for, 13:159–160, 159*f*

Pseudophakic (aphakic) bullous edema/keratopathy, after cataract surgery, 4:89–91, 90*f*, 8:384–385, 11:147, 147*f*, 167
  IOL design and, 11:167

Pseudophakic glaucoma, 10:124
  in children, 6:239

Pseudophakic refractive procedures, 13:4*t*

Pseudophakodonesis, IOL dislocation and, 11:164–165, 166

Pseudoplasticity, of ophthalmic viscosurgical device, 11:97

Pseudopolycoria, 6:230–231, 231*f*

Pseudoproptosis, 6:334, 7:23

Pseudoptosis, 5:276*f*, 281, 6:179*t*, 7:210, 211*f*
  in third nerve (oculomotor) paralysis, 6:132

Pseudoretinitis pigmentosa
  in congenital rubella, 6:183
  in congenital syphilis, 6:185

Pseudoretinoblastoma, 4:305*t*

Pseudorosettes, in retinoblastoma, 4:178–179, 179*f*

Pseudo–Roth spots, in leukemia, 4:326

Pseudostrabismus
  in epicanthus, 7:147
  in retinopathy of prematurity, 6:287, 287*f*

Pseudotumor
  benign lymphoid (pseudolymphoma). *See* Lymphoid hyperplasia
  cerebri (idiopathic intracranial hypertension), 5:123–125, 123*t*
    in children, 5:124–125, 6:312–313
    headache and, 5:123, 124, 294
  orbital. *See* Nonspecific orbital inflammation

Pseudoxanthoma elasticum, 1:153
  angioid streaks in, 12:84, 84*f*
  Bruch membrane affected in, 12:17
  peau d'orange fundus changes in, 12:84, 84*f*

PSF. *See* Point spread function

Psoriasis/psoriatic arthritis, 1:165–166, 9:123, 123*f*
  in children, 6:269*t*, 270–271
  iritis in, 9:123

PSP. *See* Progressive supranuclear palsy

PSR. *See* Sickle cell retinopathy, proliferative

Psychiatric disorders. *See* Behavioral/psychiatric disorders

Psychic drug dependence, 1:250

Psychic paralysis of gaze. *See* Ocular motor apraxia

Psychomotor seizures, 1:261

Psychophysical testing, 12:33, 45–52. *See also specific test*

Psychotic disorder. *See also* Schizophrenia
  brief, 1:247

Psychotropic drugs, tear production affected by, 8:66*t*

PT. *See* Prothrombin time

PTC. *See* Pseudotumor, cerebri
Pterygium, **4**:57, 57–58, 59*f*, **8**:332, 332*f*, 391
  conjunctival transplantation for, **8**:392*f*, 393, 393–395
  excision of, **8**:391–393, 392*f*
    bacterial scleritis after, **8**:171, 171*f*
    medial rectus muscle damage/strabismus and,
      6:143
    recurrent, after conjunctival autograft, **8**:394–395
    subconjunctival hemorrhage caused by, **8**:76*t*
Pterygoid canal, nerve of, **2**:107
Pterygoid process, of sphenoid bone, **5**:7
Pterygoid venous plexus, **2**:40*f*, **5**:24*f*, 25
  eyelids drained by, **7**:143
Pterygomaxillary area, **5**:8, 12
Pterygopalatine fossa, **5**:12, **7**:7*f*, 9
Pterygopalatine ganglion/nerves, **2**:107, **5**:60, 66*f*
PTH. *See* Parathyroid hormone
PTK. *See* Phototherapeutic keratectomy
Ptosis (blepharoptosis), **5**:277*f*, 278–281, 279*f*, 280*t*,
  6:178–179, 179*t*, **7**:201–203
  acquired, **5**:279–281, 280*t*, **6**:179*t*, **7**:201
    aponeurotic, **7**:206, 206*f*, 207*t*
    eyelid position in downgaze and, **7**:203
    mechanical, **7**:210
    myogenic, **7**:205
    neurogenic, **7**:208–209
  anophthalmic, **7**:125
  aponeurotic, **5**:280, 280*t*, **7**:206, 206*f*, 207*t*
  apparent (pseudoptosis), **5**:276*f*, 281, **7**:210, 211*f*
  apraxia of eyelid opening and, **5**:281
  in blepharophimosis syndrome, **6**:178, 179*f*, **7**:145,
    204
  in blowout fractures, **7**:101
  botulinum toxin causing, **6**:164, **7**:208
  cerebral, **5**:280
  in children, **6**:178–179, 179*t*
  in chronic progressive external ophthalmoplegia,
    5:280, 336, 336*f*, **6**:137
  classification of, **6**:179, **7**:201, 205–210
  congenital, **5**:278–279, 279*f*, **6**:178, 179*t*, **7**:201
    amblyopia in, **7**:203
    eyelid position in downgaze and, **7**:203
    mechanical, **7**:210
    myogenic, **7**:205, 205*f*, 207*t*
    neurogenic, **7**:206–208, 208*f*
  contact lenses causing, **3**:199
  as cosmetic issue, **7**:204, 210
  downgaze exacerbating, **7**:201
  enucleation and, **7**:119
  evaluation of, **5**:275–277, 276*f*, 277*f*, 278*f*, **6**:179, **7**:201
    in children, **6**:179
  as functional issue, **7**:204, 210
  in Horner syndrome, **5**:266, **7**:204, 204*f*, 207
    pharmacologic testing for, **7**:204, 204*f*
  Marcus Gunn jaw-winking, **5**:279, 279*f*, 284, **6**:180,
    7:203, 207, 208*f*
    synkinesis in, **6**:180, **7**:203, 207, 208*f*
  mechanical, **5**:280*t*, 281, **7**:210, **8**:21
  in monocular elevation deficiency (double elevator
    palsy), **6**:123, 123*f*, **7**:205
  in myasthenia gravis, **5**:276–277, 277*f*, 280, 328,
    6:137, 138*f*, 139*t*, **7**:204–205, 209
    edrophonium chloride (Tensilon) test and, **7**:209

  myogenic, **5**:280*t*, **7**:205, 205*f*, 207*t*
    in myotonic dystrophy, **5**:280, 338
  neurogenic, **5**:279–280, 280*t*, **7**:206–209, 208*f*
  neuromuscular, **5**:280*t*
  nonorganic, **5**:316
  in orbital rhabdomyosarcoma, **6**:335, 335*f*
  pharmacologic testing in, **7**:204–205, 204*f*
  physical examination of patient with, **7**:201–204, 202*f*,
    203*f*
  plexiform neuroma of eyelid causing, **6**:367, 367*f*
  reverse, lower eyelid, **7**:207
  steroid-induced, **5**:280
  synkinesis in, **6**:180, **7**:203, 207, 208*f*
  third nerve (oculomotor) palsy/paralysis causing,
    5:228, 228*f*, **6**:132, 133*f*
  traumatic, **5**:280*t*, 281, **7**:181, 210
    amblyopia and, **7**:181
  treatment of, **7**:210–213, 212*f*
    in children, **6**:179
    complications of, **7**:213
  visual field testing in, **7**:204
Ptosis, brow, **7**:227–228, 227*f*
  dermatochalasis and, **7**:222, 227
Ptosis repair, **7**:210–213, 212*f*. *See also specific procedure*
  complications of, **7**:213
PTSD. *See* Post-traumatic stress disorder
PTT. *See* Partial thromboplastin time
Pubic louse (*Phthirus pubis*), **8**:142, 142*f*
  ocular infection caused by, **8**:142, 149
    cholinesterase inhibitors for, **2**:340
Public health ophthalmology, **8**:104
PubMed, **1**:316
PUK. *See* Peripheral keratitis, ulcerative
Pulfrich phenomenon, **5**:189
Pull-over (stay) sutures, **6**:149
Pulley hindrance, **6**:24
Pulley system, **6**:21–24, 22*f*, 23*f*
  A- and V-pattern deviations and, **6**:109–110, 110*f*
  orbital muscle layer and, **6**:18, 21, 22, 22*f*, 23
  pseudo-Brown syndrome and, **6**:130
  rectus muscles and, **6**:21–22, 22*f*, 23, 23*f*
  vertical deviations and, **6**:114
Pulmicort. *See* Budesonide
Pulmonary diseases, **1**:141–146
  evaluation of, **1**:143
  irreversible, **1**:142
  obstructive, **1**:141–142
    ocular surgery in patients with, **1**:308
  pre- and postoperative considerations and, **1**:146, 308
  recent developments in, **1**:141
  restrictive, **1**:142
  reversible, **1**:142
  in sarcoidosis, **9**:174
  treatment of, **1**:143–146
    nonpharmacologic, **1**:143–144
    pharmacologic, **1**:144–146, 145*t*
  in Wegener granulomatosis, **9**:145
Pulmonary edema, in heart failure, **1**:114, 117
Pulmonary function tests, **1**:143
Pulmonary hypertension, sildenafil for, **1**:141
Pulsation, orbital, **7**:25
Pulse pressure, in shock, **1**:294
Pulsed phacoemulsification, **11**:107

Pulseless disease (Takayasu arteritis), 1:176–178, 177t
Pulvinar, 5:20f, 36, 41
Pump–leak theory, 11:18–19, 18f
Pumping, for lasers, 3:21, 23, 24f
Punch biopsy, 7:170, 170f. See also Incisional biopsy
Puncta, 2:23, 33, 34, 6:203, 7:244–245, 245f
  agenesis/dysgenesis of, 7:250
  aplasia/hypoplasia of, 7:250, 278
  atresia of, 6:203
  disorders of, 7:262–263
  duplication of, 7:277
  large, 7:262
  malposition of, 7:262–263
  stenosis and occlusion of, 6:203, 7:250, 262, 278
  supernumerary, 6:204
  surgical closure of, 7:271
Punctal occlusion. See also Punctal plugs
  for cicatricial pemphigoid, 8:203
  for dry eye, 7:271, 8:60t, 61–62, 61f, 62f
Punctal plugs
  for cicatricial pemphigoid, 8:203
  for dry eye, 7:271, 8:60t, 61–62, 62f
    canalicular obstruction and, 7:263–264, 271
    extrusion/migration of, 7:271
    nasolacrimal duct obstruction and, 7:267
Punctate epithelial defects/erosions
  conjunctival, 8:20t
  corneal, 8:20t, 25, 26f, 27t
    refractive surgery in patient with, 13:35, 36f
    in vernal keratoconjunctivitis, 8:187
Punctate epithelial keratitis/keratopathy, 8:20t, 25, 26f, 27t
  contact lens wear and, 3:198
  exposure causing, 8:80
  herpes simplex causing, 8:110
  microsporidial, 8:170
  staphylococcal blepharitis/blepharoconjunctivitis
    and, 8:145, 146f, 147
  superficial Thygeson, 8:204–207, 206f
  topical anesthetic abuse causing, 8:90
Punctate inner choroiditis/choroidopathy (PIC),
  9:148–150t, 161, 164–167, 165f, 166f, 12:186t, 192,
  192f
Punctate outer retinal toxoplasmosis (PORT), 9:230,
  231f
Punctate staining patterns (fluorescein), 8:17, 18f
Pupil. See Pupils
Pupil expansion rings, 11:194, 194f
  for intraoperative floppy iris syndrome, 11:155, 156f
Pupil-involving third nerve (oculomotor) palsy/
  paralysis, 5:229, 229f, 271–273
Pupil–optic nerve (PO) section, 4:27–28, 28f
Pupil size. See Pupils, size of
Pupil-sparing third nerve (oculomotor) palsy/paralysis,
  5:230–231, 6:132
Pupillary axis, 3:106, 107f, 6:12
Pupillary block
  absolute, 10:110
  angle closure/angle-closure glaucoma with, 10:5t, 7t,
    110–111, 111f, 120–124, 121f, 122f, 123f, 123t
    iridotomy/iridectomy for, 10:111, 201, 201f,
      202–203, 204
    uveitis and, 9:89, 296

angle closure/angle-closure glaucoma without, 10:5t,
  7t, 111, 124–137
  surgery for, 10:201
  anterior chamber intraocular lenses and, 10:124
  in aphakic/pseudophakic eye, 10:124
  after cataract surgery, flat or shallow anterior
    chamber and, 11:153–154
  after Descemet stripping automated endothelial
    keratoplasty, 8:442
  ectopia lentis and, 10:121–122
  intumescent cataract causing, phacomorphic
    glaucoma and, 11:63, 64f
  mechanism of angle closure and, 10:111, 111f, 111t
  microspherophakia causing, 10:122, 123f, 11:29
  phacomorphic glaucoma and, 10:120, 121f
  after phakic IOL insertion
    angle-supported PIOLs, 13:134–135
    posterior chamber PIOLs, 13:135
  "relative," 10:109
  retinopathy of prematurity and, 12:163
  reverse, in pigmentary glaucoma, 10:89, 90f
Pupillary capture, after cataract surgery, 11:166, 167f
  IOL decentration and, 11:163
Pupillary (central) cysts, 6:227
Pupillary defects, 5:261–274. See also specific type and
  under Pupils
  afferent
    relative. See Relative afferent pupillary defect
    in traumatic optic neuropathy, 7:105
  benign episodic mydriasis, 5:274
  examination of patient with, 5:261
  history in, 5:261
  irregularity, 5:263–264
  nonorganic, 5:316
  paradoxical reactions, 5:274
  in ptosis, 7:204
  reactivity disorders (light–near dissociation),
    5:273–274, 273t
  size/shape/location abnormalities, 5:263, 264–273,
    6:170, 228–231, 231f. See also Anisocoria
    nonorganic, 5:316
  in third nerve (oculomotor) palsy, 5:229, 229f,
    230–231, 271–273
Pupillary escape, 5:93, 94f
Pupillary light reflex (pupillary response to light), 5:262.
  See also Pupils, examination of
  in cataract surgery evaluation, 11:77
  consensual response in, 5:262
  direct response in, 5:262
  disorders of, 5:273–274, 273t
  in infant with decreased vision, 6:413, 414
  in newborn, 6:170
  nonorganic ophthalmic disorders and, 5:307
  in nystagmus evaluation, 6:319, 320t
  paradoxical, 5:274, 6:319, 319t, 414
  pathways for, 2:99
Pupillary membrane
  anterior, 11:25, 25f
  development of, 2:133f, 134, 135, 137, 138, 11:25, 25f
  persistent, 2:139f, 6:228, 229f
Pupillary near reflex. See Near reflex
Pupillary rings, 11:194, 194f
  for intraoperative floppy iris syndrome, 11:155, 156f

Pupillometers, **13**:34
Pupilloplasty, for cataracts, **11**:71
Pupils
  abnormalities of, **5**:261–274, **6**:228–231, 231*f*. *See also*
    specific type and Pupillary defects
  Adie tonic, **5**:54, 265*f*, 270–271, 271*f*, 272*f*, 316, **6**:229
    pharmacologic testing for, **2**:338, **5**:270–271, 272*f*,
     316
  Argyll Robertson, **5**:274
    in syphilis, **9**:246
  Argyll Robertson–like, **5**:274
  conjugacy of, in indirect ophthalmoscopy, **3**:246, 247*f*
  constriction of, in near and light reflexes, **2**:99, **5**:262.
    See also Pupillary light reflex
  dilation of. *See* Mydriasis/mydriatics
  displacement of (corectopia), **5**:264, **6**:230
    cataract surgery in patient with, **11**:196
    in iridocorneal endothelial (ICE) syndrome,
     10:128, 129*f*
  distance between, bifocal segment decentration and,
    3:157
  in ectopia lentis et pupillae, **11**:38
  entrance, **3**:108
    blurred retinal images and, **3**:312, 312*f*
    location effect of cylindrical lenses and, **3**:313–314,
     313*f*
    spectacle lens distance from, distortion and, **3**:311
  examination of, **5**:261–263
    before cataract surgery, **11**:77–78
    in glaucoma, **10**:28–29
    in low vision, **5**:92–95, 94*f*
     in infant, **6**:414
    in nystagmus, **6**:319–320, 320*t*
    after perforating injury, **8**:374
    in ptosis, **7**:204
    before refractive surgery, **13**:34
  fixed, dilated, **5**:316
  in infants and children, **6**:169–170
  irregular, **5**:263–264
  Marcus Gunn. *See* Marcus Gunn pupil
  ovalization of after phakic intraocular lens insertion,
    13:133*t*
    angle-supported PIOLs and, **13**:134–135
  pharmacologic testing of, **5**:263
  reactivity/response of to light. *See* Pupillary light
    reflex
  secluded, **10**:110, 130, 130*f*
  shape of, abnormalities in (dyscoria), **6**:223
  size of
    abnormalities in, **5**:263, 264–273, **6**:170, 228–230.
     See also Anisocoria
    baseline, **5**:263
    cataract surgery and, **11**:78, 194–195, 194*f*
     IOL selection and, **11**:78
     trauma and, **11**:206–207
     uveitis and, **11**:203–204
    contrast sensitivity affected by, **3**:113
    decentered ablation and, **13**:96
    evaluation of, **5**:262
     before refractive surgery, **13**:34
    glaucoma/glaucoma therapy and, **10**:28–29
    nonorganic causes of changes in, **5**:316
    perimetry variations and, **10**:56, 65, 66*f*

refractive surgery and, **3**:236–237, **13**:34
  spherical aberration and, **3**:100
  visual resolution affected by, **3**:107–108, 107*f*
  wavefront aberrations and, **13**:7, 95
springing, **5**:274
substance use/abuse and, **1**:250
tadpole, **5**:263
tonic (Adie pupil/syndrome), **5**:54, 265*f*, 270–271,
  271*f*, 272*f*, 316, **6**:229
  pharmacologic testing for, **2**:338, **5**:270–271, 272*f*,
   316
trauma affecting, **5**:263
in uveitic eye, cataract surgery and, **11**:203–204
white. *See* Leukocoria
PureVision contact lenses, **3**:177*t*
Purified neurotoxin complex, **2**:390
Purified protein derivative (PPD) test, **1**:19, **9**:35,
  259–260. *See also* Tuberculin skin test
  in HIV infection/AIDS, **9**:260
  immune response arc and, **9**:35
  uveitis associated with, **9**:128
Purine antagonists, in cancer chemotherapy, **1**:240*t*
Purine bases/purines, **2**:159
  hyperuricemia caused by disorders of metabolism
   of, **8**:325
Purite. *See* Oxychloro complex
Purkinje cells, **5**:48
Purkinje-Sanson image, in pachymetry, **3**:259
Purpura, **1**:153
  Henoch-Schönlein, **1**:177*t*
  idiopathic thrombocytopenic, **1**:154
  thrombotic thrombocytopenic, **1**:154
   choroidal perfusion abnormalities and, **12**:179
  in Wegener granulomatosis, **9**:145
Pursuit eye movements/pursuit pathways/system, **5**:41,
  42*f*, 43*f*, 198–199, 198*t*, 204, **6**:37
  assessment of, **5**:204
  dysfunction of, **5**:213
   in ataxia-telangiectasia, **5**:344
  optokinetic nystagmus and, **5**:168–169, 201
  smooth, **6**:37
   asymmetry of, **6**:91
Purtscher/Purtscherlike retinopathy, **12**:154–155, 154*f*,
  155*t*
"Pushing plus," before refractive surgery, **13**:33
Pustule, of eyelid, **8**:20*t*
Putterman müllerectomy, for ptosis correction, **7**:212
PVCs. *See* Premature ventricular complexes/
  contractions
PVD. *See* Posterior vitreous detachment
PVL. *See* Periventricular leukomalacia
PVR. *See* Vitreoretinopathies, proliferative
PXE. *See* Pseudoxanthoma elasticum
Pyoceles
  in dacryocystitis, **7**:275
  orbital invasion by, **7**:89
Pyogenic granuloma, **4**:56, 57*f*, **8**:241–242, 241*f*
  in children, **6**:351
Pyrazolones, **2**:362. *See also* Nonsteroidal anti-
  inflammatory drugs
Pyridoxine (vitamin B_6)
  for gyrate atrophy, **12**:244
  for homocystinuria, **2**:232, **6**:399, **11**:37

Pyrimethamine, 2:374
  for toxoplasmosis, 9:232, 233, 309, 12:208–209, 208t
Pyrimidine antagonists, in cancer chemotherapy, 1:240t
Pyrimidine bases/pyrimidines, 2:159
  fluorinated, 2:379t, 385
Pyruvate carboxylase, defective, 2:213t
Pyruvate dicarboxylase, defective, 2:213t
Pythagorean theorem, review of, 3:35, 35f

Q

q arm, 2:159
Q/D. See Quinupristin/dalfopristin
Q factor, 3:231–232
Q formula, Hoffer, for IOL power determination/
  selection, 11:85, 87
  refractive lens exchange/clear lens extraction and,
  13:140
Q value, 13:10
Q-wave infarction, 1:102. See also Acute coronary
  syndrome
  management of, 1:112–113
Q waves, in myocardial infarction, 1:102, 104
Quadrafoil, 13:8
Quadruple sectoranopia, lateral geniculate body lesions
  causing, 5:167, 167f
Quality of field, perimetry interpretation and, 10:59
Quality improvement, continuous, 1:344, 346, 347f
QuantiFERON-TB Gold test, 1:19, 9:259–260
Quantum optics, 3:3
Quetiapine, 1:252
Quibron. See Theophylline
Quickert sutures
  for involutional entropion, 7:195f, 196
  for spastic entropion, 7:195f
Quinapril, 1:76t, 78t
Quinidine, 1:123t
  for cardioversion, 1:125
Quinolones, 1:39, 44, 52t, 60–61. See also specific agent
Quinupristin/dalfopristin, 1:53t, 63–64
Quixin. See Levofloxacin

R

RA. See Rheumatoid arthritis
Rab escort protein 1 (REP-1/CHM) gene, mutation in,
  2:298
  in choroideremia, 2:298, 12:242
Rabies vaccination, 1:286
Rabies virus, ocular infection caused by, 8:130
Raccoon roundworm (Baylisascaris procyonis), diffuse
  unilateral subacute neuroretinitis caused by, 9:239,
  12:210
Race. See also Ethnic background
  angle closure/angle-closure glaucoma and, 10:10, 109,
  112–113
  cataract development and, 11:67
  central serous chorioretinopathy and, 12:171
  corneal thickness and, 10:74, 84, 105
  exfoliation syndrome/pseudoexfoliation and, 10:87
  eyelid crease/fold and, 7:136

genetic disorders and, 2:210–211
  glaucoma risk and, 10:8, 10, 76, 84, 109, 112–113
  hypertension and, 1:87
  ocular melanosis and, 8:238t. See also Melanosis, oculi
  open-angle glaucoma and, 10:8, 76
  optic disc size affected by, 10:46
  sickle cell hemoglobinopathies and, 12:116
  systemic lupus erythematosus and, 9:140
  vernal keratoconjunctivitis and, 8:187
  Vogt-Koyanagi-Harada (VKH) syndrome and, 4:190,
  9:183
Racemose angioma/hemangioma (Wyburn-Mason
  syndrome), 4:296, 297f, 5:339t, 345, 345f, 6:342,
  364t, 381, 381f, 12:151
Racquet (single-pedicle) flaps, 8:400
Radial incisions
  for intrastromal corneal ring segment placement, 13:57
  for keratorefractive surgery, 13:21
  for radial keratotomy, 13:44, 45f, 46f
    traumatic rupture of, 13:47, 47f
Radial keratoneuritis, in Acanthamoeba keratitis, 4:85
Radial keratotomy (RK), 13:4t, 43–48, 45f, 46f, 47f. See
  also Keratorefractive surgery
  cataract surgery after, 11:78, 13:48
  hyperopia and, 11:193–194
    IOL power calculation and, 11:86
  complications of, 13:45–47, 46f, 47f
  contact lens use after, 13:193, 193f
  corneal topography after, 13:44
  corneal transplantation after, 13:48, 191
  herpes simplex virus keratitis and, 13:166
  hyperopic shift and, 13:44, 45, 47
  IOL power calculations after, 3:220–222, 13:48
  iron lines associated with, 8:336
  keratometric power measurements affected by, 13:187
  ocular surgery after, 13:47–48
  penetrating keratoplasty after, 13:48
  refraction after, 13:44
    stability of, 13:44–45
  spherical aberration after, 3:100
  surgical technique for, 13:44, 45f, 46f
  visual acuity after, 13:44, 45–46
Radial optic neurotomy, for central retinal vein
  occlusion, 12:133
Radial perineuritis, Acanthamoeba keratitis and, 8:167
Radial peripapillary network, 12:12
Radial perivascular lattice degeneration, 4:155–156
Radial thermokeratoplasty, 13:119
Radiance (brightness), 3:18. See also Intensity
  as image characteristic, 3:19
  for medical lasers, 3:18t, 21
Radiant energy, for medical lasers, 3:18t
Radiant energy density, for medical lasers, 3:18t, 21
Radiant intensity, for medical lasers, 3:18t
Radiant power, for medical lasers, 3:18t
Radiation. See also Radiation therapy; Ultraviolet light
  anterior segment injury caused by, 8:352–353
  cancer caused by, 1:236, 237
  cataracts caused by, 11:51–53
  DNA repair after, 2:170
  eye and adnexa affected by, 1:238, 244
  fetal exposure and, 1:238
  in free-radical generation, 2:312

neuroimaging in evaluation of disorders caused by, 5:82*t*
retina affected by, **12**:151–153, 153*f*
Radiation necrosis, **5**:369
Radiation optic neuropathy, **1**:238–239, **5**:369, 369*f*
Radiation retinopathy, **1**:238, **12**:151–153, 153*f*
Radiation surgery, **5**:368
Radiation therapy, **1**:237–239, **5**:368–369
  for basal cell carcinoma of eyelid, **7**:172
  carcinogenic effects of, **1**:236, 237
  for choroidal hemangioma, **4**:292–293
  complications of, **5**:368–369
  for hemangiomas, **7**:64
  increased sensitivity to, in ataxia-telangiectasia, **6**:378
  for lacrimal gland tumors, **7**:87
  for lacrimal sac tumors, **7**:277
  for lymphoma, **4**:74, 324, **7**:83, **9**:283, 284
  for melanoma, **4**:283–285, 284*f*
    in iris, **4**:271
  for metastatic eye disease, **4**:322
  neuromyotonia after, **5**:235
  ophthalmic considerations and, **1**:238–239
  for optic nerve glioma, **5**:152, 153, **7**:71–72
  for optic nerve sheath meningioma, **5**:149–150, **7**:76
  for retinal capillary hemangioblastoma, **4**:295
  for retinoblastoma, **4**:312, **6**:358
    secondary tumors and, **4**:312, 313–314, 314*t*
  retinopathy after, **1**:238, **12**:151–153, 153*f*
  for rhabdomyosarcoma, **7**:78
  for thyroid eye disease, **5**:334, **7**:54
  for uveal lymphoid infiltration, **4**:326
RADICAL (Reduced Fluence Visudyne Anti-VEGF-Dexamethasone in Combination for AMD Lesions) study, **12**:78
Radiculitis, herpes, **5**:359
Radioactive iodine
  for hyperthyroidism, **1**:211, **7**:52–53
    orbital disease exacerbation and, **5**:333
  nasolacrimal duct obstruction and, **7**:267
  for thyroid scanning, **1**:210
  for uveal melanoma, **4**:284
Radioactive iodine uptake, **1**:209
Radioactive plaque therapy (brachytherapy)
  for choroidal hemangioma, **4**:292–293
  for melanoma, **4**:283–284, 284*f*
    of iris, **4**:271
  for metastatic eye disease, **4**:322
  for retinoblastoma, **4**:312
  retinopathy after, **12**:151–153, 153*f*
Radiofrequency
  for conductive keratoplasty, **13**:22, 120–123, 121*f*, 153–154
  for epilation, in trichiasis, **7**:200
  for punctal occlusion, **8**:62
Radiofrequency catheter ablation, for atrial fibrillation/flutter, **1**:125
Radiofrequency pulses, in MRI, **5**:72
Radiography
  chest. *See* Chest x-ray
  in foreign-body identification, **12**:325–326
  in uveitis, **9**:94*t*

Radiometry, **3**:16
  terms used in, **3**:18*t*
Radionuclide scintigraphy/scans
  in ischemic heart disease, **1**:106–107
  for lacrimal drainage evaluation, **7**:261–262
Radiosurgery, **5**:368
Radius of curvature
  corneal, **8**:6, 39
    in cornea plana, **8**:254
    instantaneous (meridional/tangential power), **8**:40, 41*f*, **13**:11, 12*f*
    keratometry in measurement of, **3**:263–265, 263*f*, 264*f*, 265*f*, 266*f*, **8**:38–39. *See also* Keratometry
  in schematic eye, **3**:105*t*
  of mirror, **3**:90
Radiuscope, **3**:169
Raeder paratrigeminal syndrome, **5**:268–269
Ragged red fibers, **5**:337, 337*f*, **12**:265
RAI. *See* Radioactive iodine
Rainbow glare, after LASIK with femtosecond flap creation, **13**:116
RAIU. *See* Radioactive iodine uptake
Raloxifene, for osteoporosis, **1**:231
Raltegravir, **1**:34
RAM. *See* Retinal Acuity Meter
Ramipril
  for heart failure, **1**:118
  for hypertension, **1**:76*t*
  for non–ST-segment elevation acute coronary syndrome, **1**:111
Ramsay Hunt syndrome, **5**:286, 287, 359
Ranbezolid, **1**:64
Random-Dot E test, **6**:87
Random-dot stereopsis tests, **6**:87
Randomization
  in clinical trials, **1**:327
  selection bias and, **1**:317
Randot test, **6**:87
Ranexa. *See* Ranolazine
Range of accommodation, **3**:117
  power of bifocal add and, **3**:146
    occupation and, **3**:157
    selection and, **3**:147
Ranibizumab, **2**:396–397
  for age-related macular degeneration/choroidal neovascularization, **12**:73–77, 75*f*, 87–88
    combination treatment and, **12**:78, 79
  for branch retinal vein occlusion, **12**:127
  for central retinal vein occlusion, **12**:131
  for macular edema, **4**:160, 169
    in diabetes mellitus, **12**:100, 101*f*
  for ocular histoplasmosis syndrome, **9**:225
Ranibizumab for Edema of the Macula in Diabetes 2 (READ-2) trial, **12**:100, 101*f*
Ranitidine, preoperative, **1**:308
Ranolazine, for angina, **1**:108
RANTES, **8**:177*t*
RAPD. *See* Relative afferent pupillary defect
Rapid plasma reagin (RPR) test, **1**:13, 279, **9**:247
  in syphilitic chorioretinitis, **12**:205
ras oncogene, **2**:171
Rathke pouch, **2**:119*f*
Ravuconazole, **1**:65

Ray tracing
   exact, **3**:55, 55*f*, 56, 56*f*
   to measure wavefront, **3**:240
   for mirrors, **3**:90, 91*f*
   paraxial
      small-angle approximation and, **3**:57–60, 57*f*, 58*f*
      through concave lenses, **3**:73–74, 73*f*, 74*f*
      through convex lenses, **3**:69–72, 71*f*
Ray-tracing model, **3**:3
Rayleigh criterion, **3**:16
Rayleigh scattering, **3**:16
Raynaud phenomenon, **1**:168*f*
   cold-induced anterior segment trauma and,
      8:351–352
   in scleroderma, **1**:173
   in systemic lupus erythematosus, **1**:168, **9**:140
Rays, **3**:28, 41, 42*f*
   divergent, **3**:62. *See also* Vergence
   paraxial, **3**:56–57, 62*f*
      approximation/tracing of, **3**:56–57, 57*f*, 58*f*. *See also* Ray tracing, paraxial
      power and, **3**:61–62, 62*f*
   as positive dysphotopsias, **3**:224
RB. *See* Reticulate body; Retinoblastoma
Rb locus, **2**:204. *See also* RB1 (retinoblastoma) gene
RB1 (retinoblastoma) gene, **2**:204–205, **4**:178, 263,
      299–300, 309, 312, 313, **6**:356
   secondary malignancies and, **4**:312, 313–314, 314*t*
RBBB. *See* Right bundle branch block
RBCD. *See* Reis-Bücklers corneal dystrophy
RBCs. *See* Red blood cells
RCFM. *See* Retrocorneal fibrous membrane
RDS/peripherin gene mutations, **2**:296, **12**:222
   in adult-onset vitelliform lesions, **12**:237
   in central areolar choroidal dystrophy, **12**:245
   in pattern dystrophies, **4**:175, **12**:240
   in retinitis pigmentosa, **12**:226, 228
   in Stargardt disease, **4**:172, **12**:234
Reactive arthritis/Reiter syndrome, **1**:164–165, **8**:209,
      9:121–123, 122*f*
   HLA association in, **1**:164, **9**:72*t*, 121
Reactive lymphoid hyperplasia. *See also* Lymphoid
   hyperplasia
   of orbit, **4**:239, **7**:81, 82
   uveal. *See* Uveal lymphoid infiltration
Reactive nitrogen products, as inflammatory mediators,
      9:31
Reactive oxygen intermediates, **2**:311. *See also* Free
   radicals
   as inflammatory mediators, **9**:30–31
READ-2 (Ranibizumab for Edema of the Macula in
   Diabetes 2) trial, **12**:100, 101*f*
Reader's Digest Large Print, **6**:418*t*
Reading
   low vision and
      computers and, **3**:303
      magnifiers for, **3**:298–299, 300*f*
      near visual acuity testing and, **3**:290
      peripheral field loss and, **3**:292
      spectacles for, **3**:295–296, 297
   position of, prismatic effects of bifocal lenses and,
      3:150
Reading add, determining, **3**:295–296, 297

Reading glasses
   for low vision/vision rehabilitation, **3**:295–296, 297
   for presbyopia, with contact lenses, **3**:176, 189
   single-vision
      for induced anisophoria, **3**:156
      for low vision/vision rehabilitation, **3**:296
REAL (Revised European American Lymphoma)
   classification, **7**:80
Real-time quantitative polymerase chain reaction
   (RT-PCR), **4**:39*t*
Reattachment surgery. *See* Retinal detachment, surgery
   for
Rebif. *See* Interferons (IFNs), β
Rebleeding, after traumatic hyphema, **8**:365–367, 367*f*,
      10:97–98
Rebound headache, analgesic, **5**:298
Rebound hyperglycemia, **1**:196–197
Rebound hypertension, **1**:87
Rebound nystagmus, **5**:248
Recall bias, **1**:323–324
Receiver operating characteristics (ROC) curve, **1**:133,
      331, 332*f*, 333*f*
Receptor agonist, **2**:331
Receptor antagonist, **2**:332
Receptor–effector coupling, **2**:261–262
Receptors, **2**:258–261, 259*t*, 264, 264*t*
   adaptive immune, **9**:36*f*, 38, 38*f*, 39*f*, 41, 47*t*, 51
   innate immune, **9**:12–13
   intracellular communication and, **2**:261–263, 262*f*,
      263*f*
   in iris–ciliary body, **2**:258–261, 259*t*
   ocular drug interactions and, **2**:331–332
   in signal transduction, **2**:258–261, 261
Recession (extraocular muscle), **6**:23*f*, 24, 148*t*. *See also*
   specific muscle
   and anteriorization, **6**:148*t*
Recession-resection procedures
   monocular, **6**:150–151, 150*t*
   for nystagmus (Kestenbaum-Anderson procedure),
      5:258, **6**:328–329, 329*t*
Recessive inheritance (recessive gene/trait), **2**:159,
      211–212
   autosomal, **2**:212–216, 213*t*, 215*t*
   disorders associated with, **2**:159, 212–216, 213*t*, 215*t*
      gene therapy for, **2**:187–188
   X-linked, **2**:218–219, 219*t*
Recessive optic atrophy, **6**:311
Recessive tumor-suppressor gene, Rb locus as, **2**:204
Recipient eye preparation
   for Descemet stripping automated endothelial
      keratoplasty, **8**:439–441, 440*f*
   for penetrating keratoplasty, **8**:418
Reciprocal innervation, Sherrington's law of, **6**:34
Reclast. *See* Zoledronic acid
Recognition, minimum angle of (MAR), **3**:109, 110*t*
   logarithm of (logMAR), **3**:109, 110*t*
      cystoid macular edema after cataract surgery and,
      11:182
Recognition disorders, **5**:192–194, 192*t*, 193*f*
Recombinant, definition of, **2**:159
Recombinant DNA, **2**:159
Recombinant tissue plasminogen activator. *See* Tissue
   plasminogen activator

Recombination, 2:150, 159
Recombination frequency, 2:180
Recombivax HB. *See* Hepatitis B vaccine
Reconstructive surgery
  for craniofacial malformations, 6:392
  eyelid, 7:181–187. *See also* Eyelids, surgery/
      reconstruction of
    after basal cell carcinoma surgery, 7:171
    for blepharophimosis syndrome, 7:145
    for epicanthus, 7:148
    for euryblepharon, 7:147
    for eyelid defects involving eyelid margin,
        7:183–186, 183f, 185f
    for eyelid defects not involving eyelid margin, 7:182
    lateral canthal defects and, 7:186
    for lower eyelid defects, 7:182, 184–186, 185f
    medial canthal defects and, 7:186–187
    after Mohs micrographic surgery, 7:171
    principles of, 7:182
    priorities in, 7:181–182
    secondary repair after trauma and, 7:180–181
    for upper eyelid defects, 7:182, 183–184, 183f
  socket, 7:124
Recording for the Blind and Dyslexic, 6:417t
Recoverin (CAR antigen), 5:115, 12:256, 257
Recruitment, 6:33
Rectal examination, in cancer screening, 1:272t
Rectilinear propagation, law of, 3:41, 42f
Rectus muscles, 2:16f, 17f, 19t, 20f, 39f, 5:10f, 55–56, 56f,
      6:13, 13–14, 14f, 16f, 17t, 18f, 7:10, 11f, 135f. *See also*
      specific muscle
  action of, 6:13, 14, 17t, 28–29, 29t
    gaze position and, 6:30, 30f, 31, 31f, 32f
    3-step test in evaluation of, 6:83–86, 85f
  anatomy of, 2:16f, 17f, 19t, 20f, 39f, 5:10f, 55–56, 56f,
      6:13, 13–14, 14f, 16f, 17t, 18f
    growth/development and, 6:170
    surgery and, 6:24
  blood supply of, 2:18–21, 19t, 37f, 38, 38f, 39f, 40f
  fascial capsules of, 6:19–20
    surgery and, 6:24
  field of action of, 6:29
  horizontal, 6:13, 14f. *See also* Lateral rectus muscles;
      Medial rectus muscles
    A-pattern deviations associated with dysfunction
        of, 6:107–108
    action of, 6:13, 28, 29t
      gaze position and, 6:30, 30f
    anatomy of, 6:13, 14f
    surgery of
        for A- and V-pattern deviations, 6:110, 111,
            111f, 112
        for nystagmus, 6:328, 329, 329t
        for third nerve (oculomotor) paralysis, 6:133
    V-pattern deviations associated with dysfunction
        of, 6:107–108
  injury of in orbital floor fractures, 6:125, 126
  insertion relationships of, 2:16, 18f, 19t, 6:16, 18f
    growth/development and, 6:170
  intermuscular septum of, 6:22
    surgery and, 6:24
  nerves supplying, 2:21, 5:54, 7:11
  origins of, 2:18, 19t

pulley system for, 6:21–22, 22f, 23, 23f
    A- and V-pattern deviations and, 6:109–110, 110f
    pseudo-Brown syndrome and, 6:130
  surgery of, 6:150, 150t, 152–154
    for A- and V-pattern deviations, 6:110, 111, 111f
    anatomy and, 6:24
    anterior segment ischemia and, 6:158–159, 158f
    for comitant vertical deviations, 6:152
    for consecutive esotropia, 6:103
    for constant exotropia, 6:103
    for convergence insufficiency, 6:106
    for dissociated vertical deviation, 6:117, 153
    for Duane syndrome, 6:129
    eyelid position changes after, 6:159, 159f, 7:214
    for hypo- and hypertropia, 6:152–153
    for infantile esotropia, 6:92
    for inferior oblique muscle paralysis, 6:122
    for intermittent exotropia, 6:102–103
    lost/slipped muscle and, 6:159–160, 160f
    for monocular elevation deficiency (double
        elevator palsy), 6:124
    for nystagmus, 6:154, 328, 329, 329t
    for orbital floor fracture, 6:126, 7:101, 102f
    for sixth nerve (abducens) paralysis, 6:135
    for superior oblique muscle paralysis, 6:120, 121
    for third nerve (oculomotor) paralysis, 6:133
    for thyroid eye disease, 6:136
  in thyroid eye disease, 4:232, 5:332f, 333, 6:135, 139t,
      7:49, 49f
  vertical, 6:14, 14f. *See also* Inferior rectus muscles;
      Superior rectus muscles
    A-pattern deviations associated with dysfunction
        of, 6:109
    action of, 6:14, 28–29, 29t
      gaze position and, 6:31, 31f, 32f
    anatomy of, 6:14, 14f
    surgery of
        for A- and V-pattern deviations, 6:111
        for comitant vertical deviations, 6:152
        for dissociated vertical deviation, 6:117, 153
        eyelid position changes after, 6:159, 159f,
            7:214
        for hypo- and hypertropia, 6:152–153
        for nystagmus, 6:329
        for superior oblique muscle paralysis, 6:120
    V-pattern deviations associated with dysfunction
        of, 6:109
Rectus subnuclei, 5:54
Recurrent corneal erosion, 8:83–85, 85f
  pain caused by, 5:300, 8:83
  posttraumatic, 8:372
Recurrent equine uveitis, 9:69
Recurrent meningeal artery, 5:14f, 15f
Recurrent pterygia, 4:57
Red blood cells, 1:147
  in anemia, 1:149–150
  development of, 1:147
Red eye. *See also* Conjunctivitis
  in children, 6:188–193, 189t
  contact lens–induced, 3:199–201
Red-glass test
  in ocular alignment assessment, 6:79
  in sensory adaptation testing, 6:53–55, 54f

Red-green color vision, 2:294
 defects in, 12:47, 49t
  gene defects causing, 2:297
  ocular findings in carriers of, 2:222t
  testing for, 12:47, 50. *See also* Red-green test
Red-green test
 duochrome/bichrome/Worth 4-dot, 3:135–136, 6:55, 55f, 87
 in binocular sensory cooperation evaluation, 6:87
 in nonorganic ophthalmic disorder evaluation
  monocular no light perception and, 5:309–310
  monocular reduced vision and, 5:311
 before refractive surgery, 13:33
 in sensory adaptation testing, 6:55, 55f
 Lancaster, 6:80
Red infarct, 12:147–148
Red lasers, 12:338
Red Maddox rod, 5:216. *See also* Maddox rod/Maddox rod testing
"Red-man syndrome," 2:377
Red oculocutaneous albinism (OCA3), 6:299t, 301
Red reflex, 3:123. *See also* Retinal reflex
 in complete cataract, 11:34
 in keratoconus, 8:297
 in lenticonus/lentiglobus, 4:121, 6:249, 11:26
 in pediatric cataract, 6:250–251
 poor, cataract surgery and, 11:195, 195f
Reduced Fluence Visudyne Anti-VEGF Dexamethasone in Combination for AMD Lesions (RADICAL) study, 12:78
Reduced schematic eye, 3:103–104, 106f
Reduced vergence, 3:63–64, 65
 image, 3:60
 magnification calculation and, 3:65
 object, 3:60
Reduced vision. *See* Low vision; Visual loss/impairment
Reduction division, in meiosis, 2:155
Reed-Sternberg cells, in Hodgkin disease, 4:239
Reese-Ellsworth Classification for Intraocular Tumors, 4:207, 308t, 6:358, 359t
Reference beam, in optical coherence tomography, 3:281, 282f
Reference sphere, wavefront analysis and, 3:238, 239f
Refixation movements, microsaccadic, 5:199
Reflectance imaging, infrared/near-infrared, 12:30–31, 31f
Reflecting power, of mirrors, 3:89–90
Reflection, light, 3:12–13, 12f
 angle of, 3:43f, 44, 44f
 applications of, 3:13
 at curved surfaces, 3:51, 52f
 diffuse, at rough optical interfaces, 3:42, 43f
 law of, 3:42–44, 43f, 44f, 45
 metallic, 3:13
 optical interface affecting, 3:42, 42f, 43f
 polarizing sunglasses in reduction of glare from, 3:11, 12, 12f, 159, 304
 specular, 3:42–44, 43f, 44f, 45
  for slit-lamp biomicroscopy, 8:12–14, 14f
  at smooth optical interfaces, 3:42, 42f
 total internal (TIR), 3:12, 13, 46–49, 48f, 49–50, 50f
  anterior chamber examination and, 3:49, 50f
Reflection coefficient, 3:44, 45

Reflex. *See specific type*
Reflex arc, neural, immune response arc compared with, 9:33, 36f
Reflex blepharospasm, 5:292
Reflex secretors, 2:241
Reflex secretory block, dry eye and, 8:50–51
Reflex tear arc, 2:106f, 7:244
 non–Sjögren syndrome disorders of, 8:65
 in Sjögren syndrome, 8:63
Reflex tearing, 2:106–107, 106f, 241, 242
 absorption of ocular medication affected by, 2:323, 327
 initiation of, 2:140
 tests of, 8:54, 54t
Reflexive saccades, in progressive supranuclear palsy, 5:208
Refractile bodies/spots
 in papilledema, 5:122, 122f
 in parafoveal/juxtafoveal retinal telangiectasia, 12:145, 146f
 in sickle cell retinopathy, 12:118, 118f, 119f
Refractile drusen, 12:59
Refracting power, 8:39. *See also* Refractive power
 in IOL power determination, 11:84
Refraction. *See also* Refractive errors
 angle of, 3:44, 45t
 clinical, 3:121–165. *See also* Visual acuity
  absorptive lenses and, 3:159–161, 160f
  accommodative problems and, 3:142–145, 143t
  aphakic lenses and, 3:158
  automated, 3:275–277, 276f
  in cataract patients
   nonsurgical management and, 11:71
   before surgery/IOL power determination, 11:76
  in children, 3:141–142
  corneal abnormalities affecting, 8:11
  cycloplegic, 3:137, 137t
   in children, 3:137, 137t, 141–142, 6:87–88, 88t
   before refractive surgery, 13:33, 73
  glass lenses and
   hi-index, 3:162–163
   standard, 3:162
  in glaucoma evaluation, 10:27
  hi-index lenses and, 3:162–163
  in low vision/vision rehabilitation, 3:294, 5:92
  manifest (noncycloplegic), 3:137
   after penetrating keratoplasty, 8:426, 427f
   refractive surgery and, 13:33, 73
  monocular diplopia and, 3:164–165
  multifocal lenses and, 3:145–157
  noncycloplegic (manifest), 3:137
   after penetrating keratoplasty, 8:426, 427f
   refractive surgery and, 13:33, 73
  objective (retinoscopy), 3:121–130, 121f, 122f. *See also* Retinoscopy
  overrefraction and, 3:138, 158
  plastic lenses and
   hi-index, 3:162–163
   high-impact, 3:162
   standard, 3:162
  prisms and, 3:163–164
  in ptosis, 7:203
  after radial keratotomy, 13:44
   stability of, 13:44–45

refractive surgery and, **13**:33
    IOL power calculation and, **13**:188
special lens materials and, **3**:161–163
special lenses and, **3**:157–161
spectacle correction of ametropias and, **3**:138–140,
    139*f*, 140*f*
subjective, **3**:130–136
    in children, **3**:141
    in low vision patient, **3**:294
at curved surfaces, **3**:51, 52*f*
law of (Snell's law), **3**:44–46, 45*f*, 46*f*, 47, 47*f*, **8**:38
    contact lens power and, **3**:167
    critical angle calculation and, **3**:47, 48
    Fermat principle and, **3**:52–53, 52*f*
    small-angle approximation and, **3**:58–60
Refractive accommodative esotropia, **6**:93
Refractive ametropia, **3**:113
Refractive astigmatism, contact lenses and, **3**:175–176
Refractive errors. *See also specific type and* Ametropia
    amblyopia caused by
        ametropic, **6**:64
        anisometropic, **3**:116, 142, **6**:63
    changes in, after strabismus surgery, **6**:155
    in children, **6**:169, 169*f*
    in cornea plana, **8**:255
    correction/treatment of, **3**:120. *See also* Contact
        lenses; Intraocular lenses (IOLs), for refractive
        errors; Refractive surgery; Spectacle lenses
        in amblyopia treatment, **6**:66
    developmental, **3**:118–119, 141–142
    emmetropization and, **3**:117
    epidemiology of, **3**:117–118
    in glaucoma, **10**:10, 27, 76, 114
    image location and, **3**:36
    optical principles/wavefront analysis and, **13**:5–9, 5*f*,
        6*f*, 7*f*, 8*f*, 9*f*
    after penetrating keratoplasty, management of,
        8:426–427, 427*f*
    perimetry variations and, **10**:27, 56
    prevention of, **3**:119–120
    in ptosis, **7**:203
    unexpected, after cataract surgery, **11**:168
Refractive index, **3**:6, 40, 40*t*
    of cornea, **8**:6, 38
    errors in IOL power calculation after corneal
        refractive surgery and, **3**:220–221
    hi-index lenses and, **3**:162–163
    of lens, **11**:7
    lens materials and, **3**:161, 162–163
    light propagation and, **3**:40–41, 40*t*
    reflection magnitude and, **3**:12
    in schematic eye, **3**:104*f*, 105*t*
    of tear (fluid) lens, **3**:174, 175, **8**:38
    wavelength and, **3**:14, 40, 49–51, 51*f*
Refractive keratotomy. *See* Keratotomy
Refractive lens exchange (clear lens extraction/refractive
    lensectomy), **13**:4*t*, 41*t*, 138–141
    advantages of, **13**:141
    complications of, **13**:141
    disadvantages/limitations of, **13**:41*t*, 141
    for hyperopia, **13**:139, 140
    indications for, **13**:138
    informed consent for, **13**:138

IOL calculations in, **13**:140–141
for myopia, **13**:138, 139–140, 140, 141
patient selection for, **13**:138–139
retinal detachment and, **13**:138, 141, 177
surgical planning/techniques for, **13**:139–140
Refractive power, **3**:61–62
    of cornea, **8**:37–38, **13**:3–4
        measurement of, **3**:263–265, 263*f*, 264*f*, 265*f*, 266*f*,
            8:38–39, **13**:3–4. *See also* Keratometry
        after refractive surgery, **13**:187
    in refractive ametropia, **3**:113
    of schematic eye, **3**:105*t*
Refractive states of eye, **3**:113–116, 113*f*, 114*f*, 115*f*. *See
    also* Refractive errors
    developmental hyperopia and, **3**:119
    developmental myopia and, **3**:118–119
    epidemiology of refractive errors and, **3**:117–118
    prevention of refractive errors and, **3**:119–120
    spherical equivalent of (binocular states of eyes),
        3:116
    treatment of refractive errors and, **3**:120
Refractive surgery. *See also specific procedure and*
    Keratorefractive surgery; Ocular (intraocular)
    surgery, refractive
    adjustable (ARS), **13**:137. *See also* Bioptics
    amblyopia and, **13**:178–181
    astigmatism and, **3**:232, 237–241, 239*f*, 241*f*
        corneal topography in detection/management of,
            8:44, **13**:12–14, 13*f*, 14*f*, 38–39, 38*f*
        penetrating keratoplasty and, **13**:169–172
    in autoimmune disease, **13**:184–185
    cataract/cataract surgery and, **11**:130–131, **13**:36–37,
        154–156, 154*f*, 155*f*
        international trends in use of, **13**:201
        IOL power calculation and, **11**:86–88, 193, **13**:189
        preoperative evaluation/planning and, **11**:75, 78
    in children, **13**:180–181
    in connective tissue diseases, **13**:31, 184–185
    contact lens use after, **3**:191, **13**:192–194, 193*f*
    corneal, **13**:3, 4*t*, 41*t*. *See also* Keratorefractive surgery
    corneal biomechanics affected by, **13**:9–10
    corneal optics and, **13**:3–5
    corneal shape and, **3**:231–235, 232*f*, 233*f*, 234*f*, 235*f*,
        13:10, 20
    corneal topography and, **8**:43–44, 44*f*, **13**:10–14, 11*f*,
        12*f*, 13*f*, 14*f*, 38–39, 38*f*, 70–71. *See also* Cornea,
        topography of
        indications for, **13**:16–17, 17*f*, 18*f*
        postoperative, **13**:17, 17*f*, 18*f*
    corneal transplant after, **13**:191–192
    in diabetes mellitus, **13**:31, 183–184
    glaucoma/ocular hypertension and, **13**:35, 172–175,
        173*f*, 194–195
    global estimates of, **13**:197–198, 198*f*
    in HIV infection/AIDS, **13**:31, 182–183
    indications for, **13**:163–164
    for induced anisophoria, **3**:156
    informed consent for, **13**:30*t*, 41–42, 41*t*, 209–217
    international perspectives in, **13**:197–202
        global estimates of surgery procedures and,
            13:197–198, 198*f*
        regulation of practices and devices and, **13**:201–202
        trends in surgery and, **13**:199–201

intraocular procedures in, **13**:125–147. *See also*
Ocular (intraocular) surgery, refractive
IOL power calculations after, **3**:220–222, **13**:187–189,
190*f*
iron lines associated with, **8**:336
irregular astigmatism and, **13**:16, 38–39, 38*f*, 171
lenticular, **3**:231. *See also specific procedure*
limitations of procedures used in, **13**:41*t*
medical history and, **13**:31
monovision and, **13**:32–33, 152–153
ocular history and, **13**:31–32
in ocular and systemic disease, **13**:163–185. *See also*
specific disorder
optical considerations/principles in, **3**:231–241,
13:5–9, 5*f*, 6*f*, 7*f*, 8*f*, 9*f*
angle kappa (κ), **3**:236
corneal shape, **3**:231–235, 232*f*, 233*f*, 234*f*, 235*f*
irregular astigmatism, **3**:237–241, 239*f*, 241*f*
pupil size, **3**:236–237
overview of procedures used in, **13**:3, 4*t*
patient age and, **13**:32–33
patient evaluation for, **13**:29–42, 30*t*. *See also*
Refractive surgery, preoperative evaluation
for
patient expectations and, **13**:29–30, 30*t*
after penetrating keratoplasty, **13**:169–172
penetrating keratoplasty after, **13**:191–192
postoperative considerations and, **13**:187–195
preoperative evaluation for, **13**:29–42, 30*t*
ancillary tests in, **13**:38–40, 38*f*
discussion of findings/informed consent and,
13:30*t*, 41–42, 41*t*, 207–217
examination in, **13**:30*t*, 33–38, 36*f*, 37*f*
history in, **13**:29–33, 30*t*
in presbyopia patient, **13**:32–33
retinal disease and, **13**:175–178
science of, **13**:3–27
social history/occupation and, **13**:30–31
spherical aberration after, **3**:99–100, 232, 233*f*
strabismus and, **13**:34–35, 178–181
postoperative, **6**:143
wavefront aberrations and, **3**:140, **13**:5–9, 5*f*, 6*f*, 7*f*, 8*f*,
9*f*, 40, 72, 74
Refsum disease/syndrome (phytanic acid storage
disease), **2**:213*t*, **12**:251*t*, 254, 261–262, 261*f*
gene defects causing, **2**:213*t*, 298
ichthyosis and, **8**:74, **12**:255
infantile, **2**:213*t*, **6**:401*t*, **12**:261
gene defects causing, **2**:213*t*, 298
pigmentary retinopathy and, **12**:251*t*, 254, 261–262,
262*f*
Regan chart, **3**:111
Regeneration, **4**:13. *See also* Wound healing/repair
aberrant nerve. *See* Aberrant nerve regeneration
Regional anesthesia, **2**:386–390, 387*t*. *See also* Topical
anesthesia
Regional enteritis (Crohn disease), **1**:165, **9**:123
Regional gigantism, **6**:367
Regional immunity, **9**:57, 58*t*. *See also* Immunologic
microenvironments
Registration, for laser centration, **13**:83–84, 84*f*
Reglan. *See* Metoclopramide
Regressed drusen, **12**:59

Regression formulas, for IOL power determination/
selection, **3**:212, 218, **11**:85, 87
Regular astigmatism, **3**:93–97, 93*f*, 94*f*, 95*f*, 96*f*, 97*f*, 98,
98*f*, 115
corneal topography in detection/management of,
13:12–13, 13*f*
retinoscopy of, **3**:125–129, 126*f*, 127*f*, 128*f*
scleral lenses for, **3**:193
wavefront aberration produced by, **13**:6, 7*f*
Regular insulin, **1**:196, 196*t*
Regulatory (suppressor) T cells, **9**:40, 41. *See also* CD8⁺
T cells; T cells
in atopy, **8**:179–180
class I MHC molecules as antigen-presenting
platform for, **9**:37, 38*f*
in external eye defense, **8**:96, 174*t*
in immune processing, **9**:40, 41
in sympathetic ophthalmia, **9**:52
Rehabilitation. *See* Vision rehabilitation
Rehabilitation teachers, **3**:305. *See also* Vision
rehabilitation
Reis-Bücklers corneal dystrophy, **8**:268*t*, 270*t*, 275–277,
276*f*
genetics of, **8**:269*t*, 276
Reiter syndrome/reactive arthritis, **1**:164–165, **8**:209,
9:121–123, 122*f*
HLA association in, **1**:164, **9**:72*t*, 121
Rejection (graft), **8**:407, 408, 427–430, 428*f*, 429*f*, 436
corneal allograft, **4**:91, 92*f*, **8**:407, 408, 427–430, 428*f*,
429*f*, 436, **9**:63, 64, 64*f*, 65
after lamellar keratoplasty, **8**:436
after penetrating keratoplasty, **8**:427–430, 428*f*,
429*f*, **9**:65
HLA/transplantation antigens and, **8**:407, **9**:65
Rejuvenation surgery, facial, **7**:230–238. *See also specific*
procedure and Facial surgery
Relafen. *See* Nabumetone
Relapsing polychondritis, **1**:175–176
eyelid manifestations of, **4**:213*t*
Relative afferent pupillary defect (Marcus Gunn pupil)
cataract surgery on patient with, **11**:77
in multiple evanescent white dot syndrome, **5**:113,
113*f*
in optic tract syndrome, **5**:167
testing for, **5**:92–95, 94*f*
in glaucoma evaluation, **10**:28, 29
in nonorganic ophthalmic disorders, **5**:308
Relative risk, **1**:270, 336
Relatives, first-degree/second-degree, **2**:159
Relaxation, in MRI, **5**:70
Relaxation times, in MRI, **5**:70, 72, **7**:26
Relaxing incisions
for anterior capsule contraction, **11**:172*f*, 173
for corneal astigmatism after penetrating keratoplasty,
8:427
limbal, **13**:4*t*, 21*f*, 49, 50–52, 50*f*, 51*t*
cataract surgery and, **11**:130–131
manual small-incision, **11**:96
instrumentation for, **13**:51
ocular surgery after, **13**:52
outcomes of, **13**:52
technique for, **13**:51
Relentless placoid chorioretinitis, **9**:157, 158*f*

Relenza. *See* Zanamivir
Reliability, **1**:339–340
Remicade. *See* Infliximab
Remodeling pathway, platelet-activating factors in, **9**:27
Remote-controlled conventional refractors, **3**:277
Renal cell carcinoma
    metastatic eye disease and, **4**:316*t*
    in von Hippel–Lindau disease, **6**:374
Renal coloboma syndrome, dysplastic optic nerve and,
    5:143
Renal disease
    congenital, retinal degeneration and, **12**:254
    diabetes mellitus and, **1**:206. *See also* Diabetic
        nephropathy
        retinopathy and, **12**:94. *See also* Diabetic
          retinopathy
    fluorescein angiography in patient with, **12**:25
    hypertension management and, **1**:79*t*, 85
    in polyarteritis nodosa/microscopic polyangiitis, **9**:143
    in scleroderma, **1**:174
    in systemic lupus erythematosus, **1**:167, 169*t*, **9**:140
    uveitis in children and, **6**:271–272
    in Wegener granulomatosis, **9**:145
Renal metabolic acidosis, carbonic anhydrase IOP
    lowering and, **2**:353
Renal–retinal dysplasias, **12**:254
Rendu-Osler-Weber disease (hereditary hemorrhagic
    telangiectasia), **1**:153, **8**:76
Renese. *See* Polythiazide
Renin-angiotensin-aldosterone system, in hypertension,
    1:71, 71*f*
Renin inhibitors, for hypertension, **1**:77*t*, 83
Renovascular hypertension, **1**:72, 72*t*
Reoperation, surgical planning and, **6**:147
ReoPro. *See* Abciximab
REP-1 (Rab escort protein 1/*CHM*) gene, mutation in,
    2:298
    in choroideremia, **2**:298, **12**:242
Repaglinide, **1**:199*t*, 201
Repair, **4**:13. *See also* Wound healing/repair
Reparative (stimulated) macrophages, **9**:20, 21*f*, 22–23
Repeat element/sequence
    Alu, **2**:148, 166
    L1, **2**:166
Reperfusion
    for angina, **1**:108–110
    for ST-segment elevation acute coronary syndrome,
        1:112–113
Repetitive nerve stimulation, electromyographic, in
    myasthenia gravis, **5**:331
Replication
    DNA, **2**:159
        origin, **2**:157
        segregation and, **2**:160, 196
        slippage, **2**:160
    microbial, as virulence factor, **8**:99
Replicative segregation, **2**:160, 173
Reproducibility, **1**:339
Requip. *See* Ropinirole
Rescue breathing, **1**:290, 291
Rescula. *See* Unoprostone
Research studies. *See* Clinical research/studies;
    Experimental (interventional) studies

Resection (extraocular muscle), **6**:23*f*, 24, 147
Reserpine, **1**:77*t*, 78*t*, 82
Residence time (of medication), **2**:323
Residual astigmatism, **3**:317, 318, 319*f*
Residual stromal bed thickness, LASIK and, **13**:40, 71–72
    corneal perforation and, **13**:104
    ectasia and, **13**:72, 114–116
Resistance (drug). *See also specific agent and specific*
    organism
    antibiotic, **1**:3, 44–56, **2**:369, 371, 375, 377
        new drug classes and, **1**:63–64
    antiretroviral, **1**:33, 34, 35, 36
    antiviral, **2**:382
    in tuberculosis, **1**:19–20, 39, **9**:261
Resistance (vascular), reduction of in heart failure
    management, **1**:118–119
Resistant hypertension, **1**:72, 72*t*
Resolution
    diffraction affecting, **3**:14–16, 14*f*, 15*f*
    minimum angle of (MAR), **3**:109, 110*t*
        logarithm of (logMAR), **3**:109, 110*t*
          cystoid macular edema after cataract surgery
            and, **11**:182
    pupil size affecting, **3**:107–108, 107*f*
Respbid. *See* Theophylline
Respimat. *See* Fenoterol, with ipratropium
Respiratory disorders. *See* Pulmonary diseases
Respiratory failure. *See* Ventilatory failure
Response accommodative convergence/accommodation
    ratio, **6**:81. *See also* Accommodative convergence/
    accommodation ratio
Restasis. *See* Cyclosporine/cyclosporine A, topical
Restimulation, of effector lymphocytes, **9**:42
Resting macrophages, **9**:20–21, 21*f*
Resting neutrophils, **9**:17, 18
ReSTOR intraocular lens, **13**:144, 155, 155*f*
Restoril. *See* Temazepam
Restriction endonucleases, **2**:151, 178–180, 179*f*
    for mutation screening, **2**:178–180, 179*f*, 184, 186–187*f*
Restriction fragment length polymorphisms (RFLPs),
    2:160, 178–180, 179*f*
Restrictive pulmonary diseases, **1**:142
Restrictive syndromes, diplopia caused by, **5**:238–241,
    240*f*, 241*f*
    paretic syndromes differentiated from, **5**:218, 219*f*
    posttraumatic, **5**:238–239
Resuscitation. *See* Cardiopulmonary resuscitation
RET oncogene
    amyloidosis and, **8**:317*t*
    mutations in, **2**:193
Retained lens material, cataract surgery and, **11**:143,
    147, 159–160, **12**:357–359, 358*t*, 359*f*
Retavase. *See* Reteplase
Retentive viscoelastics. *See also* Ophthalmic
    viscosurgical devices
    elevated intraocular pressure and, **10**:101
Reteplase, for ST-segment elevation acute coronary
    syndrome, **1**:113
Reticular degenerative retinoschisis, **4**:154, **12**:293–294
Reticular dystrophy, **12**:240, 241*f*
Reticular formation
    medullary, **5**:39, 39*f*
    paramedian pontine, **2**:104, 104*f*, **5**:39, 39*t*, 42, 46*f*, 199

Reticular peripheral cystoid degeneration, 4:154, 154*f*, 12:282, 293
Reticulate body, *Chlamydia,* 8:137
Reticulum cell sarcoma. *See* Intraocular tumors, lymphoma
Retina, 2:41*f*, 42, 71–79, 291–302, 4:145–148, 146*f*, 147*f*, 12:8–13, 9*f*, 9*t*, 10*f*, 11*f*, 13*f*, 14*f*, 15*f. See also under Retinal*
   amyloidosis affecting, 12:312
   anatomy of, 2:41*f*, 42, 71–79, 73*f*, 74*f*, 75*f*, 76*f*, 79*f*, 5:27–29, 30*f*, 12:8–13, 9*f*, 9*t*, 10*f*, 11*f*, 13*f*, 14*f*, 15*f*
   angiography in examination of, 12:20–26, 23*f*, 24*f. See also* Fluorescein angiography; Indocyanine green angiography
   antioxidants in, 2:316–318, 318*f*
   arteriovenous anastomoses/malformations in, 12:151
      in Takayasu arteritis, 1:178
   astrocytic hamartoma of, 4:305–306, 306*f*
      optic disc drusen differentiated from, 5:136, 136*f*
      retinoblastoma differentiated from, 4:305–306, 306*f*
   atrophy of
      gyrate, 2:213*t*, 12:243–244, 244*f*
      ischemia causing. *See also* Retinal ischemia
         in retinal arterial and venous occlusions, 4:157*f*, 163, 164
   biochemistry and metabolism of, 2:291–302
   blood supply of. *See* Retinal blood vessels
   capillary hemangioblastoma of, 4:294–295, 294*f*, 5:339*t*, 344, 344*f*, 6:364*t*, 374–375, 375*f*, 12:148–151, 149*f*, 150*f. See also* Retinal angiomatosis
   cavernous hemangioma of, 4:295, 296*f*, 12:151, 152*f*
   congenital disorders of, 4:148–151, 149*f*, 150*f*, 12:213–219
   contrast sensitivity in disorders of, 3:112, 12:50
   degenerations of. *See* Retinal degenerations
   detachment of. *See* Retinal detachment
   development of, 2:121, 124–126, 125*f*, 6:44, 44–45
      melanin in, 2:308
   diabetes mellitus affecting. *See* Diabetic retinopathy
   disorders of. *See specific type and* Retinal disease; Retinopathy
   dysplasia of, retinoblastoma differentiated from, 4:305*t*
   dystrophies of. *See* Retinal dystrophies
   edema of. *See* Retinal edema
   electrophysiology of, 2:301–302, 301*f*, 12:33–45. *See also specific test*
   emboli in. *See also* Emboli
      transient visual loss caused by, 5:175*f*, 176*t*, 177–183, 178*f*, 179*f*, 179*t*, 181*t*
   equatorial, 12:8
   examination of, 12:19–20
      before cataract surgery, 11:80
      imaging in, 5:81
         angiography, 12:20–26, 23*f*, 24*f. See also* Fluorescein angiography; Indocyanine green angiography
         fundus autofluorescence, 12:30
            near-infrared, 12:31
         infrared reflectance imaging, 12:30–31, 31*f*
         OCT, 12:26–29, 27*f*, 28*f*
         scanning laser ophthalmoscopy, 12:29–30
   fleck, of Kandori, 12:218

free radicals affecting, 2:315–316
gliosis of, 4:164, 165
   of peripapillary nerve fiber layer, 5:121, 121*f*
gyrate atrophy of, 2:213*t*, 12:243–244, 244*f*
hamartomas of, 4:184, 289, 289*f*, 6:352
   optic disc drusen differentiated from, 5:136, 136*f*
healing/repair of, 4:17
histologic sequelae of trauma to, 4:20
in HIV infection/AIDS. *See also* Retinitis
   in children, 6:184, 304
   progressive outer retinal necrosis and, 5:359, 9:203, 203*f*, 307–308, 308*f*, 12:201
imaging techniques in evaluation of, 5:81
   angiography, 12:20–26, 23*f*, 24*f. See also* Fluorescein angiography; Indocyanine green angiography
   fundus autofluorescence, 12:22, 30
      near-infrared, 12:31
   infrared reflectance imaging, 12:30–31, 31*f*
   OCT, 12:26–29, 27*f*, 28*f*
   scanning laser ophthalmoscopy, 12:29–30
immune response in, 9:58*t*, 64–67
infection/inflammation of, 4:151–153, 151*f*, 152*f*, 153*f*, 154*f*, 12:185–211. *See also specific disease and* Retinitis
layers of, 12:10, 11*f*
in leukemia, 4:326, 327, 327*f*
light causing injury of. *See* Retina, photic injury of
mechanical injury of, light causing, 12:332
melanoma invading, 4:198, 198*f*
nasal, 5:28*f*, 31
necrosis of
   acute, 4:151, 151*f*, 9:199–203, 200*t*, 201*f*, 12:201–202, 202*f*
   progressive outer, 9:203, 203*f*, 307–308, 308*f*, 12:201
neovascularization of. *See also* Neovascularization
   in age-related macular degeneration, 4:169–170, 171*f*
   disorders of, in retinopathy of prematurity, 4:167, 6:280–287, 12:157, 163
      screening for, 6:285, 286*t*
   ischemia causing, 4:162, 162*f*
   peripheral, 12:121, 122*t*
      vitreous hemorrhage and, 12:313, 314
   in uveitis, 9:303–304
neurosensory, 2:41*f*, 73–79, 291–298, 4:145, 145–147, 146*f*, 147*f*, 12:8–13, 9*f*, 9*t*, 10*f*, 11*f*, 13*f*, 14*f*, 15*f*
   anatomy of, 2:41*f*, 73–79, 74*f*, 75*f*, 76*f*, 77*f*, 79*f*, 12:8–13, 9*f*, 9*t*, 10*f*, 11*f*, 13*f*, 14*f*, 15*f*
   biochemistry and metabolism of, 2:291–298
   development of, 2:121, 124–126, 125*f*
   glial elements of, 2:74*f*, 77
   neuronal elements of, 2:73–77, 74*f*, 75*f*, 76*f*, 77*f*
      ischemia affecting, 4:156–157, 157*f*, 158*f*
   stratification of, 2:74*f*, 78–79, 79*f*
   vascular elements of, 2:74*f*, 78, 12:12, 15*f. See also* Retinal blood vessels
      development of, 2:138
OCT in examination of, 12:26–29, 27*f*, 28*f*
oxidative lens damage during surgery on, 11:16
peripheral (anterior), 12:8
phakomas of. *See also* Phakoma/phakomatoses
   in tuberous sclerosis, 6:372–374, 373*f*

photic injury of, **3**:19, 160–161, 206, **12**:332–334
  during cataract surgery, **11**:183–184
  in retinitis pigmentosa, **12**:231
photochemical injury of, **12**:332
  occupational light toxicity and, **12**:334
  ophthalmic instrumentation causing, **12**:333–334
  in photodynamic therapy, **12**:344
  in solar retinopathy, **12**:332–333
photocoagulation causing lesions of, **12**:342
physiology and psychophysics of, **12**:33–52
pigment epithelium of. *See* Retinal pigment
  epithelium
in primary central nervous system lymphoma, **9**:281,
  282*f*
radiation affecting, **12**:151–153, 153*f*
regional differences in, **2**:72, 73*f*
scanning laser ophthalmoscopy in evaluation of,
  12:29–30
splitting of, in shaking injury, **6**:405–406, 406*f*
systemic disease affecting, **12**:249–270, 250–251*t*
  in childhood, **6**:296–304
in systemic lupus erythematosus, **1**:170, **9**:141–142,
  141*f*, 142*f*, **12**:195–196, 195*f*
thermal injury of, light causing, **3**:19, **12**:332
thickness of, mapping with OCT, **12**:28*f*, 29
topography of, **2**:41*f*, 42, **4**:145–148, 146*f*, 147*f*
transplantation of, **9**:66
tumors of, **4**:178–184. *See also* Retinoblastoma
  glaucoma caused by, **10**:92–93, 130
  metastatic, **4**:315–316, 320, 321*f*, **9**:286–287
  pigmented, **4**:288–289, 289*f*
in uveitis, **9**:78*t*, 82, 82*t*, 83*t*, 86*t*, 89–90, 140. *See also*
  Posterior uveitis
vascular abnormalities/vascularization of. *See* Retina,
  neovascularization of; Retinal disease, vascular
vitreous attachment to, **12**:7*f*, 8
  posterior vitreous detachment and, **12**:274–276,
    274*f*, 275*f*, 297–306, 362
in von Hippel–Lindau disease. *See* Retinal
  angiomatosis
in Wegener granulomatosis, **9**:145, 146*f*
Retina International, **6**:418*t*
Retinal Acuity Meter (RAM), in cataract surgery
  evaluation, **11**:81
Retinal adhesion, retinal pigment epithelium in
  maintenance of, **2**:308
Retinal angiography, **12**:20–26, 23*f*, 24*f*. *See also*
  Fluorescein angiography; Indocyanine green
  angiography
Retinal angiomatosis (angiomatosis retinae, von Hippel/
  von Hippel–Lindau syndrome/disease), **4**:294–295,
  294*f*, **5**:339*t*, 344, 344*f*, **6**:364*t*, 374–375, 375*f*,
  12:148–151, 149*f*, 150*f*
  retinoblastoma differentiated from, **6**:358
Retinal arterial arcades, inferior/superior, **5**:16
Retinal arteriole obstruction, capillary, **12**:135–136,
  135*f*. *See also* Cotton-wool spots
Retinal arterioles, optic nerve supplied by, **10**:42–43
Retinal artery
  central, **2**:78, 90, 94, 95*f*, 96, **5**:13*f*, 14*f*, 15, 18*f*, 19*f*, 31,
    10:42, 43*f*, 44, **12**:12, 135
    angiography and, **12**:21
    optic nerve supplied by, **10**:42, 43*f*, 44

macroaneurysms of, **12**:147–148, 147*f*
  age-related macular degeneration differentiated
    from, **12**:68–69, 69*f*
microaneurysms of, **4**:160–162, 162*f*, 164
  in diabetes mellitus, **4**:166
    in children, **6**:297
    in diabetic macular ischemia, **12**:103
    in nonproliferative diabetic retinopathy, **12**:104,
      104*f*
occlusion of. *See* Retinal artery occlusion
Retinal artery occlusion, **12**:135–140
  branch, **4**:163, **12**:136–137, 136*f*, 137*f*
  central, **4**:162–163, 163*f*, **12**:138–140, 138*f*, 139*f*
    ERG in evaluation of, **12**:40*f*
    in sickle cell hemoglobinopathies, **12**:119
  in systemic lupus erythematosus, **9**:141–142, 142*f*
Retinal blood vessels, **2**:74*f*, 78, **4**:146, **12**:12, 15*f*. *See
  also specific vessel*
  angiography and, **12**:21–22, 23*f*, 24*f*
  anomalies of, **4**:149, 150*f*
  development of, **2**:138
  disease of. *See* Retinal disease, vascular
  ischemia and, **4**:158–162, 159*f*, 160*f*, 161*f*, 162*f*
Retinal breaks, **12**:271–274, 273*f*. *See also* Retinal tears
  in acute retinal necrosis/herpetic retinitis, **9**:200, 201*f*,
    202, **12**:201
  asymptomatic, treatment of, **12**:284, 284*t*
  lattice degeneration and, **12**:276
    treatment of, **12**:283, 284–285, 284*t*
  management of, **12**:289–290, 290*f*
  paving-stone (cobblestone) degeneration and, **12**:282
  photocoagulation for, **12**:283
  in posterior vitreous detachment, **12**:298, 362
  prophylactic treatment of, **12**:282–285, 284*t*
  retinal detachment and, **12**:271, 286, 288*f*, 289*f*, 362,
    363*f*
    prophylaxis of, **12**:282–285, 284*t*
  symptomatic, treatment of, **12**:283–284, 284*t*
  traumatic, **12**:272–274, 273*f*
  vitreous hemorrhage and, **12**:313
  vitreous traction and, **12**:274, 275*f*
Retinal capillary nonperfusion
  in Coats disease, **12**:143, 144*f*
  in diabetic retinopathy, **12**:90, 91*f*, 103
  in radiation retinopathy, **12**:152, 153*f*
Retinal correspondence, **6**:39–40, 40*f*
  anomalous, **6**:39, 51*f*, 52–53, 53*f*
    harmonious, **6**:55
    testing in, **6**:52, 53–59
    unharmonious, **6**:55
  normal, **6**:39
Retinal degenerations, **4**:154–177, **12**:249–270,
  250–251*t*. *See also specific type and* Pigmentary
  retinopathy; Retinal dystrophies
  in Bardet-Biedl syndrome, **12**:250*t*, 252–253, 252*f*
  in cancer, **12**:256–257, 256*f*
  in dermatologic disease, **12**:255
  drug toxicity and, **12**:266–270, 266*f*, 268*f*, 269*t*
  ERG in evaluation of, **12**:39–41, 40*f*, 41*f*
  in gastrointestinal disease, **12**:255, 255*f*
  gene defects causing, **2**:298
  hearing loss and, **12**:251*t*, 253. *See also* Usher syndrome
  infantile to early childhood–onset, **12**:251–252

ischemic, **4**:156–164. *See also* Retinal ischemia
lattice, **4**:155–156, 155*f*, **12**:276–278, 277*f*, 278*f*
  in hereditary hyaloideoretinopathies with optically
    empty vitreous, **12**:309, 309*f*
  radial perivascular, **4**:155–156
  treatment of, **12**:283, 284–285, 284*t*
in metabolic diseases, **6**:398, **12**:257–265
in neuromuscular disorders, **12**:254
paving-stone (cobblestone), **4**:156, 156*f*, **12**:281–282,
  281*f*
peripheral cystoid, **4**:154, 154*f*, **12**:282
  reticular, **4**:154, 154*f*, **12**:282, 293
  typical, **4**:154, 154*f*, **12**:282, 292
renal disease and, **12**:254
retinal pigment epithelium and, **2**:308, **12**:58
systemic disease and, **12**:249–270, 250–251*t*
Retinal detachment, **2**:72, **4**:136, 136*f*, **12**:286–292, 287*t*,
  362–368
in acute retinal necrosis/herpetic retinitis, **9**:200, 201*f*,
  202–203, **12**:201–202
angle-closure glaucoma and, **10**:133
after anterior segment trauma repair, **8**:382
after blunt trauma, in young patient, **12**:272–273
in branch retinal vein occlusion, **12**:123
after cataract surgery, **11**:143, 144*t*, 184–185, **12**:314,
  362–363, 363*f*, **13**:176–177
  family history as risk factor and, **11**:75
  Nd:YAG laser capsulotomy and, **11**:175, 184, **12**:363
  retained lens material and, **12**:357, 358
in central serous chorioretinopathy, **12**:171, 172–173,
  173*f*
in child abuse, **6**:404
choroidal/ciliary body melanoma and, **4**:168
choroidal hemangioma and, **4**:292
choroidal perfusion abnormalities and, **12**:176, 178*f*,
  179
classification of, **12**:286, 287*t*
in CMV retinitis, **9**:206, 307, **12**:201
in Coats disease, **4**:149, 150*f*, 305, 306*f*, **12**:143, 144,
  144*f*
COL2A1 gene and, **12**:310
complex, **12**:367
in diabetic retinopathy, **12**:110–111, 191, 352–353,
  353*f*
diagnostic features of, **12**:287*t*
differential diagnosis of, **12**:286, 292–294, 293*f*, 294*t*
enclosed ora bays and, **12**:280
exudative, **12**:286, 287*t*, 291–292, 292*f*
  in Coats disease, **12**:143, 144, 144*f*, 292
  photocoagulation causing, **12**:342
familial exudative vitreoretinopathy and, **12**:311
fellow eye in patient with, **12**:285
glaucoma and, **10**:133
hallucinations caused by, **5**:189
in intraocular lymphoma, **12**:199
lattice degeneration and, **4**:155, **12**:276–278, 278*f*
  treatment of, **12**:283, 284–285, 284*t*
lesions not predisposing to, **12**:281–282, 281*f*
lesions predisposing to, **12**:276–280, 277*f*, 278*f*, 279*f*,
  280*f*, 281*f*
in leukemia, **4**:327
management of, **12**:289–291, 290*f*, 362–368, 363*f*,
  365*f*, 366*f*

meridional folds and, **12**:280
metastatic eye disease and, **4**:317, 318*f*
muscarinic therapy and, **2**:335
myopia/high myopia and, **13**:138, 141, 175–176,
  176–177
after Nd:YAG laser capsulotomy, **11**:175, 184,
  12:363
nonrhegmatogenous (secondary), **12**:286, 287*t*
  angle-closure glaucoma and, **10**:133
in ocular histoplasmosis syndrome, **9**:223
in pars planitis, **9**:136, 139, 302, **12**:196
peripheral retinal excavations and, **12**:280
phakic IOLs and
  iris-fixated PIOLs, **13**:135
  posterior chamber PIOLs, **13**:136
pneumatic retinopexy for, **12**:290, 364–365, 365*f*
posterior vitreous detachment and, **2**:84, 84*f*, 85*f*,
  12:274, 275*f*, 362
  cataract surgery and, **11**:184
postoperative, **12**:314, 362–363, 363*f*
in progressive outer retinal necrosis, **9**:203
proliferative vitreoretinopathy and, **4**:136, 137*f*,
  12:286–288, 289*f*, 289*t*
  uveitis and, **9**:302
in punctate inner choroiditis/choroidopathy, **9**:165,
  12:192, 192*f*
after refractive lens exchange/clear lens extraction,
  13:138, 141, 177
refractive surgery and, **13**:175–178
in retinal angiomatosis/capillary hemangioblastoma/
  von Hippel–Lindau disease, **4**:294, **12**:148–149,
  149*f*
retinal breaks and, **12**:271, 286, 288*f*, 289*f*, 362, 363*f*
retinal pigment epithelial maintenance of adhesion
  and, **2**:308
in retinoblastoma, **4**:302, 303*f*
in retinopathy of prematurity, **6**:287, **12**:157, 158,
  160*f*, 163, 164
retinoschisis and, **12**:294, 294*t*
rhegmatogenous, **4**:136, 136*f*, **9**:288, 302, **12**:286,
  286–291, 287*t*, 288*f*, 289*f*, 289*t*, 290*f*
  angle-closure glaucoma and, **10**:133
  after cataract surgery, **11**:143, 144*t*, 184–185,
    13:176–177
    family history as risk factor and, **11**:75
    Nd:YAG laser capsulotomy and, **11**:175, 184
  management of, **12**:289–291, 290*f*, 362–368, 363*f*,
    365*f*, 366*f*
  after Nd:YAG laser capsulotomy, **11**:175
  posterior vitreous detachment and, **2**:84, 84*f*, 85*f*
    after cataract surgery, **11**:184
  in retinopathy of prematurity, **12**:164
  Schwartz (Schwartz-Matsuo) syndrome and,
    10:102–103
in sarcoidosis, **8**:74
Schwartz (Schwartz-Matsuo) syndrome and,
  10:102–103
scleral buckle for, **12**:289–290, 290*f*, 365, 366*f*
  refractive surgery after, **13**:177–178
sickle cell retinopathy and, **12**:121
  in uveitis, **9**:302
secondary (nonrhegmatogenous), **12**:286, 287*t*
  angle-closure glaucoma and, **10**:133

in sickle cell retinopathy, **12:**119, 119*f,* 121
  vitreoretinal surgery for, **12:**121
Stickler syndrome and, **12:**310
subclinical, **12:**285
surgery for, **12:**289–291, 290*f,* 362–368, 363*f,* 365*f,* 366*f*
  anatomical reattachment, **12:**290–291
  angle-closure glaucoma after, **10:**135
  in CMV retinitis, **9:**307
  LASIK and, **13:**176, 189–191
  pneumatic retinopexy, **12:**290, 364–365, 365*f*
  primary vitrectomy, **12:**290, 291, 366–368, 366*f*
  refractive surgery and, **13:**177–178
  in retinopathy of prematurity, **6:**287, **12:**170
  scleral buckle, **12:**289–290, 290*f,* 365, 366*f*
  strabismus and, **6:**143
  techniques for, **12:**364–368
  in uveitis, **9:**302
  visual acuity after, **12:**291
  in sympathetic ophthalmia, **9:**178, 179*f*
  tractional, **12:**286, 287*t,* 291, 362
    in diabetic retinopathy, **12:**110–111, 191, 352–353, 353*f*
    in pars planitis, **12:**196
    after penetrating injury, **12:**191, 324
    in retinopathy of prematurity, **12:**157, 163
  traumatic, **12:**291
    in young patient, **6:**404, **12:**272–273
      abuse and, **6:**404
  in uveal lymphoid infiltration, **4:**325
  uveitis and, **9:**302
    differential diagnosis in children and, **6:**276*t*
  vitrectomy for, **12:**290, 291, 366–368, 366*f*
    in diabetes mellitus, **12:**110–111, 352–353, 353*f*
    refractive surgery after, **13:**177–178
  vitreoretinal tufts and, **12:**278
  vitreous hemorrhage and, **12:**313, 314
  in Vogt-Koyanagi-Harada (VKH) syndrome, **9:**185, 185*f*
  in young patient, **12:**272–273
    abuse and, **6:**404
Retinal dialyses, **4:**20, **12:**271, 272, 273*f*
  treatment of, **12:**284*t*
Retinal disease, **4:**145–184. *See also specific type and* Macula, disease of; Retinitis; Retinopathy
  angiography in, **12:**20–26, 23*f,* 24*f. See also* Fluorescein angiography; Indocyanine green angiography
  after cataract surgery, **11:**181–185, 182*f*
  cataract surgery in patient with, **11:**75, 204–205
  in children, **6:**279–304
    early-onset, **6:**279–288
    hereditary, **6:**288–292
      macular dystrophies, **6:**292–294
      vitreoretinopathies, **6:**294–296
    systemic diseases and, **6:**296–304
  chloroquine/hydroxychloroquine toxicity and, **1:**185, **12:**38*f,* 266–270, 266*f,* 268*f,* 269*t*
  color vision/color vision testing and, **12:**46–50, 48*f,* 49*f*
  congenital, **4:**148–151, 149*f,* 150*f,* **12:**213–219
  contrast sensitivity testing and, **3:**112, **12:**50–52, 51*f*
  cortical evoked potentials in, **12:**44–45, 45*f*
  dark adaptation testing in, **12:**46, 47*f*

degenerative, **4:**154–177, **12:**249–270, 250–251*t. See also* Retinal degenerations
in diabetes mellitus . *See* Diabetic retinopathy
diagnostic approach to, **12:**19–32
electrically evoked potentials in, **12:**45
electro-oculogram in, **12:**42–44, 42*f,* 43*f*
electrophysiologic testing in, **5:**108–110, 110*f,* **12:**33–45. *See also specific test*
ERG in, **5:**109–110, 110*f,* **12:**33, 33–41
hallucinations caused by, **5:**189–190
hereditary, **6:**288–292
illusions caused by, **5:**188
in infant with decreased vision, **6:**415
inflammatory, **4:**151–153, 151*f,* 152*f,* 153*f,* 154*f,* **12:**185–211. *See also specific disorder and* Retinitis
  infectious, **12:**200–211
  noninfectious, **12:**185–199
in metabolic disorders, **6:**302–303, 398, **12:**257–265
neoplastic, **4:**178–184. *See also* Retinoblastoma
  glaucoma caused by, **10:**92–93, 130
  metastatic, **4:**315–316, 320, 321*f*
  pigmented, **4:**288–289, 289*f*
optical coherence tomography in, **12:**26–29, 27*f,* 28*f*
photocoagulation causing, **12:**342
psychophysical testing in, **12:**33, 45–52. *See also specific test*
refractive surgery in patient with, **13:**175–178
scanning laser ophthalmoscopy in, **12:**29–30
stationary, **12:**213–219
Th1 delayed hypersensitivity and, **9:**50*t*
tuberculous, **9:**258, 260*f*
vascular, **12:**89–112, 113–155. *See also specific type*
  angle-closure glaucoma and, **10:**135
  antiphospholipid antibody syndrome and, **1:**158, **9:**142
  arterial occlusion, **12:**135–140. *See also* Retinal artery occlusion
  Behçet disease and, **9:**193, 193*f,* 194*f,* **12:**194–195
  carotid occlusive disease and, **12:**133–135, 134*f*
  Coats disease and, **12:**143–145, 144*f*
    in children, **6:**287–288, 288*f*
  congenital, **4:**149, 150*f*
  cystoid macular edema and, **12:**142–143, 142*f*
  in diabetes mellitus . *See* Diabetic retinopathy
  ERG in evaluation of, **12:**40, 41*f*
  hypertension and, **1:**88, 88*t,* **12:**113–115, 114*f,* 116*f,* 117*f*
  in incontinentia pigmenti, **6:**380, 380*f*
  lupus vasculitis, **9:**141–142, 142*f,* **12:**195–196, 195*f*
  macroaneurysms, **12:**147–148, 147*f*
    age-related macular degeneration differentiated from, **12:**68–69, 69*f*
  microaneurysms, **4:**160–162, 162*f,* 164
    in diabetes mellitus, **4:**166
      in children, **6:**297
      in diabetic macular ischemia, **12:**103
      in nonproliferative diabetic retinopathy, **12:**104, 104*f*
  ocular ischemic syndrome, **12:**133–135, 134*f*
  parafoveal (juxtafoveal) telangiectasia, **12:**145–147, 145*f,* 146*f*
  peripheral neovascularization and, **12:**121, 122*t*

phakomatoses, **12**:148–151, 149*f*, 150*f*, 152*f*
  in children, **6**:372–374, 373*f*
Purtscher/Purtscherlike retinopathy, **12**:154–155,
  154*f*, 155*t*
radiation retinopathy, **12**:151–153, 153*f*
in retinopathy of prematurity, **6**:280–287
  screening for, **6**:285, 286*t*
in sickle cell retinopathy, **12**:115–121, 117*t*, 118*f*,
  119*f*, 120*f*
systemic hypertension and, **1**:88, 88*t*
Terson syndrome, **12**:155
Valsalva retinopathy, **12**:153–154
vasculitis and, **12**:140–141, 141*f*. *See also* Retinal
  vasculitis
venous occlusion, **12**:121–133. *See also* Retinal vein
  occlusion
in Wyburn-Mason syndrome, **6**:342, 381, 381*f*
visually evoked potentials in, **5**:108–109, **12**:44–45, 45*f*
Retinal dystrophies. *See also specific type and* Retinal
  degenerations
ERG in evaluation of, **12**:39–41, 40*f*, 41*f*
hereditary, **12**:221–248
  diagnostic and prognostic testing in, **12**:223, 224*t*
  inner, **12**:246–248
  photoreceptor (diffuse), **4**:175–177, **12**:223–234
Retinal edema, **4**:158–160, 159*f*, 160*f*. *See also* Macular
  edema
in branch retinal artery occlusion, **12**:136
in central retinal artery occlusion, **12**:138, 138*f*
in central retinal vein occlusion, **12**:128, 129*f*
in clinically significant diabetic macular edema, **12**:7,
  99*f*
cystoid macular edema, **12**:142–143, 142*f*
Retinal excavations, peripheral, **12**:280
Retinal folds
congenital, retinoblastoma differentiated from,
  4:305*t*
in shaking injury, **6**:405
Retinal ganglion cells. *See* Ganglion cells
Retinal gene therapy, **9**:66
Retinal hemorrhages
in arterial macroaneurysms, **12**:147–148
in branch retinal vein occlusion, **12**:123
in central retinal vein occlusion, **12**:128, 128*f*, 129*f*
in dengue fever, **9**:219
in diabetic retinopathy, **12**:104, 104*f*
dot-and-blot, **5**:183, 184, 184*f*
  ischemia causing, **4**:160, 161*f*
ischemia causing, **4**:160, 161*f*, 164, 165*f*
in leukemia, **4**:326, 327*f*, **6**:297
in NAION versus optic neuritis, **5**:128
in ocular ischemic syndrome, **12**:133, 134*f*
in Rift Valley fever, **9**:217
in shaking injury, **6**:405, 405*f*, **12**:330, 330*f*, 331
systemic lupus erythematosus and, **9**:141
in Terson syndrome, **12**:155
Retinal holes
atrophic, **12**:271
  lattice degeneration and, **4**:155, **12**:278, 278*f*
    treatment of, **12**:284–285, 284*t*
  treatment of, **12**:283, 284, 284*t*
lattice degeneration and, **4**:155, **12**:276, 277*f*, 278,
  278*f*

operculated, **12**:271
  treatment of, **12**:283, 284*t*
photocoagulation causing, **12**:342
retinal breaks and, **12**:271
Retinal illuminance, **3**:18*t*
Retinal image
blurred, meridional magnification and, **3**:312*f*
size of
  calculation of, **3**:103–104, 106*f*
  contact lenses and, **3**:170–172
  Knapp's law and, **3**:79–80, 80*f*
Retinal ischemia, **4**:156–164
in Behçet disease, **9**:193
cellular responses to, **4**:156–158, 157*f*, 158*f*
central and branch retinal artery and vein occlusions
  causing, **4**:162–164, 163*f*, 164*f*
inner ischemic retinal atrophy and, **4**:157, 157*f*
  in retinal arterial and venous occlusions, **4**:157*f*,
    163, 164
outer ischemic retinal atrophy and, **4**:157, 157*f*
retinopathy of prematurity and, **4**:167
vascular responses to, **4**:158–162, 159*f*, 160*f*, 161*f*,
  162*f*
Retinal locus, preferred, **3**:286, 293
Retinal migraine, **5**:184–185, 190, 297. *See also* Migraine
  headache
Retinal neovascularization. *See also* Neovascularization;
  Retinal disease, vascular
in age-related macular degeneration, **4**:169–170,
  171*f*
ischemia causing, **4**:162, 162*f*
peripheral, **12**:121, 122*t*
  vitreous hemorrhage and, **12**:313, 314
in retinopathy of prematurity, **4**:167, **6**:280–287,
  12:157, 163
  screening for, **6**:285, 286*t*
Retinal nerve fibers, **10**:41–42, 41*f*. *See also* Nerve fiber
  layer
distribution of, **10**:41–42, 41*f*
myelinated (medullated), **4**:148, **6**:306, 306*f*
quantitative measurement of, **10**:51–52, 52–53*f*
Retinal pigment epithelium (RPE), **2**:64, 65*f*, 71–73,
  73*f*, 74*f*, 75*f*, 76*f*, 303–309, 303*f*, **4**:145, 146*f*, **5**:28,
  12:14–16, 16*f*
adenomas/adenocarcinomas of, **4**:184, 288
age-related changes in, **12**:55
in age-related macular degeneration, **12**:57, 58–59,
  59*f*
anatomy of, **2**:64, 65*f*, 71–73, 73*f*, 303–304, **5**:28,
  12:14–16, 16*f*
angiography and, **12**:21
antioxidants in, **2**:315–316
atrophy of, **4**:169, 170*f*, **12**:58–59, 59*f*, 243–244, 244*f*
  photocoagulation and, **12**:342
biochemistry and metabolism of, **2**:303–309
burns of, during cataract surgery, **11**:183–184
in choroideremia, **12**:242–243, 243*f*
composition of, **2**:304–305
congenital abnormalities of, **4**:148–151, 149*f*, 150*f*
  hypertrophy of, **4**:149–151, 150*f*, **6**:352, 353*f*, **12**:255*f*,
    282
    melanoma differentiated from, **4**:150, 278, 279*f*
degeneration of, **12**:58

detachment of, **2**:72. *See also* Retinal detachment
  in age-related macular degeneration/choroidal
    neovascularization, **12**:57, 66–67
  in central serous chorioretinopathy, **12**:23, 24*f*, 171,
    173, 174
  choroidal neovascularization and, **12**:65
  drusenoid, **12**:57, 238, 239*f*
  fibrovascular, **12**:66–67
  multiple recurrent serosanguineous (polypoidal
    choroidal vasculopathy), **4**:171, 172*f*, 173*f*
    age-related macular degeneration differentiated
      from, **12**:69–70, 70*f*
    central serous retinopathy differentiated from,
      12:174, 175
development of, **2**:121, 125*f*, 127
in disease, **2**:308–309
disorders of, **4**:145–184. *See also specific type*
dystrophies of, age-related macular degeneration
  differentiated from, **12**:60, 69
electro-oculogram and, **12**:42–44, 42*f*, 43*f*
fundus autofluorescence in evaluation of, **12**:30
gene defects affecting, **2**:297
geographic atrophy of, **4**:169, 170*f*, **12**:58–59, 59*f*
  patient education/follow-up and, **12**:60
in gyrate atrophy, **12**:243–244, 244*f*
hamartoma of, **4**:184, 289, 289*f*, **6**:352
  in Gardner syndrome, **4**:151
healing/repair of, **4**:17
hyperpigmentation of, in age-related macular
  degeneration, **12**:58
hyperplasia of, **12**:282
hypertrophy of, **12**:282
  congenital, **4**:149–151, 150*f*, **6**:352, 353*f*, **12**:255*f*,
    282
    melanoma differentiated from, **4**:150, 278, 279*f*
immune response in, **9**:58*t*, 64–67
inflammation of (acute retinal pigment epitheliitis/
  ARPE/Krill disease), **9**:148–150*t*, 170, 170*f*,
  12:193–194
lipids in, **2**:305
nongeographic atrophy (degeneration) of, **12**:58
nucleic acids in, **2**:305
phagocytosis by, **2**:306–307, **12**:12, 15
physiologic roles of, **2**:71–72, 305–308
pigment granules in, **2**:307–308
in primary central nervous system lymphoma, **9**:281,
  282, 282*f*
proteins in, **2**:304
regional differences in, **2**:72, 73*f*
retinal adhesion maintained by, **2**:308
rubella (congenital) and, **9**:210
in Stargardt disease, **2**:309, **12**:234, 235*f*
subretinal space maintenance and, **2**:308
in syphilis, **9**:243
topography of, **4**:146*f*, 148
transplantation of, **9**:66
transport functions of, **2**:307
tumors of, **4**:288–289, 289*f*
  in children, **6**:352–353, 353*f*
visual pigment regeneration in, **2**:305–306
Retinal pigment epithelium–photoreceptor complex,
  in multiple evanescent white dot syndrome,
  9:168–169

Retinal reflex, **3**:122–124, 123*f*, 124*f*
  aberrations of, **3**:129
  characteristics of, **3**:124, 124*f*
    cylinder axis location and, **3**:126–127, 126*f*, 127*f*,
      128*f*
Retinal rivalry, **6**:49, 50*f*
Retinal scars, **4**:17
Retinal sclopetaria, **4**:22, 203, **12**:323, 323*f*
Retinal sheathing
  in sarcoidosis, **9**:175, 176*f*
  in toxoplasmosis, **9**:229
Retinal striae, **12**:300
Retinal tears, **4**:135–136, 135*f. See also* Retinal breaks
  COL2A1 gene and, **12**:310
  enclosed ora bays and, **12**:280
  flap (horseshoe), **12**:271, 272, 273*f*
    treatment of, **12**:283, 284, 284*t*
  focal vitreous traction and, **4**:135
  giant, **12**:271
    retained lens fragments after phacoemulsification
      and, **12**:358
  lattice degeneration and, **4**:155, **12**:278, 278*f*
    treatment of, **12**:283, 284–285, 285*t*
  meridional folds and, **12**:10*f*, 280
  muscarinic therapy and, **2**:335
  paving-stone (cobblestone) degeneration and,
    12:282
  in posterior vitreous detachment, **2**:287
  retinal breaks and, **12**:271
  Stickler syndrome and, **12**:310
  vitreous traction and, **12**:274, 275*f*
Retinal telangiectasia, **12**:143–145, 144*f. See also* Coats
  disease
  parafoveal (juxtafoveal), **12**:145–147, 145*f*, 146*f*
Retinal thickness map, OCT producing, **12**:28*f*, 29
Retinal tufts, **12**:278, 279*f*, 280*f*
Retinal vasculitis, **12**:140–141, 141*f*
  in Behçet disease, **1**:181, **9**:193, 193*f*, 194*f*,
    12:194–195
  benign (papillophlebitis), **4**:164, **5**:131–132, 132*f*,
    12:128
  HLA association in, **9**:72*t*
  in HTLV-1 infection, **9**:219
  inflammatory, **12**:194–196
  in Lyme disease, **9**:251
  neovascularization in, **9**:303
  in polyarteritis nodosa/microscopic polyangiitis,
    9:143, 144*f*
  in Rift Valley fever, **9**:217
  in syphilis, **9**:243, 245
  in systemic lupus erythematosus, **9**:141–142, 142*f*,
    12:195–196, 195*f*
  in toxoplasmosis, **9**:229
  in tuberculosis, **9**:258
  in uveitis, **9**:81*t*, 83*t*, 199. *See also* Posterior uveitis
    viral, **9**:199
  in Wegener granulomatosis, **9**:145
  in Whipple disease, **9**:265
Retinal vasospasm (migraine), **5**:184–185, 190
Retinal vein
  arcade, **5**:23
  central, **2**:40*f*, 90, 96, **5**:19*f*, 24, 24*f*, **10**:43*f*, 44
    optic nerve drained by, **10**:43*f*, 44

Retinal vein occlusion, **12**:121–133
  branch, **4**:164, **12**:121–127, 122*f*, 125*f*
    evaluation/management of, **12**:124–127, 125*f*
    neovascularization in, **4**:164, **12**:123
    risk factors for, **12**:123
    visual prognosis in, **12**:123
  central, **4**:163–164, 165*f*, **12**:127–133, 127*f*, 128*f*, 129*f*, 132*f*
    angle-closure glaucoma and, **10**:135
    neovascularization and, **10**:127
    cilioretinal artery occlusion and, **12**:137–138
    ERG in, **12**:40, 41*f*, 128
    evaluation and management of, **12**:130–131
    iris neovascularization in, **12**:128–129
    photocoagulation for, **12**:132
    ischemic/nonperfused, **4**:164, 165*f*, **12**:127, 128, 129*f*
    nonischemic/perfused, **12**:127, 128, 128*f*
    open-angle glaucoma and, **10**:77
    papillophlebitis and, **4**:164, **12**:128
    risk factors for, **12**:129–130
    treatment of, **12**:131–133, 132*f*
  hemispheric (hemicentral), **12**:127, 127*f*
  in sarcoidosis, **9**:175
  in systemic lupus erythematosus, **9**:141–142, 142*f*
Retinaldehyde, in retinal pigment epithelium, **2**:305–306, **12**:15
Retinitis, **9**:78*t*, 82
  in acute retinal necrosis, **9**:200, 201*f*
  in Behçet disease, **9**:193, 194*f*
  Candida, **9**:274–276, 275*f*
  Chikungunya, **9**:220
  CMV, **1**:3, 24, 37–38, **4**:151, 152*f*, **5**:359, **9**:204–207, 205*f*, 206*f*, 306–307, **12**:200–201, 200*f*
    acute retinal necrosis, **9**:202
    cidofovir for, **1**:24, 38, 66, **2**:381*t*, 384
    congenital (cytomegalic inclusion disease), **6**:184–185, 184*f*, **9**:204, 205, 206
    fomivirsen for, **1**:24, 38
    foscarnet for, **1**:24, 38, 66, **2**:381*t*, 384, **9**:207, **12**:200
    ganciclovir for, **1**:24, 37–38, 66, **2**:381*t*, 383–384, **9**:207, **12**:200
    in HIV infection/AIDS, **1**:3, 24, **4**:151, **5**:359, **9**:204, 205, 206, 306–307
      in children, **6**:184
    immune recovery uveitis and, **1**:41, **9**:306, **12**:201
    retinal detachment and, **9**:302, 307
  foveomacular (solar retinopathy/retinitis), **12**:332–333
  herpetic, **9**:199
    necrotizing, **4**:151, 151*f*, **9**:200, 307–308, 308*f*, **12**:201–202, 202*f*. *See also* Acute retinal necrosis; Progressive outer retinal necrosis
    nonnecrotizing (nonnecrotizing posterior uveitis), **9**:203–204
  pigmentosa. *See* Retinitis pigmentosa
  in progressive outer retinal necrosis, **9**:203, 203*f*, 307–308, 308*f*
  punctata albescens, **12**:218, 226, 226*f*
    CRALBP defects causing, **2**:297
  in Rift Valley fever, **9**:217, 217*f*
  rubella, **9**:211

solar (solar retinopathy/foveomacular retinitis), **12**:332–333
  in subacute sclerosing panencephalitis, **9**:213–214, 214*f*
  in syphilis, **9**:245, 245*f*, 247*f*
  in toxoplasmosis, **6**:181, 182, 182*f*, **9**:229, 229*f*, 308–309, 309*f*
    vitreous opacification and, **9**:302
  with uveitis, **9**:78*t*, 82, 82*t*. *See also* Posterior uveitis
  in Wegener granulomatosis, **9**:145, 146*f*
Retinitis pigmentosa, **4**:175–177, 177*f*, **6**:398, **9**:287, **12**:223–232
  autosomal dominant, **2**:217, **12**:228
    oxygen-related protein mutations causing, **2**:296
    rhodopsin mutations causing, **2**:295
  autosomal recessive, **12**:228
    retinal pigment epithelium defects in, **2**:308
    rhodopsin mutations causing, **2**:295
    rod cGMP-gated channel mutations causing, **2**:295
    rod cGMP phosphodiesterase mutations causing, **2**:295
  cataract/cataract surgery in patients with, **12**:225–226, 230
  central, **12**:228
  clinical features of, **12**:225–227, 225*f*, 226*f*
  congenital/infantile/childhood (Leber congenital amaurosis), **6**:289–291, 290*f*, **12**:229, 251–252
    gene therapy for, **9**:66
    guanylate cyclase mutations causing, **2**:296
    pleiotropism and, **2**:210
    RPE65 gene defects causing, **2**:297, **6**:290
  contrast sensitivity testing in, **12**:50
  counseling patients with, **12**:229–230
  cystoid macular edema and, **12**:225, 230, 230*f*
  definition of, **12**:223–224
  diagnosis of, **12**:225–227, 225*f*, 226*f*
  differential diagnosis of, **12**:227
  ERG in, **12**:40*f*, 226
  genetics of, **4**:175, **12**:228–229. *See also specific mutation type*
  hearing loss and, **12**:253. *See also* Usher syndrome
  management/therapy of, **12**:229–232, 230*f*
  multiplex, **12**:228
  with neuropathy and ataxia, **2**:175–176, **12**:265
    mitochondrial DNA mutations and, **2**:174*f*, 175–176
  oxygen-regulated protein defects causing, **2**:296
  pericentral, **12**:228
  primary, **12**:224
  regional variants of, **12**:227–228, 227*f*
  retinal pigment epithelium in, **2**:308, **4**:175, 177
  ROM1 gene in, **2**:296
  sectorial, **12**:227–228, 227*f*
  simplex, **12**:227
  sine pigmento, **12**:225, 225*f*
  unilateral, **12**:228
  uveitis differentiated from, **9**:287
    in children, **6**:276*t*
  visual field testing/defects in, **12**:226, 228
  X-linked, **12**:228, 229
    ocular findings in carriers of, **2**:221*f*, 222*t*, **12**:226, 228
    retinal pigment epithelium in, **2**:308

Retinoblastoma, 2:204–205, 4:178–181, 263, 299–314,
6:354–361, 9:286
chemotherapy of, 4:310–311, 311*f*, 6:358–359, 360*f*
classification of, 4:307–308, 308*t*, 6:358, 359*t*
clinical evaluation/diagnosis of, 4:301–307, 301*t*,
302*f*, 303*f*, 304*f*, 6:356–358, 356*f*, 357*f*
differential diagnosis and, 4:304–307, 305*t*, 306*f*,
307*f*, 6:358, 359*t*
Coats disease differentiated from, 4:305, 305*t*, 306*f*,
6:358
conditions associated with, 4:309
cryotherapy for, 4:312
diffuse infiltrating, 4:303, 6:355
endophytic, 6:354, 355*f*
enucleation for, 4:310, 6:358, 7:118
epidemiology of, 4:299, 299*t*
exenteration for, 7:126
exophytic, 6:355, 355*f*
extraocular, 6:360, 361
fleurettes in, 4:180, 181*f*, 6:358
genetics of, 2:204–205, 4:178, 263, 299–301, 300*f*,
6:356–357, 357*f*
counseling and, 4:299–301, 300*f*, 6:356–357, 357*f*
histologic features of, 4:178–180, 179*f*, 180*f*, 181*f*,
6:358
intracranial, 4:309
iris affected in, 4:271*t*, 303
leukocoria in, 4:301, 301*t*, 302*f*, 5:263, 6:354, 355*f*
differential diagnosis and, 6:358, 359*t*
long arm 13 deletion syndrome and, 2:204–205, 205*t*
metastatic, 4:304
monitoring patient with, 6:361
mutation rate of, 2:207
nonocular, 6:360, 361
optic nerve affected in, 4:180, 182*f*
orbit affected in, 4:304, 304*f*
pathogenesis of, 4:178
persistent fetal vasculature (persistent hyperplastic
primary vitreous) differentiated from, 4:304–305,
305*t*, 12:308
photocoagulation/hyperthermia for, 4:311, 311*f*
presenting signs and symptoms of, 4:301–304, 301*t*,
302*f*, 303*f*, 304*f*, 6:354, 355*f*
prognosis for, 4:313–314, 314*t*
progression of, 4:180–181
radiation therapy of, 4:312
secondary tumors and, 4:312, 313–314, 314*t*,
6:358
rosettes in, 4:180, 181*f*, 6:358
secondary malignancies and, 4:312, 313–314, 314*t*,
6:358, 361
spontaneous regression of, 4:313, 6:356
staging of, 4:342–344*t*
strabismus in, 6:354
targeted therapy of, 4:313
toxocariasis differentiated from, 9:237
treatment of, 4:310–313, 311*f*, 6:358–360
trilateral, 4:309, 6:360
uveitis in children differentiated from, 6:276*t*
vitreous seeding and, 4:303, 303*f*, 6:354, 355*f*
Retinoblastoma *(RB1)* gene, 2:204–205, 4:178, 263,
299–300, 309, 312, 313, 6:356
secondary malignancies and, 4:312, 313–314, 314*t*

Retinoblastoma Support News (newsletter), 6:417*t*
Retinochoroidal collaterals (optociliary shunt vessels),
5:25, 149
in optic nerve sheath meningioma, 5:149, 150*f*
in papilledema, 5:121–122
Retinochoroiditis, 9:78*t*
in congenital herpes simplex, 6:185
in cytomegalic inclusion disease, 6:184, 184*f*
Toxoplasma causing, 9:226–235, 227*f*, 229*f*, 230*f*, 231*f*,
233*f*, 308–309, 309*f*, 12:206–209, 208*f*, 208*t*
congenital, 9:228, 229*f*, 230, 233
in HIV infection/AIDS, 9:228, 232, 233–234,
308–309, 309*f*, 12:208
Retinochoroidopathies. *See also specific disorder*
birdshot (vitiliginous chorioretinitis), 9:148–150*t*,
152–155, 152*f*, 153*f*, 154*f*, 12:186*t*, 190–191, 190*f*
HLA association in, 9:72*t*, 73, 148*t*, 152, 12:190
Retinocytoma (retinoma), 4:181, 183*f*, 309, 6:356
Retinogeniculocortical pathway, 6:42, 42–44, 43*f*
development of, 6:42, 43, 43*f*, 44
abnormal visual experience affecting, 6:46–49,
47*f*, 48*f*
Retinoic acid
homeobox gene expression affected by, 2:115
ocular development/congenital anomalies and, 2:142
Retinoid-binding proteins, interphotoreceptor, 2:306,
4:178
Retinoid inhibitors, for age-related macular
degeneration, 12:63
Retinoids, for xerophthalmia/dry-eye syndrome, 8:79
Retinol, 2:306
Retinoma (retinocytoma), 4:181, 183*f*, 309, 6:356
Retinopathy. *See also specific type and* Retinitis
acute zonal occult outer (AZOOR), 9:148–150*t*,
170–172, 171*f*, 12:186*t*, 192–193, 192*f*
in antiphospholipid antibody syndrome, 1:172, 9:142
autoimmune, 12:256
cancer-associated, 5:112, 114–115, 190, 12:256–257,
256*f*
canthaxanthine, 12:268*f*, 269
of carotid occlusive disease, 12:133–135, 134*f*
central retinal vein occlusion differentiated from,
12:130, 133
central serous, 12:171–176, 173*f*
age-related macular degeneration differentiated
from, 12:60, 70, 71*f*
fluorescein angiography in, 12:23, 24*f*, 172–173, 173*f*
photocoagulation for, 12:175, 176, 341
in child abuse, 12:331
chloroquine/hydroxychloroquine causing, 1:185,
12:38*f*, 266–270, 266*f*, 268*f*, 269*t*
CMV, in children, 6:184
in congenital rubella syndrome, 6:183, 183*f*, 9:210,
210*f*
crystalline, 12:268–269, 268*f*, 269*t*
Bietti, 8:313, 12:250*t*
drug toxicity causing, 12:268–269, 268*f*, 269*t*
diabetic. *See* Diabetic retinopathy
drug-related, 12:266–270, 266*f*, 268*f*, 269*t*
eclipse (solar), 12:332–333
exudative, retinopathy of prematurity and, 12:164
hemorrhagic (severe/ischemic CRVO), 12:127, 128,
129*f*

herpetic necrotizing, **9**:200, 307–308, 308*f*. *See also* Acute retinal necrosis; Progressive outer retinal necrosis

HIV, **9**:305, 306*f*. *See also* HIV infection/AIDS, retinitis in

hypertensive, **1**:88, **12**:113–114, 114*f*, 116*f*

hyperviscosity, central retinal vein occlusion differentiated from, **12**:129–130

of incontinentia pigmenti, **6**:380, 380*f*, 381, **12**:251*t*, 255

isotretinoin, **12**:269

in leukemia, **4**:326, 327*f*, **6**:297

lupus, **9**:141–142, 141*f*, 142*f*, **12**:195–196, 195*f*

in measles, **9**:212, 213

melanoma-associated, **5**:112, 113, **12**:256, 257

in ocular ischemic syndrome, **12**:133–135, 134*f*

paraneoplastic, **5**:114–115, **12**:256–257, 256*f*

pigmentary, **12**:223–224, 249. *See also* Retinitis pigmentosa

  in Bardet-Biedl syndrome, **12**:250*t*, 252

  in congenital rubella syndrome, **9**:210, 210*f*

  hearing loss and, **12**:251*t*, 253. *See also* Usher syndrome

  in measles, **9**:212, 213

  in neuromuscular disorders, **12**:254

  secondary/systemic disease and, **12**:224, 249, 250–251*t*

  X-linked, **12**:251*t*

in polyarteritis nodosa/microscopic polyangiitis, **9**:143

of prematurity, **4**:167, **6**:280–287, **12**:157–170

  angle kappa and, **6**:287, 287*f*

  classification of, **6**:282–285, 282*t*, 283*f*, 284*f*, 285*t*, **12**:157–160, 158*t*, 159*f*, 160*f*

  conditions associated with, **12**:163–164

  diagnosis of, **6**:285

  epidemiology of, **12**:157

  extent of involvement and, **12**:160, 161*f*

  familial exudative vitreoretinopathy and, **12**:310

  fundus photography/screening in, **12**:164, 165

  glaucoma and, **12**:163

  management of, **6**:285–286, 286*f*, 286*t*, **12**:166–170

  natural course of, **12**:163

  pathogenesis of, **12**:162–164

  prevention/risk factors for, **12**:165–166

  retinoblastoma differentiated from, **4**:305*t*

  screening for, **6**:285, 286*t*, **12**:164–165

  sequelae and complications of, **6**:286–287, 287*f*, **12**:163–164

  stages of, **12**:158–160, 158*t*, 159*f*, 160*f*

  terminology used with, **12**:160–161, 161*f*

  zones of involvement and, **6**:282*t*, 283*f*, 285*t*, 286*t*, **12**:158, 158*t*, 159*f*, 161

Purtscher/Purtscherlike, **12**:154–155, 154*f*, 155*t*

radiation, **1**:238, **12**:151–153, 153*f*

in rubella (congenital), **6**:183, 183*f*, **9**:210, 210*f*

in scleroderma, **1**:174

in shaken baby syndrome, **12**:331

sickle cell. *See* Sickle cell retinopathy

solar (foveomacular/solar retinitis), **12**:332–333

surface-wrinkling, **12**:300

tamoxifen, **12**:268, 268*f*

thioridazine, **12**:267–268, 268*f*

Valsalva, **12**:153–154

venous stasis, **5**:184, **12**:127, 128, 128*f*

vitamin A deficiency, **12**:260–261

Retinopexy, pneumatic, for retinal detachment, **12**:290, 364–365, 365*f*

Retinoschisin, in X-linked retinoschisis, **12**:247

Retinoschisis, **4**:154, **12**:246, 292–294, 293*f*, 294*t*

  foveal, **6**:294

  juvenile, **6**:294–295, 295*f*

  reticular degenerative, **4**:154, **12**:293–294

  retinal detachment and, **12**:294, 294*t*

  traumatic, in shaking injury, **6**:405–406, 406*f*

  typical degenerative, **4**:154, **12**:293, 293*f*

  X-linked (congenital/juvenile), **6**:294–295, 295*f*, **12**:246–247, 246*f*

    ERG in, **12**:36*f*, 247

Retinoscopes, **3**:121, 121*f*, 122*f*. *See also* Retinoscopy

Retinoscopic reflex. *See* Retinal reflex

Retinoscopy, **3**:121–130, 121*f*, 122*f*, **8**:45

  automatic (automatic objective refractors), **3**:276, 277

  before cataract surgery, **11**:80

  in children, **3**:141–142

    cataract and, **6**:251

  conjugacy/conjugate points and, **3**:28, 29*f*

  correcting lens in, **3**:124–125, 125*f*

  fixation and fogging and, **3**:122

  irregular astigmatism and, **3**:129, **8**:45

  low vision and, **3**:294

  neutrality in, **3**:123*f*, 124, 125, 126*f*

  positioning and alignment in, **3**:122

  regular astigmatism and, **3**:125–129, 126*f*, 127*f*, 128*f*

  retinal reflex and, **3**:122–124, 123*f*, 124*f*

    aberrations of, **3**:129

  steps in performance of, **3**:129–130

Retisert. *See* Fluocinolone implant

RetNet website, **12**:221, 228, 233, 253

Retraction, eyelid, **5**:281–282, 282*t*, **7**:213–216

  after blepharoplasty, **7**:214, 215, 226

  in convergence-retraction nystagmus, **5**:256

  in dorsal midbrain (Parinaud) syndrome, **5**:211, 273, 281, **7**:214

  ptosis and, **5**:275

  seizures causing, **1**:263–264

  in thyroid eye disease, **4**:232, 233*f*, **5**:276, 278*f*, 281, 332*f*, 333, **7**:47*f*, 49, 51, 54, 213–214, 214*f*, 215

    management and, **5**:334

  proptosis differentiated from, **7**:213–214

  treatment of, **7**:215–216

Retractors, eyelid, **7**:135*f*, 138–140, 139*f*

  lower eyelid, **7**:135*f*, 140

    in involutional ectropion, repair of, **7**:193

    in involutional entropion, **7**:194–195, 196*f*

      repair of, **7**:196, 197*f*

  upper eyelid, **7**:138–140, 139*f*

Retrobulbar anesthesia. *See also* Anesthesia (anesthetics)

  adverse reactions to, **1**:298–299, 311

  agents for, **2**:387

  for cataract surgery, **11**:98–99, 99*f*

    hemorrhage and, **11**:176, 189

  for extraocular muscle surgery, **6**:160–161

  for phakic IOL insertion, **13**:129

  strabismus after, **6**:143

Retrobulbar drug administration, **2**:327

Retrobulbar hemorrhage
    after blepharoplasty, visual loss and, 7:226
    cataract surgery and, 11:144*t*, 176–177, 189
Retrobulbar optic neuritis, 5:144–146, 145*f*
    contrast sensitivity affected by, 3:113
    in cryptococcosis, 5:367
Retrochiasmal lesions, 5:165–172
    lateral geniculate body lesions, 5:167–168, 167*f*
    in multiple sclerosis, 5:324
    neuroimaging in evaluation of, 5:84
    occipital lobe lesions, 5:169–172, 170*f*, 171*f*, 172*f*
    optic tract lesions, 5:165–167, 166*f*
    parietal lobe lesions, 5:168–169
    temporal lobe lesions, 5:168, 169*f*
Retrocorneal fibrous membrane (posterior collagenous
    layer), 2:251, 4:91, 92*f*, 8:29
Retrogeniculate visual loss/cortical visual impairment,
    6:415–416. *See also* Cerebral/cortical blindness
Retroillumination, for slit-lamp biomicroscopy, 8:14–15,
    16*f*
Retrolaminar nerve/retrolaminar area of optic nerve,
    2:91, 10:42, 43*f*, 44
    blood supply of, 2:94, 95*f*
Retrolental fibroplasia. *See* Retinopathy, of prematurity
Retro-orbicularis oculi fat (ROOF), 7:141
Retro-orbital plexus, 2:106*f*, 107
Retroposon, 2:160
Retrotransposition, 2:160
Retrovir. *See* Zidovudine
Retroviruses, 8:130
    cancer association of, 1:236–237
    HIV as, 1:28–29
Rev-Eyes. *See* Dapiprazole
Revascularization procedures. *See also* Coronary artery
    bypass graft; Percutaneous coronary intervention
    for angina, 1:108–110
    for ST-segment elevation acute coronary syndrome,
        1:112–113
    troponin levels in determining need for, 1:105
Reverse Galilean telescope
    contact lens correction of aphakia and, 3:171–172
    in slit-lamp biomicroscope, 3:252
Reverse-geometry designs, orthokeratology and, 3:194,
    195
Reverse ocular bobbing, 5:259
Reverse ocular dipping, 5:259
Reverse slab-off, for induced anisophoria, 3:154–155
Reverse transcriptase, 1:28, 8:130
    viral carcinogenesis and, 1:236
Reverse transcriptase inhibitors, 1:33–34
    in HAART, 1:35
    nonnucleoside (NNRTIs), 1:34
    nucleoside (NRTIs), 1:33
Reverse transcriptase-polymerase chain reaction
    (RT-PCR), 4:39*t*
Reverse transcription, 2:160
Revised European American Lymphoma (REAL)
    classification, 7:80
Reyataz. *See* Atazanavir
ReZoom intraocular lens, 3:228, 228*f*, 13:144, 154,
    154*f*
Rezulin. *See* Troglitazone
RF. *See* Rheumatoid factor

RF-negative polyarthritis, 6:269, 269*t*
    uveitis in, 6:269
RFLPs (restriction fragment length polymorphisms),
    2:160, 178–180, 179*f*
RGCs (retinal ganglion cells). *See* Ganglion cells
RGP contact lenses. *See* Rigid gas-permeable contact
    lenses
Rhabdomyomas, in tuberous sclerosis, 6:372
Rhabdomyosarcoma
    of orbit, 4:242–244, 243*f*, 6:334–335, 335*f*, 7:76–78, 77*f*
    retinoblastoma associated with, 4:314*t*
Rhegmatogenous posterior vitreous detachment,
    12:297. *See also* Posterior vitreous detachment
Rhegmatogenous retinal detachment. *See* Retinal
    detachment
Rheopheresis (differential membrane filtration), for
    nonneovascular age-related macular degeneration,
    ineffectiveness of, 12:63
Rheumatic disorders, 1:161–187. *See also specific type*
    medical therapy for, 1:181–187, 181*t*, 183*t*
    recent developments in, 1:161
Rheumatoid arthritis, 1:161–162
    cataract surgery in patient with, corneal melting/
        keratolysis and, 11:150
    juvenile. *See* Juvenile idiopathic (chronic/rheumatoid)
        arthritis
    peripheral ulcerative keratitis and, 8:211, 212, 212*f*
    refractive surgery contraindicated in, 13:184
    scleritis/scleromalacia perforans and, 8:220, 220*f*, 222
Rheumatoid factor, 1:162
    in aqueous tear deficiency, 8:57
    in juvenile idiopathic (chronic/rheumatoid) arthritis,
        uveitis and, 6:269, 269*t*, 9:129
    in Sjögren syndrome, 8:57
    testing for, 8:182*t*
Rheumatoid nodules, 1:162
Rheumatrex. *See* Methotrexate
Rhinocerebral mucormycosis, 5:366, 366*f*
Rhinophyma, in rosacea, 8:69
Rhinosporidium seeberi (rhinosporidiosis), 8:139
    conjunctivitis caused by, 4:54
Rhinoviruses, 8:129
Rhizopus/Rhizopus infection, 8:140
    orbital, 7:45
RHO gene. *See also* Rhodopsin, gene for
    in retinitis pigmentosa, 4:175
Rhodopsin, 2:291–293, 292*f*
    gene for, mutations in, 2:182, 295, 12:222
        in congenital stationary night blindness, 12:215
        in retinitis pigmentosa, 4:175, 12:228, 231
    light affecting, 2:291–293, 292*f*
    phosphorylation of, 2:292, 292*f*, 293
    regeneration of, retinal pigment epithelium in,
        2:305–306
Rhodopsin kinase, 2:293
    mutations in, 2:295
Rhytidectomy, 7:235–236, 237*f*
Ribavirin, 1:55*t*
    for hepatitis C, 1:26
Riboflavin (vitamin B$_2$), in collagen crosslinking, 13:123
Ribonucleic acid. *See* RNA
Richner-Hanhart syndrome, 8:314
Riddoch phenomenon, 5:172, 195

Riders, 11:30
Ridley lens/Ridley intraocular lens, 3:208, 209f, 11:132–133, 132f
RIEG1 gene, 2:141, 10:11t
RIEG2 gene, 10:11t
Rieger anomaly/syndrome, 2:141, 6:213, 8:256, 10:145.
    See also Axenfeld-Rieger syndrome
    gene for, 10:11t
Rifabutin, 1:39
    endothelial pigmentation caused by, 8:349
    uveitis caused by, 9:128, 12:269
Rifadin. *See* Rifampin
Rifampin, 1:19, 39, 53t, 62–63
    ocular effects of, 1:301t
Rift Valley fever, 9:217–218, 217f
Right bundle branch block, 1:122t
Right gaze (dextroversion), 6:35
Right to Sight, 11:65
Rigid contact lenses (hard contact lenses), 3:176, 180.
    See also Contact lenses; Rigid gas-permeable contact
    lenses
    disinfection of trial lenses and, 3:201
Rigid gas-permeable contact lenses, 3:176–178, 180,
    181t. *See also* Contact lenses
    base curve of, lens fitting and, 3:183–184
    daily wear, 3:180
    diameter of, lens fitting and, 3:184t, 185
    extended-wear, 3:180
    fitting, 3:182–186, 184f, 184t, 186f, 187f
        disinfection of trial lenses and, 3:201
    in giant papillary conjunctivitis, 8:195
    for keratoconus, 3:190–191, 191f
    materials for, 3:176–178, 177t
    for myopia reduction (orthokeratology), 3:194–195,
        13:63–64
    parameters of, 3:182–185, 184t
    position of, lens fitting and, 3:184–185, 185f, 186
    power of, lens fitting and, 3:185
    after radial keratotomy, 13:193
    refractive surgery and, 13:32, 192
    soft lenses compared with, 3:181t
    tear (fluid) lens and, 3:169, 173–174, 174f, 175
        fitting and, 3:183, 185
    3 and 9 o'clock staining caused by, 3:198, 198f
Riley-Day syndrome (familial dysautonomia), 2:213t,
    6:221
    congenital corneal anesthesia and, 8:264
    neurotrophic keratopathy in, 8:87
    racial and ethnic concentration of, 2:211
Rim of optic cup, 2:123
"Rim"/RIM proteins, 2:293. *See also specific type*
    mutations in, 4:172
RimabotulinumtoxinB, 7:218–220
Rimantadine, 1:55t, 66
Rimexolone, 2:357t, 361
    for uveitis, 9:101t, 102
riMLF. *See* Rostral interstitial nucleus of medial
    longitudinal fasciculus
Ring of Elschnig, 10:42
Ring infiltrate, in *Acanthamoeba* keratitis, 4:85, 86f
Ring melanoma, 4:197, 197f, 200, 273
Ring of Schwalbe. *See* Schwalbe line/ring
Ring siderosblast, 1:149

Ring sign
    in nonspecific orbital inflammation, 7:59
    in optic nerve sheath meningioma, 5:150f
Riolan, muscle of, 2:23, 23f, 27, 7:137, 142, 142f
RIP. *See* Nucleus raphe interpositus
Rise time, in phacoemulsification, 11:104, 109, 110f
Risedronate, for osteoporosis, 1:230–231
Risk, 1:336
    relative, 1:270, 336
Risk difference, 1:336
Risk factor, 1:337. *See also specific disorder*
    in cohort studies, 1:326–327
    in cross-sectional studies, 1:325–326
    pretest probability of disease and, 1:333–334
Risk ratio, 1:337
Risley (rotary) prism, 3:88
Risorius muscle, 7:131, 133f
Risperdal. *See* Risperidone
Risperidone, 1:251
Ritipenem, 1:59
Ritonavir, 1:34
Rituxan. *See* Rituximab
Rituximab, 1:186, 9:108t, 115
    for primary central nervous system lymphoma, 9:284
    for uveitis, 9:108t, 115
Rivalry pattern, 6:49, 50f
River blindness (onchocerciasis), 8:141, 9:241–242
Rizzutti sign, in keratoconus, 8:297–298, 298f
RK. *See* Radial keratotomy
RLF (retrolental fibroplasia). *See* Retinopathy, of
    prematurity
RMS (root-mean-square) errors, magnitude of
    wavefront deviation and, 13:6
RNA
    amplification of, in polymerase chain reaction, 2:158
    heteronuclear/heterogeneous nuclear (hnRNA),
        2:153, 161
    messenger (mRNA), precursor, 2:161
    in retinal pigment epithelium, 2:305
    small interference (short interfering) (siRNA), in
        gene therapy, 2:188
    splicing of, 2:161, 168
        alternative, 2:165
    transfer (tRNA), initiator, 2:154
    virus, 8:104
RNA viruses, 8:129–130. *See also specific virus*
    cancer association of, 1:236–237
ROC (receiver operating characteristics) curve, 1:133,
    331, 332f, 333f
Rocephin. *See* Ceftriaxone
Rod cGMP-gated channel, 2:292–293
    mutations in, 2:295
Rod cGMP phosphodiesterase (rod PDE), 2:293
    mutations in, 2:295
Rod–cone dystrophies/degenerations. *See also* Retinitis
    pigmentosa
    choroideremia as, 12:242
    ERG patterns in, 12:36f
    visual field testing in, 12:223
Rod inner segments, 2:73, 76f, 292, 4:145, 146f, 12:10,
    11f, 13f. *See also* Photoreceptor inner segments;
    Rods
    free-radical leakage from, 2:315

Rod monochromatism, **12**:214*t*, 215. *See also*
    Achromatopsia
    in children, **6**:291
Rod outer segments, **2**:73, 76*f*, 291, 292, **4**:145, 146*f*,
    12:10, 11*f*, 12, 13*f*. *See also* Photoreceptor outer
    segments; Rods
    development of, **2**:126
    energy metabolism in, **2**:293
    oxidative damage to, **2**:315
    phototransduction in, **2**:291–293, 292*f*
    shed, retinal pigment epithelium phagocytosis of,
        2:306–307, **12**:12, 15
Rod PDE. *See* Rod phosphodiesterase
Rod phosphodiesterase, **2**:293
    mutations in, **2**:295
Rod response, **2**:294, 301*f*, 302, **12**:33, 34*f*, 35, 36*f*. *See
    also* Dark adaptation, testing
Rod transducin, **2**:293
    mutations in, **2**:295
Rodenstock contact lens, for slit-lamp biomicroscopy,
    3:255
Rods, **2**:73, 73–74, 76*f*, 77*f*, **4**:145, 146*f*, **5**:27, **12**:10, 12,
    13*f*, 14*f*. *See also* Rod outer segments
    abnormalities of, **12**:215–219. *See also* Night
        blindness; Night-vision abnormalities
    amacrine cells for, **2**:300
    bipolar cells for, **2**:298
    development of, **2**:126
    electrophysiologic responses of, **2**:301*f*, 302
    gene defects in, **2**:295–296
    phototransduction in, **2**:291–293, 292*f*
Rofecoxib, **2**:257–258
    withdrawal of from market, **1**:184, **9**:99
Roferon-A. *See* Interferons (IFNs), α
ROIs. *See* Reactive oxygen intermediates
ROM1 gene/ROM1 protein, **2**:293
    mutations in, **2**:296
Romazicon. *See* Flumazenil
Romycin. *See* Erythromycin
ROOF (retro-orbicularis oculi fat), **7**:141
Root-mean-square (RMS) errors, magnitude of
    wavefront deviation and, **13**:6
ROP. *See* Retinopathy, of prematurity
Ropinirole, for Parkinson disease, **1**:259
Rosacea, **8**:69–71, 70*f*, 71*f*
    blepharitis and, **8**:69, 144*t*
    cataract surgery in patient with, **11**:77, 190
    meibomian gland dysfunction and, **8**:67–68, 69, 144*t*
Rose bengal stain, **2**:392, **8**:17
    in tear-film evaluation, **8**:17, 56, 56*f*
Rosengren-Doane tear pump, **7**:246, 247*f*
Rosenmüller, valve of, **7**:245
Rosenthal, basilar vein of, **5**:26
Rosenthal fibers, in optic nerve gliomas, **4**:257, 257*f*
Roseolovirus, **1**:22
Rosette cataract, **11**:50, 50*f*
Rosettes, retinoblastoma, **4**:180, 181*f*, **6**:358
Rosiglitazone, **1**:199*t*, 201
    with metformin, **1**:201
Rostral interstitial nucleus of medial longitudinal
    fasciculus, **5**:38, 39*f*, 42, 44*f*, 46*f*, 199, 199–200
Rosuvastatin, for hypercholesterolemia/heart disease
    prevention, **1**:137*t*

Rotary (Risley) prism, **3**:88
Rotation, center of, **6**:27, 27*f*
Rotation/rotational flap
    for wound closure after pterygium excision, **8**:392*f*,
        393
    for eyelid repair, **7**:182, 184
Rotational corneal autograft, **8**:432
Roth spots, **4**:160, **9**:272
Rothmund-Thomson syndrome, **8**:324*t*
Round segment 1-piece bifocals, **3**:147, 148*f*
Roxithromycin, **1**:50*t*, 61
RP. *See* Retinitis pigmentosa
RP12 phenotype, **12**:229
RPCD. *See* Reticular peripheral cystoid degeneration
RPE. *See* Retinal pigment epithelium
RPE65 gene/RPE65 protein, **2**:304, 306
    mutations in, **2**:297
        in Leber congenital amaurosis, **2**:297, **6**:290
    retinal gene therapy and, **9**:65
RPED. *See* Retinal pigment epithelium (RPE),
    detachment of
RPR (rapid plasma reagin) test, **1**:13, 279, **9**:247
    in syphilitic chorioretinitis, **12**:205
RRD (rhegmatogenous retinal detachment). *See* Retinal
    detachment
RS1 gene, in X-linked retinoschisis, **12**:247
RSBT. *See* Residual stromal bed thickness
RT. *See* Radiation therapy
RT-PCR. *See* Real-time quantitative polymerase chain
    reaction; Reverse transcriptase-polymerase chain
    reaction
Rubella, **9**:209–211, 209*f*, 210*f*
    acquired, **9**:210–211
    congenital, **1**:283, **6**:183–184, 183*f*, **8**:130, **9**:209–210,
        209*f*, 210*f*, 211
        aphakia and, **4**:121
        cataracts and, **6**:183, **9**:210, **11**:35
        glaucoma and, **10**:142*t*
    Fuchs heterochromic iridocyclitis/uveitis and, **9**:48,
        134, 211
    immunization against, **1**:283
Rubeola (measles) virus, **8**:129, **9**:212
    immunization against, **1**:282
    ocular infection caused by, **8**:129, **9**:212–214, 214*f*
Rubeosis iridis (iris neovascularization), **4**:192, 192*t*, 193*f*
    in branch retinal vein occlusion, **12**:124
    in central retinal artery occlusion, **12**:140
    in central retinal vein occlusion, **12**:128–129
        photocoagulation for, **12**:132
    in diabetes mellitus, **4**:166, 166*f*, **12**:108–109
    glaucoma and, **4**:192, **10**:30–31, 37, 125, 125*f*, 125*t*,
        126*f*, 201. *See also* Neovascular glaucoma
        incisional surgery contraindicated in, **10**:185
        in infants and children, **10**:141*t*
        laser iridotomy contraindicated in, **10**:202
    in ocular ischemic syndrome, **12**:133, 134, 134*f*
    in retinoblastoma, **4**:179, 180*f*, 303
Ruby laser, **3**:24. *See also* Lasers
    photocoagulation for central serous
        chorioretinopathy with, **12**:175
Rud syndrome, ichthyosis in, **8**:74
Rufen. *See* Ibuprofen
Rufous oculocutaneous albinism (OCA3), **6**:299*t*, 301

Run diagrams, **1**:344–345, 346*f*
Running sutures, for penetrating keratoplasty, **8**:419, 420*f*
Rupintrivir, **1**:34
Rush (plus) disease, retinopathy of prematurity and, **4**:167, **6**:282*t*, 283, 284*f*, **12**:160, 161*f*
Russell bodies, **4**:9
Rust ring, iron foreign body causing, **8**:371, 371*f*
Ruthenium 106, for uveal melanoma, **4**:284
RVF. *See* Rift Valley fever

S

S-100 protein, in immunohistochemistry, **4**:33
in adenoid cystic carcinoma, **4**:236
S-3578, **1**:58
S-antigen
in birdshot retinochoroidopathy, **9**:152
in experimental autoimmune uveitis/sympathetic ophthalmia, **9**:69, 181
in serpiginous choroiditis, **9**:158
S cones, **2**:294
enhanced, **12**:218–219, 219*f*, 248. *See also* Goldmann-Favre disease/syndrome
horizontal cells for, **2**:299
retinal ganglion cells for, **2**:299*f*, 300
SA. *See* Sideroblastic anemia
SA node. *See* Sinoatrial (SA) node
SAARDs. *See* Slow-acting (disease-modifying) antirheumatic drugs
Sabin vaccine (oral polio vaccine/OPV), **1**:283
Sabril. *See* Vigabatrin
SAC. *See* Seasonal allergic conjunctivitis
Saccades/saccadic system, **5**:40–41, 40*f*, 46*f*, 198–199, 198*t*, 202–203, 202*f*, **6**:37
antiepileptic drugs affecting, **1**:264
assessment of, **5**:202–203, 203*f*
dysfunction of, **5**:208–213, 211*f*, 212*f*, 243. *See also* Saccadic initiation failure; Saccadic intrusions/oscillations
in Alzheimer disease, **1**:268
in ataxia-telangiectasia, **5**:344, **6**:378
gaze palsy/preference/tonic deviations and, **5**:210–213, 211*f*, 212*f*
in internuclear ophthalmoplegia, **5**:224
ocular motor apraxia and, **5**:194, 209–210, **6**:141–142
in progressive supranuclear palsy, **5**:208
hypermetric saccades and, **5**:203, 209
hypometric saccades and, **5**:203, 209
testing velocity of, **5**:203, 208–209, **6**:83
Saccadic initiation failure (ocular motor apraxia), **5**:194, 208, 209–210, **6**:141–142
Saccadic intrusions/oscillations, **5**:200, 204–205, 208, 243, 244, 254–256, 255*f*
macrosaccadic, **5**:255, 255*f*
with normal intersaccadic intervals, **5**:254–255, 255*f*
without normal intersaccadic intervals, **5**:255–256, 255*f*
Saccadic (cogwheel) pursuit, **5**:213
Saccadomania (opsoclonus), **5**:251*t*, 255–256
in children, **6**:325
neuroblastoma and, **6**:336

Saccular (berry) aneurysm, **1**:97, **5**:350
Saccule, **5**:47*f*, 48
Saethre-Chotzen syndrome, **6**:389, 390*f*
Sagittal curvature. *See* Axial curvature
Sagittal depth (vault), of contact lens, **3**:169, 169*f*
Sagittal sinus, superior, **2**:108, 108*f*, **5**:25–26, 26*f*
thrombosis in, **5**:357–358
Sagittal suture, **5**:7
SAI (surface asymmetry index), **3**:267
SAILOR trial, **12**:77
Sakacin, **1**:64
Salbutamol, **1**:144
Salicylates, **1**:183*t*, **2**:362. *See also* Nonsteroidal anti-inflammatory drugs
Salivary gland biopsy, in Sjögren syndrome, **8**:57, 59*f*, 63
Salivary (salivatory) nucleus, **2**:106, 106–107, 107, **5**:66, 66*f*
SALK. *See* Superficial anterior lamellar keratoplasty
Salk vaccine (inactivated poliovirus vaccine/IPV), **1**:283
in combination vaccines, **1**:285
Salmeterol, **1**:145
with fluticasone, **1**:145*t*
Salmon patch hemorrhages, in sickle cell disease, **12**:118, 118*f*, 119*f*
Salmon patches, in syphilitic keratitis, **6**:221, **8**:208, 208*f*
Salmonella, **8**:135
Salsalate, **1**:183*t*
Salt-and-pepper fundus/retinopathy
rubella and, **6**:183, 183*f*, **9**:210, 210*f*
syphilis and, **9**:243
in infants and children, **6**:185
Salzmann nodular degeneration, **4**:88, 88*f*, **8**:340–341, 341*f*
SAM. *See* Steeper add minus (SAM) rule
Sampaolesi line
in exfoliation syndrome, **10**:38, 86, 87*f*
in pigment dispersion syndrome/pigmentary glaucoma, **10**:88
Sample size/sampling, **1**:317–318
monitoring system and, **1**:342
Sandhoff disease (GM₂ gangliosidosis type II), **2**:213*t*, **6**:303, 401*t*
cherry-red spot in, **6**:401*t*, **12**:262
Sandimmune. *See* Cyclosporine/cyclosporine A
Sands of the Sahara (diffuse lamellar keratitis/DLK), after LASIK, **13**:108–111, 109*f*, 109*t*, 110*t*, 111*f*
glaucoma/IOP elevation and, **13**:97, 174, 195
infectious keratitis differentiated from, **13**:110–111, 110*t*, 111*f*
Sandwich technique, **12**:343
Sanfilippo syndrome, **2**:213*t*, **6**:400*t*, **8**:305–307, 306*t*, **12**:250*t*, 262
pigmentary retinopathy and, **12**:250*t*, 262
Sanger method, for DNA sequencing, **2**:184, 185*f*
SAP. *See* Standard automated perimetry
Saquinavir, **1**:34
Sarcoid granuloma, **5**:335, **8**:73–74, **9**:84, 173, 174, 174*f*, 175, 176*f*
Sarcoidosis, **5**:334–336, **7**:32, 58–59, **8**:73–74, **9**:172–177, 174*f*, 175*f*, 176*f*
anterior uveitis and, **9**:174–175
conjunctivitis and, **4**:52, 53*f*
cranial nerve VII (facial) involvement in, **5**:287, 288, 335

diagnosis and treatment of, **9**:175–177
eyelid manifestations of, **4**:213*t*
glaucoma and, **9**:175, 296
HLA association in, **9**:72*t*, 173
keratic precipitates in, **9**:86*f*
neovascularization in, **9**:303
neuro-ophthalmologic manifestations in, **5**:335
numb chin associated with, **5**:303
optic nerve involvement and, **4**:253, 253*f*, **5**:133*f*, 144, 335
orbit affected in, **7**:32, 58–59
panuveitis and, **6**:274, 274*f*, **9**:172–177, 174*f*, 175*f*, 176*f*, **12**:196–197, 197*f*
pars planitis and, **9**:136
pediatric, **6**:274, 274*f*
posterior synechiae/iris nodules in, **9**:87*f*, 175, 175*f*
retina affected in, **8**:74
uveal tract affected in, **4**:190–191, 191*f*, 272*f*, **9**:172–177, 174*f*, 175*f*, 176*f*, **12**:196–197, 197*f*
in children, **6**:274, 274*f*
Sarcoma, **4**:10*t*, 11*f*
Ewing
of orbit, **6**:337
retinoblastoma associated with, **4**:314*t*
granulocytic (chloroma), **4**:328, **6**:337, **7**:90
Kaposi. *See* Kaposi sarcoma
orbital, **4**:240
in children, **6**:334–336, 335*f*
exenteration for, **7**:126
secondary, **7**:89
staging of, **4**:348–349*t*
reticulum cell. *See* Intraocular tumors, lymphoma
retinoblastoma associated with, **4**:314, 314*t*, **6**:336
Satellite DNA, **2**:160, 166, 180
Satellite lesions, in toxoplasmosis, **6**:182
Sattler layer, **12**:17
Sattler veil (central epithelial edema), **8**:91
Saturation recovery (SR) imaging, **5**:70
SBE (subacute bacterial endocarditis). *See* Endocarditis
SCA. *See* Superior cerebellar artery
SCA7 gene, cone–rod dystrophy and, **12**:233
Scalp flap, coronal, for orbitotomy, **7**:109
Scanning laser ophthalmoscopy (SLO), **3**:251, **12**:29–30
in central visual field evaluation, **3**:286, 287*f*, 293
in fundus autofluorescence, **12**:30
in indocyanine green angiography, **12**:25
in optic disc evaluation, **10**:51, 52*f*
Scanning laser polarimetry, in retinal nerve fiber evaluation, **10**:51, 53*f*
Scanning-slit confocal microscope, **8**:36. *See also* Confocal microscopy
Scanning-slit lasers, for photoablation, **13**:25
Scanning-slit technology/topography
for anterior segment imaging, **8**:34, 35*f*
for corneal computed tomography, **13**:15, 15*f*
for pachymetry/pachometry, **8**:28, **13**:39. *See also* Pachymetry/pachymeter
Scaphocephaly, **6**:383
Scars
retinal, **4**:17
wound repair and, **4**:13, 14*f*
Scatter diagram, **1**:344, 345*f*

Scatter laser treatment. *See also* Panretinal photocoagulation; Photocoagulation
for branch retinal vein occlusion, **12**:124–125, 125*f*
for central retinal vein occlusion, **12**:132
for diabetic retinopathy, **12**:106–108, 108*f*, 109*f*
indications for, **12**:340
for nonproliferative diabetic retinopathy/macular edema, **12**:102
ETDRS, **12**:98, 102
for ocular ischemic syndrome, **12**:134
for proliferative diabetic retinopathy, **12**:106–108, 108*f*, 109*f*
DRS/ETDRS, **12**:107–108, 108*f*, 109*f*
for retinopathy of prematurity, **12**:167–168, 168*f*
for sickle cell retinopathy, **12**:120–121
Scattering, light, **3**:16
Rayleigh, **3**:16
for slit-lamp biomicroscopy, **8**:14, 15*f*
Scavenging, **9**:20–21, 21*f*
Scavenging macrophages, **9**:20–21, 21*f*
phacolytic glaucoma and, **9**:22
Scavenging receptors, **9**:21
SCD. *See* Sudden cardiac death
SCD/SCCD (Schnyder crystalline corneal dystrophy). *See* Schnyder corneal dystrophy
sCG activators. *See* Guanylate cyclase activators
Schachar theory of accommodation, **13**:150–152, 151*f*, 152*f*
Schaumann bodies, in sarcoidosis, **4**:191, **9**:173
Scheie Classification of Hypertension Retinopathy, Modified, **12**:114
Scheie syndrome, **2**:213*t*, **6**:400*t*, **8**:305, 306*f*, **12**:250*t*, 262
congenital/infantile corneal opacities and, **6**:217, **8**:263
pigmentary retinopathy and, **12**:250*t*, 262
Scheimpflug camera
for anterior segment imaging, **8**:34, 34*f*
for corneal computed tomography, **13**:15, 15*f*
for corneal power measurement in IOL power determination, **3**:217, 217*f*
for pachymetry/pachometry, **8**:28, 29*f*
Scheiner double-pinhole principle, in automated refraction, **3**:275, 276*f*
Schematic eye, **3**:103–104, 104*f*, 105*t*, 106*f*
IOL power prediction formulas based on, **3**:212–213, 212*f*
optical constants of, **3**:104*f*, 105*t*
reduced, **3**:103–104, 106*f*
Schiøtz (indentation) tonometry, **10**:19, 26
Schirmer tests, **8**:53, 54, 54*f*, 54*t*
type I, **8**:54, 54*t*
in pseudoepiphora, **7**:257
type II, **8**:54, 54*t*
Schizoaffective disorder, **1**:247
Schizophrenia, **1**:246–247
drugs for (antipsychotic drugs), **1**:251–252, 252*t*
oculogyric crisis caused by, **5**:212–213
Schizophreniform disorder, **1**:247
Schlemm canal, **2**:51*f*, 54, 55*f*, 56*f*, 57*f*, **4**:101–102, **10**:3*f*, 13, 16, 17*f*, 18
development of, **2**:136
gonioscopic visualization of, **10**:35–36, 36*f*
Schlichting dystrophy. *See* Posterior polymorphous corneal dystrophy

Schnabel, cavernous optic atrophy of, **4**:254, 255*f*
Schnyder corneal dystrophy, **8**:268*t*, 270*t*, 284–285, 285*f*,
    309
  genetics of, **8**:269*t*, 284
School-aged children. *See also* Children
  low vision in, **3**:307
Schubert-Bornschein form of congenital stationary
    night blindness, **12**:216
Schwalbe line/ring, **2**:39, 42, 49*f*, 50, 51*f*, 53, **4**:101, 102*f*,
    10:30*f*, 34
  prominent (posterior embryotoxon), **2**:141, **4**:102–103,
    103*f*, 104*f*, **6**:212, 212*f*, **8**:255, 256*f*, 261*t*
    in Axenfeld-Rieger syndrome, **4**:102–103, 103*f*,
      104*f*, **6**:212, 212*f*, 213, **8**:256, **10**:30, 146
    isolated, Axenfeld-Rieger syndrome differentiated
      from, **10**:146*t*
Schwann cells, retinal, **2**:301
Schwannoma (neurilemoma/neurinoma)
  conjunctival, **8**:240
  of orbit, **4**:244–245, 245*f*, **7**:76
    in children, **6**:343
  of uveal tract, **4**:203
Schwartz (Schwartz-Matsuo) syndrome, **9**:288,
    10:102–103
Scientific studies. *See* Clinical research/studies
Scintigraphy. *See specific type and* Radionuclide
    scintigraphy/scans
Scissors reflex, **3**:129
Sclera, **2**:41*f*, 42, 47–48, **8**:9, **12**:18. *See also* Episclera
  aging of, **4**:115, 116*f*, **8**:9, 345–346, 346*f*
  anatomy of, **2**:41*f*, 42, 47–48, **8**:9, **12**:18
  bare, wound closure after pterygium excision and,
    8:391, 392*f*
  blue, **8**:252–253
    in Ehlers-Danlos syndrome, **8**:252, 325
    in keratoglobus, **8**:302
    in Marfan syndrome, **8**:325
    in osteogenesis imperfecta, **8**:252
  congenital anomalies of, **4**:112–113, **8**:249–253
  degenerations of, **4**:115–116, 116*f*, **8**:345–346,
    346*f*
  development of, **2**:135, **8**:4
  disorders of, **4**:111–118, **8**:21*t*. *See also specific type
    and* Episcleritis; Scleritis
    immune-mediated, **8**:217–223, 218*f*, 218*t*, 219*f*,
      220*f*, 221*f*
    ionizing radiation causing, **8**:352–353
    neoplastic, **4**:116–118, 117*f*, 118*f*
    in polyarteritis nodosa/microscopic polyangiitis,
      9:143
    Th1 delayed hypersensitivity and, **9**:50*t*
  in glaucoma, **10**:29
  healing/repair of, **4**:16
  immune response/immunologic features of, **9**:58*t*
  infection/inflammation of, **4**:113–114, 113*f*, 114*f*,
    115*f*, **8**:21*t*, 28. *See also* Episcleritis; Scleritis
  innervation of, **8**:9
  perforation of
    extraocular muscle/strabismus surgery and, **6**:25,
      155–156
    repair of, **8**:377–378, 379*f*. *See also* Corneoscleral
      laceration, repair of
    traumatic, **6**:408

pigment spot of, **8**:233
rupture of, **2**:48, **12**:323
stroma of, **2**:48, **4**:112, 112*f*
topography of, **2**:41*f*, 42, **4**:111–112, 111*f*
Scleral buckle
  for retinal capillary hemangioblastoma, **4**:295
  for retinal detachment, **12**:289–290, 290*f*, 365, 366*f*
    angle-closure glaucoma after, **10**:135
    refractive surgery after, **13**:177–178
    sickle cell retinopathy and, **12**:121
    in uveitis, **9**:302
  for retinopathy of prematurity, **6**:287, **12**:170
Scleral contact lenses, **3**:191–193, 192*f*
  in dry-eye disorders, **8**:61
  for graft-vs-host disease, **8**:204, 204*f*
  for keratoconus, **3**:191, 193
  manufacture of, **3**:179
Scleral dellen, **8**:91
Scleral expansion/scleral expansion bands, for
    presbyopia, **13**:158, 158*f*
Scleral flap, for trabeculectomy, **10**:186, 188, 190*f*
  closure of, **10**:191, 192*f*
  management of, **10**:194
Scleral patch grafts, for exposure and extrusion of
    orbital implant, **7**:123
Scleral plaques, senile, **4**:115, 116*f*, **8**:9, 345–346, 346*f*
Scleral shells, for cosmesis/pain, **7**:118
Scleral spur, **2**:50, 51*f*, 52*f*, 53*f*, **4**:101, 102*f*, **10**:30*f*, 34, 35
Scleral spur cells, **2**:50
Scleral sulcus, internal, **2**:50, **4**:102
Scleral support ring, for ICCE, **11**:214
Scleral surgery. *See also specific procedure*
  infectious scleritis after, **9**:266–267
  for presbyopia, **13**:157–159, 158*f*
  for scleritis, **9**:118
Scleral tunnel incisions, for cataract surgery, **11**:111–113,
    111*f*, 112*f*
  closure of, **11**:112–113, 112*f*
Sclerectomy, for glaucoma
  deep (nonpenetrating), **10**:210–211
  in uveitis, **9**:298
Scleritis, **4**:114, 114*f*, 115*f*, **8**:21*t*, 217–223, 218*f*, 218*t*,
    219*f*, 220*f*, 221*f*
  anterior, **8**:28, 218, 218*f*, 218*t*, 219*f*
  brawny, **4**:114, 114*f*, 115*f*
  complications of, **8**:220–222, 221*f*
  corticosteroids for, **8**:222, 223, **9**:117–118, 267
    route of administration of, **2**:360*t*, **9**:117–118
  diffuse, **8**:218, 218*f*
  in herpes zoster, **8**:120, **9**:266
  immune-mediated, **8**:181, 217–223, 218*f*, 218*t*, 219*f*,
    220*f*, 221*f*
  infectious/microbial, **8**:171, 171*f*, **9**:266–267
  laboratory evaluation of, **8**:222, **9**:266
  management of, **8**:222–223, **9**:117–118, 267
  necrotizing, **4**:114, 114*f*, 115*f*, **8**:21*t*, 28, 218–220,
    218*t*, 219*f*, 220*f*, 222, 223, **9**:267*f*
    with inflammation, **8**:218*t*, 219, 219*f*
    without inflammation (scleromalacia perforans),
      4:114, **8**:218*t*, 220, 220*f*
  nodular, **8**:218, 219*f*
  noninfectious, **9**:117–118
  nonnecrotizing, **4**:114, **8**:21*t*, 28, **9**:117–118

nonspecific orbital inflammation and, 7:59
pain and, 5:300, 8:217–218, 219, 9:118, 266
posterior, 8:218t, 220, 221f
subtypes and prevalence of, 8:218t
in Wegener granulomatosis, 1:179, 7:56, 9:145
Sclerocornea, 4:81–82, 6:216–217, 216t, 8:258, 260f, 262t
cornea plana and, 4:82, 8:254, 255, 258
glaucoma and, 6:238
Scleroderma, 1:173–174
eyelid manifestations of, 4:213t
Scleroderma renal crisis, 1:174
Sclerokeratitis, 8:221–222, 221f, 223
Scleromalacia, 8:28
perforans, 4:114, 8:218t, 220, 220f
Sclerosing (morpheaform) basal cell carcinoma, 4:218, 219, 219f, 7:169, 169f. See also Basal cell carcinoma
Sclerosing nonspecific orbital inflammation, 7:60, 61. See also Nonspecific orbital inflammation
Sclerosis
multiple. See Multiple sclerosis
nuclear, 11:39
progressive systemic. See Progressive systemic sclerosis
tuberous (Bourneville disease/syndrome), 5:339t, 341, 342f, 6:364t, 371–374, 372f, 373f
glaucoma associated with, 10:28
Sclerostomy, for uveitic glaucoma, 9:298
Sclerostomy/keratectomy, in trabeculectomy, 10:189, 191f
Sclerotic (gliotic) lesions, in multiple sclerosis, 5:322
Sclerotic scatter, for slit-lamp biomicroscopy, 8:14, 15f
Sclerotomy, anterior ciliary, for presbyopia, 13:158
Sclerouveitis, 9:79
in inflammatory bowel disease, 9:123
Sclopetaria, 4:22, 203, 12:323, 323f
Scopolamine, 2:260, 341t
adverse effects of, 2:343f
for cycloplegia/cycloplegic refraction, 3:137t, 6:88, 88t
side effects of, 3:137
SCORE (Standard Care Versus Corticosteroid for Retinal Vein Occlusion) trial, 12:100, 126, 131
Scoring Tool for Assessing Risk (STAR), 10:159
Scotomata, 5:118t, 10:55
in acute zonal occult outer retinopathy, 12:192
in age-related macular degeneration, 12:64, 79
arcuate (Bjerrum), 10:68, 70f
arteriovenous malformations causing, 5:356
in central serous chorioretinopathy, 12:171
in choroideremia, 12:243
in cone–rod dystrophies, 12:234
in glaucoma, 10:68, 69f, 70f, 79
in low vision, 3:285, 286, 293
legal blindness and, 3:287, 292
in migraine aura without headache, 5:296
in migraine headache, 5:295, 295f
of monofixation syndrome, 6:59–60
Bagolini glasses in evaluation of, 6:57
4Δ base-out prism test in evaluation of, 6:57–58, 57f
Worth 4-dot test in evaluation of, 6:55
in multiple evanescent white dot syndrome, 5:113, 113f, 9:168
paracentral, 10:68, 69f, 79, 12:64, 79

in photoreceptor dystrophies, 12:223, 225f
physiologic (blind spot), 5:27
idiopathic enlargement of, 5:112–113, 12:190
in retinitis pigmentosa, 12:225f, 228
in serpiginous choroiditis/choroidopathy, 9:159, 12:188
in Stargardt disease, 12:235
suppression, diplopia after strabismus surgery and, 6:155
systemic hypoperfusion causing, 5:172, 182
in uveitis, 9:84t, 85
Scotopic/dark-adapted electroretinogram, 12:33, 34f, 35, 36f. See also Dark adaptation, testing; Electroretinogram
in hereditary retinal/choroidal dystrophies, 12:224t
Scrapie, 5:368
Scraping, for specimen collection, 8:47, 102–103
Screening/diagnostic tests, 1:269–279. See also specific test or disorder
interpretation of, 1:329–336
clinical acceptance and, 1:335
combination strategies and, 1:334–335
continuous outcome and, 1:330–332, 331f, 332f
criteria for diagnosis and, 1:332–333, 333f
generalizability and, 1:335
pretest probability and, 1:333–334, 334t
for JIA-associated uveitis, 6:270, 271t
for neonates, 6:250–251
for retinopathy of prematurity, 6:285, 286t, 12:164–165
Sculpting, instrument settings for, 11:118–119
Scurvy (vitamin C deficiency), 1:153, 8:79
SD-OCT. See Spectral-domain OCT
SE (spin echo) technique, 5:70, 72
Sea-blue histiocyte syndrome, 12:262, 263f. See also Niemann-Pick disease
Sea fan neovascularization, in sickle cell disease, 12:119, 119f, 120f
Seasonal allergic conjunctivitis, 6:198, 198t, 199t, 8:185–187
Sebaceous adenomas, 4:215t, 221, 222f, 7:161
in tuberous sclerosis, 5:341, 342f, 6:372, 372f, 10:28
Sebaceous carcinoma/adenocarcinoma, 4:215t, 221–224, 222f, 223f, 7:173–175, 174f, 8:233, 234f
Sebaceous cysts (epidermal inclusion cysts), of eyelid, 4:213, 213f, 7:158–159, 159f
Sebaceous glands of eyelid, 4:205–206, 7:160, 8:4
tumors/lesions of, 4:221–224, 221f, 222f, 223f, 8:233, 234f. See also Sebaceous adenomas; Sebaceous carcinoma/adenocarcinoma
benign, 4:221, 221f, 222f, 7:160–161
malignant, 4:221–224, 222f, 223f, 7:173–175, 174f
Sebaceous hyperplasia, 4:221, 221f, 7:160–161
Seborrheic blepharitis, 8:71–72, 143, 144t
Seborrheic keratosis, 4:214–215, 214f, 215f, 7:157–158, 157f
Secluded pupil, 10:110, 130, 130f
Second cranial nerve. See Optic nerve
Second-degree atrioventricular blocks (Wenckebach and Mobitz), 1:122t
Second-degree relatives, 2:159

Second messengers, in signal transduction, 2:262–263, 262f, 263f
Second-order neuron
  dilator muscle innervation and, 2:60
  Horner syndrome caused by lesions of, 5:267, 268f
Second sight, 11:39, 70
Secondary anophthalmia, 7:33
Secondary aphakia, 4:121, 11:26. See also Aphakia
Secondary coloboma, 11:26. See also Coloboma
Secondary deviation, 6:35
Secondary (posterior) focal point, 3:69, 70f
Secondary glaucoma. See Angle closure/angle-closure glaucoma; Glaucoma; Open-angle glaucoma
Secondary hypertension, 1:72, 72t
Secondary lens fibers, development of, 2:130, 11:23–24, 23f
  microspherophakia and, 11:29
Secondary positions of gaze, 6:27
Secondary vitreous, 2:130–132, 131f, 4:132
Secretogranin II, in aqueous humor, 2:267, 270
Secretory IgA, 8:173
  in tear film, 2:240
    in external eye defense, 8:95
Secretory lacrimal apparatus, 2:26f, 32–33, 32f, 33f, 241–244, 242f, 243f, 7:243–244. See also Lacrimal glands
  anatomy of, 7:243–244
  development of, 7:243
    abnormalities of, 7:277
  disorders of, 7:249–278
Sectoranopia, quadruple, lateral geniculate body lesions causing, 5:167, 167f
Sectral. See Acebutolol
Sedative-hypnotics/sedation, 1:253–254, 253t
  for benign essential blepharospasm, 7:220
  preoperative, 1:310–311
See-saw (vision loss) nystagmus, 5:251t, 253–254
  in children, 6:325
SEFs. See Supplementary eye fields
Segmented bifocal contact lenses, 3:189, 189f
Segregation (genetic), 2:160, 193, 196
  replicative, 2:160, 173
Seidel test, 8:17, 19f
Seizures, 1:260–264, 297–298. See also Epilepsy
  arteriovenous malformations causing, 5:354
  diagnosis of, 1:262
  etiology of, 1:261–262
  facial movements/palsy and, 5:292
  hallucinations and, 5:190
  local anesthetics causing, 1:312
  nonepileptic, 1:262
  ocular deviations caused by, 1:263, 5:211–212
  ophthalmic considerations and, 1:263–264
  transient visual loss caused by, 5:186
  treatment of, 1:262–263, 263f, 297–298
  in tuberous sclerosis, 5:341, 6:372
Selectins, in neutrophil rolling, 9:18, 19f
Selection bias, 1:317
  in case-control studies, 1:325
  in case series, 1:322
Selective estrogen receptor modulators (SERMs), for osteoporosis, 1:231
Selective laser trabeculoplasty, 10:180, 181–182

Selective serotonin reuptake inhibitors, 1:254–256, 255f
Selegiline, for Parkinson disease, 1:259
Selenium, 2:316f
  in retina and retinal pigment epithelium, 2:316–317, 318f
Selenoprotein P, in aqueous humor, 2:269
Self–blood-glucose monitoring, 1:204
Self-examination, breast, for cancer screening, 1:272t
Self-sealing incision, for cataract surgery
  beveled/biplanar, clear corneal incision and, 11:114, 115f
  scleral tunnel incisions and, 11:112, 113
Self-tolerance, T regulatory cells in, 9:40
Sella turcica, 5:5, 6f, 16
Selzentry. See Maraviroc
Semicircular canals
  hair cells of, 5:47, 47f
  peripheral vestibular nystagmus and, 5:249
Semicircular flap
  for canthal repair, 7:186
  for eyelid repair, 7:183f, 184, 185f, 186
Semiconductor diode lasers, 3:25. See also Lasers
Semilunar fold, 8:4
Semilunar ganglion (gasserian/trigeminal ganglion), 2:101, 101–102, 101f, 5:59, 59f
Senile furrow degeneration, 8:339
Senile lentigo, 7:165
Senile macular degeneration. See Age-related macular degeneration
Senile scleral/calcific plaques, 4:115, 116f, 8:9, 345–346, 346f
Senior-Loken syndrome, 6:302
Senofilcon A contact lenses, 3:177t
Sensation
  age-related changes in, 1:225
  in cornea, 8:6
    esthesiometry in evaluation of, 8:30–31
    reduction of
      in diabetes mellitus, 8:308
      in herpes simplex epithelial keratitis, 8:110
      in neurotrophic keratopathy, 8:87
Sense strand of DNA, 2:160
Sensitivity
  of screening/diagnostic test, 1:270, 329, 330
    continuous outcome and, 1:331–332, 331f, 332f
    likelihood ratio calculation and, 1:334
  spatial contrast, in low vision evaluation, 5:105
Sensitivity threshold, in perimetry, 5:100. See also Threshold stimulus
Sensitization, lymphocyte, 9:35–38, 40f. See also Activation
Sensorcaine. See Bupivacaine
Sensory defects/deprivation
  congenital nystagmus and, 6:322, 414
  esodeviation and, 6:96–97
  exotropia and, 6:104–105
  visual development affected by, 6:46–47, 47f
Sensory fusion, 6:41
Sensory nucleus
  of cranial nerve V (trigeminal), 2:100, 101f, 5:57, 57f, 59f
  of cranial nerve VII (facial), 2:105

Sensory pathways, **5:**57–60, 57*f,* 58*f,* 59*f*
Sensory root
 of cranial nerve V (trigeminal), **2:**100
 of cranial nerve V₁ (ophthalmic), **2:**14, 15*f*
 of cranial nerve VII (facial), **2:**105
Sensory visual system, **6:**39–60
 abnormalities of binocular vision and, **6:**49–50, 50*f*
 adaptations in strabismus and, **6:**50–60, 51*f*
  testing, **6:**53–59
 assessment of binocular vision and, **6:**86–87
 neurophysiological aspects of, **6:**42–49, 43*f,* 45*f,* 47*f,* 48*f*
 physiology of normal binocular vision and, **6:**39–42, 40*f,* 41*t*
Sentinel bleed, before aneurysm rupture, **5:**351
Sentinel lymph node biopsy
 in eyelid melanoma, **7:**176
 in sebaceous adenocarcinoma, **7:**174–175
Sentinel vessels, **4:**269*f,* 273, 274*f,* 275, **10:**29
Septata, keratoconjunctivitis caused by, **8:**170
Septate filamentous fungi, **8:**138, 138*f,* 138*t,* 139. *See also* Fungi
Septic shock (sepsis), **1:**294
Septic thrombosis
 cavernous sinus, **5:**357
 lateral (transverse) sinus, **5:**357
 superior sagittal sinus, **5:**357
Septo-optic dysplasia (de Morsier syndrome), **5:**141, **6:**308
Septra. *See* Trimethoprim-sulfamethoxazole
Sequence (congenital anomalies), **6:**171
Sequence-tagged sites, **2:**160
Sequencing, DNA, **2:**184, 185*f*
Ser-Ap-Es. *See* Reserpine
Serevent. *See* Salmeterol
SERMs (selective estrogen receptor modulators), for osteoporosis, **1:**231
Seroepidemiology, of HIV infection/AIDS, **1:**31–32
Serologic tests
 in syphilis, **1:**13–14, **9:**247–248
  on CSF, **5:**361, **9:**248
 in uveitis, **9:**94*t*
Seronegative spondyloarthropathies, **1:**163–167. *See also specific type and* Spondyloarthropathies/spondyloarthritis
 uveitis in, **9:**120–123, 122*f,* 123*f*
Seroquel. *See* Quetiapine
Serositis, in systemic lupus erythematosus, **1:**169*t*
Serotonin, antipsychotic mechanism of action and, **1:**251
Serotonin modulators, **1:**255*t*
Serotonin-norepinephrine reuptake inhibitors, **1:**255*t*
Serotonin reuptake inhibitors, selective, **1:**254–256, 255*f*
Serous suprachoroidal detachment, melanoma differentiated from, **4:**279–280
Serpasil. *See* Reserpine
Serpiginous choroidopathy/choroiditis (geographic/helicoid), **9:**148–150*t,* 158–161, 159*f,* 160*f,* **12:**186*t,* 188–189, 188*f*
 tuberculosis and, **9:**258, 259*f*
Serratia, **8:**135
 endogenous bacterial endophthalmitis caused by, **12:**202

Sertaconazole, **1:**65
Serum, **1:**147
Serum drops
 for dry eye, **8:**60
 for neurotrophic keratopathy, **8:**88
Serzone. *See* Nefazodone
Sessile papillomas, conjunctival, **4:**61–62
Setting sun sign, **5:**212
Seventh nerve (facial) palsy/paralysis. *See* Facial paralysis/weakness
Sex (gender)
 in glaucoma, **10:**10, 114
 osteoporosis risk and, **1:**228
Sex chromosomes, **2:**193, 194
 aneuploidy of, **2:**199
 mosaicism and, **2:**204
Sex-determining region Y (SRY/testis-determining factor/TDF), **2:**218
Sex-linked inheritance (sex-linked genes), **2:**160, 218. *See also* X-linked inheritance; Y-linked inheritance
Sexual abuse, gonococcal conjunctivitis in children and, **6:**189
SF. *See* Surgeon factor
SF₆
 for retinal detachment, **12:**367
 for submacular hemorrhage, **12:**351
SFU. *See* Subretinal fibrosis and uveitis syndrome
Shadowing, as negative dysphotopsia, **3:**224
Shafer sign ("tobacco dust"), **12:**286, 314
Shaffer gonioscopic grading system, **10:**35
Shagreen, crocodile, **8:**337
Shagreen patch, in tuberous sclerosis, **5:**341, **6:**372
Shaker-1 (sh1) gene, **2:**176
Shaking injury (shaken baby syndrome), **6:**404–407, 405*f,* 406*f,* **12:**330–331, 330*f*
Shallow anterior chamber. *See* Anterior chamber, flat or shallow
"Shape factor" of spectacle lens, meridional magnification and, **3:**311
Sharps containers, in infection control, **8:**46
Shave biopsy, **7:**170*f*
Sheathing, retinal vascular
 in sarcoidosis, **9:**175, 176*f*
 in toxoplasmosis, **9:**229
Sheathotomy, arteriovenous, for branch retinal vein occlusion, **12:**126
Sheehan syndrome (pituitary apoplexy), **1:**216, **5:**162–164, 163*f*
Sherrington's law of reciprocal innervation, **6:**34
Shield ulcer, **6:**200, **8:**187, 189*f*
Shigella, **8:**135
Shingles. *See* Herpes zoster
Shock, **1:**293–296. *See also specific type*
 assessment of, **1:**294
 classification of, **1:**293–294
 after myocardial infarction, **1:**103
 treatment of, **1:**294
Shock value, in nonorganic ophthalmic disorder evaluation, **5:**308
Short (p) arm, **2:**157
Short arm 11 deletion syndrome (11p13 syndrome), **2:**205–207
 in aniridia, **2:**205–207, **4:**188, **10:**142

Short ciliary arteries, **5:**13*f*, 14*f*, 18
  optic nerve supplied by, **10:**42, 43, 44
Short ciliary nerves, **2:**15*f*, 16, 36, 99
  ciliary muscle supplied by, **2:**64
  iris sphincter supplied by, **2:**61
  posterior, **2:**36
Short interfering (small interference) RNA (siRNA), in
  gene therapy, **2:**188
Short interspersed elements, **2:**166
  Alu repeat sequence, **2:**148, 166
Short tandem repeats, **2:**161, 180, 181*f*
Short tau inversion recovery (STIR) technique, **5:**73, 76*t*
Short-term fluctuation, in perimetry, **5:**104
Short-wavelength automated perimetry (SWAP),
  10:60–61
  in glaucoma suspect screening, **10:**82–83
Shunting surgery
  for glaucoma. *See* Glaucoma drainage devices
  for idiopathic intracranial hypertension, **5:**124
Sialic acid, in microbial adherence, **8:**98
Sialidoses, **6:**400*t*
  cherry-red spot in, **6:**400*t*, **12:**262
  dysmorphic, **8:**312
Sickle Cell Association, **6:**418*t*
Sickle cell disease (sickle cell anemia), **1:**150, **12:**115–121,
  117*t*
  genetic testing/counseling for, **1:**147, 150
  hyphema/elevated intraocular pressure and, **10:**98–99
  ophthalmic manifestations of, **12:**115–121, 117*t*, 118*f*,
    119*f*, 120*f*. *See also* Sickle cell retinopathy
    angioid streaks, **12:**84, 120
    traumatic hyphema and, **6:**409, **8:**369, **10:**98–99,
      12:120
      elevated intraocular pressure and, **10:**98–99
      surgery for, **10:**98–99
  point mutation causing, **2:**207
  preoperative screening for, **1:**305
  racial and ethnic concentration of, **2:**211, **12:**116
Sickle cell hemoglobin (SC), **12:**116, 117*t*
Sickle cell preparations, **6:**409, **12:**116
Sickle cell retinopathy, **12:**115–121, 117*t*, 118*f*, 119*f*,
  120*f*
  angioid streaks in, **12:**84, 120
  management of, **12:**120–121
  nonproliferative, **12:**118–119, 118*f*, 119*f*
  proliferative, **12:**119, 119*f*
    photocoagulation for, **12:**120–121
    vitreoretinal surgery for, **12:**121
Sickle cell thalassemia, **12:**116, 117*t*
Sickle cell trait (hemoglobin AS), **12:**116, 117*t*
SICRET (Susac) syndrome, **9:**146–147, 147*f*, **12:**141
Sideroblastic anemia, **1:**149
Siderosis/siderosis bulbi, **4:**124, **11:**53, 54*f*, **12:**328,
  328*t*
  corneal pigmentation in, **8:**337*t*
  glaucoma and, **10:**97
Siegrist streaks, **12:**114–115, 177
Siepser slipknot technique, for intraocular lens
  decentration, **11:**163, 164*f*
sIgA. *See* Secretory IgA
Sigmoid sinus, **2:**108, 108*f*, **5:**26, 26*f*
Sigmoidoscopy, in cancer screening, **1:**272*t*, 276
Signal error information, **5:**48–49

Signal transduction, **2:**261
  in iris–ciliary body, **2:**258–261
  in tear secretion, **2:**242–243, 242*f*, 243*f*
Signal transduction pathways, **2:**258–261
Significance, statistical, **1:**342. *See also P* value
Sildenafil
  ocular effects of, **1:**300, 302*t*, **5:**189, **12:**269
  in pulmonary arterial hypertension, **1:**141
Silent sinus syndrome, **7:**89
Silent visual fields, in nonorganic ophthalmic disorders,
  5:312
Silicone, refractive index of, **3:**40, 40*t*
Silicone acrylate, contact lenses made from, **3:**176–177,
  180
Silicone bands, for corneal exposure in facial palsy,
  5:288
Silicone foldable intraocular lenses, **3:**205, 206,
  11:135–136. *See also* Foldable intraocular lenses
  capsular opacification and, **11:**170
  instrumentation for handling, **11:**138
  in uveitic eye, **11:**204
Silicone oil
  cataract/cataract surgery with, **11:**205, 206
  IOL implantation in eye filled with, **3:**222–223
  for tamponade in retinal detachment, **12:**345, 366,
    366*f*, 367
    in CMV retinitis, **9:**307
    in uveitis, **9:**302
Silicone plugs, for dry eye, **7:**271, **8:**61–62, 62*f. See also*
  Lacrimal plugs
Silicone rods, for frontalis suspension, **7:**212
Silicone stent, for lacrimal intubation, **7:**252, 253. *See
  also* Lacrimal intubation
Silicone Study, **12:**367
Silicone suspension sling, for paralytic ectropion, **7:**216
Silodosin, intraoperative floppy iris syndrome and,
  11:155
Silver compounds, corneal pigmentation caused by,
  8:337*t*, 349
Silver nitrate, for ophthalmia neonatorum prophylaxis,
  6:188
  chemical conjunctivitis caused by, **6:**188
SIM K (simulated keratometry) value, **3:**267
Simcoe modified C-loop IOL, **3:**209*f*
Simple (physiologic/essential) anisocoria, **5:**264, 265*f*,
  6:229
Simple cells/neurons, **5:**34
Simple diffusion, glucose transport into lens and, **11:**13
Simple (diffuse) episcleritis, **4:**113, 113*f*, **8:**28, 216
Simple epithelial cysts. *See also* Epithelial cysts
  of orbit, **4:**229, 230
Simple hyperopic astigmatism, **3:**114, 115*f*
Simple lentigines (lentigo simplex), **7:**165
"Simple magnifier formula," **3:**244–245
Simple myopic astigmatism, **3:**114, 115*f*
Simple partial seizures, **1:**261
Simplex case/genetic disease, **2:**161, 192
Simplex retinitis pigmentosa, **12:**227
Simponi. *See* Golimumab
Simulated divergence excess exotropia, **6:**101
Simultanagnosia, **5:**194, 195*f*, 210
  in Alzheimer disease, **1:**268
Simultaneous prism and cover test, **6:**75–76

Simultaneous vision contact lenses, 3:176, 189–190, 190*f*
Simvastatin
  cataract risk and, 11:49
  for hypercholesterolemia/heart disease prevention, 1:136, 137*t*, 138
Sinemet. *See* Levodopa/carbidopa
SINEs. *See* Short interspersed elements
Single binocular vision
  Panum's area of, 6:40, 40*f*, 49
  testing field of, 6:83, 84*f*
Single-flash cone response (photopic/light-adapted electroretinogram), 12:34, 34*f*, 35, 36*f*
  in cone dystrophies, 12:232
  in hereditary retinal/choroidal dystrophies, 12:224*t*
Single-gene disorder (mendelian disorder), 2:155, 208
Single-optic intraocular lenses, 13:146. *See also* Crystalens
Single-pedicle (racquet) flaps, 8:400
Single-photon emission computed tomography (SPECT), 5:80
  in Alzheimer disease, 1:267
  in ischemic heart disease, 1:106, 271–272
Single-sided disk confocal microscope, 8:36
Single-stranded conformational polymorphism, 2:182
Single-vision reading glasses
  for induced anisophoria, 3:156
  in low vision/vision rehabilitation, 3:296
Singlet oxygen, 2:311, 312, 313, 314, 315
Singulair. *See* Montelukast
Sinoatrial (SA) node, 1:121
Sinus arrest, 1:122*t*
Sinus bradycardia, 1:122*t*
Sinus surgery, endoscopic, medial rectus laceration/strabismus and, 6:143
Sinus tachycardia, 1:124*t*
Sinus thrombosis, 2:108–109
  cavernous, 5:357
    orbital infection and, 7:43
  dural, 5:356–358
  lateral (transverse), 5:357
  superior sagittal, 5:357–358
Sinuses. *See specific type and* Paranasal sinuses
Sinusitis
  allergic aspergillosis, 7:46
  Brown syndrome caused by, 6:130
  orbital cellulitis caused by, 6:195, 196, 196*f*, 7:40, 41, 42, 42*t*
  pain distribution and, 2:13, 13*f*
  preseptal cellulitis caused by, 6:195, 7:40, 41
  silent sinus syndrome and, 7:89
  tuberculous, orbital infection and, 7:45
  in Wegener granulomatosis, 9:145
Sipple-Gorlin syndrome, enlarged corneal nerves in, 8:328–329, 329*t*
siRNA. *See* Small interference (short interfering) RNA
Sirolimus, 9:108*t*, 112
  for uveitis, 9:108*t*, 112
Sister chromatids, 2:149
SITA. *See* Swedish interactive thresholding algorithm
Sitagliptin, 1:199*t*, 202
Sixth cranial nerve. *See* Cranial nerve VI

Sixth nerve (abducens) palsy/paralysis, 5:218, 220*f*, 234–235, 6:98, 134–135, 134*f*
  diplopia and, 5:218, 220*f*, 223–224, 227, 234–235
  divergence insufficiency/paralysis and, 5:214, 222*t*, 234
  incomitant esodeviation caused by, 6:98
  Möbius syndrome/sequence and, 6:140
  in multiple sclerosis, 5:325
  surgery for, 6:153
Sjögren-Larsson syndrome, ichthyosis in, 8:74, 12:255
Sjögren syndrome, 1:174, 8:63–65, 64*t*
  aqueous tear deficiency/dry eye and, 8:50, 51*f*, 52
  cataract surgery in patient with, corneal melting/keratolysis and, 11:150
  classification of, 8:63, 64*t*
  laboratory evaluation in diagnosis of, 8:57, 59*f*, 59*t*
  lacrimal lymphocytic infiltrates and, 7:88
Sjögren Syndrome Foundation, 8:61
Skeletal disorders. *See also* Connective tissue disorders
  corneal changes in, 8:322–324*t*
Skew, of retinal reflex, in axis determination, 3:126–127, 127*f*
Skew deviation, 5:222–223, 222*t*
  alternating, 5:222, 222*t*
    periodic, 5:223
  in infants, 6:413
  inferior oblique muscle paralysis as form of, 6:121
  in multiple sclerosis, 5:325
  neuroimaging in evaluation of, 5:85
Skin
  congenital nevocellular nevi of, 6:349–350, 350*f*
  disorders of
    in Behçet disease, 1:180, 9:191–192
    cataracts associated with, 11:62
    in dermatomyositis, 1:175, 175*f*
    desquamating, ocular surface involved in, 8:74
    in incontinentia pigmenti, 6:379–380, 380*f*
    retinal degeneration and, 12:255
    in rubella, 9:210
    in scleroderma, 1:173
    in systemic lupus erythematosus, 1:167, 169*t*, 9:140, 141*t*
    in tuberous sclerosis, 6:372, 372*f*
    in uveitis, 9:86*t*
    in Wegener granulomatosis, 9:145
  eyelid, 2:22–23, 4:205, 206*f*, 7:135*f*, 136, 8:4
    tumors of, 7:155–177. *See also* Eyelids, tumors of
      medial canthal/lacrimal sac involvement and, 7:171
      metastatic eye disease and, 4:316*t*
  laser resurfacing of, 7:230–231
Skin cancer, metastatic eye disease and, 4:316*t*
Skin grafts. *See* Flaps; Grafts
Skin tags, 7:157, 157*f*
Skin tests. *See also specific type*
  tuberculin, 1:19, 278–279, 9:35, 259–260
    in HIV infection/AIDS, 9:260
    immune response arc and, 9:35
    uveitis associated with, 9:128
Skip lesions, 4:252
Skipped generation (incomplete penetrance), 2:209, 217

Skull base, **6:**383, 384*f*
  bony anatomy of, **5:**5–7, 6*f*, 7–8*f*, 9–10*f*
  suture fusion and, **6:**386, 386*f*
Skull fracture, arteriovenous fistula caused by, **7:**67
Slab-off (bicentric grinding), for induced anisophoria, **3:**154, 155*f*
  reverse, **3:**154–155
SLC4A11 gene, in congenital hereditary endothelial dystrophy, **8:**269*t*, 296
SLC45A2 gene, in OCA4, **12:**258*t*
SLE. *See* Systemic lupus erythematosus
Sleep apnea/sleep disorders, hypertension and, **1:**75*t*, 85
Sleep test, for myasthenia gravis, **5:**330, **6:**137
Sliding flap, for wound closure after pterygium excision, **8:**391, 392*f*
Slipped muscle, in extraocular muscle surgery, **6:**24, 160, 160*f*
  esodeviations and, **6:**97–98
Slit illumination, for slit-lamp biomicroscopy, **8:**12, 13*f*
Slit-lamp biomicroscopy/examination, **3:**251–255, 251*f*, 253*f*, 254*f*, 255*f*, 256*f*, **8:**12–16
  astronomical (Keplerian) telescope in, **3:**82*f*
  binocular viewing system of, **3:**253
  before cataract surgery, **11:**78–80
    limitations of, **11:**80
  in choroidal/ciliary body melanoma, **4:**275
  clinical procedure for, **8:**15–16
  in contact lens selection, **3:**179–180
  in diabetic macular edema, **12:**95
  fundus lenses for, **3:**253–255, 254*f*, 255*f*, 256*f*
  Galilean telescope in, **3:**81, 81*f*, 251*f*, 252
  in glaucoma, **10:**29–32, 46
    congenital/infantile, **6:**236–237
  illumination system of, **3:**252–253, 253*f*
    direct illumination methods and, **8:**12–14, 13*f*, 14*f*
    indirect illumination methods and, **8:**14–15, 15*f*, 16*f*
  inverting prism in, **3:**251*f*, 252
  in iris nevus, **4:**266
  in macular holes, **12:**304
  objective lens for, **3:**251*f*, 252
  in ocular trauma, **12:**318
  in optic disc evaluation, **10:**32, 46
  in pediatric cataract, **6:**252–253
  in posterior vitreous detachment, **12:**276, 297–298
  in pupillary examination, **5:**262
  in recurrent corneal erosions, **8:**83
  before refractive surgery, **13:**35–37, 36*f*, 37*f*
  in retinal examination, **12:**19–20
  in striae in LASIK flaps, **13:**105, 107*t*
Slit-lamp delivery systems, for photocoagulation, **12:**340
Slit-lamp photography, **8:**31. *See also* Slit-lamp biomicroscopy/examination
SLK. *See* Superior limbic keratoconjunctivitis
SLN. *See* Sentinel lymph node biopsy
SLO. *See* Scanning laser ophthalmoscopy
Slo-Phyllin. *See* Theophylline
Sloan achromatopsia test, **12:**50
Slow-acting (disease-modifying) antirheumatic drugs, **1:**162, 186
Slow-channel calcium-blocking agents, for angina, **1:**108
Slow inactivators, isoniazid use in, **2:**229

Slow-reacting substance of anaphylaxis, **8:**179*t*
  leukotrienes in, **2:**258
Slow twitch (tonic) fibers, **2:**21, 21*t*, **5:**55
SLT. *See* Selective laser trabeculoplasty
Sly syndrome, **6:**400*t*
Small-angle approximation, **3:**57–60, 57*f*, 58*f*
Small-gauge vitrectomy, **12:**346
Small-incision cataract surgery, manual, **11:**96
Small interference (short interfering) RNA (siRNA), in gene therapy, **2:**188
Small-molecule inhibition, for retinoblastoma, **4:**313
Smallest region of overlap, **2:**161
Smallpox vaccination, ocular complications of, **8:**128
Smart System II PC Plus test, **6:**87
SmartLens, **13:**160
SmartSight patient handout/website, **1:**220, **6:**330, 417, **9:**304, **11:**71, **12:**60, 231
SMAS. *See* Superficial musculoaponeurotic system
SMAS (Specular Microscopy Ancillary Study), **8:**411
Smith-Indian operation, **11:**92
Smith-Lemli-Opitz syndrome, **6:**398
Smokestack, in central serous chorioretinopathy, **12:**172, 173*f*
Smoking
  cancer and, **1:**274, 275
  cataract development and, **11:**58–59, 67–68
  cessation of, **1:**107, 109*t*, 143
  heart disease and, **1:**99, 100, 107, 109*t*, 133*t*
  hypertension and, **1:**74
  optic neuropathy and, **5:**154
  pulmonary disease and, **1:**143
  thyroid disease and, **1:**211, **5:**333, **6:**135, **7:**52
Smooth muscle tumors, **8:**240
Smooth pursuit eye movements/system, **5:**41, 42*f*, 43*f*, 198–199, 198*t*, 204, **6:**37. *See also* Pursuit eye movements/pursuit pathways/system
  asymmetry of, **6:**91
SNAP protein receptor (SNARE), botulinum toxin affecting, **7:**219*f*
Snapback test, **7:**195
SNARE. *See* SNAP protein receptor
Snellen acuity, **3:**109–110, 109*f*, 110*t*. *See also* Visual acuity
  in children, **6:**72*t*, 73
    in strabismic amblyopia, **6:**62
  contrast sensitivity and, **3:**111
  in low vision, **3:**289–290
  spatial frequency and, **3:**111
Snellen charts, **3:**109–110, 109*f*
  for bottom-up acuity testing, **5:**311
  in children, **6:**72*t*, 73
    monofixation assessment and, **6:**60
  optotypes of, **3:**109, 109*f*
  polarized letters for, **3:**11
  for potential acuity meter, **3:**277–278
Snell's law (law of refraction), **3:**44–46, 45*f*, 46*f*, 47, 47*f*, **8:**38
  contact lens power and, **3:**167
  critical angle calculation and, **3:**47, 48
  Fermat principle and, **3:**52–53, 52*f*
  small-angle approximation and, **3:**58–60
Snow blindness, **8:**352

Snowballs
  in intermediate uveitis/pars planitis, **9**:89, 134, 135, 135*f*, **12**:196
  in sarcoidosis, **9**:175, **12**:197
Snowbanks
  in intermediate uveitis/pars planitis, **9**:89, 134, 135, **12**:196
  in sarcoidosis, **12**:197
Snowflake cataract, **2**:279, **11**:55, 56*f*
Snowflakes, in typical degenerative retinoschisis, **12**:293
SNP oligonucleotide microarray analysis (SOMA), **4**:38*t*
SNRPN gene, imprinting of, **2**:169
SO. *See* Superior oblique muscles; Sympathetic ophthalmia
Social history
  cataract surgery evaluation and, **11**:75
  refractive surgery evaluation and, **13**:30–31, 30*t*
  in uveitis, **9**:315
Socket contraction, **7**:124, 124*f*. *See also* Anophthalmic socket
SOD. *See* Superoxide dismutase
Sodium
  in aqueous humor, **2**:255, 266*t*, 267
  dietary
    congestive heart failure and, **1**:120
    hypertension management and, **1**:74, 75*t*
  in lens, **2**:278, **11**:18–19, 18*f*
  in tear film, **2**:238*t*, 240
  transport of, **2**:307
    aqueous humor secretion and, **2**:351
    carbonic anhydrase inhibitors affecting, **2**:351
  in vitreous, **2**:266*t*, 286
Sodium balance, in lens, pump–leak theory of maintenance of, **11**:18–19, 18*f*
Sodium bicarbonate. *See* Bicarbonate
Sodium borate transporter, member 11 *(SLC4A11)* gene, in congenital hereditary endothelial dystrophy, **8**:269*t*, 296
Sodium chloride, for ocular edema, **2**:391
Sodium citrate, for chemical injuries, **8**:358
Sodium fluorescein. *See* Fluorescein
Sodium hyaluronate, as viscoelastic, **2**:393, **11**:96
  elevated intraocular pressure and, **10**:101
Sodium perborate, as ocular medication preservative, **2**:323
Sodium-potassium-calcium exchanger (Na$^+$,K$^+$-Ca exchanger), in rods, **2**:292
Sodium-potassium pump (Na$^+$,K$^+$-ATPase)
  in aqueous humor secretion/suppression, **2**:351, **10**:15
  corneal hydration and, **8**:8
  in Fuchs endothelial corneal dystrophy, **8**:291
  in lens active transport, **11**:18
    pump–leak theory and, **11**:18–19, 18*f*
  in lens ionic balance, **2**:278
  in retinal pigment epithelium, **2**:304, 307
  in rods, **2**:292
Soemmering ring/Soemmering ring cataract, **4**:126, 126*f*, **11**:170
Soft (flexible) contact lenses, **3**:178, 180, 181*t*. *See also* Contact lenses
  astigmatism correction with, **3**:186–188, 187*t*, 188*f*
  care of, teaching, **3**:182
  conjunctivitis caused by, **8**:193–195

  as corneal bandages, **3**:193–194
  daily wear, **3**:180
  extended-wear, **3**:180
    as bandage lenses, **3**:193–194
    materials for, **3**:178
  fitting, **3**:182, 183*t*
    disinfection of trial lenses and, **3**:201
  giant papillary conjunctivitis caused by, **8**:193–195
  hydrogel polymers for, **3**:177*t*, 178
  for keratoconus, **3**:190
  after LASIK, **13**:194
  manufacture of, **3**:178–179
  materials for, **3**:177*t*, 178
  neovascularization associated with, **8**:92
  for orthokeratology, **3**:195
  parameters of, **3**:180, 181*t*, 182
  after radial keratotomy, **13**:193
  refractive surgery and, **13**:192
  rigid gas-permeable lenses compared with, **3**:181*t*
  after surface ablation, **13**:193
  tonometry accuracy and, **10**:23–24
  toric, **3**:186–188, 187*t*, 188*f*
Soft drusen, **4**:169, 169*f*, **12**:57, 57*f*, 58
  drusenoid RPE detachment and, **12**:57, 238, 239*f*
Soft exudates. *See* Cotton-wool spots
Soft-tissue histiocytosis. *See* Histiocytosis
Soft-tissue sarcoma
  of orbit, **4**:240
  retinoblastoma associated with, **4**:314, 314*t*, **6**:336
Soft-tissue tumors, **4**:10*t*, 11*f*
  of orbit, **4**:240
Soil contamination, *Bacillus* endophthalmitis and, **8**:375
Solar elastosis, of eyelid, **4**:217, 218*f*
Solar lentigo, **7**:165
Solar retinopathy/retinitis (foveomacular retinitis), **12**:332–333
Solid-state laser, **3**:24, 25. *See also* Lasers
  for photoablation, **13**:23. *See also* Photoablation
Solitary fibrous tumor, of orbit, **7**:78
Solitary idiopathic choroiditis, **12**:194
Solu-Cortef. *See* Hydrocortisone sodium succinate
SOMA. *See* SNP oligonucleotide microarray analysis
Somatic afferent fibers, **2**:105
Somatic motor nerves, cholinergic drug action and, **2**:334, 335*f*
Somatization disorder, **1**:248
Somatoform disorders, **1**:248–249
Somatoform pain disorder, **1**:248
Somatostatin, **1**:214*t*
Somatotroph adenomas, **1**:215
Somogyi phenomenon, **1**:196–197
Sonata. *See* Zaleplon
Sondermann channels, **2**:57*f*
Sonic hedgehog mutations, **2**:141, 142
  cyclopia caused by, **2**:141
Sonography. *See* Ultrasonography
SOOF (suborbicularis oculi fat), **7**:135*f*, 141
SOOF lift, **7**:233, 234*f*
Sorbitol/sorbitol pathway
  in cataract formation, **2**:280, 281, **11**:15
  diabetic retinopathy and, **2**:301
  in lens glucose/carbohydrate metabolism, **2**:280, 280*f*, **11**:14*f*, 15

Sorsby macular dystrophy, **12**:241–242, 242*f*
   retinal pigment epithelium in, **2**:308
   TIMP3 defects causing, **2**:182, 297, **12**:241
SOS. *See* Sands of the Sahara
Sotalol, **1**:123*t*
Sotret. *See* Isotretinoin
Southern blot analysis, **2**:161, 179*f*
   in mutation screening, **2**:179*f*, 184, 187*f*
SP. *See* Swelling pressure
Space maintenance, by ophthalmic viscosurgical device, **11**:98
Spaeth gonioscopic grading system, **10**:35, 36*f*
Sparfloxacin, **1**:52*t*, 61
Spasm
   of accommodation (ciliary muscle spasm), **5**:316
      accommodative excess caused by, **3**:143
   of convergence, **5**:214
   essential blepharospasm, **5**:289–290, 289*t*, 290*f*, **7**:218–220, 219*f*
   of fixation. *See* Ocular motor apraxia
   habit, **5**:292
   hemifacial, **5**:289*t*, 291, 292*f*, **7**:221
   of near reflex, **3**:143, **5**:315
      esotropia and, **6**:97
Spasmus nutans/spasmus nutans syndrome, **5**:247, **6**:324–325
Spastic entropion, **7**:194, 195*f*
Spastic paretic facial contracture, **5**:291–292
Spatial (lateral) coherence, **3**:8, 8*f*
Spatial frequency, **3**:111
   contrast sensitivity testing and, **5**:105, **12**:50, 51*f*
Spatial localization, errors in, distortion and, **3**:174–175, 310. *See also* Distortion
   adaptation and, **3**:320–321
"Special cause" variance, **1**:346
Specific (adaptive) immunity, **1**:4. *See also* Adaptive immune response
Specific gravity, lens materials and, **3**:161, 162–163
Specificity, of screening/diagnostic test, **1**:270, 330
   continuous outcome and, **1**:331–332, 331*f*, 332*f*
   likelihood ratio calculation and, **1**:334
Specimen collection/handling, **4**:25–30, 31*t*
   communication with health care team and, **4**:25–26
   gross dissection and, **4**:27–28, 28*f*
   for ocular cytology, **8**:47–48
   for ocular microbiology, **8**:100–103, 101*t*, 102*f*
   orientation of globe and, **4**:26, 26*f*
   processing/staining tissues and, **4**:28–30, 29*t*, 30*f*, 31*t*
   special procedures and, **4**:33–45, 34*t*
   transillumination and, **4**:26–27, 27*f*
Speckle, laser, **3**:20
SPECT. *See* Single-photon emission computed tomography
Spectacle blur, contact lens–induced corneal changes causing, **3**:199
Spectacle crown glass, refractive index of, **3**:40*t*
Spectacle lenses (spectacles). *See also* Lenses
   absorptive, **3**:159–161, 160*f*. *See also* Sunglasses
   accommodation affected by, **3**:144–145
   anophthalmic socket camouflage and, **7**:125
   aphakic. *See* Aphakic spectacles
   after cataract surgery in children, **6**:258, 259
   for consecutive esotropia, **6**:103

convergence affected by, **3**:144–145, 173
for convergence insufficiency, **6**:106
cylindrical correcting, **3**:139–140. *See also* Cylinders
distance, **3**:295
for dry eye, **8**:61
frames for, anophthalmic socket camouflage and, **7**:125
glass
   hi-index, **3**:162–163
   standard, **3**:162
hi-index, **3**:162–163
for high accommodative convergence/accommodative esotropia, **6**:94, 95
high-impact, **3**:162
for intermittent exotropia, **6**:102
iseikonic, **3**:140, 321
for low vision/vision rehabilitation
   distance spectacles and, **3**:295–296, 297
   near (reading) spectacles and, **3**:295–296, 297
magnification for near vision with, **3**:295–296, 297
minus cylinder (posterior toric), **3**:316
monocular distortion and, **3**:311
near (reading), **3**:176, 189
   for low vision/vision rehabilitation, **3**:295–296, 297
   for presbyopia, with contact lenses, **3**:176, 189
   single-vision, for induced anisophoria, **3**:156
for partially accommodative esotropia, **6**:95
plastic
   bifocal, **3**:147, 148*f*
      reverse slab-off and, **3**:155
   hi-index, **3**:162–163
   high-impact, **3**:162
   prism calibration for, **3**:85, 86*f*
   standard, **3**:162
plus cylinder (anterior toric), distortion and, **3**:311, 316
power of
   bifocal segment decentration and, **3**:157, 164
   lensmeters in measurement of, **3**:268–272, 269*f*, 270*f*, 271*f*
   prisms incorporated into, **3**:83, 87, 164. *See also* Prisms
   protective, lens materials for, **3**:162
for refractive accommodative esotropia, **6**:93
"shape factor" of, meridional magnification and, **3**:311
special materials used for, **3**:161–163
spherical correcting, **3**:138–139, 139*f*
vertex distance and, **3**:139, 140*f*
Spectacle-mounted telescopes, **3**:300
Spectinomycin, for gonococcal conjunctivitis, **8**:152
Spectracef. *See* Cefditoren
Spectral-domain OCT, **12**:27
   in central serous chorioretinopathy, **12**:173
   near-infrared spectrum scanning laser and, **12**:30–31, 31*f*
   in retinal nerve fiber evaluation, **10**:52
   in uveitis, **9**:95–96
Spectroscopy, magnetic resonance (MRS), **5**:69, 80
Specular Microscopy Ancillary Study (SMAS), **8**:411
Specular microscopy/photomicroscopy, **3**:260–261, 261*f*, **8**:14, 31–33, 32*f*
   before cataract surgery, **11**:84
   in iridocorneal endothelial (ICE) syndrome diagnosis, **10**:129–130

in optical focusing technique for pachymetry, 3:259
before phakic intraocular lens insertion, 13:129
Specular reflection, 3:42–44, 43*f*, 44*f*, 45
for slit-lamp biomicroscopy, 8:12–14, 14*f*
at smooth optical interfaces, 3:42, 42*f*
Specular transmission, 3:44–46, 45*f*, 46*f*, 47, 47*f*
at smooth optical interfaces, 3:42, 42*f*
Speed of light, 3:4, 40
Speed of retinal reflex, 3:124, 124*f*
Sperm, 2:196
Sphenocavernous (parasellar) syndrome, 5:236
Sphenoethmoidal recess, 7:18
Sphenoid bone, 5:5, 6, 6*f*, 7, 7*f*, 8*f*, 9*f*, 10, 7:6*f*, 7*f*
in metastatic disease, 7:91, 92*f*
pterygoid process of, 5:7
Sphenoid sinuses, 2:9*f*, 12, 13*f*, 14*f*, 5:7, 8, 11*f*, 7:7*f*, 18*f*, 19
Sphenoid wings, 5:6, 6*f*, 7*f*, 8*f*, 9*f*, 7:6*f*, 7*f*
meningiomas of, 7:73, 74, 74*f*, 75
Sphenopalatine ganglion, 5:67
Spheres
amplitude of accommodation measured with, 3:146
power of
fogging in determination of, 3:136
optimal value for, 3:320
refining, in subjective refraction, 3:135–136
Spherical aberration, 3:99–100, 100, 101*f*, 231, 233*f*, 238, 239*f*, 13:7, 8*f*
keratorefractive surgery and, 3:99–100, 232, 233*f*
after LASIK, 13:7, 95
after surface ablation, 13:8*f*, 95
Spherical equivalent, 3:94
Spherical lenses
concave, paraxial ray tracing through, 3:73–74, 73*f*, 74*f*
convex, paraxial ray tracing through, 3:69–72, 71*f*
correcting, 3:138–139, 139*f*
vertex distance and, 3:139, 140*f*
prismatic effect of, 3:87, 87*f*. See also Prentice rule
Spherocylindrical lenses, 3:94–95, 95–97, 96*f*, 97*f*, 98, 98*f*. See also Cylinders
combination of at oblique axes, 3:99
conoid of Sturm and, 3:93, 93*f*
images formed by, 3:94, 94*f*
transposition and, 3:97–99
Spherocytosis
corneal deposits and, 8:328
hereditary, 1:149–150
Spheroidal degeneration (actinic/Labrador keratopathy), 4:88–89, 90*f*, 8:334–335, 335*f*
Spherophakia, 6:260, 260*f*
Spherule (synaptic body), of rod, 2:74, 77*f*
Sphincter muscle, 2:58*f*, 59*f*, 61, 258, 259, 4:186, 186*f*
damage to
anisocoria and, 5:269–270
cataract surgery in patient with, 11:207–208
pupil irregularity and, 5:263
development of, 2:61, 137
miotics affecting, 2:259, 259*t*, 335
muscarinic drugs affecting, 2:335, 340
mydriatics affecting, 2:259*t*, 260, 340
testing, pharmacologic anisocoria and, 5:270

Sphingolipidoses, 8:310–311
corneal changes in, 8:310–311, 311*f*
Sphingomyelinase, defective, 2:213*t*
Spielmeyer-Vogt disease, 6:401*t*
pigmentary retinopathy in, 12:251*t*, 260
Spin echo (SE) technique, 5:70, 72
Spin-lattice/longitudinal relaxation time (T1), 5:70, 72, 7:26–27
Spin-spin/transverse relaxation time (T2), 5:70, 72, 7:27–28
Spina Bifida (toll-free telephone), 6:418*t*
Spinal nucleus and tract, of cranial nerve V (trigeminal), 2:100–102, 101*f*, 5:57–59, 57*f*
Spindle cell carcinoma, 4:64, 8:233
Spindle cells
in choroidal/ciliary body melanoma, 4:196, 196*f*, 199
in choroidal/ciliary body nevus, 4:195, 195*f*
in iris melanoma, 4:194
in iris nevus, 4:193
in nodular fasciitis, 4:118, 118*f*
in rhabdomyosarcoma, 4:243
Spindle pattern, in pigment dispersion syndrome, 10:87–88, 88*f*
Spinocerebellar degenerations
cone–rod dystrophy and, 12:233
pigmentary retinopathy and, 12:254
Spiradenoma, eccrine, 7:161
Spiral (helical) computed tomography
chest, in cancer screening, 1:275
in orbital evaluation, 7:26
Spiral of Tillaux, 2:16, 18*f*, 5:55, 6:16, 18*f*
Spiramycin, 1:50*t*, 61
for toxoplasmosis, 9:233
Spiriva. See Tiotropium
Spirochetes, 8:137
Spironolactone
for heart failure, 1:118
for hypertension, 1:76*t*, 78*t*
Spitz nevus, 4:226
SPK. See Thygeson superficial punctate keratitis
Splice junction site, 2:148, 161
Spliceosome, 2:161, 168
Splicing, 2:161, 168
alternative, 2:165, 168
Split bifocal intraocular lens, 3:226, 227*f*
Split lens bifocal, 3:147, 148*f*
Spondylitis, ankylosing, 1:163–164, 9:119*f*, 121
cataract surgery in patient with, 11:188, 189*f*
glaucoma and, 9:296
HLA in, 1:163–164, 9:72, 121
juvenile, 1:166, 6:271
Spondyloarthropathies/spondyloarthritis, 1:163–167. See also specific type
juvenile, 1:166
undifferentiated, 1:163
uveitis in, 1:163, 164, 165, 166, 9:120–123, 122*f*, 123*f*
Spongiform encephalopathies, transmissible, 5:368
Spongiosis, definition of, 4:206
Spontaneous emission, in lasers, 3:21, 21–23, 23*f*
Spontaneous hyphema, 8:365
Spontaneous nystagmus
fixation and, 5:200
vestibular imbalance and, 5:200–201, 205

Spontaneous vitreous hemorrhage, 12:313–314
Sporadic, definition of, 2:161
Sporadic Alzheimer disease, 1:266
Sporanox. *See* Itraconazole
Spore-forming intestinal protozoa, gastrointestinal infection in HIV/AIDS and, 1:38
Spread of comitance, 5:219
in superior oblique muscle paralysis, 6:120
Spreading depression of Leão, 5:191
Springing pupils, 5:274
Sputnik intraocular lens, 3:207, 208*f*
Sputum cytology, in cancer screening, 1:272*t*, 275
Squamous cell carcinoma
of conjunctiva, 8:226*t*, 231–232, 232*f*
in situ, 4:63–64, 64*f*
invasive, 4:63*f*, 64, 64*f*
of eyelid, 4:219, 220*f*, 7:172, 173*f*
actinic keratosis and, 4:216–217, 217*f*, 218*f*, 7:166, 172
Bowen disease, 7:167
well-differentiated keratinizing (keratoacanthoma), 4:215*t*, 216, 216*f*, 7:167–168, 167*f*
of lacrimal sac, 7:276–277
of orbit, secondary, 7:89, 90*f*
retinoblastoma associated with, 4:314*t*
Squamous cell papilloma
of conjunctiva, 4:61–62, 61*f*
of eyelid, 7:157, 157*f*
of lacrimal sac, 7:276–277
Squamous dysplasia, of conjunctiva, 8:228. *See also* Squamous neoplasia, ocular surface
Squamous neoplasia, ocular surface, 4:62–64, 63*f*, 64*f*
Square-wave jerks, 5:200, 205, 254, 255*f*
Square waves, 5:199
SR. *See* Superior rectus muscles
SR (saturation recovery) imaging, 5:70
SRI (surface regularity index), 3:267
SRK formulas, for IOL power determination/selection, 3:212–213, 217, 219, 11:85
refractive lens exchange/clear lens extraction and, 13:140
SRO. *See* Smallest region of overlap
SRY. *See* Sex-determining region Y
SS. *See* Sickle cell disease; Sigmoid sinus; Sjögren syndrome
SSA antigen, antibodies to (anti-Ro antibodies)
in aqueous tear deficiency, 8:57
in Sjögren syndrome, 1:174, 8:57, 64*t*
in systemic lupus erythematosus, 9:140
SSB antigen, antibodies to (anti-La antibodies)
in aqueous tear deficiency, 8:57
in Sjögren syndrome, 1:174, 8:57, 64*t*
in systemic lupus erythematosus, 9:140
SSCM. *See* Scanning-slit confocal microscope
SSCP. *See* Single-stranded conformational polymorphism
SSPE. *See* Subacute sclerosing panencephalitis
SSRIs. *See* Selective serotonin reuptake inhibitors
SSS. *See* Superior sagittal sinus
SST (Submacular Surgery Trials), 9:225, 12:79, 249–250
St John's wort (*Hypericum perforatum*), perioperative use of, 1:306
ST-segment changes, in ischemic heart disease, 1:102, 104

ST-segment elevation MI (STEMI), 1:102. *See also* Acute coronary syndrome
management of, 1:109*t*, 112–113
STAAR toric IOL, 13:142, 142*f*, 143, 144
Stabbing headache, idiopathic, 5:299
Stable angina pectoris, 1:101
hypertension management and, 1:84
management of, 1:108–110, 109*t*
Staining, fluorescein, 12:23, 23*f*, 24*f*. *See also* Hyperfluorescence
Stains/staining techniques, 4:30, 30*f*, 31*t*, 8:17, 18*f*, 19*f*
immunohistochemical, 4:33–36, 35*f*
for microbial keratitis, 8:103*t*
Staircase strategy, in perimetry, 10:56–57, 57*f*
Stallard-Wright incision, for orbitotomy, 7:108*f*, 112
Stamler lid splint, 8:391
Stand magnifiers, 3:299, 300*f*
Standard automated perimetry (SAP), 10:54, 73
Standard Care Versus Corticosteroid for Retinal Vein Occlusion (SCORE) trial, 12:100, 126, 131
Standard (field) lens, in manual lensmeter, 3:269, 269*f*
Standing potential, 12:42, 42*f*
Stapedial artery, 2:138
Stapedial/stapedius nerve, 2:106, 5:61
Staphylococcus, 1:5–6, 8:132–133
aureus, 1:5–6
blepharitis/blepharoconjunctivitis caused by, 8:143–148, 144*f*, 144*t*, 146*f*, 150
chalazion caused by, 7:152–153
endogenous bacterial endophthalmitis caused by, 9:272, 12:202
hordeolum caused by, 8:148
keratitis caused by, 8:145–146, 146*f*
after photoablation, 13:98
as normal ocular flora, 8:96, 97*t*
orbital cellulitis in children caused by, 6:195
postoperative endophthalmitis caused by, 11:180, 12:354
preseptal cellulitis caused by, 7:41
in children, 6:195
blepharitis/blepharoconjunctivitis caused by, 8:101*t*, 143–148, 144*f*, 144*t*, 146*f*, 150
keratitis and, 8:145–146, 146*f*
marginal infiltrates in, 8:145, 146*f*, 147, 210
cellulitis caused by
orbital, in children, 6:195
preseptal, 7:41
in children, 6:194, 195
chalazion caused by, 7:152–153
conjunctivitis in children caused by, 6:189
endocarditis prophylaxis and, 1:7, 8*t*
endophthalmitis caused by
endogenous bacterial, 9:272, 12:202
postoperative, 9:126, 269, 11:180, 12:354
epidermidis, 1:6
chronic uveitis after cataract surgery caused by, 11:158
as normal ocular flora, 8:96, 97*t*
postoperative endophthalmitis caused by, 9:126, 269, 11:180
hordeolum caused by, 8:148
keratitis caused by, 8:145–146, 146*f*, 13:98
as normal ocular flora, 8:96, 97*t*

ocular infection caused by, **8**:143–148, 144*f*, 144*t*, 146*f*, 150. *See also specific type*
resistant strains of, **1**:3, 5–6, 57, 60
uveitis caused by, chronic, after cataract surgery, **11**:158
Staphylomas
axial length measurement for IOL power determination and, **3**:213, **13**:140
in children, **4**:116, **6**:310, 415
congenital, **8**:258–260, 262*t*, 263*f*
corneal, **8**:258–260, 262*t*, 263*f*
peripapillary, **6**:310, 415
scleral, **4**:116, 116*f*
in scleritis, **4**:114, 115*f*, 116
in scleromalacia perforans, **8**:220
STAR (Scoring Tool for Assessing Risk), **10**:159
Starbursts, scattering causing, **3**:16
"Stare test," **8**:56
Starfish cataract, in children, **6**:251*f*
Stargardt disease (juvenile macular degeneration/ fundus flavimaculatus), **4**:172, 174*f*, **6**:292–293, 293*f*, **12**:234–236, 235*f*, 236*t*
ABC/ABCR transporter mutations causing, **2**:296, **4**:172, **6**:293, **12**:233, 234
cone–rod dystrophy and, **6**:293, **12**:233, 235
gene for, **12**:222, 233, 234
retinal pigment epithelium in, **2**:309, **12**:234, 235*f*
Starlix. *See* Nateglinide
Static perimetry, **5**:99, 99–100, **10**:54*f*, 55
automated. *See* Automated perimetry
for peripheral visual field assessment, **3**:292
Statins, **1**:136–138, 137*t*
age-related macular degeneration and, **1**:139, 325
Alzheimer disease prevention and, **1**:267
cataracts and, **1**:139, **11**:49
heart disease prevention and, **1**:99, 107, 131, 136–138, 137*t*
for hypercholesterolemia, **1**:131, 136–138, 137*t*
stroke prevention and, **1**:91, **5**:182
Stationary night blindness, congenital, **6**:291–292, **12**:215–217, 216*f*, 217*f*
ERG patterns in, **6**:291, **12**:36*f*, 216, 217, 217*f*
with myopia, ocular findings in carriers of, **2**:222*t*
Stationary nyctalopia, rod-specific mutations causing, **2**:295, 296
Stationary retinal disease, **12**:213–216
Statistics, **1**:315–348
clinical practice applications and, **1**:338–348
data presentation and, **1**:343–346, 344*f*, 345*f*, 346*f*
measurement system design and, **1**:339–340
monitoring system implementation and, **1**:340–342
quality improvement and, **1**:346, 347*f*
results analysis and, **1**:342–343
interpreting results of studies for patients and, **1**:336–338
research study evaluation and, **1**:315–320
clinical relevance and, **1**:319–320
intervention issues and, **1**:318
outcome issues and, **1**:318–319
participants and setting and, **1**:316–317
sample size and, **1**:317–318
validity and, **1**:319, 339

study designs and, **1**:320–329, 321*f*. *See also specific type of study*
case-control studies, **1**:321*f*, 323–325, 324*f*
case reports, **1**:321, 321*f*
case series, **1**:321*f*, 322–323
clinical trials, **1**:327–328, 327*f*
systematic reviews/meta-analyses of, **1**:328–329
cohort studies, **1**:321*f*, 324*f*, 326–327
cross-sectional studies, **1**:325–326
test interpretation and, **1**:329–336
STATPAC program (Humphrey), **10**:59, 60, 60*f*, 63
Status epilepticus, **1**:297–298
Status epilepticus amauroticus, **5**:186
Stavudine (d4T), **1**:33
Stay (pull-over) sutures, **6**:149
Stearate/stearic acid
in retinal pigment epithelium, **2**:305, 306
in vitreous, **2**:286
Steepening, in hyperopia surgery, **13**:20
Steeper add minus (SAM) rule, **3**:174, 175, 185
Steeper than K (apical clearance) fit, for rigid gas-permeable contact lenses, **3**:184, 184–185
Steinert disease, pigmentary retinopathy and, **12**:250*t*
Stellate (sutural) cataracts, **11**:33, 33*f*
Stem cell biology, in cancer management, **1**:235
Stem cell transplantation. *See* Limbal transplantation
Stem cells, **8**:5, 6, 9, 92–93. *See also* Limbal stem cells
blood cell formation and, **1**:147
conjunctival, **8**:92
corneal, **8**:5, 6, 9, 92–93, 389
in corneal and conjunctival wound healing/repair, **8**:388
Stent placement
for canalicular obstruction, **7**:264
for canalicular trauma, **7**:254*f*, 272–273
carotid artery, **5**:182–183
for ocular ischemic syndrome, **12**:134–135
coronary, **1**:99, 103, 108–109
for angina, **1**:108–109
in myocardial infarction management, **1**:99, 112–113
for nasolacrimal duct obstruction, **7**:267
Steradian, **3**:18*t*
Stereo Fly test, **6**:87
Stereoacuity
development of, **6**:170–171
testing, **6**:87
in monofixation syndrome, **6**:60
Stereophotography, for recording optic disc evaluation, **10**:51, 75, 81
Stereopsis, **6**:40–41, 40*f*, 41–42
chromostereopsis, **3**:41, 41*f*
depth perception differentiated from, **6**:42
in intermittent exotropia, **6**:101
in monofixation syndrome, **6**:60
testing, **6**:87
in nonorganic ophthalmic disorder evaluation
monocular no light perception and, **5**:310
monocular reduced vision and, **5**:311, 311*t*
Sterile (noninfectious) endophthalmitis, **9**:269

Sterile infiltrates
  contact lenses causing, 3:198
  after surface ablation, 13:100, 100*f*
Sterile interface inflammation (diffuse lamellar keratitis/
    DLK), after LASIK, 13:108–111, 109*f*, 109*t*, 110*t*,
    111*f*
  glaucoma/IOP elevation and, 13:97, 174, 195
  infectious keratitis differentiated from, 13:110–111,
    110*t*, 111*f*
Steroids. *See* Corticosteroids
Stevens-Johnson syndrome (erythema multiforme
    major), 8:195–198, 196*t*, 197*f*, 198*f*
  in children, 6:200–201, 201*f*
  mucous membrane grafting for, 8:198, 401
STGD4 gene, in Stargardt disease, 4:172, 12:234
Stickler syndrome (hereditary progressive arthro-
    ophthalmopathy), 6:295, 12:250*t*, 309, 309*f*, 310
  Pierre Robin sequence (anomaly/deformity) and,
    12:310
  pigmentary retinopathy and, 12:250*t*, 309*f*
  vitreous collapse in, 2:288
Stigmatic image/imaging, 3:37, 39*f*
  single refractive surface and, 3:53–55, 54*f*
  wavefront analysis and, 3:238
Stiles-Crawford effect, 8:37
Still disease (systemic-onset juvenile idiopathic
    [chronic/rheumatoid] arthritis), 1:167, 9:129
  eye examination schedule for children with, 9:131*t*
Stimulated emission, in lasers, 3:21, 21–23, 23*f*
Stimulated (reparative/inflammatory) macrophages,
    9.20, 21*f*, 22–23
Stimulatory hypersensitivity (type V) reaction, 9:44, 44*t*
Stimulus, as perimetry variable
  luminance and, 10:56
  size and, 10:56
  speed of movement of, 10:56
  wavelength and, 10:56
Stimulus accommodative convergence/accommodation
    ratio, 6:81. *See also* Accommodative convergence/
    accommodation ratio
Stimulus deprivation amblyopia, 6:64
  eye trauma and, 6:403
  visual development affected by, 6:46–47, 47*f*, 61–62
STIR (short tau inversion recovery) technique, 5:73,
    76*t*
Stocker-Holt variant Meesmann corneal dystrophy,
    8:272. *See also* Meesmann corneal (juvenile
    hereditary epithelial) dystrophy
Stocker lines, 8:332, 337*t*
Stomach cancer, 1:275
Stomodeum, 2:119*f*
Stool guaiac slide test, in cancer screening, 1:272*t*, 276
Stool for ova and parasites, in uveitis, 9:95*t*
"Stop and chop" phaco, 11:122–123, 124*f*
Stop codon (termination codon), 2:161
  frameshift mutation and, 2:152
STOP-ROP (Supplemental Therapeutic Oxygen for
    Prethreshold ROP) study, 6:281, 12:166
Storiform pattern, in fibrous histiocytoma, 4:117, 240,
    242*f*
Strabismic amblyopia, 6:62–63, 63*f*
  visual development and, 6:48–49, 48*f*, 61–62

Strabismus, 6:9–164. *See also* Deviations; Diplopia
  A-pattern, 6:107–112, 109*f*. *See also* A-pattern
    deviations
  acquired, 6:11
  age of onset and, 6:11, 71, 100
  amblyopia and, 6:62–63, 63*f*. *See also* Amblyopia
    visual development and, 6:48–49, 48*f*, 61–62
  anomalous retinal correspondence in, 6:51*f*, 52–53, 53*f*
    testing for, 6:52, 53–59
  botulinum toxin for, 6:163–164
  in Brown syndrome, 6:122*t*, 130–132, 131*f*
  childhood glaucoma and, 10:158
  in chronic progressive external ophthalmoplegia,
    6:137, 139*t*
  classification of, 6:10–11
  comitant/incomitant deviations in, 5:219, 220*f*
  congenital, 6:11
  in congenital fibrosis syndrome, 6:138–140
  convergent, 6:9
  cover tests in, 6:74–76, 75*f*, 76*f*
  in craniosynostosis, 6:390–391, 391*f*
  cyclovertical, surgery planning and, 6:146
  definition of, 6:9
  diagnosis of, 5:216, 216*f*, 6:71–88. *See also* Ocular
    motility, assessment of
    screening tests in, 1:329–330, 329*t*, 330*t*
  diagnostic positions of gaze and, 6:80, 80*f*
  dissimilar image tests in, 6:78–79, 79*f*
  dissimilar target tests in, 6:79–80
  dissociated. *See* Dissociated horizontal deviation;
    Dissociated vertical deviation
  divergent, 6:9
  in Duane syndrome, 6:127–130, 128*f*
  esodeviations, 6:89–98, 90*t*
  exodeviations, 6:99–106
  extorsional, 6:10
  extraocular muscle anatomy and, 6:13–25, 14*f*, 16*f*, 17*t*
  extraocular muscle field of action and, 6:29
  fixus, 6:139
  full-time patching for amblyopia and, 6:66
  in Graves eye disease. *See* Strabismus, in thyroid eye
    disease
  high myopia and, 6:141
  history/presenting complaint in, 6:71
  infantile, 6:11
  infantile esotropia and, 6:90
  in inferior oblique muscle paralysis, 6:122*t*
  in internuclear ophthalmoplegia, 6:141
  intorsional, 6:10
  light reflex tests in, 6:76–78, 77*f*, 78*f*
  manifest, 6:9
  in Möbius syndrome, 6:140–141, 140*f*
  monofixation syndrome in, 6:59
  motor physiology and, 6:27–37
  motor tests in evaluation of, 6:83
  in myasthenia gravis, 6:137–138, 138*f*, 139*t*
  nanophthalmos and, 8:251
  nystagmus surgery and, 6:329
  ocular alignment tests in, 6:74–80
  in ocular motor apraxia, 6:141–142
  in optic nerve hypoplasia, 6:308, 414–415
  paralytic, Hering's law and, 6:35

in pediatric cataract, **6**:252
in pregeniculate visual loss, **6**:414
prescribing guidelines in children and, **3**:141
prism adaptation test in, **6**:86
pulley system pathology and, **6**:23, 109–110, 110*f*
pseudo-Brown syndrome and, **6**:130
refractive surgery and, **13**:34–35, 178–181
in retinoblastoma, **4**:301, 301*t*, 302*f*, **6**:354
secondary, botulinum toxin injections causing, **6**:164
sensory adaptations in, **6**:50–60, 51*f*
testing for, **6**:53–59
sensory physiology/pathology and, **6**:39–60
in sixth nerve (abducens) paralysis, **6**:98, 134–135,
134*f*
in superior oblique myokymia, **6**:142–143
suppression in, **5**:219, **6**:50–52, 51*f*
testing for, **6**:51, 53–59
terminology related to, **6**:9–11
in third nerve (oculomotor) paralysis, **6**:132–134, 133*f*
3-step test in, **6**:83–86, 85*f*
in thyroid eye disease, **5**:238, **6**:135–136, 136*f*, 139*t*,
7:49
treatment of
chemodenervation (botulinum toxin), **6**:163–164
surgical. *See* Strabismus surgery
V-pattern, **6**:107–112, 108*f*. *See also* V-pattern
deviations
vertical, **6**:10. *See also* Vertical deviations
visual acuity testing in, **6**:71–74, 72*t*
visual development affected by, **6**:48–49, 48*f*
Strabismus surgery, **6**:145–162. *See also specific type or
disorder and* Extraocular muscle surgery
acuity considerations and, **6**:145–146
adjustable sutures used in, **6**:148–149
anesthesia for, **6**:160–162
complications of, **6**:154–160
cyclovertical strabismus and, **6**:146–147
for dissociated vertical deviation, **6**:117, 153
for esodeviations and exodeviations, **6**:150–151, 150*t*
extraocular muscle anatomy and, **6**:23*f*, 24–25
in glaucoma, **10**:158
guidelines for, **6**:149–154, 150*t*
for hypo- and hypertropia, **6**:152–153
incisions for, **6**:154
incomitance and, **6**:146
indications for, **6**:145
infections after, **6**:156, 156*f*
monocular recession-resection procedures in,
6:150–151, 150*t*
oblique muscle procedures and, **6**:148*t*, 151–152
planning, **6**:145–147
posterior fixation in, **6**:148*t*, 149
prior surgery and, **6**:147
pull-over (stay) sutures used in, **6**:149
rectus muscle procedures and, **6**:152–154
strengthening procedures in, **6**:147–148, 152
symmetric, **6**:150, 150*t*
techniques for, **6**:147–149, 148*t*
for thyroid eye disease, **7**:53, 54
transposition procedures in, **6**:149, 153
weakening procedures in, **6**:147, 148*t*, 151–152. *See
also* Weakening procedures
Straddling, in axis determination, **3**:127, 128*f*

Straight sinus, **2**:108, 108*f*, **5**:26, 26*f*
Strampelli anterior chamber IOL, **3**:210, 210*f*
Stratum album profundum, **5**:41
Stratum griseum profundum, **5**:41
Strawberry hemangioma. *See* Hemangiomas
Streak projection system, for retinoscope, **3**:121, 121*f*
Streak reflex. *See* Retinal reflex
Streaks, as positive dysphotopsias, **3**:223, **11**:168
Strengthening procedures (extraocular muscle),
6:147–148, 152
Streptococcus, **1**:6–8, **8**:133, 133*f*
α-hemolytic, endocarditis and, **1**:7, 8*t*
β-hemolytic. *See Streptococcus*, *pyogenes*
in bleb-associated endophthalmitis, **12**:354, 357
cellulitis caused by
orbital, in children, **6**:195
preseptal, in children, **6**:194, 195
conjunctivitis caused by, **8**:101*t*, 149–150
in children, **4**:53, **6**:189
endophthalmitis caused by
bleb-associated, **12**:354
endogenous bacterial, **9**:272, **12**:202
postoperative, **11**:180, **12**:354
keratitis caused by, **8**:159, 160*f*
after penetrating keratoplasty, **8**:425
after photoablation, **13**:98
necrotizing fasciitis caused by, **7**:44
as normal ocular flora, **8**:96, 97*t*
ocular infection caused by, **8**:101*t*, 133, 149–150. *See
also specific type*
persistence and, **8**:99
pneumoniae (pneumococcus), **1**:7, 284, **8**:133, 133*f*
conjunctivitis caused by, **8**:149–150
in children, **4**:53, **6**:189
immunization against, **1**:284–285
keratitis after photoablation caused by, **13**:98
as normal ocular flora, **8**:96
orbital cellulitis caused by, in children, **6**:195
preseptal cellulitis caused by, in children, **6**:195
in postoperative endophthalmitis, **12**:354
pyogenes (group A β-hemolytic), **1**:6, **8**:133, 149
orbital cellulitis in children caused by, **6**:195
orbital necrotizing fasciitis caused by, **7**:44
viridans, keratitis after photoablation caused by, **13**:98
Streptogramins, **1**:53*t*, 63–64
Streptokinase, **1**:159, **2**:393
for ST-segment elevation acute coronary syndrome,
1:113
Streptolysin, **8**:133
Streptomycin, **1**:19, 39, 51*t*, 61–62, **2**:376
ototoxicity of, mitochondrial DNA mutations and,
2:176
Stress (exercise) tests, in ischemic heart disease, **1**:106
echocardiography, **1**:106
Striae
after conductive keratoplasty, **13**:120, 121*f*
in LASIK flaps, **13**:105–108, 106*t*, 107*f*
retinal, **12**:300
Striate cortex (Brodmann area 17), **5**:28*f*, 34, 35*f*, **6**:42.
See also Visual (calcarine/occipital) cortex
development of, **6**:44, 45*f*
abnormal visual experience affecting, **6**:46–49,
47*f*, 48*f*

Striate keratopathy, intraocular surgery causing, **8**:383
Striate melanokeratosis, **4**:67, **8**:234
"String sign," in internal carotid artery aneurysm, **5**:269*f*
Stroke, **1**:91
  arterial dissection causing, **5**:353
  carotid artery disease and, **1**:96. *See also* Carotid occlusive disease
    clinical/laboratory evaluation and, **5**:180
    prognosis and, **5**:181, 181*t*
    transient visual loss and, **5**:177–183, 179*f*
    treatment and, **5**:181–183
  completed, **1**:92
  dementia after, **1**:265
  in diabetes mellitus, **1**:207
  diagnosis of, **1**:93–94
  evolving, **1**:93
  gaze palsy/preference and, **5**:210
  hemorrhagic, **1**:91
  homonymous hemianopia caused by, **5**:165, 168, 171, 172*f*
  hypertension management and, **1**:79*t*, 85, 94
  incidence of, **1**:91
  internuclear ophthalmoplegia caused by, **5**:225
  ischemic, **1**:91, 92
  ocular ischemic syndrome and, **12**:134
  risk factors for, **1**:93, **5**:181, 181*t*
  severity of, **1**:93
  treatment of, **1**:94–95
    emergency transport and, **1**:289, 291
    recent developments in, **1**:91
Stroke Association, **1**:93
Stroke (phacoemulsification), **11**:103
Stroke scale, **1**:93
Stroma
  choroidal, **4**:187
    development of, **2**:133
  ciliary body, **2**:61–63, 62*f*
  conjunctival (substantia propria), **4**:47, 48*f*, **8**:5–6, **9**:57
    age-related/involutional changes in, **8**:331
    in external eye defense, **8**:96
    immune and inflammatory cells in, **8**:173, 174*t*, **9**:59
  corneal, **2**:45, 46*f*, 247*f*, 249–250, **4**:77, 78*f*, **8**:7–8, 7*f*, 8*f*
    anatomy of, **2**:45, 46*f*, 247*f*, **8**:7–8, 7*f*, 8*f*
    biochemistry and metabolism of, **2**:249–250
    development of, **2**:133–135, 134*f*, **8**:4
    healing/repair of, **4**:14
    inflammation of, **8**:25, 27*f*, 27*t*
      in systemic infections, **8**:169–170
    neovascularization of, contact lenses causing, **8**:92
    pigmentation of, **8**:348–349
      drug-induced, **8**:347*t*
    refractive index of, **8**:38
    wound healing/repair and, **4**:14
  iris, **2**:56, 60*f*, **4**:185–186
    cysts of, **6**:227
    wound healing/repair and, **4**:16
  scleral, **2**:48, **4**:112, 112*f*
Stromal bed, preparation of for LASIK, **13**:77–83, 78*f*, 79*f*, 81*f*, 82*f*, 83*t*

Stromal bed thickness, residual, LASIK and, **13**:40, 71–72
  corneal perforation and, **13**:104
  ectasia and, **13**:72, 114–116
Stromal corneal dystrophies, **4**:96–97, 97*f*, 97*t*, 98*f*, 99*f*, **8**:268*t*, 278–290, 278*t*. *See also specific type*
  Avellino (granular type 2), **4**:97, 97*t*, 99*f*, **8**:268*t*, 269*t*, 270*t*, 278*t*, 282, 282*f*
    genetics of, **4**:97, **8**:269*t*, 282
    refractive surgery and, **13**:35
  central cloudy of François, **8**:268*t*, 270*t*, 289–290, 289*f*
    genetics of, **8**:269*t*, 289
  congenital/congenital hereditary, **6**:216*t*, 219, **8**:260, 268*t*, 270*t*, 286–287, 286*f*
    genetics of, **8**:269*t*, 286
  Fleck, **8**:268*t*, 270*t*, 287, 287*f*
    genetics of, **8**:269*t*, 287
  genetics of, **4**:96
  granular, **8**:268*t*, 278*t*. *See also* Granular corneal dystrophy
    type 1 (classic/GCD1), **4**:96, 97*t*, 98*f*, **8**:268*t*, 270*t*, 280–281, 281*f*
    type 2 (granular-lattice/GCD2), **4**:97, 97*t*, 99*f*, **8**:268*t*, 269*t*, 270*t*, 278*t*, 282, 282*f*, **13**:35
    type 3 (Reis-Bücklers), **8**:268*t*, 269*t*, 270*t*, 275–277, 276*f*
  lattice, **4**:96–97, 97*t*, 99*f*, **8**:268*t*, 278*t*. *See also* Lattice corneal dystrophy
  macular, **4**:96, 97*f*, 97*t*, **8**:268*t*, 270*t*, 278*t*, 283–284, 284*f*
    genetics of, **8**:269*t*, 283
  nomenclature of, **4**:96
  non–TGFBI-associated, **8**:268*t*, 283–290
  posterior amorphous, **8**:268*t*, 270*t*, 288–289, 288*f*
    genetics of, **8**:269*t*, 288
  pre-Descemet, **8**:268*t*, 269*t*, 270*t*, 290, 290*f*
    genetics of, **8**:269*t*, 290
  Schnyder, **8**:268*t*, 270*t*, 284–285, 285*f*, 309
    genetics of, **8**:269*t*, 284
  TGFBI-associated, **8**:268*t*, 278–282, 278*t*
Stromal degenerations, **8**:336–344
  age-related/involutional changes and, **8**:336–338, 338*f*, 339*f*
  peripheral, **8**:339–340, 340*f*
  postinflammatory changes and, **8**:340–344, 341*f*, 342*f*, 343*f*
Stromal edema, **8**:29
  after cataract surgery, **11**:146–148
Stromal graft rejection, **8**:429. *See also* Rejection
Stromal keratitis, **8**:21*t*, 25, 27*f*, 27*t*
  in Cogan syndrome, **8**:209, 210
  Epstein-Barr virus causing, **8**:122–123, 123*f*
  herpes simplex virus causing, **4**:82, 84*f*, **8**:108*t*, 113–116, 114*f*, 115*f*
    penetrating keratoplasty for, **8**:117
  in herpes zoster ophthalmicus, **8**:120
  microsporidial, **8**:170
  necrotizing, **8**:25
  nonnecrotizing, **8**:27*f*
  nonsuppurative, **8**:21*t*, 25, 27*f*, 27*t*
    systemic infections and, **8**:169–170
  pressure-induced (PISK), after LASIK, **13**:112, 112*f*
  scleritis and, **8**:221

suppurative, **8**:21*t*, 25, 27*f*, 27*t*
syphilitic, **8**:207, 208
Stromal micropuncture, for recurrent corneal erosions, **8**:84, 85*f*
Stromal nevi, **4**:65
STRs. *See* Short tandem repeats
Structure, care system, **1**:338
monitoring system and, **1**:340–342
STSs. *See* Sequence-tagged sites
Student *t* test, **1**:320
Sturge-Weber syndrome (cerebrofacial/ encephalotrigeminal/encephalofacial angiomatosis), **5**:339*t*, 341–342, 343*f*, **6**:342, 364*t*, 375–378, 376*f*, 377*f*, **10**:28, 147–148
choroidal hemangioma in, **4**:200, 292, **6**:377, 377*f*, **12**:181
glaucoma associated with, **5**:341, 343*f*, **10**:28, 147–148
in children, **5**:341, 343*f*, **6**:238, 377, 378, **10**:147–148
port-wine stain (nevus flammeus) in, **5**:341, 343*f*, **6**:238, 342, 375, 376, 376*f*, **8**:241, **10**:28, 147
Sturm, conoid of, **3**:93, 93*f*
astigmatic dial refraction and, **3**:130
Stye (external hordeolum), **4**:208, **7**:154, **8**:148
Subacute bacterial endocarditis. *See* Endocarditis
Subacute granulomatous thyroiditis, **1**:212–213
Subacute lymphocytic ("painless") thyroiditis, **1**:213
Subacute sclerosing panencephalitis, **8**:129, **9**:213–214, 214*f*
Subarachnoid hemorrhage, **1**:97, 98. *See also* Intracranial hemorrhage
arteriovenous malformations causing, **5**:354
ocular hemorrhage with, **5**:351
in shaking injury, **6**:405, 406
Subarachnoid space, optic nerve in, **2**:91, **4**:249, 250*f*
Subarachnoid surgical space, **7**:107*f*, 108
Sub-brow fat pads, **7**:135*f*, 141
Subcapsular cataract
anterior (subcapsular fibrous plaques), **4**:124, 125*f*
posterior, **4**:124–125, 125*f*, **11**:42–44, 47*f*
in children, **6**:249, 250*t*
corticosteroids causing, **11**:47–48
ischemia causing, **11**:64
in myotonic dystrophy, **11**:57
retinoblastoma differentiated from, **4**:305*t*
silicone oil use and, **11**:205
uveitis and, **11**:59
visual acuity and, **11**:43, 70, 70*t*
Subciliary incision, for orbitotomy, **7**:108*f*, 110
Subclavian artery, **5**:21
Subclavian steal, **5**:349
Subclinical retinal detachment, **12**:285
Subconjunctival arteries, **5**:14*f*
Subconjunctival carboplatin, for retinoblastoma, **4**:311
Subconjunctival drug administration, **2**:327
lidocaine, for cataract surgery, **11**:101
Subconjunctival fibrosis, medications causing, **8**:360–361
Subconjunctival hemorrhage, **8**:75, 76, 76*t*, 362–363
in child abuse, **6**:404
in dengue fever, **9**:219
Subcutaneous fat/tissue, eyelid, **7**:135*f*, 136

Subcutaneous nodules
in rheumatoid arthritis, **1**:162
in sarcoidosis, **4**:191, 191*f*
Subcutaneous rhytidectomy
classic, **7**:236
with SMAS, **7**:236, 237*f*
Subendocardial (NSTEMI/nontransmural) infarction, **1**:102
Subepithelial corneal degenerations, **8**:334–336, 335*f*
Subepithelial corneal dystrophies. *See* Epithelial/ subepithelial dystrophies
Subepithelial corneal infiltrate, **8**:21*t*
Subepithelial graft rejection, **8**:428–429, 428*f*. *See also* Rejection
Subepithelial nevi, **4**:65
Subjective refraction, **3**:130–136
astigmatic dial technique for, **3**:130–132, 131*f*
with automated refractors, **3**:277
binocular balance and, **3**:136
in children, **3**:141
cross-cylinder technique for, **3**:132–135, 133*f*, 134*f*
in low vision patient, **3**:294
sphere refining and, **3**:135–136
Sublimaze. *See* Fentanyl
Subluxation, intraocular lens, **11**:143, 144*t*, 162–166, 163*f*, 164*f*, 165*f*
Subluxed/subluxated lens, **6**:261, 262*t*, **11**:35, 36*f*. *See also* Ectopia lentis
angle closure and, **10**:112, 122, 123*f*
cataract surgery in patient with, **11**:197–199, 198*f*
traumatic, **11**:36, 50–51, 50*f*
child abuse and, **6**:404
Submacular hemorrhage, **12**:349–351, 350*f*
Submacular surgery
for age-related macular degeneration, **12**:79
for hemorrhage, **12**:349–351, 350*f*
for ocular histoplasmosis syndrome, **9**:225–226, 225*f*, **12**:82, 351
Submacular Surgery Trials (SST), **9**:225, **12**:79, 349–350
Submandibular ganglion, **5**:66*f*
Suborbicularis fat pads (suborbicularis oculi fat/SOOF), **7**:135*f*, 141
midface rejuvenation surgery and (SOOF lift), **7**:233, 234*f*
Subperiorbital (subperiosteal) surgical space, **7**:107, 107*f*
Subperiosteal abscess, in orbital cellulitis, **6**:195, 196, 196*f*
Subperiosteal route
for midface lift, **7**:234, 235*f*
for orbitotomy
inferior approach, **7**:110
superior approach, **7**:108–109
Subretinal fibrosis and uveitis syndrome (SFU), **9**:148–150*t*, 161, 167–168, 167*f*
Subretinal fluid, in central serous chorioretinopathy, **12**:172, 173, 173*f*, 174
Subretinal neovascular membranes. *See also* Neovascularization
in age-related macular degeneration, **4**:169–170, 171*f*
Subretinal space, **2**:72, 74*f*
biopsy of in intraocular lymphoma, **4**:324
development of, **2**:123
retinal pigment epithelium in maintenance of, **2**:308

Substance abuse disorders, 1:250–251. *See also specific substance*
 endogenous mold *(Aspergillus)* endophthalmitis and, 12:203
 ophthalmic considerations and, 1:250–251
Substance P, 8:177t, 9:29t
 in iris–ciliary body, 2:259
 in tear secretion, 2:240
Substantia nigra, 5:40f
 in Parkinson disease, 1:258
Substantia propria
 conjunctival (conjunctival stroma), 4:47, 48f, 8:5–6, 9:57
  age-related/involutional changes in, 8:331
  in external eye defense, 8:96
  immune and inflammatory cells in, 8:173, 174t, 9:59
 corneal. *See* Stroma, corneal
Sub-Tenon drug administration, 2:327
 corticosteroid, 9:102–103, 102f
  in cystoid macular edema
   after cataract surgery, 11:183
   in uveitis, 9:300
  in pars planitis, 9:137
 lidocaine, for cataract surgery, 11:101, 101f
 local anesthetic, 2:389
Sub-Tenon (episcleral) surgical space, 7:107f, 108
Succinate, for Leber hereditary optic neuropathy, 5:138
Succinylcholine, 2:344
 adverse effects of, 2:343f
 malignant hyperthermia caused by, 6:161
 in patients taking cholinesterase inhibitors, 2:340
 pharmacogenetics and, 2:229–230
Suction ring
 for femtosecond laser flap creation, 13:80–81, 81f
 filtering bleb affecting placement of, 13:174–175
 for microkeratome flap creation, 13:77–78, 78f, 79f
Sudden cardiac death, 1:102–103, 103–104
Sufenta. *See* Sufentanil
Sufentanil, perioperative, 1:309t, 310
"Sugar" cataracts, 2:279–281
 aldose reductase in development of, 2:280–281, 11:15
Sugiura sign, 9:185, 186f, 12:197
Suicide
 in older patients, 1:226
 SSRI use and, 1:256
Suicide induction (cell), by cytotoxic T lymphocytes, 9:51, 53f
Sulamyd. *See* Sulfacetamide
Sular. *See* Nisoldipine
Sulbactam, 1:59. *See also specific antibiotic combination*
Sulcus
 intermarginal (gray line), 2:23, 26f, 237, 7:136, 142
 internal scleral, 2:50, 4:102
Sulcus-supported intraocular lenses, 13:127t
Sulfacetamide, 2:372t, 374
 in combination preparations, 2:373t
Sulfadiazine, 2:374
 for toxoplasmosis, 9:232, 309, 12:208–209, 208t
Sulfasalazine, 1:162, 185
 for ankylosing spondylitis, 9:121
Sulfatase deficiency, multiple, 8:310
Sulfisoxazole, 1:45t

Sulfite oxidase deficiency, 2:213t, 6:264
Sulfoiduronate sulfatase, defective, 2:213t
Sulfonamides, 1:44, 45t, 2:374. *See also specific agent*
 protein binding of, 2:329
 for toxoplasmosis, 9:233
 uveitis caused by, 9:128
Sulfonylureas, 1:198–200, 199t
Sulfur metabolism, in sulfite oxidase deficiency, 6:264
Sulindac, 1:183t, 2:362t
Sumatriptan, refractive surgery in patient taking, 13:31
SUN Working Group, uveitis classification of, 9:78, 78t, 79t
Sunburst lesions, black, in sickle cell disease, 12:118, 119f
SUNCT, 5:299
Sunflower cataract, in chalcosis/Wilson disease, 8:327, 11:54, 57, 12:327
Sunglasses, 3:159–161, 160f, 304
 chromatic aberrations affected by, 3:101–102
 photochromic lenses and, 3:159–160
 polarizing (polarized/Polaroid lenses), 3:11, 12, 12f, 159, 304
 ultraviolet-absorbing lenses and, 3:160–161
  cataract prevention and, 11:53
 visual functions improved by, 3:159, 160f, 304
Sunlight. *See* Ultraviolet light
Sunset-glow fundus, in Vogt-Koyanagi-Harada (VKH) syndrome, 9:184, 185, 186f, 12:197
"Sunsetting," in infants, 6:413
Superficial anterior lamellar keratoplasty (SALK), 8:413, 415–416t, 435
 advantages of, 8:416t
 complications of
  intraoperative, 8:415t
  postoperative, 8:415t
 disadvantages of, 8:416t
 indications for, 8:415t
 penetrating/selective keratoplasty compared with, 8:415–416t
 surgical technique for, 8:435
Superficial basal cell carcinoma, 7:169. *See also* Basal cell carcinoma
Superficial granular corneal dystrophy. *See* Reis-Bücklers corneal dystrophy
Superficial keratectomy, 8:402–403
Superficial mimetic muscles, 7:131, 133f
Superficial musculoaponeurotic system (SMAS), 7:131, 132f
 cosmetic surgery and, 7:131, 236, 237f
Superficial petrosal nerve, greater, 2:106, 107, 5:16, 61
Superficial punctate keratitis of Thygeson, 8:204–207, 206f
Superficial temporal artery, 5:12, 14f, 15f, 19
Superficial temporal fascia (temporoparietal fascia), 7:131, 132f
Superior cerebellar artery, 5:20f, 22f, 23
 cranial nerve relationship and, 5:52f
Superior cervical ganglion, 2:15, 60
 dilator muscle innervation and, 2:258
Superior colliculus, 5:39f, 40f, 41, 61
Superior displacement of globe, in orbital disorders, 7:23
Superior limbic keratoconjunctivitis, 8:81–82, 82f
Superior marginal arcade, 5:14f
Superior muscular artery, 5:18

Superior oblique muscles, 2:16*f*, 17*f*, 18, 19*t*, 20*f*, 38*f*, 39*f*, 5:10*f*, 55, 56*f*, 6:14–15, 14*f*, 15*f*, 16*f*, 17*t*, 18*f*, 7:10, 11*f*, 135*f*
  action of, 6:15, 17*t*, 29, 29*t*
    gaze position and, 6:31–32, 33*f*
    3-step test in evaluation of, 6:83–86, 85*f*
  anatomy of, 2:16*f*, 17*f*, 18, 19*t*, 20*f*, 38*f*, 39*f*, 5:10*f*, 6:14–15, 14*f*, 15*f*, 16*f*, 17*t*, 18*f*
    surgery and, 6:24
  field of action of, 6:29
  insertion relationships of, 2:17, 18*f*, 19*t*
  myokymia affecting, 6:142–143
  nerves supplying, 2:21, 7:11
  overaction of
    A-pattern deviations associated with, 6:107, 109*f*
    in inferior oblique muscle paralysis, 6:122*t*
    vertical deviations caused by, 6:113, 115–116, 115*f*
  paralysis (paresis/palsy) of, 6:118–121, 119*f*
    Hering's law and, 6:35, 36*f*
    after tenotomy for Brown syndrome, 6:131–132
  surgery of, 6:152
    for A- and V-pattern deviations, 6:110, 111
    for inferior oblique muscle paralysis, 6:122
    for superior oblique myokymia, 6:142–143
    for vertical deviation, 6:116
Superior oblique myokymia, 5:256–257, 6:142–143
Superior oblique tendon, 6:14–15, 15*f*, 16*f*
  fossa for trochlea of, 7:5–6
  tucking procedure on, 6:120, 152
Superior oblique tendon sheath syndrome (Brown syndrome), 5:239–240, 240*f*
Superior oblique tenotomy
  for Brown syndrome, 6:131–132
  for superior oblique myokymia, 6:142–143
  for third nerve (oculomotor) paralysis, 6:133
Superior ophthalmic vein, 5:10*f*, 24–25, 24*f*, 27*f*, 7:11*f*, 12*f*, 13, 13*f*, 14*f*, 15*f*
Superior orbital fissure, 2:7*f*, 10, 11*f*, 12*f*, 5:6, 6*f*, 7*f*, 9*f*, 10, 7:6*f*, 7*f*, 9
  ophthalmoplegia caused by lesions of, 5:236–238
Superior orbital vein, 6:18
Superior palpebral vein, 5:25*f*
Superior peripheral arcade, 5:14*f*
Superior petrosal sinus, 2:108*f*, 5:26, 27*f*
Superior punctum, 2:23, 33. *See also* Puncta
Superior rectus muscles, 2:16*f*, 17*f*, 19*t*, 20*f*, 37*f*, 38, 38*f*, 39*f*, 40*f*, 5:10*f*, 55, 56*f*, 6:14, 14*f*, 16*f*, 17*t*, 18*f*, 7:10, 135*f*
  action of, 6:14, 17*t*, 29*t*
    gaze position and, 6:31, 31*f*
    3-step test in evaluation of, 6:83–86, 85*f*
  anatomy of, 2:16*f*, 17*f*, 19*t*, 20*f*, 37*f*, 38, 38*f*, 39*f*, 40*f*, 5:10*f*, 6:14, 14*f*, 16*f*, 17*t*, 18*f*
    surgery and, 6:23*f*, 24–25
  insertion relationships of, 2:16, 18*f*, 19*t*
  nerves supplying, 2:21, 7:11, 139
  surgery of
    for A-pattern deviation, 6:111
    for dissociated vertical deviation, 6:153
    eyelid position changes after, 6:159
    for inferior oblique muscle paralysis, 6:122
    for nystagmus, 6:329
    for orbital floor fracture, 6:126
    for superior oblique muscle paralysis, 6:120

Superior rectus subnucleus, 5:54
Superior sagittal sinus, 2:108, 108*f*, 5:25–26, 26*f*
  thrombosis in, 5:357–358
Superior segmental hypoplasia, 5:142
Superior sulcus deformity, anophthalmic socket and, 7:122, 122*f*
Superior tarsal muscle of Müller, 2:23*f*, 25*f*, 28, 4:186, 205, 5:63, 64, 64*f*, 7:135*f*, 138, 139–140
  in Horner syndrome, 5:266, 7:207
  internal (transconjunctival) resection of, for ptosis correction, 7:212
Superior transverse (Whitnall) ligament, 2:25*f*, 28, 7:135*f*, 138, 139*f*, 244
Superior vena cava syndrome, glaucoma associated with, 10:28
Supernumerary puncta, 6:204
Superoxide, 2:311, 312*f*, 9:30. *See also* Free radicals
Superoxide dismutase, 2:312*f*, 317, 9:30
  in lens, 2:314, 11:16
  in retina and retinal pigment epithelium, 2:317
Supplemental Therapeutic Oxygen for Prethreshold ROP (STOP-ROP) study, 6:281, 12:166
Supplementary eye fields, 5:40, 40*f*
Support groups
  genetic disorders and, 2:232
  low vision/vision rehabilitation and, 3:305
Suppression, 5:219, 6:50–52, 51*f*
  testing in, 6:51, 53–59, 87
Suppression scotoma, diplopia after strabismus surgery and, 6:155
Suppressor T cells. *See* Regulatory (suppressor) T cells
Supracapsular phacoemulsification, 11:121
Suprachoroidal/choroidal hemorrhage, 4:18–19, 19*f*, 12:360–361, 362*f*
  angle-closure glaucoma and, 10:133
  cataract surgery and, 11:144*t*, 177–179, 189
    delayed, 11:178–179
    expulsive, 11:178
    flat or shallow anterior chamber and, 11:152
  expulsive, 4:18–19, 19*f*
    cataract surgery and, 11:178
  postoperative, 12:360–361, 362*f*
Suprachoroidal detachment, melanoma differentiated from, 4:279–280
Suprachoroidal effusion
  angle-closure glaucoma and, 10:133
  cataract surgery and, 11:177–178
    flat or shallow anterior chamber and, 11:152
  after filtering surgery, 10:197–198
Supraduction. *See* Elevation of eye
Supranuclear palsy, progressive
  convergence insufficiency in, 5:213
  facial weakness/paralysis in, 5:285
  pursuit dysfunction in, 5:213
  saccadic dysfunction in, 5:208
    intrusions, 5:200
Supranuclear (cortical) pathways, 5:37, 38–41, 38*f*, 39*f*, 40*f*, 42*f*, 43*f*, 197, 6:37
  disorders of, 5:197–214
    diplopia and, 5:220–223, 222*t*
    facial weakness/paralysis caused by, 5:284–285
  saccades/saccadic system and, 5:40–41, 40*f*
  smooth pursuit system and, 5:41, 42*f*, 43*f*

Supraorbital artery, **2**:20*f*, 37*f*, **5**:13*f*, 14*f*, 15*f*, 16
  eyelids supplied by, **7**:143
Supraorbital ethmoids, **7**:18
Supraorbital foramen/notch, **2**:5, 6*f*, 7*f*, 10, **5**:12, **7**:6, 6*f*
Supraorbital nerve, **2**:103, **5**:59*f*, 60
Supraorbital vein, **2**:40*f*, **5**:25*f*
Supratarsal corticosteroid injections, for vernal
  keratoconjunctivitis, **8**:189
Suprathreshold stimulus/testing (perimetry), **10**:54
Supratrochlear artery, **2**:37*f*, **5**:13*f*, 14*f*, 15*f*, 16
Supratrochlear nerve, **2**:103, **5**:60
Supratrochlear vein, **5**:25*f*
Supraventricular tachycardias, **1**:123–124, 124*t*
  paroxysmal, **1**:124*t*
Suprax. *See* Cefixime
Suprofen, **2**:257
Surface ablation, **13**:4*t*, 24, 41*t*, 65, 67–68. *See also
  specific procedure*
  aberrations and, **13**:7, 95
  application of laser treatment and, **13**:83–84, 84*f*
  arcuate keratotomy and, **13**:52
  bandage contact lenses after, **13**:85, 86, 193
    sterile infiltrates and, **13**:100, 100*f*
  calibration of excimer laser for, **13**:73
  central islands and, **13**:94–95, 94*f*
  complications/side effects of, **13**:93–99, 100–102
  contact lens use after, **13**:193
  contraindications to, **13**:70
  corneal haze and, **13**:101, 101*f*
  corneal preparation for, **13**:75–77, 76*f*
  corneal sensation affected by, **13**:97–98
  corneal transplantation after, **13**:191
  corticosteroids after, **13**:85, 86
    complications associated with, **13**:96–97
  decentered ablation and, **13**:95–96, 97*f*
  dry eye after, **13**:97–98, 164–165
  endothelial effects of, **13**:97
  epithelial debridement for, **13**:75, 76*f*
  epithelial preservation techniques for, **13**:75–77
  glaucoma/ocular hypertension and, **13**:96–97,
    172–175, 173*f*, 194–195
  herpes simplex virus keratitis and, **13**:166, 167
  infectious keratitis and, **13**:98–99
  international trends in use of, **13**:199
  for LASIK enhancement, **13**:90–91
  limbal relaxing incisions and, **13**:52
  limitations of, **13**:41*t*
  outcomes of, **13**:87–89
  overcorrection and, **13**:93–94
  patient selection for, **13**:70–71
  persistent epithelial defects after, **13**:100
  postoperative care for, **13**:86
    immediate postablation measures, **13**:84–85
  preoperative patient preparation for, **13**:74–75
  preoperative planning/laser programming for,
    13:73–74
  re-treatment (enhancements) and, **13**:89–91, 90*f*
  sterile infiltrates and, **13**:100, 100*f*
  surgical technique for, **13**:73–87
  tracking/centration/ablation and, **13**:83–84, 84*f*
  undercorrection and, **13**:94
  wavefront-guided. *See* Wavefront-guided laser
    ablation
Surface asymmetry index (SAI), **3**:267

Surface dyslexia, in Alzheimer disease, **1**:268
Surface ectoderm, lens development and, **11**:21, 22*f*
Surface markers, **9**:12
Surface normal, **3**:42, 42*f*, 44, 44*f*, 45*f*, 46, 46*f*
  determination of position of, **3**:51, 52*f*
Surface regularity index (SRI), **3**:267
Surface tension, of ophthalmic viscosurgical device,
  11:97
Surface-wrinkling retinopathy, **12**:300
Surfactants, in eyedrops, absorption and, **2**:326–327
Surge, in phacoemulsification, **11**:104
Surgeon factor, in IOL power determination/power
  prediction formulas, **3**:218
Surgery. *See also specific procedure and* Ocular
  (intraocular) surgery
  diabetes mellitus and, **1**:305, 307–308
  endophthalmitis after, **9**:126. *See also* Postoperative
    endophthalmitis
    acute-onset, **9**:269
    chronic (delayed-onset), **9**:269–271, 270*f*
  in older patients, **1**:224–225
  pulmonary disease and, **1**:308
Surgical (consecutive) esodeviation, **6**:97–98
  management of, **6**:103
Surgical instruments
  for arcuate keratotomy, **13**:51
  for intrastromal corneal ring segment placement,
    13:57
  for limbal relaxing incisions, **13**:51
  for phacoemulsification, **11**:104–106, 105*f*, 106*f*,
    107*f*
    settings for, **11**:118–119
Surgical spaces, orbital, **7**:107–108, 107*f*
Sursumduction/sursumversion. *See* Elevation of eye
Susac (SICRET) syndrome, **9**:146–147, 147*f*, **12**:141
Susceptibility testing, antimicrobial, **1**:56
Suspensory ligament of Lockwood, **2**:35, 36*f*, **6**:22, 23*f*,
  7:138, 140
Suspensory ligaments of lens. *See* Zonules
Sussman goniolens, **10**:34
SUSTAIN trial, **12**:77
Sustained-release preparations
  oral, **2**:329
  for topical administration, **2**:330–331
Sustiva. *See* Efavirenz
Sutural cataracts, **11**:33, 33*f*
Sutures (lens), **2**:69*f*, 70, **11**:9
  development of, **2**:130, **11**:23*f*, 24–25, 24*f*
  opacification of (sutural/stellate cataract), **11**:33, 33*f*
Sutures (surgical)
  adjustable, for strabismus surgery, **6**:148–149
  allergic reaction to, **6**:156, 157*f*
  for cataract surgery
    astigmatism and, **11**:150, 212–213
    manual small-incision cataract surgery and, **11**:96
    posterior chamber IOL implantation and, **11**:139
  interrupted, "clover-shaped" aberration caused by,
    3:240
  McCannel, for intraocular lens decentration,
    11:163–164, 164*f*
  for penetrating keratoplasty, **8**:418–419, 419*f*, 420*f*
    postoperative problems and, **8**:423–425, 424*f*
    removal of in children, **8**:431, 431*t*
  pull-over (stay), for strabismus surgery, **6**:149

Quickert
for involutional entropion, 7:195*f*, 196
for spastic entropion, 7:195*f*
removal of
after corneoscleral laceration repair, 8:382
after pediatric corneal transplantation, 8:431, 431*t*
for trabeculectomy, laser lysis of, 10:186, 191
scleral flap closure and, 10:191, 194
Swabbing, for specimen collection, 8:47, 100–102
SWAP. *See* Short-wavelength automated perimetry
Sweat glands, of eyelid, 2:23, 23*f*, 27*t*, 4:205, 207*t*, 7:160,
8:4
tumors arising in, 7:161–162, 161*f*, 162, 162*f*
Swedish interactive thresholding algorithm (SITA)
(perimetry), 5:101, 10:57, 58
SWAP using, 10:61
Sweep VEP, 6:171
Swelling pressure, 8:8
Swinging flashlight test, for relative afferent pupillary
defect, 5:93, 94*f*
before cataract surgery, 11:77
Switch flap, for eyelid repair, 7:183*f*
SWJs. *See* Square-wave jerks
SWS. *See* Sturge-Weber syndrome
Symadine. *See* Amantadine
Symblepharon, 7:199–200
in cicatricial pemphigoid, 8:200, 202, 210*f*
in Stevens-Johnson syndrome, 6:201, 8:197, 198*f*
Symlin. *See* Pramlintide
Symmetrel. *See* Amantadine
Symmetric surgery, 6:150, 150*t*
Sympathetic nerves/pathway, 5:63–65, 64*f*
adrenergic drug action and, 2:346
cholinergic drug action and, 2:334, 335*f*
in ciliary ganglion, 2:14, 15–16, 15*f*
ciliary muscle innervation and, 2:64
dilator muscle innervation and, 2:60, 258
orbit supplied by, 7:17
sphincter muscle innervation and, 2:61
in tear secretion, 2:237, 240, 242, 242*f*
Sympathetic ophthalmia, 4:189, 189*f*, 190*f*, 9:52–53,
178–183, 179*f*, 180*f*, 181*f*, 182*t*, 12:198–199,
329–330
corticosteroids for, 9:182–183
route of administration of, 2:360*t*
enucleation in prevention of, 4:189, 7:117, 118, 8:376,
9:182, 12:198–199, 329
evisceration and, 7:120, 9:182, 12:329
experimental autoimmune uveitis as model for, 9:69
glaucoma/glaucoma surgery and, 9:296, 10:185
histologic/histopathologic features of, 4:189, 189*f*,
190*f*, 9:180, 181*f*
HLA association in, 9:72*t*, 181
surgical procedures/injuries leading to, 4:189, 189*f*,
190*f*, 9:178, 182*t*, 12:198
Sympathetic root, in ciliary ganglion, 2:14, 15*f*
Sympathizing eye, 9:178, 179, 179*f*, 180, 182. *See also*
Sympathetic ophthalmia
Sympatholytics, for hypertension, 1:82
Sympathomimetic activity, intrinsic, β-blockers with,
1:76*t*, 80–81
Synaptic body
of cone (pedicle), 2:74, 77*f*
of rod (spherule), 2:73–74, 77*f*

Synaptophysin, in immunohistochemistry, 4:34
Synchesis. *See* Synchysis
Synchrony intraocular lens, 13:160
Synchysis, 12:297
in cholesterolosis (synchysis scintillans), 4:138,
12:311–312
in hereditary hyaloideoretinopathies with optically
empty vitreous, 12:309
Synchysis scintillans, 4:138, 12:311–312
Syndactyly
in Apert syndrome, 6:388, 389*f*
in Fraser syndrome, 6:175
in Saethre-Chotzen syndrome, 6:388, 390*f*
Syndrome (genetic), definition of, 6:171
Syndrome X. *See* Metabolic syndrome
Synechiae
anisocoria and, 5:266
anterior
in glaucoma
angle closure and, 10:109, 113, 117
inflammation and, 10:130, 131, 131*f*
anterior segment/iris neovascularization and,
10:37, 37*f*, 124, 125, 126*f*
chamber deepening/goniosynechialysis in
management of, 10:204
flat anterior chamber and, 10:136
gonioscopy in identification of, 10:37, 37*f*
iridocorneal endothelial (ICE) syndrome and,
4:105, 105*f*, 10:128, 128*f*
plateau iris and, 10:120
uveitis and, 9:296
in sarcoidosis, 9:175
in uveitis, 9:85, 88
glaucoma and, 9:296
posterior
anisocoria and, 5:266
in children, 6:231
in glaucoma
inflammation and, 10:130, 130*f*
pupillary block/angle closure and, 10:110–111
uveitis and, 9:296
mydriasis in prevention of, 2:341
in pars planitis, 9:136
in sarcoidosis, 9:87*f*, 175
in sympathetic ophthalmia, 9:178, 179*f*
in uveitis, 9:85, 87*f*, 88
glaucoma and, 9:296
lens changes/cataract and, 11:59
pupil irregularity and, 5:263
in sarcoidosis, 9:87*f*, 175
in uveitis, 9:85, 87*f*, 88
Synechiolysis, with penetrating keratoplasty, 8:419–420
Synercid. *See* Quinupristin/dalfopristin
Syneresis, 4:134, 134*f*, 12:297
in posterior vitreous detachment, 12:274
in young eyes, 12:272
SynergEyes-PS, 3:191
Synergist (muscle), 6:34
Synergistins (streptogramins), 1:53*t*, 63–64
Synkinesis, 7:203, 207, 208*f*
facial, 5:284*f*, 286
in Marcus Gunn jaw-winking ptosis, 6:180, 7:203,
207, 208*f*
near reflex and. *See* Near reflex

Synkinetic near reflex. *See* Near reflex
Synteny/syntenic traits, **2:**161, 176–177, 197
Syphilis, **1:**12–14, 14*t*, 279, **8:**137, **9:**242–249, 244*f*, 245*f*,
    246*f*, 247*f*, 248*t*
    acquired, **9:**244–246, 245*f*, 246*f*, 247*f*
    chorioretinitis in, **9:**243, 245, 245*f*, 309–310,
        12:205–206, 207*f*
        posterior placoid, **9:**245, 246*f*, 309–310
    congenital/intrauterine, **1:**12, 279, **6:**185–186, 221,
        9:243–244, 244*f*, 248*t*, 249
    corneal manifestations of, **4:**87, 87*f*, **6:**185, 186,
        221, **8:**207–209, 208*f*, 264, **9:**243–244, 244*f*
    diagnosis/screening/testing for, **1:**13–14, 279, **9:**243,
        247–248
    false-positive treponemal tests for, **1:**13, **9:**247
    in HIV infection/AIDS, **1:**14, **5:**361, **9:**246, 247, 248,
        249, 309–310
    keratitis in, **4:**87, 87*f*, **6:**185, 186, 221, **8:**207–209, 208*f*,
        264, **9:**243, 244*f*
    latent, **1:**12–13, **9:**244, 248*t*
    optic nerve involvement and, **5:**144
    pars planitis and, **9:**136
    primary, **1:**12, **9:**244, 247, 248*t*
    secondary, **1:**12, **9:**244, 248*t*
    tertiary, **1:**13, **9:**244, 248*t*
    treatment of, **1:**14, 14*t*, **9:**248–249, 248*t*
Syphilitic posterior placoid chorioretinitis, **9:**245, 246*f*,
    309–310
Syringomas, **4:**221, 221*f*, **7:**161, 161*f*
Systemic drug therapy, for ocular disorders, **2:**328–330
    corticosteroids for uveitis and, **9:**104–105
Systemic lupus erythematosus, **1:**167–170, 168*f*, 169*t*,
    9:140–143, 141*f*, 141*t*, 142*f*
    choroidal perfusion abnormalities and, **12:**179
    eyelid manifestations of, **4:**213*t*
    HLA association in, **1:**167, **9:**140
    optic nerve involvement and, **5:**144
    refractive surgery contraindicated in, **13:**184
    retinal manifestations of, **9:**141–142, 141*f*, 142*f*,
        12:195–196, 195*f*
Systemic sclerosis, progressive (scleroderma),
    1:173–174
    eyelid manifestations of, **4:**213*t*
Systemic/visceral/nodal lymphoma. *See also*
    Lymphomas
    eye involvement and, **4:**140–142, 141*f*, 142*f*, 143*f*,
        323–325, 323*f*, 325*f*
Systole (systolic phase), **1:**117
Systolic dysfunction, **1:**117
    causes of, **1:**116
    management of, **1:**118–119

T

T. *See* Transducin
T1 (spin-lattice/longitudinal relaxation time), **5:**70, 72,
    7:26–27
T1-weighted images, **5:**72, 73*f*, 73*t*, 74*f*, 75*f*, 76*f*, 76*t*,
    7:27*f*, 28
T2 (spin-spin/transverse relaxation time), **5:**70, 72,
    7:27–28
T2-weighted images, **5:**72, 72–73, 73*f*, 73*t*, 74*f*, 75*f*, 76*t*,
    77*f*, 78*f*, **7:**28

T$_3$. *See* Triiodothyronine
T$_4$. *See* Thyroxine
T4/T8 ratio, in HIV infection/AIDS, **1:**29. *See also* CD4$^+$
    T cells; CD8$^+$ T cells
T-20. *See* Enfuvirtide
T-cell lymphomas
    intraocular, **9:**281. *See also* Primary intraocular/
        central nervous system lymphomas
    orbital, **4:**24, **7:**80. *See also* Lymphomas
T-cell signaling inhibitors, for uveitis, **9:**108*t*, 111–112
T cells (T lymphocytes), **1:**5, **4:**9, **9:**12. *See also specific
    type*
    activation of, **9:**37–38, 40*f*, 42
    in anaphylactic/atopic (type I) reactions, **8:**179–180
    in cell-mediated immunity, **1:**5, **8:**180, **9:**48–51, 49*f*,
        50*t*. *See also* Lymphocyte-mediated immune
        effector responses
    class I MHC molecules as antigen-presenting
        platform for, **9:**37, 38*f*
    class II MHC molecules as antigen-presenting
        platform for, **9:**37, 39*t*
    cytotoxic, **9:**42*f*, 43, 51, 53*f*
        in viral conjunctivitis, **9:**60
    delayed hypersensitivity (DH), **9:**42–43, 42*f*, 48–51,
        49*f*, 50*t*
    differentiation of, **9:**39–41
    in external eye, **8:**96, 174*t*
    helper. *See* T helper cells
    in herpetic stromal keratitis, **8:**114
    in HIV infection/AIDS, **1:**29, **8:**130, **9:**305
    in immune processing, **9:**38–39, 40*f*
    killer, **8:**180. *See also* Killer cells
    in poison ivy, **9:**34, 35
    primary versus secondary immune response and,
        9:43–44
    regulatory (suppressor). *See* Regulatory (suppressor)
        T cells
    in Sjögren syndrome, **8:**63
    in sympathetic ophthalmia, **9:**52–53, 181
    in tuberculosis, **9:**35
    in viral conjunctivitis, **9:**60
    in Vogt-Koyanagi-Harada (VKH) syndrome,
        9:183
T helper cells. *See also specific type*
    in anaphylactic/atopic (type I) reactions, **8:**179
    class II MHC molecules as antigen-presenting
        platform for, **9:**37, 39*f*
    in delayed hypersensitivity (type IV) reactions, **8:**180,
        9:42–43, 42*f*, 48–51, 49*f*, 50*t*
        sympathetic ophthalmia and, **9:**52–53
        Toxocara granuloma and, **9:**52
    differentiation of, **9:**39–41
    in external eye, **8:**174*t*
    in HIV infection/AIDS, **1:**29, **9:**305
    in immune processing, **9:**38–39, 40*f*
    in Vogt-Koyanagi-Harada (VKH) syndrome,
        9:183
T helper-0 cells, **9:**39
T helper-1 cells, **8:**177, **9:**39
    in delayed hypersensitivity (type IV) reactions, **8:**180,
        9:43, 50, 50*t*
        sympathetic ophthalmia and, **9:**52–53
    in Vogt-Koyanagi-Harada (VKH) syndrome,
        9:183

T helper-2 cells, **9**:39–40
    in anaphylactic/atopic (type I) reactions, **8**:179
    in delayed hypersensitivity (type IV) reactions, **9**:43,
        50
        Toxocara granuloma and, **9**:52
T helper-17 cells, **9**:40
T-lymphocyte antigen receptors, **9**:38, 38*f*, 39*f*, 51
T lymphocytes. *See* T cells
T pallidum hemagglutination assay (TPHA), **1**:13
t test (Student *t* test), **1**:320
T waves, in ischemic heart disease, **1**:102, 104
TABO convention, **3**:97*f*
Taches de bougie, in sarcoidosis, **9**:175
Tachyarrhythmias, **1**:123–127
    heart failure and, **1**:120
    supraventricular, **1**:124*t*
    ventricular, **1**:125–127
Tachycardia, **1**:123
    junctional, **1**:124*t*
    narrow-complex, **1**:123
    sinus, **1**:124*t*
    supraventricular, **1**:123–124, 124*t*
    ventricular, **1**:123, 125–126, 126*t*
    wide-complex, **1**:123
Tachyphylaxis
    with α-agonists, **10**:169
    with β-blockers, **10**:167
Tachyzoites, in toxoplasmosis transmission, **6**:181
Tacrolimus, **1**:187, **9**:108*t*, 112
    for allergic conjunctivitis, **8**:187
    for atopic dermatitis, **8**:185
    for Behçet disease, **9**:195
    for corneal graft rejection, **8**:430
    for graft-vs-host disease, **8**:203
    for Thygeson superficial punctate keratitis, **8**:206
    for uveitis, **9**:108*t*, 112
TACSTD2 gene, in gelatinous droplike corneal
    dystrophy, **8**:269*t*, 274
Tactile aids, for low vision patient, **3**:301
Tactile tension, for intraocular pressure estimation, **10**:26
Tadalafil, ocular effects of, **1**:302*t*
Tadpole pupil, **5**:263
Taenia solium (pork tapeworm), **8**:142, **9**:237
    orbital infection caused by, **4**:235, **7**:47
Tafluprost, **10**:162*t*, 166
Takayasu arteritis (aortic arch arteritis/aortitis
    syndrome/pulseless disease), **1**:176–178, 177*t*
Tambocor. *See* Flecainide
Tamiflu. *See* Oseltamivir
Tamoxifen, **1**:242*t*
    cataract risk and, **11**:49
    ocular effects of, **1**:302*t*
    retinopathy caused by, **12**:268, 268*f*
Tamsulosin
    intraoperative floppy iris syndrome and, **11**:74, 154,
        155
    ocular effects of, **1**:301*t*
Tandem repeats
    short, **2**:161, 180, 181*f*
    variable/variable number of (minisatellites), **2**:156,
        166, 180
Tandem scanning confocal microscopy, **8**:36. *See also*
    Confocal microscopy

Tangent screen, **5**:99
    for central visual field assessment, **3**:292, 293
    in nonorganic ophthalmic disorder evaluation,
        5:313–314, 315*f*
    in strabismus/amblyopia evaluation, **6**:83
Tangential incisions, for keratorefractive surgery, **13**:21,
    21*f*
Tangential power (instantaneous radius of curvature),
    8:40, 41*f*, **13**:11, 12*f*
Tangier disease, **8**:310
TAO (thyroid-associated orbitopathy). *See* Thyroid eye
    disease
Tap biopsy of vitreous. *See* Vitreous biopsy
TAP (Treatment of Age-Related Macular Degeneration
    with Photodynamic Therapy) Study, **12**:72, 75*f*,
    344
Tapazole. *See* Methimazole
Tapetal retinal reflex, in cone dystrophies, **12**:232, 233
Tapeworms
    dog *(Echinococcus granulosus)*, orbital infection
        caused by, **4**:235, **7**:47
    eye invaded by, **7**:47, **9**:237–239, 238*f*
    pork *(Taenia solium)*, **8**:142, **9**:237
        orbital infection caused by, **4**:235, **7**:47
Tapioca melanoma, **4**:271*t*
Tarantula hairs, ocular inflammation caused by, **8**:362
Tardive dyskinesia
    blepharospasm and, **5**:289
    facial movements and, **5**:292
Target, in microarray, **4**:41
Target recognition/selection, smooth pursuit
    movements and, **5**:41
Targocid. *See* Teicoplanin
Tarka. *See* Verapamil
Tarsal conjunctiva, **8**:4. *See also* Conjunctiva
    in superior limbic keratoconjunctivitis, **8**:81, 82
Tarsal ectropion, **7**:193
Tarsal fracture operation, for cicatricial entropion,
    7:198–199, 199*f*
Tarsal glands, **2**:23, 23*f*, 28, 29*f*, 237, 239*f*. *See also*
    Glands of Wolfring; Meibomian glands
Tarsal kink, **6**:176–177, **7**:150
Tarsal muscles
    inferior, **7**:140
    superior (Müller), **2**:23*f*, 25*f*, 28, **4**:186, 205, **5**:63, 64,
        64*f*, **7**:135*f*, 138, 139–140
        in Horner syndrome, **5**:266, **7**:207
        internal (transconjunctival) resection of, for ptosis
           correction, **7**:212
Tarsal plates/tarsus, **2**:25*f*, 27, 28, 29*f*, **4**:205, 206*f*, **7**:135*f*,
    140–141, 140*f*, **8**:4, 5*f*
    sebaceous adenocarcinoma arising in, **4**:221, **7**:173,
        174
Tarsal strip procedure
    for cicatricial ectropion, **7**:193
    for involutional ectropion, **7**:190, 192, 192*f*
    for involutional entropion, **7**:196
Tarsoconjunctival grafts
    for chemical injuries, **8**:358
    for cicatricial entropion, **7**:199
    for eyelid repair, **7**:180, 183*f*, 184, 185*f*, 186
Tarsoconjunctival müllerectomy (Fasanella-Servat
    procedure), for ptosis correction, **7**:212

Tarsorrhaphy, 8:390–391
  for chemical injuries, 8:358
  for craniosynostosis-induced corneal exposure,
    6:389
  for dry eye, 8:60t, 62
  for exposure keratopathy, 8:80
  for eyelid burns, 7:181
  for eyelid retraction, 7:215
  for neurotrophic keratopathy, 8:88
  for paralytic ectropion, 7:216, 217f
  for persistent corneal epithelial defects, 8:87
  in thyroid eye disease, 5:334, 7:215
Tarsotomy
  for cicatricial entropion, 7:198–199, 199f
  for trichiasis, 8:89
Tarsus. See Tarsal plates/tarsus
Task analysis, in low vision assessment, 3:289
TASS. See Toxic anterior segment syndrome
TATA box, 2:161
Tattoo, corneal, 8:337t, 405
τ (implicit time), in electroretinogram, 12:34, 34f
Tau proteins, in Alzheimer disease, 1:267
Taxol. See Paclitaxel
Taxon-specific crystallins, 2:276
Tay-Sachs disease (GM$_2$ gangliosidosis type I), 2:213t,
  6:303, 398, 401t, 8:310, 12:262, 263f
  racial and ethnic concentration of, 2:210–211
  retinal degeneration and, 12:262, 263f
Tazicef. See Ceftazidime
Tazidime. See Ceftazidime
Tazobactam, 1:59. See also specific antibiotic
  combination
Tazolol, 2:259t
TB. See Tuberculosis
TBCD. See Thiel-Behnke corneal dystrophy
TBG. See Thyroxine-binding globulin
TBII. See Thyroid-binding inhibitory immunoglobulins
TBUT. See Tear breakup time
3TC. See Lamivudine
Tc-99. See under Technetium-99
TCA cycle. See Tricarboxylic acid (TCA) cycle
TCF8, in posterior polymorphous corneal dystrophy,
  8:293
TCOF1 gene, in Treacher Collins syndrome, 6:394
Td vaccine, 1:284
  in combination vaccines, 1:285
Tdap vaccine, 1:269, 284
TDF. See Testis-determining factor
TE (time to echo), 5:70, 72
Tear breakup, 8:52
Tear breakup time, 8:52–53
  fluorescein in evaluation of, 7:257, 8:17, 52–53
  in pseudoepiphora evaluation, 7:257
  refractive surgery and, 13:35, 36f
Tear deficiency states, 2:244–246, 245f, 246f. See also
  specific type and Dry-eye syndrome
  aqueous, 2:244–245, 8:49–50, 50f, 51, 51f, 52,
    55–65
  evaporative tear dysfunction, 8:51, 51f, 52, 65–75
  mucin, 2:241, 244
  refractive surgery and, 13:35, 36f
  rose bengal in evaluation of, 8:17
  tests of, 8:53–54, 54f, 54t

Tear film (tears), 2:237–246, 238f, 238t, 239f, 8:175–177,
  177t
  aqueous layer of, 2:42, 237, 238f
    secretion of, 2:239–240, 239f
  biochemistry and metabolism of, 2:237–246
  bloody, 8:76
  composition of, 7:244
    assays of, 8:54–55
  contact lens optics and, 3:169
  dysfunction/alterations of, 2:244–246, 245f, 246f. See
    also Tear deficiency states
    decreased vision/transient visual loss and, 5:111,
      175
    illusions caused by, 5:188
  evaluation of, 8:52–55, 53f, 54f, 54t
    fluorescein for, 8:17
    in ptosis, 6:179, 7:202
  in external eye defense, 8:3, 95
  hypersecretion of (lacrimation), 7:256. See also Tearing
  immune response/immunologic features of,
    8:175–177, 177t
  inspection in evaluation of, 8:52–53, 53f
  instability of, 8:48–49, 49–50, 50f
  lipid layer of, 2:42, 237–239, 238f, 238t, 239f
  mucin layer of, 2:42, 238f
  osmolarity of, 8:54
  pH of, 2:238t, 240
  precorneal, 2:42, 237
  preocular, 2:237
  refractive index of, 8:38
  secretion of, 2:239–240, 239f, 241–244, 242f, 243f
    tests of, 8:53–54, 54f, 54t
  solutes in, 2:240
  thickness of, 2:237, 238f, 238t
Tear hyperosmolarity, dry eye and, 8:49–50, 50f
Tear (fluid) lens, contact lenses and, 3:169, 173–174,
  174f, 175
  fitting and, 3:183, 185
Tear meniscus (marginal tear strip), 2:237
  inspection of, 8:52
  in pseudoepiphora evaluation, 7:257
Tear pump, 7:136, 246, 247f
  evaluation of function of, 7:258
  ocular medication absorption affected by, 2:324
Tear sac. See Lacrimal sac
"Tear star," 8:336
Tearing/epiphora, 7:256, 257. See also specific cause
  acquired, 7:256–270
    evaluation of, 7:256–262, 259f, 260f, 261f
  in canalicular disorders
    acquired, 7:263–265
    congenital, 7:250
  chewing causing (crocodile tears), 5:285
  congenital, 6:203, 206, 7:249–256
    evaluation of, 6:206, 7:249
  conjunctival inflammation causing, 8:20t
  in craniosynostosis, 6:391–392
  in dacryocystocele, 7:255–256, 256f
  diagnostic tests for evaluation of, 7:258–262, 259f,
    260f, 261f
  examination in patient with, 7:257–258
  history in patient with, 7:256–257
  lacrimal outflow evaluation in patient with, 7:258

in nasolacrimal duct obstruction
    acquired, 7:266–270, 269f, 270f
    congenital, 6:206, 208, 7:250–255, 252f, 253f, 254f
in primary congenital glaucoma, 6:203, 234, 235t,
    10:143
    differential diagnosis and, 10:144, 144t
pseudoepiphora evaluation and, 7:257–258
in punctal disorders, 6:203
    acquired, 7:262–263
    congenital, 7:250
reflex, 2:106–107, 106f, 241, 242
    absorption of ocular medication affected by, 2:323,
        327
    initiation of, 2:140
    in uveitis, 9:84, 84t
Tears (artificial), 2:245, 390–391. See also Lubricants
    for allergic conjunctivitis, 8:186
    for corneal exposure in facial palsy, 5:288
    for dry eye, 2:245, 390–391, 8:57, 58, 60t
    for exposure keratopathy, 8:80
    for paralytic ectropion, 7:216
    for Stevens-Johnson syndrome, 6:201, 8:196
    for Thygeson superficial punctate keratitis, 8:206
Tears (retinal). See Retinal tears
Technetium-99 pyrophosphate scintigraphy, in ischemic
    heart disease, 1:106
Technetium-99m sestamibi scintigraphy, in ischemic
    heart disease, 1:106
Technetium-99m thyroid scanning, 1:210
Tecnis intraocular lens, 3:228, 13:144, 155
Tectonic graft, lamellar, for keratoglobus, 8:303
Tectonic penetrating keratoplasty
    for herpetic eye disease complications, 8:117
    for peripheral ulcerative keratitis, 8:213
Teczem. See Diltiazem
TED. See Thyroid eye disease
Teenagers. See Adolescents
Tegopen. See Cloxacillin
Tegretol/Tegretol XR. See Carbamazepine
Teichoic acid, in bacterial cell wall, 8:132
Teicoplanin, 1:51t, 60
Tekturna. See Aliskiren
Telangiectasias
    in ataxia-telangiectasia (Louis-Bar syndrome), 5:344,
        345f, 6:378–379, 379f, 8:77
    capillary, 1:97
    conjunctival, 5:344, 345f, 6:378, 379f
    hereditary hemorrhagic (Osler-Weber-Rendu
        disease), 1:153, 8:76
    retinal, 12:143–145, 144f. See also Coats disease
        parafoveal (juxtafoveal), 12:145–147, 145f, 146f
    in rosacea, 8:69
    in scleroderma, 1:173
Telecanthus, 6:174, 386, 7:22
    in blepharophimosis syndrome, 6:178, 179f, 7:145
Telecentricity, 3:80
Teleopsia, 5:189
Telescopes
    as afocal systems, 3:81–83, 81f, 82f, 83f
    astronomical (Keplerian), 3:81–83, 82f, 83f, 252
        in operating microscope, 3:262, 262f
        in slit-lamp biomicroscope, 3:82f, 252
    binocular, 3:300, 301f

diffraction and, 3:14
Galilean, 3:81–83, 81f, 83f, 252
    contact lens correction of aphakia and, 3:171,
        171–172
    in operating microscope, 3:262, 262f, 263
    reverse
        contact lens correction of aphakia and, 3:171,
            171–172
        in slit-lamp biomicroscope, 3:252
    in slit-lamp biomicroscope, 3:81, 81f, 251f, 252
Keplerian. See Telescopes, astronomical
lenses for, 3:81, 81f, 82, 82f
    in low vision/vision rehabilitation, 3:299–300, 301f
    monocular, 3:299–300
    in operating microscope, 3:262, 262f, 263
    in slit-lamp biomicroscope, 3:81, 81f, 251f, 252
    spectacle-mounted, 3:300
Television, closed-circuit, 3:302–303, 302f
Telithromycin, 1:50t, 61, 64
Teller acuity cards, 6:62, 63f, 73, 170
Telmisartan, 1:76t, 78t
Telomeres/telomeric DNA, 2:162, 166
Telorbitism (hypertelorism), 6:173, 384, 7:22
    in craniosynostosis, 7:35
Telzir. See Fosamprenavir
Temafloxacin, 1:52t, 61, 2:371
Temazepam, 1:254
Temperature
    anterior segment injury and, 8:351–352
    refractive index affected by, 3:40
Temporal approach clear ("near clear") technique, for
    cataract surgery, 11:114
Temporal (giant cell) arteritis. See Arteritis, giant cell
Temporal artery
    deep, 5:15f
    eyelids supplied by, 7:143
    posterior, 5:22f
    superficial, 5:12, 14f, 15f, 19
Temporal bone, 5:7
Temporal (longitudinal) coherence, 3:8, 8f
Temporal crescent, 5:34, 35f, 169, 171, 172f
Temporal fascia
    deep, 7:132f, 134
    superficial, 7:131, 132f
Temporal fossa, 5:7, 11f
Temporal lobe, 5:28f
    lesions of, 5:103f, 168, 169f
        epilepsy and, 1:261
        hallucinations and, 5:190–191
        resection of, for seizures, 1:263
        visual field defects and, 5:168
Temporal lobe seizures, 1:261
Temporal nerve, 5:61, 7:133, 134f. See also Frontal/
    temporal nerve
Temporal veins, eyelids drained by, 7:143
Temporal wedge, in glaucoma, 10:68
Temporalis muscle, 7:132f, 133, 133f
Temporin A/temporin L, 1:64
Temporofacial trunk, of cranial nerve VII (facial), 2:106,
    5:61
Temporomandibular joint disease, 5:302
Temporoparietal fascia (superficial temporal fascia),
    7:131, 132f

TEN. *See* Toxic epidermal necrolysis
Tenacious proximal fusion, in intermittent exotropia, 6:100–101
Tendency-oriented perimeter (TOP) algorithm, 10:57
Tenecteplase, for ST-segment elevation acute coronary syndrome, 1:113
Tenectomy, 6:148t
Tenex. *See* Guanfacine
Teniposide, 1:239
Tenofovir, 1:33, 34
Tenon capsule, 2:35, 4:47, 6:19, 20, 20f, 21f
    extraocular muscle surgery and, 6:25
        advancement of, 6:157
            excessive, 6:157
        scarring of (adherence syndrome), 6:158
Tenoretic. *See* Atenolol
Tenormin. *See* Atenolol
Tenotomy, 6:148t
    superior oblique
        for Brown syndrome, 6:131–132
        for superior oblique myokymia, 6:142–143
        for third nerve (oculomotor) paralysis, 6:133
Tensilon. *See* Edrophonium
Tensilon test. *See also* Edrophonium
    for myasthenia gravis diagnosis, 2:342–343, 5:239–240, 6:138, 138f, 139t, 7:209
Tension rings, capsular, for zonular incompetence, 11:198, 199
Tension-type headache, 5:298, 299
Tensor fascia lata, autogenous and banked, for frontalis suspension, 6:179, 7:212
Tentorium, inferior hypophyseal artery of, 5:16
Tenzel semicircular rotation flap/modified Tenzel flap, in lower eyelid repair, 7:184, 186
Tequin. *See* Gatifloxacin
Terak. *See* Oxytetracycline, with polymyxin B
Teratogens, 2:141
    congenital anomalies caused by, 2:141–143, 142f
Teratoid medulloepitheliomas, 4:184
Teratomas, 4:6, 7f
    orbital, 7:37
        in children, 6:344–345, 345f
Terazosin, 1:77t
    intraoperative floppy iris syndrome and, 11:74, 155
Terbinafine, 1:54t, 65
Terbutaline, 1:144, 145t
Teriparatide, for osteoporosis, 1:231
Terminal web, 2:46f, 47, 65f
Termination codon (stop codon), 2:161
    frameshift mutation and, 2:152
Terrien marginal degeneration, 8:339–340, 340f
Terson syndrome, 5:351, 351f, 12:155
Tertiary positions of gaze, 6:28
Tertiary vitreous, 2:132, 4:132
Tesla, 5:70
Test–retest reliability, 1:339
Testing distance, 3:109, 109f
Testis-determining factor (TDF/sex-determining region Y/SRY), 2:218
Tetanic cataract, 11:57
Tetanus, immunization against, 1:284
Tetanus and diphtheria toxoid vaccine (Td vaccine), 1:284
    in combination vaccines, 1:285

Tetanus immunoglobulin, 1:284
Tetracaine, 2:387t, 389
    for cataract surgery, 11:99
    maximum safe dose of, 1:298t
Tetracyclines, 1:44, 51t, 62, 2:374–375. *See also specific agent*
    for chemical injuries, 8:358
    for chlamydial conjunctivitis, 8:157
    intravenous administration of, 2:329
    for meibomian gland dysfunction, 8:68
    ocular effects of, 1:301t
    for ophthalmia neonatorum prophylaxis, 6:188
    for persistent corneal defects/neurotrophic keratopathy, 8:86, 88
    for recurrent corneal erosions, 8:84
    for rosacea, 8:69–70
    for trachoma, 8:156
Tetrafilcon, for contact lenses, 3:177t
Tetrahydrotriamcinolone, anti-inflammatory/pressure-elevating potency of, 2:360t
Tetrahydrozoline, 2:392
Tetravac. *See* DTacP-IPV vaccine
Tetravisc. *See* Tetracaine
Teveten. *See* Eprosartan
TGF-βs. *See* Transforming growth factor βs
TGFBI gene, corneal dystrophies associated with, 8:268t, 269t
    epithelial basement membrane, 8:269t, 270
    granular type 1, 4:96, 8:281
    granular type 2, 8:269t, 282
    lattice, 4:97, 8:269t, 278
    Reis-Bücklers, 8:269t, 276
    stromal, 8:278–282, 278t
    Thiel-Behnke, 8:269t, 277
Th0 cells. *See* T helper-0 cells
Th1 cells. *See* T helper-1 cells
Th2 cells. *See* T helper-2 cells
Th17 cells. *See* T helper-17 cells
Thalamic esodeviations, 5:222t, 223
    esotropia, convergence spasm and, 5:214
Thalamostriate arteries, 5:23
Thalamus, 5:28f, 39f, 41
Thalassemia, 1:148–149
    α, 1:148
    β, 1:148
        angioid streaks in, 12:84
        bone marrow transplantation for, 1:147, 148–149
    sickle cell, 12:116, 117t
Thalidomide, for HIV infection/AIDS, 1:36
Thallium-201 myocardial scintigraphy, 1:106
The Arc of the United States, 6:418t
Theo-Cap/Theo-Dur/Theo-Time. *See* Theophylline
Theochron. *See* Theophylline
Theophylline, 1:144, 145t
Theoretical formulas, for IOL power determination, 3:212–213, 212f, 217–219. *See also* Power prediction formulas, for IOLs
    errors in, 3:221
    for postkeratorefractive eye, 3:221–222
Theques, 4:65
Therapeutic contact lenses, 3:193–194. *See also* Bandage contact lenses

Therapeutic lifestyle changes (TLCs). *See* Lifestyle modification
Thermal cautery
  for involutional ectropion, **7**:190
  for involutional entropion, **7**:196
  for punctal occlusion, **7**:271, **8**:61, 61*f*, 62
Thermal injury (burns)
  anterior segment, **8**:351–352
  cataract surgery incision, **11**:149
  in children, **6**:407
  eyelid, **7**:181
  retinal, light causing, **12**:332
Thermal laser photocoagulation. *See* Photocoagulation
Thermokeratoplasty, **13**:22, 22*f*, 119
  corneal transplantation after, **13**:192
  laser, **13**:4*t*, 22, 22*f*, 120
  radial, **13**:119
Thermotherapy, transpupillary, **12**:343
  for age-related macular degeneration/choroidal neovascularization, **12**:79, 343
  for melanoma, **4**:285, **12**:343
  for metastatic eye disease, **4**:322
Thiabendazole, for diffuse unilateral subacute neuroretinitis, **9**:241
Thiamine deficiency, optic neuropathy caused by, **5**:154
Thiazide diuretics
  for heart failure, **1**:118, 119
  for hypertension, **1**:69, 75, 76*t*, 80
  ocular effects of, **1**:302*t*
Thiazolidinediones, **1**:199*t*, 201
Thick lenses, **3**:76–78, 78*f*
Thickness of retinal reflex, **3**:124, 124*f*
  in axis determination, **3**:126, 127*f*
Thiel-Behnke corneal dystrophy, **8**:268*t*, 270*t*, 277–278, 278*f*
  genetics of, **8**:269*t*, 277
Thimerosal
  allergic/sensitivity/toxic reactions and, **2**:322, **8**:92, 360
  in MMR vaccine, **1**:282
Thin-lens approximation, **3**:66
Thin-lens equation (TLE), **3**:66
Thin lenses, **3**:66
  in afocal system, **3**:80–81
  negative, **3**:72*f*, 73
Thioflavin T stain, **4**:31*t*
Thiopental, perioperative, **1**:311
Thiopurine S-methyltransferase (TPMT), azathioprine response and, **9**:109–110
Thioridazine
  lens changes caused by, **11**:49
  ocular side effects of, **1**:252
  retinal degeneration caused by, **12**:267–268, 268*f*
Third cranial nerve. *See* Cranial nerve III
Third-degree atrioventricular block, **1**:122*t*
Third nerve (oculomotor) palsy/paralysis, **5**:228–232, 228*f*, **6**:132–134, 133*f*
  aberrant nerve regeneration and, **5**:232, 232*f*, **6**:132
  aneurysm and, **5**:228–232, 228*f*, 229*f*, 273, 351
  anisocoria and, **5**:265*f*, 271–273
  diplopia and, **5**:223, 227
  divisional, **5**:231
  inferior oblique muscle paralysis caused by, **6**:121

  partial, **5**:230
  ptosis in, **7**:207, 208
  pupil-involving, **5**:229, 229*f*, 271–273
  pupil-sparing, **5**:230–231, **6**:132
  superior oblique muscle paralysis caused by, **6**:118
  surgery for, **6**:153
  in younger patients, **5**:231–232, **6**:132–134, 133*f*
Third-order neurons
  dilator muscle innervation and, **2**:60
  Horner syndrome caused by lesions of, **5**:267
13q14 (long arm 13 deletion) syndrome, **2**:204–205, 205*t*
30° test, **5**:135
30-Hz flicker response, **12**:34, 34*f*, 35, 36*f*
  vascular disease and, **12**:40, 41*f*
Thorazine. *See* Chlorpromazine
Three cone opsins, **2**:294. *See also* Color vision
Three-dimensional computed tomography, in orbital evaluation, **7**:26, 27*f*
3-mirror contact lens, Goldmann, for slit-lamp biomicroscopy, **3**:253, 254*f*
3 o'clock and 9 o'clock staining, **3**:185, 198, 198*f*
Three-point touch, for keratoconus, **3**:190, 191*f*
3-step test, **6**:83–86, 85*f*
  in fourth nerve (trochlear) palsy, **5**:233
  in inferior oblique muscle paralysis, **6**:121
  in superior oblique muscle paralysis, **6**:118, 119
3-zone bifocal intraocular lens, **3**:227
Threshold
  contrast, **3**:111, **5**:105
  genetic, **2**:162
    polygenic traits with, **2**:225
  minimum legible, **3**:108
  minimum separable, **3**:108
  minimum visible, **3**:108
  sensitivity, **5**:100
Threshold disease, in retinopathy of prematurity, **6**:283, 284*f*, **12**:163
  treatment criteria and, **6**:285–286, 286*f*
Threshold stimulus/testing (perimetry), **5**:100, **10**:54, 57, 58, 58*f*
Thrombi/thrombus. *See* Thrombosis/thrombotic disorders
Thrombin, **1**:152, **2**:393–394, **9**:24
Thrombin inhibitors, for non–ST-segment elevation acute coronary syndrome, **1**:111–112
Thrombocytopenia, **1**:154
  capillary hemangiomas and (Kasabach-Merritt syndrome), **6**:339, **7**:63
Thrombocytopenic purpura
  idiopathic, **1**:154
  thrombotic, **1**:154
    choroidal perfusion abnormalities and, **12**:179
Thrombolytic therapy, **1**:159
  for acute ischemic stroke, **1**:94
    emergency transport and, **1**:289, 291
  for ST-segment elevation acute coronary syndrome, **1**:113
Thrombophilia, **1**:157. *See also* Hypercoagulable states; Thrombosis/thrombotic disorders
  fetal loss/preeclampsia and, **1**:147
Thromboplastin time, activated partial (aPTT), **1**:152

Thrombopoietin, **1**:147
Thrombosis/thrombotic disorders, **1**:157. *See also* Hypercoagulable states
    antiphospholipid antibody syndrome and, **1**:158, 170, 171
    atrial fibrillation and, **1**:125
    branch retinal artery occlusion and, **12**:136–137, 136*f*, 137*f*
    central retinal artery occlusion and, **12**:139
    cerebral venous and dural sinus, **5**:356–358. *See also* Sinus thrombosis
    choroidal perfusion abnormalities and, **12**:179
    fetal loss/preeclampsia and, **1**:147, 158
    after PCI with stenting, **1**:109
    retinal vasculitis and, **12**:141
    stroke and, **1**:92
        in diabetes mellitus, **1**:207
    in thrombotic thrombocytopenic purpura, **1**:154
Thrombospondin I, in vitreous, **2**:287
Thrombotic thrombocytopenic purpura, **1**:154
    choroidal perfusion abnormalities and, **12**:179
Thromboxanes, **2**:255, 256, 257
    aspirin affecting, **2**:362
ThT (thioflavin T) stain, **4**:31*t*
Thygeson superficial punctate keratitis, **8**:204–207, 206*f*
Thymectomy, for myasthenia gravis, **5**:331
Thymoxamine, **2**:259*t*, 260, 348
    angle closure prevention and, **10**:119
Thyroglobulin, **1**:208
    antibodies to, **1**:210
Thyroid-associated ophthalmopathy/orbitopathy. *See* Thyroid eye disease
Thyroid-binding inhibitory immunoglobulins, in thyroid eye disease, **7**:48
Thyroid biopsy, **1**:210
Thyroid carcinoma, **1**:213–214
    retinoblastoma associated with, **4**:314*t*
Thyroid disease, **1**:208–214. *See also* Thyroid eye disease
    hyperthyroidism, **1**:210–212
    hypothyroidism, **1**:212
    in older patients, **1**:233
    physiology of, **1**:208
    screening/testing for, **1**:208–210, **7**:32
    smoking and, **1**:211, **5**:333, **6**:135, **7**:52
    thyroiditis, **1**:212–213, **7**:47, 48, 51
    tumors, **1**:213–214
Thyroid eye disease, **1**:211, **4**:232, 233*f*, **5**:331–334, 332*f*, **6**:135–136, 136*f*, 139*t*, **7**:47–55, 47*f*, 48*f*, 52*t*, 53*t*, 56
    antithyroid antibodies and, **1**:211, **7**:48, 50
    in children, **6**:135–136, 136*f*, 139*t*
    clinical presentation and diagnosis of, **7**:47, 47*f*, 48–49, 48*f*, 49*f*, 51
    diplopia caused by, **5**:238, 333, 334
    epidemiology of, **7**:50–51
    extraocular myopathy in, **4**:232, **5**:332*f*, 333, **6**:135, **7**:49, 49*f*, 51
    eye movements affected in, **4**:232, **5**:238, **7**:23–24
    eyelid abnormalities and, **5**:332, 332*f*, **7**:24, 47, 47*f*, 51
        management and, **5**:334, **7**:53, 53*t*, 54, 55
        retraction, **4**:232, 233*f*, **5**:276, 278*f*, 281, 332, 332*f*, **7**:47*f*, 49, 51, 54, 213–214, 214*f*, 215

    glaucoma and, **10**:28
    myasthenia gravis and, **7**:51, 209
    neuroimaging in evaluation of, **5**:82*t*, 332*f*, 333
    neuro-ophthalmic signs of, **5**:331–334, 332*f*
    in older patients, **1**:233
    optic neuropathy in, **5**:147–149, 148*f*, 333, **7**:49, 51, 53–54
    pathogenesis of, **4**:232, **7**:50
    prognosis of, **7**:52–55
    proptosis and, **4**:232, 233*f*, **5**:332, 332*f*, **7**:23, 47*f*, 49
        in children/adolescents, **6**:135, 136, 136*f*, 346, 347*f*
        eyelid retraction differentiated from, **7**:213–214
        radioactive iodine treatment affecting, **7**:52–53
            orbital disease exacerbation and, **5**:333
        smoking and, **1**:211, **5**:333, **6**:135, **7**:52
        strabismus and, **5**:238, **6**:135–136, 136*f*, 139*t*
        superior limbic keratoconjunctivitis and, **8**:81–82, 82*f*
        thyroid function tests in, **5**:333, **7**:32
        treatment of, **5**:333–334, **7**:52–55, 52*t*, 53*t*
        von Graefe sign in, **7**:24
Thyroid follicles, **1**:208
Thyroid function tests, **5**:333, **7**:32
Thyroid hormone–binding protein tests, **1**:209
Thyroid hormones, **1**:208
    measurement of, **1**:208–209
Thyroid medications, in perioperative setting, **1**:306
Thyroid microsomal (antimicrosomal) antibody
    testing for, **1**:210
    in thyroid eye disease, **7**:48
Thyroid nodules, **1**:213
Thyroid ophthalmopathy/orbitopathy/thyroid-related
    immune orbitopathy. *See* Thyroid eye disease
Thyroid scanning, **1**:210
    for thyroid tumor identification, **1**:213
Thyroid-stimulating hormone. *See* Thyrotropin
Thyroid-stimulating immunoglobulins, in thyroid eye
    disease, **7**:48
Thyroid storm, **1**:210
Thyroid tumors, **1**:213–214
Thyroid ultrasound, **1**:210
Thyroiditis, **1**:212–213. *See also specific type*
    Hashimoto, thyroid eye disease and, **7**:47, 48, 51
Thyrotoxic exophthalmos. *See* Thyroid eye disease
Thyrotoxicosis. *See* Hyperthyroidism
Thyrotroph adenomas, **1**:215
Thyrotropin (thyroid-stimulating hormone/TSH), **1**:208
    receptor for
        antibodies to, **1**:210, 211
            in thyroid eye disease, **4**:232, **7**:48, 50
        in thyroid eye disease, **4**:232, **7**:50
            radioactive iodine treatment and, **7**:53
    serum levels of, **1**:209, **7**:32
Thyrotropin-releasing hormone, **1**:208, 214*t*
Thyroxine (T$_4$), **1**:208
    serum levels of, **1**:208–209, **7**:32
Thyroxine-binding globulin (TBG), **1**:208
    serum levels of, **1**:209
TI (interpulse time), **5**:70
Tiagabine, **1**:263*t*
TIAs. *See* Transient ischemic attacks

Tiazac. *See* Diltiazem
Tibia bone tissue keratoprosthesis, 8:432
Tic, facial (habit spasm), 5:292
Tic douloureux (trigeminal neuralgia), 5:59, 301–302
Ticar. *See* Ticarcillin
Ticarcillin, 1:46*t*, 57, 2:368*t*, 370
  with clavulanic acid, 1:59
Ticks, Lyme disease transmitted by, 1:14–15, 8:137,
  9:250, 12:210
Tigacyl. *See* Tigecycline
Tigecycline, 1:64
Tight junctions (zonulae occludentes)
  in ciliary body epithelium, 2:62, 265
  in corneal endothelium, 2:135
  in corneal epithelium, 8:6
  in retinal blood vessels, 2:78
  in retinal pigment epithelium, 2:72, 12:14
Tight lens syndrome, 3:199
Tight orbit, 7:105
TIGR/myocilin (TIGR/MYOC) gene, 10:11, 11*t*, 142
  in pediatric glaucoma, 6:233
TIGR protein, 10:11
Tilade. *See* Nedocromil
Tillaux, spiral of, 2:16, 18*f*, 5:55, 6:16, 18*f*
Tilted disc syndrome (Fuchs coloboma), 5:142–143,
  142*f*, 6:307, 307*f*
Time to echo (TE), 5:70, 72
Time to repetition (TR), 5:70, 72
Timentin. *See* Ticarcillin, with clavulanic acid
Timolide. *See* Timolol
Timolol, 2:259*t*, 350, 350*t*, 10:162*t*
  in children, 10:156
  cholesterol levels affected by, 1:139
  in combination preparations, 2:347*t*, 350, 352–353,
    352*t*, 355, 10:165*t*, 167, 173
  for glaucoma, 2:350, 350*t*, 352*t*, 10:162*t*, 168
    in children, 6:242, 10:156
    in combination preparations, 10:165*t*, 167, 173
  for hypertension, 1:76*t*, 78*t*
  during pregnancy/lactation, 10:176
  sustained-release preparation of, 2:330
  systemic absorption of, 2:325*f*
Timoptic. *See* Timolol
TIMP3 gene/TIMP3 protein mutation, 2:182, 297
  in Sorsby dystrophy, 12:241
Tinnitus, vestibular nystagmus and, 5:248, 249*t*, 250
TINU. *See* Tubulointerstitial nephritis and uveitis
  (TINU) syndrome
Tiotropium, 1:145, 145*t*
Tipranivir, 1:34
TIR. *See* Total internal reflection
Tirofiban, for ischemic heart disease, 1:109, 109*t*
  non–ST-segment elevation acute coronary syndrome,
    1:112
Tissue addition/subtraction techniques, 13:21, 22*f*, 53.
  See also specific procedure
Tissue adhesives
  cyanoacrylate, 8:403–404. *See also* Cyanoacrylate
    adhesives
  fibrin, for corneal autograft fixation, 8:394
Tissue factor pathway inhibitor, 1:152
Tissue–laser interactions, 3:25–26, 26*f*, 13:23
Tissue microarrays, 4:41, 42*f*

Tissue plasminogen activator, 1:91, 159, 2:334, 393, 9:24
  for acute ischemic stroke, 1:91, 94
  for central retinal vein occlusion, 12:133
  intraocular administration of, 2:328
  for ST-segment elevation acute coronary syndrome,
    1:113
  for submacular hemorrhage, 12:350, 350*f*
  in vitreous, 2:285
Tissue preparation
  for pathologic examination, 4:28–30, 29*t*, 30*f*, 31*t*
    fixatives for, 4:28–29, 29*t*
    processing and, 4:29
    special procedures and, 4:33–45, 34*t*
    staining and, 4:30, 30*f*, 31*t*
Tissue-resident macrophages, 9:11
Titmus test, in nonorganic ophthalmic disorder evaluation
  monocular no light perception and, 5:310
  monocular reduced vision and, 5:311, 311*t*
TK. *See* Transverse keratotomy
TKPro. *See* Tibia bone tissue keratoprosthesis
TLCs (therapeutic lifestyle changes). *See* Lifestyle
  modification
TLE. *See* Thin-lens equation
TLR2, 9:14
  in lipopolysaccharide-induced uveitis, 9:15
TLR4, 9:14
TMAb. *See* Thyroid microsomal (antimicrosomal)
  antibody
TMAs. *See* Tissue microarrays
TMC-125. *See* Etravirine
TMJ disease. *See* Temporomandibular joint disease
TMP-SMX. *See* Trimethoprim-sulfamethoxazole
TMVL. *See* Transient visual loss, monocular
TNF. *See* Tumor necrosis factor
TNKase. *See* Tenecteplase
TNM staging system
  for conjunctival carcinoma, 4:332–333*t*
  for conjunctival melanoma, 4:334–336*t*
  for eyelid carcinoma, 4:329–331*t*
  for lacrimal gland carcinoma, 4:345–347*t*
  for orbital sarcoma, 4:348–349*t*
  for retinoblastoma, 4:342–344*t*
  for uveal melanoma, 4:337–341*t*
TNO test, 6:87
"Tobacco dust" (Shafer sign), 12:286, 314
Tobacco use. *See also* Smoking
  cataract development and, 11:58–59, 67–68
  esophageal cancer and, 1:275
  optic neuropathy and, 5:154
  thyroid disease and, 5:333
Tobralcon. *See* Tobramycin
Tobramycin, 1:51*t*, 61–62, 2:368*t*, 372*t*, 375–376
  for bacterial keratitis, 8:162*t*
  in combination preparations, 2:373*t*
  ototoxicity of, mitochondrial DNA mutations and,
    2:176
Tobrasol. *See* Tobramycin
Tobrex. *See* Tobramycin
Tocainide, 1:123*t*
Tocilizumab, 1:186
α-Tocopherol. *See* Vitamin E
Todd paralysis, 1:262, 5:292
Tofranil. *See* Imipramine

Togaviruses, **8**:129
Tolbutamide, **1**:199*t*
Tolectin. *See* Tolmetin
Tolerance (drug), **1**:250
Tolerance (immunologic)
 corneal transplantation and, **8**:175, 408
 T regulatory cells in, **9**:40, 41
Toll-like receptors, **9**:14
 in lipopolysaccharide-induced uveitis, **9**:15
Tolmetin, **1**:183*t*, **2**:362*t*
 for uveitis in children, **6**:277
Tolosa-Hunt syndrome, **5**:236–237, 301
Tomato ketchup fundus, **4**:292, 293*f*
Tomography
 computed. *See* Computed tomography
 myocardial perfusion, **1**:106
 optical coherence. *See* Optical coherence
 tomography/biometry
Tomopenem, **1**:59
Tonic cells, **2**:298, 299*f*, 300
Tonic-clonic seizures, **1**:261
Tonic convergence, **6**:36
Tonic eye deviations, **5**:211–213
Tonic (slow twitch) fibers, **2**:21, 21*t*, **5**:55
Tonic pupil (Adie pupil), **5**:54, 265*f*, 270–271, 271*f*, 272*f*,
 316, **6**:229
 pharmacologic testing for, **2**:338, **5**:270–271, 272*f*, 316
Tono-Pen, **10**:26
 in infants and children, **10**:151
 for IOP measurement in children, **6**:236
 for IOP measurement after refractive surgery, **13**:97,
 112, 174, 194
Tonography, in aqueous outflow measurement, **10**:19
Tonometry (tonometer), **10**:22–26
 applanation. *See* Applanation tonometer/tonometry;
 Goldmann applanation tonometry
 corneal thickness affecting, **8**:30, **10**:24–25, 84, **13**:35,
 173, 194
 dynamic contour, **3**:258–259, 259*f*, **10**:25
 Goldmann, **10**:22–23, 23*f*, 24*f*
 in infants and children, **6**:236, **10**:150–151
 infection control and, **8**:46, **10**:26
 noncontact (air-puff), **10**:25
 infection control and, **10**:26
 Perkins, **10**:23
 in infants and children, **6**:236, **10**:151
 pneumatic (pneumotonometry/pneumotonometer),
 10:26
 in infants and children, **10**:151
 for IOP measurement after refractive surgery,
 13:97, 112, 174, 194
 after refractive surgery, **13**:35, 97, 112, 174, 194
 LASIK, **13**:35, 97, 112
 surface ablation, **13**:35, 97
 Schiøtz (indentation), **10**:19, 26
 sources of error in, **10**:23, 24*t*
TOP. *See* Tendency-oriented perimeter (TOP) algorithm
Topamax. *See* Topiramate
Topical anesthesia, **2**:386–390, 387*t*. *See also* Anesthesia
 (anesthetics), local
 for anterior segment surgery, **2**:389–390
 for cataract surgery, **11**:99–100
 for extraocular muscle surgery, **6**:160

 for foreign-body removal in children, **6**:5
 for phakic IOL insertion, **13**:129
 after surface ablation, **13**:86
Topical medications, **2**:323–327, 324*f*, 325*f*. *See also*
 Eyedrops
 sustained-release devices for, **2**:330–331
Topiramate, **1**:263*t*
 for idiopathic intracranial hypertension, **5**:124
 for migraine headache, **5**:298
 ophthalmic side effects of, **1**:245, 264, 301*t*
 glaucoma and, **6**:239, **10**:136–137, 137*f*
Topographical method, for IOL power calculation after
 refractive surgery, **11**:87
Topography, **2**:41–42, 41*f*, **4**:6
 anterior chamber, **2**:41–42, 41*f*, **4**:101–102, 101*f*,
 102*f*
 choroidal, **4**:186–187, 187*f*
 ciliary body, **2**:41*f*, **4**:186, 187*f*
 conjunctival, **4**:47, 48*f*
 corneal, **2**:41*f*, 42, 43, **3**:265–268, 266*f*, 267*f*, 268*f*,
 4:77–78, 78*f*, **8**:36–45, **9**:63, 63*f*, **13**:10–14,
 11*f*, 12*f*, 13*f*, 14*f*, 38–39, 38*f*. *See also* Cornea,
 topography of
 eyelid, **4**:205–206, 206*f*, 207*t*
 iris, **2**:41*f*, **4**:185–186, 186*f*
 lens, **2**:41*f*, **4**:119–120, 119*f*, 120*f*
 optic disc, **10**:50
 optic nerve, **4**:249, 250*f*
 orbital, **4**:229, **7**:5–8, 6*f*, 7*f*, 8*f*
 retinal, **2**:41*f*, 42, **4**:145–148, 146*f*, 147*f*
 retinal pigment epithelium, **4**:146*f*, 148
 scleral, **2**:41*f*, 42, **4**:111–112, 111*f*
 trabecular meshwork, **4**:101–102, 101*f*, 102*f*
 uveal tract, **2**:42, **4**:185–187, 185*f*, 186*f*, 187*f*
 vitreous, **2**:41*f*, 42, **4**:131–132
Toprol-XL. *See* Metoprolol
Toradol. *See* Ketorolac
TORCHES, **6**:181. *See also specific disorder*
 lymphocytic choriomeningitis virus causing,
 9:211–212
Torcular Herophili, **5**:26
Toric intraocular lenses, **3**:225, **11**:131, **13**:4*t*, 126,
 141–144, 142*f*
 complications associated with, **11**:169
Toric soft contact lenses, **3**:186–188, 187*t*, 188*f*
Toric spectacle lenses
 anterior (plus cylinder), **3**:311, 316
 posterior (minus cylinder), **3**:316
Toric surfaces, **3**:95–97, 96*f*
Torsades de pointes, **1**:125, 126*t*
Torsemide
 for heart failure, **1**:118
 for hypertension, **1**:76*t*
Torsion, **6**:29
Torsional deviations, **6**:11
Torsional fusional vergence, **6**:82
Torsional nystagmus, **5**:252
Torticollis, spasmus nutans and, **5**:247
Torulopsis candida, endophthalmitis caused by, **9**:270
Total cataract, **11**:34
Total internal reflection (TIR), **3**:12, 13, 46–49, 48*f*,
 49–50, 50*f*
 anterior chamber examination and, **3**:49, 50*f*

Total T$_4$, **1**:208, 209

Tourette syndrome, facial twitching and, **5**:292

Touton giant cells, **4**:7, 9*f*
  in juvenile xanthogranuloma, **4**:191, 191*f*, **6**:351, **9**:286

Toxemia of pregnancy. *See* Eclampsia; Preeclampsia

Toxic anterior segment syndrome (TASS), **11**:147, 151–152

Toxic conjunctivitis/keratoconjunctivitis
  contact lens solutions causing, **8**:92
  medications causing, **8**:359–361, 359*t*, 361*f*

Toxic dementia, **1**:265

Toxic epidermal necrolysis, **8**:196, 196*t*

Toxic goiter
  diffuse, **1**:211. *See also* Thyroid eye disease
  nodular, **1**:212

Toxic keratitis, **8**:360. *See also* Toxic conjunctivitis/keratoconjunctivitis

Toxic optic neuropathy, **1**:250, **5**:154–156, 155*f*

Toxic solutions, exposure to during cataract surgery, corneal edema caused by, **11**:147, 151–152

Toxic ulcerative keratopathy, **8**:86, 88

Toxicity
  drug therapy, **2**:321, 322–323
    aging and, **2**:323
    tissue binding and, **2**:327
  light. *See* Light toxicity/photic damage/phototoxicity

Toxocara (toxocariasis), **4**:305, **6**:273–274, **8**:142, **9**:235–237, 236*f*, 236*t*, 237*f*, **12**:209–210, 209*f*
  canis, **6**:273, **8**:142, **9**:52, 235, 239, **12**:209
  cati, **8**:142, **9**:235
  diffuse unilateral subacute neuroretinitis caused by, **9**:239, **12**:210
  granuloma caused by, **9**:52, 136, 235, 236*f*, 236*t*
  pars planitis and, **9**:136, 235
  retinoblastoma differentiated from, **4**:305, 305*t*
  uveitis in children caused by, **6**:273–274, 273*f*

Toxoplasma (toxoplasmosis), **1**:21–22, **6**:181–183, 182*f*, **8**:141, **9**:226–235, 227*f*, 229*f*, 230*f*, 231*f*, 233*f*
  acquired, **9**:228–229
  in children, **6**:181–183, 182*f*
  chorioretinitis caused by, **12**:206–209, 208*f*, 208*t*
  congenital, **1**:21, **6**:182, 182*f*, **9**:228, 229*f*, 230, 233, **12**:206–207
  Fuchs heterochromic iridocyclitis/uveitis in, **9**:134
  gondii, **1**:21, **6**:181, **8**:141, **9**:226–228, 227*f*, 230, 309, **12**:206
  in HIV infection/AIDS, **1**:39, **5**:362, **9**:228, 232, 233–234, 308–309, 309*f*, **12**:208
  ocular infection/inflammation caused by, **1**:21, **4**:153, 154*f*, **8**:141, **9**:226–235, 227*f*, 229*f*, 230*f*, 231*f*, 233*f*, 308–309, 309*f*
  during pregnancy, **1**:21, **9**:228, 233
  punctate outer retinal (PORT), **9**:230, 231*f*
  retinal, **4**:153, 154*f*, **12**:206–209, 208*f*, 208*t*
  transmission of, **9**:227–228
  treatment of, **1**:21, **12**:208–209, 208*t*
  uveitis in, **1**:21, **9**:226–235, 227*f*, 229*f*, 230*f*, 231*f*, 233*f*
  vitreous opacification and, **9**:302

Toys, for pediatric examination, **6**:3, 4*f*

tPA. *See* Tissue plasminogen activator

TPCD. *See* Typical peripheral cystoid degeneration

TPHA (*T pallidum* hemagglutination assay), **1**:13

TPMT. *See* Thiopurine S-methyltransferase

TR (time to repetition), **5**:70, 72

Trabectome, **10**:200

Trabecular meshwork, **2**:49*f*, 51*f*, 53–55, 53*f*, 55*f*, 56*f*, **10**:3*f*, 13, 17–18, 17*f*
  chemical injury of, glaucoma and, **10**:97
  congenital anomalies of, **4**:102–103, 103*f*, 104*f*
  corneoscleral, **2**:53, 54
  degenerations of, **4**:104–109, 110*f*
  development of, **2**:135, 136
  disorders of, **4**:101–109, 110*f*. *See also specific type*
  endothelial, **2**:54
  in exfoliation syndrome/pseudoexfoliation, **10**:38, 86
  in glaucoma, **4**:106–109, 110*f*, **10**:87, 88, 88*f*, 89, 97
  neovascularization and, **10**:125
  pigment in, **4**:109, 109*f*, 110*f*, **10**:17, 37–38
    in exfoliation syndrome/pseudoexfoliation, **4**:106, 106*f*, 107*f*, **10**:38, 86
    in pigment dispersion syndrome/pigmentary glaucoma, **4**:109, 109*f*, 110*f*, **10**:87, 88, 88*f*, 89
    in pseudoexfoliation, **4**:106, 106*f*, 107*f*
  secondary, **4**:315–322
  topography of, **4**:101–102, 101*f*, 102*f*
  uveal, **2**:53, 54
  in uveitis, **9**:89, 296

Trabecular outflow, **10**:16–18, 17–18*f*

Trabeculectomy, **10**:107–108, 183–198. *See also* Filtering procedures
  antifibrotic agents used with, **10**:186, 193–194, 195*f*
  bleb-related endophthalmitis and, **10**:196
  with cataract surgery, **10**:199–200
  in children, **6**:241, **10**:153, 155
    uveitic glaucoma and, **6**:278
  complications of, **10**:196–198, 196*t*, 197*f*
  contraindications to, **10**:185
  failed, glaucoma drainage device implantation after, **10**:206
  flap management in, **10**:194
  indications for, **10**:184–185
  postoperative considerations in, **10**:194–195
  preoperative evaluation for, **10**:185–186
  technique for, **10**:186–193
    for conjunctival flap, **10**:187–188, 188*f*, 189*f*
      closure and, **10**:191–192, 193*f*
      management and, **10**:194
    for exposure, **10**:187, 187*f*
    for iridectomy, **10**:189–190, 191*f*
    for paracentesis, **10**:188, 190*f*
    for scleral flap, **10**:186, 188, 190*f*
      closure and, **10**:191, 192*f*
      management and, **10**:194
    for sclerostomy/keratectomy, **10**:189, 191*f*
  uveitic glaucoma and, **9**:298
    in children, **6**:278

Trabeculitis, **9**:89, 296
  in glaucomatocyclitic crisis (Posner-Schlossman syndrome), **10**:94
  herpetic infection causing, **9**:199

Trabeculocytes, **2**:53, 54

Trabeculodialysis, for uveitic glaucoma, **9**:298

Trabeculoplasty
  for exfoliation glaucoma, **10**:87
  for open-angle glaucoma, **10**:82, 107–108, 180–183, 182*f*

for pigmentary glaucoma, **10**:89
selective, **10**:180, 181–182
in uveitic glaucoma, **9**:298
Trabeculotomy, for childhood glaucoma, **6**:240–241,
10:152–153, 154, 154*f*, 155
Tracheotomy, for anaphylaxis, **1**:295
Trachipleistophora, **8**:141
Trachoma, **4**:54, **8**:154–156, 155*f*, 156*f*
in children, **6**:190
Trachoma-inclusion conjunctivitis (TRIC) agent, **6**:187
Tracking devices (excimer laser), **13**:83–84
Traction retinal tufts, zonular, **12**:278, 280*f*
Traction test, in blowout fractures, **7**:101
surgery and, **7**:102
Tractional retinal detachment. *See* Retinal detachment
Trait, **2**:211
holandric, **2**:218
Tram-track sign, in optic nerve sheath meningioma,
5:150*f*, 150*t*, **7**:74
Trandate. *See* Labetalol
Trandolapril, **1**:76*t*, 78*t*
Tranexamic acid, **2**:394
for hyphema, **6**:410, **8**:368
Tranquilizers. *See* Antipsychotic drugs
11-*trans*-retinaldehyde, **12**:15
Transbronchial biopsy, **1**:143
Transcaruncular route, for orbitotomy, **7**:108*f*, 112
Transconjunctival route
for lower blepharoplasty, **7**:225
for orbital decompression, **7**:113–114, 113*f*
for orbitotomy
inferior approach, **7**:110, 111*f*
medial approach, **7**:111
superior approach, **7**:109
for ptosis repair, **7**:212
Transconjunctival vitrectomy technique, **12**:346
Transcranial Doppler, in cerebral ischemia/stroke, **1**:93
Transcranial magnetic stimulation, for depression, **1**:256
Transcribed strand of DNA (antisense DNA), **2**:148
Transcription (gene), **2**:162, 166–169, 167*f*
reverse, **2**:160
Transcription factors, **2**:166–168, 167*f*
Transcutaneous routes
for orbitotomy
inferior approach, **7**:110, 110*f*
medial approach, **7**:110–111
superior approach, **7**:108–109
for ptosis correction, **7**:211
Transducin, rod, **2**:293
mutations in, **2**:295
Transendothelial osmotic force, **8**:8
Transepithelial ablation, **13**:75
Transesophageal Doppler echocardiography, in cerebral
ischemia/stroke, **1**:94
Transfer RNA (tRNA), initiator, **2**:154
Transferrin
in aqueous humor, **2**:268, 270
in vitreous, **2**:285
Transforming growth factor β–induced gene. *See TGFBI*
gene
Transforming growth factor β–induced (TGFBI)
keratoepithelin, in Reis-Bücklers corneal dystrophy,
8:276

Transforming growth factor βs, **2**:114, 396, **8**:177*t*,
9:29*t*
in aqueous humor, **2**:270
in exfoliation syndrome/pseudoexfoliation, **11**:61–62
homeobox gene expression affected by, **2**:115
in ocular development, **2**:114
in Sjögren syndrome, **8**:63
in tear film, **2**:241
Transfusion-transmitted virus (TTV), **1**:26
Transient amplifying cells, in corneal epithelium, **2**:43
Transient ischemic attacks, **1**:92
carotid artery disease causing, **1**:96, 97, **5**:181
central retinal artery occlusion and, **12**:139
diagnosis/management of, **1**:92–95
stroke following, **5**:181, 181*f*
vertebrobasilar, **5**:347–349
Transient nerve fiber layer of Chievitz, **2**:126
Transient obscurations of vision, **5**:174, 176. *See also*
Transient visual loss
Transient visual loss, **5**:173–186. *See also* Amaurosis,
fugax
age of patient and, **5**:173
binocular, **5**:173, 185–186
carotid artery disease causing, **1**:96, **5**:173, 174,
177–183, 179*f*, 183–184
in central retinal artery occlusion, **12**:139
cerebrovascular disease causing, **5**:173, 176*t*, 347
duration of, **5**:173–174
examination of patient with, **5**:174–175, 175*f*
migraine causing, **5**:174, 184–185, 185
monocular, **5**:173, 175–185, 176*t*, 178*f*, 179*f*, 179*t*,
181*t*. *See also* Monocular transient visual loss
carotid artery disease causing, **1**:96
pattern of, **5**:174
recovery pattern and, **5**:174
signs and symptoms associated with, **5**:174
Transillumination, **4**:26–27, 27*f*
in choroidal/ciliary body melanoma diagnosis, **4**:277,
277*f*
iris, **6**:231
in albinism, **4**:148*f*, **6**:231, 298, 301*f*
in pathologic examination, **4**:26–27, 27*f*
in retinal examination, **12**:20
Transit amplification, in stem cell differentiation, **8**:93
Transitional zone (peripheral zone), **8**:37, 37*f*
Transketolase, in cornea, **2**:248
Translated strand of DNA (antisense DNA), **2**:148
Translation, **2**:162, 166
gene product changes/modification after
(posttranslational modification), **2**:158
of lens proteins, **2**:277
Translocation, chromosome, **2**:162
Down syndrome caused by, **2**:201–202
Transmigration, in neutrophil recruitment and
activation, **9**:18, 19*f*
Transmissibility (oxygen), of contact lens, **3**:168,
176–178, 177*t*. *See also* Gas-permeability constant
corneal hypoxia and, **3**:200
orthokeratology and, **3**:194
rigid contact lenses and, **3**:176–178
scleral contact lenses and, **3**:192
soft (flexible) contact lenses and, **3**:178, 181*t*
Transmissible spongiform encephalopathies, **5**:368

Transmission, light, **3**:13
angle of, **3**:44, 45*t*
critical angle and, **3**:47–48, 48*f*
wavelength and, **3**:50, 51*f*
diffuse, at rough optical interfaces, **3**:42, 43*f*
specular, **3**:44–46, 45*f*, 46*f*, 47, 47*f*
at smooth optical interfaces, **3**:42, 42*f*
Transmission (window) defect, of fluorescence, **12**:23,
23*f. See also* Hyperfluorescence
in angioid streaks, **12**:84
in macular holes, **12**:305
Transmural (subendocardial/NSTEMI) infarction, **1**:102
Transplant rejection. *See* Rejection
Transplantation. *See also specific type*
amniotic membrane, **8**:389
for chemical injuries, **8**:358
indications for, **8**:387*t*
conjunctival, **8**:392*f*, 393–395
for chemical injuries, **8**:358
indications for, **8**:387*t*, 395
for wound closure after pterygium excision, **8**:392*f*,
393, 393–395
corneal, **8**:407–411, 413–445. *See also* Donor cornea;
Keratoplasty
autograft procedures for, **8**:413, 431–432
basic concepts of, **8**:407–411
cataract/cataract surgery following, **11**:193
for chemical injuries, **8**:358
clinical approach to, **8**:413–445
comparison of procedures for, **8**:415–416*t*
donor selection and, **8**:408–411, 410*t*
eye banking and, **8**:408–411, 410*t*
histocompatibility antigens and, **8**:407
immune privilege and, **8**:175, 407–408
immunobiology of, **8**:407–408
IOL power calculations after, **3**:222
lamellar keratoplasty for, **8**:413, 433–437, 434*f*
pediatric, **6**:219, **8**:430–431, 431*t*
penetrating keratoplasty for, **8**:413, 415–416*t*,
417–430
preoperative evaluation/preparation and,
8:414–417
rabies virus transmission and, **8**:130
after refractive surgery, **13**:191–192
rejection and, **4**:91, 92*f*, **8**:407, 408, 427–430, 428*f*,
429*f*, 436, **9**:63, 64, 64*f*, 65. *See also* Rejection
in triple procedure, **11**:141, 192
histocompatibility antigens and, **8**:407
immune privilege and, **8**:174–175, 407–408
immunobiology of, **8**:407–408
limbal, **8**:94, 389, 395–398, 396–397*f*
for chemical injuries, **8**:94, 358
indications for, **8**:387*t*
mucous membrane, **8**:389
indications for, **8**:387*t*
organ
endogenous mold *(Aspergillus)* endophthalmitis
after, **12**:203
for enzyme deficiency disease, **2**:231
regional immunity and, **9**:57
rejection and. *See* Rejection
retinal/retinal pigment epithelium, **9**:66
Transplantation antigens, **8**:407

Transport mechanisms
in aqueous humor dynamics, **2**:254–255, **10**:14
lens, **2**:277–278, **11**:17–19, 18*f*
retinal pigment epithelium, **2**:307
Transposition, of spherocylindrical lens notation,
3:97–99
Transposition flaps
for canthal repair, **7**:186
for eyelid repair, **7**:182
Transposition procedures, extraocular muscle, **6**:149,
153
Transpupillary thermotherapy, **12**:343
for age-related macular degeneration/choroidal
neovascularization, **12**:79, 343
for melanoma, **4**:285, **12**:343
for metastatic eye disease, **4**:322
Transpupillary Thermotherapy for Choroidal
Neovascularization (TTT4CNV) study, **12**:79
Transrectal ultrasonography, in prostate cancer, **1**:274
Trans-RPE potential, electro-oculogram and, **2**:307
Transscleral diathermy, contraindications to, **4**:285
Transscleral laser cycloablation, **10**:210
for childhood glaucoma, **6**:241, **10**:155
Transseptal injection, for periocular corticosteroids,
9:103, 103*f*
Transthyretin (prealbumin), **1**:208
amyloidosis/amyloid deposits and, **4**:140, 212, **8**:317*t*,
319, **12**:312, 313*f*
serum levels of, **1**:209
Transverse keratotomy, **13**:49
Transverse ligament, superior (Whitnall), **2**:25*f*, 28,
7:135*f*, 138, 139*f*, 244
Transverse magnification, **3**:32–36, 33*f*, 34*f*, 64–65, 65*f*
in afocal system, **3**:80, 82
calculation of, **3**:32, 64–65, 65*f*
Transverse/spin-spin relaxation time (T2), **5**:70, 72,
7:27–28
Transverse sinus, **2**:108, 108*f*, **5**:26, 26*f*
thrombosis in, **5**:357
Trauma, **12**:317–334. *See also under Traumatic and*
Blunt trauma; Lacerations; Penetrating injuries;
Wound healing/repair
angle recession/angle-recession glaucoma and, **4**:18,
19*f*, 109, **10**:38–39, 38*f*, 39*f*, 100–101, 100*f*, 135
animal and plant substances causing, **8**:361–362
anterior segment, **8**:351–385, **10**:38–39, 38*f*, 39*f*,
96–102. *See also* Anterior segment, trauma to
assessment of, **11**:206
blunt. *See* Blunt trauma
canalicular, **7**:179, 272–273
obstruction caused by, **7**:264
canthal soft tissue, **7**:178–180
cataract surgery after, **11**:206–209, 207*f*
cellulitis caused by
orbital, **7**:42–43
preseptal, **7**:40, 41
chemical injuries, **8**:353–359, 353*t*, 354*f*, 356*t*, 357*f*
in children, **6**:407
in children, **6**:403–411, **12**:272–273, 330–331, 330*f*
abuse and, **6**:404–407, 405*f*, 406*f*, **12**:330–331, 330*f*
blunt injury and, **6**:409–411, 410*f*, 411*f*
cataract caused by, **6**:251*f*
chemical injuries and, **6**:407

hyphema and, **6:**409–411, 410*f*
management of, **6:**403
orbital fractures and, **6:**124–126, 125*f*, 411, 411*f*
penetrating injury and, **6:**408–409, 408*f*
retinal breaks and, **12:**272–273
shaking injury and, **6:**404–407, 405*f*, 406*f*,
    12:330–331, 330*f*
superficial injury and, **6:**407–408
concussive, **8:**362–369, 364*f*, 365*f*, 366*f*, 367*f*, 369*t*
convergence insufficiency caused by, **5:**213
corneal blood staining and, **8:**366–367, 367*f*, **10:**96,
    97*f*
dementia associated with (dementia pugilistica/
    boxer's syndrome), **1:**265
diplopia after, **5:**238–239
ectopia lentis caused by, **11:**36
child abuse and, **6:**404
endophthalmitis after, **12:**328–329
ERG in evaluation of, **12:**41
eyelid, **7:**177–181. *See also* Eyelids, trauma to
repair of. *See* Eyelids, surgery/reconstruction of
foreign bodies and, **12:**325–328, 326*f*, 328*t*
fourth nerve (trochlear) palsy caused by, **5:**234
glaucoma associated with, **4:**107–109, 108*f*, **10:**38–39,
    38*f*, 39*f*, 96–102, 135
angle closure/angle-closure glaucoma and, **10:**135
fibrous ingrowth and, **10:**134, 134*f*
angle recession and, **4:**18, 109, **10:**38–39, 38*f*, 39*f*,
    100–101, 100*f*
in children, **10:**141*t*
lens particle glaucoma and, **10:**91–92
open-angle glaucoma and, **10:**38–39, 38*f*, 39*f*
phacoantigenic glaucoma and, **10:**92
histologic sequelae of, **4:**18–22, 18*f*, 19*f*, 20*f*, 21*f*, 22*f*,
    23*f*
hypercoagulability associated with, **1:**158
hyphema and. *See* Traumatic hyphema
innate immune response and, **9:**17
lacrimal system, **7:**272–273
LASIK flap dislocation and, **13:**108
lens damage/cataracts caused by, **4:**20, **11:**50–54, 50*f*,
    51*f*, 52*f*, 54*f*, 55*f*, 206–209, 207*f*
child abuse and, **6:**404
glaucoma and, **10:**91–92, **11:**63
phacoantigenic uveitis and, **4:**122, **11:**62
surgery for, **11:**206–209, 207*f*
macular holes associated with, **12:**321–322, 322*f*
nasolacrimal duct obstruction caused by, **7:**266–267,
    273
neuroimaging in evaluation of, **5:**82*t*
nonperforating mechanical, **8:**369–372, 370*f*, 371*f*
ocular infection and, **8:**99
optic disc avulsion and, **12:**331–332, 331*f*
optic neuropathy caused by, **2:**93, **5:**156–157, 156*f*,
    7:105–106
orbital, **7:**95–106. *See also specific type and* Orbit,
    trauma to
patient evaluation after, **11:**206, **12:**317–318
penetrating. *See* Penetrating injuries
perforating. *See* Perforating injuries
photic damage and, **12:**332–334
posterior segment, **12:**317–334. *See also* Posterior
    segment, trauma to

ptosis caused by, **5:**280*t*, 281, **7:**181, 210
amblyopia and, **7:**181
pupil irregularity caused by, **5:**263
Purtscher retinopathy and, **12:**154–155, 154*f*, 155*t*
retinal breaks caused by, **12:**272–274, 273*f*
retinal detachment and, **12:**291
in young patients, **12:**272–273
scleritis after, **9:**266–267
seventh nerve (facial) palsy caused by, **5:**287
spheroidal degeneration and, **8:**335
subconjunctival hemorrhage caused by, **8:**76*t*,
    362–363
child abuse and, **6:**404
surgical, **8:**382–385, 384*f*
open-angle glaucoma and, **10:**101–102
sympathetic ophthalmia and, **4:**189, 189*f*, 190*f*,
    9:52–53, 178, 180, 181, 182*t*, **12:**198, 329–330
enucleation in prevention of, **4:**189, **7:**118, **9:**182
temperature and radiation causing, **8:**351–353
toxic reactions to medications and, **8:**359–361, 359*t*,
    361*f*
uveal tract, **4:**203
Traumatic corneal endothelial rings, **8:**363
Traumatic hyphema, **8:**365–369, 365*f*, 366*f*, 367*f*, 369*t*
glaucoma/elevated intraocular pressure and, **10:**97–99,
    97*f*
in infants and children, **6:**409–411, 410*f*
medical management of, **8:**367–368
rebleeding after, **8:**365–367, 367*f*, **10:**97–98
sickle cell disease and, **6:**409, **8:**369, **10:**98–99,
    12:120
elevated intraocular pressure and, **10:**98–99
surgery for, **8:**368, 369*t*, **10:**98–99
Traumatic iritis, **8:**363
Traumatic miosis, **8:**363
Traumatic mydriasis, **8:**363
Traumatic posterior annular keratopathy, **8:**363
Traumatic recession of anterior chamber angle, **4:**18,
    19*f*, 109
glaucoma and, **4:**18, 109, **10:**38–39, 38*f*, 39*f*, 100–101,
    100*f*, 135
Traumatic retinal breaks, **12:**272–274, 273*f*
Traumatic retinoschisis, in shaking injury, **6:**405–406,
    406*f*
Traumatic visual loss with clear media, **7:**104–106
Travatan/Travatan Z. *See* Travoprost
Travel immunizations, **1:**286
Travoprost, **2:**354, 354*t*, **10:**162*t*, 166
for childhood glaucoma, **6:**242–243
in combination preparations, **10:**165*t*, 173
Trazodone, **1:**256
Treacher Collins/Treacher Collins–Franceschetti
    syndrome (mandibulofacial dysostosis), **6:**393–394,
    394*f*, **7:**34, 34*f*, **8:**324*t*
eyelid manifestations of, **4:**213*t*
palpebral fissure slanting in, **6:**178, 393–394, 394*f*
Treatment of Age-Related Macular Degeneration
    with Photodynamic Therapy (TAP) Study, **12:**72,
    75*f*, 344
Tree sap, ocular injuries caused by, **8:**362
Trefoil, **3:**233*f*, **13:**7, 9*f*
Treg cells. *See* Regulatory (suppressor) T cells
Tremor, in Parkinson disease, **1:**258

Trephination/trephines
for deep anterior lamellar keratoplasty, 8:436
for penetrating keratoplasty, 8:417, 418
for superficial anterior lamellar keratoplasty, 8:435
Treponema pallidum, 1:12–14, 6:185, 8:137, 9:242. *See also* Syphilis
Treponemal tests, for syphilis, 1:13, 279, 9:247–248
TRH. *See* Thyrotropin-releasing hormone
Trial contact lens fitting
disinfection and, 1:41, 3:201, 8:46
for rigid gas-permeable contact lenses, 3:182–186, 184f, 184t, 186f, 187f
for soft (flexible) contact lenses, 3:182, 183t
Trial frames
for astigmatic spectacle correction, 3:140
for prism correction, 3:163–164
for refraction
in aphakia, 3:158
in low vision/vision rehabilitation, 3:294
Trial lens clips
for overrefraction, 3:138, 158
for prism correction, 3:163–164
for refraction, in aphakia, 3:158
Triamcinolone, 1:181t
for chalazion, 8:73
for corneal graft rejection, 8:429
for cystoid macular edema, 12:143, 360
in uveitis, 9:105, 300
intravitreal (IVTA)
for branch retinal vein occlusion, 12:126
for central retinal vein occlusion, 12:131
for macular edema, 4:158–160, 12:100
with photodynamic therapy, 12:344
for ocular histoplasmosis syndrome, 9:225
for pars planitis, 9:137
with photodynamic therapy, 12:344
for pulmonary diseases, 1:145t
PVD visualization in vitrectomy and, 12:298, 301f
for uveitis, 9:101t, 102, 105, 300
for vernal keratoconjunctivitis, 8:189
Triamterene
for heart failure, 1:118
for hypertension, 1:76t, 78t
Triazolam, 1:254
Triazoles, 1:65, 2:379t, 380
for *Acanthamoeba* keratitis, 8:169
TRIC (trachoma-inclusion conjunctivitis) agent, 6:187
Tricarboxylic acid (TCA) cycle, in corneal glucose metabolism, 2:248
Trichiasis, 2:29, 7:200, 8:89
in anophthalmic socket, 7:125
in cicatricial entropion, 7:198, 200
in involutional entropion, 7:195, 200
in staphylococcal blepharitis, 8:145
Trichilemmal (pilar) cyst, 7:159
Trichilemmomas, 4:215t, 7:163
Trichinella spiralis (trichinosis), orbital infection caused by, 7:47
Trichoepithelioma, 7:162–163, 163f
Trichofolliculoma, 7:163
Trichotillomania, 6:177, 7:155
Trichromatism/trichromacy, 12:213, 214t
anomalous, 12:213, 213–214

Tricor. *See* Fenofibrate
Tricyclic antidepressants, 1:255t, 256
apraclonidine/brimonidine interactions and, 2:348, 10:170
Triesence, 2:361
Trifluridine, 2:380, 381t
for herpes simplex virus infections, 8:109t
epithelial keratitis, 8:112
stromal keratitis, 8:108t, 115
Trifocal lenses, 3:147, 149
progressive addition, 3:147–150, 150f
Trigeminal autonomic cephalgias, 5:299
Trigeminal dermatomes, herpes zoster involving, 5:302–303, 303f
Trigeminal ganglion (gasserian/semilunar ganglion), 2:101, 101–102, 101f, 5:59, 59f
Trigeminal nerve. *See* Cranial nerve V
Trigeminal neuralgia (tic douloureux), 5:59, 301–302
Trigeminal nucleus, 5:57, 57f. *See also* Cranial nerve V
Triglycerides, 1:132, 132t
drugs affecting metabolism of, 1:137t
lowering levels of, 1:134, 137t. *See also* Lipid-lowering therapy
risk assessment and, 1:132–133, 133t
Trigonometry, review of, 3:34–35, 35f
Trihexyphenidyl, for Parkinson disease, 1:259
Triiodothyronine (T$_3$), 1:208
serum levels of, 1:209, 7:32
Triiodothyronine (T$_3$) resin uptake test, 1:209
Trilateral retinoblastoma, 4:309
Trileptal. *See* Oxcarbazepine
Trilisate. *See* Choline magnesium trisalicylate
Trimethaphan, adverse effects of, 2:343f
Trimethoprim, 1:44
with sulfonamides, 2:374. *See also* Trimethoprim-sulfamethoxazole
Trimethoprim-polymyxin B, 2:372t
Trimethoprim-sulfamethoxazole, 1:45t, 63
for *Pneumocystis jiroveci* (*Pneumocystis carinii*) choroiditis, 9:310
for *Pneumocystis jiroveci* (*Pneumocystis carinii*) pneumonia, 1:37
for *Pneumocystis jiroveci* (*Pneumocystis carinii*) prophylaxis, alkylating agent treatment and, 9:109, 113
for toxoplasmosis, 9:232–233, 234, 12:209
for Wegener granulomatosis, 1:179
Trinucleotide repeats, 2:155
expansion/contraction of, 2:162
anticipation and, 2:148, 162, 208–209
TRIO (thyroid-related immune orbitopathy). *See* Thyroid eye disease
Triple procedure, 11:141, 192
Triplet, 2:150
Tripod ("Pregnant 7") anterior chamber IOL, 3:211, 211f
Tripod (zygomaticomaxillary complex) fractures, 7:95–97, 97f
Trisomy, 2:199
Trisomy 21 (Down syndrome/trisomy G syndrome), 2:201–203, 202t
Brushfield spots in, 4:270t, 272f, 6:227
congenital ectropion and, 7:146

mosaicism in, 2:204
pharmacogenetics and, 2:229
pseudopapilledema in, 6:314
Trisomy 21 mosaicism, 2:204
Tritan defects (tritanopia/blue-yellow color confusion),
    12:47, 213, 214t
    in dominant optic atrophy, 5:139
    tests for, 12:49
Tritan plates, Lanthony, in low vision evaluation, 5:105
Tritanomalous congenital defects, 12:213, 214t
Trivariant color vision, 2:294–295. See also Color vision
Trivex plastic lenses, 3:162
Trizivir, 1:33
tRNA. See Transfer RNA
Trochlea, 2:7, 6:14–15, 16f
    in Brown syndrome, 6:130
Trochlear fossa, 2:7
Trochlear nerve. See Cranial nerve IV
Trochlear nerve palsy/paralysis. See Fourth nerve
    (trochlear) palsy/paralysis
Troglitazone, withdrawal of from market, 1:201
Trolands, 3:18t
Tropheryma whipplei (Tropheryma whippelii), 5:257,
    9:265
Trophoblast, 2:117
-tropia (suffix), 6:10
Tropias, 6:10. See also Heterotropias
    induced, testing visual acuity and, 6:72–73
    intermittent, 6:10
        esotropia, 6:89
        exotropia, 6:99–103
    refractive surgery and, 13:34
Tropicalyl. See Tropicamide
Tropicamide, 2:260, 341t
    for cycloplegia/cycloplegic refraction, 3:137t, 6:88,
        88t
    for uveitis, 9:120
Troponins, cardiac-specific (troponins T and I), in acute
    coronary syndrome, 1:105
Trovafloxacin, 1:52t, 61
Trovan. See Trovafloxacin
True divergence excess exotropia, 6:101
Trusopt. See Dorzolamide
Truvada, 1:34
Trypan blue, 2:392
Trypan blue dye, for capsule staining, 11:195, 195f, 196
Tryptase, 8:179t
TS. See Transverse sinus; Tuberous sclerosis
TSC1/TSC2 genes, in tuberous sclerosis, 5:341, 6:371
TSCM. See Tandem scanning confocal microscopy
TSH (thyroid-stimulating hormone). See Thyrotropin
TSH-R. See Thyrotropin (thyroid-stimulating hormone/
    TSH), receptor for
TSI. See Thyroid-stimulating immunoglobulins
TTP. See Thrombotic thrombocytopenic purpura
TTR. See Transthyretin
TTT. See Transpupillary thermotherapy
TTT4CNV (Transpupillary Thermotherapy for
    Choroidal Neovascularization) study, 12:79
TTV. See Transfusion-transmitted virus
Tube–cornea touch, after glaucoma drainage device
    implantation, 10:207–208, 208t
Tube Versus Trabeculectomy study, 10:205–206

Tubercles
    choroidal, in tuberculosis, 9:258, 259f, 12:205
    "hard," 4:7, 8f
    in sarcoidosis, 4:52, 53f, 9:173
Tuberculin hypersensitivity, 9:35
Tuberculin skin test, 1:19, 278–279, 9:35, 259–260
    in HIV infection/AIDS, 9:260
    immune response arc and, 9:35
    uveitis associated with, 9:128
Tuberculosis, 1:18–20, 278–279, 9:256–262, 258f, 259f,
    260f, 262f
    diagnosis/screening/testing for, 1:19, 278–279, 9:35,
        259–261
    in HIV infection/AIDS, 1:19, 39, 5:360, 9:256–257,
        257, 258, 313–314
    immune response to, 9:35
    miliary, 9:257
    multidrug-resistant, 1:19–20, 39, 9:261
    ocular involvement in, 9:257–258, 258f, 259f, 260f, 262f
        choroidal, 9:258, 259f, 12:204–205, 205f
        dacryoadenitis, 7:273
        orbital, 7:45
        primary, 9:257
        secondary, 9:257
        uveitis, 9:256, 257, 257–258, 258f, 261–262, 262f
    in older patients, 1:232–233
    treatment of, 1:19–20, 9:261–262, 262f
        in HIV infection/AIDS, 1:39
    vaccine for, 1:279
Tuberculous choroiditis, 9:258, 259f
Tuberculous meningitis, neuro-ophthalmic signs of, 5:360
Tuberculous uveitis, 9:256, 257, 257–258, 258f, 261–262,
    262f
Tuberin, 5:341
Tuberous sclerosis (Bourneville disease/syndrome),
    5:339t, 341, 342f, 6:364t, 371–374, 372f, 373f
    glaucoma associated with, 10:28
Tubocurarine, 2:259t
    adverse effects of, 2:343f
Tubulin, 2:277
Tubulointerstitial nephritis and uveitis (TINU)
    syndrome, 6:271–272, 9:72t, 119, 124
Tucking procedure, 6:120, 152
Tumor-associated calcium signal transducer 2
    (TACSTD2) gene, in gelatinous droplike corneal
    dystrophy, 8:269t, 274
Tumor necrosis factor
    α, 1:186, 8:177, 177t, 9:28t, 30
        in cicatricial pemphigoid, 8:199
        for rheumatic disorders, 1:161
        in Sjögren syndrome, 8:63
        in tear film, 2:241
    β, 9:28t
        in delayed hypersensitivity, 9:49f, 50
Tumor necrosis factor inhibitors
    adverse effects of, 9:109, 114, 115
    anti-idiotype antibodies and, 9:46
    for juvenile idiopathic (chronic/rheumatoid) arthritis,
        9:131
    for rheumatic disorders, 1:161, 186
    for scleritis, 8:222
    for uveitis, 9:109, 114–115
        in children, 6:278

Tumor-suppressor genes, **1**:235–236, **2**:162, 170,
   171–173. *See also specific type*
   in DNA repair, **2**:170
   recessive, Rb locus as, **2**:204
   Wilms tumor, imprinting of, **2**:154
Tumors. *See also specific type and structure or organ
      affected and* Cancer; Intraocular tumors;
      Neoplasia
   of anterior chamber and trabecular meshwork, **4**:109,
      110*f*
   canalicular obstruction and, **7**:264
   in children, **6**:331–361, 332–333*t*
      classification of, **6**:332–333*t*
      eyelid/epibulbar, **6**:333*t*, 347–351
      intraocular, **6**:351–361
      orbital, **6**:331–347, 332–333*t*
   of choroid and ciliary body, **4**:195–200
   conjunctival, **4**:61–75
   corneal, **4**:100
   eyelid, **4**:214–227
   iris, **4**:193–194, 194*f*
   nasolacrimal duct obstruction and, **7**:267
   neuroimaging in evaluation of, **5**:82*t*
   ocular surface, **8**:225–247
      of epithelial origin, **8**:226–233, 226*t*
      of neuroectodermal origin, **8**:233–240, 234*t*
   optic disc/nerve, **4**:256–258, 256*f*, 257*f*, 258*f*,
      259*f*
   of orbit, **4**:235–247
   scleral, **4**:116–118, 117*f*, 118*f*
   secondary, **4**:315–322. *See also* Metastatic eye
      disease
      orbital, **4**:247
      retinoblastoma and, **4**:312, 313–314, 314*t*
   uveal tract, **4**:193–203
   of vitreous, **4**:140–142, 141*f*, 142*f*, 143*f*
Tunica vasculosa lentis, **2**:137, **11**:25, 25*f*
   remnant of, **2**:138, **12**:307
      epicapsular star, **11**:27, 28*f*
      Mittendorf dot, **2**:85, 85*f*, **4**:133, **6**:307, **11**:25, 27,
         12:307
Tuning, in phacoemulsification, **11**:103
Turban tumors, **7**:162
Turbinates (conchae), nasal, **7**:18, 245*f*, 246
   inferior, **7**:18, 245*f*, 246
   infracture of, for congenital nasolacrimal duct
      obstruction, **6**:208–209, **7**:255
Turkey gobbler defect, **7**:229
Turribrachycephaly, **6**:387*f*, 389*f*
Turricephaly, **6**:383
Twin studies
   in age-related cataract, **11**:37–38
   in glaucoma, **10**:12
Twinrix, **1**:281
TWIST gene, **6**:387
   in Saethre-Chotzen syndrome, **6**:388
Twitch-type fibers, **2**:21, 21*t*, **5**:55
2 × 2 table, **1**:329–330, 329*t*, 330*t*
2-hit hypothesis, **2**:173
TXA. *See* Thromboxanes
Tympanic segment of cranial nerve VII (facial),
   2:105–106, **5**:61

Tyndall effect, **3**:16
Typhoid immunization, **1**:286
Typical degenerative retinoschisis, **4**:154, **12**:293,
   293*f*
Typical peripheral cystoid degeneration, **4**:154, 154*f*,
   12:282, 292
TYR gene mutations, in albinism, **2**:195, 213*t*, 308,
   6:298, 299*t*
Tyr402His
   in age-related macular degeneration, **12**:56
   in basal laminar/cuticular drusen, **12**:239–240
Tyrosinase activity, in albinism, **2**:195, 213*t*, 308, **6**:298,
   299*t*, 300
Tyrosinase gene mutations, in albinism, **2**:195, 213*t*,
   308, **6**:298, 299*t*, **12**:258, 258*t*
Tyrosine aminotransferase, defective, **2**:213*t*, **8**:315
Tyrosinemia, **2**:213*t*, **8**:314–315, 314*t*
Tyrosinosis, **2**:213*t*
Tyrosinuria, **8**:315
TYRP1 gene, in OCA3, **6**:299*t*, 301, **12**:258*t*
Tysabri. *See* Natalizumab

U

UbiA prenyltransferase domain-containing protein 1
   (UBIAD1), in Schnyder corneal dystrophy, **8**:269*t*,
   284
UBM. *See* Ultrasound biomicroscopy
UC. *See* Uncentral fixation/acuity
UCVA. *See* Uncorrected visual acuity
UDP galactose 4-epimerase deficiency, galactosemia/
   cataract formation and, **11**:56
UGH syndrome. *See* Uveitis-glaucoma-hyphema
   (UGH) syndrome
Uhthoff symptom, **5**:174, 323
UKPDS (United Kingdom Prospective Diabetes Study),
   1:203, **12**:91, 92, 93
Ulcerative basal cell carcinoma, **7**:169*f*. *See also* Basal
   cell carcinoma
Ulcerative colitis, **1**:165, **9**:123
Ulcerative keratitis. *See also* Keratitis
   peripheral, **8**:211–213, 211*t*, 212*f*, 339
      differential diagnosis of, **8**:211*t*
      in systemic immune-mediated diseases, **8**:211–213,
         211*t*, 212*f*
   in rosacea, **8**:70
Ulcerative keratopathy, toxic, **8**:86, 88
Ulcers
   conjunctival, **8**:22*t*
   corneal. *See* Corneal ulcers; Keratitis
   eyelid, **8**:20*t*
   genital and oral, in Behçet disease, **1**:180, **9**:191, 192,
      192*f*
   Mooren, **8**:213–216, 215*f*
   neurotrophic, herpetic keratitis and, **4**:83, 84*f*, **8**:87,
      88, 117
Ultex-type bifocal, **3**:148*f*, 157
Ultrafiltration, in aqueous humor dynamics/formation,
   2:254–255, **10**:14
Ultralente insulin, **1**:196
Ultrasonic, definition of, **11**:104

Ultrasonography/ultrasound (echography), 3:272–275, 273f, 274f, 5:81
A-scan, 3:273, 273f, 274f, 275. *See also* A-scan ultrasonography
  for axial length measurement
    in IOL power determination/selection, 3:213–214, 214f, 215f
    in primary congenital glaucoma, 10:152
anterior segment (ultrasound biomicroscopy), 2:50, 52f, 8:33, 33f
  before corneal transplantation, 8:417
  in glaucoma, 10:70, 72f
  in pars planitis, 9:136
  in uveitic glaucoma, 9:296
B-scan, 3:274–275, 274f. *See also* B-scan ultrasonography
  for axial length measurement in IOL power determination/selection, 3:213
  in primary congenital glaucoma evaluation, 10:152
in carotid artery evaluation, 5:81, 180
before cataract surgery, 11:80–81, 82–83, 83f
in cerebral ischemia/stroke, 1:93
in choroidal/ciliary body melanoma, 4:276–277, 276f
in choroidal hemangioma, 4:291f, 292
in cysticercosis, 9:239
diagnostic, 3:272–275, 273f, 274f
in drusen versus papilledema differentiation, 5:134–135, 135f
in foreign-body identification, 12:325, 326, 326f
high-resolution, in corneal imaging, 8:29
in IOL power determination/selection, 3:213–214, 214f, 215f, 11:82–83, 83f, 84, 84–85
in iris melanoma, 4:269, 273f
in ischemic heart disease, 1:105–106, 107
in lymphoma, 4:323–324, 9:282
in metastatic eye disease, 4:319
in ocular ischemic syndrome, 9:288
in ocular trauma, 12:318
in orbital evaluation, 5:81, 7:29–30
  hemangioma diagnosis and, 6:340
for pachymetry/pachometry, 3:259, 8:28. *See also* Pachymetry/pachymeter
  for intrastromal corneal ring segment placement, 13:57
  before refractive surgery, 13:39–40
for phacoemulsification
  linear, 11:106
  panel control, 11:106
  terminology related to, 11:102–104
in posterior vitreous detachment, 12:276, 298
principles of, 3:272–275, 273f, 274f
in retinoblastoma, 4:303, 6:356
thyroid, 1:210
transrectal, in prostate cancer, 1:274
in uveal lymphoid infiltration, 4:326
in uveitic glaucoma, 9:296
in uveitis, 9:95
in vitreous hemorrhage, 12:110, 314
in Vogt-Koyanagi-Harada (VKH) syndrome, 9:188, 12:198

Ultrasound biomicroscopy, 2:50, 52f, 8:33, 33f
  before corneal transplantation, 8:417
  in glaucoma evaluation, 10:70, 72f
  in pars planitis, 9:136
  in uveitic glaucoma, 9:296
Ultraviolet-absorbing lenses, 3:160–161. *See also* Sunglasses
  cataract prevention and, 11:53
Ultraviolet blue phototoxicity, 2:316
Ultraviolet chromophores/filters, intraocular lenses with, 3:206, 11:138
Ultraviolet light (ultraviolet radiation)
  basal cell carcinoma and, 4:217–219, 218f, 219f, 7:168
  in collagen crosslinking, 13:123, 168
  eye disorders/injury associated with, 2:313, 316, 3:19, 160–161, 206, 12:332–334. *See also* Light toxicity/ photic damage/phototoxicity
    actinic keratosis, 4:216–217, 217f, 218f, 7:166, 167f
    age-related macular degeneration, 12:63
    ambient exposure and, 12:334
    anterior segment injury, 8:352
    cataracts, 11:53
    conjunctival intraepithelial neoplasia, 8:228
    corneal haze after surface ablation and, 13:101
    eyelid tumors, 4:218–219, 218f, 219f, 220f, 7:168
    lentigines, 7:165
    melanoma, 7:175
    pinguecula, 4:56, 8:331–332
    pterygium, 8:332
    in retinitis pigmentosa, 12:231
    solar retinopathy, 12:332–333
    spheroidal degeneration (Labrador/actinic keratopathy), 4:88–89, 90f, 8:334–335, 335f
  lenses absorbing, 3:160–161. *See also* Sunglasses
    cataract prevention and, 11:53
  melanoma caused by, 1:277, 7:175
  ocular surface squamous neoplasia and, 4:62
  squamous cell carcinoma and, 4:219, 220f
Ultra-wide-angle fundus photography, for screening in retinopathy of prematurity, 12:165
UM. *See* Unmaintained fixation/acuity
Umbo, 2:80f, 12:8, 9f, 9t
Unasyn. *See* Ampicillin, with sulbactam
Uncentral fixation/acuity, 6:72
Uncorrected visual acuity (UCVA), refractive surgery and, 13:33
Uncrossed diplopia, 6:54, 54t
Uncus, 5:54
Undercorrection, with photoablation, 13:94
Undifferentiated spondyloarthropathy, 1:163
Unequal crossing over, 2:162
  color vision defects and, 2:295
Unformed hallucinations, 5:172, 189, 190. *See also* Hallucinations
Unharmonious anomalous retinal correspondence, 6:55
Unifocal eosinophilic granuloma of bone, 7:84
Unilateral aphakia, 3:116
Unilateral visual loss
  in low vision evaluation, 5:91
  in nonorganic disorders, 5:310–311, 311t
Uniparental disomy, 2:162, 169
Unipen. *See* Nafcillin

Uniphyl. *See* Theophylline
Uniretic. *See* Moexipril
Unit magnification, planes of (principal planes), 3:75, 75*f*
United Cerebral Palsy Association, 6:418*t*
United Kingdom Prospective Diabetes Study (UKPDS),
    1:203, 12:91, 92, 93
Univasc. *See* Moexipril
Universal precautions, 8:45–46, 9:314
Universal Protocol of the Joint Commission on
    Accreditation of Healthcare Organizations, 1:303,
    306–310
Unmaintained fixation/acuity, 6:72
Unoprostone, 2:354, 354*t*
Unpolarized light, 3:10
Unstable angina, 1:101–102
    hypertension management and, 1:84
Unsteady fixation/acuity, 6:72
Untranslated region, 2:162–163, 165
Upbeat nystagmus, 5:251*t*, 252
Upgaze. *See* Elevation of eye
Upper eyelid. *See* Eyelids, upper
Urea
    in aqueous humor, 2:268
    as hyperosmotic agent, 2:355, 356, 356*t*
    in tear film, 2:240
Urea-insoluble (membrane structural) lens proteins,
    2:277, 11:11*f*, 12
Urea-soluble (cytoskeletal) lens proteins, 2:277, 11:11*f*, 12
Ureaphil. *See* Urea
Urinalysis
    in immune-mediated disease, 8:182*t*
    in uveitis, 9:94*t*
Urinary sphincter disturbances, in multiple sclerosis,
    5:323
Urinary tract stones, acetazolamide use and, 2:353
Urokinase, 1:159, 2:393
    uveitis caused by, 9:128
Urologic cancer, screening for, 1:274
Uroxatral. *See* Alfuzosin
Urticaria (hives), from fluorescein angiography, 12:24, 25
Urticating hairs, ocular inflammation caused by, 8:362
Urushiol (poison ivy toxin), immune response to, 9:34–35
US. *See* Unsteady fixation/acuity
US National Cholesterol Education Program (NCEP),
    1:131
USH1B gene, 2:176
USH2A gene, 12:222
USH3A gene, 12:253
Usher syndrome, 12:251*t*, 253
    gene for, 2:176, 12:222, 253
    myosin VIIA gene in, 2:176, 296
    retinal pigment epithelium in, 2:308
    synteny and, 2:176
Usherin, in Usher syndrome, 12:253
UTR. *See* Untranslated region
Utricle, 5:47*f*, 48
UV light/radiation. *See* Ultraviolet light
Uvea (uveal tract), 2:42, 55–66, 253, 9:77. *See also*
    specific structure
    bilateral diffuse melanocytic proliferation of, 9:287,
        12:183, 183*f*
    congenital anomalies of, 4:188
    degenerations of, 4:192–193, 192*t*, 193*f*

disorders of, 4:185–203. *See also specific type*
    neoplastic, 4:193–203. *See also* Uvea (uveal tract),
        tumors of
    Th1 delayed hypersensitivity and, 9:50*t*
healing/repair of, 4:16–17
immune response in, 9:58*t*, 59–63
infection/inflammation of, 4:188–191, 189*f*, 190*f*,
    191*f*, 9:77–116. *See also* Endophthalmitis; Uveitis
lymphoid infiltration and, 4:202, 325–326
lymphoid proliferation and, 4:202, 202*f*
    masquerade syndromes secondary to, 9:285
lymphoma of, 4:202, 202*f*, 323
melanocytoma of, 4:195, 268
melanoma of, 4:195–200, 196*f*, 197*f*, 198*f*, 199*f*, 263,
    273–288, 9:285–286. *See also* Choroidal/ciliary
    body melanoma; Iris, melanoma of
in neurofibromatosis, melanocytic tumors and,
    6:365–366, 366*f*
retinoblastoma involving, 4:180–181
sarcoidosis involving, 4:190–191, 191*f*, 272*f*
topography of, 2:42, 4:185–187, 185*f*, 186*f*, 187*f*
traumatic injury of, 4:203
tumors of, 4:193–203. *See also specific tumor*
    metastatic, 4:200, 201*f*, 316–317, 316*f*, 317*f*,
        321–322, 9:286
    miscellaneous, 4:200–203, 201*f*, 202*f*
    pigmented, 4:288–289, 289*f*
Uveal (posterior) bleeding syndrome (polypoidal
    choroidal vasculopathy), 4:171, 172*f*, 173*f*
    age-related macular degeneration differentiated from,
        12:69–70, 70*f*
    central serous retinopathy differentiated from,
        12:174, 175
Uveal effusions/uveal effusion syndrome, 12:182–183,
    182*f*
    angle-closure glaucoma and, 10:131, 133
    central serous chorioretinopathy differentiated from,
        12:174
Uveal lymphoid infiltration, 4:202, 325–326
Uveal meshwork, 2:53, 54
Uveal prolapse, 4:203
Uveitic glaucoma, 9:294, 295–297, 295*t*
    angle-closure, 10:130*f*, 131
    glaucoma drainage device implantation and, 10:206
    open-angle, 10:93–95
    surgery in children and, 6:278
Uveitic ocular hypertension, 9:294, 295
Uveitis, 4:188–191, 9:77–116. *See also specific type and*
    Endophthalmitis
    acute, 9:79*t*, 83, 119–128
    in AIRE-deficient mice, 9:69–70
    animal models of, 9:69–70
    in ankylosing spondylitis, 1:164
    anterior. *See* Anterior uveitis; Iridocyclitis; Iritis
    in bartonellosis/cat-scratch disease, 9:263–264
    in Behçet disease, 1:180, 9:190–196, 190*f*, 191*t*, 192*f*,
        193*f*, 194*f*, 12:194
    calcific band-shaped keratopathy and, 9:85, 291
    cataracts and, 9:125, 291–294, 11:59, 60*f*, 203–204
        after cataract surgery, 11:158–159
        surgery in patients with, 9:291–294, 11:75, 158,
            203–204, 206–207
        children, 6:278

in Chikungunya fever, **9**:220
in children, **6**:267–278
 anterior, **6**:267, 267–272, 270*f*, 271*t*
 classification of, **6**:267, 268*t*
 diagnosis/differential diagnosis of, **6**:268*t*, 275, 277*t*
 intermediate/pars planitis, **6**:267, 268*t*, 272, 273*f*
 laboratory tests for, **6**:275, 277*t*
 masquerade syndromes and, **6**:275, 276*t*
 panuveitis, **6**:267, 268*t*, 274–275, 274*f*
 posterior, **6**:267, 272–274, 273*f*
  differential diagnosis of, **6**:268*t*
 treatment of, **6**:275–278
chronic, **9**:79*t*, 83, 84, 128–134
classification of, **9**:78–84, 78*t*, 79*t*
 in children, **6**:267, 268*t*
clinical approach to, **9**:77–116
CMV, **9**:204–208. *See also* Retinitis, CMV
coccidioidal, **9**:279–280
in collagen vascular diseases, **9**:140–146
complications of, **9**:291–304. *See also specific type*
corticosteroids for, **9**:100–106, 101*t*, 102*f*, 103*f*, 119–120, 120*f*, 300
 route of administration of, **2**:360*t*
cystoid macular edema and, **9**:300–301
in cytomegalic inclusion disease, **6**:184, **9**:204, 205, 206
diagnosis of, **9**:315–319
 in children, **6**:268*t*, 275, 277*t*
differential diagnosis of, **9**:91
 in children, **6**:268*t*
diffuse. *See* Panuveitis
diffuse unilateral subacute neuroretinitis and, **9**:239–241, 240*f*, 241*f*
drug-induced, **9**:128
epidemiology of, **9**:91–93, 92*t*
experimental
 autoimmune, **9**:69
 immune, **9**:15, 69
familial juvenile systemic granulomatosis (Blau syndrome) and, **6**:274–275
fibrin deposition in, **9**:24, 85, 88, 119, 119*f*
flowchart for evaluation of, **9**:80–81*t*
Fuchs heterochromic iridocyclitis (Fuchs uveitis syndrome) and, **9**:132–134, 133*f*
 cataracts/cataract surgery in, **9**:133, 134, **11**:59, 60*f*
 glaucoma and, **9**:133, 134, **10**:94–95, 95*f*
 rubella reactivation and, **9**:48, 134, 211
glaucoma and, **9**:17, 84, 294–299, 295*t*, **10**:93–95, 130*f*, 131. *See also* Uveitic glaucoma; Uveitis-glaucoma-hyphema (UGH) syndrome
 glaucoma drainage device implantation for, **10**:206
 in infants and children, **10**:141*t*
granulomatous, **9**:84
 lens-associated, **9**:126
 tuberculous, **9**:257–258, 258*f*
herpetic, **9**:197–209
historical factors in diagnosis of, **9**:90, 90*t*, 315–319
in HIV infection/AIDS, **9**:305
HLA association in, **1**:163, 164, 165, 166, **6**:269, 271, **9**:71, 72*t*, 119*f*, 120–123, 122*f*, 123*f*
HTLV-1 causing, **9**:218–219
hypotony and, **9**:299–300
immune recovery, **1**:41, **9**:306, **12**:201

incidence of, **9**:91
infectious. *See also specific causative agent*
 bacterial, **9**:242–266
 fungal, **9**:221–226
 helminthic, **9**:235–242
 masquerade syndromes and, **9**:289
 protozoal, **9**:226–235
 retinal detachment and, **9**:302
 viral, **9**:197–220
inflammatory chorioretinopathies (white dot syndromes) and, **9**:147–172, 148–150*t*, 151*t*
intermediate. *See* Intermediate uveitis
intraocular lenses and, **9**:127, 291, 292–293, 294
 postoperative inflammation and, **9**:126–127, 127*f*, 294
intraocular lymphoma and, **4**:323
ischemic, **5**:184
in juvenile idiopathic (chronic/rheumatoid) arthritis, **6**:268–271, 270*f*, 271*t*, **9**:128–132, 130*f*, 131*t*
 cataracts and, **9**:129, 130, 130*f*, 131–132, 293
in Kawasaki disease, **6**:202
laboratory/medical evaluation of, **9**:80–81*t*, 93–98, 94–95*t*, 96*f*
 in children, **6**:275, 277*t*
lens-associated/phacoantigenic, **4**:122, 122*f*, 123*f*, **9**:125–126, 125*f*, **11**:62
 sympathetic ophthalmia and, **9**:182
in leptospirosis, **9**:255, 256
lipopolysaccharide-induced, **9**:15
Lyme, **8**:137, **9**:251
lymphocytic choriomeningitis virus infection and, **9**:211–212
masquerade syndromes and, **9**:281–289, 282*f*, 283*f*, **12**:199, 199*f*
 in children, **6**:275, 276*t*
in measles (rubeola), **9**:212–214, 214*f*
in multiple sclerosis, **9**:136, 139
nongranulomatous, **9**:84
noninfectious (autoimmune)
 anterior uveitis, **9**:118–134
 experimental, **9**:69
 intermediate uveitis, **9**:134–140
 panuveitis, **9**:172–196
 posterior uveitis, **9**:140–172
 vitreous infiltrate in, **4**:133
in onchocerciasis, **9**:242
onset/duration/course of, **9**:83–84
peripheral. *See* Pars planitis
phacotoxic, **9**:125. *See also* Uveitis, lens-associated/phacoantigenic
posterior. *See* Posterior uveitis
postoperative
 infections and, **9**:126
 IOL-associated inflammation and, **9**:125*f*, 126–127, 127*f*
 lens-associated, **9**:125, 125*f*
prevalence of, **9**:91
Propionibacterium acnes causing, **9**:126
prostaglandin analogues causing, **10**:166
in psoriatic arthritis, **1**:166, **6**:270–271
in reactive arthritis, **1**:165
recurrent, **9**:84
 equine, **9**:69

retinal detachment and, **9**:302
retinoblastoma differentiated from, **4**:305*t*, **6**:276*t*
in Rift Valley fever, **9**:217–218, 217*f*
in rubella, **9**:209–211, 209*f*, 210*f*
sarcoidosis and, **4**:190–191, 191*f*, **6**:274, 274*f*, **8**:74,
  9:172–177, 174*f*, 175*f*, 176*f*, **12**:196–197, 197*f*
scleritis and, **8**:220, 220–221
signs of, **9**:85–90, 86*f*, 86*t*, 87*f*, 88*t*
in spondyloarthropathies/spondyloarthritis, **1**:163,
  164, 165, 166, **6**:271
subretinal fibrosis and (SFU), **9**:148–150*t*, 161,
  167–168, 167*f*
sympathetic ophthalmia and, **4**:189, 189*f*, 190*f*,
  9:52–53, 178–183, 179*f*, 180*f*, 181*f*, 182*t*
symptoms of, **9**:84–85, 84*t*
syphilitic, **9**:242–249, 244*f*, 245*f*, 246*f*, 247*f*, 248*t*
systemic disease associations and, **9**:90, 90*t*
terminology associated with, **9**:79*t*
Th1 delayed hypersensitivity and, **9**:50*t*
in toxocariasis, **6**:273–274, 273*f*, **12**:209
in toxoplasmosis, **1**:21, **9**:226–235, 227*f*, 229*f*, 230*f*,
  231*f*, 233*f*, **12**:206
treatment of, **9**:98
  in children, **6**:275–278
  medical, **9**:98–116, 101*t*, 108*t*
  surgical, **9**:116
tuberculous, **9**:256, 257, 257–258, 258*f*, 261–262, 262*f*
tubulointerstitial nephritis and, **6**:271–272, **9**:72*t*,
  119, 124
varicella-zoster infection and, **9**:197–199, 198*f*
vitreous opacification and vitritis and, **9**:302
Vogt-Koyanagi-Harada (VKH) syndrome and,
  4:189–190, **9**:183–190, 185*f*, 186*f*, 187*t*, 188*f*,
  12:197–198, 198*f*
  in children, **6**:275
Wegener granulomatosis and, **9**:145–146
West Nile virus infection and, **9**:214–217, 215*f*, 216*f*
in Whipple disease, **9**:265
Uveitis-glaucoma-hyphema (UGH) syndrome, **9**:17,
  126–127, **10**:102
  intraocular lens implantation and, **3**:210, **9**:17,
    126–127, **11**:167
  decentration and, **11**:163
  transient visual loss and, **5**:175–176
Uveoparotid fever (Heerfordt syndrome), **8**:73, **9**:174
Uveoscleral drainage/outflow, **2**:50, **10**:3*f*, 16, 19
Uvula, ventral, **5**:48

V

V1 to V6 areas of brain. *See* Visual (calcarine/occipital)
  cortex
V-neck sign, in dermatomyositis, **1**:175
V-number (Abbe number), **3**:50–51
  lens materials and, **3**:161, 162–163
V-pattern deviations, **6**:107–112, 108*f*
  in Brown syndrome, **6**:122*t*, 131
  in craniosynostosis, **6**:391, 391*f*
  definition of, **6**:107
  esotropia, **6**:107–112, 108*f*
    treatment of, **6**:112
  exotropia, **6**:107–112, 108*f*
    treatment of, **6**:112

pulley system pathology and, **6**:23, 109–110, 110*f*
  in superior oblique muscle paralysis, **6**:119
  surgical treatment of, **6**:110–111, 111*f*, 112
Vaccine-associated paralytic poliomyelitis, **1**:283
Vaccine development, **1**:269, 286. *See also*
  Immunization
  for cancer, **1**:244
  for HIV, **1**:36
Vaccinia/vaccinia infection, **8**:128
Vaccinia-immune globulin, **8**:128
Vacuum (phacoemulsification)
  definition of, **11**:104
  settings for, **11**:118, 119
  terminology related to, **11**:104
Vacuum rise time (phacoemulsification), **11**:104, 109,
  110*f*
Vagus nerve stimulation
  for depression, **1**:256
  for seizures, **1**:263
Valacyclovir, **1**:55*t*, **2**:329, 381*t*, 383
  for acute retinal necrosis, **9**:202, **12**:201
  for epithelial keratitis, **8**:113
  for herpes simplex virus infections, **1**:23, **8**:109*t*,
    9:199, **12**:201
    anterior uveitis, **9**:199
  for herpes zoster virus infections, **1**:23, **2**:381*t*, 383,
    8:121, **12**:201
  for stromal keratitis, **8**:115
Valcyte. *See* Valganciclovir
Valdecoxib, **2**:258
  withdrawal of from market, **1**:184, **9**:99
Valganciclovir, **1**:55*t*, 66
  for CMV retinitis, **1**:24, 38, 66, **9**:207, **12**:200
Validity, **1**:319, 339
Valium. *See* Diazepam
Valproate/valproic acid
  as mood stabilizer, **1**:257
  for seizures, **1**:263*t*
Valsalva retinopathy, **12**:153–154
Valsartan
  for heart failure, **1**:118
  for hypertension, **1**:76*t*, 78*t*
Valtrex. *See* Valacyclovir
Valve of Hasner, **7**:245*f*, 246
  nasolacrimal duct obstruction and, **7**:243, 246, 250
Valve of Rosenmüller, **7**:245
Valved glaucoma drainage devices, **10**:205, 205*t*, 207
Van Herick method, **10**:30
Vanceril. *See* Beclomethasone
Vancocin. *See* Vancomycin
Vancomycin, **1**:5, 50*t*, 59–60, **2**:368*t*, 376–377
  for bacterial keratitis, **8**:162*t*
  for *C difficile* colitis, **1**:8–9
  for endophthalmitis, **9**:271, **12**:356
    after cataract surgery, **11**:181
  resistance and, **1**:3, 5, 60
Vancomycin-intermediate *S aureus* (VISA), **1**:5
Vancomycin-resistant enterococci (VRE), **1**:3, 5, 60
Vancomycin-resistant *S aureus* (VRSA), **1**:3, 5, 60
Vantin. *See* Cefpodoxime
Vaporization, **12**:339
Variability, in genetic disease, **2**:208–209
Variable/variable number of tandem repeats (variable
  tandem repeats/minisatellite), **2**:156, 166, 180

Variance (statistical), 1:343
  "special cause," 1:346
Variant (Prinzmetal) angina, 1:101
Variant Creutzfeldt-Jakob disease, 5:368
Varicella (chickenpox), 1:23, 8:117, 118, 9:198f. *See also*
    Varicella-zoster virus
  conjunctivitis in, 6:192–193, 193f, 8:118
  iritis/iridocyclitis in, 9:197
Varicella vaccine (Varivax; Zostavax), 1:23, 233, 282
Varicella-zoster sine herpete, 5:302, 9:197
Varicella-zoster virus, 1:23–24. *See also* Herpes zoster
  acute retinal necrosis/progressive outer retinal
      necrosis/nonnecrotizing herpetic retinitis caused
      by, 9:199–204, 200t, 201f, 203f, 307
  anterior uveitis caused by, 9:197–199, 198f
  conjunctivitis caused by, 6:192–193, 193f,
      8:117–119
  immunization against, 1:23, 233, 282, 8:119, 121
  infection in older patients and, 1:233
  ocular infection caused by, 8:117–122, 118t, 119f,
      120f, 121f
    herpes simplex virus infection differentiated from,
        8:118t
Varices, orbital, 7:66–67
  in children, 6:342
  glaucoma associated with, 10:28
Varivax. *See* Varicella vaccine
Vascular dementia, 1:227, 265
Vascular endothelial growth factor (VEGF), 2:396,
    8:177t
  in age-related macular degeneration/choroidal
      neovascularization, 12:72–73
  agents inhibiting. *See* Anti-VEGF agents
  alternative splicing and, 2:168
  antibodies against, in cancer therapy, 1:243
  in aqueous humor, 2:270, 271
  in diabetic retinopathy, 1:205, 12:104
  in retinal ischemia, 4:158
  retinopathy of prematurity and, 6:281
  in vitreous, 2:287
Vascular endothelial growth factor (VEGF) inhibitors.
    See Anti-VEGF agents
Vascular filling defect, 12:22
Vascular loops, 2:85
  prepapillary, 4:133, 12:307, 307f
Vascular malformations. *See also* Cavernous
    hemangioma
  intracranial hemorrhage caused by, 1:97
  orbital, 6:341–342, 341f, 7:63–69
Vascular resistance, reduction of in heart failure
    management, 1:118–119
Vascular stroke. *See* Stroke
Vascular system
  anatomy of, 5:12–27, 13–14f, 15f, 17f, 19f, 20f, 22f
    arterial, 5:12–23, 13–14f, 15f, 17f, 19f, 20f, 22f,
        23f
    venous, 5:23–27, 24–25f, 27f
  of anterior optic nerve, 10:42–44, 43f
  of choroid, 2:64, 65f, 66, 66f, 67
    development of, 2:132–133
  of ciliary body, 2:62–63
    development of, 2:137–138, 139f
  disorders of, 1:153. *See also* Vasculitis
    in diabetes mellitus, 1:205, 207

  of extraocular muscles, 2:18–21, 19t, 38, 38f, 6:16–18
    surgery and, 6:25
  of eyelids, 2:29–30, 30f, 7:143
  imaging of, 5:74–81, 79f
    selecting modality for, 5:82t
  of iris, 2:58, 59f
  of orbit, 7:12–13, 13f, 14f, 15f
    anatomy of, 2:36–40, 37f, 38f, 39f, 40f, 5:10, 13–14f,
        15–18, 24–25f, 7:12–13, 13f, 14f, 15f
    development of, 2:138
  of retina. *See* Retinal blood vessels
  tumors arising in. *See* Vascular tumors
Vascular tufts, papillary conjunctivitis causing, 8:22,
    22f, 23f
Vascular tumors
  of eyelid and conjunctiva, 8:240–242, 241t
    benign, 8:240–241
    inflammatory, 8:241–242, 241f
    malignant, 8:242, 243f
  of orbit, 4:240, 241f, 7:63–69
    in children, 6:332t, 338–342, 339f, 341f
Vasculitis, 1:176–180, 177t. *See also specific type and*
    Arteritis
  in Behçet disease, 1:180–181, 9:190, 190f, 192
  connective tissue disorders associated with, 7:58
  essential cryoglobulinemic, 1:177t
  giant cell (temporal) arteritis. *See* Arteritis, giant
      cell
  large vessel, 1:176–178, 177t
  lupus, 9:141–142, 142f, 12:195–196, 195f
    choroidal perfusion abnormalities and, 12:179
  medium-sized vessel, 1:177t, 178
  optic disc (papillophlebitis), 4:164, 5:131–132, 132f,
      12:128
  optic neuritis and, 5:144
  orbital manifestations of, 7:39t, 55–58, 57f
  retinal, 12:140–141, 141f
    in Behçet disease, 9:193, 193f, 194f, 12:194–195
    HLA association in, 9:72t
    in HTLV-1 infection, 9:219
    idiopathic, aneurysms and neuroretinitis and
        (IRVAN), 12:141
    inflammatory, 12:194–196
    in Lyme disease, 9:251
    in polyarteritis nodosa/microscopic polyangiitis,
        9:143, 144f
    in Rift Valley fever, 9:217
    in syphilis, 9:243, 245
    in systemic lupus erythematosus, 9:141–142, 142f,
        12:195–196, 195f
    in toxoplasmosis, 9:229
    in tuberculosis, 9:258
    in uveitis, 9:81t, 83t, 199. *See also* Posterior uveitis
      viral, 9:199
    in Wegener granulomatosis, 9:145
    in Whipple disease, 9:265
  rheumatoid, 1:162
  small vessel, 1:177t, 179–180
  Takayasu arteritis, 1:176–178, 177t
  transient visual loss caused by, 5:176t, 183
  Wegener granulomatosis. *See* Wegener
      granulomatosis
Vasculogenesis, in retinopathy of prematurity,
    12:162

Vasculopathy
  polypoidal choroidal (posterior uveal bleeding
    syndrome), 4:171, 172f, 173f
    age-related macular degeneration differentiated
      from, 12:69–70, 70f
    central serous chorioretinopathy differentiated
      from, 12:174, 175
  primary occlusive, 12:141
Vasculotropin. See Vascular endothelial growth factor
Vaseretic. See Captopril; Enalapril
Vasoactive amines, 8:177t
Vasoactive intestinal polypeptide (VIP), 9:29t
  outflow facility affected by, 2:50
  in tear secretion, 2:237, 240, 243, 243f
Vasocon-A. See Naphazoline/antazoline
Vasoconstrictors, for allergic conjunctivitis, 6:198, 199t,
  8:186
Vasodilators
  for heart failure, 1:119
  for hypertension, 1:77t, 82–83
Vasopressin (antidiuretic hormone), 1:214
Vasopressors, for shock, 1:294
Vasoproliferative tumor, 12:148
Vasospasm
  retinal (migraine), 5:184–185, 190, 297
  transient visual loss and, 5:174, 176t, 184–185
Vasotec. See Enalapril
Vasurfilcon, for contact lenses, 3:177t
Vaughan Williams classification, of antiarrhythmic
  drugs, 1:123t
Vault, of contact lens, 3:169, 169f
vCJD. See Variant Creutzfeldt-Jakob disease
VCTS (Vision Contrast Test System), 3:292
VDA (Visual Disability Assessment), 11:71
VDRL (Venereal Disease Research Laboratory) test,
  1:13, 279, 5:361, 9:247, 248
  in syphilitic chorioretinitis, 12:205
VECAT (Vitamin E, Cataract and Age-Related
  Maculopathy Trial), 2:314–315
VECP. See Visually evoked cortical potentials
Vectograph slide test, 6:87
Vector, 2:163
  cloning, 2:149–150
  cosmid, 2:150
  in gene therapy, 2:187
Vector addition of prisms, 3:88, 88f
Vegetation/plants, ocular injuries caused by, 8:362
  corneal foreign body, 8:371
VEGF. See Vascular endothelial growth factor
VEGF Inhibition Study in Ocular Neovascularization
  (VISION), 12:75f
VEGF Trap
  for age-related macular degeneration/choroidal
    neovascularization, 12:77–78
  for central retinal vein occlusion, 12:131
VEGF Trap-Eye: Investigation of Efficacy and Safety
  in Wet Age-Related Macular Degeneration 1 and 2
  (VIEW 1 and 2) studies, 12:77–78
Vein of Galen, 5:26
Vein of Labbé, 5:26
Veins. See also specific vein
  anatomy of, 5:23–27, 24–25f, 27f
  extraocular muscles supplied by, 6:18
    surgery and, 6:25

Velban. See Vinblastine
Velocardiofacial syndrome, posterior embryotoxon in,
  6:212
Velocity
  of light, 3:6
  saccadic system evaluation and, 5:203, 208–209,
    6:83
Velosef. See Cephradine
Vena vorticosa, 5:24f
Venereal Disease Research Laboratory (VDRL) test,
  1:13, 279, 5:361, 9:247, 248
  in syphilitic chorioretinitis, 12:205
Venlafaxine, 1:256
Venodilation, for heart failure, 1:119
Venography
  magnetic resonance (MRV), 5:77–78, 79f
    in idiopathic intracranial hypertension, 5:123
  in orbital evaluation, 7:31
Venomous insect stings, ocular injury/infection caused
  by, 8:361–362
Venous angiomas, 1:97–98
Venous beading, in diabetic retinopathy, 12:104, 104f
Venous capacitance, increase in for heart failure, 1:119
Venous malformations (varices), orbital, 7:66–67
  in children, 6:342
  glaucoma associated with, 10:28
Venous occlusive disease, retinal, 12:121–133. See also
  Retinal vein occlusion
  branch retinal vein occlusion, 4:164, 12:121–127,
    122f, 125f
  central retinal vein occlusion, 4:163–164, 165f,
    12:127–133, 127f, 128f, 129f, 132f
    angle-closure glaucoma and, 10:135
    neovascularization and, 10:127
    open-angle glaucoma and, 10:77
    photocoagulation for, 12:340
Venous outflow disorders, choroidal perfusion
  abnormalities and, 12:176
Venous retrobulbar hemorrhage, cataract surgery and,
  11:176
Venous sinuses, 2:108–109, 108f
  thrombosis of, 5:78, 79f
Venous stasis retinopathy, 5:184, 12:127, 128, 128f, 133
Venous system. See also specific vein
  of extraocular muscles, 6:18
    surgery and, 6:25
Venous thrombosis. See also Thrombosis/thrombotic
  disorders
  anticoagulation therapy in prevention of, 1:152
  cerebral, 5:356–358
Ventilatory failure
  local anesthetic administration causing, 1:311, 312
  in shock, 1:293, 294
Ventilatory support, noninvasive, 1:144
Venting, in phacoemulsification, 11:104
Ventolin. See Albuterol
Ventral medial rectus subnucleus, 5:54
Ventral uvula, 5:48
Ventricular assist devices, for heart failure, 1:120
Ventricular complexes/contractions, premature (PVCs),
  1:121, 122t, 123
Ventricular fibrillation, 1:125, 126–127, 126t
  emergency management of, 1:289, 292
Ventricular flutter, 1:125, 126t

Ventricular hypertrophy, hypertension and, 1:85
Ventricular septal rupture, after myocardial infarction, 1:103
Ventricular tachyarrhythmias, 1:125–127
Ventricular tachycardia, 1:123, 125–126, 126t
Ventriculography, coronary, 1:107
Ventriculoperitoneal shunting, for idiopathic intracranial hypertension, 5:124
Venturi pump, for phacoemulsification aspiration, 11:109, 109f
    vacuum rise time for, 11:109, 110f
VEP/VER. See Visually evoked cortical potentials (visual evoked response)
VePesid. See Etoposide
Verapamil
    for arrhythmias, 1:123t
    for hypertension, 1:77t, 78t
    for ischemic heart disease
        angina, 1:108
        non–ST-segment elevation acute coronary syndrome, 1:111
Verelan. See Verapamil
Vergence change on transfer, 3:66
Vergence (optics), 3:62–64, 63f, 65
    calculation of, for mirrors, 3:90–92, 92f
    reduced, 3:63–64, 65
        image, 3:60
        magnification calculation and, 3:65
        object, 3:60
Vergences/vergence system (eye movements), 5:198–199, 198t, 204, 6:34, 35–37. See also specific type
    assessment of, 5:204, 6:86–87
    disorders of, 5:213–214
    fusional, 6:41, 41t, 82–83
        assessment of, 6:82
    in infants, 6:413
    supranuclear control and, 6:37
Verhoeff–van Gieson stain, 4:31t
Vermis, dorsal, 5:43f, 48–49
Vernal conjunctivitis/keratoconjunctivitis, 8:187–190, 188f, 189f
    atopic keratoconjunctivitis differentiated from, 8:190, 191f
    in children, 6:198–200, 199f
Vernier acuity, 3:109
Verocay bodies, 4:245
Verrucae (warts)
    papillomavirus causing, 7:158, 158f, 8:128, 129
    vulgaris, of eyelid, 4:209, 209f, 7:158, 158f
Versed. See Midazolam
Versican, in vitreous, 2:283
Versions, 5:215, 6:34, 35, 36f. See also specific type
    assessment of, 6:81
    development of, 6:170
Vertebral artery, 2:109, 5:12, 13f, 21, 22f
    aneurysms of, 5:350f
    dissection of, 5:353, 354
Vertebral fracture, osteoporosis and, 1:229
Vertebrobasilar system, 5:22f. See also Basilar artery; Vertebral artery
    arterial dissections in, 5:353, 354
    disorders of, 5:347–349, 348f
        transient visual loss caused by, 5:186, 347–348

Verteporfin, photodynamic therapy with, 12:343–344
    in age-related macular degeneration/choroidal neovascularization, 12:72, 78, 79
    in central serous chorioretinopathy, 12:175
    in choroidal hemangioma, 4:292, 12:182
    combination treatment and, 12:72, 78, 79
    in ocular histoplasmosis syndrome, 9:223, 224
    in retinal hemangioblastoma, 4:295, 12:150
Verteporfin in Photodynamic Therapy (VIP) Trial, 12:72, 344
Vertex distance
    correcting lenses and, 3:139, 140f
    measurement of before refractive surgery, 13:33
    meridional magnification as function of, 3:311, 312f
        minimizing, 3:316–317
Vertex power, lensmeter in measurement of, 3:167, 270, 270f, 271
Vertical chopping techniques, in phacoemulsification, 11:123
Vertical deviations, 6:10, 11, 113–126. See also specific type
    in blowout fractures, 6:124–126, 125f, 7:100–101
        surgery and, 7:102
    botulinum toxin causing, 6:164
    comitant, 6:113
        surgery for, 6:152
    dissociated, 6:116–118, 117f
        surgery for, 6:117, 153
    incomitant (noncomitant), 6:113
        strabismus surgery planning and, 6:146
    inferior oblique muscle overaction and, 6:113, 113–115, 114f
    superior oblique muscle overaction and, 6:113, 115–116, 115f
Vertical eyelid splitting, for orbitotomy, 7:108f, 109
Vertical fusional vergence, 6:41t, 82
Vertical gaze, 5:42–44, 44f
Vertical gaze palsy, 5:210–211, 212f
Vertical heterophoria/phoria
    prismatic effects of bifocal lenses and, 3:151, 152f
    prisms for, 3:163
Vertical incomitance, 6:113
    strabismus surgery planning and, 6:146
Vertical interpalpebral fissure height, 5:275, 276f
    in ptosis, 6:179, 7:202, 202f
Vertical prism dissociation test, in nonorganic ophthalmic disorders, 5:309, 310f
Vertical rectus muscles, 6:14, 14f. See also Inferior rectus muscles; Superior rectus muscles
    A-pattern deviations associated with dysfunction of, 6:109
    action of, 6:14, 28–29, 29t
        gaze position and, 6:31, 31f, 32f
    anatomy of, 6:14, 14f
    surgery of
        for A- and V-pattern deviations, 6:111
        for comitant vertical deviations, 6:152
        for dissociated vertical deviation, 6:117, 153
        eyelid position changes after, 6:159, 159f, 7:214
        for hypo- and hypertropia, 6:152–153
        for nystagmus, 6:329
        for superior oblique muscle paralysis, 6:120
    V-pattern deviations associated with dysfunction of, 6:109

Vertical retraction syndrome, 6:140
Vertical strabismus. *See* Vertical deviations
Vertical vergence, 6:36
Verticillium, endophthalmitis caused by, 9:270
Vertigo
  benign paroxysmal positional, nystagmus and, 5:249*t*, 250
  transient ischemic attacks causing, 5:347
Vertometer. *See* Lensmeters
Very-low-density-lipoproteins, 1:131
Vesicle
  of eyelid, 8:20*t*
  lens, formation of, 2:121, 129, 129*f*, 11:21, 22*f*
  optic, 2:121, 121*f*, 123*f*, 124*f*, 8:4
    lens development and, 2:128–129, 11:21, 22*f*
Vestibular artery, anterior/posterior, 5:21
Vestibular nerve/nuclei, 5:39, 44*f*, 45*f*, 46, 47–48, 200
  disruption to, 5:205
    nystagmus and, 5:249–250
Vestibular nystagmus, 5:200–201, 205, 244*f*, 248–253, 249*t*
  central, 5:249*t*, 250–253, 251*t*, 252*f*
    instability (periodic alternating), 5:251*t*, 252–253, 6:322
  peripheral, 5:248–250, 249*t*
Vestibular ocular reflex, 5:49*f*, 198–199, 198*t*, 200
  assessment of, 5:200–201
  disorders of, 5:205–207, 206*f*, 207*f*
  suppression of, 5:206–207, 207*f*
Vestibular ocular reflex gain, 5:201
Vestibular ocular system, 5:47–48, 47*f*, 49*f*. *See also* Vestibular nerve/nuclei; Vestibular ocular reflex
  disorders of, 5:205–207, 206*f*, 207*f*
  nystagmus and. *See* Vestibular nystagmus
Vestibulocerebellum, 5:48–49
Vexol. *See* Rimexolone
VF. *See* Ventricular fibrillation
VF-14. *See* Visual Function Index
Vfend. *See* Voriconazole
VHL. *See* von Hippel–Lindau disease
Viagra. *See* Sildenafil
Vibramycin. *See* Doxycycline
Vicriviroc, 1:34
Vidarabine, 2:380, 381*t*
  for herpes simplex virus infections, 1:23, 8:109*t*
Video ophthalmoscopy, 3:251
Video specular microscopy, 3:261
Videokeratography
  IOL power determination/selection after refractive surgery and, 11:86
  in keratoconus, 8:299, 300*f*
Videokeratoscopy, 3:267, 267*f*, 268*f*, 8:39, 39*f*
  in keratoconus, 8:298
  tear breakup evaluated with, 8:53
Videophotography, 8:31
Videx. *See* Didanosine
Vidian canal, 5:8
Vidian nerve, 5:63
Vieth-Müller circle, 6:39, 40*f*
VIEW 1 and 2 (VEGF Trap-Eye: Investigation of Efficacy and Safety in Wet Age-Related Macular Degeneration 1 and 2) studies, 12:77–78

Vifilcon, for contact lenses, 3:177*t*
VIG. *See* Vaccinia-immune globulin
Vigabatrin, 1:263*t*
  ophthalmic side effects of, 1:245, 264
Vigamox. *See* Moxifloxacin
VIM (Visudyne in Minimally Classic CNV) Trial, 12:72
Vimentin, 2:277, 11:12
Vinblastine, 1:239, 241*t*
Vinca alkaloids, in cancer chemotherapy, 1:239, 241*t*
Vincristine, 1:239, 241*t*
  for hemangiomas, in children, 6:340
Vioxx. *See* Rofecoxib
VIP. *See* Vasoactive intestinal polypeptide
VIP Pathologic Myopia Trial, 12:86
VIP (Verteporfin in Photodynamic Therapy) Trial, 12:72, 344
Vira-A. *See* Vidarabine
Viracept. *See* Nelfinavir
Viral capsid, 8:104
Viral load, testing, in HIV infection/AIDS, 1:33
Viramune. *See* Nevirapine
Virazole. *See* Ribavirin
Virchow's law, 6:383, 385*f*
Viread. *See* Tenofovir
Virology, 8:104–130. *See also* Viruses
Viroptic. *See* Trifluridine
Virtual colonoscopy, in cancer screening, 1:269, 272*t*, 276
Virtual images, 3:67–68, 67*f*, 69*f*
  displacement of by prisms, 3:86–87, 86*f*
Virtual objects, 3:67–68, 67*f*, 69*f*
Virulence (microbial), 8:98–99
  mechanisms of, 1:4
Viruses, 8:104. *See also specific organism or type of infection*
  cancer etiology and, 1:236–237
  conjunctivitis caused by, 4:53–54, 55*f*
    in children, 6:190–193
    immune response to, 9:60–61
    in neonates, 6:188
  eyelid infection caused by, 4:209–210, 209*f*, 210*f*
  ocular infection/inflammation caused by, 8:104–130
    adherence and, 8:98
    invasion and, 8:99
    isolation techniques for diagnosis of, 8:103
    specimen collection for diagnosis of, 8:101*t*
  optic nerve infection caused by, 4:252, 5:144, 6:311–312
  retinal infection caused by, 4:151, 151*f*, 152*f*
  Sjögren-like syndromes caused by, 8:63
  treatment of infection caused by. *See* Antiviral agents
  uveitis caused by, 9:197–220. *See also specific virus*
VISA. *See* Vancomycin-intermediate *S aureus*
Visceral afferent fibers, 2:105
Visceral efferent fibers, 2:105
Visceral larval/larvae migrans, 6:273, 8:142, 9:235. *See also Toxocara* (toxocariasis)
Viscocanalostomy, 10:211
  for uveitic glaucoma, 9:298
Viscodissection. *See* Viscoelastic agents (ophthalmic viscosurgical devices)

Viscoelastic agents (ophthalmic viscosurgical devices),
  2:393, 11:96–98, 97t
  for cataract surgery, 11:96–98, 97t
    advanced cataract extraction and, 11:196
    aniridia and, 11:200
    capsular rupture and, 11:160, 161
    ECCE, 11:94, 212
    high hyperopia and, 11:200–201
    inflamed eye and, 9:292, 11:207
    intraoperative floppy iris syndrome and, 11:155
    intumescent cataract extraction and, 11:196
    IOL implantation and, 11:138, 139, 140, 141,
      13:129, 130
    phacoemulsification, 11:102, 110, 117, 126
    pupil expansion and, 11:98, 194
    traumatic cataract and, 11:208
    uveitis and, 9:292, 11:207
  characteristics of, 11:98
  elevated intraocular pressure and, 10:101, 11:154
  for goniotomy and trabeculotomy, in children, 10:155
  for penetrating keratoplasty, 8:418
  physical properties of, 11:97–98, 97t
Viscoelasticity, of ophthalmic viscosurgical device,
  11:97
Viscomydriasis, 11:98
Viscosity
  ocular medication absorption affected by, 2:236
  of ophthalmic viscosurgical device, 11:97
Viscosurgical devices, ophthalmic. See Viscoelastic
  agents
Vision
  awareness of, disorders of, 5:195–196
  binocular. See Binocular vision
  color. See Color vision
  decreased. See Low vision; Visual loss/impairment
  development of, 6:44–46, 45f, 413
    abnormal visual experience affecting, 6:46–49,
      47f, 48f
    delayed, 6:416
  diurnal variation in, after radial keratotomy, 13:44–45
  double. See Diplopia
  line of, principal, 3:106
  loss of/low. See Blindness; Low vision; Visual loss/
    impairment
  neurophysiology of, 6:42–49, 43f, 45f, 47f, 48f
  physiology of, 6:39–42, 40f, 41t
VISION (VEGF Inhibition Study in Ocular
  Neovascularization), 12:75f
VISION 2020, 11:65
Vision Contrast Test System (VCTS), 3:292
Vision loss (see-saw) nystagmus, 5:251t, 253–254
  in children, 6:325
Vision rehabilitation, 3:283–307, 284f
  in age-related macular dystrophy, 12:79
  in cataracts, 11:71
    ocular trauma and, 11:208
  central visual field and, 3:292–293
  in children, 3:306–307, 6:330, 416–417
  classification of deficits and, 3:286–288. See also
    Visual deficits
  color vision and, 3:294
  computers in, 3:303–304

in cone dystrophies, 12:232
contrast enhancement in, 3:304
contrast sensitivity testing and, 3:291–292, 292
counseling and support groups in, 3:305
distance visual acuity and, 3:289
electronic magnification in, 3:302–303, 302f
epidemiology of vision impairment and, 3:284
functional history and, 3:288–289
functional improvement and, 3:294–304
glare and, 3:293, 304
high-plus aspheric lenses in, 3:297–298
instruction and training for, 3:304–305
legal blindness and, 3:284
lighting and glare control in, 3:304
  contrast sensitivity and, 3:291
low vision definitions and, 3:284–286
magnifiers (handheld and stand) in, 3:298–299, 300f
near visual acuity assessment and, 3:290–291
nonoptical aids in, 3:301–304, 302f
nonvisual assistance in, 3:301–302
for nystagmus, in children, 6:330
optical aids used in, 3:295–301
patient assessment in, 3:288–294. See also Low vision,
  assessment of
patient well-being and, 3:289
peripheral visual field and, 3:288, 292
prisms in, 3:300–301
professionals providing, 3:305
refraction in, 3:294
in retinitis pigmentosa, 12:230
services available for, 3:305, 305–306
spectacles in
  distance, 3:295
  for magnification/reading, 3:295–298, 298f
telescopes in, 3:299–300, 301f
in uveitis, 9:304
visual function and, 3:285
visual function measurement and, 3:289–294
Vision Rehabilitation for Adults, 1:220
Vision substitution skills, 3:301–302
Visken. See Pindolol
Vistide. See Cidofovir
Visual acuity, 3:108–111, 109f, 110f, 110t. See also
  Distance visual acuity; Near visual acuity
  in acute macular neuroretinopathy, 12:193
  in acute posterior multifocal placoid pigment
    epitheliopathy (APMPPE), 12:187
  in age-related macular degeneration, 12:55, 79
  in albinism, 6:298, 12:258
  in amblyopia, 6:62, 65, 71–74, 72t
  in astigmatic dial refraction, 3:131
  in autosomal dominant optic atrophy, 5:139, 6:310
  after bioptics, 13:137
  in birdshot retinochoroidopathy, 12:190
  in branch retinal vein occlusion, 12:123, 124, 127
  in cataract, 11:69–70, 70t
    preoperative evaluation and, 11:75, 76
  after cataract surgery, 11:141
    in children, 6:260
    cystoid macular edema and, 11:182
    with ECCE, 11:213
    endophthalmitis and, 11:181

with ICCE, **11**:215
  incorrect lens power and, **11**:168
in central areolar choroidal dystrophy, **12**:245
in central retinal artery occlusion, **12**:138
in central retinal vein occlusion, **12**:128, 131
in central serous chorioretinopathy, **12**:171, 175
in choroidal neovascularization, **12**:65, 79
clinical measurement of. *See* Refraction, clinical;
  Visual acuity, testing
after conductive keratoplasty, **13**:120–121
  for presbyopia, **13**:121, 154
in cone dystrophies, **12**:232
in congenital glaucoma, **6**:233, 243, **10**:150
in congenital stationary night blindness, **12**:215
contrast sensitivity/contrast sensitivity function and,
  3:111–113, 112*f*
development of, **6**:170–171
in diabetic retinopathy/diabetic macular edema, after
  photocoagulation, **12**:102
diffraction affecting, **3**:14, 14*f*
dynamic, vestibular ocular reflex and, **5**:201
in epiretinal membrane, **12**:301, 346
fusional vergences and, **6**:82
in giant cell arteritis/AAION, **5**:125, 126*t*
after intrastromal corneal ring segment placement,
  13:60
  for keratoconus, **13**:59, 62
  for myopia, **13**:58
after LASIK, **13**:87–89
  in diabetes mellitus, **13**:183
  for hyperopia/hyperopic astigmatism, **13**:88
  for low myopia, **13**:87
  for mixed astigmatism, **13**:89
  striae and, **13**:105
in Leber congenital amaurosis, **6**:289, **12**:229
legally blind definition and, **3**:284
in low vision
  assessment and, **3**:289, 289–291
  best-corrected, **5**:92
  definition and, **3**:285
in macular holes, **12**:304, 349
with monovision, **13**:153
after multifocal IOL insertion, **13**:145, 155
in multiple evanescent white dot syndrome, **12**:189
in NAION, **5**:126*t*, 127
in North Carolina macular dystrophy, **12**:246
in ocular histoplasmosis syndrome, **12**:81
in optic nerve hypoplasia, **6**:308
in optic neuritis, **5**:144, 145
periocular trauma and, **7**:104–106
after phakic intraocular lens implantation, **13**:131–134,
  132*t*
pinhole, **3**:108
posterior segment trauma evaluation and, **12**:318
after PRK
  hyperopic, **13**:88
  mixed astigmatic, **13**:89
  myopic, **13**:87
in ptosis, **7**:203
after radial keratotomy, **13**:44, 45–46
after refractive lens exchange/clear lens extraction,
  13:138, 141
after retinal detachment surgery, **12**:291

in rod monochromatism, **12**:215
spherical aberration affecting, **3**:100
in Stargardt disease, **6**:293, **12**:236
in strabismic amblyopia, **6**:62
after strabismus surgery, **6**:155
strabismus surgery planning and, **6**:145–146
testing, **3**:108–111, 109*f*, 110*f*, 110*t*, **6**:71–74, 72*t*, **8**:11.
  See also Refraction, clinical
  in amblyopia, **6**:65, 71–74, 72*t*
   refractive surgery and, **13**:178, 179
  before cataract surgery, **11**:75, 76
  in central visual field deficits, **3**:287
  in children, **6**:71–74, 72*t*, **10**:150
  in low vision/vision rehabilitation, **3**:289, 289–291,
   5:92
  in nonorganic ophthalmic disorders, **5**:307–314,
   308*f*, 309*f*, 310*f*, 311*t*, 313*f*, 314*f*, 315*f*
   bottom-up testing and, **5**:311
  in nystagmus, **6**:73, 318–319
  after perforating injury, **8**:374, 382
  in peripheral visual field deficits, **3**:288
  before refractive surgery, **13**:33
  Snellen chart for, **3**:109–110, 109*f*, 110*t*, 289–290
   in children, **6**:72*t*, 73
  in strabismus, **6**:71–74, 72*t*
  after toric IOL implantation, **13**:143
  uncorrected, refractive surgery and, **13**:33
  after wavefront-guided/wavefront-optimized
   ablation, **13**:26, 88–89
"Visual aids," in nonorganic ophthalmic disorder
  evaluation, **5**:312
Visual allesthesia, **5**:195
Visual aura. *See* Aura
Visual axis, **3**:87, 103, 106, 107*f*, **6**:12, 14*f*, 39
  accommodative convergence and, **6**:37
  muscle action/gaze position and, **6**:30
  Nd:YAG laser capsulotomy location and, **11**:172
Visual confusion, **6**:49, 50*f*
Visual (calcarine/occipital) cortex, **2**:97, **5**:34–37, 35*f*,
  36*f*, **6**:42
  development of, **6**:44, 45*f*
   abnormal visual experience affecting, **6**:46–49,
    47*f*, 48*f*
  disorders of, **5**:191–196, 192*t*
   hallucinations and, **5**:172, 190–191
   illusions and, **5**:189
   recognition disorders and, **5**:192–194, 192*t*, 193*f*
   vision/visual deficit awareness disorders and,
    5:192*t*, 195–196
   visual–spatial relationship disorders and, **5**:192*t*,
    194–195, 195*f*
  eye movement control and, **5**:37, 38–41, 38*f*, 39*f*, 40*f*,
   42*f*, 43*f*
Visual deficits. *See also* Low vision; Visual loss/
  impairment
  awareness of, disorders of, **5**:195–196
  central visual field, **3**:286–287, 287*f*, 292–293
  classification of, **3**:286–288
  cloudy media, **3**:286
  peripheral visual field, **3**:288, 292
   in glaucoma, **10**:68, 72*f*
Visual disability, **3**:283, 284*f*. *See also* Low vision
Visual Disability Assessment (VDA), **11**:71

Visual disorder, **3**:283, 284*f. See also* Low vision
Visual evoked potential/response. *See* Visually evoked cortical potentials
Visual field, **10**:53, 54*f. See also* Visual field defects
clinical evaluation of. *See* Visual field testing
cloverleaf, **10**:61, 62*f*
contact lens use and, **3**:170
Visual field defects, **2**:93, 94*f*
in acute zonal occult outer retinopathy, **9**:171, 172, **12**:192, 193
arteriovenous malformations causing, **5**:355*f*, 356
in branch retinal artery occlusion, **12**:136
central, **3**:286–287, 287*f*, 292–293
chiasmal lesions causing
bitemporal patterns and, **5**:159–162, 160*f*, 161*f*
parasellar lesions and, **5**:162–165, 163*f*
in chloroquine/hydroxychloroquine toxicity, **12**:266
in chronic papilledema, **5**:122, 122*f*
in cone dystrophies, **12**:232
in cone–rod dystrophies, **12**:223, 232
in congenital tilted disc syndrome, **5**:142, 142*f*
congruous, retrochiasmal lesions producing, **5**:165
cortical lesions causing, **5**:34
evaluation of, **5**:97–104, 101*f*, 102*f*, 103*f. See also* Visual field testing
in glaucoma, **10**:68, 69*f*, 70*f*, 71*f*, 72*f*, 73, 75, 79
cataract/media opacities and, **11**:201, 202*f*
evaluation of, **10**:53–68. *See also* Perimetry; Visual field testing
serial fields and, **10**:62–68, 64*f*, 65*f*, 66*f*, 67*f*
single field and, **10**:59–62, 60*f*, 62*f*, 63*f*
indications for surgery and, **10**:179
normal-tension glaucoma and, **10**:79, 81–82
optic disc changes correlated with, **10**:66–67, 75
peripheral, **10**:68, 72*f*
primary open-angle glaucoma (POAG) and, **10**:73, 75
progression of, **10**:65–66, 65*f*, 66*f*, 67*f*
screening tests for, **10**:58
incongruous, retrochiasmal lesions producing, **5**:165
lateral geniculate body lesions causing, **5**:167–168, 167*f*
in Leber hereditary optic neuropathy, **5**:137, 137*f*, 138
in low vision patients, **3**:285, 286, 286–287, 287*f*, 288
in migraine aura without headache, **5**:296, 297
in migraine headache, **5**:295, 295*f*, 297
in multiple sclerosis, **5**:324
in NAION, **5**:128*t*
neuroimaging in evaluation of, **5**:84, 84*f*
as nonorganic disorders, **5**:312–314, 313*f*, 314*f*, 315*f*
occipital lobe lesions causing, **5**:169–172, 170*f*, 171*f*, 172*f*
optic disc drusen causing, **5**:133
in optic nerve hypoplasia, **6**:308
in optic neuritis, **5**:128*t*, 144, 145*f*
in optic neuropathy, **5**:116, 117*f*, 118*t*, 119*f*
optic tract lesions causing, **5**:32–33, 165–167, 166*f*
parietal lobe lesions causing, **5**:168–169
perimetric terms and, **5**:118*t*
peripheral, **3**:288, 292
in glaucoma, **10**:68, 72*f*
in photoreceptor dystrophies, **12**:223, 225*f*
in retinitis pigmentosa, **12**:225*f*, 228

in retrochiasmal lesions, **5**:165–172
in Stargardt disease, **12**:235
temporal lobe lesions causing, **5**:103*f*, 168, 169*f*
vigabatrin causing, **1**:245, 264
Visual field testing, **5**:97–104, 101*f*, 102*f*, 103*f*
Amsler grid, **5**:98–99
before cataract surgery, **11**:81–82
in chloroquine/hydroxychloroquine toxicity screening, **12**:267
in cone dystrophies, **12**:232
confrontation testing, **5**:98, 312–313
in glaucoma, **10**:53–68
artifacts and, **10**:56, 61–62, 62*f*, 63*f*
interpretation in
of serial fields, **10**:62–68, 64*f*, 65*f*, 66*f*, 67*f*
of single field, **10**:59–62, 60*f*, 62*f*, 63*f*
optic disc changes correlated with, **10**:66–67, 75
perimetry in, **10**:53–68. *See also* Perimetry
progression of defect and, **10**:65–66, 65*f*, 66*f*, 67*f*
screening tests in, **10**:58
ultrasound biomicroscopy in, **10**:70, 72*f*
Goldmann perimetry, **5**:99–100. *See also* Goldmann perimetry
in children, **6**:83
in hereditary retinal and choroidal dystrophies, **12**:223, 225
in inflammatory chorioretinopathies, **9**:150*t*
in low vision patients/vision rehabilitation, **3**:292–293, **5**:97–104, 101*f*, 102*f*, 103*f*
in measles, **9**:213
perimetry, **5**:99–104, 101*f*, 102*f*, 103*f. See also* Perimetry
in photoreceptor dystrophies, **12**:223, 225*f*
in ptosis, **7**:204
in retinitis pigmentosa, **12**:225*f*, 226
silent, in nonorganic ophthalmic disorder evaluation, **5**:312
Visual function, **3**:283, 284*f*, 285
improving, **3**:294–304. *See also* Vision rehabilitation
measuring, **3**:285, 289–294. *See also* Low vision, assessment of
in cataract evaluation, **11**:71
after surgery, **11**:141
before surgery, **11**:71, 76–77
contrast sensitivity testing and, **3**:291
reduced/deficits in. *See* Low vision; Visual deficits; Visual loss/impairment
sunglasses affecting, **3**:159, 160*f*, 304
Visual Function Index (VF-14), **11**:71
Visual handicap, **3**:283, 284*f. See also* Low vision
Visual impairment, **3**:283, 284*f. See also* Low vision; Visual loss/impairment
Visual indices, in perimetry, **10**:59, 63
Visual loss/impairment, **3**:283, 284*f. See also specific type and* Blindness; Low vision; Visual acuity
in acute macular neuroretinopathy, **12**:193
in acute posterior multifocal placoid pigment epitheliopathy (APMPPE), **9**:148*t*, 155, 157, **12**:185, 187
in acute retinal necrosis, **9**:200
in acute zonal occult outer retinopathy, **9**:148*t*, 171, 172, **12**:192, 193
in albinism, **6**:298

in Alzheimer disease, **1**:268
amblyopia causing, **5**:116, **6**:61–69
in *Aspergillus* endophthalmitis, **9**:276, 278
assessment of, **5**:91–110. *See also* Low vision,
    assessment of
awareness of, disorders of, **5**:195–196
in *Bartonella*-associated neuroretinitis, **9**:263–264
in Behçet disease, **9**:192, 195–196
bilateral/binocular, **5**:91
in birdshot retinochoroidopathy, **9**:148*t*, 153, **12**:190
after blepharoplasty, **7**:226
in blowout fractures, **7**:101
in branch retinal vein occlusion, **12**:123
in *Candida* chorioretinitis/endophthalmitis, **9**:274
carotid dissection and, **5**:353
cataract and, **11**:65, 65*t*, 71
    in children, **6**:252
in central retinal artery occlusion, **12**:138
in central retinal vein occlusion, **12**:128
in central serous chorioretinopathy, **12**:171, 175
chiasmal lesions causing, **5**:159–165
classification and management of, **5**:111–172. *See also*
    specific causative factor
in coccidioidomycosis, **9**:280
in cone dystrophies, **12**:232
craniosynostosis and, **6**:390
in cysticercosis, **9**:238, 239
in dengue fever, **9**:219
in diabetic retinopathy, **12**:95
in diffuse unilateral subacute neuroretinitis,
    9:239–240
in endophthalmitis, **9**:272
epidemiology of, **3**:284
functional. *See* Visual loss/impairment, nonorganic
in glaucoma, **10**:3–4, 8, 78, 109, 117. *See also* Visual
    field defects, in glaucoma
    in children, **6**:233, 243, **10**:158
    after trabeculectomy, **10**:186
in hereditary retinal disease, **6**:289
in Leber congenital amaurosis, **12**:229
in leukemia, **6**:297
in macroaneurysms, **12**:147–148
in macular holes, **12**:304, 349
maculopathies causing, **5**:112–115
in measles, **9**:213
media abnormality causing, **5**:111–112
in meningioma, **7**:74
in multifocal choroiditis and panuveitis syndrome,
    9:148*t*, 161
in multiple evanescent white dot syndrome, **9**:148*t*,
    168, **12**:189
nonorganic, **1**:248, 257, **5**:305–317
    afferent visual pathways and, **5**:307–314, 308*f*, 309*f*,
        310*f*, 311*t*, 313*f*, 314*f*, 315*f*
    categories of, **5**:305
    examination in, **5**:307–317, 308*f*, 309*f*, 310*f*, 311*t*,
        313*f*, 314*f*, 315*f*
    eyelid position/function and, **5**:316–317
    management of, **5**:317
    ocular motility/alignment and, **5**:314–315
    pupils/accommodation and, **5**:316
in nystagmus, **6**:318–319
in ocular histoplasmosis syndrome, **9**:223, 225, **12**:81

in ocular ischemic syndrome, **12**:133
in older patients, **1**:221, 227
    ADLs/function affected by, **1**:219, 220, 224, **3**:284
    depression and, **1**:248
in onchocerciasis (river blindness), **9**:241–242
optic neuropathy causing, **5**:116–159. *See also* Optic
    neuropathy
after orbital surgery, **7**:116
after parasellar tumor therapy, **5**:164
in pars planitis, **12**:196
after photodynamic therapy, **12**:344
in progressive outer retinal necrosis, **9**:203
in ptosis, **7**:201, 203–204
in punctate inner choroiditis, **9**:148*t*, 164–165
in retinitis pigmentosa, **12**:225*f*, 228, 229, 230, 231
in retinopathy of prematurity, **6**:286–287, 287*f*,
    12:157
retrochiasmal lesions causing, **5**:165–172
in Rift Valley fever, **9**:218
in sarcoidosis, **5**:335
in serpiginous choroiditis/choroidopathy, **9**:148*t*, 159,
    12:188
in sickle cell retinopathy, **12**:117
in Stargardt disease, **12**:235
in sympathetic ophthalmia, **9**:179, 182–183
symptoms associated with, **5**:91–92
in thyroid eye disease, **5**:148, **7**:51
time course of, **5**:91
in toxocariasis, **9**:235, 236
in toxoplasmosis, **9**:229, **12**:207
after trabeculectomy, **10**:186
transient, **5**:173–186. *See also* Transient visual loss
traumatic, with clear media, **7**:104–106
unilateral, **5**:91
in uveal lymphoid infiltration, **4**:325
in uveitis, **9**:84, 84*t*, 85, 119, 304
    cataract and, **9**:291
    cystoid macular edema and, **9**:300
in Vogt-Koyanagi-Harada (VKH) syndrome, **9**:185,
    189
in Wegener granulomatosis, **9**:145
in West Nile virus chorioretinitis, **9**:215, 216
Visual pathways, **2**:93, 94*f*, **5**:5–67. *See also*
    Retinogeniculocortical pathway
    afferent, **5**:27–37. *See also* Afferent visual pathways
    autonomic pathways and, **5**:63–67
        parasympathetic, **5**:65–67, 65*f*, 66*f*
        sympathetic, **5**:63–65, 64*f*
    bony anatomy of head and, **5**:5–7, 6*f*, 7–8*f*, 9–10*f*
    development of, **6**:45–46
    efferent (ocular motor), **5**:37–56. *See also* Ocular
        motility, control of; Ocular motor pathways
    neuroimaging in evaluation of, **5**:84
    sensory and facial motor fibers and, **5**:56–62
    vascular anatomy and, **5**:12–27
Visual pigments, **12**:15
    absorption spectra of, **12**:337, 338*f*
    regeneration of, retinal pigment epithelium in,
        2:305–306
Visual processing stream, dorsal, **5**:204
Visual (optic) radiations (geniculocalcarine pathways),
    2:93, 94*f*, 96, **5**:20*f*, 21, 28*f*, 34
    lesions of, **5**:165–172

Visual reaction time (latency)
  perimetry variations and, **10**:56
  saccadic system evaluation and, **5**:203, 208
Visual rehabilitation. *See* Vision rehabilitation
Visual resolution. *See* Resolution
Visual–spatial relationships, disorders of, **5**:192*t*,
  194–195, 195*f*
Visually evoked cortical potentials (visual evoked
  response), **12**:44–45, 45*f*
  in infants and children, **6**:72*t*, 171, 413
  in low vision, **5**:108–109
  in nonorganic ophthalmic disorders, **5**:308
Visudyne in Minimally Classic CNV (VIM) Trial, **12**:72
Visuscope, for strabismic amblyopia testing, **6**:63
VIT1, in vitreous, **2**:283, 285–286
Vital capacity, forced (FVC), **1**:143
Vitamin A
  for abetalipoproteinemia, **2**:232, **12**:260
  for cicatricial pemphigoid, **8**:202
  deficiency of, **5**:114, **8**:77–79, 77*t*, 78*f*
    Corynebacterium xerosis and, **8**:134
    retinopathy caused by, **12**:260–261
  metabolism of, **8**:77*t*
  ocular development/congenital anomalies and, **2**:115,
    142
  in retinal pigment epithelium, **2**:305, 306
  for retinitis pigmentosa, **12**:231
  in visual cycle, **2**:305–306
Vitamin B$_2$ (riboflavin), in collagen crosslinking, **13**:123
Vitamin B$_6$ (pyridoxine)
  for gyrate atrophy, **12**:244
  for homocystinuria, **2**:232, **6**:399, **11**:37
Vitamin B$_{12}$ deficiency, **1**:149
  in older patients, **1**:232
  optic neuropathy caused by, **5**:154
Vitamin B$_{12}$ supplements, for homocystinuria, **6**:399
Vitamin C (ascorbic acid)
  for age-related macular degeneration, **12**:61–62
  antioxidant effect of, **2**:317–318
    in lens, **2**:314–315
    in retina and retinal pigment epithelium,
      2:317–318
  in aqueous humor, **2**:255, 266*t*
  for chemical injuries, **8**:79, 358
  corneal wound healing and, **13**:27
  deficiency of (scurvy), **1**:153, **8**:79
  oral supplements and, **2**:314–315
  in tear film, **2**:240
  in vitreous, **2**:266*t*
Vitamin D, for osteoporosis, **1**:230
Vitamin E
  abetalipoproteinemia and, **2**:232, **12**:260
  age-related macular degeneration and, **12**:61–62
  antioxidant effect of, **2**:312, 314*f*, 317
    in lens, **2**:314–315
    oral supplements and, **2**:314–315
    in retina and retinal pigment epithelium, **2**:317,
      318*f*
  perioperative use of, **1**:306
  for retinitis pigmentosa, **12**:231
Vitamin E, Cataract and Age-Related Maculopathy Trial
  (VECAT), **2**:314–315
Vitamin K deficiency, coagulation disorders and, **1**:156

Vitamins
  deficiencies of
    cataracts caused by, **11**:57–58
    optic neuropathy caused by, **5**:154–155
  supplementary, **2**:395
    in age-related macular degeneration management,
      12:61–63
    cataract prevention and, **11**:58
    in genetic disorders, **2**:232
    in retinitis pigmentosa management, **12**:231
Vitelliform/vitelliruptive degeneration/dystrophy,
  12:236–238. *See also* Adult-onset vitelliform lesions;
  Best disease
Vitelliform exudative macular detachment, **12**:238,
  238*f*
Vitelliform macular dystrophy, juvenile-onset. *See* Best
  disease
Vitelliform macular dystrophy *(VMD2/Best1)* gene,
  4:174–175, **6**:294, **10**:11*t*, **12**:236
Vitiliginous chorioretinitis (birdshot
  retinochoroidopathy), **9**:148–150*t*, 152–155, 152*f*,
  153*f*, 154*f*, **12**:186*t*, 190–191, 190*f*
  HLA association in, **9**:72*t*, 73, 148*t*, 152, **12**:190
Vitiligo, in Vogt-Koyanagi-Harada (VKH) syndrome,
  9:185, 186*f*, **12**:197
Vitrasert. *See* Ganciclovir
Vitravene. *See* Fomivirsen
Vitrectomy, **12**:345–368
  for amyloidosis, **12**:312–313, 313*f*
  angle-closure glaucoma after, **10**:135
  anterior
    for capsular rupture during cataract surgery,
      11:160
    for vitreous prolapse, **11**:162
  for aqueous misdirection (malignant/ciliary block
    glaucoma), **10**:133
  for branch retinal vein occlusion, **12**:126
  for capsular rupture during cataract surgery,
    11:160–161, 161
  with capsulectomy, for pediatric cataract
    lensectomy with intraocular lens implantation and,
      6:258
    lensectomy without intraocular lens implantation
      and, **6**:256, 257*f*
  cataract/cataract surgery after, **11**:16, 60, 75, 205–206,
    12:368
  for choroidal neovascularization, **12**:351, 351*f*
    uveitic, **9**:303
  for CMV retinitis, **12**:201
  for coccidioidomycosis, **9**:280
  complications of, **12**:368, 368*t*
  for cystoid macular edema, **12**:143
    postoperative, **12**:360, 360*f*
      after cataract surgery, **11**:183
    in uveitis, **9**:301
  for diabetic retinopathy complications, **12**:109–111,
    352–353, 353*f*
    macular edema, **12**:103, 353
    tractional retinal detachment, **12**:110–111,
      352–353, 353*f*
    vitreous hemorrhage, **12**:110, 352
  for dislocated posterior chamber intraocular lenses,
    12:359–360

for endophthalmitis
    Aspergillus/mold, 9:277, 278, 12:204
    Candida/yeast, 9:275, 12:203
    postoperative, 9:271, 11:181, 12:354–357, 355*f*,
        356*f*, 357*f*
        acute-onset, 12:354, 354–356, 355*f*
        bleb-associated, 12:354, 356–357, 357*f*
        chronic (delayed-onset), 12:355, 356, 356*f*
endophthalmitis after, 12:368
in endophthalmitis diagnosis, 9:272–273, 275
for epiretinal membranes, 12:301, 346, 347*f*, 348*f*
for foreign-body removal, 12:327
for Fuchs heterochromic iridocyclitis/uveitis, 9:134
for hemolytic/ghost cell glaucoma, 10:100
for idiopathic macular hole, 12:305–306, 349, 350*f*
intraocular lens condensation and, 3:206
in intraocular lymphoma, 4:142, 324, 9:282, 283
for macular diseases, 12:346–352
after needle penetration/perforation of globe, 12:362,
    363*f*
ocular physiologic changes after, 2:287–288
open-angle glaucoma after, 12:368
oxidative lens damage and, 11:16
pars plana. *See* Pars plana vitrectomy
for pars planitis, 9:138, 12:196
after penetrating injury, 12:324
after perforating injury, 12:325
with phacoemulsification, in uveitis, 9:293
phototoxicity and, 12:333
for posterior segment complications of anterior
    segment surgery, 12:354–362
for posterior vitreous detachment, 12:276, 289, 301*f*
for postoperative endophthalmitis, 12:354–357, 355*f*,
    356*f*, 357*f*
primary, 12:366–368, 366*f*
in primary central nervous system lymphoma, 4:142,
    324, 9:282, 283
for retained lens fragments after phacoemulsification,
    11:159–160, 12:357–359, 358*t*, 359*f*
for retinal detachment, 12:290, 291, 366–368, 366*f*
    in acute retinal necrosis, 9:202, 302
    in CMV retinitis, 9:307
    complex detachment, 12:367
    in diabetes mellitus, 12:110–111, 352–353, 353*f*
    refractive surgery after, 13:177–178
    in retinopathy of prematurity, 6:287, 12:170
    tractional, 12:110–111, 191
    in uveitis, 9:302
for retinopathy of prematurity, 6:287, 12:170
in sickle cell retinopathy, 12:121
small gauge technique for, 12:346
for subfoveal choroidal neovascularization, 12:351, 351*f*
for submacular hemorrhage, 12:349–351, 350*f*
for suprachoroidal hemorrhage, 12:360–361, 362*f*
sympathetic ophthalmia and, 9:178, 12:329
transconjunctival technique for, 12:346
for uveal lymphoid infiltration diagnosis, 4:326
for uveitic neovascularization, 9:303
for uveitis, 9:292, 293, 301
    juvenile idiopathic (chronic/rheumatoid) arthritis–
        associated, 9:131
    vitreous biopsy and, 9:97

for vitreocorneal adherence/persistent corneal edema,
    11:148
for vitreomacular traction syndrome, 12:302–303,
    346–347, 348*f*
for vitreous opacification/vitritis, 9:302
for vitreous prolapse, 11:162
Vitrectorhexis, in infants and children, 6:255
Vitreocorneal adherence, after cataract surgery, 8:384,
    11:148
Vitreolysis
    enzymatic, 2:289
    Nd:YAG laser, for vitreous prolapse in anterior
        chamber, 11:162
Vitreomacular traction syndrome, 12:298, 302–304,
    303*f*, 346–347, 348*f*
    vitrectomy for, 12:302–303, 346–347, 348*f*
Vitreoretinal dystrophies, 12:246–248
    in children, 6:294–296
    Goldmann-Favre, 6:296, 12:219, 248
Vitreoretinal interface, diseases of, 12:297–315. *See also*
    specific type
Vitreoretinal/retinal (primary intraocular) lymphoma,
    1:244, 4:140–142, 141*f*, 142*f*, 143*f*, 323–325, 323*f*,
    325*f*, 9:136, 281–284, 282*f*, 283*f*, 12:199, 199*f*
    central serous retinopathy differentiated from, 12:174
    in HIV infection/AIDS, 9:314
    uveitis differentiated from, 9:91, 136, 281–283
        in children, 6:276*t*
Vitreoretinal surgery, 12:345–368. *See also* Vitrectomy
    angle-closure glaucoma after, 10:135
    for cysticercosis, 9:239
    in sickle cell retinopathy, 12:121
    sympathetic ophthalmia and, 9:178
Vitreoretinal traction, in retinopathy of prematurity,
    6:281
Vitreoretinal tufts, 12:278, 279*f*, 280*f*
Vitreoretinopathies. *See also specific type*
    cataract surgery in patient with, 11:205
    familial exudative, 6:296, 12:310–311, 310*f*
    hereditary, 6:294–296, 12:246–248
    proliferative, 4:20, 21*f*, 136, 137*f*, 12:286–288, 289*f*,
        289*t*
        rhegmatogenous retinal detachment and,
            12:286–288, 289*f*, 289*t*
    uveitis and, 9:302
Vitreoschisis. *See* Vitreous detachment
Vitreous, 2:41*f*, 42, 82–85, 283–289, 12:7–8, 7*f*
    aging affecting, 2:84, 84*f*, 286–289
    amyloidosis involving, 4:139–140, 140*f*, 141*f*,
        12:312–313, 313*f*
    anatomy of, 2:41*f*, 42, 82–85, 83*f*, 84*f*, 85*f*, 12:7–8, 7*f*
    as angiogenesis inhibitor, 2:287
    biochemistry and metabolism of, 2:283–289
    biopsy of
        for endophthalmitis after cataract surgery, 11:181
        for intraocular (primary central nervous system)
            lymphoma, 4:324, 9:282, 283
        for specimen collection, 12:354
        for uveitis, 9:97
    cataract surgery complications and, 11:144*t*, 12:314
        with ICCE, 11:214
        posterior vitreous detachment, 11:184, 12:275, 297

prolapse, 11:162
vitreocorneal adherence, 11:148
collagen in, 2:82–83, 83f, 130, 132, 283, 283–284,
    284f, 4:131
    liquefaction and, 2:286
composition of, 2:283–286
congenital anomalies of, 4:132–133, 132f
cortex of, 4:131
cysts of, 4:133
degenerations of, 4:134–140
detachment of. See Vitreous detachment
development of, 2:85, 130–132, 131f, 4:131–132
    abnormalities of, 4:132–133, 132f, 12:307–309,
        307f, 308f
disorders of, 4:131–142, 143f, 12:297–315. See also
    specific type
    biochemical changes associated with, 2:286–289
    in children, 6:279–304
    decreased vision and, 5:112
    neoplastic, 4:140–142, 141f, 142f, 143f
genetic disease involving, 2:288
healing/repair of, 4:17
hyaluronan/hyaluronic acid in, 2:83f, 130–132, 283,
    284–285, 12:7, 297
immune response in, 9:58t, 59–63
infection/inflammation of, 2:288, 4:133, 134f. See also
    Endophthalmitis; Intermediate uveitis; Vitritis
injury to, 2:288
in leukemia, 4:326
lipids in, 2:286
liquefaction of, 2:286
    injury/hemorrhage/inflammation and, 2:288
macular attachment to, 12:7f, 8
    posterior vitreous detachment and, 12:298,
        302–304, 303f
macular hole formation and, 2:288
myopia caused by changes in, 2:286, 287
opacification of, 12:311–314
    in amyloidosis, 4:140, 12:312–313, 313f
    in asteroid hyalosis, 12:311, 312f
    in cholesterolosis, 12:311–312
    hemorrhage causing, 12:313–314
    pigment granules and, 12:314
    in uveitis, 9:302
optically empty, hereditary hyaloideoretinopathies
    with, 12:309–310, 309f
pigment granules in ("tobacco dust"/Shafer sign),
    12:286, 314
primary, 2:130, 131f, 4:132
    persistent hyperplasia of. See Persistent fetal
        vasculature
proteins in, 2:283, 285–286, 4:131
refractive index of, 3:40t, 104f, 105t
retinal attachment to, 12:7f, 8
    posterior vitreous detachment and, 12:274–276,
        274f, 275f, 297–306, 362
in sarcoidosis, 9:175
secondary, 2:130–132, 131f, 4:132
specimen collection from, 12:354
tap biopsy of. See Vitreous biopsy
tertiary, 2:132, 4:132
topography of, 2:41f, 42, 4:131–132

Toxocara larvae in, 9:237, 237f
    in uveitis, 9:78t, 79, 86t, 89, 134. See also Intermediate
        uveitis
    zonular fibers in, 2:286, 4:132
Vitreous base, 2:83, 12:7, 7f, 274
    avulsion of, 12:272, 273f
    posterior vitreous detachment and, 12:297
Vitreous biopsy
    for endophthalmitis after cataract surgery, 11:181
    for intraocular (primary central nervous system)
        lymphoma, 4:324, 9:282, 283
    for specimen collection, 12:354
    for uveitis, 9:97
Vitreous cellular reaction, in uveitis, 9:85, 89, 119
Vitreous detachment
    anterior, 12:297
    hallucinations and, 5:189
    posterior, 2:84, 84f, 85f, 286–287, 4:134–135, 135f,
        12:200f, 274–276, 274f, 275f, 297–306, 299f, 301f,
        362
        in diabetic retinopathy, 12:110
        epiretinal membranes and, 12:298–301, 302f
        macular holes and, 12:298, 304–306, 305–306f
        perifoveal, 12:298
        retinal detachment after cataract surgery and, 11:184
        vitreomacular traction syndrome and, 12:298,
            302–304, 303f
        vitreous hemorrhage and, 12:275, 313
Vitreous hemorrhage, 2:288, 4:137–138, 139f,
    12:313–314, 319
    blunt trauma causing, 12:319
    branch retinal vein occlusion and, 12:123, 125, 126
    central retinal vein occlusion and, 12:130
    diabetic retinopathy and, 12:105, 106f, 110, 313, 352
    hemolytic/ghost cell glaucoma and, 10:99–100
    pars planitis and, 9:139, 12:196
    posterior vitreous detachment and, 12:275, 313
    retinal cavernous hemangioma and, 12:151
    retinoblastoma differentiated from, 4:305t
    retinopathy of prematurity and, 12:157, 163, 164
    shaking injury and, 6:405, 407
    spontaneous, 12:313–314
    systemic lupus erythematosus and, 9:141
    vitrectomy for, in diabetes mellitus, 12:110, 352
Vitreous membrane, tractional retinal detachment and,
    12:291
Vitreous opacities. See Vitreous, opacification of
Vitreous pocket, precortical, 12:7f, 8
Vitreous pressure, positive, flat or shallow anterior
    chamber and, 11:152
Vitreous seeds, in retinoblastoma, 4:303, 303f, 6:354, 355f
Vitreous tap, for specimen collection, 12:354
Vitreous traction
    in posterior vitreous detachment, 12:298, 302–304,
        303f, 362
    in retinal break/tear formation, 12:274, 275f
    retinal cavernous hemangioma and, 12:151
Vitreous wick syndrome, 11:162
Vitritis, 4:133, 9:119, 302. See also Endophthalmitis
    in acute posterior multifocal placoid pigment
        epitheliopathy (APMPPE), 9:156
    in acute zonal occult outer retinopathy, 12:192

Aspergillus causing, **9**:277
in *Bartonella*-associated neuroretinitis, **9**:264
in birdshot retinochoroidopathy, **9**:152, **12**:190
chorioretinitis with/without, flowchart for evaluation
    of, **9**:80*t*
in choroidal metastasis, **9**:286
in CMV retinitis, **6**:184
in cystoid macular edema, **12**:142
in HTLV-1 infection, **9**:219
in intraocular (primary central nervous system)
    lymphoma, **4**:141, 141*f*, 323, 323*f*, **9**:136, 281
in leptospirosis, **9**:255
in Lyme disease, **9**:251, 252*f*, **12**:210
in multifocal choroiditis and panuveitis syndrome,
    9:161, **12**:191
in nocardiosis, **9**:256
in pars planitis, **12**:196
in Rift Valley fever, **9**:217
in subretinal fibrosis and uveitis syndrome (SFU),
    9:167
in sympathetic ophthalmia, **9**:178, 179*f*
in syphilis, **9**:245, 310
in uveitis, **9**:119, 302
in Vogt-Koyanagi-Harada (VKH) syndrome, **9**:184,
    12:197
in Wegener granulomatosis, **9**:145
in Whipple disease, **9**:265
Vittaforma/Vittaforma corneae, **8**:141, 170
VKC. *See* Vernal conjunctivitis/keratoconjunctivitis
VKH. *See* Vogt-Koyanagi-Harada (VKH) syndrome
VLDL. *See* Very-low-density-lipoproteins
VLM. *See* Visceral larval/larvae migrans
VM-26. *See* Teniposide
VMD2 (vitelliform macular dystrophy/*Best1*) gene,
    4:174–175, **6**:294, **10**:11*t*, **12**:236
VMT. *See* Vitreomacular traction syndrome
VNS. *See* Vagus nerve stimulation
VNTRs. *See* Variable/variable number of tandem
    repeats
Vogt
    palisades of, **8**:5
    white limbal girdle of, **8**:336
Vogt-Koyanagi-Harada (VKH) syndrome, **4**:189–190,
    9:183–190, 185*f*, 186*f*, 187*f*, 188*f*, **12**:197–198,
    198*f*
    central serous chorioretinopathy differentiated from,
        12:174
    in children, **6**:275
    diagnosis/differential diagnosis of, **9**:187–189, 187*t*
    glaucoma and, **9**:189, 296
    histologic findings in, **9**:184
    HLA association in, **9**:72*t*, 184, **12**:197
Vogt lines, in keratoconus, **8**:298
Vogt triad, in tuberous sclerosis, **6**:371
Volkmann type cataract, **6**:247*t*
Voltaren. *See* Diclofenac
Volume expansion
    for anaphylaxis, **1**:295
    for shock, **1**:294
Volume overload, **1**:117
Voluntary convergence, **6**:37
Voluntary nystagmus, **5**:256, 314–315
Vomiting. *See* Nausea and vomiting

von Basedow disease. *See* Hyperthyroidism; Thyroid
    eye disease
von Graefe knife, **11**:92
von Graefe sign, **7**:24
von Helmholtz keratometers, **3**:264, 265*f*
von Hippel, internal ulcer of, **4**:81, 81*f*
    intrauterine inflammation and, **8**:263–264
von Hippel disease/syndrome, **4**:294, **5**:339*t*, 344, 344*f*,
    6:364*t*, 374–375, 375*f*, **12**:148–151, 149*f*, 150*f*. *See
    also* Retinal angiomatosis
    with hemangioblastomas. *See* von Hippel–Lindau
        disease/syndrome
von Hippel lesions, **12**:150
von Hippel–Lindau disease/syndrome, **4**:294–295,
    5:339*t*, 344, **6**:364*t*, 374–375, 375*f*, **12**:150, 150*f*. *See
    also* Retinal angiomatosis
    retinoblastoma differentiated from, **6**:358
von Kossa stain, **4**:31*t*
von Recklinghausen disease/neurofibromatosis. *See*
    Neurofibromatosis, von Recklinghausen
von Willebrand disease, **1**:155–156
von Willebrand factor, **1**:155–156
VOR. *See* Vestibular ocular reflex
Voriconazole, **1**:54*t*, 65
    for fungal endogenous endophthalmitis
        Aspergillus/mold, **9**:278, **12**:204
        Candida/yeast, **9**:275, **12**:203
        coccidioidomycosis, **9**:280
    for fungal keratitis, **8**:166
Vortex (hurricane) keratopathy (cornea verticillata),
    8:310, 311*f*, 346–348, 347*f*, 348*f*, 360
    in Fabry disease, **12**:263, 264*f*
Vortex veins, **2**:38–40, 38*f*, 40*f*, 64, **5**:14*f*, 24, **6**:18, **12**:18
    extraocular muscle surgery and, **6**:25
Vorticose veins, **5**:24*f*
VoSpire ER. *See* Albuterol
Vossius ring, **4**:20, **11**:50
Voxel, **5**:70
VP-16. *See* Etoposide
VRE. *See* Vancomycin-resistant enterococci
VRSA. *See* Vancomycin-resistant *S aureus*
VSR. *See* Venous stasis retinopathy
VT. *See* Ventricular tachyarrhythmias; Ventricular
    tachycardia
VTRs. *See* Variable/variable number of tandem repeats
VZV. *See* Varicella-zoster virus

W

Waardenburg-Jonkers corneal dystrophy. *See* Thiel-
    Behnke corneal dystrophy
Waardenburg syndrome, **2**:166, 216, **6**:175, 175*f*
    dystopia canthorum in, **6**:175, 175*f*
    pigmentary retinopathy and, **12**:250*t*
Wagner disease/Wagner hereditary vitreoretinal
    degeneration, **12**:250*t*, 309
WAGR syndrome, **2**:206, **6**:224, **10**:147, **11**:29
Waite-Beetham lines, **8**:30, 308
Waldenström macroglobulinemia, corneal deposits in,
    8:320
Wall-eyed bilateral internuclear ophthalmoplegia
    (WEBINO), **5**:225, 225*f*

Wallenberg syndrome (Wallenberg lateral medullary
    syndrome), 5:21, 195, 205–206
  Horner syndrome and, 5:267
  MR imaging in, 5:75f
Wallerian degeneration, optic nerve, 4:253–254
Warfarin/warfarin derivatives, 1:159
  for antiphospholipid antibody syndrome, 1:171
  cataract surgery in patient taking, 11:189
  DNA tests in dosage determination, 1:153
  for heart failure, 1:120
  ocular effects of, 1:302t
  in perioperative setting, 1:306, 307
Warts (verrucae)
  of eyelid, 4:209, 209f, 7:158, 158f
  papillomavirus causing, 4:209, 209f, 7:158, 158f,
    8:128, 129
Wasp stings, ocular injury caused by, 8:361–362
Water, refractive index of, 3:40t
Water and electrolyte balance, in lens, maintenance of,
    11:17–19, 18f
Water channels (aquaporins), 11:12, 17
Water-insoluble lens proteins, 11:11, 11f, 12
  aging affecting, 11:13
Water-soluble lens proteins, 11:11, 11f. See also
    Crystallins
  conversion of to water-insoluble, 11:13
Watershed zone, 2:94
Watt, 3:16
  laser power reading in, 3:18t, 21
Wave theory, 3:3, 3–7, 4f, 5f, 6f. See also Light waves
Wavefront, geometric, 3:238
Wavefront aberrations, 3:93–100, 238, 239f. See also
    specific type and Aberrations; Wavefront analysis
  "clover-shaped," 3:240
  coma, 13:7, 8f
  combining spherocylindrical lenses and, 3:99
  custom contact lenses for, 3:195–196
  first-order, 13:6
  graphical representations of, 13:5–6, 5f
  higher-order, 3:93, 115–116, 240, 13:7–8, 8f, 9f
    contact lens masking of, 3:190
    custom contact lenses for, 3:195–196
    after LASIK, 13:7, 95, 96f
    after surface ablation, 13:7, 95
    wavefront-guided/wavefront-optimized ablation
      and, 13:7, 8, 25, 69, 95
  hyperopia producing (negative defocus), 3:238, 13:6
  irregular astigmatism, 3:93, 115–116, 164, 13:9
  keratorefractive surgery and, 3:140, 13:5–9, 5f, 6f, 7f,
    8f, 9f, 40, 72, 74
  lower-order, 13:6, 6f, 7f
  measurement of, 13:5–6, 5f
    before LASIK, 13:72
  myopia producing (positive defocus), 3:238, 13:6, 6f
  piston, 13:7
  prisms, 13:6
  quadrafoil, 13:8
  regular astigmatism, 3:93–97, 93f, 94f, 95f, 96f, 97f,
    98, 98f, 13:6, 7f
  secondary astigmatism, 13:8
  spherical, 13:7, 8f
    after LASIK, 13:7, 95
    after surface ablation, 13:8f, 95

trefoil, 13:7, 9f
zero-order, 13:6
Wavefront aberrometers, 3:279–281, 280f
  custom contact lens fitting and, 3:195–196
Wavefront analysis, 3:237–240, 239f, 13:5–9, 5f, 6f, 7f,
    8f, 9f, 40, 72, 74. See also Irregular astigmatism;
    Wavefront aberrations
  contact lenses and, 3:195–196
  dry eye and, 8:55
  geometric wavefront and, 3:238
  graphical representations and, 13:5–6, 5f
  irregular astigmatism and, 13:9
  before LASIK, 13:72
  reference sphere and, 3:238, 239f
  before wavefront-guided ablation, 13:25, 40, 72, 74
Wavefront-guided laser ablation, 13:25, 26, 40, 69, 72
  higher-order aberrations and, 13:7, 8, 69, 95
  international trends in use of, 13:199
  for LASIK re-treatment/enhancement, 13:91
  outcomes of, 13:88–89
  overcorrection and, 13:94
  preoperative planning/laser programming for, 13:72,
    74
Wavefront-guided lasers, 13:25, 74
Wavefront-optimized laser ablation, 13:25, 26, 69. See
    also Wavefront-guided laser ablation
  higher-order aberrations and, 13:7, 8, 25, 69
  outcomes of, 13:88–89
Wavelength, 3:3, 4f
  chromatic aberrations and, 3:100–102, 102f
  color perception and, 3:19
  illuminance determination and, 3:17, 17f
  laser, 3:20, 26f
    for photocoagulation, 12:337–339
  refraction/refractive index and, 3:14, 40, 49–51, 51f
  relationship of to frequency, 3:4, 7
WDR36 gene, 10:11t
Weakening procedures (extraocular muscle), 6:147,
    148t, 151–152
  inferior oblique muscle, 6:151–152
    for superior oblique muscle paralysis, 6:120
    for V-pattern deviations, 6:110, 112
    for vertical deviations, 6:114–115
  superior oblique muscle, 6:152
    for A-pattern deviations, 6:110, 111, 112
    for vertical deviation, 6:116
Wear-and-tear pigment (lipofuscin granules), 2:72
  accumulation of in Best disease, 12:236
Weber syndrome, 5:226
WEBINO. See Wall-eyed bilateral internuclear
    ophthalmoplegia
Wedl (bladder) cells, 4:125, 125f, 11:44, 170
Wegener granulomatosis, 1:177t, 179, 7:32, 56–58, 57f,
    9:145–146, 146f
  choroidal perfusion abnormalities and, 12:179, 180f
  eyelid manifestations of, 4:213t
  scleritis/retinal vasculitis and, 7:56, 9:145, 146f
Weight, IGF, neonatal ROP (WINROP) algorithm,
    12:166
Weight reduction
  cardiovascular disease risk modification and, 1:133t
  diabetes mellitus prevention/management and, 1:189,
    194, 195

hypercholesterolemia management and, 1:133*t*, 134, 134*f*
hypertension management and, 1:75*t*
for idiopathic intracranial hypertension, 5:124
Weil disease, 9:254–255
Weill-Marchesani syndrome, 6:264
microspherophakia in, 6:264, 11:29
Weiss ring, 12:274, 274*f*, 297–298, 304
Welch-Allyn retinoscope, 3:121, 122, 127
Welding, occupational light injury and, 12:334
Well-being, assessment of in low vision patient, 3:289
Wellbutrin. *See* Bupropion
Wenckebach atrioventricular block, 1:122*t*
Werner syndrome, 8:324*t*
Wernicke disease, 1:250
WESDR (Wisconsin Epidemiologic Study of Diabetic Retinopathy), 12:90
Wessely immune ring, 8:181
West Nile virus, 9:214–217, 215*f*, 216*f*
chorioretinitis caused by, 9:215, 215*f*, 216*f*, 12:211
Western blot analysis, 2:163
in HIV infection/AIDS, 1:31
in Lyme disease, 1:16, 5:364, 9:252
Wetting angle, of contact lens, 3:169, 170*f*
WFVA. *See* Wavefront analysis
Wheezing, 1:141
WHI. *See* Women's Health Initiative
Whipple disease, 9:265–266
eye movement abnormalities in, 5:257
White blood cells, 1:147, 9:9–12. *See also specific type*
White coat hypertension, 1:70
White dot syndromes, 9:147–172, 148–150*t*, 151*t*, 12:185–193, 186*t*. *See also specific type*
multiple evanescent (MEWDS), 5:113–114, 113*f*, 9:148–150*t*, 168–170, 168*f*, 169*f*, 12:186*t*, 189–190, 189*f*
White-eyed blowout fracture, 6:125, 7:100
White infarct, 12:147
White limbal girdle, 8:336
White Maddox rod, 5:216. *See also* Maddox rod/ Maddox rod testing
White matter lesions
in multiple sclerosis, 5:324
neuroimaging in evaluation of, 5:82*t*, 84
White pupil. *See* Leukocoria
White ring, Coats, 8:334, 335*f*
"White spot" (hypopigmented macule/ash-leaf spot), in tuberous sclerosis, 5:341, 342*f*, 6:372, 372*f*, 10:28
Whitnall ligament (superior transverse ligament), 2:25*f*, 28, 7:135*f*, 138, 139*f*, 244
Whitnall tubercle, 2:9, 7:6, 6*f*, 7*f*
WHO (World Health Organization), 1:245
cataract epidemiology and, 11:65, 65*t*
Wide-angle fundus camera, 3:250
for screening in retinopathy of prematurity, 12:165
Wide-complex tachycardias, 1:123
Wide-field specular microscopy, 3:261
Wide-temple sunglasses, for glare reduction, 3:159, 304
Width (thickness) of retinal reflex, 3:124, 124*f*
in axis determination, 3:126, 127*f*
Wieger ligament, 12:7, 7*f*
Wilbrand knee, 2:96, 5:31, 161

Wilcoxon rank sum test, 1:320
Wild type, 2:163
Wildervanck syndrome, Duane syndrome and, 6:127
Willis, circle of, 2:93, 94*f*, 109, 109*f*, 5:20
Wilms tumor, aniridia and, 4:188, 6:224, 10:147, 11:29
Wilms tumor *(WT1)* gene, aniridia and, 6:224, 10:147
Wilms tumor–suppressor gene, imprinting of, 2:154, 169
Wilson disease (hepatolenticular degeneration), 2:231, 6:220–221, 398, 8:327–328, 327*f*, 11:57
cataracts associated with, 6:247*t*, 8:327, 11:57
oculogyric crisis in, 5:212–213
penicillamine for, 2:231, 8:327–328
Window (transmission) defect, of fluorescence, 12:23, 23*f*. *See also* Hyperfluorescence
in angioid streaks, 12:84
in macular holes, 12:305
"Wing" cells, 2:43, 44*f*
WINROP (weight, IGF, neonatal ROP) algorithm, 12:166
Wipeout, after trabeculectomy, 10:186
Wisconsin Epidemiologic Study of Diabetic Retinopathy (WESDR), 12:90
With motion, in retinoscopy, 3:123*f*, 124
neutrality and, 3:124, 125, 126*f*
With-the-rule astigmatism, 3:115
Withdrawal (abstinence) syndrome, 1:250. *See also specific drug*
hypertension and, 1:87
WNV. *See* West Nile virus
Wofflin nodules, 6:227
Wolff-Parkinson-White syndrome, 1:124*t*
Wolfram (DIDMOAD) syndrome
in children, 6:297
pleiotropism in, 2:210
Wolfring, glands of, 2:23*f*, 26*f*, 27*t*, 33, 240, 4:205, 207*t*, 7:135*f*, 141, 244
Women's Health Initiative (WHI), 1:230, 274
Working distance
bifocal segment decentration and, 3:157
for operating microscope, 3:262
in retinoscopy, 3:28, 29*f*, 125
"Working distance" lens, in retinoscopy, 3:125
World Health Organization (WHO), 1:245
cataract epidemiology and, 11:65, 65*t*
Worm's-eye view position, 7:23, 24*f*
Worst "iris claw" (Artisan) lens, 3:207, 208*f*
Worth 4-dot (red-green/duochrome) test, 3:135–136, 6:55, 55*f*, 87
in binocular sensory cooperation evaluation, 6:87
in nonorganic ophthalmic disorder evaluation
monocular no light perception and, 5:309–310
monocular reduced vision and, 5:311
before refractive surgery, 13:33
in sensory adaptation testing, 6:55, 55*f*
Wound closure, after cataract surgery
complications associated with, 11:148–149
after ECCE, 11:212–213
postoperative endophthalmitis and, 11:180
scleral tunnel incisions and, 11:112–113, 112*f*
Wound contraction, 4:13, 14*f*
Wound dehiscence/rupture, after cataract surgery, 11:149

Wound healing/repair, **4**:13–23. *See also specific tissue*
  of conjunctiva, **8**:388
  of cornea, **4**:13–16, 15*f*, **8**:387–388
    keratorefractive surgery and, **13**:26–27
      delays in, **13**:86, 100
  of eyelid/orbit/lacrimal tissues, **4**:17–18
  general aspects of, **4**:13, 14*f*
  histologic sequelae of trauma and, **4**:18–22, 18*f*, 19*f*,
    20*f*, 21*f*, 22*f*, 23*f*
  of lens, **4**:17
  of limbus, **4**:16
  ocular surface response to, **8**:388–389
  promotion of, in chemical injuries, **8**:358
  of retina, **4**:17
  of sclera, **4**:16
  of uvea, **4**:16–17
  of vitreous, **4**:17
Wound leaks
  after cataract surgery, **11**:144*t*, 148–149
    flat anterior chamber and, **11**:153
      angle-closure glaucoma and, **10**:136
  after penetrating keratoplasty, **8**:421
WPW syndrome. *See* Wolff-Parkinson-White
  syndrome
Writing, computers for low vision and, **3**:304
Wrong site/wrong procedure surgery, Universal
  Protocol in avoidance of, **1**:309–310
WT1 (Wilms tumor) gene, aniridia and, **6**:224, **10**:147
Wyburn-Mason syndrome (racemose angioma/
  hemangioma), **4**:296, 297*f*, **5**:339*t*, 345, 345*f*, **6**:342,
  364*t*, 381, 381*f*, **12**:151

X

x-axis of Fick, **6**:27, 27*f*
X chromosome, **2**:193, 194, 195
  genes for color vision on, **2**:294–295
  inactivation of (Lyonization/Barr body), **2**:149, 155,
    168–169, 220–224
    ocular findings in carrier states and, **2**:220–224,
      221–222*f*, 222*t*
X-linked disorders, **2**:219–220. *See also specific disorder
  and* X-linked inheritance
  Aicardi syndrome, **6**:292, 292*f*
  albinism (Nettleship-Falls), **6**:298, 300*t*, 301, **12**:258
    ocular findings in carriers of, **2**:222*f*, 223, **12**:258
  Alport syndrome, **6**:302
  blue-cone monochromatism/monochromacy, **6**:291,
    12:214*t*, 215
    ocular findings in carriers of, **2**:222*t*
  choroideremia, ocular findings in carriers of, **12**:243
  color vision deficiency, **12**:214, 214*t*, 215
  cone dystrophies, **12**:233
  congenital stationary night blindness, **6**:291, **12**:215
  dominant, **2**:219–220
  Fabry disease, **8**:305, 310
  familial exudative vitreoretinopathy, **6**:296, **12**:310, 311
  gene therapy for, **2**:187–188
  Hunter syndrome, **8**:305, 306*t*
  ichthyosis, **8**:74
  incontinentia pigmenti (Bloch-Sulzberger syndrome),
    6:379

Lisch corneal dystrophy, **8**:273
Lowe syndrome, **6**:302
megalocornea, **8**:253–254, 254*f*
Norrie disease, **6**:296
  ocular findings in carriers of, **2**:220, 221–222*f*, 222*t*
  pigmentary retinopathies, **12**:251*t*
  retinitis pigmentosa, **12**:228, 229
    ocular findings in carriers of, **2**:221*f*, 222*t*, **12**:226,
      228
  retinoschisis (congenital/juvenile retinoschisis),
    6:294–295, 295*f*, **12**:246–247, 246*f*
    ERG in, **6**:295, **12**:36*f*, 247
X-linked inheritance (X-linked genes), **2**:163, 185. *See
  also* X-linked disorders
  dominant, **2**:219, 219*t*
  recessive, **2**:218–219, 219*t*
X-pattern exotropia, **6**:23
Xalatan. *See* Latanoprost
Xanax. *See* Alprazolam
Xanthelasma. *See also* Xanthomas
  in dyslipoproteinemia/hyperlipoproteinemia, **4**:211,
    211*f*, 213*t*, **7**:160, 160*f*, **8**:308, 309*t*
  of eyelid, **4**:211, 211*f*, 213*t*, **7**:160, 160*f*
Xanthine derivatives, for pulmonary diseases, **1**:145*t*
Xanthocoria, in Coats disease, **12**:143
Xanthogranuloma
  juvenile, **6**:226, 351, 352*f*, **7**:85, **8**:242, **9**:286
    glaucoma associated with, **6**:351, **10**:28
    of iris, **4**:191, 270*t*, **6**:226, 351, 352*f*
    of uveal tract, **4**:191, 191*f*
    uveitis in children differentiated from, **6**:276*t*
  necrobiotic, **7**:85, **8**:242
  of orbit, **7**:85
Xanthomas
  fibrous (fibrous histiocytoma), **8**:242
    malignant (atypical fibroxanthoma), **4**:117–118,
      240–242
  orbital, **4**:240–242, 242*f*, **7**:78
  scleral, **4**:117–118, 117*f*
  in hyperlipoproteinemias, **4**:211, 211*f*, 213*t*
Xanthophylls (carotenoids)
  absorption spectrum for, **12**:337, 338*f*
  cataract risk affected by, **11**:58
  in lens, **2**:314–315, 314*f*
  in macula, **4**:147, 12:8
    age-related macular degeneration and, **12**:62
  in retina, **2**:81, 318, 318*f*
Xenon arc laser therapy, for retinoblastoma, **4**:311
Xenon fluoride excimer laser, **3**:25. *See also* Lasers
Xeomin (incobotulinumtoxinA). *See* Botulinum toxin,
  type A
Xeroderma pigmentosum, **2**:170, **7**:168, **8**:75
Xerophthalmia, **8**:77–78, 79. *See also* Vitamin A,
  deficiency of
Xerophthalmic fundus, **8**:78
Xerosis
  Corynebacterium xerosis and, **8**:134
  in vitamin A deficiency, **8**:77, 78, 134
  in vitamin C deficiency, **8**:79
Xibrom. *See* Bromfenac
Xigris. *See* Drotrecogin
XLM. *See* External limiting membrane
XLRP. *See* X-linked disorders, retinitis pigmentosa

XLRS. *See* X-linked disorders, retinoschisis
XP. *See* Xeroderma pigmentosum
Xylocaine. *See* Lidocaine

Y

y-axis of Fick, **6**:27, 27*f*
Y chromosome, **2**:193, 194
   inheritance/traits determined by (holandric
      inheritance/trait), **2**:218
Y-group cells, **5**:39
Y-linked inheritance (Y-linked genes), **2**:163
Y-sutures, lens, **2**:69*f*, 70, **11**:9
   development of, **2**:130, **11**:24–25, 24*f*
   opacification of (sutural/stellate cataract), **11**:33, 33*f*
Y-V-plasties
   for blepharophimosis syndrome, **7**:145
   for epicanthus, **7**:148
YAC. *See* Yeast artificial chromosome
Yeast artificial chromosome (YAC), **2**:163
Yeasts, **5**:364, **8**:138, 138*t*, 139, 139*f*
   Candida, **1**:20, **9**:273, 274–276, 275*f*
   endogenous endophthalmitis caused by, **9**:273–274,
      274–276, 275*f*, **12**:203, 204*f*
   keratitis caused by, **8**:166
   as normal ocular flora, **8**:97*t*
Yellow fever vaccination, **1**:286
Yellow lasers, **12**:338
Yohimbine, **2**:259*t*
Yoke muscles, **6**:35
   cardinal positions of gaze and, **6**:28*f*, 35, 80
   Hering's law of motor correspondence and, **6**:35

Z

z-axis of Fick, **6**:27, 27*f*
z-height/z-maps, **8**:42, **13**:15–16, 16*f*
Z-plasties
   for blepharophimosis syndrome, **7**:145
   for epicanthus, **7**:148
   for eyelid repair, **7**:180
   for symblepharon, **7**:199
Z syndrome, **11**:169
Zaditor. *See* Ketotifen
Zafirlukast, **1**:145*t*
Zagam. *See* Sparfloxacin
Zaleplon, **1**:254
Zanamivir, **1**:55*t*, 66, 282
Zarontin. *See* Ethosuximide
Zaroxolyn. *See* Metolazone
Zeaxanthin, **2**:81
   antioxidant effect of, **2**:316
   cataract risk affected by, **11**:58
   in macula, **12**:8
      age-related macular degeneration and, **12**:62
ZEB1 gene, in posterior polymorphous corneal
   dystrophy, **8**:269*t*
Zebeta. *See* Bisoprolol
Zefazone. *See* Cefmetazole
Zeftera. *See* Ceftobiprole

Zeis, glands of, **2**:23, 23*f*, 26*f*, 27*t*, **4**:205, **7**:142*f*, 160,
   8:4, 5*f*
   chalazion caused by obstruction of, **4**:210–211, 211*f*,
      8:72
   hordeolum caused by infection of, **4**:208, **7**:154
   sebaceous adenocarcinoma arising in, **4**:221–222,
      7:173
   in tear-film lipids/tear production, **2**:237
Zeiss 4-mirror goniolens
   for gonioscopy, **10**:34
   for slit-lamp biomicroscopy, **3**:253, 255*f*
Zellweger (cerebrohepatorenal) syndrome, **6**:398,
   12:251*t*, 254, 261
   pigmentary retinopathy and, **12**:251*t*, 254, 261
Zenapax. *See* Daclizumab
Zenker acetic tissue fixative, **4**:29*t*
Zentmayer line, **10**:88, 89*f*
Zerit. *See* Stavudine
Zernike polynomials, **3**:116, 240, **13**:6, 6*f*, 7*f*, 8*f*, 9*f*
Zero-order aberrations, **13**:7
Zestoretic. *See* Lisinopril
Zestril. *See* Lisinopril
Zeta (ξ)-crystallins, **2**:115
Ziac. *See* Bisoprolol
Ziagen. *See* Abacavir
Zidovudine, **1**:33, **2**:381*t*, 384–385
   with lamivudine, **1**:33
Ziehl-Neelsen stain, **4**:31*t*
Zileuton, **1**:145*t*
Zimmerman tumor (phakomatous choristoma), **4**:20*f*,
   207, **8**:247
Zinacef. *See* Cefuroxime
Zinc
   in age-related macular degeneration management,
      12:61–62
   in aqueous humor, **2**:267
   foreign body of, **12**:327
Zinc deficiency, vitamin A deficiency and, **5**:114
Zinc finger motif, **2**:166, 167*f*
Zinn
   annulus of, **2**:10, 16*f*, 17*f*, 18, 19*t*, 91, **5**:10*f*, 31, **7**:11, 12*f*
   zonules of (zonular fibers), **2**:41*f*, 51*f*, 52*f*, 61, 69*f*, 70,
      273, 286, **4**:120, 120*f*, **11**:5, 6*f*, 7–8
      absent/abnormal, cataract surgery and, **11**:117, 118
      in glaucoma, **10**:112, **11**:202
         iris coloboma/corectopia and, **11**:196, 197*f*
      in accommodation, **13**:149–152, 150*f*, 151*f*
      development of, **2**:129*f*, 130, **11**:25
      evaluation of, before cataract surgery, **11**:79
      tertiary vitreous, **2**:132, **4**:132
Zinn-Haller, circle of, **2**:94, **5**:19, **10**:42, 43, 44
Ziracin. *See* Evernimicin
Zithromax. *See* Azithromycin
ZMC fractures. *See* Zygomaticomaxillary complex
   (ZMC) fractures
Zocor. *See* Simvastatin
Zofran. *See* Ondansetron
Zoledronic acid, for osteoporosis, **1**:230–231
Zollinger-Ellison syndrome, **1**:216
Zolpidem, **1**:254
Zonal granuloma, **4**:122
Zonegran. *See* Zonisamide

Zones of discontinuity, 2:70
Zonisamide, 1:263t
Zonulae adherentes, in retinal pigment epithelium, 2:72
Zonulae occludentes (tight junctions)
in ciliary body epithelium, 2:62, 265
in corneal endothelium, 2:135
in corneal epithelium, 8:6
in retinal blood vessels, 2:78
in retinal pigment epithelium, 2:72, 12:14
Zonular apparatus, 2:286
Zonular (lamellar) cataracts, 6:247f, 247t, 248, 248f, 250t, 11:30, 32f
pulverulent, 6:247t
Zonular dehiscence
angle closure and, 10:112
cataract surgery and, 11:197–199, 198f
in glaucoma, 11:202
iris coloboma/corectopia and, 11:196, 197f
Zonular fibers
lens (zonules of Zinn), 2:41f, 51f, 52f, 61, 69f, 70, 273, 286, 4:120, 120f, 11:5, 6f, 7–8
absent/abnormal, cataract surgery and, 11:117, 118
in glaucoma, 10:112, 11:202
iris coloboma/corectopia and, 11:196, 197f
in accommodation, 13:149–152, 150f, 151f
development of, 2:129f, 130, 11:25
evaluation of, before cataract surgery, 11:79
vitreous, 2:286
tertiary, 2:132, 4:132
Zonular lamella, 11:/
Zonular rupture, cataract surgery and, 11:144t
Zonular traction retinal tufts, 12:278, 280f
Zonules
occluding, corneal, 2:43
of Zinn (zonular fibers/suspensory ligaments), 2:41f, 51f, 52f, 61, 69f, 70, 273, 286, 4:120, 120f, 11:5, 6f, 7–8
absent/abnormal, cataract surgery and, 11:117, 118
in glaucoma, 11:202
iris coloboma/corectopia and, 11:196, 197f
in accommodation, 13:149–152, 150f, 151f
development of, 2:129f, 130, 11:25
evaluation of, before cataract surgery, 11:79
tertiary vitreous, 2:132, 4:132
Zoom Galilean telescopes, in operating microscope, 3:262, 263
Zostavax. See Varicella vaccine
Zoster. See Herpes zoster
Zoster sine herpete, 5:302, 9:197
Zosyn. See Piperacillin, with tazobactam
Zovirax. See Acyclovir
Zyflo. See Zileuton
Zygomatic artery, 5:13f
Zygomatic bone, 5:5, 7, 7f, 8f, 7:6f, 7f
fractures of, 7:95–97, 97f
Zygomatic foramen, 2:10
Zygomatic nerve, 5:10f, 59f, 60, 61, 7:133, 134f
in reflex tear arc, 7:244
Zygomaticofacial artery, 2:39f, 5:14f, 15f
Zygomaticofacial canal, 7:9
Zygomaticofacial foramen, 7:6f
Zygomaticofacial nerve, 5:60
Zygomaticomaxillary complex (ZMC) fractures (tripod fractures), 7:95–97, 97f
Zygomaticomaxillary suture, 5:9
Zygomaticotemporal artery, 2:39f, 5:15f, 16
Zygomaticotemporal canal, 7:6f, 9
Zygomaticotemporal foramen, 5:12
Zygomaticotemporal nerve, 5:60
in reflex tear arc, 7:244
Zygomaticus muscles, 7:131, 133f
Zygomycetes (zygomycosis/mucormycosis/phycomysosis), 5:366–367, 366f, 8:140
cornea involved in (keratitis), 4:83
optic nerve involved in, 4:251
orbit involved in, 4:234, 6:197, 197f, 7:45–46
exenteration in management of, 7:45, 126
Zygote, 2:196
Zylet. See Loteprednol
Zymar. See Gatifloxacin
Zymaxid. See Gatifloxacin
Zyprexa. See Olanzapine
Zyvox. See Linezolid